PERSONAL FINANCIAL PLANNING

Lawrence J. Gitman, CFP® · *San Diego State University*
Michael D. Joehnk, CFA · *Arizona State University*

11e

THOMSON

SOUTH-WESTERN

Australia · Brazil · Canada · Mexico · Singapore · Spain · United Kingdom · United States

THOMSON

SOUTH-WESTERN

Personal Financial Planning, Eleventh Edition
Lawrence J. Gitman and Michael D. Joehnk

VP/Editorial Director:
Jack W. Calhoun

VP/Editor-in-Chief:
Alex von Rosenberg

Sr. Developmental Editor:
Susanna C. Smart

Marketing Manager:
Jason Krall

Content Project Manager:
Starratt Alexander

Manager of Technology, Editorial:
John Barans

Sr. Technology Project Editor:
Matt McKinney

Manufacturing Coordinator:
Sandee Milewski

Production House:
Lachina Publishing Services

Printer:
China Translation &
Printing Services Ltd.

Art Director:
Bethany Casey

Cover & Internal Designer:
Ann Small, A Small Design Studio

Cover & Internal Illustrations:
Peter McDonnell Illustration

Photography Manager:
Deanna Ettinger

Photo Researcher:
Deanna Ettinger

ISBN 13:
978-0-324-42286-3

ISBN 10:
0-324-42286-5

Library of Congress Control Number:
2006909335

For more information about our p
roducts, contact us at:
Thomson Learning Academic
Resource Center
1-800-423-0563

Thomson Higher Education
5191 Natorp Boulevard
Mason, OH 45040
USA

For our children:
Zachary, Jessica, and Caren
LJG

For the twins,
Grace Hesketh Joehnk
and
Rhett Weaver Joehnk,
because they're so special
MDJ

CONTENTS

PART 3 MANAGING CREDIT, 173

PART 4 MANAGING INSURANCE NEEDS, 239

APPENDICES

"Feds Hold Firm on Interest Rates as Inflation Remains in Check"
"Rate of Increase in Home Prices Drops Sharply"
"Dow Jones Industrial Average Nears All-Time High"
"30-year Fixed Rate Mortgages Fall Below 6%"
"Pension Protection Act of 2006 Signed Into Law"
"Economy Picks Up Steam as Jobless Claims Fall Again"
"NYSE Incorporates, Lists Its Stock on, Where Else, the NYSE"
"Credit Card Issuers Target Both College and High School Students"

At one time or another, chances are we've all read these kinds of headlines, or seen the stories on television. They highlight the ever-changing nature of the financial environment in which we live. Indeed, it is these changes in the financial environment, along with changes in our own lives—family, health, job—that make personal financial planning both necessary and challenging. This book, *Personal Financial Planning, Eleventh Edition,* provides the framework and tools for preparing personal financial plans that serve as road maps for goal achievement. *Personal Financial Planning* emphasizes the dynamics of the financial planning process by considering the impact of life changes—birth, marriage, divorce, job and career, and death.

Personal Financial Planning addresses all of the major financial planning issues and problems that individuals and families encounter. It is built around a model that links together all of the major elements of effective money management. All of the latest financial planning tools and techniques are discussed. This comprehensive text is written in a low-key, personal style and uses state-of-the-art pedagogy to present the key concepts and procedures used in sound personal financial planning and effective money management. The roles of various financial decisions in the overall personal financial planning process are clearly delineated.

The book serves individuals who are, or will be, actively developing their own personal financial plans. It meets the needs of instructors and students in the first course in personal financial planning (often called "personal finance") offered at colleges and universities, junior and community colleges, professional certification programs, and continuing education courses. The experiences of individuals and families are used to demonstrate successes and failures in various aspects of personal financial planning. A conversational style and liberal use of examples and worksheets guide students through the material and emphasize important points. Clearly the benefits of the book's readability accrue not only to students but also to their instructors.

MAJOR CHANGES IN THE ELEVENTH EDITION

The eleventh edition has been thoroughly updated to reflect the cutting edge of contemporary personal financial planning. It reflects feedback from past users as well as nonusers,

Worksheet 5.1 Comparing Mary Dixon's Automobile Lease versus Purchase Costs

This worksheet illustrates Mary Dixon's lease versus purchase analysis for a new Toyota Scion xA costing $15,000. The 3-year closed-end lease requires an initial payment of $1,800 ($1,500 down payment + $300 security deposit) and monthly payments of $300. Purchasing requires a $2,500 down payment, sales tax of 5 percent ($750), and 36 monthly payments of $392. The trade-in value of the new car at the end of 3 years is estimated to be $8,000. *Because the total cost of leasing of $12,516 is greater than the $9,662 total cost of purchasing, Mary should purchase rather than lease the car.*

AUTOMOBILE LEASE VERSUS PURCHASE ANALYSIS*

Name Mary Dixon   Date March 4, 2008

Item Description		Amount
LEASE		
1	Initial payment:	
	a. Down payment (capital cost reduction) $ 1,500	
	b. Security deposit 300	$ 1,800
2	Term of lease and loan (years)*	3
3	Term of lease and loan (months) (Item 2 × 12)	36
4	Monthly lease payment	$ 300
5	Total payments over term of lease (Item 3 × Item 4)	$ 10,800
6	Interest rate earned on savings (in decimal form)	.04
7	Opportunity cost of initial payment (Item 1 × Item 2 × Item 6)	$ 216
8	Payment/refund for market value adjustment at end of lease ($0 for closed-end leases) and/or estimated end-of-term charges	$ 0
9	**Total cost of leasing (Item 1a + Item 5 + Item 7 + Item 8)**	$ 12,516
PURCHASE		
10	Purchase price	$ 15,000
11	Down payment	$ 2,500
12	Sales tax rate (in decimal form)	.05
13	Sales tax (Item 10 × Item 12)	$ 750
14	Monthly loan payment (Terms: 12,500 , 36 months, 8 %)	$ 392
15	Total payments over term of loan (Item 3 × Item 14)	$ 14,112
16	Opportunity cost of down payment (Item 2 × Item 6 × Item 11)	$ 300
17	Estimated trade-in value of car at end of loan	$ 8,000
18	**Total cost of purchasing (Item 11 + Item 13 + Item 15 + Item 16 − Item 17)**	$ 9,662

DECISION

If the value of Item 9 is less than the value of Item 18, leasing is preferred; otherwise the *purchase alternative is preferred.*

*Note: This form is based on assumed equal terms for the lease and the installment loan, which is assumed to be used to finance the purchase.

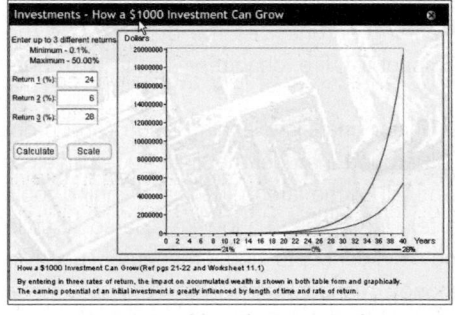

Investments – How a $1000 Investment Can Grow

How a $1000 Investment Can Grow (Ref pgs 21-22 and Worksheet 11.1)

By entering in three rates of return, the impact on accumulated wealth is shown in both table form and graphically. The earning potential of an initial investment is greatly influenced by length of time and rate of return.

practicing financial planners, students, and our own research. It provides helpful new approaches, expanded coverage in certain areas, streamlined coverage in others, and enhanced pedagogy anchored by a state-of-the-art integrated learning system. The basic organizational structure, topical coverage, superior readability, and useful instructional aids that marked the success of the first ten editions have been retained. Important changes in this edition are described below, first as general changes and then as specific chapter-by-chapter changes.

General Changes

- The highly regarded *Worksheets* continue to be included with this edition, and as with the previous edition, they are also available online as part of the Gitman/Joehnk ThomsonNOW product. As such, students have the option to use the Worksheets multiple times and have some of the calculations within the Worksheets completed electronically. The expanded and revised Worksheets are separately labeled and numbered as "Worksheet *X.Y.*" The labels make text references to the worksheets much clearer. All end-of-chapter problems that can be solved using a given worksheet have an identifying icon and provide the worksheet reference, which directs the student to its application.

- In addition to the Worksheets, *Personal Financial Planning Software* is available with each new text as part of ThomsonNOW. Students will find that the chapter concepts, Worksheets, problems, and cases can be solved with the use of the software. Given the ease of using the *Personal Financial Planning Software*, we believe students will be more inclined to begin and continue their own financial planning.

- *Web-based part-ending cases* are part of the package, one for each of the six major parts of the text. These cases are provided online as part of ThomsonNOW. They have been developed to challenge readers to integrate and develop plans with regard to the major topics covered in the corresponding part.

- Also available are *CFP®* Exam Questions as part of ThomsonNOW. For each Part, 12 to 15 actual exam questions are included from previous years' *CFP®* exams. These questions should help students gain insight into the *CFP®* program and the level of study required to earn this widely respected certification.

- The *book has been completely updated and redesigned* to allow improved presentation of each of the text's pedagogical features.

- The eleventh edition continues to place emphasis on *the use of the Internet*. A number of features that either link students to relevant Internet sites or describe how the Internet can be incorporated into the personal financial planning process are included. The Internet feature, *Money Online,* can now be found on the text Web site at **http://www.thomsonedu.com/finance/gitman.** Each *Money Online* has two parts: The first part includes eight to ten Web addresses followed by a brief paragraph that chal-

MONEY ONLINE   www.thomsonedu.com/finance/gitman

MONEY ONLINE • MONEY ONLINE • MONEY ONLINE • MONEY ONLINE • MONEY ONLINE • MONEY ONLINE • MONEY ONLINE • MONEY

lenges the reader to go to the site and either research specific information or review the resources available there. All of the Web topics presented within the chapter are intended to reinforce—as well as expand—the reader's practical grasp of the key concepts, tools, and techniques presented in the chapter. The second part of *Money Online*—"Just for Fun!"—includes one to three Web addresses followed by brief paragraphs that direct the reader to interesting, and often entertaining, sites to obtain information, perform an activity, or answer specific questions.

Each chapter also includes a number of *Smart.Sites,* margin notes that direct students to specific sites related to the topics under discussion. This element helps keep readers in touch with the Web while they read and study the chapter. In addition, many Web addresses are embedded in the text and exhibits. These Web links are included when referencing a specific company, information provider, or organization, and provide the reader with a convenient way to learn more about the topic, obtain information, or make inquiries or transactions.

Another source of additional Internet insights is the *Money in Action* boxes (described in detail below); some of these features focus on technology and include descriptions and links to useful sites on the Internet. Clearly, this edition's emphasis on the Internet is significant and widely present both in the chapter and in the end-of-chapter materials.

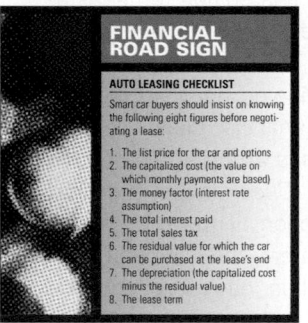

- The *focus of the text has been improved* by eliminating certain noncritical discussions and elements, tightening and streamlining wherever possible, and moving material to the text's Web site. Clearer focus on the dynamics of the personal financial planning process and the concepts, tools, and techniques used to implement this process are embodied in the eleventh edition. Specific changes include concise *Money in Action* boxes with *Critical Thinking Questions;* revised and redesigned *Concept Check* questions at the end of each major chapter section; revised and redesigned *Financial Road Signs* that add interesting and useful sidebar information; and the refining of certain discussions by tightening the writing. In addition, excessive detail has been eliminated in response to user and reviewer suggestions. Some of the discussions have been restructured to eliminate the need to reintroduce topics that were presented in previous chapters. All of these changes are believed to clarify and enhance reader understanding and comprehension of the text's content.

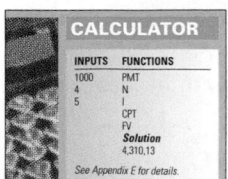

- Step-by-step *use of a hand-held financial calculator* to make time value calculations continues to be integrated into relevant discussions in this edition. To improve understanding, relevant keystrokes are highlighted in these demonstrations. The basics of time value of money are introduced in Chapter 2, *Developing Your Financial Statements and Plans,* and an explanation of how to use financial calculators to conveniently make time value calculations now appears in text Appendix E. The use of a financial calculator is reinforced in later chapters where time value techniques are applied. For example, the use of a calculator to find the future value of a deposit given various compounding periods is shown in Chapter 4, *Managing Your Cash and Savings,* and in Chapter 14, *Planning for Retirement,* to find estimates for future retirement needs. The inclusion of calculator keystrokes should help the reader learn how to more effectively develop financial plans using an important tool of the trade.

- This edition also includes one *Money in Action* feature for each chapter. Most of these features are new to this edition, some have been revised and updated from the previous edition, and all are drawn from recent articles in the popular press—providing both relevant and timely information. The *Money in Action* features address a variety of

MONEY IN ACTION

IN ACTION • MONEY IN ACTION • MONEY IN ACTION • MONEY IN ACTION • MONEY IN ACTION • N

WILL THAT BE A DEBIT OR CREDIT CARD?

The U.S. is saturated with literally millions of credit and debit cards. Young people are shifting to debit cards because these cards have no annual fee or monthly balances. You pay as you go. Debit card charges represent 60 percent of the transactions processed by Visa. You may not know that when you use your *debit* card, you don't have to choose debit and enter your PIN (PIN transaction). Instead, you can choose *credit* and sign the receipt (signature transaction). A 2004 MasterCard survey showed that 70 percent of people didn't realize that a debit card could be used for a signature transaction. Here are some benefits of choosing *credit* instead of *debit*:

- **Avoid fees:** Banks never charge for signature transactions, but 14 percent charge fees for PIN transactions.
- **Rewards points:** Some debit cards have rewards programs, but sometimes a signature transaction is required to earn points, or you may earn more points with a signature transaction than a PIN transaction.
- **Liability protection:** Signature transactions go through Visa or MasterCard networks that offer protection from fraudulent use. PIN transactions are processed through electronic funds transfer systems, such as NYCE or STAR, that don't offer liability protection.

One point to remember is that if you choose *debit* the money is removed from your account that day;

but if you choose *credit* it will be two to three days before the money is deducted. In any case, it's important to keep your receipts and update your checkbook.

So, why would you ever use your PIN to complete a transaction? If you want cash back, then you should use your PIN. It's better to get cash back from a debit transaction than to use an ATM that doesn't belong to your bank. Both the ATM and your bank will charge fees that outweigh any benefit of signing for the transaction.

Critical Thinking Questions

1. What are the benefits to using a debit card over a credit card?
2. Explain why it is better to choose *credit* rather than *debit* when using a debit card.

Sources: Carolyn Bigda, "Debit or Credit? The Savvy Answer Is...," *Money*, October 2005, p. 40c; Robin Sidel, "American Express Tries to Find Its Place with a Younger Crowd," *Wall Street Journal*, September 22, 2005, p. A1; "Debit Cards," *Bankrate.com*, May 1, 2006.

IN ACTION • MONEY IN ACTION • MONEY IN ACTION • MONEY IN ACTION • MONEY IN ACTION • N

informative topics to help ground the text discussions to actual financial planning ideas, experiences, practices, and events—all intended to fully engage readers in the personal financial planning process. Examples of *Money in Action* include How Americans Feel About Money (Chapter 1), Online Bill Payment: How and Why? (Chapter 4), Clicking the Tires (Chapter 5), Health Insurance: Don't Leave School Without It (Chapter 9), and How to Build a Portfolio When You're Just Starting Out (Chapter 11). Each feature contains *Critical Thinking Questions* that can be used to improve reader understanding. As an added bonus, many of the relevant and interesting *Money in Action* features from the previous edition were revised and updated, as necessary, and then moved to our Web site at **http://www.thomsonedu.com/ finance/gitman;** one example is "Anatomy of a Market Meltdown," which explores in some detail the factors that led up to the big bear market of 2000–2002.

- The *integrated learning system* has been refined even more in this edition to help students better anchor their study to a set of chapter learning goals. Each chapter begins with a list of six numbered learning goals, LG1 through LG6. The learning goal numbers are tied to major chapter headings and restated and reviewed point by point in the end-of-chapter summary, financial planning exercises, and *Critical Thinking Cases*. Another element of this system is the *Concept Check* questions that appear at the end of each section of the chapter. As students read through the chapters, they can test their understanding of the material in each section. The most effective advanced pedagogical features from the previous edition—marginal glossary, exhibits and worksheets, and end-of-chapter financial planning exercises and *Critical Thinking Cases* have also been retained and improved as part of the integrated learning system. Also included at the end of each chapter is *Applying Personal Finance—* features that present a challenging out-of-class exercise dealing with at least one of the main topics presented in the chapter.

Concept Check

CONCEPT CHECK • CONCEPT CHECK • CONCEPT CHECK • CONCEPT CHECK • CONCEPT CHECK

5-19	Describe the various sources of mortgage loans. hat role might a *mortgage broker* play in obtaining mortgage financing
5-20	riefly escribe the two basic types of mortgage loans. hich has the lowest initial rate of interest hat is *negative amortization*, an which type of mortgage can experience it Discuss the a vantages an isa vantages of each mortgage type.
5-21	Differentiate among conventional, insure, an guarantee mortgage loans.
5-22	hat factors shoul you consi er when eci ing whether to refinance your mortgage to re uce the monthly payment ow can the refinancing ecision be ma e

Specific Chapter-by-Chapter Changes

Because users often like to know where new material appears, the significant changes that have been made in the eleventh edition are summarized below, on a chapter-by-chapter basis.

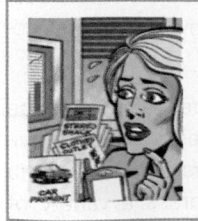

Chapter 1 on understanding the financial planning process has been carefully streamlined to focus on the most important topics and enhance readability. All discussions, including exhibits, *Financial Road Rigns,* and *SmartSites* have been refreshed and updated. The result is a shorter, more focused and engaging introduction to the financial planning process. Sidebar material focuses on assessing current wealth and monitoring it in the future, personal finance tips, Americans' opinions about money, statistics on student debt, comparing housing costs in the U.S., and avoiding online job-search mistakes.

Chapter 2 on developing your financial statements has been restructured to improve its flow. All discussions have been streamlined and updated. The discussion of the time value of money now follows the discussion of cash financial statements and budgeting. Calculator keystrokes and time lines now appear in the time value of money discussions. Special planning concerns are now discussed at the end of the chapter to achieve a more logical flow of topics. Sidebar discussions include tips for eliminating documents that you don't need, budgeting hints, reducing spending to create more savings, and major life situations that require extra planning attention.

Chapter 3 on preparing your taxes has been completely updated to reflect the changes in tax laws (including those resulting from the *Working Families Tax Relief Act of 2004*), rates, procedures, and forms in effect at the time we revised the chapter. The material has been streamlined considerably to emphasize current tax practices and clarify discussions of progressive tax rates, average tax rates, itemized deductions, IRAs, and other types of taxes. The chapter continues to provide readers with sidebar advice on finding missing deductions, avoiding common tax form errors, tax tips, audit triggers, and choosing a tax preparer.

Chapter 4 on managing your cash and savings has been restructured by moving the section on maintaining a checking account forward to follow the descriptive discussions of cash management products. Many discussions, including the types of financial institutions, have been streamlined to improve clarity. The chapter includes the latest return and institutional data that accurately reflects current market rates and structure. Calculator keystrokes are now shown in the discussion of earning interest on your money. Practical sidebar discussions of protecting your personal financial information online, online bill payment, saving money in a crunch, the safety of online banking, renting a safe-deposit box, determining interest on savings, and choosing a bank are included in the chapter.

Chapter 5 on making automobile and housing decisions has been streamlined and reorganized to improve the flow of the material. The automobile affordability section now includes a discussion of gas, diesel, or hybrid cars. Calculator keystrokes have been added to the computations demonstrated within the chapters. The information on using the Internet to shop for and buy a car has been updated. The mortgage loan section has been revised to better coordinate with the savings discussions in Chapter 4. Sidebar discussions focus on alternative sources of used cars, online new car shopping, a checklist for negotiating an auto lease, factors to consider about an auto lease, markets with the greatest real estate growth, and questions to consider before buying a home.

Chapter 6 on consumer credit and credit cards emphasizes the positive aspects of using credit, and what it takes to build and maintain a strong credit history. In addition to the usual chapter updating and streamlining, considerable attention is devoted to eliminating or sharply curtailing detail on bankruptcy proceedings. Instead, we greatly expanded the discussion of FICO scores, including how they're used, what goes into them, and steps you can take to build up your own FICO score. Also added to this edition is discussion of the new uniform credit-scoring system (VantageScore) that was introduced by the big-3 national credit bureaus in 2006, and a new *Money in Action* box on how to get some of the benefits of a credit card from your debit card.

Chapter 7 on using consumer loans focuses on the benefits and uses of consumer credit, in the forms of both single-payment and installment loans. The discussion concentrates on the key issues surrounding the decision to use these types of loans, including loan provisions, finance charges, and other credit considerations. As part of the revision process, the discussion of student loans is updated and expanded to provide more detail about the terms and provisions of federally sponsored student loans, including a new table that compares the key provisions of these programs. At the same time, the material on sources of consumer loans is tightened-up considerably to provide focused discussion of the major lenders.

Chapter 8 on insuring your life has been thoroughly updated and refined to improve readability and comprehension. The needs analysis demonstration and related worksheet have been relabeled to make the process easier to follow. Practical sidebar material appearing in this chapter includes questions to ask before buying insurance, the effect of insurance company ownership on premiums, expectations for a life insurance medical exam, how to understand an insurance illustration, and how to file a life insurance claim. Descriptions of Internet resources and advice on buying life insurance online have been updated.

Chapter 9 on insuring your health includes the latest industry and policy data that focuses on the growing cost of health insurance and how to minimize healthcare costs. A brief discussion of the new Medicare prescription drug coverage has been added. Some exhibits have been eliminated and other discussions streamlined to better focus the chapter on the most important material. Practical sidebar material includes the pricing of student health insurance, key questions for choosing a healthcare plan, data on workers taking health care benefits offered by employers, filling the health insurance gap when changing group carriers or starting a new job, standards for a good long-term care policy, and tips for reducing the cost of disability income insurance.

Chapter 10 on protecting your property has been streamlined for improved readability. The exhibit that illustrates the calculation of replacement cost has been updated to reflect current values. The sample auto policy has also been updated. A new discussion of underinsured motorists coverage has been added to the section on uninsured motorists coverage. Practical sidebar discussions offer tips and strategies for lowering property and liability insurance premiums data on high-risk cars, and advice on what to do when a claim is denied. We continue to emphasize practical advice for reducing homeowner's insurance premiums, filing auto insurance claims, preventing auto theft, and obtaining discounts for auto safety and good driving.

Chapter 11 on investment planning is thoroughly revised and updated to reflect the many ongoing developments in this area. Added to the material on securities markets is a new section on *Broker Markets and Dealer Markets;* this material looks at the secondary markets from the perspective of how trades are executed, rather than whether the trading takes place on listed exchanges, NASDAQ, or OTC markets. The NASDAQ and OTC markets are now treated as totally separate entities; as a result, the discussion covers key trading mechanisms and basic operating procedures for each market, including, for example, the new NASDAQ Global Select market and the OTC Bulletin Board. We also added new *Financial Road Signs* features that looks at the continued decline in the number of individuals investing directly in stocks, rather than through mutual funds and the like, and another that describes different types of limit orders.

Chapter 12 on investing in stocks and bonds continues to emphasize the risk/return characteristics of these securities. As part of the revision process, all the return behavior and security performance material for both stocks and bonds is updated. In addition, we've added a new section on stock valuation showing the worksheet approach used by investment clubs, as well as a new *Money in Action* box on what to look for in annual reports. In the material on bonds, we now show how to find the yield to maturity on bonds using semiannual compounding, and we've also added a section on how bonds are priced in the marketplace.

Chapter 13 on investing in mutual funds is expanded to include *real estate.* Now titled "Investing in Mutual Funds and Real Estate," the chapter provides readers with a new section on the principles and properties of investing in real estate, including the widespread use of leverage, and various ways of investing in income-producing properties, from commercial and residential properties to buying homes as investment vehicles. We end this material by looking at two alternatives to directly investing in real estate: real estate limited partnerships and real estate investment trusts (REITs). Most of this chapter still deals with mutual funds, and all the material is condensed significantly so as to enhance readability. Also, all market statistics and performance data are updated, as necessary. In addition, a new *Money in Action* box addresses the issue of how to select mutual funds to include in company-sponsored pension programs, like 401(k)s.

Chapter 14 on planning for retirement is thoroughly updated and streamlined for improved clarity; also, each of the various retirement/pension programs (including Social Security, company-sponsored plans, and self-directed programs) is carefully updated to reflect the latest guidelines, limitations, and requirements, including those contained in the Pension Protection Act of 2006. In addition, new material is added on the latest type of company-sponsored pension plan, the so-called Roth 401(k). We also expanded the discussion of cash balance plans, in light of the much bigger role that these types of plans will likely play in the future. And for much the same reason, we added some discussion and a new *Money in Action* box that address the growing problem of pension freezes and defaults, and the role that the Pension Benefit Guarantee Corporation plays in these situations.

Chapter 15 on preserving your estate has been updated to reflect the most recent estate tax laws and tax rates. The coverage has been improved to make this important technical subject more accessible. The worksheet for computing federal estate tax due has been changed to reflect the current calculation, and the table of federal estate tax credits has been correspondingly eliminated. Valuable links include a comprehensive guide on what to do when a loved one dies and additional information on ethical wills and trusts. Useful sidebar material covers discussing end-of-life issues with family members, the excuses people use to avoid estate planning, tips for choosing a guardian for children, will-writing pointers, and how to use trusts effectively.

ORGANIZATION OF THE BOOK

Personal Financial Planning is divided into six parts. Part One presents the foundations of personal financial planning, beginning with the financial planning process and then covering financial statements and plans, and taxes. Part Two concerns the management of basic assets, including cash and savings instruments, automobiles, and housing. Part Three covers credit management, including the various types of open account borrowing and consumer loans. Part Four deals with managing insurance needs, and considers life insurance, health-care insurance, and property insurance. Part Five covers investments, including stocks, bonds, mutual funds, and real estate, and how to make transactions in securities markets. Part Six is devoted to retirement and estate planning. Web-based part cases and CFP® exam questions are available online as part of the Gitman/Joehnk ThomsonNOW product.

PEDAGOGY

Each chapter opens with six learning goals that link the material covered to specific learning outcomes and, as noted earlier, anchor the text's *integrated learning system*. Then, at the end of each of the major sections are *Concept Check* questions that allow readers to confirm their understanding of the material before moving on to the next section.

Each chapter contains a *Money in Action* feature that consists of brief discussions of relevant personal financial planning material that serve to enrich the topical coverage. At the end of each of these features are *Critical Thinking Questions*. Also in each chapter are three or four *Financial Road Signs,* which provide important hints or suggestions to consider when implementing certain parts of a financial plan, such as "Should You Buy or Lease Your Next Car," "Five Questions to Ask Before Buying a Mutual Fund," "Keeping Up Your FICO Score," and "No Payments, No Interest—What a Deal." *Worksheets,* which are typically filled in and discussed, are included to simplify demonstration of various calculations and procedures and to provide students with helpful materials they can use in managing their own personal finances. The worksheets are numbered to provide convenient reference to them in the end-of-chapter problems, and they include descriptive captions. Numerous exhibits, each containing descriptive captions, are used throughout to more fully illustrate key points in the text. Also included in each chapter is a *running glossary* that appears in the margin and provides brief definitions of all highlighted terms in the accompanying text.

Most chapters contain discussions and illustrations of how both the Internet and the personal computer can be used in various phases of personal financial planning. In addition, each chapter contains as many as six to eight *Smart Sites,* each of which directs the reader to specific Internet sites that deal with the topic(s) being discussed at that point, and that enable the reader to broaden his or her understanding of key financial planning concepts. End-of-chapter material includes a *Summary* that restates each learning goal and follows it with a brief paragraph that summarizes the material related to it. The next element is *Financial Planning Exercises,* which include questions and problems that students can use to test their grasp of the material. That's followed by *Applying Personal Finance,* which generally involves some type of outside project or exercise. Two *Critical Thinking Cases* highlighting the important analytical topics and concepts are also supplied. Following the cases is the new and improved *Money Online* element that provides links to helpful Web addresses, home page descriptions, and a series of Web-related interactive exercises.

SUPPLEMENTARY MATERIALS

Recognizing the importance of outstanding support materials to the instructor and the student, we have continued to improve and expand our supplements package.

Instructor Supplements

ThomsonNOW

Designed by the instructor for the instructor, **ThomsonNOW for Finance** is the most reliable, flexible, and easy-to-use online suite of services and resources. **ThomsonNOW for Finance** takes the best of current technology tools including online homework management, an electronic test bank, and course support materials such as online quizzing and tutorials to support your course goals and save you significant preparation and grading time!

- **Plan** student assignments with an easy online homework management component.
- **Manage** your grade book with ease.
- **Teach** today's student using valuable course support materials.
- **Reinforce** student comprehension with Personalized Study.
- **Test** with an electronic test bank.
- **Grade** automatically for seamless, immediate results.

This powerful, fully integrated online teaching and learning system provides you with the ultimate in flexibility, ease of use, and efficient paths to success to deliver the results you want—NOW!

For more information visit **http://www.thomsonedu.com/thomsonnow** today!

Instructor's Manual and Test Bank

A comprehensive *Instructor's Manual* has been prepared to assist the instructor. For each chapter, the manual includes

- An outline
- Discussion of major topics
- A list of key concepts
- Solutions to all *Concept Check* questions, end-of-chapter financial planning exercises, and cases

The *Test Bank* has been revised, updated, and expanded. It includes true-false and multiple-choice questions, as well as four to six short problems for nearly every chapter. Both the Instructor's Manual and the Test Bank are revised by Peggy Ward at Wichita State University.

Computerized Test Bank

A computerized version of the printed test bank is available in Windows Microsoft Word® featuring Thomson South-Western's computerized test bank program, ExamView, which has many features that allow the instructor to modify test questions, select items by key words, and scramble tests for multiple class sections online. There is also the option to create your own questions or instructions and print out answer sheets. You can also create and administer quizzes online, using the Internet, local-area networks, or wide-area networks.

PowerPoint®

For instructors who enjoy working with computerized presentations, we have a complete lecture presentation in PowerPoint. Available to instructors on the text Web site, each chapter's file consists of a general outline that includes key concepts and key figures and tables from the book. Instructors can easily modify the presentations using PowerPoint's many features.

Student Supplements

Gitman/Joehnk ThomsonNOW Web site—
http://www.thomsonedu.com/thomsonnow

Access to the Gitman/Joehnk ThomsonNOW Web site may be included via a unique serial number with each new copy of the textbook. The Gitman/Joehnk ThomsonNOW site provides a wealth of study tools using some of the most advanced technology features available in the personal financial planning course area, integrated in one location and organized by chapter. It includes the Personal Financial Planning Software, electronic Worksheets, End of Part Cases, CFP® Exam Questions, and Pre- and Post-Tests. Used book buyers may purchase access to the Gitman/Joehnk ThomsonNOW Web site online.

Personal Financial Planning Software

The Personal Financial Planning software, available online as part of the Gitman/Joehnk ThomsonNOW site, performs like many of the widely used commercially available software packages and is completely interactive. Best of all, being user-friendly, it streamlines the record-keeping and problem-solving activities presented in the text. Most of the worksheets used in the text correspond to the software to provide assistance in applying some of the complex procedures, ranging from financial statement and budget preparation to investment management and retirement planning. In addition to various interactive calculations performed by the software, the program also contains cutting-edge applications that differentiate it from more generic personal financial planning software. These applications include *graphing capabilities* (with several of the time value and asset valuation computations) that allow the user to immediately see the impact of changes to the input variables.

Interactive Worksheets

Interactive *Worksheets* identical to those presented in the text are on the Gitman/Joehnk ThomsonNOW site. Each worksheet provides a logical format for dealing with some aspect of personal financial planning such as preparation of a cash budget, home affordability analysis, or an automobile lease versus purchase analysis. Providing worksheets electronically allows students to complete them multiple times for mastery, and many of the worksheets can actually be used to calculate figures needed to make financial decisions.

Product Support Web Site

The product support Web site at **http://www.thomsonedu.com/finance/gitman** includes relevant Internet exercises and URLs presented in the text, along with supplements available for download for qualified instructors. It also contains links to a wealth of finance resources available from Thomson South-Western, such as NewsWire: Finance in the News, ThomsonNOW, and more.

ACKNOWLEDGMENTS

In addition to the many individuals who made significant contributions to this book by their expertise, classroom experience, guidance, general advice, and reassurance, we also appreciate the students and faculty who used the book and provided valuable feedback on it, confirming our conviction that a truly teachable personal financial planning text could be developed.

Of course, we are indebted to all the academicians and practitioners who have created the body of knowledge contained in this text. We particularly wish to thank several people who gave the most significant help in developing and revising it. They include attorney Robert J. Wright of Wright & Wright, CPAs, for his assistance in the chapter on taxes, John C. Bost Esq., of San Diego State University, for his help in revising and updating the estate planning chapter, and Marlene Bellamy of Writeline Associates, for her help with the real estate material.

Thomson South-Western shared our objective of producing a truly teachable text and relied on the experience and advice of numerous excellent reviewers for the eleventh edition: Wayne H. Gawlick, MBA, M.Ed., Joliet Junior College; Henry C. Hill, Blinn College; Gordon Karels, University of Nebraska–Lincoln; Aaron L. Phillips, California State University–Bakersfield; Margaret P. Reed, University of Cincinnati; Dr. Frank A. Thompson, University of Northern Iowa; Dick Verrone, University of North Carolina–Wilmington; Peggy Bergmeier Ward, Wichita State University; Brock Williams, Metropolitan Community College–Fort Omaha.

We also appreciate the many suggestions from previous reviewers, all of whom have had a significant impact on the earlier editions of this book. Our thanks go to the following: Linda Afdahl, Micheal J. Ahern III, Robert J. Angell, H. Kent Baker, Harold David Barr, Catherine L. Bertelson, Steve Blank, Kathleen K. Bromley, D. Gary Carman, Dan Casey, P. R. Chandy, Tony Cherin, Larry A. Cox, Maurice L. Crawford, Carlene Creviston, Rosa Lea Danielson, William B. Dillon, David Durst, Jeanette A. Eberle, Mary Ellen Edmundson, Ronald Ehresman, Jim Farris, Stephen Ferris, Eric W. Hayden ,Sharon Hatten Garrison, Alan Goldfarb, Carol Zirnheld Green, Joseph D. Greene, C. R. Griffen, John L. Grimm, Chris Hajdas, James Haltman, Vickie L. Hampton, Forest Harlow, Kendall B. Hill, Darrell D. Hilliker, Arlene Holyoak, Marilynn E. Hood, Frank Inciardi, Ray Jackson, Kenneth Jacques,

Dixie Porter Johnson, Ted Jones, William W. Jones, Judy Kamm, Peggy Keck, Gary L. Killion, Earnest W. King, Karol Kitt, George Klander, Xymena S. Kulsrud, Carole J. Makela, Paul J. Maloney, David Manifold, Charles E. Maxwell, Charles W. McKinney, Robert W. McLeod, George Muscal, Robert Nash, Ed Nelling, Charles O'Conner, Albert Pender, Armand Picou, Franklin Potts, Fred Power, Alan Raedels, Charles F. Richardson, Arnold M. Rieger, Vivian Rippentrop, Gayle M. Ross, Kenneth H. St. Clair, Brent T. Sjaardema, Thomas M. Springer, Rosemary Walker, Tom Warschauer, Gary Watts, Grant J. Wells, Janet Bear Wolverton, Betty Wright, and R. R. Zilkowski.

Because of the wide variety of topics covered in this book, we called on many experts for whose insight on recent developments we are deeply grateful. We would like to thank them and their firms for allowing us to draw on their knowledge and resources, particularly Robert Andrews; Willis M. Allen Co. Realtors; Bill Bachrach, Bachrach & Associates; Mark D. Erwin, Commonwealth Financial Network; Robin Gitman, Willis M. Allen Co. Realtors; Craig Gussin, CLU, Auerbach & Gussin; John Markese, President of the American Association of Individual Investors; Frank Hathaway, CFA, Chief Economist, NASDAQ; Aaron Kohn, CFM, Merrill Lynch Global Private Client Group, Mark Nussbaum, CFP®, UBS Financial Services, Inc.; Sherri Tobin, Farmers Insurance Group; Fred Weaver, Washington Mutual; Karen Weston, Coldwell Banker Realtors; Keith Wibel, CFA, Foothills Asset Management; and Lynn Yturri, CFA, Bank One Investment Management. We would like to thank Cynthia Arnold for her assistance with updating and creating new *Money in Action* features, Wayne Gawlik of Joliet Junior College for his extensive work on materials for the ThomsonNOW online product, and Ellen Marsden for her revision of the online quiz material.

The editorial staff of Thomson South-Western has been most helpful in our endeavors. We wish to thank Starratt Alexander, Content Project Manager; Matt McKinney, Sr. Technology Project Editor; Jason Krall, Marketing Manager; and Adele Scholtz, Editorial Assistant. Special thanks go to Steve Momper, Publisher, and Susan Smart, Senior Developmental Editor, without whose support this revision would not have been as lively and contemporary in approach as we believe it is and whose expert management of the writing and reviewing of the text proved invaluable. We are also grateful to Lori Kozey of Lachina Publishing Services, who ably assured the book's timely and accurate production.

Finally, our wives, Robin and Charlene, have provided needed support and understanding during the writing of this book. We are forever grateful to them.

Lawrence J. Gitman, CFP®
La Jolla, California

Michael D. Joehnk, CFA
Flagstaff, Arizona
January 2007

Lawrence J. Gitman is an emeritus professor of finance at San Diego State University. He received his bachelor's degree from Purdue University, his M.B.A. from the University of Dayton, and his Ph.D. from the University of Cincinnati. Professor Gitman is a prolific textbook author and has more than fifty articles appearing in *Financial Management*, the *Financial Review*, the *Journal of Financial Planning*, the *Journal of Risk and Insurance*, the *Financial Services Review*, the *Journal of Financial Research, Financial Practice and Education*, the *Journal of Financial Education*, and other scholarly publications.

His major textbooks include *The Future of Business*, Sixth Edition, and *The Future of Business: The Essentials, Third Edition*, which are both coauthored with Carl McDaniel; *Fundamentals of Investing*, Tenth Edition, which is coauthored with Michael D. Joehnk. Gitman and Joehnk also wrote *Investment Fundamentals: A Guide to Becoming a Knowledgeable Investor*, which was selected as one of 1988's ten best personal finance books by *Money* magazine; *Corporate Finance*, Second Edition, which is coauthored with Scott B. Smart and William L. Megginson; *Principles of Managerial Finance*, Fourth Brief Edition; *Principles of Managerial Finance*, Eleventh Edition; *Foundations of Managerial Finance*, Fourth Edition; and *Introduction to Finance*, which is coauthored with Jeff Madura.

An active member of numerous professional organizations, Professor Gitman is past president of the Academy of Financial Services, the San Diego Chapter of the Financial Executives Institute, the Midwest Finance Association, and the FMA National Honor Society. In addition, he is a Certified Financial Planner® (CFP®). Gitman formerly served as a Director on the CFP® Board of Governors, as Vice-President–Financial Education for the Financial Management Association, and as Director of the San Diego MIT Enterprise Forum. He has two grown children and lives with his wife in La Jolla, California, where he is an avid bicyclist.

Michael D. Joehnk is an emeritus professor of finance at Arizona State University. In addition to his academic appointments at ASU, Professor Joehnk spent a year (1999) as a visiting professor of finance at the University of Otago in New Zealand. He received his bachelor's and Ph.D. degrees from the University of Arizona and his M.B.A. from Arizona State University. A Chartered Financial Analyst (CFA), he has served as a member of the Candidate Curriculum Committee and of the Council of Examiners of the Institute of Chartered Financial Analysts. He has also served as a director of the Phoenix Society of Financial Analysts, secretary-treasurer of the Western Finance Association, and was elected to two terms as a vice-president of the Financial Management Association. Professor Joehnk is the author or coauthor of some fifty articles, five books, and numerous monographs. His articles have appeared in *Financial Management*, the *Journal of Finance*, the *Journal of Bank Research*, the *Journal of Portfolio Management*, the *Journal of Consumer Affairs*, the *Journal of Financial and Quantitative Analysis*, the *AAII Journal*, the *Journal of Financial Research*, the *Bell Journal of Economics*, the *Daily Bond Buyer, Financial Planner*, and other publications.

In addition to coauthoring several books with Lawrence J. Gitman, Professor Joehnk was the author of a highly successful paperback trade book, *Investing for Safety's Sake*. In addition, Dr. Joehnk was the editor of *Institutional Asset Allocation*, which was sponsored by the Institute of Chartered Financial Analysts and published by Dow Jones-Irwin. He also was a contributor to the *Handbook for Fixed Income Securities*, and *Investing and Risk Management*—Vol. 1 of the Library of Investment Banking. In addition, he served a 6-year term as executive co-editor of the *Journal of Financial Research*. He and his wife live in Flagstaff, Arizona, where they enjoy hiking and other activities in the nearby mountains and canyons.

PART 1 > Foundations of Financial Planning

Understanding the Financial Planning Process

LG1	●	Identify the benefits of using personal financial planning techniques to manage your finances.	p. 2
LG2	●	Describe the personal financial planning process and define your goals.	p. 6
LG3	●	Explain the life cycle of financial plans and their role in achieving your financial goals.	p. 13
LG4	●	Examine the economic environment's influence on personal financial planning.	p. 18
LG5	●	Evaluate the impact of age, education, and geographic location on personal income.	p. 22
LG6	●	Understand the importance of career choices and their relationship to personal financial planning.	p. 22
	●		

LG1 THE REWARDS OF SOUND FINANCIAL PLANNING

What does living "the good life" mean to you? Is it owning a home in a certain part of town, starting a company, being debt free, driving a particular type of car, taking luxury vacations, or having a large investment portfolio? Today's complex, fast-paced world offers a bewildering array of choices. Add to this a rapidly changing economic, political, technological, and social environment, and it's easy to see why developing solid financial strategies, guaranteed to improve your lifestyle, is increasingly difficult. Today a couple may need two incomes just to maintain an acceptable standard of living, and they may have to wait longer to buy a home. Clearly, no matter how you define it, the good life requires sound planning to turn financial goals into reality.

The best way to achieve financial objectives is through *personal financial planning*. It helps us define our financial goals and develop appropriate strategies to reach them. We can no longer depend on employee or government benefits such as steady salary increases, or adequate funding from employer-paid pensions or Social Security, to retire comfortably. Creating flexible plans and regularly revising them is the key to building a sound financial future. And successful financial planning brings rewards, such as an improved standard of living, wise spending habits, and increased wealth. Of course, planning alone does not guarantee success; but having an effective, consistent plan can help you use your resources wisely.

The goal of this book is to remove the mystery from the personal financial planning process and replace it with the tools you need to take charge of your personal finances and your life. To organize this process, the text is divided into six parts:

- **Part 1:** Foundations of Financial Planning
- **Part 2:** Managing Basic Assets
- **Part 3:** Managing Credit
- **Part 4:** Managing Insurance Needs
- **Part 5:** Managing Investments
- **Part 6:** Retirement and Estate Planning

Each part explains a different aspect of personal financial planning as shown in Exhibit 1.1. This organizational scheme revolves around financial decision making that's firmly based on an operational set of financial plans. We believe that through sound financial planning, individuals can make decisions that will produce their desired results. Starting with Part 1, where we look at personal financial statements, plans, and taxes, we move through the various types of decisions you'll make when implementing a financial plan.

Improving Your Standard of Living

With personal financial planning we learn to acquire, use, and control our financial resources more efficiently. It allows us to gain more enjoyment from our income and thus improve our **standard of living**—the necessities, comforts, and luxuries we have or desire.

Americans view standards of living and what constitutes necessities and luxuries differently depending on their level of affluence. For example, 45 percent of Americans consider a second or vacation home the ultimate symbol of affluence, while others see taking two or more annual vacations or living in an exclusive neighborhood as an indicator of wealth.

So our quality of life is closely tied to our standard of living. Although other factors— geographic location, public facilities, local cost of living, pollution, traffic, and population density—also affect quality of life, wealth is commonly viewed as its primary determinant. The presence or absence of material items such as a house, car, and clothing, and having money available for healthcare, education, art, music, travel, and entertainment, contribute to our quality of life. Of course, many so-called wealthy people live "plain" lives, choosing to save or invest or support philanthropic organizations with their money, rather than indulge themselves with luxuries.

standard of living The necessities, comforts, and luxuries enjoyed or desired by an individual or family.

One trend with a profound effect on our standard of living is the *two-income family*. What was relatively rare in the early 1970s has become commonplace today, and the

EXHIBIT 1.1   Organizational Planning Model

This text emphasizes making financial decisions regarding assets, credit, insurance, investments, and retirement and estates.

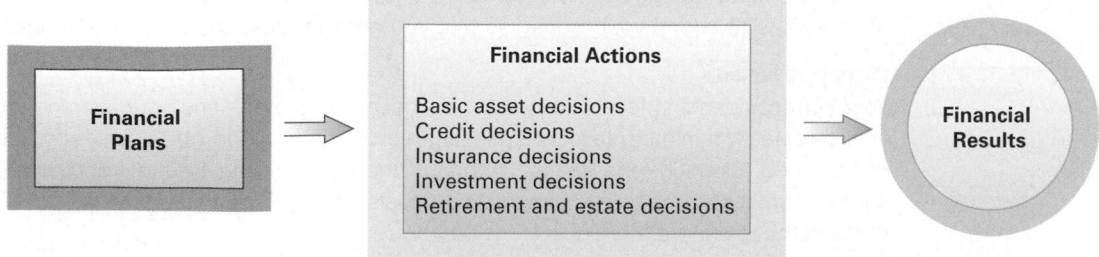

Financial Plans → **Financial Actions**: Basic asset decisions, Credit decisions, Insurance decisions, Investment decisions, Retirement and estate decisions → **Financial Results**

HOW AMERICANS FEEL ABOUT MONEY

Since World War II, inflation-adjusted income has nearly tripled and the size of new homes has more than doubled. Yet polls show that the wealthiest Americans aren't any happier than those with less money. At an annual income of about $50,000, the happiness curve flattens out. However, a sense of control over finances does correlate with happiness. To feel secure (and happy), Americans need to have enough money to retire, buy things they want, and cope with a financial setback. These and other poll findings offer insights into our attitudes toward money matters.

According to a recent survey on Americans and their money, 54 percent of adults said one of their biggest money pressures right now is just meeting their bills. Their top financial priority was getting out of debt (71 percent). Owning a home free and clear (52 percent) and taking one luxury vacation every year (33 percent) were two other important goals.

The rich are not so different from the average American. They want bigger financial cushions (85 percent) and have significant debt loads (42 percent are spending less so they can pay off bills). Their most pressing financial concerns were retirement planning (34 percent), wealth accumulation (19 percent), and supporting their families (18 percent). Most of the rich consider themselves middle class, not wealthy. They say they need $2.5 million to feel wealthy and the best ways to increase wealth are to invest in real estate (19 percent), get a professional degree (15 percent), inherit money (14 percent), invest in stock (12 percent), or start a business (12 percent).

Gender differences also affect the way Americans think about money. Most married adults share all their money, but 28 percent of women and 20 percent of men maintain separate accounts. Women tend to be more conservative and less confident than male investors, but 80 percent of women say they're more knowledgeable about investing than they were 5 years ago. Historically most women weren't involved in their families' financial planning, but their role is evolving as more (63 percent) participate in investment decisions.

Critical Thinking Questions

1. What, if any, is the correlation between income and happiness?
2. What are some common financial concerns of Americans today?
3. What role does gender play in how Americans think about money?

Sources: Marion Asnes with Andy Borinstein and Douglas King, "The Changing Face of Affluence," *Money*, September 27, 2002, p. 42; Gini Kopecky Wallace, "Can Money Buy Happiness?" *Family Circle*, April 15, 2003, pp. 64–68; Jean Sherman Chatzky, "Women & Money," *Money*, June 1, 2002, p. 150; Jean Sherman Chatzky, "The 10 Commandments of Financial Happiness," *Money*, October 1, 2003, p. 113.

incomes of millions of families have risen sharply as a result. Seventy-five percent of married adults say they and their mate share all their money, while some partners admit to having a secret stash of cash. Two incomes buy more but also require greater responsibility to manage the money wisely and coordinate the partners' financial and career goals.

Spending Money Wisely

Using money wisely is a major benefit of financial planning. Whatever your income, you can either spend it now or save some of it for the future. Determining your current and future spending patterns is an important part of personal money management. The goal, of course, is to spend your money so that you get the most satisfaction from each dollar.

Current Needs

Your current spending level is based on the necessities of life and your average propensity to consume. A minimum level of spending would allow you to obtain only the necessities of life: food, clothing, and shelter. Although the quantity and type of food, clothing, and shelter purchased may differ among individuals depending on their wealth, we all need these items to survive.

Average propensity to consume refers to the percentage of each dollar of income, on average, that is spent for current needs rather than savings. Some people with high average propensities to consume earn low incomes and spend a large portion of it for basic necessities. On the other hand, many "ultraconsumers" choose to splurge on a few items and scrimp elsewhere. These people also exhibit high average propensities to consume. Conversely, individuals earning large amounts quite often have low average propensities to consume, because the cost of necessities represents only a small part of their income.

Still, it's not unusual to find two people with significantly different incomes but the same average propensity to consume due to differences in their standard of living. The person making more money may believe it is essential to buy better-quality items or more items and will thus, on average, spend the same percentage of each dollar of income as the person making far less. The *Money in Action* box on page 4 reveals some of our attitudes toward getting and keeping wealth.

Future Needs

In any carefully developed financial plan, you should set aside a portion of current income for deferred, or future, spending. Placing these funds in various savings and investment vehicles allows you to generate a return on your funds until you need them. For example, you may want to build up a retirement fund to maintain a desirable standard of living in your later years. Instead of spending the money now, you defer actual spending until the future when you retire.

Thirty-four percent of Americans say retirement planning is their most pressing financial concern. Other examples of deferred spending include saving for a child's education, a primary residence or vacation home, a major acquisition (such as a car or home entertainment center), or even a vacation.

The portion of current income we commit to future needs is a function of how much we earn and our average propensity to consume. Forty-five percent of affluent Americans say they need at least $2.5 million to feel rich. The more we earn and the less we devote to current spending, the more we can commit to meeting future needs. In any case, some portion of current income should be set aside regularly for future use. This practice creates good saving habits.

average propensity to consume The percentage of each dollar of income, on average, that a person spends for current needs rather than savings.

wealth The total value of all items owned by an individual, such as savings accounts, stocks, bonds, home, and automobiles.

financial assets Intangible assets, such as savings accounts and securities, that are acquired for some promised future return.

tangible assets Physical assets, such as real estate and automobiles, that can be held for either consumption or investment purposes.

Accumulating Wealth

In addition to using current income to pay the everyday expenses of living, we spend it to acquire assets such as cars, a home, or stocks and bonds. Our assets largely determine how wealthy we are. Personal financial planning plays a critical role in the accumulation of wealth by helping to direct our financial resources to the most productive areas.

As a rule, a person's **wealth** is a function of the total value of all the items he or she owns. Wealth consists of financial and tangible assets. **Financial assets** are intangible, paper assets, such as savings accounts and securities (stocks, bonds, mutual funds, and so forth). They are *earning assets* that are held for the returns they promise. **Tangible assets,** in contrast, are physical assets, such as real estate and automobiles, that can be held for either consumption (like your home, car, artwork, or jewelry) or investment purposes (like the duplex you bought for rental purposes). In general, the goal of most people is to accumulate as much wealth as possible while maintaining current consumption at a level that provides a desired standard of living. To see how you compare with the typical American in financial terms, check out the statistics in Exhibit 1.2.

EXHIBIT 1.2

The Average American, Financially Speaking

This financial snapshot of the "average American" gives you an idea of where you stand in terms of income, net worth, and other measures. It should help you set some goals for the future.

	Income and Assets
What Do We Earn? (*average*)	
All familes	$ 70,700
Self-employed	141,500
Retired	43,200
What Are We Worth? (*average*)	
All familes	$ 448,200
Self-employed	1,423,200
Retired	469,000
Home Ownership (*average*)	
Value of primary residence	$246,800
Equity in primary residence	61,200
Mortgage on primary residence	185,600
How Much Savings Do We Have? (*average*)	
Mutual funds	$14,700
Individual stocks	17,600
Bank accounts	13,200
Retirement accounts	32,000

Source: Adapted from Brian K. Buck, Arthur B. Kennickell, and Kevin B. Moore, "Recent Changes in U.S. Family Finances: Evidence from the 2001 and 2004 Survey of Consumer Finances," *Federal Reserve Bulletin*, Board of Governors of the Federal Reserve System, Washington, D.C., February 2006, http://www.federalreserve.gov/pubs/oss/oss2/2004/bullo206.pdf.

❚❚ Concept Check

CHECK • CONCEPT CHECK • CONCEPT CHECK • CONCEPT CHECK • CONCEPT CHECK • CONCEPT CHECK • CONCEPT

1-1	What is a *standard of living*? What factors affect the quality of life?
1-2	Are consumption patterns related to quality of life? Explain.
1-3	What is *average propensity to consume*? Is it possible for two people with very different incomes to have the same average propensity to consume? Why?
1-4	Discuss the various forms in which wealth can be accumulated.

LG2   THE PERSONAL FINANCIAL PLANNING PROCESS

Many people erroneously assume that personal financial planning is only for the wealthy when nothing could be further from the truth. Whether you have a lot of money or not enough, you still need personal financial planning. If you have enough money, planning can help you spend and invest it wisely. If your income seems inadequate, taking steps to plan your financial activities will lead to an improved lifestyle. This is what **personal financial planning** is: a systematic process that considers the important elements of an individual's financial affairs and is aimed at fulfilling his or her financial goals.

Everyone needs to develop a personal financial plan—including recent college graduates, single professionals, young married couples, single parents, mid-career married breadwinners, and senior corporate executives. Knowing what you need to accomplish financially, and how you intend to do it, gives you an edge over someone who merely reacts to financial events as they unfold.

For example, purchasing a new car immediately after graduation may be an important goal for you. But buying a car is a major expenditure involving a large initial cash outlay and additional consumer debt that must be repaid over time. Therefore it warrants careful planning. Evaluating, and possibly even arranging, financing before your shopping trip, as opposed to simply accepting the financing arrangements offered by an auto dealer, might save you a considerable amount of money. Moreover, some dealers advertise low-interest loans but charge higher prices for their cars, so knowing all your costs in advance can help you identify the best deal. Using personal financial planning concepts to reach all your financial goals will bring similar positive benefits.

Steps in the Financial Planning Process

Take a closer look at financial planning, and you'll see that the process translates personal financial goals into specific financial plans and then helps you implement those plans through financial strategies. The financial planning process involves the six steps shown in Exhibit 1.3.

In effect, the financial planning process runs full circle. You start with financial goals, formulate and implement financial plans and strategies to reach them, monitor and control progress toward goals through budgets, and use financial statements to evaluate the plan and budget results. This leads you back to redefining your goals to better meet your current needs, and to revising your financial plans and strategies accordingly.

personal financial planning A systematic process that considers important elements of an individual's financial affairs in order to fulfill financial goals.

EXHIBIT 1.3   The Six-Step Financial Planning Process

The financial planning process translates personal financial goals into specific financial plans and strategies, implements them, and then uses budgets and financial statements to monitor, evaluate, and revise plans and strategies as needed. This process typically involves the six steps shown in sequence here.

1. Define financial goals.

2. Develop financial plans and strategies to achieve goals.

3. Implement financial plans and strategies.

4. Periodically develop and implement budgets to monitor and control progress toward goals.

5. Use financial statements to evaluate results of plans and budgets, taking corrective action as required.

6. Redefine goals and revise plans and strategies as personal circumstances change.

Let's now look at how goal setting fits into the planning process. In Chapters 2 and 3, we'll consider other information essential to creating your financial plans: personal financial statements, budgets, and taxes.

Defining Your Financial Goals

Financial goals are results that an individual wants to attain, such as buying a home, building a college fund, or achieving financial independence. What are your financial goals? Have you spelled them out? Without financial goals, it's impossible to effectively manage your financial resources. We need to know where we are going, in a financial sense, to effectively direct the major financial events in our lives. Perhaps achieving financial independence at a relatively early age is important to you. If so, then activities such as saving, investing, and retirement planning will be an important part of your financial life. Your financial goals or preferences must be stated in monetary terms because money, and the *utility* (defined later) it buys, is an integral part of financial planning.

The Role of Money

About 80 percent of Americans believe that money is power, and about 75 percent say that it is freedom. **Money** is the medium of exchange used as a measure of value in financial transactions. Without the standard unit of exchange provided by the dollar, it would be difficult to set specific personal financial goals and measure progress toward achieving them. Money, as we know it today, is the key consideration in establishing financial goals, yet it's not money as such that most people want. We want the **utility,** the amount of satisfaction received from buying certain types or quantities of goods and services, that money makes possible. People may choose one item over another because of a special feature that provides additional utility. For example, many people will pay more for a car with satellite radio than one with only a CD player. The added utility may result from the actual usefulness of the special feature, or from the "status" it's expected to provide, or both. Regardless, people receive varying levels of satisfaction from similar items, and their satisfaction isn't necessarily related to the cost of the items. When evaluating alternative qualities of life, spending patterns, and forms of wealth accumulation, we need to consider utility along with cost.

The Psychology of Money

Money and its utility are not only economic concepts; they're also closely linked to the psychological concepts of values, emotion, and personality. Your personal value system—the ideals and beliefs you hold important and use to guide your life—will also shape your attitude toward money and wealth accumulation. If status and image are important to you, you may spend a high proportion of your current income to acquire luxuries. If you place a high value on family life, you may choose a career that offers regular hours and less stress, or an employer who offers flextime rather than a higher-paying position requiring travel and lots of overtime. You may have plenty of money but choose to live frugally and do things yourself rather than hire someone to do them for you. Clearly then, financial goals and decisions are consistent with your personal values. By identifying your values, you can formulate financial plans that provide the greatest personal satisfaction and quality of life.

Money is a primary motivator of personal behavior because it has a strong effect on self-image. Each person's unique personality and emotional makeup determine the importance and role of money in his or her life. Depending on timing and circumstances, emotional responses to money may be positive—such as love, happiness, and security—or negative—such as fear, greed, and insecurity. For example, some people feel satisfaction in their work when they receive a paycheck. Others feel relief in knowing that they can pay past-due bills. Still others worry over what to do with the money. Some young people have a negative attitude toward money. You should become aware of your own attitudes toward money because they are the basis of your "money personality" and money management style. Exhibit 1.4 explores American attitudes toward money.

FINANCIAL ROAD SIGN

GETTING YOUR FINANCIAL ACT TOGETHER

Will this be the year you finally straighten out your finances? Here are five important things you can do to get your financial act together:
1. Start keeping good financial records.
2. Put together a realistic budget you can live with.
3. Save for a specific goal by paying yourself first.
4. Begin saving seriously for retirement.
5. Set up an emergency fund.

financial goals Results that an individual wants to attain, such as buying a home, building a college fund, or achieving financial independence.

money The medium of exchange used as a measure of value in financial transactions.

utility The amount of satisfaction received from purchasing certain types or quantities of goods and services.

EXHIBIT 1.4   Does Money Equal Happiness?

Money. Would life be sweeter if we had more of it? The answer is . . . maybe.

- 77 percent of adults believe that America is the land of financial opportunity.
- 85 percent agree that the rich get richer and the poor get poorer.
- 94 percent believe that corporate greed is out of control.
- 76 percent of Americans believe that money can't buy happiness.
- 84 percent of adults believe that Americans worship money.
- 70 percent say the love of money is the root of all evil.
- 29 percent chose being healthy over being rich.
- 70 percent of adults say it's as easy to love a rich person as a poor one.
- 69 percent say they are doing better than their parents did.
- 40 percent of seniors say they feel financially secure.

Source: Reprinted with permission of FAMILY CIRCLE magazine.

Some questions to ask yourself are: How important is money to you? Why? What types of spending give you satisfaction? Are you a risk taker? Do you need large financial reserves to feel secure? Knowing the answers to these questions is a prerequisite to developing realistic and effective financial goals and plans. For example, if you prefer immediate satisfaction, you will find it more difficult to achieve long-term net worth or savings goals than if you are highly disciplined and primarily concerned with achieving a comfortable retirement at an early age. Clearly, trade-offs between current and future benefits are strongly affected by values, emotions, and personality. Effective financial plans are both economically and psychologically sound. They must not only consider your wants, needs, and financial resources but also realistically reflect your personality and emotional reactions to money.

Money and Relationships

The average couple spends between 250 and 700 hours planning their wedding, and they spend an average of about $20,000 on the big day. But with all the hoopla surrounding the wedding day, many couples overlook one of the most important aspects of marriage—financial compatibility. Money can be one of the most emotional issues in any relationship, whether with a partner, your parents, or children. Most people are uncomfortable talking about money matters and avoid such discussions, even with their partners. However, differing opinions of how to spend money may threaten the stability of a marriage or cause arguments between parents and children. Learning to communicate with your partner about money is a critical step in developing effective financial plans.

© STOCKBYTE SILVER/GETTY IMAGES

Your parents will play an important role in your financial planning. As they age, you may have to assume greater responsibility for their care. Do you know what healthcare coverage and financial plans they have in place? Where do they keep important financial and legal documents? What preferences do they have for healthcare should they become incapacitated? Asking these questions may be difficult, but having the answers will save you many headaches.

As we noted earlier, there are many distinct money personality types. One person may be analytical and see money as a means of control, another may use it to express affection, and yet another may use it to boost self-esteem. When couples have very different attitudes toward money—for example, if one person likes to prepare detailed budgets but the other is an impulse shopper—conflicts are bound to arise.

The best way to resolve money disputes is to be aware of your partner's financial style, keep the lines of communication open, and be willing to compromise. It's highly unlikely that you can change your partner's style—or your own, for that matter—but you can work out your differences. Financial planning is an especially important part of the conflict resolution process.

To gain a better understanding of your differences, work together to establish a set of financial goals that takes into account each person's needs and values. For instance, you may be a risk taker who likes to speculate in the stock market, while your more cautious partner wants to put all your money into a savings account in case one of you loses your job. If you can agree on the amount of money you should have readily available in low-risk investments and savings accounts, you can then allocate a specific portion of your funds to riskier investments.

Types of Financial Goals

Financial goals cover a wide range of financial desires—from controlling living expenses to meeting retirement needs, from setting up a savings and investment program to minimizing your taxes. Other important financial goals include having enough money to live as well as possible now, being financially independent, sending children to college, and providing for retirement.

Financial goals should be defined as specifically as possible. Saying that you want to save money next year is not a specific goal. How much do you want to save, and for what purpose? A goal such as "save 10 percent of my take-home pay each month to start an investment program" states clearly what you want to do and why.

Because they're the basis of your financial plans, your goals should be realistic and attainable. If you set your savings goals too high—for example, 25 percent of your take-home pay when your basic living expenses already account for 85 percent of your take-home pay—your goal is unattainable and there's no way to meet it. But if savings goals are set too low, you may not accumulate enough for a meaningful investment program. If your goals are pipe dreams, they'll put the basic integrity of your financial plan at risk and be a source of

---

EXHIBIT 1.5 Financial Planning Reality Check

How realistic are your assumptions about your financial future? Take this reality check and see.

Assumption 1: You need only 75 percent of your preretirement income to maintain a comfortable lifestyle after you retire.

Reality: That figure is more likely to be 100 percent, because health costs are increasing, outpacing any savings gained by eliminating work-related expenses.

Assumption 2: You'll cover 50 percent or more of your living expenses with your pension and Social Security.

Reality: Social Security and company pension plan payments are decreasing, so anticipate using your 401(k) and other retirement savings for living expenses.

Assumption 3: You can retire at 60.

Reality: You'll need more savings than you think to stretch your retirement nest egg over your life expectancy. If you can't save more, you'll need to retire later or work part-time after retirement.

Assumption 4: It takes a few thousand dollars a year to accumulate enough to finance your child's college education.

Reality: College costs are climbing faster than inflation. You'll need to save at least $260,000 to fund your newborn's private college education. Investigate state-sponsored 529 college savings plans or expect to use loans.

Assumption 5: A 3-month emergency fund provides enough financial cushion.

Reality: Six months is the minimum, and a year is better, especially if your industry is prone to layoffs. It takes more than 4 months on average to find a new job.

Source: Adapted from Janice Revell, "Your Financial Reality Checkup," *Fortune,* June 16, 2003, pp. 90–96.

ongoing financial frustration. You must also use realistic assumptions when setting goals. Exhibit 1.5 will help you do a reality check.

It's important to involve your immediate family in the goal-setting process. When family members "buy into" the goals, it eliminates the potential for future conflicts and improves the family's chances for financial success. After defining and approving your goals, you can prepare appropriate cash budgets. Finally, you should assign priorities and a time frame to financial goals. Are they short-term goals for the next year, or intermediate or long-term goals, not to be realized for many more years? For example, saving for a vacation might be a medium-priority short-term goal, whereas buying a larger home may be a high-priority intermediate goal, and purchasing a vacation home a low-priority long-term goal. Normally, long-term financial goals are set first, followed by a series of corresponding short-term and intermediate goals. Your goals will continue to change with your life situation, as exhibit 1.6 demonstrates.

Putting Target Dates on Financial Goals

goal dates Target dates in the future when certain financial objectives are expected to be completed.

Financial goals are most effective when set with goal dates. **Goal dates** are target points in the future when you expect to achieve or complete certain financial objectives. They may serve as progress checkpoints toward some longer-term financial goals, or as deadlines for others. One goal may be to purchase a boat in 2012 (the goal date), another to

---

EXHIBIT 1.6   How Financial Goals Change With a Person's Life Situation

Financial goals are not static, but change continually over a lifetime. Here are some typical long-term, intermediate, and short-term goals for a number of different personal situations.

Personal Situation	Long-Term Goals (6+ years)	Intermediate Goals (2–5 years)	Short-Term Goals (1 year)
College senior	Begin an investment program Buy a condominium Earn a master's degree	Repay college loans Trade in car and upgrade to a nicer model Buy new furniture	Find a job Rent an apartment Get a bank credit card Buy a new stereo
Single, mid-20s	Begin law school Build an investment portfolio Save enough for a down payment on a home	Begin regular savings program Take a Caribbean vacation Buy life insurance Start a retirement fund	Prepare a budget Buy a new flat-screen television and TiVo Get additional job training Build an emergency fund Reduce expenses 10%
Married couple with children, late 30s	Diversify investment portfolio Buy a larger home	Buy a second car Increase college fund contributions Increase second income: from part time to full time	Repaint house Get braces for children Review life and disability insurance
Married couple with grown children, mid-50s	Decide whether to relocate when retired Retire at age 62 Travel to Europe and the Far East	Take cruise Shift investment portfolio into income-producing securities Sell house and buy smaller residence	Buy new furniture Review skills for possible career change

accumulate a net worth of $200,000 by 2023—goal dates of 2013 and 2018 could be set for the attainment of net worth of $10,000 and $110,000, respectively.

Long-Term Goals

Long-term financial goals should indicate wants and desires for a period covering about 6 years out to the next 30 or 40 years. Although it's difficult to pinpoint exactly what you will want 30 years from now, it's useful to establish some tentative long-term financial goals. Recognize, though, that long-term goals will change over time, and you'll need to revise them accordingly. If the goals seem too ambitious, you'll want to make them more realistic. If they're too conservative, you'll want to adjust them to a level that will encourage you to make financially responsible decisions rather than squander surplus funds.

Short-Term and Intermediate Goals

Short-term financial goals are set each year and cover a 12-month period. They include making substantial, regular contributions to savings or investments to accumulate your desired net worth. Intermediate goals bridge the gap between short- and long-term goals. Both should be consistent with established long-term goals. Short-term goals become the key input for the cash budget, a tool used to plan for short-term income and expenses. To define your short-term goals, consider your immediate goals, expected income for the year, and long-term goals. Short-term planning should also include establishing an emergency fund with 3 to 6 months' worth of income. This special savings account serves as a safety valve in case of financial emergencies such as a temporary loss of income.

Unless you attain your short-term goals, you probably won't achieve your intermediate or long-term goals. It's tempting to let the desire to spend now take priority over the need to save for the future. But, by making some short-term sacrifices now, you're more likely to have a comfortable future. If you don't realize this for another 10 or 20 years, you may discover that it's too late to reach some of your most important financial goals.

Worksheet 1.1 is a convenient way to summarize your personal financial goals. It groups them by time frame (short-term, intermediate, or long-term) and lists a priority for each goal (high/medium/low), a target date to reach the goal, and estimated cost.

We have filled out the form showing the goals Tim and Andrea Shepard set in December 2007. The Shepards were married in 2004, own a condominium in a midwestern suburb, and have no children. Because Tim and Andrea are 28 and 26 years old, they have set their longest-term financial goal 33 years from now, when they want to retire. Tim has just completed his fifth year as a marketing representative for a large auto products manufacturer. Andrea, a former elementary school teacher, finished her MBA in May 2007 and began working at a local advertising agency. Tim and Andrea love to travel and ski. They plan to start a family in a few years, but for now they want to develop some degree of financial stability and independence. Their goals include purchasing assets (clothes, stereo, furniture, car), reducing debt, reviewing insurance, increasing savings, and planning for retirement.

❚❚ Concept Check

1-5	What is the role of money in setting financial goals? What is the relationship of money to utility?
1-6	Explain why financial plans must be psychologically as well as economically sound. What is the best way to resolve money disputes in a relationship?
1-7	Explain why it is important to set realistically attainable financial goals. Select one of your personal financial goals and develop a brief financial plan for achieving it.
1-8	Distinguish between long-term, intermediate, and short-term financial goals. Give examples of each.

Set financial goals carefully and realistically, as they form the basis for your personal financial plans. Each goal should be clearly defined and have a priority, time frame, and cost estimate.

Personal Financial Goals

Name(s) __Tim and Andrea Shepard__   Date __December 27, 2007__

Short-Term Goals (1 year or less)

Goal	Priority	Target Date	Cost Estimate
Buy new tires and brakes for Ford Focus	High	Feb. 2008	$ 500
Buy career clothes for Andrea	High	May 2008	1,200
Take Colorado ski trip	Medium	Mar. 2008	1,800
Replace stereo components	Low	Sept. 2008	1,100
Buy new work clothes for Tim	Medium	June 2008	750

Intermediate Goals (2 to 5 years)

Goal	Priority	Target Date	Cost Estimate
Start family	High	2010	–
Repay all loans except mortgage	High	2011	$ 7,500
Trade Focus and buy larger car	High	2011	10,000
Buy new bedroom furniture	Low	2012	4,000
Take 2-week Hawaiian vacation	Medium	2009–10	5,000
Review insurance needs	High	2010	–
Accumulate $100,000 net worth	High	2012	–

Long-Term Goals (6+ years)

Goal	Priority	Target Date	Cost Estimate
Begin college fund	High	2013	?/year
Diversify/increase investment portfolio	High	2014	Varies
Buy larger home	High	2016	$250,000
Take European vacation	Low	2015	$ 10,000
Retire from jobs	High	2040	?
Increase college fund contributions	High	2015	–

LG3 FROM GOALS TO PLANS: A LIFETIME OF PLANNING

How will you achieve the financial goals you set for yourself? The answer, of course, lies in the financial plans you establish. Financial plans provide the roadmap for achieving your financial goals. The six-step financial planning process (introduced in Exhibit 1.3 on page 7) results in separate yet interrelated components covering all the important financial elements in your life. Some elements deal with the more immediate aspects of money management, such as preparing a budget to help manage spending. Others focus on acquiring major assets, controlling borrowing, reducing financial risk, providing for emergency funds and future wealth accumulation, taking advantage of and managing employer-sponsored benefits, deferring and minimizing your taxes, providing for financial security when you stop working, and ensuring an orderly and cost-effective transfer of assets to your heirs.

In addition to discussing your financial goals and attitudes toward money with your partner, you must allocate responsibility for money management tasks and decisions. Many couples make major decisions jointly and divide routine financial decision making on the basis of expertise and interest. Others, such as Anne and John North, believe it is important for their entire family to work together as a team to manage the family finances. They hold family financial meetings once every few months to help their children understand how the household money is spent. These meetings also serve as a forum for their children to request a raise in allowance, a new bike, or funds for a school trip. The entire family is involved in the decision-making process on how surplus funds will be allocated.

Giving children an allowance is a good way to start teaching them to budget and save. By setting their own financial goals and taking steps to reach them, they will develop their own money management skills.

The Life Cycle of Financial Plans

Financial planning is a dynamic process. As you move through different stages of your life, your needs and goals will change. But certain financial goals are important regardless of age. Having extra resources to fall back on in an economic downturn or period of unemployment should be a priority whether you are 25, 45, or 65. Some changes—a new job, marriage, children, moving to a new area—may be part of your original plan.

However, more often than not, you'll face unexpected "financial shocks" during your life: loss of a job, a car accident, divorce or death of a spouse, a long illness, or the need to support adult children or aging parents. With careful planning, you can get through tough times and prosper in good times. To weather life's financial storms, you need to plan ahead and take steps—for example, setting up an emergency fund or reducing monthly expenses—that will protect you and your family financially if a setback occurs.

As we move from childhood to retirement age, we traditionally go through different life stages. Exhibit 1.7 illustrates the various components of a typical *personal financial planning life cycle* as they relate to these different life stages. As we pass from one stage of maturation to the next, our patterns of income, home ownership, and debt also change. From early childhood, when we relied on our parents for support, to early adulthood, when we held our first jobs and started our families, we can see a noticeable change in income patterns. For example, those age 45–64 tend to have higher income than those younger than age 45. Thus, as our emphasis in life changes, so do the kinds of financial plans we need to pursue.

Today new career strategies—planned and unplanned job changes, or several different careers over a lifetime, for example—are common and may require revising financial plans. Many young people wait to marry and have children, first focusing on their careers and building a financial base. The families of women who interrupt their careers to stay home with their children, whether for 6 months or 6 years, will experience periods of reduced income. A divorce, a spouse's death, and remarriage can also drastically change your financial circumstances. Many people in their thirties, forties, and fifties may find themselves in the "sandwich generation," supporting their elderly parents while still raising their children and paying for college. And some people must cope with reduced income through lost jobs due to corporate downsizing or early retirement. We'll look at these and other special planning concerns in Chapter 2.

Plans to Achieve Your Financial Goals

As discussed earlier, financial goals can range from short-term goals such as saving for a new stereo to long-term goals such as saving enough to start your own business. Reaching your particular goals requires different types of financial planning. Let's take a brief look at what each major plan category includes.

Asset Acquisition Planning

One of the first categories of financial planning we typically encounter is asset acquisition. We accumulate *assets*—things we own—throughout our lives. These include *liquid assets* (cash, savings accounts, and money market funds) used to pay everyday expenses, *investments* (stocks, bonds, and mutual funds) acquired to earn a return, *personal property* (movable property such as automobiles, household furnishings, appliances, clothing, jew-

EXHIBIT 1.7   The Personal Financial Planning Life Cycle

As you move through life and your income patterns change, you'll typically have to pursue a variety of financial plans. For instance, when you graduate from college, you'll be focused on buying a car and a house, and you'll be concerned about health and automobile insurance to protect against loss.

elry, home electronics, and similar items), and *real property* (immovable property; land and anything fixed to it, such as a house). Chapters 4 and 5 focus on important considerations for managing liquid assets and other major assets such as automobiles and housing.

Liability and Insurance Planning

Another category of financial planning is liability planning. A *liability* is something we owe and is represented by the amount of debt we incur. We create liabilities by borrowing money. By the time most of us graduate from college, we have debts of some sort: education loans, car loans, credit card balances, and so on. Our borrowing needs typically increase as we acquire other assets such as a home, furnishings, and appliances. Whatever the source of credit, such transactions have one thing in common: *the debt must be repaid at some future time.* How we manage our debt burden is just as important as how we manage our assets. Managing credit effectively requires careful planning and is the topic of Chapters 6 and 7.

Obtaining adequate *insurance coverage* is also essential. Like borrowing money, obtaining insurance is generally something that's introduced relatively early in our life cycle (usually early in the family formation stage). Insurance is a way to reduce financial risk and protect both income (life, health, and disability insurance) and assets (property and liability insurance). Most consumers regard insurance as absolutely essential, and for good reason. One serious illness or accident can wipe out everything you have accumulated over years of hard work. But, having the wrong amount of insurance can be costly, too. We'll examine how to manage your insurance needs in Chapters 8, 9, and 10.

Savings and Investment Planning

As your income begins to increase, so does the importance of savings and investment planning. Initially, people save to establish an emergency fund for meeting unexpected expenses. Eventually, however, they devote greater attention to investing excess income as a means of accumulating wealth, either for major expenditures such as a child's college education or for retirement. They acquire wealth through savings and subsequent investing of funds in various investment vehicles—common or preferred stocks, government or corporate bonds, mutual

Smart.Sites

Link to the Learning Center at **http://www .thomsonedu.com/ finance/gitman** for helpful information on insurance coverage.

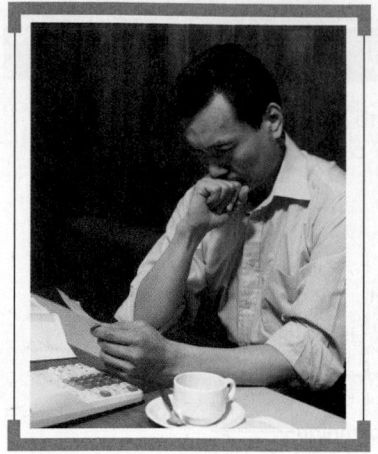

© DANIEL MACKIE/STONE

funds, real estate, and so on. The higher the returns on investments of excess funds, the greater wealth they accumulate.

Exhibit 1.8 shows the impact of alternative rates of return on accumulated wealth. The graph shows that if you had $1,000 today and could keep it invested at 8 percent, you would accumulate a considerable sum of money over time. For example, at the end of 40 years, you'd have $21,725 from your original $1,000. Earning a higher rate of return has even greater rewards. Some might assume that earning, say, 2 percentage points more—that is, 10 rather than 8 percent—would not matter a great deal. But it certainly would! Note that if you could earn 10 percent over the 40 years, you'd accumulate $45,259, or more than twice as much as you'd accumulate at 8 percent.

How long you keep your money invested is just as important as the rate of return you earn on your investments. With either rate of return, you can accumulate more than twice as much capital by investing for 40 rather than 30 years. This is the magic of compound interest, which explains why it's so important to create strong savings and investment habits early in life. We'll more fully examine compounding in Chapter 2, savings in Chapter 4, and investments in Chapters 11, 12, and 13.

Employee Benefit Planning

Your employer may offer a wide variety of employee benefit plans, especially if you work for a large firm. These could include life, health, and disability insurance; tuition reimbursement programs for continuing education; pension and profit-sharing plans, and 401(k) retirement plans; flexible spending accounts for child care and healthcare expenses; stock options; sick leave, personal time, and vacation days; and miscellaneous benefits such as employee discounts and subsidized meals or parking. Many of these plans are more fully described in later chapters.

Managing your employee benefit plans and coordinating them with your other plans is an important part of the overall financial planning process. For example, such benefits as

---

EXHIBIT 1.8　How a $1,000 Investment Grows over Time

Eight percent, 10 percent. What's the big deal? The deal is more than twice the money over a 40-year period! Through the power of compound interest, a higher return means dramatically more money as time goes on.

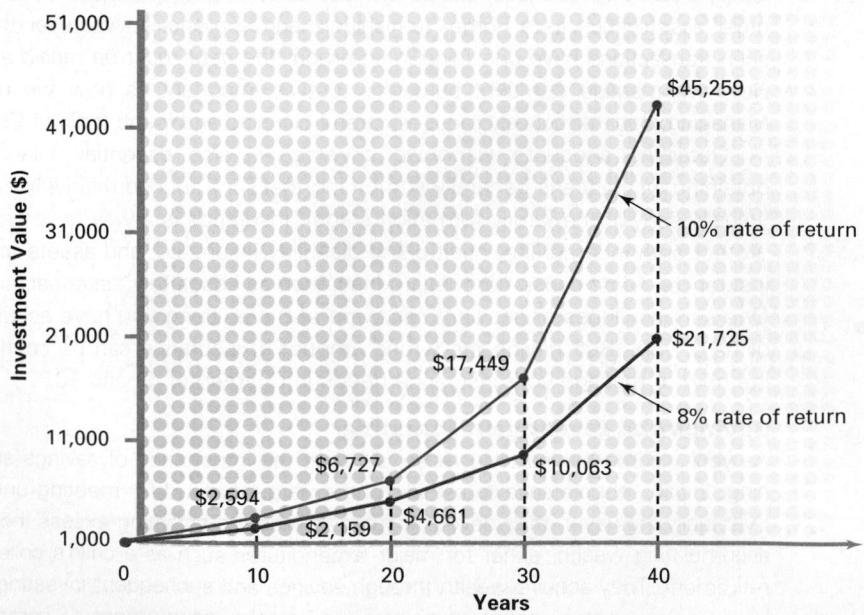

tax-deferred retirement plans and flexible spending accounts offer tax advantages. Some retirement plans allow you to borrow against them. Employer-sponsored insurance programs may need to be supplemented with personal policies. In addition, in today's volatile labor market, you can no longer assume that you'll be working at the same company for many years. If you change jobs, your new company may not offer the same benefits. Your personal financial plans should include contingency plans to replace employer-provided benefits as required. We'll discuss employee benefits in greater detail in Chapters 2 (planning); 3 (taxes); 8, 9, and 10 (insurance); and 14 (retirement).

Tax Planning

Despite all the talk about tax reform, our tax code remains highly complex. Income can be taxed as active (ordinary), portfolio (investment), passive, tax-free, or tax-deferred. Then there are tax shelters, which use various aspects of the tax code (such as depreciation expenses) to legitimately reduce an investor's tax liability. Tax planning considers all these factors and more. It involves looking at your current and projected earnings and developing strategies that will defer and minimize taxes. Tax plans are closely tied to investment plans and will often specify certain investment strategies. Although tax planning is most common among individuals with high incomes, sizable savings can also result for people with lower levels of income. We'll examine taxes and tax planning in Chapter 3.

Retirement and Estate Planning

While you're still working, you should be managing your finances to attain those goals you feel are important after you retire. These might include maintaining your standard of living, extensive travel, plans for visiting children, frequent dining at better restaurants, and perhaps a vacation home or boat. Retirement planning actually begins long before you retire. As a rule, most people don't start thinking about retirement until well into their forties or fifties. This is unfortunate, because it usually results in a substantially reduced level of retirement income. The sooner you start, the better off you'll be. Take, for instance, the IRA (individual retirement arrangement), in which certain wage earners are allowed to invest up to $4,000 per year (in 2007, increasing to $5,000 in 2008). If you start investing for retirement at age 40, put only $2,000 per year in an IRA for 25 years, and earn 10 percent, your account will grow to $196,694 at age 65. However, if you start your retirement program 10 years earlier (at age 30), your IRA will grow to a whopping $542,049 at age 65. Although you're investing only $20,000 more ($2,000 per year for an extra 10 years), your IRA will nearly triple in size. We'll look at IRAs and other aspects of retirement planning in Chapter 14.

Accumulating assets to enjoy in retirement is only part of the long-term financial planning process. As people grow older, they must also consider how they can most effectively pass their wealth on to their heirs, an activity called *estate planning*. We'll examine this complex subject, which includes such topics as wills, trusts, and the effects of gift and estate taxes, in Chapter 15.

Technology in Financial Planning

Using personal computers and the Internet streamlines the number crunching and information gathering involved in budgeting, tax planning, and investment management. Many reasonably priced, user-friendly programs are available for personal financial planning and money management, including the popular Microsoft Money and Quicken packages.

The Internet puts a wealth of financial information literally at your fingertips. Several comprehensive sites that consistently get rave reviews are Yahoo! Finance (**http://finance .yahoo.com),** Microsoft's MSN MoneyCentral (**http://moneycentral.msn.com),** and Intuit's Quicken.com (**http://www.quicken.com).** To help you find useful online resources, every chapter includes numerous "smart.sites," links to relevant financial planning Web sites. The *Money Online* feature at the end of each chapter connects you to a list of links to relevant Web sites, each accompanied by a brief description of its content. Also included are links to companion exercises to help you effectively use the Web in financial planning. By bookmarking (saving) these sites, you'll build up a valuable library of personal financial Web sites.

Where applicable, we'll point out ways to use the computer and Internet to simplify and reduce the time required to manage your personal finances. We also include a simple, computer program to use with many of the analytical and computational procedures addressed in the text. ThomsonNOW is keyed to various sections of this book, and it offers short programs that perform many of the routine financial calculations and procedures used in the text. ThomsonNOW also automates the completion of most of the chapter worksheets.

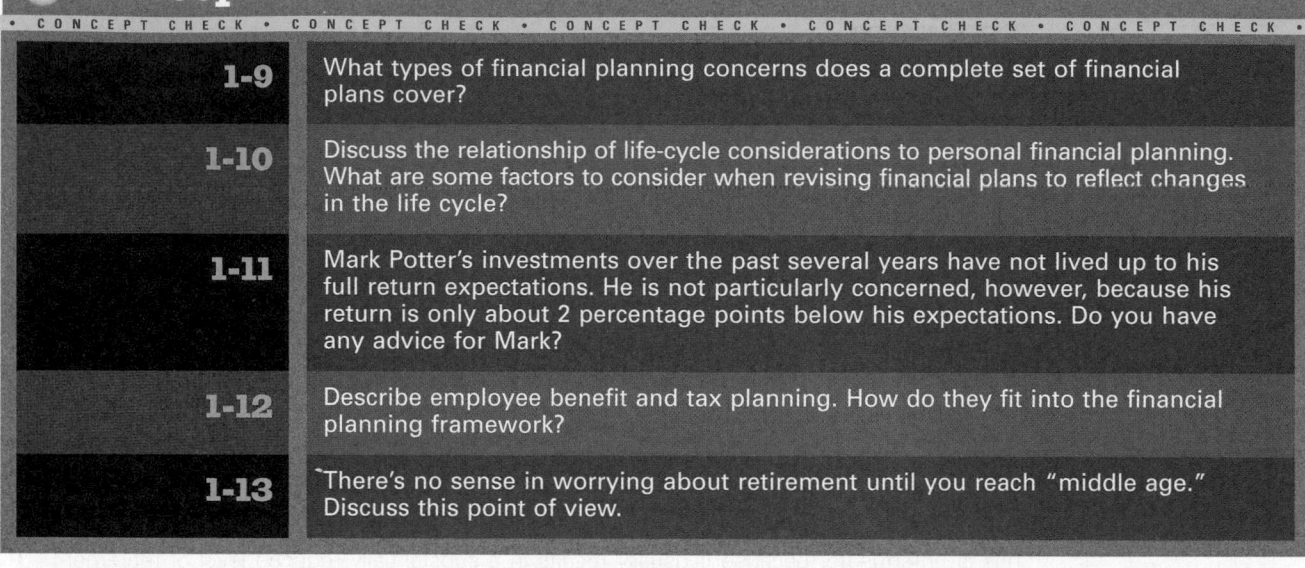

CHECK • CONCEPT CHECK • CONCEPT CHECK • CONCEPT CHECK • CONCEPT CHECK • CONCEPT CHECK • CONCEPT

Ⅱ Concept Check

1-9	What types of financial planning concerns does a complete set of financial plans cover?
1-10	Discuss the relationship of life-cycle considerations to personal financial planning. What are some factors to consider when revising financial plans to reflect changes in the life cycle?
1-11	Mark Potter's investments over the past several years have not lived up to his full return expectations. He is not particularly concerned, however, because his return is only about 2 percentage points below his expectations. Do you have any advice for Mark?
1-12	Describe employee benefit and tax planning. How do they fit into the financial planning framework?
1-13	"There's no sense in worrying about retirement until you reach "middle age." Discuss this point of view.

LG4   THE PLANNING ENVIRONMENT

Financial planning takes place in a dynamic economic environment created by the actions of government, business, and consumers. Your purchase, saving, investment, and retirement plans and decisions are influenced by both the present and future state of the economy. Understanding the economic environment will allow you to make better financial decisions.

For example, a strong economy can lead to high returns in the stock market, which can positively affect your investment and retirement programs. The economy can also affect the interest rates you pay on your mortgage and credit cards as well as those you earn on savings accounts and bonds. Periods of high inflation can lead to rapid price increases that make it difficult to make ends meet. Here we look at two important aspects of the planning environment: the major financial planning players and the economy.

The Players

The financial planning environment contains various interrelated groups of players, each attempting to fulfill certain goals. Although their objectives are not necessarily incompatible, they do impose some constraints on one another. There are three vital groups: government, business, and consumers. Exhibit 1.9 shows the relationships among these groups.

Government
The federal, state, and local governments provide us with many essential public goods and services, such as police and fire protection, national defense, highways, public education, and healthcare. The federal government plays a major role in regulating the level of economic activity. Government is also a customer of business and an employer of consumers, so it's a source of revenue for business and of wages for consumers. The two major constraints from the perspective of personal financial planning are taxation and regulation.

Taxation. The federal government levies taxes on income, state governments levy taxes on sales and income, and local governments levy taxes primarily on real estate and personal property. The largest tax bite for consumers is federal income taxes, which are somewhat progressive because (up to a point) the greater the taxable income, the higher the tax rate. Changes in tax rates and procedures will increase or decrease the amount of income consumers have to spend, so you should factor the effects of taxes into your personal money management activities. Due to tax structure constraints and the potential magnitude of taxes, financial decisions should be evaluated on an "after-tax" basis. (Taxes are discussed in Chapter 3.)

Regulation. Federal, state, and local governments place many regulations on activities that affect consumers and businesses. Aimed at protecting the consumer from fraudulent and undesirable actions by sellers and lenders, these regulations require certain types of businesses to have licenses, maintain specified hygiene standards, adequately disclose financial charges, and warrant their goods and services. Other laws protect sellers from adverse activities by consumers—for example, shoplifting and nonpayment for services rendered. Certainly, decisions related to achieving personal financial goals should consider the legal requirements that protect consumers and those that constrain their activities.

Business

As Exhibit 1.9 shows, business provides consumers with goods and services and in return receives payment in the form of money. To produce these goods and services, firms must hire labor and use land and financial capital (economists call these *factors of production*). In return, firms pay out wages, rents, interest, and profits to the various factors of production. Thus, businesses are an important part of the circular flow of income that sustains our free enterprise system. In general, they create a competitive environment in which consumers may select from an array of goods and services. As noted earlier, all businesses are limited in some way by federal, state, and local laws.

Consumers

The consumer is the central player in the financial planning environment. Consumer choices ultimately determine the kinds of goods and services businesses will provide. The

EXHIBIT 1.9   The Financial Planning Environment

Government, business, and consumers are the major players in our economic system. They all interact with one another to produce the environment in which we carry out our financial plans.

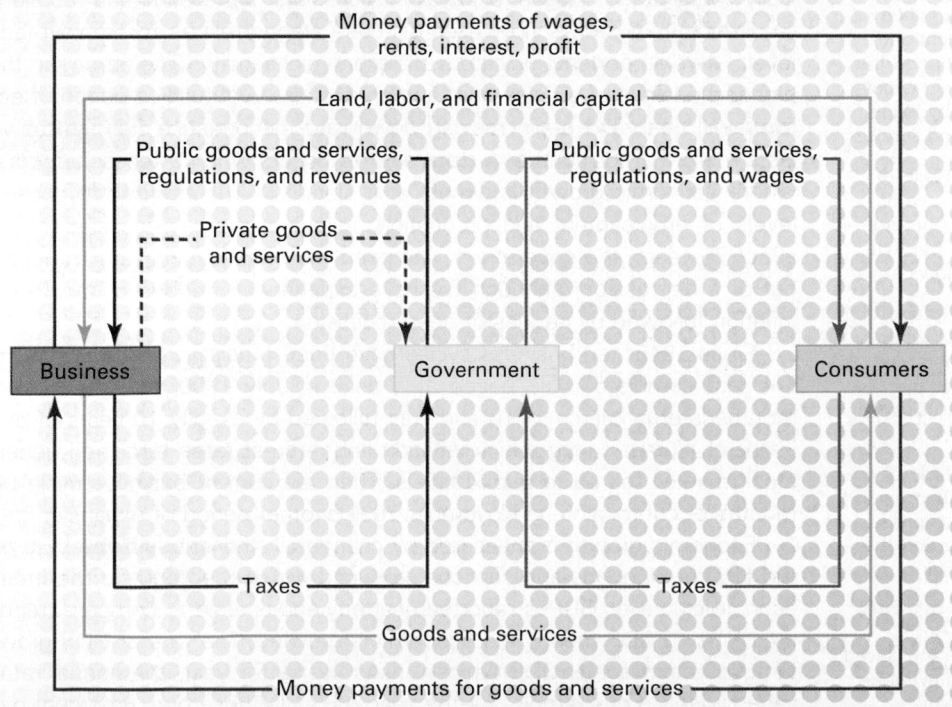

consumer's choice of whether to spend or save also has a direct impact on the present and future circular flows of money. Cutbacks in consumer spending are usually associated with a decline in economic activity, while an increase helps the economy to recover.

Consumers are often thought to have free choices in the marketplace, but they must operate within an environment that interacts with government and business. Although they can affect these parties through their elected officials and by their purchasing actions, consumers need lobbyists and consumer groups in order to create any real impact. The individual consumer should not expect to change government or business, but rather plan transactions within the existing financial environment.

The Economy

Our economy is influenced by interaction between government, business, and consumers as well as by world economic conditions. Through specific policy decisions, the government's goal is to manage the economy to provide economic stability and high levels of employment. These government decisions have a major impact on the economic and financial planning environment. The federal government's *monetary policy*—programs for controlling the amount of money in circulation (the money supply)—is used to stimulate or contract economic growth. For example, increases in the money supply tend to lower interest rates. This typically leads to a higher level of consumer and business borrowing and spending that increases overall economic activity. The reverse is also true. Reducing the money supply raises interest rates, reducing consumer and business borrowing and spending and slowing economic activity.

The government's other principal tool for managing the economy is *fiscal policy*—its programs of spending and taxation. Increased spending for social services, education, defense, and other programs stimulates the economy, while decreased spending slows economic activity. Increasing taxes, on the other hand, gives businesses and individuals less to spend and, as a result, negatively affects economic activity. Conversely, decreasing taxes stimulates the economy.

Economic Cycles

Although the government uses monetary and fiscal policy to manage the economy and provide economic stability, the level of economic activity changes constantly. The upward and downward movement creates *economic cycles* (also called *business cycles*). These cycles vary in length and in how high or low the economy moves. An economic cycle typically contains four stages: *expansion, recession, depression,* and *recovery*.

Exhibit 1.10 shows how each of these stages relates to employment and production levels, two important indicators of economic activity. The stronger the economy, the higher the levels of employment and production. Eventually a period of economic **expansion** will peak and begin moving downward, becoming a **recession** when the decline lasts more than 6 months. A **depression** occurs when a recession worsens to the point where economic growth is almost at a standstill. The **recovery** phase, with increasing levels of employment and production, follows either a recession or a depression. For about 75 years, the government has been reasonably successful in keeping the economy out of a depression, although we have experienced periods of rapid expansion and high inflation followed by periods of deep recession.

Since 1945, ten business cycles have been officially recognized in the United States. The last complete cycle began at a peak in July 1990, contracted and hit a trough 8 months later in March 1991, and was followed by exactly 10 years of expansion (peaking in March 2001), during which inflation and interest rates remained generally low and the stock market soared to record levels. Then the current business cycle began and after 8 months of contraction, in November 2001 another period of expansion began.

Economic growth is measured by changes in the **gross domestic product (GDP),** the total of all goods and services produced within the country. The broadest measure of economic activity, GDP is reported quarterly and is used to compare trends in national output. A rising GDP means the economy is growing. The *rate* of GDP growth is also important. Although actual GDP typically rises year after year, the annual rate of GDP growth varies widely. For example, for the year 2005 GDP rose by 1.8 percent over 2004.

expansion The phase of the economic cycle when levels of employment and production are high and the economy is growing, generally accompanied by rising prices for goods and services.

recession The phase of the economic cycle when levels of employment and production fall and growth of the economy slows.

depression The phase of the economic cycle when levels of employment and production are low and economic growth is at a virtual standstill.

recovery The phase of the economic cycle when levels of employment and production are improving and the economy is growing.

gross domestic product (GDP) The total of all goods and services produced in a country; used to monitor economic growth.

The economy goes through various stages over time, although real depressions are extremely rare. These stages tend to be cyclical and directly affect the levels of employment and production.

How is the U.S. economy doing this month? Link to the Bureau of Labor Statistics "Economy at a Glance" page at **http://www .thomsonedu.com/ finance/gitman.**

inflation A state of the economy in which the general price level is increasing.

consumer price index (CPI) A measure of inflation based on changes in the cost of consumer goods and services.

purchasing power The amount of goods and services each dollar buys at a given time.

Another important measure of economic health is the *unemployment rate*. The swings in unemployment from one phase of the cycle to the next can be substantial. For example, since 1960 the unemployment rate has fluctuated between a low of 4 percent and a high of nearly 10 percent. In 2005 it was 5.1 percent. In addition to GDP growth and the unemployment rate, numerous economic statistics such as inflation, interest rates, bank failures, corporate profits, taxes, and government deficits directly and profoundly affect our financial well-being. These factors in turn affect our financial plans—our level of income, investment returns, interest earned and paid, taxes paid, and, in general, prices paid for goods and services we buy.

Inflation, Prices, and Planning

As we've discussed, our economy is based on the exchange of goods and services between businesses and their customers—consumers, government, and other businesses—for a medium of exchange called money. The mechanism that facilitates this exchange is a system of *prices*. Technically speaking, the price of something is *the amount of money the seller is willing to accept in exchange for a given quantity of some good or service*—for instance, $3 for a pound of meat or $10 for an hour of work. When the general level of prices *increases* over time, the economy is said to be experiencing a period of **inflation.** The most common measure of inflation, the **consumer price index (CPI),** is based on changes in the cost of consumer goods and services. At times, the rate of inflation has been substantial. In 1980, for instance, prices went up by 13.5 percent. Fortunately, inflation has dropped dramatically in this country, and the annual rate of inflation has remained below 5 percent every year since 1983, except in 1990 when it was 5.4 percent. Since 2000, the rate of inflation has ranged between 2 percent and 3.5 percent; for 2005 it was 3.39 percent.

Inflation is of vital concern to financial planning. It affects not only what we pay for our goods and services but also what we earn in our jobs. Inflation tends to give an illusion of something that doesn't exist. That is, though we seem to be making more money, we really aren't. As prices rise, we need more income because our **purchasing power**—the amount of goods and services each dollar buys at a given time—declines. For example, assume that you earned $45,000 in 2003 and received annual raises so that your salary was $48,000 by 2006. That represents an annual growth rate of 2.2 percent. If inflation averaged 2.8 percent per year, however, your purchasing power would have decreased, even though your income rose. You'd need $48,887 just to keep pace with inflation. So be sure to look at what you earn in terms of its purchasing power, not just in absolute dollars.

Inflation also directly affects interest rates. High rates of inflation drive up the cost of borrowing money as lenders demand compensation for their eroding purchasing power. Higher interest rates mean higher mortgage payments, higher monthly car payments, and so on. High inflation rates also have a detrimental effect on stock and bond prices. Finally, sustained high rates of inflation can have devastating effects on retirement plans and other long-term financial goals. Indeed, for many people it can put such goals out of reach. Clearly, low inflation is good for the economy, for interest rates and stock and bond prices, and for financial planning in general.

⏸ Concept Check

CHECK • CONCEPT CHECK • CONCEPT CHECK • CONCEPT CHECK • CONCEPT CHECK • CONCEPT CHECK • CONCEPT C

1-14	Discuss the following statement: "It is the interaction among government, business, and consumers that determines the environment in which personal financial plans must be made."
1-15	What are the stages of an economic cycle? Explain their significance for your personal finances.
1-16	What is *inflation*, and why should it be a concern in financial planning?

LG5, LG6 WHAT DETERMINES YOUR PERSONAL INCOME?

An obvious and important factor in determining how well we live is the amount of income we earn. In the absence of any inheritance or similar financial windfall, your income will largely depend on such factors as your age, marital status, education, geographic location, and choice of career. Making a lot of money isn't easy, but it can be done! A high level of income—whether derived from your job, your own business, or your investments—is within your reach if you have the necessary dedication, commitment to hard work, and a well-thought-out set of financial plans. The data in Exhibit 1.11 shows how income changes with age and education.

Demographics and Your Income

Typically, people with low incomes fall into the very young or very old age groups, with the highest earnings generally occurring between the ages of 45 and 64. Those below age 45 are developing trades or beginning to move up in their jobs, and many over 64 are working only part-time or are completely retired. In the 35–44 age group, the average income of the heads of household is about $73,800, which jumps to over $94,000 for those in the 45–54 age group, and then falls sharply to about $60,000 in the 65–74 age group. Your own income will vary over time, too, so you need to incorporate anticipated shifts in earnings into your financial plans.

Your Education

Your level of formal education is a controllable factor that significantly affects your income. As Exhibit 1.11 illustrates, heads of household who have more formal education earn higher annual incomes than do those with lesser degrees. In a recent study of affluent Americans, defined as those earning $75,000 or more, 62 percent had college and/or postgraduate degrees, while only 11 percent had a high-school diploma or less. According to data from the *Survey of Consumer Finances*, the median salary of a high-school graduate in 2004 was about $35,600, compared with $73,000 for a college graduate. Add a PhD or other professional degrees, and earnings rise substantially. Over a lifetime, these differences really add up! Education alone cannot guarantee a high income, but these statistics suggest that a solid formal education greatly enhances your earning power.

Where You Live

Geographic factors can also affect your earning power. Salaries vary regionally, tending to be higher in the Northeast and West than in the South. Typically, your salary will also be higher if you live in a large metropolitan area rather than a small town or rural area. Such factors as economic conditions, labor supply, and industrial base also affect salary levels in different areas.

Living costs also vary considerably throughout the country. You'd earn more in Los Angeles than Memphis, Tennessee; but your salary would probably not go as far due to the much higher cost of living in Los Angeles. Like many others, you may decide that lifestyle considerations take priority over earning potential. Your local chamber of commerce or the Internet can provide an intercity cost-of-living index that shows living costs in major cities and serves as a useful resource for comparing jobs in different areas. (See the *Financial Road Sign* "Calculate That Move" for more information.) The overall index is

---

EXHIBIT 1.11	How Age and Education Affect Annual Income

The amount of money you earn is closely tied to your age and education. Generally, the closer you are to middle age (45–64) and the more education you have, the greater your income will be.

ANNUAL INCOME (HEAD OF HOUSEHOLD)

Age	Average Income
35 and under	$ 45,100
35–44	73,800
45–54	94,400
55–64	100,300
65–74	59,600
75 and over	40,900

Education	Average Income
No high-school diploma	$ 25,900
High-school diploma	44,800
Some college	56,000
College graduate	117,500

Source: Adapted from Brian K. Bucks, Arthur B. Kennickell, and Kevin B. Moore, "Recent Changes in U.S. Family Finances: Evidence from the 2001 and 2004 Survey of Consumer Finances," *Federal Reserve Bulletin*, Board of Governors of the Federal Reserve System, Washington, D.C., February 2006, http://www.federalreserve.gov/pubs/035/0552/2004/bull0206.pdf.

developed by tracking costs in six major categories: groceries, housing, utilities, transportation, healthcare, and miscellaneous goods and services.

Your Career

A critical factor in how much you earn over your lifetime is your career. The career you choose is closely related to your level of education and your particular skills, interests, lifestyle preferences, and personal values. Social, demographic, economic, and technological trends also influence your decision as to what fields offer the best opportunities for your future. It's not a prerequisite for many types of careers, such as sales, service, and certain types of manufacturing and clerical work, but a formal education generally leads to greater decision-making responsibility—and consequently increased income potential—within a career. Exhibit 1.12 presents a list of representative salaries for entry-level, mid-level, and managerial positions for various careers.

Planning Your Career

Career planning and personal financial planning are closely related activities, so the decisions you make in one area affect the other. Like financial planning, career planning is a lifelong process that includes short- and long-term goals. Since your career goals are likely to change several times, you should not expect to stay in one field, or remain with one company, your whole life.

You might graduate with a computer science degree and accept a job with a software company. Your financial plan might include furnishing your apartment, saving for a vacation or new car, and starting an investment program. If 5 years later you decide to go to law school, you'll have to revise your financial plan to include strategies to cover living expenses and finance your tuition. You may decide that you need to go to school at night while earning a living during the day.

The average American starting a career today can expect to have at least 10 jobs with five or more employers, and many of us will have three, four, or even more

Smart Sites

One of the first steps in the job-search process is to assess your personality. At **http://www.thomsonedu.com/finance/gitman,** link to the Keirsey Temperament Sorter®-11 as a starting point.

Smart Sites

The U.S. News & World Report Career Center has material on a variety of career topics, from internships and resumes to the hottest careers and benefits: Link to it at **http://www.thomsonedu.com/finance/gitman.**

EXHIBIT 1.12 — Representative Salaries for Selected Careers

Professional and managerial workers, who typically have a college degree, tend to earn the highest salaries.

	SALARY		
Career	Entry-Level	Midlevel	Managerial
Accountant, public	$ 43,000	$ 69,000	$133,000
Computer programmer	40,000	59,000	99,000
Engineer	52,000	75,000	120,000
Family practice medical doctor	137,000	156,000	n/a
Financial manager	60,000	82,000	140,000
Human resources manager	30,000	82,000	137,000
Lawyer	75,000	95,000	145,000
Paralegal	26,000	40,000	62,000
Pharmacist	n/a	85,000	n/a
Police officer	36,000	45,000	77,000
Psychologist	33,000	70,000	93,000
Registered nurse	37,000	52,000	75,000
Systems analyst	42,000	66,000	99,000
Teacher, K–12	32,000	45,000	68,000

Source: *Occupational Outlook Handbook* 2006–2007 Edition, U.S. Bureau of Labor Statistics, http://www.bls.gov/oco, downloaded March 23, 2006.

FINANCIAL ROAD SIGN

AVOIDING ONLINE JOB-SEARCH MISTAKES

These tips will help you use online job-search resources wisely.

Format: Use ASCII format, not Word, to create an online résumé. Use only plain text (no bold, underlines) and keyboard symbols (asterisks, not bullets). Cut and paste your résumé into an e-mail; don't attach it.

Limit postings: Post your résumé on sites where employers browse for free, such as **http://hotjobs.com** or **http://www.monster.com,** and on sites specializing in your field.

Follow up: If you use a service like **http://www.resumemachine.com** to send résumés to human resources (HR) departments, follow up by phone with companies that received it.

Avoid ads: If you post your résumé on a personal Web page, keep it simple and don't use a free Web-hosting site where employers see the site's ads as well.

Try other useful sites: You can also use **http://www.hotjobs.com** and **http://www.monster.com** for job postings, as well as **http://www.careerjournal.com,** a career service offered by *The Wall Street Journal.*

Source: Adapted and updated from Joellen Perry, "Avoid a Comedy of E-Errors," *U.S. News & World Report,* November 6, 2000, from http://www.usnews.com.

careers during our lifetimes. Some of these changes will be based on personal decisions; others may result from layoffs due to corporate downsizing. For example, a branch manager for a regional bank who feels that bank mergers have reduced her job prospects in banking may buy a quick-print franchise and become her own boss. Job security is practically a thing of the past, and corporate loyalty has given way to a more self-centered career approach that requires new career strategies.

Through careful career planning, you can improve your work situation to gain greater personal and professional satisfaction. Some of the steps are similar to the financial planning process described earlier:

• Identify your interests, skills, needs, and values.
• Set specific long- and short-term career goals.
• Develop and use an action plan to achieve those goals.
• Review and revise your career plans as your situation changes.

Your action plan depends on your job situation. For example, if you're unemployed, it will focus on your job search. If you have a job but want to change careers, it might include researching career options, networking to develop a broad base of contacts, listing companies to contact for information, and getting special training to prepare for your chosen career.

A personal portfolio of skills, both general and technical, will protect your earning power during economic downturns and advance it during prosperous times. Employers need flexible, adaptable workers as companies restructure and pare down their operations. It's important to keep your skills current with on-the-job training programs and continuing education. Adding proficiency in technology or languages puts you ahead of the pack in keeping up with changing workplace requirements. It's a good idea to broaden your contacts within your industry and among your colleagues, who know which industries have potential, which are in trouble, and what skills are in demand in your field.

Good job-hunting skills will serve you well throughout your career. Learn how to research new career opportunities and investigate potential jobs, taking advantage of online resources as well as traditional ones. Develop a broad base of career resources, starting with your college placement office, public library, and personal contacts such as family and friends. Know how to market your qualifications to your advantage in your résumé and cover letters, on the phone, and in person during a job interview.

⑪ Concept Check

CHECK • CONCEPT CHECK • CONCEPT CHECK • CONCEPT CHECK • CONCEPT CHECK • CONCEPT CHECK • CONCEPT

1-17	"All people who have equivalent formal education earn similar incomes." Do you agree or disagree with this statement? Explain your position.
1-18	Discuss the need for career planning throughout the life cycle and its relationship to financial planning. What are some of your personal career goals?

SUMMARY

LG1 **Identify the benefits of using personal financial planning techniques to manage your finances.** Personal financial planning helps you marshal and control your financial resources. It should allow you to improve your standard of living, get more enjoyment from your money by spending it wisely, and accumulate wealth. By setting short- and long-term financial goals, you'll enhance your quality of life both now and in the future. The ultimate result will be an increase in wealth.

LG2 **Describe the personal financial planning process and define your goals.** Personal financial planning is a six-step process that helps you achieve your financial goals: (1) define financial goals; (2) develop financial plans and strategies to achieve goals; (3) implement financial plans and strategies; (4) periodically develop and implement budgets to monitor and control progress toward goals; (5) use financial statements to evaluate results of plans and budgets, taking corrective action as required; and (6) redefine goals and revise plans and strategies as personal circumstances change. Before you can manage your financial resources, you must realistically spell out your short-term, intermediate, and long-term financial goals. Your goals, which reflect your values and circumstances, may change due to personal circumstances. State them specifically in terms of the desired results.

LG3 **Explain the life cycle of financial plans and their role in achieving your financial goals.** In moving through various life-cycle stages, you must revise your financial plans to include goals and strategies appropriate to each stage. Income and expense patterns change with age. Changes in your life due to marriage, children, divorce, remarriage, and job status also necessitate adapting financial plans to meet current needs. Although these plans change over time, they are the roadmap that you'll follow to achieve your financial goals. After defining your goals, you can develop and implement an appropriate personal financial plan. A complete set of financial plans covers asset acquisition, liability and insurance, savings and investments, employee benefits, taxes, and retirement and estate planning. Review these plans regularly and revise them as necessary.

LG4 **Examine the economic enviroment's influence on personal financial planning.** Financial planning occurs in an environment where the government, business, and consumers are all influential participants. Government provides certain essential services and the structure within which businesses and consumers function. Businesses provide goods and services to consumers, whose choices influence the products and services businesses offer. Personal financial decisions are affected by economic cycles (expansion, recession, depression, and recovery) and the impact of inflation on prices (purchasing power and personal income).

LG5 **Evaluate the impact of age, education, and geographic location on personal income.** Demographics, education, and career are all important factors affecting your income level. As a rule, people age 45 to 64 tend to earn more than others, as do those who are married. Equally important, statistics show a direct correlation between level of education and income. Where you live is an additional consideration—salaries and living costs are higher in some areas than in others. Career choices also affect your level of income—those in professional and managerial positions tend to earn the highest salaries.

LG6 **Understand the importance of career choices and their relationship to personal financial planning.** Career planning is a lifetime process that involves goal setting and career development strategies. A career plan should be flexible and able to adapt to new workplace requirements. Use continuing education and on-the-job training to facilitate changes in job, employer, and even career. When making career plans, identify your interests, skills, needs, and values; set specific long- and short-term career goals; develop and use an action plan to achieve your goals; and review and revise your career plans as your situation changes. Most career decisions have monetary implications, so coordinate your career plans with your personal financial plans.

FINANCIAL PLANNING EXERCISES

LG1 1. How can using personal financial planning tools help you improve your financial situation? Describe changes you can make in at least three areas.

LG2, 3 2. ***Use Worksheet 1.1.*** Describe your current status based on the personal financial planning life cycle shown in Exhibit 1.7. Fill out Worksheet 1.1, "Summary of Personal Financial Goals," with goals reflecting your current situation and your expected life situation in 5 and 10 years. Discuss the reasons for the changes in your goals and how you'll need to adapt your financial plans as a result. Which types of financial plans do you need for your current situation, and why?

LG2 3. Recommend three financial goals and related activities for someone in each of the following circumstances:
   a. Junior in college
   b. 25-year-old computer programmer who plans to earn a master's degree in business administration
   c. Couple in their thirties with two children, ages 3 and 6
   d. Divorced 45-year-old man with a 15-year-old child and a 75-year-old father who is ill

LG4 4. Summarize current and projected trends in the economy with regard to GDP growth, unemployment, and inflation. How should you use this information to make personal financial and career planning decisions?

LG6 5. Assume that you graduated from college with a major in marketing and took a job with a large consumer-products company. After 3 years, you are laid off when the company downsizes. Describe the steps you'd take to "repackage" yourself for another field.

APPLYING PERSONAL FINANCE

Watch Your Attitude!

Many people's *attitude* toward money has as much or more to do with their ability to accumulate wealth as it does with the *amount* of money they earn. Attitude influences the entire financial planning process and often determines whether financial goals become reality or end up being pipe dreams. This project will help you examine your attitude toward money and wealth so that you can formulate realistic goals and plans.

Use the following questions to stimulate your thought process.

1. Am I a saver, or do I spend almost all the money I receive?
2. Does it make me feel good just to spend money, regardless of what it's for?
3. Is it important for me to have new clothes or a new car just for the sake of having them?
4. Do I have clothes hanging in my closet with the price tags still on them?
5. Do I buy things because they are a bargain or because I need them?
6. Do I save for my vacations, or do I charge everything and take months paying off my credit card at high interest?
7. If I have a balance on my credit card, without looking at my statement can I recall what the charges were for?
8. Where do I want to be professionally and financially in 5 years? In 10 years?
9. Will my attitude toward money help get me there? If not, what do I need to do?
10. If I dropped out of school today or lost my job, what would I do?

Does your attitude toward money help or hinder you? How can you adjust your attitude so that you are more likely to accomplish your financial goals?

CRITICAL THINKING CASES

LG1, 2, 3, 4   ## 1.1   Nathan's Need to Know: Personal Finance or Tennis?

During the Christmas break of his final year at Western State University, Nathan Strong plans to put together his résumé in order to seek full-time employment as a medical technician during the spring semester. To help Nathan prepare for the job interview process, his older brother has arranged for him to meet with a friend, Alicia Nolan, who has worked as a medical technician since her graduation from Western State 2 years earlier. Alicia gives him numerous pointers on résumé preparation, the interview process, and possible job opportunities.

After answering Nathan's many questions, Alicia asks Nathan to bring her up to date on Western State. As they discuss courses, Alicia indicates that of all the electives she has taken, the personal financial planning course was most useful. Nathan says that although he had considered personal financial planning for his last elective, he's currently leaning toward a beginning tennis course. He feels that the course will be fun because some of his friends are taking it. He points out that he doesn't expect to get rich and already knows how to balance his checkbook. Alicia tells him that personal financial planning involves much more than balancing a checkbook and that the course was highly relevant regardless of income level. She strongly believes that the personal financial planning course will benefit Nathan more than beginning tennis—a course that she also took while at Western State University.

Critical Thinking Questions

1. Describe to Nathan the goals and rewards of the personal financial planning process.
2. Explain to Nathan what is meant by financial planning and why it is important regardless of income.
3. Describe the financial planning environment to Nathan. Explain the role of the consumer and the impact of economic conditions on financial planning.
4. What arguments would you present to convince Nathan that the personal financial planning course would benefit him more than beginning tennis?

LG5, 6   ## 1.2   Tony's Dilemma: Finding a New Job

Anthony Como, a 47-year-old retail store manager earning $75,000 a year, has worked for the same company during his entire 28-year career. A major economic recession has caused massive layoffs throughout the retail industry, and Tony is among the unlucky people who lost their jobs. Ten months later, he is still unemployed, and his 10 months' severance pay and 6 months' unemployment compensation have run out. Fortunately, when he first became a store manager, Tony took a personal financial planning course offered by the local university. Because he then adopted careful financial planning practices, he now has sufficient savings and investments to carry him through several more months of unemployment. His greatest financial need is to find a job.

Tony actively seeks work but finds himself overqualified for available lower-paying jobs and underqualified for higher-paying, more desirable positions. There are no openings for positions equivalent to the manager's job he had lost. Although Tony attended college for 2 years after high school, he didn't earn a degree. He lost his wife several years earlier and is very close to his two grown children, who live in the same city.

Tony has these options:

- Wait out the recession until another retail store manager position opens up.
- Move to another area of the country where store manager positions are still available.
- Accept a lower-paying job for 2 or 3 years and go back to school evenings to finish his college degree and qualify for a better position.
- Consider other types of jobs that could benefit from his managerial skills.

Critical Thinking Questions

1. What important career factors should Tony consider when evaluating his options?
2. What important personal factors should Tony consider when deciding among his career options?
3. What recommendations would you give Tony in light of both the career and personal dimensions of his options noted in Questions 1 and 2?

Visit **http://www.thomsonedu.com/finance/gitman** for some additional Web-based exercises and hot links (with annotations) to a variety of resources relevant to the topics covered in this chapter.

Developing Your Financial Statements and Plans

LG1	●	Understand the interlocking network of financial plans and statements.	p. 30
LG2	●	Prepare a personal balance sheet.	p. 32
LG3	●	Generate a personal income and expense statement.	p. 37
LG4	●	Develop a good recordkeeping system and use ratios to interpret personal financial statements.	p. 42
LG5	●	Construct a cash budget and use it to monitor and control spending.	p. 45
LG6	●	Describe the use of *time value of money* concepts to put a monetary value on financial goals and the role of special planning concerns.	p. 52, 55
	●		

LG1 · · MAPPING OUT YOUR FINANCIAL FUTURE

On your journey to financial security, you need navigational tools to guide you to your destination: the fulfillment of your financial goals. Operating without a plan is like traveling through an unfamiliar state without a roadmap. Financial plans, financial statements, and budgets provide direction by helping you work toward specific financial goals. *Financial plans* are the roadmaps that show you the way, whereas *personal financial statements* let you know where you stand financially. *Budgets,* detailed short-term financial forecasts that compare estimated income with estimated expenses, allow you to monitor and control expenses and purchases consistent with your financial plans. All three are essential to sound personal financial management and the achievement of goals. They provide control by bringing the various dimensions of your personal financial affairs into focus.

The Role of Financial Statements in Financial Planning

personal financial statements *Balance sheets* and *income and expense statements* that serve as planning tools that are essential to developing and monitoring personal financial plans.

Before you can set realistic goals, develop your financial plans, and effectively manage your money, you must take stock of your current financial situation. You'll also need tools to monitor your progress. **Personal financial statements** are planning tools that provide an up-to-date evaluation of your financial well-being, help you identify potential financial problems, and help you make better-informed financial decisions. They measure your financial condition so you can establish realistic financial goals and evaluate your progress toward those goals. Knowing how to prepare and interpret personal financial statements is a cornerstone of personal financial planning.

Two types of personal financial statements—the *balance sheet* and *income and expense statement*—are essential to developing and monitoring personal financial plans. They show your financial position as it *actually* exists and report on financial transactions that have *really* occurred.

The **balance sheet** describes your financial position—the assets you hold, less the debts you owe, equal your net worth (general level of wealth)—at a *given point* in time. This planning tool helps you track the progress you're making in building up your assets and reducing your debt.

In contrast, the **income and expense statement** measures financial performance *over* time. It tracks income earned, as well as expenses made, during a given period (usually a month or a year). You use this tool to compare your actual expenses and purchases with the amounts budgeted and then make the necessary changes to correct discrepancies between the actual and budgeted amounts. This information helps you control your future expenses and purchases so you'll have the funds needed to carry out your financial plans.

Budgets, another type of financial report, are *forward* looking. Because they are based on expected income and expenses, budgets allow you to monitor and control spending.

Exhibit 2.1 summarizes the various financial statements and reports and their relationship to each other in the personal financial planning process. Note that *financial plans* provide direction to annual budgets. Budgets directly affect your balance sheet and income and expense statement. As you move from plans to budgets to actual statements, you can compare your actual results with your plans. This will show you how well you are meeting your financial goals and staying within your budget.

balance sheet A financial statement that describes a person's financial position at a *given point* in time.

income and expense statement A financial statement that measures financial performance *over* time.

budget A detailed financial report that looks *forward*, based on expected income and expenses.

Assessing Your Financial Situation, Plans, and Goals

As you learned in Chapter 1, the financial planning process includes six steps that translate personal financial goals into specific financial plans and the strategies to achieve these

---

EXHIBIT 2.1   The Interlocking Network of Financial Plans and Statements

Personal financial planning involves a network of financial reports that link future goals and plans with actual results. Such a network provides direction, control, and feedback.

- Evaluate and plan major outlays
- Manage credit
- Secure adequate insurance coverage
- Establish savings/investment programs
- Manage employee benefits
- Reduce taxes
- Implement retirement program
- Minimize estate taxes

Financial plans

Feedback

- Monitor and control income, living expenses, purchases, and savings on a monthly basis

Budgets

Feedback

Actual financial results:
- Balance sheet
- Income and expense statement

Financial statements

goals. In addition to clearly defining your financial goals in measurable terms, you need to put target dates and a monetary value on your short-term, intermediate, and long-term goals. In the following parts of this chapter, we'll discuss the various types of financial statements and plans. Then we'll look at how to use time value of money concepts to calculate the value of a financial goal that occurs several years into the future. At the end of the chapter, we explain some special planning concerns, such as using professional financial planners.

❚❚ Concept Check

2-1 What are the two types of *personal financial statements*? What is a *budget*, and how does it differ from personal financial statements? What role do these reports play in a *financial plan*?

LG2   THE BALANCE SHEET: HOW MUCH ARE YOU WORTH TODAY?

Because you should track your progress toward your financial goals, you need a starting point that shows how much you're worth today. Preparing a personal *balance sheet*, or *statement of financial position*, will give you this important information. This financial statement represents a person's (or family's) financial condition at a certain *point in time*. Think of a balance sheet as a snapshot taken of your financial position on one day out of the year.

A balance sheet has three parts that, taken together, summarize your financial picture:

- **Assets:** What you own
- **Liabilities, or debts:** What you owe
- **Net worth:** The difference between your assets and liabilities

The accounting relationship among these three categories is called the *balance sheet equation* and is expressed as follows:

$$\textbf{Total assets} = \textbf{Total liabilities} + \textbf{Net worth}$$
$$\textbf{or}$$
$$\textbf{Net worth} = \textbf{Total assets} - \textbf{Total liabilities}$$

Let's now look at the components of each section of the balance sheet.

Assets: The Things You Own

Assets are the items you own. An item is classified as an asset no matter if it was purchased for cash or financed with debt. In other words, even if you haven't fully paid for an asset, you should list it on the balance sheet. An item that's leased, in contrast, is not shown as an asset, because someone else actually owns it.

A useful way to group assets is on the basis of their underlying characteristics and uses. This results in four broad categories: liquid assets, investments, real property, and personal property.

assets Items that one owns.

liquid assets Assets that are held in the form of cash or can readily be converted to cash with little or no loss in value.

investments Assets such as stocks, bonds, mutual funds, and real estate that are acquired in order to earn a return rather than provide a service.

- **Liquid assets:** Low-risk financial assets held in the form of cash or instruments that can readily be converted to cash with little or no loss in value. They help us meet the everyday needs of life and provide for emergencies and unexpected opportunities. Cash on hand or in a checking or savings account, money market deposit accounts, money market mutual funds, or certificates of deposit that mature within 1 year are all examples of liquid assets.
- **Investments:** Assets acquired to earn a return rather than provide a service. These assets are mostly intangible *financial assets* (stocks, bonds, mutual funds, and other types of securities), typically acquired to achieve long-term personal financial goals. Business ownership, the cash value of life insurance and pensions, retirement funds such as IRAs and 401(k) plans, and other investment vehicles such as commodities, financial futures, and options represent still other forms of investment assets. (For retirement fund

© DIGITAL VISION/GETTY IMAGES

accounts, *only those balances that are eligible to be withdrawn should be shown as an asset on the balance sheet.*) They vary in marketability (the ability to sell quickly) from high (stocks and bonds) to low (real estate and business ownership investments).

- **Real and personal property:** Tangible assets that we use in our everyday lives. **Real property** refers to immovable property: land and anything fixed to it, such as a house. Real property generally has a relatively long life and high cost, and it may *appreciate*, or increase in value. **Personal property** is movable property, such as automobiles, recreational equipment, household furnishings and appliances, clothing, jewelry, home electronics, and similar items. Most types of personal property *depreciate*, or decline in value, shortly after being put into use.

About 40 percent of the average household's assets consists of financial assets (liquid assets and investments); nearly half is real property (including housing); and the rest is other nonfinancial assets. The first section of Worksheet 2.1 on page 34 lists some of the typical assets you'd find on a personal balance sheet.

All assets, regardless of category, are recorded on the balance sheet at their current **fair market value,** which may differ considerably from their original purchase price. Fair market value is either the actual value of the asset (such as money in a checking account) or the price that the asset can reasonably be expected to sell for in the open market (such as a used car or a home).

Those of you who have taken accounting will notice a difference between the way assets are recorded on a personal balance sheet and a business balance sheet. Under generally accepted accounting principles (GAAP), the accounting profession's guiding rules, assets appear on a company's balance sheet at *cost*, not *fair market value*. One reason for the disparity is that in business, an asset's value is often subject to debate and uncertainty. The user of the statements may be an investor, and accountants like to be conservative in their measurement. For purposes of personal financial planning, the user and the preparer of the statement are one and the same. Besides, most personal assets have market values that can be easily estimated.

Liabilities: The Money You Owe

Liabilities represent an individual's or family's debts. They could result from department store charges, bank credit card charges, installment loans, or mortgages on housing and other real estate. A liability, regardless of its source, is something that you owe and must repay in the future.

Liabilities are generally classified according to maturity:

- **Current,** or **short-term, liability:** Any debt currently owed and due within 1 year of the date of the balance sheet. Examples include charges for consumable goods, utility bills, rent, insurance premiums, taxes, medical bills, repair bills, and total **open account credit obligations**—the outstanding balances against established credit lines (usually through credit card purchases).
- **Long-term liability:** Debt due 1 year or more from the date of the balance sheet. These liabilities typically include real estate mortgages, most consumer installment loans, education loans, and margin loans used to purchase securities.

You must show all types of loans on your balance sheet. Although most loans will fall into the category of long-term liabilities, *any loans that come due within a year should be shown as current liabilities.* Examples of short-term loans include a 6-month, single-payment bank loan and a 9-month consumer installment loan for a refrigerator.

Regardless of the type of loan, *only the latest outstanding loan balance should be shown as a liability on the balance sheet,* because at any given time it is the balance still due—not

real property Tangible assets that are immovable: land and anything fixed to it, such as a house.

personal property Tangible assets that are movable and used in everyday life.

fair market value The actual value of an asset, or the price that it can reasonably be expected to sell for in the open market.

liabilities Debts, such as credit card charges, loans, and mortgages.

current (short-term) liability Any debt due within 1 year of the date of the balance sheet.

open account credit obligations Current liabilities that represent the balances outstanding against established credit lines.

long-term liability Any debt due 1 year or more from the date of the balance sheet.

the initial loan balance—that matters. Another important and closely related point is that *only the principal portion of a loan or mortgage should be listed as a liability on the balance sheet.* In other words, you should not include the interest portion of your payments as part of your balance sheet debt. The *principal* defines the amount of debt you owe at a given time and does not include any future interest payments.

Lenders evaluate a prospective borrower's liabilities carefully. High levels of debt and overdue debts are both viewed with disfavor. On Worksheet 2.1, you'll find the most common categories of liabilities.

Worksheet 2.1   Balance Sheet for Tim and Andrea Shepard

A balance sheet is set up to show what you own on one side (your assets) and how you pay for them on the other (debt or net worth). As you can see, the Shepards have more assets than liabilities.

BALANCE SHEET

Name(s) Tim and Andrea Shepard   Date December 31, 2007

ASSETS			LIABILITIES AND NET WORTH		
Liquid Assets			**Current Liabilities**		
Cash on hand	$ 90		Utilities	$ 120	
Checking accounts	575		Rent		
Savings accounts	760		Insurance premiums		
Money market deposits and funds	800		Taxes		
			Medical/dental bills	75	
Certificates of deposit (<1 yr. to maturity)			Repair bills		
			Bank credit card balances	395	
Total Liquid Assets		$ 2,225	Dept. store credit card balances	145	
			Travel and entertainment card balances	125	
Investments					
Stocks	$ 1,250		Gas and other credit card balances		
			Bank line of credit balances		
Bonds Corp.	1,000		Other current liabilities	45	
Certificates of deposit (>1 yr. to maturity)					
Mutual funds	1,500		**Total Current Liabilities**	$	905
			Long-Term Liabilities		
Real estate			Primary residence mortgage	$ 92,000	
Retirement funds, IRA	2,000				
Other			Second home mortgage		
Total Investments		$ 5,750	Real estate investment mortgage		
Real Property			Auto loans	4,250	
Primary residence	$120,000		Appliance/furniture loans	800	
Second home			Home improvement loans		
Other			Single-payment loans		
Total Real Property		$ 120,000	Education loans	3,800	
Personal Property			Margin loans used to purchase securities		
Auto(s): '05 Toyota Corolla	$ 9,500		Other long-term loans (from parents)	4,000	
Auto(s): '02 Ford Focus	4,500		**Total Long-Term Liabilities**		$ 104,850
Recreational vehicles			**(II) Total Liabilities**		$105,755
Household furnishings	3,700				
Jewelry and artwork	1,500				
Other			**Net Worth [(I) – (II)]**		$ 41,420
Other					
Total Personal Property		$ 19,200			
(I)Total Assets		$ 147,175	**Total Liabilities and Net Worth**		$ 147,175

Net Worth: A Measure of Your Financial Worth

Now that you've listed what you own and what you owe, you can calculate your **net worth,** the amount of actual wealth or **equity** that an individual or family has in owned assets. It represents the amount of money you'd have left after selling all your owned assets at their estimated fair market values and paying off all your liabilities (assuming there are no transaction costs). As noted earlier, every balance sheet must "balance" so that total assets equal total liabilities plus net worth. Rearranging this equation, we see that net worth equals total assets minus total liabilities. Once you establish the fair market value of assets and the level of liabilities, you can easily calculate net worth by subtracting total liabilities from total assets. If net worth is less than zero, the family is *technically insolvent*. Although this form of **insolvency** doesn't mean that the family will end up in bankruptcy proceedings, it does show a lack of financial planning.

Net worth typically increases over the life cycle of an individual or family, as Exhibit 2.2 on page 36 illustrates. For example, the balance sheet of a college student will probably be fairly simple. Assets would include modest liquid assets (cash, checking, and savings accounts) and personal property, which may include a car. Liabilities might include utility bills, perhaps some open account credit obligations, and automobile and education loans. At this point in life, net worth would typically be low, because assets are small in comparison with liabilities. A 29-year-old, single school teacher would have more liquid assets and personal property, may have started an investment program, and may have purchased a condominium. Net worth would be rising but may still be low due to the increased liabilities associated with real and personal property purchases. The higher net worth of a two-career couple in their late thirties with children would reflect a greater proportion of assets relative to liabilities as they save for college expenses and retirement.

In the long-term financial planning process, the level of net worth is important. Once you have established a goal of accumulating a certain level or type of wealth, you can track progress toward that goal by monitoring net worth.

Balance Sheet Format and Preparation

You should prepare your personal balance sheet at least once a year, preferably every 3 to 6 months. Here's how to do it, using the categories in Worksheet 2.1 as a guide:

Smart.Sites

What's the fair market value of your car? The personal watercraft your uncle gave you? Go to the link at **http://www .thomsonedu.com/finance/ gitman** to find out.

1. **List your assets at their fair market value as of the date you are preparing the balance sheet.** You'll find the fair market value of liquid and investment assets on checking and savings account records and investment account statements. Estimate the values of homes and cars using published sources of information, such as advertisements for comparable homes and the *Kelley Blue Book* for used car values. Certain items—for example, homes, jewelry, and artwork—may appreciate, or increase in value, over time. The values of assets like cars and most other types of personal property will depreciate, or decrease in value, over time.
2. **List all current and long-term liabilities.** Show all outstanding charges, *even if you haven't received the bill*, as current liabilities on the balance sheet. For example, assume that on June 23 you used your Visa card to charge $320 for a set of tires. You typically receive your Visa bill around the 10th of the following month. If you were preparing a balance sheet dated June 30, you should include the $320 as a current liability, even though the bill won't arrive until July 10. Remember to list only the principal balance of any loan obligation.
3. **Calculate net worth.** Subtract your total liabilities from your total assets. This is your net worth, which reflects the equity you have in your total assets.

net worth An individual's or family's actual wealth; determined by subtracting total liabilities from total assets.

equity The actual ownership interest in a specific asset or group of assets.

insolvency The financial state in which net worth is less than zero.

A Balance Sheet for Tim and Andrea Shepard

What can you learn from a balance sheet? Let's examine a hypothetical balance sheet as of December 31, 2007, prepared for Tim and Andrea Shepard, the young couple (ages 28 and 26) we met in Chapter 1 (see Worksheet 2.1 on page 34). Assets are listed on the left

EXHIBIT 2.2   Median Net Worth by Age

Net worth starts to build in the 25–34 age bracket and continues to climb, peaking in the age 55–64 bracket. It declines once a person retires and begins to use assets to meet living expenses, usually at about age 65.

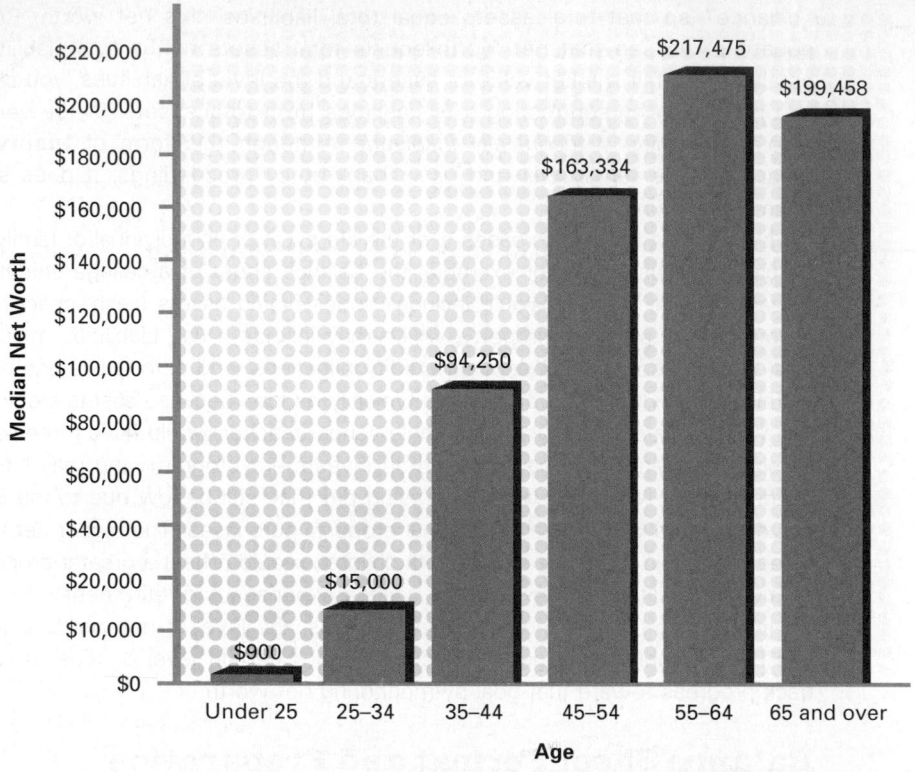

Source: Claritas Inc. Market Audit Data, December 2003.

side, the most liquid first; liabilities are on the right, starting with the most recent. The net worth entry is at the bottom right of the statement, just below the liabilities. The statement should *balance*: total assets equal the sum of total liabilities and net worth, as in the balance sheet equation on page 32. Here's what this financial statement tells us about the Shepards' financial condition:

- **Assets:** Given their ages, the Shepards' asset position looks quite good. Their dominant asset is their condo. They also have $5,750 in investments, which include retirement funds, and appear to have adequate liquid assets to meet their bill payments and cover small, unexpected expenses.
- **Liabilities:** The Shepards' primary liability is the $92,000 mortgage on their condo. Their equity, or actual ownership interest, in the condo is approximately $28,000 ($120,000 market value minus $92,000 outstanding mortgage loan). Their current liabilities are $905, with other debts of $12,850 representing auto, furniture, and education loans, as well as a loan from their parents to help with the down payment on their home.
- **Net worth:** The Shepards' net worth ($147,175 in total assets minus total liabilities of $105,755) is $41,420—considering their ages, a respectable amount that is well above the median shown in Exhibit 2.2.

Comparing the Shepards' total liabilities to their total assets gives a more realistic view of their current wealth position than merely looking at just assets or just liabilities. By calculating their net worth at specific times, they can measure their progress toward achieving their financial goals.

2-2	Describe the balance sheet, its components, and how you would use it in personal financial planning. Differentiate between investments and real and personal property.
2-3	What is the balance sheet equation? Explain when a family may be viewed as *technically insolvent*.
2-4	Explain two ways in which net worth could increase (or decrease) from one period to the next.

LG3 THE INCOME AND EXPENSE STATEMENT: WHAT WE EARN AND WHERE IT GOES

When confronted with a lack of funds, the first question people ask themselves is, "Where does all the money go?" Preparing an *income and expense statement* would answer this question. Whereas the balance sheet describes a person's or family's financial position at a given time, the income and expense statement captures the various financial activities that have occurred over time—normally over the course of a year, although it technically can cover any time period (month, quarter, and so on). Think of this statement as a motion picture that not only shows actual results over time but also lets you compare them with budgeted financial goals. Equally important, the statement allows you to evaluate the amount of saving and investing during the period it covers.

Like the balance sheet, the income and expense statement has three major parts: *income*, *expenses*, and *cash surplus* (or *deficit*). A cash surplus (or deficit) is merely the difference between income and expenses. The statement is prepared on a **cash basis,** which means that *only transactions involving actual cash receipts or actual cash outlays are recorded*. The term *cash* is used in this case to include not only coin and currency but also checks and debit card transactions drawn against checking and certain types of savings accounts.

Income and expense patterns change over the individual's or family's life cycle. Income and spending levels rise steadily to a peak in the 45–54 age bracket. On average, people in this age group, whose children are typically in college or no longer at home, have the highest level of income. They also spend more than other age groups on entertainment, dining out, transportation, education, insurance, and charitable contributions. Families in the 35–44 age bracket have slightly lower average levels of income and expenses but very different spending patterns. Because they tend to have school-age children, they spend more on groceries, housing, clothing, and other personal needs. The average percentage of pretax income spent, however, is about the same: 75 to 80 percent for all age brackets through age 64. It rises sharply to about 97 percent, however, for persons age 65 and over.

Income: Cash In

Common sources of **income** include earnings received as wages, salaries, self-employment income, bonuses, and commissions; interest and dividends received from savings and investments; and proceeds from the sale of assets such as stocks and bonds or an auto. Other income items include pension or annuity income; rent received from leased assets; alimony and child support; scholarships, grants, and Social Security received; tax refunds; and miscellaneous types of income. Worksheet 2.2 on page 38, Tim and Andrea Shepard's Income and and Expense Statement, has general categories for recording income.

Note also that the proper figure to use is *gross* wages, salaries, and commissions, which constitute the amount of income you receive from your employer *before* taxes and other payroll deductions. The gross value is used because the taxes and payroll deductions will be itemized and deducted as expenses later in the income and expense statement. Therefore, you

cash basis A method of preparing financial statements in which only transactions involving actual cash receipts or actual cash outlays are recorded.

income Earnings received as wages, salaries, bonuses, commissions, interest and dividends, and proceeds from the sale of assets.

The income and expense statement essentially shows what you earned, how you spent your money, and how much you were left with (or, if you spent more than you took in, how much you went "in the hole").

INCOME AND EXPENSE STATEMENT

Name(s) Tim and Andrea Shepard

For the Year _____ Ended December 31, 2007

INCOME

Wages and salaries	Name: Tim Shepard	$	55,000
	Name: Andrea Shepard		15,450
	Name:		
Self-employment income			
Bonuses and commissions	Tim-sales commissions		2,275
Investment income	Interest received		195
	Dividends received		120
	Rents received		
	Sale of securities		
	Other		
Pensions and annuities			
Other income			
	(I) Total Income	**$**	**73,040**

EXPENSES

Housing	Rent/mortgage payment (include insurance and taxes, if applicable)	$	16,864
	Repairs, maintenance, improvements		1,050
Utilities	Gas, electric, water		1,750
	Phone		480
	Cable TV and other		240
Food	Groceries		2,425
	Dining out		3,400
Transportation	Auto loan payments		2,520
	License plates, fees, etc.		250
	Gas, oil, repairs, tires, maintenance		2,015
Medical	Health, major medical, disability insurance (payroll deductions or not provided by employer)		1,200
	Doctor, dentist, hospital, medicines		305
Clothing	Clothes, shoes, and accessories		1,700
Insurance	Homeowner's (if not covered by mortgage payment)		425
	Life (not provided by employer)		260
	Auto		695
Taxes	Income and social security		15,430
	Property (if not included in mortgage)		1,000
Appliances, furniture, and other major purchases	Loan payments		800
	Purchases and repairs		450
Personal care	Laundry, cosmetics, hair care		700
Recreation and entertainment	Vacations		2,000
	Other recreation and entertainment		2,630
Other items	Tuition and books: Andrea		1,400
	Gifts		215
	Loan payments: Education loans		900
	Loan payments: Parents		600
	(II) Total Expenses	**$**	**61,704**
	CASH SURPLUS (OR DEFICIT) [(I) − (II)]	**$**	**11,336**

should not use *take-home* pay, because it understates your income by the amount of these deductions.

Expenses: Cash Out

Expenses represent money used for outlays. Worksheet 2.2, Tim and Andrea Shepard's Income and and Expense Statement, categorizes them by the types of benefits they provide: (1) living expenses (such as housing, utilities, food, transportation, medical, clothing, and insurance), (2) tax payments, (3) asset purchases (such as autos, stereos, furniture, appliances, and loan payments on them), and (4) other payments for personal care, recreation and entertainment, and other expenses. Some are **fixed expenses**—usually contractual, predetermined, and involving equal payments each period (typically each month). Examples include mortgage and installment loan payments, insurance premiums, professional or union dues, club dues, monthly savings or investment programs, and cable TV fees. Others (such as food, clothing, utilities, entertainment, and medical expenses) are **variable expenses,** because their amounts change from one time period to the next.

Exhibit 2.3 on page 40 shows the average annual expenses by major category as a percentage of after-tax income. It's a useful benchmark to see how you compare with national averages. However, your own expenses will vary according to your age, lifestyle, and where you live. For example, it costs considerably more to buy a home in San Diego than in Indianapolis. If you live in the suburbs, your commuting expenses will be higher than those of city dwellers.

Cash Surplus (or Deficit)

The third component of the income and expense statement shows the net result of the period's financial activities. Subtracting total expenses from total income gives you the cash surplus (or deficit) for the period. At a glance, you can see how you did financially over the period. A positive figure indicates that expenses were less than income, resulting in a **cash surplus.** A value of zero indicates that expenses were exactly equal to income for the period, while a negative value means that your expenses exceeded income and you have a **cash deficit.**

You can use a cash surplus for savings or investment purposes, to acquire assets, or to reduce debt. Adding to savings or investments should increase your future income and net worth, and making payments on debt affects cash flow favorably by reducing future expenses. In contrast, when a cash deficit occurs, you must cover the shortfall from your savings or investments, reduce assets, or borrow. All of these strategies will reduce net worth and negatively affect your financial future.

One final point: a cash surplus does not necessarily mean that funds are simply lying around waiting to be used. Because the income and expense statement reflects what has actually occurred, the disposition of the surplus (or deficit) is shown in the asset, liability, and net worth accounts on the balance sheet. For example, if you used the surplus to make investments, this would increase the appropriate asset account. If you used the surplus to pay off a loan, the payment would reduce that liability account. Of course, if you used the surplus to increase cash balances, you'd have the funds to use. In each case, your net worth *increases*. Surpluses *increase* net worth; deficits *decrease* it, whether the shortfall is financed by reducing an asset (for example, drawing down a savings account) or by borrowing.

Preparing the Income and Expense Statement

As shown in Worksheet 2.2, the income and expense statement is dated to define the period covered. To prepare the statement, follow these steps:

1. **Record your income from all sources for the chosen period.** Use your paycheck stubs to verify your gross pay for the period, and be sure to include bonuses, commission checks, and overtime pay. You'll find interest earned, securities bought and sold, interest and dividends received, and other investment matters on your bank and investment account statements. Keep a running list of other income sources, such as rents, tax refunds, and asset sales.

expenses Money spent on living expenses and to pay taxes, purchase assets, or repay debt.

fixed expenses Contractual, predetermined expenses involving equal payments each period.

variable expenses Expenses involving payment amounts that change from one time period to the next.

cash surplus An excess amount of income over expenses that results in *increased* net worth.

cash deficit An excess amount of expenses over income, resulting in insufficient funds as well as in *decreased* net worth.

EXHIBIT 2.3   How We Spend Our Income

Just three categories account for almost two-thirds of spent after-tax income: food, housing, and transportation.

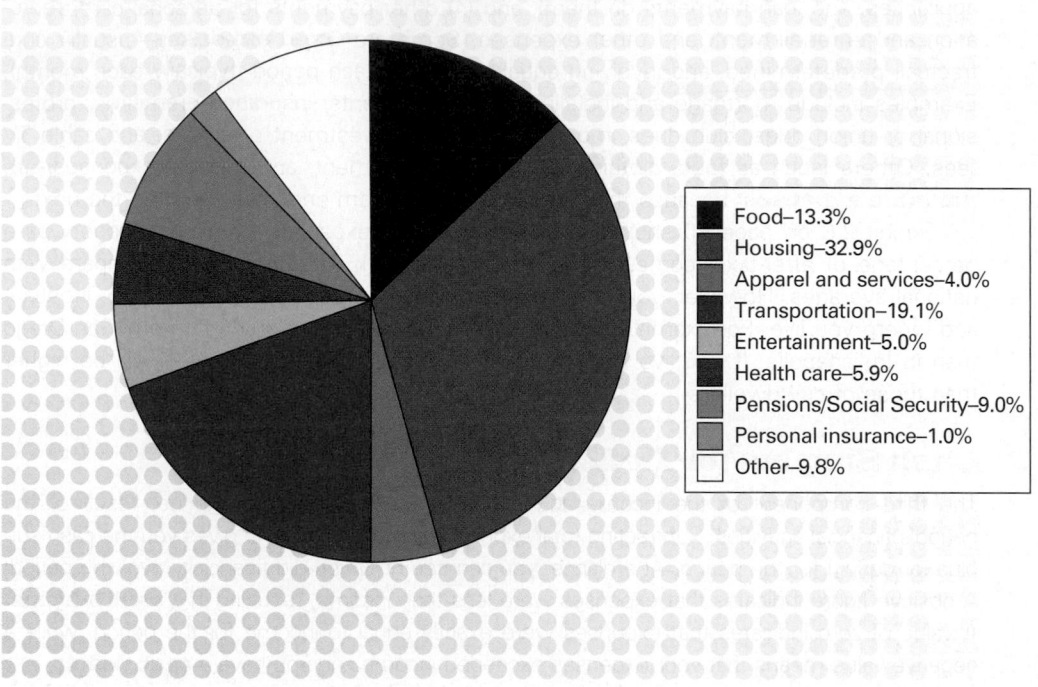

- Food–13.3%
- Housing–32.9%
- Apparel and services–4.0%
- Transportation–19.1%
- Entertainment–5.0%
- Health care–5.9%
- Pensions/Social Security–9.0%
- Personal insurance–1.0%
- Other–9.8%

Source: "Consumer Expenditures in 2003," Washington, D.C.: U.S. Department of Labor, Bureau of Labor Statistics Report 986, June 2005, p. 8.

2. **Establish meaningful expense categories.** Those shown on Worksheet 2.2 are a good starting point. Information on monthly house (or rent) payments, loan payments, and other fixed payments (such as insurance premiums and cable TV) is readily available from either the payment book or your checkbook (or, in the case of payroll deductions, your check stubs). (*Note:* Be careful with so-called *adjustable-rate loans,* because the amount of monthly loan payments will change when the interest rate changes.)

3. **Subtract total expenses from total income to get the cash surplus (a positive number) or deficit (a negative number).** This "bottom line" summarizes the *net cash flow* resulting from your financial activities during the period.

You'll probably pay for most major variable expenses by check, debit card, or credit card, so it's easy to keep track of them. It's harder to keep tabs on all the items in a month that you pay with cash, such as parking, lunches, movies, and incidentals. Most of us don't care to write down every little expense to the penny. You might try counting the cash in your wallet at the beginning of the month, then count again after a week goes by to see how much money is missing. Try to remember what you spent during the week, and write it down on your calendar to the nearest $5. If you can't remember, then try the exercise over shorter and shorter periods until you can.

Just as you show only the amounts of cash actually received as income, record only the amounts of money you actually pay out in cash as expenses. If you borrow to acquire an item, particularly an asset, include only the *actual cash payment—purchase price minus amount borrowed*—as an expense, as well as *payments on the loan* in the period you actually make them. You show credit purchases of this type as an asset and corresponding liability *on the balance sheet*. Record only the cash payments on loans, not the actual amounts of the loans themselves, on the income and expense statement.

For example, assume that you purchase a new car for $20,000 in September. You make a down payment of $3,000 and finance the remaining $17,000 with a 4-year, 7.5 percent installment loan. Your September 30 income statement would show a cash expenditure of $3,000, and each subsequent monthly income statement would include your monthly loan payment of $411. Your September 30 balance sheet would show the car as an asset valued at $20,000 and the loan balance as a $17,000 long-term liability. The market value of the car and the loan balance would be adjusted on future balance sheets.

Finally, when making your list of expenses for the year, remember to include the amount of income tax and Social Security taxes withheld from your paycheck as well as any other payroll deductions (health insurance, savings plans, retirement and pension contributions, and professional/union dues). These deductions (from gross wages, salaries, bonuses, and commissions) represent personal expenses, even if they don't involve a direct cash payment.

You might be shocked when listing what's taken out of your paycheck. Even if you're in a fairly low federal income tax bracket, your paycheck could easily be reduced by more than 25 percent for taxes alone. Your federal tax could be withheld at 15 percent, your state income tax could be withheld at 5 percent, and your Social Security and Medicare tax could be withheld at 7.65 percent. That doesn't even count health and disability income insurance.

Preparing income and expense statements can involve a lot of number crunching. Fortunately, some good computer software packages, such as Quicken and Microsoft Money, can simplify the job of preparing personal financial statements and doing other personal financial planning tasks.

An Income and Expense Statement for Tim and Andrea Shepard

Tim and Andrea Shepard's balance sheet in Worksheet 2.1 showed us their financial condition as of December 31, 2007. Their income and expense statement for the year ended December 31, 2007, in Worksheet 2.2, was prepared using the background material presented earlier, along with the Shepards' balance sheet. This statement shows how cash flowed into and out of their "pockets":

- **Income:** Total income for the year ended December 31, 2007, is $73,040. Tim's wages clearly represent the family's chief source of income, although Andrea has finished her MBA and will now be making a major contribution. Other sources of income include $195 in interest on their savings accounts and bond investments and $120 in dividends from their common stock holdings.
- **Expenses:** Total expenses for the year of $61,704 included their home mortgage, food, auto loan, clothing, and income and Social Security taxes. Other sizable expenses during the year include home repairs and improvements, gas and electricity, auto license and operating expenses, insurance, tuition, and education loan payments.

ⓘ Concept Check

CHECK • CONCEPT CHECK • CONCEPT CHECK • CONCEPT CHECK • CONCEPT CHECK • CONCEPT CHECK • CONCEPT C

2-5	What is an *income and expense statement?* What role does it serve in personal financial planning?
2-6	Explain what *cash basis* means in this statement: "An income and expense statement should be prepared on a cash basis." How and where are credit purchases shown when statements are prepared on a cash basis?
2-7	Distinguish between *fixed* and *variable expenses,* and give examples of each.
2-8	Is it possible to have a *cash deficit* on an income and expense statement? If so, how?

Developing Your Financial Statements and Plans

- **Cash surplus:** The Shepards end the year with a cash surplus of $11,336 (total income of $73,040 minus total expenses of $61,704).

The Shepards can use their surplus to increase savings, invest in stocks, bonds, or other vehicles, or make payments on some outstanding debts. The best strategy depends on their financial goals. If they had a cash deficit, the Shepards would have to withdraw savings, liquidate investments, or borrow an amount equal to the deficit to meet their financial commitments (that is, "make ends meet"). With their surplus of $11,336, the Shepards have made a positive contribution to their net worth.

LG4 · USING YOUR PERSONAL FINANCIAL STATEMENTS

Whether you're just starting out and have a minimal net worth or are further along the path toward achieving your goals, your balance sheet and income and expense statement provide insight into your current financial status. You now have the information you need to examine your financial position, monitor your financial activities, and track the progress you're making. Let's now look at ways to help you create better personal financial statements and analyze them to better understand your financial situation.

Keeping Good Records

Although recordkeeping doesn't rank high on most "to do" lists, a good recordkeeping system helps you manage and control your personal financial affairs. With organized, up-to-date financial records, you'll prepare more accurate personal financial statements and budgets, pay less to your tax preparer, not miss any tax deductions, and save on taxes when you sell a house or securities or withdraw retirement funds. Also, good records make it easier for a spouse or relative to manage your financial affairs in an emergency. To that end, you should prepare a comprehensive list of these records, their locations, and your key advisors (financial planner, banker, accountant, attorney, doctors) for family members.

Prepare your personal financial statements at least once each year, ideally when drawing up your budget. Many people update their financial statements every 3 or 6 months. You may want to keep a *ledger*, or financial record book, to summarize all your financial transactions. The ledger has sections for assets, liabilities, sources of income, and expenses; these sections contain separate accounts for each item. Whenever any accounts change, make an appropriate ledger entry. For example, if you buy an iPod nano for $250 cash, you'd show the iPod nano on your balance sheet as an asset (at its fair market value) and as a $250 expenditure on your income and expense statement. If you borrowed to pay for the iPod nano, the loan amount would be a liability on the balance sheet, and any loan payments made during the period would be shown on the income and expense statement. You'd keep similar records for asset sales, loan repayments, income sources, and so on.

Organizing Your Records

Your system doesn't have to be fancy to be effective. You'll need a bank safe-deposit box, the ledger book described earlier, and a set of files with general categories such as banking and credit cards, taxes, home, insurance, investments, and retirement accounts. An expandable file, with a dozen or so compartments for incoming bills, receipts, paycheck stubs, or anything you might need later, works well.

Start by taking an inventory. Make a list of everything you own and owe. Check it at least once a year to make sure it's up to date and to review your financial progress. Then, record transactions manually in your ledger or with financial planning software. Exhibit 2.4 offers general guidelines for keeping and organizing your personal financial records.

You'll want to set up separate files for tax-planning records, with one for income (paycheck stubs, interest on savings accounts, and so on) and another for deductions, as well as for individual mutual fund and brokerage account records. Once you set up your files, be sure to go through them at least once a year and throw out unnecessary items.

Tracking Financial Progress: Ratio Analysis

Each time you prepare your financial statements, you should analyze them to see how well you're doing on your financial goals. For example, with an income and expense statement, you can compare actual financial results with budgeted figures to make sure that your spending is under control. Likewise, comparing a set of financial plans with a balance sheet will reveal whether you're meeting your savings and investment goals, reducing your debt, or building up a retirement reserve. You can compare current performance with historical performance to find out if your financial situation is improving or getting worse.

Calculating certain financial ratios can help you evaluate your financial performance over time. What's more, if you apply for a loan, the lender probably will look at these ratios to judge your ability to carry additional debt. Four important money management ratios are (1) solvency ratio, (2) liquidity ratio, (3) savings ratio, and (4) debt service ratio. The first two are associated primarily with the balance sheet; the last two relate primarily to the income and expense statement. Exhibit 2.5 on page 44 defines these ratios and illustrates their calculation for Tim and Andrea Shepard.

Balance Sheet Ratios

solvency ratio Total net worth divided by total assets; measures the degree of exposure to insolvency.

liquidity ratio Total liquid assets divided by total current debts; measures the ability to pay current debts.

When evaluating your balance sheet, you should be most concerned with your net worth at a given time. As explained earlier in this chapter, you are *technically insolvent* when your total liabilities exceed your total assets—that is, when you have a negative net worth. The **solvency ratio** shows, as a percentage, your degree of exposure to insolvency, or how much "cushion" you have as a protection against insolvency. Tim and Andrea's solvency ratio

---

EXHIBIT 2.4 — Organizing Your Financial Records

Confused about what to keep, where to keep it, and when to toss it? Here are some general rules.

Permanent papers: *Place in a fireproof box (which won't protect documents from charring at high heat) or, preferably, a safe-deposit box at the bank.*

Birth, marriage, and death certificates; separation or divorce agreements; adoption papers; passports; military service records; wills, healthcare proxy (giving someone legal right to make medical decisions if you become incapacitated), powers of attorney; copies of IRAs and 401(k)s; all current insurance policies and the names of the agents; securities certificates, deeds, and purchase and sale documents on all homes you've owned; other documents relating to property ownership such as a car title; retirement fund records (pension plans, IRAs, and so on) to know which portions of them are tax deferred and therefore not subject to tax until funds are withdrawn.

Keep original wills, proxies, and powers of attorney at home because a safe-deposit box may be sealed at your death. Make copies of all other permanent papers to keep at home. Shred prior wills to avoid confusion.

Long-term papers: *Keep for 7 years in a file cabinet or file boxes.*

Federal and state income tax returns and all supporting documentation (receipts, charitable contributions, canceled checks for tax-deductible expenses, casualty losses); household papers such as receipts, instruction manuals, warranties, and records of home capital improvements.

After 7 years, transfer copies of tax returns to permanent storage—dispose of supporting documentation by shredding.

Keep the following at least 3 years after the due date of the tax return in which you report the sale, the period the IRS has to challenge your return: security purchase and sale confirmations, dividend reinvestment notices, and records of stock splits; home-related documents.

Keep product warranties until they expire.

Short-term papers: *Keep in a file cabinet or a file box at home.*

Monthly bank, brokerage, mutual fund, 401(k) statements, paycheck stubs: *Shred when you receive your year-end statement, and keep year-end statements for at least 3 years.*

Credit card statements, utility, and telephone bills: *Shred when paid.*

ATM receipts and deposit slips: *Shred when transaction appears on your bank statement.*

Other papers worth keeping: In case of emergency, you should have photos and fingerprints of your children. Medical records are also good to keep.

EXHIBIT 2.5   Ratios for Personal Financial Statement Analysis

Ratio	Formula	2007 Calculation for the Shepards
Solvency ratio	$\dfrac{\text{Total net worth}}{\text{Total assets}}$	$\dfrac{\$41,420}{\$147,175} = 0.281$, or 28.1%
Liquidity ratio	$\dfrac{\text{Total liquid assets}}{\text{Total current debts}}$	$\dfrac{\$2,225}{\$22,589^{(a)}} = 0.099$, or 9.9%
Savings ratio	$\dfrac{\text{Cash surplus}}{\text{Income after taxes}}$	$\dfrac{\$11,336}{\$73,040 - \$15,430} = \dfrac{\$11,336}{\$57,610} = 0.197$, or 19.7%
Debt service ratio	$\dfrac{\text{Total monthly loan payments}}{\text{Monthly gross (before tax) income}}$	$\dfrac{\$1,807^{(b)}}{\$6,807^{(c)}} = 0.266$, or 26.6%

(a) You'll find the Shepards' total liquid assets ($2,225) and total current liabilities ($905) on Worksheet 2.1. The total current debt (from Worksheet 2.2) totals $22,589: current liabilities of $905 + loan payments due within 1 year of $21,684 − $16,864 in mortgage payments + $2,520 in auto loan payments + $800 in furniture loan payments + $900 in education loan payments + $600 in loan payments to parents.

(b) On an *annual* basis, the Shepards' debt obligations total $21,684 ($16,864 in mortgage payments, $2,520 in auto loan payments, $800 in furniture loan payments, $900 in education loan payments, and $600 in loan payments to parents, from Worksheet 2.2). The Shepards' total *monthly* loan payments are about $1,807 ($21,684 ÷ 12 months).

(c) Dividing the Shepards' *annual* gross income, also found in Worksheet 2.2, of $73,040 by 12 equals $6,087 monthly ($73,040 ÷ 12).

FINANCIAL ROAD SIGN

DECLUTTER YOUR LIFE!

Too much paper in your house? Here are tips to eliminate what you don't need.
1. Be selective to avoid information overload; you don't need to know everything.
2. Set up a regular weekly time to read the key materials you select.
3. Sort mail daily into a mail basket for each person, tossing obvious junk immediately.
4. Don't procrastinate. Sort one pile at a time and take some action *now.*
5. Don't make copies "just in case."
6. File only the essentials. Eighty percent of paper filed is rarely used.
7. Purge files and other papers regularly to make room for new information.
8. Give away recent magazines, catalogs, or books when they're still useful.
9. Buy a shredder and use it to shred any paper with any personal identification and account numbers, including unsolicited credit card offers. This will minimize the risk of identity theft.

is 28.1 percent, which means that they could withstand only about a 28 percent decline in the market value of their assets before they would be insolvent. The low value for this ratio suggests they should consider improving it in the future.

Although the solvency ratio indicates the potential to withstand financial problems, it does not deal directly with the ability to pay current debts. This issue is addressed with the **liquidity ratio,** which shows how long you could continue to pay current debts (any bills or charges that must be paid *within 1 year*) with existing liquid assets in the event of income loss.

This ratio indicates that the Shepards can cover only about 10 percent of their existing 1-year debt obligations with their current liquid assets. In other words, they have slightly over 1 month (1 month is $^1/_{12}$, or 8.3 percent) of coverage. If an unexpected event cut off their income, their liquid reserves would quickly be exhausted. Although there's no hard-and-fast rule for what this ratio should be, it seems too low for the Shepards. They should consider strengthening it along with their solvency ratio. They should be able to add to their cash surpluses now that Andrea is working full-time.

The amount of liquid reserves will vary with your personal circumstances and "comfort level." Another useful liquidity guideline is to have a reserve fund equal to 3 to 6 months of after-tax income available to cover living expenses. The Shepards' after-tax income for 2007 was $4,801 per month ([$73,040 total income − $15,430 income and Social Security taxes] ÷ 12). Therefore, this guideline suggests they should have between $14,403 and $28,806 in total liquid assets—considerably more than the $2,225 on their latest balance sheet. If you feel that your job is secure or you have other potential sources of income, you may be comfortable with 3 or 4 months in reserve. If you tend to be cautious financially, you may want to build a larger fund. In troubled economic times, you may want to keep 6 months or more of income in this fund as protection should you lose your job.

Income and Expense Statement Ratios

When evaluating your income and expense statement, you should be concerned with the bottom line, which shows the cash surplus (or deficit) resulting from the period's activities. You can relate the cash surplus (or deficit) to income by calculating a **savings ratio,** which is done most effectively with after-tax income.

Tim and Andrea saved about 20 percent of their after-tax income, which is on the high side (American families, on average, save about 5 to 8 percent). How much to save is a personal choice. Some families would plan much higher levels, particularly if they're saving to achieve an important goal, such as buying a home.

While maintaining an adequate level of savings is obviously important to personal financial planning, so is the ability to pay debts promptly. In fact, debt payments have a higher priority. The **debt service ratio** allows you to make sure you can comfortably meet your debt obligations. This ratio excludes current liabilities and considers only mortgage, installment, and personal loan obligations.

Monthly loan payments account for about 27 percent of Tim and Andrea's monthly gross income. This relatively low debt service ratio indicates that the Shepards should have little difficulty in meeting their monthly loan payments. In your financial planning, try to keep your debt service ratio somewhere under 35 percent or so, because that's generally viewed as a manageable level of debt—and, of course, the lower the debt service ratio, the easier it is to meet loan payments as they come due.

❚❚ Concept Check

CHECK • CONCEPT CHECK • CONCEPT CHECK • CONCEPT CHECK • CONCEPT CHECK • CONCEPT CHECK • CONCEPT C

2-9	How can accurate records and control procedures be used to ensure the effectiveness of the personal financial planning process?
2-10	Describe some of the areas or items you would consider when evaluating your balance sheet and income and expense statement. Cite several ratios that could help in this effort.

LG5   CASH IN/CASH OUT: PREPARING AND USING BUDGETS

Many of us avoid budgeting as if it were the plague. After all, do you really want to know that 30 percent of your take-home pay is going to restaurant meals? Yet preparing, analyzing, and monitoring your personal budget are essential steps for successful personal financial planning.

savings ratio Cash surplus divided by net income (after tax); indicates relative amount of cash surplus achieved during a given period.

debt service ratio Total monthly loan payments divided by monthly gross (before-tax) income; provides a measure of the ability to pay debts promptly.

After defining your short-term financial goals, you can prepare a cash budget for the coming year. Recall that a *budget* is a short-term financial planning report that helps you achieve your short-term financial goals. By taking the time to evaluate your current financial situation, spending patterns, and goals, you can develop a realistic budget consistent with your personal lifestyle, family situation, and values. A cash budget is a valuable money management tool that helps you:

1. Maintain the necessary information to monitor and control your finances
2. Decide how to allocate your income to reach your financial goals
3. Implement a system of disciplined spending—as opposed to just existing from one paycheck to the next

FINANCIAL ROAD SIGN

4. Reduce needless spending so you can increase the funds allocated to savings and investments
5. Achieve your long-term financial goals

Just as your goals change over your lifetime, so will your budget as your financial situation becomes more complex. Typically, the number of income and expense categories increases as you accumulate more assets and debts and have more family responsibilities. For example, the budget of a college student should be quite simple, with limited income from part-time jobs, parental contributions, and scholarships and grants. Expenses might include room and board, clothes, books, auto expenses, and entertainment. Once a student graduates and goes to work full-time, his or her budget will include additional expenses such as rent, insurance, work clothes, and commuting costs. Not until retirement can you expect this process to perhaps become simpler.

The Budgeting Process

Like the income and expense statement, *a budget should be prepared on a cash basis;* thus, we call this document a **cash budget** because it deals with estimated cash receipts and cash expenses, including savings and investments, that are expected to occur in the coming year. Because you receive and pay most bills monthly, you'll probably want to estimate income as well as expenses on a monthly basis.

The cash budget preparation process has three stages: estimating income, estimating expenses, and finalizing the cash budget. When you're estimating income and expenses, take into account any anticipated changes in the cost of living and their impact on your budget components. If your income is fixed—not expected to change over the budgetary period—increases in various expense items will probably decrease the purchasing power of your income. Worksheet 2.3, the Shepards' "Annual Cash Budget by Month," has separate sections to record income (cash receipts) and expenses (cash expenses) and lists the most common categories for each.

Estimating Income

The first step in preparing your cash budget is to estimate your income for the coming year. Include all income expected for the year: the take-home pay of both spouses, expected bonuses or commissions, pension or annuity income, and investment income—interest, dividend, rental, and asset (particularly security) sale income. When estimating income, keep in mind that *any item you receive for which repayment is required is not considered income.* For instance, loan proceeds are treated not as a source of income but as a *liability* for which scheduled repayments are required.

Note also that unlike the income and expense statement, in the cash budget you should use *take-home pay* (rather than gross income). Your cash budget focuses on those areas that you can control—and most people effectively have limited control over things like taxes withheld, contributions to company insurance and pension plans, and the like. In effect, take-home pay represents the amount of *disposable income* you receive from your employer.

Estimating Expenses

The second step in the cash budgeting process is by far the most difficult: preparing a schedule of estimated expenses for the coming year. This is usually done using actual expenses from previous years (as found on income and expense statements and in supporting information for those periods), along with predetermined short-term financial goals. Good financial records, as discussed earlier, make it easier to develop realistic expense estimates. If you do not have past expense data, you could reexamine old checkbook registers and credit card statements to approximate expenses, or take a "needs approach" and attach dollar values to projected expenses. Pay close attention to expenses associated with medical disabilities, divorce and child support, and similar special circumstances.

cash budget A budget that takes into account estimated monthly cash receipts and cash expenses for the coming year.

The Shepards' annual cash budget shows several months in which substantial cash deficits are expected to occur; they can use this information to develop plans for covering those monthly shortfalls.

ANNUAL CASH BUDGET BY MONTH

Name(s) _Tim and Andrea Shepard_

For the _Year_ _____ Ended _December 31, 2008_

INCOME	Jan.	Feb.	Mar.	April	May	June	July	Aug.	Sep.	Oct.	Nov.	Dec.	Total for the Year
Take-home pay	$4,775	$4,775	$4,775	$4,965	$4,965	$5,140	$5,140	$5,140	$5,140	$5,140	$5,140	$5,140	$60,235
Bonuses and commissions						1,350						1,300	2,650
Pensions and annuities													
Investment income		90				90			90			90	360
Other income													
(I) Total Income	$4,775	$4,775	$4,865	$4,965	$4,965	$6,580	$5,140	$5,140	$5,230	$5,140	$5,140	$6,530	$63,245
EXPENSES													
Housing (rent/mtge., repairs)	$1,506	$1,856	$1,506	$1,506	$1,505	$1,505	$1,505	$1,505	$1,505	$1,505	$1,505	$1,505	$18,414
Utilities (phone, elec., gas, water)	245	245	245	175	180	205	230	245	205	195	230	250	2,650
Food (home and away)	575	575	575	575	575	575	575	575	575	575	575	575	6,900
Transportation (auto/public)	370	620	370	540	370	370	575	370	370	450	370	370	5,145
Medical/dental, incl. insurance	30	30	30	30	30	45	30	30	30	30	30	30	375
Clothing	150	150	500	400	200	200	300	500	200	300	300	300	3,500
Insurance (life, auto, home)				225	370		300			225	370		1,490
Taxes (property)		550						550					1,100
Appliances, furniture, and other (purchases/loans)	60	60	30			750			300	300	300		1,800
Personal care	100	100	100	100	100	100	100	100	100	100	100	100	1,200
Recreation and entertainment	250	250	3,200	200	200	300	300	200	200	200	200	2,050	7,550
Savings and investments	375	375	375	375	375	375	375	375	375	375	375	375	4,500
Other expenses	135	250	235	135	610	180	135	285	245	135	605	385	3,335
Fun money	230	230	230	230	230	230	230	230	230	230	230	230	2,760
(II) Total Expenses	$4,026	$5,291	$7,396	$4,491	$4,745	$4,835	$4,655	$4,965	$4,335	$4,620	$5,190	$6,170	$60,719
CASH SURPLUS (OR DEFICIT) [(I) − (II)]	$749	$(516)	$(2,531)	474	220	$1,745	485	175	895	520	(50)	360	2,526
CUMULATIVE CASH SURPLUS (OR DEFICIT)	$749	$233	$(2,298)	$(1,824)	$(1,604)	141	626	801	1,696	2,216	2,166	$2,526	2,526

Whether or not you have historical information, when preparing your budget *be aware of your expenditure patterns and how you spend money*. After tracking your expenses over several months, study your spending habits to see if you are doing things that should be eliminated (like going to the ATM too often or using credit cards too freely).

You'll probably find it easier to budget expenses if you group them into several general categories, rather than trying to estimate each item. Worksheet 2.3 is an example of one such grouping scheme, patterned after the categories used in the income and expense statement. You may also want to refer to the average expense percentages given in Exhibit 2.3. Choose categories that reflect your priorities and allow you to monitor areas of concern.

Initially, your expense estimates should include the transactions necessary to achieve your short-term goals. You should also quantify any current or short-term contributions toward your long-term goals and schedule them into the budget. Equally important are scheduled additions to savings and investments, because planned savings should be high on everyone's list of goals. If your budget doesn't balance with all these items, you will have to make some adjustments in the final budget.

Base estimated expenses on current price levels and then increase them by a percentage that reflects the anticipated rate of inflation. For example, if you estimate the monthly food bill at $350 and expect 4 percent inflation, you should budget your monthly food expenditure at $364, or $350 + $14 (4 percent × $350).

Don't forget an allowance for "fun money," which family members spend as they wish. This gives each person some financial independence and helps to form a healthy family budget relationship.

Finalizing the Cash Budget

After estimating income and expenses, finalize your budget by comparing projected income to projected expenses. Show the difference in the third section as a surplus or deficit. In a *balanced budget*, the total income for the year equals or exceeds total expenses. If you find that you have a deficit at year end, you'll have to *go back and adjust your expenses*. If you have several months of large surpluses, you should be able to cover any shortfall in a later month, as explained later. Budget preparation is complete once all monthly deficits are resolved and the total annual budget balances.

Admittedly, there's a lot of number crunching in personal cash budgeting. As discussed earlier, personal financial planning software can greatly streamline the budget preparation process.

Dealing with Deficits

Even if the annual budget balances, in certain months expenses may exceed income, causing a monthly budget deficit. Likewise, a budget surplus occurs when income in some months exceeds expenses. Two remedies exist:

- Shift expenses from months with budget deficits to months with surpluses (or, conversely, transfer income, if possible, from months with surpluses to those with deficits).
- Use savings, investments, or borrowing to cover temporary deficits.

Because the budget balances for the year, the need for funds to cover shortages is only temporary. In months with budget surpluses, you should return funds taken from savings or investments or repay loans. Either remedy is feasible for curing a monthly budget deficit in a balanced annual budget, although the second is probably more practical.

What can you do if your budget shows an annual budget deficit, even after you've made a few expense adjustments? You have three options:

- **Liquidate enough savings and investments or borrow enough to meet the total budget shortfall for the year.** Obviously, this option is not recommended, because it violates the objective of budgeting: to set expenses at a level that allows you to enjoy a reasonable standard of living *and* progress toward achieving your long-term goals. Reducing savings and investments or increasing debt to balance the budget reduces net worth. People who use this approach are *not* living within their means.
- **Cut low-priority expenses from the budget.** This option is clearly preferable to the first one. It balances the budget without using external funding sources by eliminating expenses associated with your least important short-term goals, such as flexible, or discretionary, expenses for nonessential items (such as recreation, entertainment, and some clothing). The *Money in Action* box on page 49 can help you find easy ways to spend less.
- **Increase income.** Finding a higher-paying job or perhaps a second, part-time job is the most difficult option; it takes more planning and may result in lifestyle changes. However, people who can't liquidate savings or investments or borrow funds to cover necessary expenses may have to choose this route to balance their budgets.

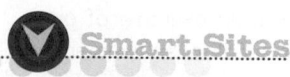
A Cash Budget for Tim and Andrea Shepard

Using their short-term financial goals (Worksheet 1.1 in Chapter 1) and past financial statements (Worksheets 2.1 and 2.2), Tim and Andrea Shepard have prepared their cash budget for the 2008 calendar year. Worksheet 2.3 shows the Shepards' estimated total 2008 annual income and expenses by month, as well as the monthly and annual cash surplus or deficit.

The Shepards list their total 2008 income of $63,245 by source for each month. By using take-home pay, they eliminate the need to show income-based taxes, Social Security

MONEY IN ACTION

SMALL SAVINGS MEAN BIG BUCKS!

It should be obvious: spend less than you earn, so you'll have money to invest. Yet so many people don't recognize this simple fact. They run up large credit card bills and take out loans instead of building a nest egg for the future.

Where to start? How about with the little stuff? You'd be amazed at how reducing even your smallest expenses can lead to big savings! Here are some examples of how reducing your discretionary spending now will yield big payoffs later, thanks to the large impact of compound interest (discussed later):

- Instead of buying 40 $5 lottery tickets a year, invest the $200 at the end of each year at 8 percent. If you start at age 18, you'll have $106,068 by the time you reach age 67!
- Buy a used car instead of a new one and invest the amount you saved at 8 percent for 40

years. If you saved $9,000 buying a used car, you'd have more than $195,000 available for your retirement fund!

- Stop the money drain into vending machines, espresso stands, and restaurant or fast-food lunches. Buy a regular cup of coffee rather than a latte or espresso, avoid the vending machines, and take a brown-bag lunch to work several days a week. If you save $22 a week for 50 weeks a year at 8 percent for 40 years, your savings will grow by more than $284,000!
- Use less of things like shampoo, detergent, and toothpaste. Try cutting the amount you use in half. Then look for other areas where you can do this.
- Pay attention to how you spend your loose change. Limit the amount of cash and coins you carry, and you'll plug one of the biggest financial leaks in most Americans' pockets.

You'll soon find many other ways to "save small," such as taking public transportation, comparing prices before you buy, reading books and magazines from the library instead of buying them, and using coupons to buy groceries.

Then, make saving a given, not something you do when you have money left over. Pay yourself first. Have your employer deposit the maximum amount in your 401(k) plan each pay period. It will grow even faster if your employer matches your contributions. You can also authorize withdrawals from your checking account to an investment account or to a mutual fund.

Critical Thinking Questions

1. List three small savings you can make, and show how they'll grow over time.
2. What is meant by "paying yourself first"? Why is it important?.

Sources: Scott Burns, "You Have a Fortune, You Just Have to Find It," *Dallas Morning News*, January 3, 1999, http://www.scottburns.com; "Escape from Affluenza," *PBS*, downloaded from http://www.pbs.org/kcts/affluenza/escape/action/index.html.

payments, and other payroll deductions as expenses. The take-home pay increases in April and June reflect Tim's and Andrea's expected salary increases.

In estimating annual expenses for 2008, the Shepards anticipate a small amount of inflation and have factored some price increases into their expense projections. They have also allocated $4,500 to savings and investments, a wise budgeting strategy, and included an amount for fun money, divided between them.

During their budgeting session, Tim and Andrea discovered that their first estimate resulted in expenses of $63,459, compared with their estimated income of $63,245. To eliminate the $214 deficit to balance their budget and allow for unexpected expenses, Tim and Andrea made these decisions:

- Omit some low-priority goals: spend less on stereo components, take a shorter Hawaiian vacation instead of the Colorado ski trip shown in Worksheet 1.1.

- Reschedule $200 of the loan repayment to their parents.
- Reduce their fun money slightly.

These reductions of $2,740 lower Tim and Andrea's total scheduled expenses to $60,719, giving them a surplus of $2,526 ($63,245 − $60,719) and more than balancing the budget on an annual basis. Of course, the Shepards can reduce other discretionary expenses to further increase the budget surplus and have a cushion for unexpected expenses.

The Shepards' final step is to analyze monthly surpluses and deficits and determine whether to use savings, investments, or borrowing to cover monthly shortfalls. The bottom line of their annual cash budget lists the cumulative, or running, totals of monthly cash surpluses and deficits. Despite their $2,526 year-end cumulative cash surplus, they have cumulative deficits in March, April, and May, primarily because of their March Hawaiian vacation. To cover these deficits, Tim and Andrea have arranged an interest-free loan from their parents. If they had dipped into savings to finance the deficits, they would have lost some interest earnings, included as income. They could delay clothing and recreation and entertainment expenses until later in the year to reduce the deficits more quickly. If they weren't able to obtain funds to cover the deficits, they would have to reduce expenses further or increase income. At year end, they should use their surplus to increase savings or investments or repay part of a loan.

Using Your Budgets

In the final analysis, a cash budget has value only if (1) you use it and (2) you keep careful records of actual income and expenses. These records show whether you are staying within budget limits. Record this information in a budget record book often enough so you don't overlook anything significant, yet not so often that it becomes a nuisance. A loose-leaf binder with separate pages for each income and expense category works quite well. Rounding entries to the nearest dollar simplifies the arithmetic.

At the beginning of each month, record the budgeted amount for each category and enter income received and money spent on the appropriate pages. At month-end, total each account and calculate the surplus or deficit. Except for certain income accounts (such as salary) and fixed expense accounts such as mortgage or loan payments, most categories will end the month with a positive or negative variance, indicating a cash surplus or deficit. You can then transfer your total spending by category to a **budget control schedule** that compares actual income and expenses with the various budget categories and shows the variances.

This monthly comparison makes it easy to identify major budget categories where income falls far short or spending far exceeds desired levels (variances of 5 to 10 percent or more). After pinpointing these areas, you can take corrective action to keep your budget on course. Don't just look at the size of the variances. Analyze them, particularly the larger ones, to discover *why* they occurred. An account deficit that occurs in only one period is obviously less of a problem than one that occurs in several periods. If recurring deficits indicate that an account was underbudgeted, you may need to adjust the budget to cover the outlays, reducing overbudgeted or nonessential accounts. Only in exceptional situations should you finance budget adjustments with savings and investments or borrowing.

Looking at the Shepards' budget control schedule for January, February, and March 2008, on Worksheet 2.4, you can see that actual income and expense levels are reasonably close to their targets and have a positive variance for the months shown (their surpluses exceed the budgeted surplus amounts). The biggest variances were in food and transportation expenses, but neither was far off the mark. Thus, for the first 3 months of the year, the Shepards seem to be doing a good job of controlling their income and expenses. They have, in fact, achieved a cumulative cash deficit of $419, smaller than the budgeted deficit (actual of −$1,879 versus budget of −$2,298) by cutting discretionary spending.

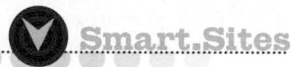

Smart Sites

Get more budgeting advice from CNNMoney's budgeting tutorial by clicking on "Evaluating them" for an interactive budget worksheet.
Go there through
http://www.thomsonedu.com/finance/gitman.

budget control schedule
A summary that shows how actual income and expenses compare with the various budget categories and where variances (surpluses or deficits) exist.

The budget control schedule provides important feedback on how the actual cash flow is stacking up relative to the forecasted cash budget. If the variances are significant enough and/or continue month after month, the Shepards should consider altering either their spending habits or their cash budget.

BUDGET CONTROL SCHEDULE

Name(s) __Tim and Andrea Shepard__

For the __3__ _____ Months Ended __March 31, 2008__

	Month: January				Month: February				Month: March			
INCOME	Budgeted Amount (1)	Actual (2)	Monthly Variance (3)	Year-to-Date Variance (4)	Budgeted Amount (5)	Actual (6)	Monthly Variance (7)	Year-to-Date Variance (8)	Budgeted Amount (9)	Actual (10)	Monthly Variance (11)	Year-to-Date Variance (12)
Take-home pay	$4,775	$4,792	$17	$17	$4,775	$4,792	$17	$34	$4,775	$4,792	$17	$51
Bonuses and commissions												
Pensions and annuities												
Investment income									90	86	(4)	(4)
Other income												
(I) Total Income	$4,775	$4,792	$17	$17	$4,775	$4,792	$17	$34	$4,865	$4,878	$13	$47
EXPENSES												
Housing (rent/mtge, repairs)	$1,506	$1,506	$0	$0	$1,856	$1,856	$0	$0	$1,506	$1,506	$0	$0
Utilities (phone, elec., gas, water)	245	237	(8)	(8)	245	252	7	(1)	245	228	(17)	(18)
Food (home and away)	575	559	(16)	(16)	575	548	(27)	(43)	575	450	(125)	(168)
Transportation (auto/public)	370	385	15	15	620	601	(19)	(4)	370	310	(60)	(64)
Medical/dental, incl. insurance	30	0	(30)	(30)	30	45	15	(15)	30	0	(30)	(45)
Clothing	150	190	40	40	150	135	(15)	25	500	475	(25)	0
Insurance (life, auto, home)												
Taxes (property)					550	550	0	0				0
Appliances, furniture, and other (purchases/loans)	60	60	0	0	60	60	0	0	30	30	0	0
Personal care	100	85	(15)	(15)	100	120	20	5	100	75	(25)	(20)
Recreation and entertainment	250	210	(40)	(40)	250	240	(10)	(50)	3,200	3,285	85	35
Savings and investments	375	375	0	0	375	375	0	0	375	375	0	0
Other expenses	135	118	(17)	(17)	250	245	(5)	(22)	235	200	(35)	(57)
Fun money	230	200	(30)	(30)	230	225	(5)	(35)	230	230	0	(35)
(II) Total Expenses	$4,026	$3,925	$(101)	$(101)	$5,291	$5,252	$(39)	$(140)	$7,396	$7,164	$(232)	$(372)
CASH SURPLUS (OR DEFICIT) [(I) − (II)]	$749	$867	$118	$118	$(516)	$(460)	$56	$174	$(2,531)	$(2,286)	$245	$419
CUMULATIVE CASH SURPLUS (OR DEFICIT)	$749	$867	$	$118	$233	$407	$	$174	$(2,298)	$(1,879)	$	$419

Key: Col. (3) = Col. (2) − Col. (1); Col. (7) = Col. (6) − Col. (5); Col. (11) = Col. (10) − Col. (9); Col. (4) = Col. (3); Col. (8) = Col. (4) + Col. (7); Col. (12) = Col. (8) + Col. (11).

Concept Check

2-11	Describe the *cash budget* and its three parts. How does a budget deficit differ from a budget surplus?
2-12	The Smith family has prepared their annual cash budget for 2008. They have divided it into 12 monthly budgets. Although only one monthly budget balances, they have managed to balance the overall budget for the year. What remedies are available to the Smith family for meeting the monthly budget deficits?
2-13	Why is it important to analyze actual budget surpluses or deficits at the end of each month?

THE TIME VALUE OF MONEY: PUTTING A DOLLAR VALUE ON FINANCIAL GOALS

Assume that one of your financial goals is to buy your first home in 6 years. Then your first question is how much to spend. Let's say you've done some "window shopping" and feel that, taking future inflation into consideration, you can buy a townhouse condominium for about $150,000 in 6 years. Of course, you won't need the full amount, but assuming that you'll make a 20 percent down payment of $30,000 (.20 × $150,000 = $30,000) and pay $5,000 in closing costs, you need around $35,000. You now have a fairly well-defined long-term financial goal: *To accumulate $35,000 in 6 years to buy a home costing about $150,000.*

The next question is how to get all that money. You'll probably accumulate it by saving or investing a set amount each month or year. You can easily estimate how much to save or invest each year if you know your goal and what you expect to earn on your savings or investments. In this case, if you have to start from scratch (that is, have nothing saved today) and estimate that you can earn about 10 percent on your money, you'll have to save or invest about $4,540 per year for each of the next 6 years to accumulate $35,000 over that time. Now you have another vital piece of information: *You know what you must do over the next 6 years to reach your financial goal.*

How did we arrive at the $4,540 figure? We used a concept called the **time value of money,** the idea that a dollar today is worth more than a dollar received in the future. With time value concepts, we can correctly compare dollar values occurring at different points in time. As long as you can earn a positive rate of return (interest rate) on your investments (ignoring taxes and other behavioral factors), in a strict financial sense you should always prefer to receive equal amounts of money sooner rather than later. The two key time value concepts, future value and present value, are discussed separately next. We'll use **timelines,** graphical presentations of cash flows, to visually depict the time value calculations. They will appear in the text margin near the related discussion. (*Note:* The time value discussions and demonstrations initially rely on the use of financial tables. Appendix E explains how to use financial calculators, which have tables built into them, to conveniently make time value calculations.) The calculator keystrokes for each calculation are shown in the text margin near the related discussion. Because of rounding in the tables, the calculator values will always be more precise.

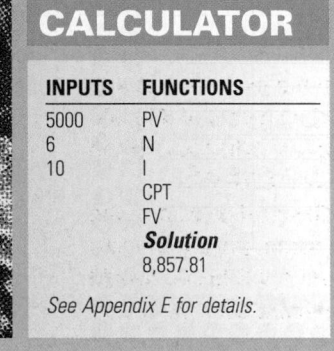

CALCULATOR

INPUTS	FUNCTIONS
5000	PV
6	N
10	I
	CPT
	FV
	Solution
	8,857.81

See Appendix E for details.

time value of money The concept that a dollar today is worth more than a dollar received in the future.

timeline A graphical presentation of cash flows.

future value The value to which an amount today will grow if it earns a specific rate of interest over a given period.

compounding When interest earned each year is left in the account and becomes part of the balance (or principal) on which interest is earned in subsequent years.

Future Value

To calculate how much to save to buy the $150,000 condominium, we used **future value,** the value to which an amount today will grow if it earns a specific rate of interest over a given period. Assume, for example, that you make annual deposits of $2,000 into a savings account that pays 5 percent interest per year. At the end of 20 years, your deposits would total $40,000 (20 × $2,000). If you made no withdrawals, your account balance would have increased to $66,132! This growth in value occurs not only because of earning interest, but because of **compounding**—the interest earned each year is left in the account and becomes part of the balance (or principal) on which interest is earned in subsequent years.

Future Value of a Single Amount

To demonstrate future value, let's return to the goal of accumulating $35,000 for a down payment to buy a home in 6 years. You might be tempted to solve this problem by simply dividing the $35,000 goal by the 6-year period: $35,000/6 = $5,833. Unfortunately, this procedure would be incorrect, because it would fail to take into account *the time value of money.* The correct way to approach this problem is to use the *future value* concept. For instance, if you can invest $100 today at 10 percent, you will have $110 in a year: You will earn $10 on your investment (.10 × $100 = $10), plus get your original $100 back. Once you know the length of time and rate of return involved, you can find the future value of any investment by using the following simple formula:

Future value = Amount invested × Future value factor

Get another lesson on time value concepts—at **http://www.thomsonedu .com/finance/gitman.**

annuity A fixed sum of money that occurs annually.

rule of 72 A useful formula for estimating about how long it will take to double a sum at a given interest rate.

Tables of future value factors simplify the computations in this formula (see Appendix A). The table is easy to use; simply find the factor that corresponds to a given year and interest rate. Referring to Appendix A, you will find the future value factor for a 6-year investment earning 10 percent is 1.772 (the factor that lies at the intersection of 6 years and 10 percent).

Returning to the problem at hand, let's say you already have accumulated $5,000 toward the purchase of a new home. To find the future value of that investment in 6 years earning 10 percent, you can use the above formula as follows:

$$\text{Future value} = \$5,000 \times 1.772 = \$8,860$$

In 6 years, then, you will have $8,860 if you invest the $5,000 at 10 percent. Because you feel you are going to need $35,000, you are still $26,140 short of your goal.

Future Value of an Annuity

How are you going to accumulate the additional $26,140? You'll again use the future value concept, but this time you'll use the *future value annuity factor*. An **annuity** is a fixed sum of money that occurs annually; for example, a deposit of $1,000 per year for each of the next 5 years, with payment to be made at the end of each year. To find out how much you need to save each year to accumulate a given amount, use this equation:

$$\text{Yearly savings} = \frac{\text{Amount of money desired}}{\text{Future value annuity factor}}$$

When dealing with an annuity you need to use a different table of factors, such as that in Appendix B. Note that it's very much like the table of future value factors and, in fact, is used in exactly the same way: The proper future value annuity factor is the one that corresponds to a given year *and* interest rate. For example, you'll find in Appendix B that the future value annuity factor for 6 years and 10 percent is 7.716. Using this factor in the above equation, you can find out how much to save each year to accumulate $26,140 in 6 years, given a 10 percent rate of return, as follows:

$$\text{Yearly savings} = \frac{\$26,140}{7.716} = \$3,387.77$$

You'll need to save about $3,390 a year to reach your goal. Note in the example that you must add $3,390 each year to the $5,000 you initially invested to build up a pool of $35,000 in 6 years. At a 10 percent rate of return, the $3,390 per year will grow to $26,140 and the $5,000 will grow to $8,860, so in 6 years you'll have $26,140 + $8,860 = $35,000.

How much, you may ask, would you need to save each year if you didn't have the $5,000 to start with? In this case, your goal would still be the same (to accumulate $35,000 in 6 years), but because you'd be starting from scratch, the full $35,000 would need to come from yearly savings. Assuming you can still earn 10 percent over the 6-year period, you can use the same future value annuity factor (7.716) and compute the amount of yearly savings as follows:

$$\text{Yearly savings} = \frac{\$35,000}{7.716} = \$4,536.03$$

or approximately $4,540. Note that this amount corresponds to the $4,540 figure cited earlier.

Using the future value concept, you can readily find either the future value to which an investment will grow over time or the amount that you must save each year to accumulate a given amount of money by a specified future date. In either case, the procedures allow you to put monetary values on long-term financial goals.

The Rule of 72

Suppose that you don't have access to time value of money tables or a financial calculator but want to know how long it takes for your money to double. There's an easy way to approximate this using the **rule of 72.** Simply divide the number 72 by the percentage rate you're earning on your investment:

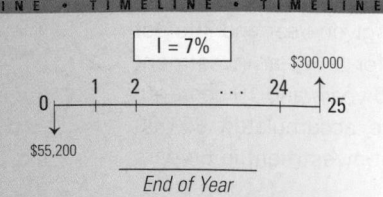

I = 7%

$300,000

0   1   2   ...   24   25

$55,200

End of Year

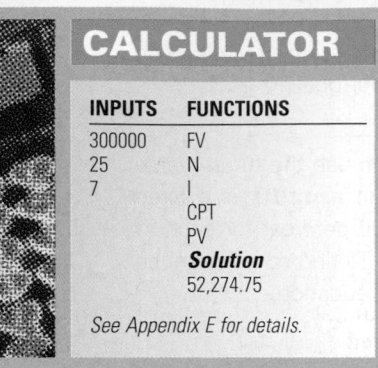

CALCULATOR

INPUTS	FUNCTIONS
300000	FV
25	N
7	I
	CPT
	PV
	Solution
	52,274.75

See Appendix E for details.

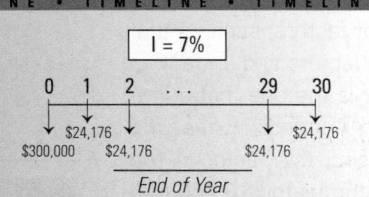

I = 7%

0   1   2   ...   29   30

↓ $24,176   ↓   ↓ $24,176
$300,000 $24,176 $24,176

End of Year

CALCULATOR

INPUTS	FUNCTIONS
300000	PV
30	N
7	I
	CPT
	PMT
	Solution
	24,175.92

See Appendix E for details.

present value The value today of an amount to be received in the future; it's the amount that would have to be invested today at a given interest rate over a specified time period to accumulate the future amount.

discounting The process of finding present value; the inverse of *compounding* to find future value.

$$\text{Number of years to double money} = \frac{72}{\text{Annual compound interest rate}}$$

For example, assume that you recently opened a savings account with $1,000 that earns an annual compound rate of interest of 4.5 percent. Your money will double in 16 years (72 ÷ 4.5 = 16). If you can find a $1,000 investment that earns 6.25 percent, you'll have $2,000 in about 11.5 years (72 ÷ 6.25 = 11.5).

The rule of 72 also applies to debts. Your debts can quickly double with high interest rates, such as those charged on most credit card accounts. So keep the rule of 72 in mind whether you invest or borrow!

Present Value

Lucky you! You've just won $100,000 in your state lottery. You want to spend part of it now, but because you're 30 years old, you also want to use part of it for your retirement fund. Your goal is to accumulate $300,000 in the fund by the time you're age 55 (25 years from now). How much do you need to invest if you estimate that you can earn 7 percent annually on your investments during the next 25 years?

Using **present value,** the value today of an amount to be received in the future, you can calculate the answer. It represents the amount you'd have to invest today at a given interest rate over the specified time period to accumulate the future amount. The process of finding present value is called **discounting,** which is the inverse of *compounding* to find future value.

Present Value of a Single Amount

Assuming you wish to create the retirement fund (future value) by making a single lump-sum deposit today, you can use this formula to find the amount you need to deposit:

Present value = Future value × Present value factor

Tables of present value factors make this calculation easy (see Appendix C). First, find the present value factor for a 25-year investment at a 7 percent discount rate (the factor that lies at the intersection of 25 years and 7 percent) in Appendix C; it is .184. Then, substitute the future value of $300,000 and the present value factor of .184 into the formula as follows:

Present value = $300,000 × .184 = $55,200

The $55,200 is the amount you'd have to deposit today into an account paying 7 percent annual interest to accumulate $300,000 at the end of 25 years.

Present Value of an Annuity

You can also use present value techniques to determine how much you can withdraw from your retirement fund each year over a specified time horizon. This calls for the *present value annuity factor.* Assume that at age 55 you wish to begin making equal annual withdrawals over the next 30 years from your $300,000 retirement fund. At first, you might think you could withdraw $10,000 per year ($300,000/30 years). However, the funds still on deposit would continue to earn 7 percent annual interest. To find the amount of the equal annual withdrawal, you again need to consider the time value of money. Specifically, you would use this formula:

$$\text{Annual withdrawal} = \frac{\text{Initial deposit}}{\text{Present value annuity factor}}$$

Use the present value annuity factors in Appendix D at the end of this text for this calculation. Substituting the $300,000 initial deposit and the present value annuity factor for 30 years and 7 percent of 12.409 (from Appendix D) into the equation above, we get

$$\text{Annual withdrawal} = \frac{\$300,000}{12.409} = \$24,176$$

Therefore, you can withdraw $24,176 each year for 30 years. This value is clearly much larger than the $10,000 annual withdrawal mentioned earlier.

$I = 8\%$

$$\$700 \quad \$700 \quad \$700$$

0   $700 \quad \$700 \quad \$700$

    1   2   3   4   5

$2,795.10

End of Year

CALCULATOR

INPUTS	FUNCTIONS
700	PMT
5	N
8	I
	CPT
	PV
	Solution
	2,794.90

See Appendix E for details.

Other Applications of Present Value

You can also use present value techniques to analyze investments. Suppose that you have an opportunity to purchase an annuity investment that promises to pay you $700 per year for 5 years. You know that you'll receive a total of $3,500 ($700 × 5 years) over the 5-year period. However, you wish to earn a minimum annual return of 8 percent on your investments. What's the most you should pay for this annuity today? You can answer this question by rearranging the terms in the equation above to get

Initial deposit = Annual withdrawal × Present value annuity factor

Adapting the equation to this situation, "initial deposit" represents the maximum price to pay for the annuity, and "annual withdrawal" represents the annual annuity payment of $700. The present value annuity factor for 5 years and 8 percent (found in Appendix D) is 3.993. Substituting this into the equation, we get:

Initial deposit = $700 × 3.993 = $2,795.10

The most you should pay for the $700, 5-year annuity, given your 8 percent annual return, is $2,795.10. At this price, you'd earn exactly 8 percent on the investment.

Using the present value concept, you can easily determine the present value of a sum to be received in the future, equal annual future withdrawals available from an initial deposit, and the initial deposit that would generate a given stream of equal annual withdrawals. These procedures, like future value concepts, allow you to place monetary values on long-term financial goals.

❙❙ Concept Check

CHECK • CONCEPT CHECK • CONCEPT CHECK • CONCEPT CHECK • CONCEPT CHECK • CONCEPT CHECK • CONCEPT CHECK • CONCEPT C

2-14	Why is it important to use *time value of money* concepts in setting personal financial goals?
2-15	What is *compounding*? Explain the *rule of 72*.
2-16	When might you use *future value*? *Present value*? Give specific examples.

LG6   SPECIAL PLANNING CONCERNS

As a student, you may not think you need to spend much time on financial planning yet. The sooner you start, however, the better prepared you'll be to adapt your plans to changing personal circumstances. Changing job status, relocating to a new state, getting married, having children, being in a serious car accident, getting a chronic illness, losing a spouse through divorce or death, retiring, taking responsibility for dependent parents—these and other stressful events are "financial shocks" that require reevaluation of your financial goals and plans.

However, don't rush to make major financial decisions at these times, when you're most vulnerable. Postpone any action until you have had time to recover from the event and evaluate all your options carefully. This can be difficult, because some financial salespeople will rush to contact you in these circumstances. For example, when you have a child, insurance agents, financial planners, and stockbrokers actively encourage you to buy insurance and start investing in a college fund. Although these are valid objectives, don't be pushed into any expensive decisions. People who get large sums of money—from severance packages, retirement benefits, or insurance policies when a loved one dies—are also likely to hear from financial salespeople eager to help them invest the funds. This is another time to wait. These brokers may have a greater interest in selling their own products than advising you on the best strategy for your needs.

Managing Two Incomes

Did you know that the earnings of the average dual-income family will add up to more than $1 million over the wage earners' lives? It may seem like a fortune, yet when you

Smart.Sites

The Genworth Center for Financial Learning Web site provides links to other Web sites that will help you plan for changing life situations, with planning tools, online courses, and advice geared to different life stages. Get there through **http://www.thomsonedu .com/finance/gitman**.

spread it over 25 or more years, it isn't that much. Today, two-income couples account for the majority of U.S. households, and many depend on the second income to make ends meet. For others, it provides financial security and a way to afford "extras." Often, how-ever, a second income doesn't add as much as expected to the bottom line. Higher expenses such as child care, taxes, clothing, dry cleaning, transportation, and lunches may consume a large part of the second paycheck. And two-income families tend to spend what they earn rather than save it.

When Ariana Diaz was offered a job as a credit analyst, she and her husband Marcos filled out Worksheet 2.5 to assess the net monthly income from her paycheck, both with and without the impact of employer-paid benefits. Ariana had been staying home with their three children, but now two were in school all day. The couple listed only those expenses that *directly relate to the second job* and made sure not to include personal expenses that would exist even without the second job. Ariana's job offer included good employer-paid benefits, with a better health insurance plan than the one Marcos's employer offered. Taking these benefits and the job-related expenses into account, the Diaz's net monthly income would increase by $3,440 a month, or $41,280 a year. Without benefits, this amount drops to $1,808, or $21,696 a year. These numbers provided the information for the Diazes to discuss the pros and cons of Ariana's job offer. They took into account not just the higher total income and out-of-pocket costs but also the intangible costs (additional demands on their lives, less time with family, and higher stress) and benefits (career devel-opment, job satisfaction, and sense of worth). They decided that the timing was right and agreed that they'd use the second income to increase their college savings accounts and build up their other investments. This would provide greater financial security in these uncertain times if Marcos were laid off from his research job at a biotechnology company.

Like the Diazes, partners in two-income households need to approach discussions on finan-cial matters with an open mind and be willing to compromise. Spouses need to decide together how to allocate income to household expenses, family financial goals, and personal spending goals. Will you use a second income to meet basic expenses, afford a more luxurious lifestyle, save for a special vacation, or invest in retirement accounts? You may need to try sev-eral money management strategies to find the one that works best for you. Some couples place all income into a single joint account. Others have each spouse contribute *equal* amounts into a joint account to pay bills, but retain individual discretion over remaining income. Still oth-ers contribute a *proportional* share of each income to finance joint expenses and goals. In any case, both spouses should have money of their own to spend without accountability.

Managing Employee Benefits

As we discussed in Chapter 1, if you hold a full-time job, your employer probably provides various employee benefits, ranging from health and life insurance to pension plans. As we saw in the Diaz's analysis, these can have a major financial impact on family income. Most American families depend solely on employer-sponsored group plans for their health insur-ance coverage and a big piece of their life insurance coverage and retirement needs.

Today's well-defined employee benefits packages cover a full spectrum of benefits that may include

- Health and life insurance
- Disability insurance
- Long-term care insurance
- Pension and profit-sharing plans
- Supplemental retirement programs, such as 401(k) plans
- Dental and vision care
- Child care, elder care, and educational assistance programs
- Subsidized employee food services

Each company's benefit package is different. Some companies and industries are known for generous benefit plans; others offer far less attractive packages. In general, large firms can afford more benefits than small ones can. Because employee benefits can increase your total compensation by 30 percent or more, you should thoroughly investi-

Developing Your Financial Statements and Plans

Use this worksheet to estimate the contribution of a second paycheck. Without the employer-paid benefits of $1,632 (line 2), the Diazes would realize a net monthly income of $1,808 (line 1 − line 3); and with them, their net monthly income would be $3,440 (line 4).

Second Income Analysis

Name(s) _Ariana and Marcos Diaz_   Date _December 27, 2007_

MONTHLY CASH INCOME

Gross pay	$5,000
Pretax employer contributions (401(k) plans, dependent-care reimbursement account(s)	400
Additional job-related income (bonuses, overtime, commissions)	0
(1) Total Cash Income	$5,400

EMPLOYER-PAID BENEFITS

Health insurance	$550
Life insurance	100
Pension contributions	600
Thrift-plan contributions	0
Social Security	382
Profit sharing	0
Other deferred compensation	0
(2) Total Benefits	$1,632

MONTHLY JOB-RELATED EXPENSES

Federal income tax	$1,500
Social Security tax	382
State income tax	250
Child care	640
Clothing; personal care; dry cleaning	400
Meals away from home	200
Public transportation	0
Auto-related expenses (gas, parking, maintenance)	220
Other	0
(3) Total Expenses	$3,592
(4) Net Income (Deficit) [(1) + (2) − (3)]	$3,440

Source: Adapted from Kevin McManus, "How to Get the Most from Two Incomes," *Changing Times*, July 1989, p. 24.

gate your employee benefits to choose those appropriate for your personal situation. Be sure to coordinate your benefits with your partner's to avoid paying for duplicate coverage. Companies change their benefit packages often and today are shifting more costs to employees. Although an employer may pay for some benefits in full, typically employees pay for part of the cost of group health insurance, supplemental life insurance, long-term care insurance, and participation in voluntary retirement programs.

Due to the prevalence of two-income families and an increasingly diverse workforce, many employers today are replacing traditional programs, where the company sets the type and amount of benefits, with **flexible-benefit (cafeteria) plans.** In flexible-benefit programs, the employer allocates a certain amount of money to each employee and then lets the employee "spend" that money for benefits that suit his or her age, marital status, number of dependent children, level of income, and so on. These plans usually cover everything from child care to retirement benefits, offer several levels of health and life insurance coverage, and have some limits on the minimum and maximum amount of coverage. Within these constraints, you can select the benefits that do you the most good. In some plans, you can even take part of the benefits in the form of more take-home pay or extra vacation time!

Along with greater choice comes the responsibility to manage your benefits carefully. You should periodically assess the benefits package you have at work relative to your own individual/family needs, supplementing any shortfall in company benefits with personal coverage. Except perhaps for group medical coverage, don't rely on your employer as the sole source of financial security. Your coverage may disappear if you change jobs or become unemployed, and, especially with life insurance and retirement plans, most employee benefits fall short of your total financial needs.

Adapting to Other Major Life Changes

Other situations that require special consideration include changes in marital status and the need to support grown children or elderly relatives. The marriage, divorce, or death of a spouse results in the need to revise financial plans and money management strategies.

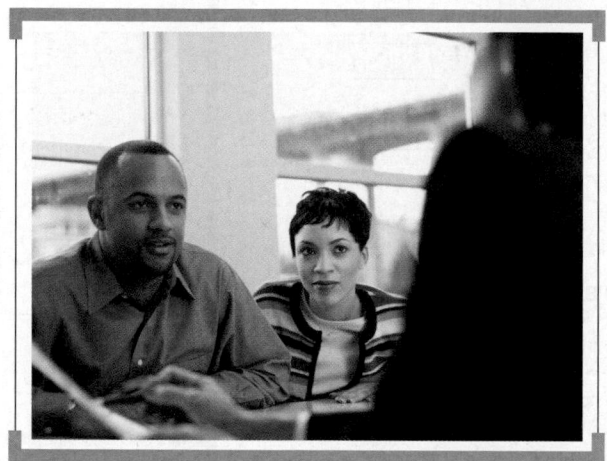

© PHOTODISC/GETTY IMAGES

As mentioned earlier, couples should discuss their money attitudes and financial goals and decide how to manage joint financial affairs before they get married. Take an inventory of your financial assets and liabilities, including savings and checking accounts; credit card accounts and outstanding bills; auto, health, and life insurance policies; and investment portfolios. You may want to eliminate some credit cards if there is overlap. Too many cards can hurt your credit rating, and most people need only one or two. Each partner should have a card in his or her name to establish a credit record. Compare employee benefit plans to figure out the lowest-cost source of health insurance coverage, and coordinate other benefits. Change the beneficiary on your life insurance policies. Adjust withholding amounts as necessary based on your new filing category.

In event of divorce, income may decrease because alimony and child-support payments cause one salary to be divided between two households. Single parents may have to stretch limited financial resources farther to meet added expenses such as child care. Remarriage brings additional financial considerations, including decisions involving children from prior marriages and managing the assets that each spouse brings to the marriage. Some couples develop a prenuptial contract that outlines their agreement on financial matters, such as the control of assets, their disposition in event of death or divorce, and other important money issues.

Death of a spouse is another change that greatly affects financial planning. The surviving spouse is typically faced with decisions on how to receive and invest life insurance proceeds and manage other assets. In families where the deceased made most of the financial decisions with little or no involvement of the surviving spouse, the survivor may be overwhelmed by the need to take on financial responsibilities. Advance planning can minimize many of these problems.

Couples should regularly review all aspects of their finances. Each spouse should understand what is owned and owed, participate in formulating financial goals and investment strategies, and fully understand estate plans (covered in detail in Chapter 15).

flexible-benefit (cafeteria) plan A type of employee benefit plan wherein the employer allocates a certain amount of money, and the employee "spends" that money for benefits selected from a menu covering everything from child care to health and life insurance to retirement benefits.

professional financial planner An individual or firm that helps clients establish financial goals and develop and implement financial plans to achieve those goals.

Using Professional Financial Planners

Does developing your own financial plans seem like an overwhelming task? Help is at hand! **Professional financial planners** will guide you through establishing goals, plan preparation, and the increasingly complex maze of financial products and investment opportunities. This field has experienced tremendous growth, and there are now more than 200,000 financial planners in the United States.

Financial planners offer a wide range of services, including preparing comprehensive financial plans that evaluate a client's total personal financial situation or abbreviated plans focusing on a specific concern, such as managing a client's assets and investments and retirement planning. Where once only the wealthy used professional planners, now financial firms such as H&R Block's Financial Advisors and the Personal Advisors of Ameriprise Financial compete for the business of middle-income people as well.

Why do people turn to financial advisers? A recent survey indicated that retirement needs motivated 50 percent, while 23 percent were unhappy with the results of trying to manage their own finances. Estate and inheritance planning caused another 13 percent to seek help; saving for college and tax issues were also mentioned.

Types of Planners

Most financial planners fall into one of two categories based on how they get paid: commissions or fees. *Commission-based planners* earn commissions on the financial products they sell, whereas *fee-only planners* charge fees based on the complexity of the plan they prepare. Many financial planners take a hybrid approach and charge fees and collect commissions on products they sell, offering lower fees if you make product transactions through them.

Insurance salespeople and securities brokers who continue to sell the same financial products (life insurance, stocks, bonds, mutual funds, and annuities) often now call themselves "financial planners." Other planners work for large, established financial institutions that recognize the enormous potential in the field and train their planners to compete with the best financial planners. Still others work in small firms, promising high-quality advice for a flat fee or an hourly rate. Regardless of their affiliation, full-service financial planners help their clients articulate their long- and short-term financial goals, systematically plan for their financial needs, and help implement various aspects of the plans. Exhibit 2.6 on page 60 provides a guide to some of the different planning designations.

In addition to one-on-one financial planning services, some institutions offer computerized financial plans. Merrill Lynch, Ameriprise Financial, T. Rowe Price, and other major investment firms provide these computerized plans on the Internet to help clients develop plans to save for college or retirement, reduce taxes, or restructure investment portfolios. You can even turn to the Internet for financial planning help, as discussed in the *Money in Action* box, "Planning on Online Financial Advice," on our Web site, http://www .thomsonedu.com/ finance/gitman.

Personal finance programs such as Quicken and Microsoft Money also have a financial planning component that can help you set a path to your goals and do tax and retirement planning. As you'll see in later chapters, some Web sites provide planning advice on one topic, such as taxes, insurance, or estate planning. Although these plans are relatively inexpensive or even free, they tend to be somewhat impersonal. However, they are a good solution for those who need help getting started and for do-it-yourself planners who want some help.

EXHIBIT 2.6   Financial Planning Designations

Confused about what the letters after a financial adviser's name signify? Here's a summary of the most common certifications so you can choose the one that best suits your needs.

Credential	Description	Web address
Chartered Financial Analyst (CFA)	Focuses primarily on securities analysis not financial planning	http://www.cfainstitute.org
Certified Financial Planner® (CFP®)	Requires a comprehensive education in financial planning	http://www.cfp.net
Chartered Financial Consultant (ChFC)	Financial planning designation for insurance agents	http://www.theamericancollege.edu/advance/chfc/default.asp?section=5
Certified Public Accountant (CPA)	Accounting degree; see PFS below	http://www.aicpa.org/index.htm
Certified Trust & Financial Advisor (CTFA)	Estate planning and trusts expertise, found mostly in the banking industry	http://www.qbd.com/ICBCertifications/CTFA.htm
Personal Financial Specialist (PFS)	Comprehensive planning credential only for CPAs	http://www.pfp.aicpa.org
Chartered Life Underwriter (CLU)	Insurance agent designation, often accompanied by the ChFC credential	http://www.theamericancollege.edu/advance/clu/default.asp?section=4
Certified Investment Management Analyst	Consulting designation for professional investment managers	http://www.imca.org/certify
Registered Financial Associate (RFA)	Designation granted only to recent graduates of an approved academic curriculum in financial services	http://www.iarfc.org/content/asp?n=1

Source: Adapted from "What the Titles Mean," *Business Week*, November 25, 2002, p. 148.

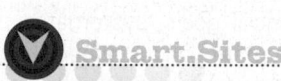
Smart.Sites

At **http://thomsonedu .com/finance/gitman** you can link to the Certified Financial Planner Board site for "10 Questions to Ask When Choosing a Financial Planner," an interview checklist, and other advice on choosing and working with a financial planner.

The cost of financial planning services depends on the type of planner, the complexity of your financial situation, and the services you want. The cost may be well worth the benefits, especially for people who have neither the time, inclination, discipline, nor expertise to plan on their own. Remember, however, that the best advice is worthless if you're not willing to change your financial habits.

Choosing a Financial Planner

Planners who have completed the required course of study and earned the Certified Financial Planner® (CFP®) or Chartered Financial Consultant (ChFC) designation are often a better choice than the many self-proclaimed financial planners. Of course, CPAs, attorneys, investment managers, and other professionals without such certifications in many instances do provide sound financial planning advice.

Unlike accounting and law, the field is still largely unregulated, and almost anyone can call themselves a financial planner. Most financial planners are honest and reputable, but there have been cases of fraudulent practice. So it's critical to thoroughly check out a potential financial advisor—and preferably interview two or three.

The way a planner is paid—commissions, fees, or both—should be one of your major concerns. Obviously, you need to be aware of potential conflicts of interest when using a planner with ties to a brokerage firm, insurance company, or bank. Many planners now provide clients with disclosure forms outlining fees and commissions for various transactions. In addition to asking questions of the planner, you should also check with your state securities department and the Securities and Exchange Commission (for planners registered to sell securities). Ask if the planner has any pending lawsuits, complaints by state or federal regulators, personal bankruptcies, or convictions for investment-related crimes. However, even these agencies may not have accurate or current information; simply being properly registered and not providing a record of disciplinary actions doesn't guarantee that their track record is good. You may also want to research the planner's reputation within the local financial community. Clearly, you should do your homework before engaging the services of a professional financial planner.

❚❚ Concept Check

2-17	Discuss briefly how the following situations affect personal financial planning:
	a. Being part of a dual-income couple
	b. Major life changes, such as marriage or divorce
	c. Death of a spouse
2-18	What is a *professional financial planner*? Does it make any difference whether the financial planner earns money from commissions made on products sold as opposed to the fees he or she charges?

« SUMMARY

LG1 **Understand the interlocking network of financial plans and statements.** Preparing and using personal financial statements—the balance sheet and the income and expense statement—is important to personal financial planning. These tools help you to keep track of your current financial position and monitor progress toward achieving financial goals. Also important is a budget, which allows you to monitor and control your spending in light of your financial plans.

LG2 **Prepare a personal balance sheet.** A balance sheet reports on your financial position at a specific time. It summarizes the things you own (assets), the money you owe (liabilities), and your financial worth (net worth). Assets include liquid assets, investments, and real and personal property. Liabilities include current liabilities that are due in less than 1 year (unpaid bills, open account credit obligations) and long-term liabilities (real estate mortgages, consumer installment loans, education loans). Net worth represents your actual wealth and is the difference between your total assets and total liabilities.

LG3 **Generate a personal income and expense statement.** The income and expense statement summarizes the income you received and the money you spent over a specific period. It's prepared on a cash basis and thus reflects your actual cash flow. Expenses consist of cash outflows to (1) meet living expenses, (2) pay taxes, (3) purchase various kinds of assets, and (4) pay debts. A cash surplus (or deficit) is the difference between income and expenses. A cash surplus can be used to increase assets or reduce debts, and therefore has a positive effect on the balance sheet's net worth account. A cash deficit, in contrast, reduces assets or increases debts, acting to reduce net worth.

LG4 **Develop a good recordkeeping system and use ratios to interpret personal financial statements.** Good records make it easier to prepare accurate personal financial statements. Organized records also simplify tax return preparation and provide the necessary documentation for tax deductions. Ratio analysis allows you to interpret your personal financial statements to assess how well you are doing relative to your past performance. Four important financial ratios are the solvency, liquidity, savings, and debt service ratios.

LG5 **Construct a cash budget and use it to monitor and control spending.** A cash budget helps you to carry out a system of disciplined spending. By curbing needless spending, a budget can increase the amount of funds allocated to savings and investments. Household budgets identify planned monthly cash income and cash expenses for the coming year. The objective is to take in more money than you spend, so you'll save money and add to your net worth over time. The final step in the budgeting process is to compare actual income and expenses with budgeted figures to learn whether you're living within your budget and, if not, to make appropriate adjustments.

LG6. Describe the use of *time value of money* concepts to put a monetary value on financial goals and the role of special plan-

ning concerns. When putting a dollar value on financial goals, be sure to consider the time value of money and, if appropriate, use the notion of future value or present value to prepare your estimates. These techniques explicitly recognize that a dollar today is worth more than a dollar in the future. Situations that require special attention include managing two incomes, managing employee benefits, and adapting to changes in your personal situation, such as marital status or taking responsibility for elderly relatives' care. Professional financial planners can help you with the planning process. Investigate a prospective financial planner's background carefully and understand how he or she is paid (commissions, fees, or both).

FINANCIAL PLANNING EXERCISES

LG2, 3

1. Chris Jones is preparing his balance sheet and income and expense statement for the year ending June 30, 2007. He is having difficulty classifying six items and asks for your help. Which, if any, of the following transactions are assets, liabilities, income, or expense items?

   a. He rents a house for $950 a month.

   b. On June 21, 2007, he bought diamond earrings for his wife and charged them using his Visa card. The earrings cost $600, but he hasn't yet received the bill.

   c. He borrowed $2,000 from his parents last fall, but so far he has made no payments to them.

   d. He makes monthly payments of $120 on an installment loan; about half of it is interest, and the balance is repayment of principal. He has 20 payments left, totaling $2,400.

   e. He paid $2,800 in taxes during the year and is due a tax refund of $450, which he hasn't yet received.

   f. He invested $1,800 in some common stock.

LG2, 3

2. Put yourself 10 years into the future. Construct a fairly detailed and realistic balance sheet and income and expense statement reflecting what you would like to achieve by that time.

LG2, 4

3. *Use Worksheet 2.1.* Elizabeth Walker's banker has asked her to submit a personal balance sheet as of June 30, 2007, in support of an application for a $3,000 home improvement loan. She comes to you for help in preparing it. So far, she has made the following list of her assets and liabilities as of June 30, 2007:

Cash on hand		$ 70
Balance in checking account		180
Balance in money market deposit account with Mid-American Savings		650
Bills outstanding:		
Telephone	$ 20	
Electricity	70	
Charge account balance	190	
Visa	180	
MasterCard	220	
Taxes	400	
Insurance	<u>220</u>	1,300

Condo and property		68,000
Condo mortgage loan		52,000
Automobile: 2003 Honda Civic		10,000
Installment loan balances:		
Auto loans	3,000	
Furniture loan	<u>500</u>	3,500
Personal property:		
Furniture	1,050	
Clothing	<u>900</u>	1,950
Investments:		
U.S. government savings bonds	500	
Stock of WIMCO Corporation	<u>3,000</u>	3,500

From the data given, prepare Elizabeth Walker's balance sheet, dated June 30, 2007 (follow the balance sheet form shown in Worksheet 2.1). Then evaluate her balance sheet relative to the following factors: (a) solvency, (b) liquidity, and (c) equity in her dominant asset.

LG3

4. *Use Worksheet 2.2.* Chuck and Judy Schwartz are about to construct their income and expense statement for the year ending December 31, 2007. They have put together the following income and expense information for 2007:

Judy's salary	$37,000
Reimbursement for travel expenses	1,950
Interest on:	
Savings account	110
Bonds of Alpha Corporation	70
Groceries	4,150
Rent	9,600
Utilities	960
Gas and auto expenses	650
Chuck's tuition, books, and supplies	3,300
Books, magazines, and periodicals	280
Clothing and other miscellaneous expenses	2,700
Cost of photographic equipment purchased with charge card	2,200
Amount paid to date on photographic equipment	1,600
Judy's travel expenses	1,950
Purchase of a used car (cost)	9,750
Outstanding loan balance on car	7,300
Purchase of bonds in Alpha Corporation	4,900

Using the information provided, prepare an income and expense statement for the Schwartzes for the year ending December 31, 2007 (follow the form shown in Worksheet 2.2).

LG5

5. Dave and Betty Williamson are preparing their 2008 cash budget. Help the Williamsons reconcile the following differences, giving reasons to support your answers:

a. Their only source of income is Dave's salary, which amounts to $3,000 a month before taxes. Betty wants to show the $3,000 as their monthly income, whereas Dave argues that his take-home pay of $2,350 is the correct value to show.

b. Betty wants to make a provision for *fun money*, an idea that Dave cannot understand. He asks, "Why do we need fun money when everything is provided for in the budget?"

LG5

6. Here is a portion of Jeffrey Cook's budget record for April 2008. Fill in the blanks in columns 5 and 6.

Item (1)	Amount Budgeted (2)	Amount Spent (3)	Beginning Balance (4)	Monthly Surplus (Deficit) (5)	Cumulative Surplus (Deficit) (6)
Rent	$350	$360	$20	$____	$____
Utilities	150	145	15	____	____

Item (1)	Amount Budgeted (2)	Amount Spent (3)	Beginning Balance (4)	Monthly Surplus (Deficit) (5)	Cumulative Surplus (Deficit) (6)
Food	310	275	−15	_____	_____
Auto	25	38	−5	_____	_____
Recreation and entertainment	50	60	−50	_____	_____

LG5

7. **Use Worksheet 2.3.** Prepare a record of your income and expenses for the last 30 days; then prepare a personal cash budget for the next 3 months. (Use the format in Worksheet 2.3 but fill out only 3 months and the Total column.) Use the cash budget to control and regulate your expenses during the next month. Discuss the impact of the budget on your spending behavior, as well as any differences between your expected and actual spending patterns.

LG6

8. Use future or present value techniques to solve the following problems:

a. Starting with $10,000, how much will you have in 10 years if you can earn 15 percent on your money? If you can earn only 8 percent?

b. If you inherited $25,000 today and invested all of it in a security that paid a 10 percent rate of return, how much would you have in 25 years?

c. If the average new home costs $125,000 today, how much will it cost in 10 years if the price increases by 5 percent each year?

d. You think that in 15 years it will cost $75,000 to give your child a college education. Will you have enough if you take $25,000 *today* and invest it for the next 15 years at 8 percent? If you start *from scratch*, how much will you have to save *each year* to have $75,000 in 15 years if you can earn an 8 percent rate of return on your investments?

e. If you can earn 12 percent, how much will you have to save *each year* if you want to retire in 35 years with $1 million?

f. You plan to have $750,000 in savings and investments when you retire at age 60. Assuming that you earn an average of 9 percent on this portfolio, what is the maximum annual withdrawal you can make over a 25-year period of retirement?

LG6

9. Over the past several years, Helen Chang has been able to save regularly. As a result, today she has $14,188 in savings and investments. She wants to establish her own business in 5 years and feels she will need $50,000 to do so.

a. If she can earn 12 percent on her money, how much will her $14,188 savings/investments be worth in 5 years? Will Helen have the $50,000 she needs? If not, how much more money will she need?

b. Given your answer to part **a**, how much will Helen have to save *each year* over the next 5 years to accumulate the additional money, assuming she can earn interest at a rate of 12 percent?

c. If Helen can afford to save only $2,000 a year, given your answer to part **a**, will she have the $50,000 she needs to start her own business in 5 years?

LG6

10. Bill Shaffer wishes to have $200,000 in a retirement fund 20 years from now. He can create the retirement fund by making a single lump-sum deposit today.

a. If he can earn 10 percent on his investments, how much must Bill deposit today to create the retirement fund? If he can earn only 8 percent on his investments? Compare and discuss the results of your calculations.

b. If upon retirement in 20 years Bill plans to invest the $200,000 in a fund that earns 11 percent, what is the maximum annual withdrawal he can make over the following 15 years?

c. How much would Bill need to have on deposit at retirement to annually withdraw $35,000 over the 15 years if the retirement fund earns 11 percent?

d. To achieve his annual withdrawal goal of $35,000 calculated in part **c,** how much more than the amount calculated in part **a** must Bill deposit today in an investment earning 10 percent annual interest?

APPLYING PERSONAL FINANCE

What's Your Condition?

Financial statements reflect your financial condition. They help you measure where you are now. Then, as time passes and you prepare your financial statements periodically, you can use them to track your progress toward financial goals. Good financial statements are also a must when you apply for a loan. This project will help you to evaluate your current financial condition.

Look back at the discussion in this chapter on balance sheets and income and expense statements, and prepare your own. If you're doing this for the first time, it may not be as easy as it sounds! Use these questions to help you along:

1. Have you included all your assets at fair market value (not historical cost) on your balance sheet?

2. Have you included all your debt balances as liabilities on your balance sheet? (Don't take your monthly payment amounts multiplied by the number of payments you have left—this total includes future interest.)

3. Have you included all items of income on your income and expense statement? (Remember, your paycheck is income and not an asset on your balance sheet.)

4. Have you included all debt payments as expenses on your income and expense statement? (Your phone bill is an expense for this month if you've already paid it. If the bill is still sitting on your desk staring you in the face, it's a liability on your balance sheet.)

5. Are there occasional expenses that you've forgotten about, or hidden expenses such as entertainment that you have overlooked? Look back through your checkbook, spending diary, or any other financial records to find these occasional or infrequent expenses.

6. Remember that items go on either the balance sheet or the income and expense statement, but not on both. For example, the $350 car payment you made this month is an expense on your income and expense statement. The remaining $15,000 balance on your car loan is a liability on your balance sheet, while the fair market value of your car at $17,500 is an asset.

After completing your statements, calculate your solvency, liquidity, savings, and debt service ratios. Now, use your statements and ratios to assess your current financial condition. Do you like where you are? If not, how can you get where you want to be? Use your financial statements and ratios to help you formulate plans for the future.

CRITICAL THINKING CASES

LG1, 2, 3, 4

2.1 The Sullivans' Version of Financial Planning

John and Lisa Sullivan are a married couple in their mid-twenties. John is a bank trainee, and Lisa works as a sales representative. Since their marriage 4 years ago, John and Lisa have been living comfortably. Their income has exceeded their expenses, and they have accumulated a net worth of nearly $45,000. This includes the $10,000 that they have built up in savings and investments. Because their income has always been more than enough for them to have the lifestyle they desire, the Sullivans have done no financial planning.

Lisa has just learned that she's 2 months pregnant. She's concerned about how they'll make ends meet if she quits work after their child is born. Each time she and John discuss the matter, John tells her not to worry because "we've always managed to pay our bills on time." Lisa can't understand his attitude, because her income will be completely eliminated. To convince Lisa there's no need for concern, John points out that their expenses for necessities last year were $24,885, which just about equaled his take-home pay of $26,480. With an anticipated promotion to a managerial position and an expected 10 percent pay raise, his income next year should exceed this amount. John also points out that they can reduce luxuries (trips, recreation, and entertainment) and can always draw down their savings or sell some of their stock if they get in a bind. When Lisa asks about the long-run implications for their finances, John says there will be "no problems" because his boss has assured him that he has a bright future with the bank. John also emphasizes that Lisa can go back to work in a few years if necessary.

Despite John's somewhat convincing arguments, Lisa feels that they should carefully examine their financial condition in order to do some serious planning. She has gathered the following financial information for the year ending December 31, 2007:

Salaries	Take-home Pay	Gross Salary
John	$26,480	$38,350
Lisa	18,090	26,000

Item Amount	
Food	$ 4,200
Clothing	2,300
Mortgage payments, including property taxes of $1,400	9,400
Travel and entertainment card balances	2,000
Gas, electric, water expenses	1,990
Household furnishings	4,500
Telephone	640
Auto loan balance	2,650
Common stock investments	7,500
Bank credit card balances	675
Income taxes	16,940
Credit card loan payments	2,210
Cash on hand	85
2004 Nissan Sentra	7,000
Medical expenses (unreimbursed)	600
Homeowner's insurance premiums paid	400
Checking account balance	485
Auto insurance premiums paid	800
Transportation	2,800
Cable television	480
Estimated value of home	98,000
Trip to Europe	5,000
Recreation and entertainment	4,000
Auto loan payments	2,150
Money market account balance	2,500
Purchase of common stock	7,500
Addition to money market account	500
Mortgage on home	70,000

Critical Thinking Questions

1. Using this information and Worksheets 2.1 and 2.2, construct the Sullivans' December 31, 2007, balance sheet and income and expense statement for the year ending December 31, 2007.

2. Comment on the Sullivans' financial condition regarding (a) solvency, (b) liquidity, (c) savings, and (d) ability to pay debts promptly. If the Sullivans continue to manage their finances as described, what do you expect the long-run consequences to be? Discuss.

3. Critically evaluate the Sullivans' approach to financial planning. Point out any fallacies in John's arguments, and be sure to mention (a) implications for the long term, (b) the potential impact of inflation, and (c) the impact on their net worth. What procedures should they use to get their financial house in order? Be sure to discuss the role that long- and short-term financial plans and budgets might play.

2.2 Joe Garcia Learns to Budget

Joe Garcia graduated from college in 2006 and moved to Atlanta to take a job as a market research analyst. He was pleased to be financially independent and was sure that, with his $35,000 salary, he could cover his living expenses and have plenty of money left over to furnish his studio apartment and enjoy the wide variety of social and recreational activities available in Atlanta. He opened several department-store charge accounts and obtained a bank credit card.

For awhile Joe managed pretty well on his monthly take-home pay of $2,250; but by the end of 2007, he was having trouble fully paying all his credit card charges each month. Concerned that his spending had gotten out of control and that he was barely making it from paycheck to paycheck, he decided to list his expenses for the past calendar year and develop a budget. He hoped not only to reduce his credit card debt but also to begin a regular savings program.

Joe prepared the following summary of expenses for 2007:

Item	Annual Expenditure
Rent	$9,600
Auto insurance	520
Auto loan payments	3,340
Auto expenses (gas, repairs, fees, and so on)	1,560
Clothing	2,200
Installment loan for stereo	540
Personal care	240
Phone	600
Cable TV	240
Gas and electricity	960
Medical care	120
Dentist	70
Groceries	2,500
Dining out	2,000
Furniture purchases	900
Recreation and entertainment	1,900
Other expenses	600

After reviewing his 2007 expenses, Joe made the following assumptions about his expenses for 2008:

1. All expenses will remain at the same levels, with these exceptions:
    a. Auto insurance, auto expenses, gas and electricity, and groceries will increase 5 percent.
    b. Clothing purchases will decrease to $1,850.
    c. Phone and cable TV will increase $5 per month.
    d. Furniture purchases will decrease to $660, most of which is for a new television.
    e. He will take a 1-week vacation to Lake Tahoe in July at a cost of $1,100.

2. All expenses will be budgeted in equal monthly installments except for the vacation and these items:
    a. Auto insurance is paid in two installments due in June and December.
    b. He plans to replace the brakes on his car in February at a cost of $120.
    c. Visits to the dentist will be made in March and September.

3. He will eliminate his bank credit card balance by making extra monthly payments of $75 during each of the first 6 months.

4. Regarding his income, Joe has just received a small raise, so his take-home pay will be $2,375 per month.

Critical Thinking Questions

1. a. Prepare a preliminary cash budget for Joe for the year ending December 31, 2008, using the format shown in Worksheet 2.3.
    b. Compare Joe's estimated expenses with his expected income, and make recommendations that will help him balance his budget.

2. Make any necessary adjustments to Joe's estimated monthly expenses, and revise his annual cash budget for the year ending December 31, 2008, using Worksheet 2.3.

3. Analyze the budget and advise Joe on his financial situation. Suggest some long-term, intermediate, and short-term financial goals for Joe, and discuss some steps he can take to reach them.

Preparing Your Taxes

LEARNING GOALS

• CHAPTER 3 • CHAPTER 3 • CHAPTER 3 • CHAPTER 3 • CHAPTER 3 • CHAPTER 3 • CHAPTER 3 • CHAPTER 3 • CH

LG1 UNDERSTANDING FEDERAL INCOME TAX PRINCIPLES

Taxes are dues we pay for membership in our society; they're the cost of living in this country. Federal, state, and local tax receipts fund government activities and a wide variety of public services, from national defense to local libraries. Administering and enforcing federal tax laws is the responsibility of the IRS, a part of the U.S. Department of Treasury.

Because federal income tax is generally the largest tax you'll pay, you are wise to make tax planning an important part of personal financial planning. A typical American family currently pays *about one-third of its gross income in taxes:* federal income and Social Security taxes and numerous state and local income, sales, and property taxes. Although you may think of tax planning as an activity to do between January, when tax forms arrive in the mail, and April 15, the filing deadline, you should make tax planning a year-round activity. You should always consider tax consequences when preparing and revising your financial plans and making major financial decisions, such as buying a home and investing.

The overriding objective of tax planning is simple: *to maximize the amount of money you keep by minimizing the amount of taxes you pay.* As long as it's done honestly and within the tax codes, there is nothing immoral, illegal, or unethical about trying to minimize

taxes The dues paid for membership in our society; the cost of living in this country.

How long does the average American have to work this year to pay federal, state, and local taxes? Find this year's date of "Tax Freedom Day" at the Tax Foundation Web site. Link to it at **http://www .thomsonedu.com/finance/ gitman.** You'll also find information there about tax policy, tax rates, tax collections, and the economics of taxation.

your tax bill. Most tax planning centers on ways to minimize income and estate (see Chapter 15) taxes. In this chapter we concentrate on income taxes paid by individuals—particularly the federal income tax, the largest and most important tax for most taxpayers. Although you may currently pay little or no taxes, we use a mid-career couple to demonstrate the key aspects of individual taxation. This approach will give you a good understanding of your future tax situation and allow you to develop realistic financial plans.

In addition to federal income tax, there are other forms of taxes to contend with. For example, additional federal taxes may be levied on income and on certain types of transactions. At the state and local levels, sales transactions, income, property ownership, and licenses may be taxed. Because most individuals have to pay many of these other types of taxes, you should evaluate their impact on your financial decisions. Thus, a person saving to purchase a new automobile costing $25,000 should realize that the state and local sales taxes, as well as the cost of license plates and registration, may add another $2,200 or more to the total cost of the car.

Because tax laws are complicated and subject to frequent revision, we'll present key concepts and show how they apply to common tax situations. Provisions of the tax code may change annually for tax rates, amounts and types of deductions and personal exemptions, and similar items. Often these changes aren't finalized until late in the year. The tax tables, calculations, and sample tax returns presented in this chapter are based on the tax laws applicable to the calendar year 2005—those in effect at the time this book was being revised. *Although tax rates and other provisions will change, the basic procedures will remain the same.* Before preparing your tax returns, be sure to review the current regulations; IRS publications and other tax preparation guides may be helpful.

The Economics of Income Taxes

Not surprisingly, most people simply don't like to pay taxes. Some of this feeling likely stems from the widely held perception that a lot of government spending amounts to little more than bureaucratic waste. But a good deal of this feeling is probably because taxpayers get nothing tangible in return for their money. After all, paying taxes isn't like spending $7,000 on furniture, a boat, or a European vacation. The fact is, we too often tend to overlook or take for granted the many services provided by the taxes we pay—public schools and state colleges, roads and highways, and parks and recreational facilities, not to mention police and fire protection, retirement benefits, and many other health and social services.

Income taxes are the major source of revenue for the federal government. Personal income taxes are scaled on progressive rates. To illustrate how this **progressive tax structure** works, we'll use the following data for single taxpayers filing 2005 returns:

Taxable Income	Tax Rate
$1 to $7,300	10%
$7,301 to $29,700	15%
$29,701 to $71,950	25%
$71,951 to $150,150	28%
$150,151 to $326,450	33%
Over $326,450	35%

income taxes A type of tax levied on taxable income by the federal government and many state and local governments.

progressive tax structure A tax structure in which the larger the amount of taxable income, the higher the rate at which it is taxed.

Of course, any nontaxable income can be viewed as being in the 0 percent tax bracket. As taxable income moves from a lower to a higher bracket, the higher rate applies *only to the additional taxable income in that bracket* and not to the entire taxable income. For example, consider two single brothers, Jason and David, whose taxable incomes are $40,000 and $80,000:

Name	Taxable Income	Tax Calculation	Tax Liability
Jason	$40,000	= [($40,000 − $29,700) × .25] + [$29,700 − $7,300] × .15] + [$7,300 × .10] = $2,575 + $3,360 + $730 =	$6,665
David	$80,000	= [($80,000 − $71,950) × .28] + [($71,950 − $29,700) × .25] + [($29,700 − $7,300) × .15] + [$7,300 × .10] = $2,254 + $10,563 + $3,360 + $730 =	$16,907

Note that Jason pays the 25 percent rate only on that portion of the $40,000 in taxable income that exceeds $29,700. Due to this kind of progressive scale, the more money you make, the progressively more you pay in taxes: Although David's taxable income is twice that of Jason's, his income tax is about 2.5 times higher than his brother's.

The tax rate for each bracket—10 percent, 15 percent, 25 percent, 28 percent, 33 percent, and 35 percent—is called the **marginal tax rate,** or the rate applied to the next dollar of taxable income. When you relate the tax liability to the level of taxable income earned, the tax rate, called the **average tax rate,** drops considerably. Jason's average tax rate, calculated by dividing the tax liability by taxable income, is about 16.7 percent ($6,665/$40,000). David's average tax rate is about 21.1 percent ($16,907/ $80,000). Clearly, taxes are still progressive, and the average size of the bite is not as bad as the stated tax rate might suggest.

Your Filing Status

The taxes you pay depend in part on your *filing status*, which is based on your marital status and family situation on the last day of your tax year (usually December 31). Filing status affects whether you're required to file an income tax return, the amount of your standard deduction, and your tax rate. If you have a choice of filing status, you should calculate your taxes both ways and choose the status that results in the lower tax liability. There are five different filing status categories:

- **Single taxpayers:** Unmarried or legally separated from their spouses by either a separation or final divorce decree.
- **Married filing jointly:** Married couples who combine their income and allowable deductions and file one tax return.
- **Married filing separately:** Each spouse files his or her own return, reporting only his or her income, deductions, and exemptions.
- **Head of household:** A taxpayer who is unmarried or considered unmarried and pays more than half of the cost of keeping up a home for himself or herself and an eligible dependent child or relative.
- **Qualifying widow or widower with dependent child:** A person whose spouse died within 2 years of the tax year (for example, in 2003 or 2004 for the 2005 tax year) and who supports a dependent child may use joint return tax rates and is eligible for the highest standard deduction. (After the 2-year period, such a person may file under the head of household status if he or she qualifies.)

marginal tax rate The tax rate you pay on the next dollar of taxable income.

average tax rate The rate at which each dollar of taxable income is taxed on average; calculated by dividing the tax liability by taxable income.

In general, married taxpayers who file jointly have a lower tax liability than if they file separately. However, sometimes these married couples pay more in total taxes than if they were single taxpayers. Combining the two incomes results in *bracket creep*—it pushes the couple into a higher tax bracket resulting in a "marriage tax." To eliminate the marriage tax, the 15 percent bracket is now twice as large for couples compared with singles. There isn't too much you can do if you're in a situation where filing jointly results in paying a marriage penalty, because it's illegal for married people to use the single filing status. But a couple planning a December wedding may reap considerable tax savings by postponing their wedding until January!

The tax brackets (rates) and payments for married couples filing separately are typically higher than for joint filers because the spouses rarely account for equal amounts of taxable income. In some cases, however, it may be advantageous for spouses to file separate returns. For instance, if one spouse has a moderate income and substantial medical expenses, and the other has a low income and no medical expenses, filing separately may provide a tax savings. It's worth your time to calculate your taxes using both scenarios to see which results in the lower amount.

Every individual or married couple who earns a specified level of income is required to file a tax return. For example, for those under 65, a single person who earned more than $8,200, and a married couple with a combined income of more than $16,400 must file a tax return (for 2005). Like the personal tax rates, these minimums are adjusted annually based on the annual rate of inflation, and they're published in the instructions accompanying each year's tax forms. If your income falls below the current minimum levels, you're not required to file a tax return. But, if you had any tax withheld during the year, you must file a tax return—even if your income falls *below* minimum filing amounts—to receive a refund of these funds.

Your Take-Home Pay

Although many of us don't give much thought to taxes until April 15 approaches, we actually pay taxes as we earn income throughout the year. Under this *pay-as-you-go* system, your employer withholds (deducts) a portion of your income every pay period and periodically sends it to the IRS. Self-employed persons must likewise deduct and forward part of their income to the IRS at four dates each year. The amounts withheld are based on a taxpayer's estimated tax liability. After the close of the taxable year, you calculate the actual taxes you owe and file your tax return. When you file, you receive full credit for the amount of taxes withheld from your income during the year and either (1) receive a refund from the IRS (if too much tax was withheld from your paycheck) or (2) have to pay additional taxes (if the amount withheld didn't cover your tax liability). Your employer normally withholds funds not only for federal income taxes but also for FICA (or Social Security) taxes and, if applicable, state and local income taxes. In addition to taxes, you may have other deductions for items such as life and health insurance, savings plans, retirement programs, professional or union dues, or charitable contributions—all of which lower your take-home pay. Your *take-home pay* is what you're left with after subtracting the amount withheld from your *gross earnings*.

Federal Withholding Taxes

The amount of **federal withholding taxes** deducted from your gross earnings each pay period depends on both the level of your earnings and the number of withholding allowances you have claimed on a form called a *W-4*, which you must complete for your employer. Withholding allowances reduce the amount of taxes withheld from your income. A taxpayer is entitled to one allowance for himself or herself, one for a spouse (if filing jointly), and one for each dependent claimed. In addition, you qualify for a *special allowance* if (1) you're single and have one job; (2) you're married, have only one job, and have a nonworking spouse; or (3) your wages from a second job or your spouse's wages (or the total of both) are $1,000 or less. *Additional withholding allowances* can be claimed by (1) heads of households, (2) those with at least $1,500 of child or dependent care expenses for which they plan to claim a credit, and (3) those with an unusually large amount of deductions. Likewise, taxpayers may have to increase their withholding allowances during the tax year if they get a part-time job, get divorced, have a child who turns 19 years old, and so on. Of course, you can elect to have your employer withhold amounts greater than those prescribed by the withholding tables.

If you know you'll work less than 8 months during a year—for example, if you're a college graduate starting your first job in the summer—you can ask your employer to calculate withholding using the part-year method. This method calculates withholding on what you actually earn in the tax year, rather than on your annual salary. For example, if you began a $45,000 per-year job on September 1, your withholding would be based not on the entire year's salary but rather on the $15,000 you'd earn during the rest of that calendar year, resulting in substantially lower withholding.

federal withholding taxes Taxes—based on the level of earnings and the number of withholding allowances claimed—an employer deducts from the employee's gross earnings each pay period.

FICA and Other Withholding Taxes

In addition to withholding on earnings, all employed workers (except certain federal employees) have to pay a combined old-age, survivor's, disability, and hospital insurance tax under provisions of the **Federal Insurance Contributions Act (FICA).** Known more commonly as the **Social Security tax,** it is paid equally by employer and employee. In 2005, the Social Security tax rate was 15.3 percent, and allocated 12.4 percent to Social Security and 2.9 percent to Medicare. The 12.4 percent applies only to the first $90,000 of an employee's earnings (this number rises with national average wages), while the Medicare component is paid on all earnings. In 2005, the employer and employee each pay 7.65 percent—one-half of the 15.3 percent rate; self-employed persons pay the full 15.3 percent tax and can deduct 50 percent of it on their tax returns.

Most states have their own income taxes, which differ from state to state. Some cities assess income taxes as well. These state and local income taxes will also be withheld from earnings. They are deductible on federal returns, but deductibility of federal taxes on the state or local return depends on state and local laws.

⏸ Concept Check

CHECK • CONCEPT CHECK • CONCEPT CHECK • CONCEPT CHECK • CONCEPT CHECK • CONCEPT CHECK • CONCEPT C

3-1 What is a *progressive tax structure* and the economic rationale for it?

3-2 Briefly define the five filing categories available to taxpayers. When might married taxpayers choose to file separately?

3-3 Distinguish between *gross earnings* and *take-home pay*. What does the employer do with the difference?

3-4 What two factors determine the amount of federal withholding taxes that will be deducted from gross earnings each pay period? Explain.

LG2 IT'S TAXABLE INCOME THAT MATTERS

As you've no doubt gathered by now, paying your income taxes is a complex process involving several steps and many calculations. Exhibit 3.1 on page 74 depicts the procedure to compute your **taxable income** and total tax liability owed. It looks simple enough—just subtract certain adjustments from your gross income to get your adjusted gross income; then subtract either the standard deduction or your itemized deductions and your total personal exemptions to get taxable income; and finally, calculate your taxes, subtract any tax credits from that amount, and add any other taxes to it to get you total tax liability. This isn't as easy as it sounds, however! Various sections of the Internal Revenue Code place numerous conditions and exceptions on the tax treatment and deductibility of certain income and expense items and define certain types of income as tax exempt. As we'll see, some problems can arise in defining what you may subtract.

Federal Insurance Contributions Act (FICA), or Social Security tax The law establishing the combined old-age, survivor's, disability, and hospital insurance tax levied on both employer and employee.

taxable income The amount of income subject to taxes; it is calculated by subtracting adjustments, the larger of itemized or standard deductions, and exemptions from gross income.

gross income The total of all of a taxpayer's income (before any adjustments, deductions, or exemptions) subject to federal taxes; it includes active, portfolio, and passive income.

Gross Income

Basically, **gross income** includes any and all income subject to federal taxes. Here are some common forms of gross income:

* Wages and salaries
* Bonuses, commissions, and tips
* Interest and dividends received
* Alimony received
* Business and farm income
* Gains from the sale of assets
* Income from pensions and annuities
* Income from rents and partnerships
* Prizes, lottery, and gambling winnings

EXHIBIT 3.1

Calculating Your Taxable Income and Total Tax Liability Owed

To find taxable income, you must first subtract all adjustments to gross income and then subtract deductions and personal exemptions. Your total tax liability owed includes tax on this taxable income amount, less any tax credits, plus other taxes owed.

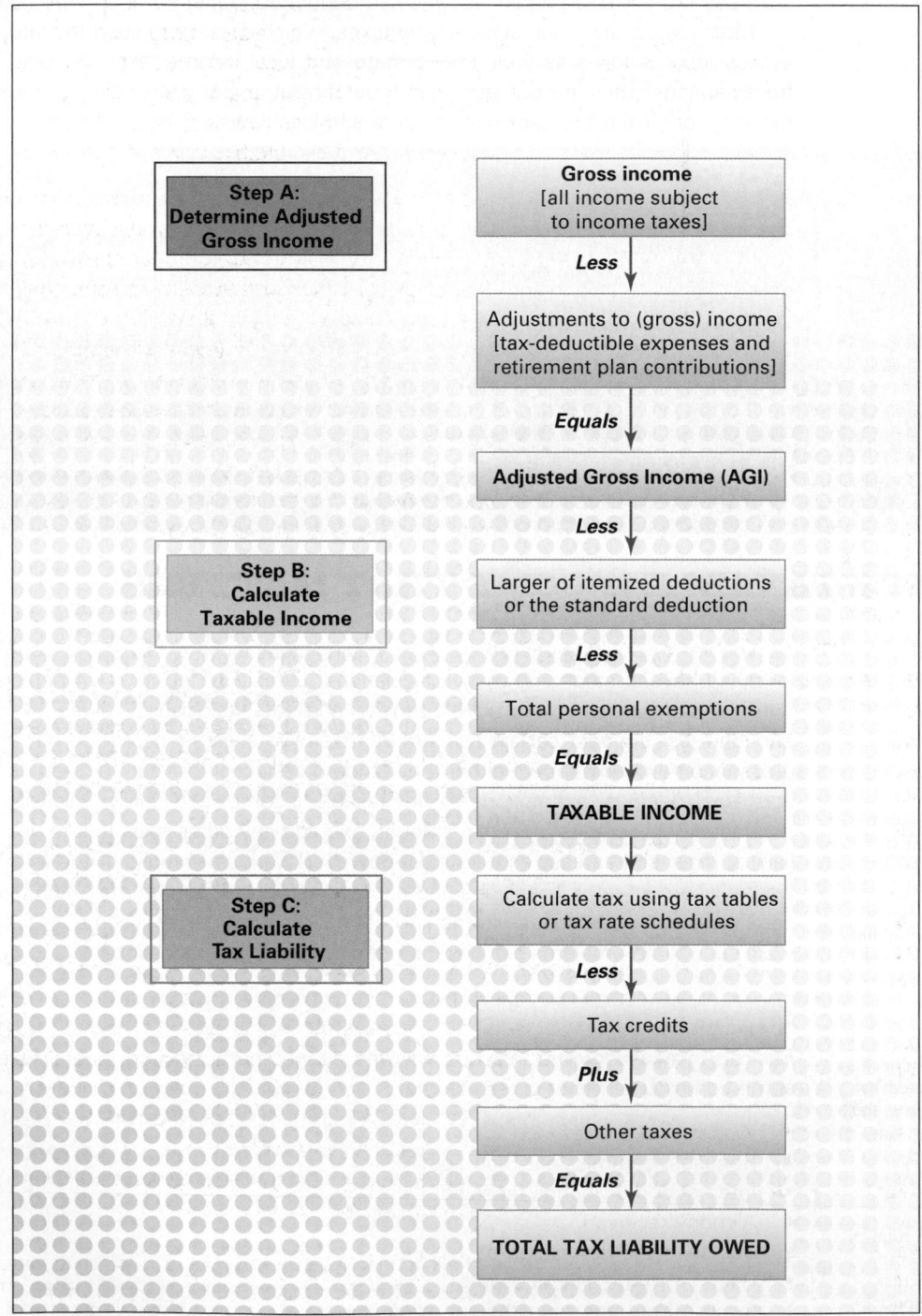

In addition to these sources of income, some types of income are considered *tax exempt* and as such are excluded—totally or partially—from gross income. Tax-exempt income doesn't even have to be listed on the tax return. Common types of tax-exempt income include child-support payments; certain types of employee fringe benefits; compensation from accident, health, and life insurance policies; federal income tax refunds; gifts, inheritances, scholarships, and fellowships (limited as to amount and time); and veterans' benefits.

Three Kinds of Income

Individual income falls into one of three basic categories:

- **Active income:** Income *earned* on the job, such as wages and salaries, bonuses and tips; most other forms of *noninvestment* income, including pension income and alimony
- **Portfolio income:** Earnings (interest, dividends, and capital gains [profits on the sale of investments]) generated from most types of investment holdings; includes savings accounts, stocks, bonds, mutual funds, options, and futures
- **Passive income:** A special category that includes income derived from real estate, limited partnerships, and other forms of tax shelters

These categories limit the amount of deductions and write-offs that taxpayers can take. Specifically, the amount of allowable, deductible expenses associated with portfolio and passive income *is limited t.o the amount of income derived from these two sources*. For example, if you had a total of $380 in portfolio income for the year, you could write off no more than $380 in portfolio-related interest expense. But, if you have more portfolio expenses than income, you can "accumulate" the difference and write it off in later years (when you have sufficient portfolio income) or when you finally sell the investment.

For deduction purposes, you cannot combine portfolio and passive income with each other or with active income. *Investment-related expenses can be used only with portfolio income*, and with a few exceptions, *passive investment expenses can be used only to offset the income from passive investments*. All the other allowances and deductions we'll describe later are written off against the total amount of *active* income the taxpayer generates.

Capital Gains

Technically, a *capital gain* occurs whenever an asset (such as a stock, a bond, or real estate) is sold for more than its original cost. So, if you purchased stock for $50 per share and sold it for $60, you'd have a capital gain of $10 per share.

Capital gains are taxed at different rates, depending on the holding period. Exhibit 3.2 on page 76 shows the different holding periods and applicable tax rates based on the 2005 tax brackets. As a rule, taxpayers include most capital gains as part of *portfolio income*. They will add any capital gains to the amount of dividends, interest, and rents they generate to arrive at total investment income.

Although there are no limits on the amount of capital gains taxpayers can generate, the IRS imposes some restrictions on the amount of capital losses taxpayers can take in a given year. Specifically, a taxpayer can write off capital losses, dollar for dollar, against any capital gains. For example, a taxpayer with $10,000 in capital gains can write off up to $10,000 in capital losses. After that, he or she can write off a maximum of $3,000 in additional capital losses against other (active, earned) income. Thus, if the taxpayer in our example had $18,000 in capital losses in 2005, only $13,000 could be written off on 2005 taxes: $10,000 against the capital gains generated in 2005 and another $3,000 against active income. The remainder—$5,000 in this case—will have to be written off in later years, in the same order as just indicated: first against any capital gains and then up to $3,000 against active income. (*Note:* To qualify as a deductible item, the capital loss *must result from the sale of some income-producing asset*, such as stocks and bonds. The capital loss on a non-income-producing asset, such as a car or TV, does *not* qualify for tax relief.)

Selling Your Home: A Special Case. Homeowners, for various reasons, receive special treatment in the tax codes, including the taxation of capital gains on the sale of a home. Under current law, single taxpayers can exclude from income the first $250,000 of gain on the sale of a principal residence. Married taxpayers can exclude the first $500,000. To get this favorable tax treatment, the taxpayer must own and occupy the residence as a principal

Smart.Sites

At **http://www .thomsonedu.com/ finance/gitman,** link to *Capital Gains and Losses* to help you understand the tax treatment of securities sales. It's just one of many tax guides you'll find at the site's *Tax Guide for Investors.*

EXHIBIT 3.2 Capital Gains Tax Categories as of 2005

Capital gains tax rates are as low as 5 or 15 percent for holding periods over 12 months, depending on the tax bracket (year 2005).

Holding Period	Tax Brackets (2005)	Tax on Capital Gains
Less than 12 months	All (10%, 15%, 25%, 28%, 33%, and 35%)	Same as ordinary income
Over 12 months	10%, 15%	5%
	25%, 28%, 33%, 35%	15%

residence for at least 2 of the 5 years prior to the sale. For example, the Greenmans (married taxpayers) just sold their principal residence for $475,000. They had purchased their home 4 years earlier for $325,000. They may exclude their $150,000 gain ($475,000 − $325,000) from their income because they occupied the residence for more than 2 years, and the gain is less than $500,000.

This exclusion is available on only one sale every 2 years. A loss on the sale of a principal residence is not deductible. Generally speaking, this law is quite favorable to homeowners.

Adjustments to (Gross) Income

Now that you've totaled your gross income, you can deduct your **adjustments to (gross) income.** These are allowable deductions from gross income, including certain employee, personal retirement, insurance, and support expenses. Most of these deductions are nonbusiness in nature. Here are some items that can be treated as adjustments to income:

- Educator expenses (limited)
- IRA contributions (limited)
- Self-employment taxes paid (limited to 50 percent of amount paid)
- Self-employed health insurance payments
- Penalty on early withdrawal of savings
- Alimony paid
- Moving expenses (some limits)

(*Note*: The limitations on deductions for self-directed retirement plans, such as IRAs and SEPs, are discussed in Chapter 14.)

After subtracting the total of all allowable adjustments to income from your gross income, you're left with **adjusted gross income (AGI).** AGI is an important value, because it's used to calculate limits for certain itemized deductions.

Deductions: Standard or Itemized?

As we see from Exhibit 3.1, the next step in calculating your taxes is to subtract allowable deductions from your AGI. This may be the most complex part of the tax preparation process. You have two options: take the *standard deduction*, a fixed amount that depends on your filing status, or list your *itemized deductions* (specified tax-deductible personal expenses). Obviously, you should use the method that results in larger allowable deductions.

Standard Deduction

Instead of itemizing personal deductions, a taxpayer can take the **standard deduction,** a blanket deduction that includes the various deductible expenses that taxpayers normally incur. People whose total itemized deductions are too small take the standard deduction, which varies depending on the taxpayer's filing status (single, married filing jointly, and so on), age (65 or older), and vision (blind). In 2005, the standard deduction ranged from $5,000 to $14,000. For single filers, it was $5,000; and for married people filing jointly,

adjustments to (gross) income Allowable deductions from gross income, including certain employee, personal retirement, insurance, and support expenses.

adjusted gross income (AGI) The amount of income remaining after subtracting all allowable adjustments to income from gross income.

standard deduction A blanket deduction that depends on the taxpayer's filing status, age, and vision and can be taken by a taxpayer whose total itemized deductions are too small.

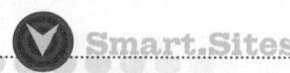

Smart.Sites

Link to About.com's Topics page at **http://www.thomsonedu.com/finance/gitman.** It offers help on tax topics, including how to find all the possible deductions for which you qualify.

itemized deductions
Personal expenditures that can be deducted from AGI when determining taxable income.

$10,000. Those over 65 and those who are blind are eligible for a higher standard deduction. Each year the standard deduction amounts are adjusted in response to changes in the cost of living.

Itemized Deductions

Itemized deductions allow taxpayers to reduce their AGI by the amount of their allowable personal expenditures. The Internal Revenue Code defines the types of nonbusiness items that can be deducted from AGI. Here are some of the more common ones:

- Medical and dental expenses (in *excess* of 7.5 percent of AGI)
- State, local, and foreign income and property taxes; state and local personal property taxes
- Residential mortgage interest and investment interest (limited)
- Charitable contributions (limited to 50 percent, 30 percent, or 20 percent of AGI depending on certain factors)
- Casualty and theft losses (in excess of 10 percent of AGI; reduced by $100 per loss)
- Job and other expenses (in excess of 2 percent of AGI)
- Moving expenses (some restrictions; also deductible for those who don't itemize)

Read the instructions accompanying the tax forms for detailed descriptions of allowable deductions in each category.

Taxpayers with AGI over a specified amount, adjusted upward annually, lose part of their itemized deductions. In 2005, the level of AGI at which the phase-out began was $72,975 for single taxpayers and $145,950 for married persons filing jointly. This limitation applies to certain categories of deductions, including other types of taxes, home mortgage interest, charitable contributions, unreimbursed employee expenses, moving expenses, and other miscellaneous deductions subject to the 2 percent limit. Medical expenses, casualty and theft losses, and investment interest are exempt from this limit on deductions; the amount of the total reduction in itemized deductions cannot be more than 80 percent of the total deductions to which the limitation applies. These total itemized deductions are reduced by the smaller of 3 percent of AGI over $145,950 (or $72,975 for married taxpayers filing separately) or 80 percent of the deductions to which the limitation applies. In 2006 this reduction started to be phased out, and it will be eliminated by 2010.

For example, assume that you're married, filing a joint return, and your AGI is $160,000. Your deductions (in excess of any specified percentages of AGI) affected by the income limitation total $45,000, and other deductions total $10,000. You must reduce deductions by $422 [($160,000 AGI − $145,950) × .03 = $422]. Therefore, you would subtract $422 from your $55,000 total itemized deductions, for an allowed deduction of $54,578. This loss of itemized deductions has the effect of raising the tax rate applied to your top bracket (in this case) from 28 percent to 28.84 percent [28.00 percent + (3 percent × 28 percent)]. Married taxpayers with combined income over the AGI deduction threshold and high itemized deductions that can be allocated to one spouse (such as medical expenses) may find that by filing separately, they can avoid this limit on deductions.

Choosing the Best Option

Your decision to take the standard deduction or itemize deductions may change from year to year, or even in the same year. Taxpayers who find they've chosen the wrong option and paid too much may recalculate their tax using the other method and claim a refund for the difference. For example, suppose that you computed and paid your taxes, which amounted to $2,450, using the standard deduction. A few months later you find that had you itemized your deductions, your taxes would have been only $1,950. Using the appropriate forms, you can file an *amended return (Form 1040X)* showing a $500 refund ($2,450 − $1,950). To avoid having to file an amended return due to using the wrong deduction technique, estimate your deductions using both the standard and itemized deduction amounts and then choose the one that results

© STOCKBYTE PLATINUM/GETTY IMAGES

in lower taxes. Interestingly, most taxpayers use the standard deduction; but homeowners who pay home mortgage interest and property taxes generally itemize because those expenses alone typically exceed the allowable standard deduction.

Exemptions

There's one more calculation for determining your taxable income. Deductions from AGI based on the number of persons supported by the taxpayer's income are called **exemptions.** A taxpayer can claim an exemption for himself or herself, his or her spouse, and any *dependents*—children or other relatives earning less than a stipulated level of income ($3,200 in 2005), for whom the taxpayer provides more than half of their total support. This income limitation is waived for children under the age of 24 (at the end of the calendar year) who are full-time students. So a college student, for example, could earn $8,000 and still be claimed as an exemption by his or her parents as long as all other dependency requirements are met. In 2005, each exemption claimed was worth $3,200. The personal exemption amount is tied to the cost of living and changes annually based on the prevailing rate of inflation.

Exemptions are phased out and eliminated altogether for taxpayers with high levels of AGI. After adjusting for inflation, it applies to single taxpayers with 2005 AGI over $145,950 and married couples filing jointly with 2005 AGI over $218,950. As with itemized deductions, in 2006 the reduction of exemptions began to be phased out, and it will be eliminated by 2010.

A personal exemption can be claimed only once. If a child is *eligible* to be claimed as an exemption by her parents, then she doesn't have the choice of using a personal exemption on her own tax return regardless of whether the parents use her exemption.

In 2005, a family of four could take total exemptions of $12,800—that is, 4 × $3,200. Subtracting the amount claimed for itemized deductions (or the standard deduction) and exemptions from AGI results in the amount of *taxable income*, which is the basis on which taxes are calculated. A taxpayer who makes $50,000 a year may have only, say, $30,000 in taxable income after adjustments, deductions, and exemptions. It is the *lower*, taxable income figure that determines how much tax an individual must pay.

❚❚ Concept Check

3-5	Define and differentiate between *gross income* and *AGI*. Name several types of tax-exempt income. What is *passive income?*
3-6	What is a *capital gain*, and how is it treated for tax purposes?
3-7	If you itemize your deductions, you may include certain expenses as part of your itemized deductions. Discuss five types of itemized deductions and the general rules that apply to them.
3-8	Larry Torrelli was married on January 15, 2007. His wife, Rebecca, is a full-time student at the university and earns $225 a month working in the library. How many personal exemptions will Larry and Rebecca be able to claim on their joint return? Would it make any difference if Rebecca's parents paid for more than 50 percent of her support? Explain.

LG3 CALCULATING AND FILING YOUR TAXES

exemptions Deductions from AGI based on the number of persons supported by the taxpayer's income.

Now that we've reviewed the general principles of federal income taxes and the components of taxable income, we can direct our attention to calculating the amount of income tax due. To do this, we need to address several key aspects of measuring taxable income and taxes: (1) the tax rates applicable to various types of personal income, (2) tax credits, (3) the basic tax forms and schedules, and (4) the procedures for determining tax liability.

Tax Rates

As we saw earlier in this chapter, to find the amount of *taxable income* we subtract item-ized deductions (or the standard deduction for nonitemizers) *and* personal exemptions from AGI. *Both itemizers and non-itemizers* use this procedure, which is a key calculation in determining your tax liability. It is *reported taxable income* that determines the amount of income subject to federal income taxes. Once you know the amount of your taxable income, you can refer to *tax rate tables* to find the amount of taxes you owe. (When actu-ally filing a tax return, taxpayers with taxable income of more than $100,000 must use the tax rate schedules.)

Tax rates vary not only with the amount of reported taxable income but also with filing status. Thus different tax rate schedules apply to each filing category, as shown in Exhibit 3.3 on page 80. The vast majority of taxpayers fall into the first three brackets and are sub-ject to tax rates of either 10, 15, or 25 percent.

To see how the tax rates in Exhibit 3.3 work, consider two single taxpayers: one has taxable income of $12,500, the other of $35,600. Here's how we would calculate their respective tax liabilities:

- For taxable income of $12,500: $730 + [($12,500 − $7,300) × .15] = $730 + $780 = $1,510
- For taxable income of $35,600: $4,090 + [($35,600 − $29,700) × .25] = $4,090 + $1,475 = $5,565

The income of $12,500 is partially taxed at the 10 percent rate and partially taxed at the 15 percent rate. The first $7,300 of the $35,600 is taxed at 10 percent, the next $22,400 at 15 percent, and the remaining $5,900 at 25 percent. Keep in mind that tax-payers use the same procedures at this point whether they itemize or not. To show how the amount of tax liability will vary with the level of taxable income, Exhibit 3.4 lists the taxes due on a range of taxable incomes, from $1,500 to $350,000, for individual and joint returns.

Recall from our earlier discussions that the average tax rate is found by dividing your tax liability by the amount of reported taxable income. Returning to our example involving the taxpayer with an income of $35,600, we see that this individual had an average tax rate of 15.6 percent ($5,565 4 $35,600), which is considerably less than the stated tax rate of 25 percent. Actually, the 25 percent represents the taxpayer's *marginal tax rate*—the rate at which the next dollar of taxable income is taxed. Notice in our calculations that the marginal 25 percent tax rate applies only to that portion of the single person's income that exceeds $29,700, or $5,900, in the above example.

Some taxpayers are subject to the *alternative minimum tax (AMT)*, currently 26 per-cent of the first $175,000 and 28 percent of the excess. A taxpayer's tax liability is the higher of the AMT or the regular tax. The AMT is designed to ensure that high-income tax-payers with many deductions and tax shelter investments that provide attractive tax write-offs are paying their fair share of taxes. The AMT includes in taxable income certain types of deductions otherwise allowed, such as state and local income and property taxes, mis-cellaneous itemized deductions, unreimbursed medical expenses, and depreciation. Therefore, taxpayers with moderate levels of taxable income, including those living in states with high tax rates and self-employed persons with depreciation deductions, may be subject to the AMT.

Tax Credits

After determining your taxable income and calculating the *tax liability*, or amount of taxes you owe, you have one final step to determine the amount of taxes due. Some taxpayers are allowed to take certain deductions, known as **tax credits,** directly from their tax liability.

A tax credit is much more valuable than a deduction or an exemption because it directly reduces, dollar for dollar, the amount of *taxes due*, whereas a deduction or an exemption merely reduces the amount of *taxable income*. In Exhibit 3.5 on page 81 we see how this difference affects the tax liability of two single taxpayers with $34,000 of gross income and $6,000 of other deductions/exemptions (in the 15 percent tax bracket).

tax credits Deductions from a taxpayer's tax liability that directly reduce his or her *taxes due* rather than *taxable income*.

EXHIBIT 3.3   Sample Tax Rate Schedules

Tax rates levied on personal income vary with the amount of reported taxable income and the taxpayer's filing status.

2005 Tax Rate Schedules

Schedule X—If your filing status is Single

If your taxable income is: Over—	But not over—	The tax is:	of the amount over—
$0	$7,300	------ 10%	$0
7,300	29,700	$730.00 + 15%	7,300
29,700	71,950	4,090.00 + 25%	29,700
71,950	150,150	14,652.50 + 28%	71,950
150,150	326,450	36,548.50 + 33%	150,150
326,450	------	94,727.50 + 35%	326,450

Schedule Y-1—If your filing status is Married filing jointly or Qualifying widow(er)

If your taxable income is: Over—	But not over—	The tax is:	of the amount over—
$0	$14,600	------ 10%	$0
14,600	59,400	$1,460.00 + 15%	14,600
59,400	119,950	8,180.00 + 25%	59,400
119,950	182,800	23,317.50 + 28%	119,950
182,800	326,450	40,915.50 + 33%	182,800
326,450	------	88,320.00 + 35%	326,450

Schedule Y-2—If your filing status is Married filing separately

If your taxable income is: Over—	But not over—	The tax is:	of the amount over—
$0	$7,300	------ 10%	$0
7,300	29,700	$730.00 + 15%	7,300
29,700	59,975	4,090.00 + 25%	29,700
59,975	91,400	11,658.75 + 28%	59,975
91,400	163,225	20,457.75 + 33%	91,400
163,225	------	44,160.00 + 35%	163,225

Schedule Z—If your filing status is Head of household

If your taxable income is: Over—	But not over—	The tax is:	of the amount over—
$0	$10,450	------ 10%	$0
10,450	39,800	$1,045.00 + 15%	10,450
39,800	102,800	5,447.50 + 25%	39,800
102,800	166,450	21,197.50 + 28%	102,800
166,450	326,450	39,019.50 + 33%	166,450
326,450	------	91,819.50 + 35%	326,450

Source: Internal Revenue Service.

One has $1,000 in deductions, and the other has a $1,000 tax credit. Look at what happens to the amount of taxes due. In effect, the tax credit in this example has reduced taxes (and therefore *increased* after-tax income) by $850 ($3,685 − $2,835).

An often-used tax credit is for *child and dependent care expenses*. This credit is based on the amount spent for dependent care while a taxpayer (and spouse, if married) works or goes to school. The qualifying dependent must be less than 13 years old, except in the case of a disabled dependent or spouse. The amount of the credit is based on up to $3,000 in care expenses for one qualifying dependent and $6,000 for two or more qualifying dependents. The actual amount of the credit is a percentage of the amount spent or of the limit, whichever is less. The maximum possible credit for one child ranges from $600 to $1,050; for two or more children the range is $1,200 to $2,100. The percentages range from 20 to 35 percent, depending on the taxpayer's AGI. For example, a couple with AGI of $24,000 who spent $3,000 on child-care expenses for their two young children would receive a dependent-care credit of $900 (.30 × $3,000).

EXHIBIT 3.4

Taxable Income and the Amount of Income Taxes Due (2005)

Given the progressive tax structure used in this country, it follows that the larger your income, the more you can expect to pay in taxes.

Taxable Income	Taxes Due (rounded)	
	Individual Returns	Joint Returns
$ 1,500	$ 150[a]	$ 150[a]
8,000	835[b]	800
15,000	1,885	1,520[b]
30,000	4,165[c]	3,770
60,000	11,665	8,330[c]
100,000	22,507[d]	18,330
180,000	46,399[e]	40,132[d]
350,000	102,970[f]	96,563[f]

[a] Income is taxed at 10 percent.
[b] 15% tax rate now applies.
[c] 25% tax rate now applies.
[d] 28% tax rate now applies.
[e] 33% tax rate now applies.
[f] 35% tax rate now applies.

An *adoption tax credit* of up to $10,630 is available for the qualifying costs of adopting a child under age 18. Only taxpayers with AGI under $199,450 are eligible for the adoption tax credit. Taxpayers with dependent children under age 17 are entitled to a *child tax credit* which in 2005 was $1,000 per qualifying child. The credit is phased out for married couples with AGI above $110,000, $75,000 for single filers, and $55,000 for married persons filing separately. Here are some other common tax credits:

- Credit for the elderly or the disabled
- Foreign tax credit
- Credit for prior year minimum tax
- Mortgage interest credit
- Credit for qualified electric vehicle

EXHIBIT 3.5

How Deductions and Tax Credits Affect Taxes Due

As this example shows, a $1,000 tax credit reduces taxes due by far more than a $1,000 tax deduction.

Calculation	$1,000 Deduction	$1,000 Tax Credit
Gross income	$34,000	$34,000
Less: Other deductions/exemptions	6,000	6,000
Less: $1,000 deduction	1,000	—
Taxable income	$27,000	$28,000
Tax liability*	3,685	3,835
Less $1,000 tax credit	—	1,000
Taxes due	$ 3,685	$ 2,835

*Tax liability is figured as follows: the first $7,300 of taxable income is taxed at 10 percent, the balance at 15 percent.

To receive one of these credits, the taxpayer must file a return, along with a separate schedule in support of the tax credit claimed.

Tax Forms and Schedules

The IRS requires taxpayers to file their returns using certain specified tax forms. As noted earlier, these forms and various instruction booklets on how to prepare them are available to taxpayers free of charge. Generally, all persons who filed tax returns in the previous year are automatically sent a booklet containing tax forms and instructions for preparing returns for the current year. Inside the booklet is a form that can be used to obtain additional tax forms for filing various tax-related returns and information. Exhibit 3.6 provides a list of commonly used tax forms and schedules.

Variations of Form 1040

All individuals use some variation of Form 1040 to file their tax returns. *Form 1040EZ* is a simple, one-page form. You qualify to use this form if you are single or married filing a joint return; under age 65 (both if filing jointly); not blind; do not claim any dependents; have taxable income of less than $100,000 from only wages, salaries, tips, or taxable scholarships or grants; have interest income of less than $1,500; and do not claim any adjustments to income, itemize deductions, or claim any tax credits. Worksheet 3.1 shows the Form 1040EZ filed in 2005 by Yoshio Ohno, a full-time graduate student at Anystate University. His sources of income include a $10,000 scholarship, of which $1,900 was used for room and board; $7,600 earned from part-time and summer jobs; and $50 interest earned on a savings account deposit. Because scholarships used for tuition and fees are not taxed, he must include as income only the portion used for room and board. He had a total of $475 withheld for federal income taxes during the year.

EXHIBIT 3.6   Commonly Used Tax Forms and Schedules

Several types of 1040 tax return forms are available. If you use the standard Form 1040, you may need to include one or more schedules and forms with the tax return, depending on the amount and types of deductions claimed. Some of the more common ones are listed below the 1040s.

1040	Standard tax return, used with itemized deductions
1040A	Short-form tax return
1040EZ	Short-form tax return for single persons with no dependents
1040X	Amended U.S. individual tax return
1040-ES	Estimated tax for individuals
Schedule A	Itemized deductions
Schedule B	Interest and ordinary dividends
Schedule C	Profit or loss from business
Schedule D	Capital gains and losses
Schedule E	Supplemental income and loss
Schedule EIC	Earned income credit
Schedule F	Profit and loss from farming
Schedule R	Credit for the elderly or disabled
Schedule SE	Self-employment tax
2106	Employee business expenses
2119	Sale of your home
2441	Child and dependent care expenses
3903	Moving expenses
4562	Depreciation and amortization
4684	Casualties and thefts
4868	Application for automatic extension of time to file U.S. individual tax return
8829	Expenses for business use of your home
8839	Qualified adoption expenses

Form 1040EZ is easy to use, and most of the instructions are printed on the form itself. Yoshio Ohno qualifies to use it because he is single, under age 65, not blind, and meets its income and deduction restrictions.

Form 1040EZ

Department of the Treasury—Internal Revenue Service

Income Tax Return for Single and Joint Filers With No Dependents (99) **2005**

OMB No. 1545-0074

Label
(See page 11.)
Use the IRS label. Otherwise, please print or type.

Your first name and initial: Yoshio
Last name: Ohno

If a joint return, spouse's first name and initial
Last name

Home address (number and street). If you have a P.O. box, see page 11.
1000 State University Drive
Apt. no. 14 A

City, town or post office, state, and ZIP code. If you have a foreign address, see page 11.
Anytown, Anystate   10001

Your social security number: 123 : 45 : 6789
Spouse's social security number

▲ You **must** enter your SSN(s) above. ▲

Presidential Election Campaign (page 12) ▶

Checking a box below will not change your tax or refund.

Check here if you, or your spouse if a joint return, want $3 to go to this fund? ▶ ☑ **You**   ☐ **Spouse**

Income

Attach Form(s) W-2 here.
Enclose, but do not attach, any payment.

1	Wages, salaries, and tips. This should be shown in box 1 of your Form(s) W-2. Attach your Form(s) W-2.	1 9,500 00
2	Taxable interest. If the total is over $1,500, you cannot use Form 1040EZ.	2 50 00
3	Unemployment compensation and Alaska Permanent Fund dividends (see page 13).	3
4	Add lines 1, 2, and 3. This is your **adjusted gross income.**	4 9,550 00
5	If someone can claim you (or your spouse if a joint return) as a dependent, check the applicable box(es) below and enter the amount from the worksheet on back. ☐ You ☐ Spouse If someone cannot claim you (or your spouse if a joint return), enter $8,200 if **single;** $16,400 if **married filing jointly.** See back for explanation.	5 8,200 00
6	Subtract line 5 from line 4. If line 5 is larger than line 4, enter -0-. This is your **taxable income.** ▶	6 1,350 00

Payments and tax

7	Federal income tax withheld from box 2 of your Form(s) W-2.	7 475 00
8a	Earned income credit (EIC).	8a 0
b	Nontaxable combat pay election. 8b	
9	Add lines 7 and 8a. These are your **total payments.** ▶	9 475 00
10	**Tax.** Use the amount on **line 6 above** to find your tax in the tax table on pages 24–32 of the booklet. Then, enter the tax from the table on this line.	10 136 00

Refund

Have it directly deposited! See page 18 and fill in 11b, 11c, and 11d.

11a	If line 9 is larger than line 10, subtract line 10 from line 9. This is your **refund.** ▶	11a 339 00
▶ b	Routing number	▶ c Type: ☐ Checking ☐ Savings
▶ d	Account number	

Amount you owe

12	If line 10 is larger than line 9, subtract line 9 from line 10. This is the **amount you owe.** For details on how to pay, see page 19. ▶ 12

Third party designee

Do you want to allow another person to discuss this return with the IRS (see page 19)? ☐ **Yes.** Complete the following. ☑ **No**

Designee's name ▶
Phone no. ▶ (   )
Personal identification number (PIN) ▶

Sign here

Under penalties of perjury, I declare that I have examined this return, and to the best of my knowledge and belief, it is true, correct, and accurately lists all amounts and sources of income I received during the tax year. Declaration of preparer (other than the taxpayer) is based on all information of which the preparer has any knowledge.

Joint return? See page 11.
Keep a copy for your records.

Your signature	Date	Your occupation	Daytime phone number
Yoshio Ohno	9/1/06	student	(555)555-1111
Spouse's signature. If a joint return, **both** must sign.	Date	Spouse's occupation	

Paid preparer's use only

Preparer's signature ▶	Date	Check if self-employed ☐	Preparer's SSN or PTIN
Firm's name (or yours if self-employed), address, and ZIP code ▶		EIN	
		Phone no. ( )	

For Disclosure, Privacy Act, and Paperwork Reduction Act Notice, see page 23.   Cat. No. 11329W   Form **1040EZ** (2005)

To use *Form 1040A*, a two-page form, your income must be less than $100,000 and derived only from specified sources. Using this form, you may deduct certain IRA contributions and claim certain tax credits, but you cannot itemize your deductions. If your income is over $100,000 or you itemize deductions, you must use the standard Form 1040 along with appropriate schedules, listed in Exhibit 3.6.

The use of these schedules, which provide detailed guidelines for calculating certain entries on the first two pages of *Form 1040*, varies among taxpayers depending on the relevance of these entries to their situations. Pages 1 and 2 of Form 1040, which summarize all items of income and deductions detailed on the accompanying schedules, are used to determine and report the taxable income and associated tax liability.

Despite detailed instructions that accompany the tax forms, taxpayers make many blunders when filling them out. Common errors include missing information and arithmetic errors. So check and recheck your forms before submitting them to the IRS.

The 2005 Tax Return of Terry and Evelyn Becker

Let's now put all the pieces of the tax preparation puzzle together to see how Terry and Evelyn Becker calculate and file their income taxes. The Beckers own their own home and are both 35 years old. Married for 11 years, they have three children—Tom (age 9), Dick (age 7), and Jessica (age 3). Terry is a cost accountant for a major oil company headquartered in their hometown of Anytown, Anystate. Evelyn has $1\frac{1}{2}$ years of college and works part-time as a sales clerk in a major department store. During 2005, Terry's salary totaled $60,415, while Evelyn earned $9,750. Terry's employer withheld taxes of $6,260, and Evelyn's, $1,150. During the year, the Beckers earned $800 interest on their joint savings account and realized $1,250 in capital gains on the sale of securities they had owned for 11 months. In addition, Terry kept the books for his brother's car dealership, from which he netted $5,800 during the year. Because no taxes were withheld from any of their outside income, during the year they made estimated tax payments totaling $1,000. The Beckers' records indicate they had $14,713 of potential itemized deductions during the year. Finally, the Beckers plan to contribute $4,000 to Evelyn's traditional IRA account. Beginning in 2006, the Beckers plan to switch Evelyn's account to a Roth IRA (see Chapter 14).

Finding the Beckers' Tax Liability: Form 1040

Look at the Beckers' 2005 tax return (Worksheet 3.2 on pages 86–87) to see the basic calculations required in preparing Form 1040. Although we don't include the supporting schedules here, we illustrate the basic calculations they require. The Beckers have detailed records of their income and expenses, which they use not only for tax purposes but as an important input into their budgeting process. Using this information, the Beckers intend to prepare their 2005 tax return so that their total tax liability is as low as possible. Like most married couples, the Beckers file a *joint return*.

Gross Income. The Beckers' gross income in 2005 amounted to $78,015—the amount shown as "total income" on line 22 of their tax return. They have both active income and portfolio income, as follows:

Active Income		
Terry's earnings	$60,415	
Evelyn's earnings	9,750	
Terry's business income (net)	5,800	
Total active income		$75,965

Interest from savings account	$ 800
Capital gains realized*	1,250
Total portfolio income	2,050
Total income ($75,965 + $2,080)	$78,015

* Because this gain was realized on stock held for less than 12 months, the full amount is taxable as ordinary income.

They have no investment expenses to offset their portfolio income, so they'll be liable for taxes on the full amount of portfolio income. Although they have interest income, the Beckers don't have to file Schedule B (for interest and dividend income) with the Form 1040, because the interest is less than $1,500 and they earned no dividends. (If they receive dividends on stock in the future, they will have to complete a Qualified Dividends and Capital Gains Tax Worksheet, provided in the Form 1040 instruction booklet. Qualified dividends are taxed at the lower capital gains rates.) In addition, Terry will have to file Schedule C, detailing the income earned and expenses incurred in his bookkeeping business, and Schedule D to report capital gains income.

Adjustments to Gross Income. The Beckers have only two adjustments to income: Evelyn's IRA contribution and 50 percent of the self-employment tax on Terry's net business income. Because Evelyn isn't covered by a retirement plan, and Terry's and her combined modified AGI is below $150,000, they can deduct her entire $4,000 maximum contribution to an IRA account even though Terry is already covered by a company-sponsored retirement program (see Chapter 14). Terry's self-employment tax will be 15.3 percent of his $5,800 net business income, and he will be able to deduct one-half that amount— $443.70 [(.153 × $5,800)/2]—on line 27.

Adjusted Gross Income. After deducting the $443.70 self-employment tax and Terry's $4,000 IRA contribution from their gross income, the Beckers are left with an AGI of $73,571.30, as reported on line 37.

Itemized Deductions or Standard Deduction? The Beckers are filing a joint return, and neither is over age 65 or blind; so according to the box on page two of Form 1040, they are entitled to a standard deduction of $10,000. However, they want to evaluate their itemized deductions before deciding which type of deduction to take—obviously they'll take the highest deduction, because it will result in the lowest amount of taxable income and keep their tax liability to a minimum. Their preliminary paperwork resulted in the following deductions:

Medical and dental expenses	$ 1,223
State income and property taxes paid	2,560
Mortgage interest	7,893
Charitable contributions	475
Job and other expenses	2,522
Total	$14,673

The taxes, mortgage interest, and charitable contributions are deductible in full; so at the minimum, the Beckers will have itemized deductions amounting to $10,928 ($2,560 + $7,893 + $475). However, to be deductible, the medical and dental expenses and job and other expenses must exceed stipulated minimum levels of AGI—only that portion which exceeds the specified minimum levels of AGI can be included as part of their itemized deductions. For medical and dental expenses the minimum is 7.5 percent of AGI, and for job and other expenses it is 2 percent of AGI. Because 7.5 percent of the Beckers' AGI is $5,517.85 (.075 × $73,571.30), they fall short of the minimum and cannot deduct any medical and dental expenses. In contrast, because 2 percent of the Beckers' AGI is $1,471.43 (.02 × $73,571.30), they can deduct any job and other expenses exceeding that amount, or $2,522 − $1,471.43 = $1,050.57. Adding that amount to their other allowable deductions ($10,928) results in total itemized deductions of $11,978.57. This amount exceeds the standard deduction of $10,000 by nearly 20 percent, so the Beckers itemize their deductions. They would enter the details of these deductions on Schedule A and attach it to their Form 1040. (The total amount of the Beckers' itemized deductions is listed on line 40 of Form 1040.)

Because they itemize deductions, the Beckers use standard Form 1040 to file their tax return. When filed with the IRS, their return will include not only Form 1040 but also other schedules and forms detailing many of their expenses and deductions.

Form 1040

Department of the Treasury—Internal Revenue Service

U.S. Individual Income Tax Return 2005 (99)   IRS Use Only—Do not write or staple in this space.

For the year Jan. 1–Dec. 31, 2005, or other tax year beginning , 2005, ending , 20   OMB No. 1545-0074

Label (See instructions on page 16.) **Use the IRS label.** Otherwise, please print or type.

Your first name and initial: Terry B.	Last name: Becker
If a joint return, spouse's first name and initial: Evelyn A.	Last name: Becker
Home address (number and street). If you have a P.O. box, see page 16.: 125 Laughing Lane	Apt. no.
City, town or post office, state, and ZIP code. If you have a foreign address, see page 16.: Anytown, Anystate 10001	

Your social security number: 123 : 45 : 6789
Spouse's social security number: 987 : 65 : 4321

▲ You **must** enter your SSN(s) above. ▲

Checking a box below will not change your tax or refund.

Presidential Election Campaign ▶ Check here if you, or your spouse if filing jointly, want $3 to go to this fund (see page 16) ▶ ☑ You ☑ Spouse

Filing Status
Check only one box.

1 ☐ Single
2 ☑ Married filing jointly (even if only one had income)
3 ☐ Married filing separately. Enter spouse's SSN above and full name here. ▶
4 ☐ Head of household (with qualifying person). (See page 17.) If the qualifying person is a child but not your dependent, enter this child's name here. ▶
5 ☐ Qualifying widow(er) with dependent child (see page 17)

Exemptions

6a ☑ **Yourself.** If someone can claim you as a dependent, **do not** check box 6a
b ☑ **Spouse**

c Dependents:

(1) First name Last name	(2) Dependent's social security number	(3) Dependent's relationship to you	(4) ✔ if qualifying child for child tax credit (see page 19)
Thomas T. Becker	065 : 01 : 2347	son	☑
Richard L. Becker	012 : 34 : 5678	son	☑
Jessica M. Becker	034 : 65 : 1234	daughter	☑
	: :		☐

If more than four dependents, see page 19.

Boxes checked on 6a and 6b: 2
No. of children on 6c who:
• lived with you: 3
• did not live with you due to divorce or separation (see page 20):
Dependents on 6c not entered above:
Add numbers on lines above ▶: 5

d Total number of exemptions claimed

Income

Attach Form(s) W-2 here. Also attach Forms W-2G and 1099-R if tax was withheld.

If you did not get a W-2, see page 22.

Enclose, but do not attach, any payment. Also, please use Form 1040-V.

7	Wages, salaries, tips, etc. Attach Form(s) W-2	7	70,165 00
8a	**Taxable** interest. Attach Schedule B if required	8a	800 00
b	**Tax-exempt** interest. **Do not** include on line 8a	8b	
9a	Ordinary dividends. Attach Schedule B if required	9a	
b	Qualified dividends (see page 23)	9b	
10	Taxable refunds, credits, or offsets of state and local income taxes (see page 23)	10	
11	Alimony received	11	
12	Business income or (loss). Attach Schedule C or C-EZ	12	5800 00
13	Capital gain or (loss). Attach Schedule D if required. If not required, check here ▶ ☐	13	1250 00
14	Other gains or (losses). Attach Form 4797	14	
15a	IRA distributions 15a b Taxable amount (see page 25)	15b	
16a	Pensions and annuities 16a b Taxable amount (see page 25)	16b	
17	Rental real estate, royalties, partnerships, S corporations, trusts, etc. Attach Schedule E	17	
18	Farm income or (loss). Attach Schedule F	18	
19	Unemployment compensation	19	
20a	Social security benefits 20a b Taxable amount (see page 27)	20b	
21	Other income. List type and amount (see page 29)	21	
22	Add the amounts in the far right column for lines 7 through 21. This is your **total income** ▶	22	78,015 00

Adjusted Gross Income

23	Educator expenses (see page 29)	23	
24	Certain business expenses of reservists, performing artists, and fee-basis government officials. Attach Form 2106 or 2106-EZ	24	
25	Health savings account deduction. Attach Form 8889	25	
26	Moving expenses. Attach Form 3903	26	
27	One-half of self-employment tax. Attach Schedule SE	27	443 70
28	Self-employed SEP, SIMPLE, and qualified plans	28	
29	Self-employed health insurance deduction (see page 30)	29	
30	Penalty on early withdrawal of savings	30	
31a	Alimony paid b Recipient's SSN ▶	31a	
32	IRA deduction (see page 31)	32	4000 00
33	Student loan interest deduction (see page 33)	33	
34	Tuition and fees deduction (see page 34)	34	
35	Domestic production activities deduction. Attach Form 8903	35	
36	Add lines 23 through 31a and 32 through 35	36	4443 70
37	Subtract line 36 from line 22. This is your **adjusted gross income** ▶	37	73,571 30

For Disclosure, Privacy Act, and Paperwork Reduction Act Notice, see page 78.   Cat. No. 11320B   Form **1040** (2005)

Tax and Credits

38	Amount from line 37 (adjusted gross income)	38	73,571 30

39a Check if: ☐ **You** were born before January 2, 1941, ☐ Blind. **Total boxes** ☐ **Spouse** was born before January 2, 1941, ☐ Blind. checked ▶ 39a

b If your spouse itemizes on a separate return or you were a dual-status alien, see page 35 and check here ▶39b ☐

Standard Deduction for—

- People who checked any box on line 39a or 39b **or** who can be claimed as a dependent, see page 36.

- All others:

Single or Married filing separately, $5,000

Married filing jointly or Qualifying widow(er), $10,000

Head of household, $7,300

40	**Itemized deductions** (from Schedule A) **or** your **standard deduction** (see left margin) .	40	11,978 57
41	Subtract line 40 from line 38	41	61,592 73
42	If line 38 is over $109,475, or you provided housing to a person displaced by Hurricane Katrina, see page 37. Otherwise, multiply $3,200 by the total number of exemptions claimed on line 6d	42	16,000 00
43	**Taxable income.** Subtract line 42 from line 41. If line 42 is more than line 41, enter -0-	43	45,592 73
44	**Tax** (see page 37). Check if any tax is from: **a** ☐ Form(s) 8814 **b** ☐ Form 4972 . .	44	6108 91
45	**Alternative minimum tax** (see page 39). Attach Form 6251	45	0
46	Add lines 44 and 45 . . . . ▶	46	6108 91
47	Foreign tax credit. Attach Form 1116 if required . . .	47	
48	Credit for child and dependent care expenses. Attach Form 2441	48	
49	Credit for the elderly or the disabled. Attach Schedule R .	49	
50	Education credits. Attach Form 8863	50	
51	Retirement savings contributions credit. Attach Form 8880 .	51	
52	Child tax credit (see page 41). Attach Form 8901 if required	52	3000 00
53	Adoption credit. Attach Form 8839	53	
54	Credits from: **a** ☐ Form 8396 **b** ☐ Form 8859 .	54	
55	Other credits. Check applicable box(es): **a** ☐ Form 3800 **b** ☐ Form 8801 **c** ☐ Form _____	55	
56	Add lines 47 through 55. These are your **total credits**	56	3000 00
57	Subtract line 56 from line 46. If line 56 is more than line 46, enter -0- . . . . . ▶	57	3108 91

Other Taxes

58	Self-employment tax. Attach Schedule SE	58	887 40
59	Social security and Medicare tax on tip income not reported to employer. Attach Form 4137	59	
60	Additional tax on IRAs, other qualified retirement plans, etc. Attach Form 5329 if required .	60	
61	Advance earned income credit payments from Form(s) W-2	61	
62	Household employment taxes. Attach Schedule H	62	
63	Add lines 57 through 62. This is your **total tax** . . . . ▶	63	3996 31

Payments

If you have a qualifying child, attach Schedule EIC.

64	Federal income tax withheld from Forms W-2 and 1099 .	64	7410 00
65	2005 estimated tax payments and amount applied from 2004 return	65	1000 00
66a	**Earned income credit (EIC)**	66a	
b	Nontaxable combat pay election ▶ 66b		
67	Excess social security and tier 1 RRTA tax withheld (see page 59)	67	
68	Additional child tax credit. Attach Form 8812	68	
69	Amount paid with request for extension to file (see page 59) .	69	
70	Payments from: **a** ☐ Form 2439 **b** ☐ Form 4136 **c** ☐ Form 8885	70	
71	Add lines 64, 65, 66a, and 67 through 70. These are your **total payments** . . . ▶	71	8410 00

Refund

Direct deposit? See page 59 and fill in 73b, 73c, and 73d.

72	If line 71 is more than line 63, subtract line 63 from line 71. This is the amount you **overpaid**	72	4413 69
73a	Amount of line 72 you want **refunded to you** . . . . ▶	73a	4413 69

▶ b Routing number ☐☐☐☐☐☐☐☐☐ ▶ c Type: ☐ Checking ☐ Savings

▶ d Account number ☐☐☐☐☐☐☐☐☐☐☐☐☐☐☐☐☐

74 Amount of line 72 you want **applied to your 2006 estimated tax** ▶ 74

Amount You Owe

75	**Amount you owe.** Subtract line 71 from line 63. For details on how to pay, see page 60 ▶	75	
76	Estimated tax penalty (see page 60)	76	

Third Party Designee

Do you want to allow another person to discuss this return with the IRS (see page 61)? ☐ **Yes.** Complete the following. ☐ **No**

Designee's name ▶ _____ Phone no. ▶ ( ) _____ Personal identification number (PIN) ▶ ☐☐☐☐☐

Sign Here

Joint return? See page 17.
Keep a copy for your records.

Under penalties of perjury, I declare that I have examined this return and accompanying schedules and statements, and to the best of my knowledge and belief, they are true, correct, and complete. Declaration of preparer (other than taxpayer) is based on all information of which preparer has any knowledge.

Your signature	Date	Your occupation	Daytime phone number
Terry B. Becker	4/10/06	Cost Accountant	(555) 555-1234
Spouse's signature. If a joint return, **both** must sign. Date		Spouse's occupation	
Evelyn A. Becker	4/10/06	Sales Clerk	

Paid Preparer's Use Only

Preparer's signature ▶	Date	Check if self-employed ☐	Preparer's SSN or PTIN
Firm's name (or yours if self-employed), address, and ZIP code ▶		EIN	
		Phone no. ( )	

Form **1040** (2005)

♻ *Printed on recycled paper*

Personal Exemptions. The Beckers are entitled to claim two exemptions for themselves and another three exemptions for their three dependent children, for a total of five (see line 6d). Because each exemption is worth $3,200, they receive a total personal exemption of $16,000 (5 × $3,200), which is the amount listed on line 42 of their Form 1040.

The Beckers' Taxable Income and Tax Liability. Taxable income is found by subtracting itemized deductions and personal exemptions from AGI. In the Beckers' case, taxable income amounts to $73,571.30 − $11,978.57 − $16,000 = $45,592.73, as shown on line 43. Given this information, the Beckers can now refer to the tax rate schedule (like the one in Exhibit 3.3) to find their appropriate tax rate and, ultimately, the amount of taxes they'll have to pay. (Because the Beckers' taxable income is less than $100,000, they could use the *tax tables* [not shown] to find their tax. For clarity and convenience, we use the schedules here.) As we can see, the Beckers' $45,592.73 in taxable income places them in the 15 percent tax bracket. Using the schedule in Exhibit 3.3, they calculate their tax as follows: $1,460 + [.15 × ($45,592.73 − $14,600)] = $6,108.91. They enter this amount on line 44. (*Note:* Had the tax tables been used, the tax would have been $6,106.)

The Beckers also qualify for the child tax credit: $1,000 for each child under age 17. They enter $3,000 on lines 52 and 56 and subtract that amount from the tax on line 46, entering $3,108.91 on line 57. In addition, the Beckers owe self-employment (Social Security) tax on Terry's $5,800 net business income. This will increase their tax liability by $887.40 (.153 × $5,800) and would be reported on Schedule SE and entered on line 58 of Form 1040. (Remember, the Beckers deducted 50 percent of this amount—$443.70—on line 27 as an adjustment to income.) The Beckers enter their total tax liability on line 63: $3,996.31 ($3,108.91 + $887.40).

Do They Get a Tax Refund? Because the total amount of taxes withheld of $7,410 ($6,260 from Terry's salary and $1,150 from Evelyn's wages) shown on line 64 plus estimated tax payments of $1,000 shown on line 65 total $8,410 as shown on line 71, the Beckers' total tax payments exceed their tax liability. As a result, they are entitled to a refund of $4,413.69: the $8,410 withholding less their $3,996.31 tax liability. (About 65 percent of all taxpayers receive refunds each year.) Instead of paying the IRS, they'll be getting money back. (Generally, it takes 1 to 2 months after a tax return has been filed to receive a refund check.)

All the Beckers have to do now is sign and date their completed Form 1040 and send it, along with any supporting forms and schedules, to the nearest IRS district office on or before April 15, 2006.

One reason for the Beckers' large refund was the child tax credit. With such a sizable refund, the Beckers may want to stop making estimated tax payments because their combined withholding more than covers the amount of taxes they owe. Another option is to change their withholding to reduce the amount withheld.

Note that if total tax payments had been less than the Beckers' tax liability, they would have owed the IRS money—the amount owed is found by subtracting total tax payments made from the tax liability. If they owed money, they would include a check in the amount due with Form 1040 when filing their tax return.

FINANCIAL ROAD SIGN

TIME FOR TAXES

To minimize tax hassles, follow these tips:
1. File on time, even if you can't pay what you owe.
2. Don't overlook tax-free income, such as an inheritance, tuition, scholarships, and gifts of money (limited to $10,000 per year from any one person in 2005 and increased to $12,000 in 2006).
3. Don't forget to sign your return, even if you file online.
4. Use direct deposit to get your refund faster.
5. Pay in installments if you can't pay your whole tax bill (file Form 9465).
6. Pay what you think you'll owe even if you get an extension.
7. Include receipts for all noncash charitable gifts valued at more than $500 with Form 8283.

Concept Check

3-9 Define and differentiate between the *average tax rate* and the *marginal tax rate.* How does a *tax credit* differ from an *itemized deduction*?

3-10 Explain how the following are used in filing a tax return: (a) Form 1040, (b) various schedules that accompany Form 1040, and (c) tax rate schedules.

Preparing and filing your tax returns involves more than merely filling out and filing a form on or before April 15. Other considerations include the need to pay estimated taxes, file for extensions, or amend the return; the possibility of a tax audit; and whether to use a tax preparation service or computer software to assist you in preparing your return.

Estimates, Extensions, and Amendments

Like Terry Becker, who provided accounting services to his brother's business, you may have income that's not subject to withholding. You may need to file a declaration of estimated taxes with your return and to pay quarterly taxes. Or perhaps you are unable to meet the normal April 15 filing deadline or need to correct a previously filed return. Let's look at the procedures for handling these situations.

Estimated Taxes

Because federal withholding taxes are regularly taken only from employment income, such as that paid in the form of wages or salaries, the IRS requires certain people to pay **estimated taxes** on income earned from other sources. This requirement allows the pay-as-you-go principle to be applied not only to employment income subject to withholding but also to other sources of income. Four payments of estimated taxes are most commonly required of investors, consultants, lawyers, business owners, and various other professionals who are likely to receive income in a form that is not subject to withholding. Generally, if all your income is subject to withholding, you probably do not need to make estimated tax payments.

The declaration of estimated taxes (Form 1040-ES) is normally filed with the tax return. Estimated taxes must be paid in four installments on April 15, June 15, and September 15 of the current year, and January 15 of the following year. Failure to estimate and pay these taxes in accordance with IRS guidelines can result in a penalty levied by the IRS.

April 15: Filing Deadline

As we've seen from the Becker family example, at the end of each tax year those taxpayers required to file a return must determine the amount of their *tax liability*—the amount of taxes they owe due to the past year's activities. The tax year corresponds to the calendar year and covers the period January 1 through December 31. Taxpayers may file their returns any time after the end of the tax year and *must* file no later than April 15 of the year immediately following the tax year (or by the first business day after that date if it falls on a weekend or federal holiday). If you have a computer, a modem, and tax preparation software, you can probably use the IRS's *e-file* and *e-pay* to file your return and pay your taxes electronically either by using a credit card or by authorizing an electronic withdrawal from your checking or savings account. You can use an "Authorized *e-file* Provider," who may charge a fee to file for you, or do it yourself using commercial tax preparation software. (We'll discuss computer-based tax returns in greater detail later.)

Depending on whether the total of taxes withheld and any estimated tax payments is greater or less than the computed tax liability, the taxpayer either receives a refund or has to pay additional taxes. For example, assume that you had $2,000 withheld and paid estimated taxes of $1,200 during the year. After filling out the appropriate tax forms, you find your tax liability is only $2,800. In this case, you have overpaid your taxes by $400 ($2,000 + $1,200 − $2,800) and will receive a $400 refund from the IRS. On the other hand, if your tax liability had amounted to $4,000, you would owe the IRS an additional $800 ($4,000 − $2,000 − $1,200). Taxpayers can pay their taxes using a credit card; however, because the IRS cannot pay credit card companies an issuing fee, taxpayers must call a special provider and pay a service charge to arrange for the payment.

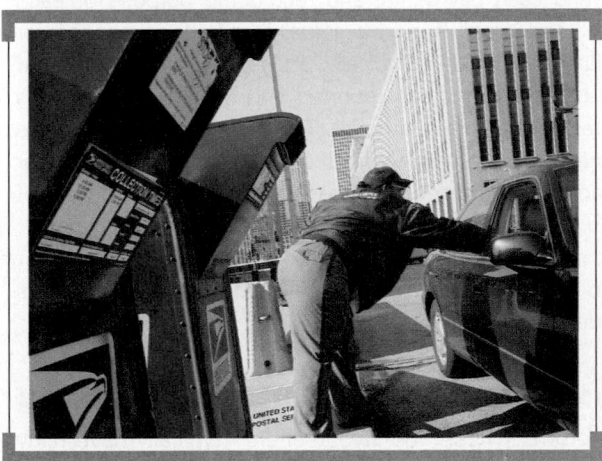

© GETTY IMAGES

estimated taxes Tax payments required on income not subject to withholding that are paid in four installments.

Filing Extensions and Amended Returns

It's possible to receive an extension of time for filing your federal tax return. You can apply for an automatic 6-month **filing extension,** which makes the due date October 15, simply by submitting Form 4868. In filing for an extension, however, the taxpayer must estimate the taxes due and remit that amount with the application. The extension does *not* give taxpayers more time to pay their taxes.

After filing a return, you may discover that you overlooked some income or a major deduction or made a mistake, so you paid too little or too much in taxes. You can easily correct this by filing an **amended return** (Form 1040X) showing the corrected amount of income or deductions and the amount of taxes you should have paid, along with the amount of any tax refund or additional taxes owed. You generally have 3 years from the date you file your original return or 2 years from the date you paid the taxes, whichever is later, to file an amended return. If you prepare and file your amended return properly and it reflects nothing out of the ordinary, it generally won't trigger an audit. By all means, don't "correct" an oversight in 1 year by "adjusting" next year's tax return— the IRS frowns on that.

Audited Returns

Because taxpayers themselves provide the key information and fill out the necessary tax forms, the IRS has no proof that taxes have been correctly calculated. In addition to returns that stand out in some way and warrant further investigation, the IRS also randomly selects some returns for a **tax audit**—an examination to validate the return's accuracy. The odds of being audited are actually quite low; the IRS audits fewer than 1 percent of returns. However, higher-income earners tend to have a greater chance of audit. For example, those with incomes between $25,000 and $50,000 have less than a 1 percent chance of being audited, but the chance of audit jumps to nearly 5 percent for those with incomes over $100,000. The outcome of an audit is not always additional tax owed to the IRS. In fact, about 5 percent of all audits result in a refund to the taxpayer, and in 15 percent of all audits the IRS finds that returns are correctly prepared.

It's particularly important to keep good, complete tax records because some day you may be audited by the IRS. Keep track of the source or use of all cash receipts and cash payments, and record the purpose of each expense. You'll also need proof that you actually had the expenses for which you have claimed deductions. Typically, audits question (1) whether all income received has been properly reported and (2) if the deductions claimed are legitimate and the correct amount. The IRS can take as many as 3 years—and in some cases, 6 years—from the date of filing to audit your return, so you should retain records and receipts used in preparing returns for a number of years. Severe financial penalties—even prison sentences—can result from violating tax laws.

In sum, while you should take advantage of all legitimate deductions to minimize your tax liability, you must also be sure to properly report all items of income and expense as required by the Internal Revenue Code.

Tax Preparation Services: Getting Help on Your Returns

Many people prepare their own tax returns. These "do-it-yourselfers" typically have fairly simple returns that can be prepared without much difficulty. Of course, some taxpayers with quite complicated financial affairs may also invest their time in preparing their own returns. The IRS offers many informational publications to help you prepare your tax return. You can order them directly from the IRS by mail, from the IRS Web site **(http://www.irs.gov),** or by calling the IRS's toll-free number (1-800-829-3676 or special local numbers in some areas). You can also download most of them from the IRS Web site. An

---

FINANCIAL ROAD SIGN

BE AWARE OF THESE AUDIT TRIGGERS

Despite the low risk of being audited, certain items are a red flag to the IRS. If any of these situations apply to you, your chances of being audited increase:

- An unusual increase in income
- Income that isn't properly documented
- Income that's lower than the amount reported on Forms 1099 submitted by financial institutions
- Returns that are missing signatures, Social Security numbers, or required forms
- Math errors
- Owning a small business (Filing Schedule C significantly raises the chance of an audit)
- Itemized deductions that are much higher than the averages for your income bracket
- Taking the home-office deduction
- Casualty losses

Some of these triggers are unavoidable, but you can make sure that your numbers add up properly, you've included all required information and forms, and you've signed your returns.

---

filing extension An extension of time beyond the April 15 deadline during which taxpayers, with the approval of the IRS, can file their returns without incurring penalties.

amended return A tax return filed to adjust for information received after the filing date of the taxpayer's original return or to correct errors.

tax audit An examination by the IRS to validate the accuracy of a given tax return.

excellent (and free) comprehensive tax preparation reference book is IRS *Publication 17, Your Federal Income Tax.* Other publications cover special topics, such as the earned income credit, self-employment taxes, and business use of your home. Each form and schedule comes with detailed instructions to guide you, step-by-step, in completing the form accurately. Other IRS information services are *TeleTax,* which provides recorded phone messages on selected tax topics via a toll-free number (1-800-829-4477), and FaxBack, which will fax many forms and instructions to you when you call 1-703-368-9694.

Help from the IRS

The IRS, in addition to issuing various publications for use in preparing tax returns, also provides direct assistance to taxpayers. The IRS will compute taxes for those whose taxable income is less than $100,000 and who do not itemize deductions. Persons who use this IRS service must fill in certain data, sign and date the return, and send it to the IRS on or before April 15 of the year immediately following the tax year. The IRS attempts to calculate taxes to result in the "smallest" tax bite. It then sends taxpayers a refund, if their withholding exceeds their tax liability, or a bill, if their tax liability is greater than the amount of withholding. People who either fail to qualify for or do not want to use this total tax preparation service can still obtain IRS assistance in preparing their returns from a toll-free service. Consult your telephone directory for the toll-free number of the IRS office closest to you.

Private Tax Preparers

More than half of all taxpayers believe that the complexity of the tax forms makes preparation too difficult and time-consuming. They prefer to use professional *tax preparation services* to improve accuracy and minimize their tax liability as much as possible. The fees charged by professional tax preparers range from about $100 for very simple returns to $1,000 or more for complicated returns that include many itemized deductions, partnership income or losses, or self-employment income. You can select from various types of tax preparation services:

*   **National and local tax services:** These include national services such as H&R Block and independent local firms. These are best for taxpayers with relatively common types of income and expenditures.
*   **Certified Public Accountants (CPAs):** Tax professionals who prepare returns and can advise taxpayers on planning.
*   **Enrolled Agents (EAs):** Federally licensed individual tax practitioners who have passed a difficult, 2-day, IRS-administered exam. They are fully qualified to handle tax preparation at various levels of complexity.
*   **Tax attorneys:** Lawyers who specialize in tax planning.

The services of CPAs, EAs, and tax attorneys can be expensive and are most suited to taxpayers with relatively complicated financial situations. The *Money in Action* box on page 92 will help you find the right preparer for your needs.

Always check your own completed tax returns carefully before signing them. Remember that *taxpayers themselves must accept primary responsibility for the accuracy of their returns.* The IRS requires professional tax preparers to sign each return as the preparer, enter their own Social Security number and address, and give the taxpayer a copy of the return being filed. Tax preparers with the necessary hardware and software can electronically file their clients' tax returns so that eligible taxpayers can more quickly receive refunds.

There's no guarantee that your professional tax preparer will correctly determine your tax liability. Even the best preparers may not have all the answers at their fingertips. In a recent *Money* magazine annual tax return test, none of the 45 experienced tax preparers who were contacted prepared the tax return for a fictional family correctly; and only 24 percent of them calculated a tax liability that was within $1,000 of the correct amount of $42,336. To reduce the chance of error, you should become familiar with the basic tax principles and regulations, check all documents (such as *W-2s* and *1099s*) for accuracy, maintain good communication with your tax preparer, and request an explanation of any entries on your tax return that you don't understand.

MONEY IN ACTION

WHICH TAX PREPARER IS RIGHT FOR YOU?

More than 60 percent of taxpayers use a professional tax preparer. It's critical to choose a reputable tax preparer, because *taxpayers themselves must accept primary responsibility for the accuracy of their returns.* As tax regulations become more complex, even the professionals make more errors.

There are four types of tax preparers. The appropriate tax preparer for you depends on the complexity of your return:

- **Nonlicensed tax preparers:** They're best for simple returns since they have minimal training. To determine if a tax preparer is reputable, be sure they operate year-round and that they stand by their work. They're usually inexpensive. The average cost at H&R Block is $140 for state and federal returns.
- **CPAs:** CPAs provide ongoing tax advice and can suggest tax-saving strategies. Be sure to choose a CPA who is a tax specialist. Check your State Board of Accountancy to make sure the CPA is licensed and not subject to any disciplinary actions.

- **Enrolled agents:** EAs are licensed by the IRS. They specialize in preparing returns and offering tax advice for individuals. Fees to use an EA are about one-third lower than CPA fees. There's no state regulation of EAs, so you'll have to do your own background checks.
- **Tax attorneys:** Tax attorneys are best reserved for those who have complex tax situations that could result in legal issues, such as a complicated sale of a small business, not filing taxes in the past, or estate and trust tax issues.

After deciding which type of tax preparer is right for you, ask for referrals from your lawyer, financial planner, and friends. Then interview your candidates before trusting anyone with your financial records. Here are some areas to probe:

1. The tax and other services offered, and areas of specialization
2. Training and experience of the tax preparer, and involvement in continuing education
3. Credentials and professional affiliations
4. Who prepares your actual return and the system for checking the accuracy of your return

5. Whether their approach to tax law is conservative or aggressive
6. Familiarity of tax law in other states, if applicable to your return
7. Audit experience
8. Fee structure
9. Amount of liability insurance
10. References of clients with similar tax situations

Avoid tax preparers who claim they can get you larger returns, base their fee on the amount of the return, or refuse to sign your return. Be aware that "refund anticipation loans" come with high interest rates and large fees. Because of these and other abuses, the federal government has proposed legislation to further regulate the tax preparation industry.

Critical Thinking Questions
1. Compare the qualifications, licensing requirements, and relative costs of a nonlicensed tax preparer, a CPA, an EA, and a tax attorney.
2. Describe a situation that's appropriate for each type of tax preparer.
3. Why is it important to understand your tax returns, even if they're prepared by a professional?

Sources: Stephanie AuWerter, "Looking for a Tax Pro?" *SmartMoney Tax Guide*, June 23, 2006, from http://www.smartmoney.com; Gerri Willis, "Sneaky Accountant Tricks," *CNNMoney.com*, March 17, 2006; Tom Herman and Robert Guy Matthews, "Tax Preparers Come Under Fire," *Wall Street Journal*, April 5, 2006, p. D2; Larry Getlen, "Questions to Ask Your Tax Preparer," *Bankrate.com*, March 4, 2004.

Computer-Based Tax Returns

Many people use their personal computers to help with tax planning and preparing tax returns. Several good tax software packages will save hours when you're filling out the forms and schedules involved in filing tax returns. The programs often identify tax-saving opportunities you might otherwise miss. These computer programs aren't for everyone, however. Very simple returns, like the 1040EZ, don't require them. And for very complex returns, there's no substitute for the skill and expertise of a tax accountant or attorney. Tax preparation software will be most helpful for taxpayers who itemize deductions but don't need tax advice.

Basically there are two kinds of software: tax planning and tax preparation. Planning programs such as Quicken let you experiment with different strategies to see their effects on the amount of taxes you must pay. The other category of tax software focuses on helping you complete and file your tax return. These programs take much of the tedium out of tax preparation, reducing the time you spend from days to hours. If you file the long Form 1040 and some supporting forms, invest in the stock market, own real estate, or have foreign income or a home-based business, you'll probably benefit from using tax preparation programs. It's even easier and faster if you use a personal finance program to keep tabs on your income and expenses, because the tax software can extract the appropriate data. The programs automate much of the process; they know that X percent of the amount you entered on Line K has to be transferred to Line Q, saving you the task of remembering to do it yourself. The programs are updated annually to include the hundreds of changes in tax laws. Another advantage is that the programs feed your data to state tax returns, so you only have to enter it once.

The two major software players are Intuit's TurboTax and Block Financial Software's TaxCut, both available for either Windows or Macintosh. TurboTax even has a Web-based version that lets you work on your returns from any computer. Both major companies also offer an add-on program that accurately assigns fair market value to the household items most commonly donated to charity. Both programs feature a clean interface and guide you through the steps in preparing your return by asking you the questions that apply to your situation. In addition to the primary tax-form preparation section, they include extensive resources and links to additional Web references, video clips to make tricky concepts easier to understand, tax-planning questionnaires, deduction finders, and more. They may warn you if a number you've typed looks incorrect. The basic version of each program costs under $40 for the regular CD-ROM versions. State tax return packages cost more. Both TurboTax and TaxCut guarantee their calculations and will pay any penalties you incur due to program errors.

In certain situations, you may want to let a professional rather than a PC prepare your return. These include major life changes such as marriage, divorce, remarriage, and inheritance. The tax treatment of stock options, an increasingly common employee benefit, is tricky to figure out. Self-employed persons may want the advice of a tax professional when it comes to deciding where to draw the line between business and personal expenses.

The IRS recently introduced "fill-in forms," which allow you to enter information while the form is displayed on your computer by Adobe Acrobat Reader (free software readily available on the Web). After entering the requested information, you can print out the completed form. Fill-in forms give you a cleaner, crisper printout for your records and for filing with the IRS. Unlike tax preparation software, these fill-in forms have no computational capabilities, so you must do all your calculations before starting. In addition, you should be ready to enter all the data at once, because Acrobat Reader doesn't save your completed forms. (If you purchase the complete Acrobat suite, you can save your forms to disk.) These forms are labeled "Fill-in forms" at the IRS Web site.

❚❚ Concept Check

CHECK • CONCEPT CHECK • CONCEPT CHECK • CONCEPT CHECK • CONCEPT CHECK • CONCEPT CHECK • CONCEPT C

3-11	Define *estimated taxes,* and explain under what conditions such tax payments are required.
3-12	What is the purpose of a *tax audit*? Describe some things you can do to be prepared if your return is audited.
3-13	What types of assistance and tax preparation services does the IRS provide?
3-14	What are the advantages of using tax preparation software?

3 : 93

Preparing Your Taxes

There's more to taxes than filing returns annually. By keeping good records and thinking about tax implications of financial transactions, you can make *tax planning* a key ingredient of your overall personal financial planning. The overriding objective of effective tax planning is to maximize total after-tax income by reducing, shifting, and deferring taxes to as low a level as legally possible.

Keep in mind that *avoiding taxes* is one thing, but *evading* them is another matter altogether. By all means, don't confuse tax avoidance with tax evasion, which includes such illegal activities as omitting income or overstating deductions. **Tax evasion,** in effect, involves a failure to accurately report income or deductions and, in extreme cases, a failure to pay taxes altogether. Persons found guilty of tax evasion are subject to severe financial penalties and even prison terms. **Tax avoidance,** in contrast, focuses on reducing taxes in ways that are legal and compatible with the intent of Congress.

Fundamental Objectives of Tax Planning

Tax planning basically involves the use of various investment vehicles, retirement programs, and estate distribution procedures to (1) reduce, (2) shift, and (3) defer taxes. You can *reduce* taxes, for instance, by using techniques that create tax deductions or credits, or that receive preferential tax treatment—such as investments that produce depreciation (such as real estate) or that generate tax-free income (such as municipal bonds). You can *shift* taxes by using gifts or trusts to shift some of your income to other family members who are in lower tax brackets and to whom you intend to provide some level of support anyway, such as a retired, elderly parent.

The idea behind *deferring* taxes is to reduce or eliminate your taxes today by postponing them to some time in the future when you may be in a lower tax bracket. Perhaps more important, *deferring taxes gives you use of the money that would otherwise go to taxes*—thereby allowing you to invest it to make even more money. Deferring taxes is usually done through various types of retirement plans, such as IRAs, or by investing in certain types of annuities, variable life insurance policies, or even Series EE bonds (U.S. savings bonds).

The fundamentals of tax planning include making sure that you take all the deductions you're entitled to and taking full advantage of the various tax provisions that will minimize your tax liability. Thus comprehensive tax planning is an ongoing activity with both an immediate and a long-term perspective. *It plays a key role in personal financial planning*—in fact, a major component of a comprehensive personal financial plan is a summary of the potential tax impacts of various recommended financial strategies. Tax planning is closely interrelated with many financial planning activities, including investment, retirement, and estate planning.

Some Popular Tax Strategies

Managing your taxes is a year-round activity. Because Congress considers tax law changes throughout the year, you may not know all the applicable regulations until the middle of the year or later. Like other financial goals, tax strategies require review and adjustment when regulations and personal circumstances change.

Tax planning can become complex at times and may involve rather sophisticated investment strategies. In such cases, especially those involving large amounts of money, you should seek professional help. Many tax strategies are fairly simple and straightforward and can be used by the average middle-income taxpayer. You certainly don't have to be in the top income bracket to enjoy the benefits of many tax-saving ideas and procedures. For example, the interest income on Series EE bonds is free from state income tax, and the holder can elect to delay payment of federal taxes until (1) the year the bonds are redeemed for cash or (2) the year in which they finally mature, whichever occurs first. This feature makes Series EE bonds an excellent vehicle for earning tax-deferred income.

tax evasion The illegal act of failing to accurately report income or deductions and, in extreme cases, failing to pay taxes altogether.

tax avoidance The act of reducing taxes in ways that are legal and compatible with the intent of Congress.

There are other strategies that can cut your tax bill. Accelerating or bunching deductions into a single year may permit itemizing deductions. Shifting income from one year to another is one way to cut your tax liability. If you expect to be in the same or a higher income tax bracket this year than you will be next year, defer income until next year and shift expenses to this year so you can accelerate your deductions and reduce taxes this year.

Maximizing Deductions

Review a comprehensive list of possible deductions for ideas, because even small deductions can add up to big tax savings. Accelerate or bunch deductions into one tax year if it allows you to itemize rather than take the standard deduction. For example, make your fourth-quarter estimated state tax payment before December 31 rather than on January 15 to deduct it in the current taxable year. Group miscellaneous expenses, and schedule non-reimbursed elective medical procedures to fall into one tax year to exceed the required "floor" for deductions (2 percent of AGI for miscellaneous expenses; 7.5 percent of AGI for medical expenses). Increase discretionary deductions such as charitable contributions.

Income Shifting

One way of reducing income taxes is to use a technique known as **income shifting.** Here the taxpayer shifts a portion of his or her income—and thus taxes—to relatives in lower tax brackets. This can be done by creating trusts or custodial accounts or by making outright gifts of income-producing property to family members. For instance, parents with $125,000 of taxable income (28 percent marginal tax rate) and $18,000 in corporate bonds paying $2,000 in annual interest might give the bonds to their 15-year-old child—with the understanding that such income is to be used ultimately for the child's college education. The $2,000 would then belong to the child, who would probably have to pay $120 (0.10 × [$2,000 − $800 minimum standard deduction for a dependent]) in taxes on this income, and the parents' taxable income would be reduced by $2,000, reducing their taxes by $560 (0.28 × $2,000).

Unfortunately, this strategy is not as simple as it might seem. Under current (2005) tax laws, investment income of a minor (under the age of 14) is taxed at the same rate as the parents' *to the extent that it exceeds $1,600*. For example, if a 5-year-old girl received $2,500 from a trust set up for her by her parents, the first $1,600 of that income (subject to a minimum $800 standard deduction) would be taxed at the child's rate, and the remaining $900 would be subject to the parents' (higher) tax rate. These restrictions do not apply to children 14 and over, so it's possible to employ such techniques with older children (and presumably with other older relatives, such as elderly parents).

Parents need to be aware that shifting assets into a child's name to save taxes could affect the amount of college financial aid for which the child qualifies. Most financial aid formulas expect students to spend 35 percent of assets held in their own name, compared with only 5.6 percent of the parents' nonretirement assets. Additional tax implications of gifts to dependents are discussed in Chapter 15.

Tax-Free and Tax-Deferred Income

income shifting A technique used to reduce taxes in which a taxpayer shifts a portion of income to relatives in lower tax brackets.

tax deferred Income that is not subject to taxes immediately but that will later be subject to taxes.

Some investments provide tax-free income; in most cases, however, the tax on the income is only deferred (or delayed) to a later day. Although there aren't many forms of tax-free investments left today, probably the best example would be the *interest* income earned on *municipal bonds*. Such income is free from federal income tax. No matter how much municipal bond interest income you earn, you don't have to pay any taxes on it. (Tax-free municipal bonds are discussed in Chapter 12.) Income that is **tax deferred,** in contrast, only delays the payment of taxes to a future date. Until that time arrives, however, tax-deferred investment vehicles allow you to *accumulate tax-free earnings*. This results in much higher savings than would occur in a taxed account. A good example of tax-deferred income would be income earned in a *traditional IRA*. See Chapter 14 for a detailed discussion of this and other similar arrangements.

For still more tips and long-term tax planning strategies, head to SmartMoney's Tax Guide for tax advice and articles on various tax topics. Link at **http://www.thomsonedu.com/finance/gitman**.

Basically, any wage earner can open an IRA and contribute up to $4,000 a year to the account (in 2005). This amount increases to $5,000 in 2008. Of course, as noted earlier in this chapter, although any employed person can contribute to an IRA, only those people meeting certain pension and/or income constraints can deduct the annual contributions from their tax returns. If you fail to meet these restrictions, you can still have an IRA, but you can't deduct the $4,000 annual contribution from your income. So why have an IRA? *Because all the income you earn in your IRA accumulates tax free.* This is a *tax-deferred* investment, so you'll eventually have to pay taxes on these earnings, but not until you start drawing down your account. *Roth IRAs* provide a way for people with AGI below a given level to contribute after-tax dollars. Not only do earnings grow tax free, but so do withdrawals if the account has been open for five or more years and the individual is over $59\frac{1}{2}$. In addition to IRAs, tax-deferred income can also be obtained from other types of pension and retirement plans and annuities. See Chapter 14 for more information on these financial products and strategies.

‖ Concept Check

CHECK • CONCEPT CHECK • CONCEPT CHECK • CONCEPT CHECK • CONCEPT CHECK • CONCEPT CHECK • CONCEPT CHECK • CONCEPT

3-15   Differentiate between *tax evasion* and *tax avoidance.*

3-16   Explain each of the following strategies for reducing current taxes: (a) maximizing deductions, (b) income shifting, (c) tax-free income, and (d) tax-deferred income.

Y • SUMMARY • SUMMARY • SUMMARY • SUMMARY • SUMMARY • SUMMARY • SUMMARY • SUMMARY • SUMMARY •

 ## SUMMARY

LG1 **Discuss the basic principles of income taxes and determine your filing status.** Because taxes have an impact on most individuals and families, understanding them is essential for effective personal financial planning and intelligent money management. The dominant tax in our country today is the federal income tax, a levy that provides the government with most of the funds it needs to cover its operating costs. Federal income tax rates are progressive, so that your tax rate increases as your income rises. Other types of taxes include state and local income taxes, sales taxes, and property taxes. The administration and enforcement of federal tax laws is the responsibility of the IRS, a part of the U.S. Department of the Treasury. The amount of taxes you owe depends on your filing status—single, married filing jointly, married filing separately, head of household, or qualifying widow(er) with dependent child—and the amount of taxable income you report. Because the government operates on a pay-as-you-go basis, employers are required to withhold taxes from their employees' paychecks.

LG2 **Describe the sources of gross income and adjustments to income, differentiate between standard and itemized deductions and exemptions, and calculate taxable income.** Gross income includes active

income (such as wages, bonuses, pensions, alimony), portfolio income (dividends, interest, and capital gains), and passive income (income derived from real estate, limited partnerships, and other tax shelters). You must decide whether to take the standard deduction or itemize your various deductions. Some allowable deductions for those who itemize include mortgage interest, medical expenses over 7.5 percent of AGI, and certain job-related expenses. To calculate taxable income, deduct allowable adjustments, such as IRA contributions and alimony paid, from gross income to get AGI; then subtract from AGI the amount of deductions and personal exemptions claimed.

LG3 **Prepare a basic tax return using the appropriate tax forms and rate schedules.** After determining your taxable income, you can find the amount of taxes owed using either the tax rate tables or, if your taxable income is over $100,000, the tax rate schedules. Tax rates vary with the level of taxable income and filing status. Personal tax returns are filed using one of these forms: 1040EZ, 1040A, or 1040. Certain taxpayers must include schedules with their Form 1040.

LG4 **Explain who needs to pay estimated taxes, when to file or amend your return, and how to handle an audit.** Persons with income not subject to withholding may need to file a declaration of estimated taxes and make tax payments in four installments. Annual returns must be filed on or before April 15, unless the taxpayer requests an automatic 6-month filing extension. The IRS audits selected returns to confirm their validity by carefully examining the data reported in them.

LG5 **Know where to get help with your taxes and how software can streamline tax return preparation.** Assistance in preparing returns is available from the IRS and private tax preparers such as national and local tax firms, certified public accountants, enrolled agents, and tax attorneys. Computer programs can help do-it-yourselfers with both tax planning and tax preparation.

LG6 **Implement an effective tax-planning strategy.** Effective tax planning is closely tied to other areas of personal financial planning. The objectives of tax planning are to reduce, shift, or defer taxes so the taxpayer gets maximum use of and benefits from the money he or she earns. Some of the more popular tax strategies include maximizing deductions, shifting income to relatives in lower tax brackets, investing in tax-exempt municipal bonds, setting up IRAs, and using other types of pension and retirement plans and annuities to generate tax-deferred income.

FINANCIAL PLANNING EXERCISES

LG2, 3 1. Mary Parker is 24 years old, single, lives in an apartment, and has no dependents. Last year she earned $38,700 as a sales assistant for Texas Instruments; $3,150 of her wages were withheld for federal income taxes. In addition, she had interest income of $142. Estimate her taxable income, tax liability, and tax refund or tax owed.

LG2 2. Tina Marcelle received the following items and amounts of income during 2007. Help her calculate (a) her gross income and (b) that portion (dollar amount) of her income that is tax exempt.

Salary	$33,500
Dividends	800
Gift from mother	500
Child support from ex-husband	3,600
Interest on savings account	250
Rent	900
Loan from bank	2,000
Interest on state government bonds	300

LG2 3. If Jenny Perez is single and in the 28 percent tax bracket, calculate the tax associated with each of the following transactions using the IRS regulations for capital gains in effect in 2005:
   a. She sold stock for $1,200 that she purchased for $1,000 5 months earlier.
   b. She sold bonds for $4,000 that she purchased for $3,000 3 years earlier.
   c. She sold stock for $1,000 that she purchased for $1,500 15 months earlier.

LG3 4. Demonstrate the differences resulting from a $1,000 tax credit versus a $1,000 tax deduction for a single taxpayer in the 25 percent tax bracket with $40,000 of pretax income.

LG3 5. *Use Worksheets 3.1 and 3.2.* John Otsubo graduated from college in 2005 and began work as a systems analyst in July 2005. He is preparing to file his income tax return for 2005 and has collected the following financial information for calendar year 2005:

Tuition, scholarships, and grants	$ 5,750
Scholarship, room, and board	1,850
Salary	30,250
Interest income	185
Deductible expenses, total	3,000
Income taxes withheld	2,600

   a. Prepare John's 2005 tax return, using a $5,000 standard deduction, a personal exemption of $3,200, and the tax rates given in Exhibit 3.3. Which tax form should John use, and why?

b. Prepare John's 2005 tax return using the data in part **a** along with the following information:

IRA contribution	$4,000
Cash dividends received	150

Which tax form should he use in this case? Why?

LG2, 3

6. Ron and Lisa Ballard are married and have one child. Ron is putting together some figures so he can prepare the Ballards' joint 2005 tax return. He can claim three personal exemptions (including himself). So far, he's been able to determine the following with regard to income and possible deductions:

Total unreimbursed medical expenses incurred	$ 1,155
Gross wages and commissions earned	50,770
IRA contribution	4,000
Mortgage interest paid	5,200
Capital gains realized on assets held less than 12 months	1,450
Income from limited partnership	200
Job expenses and other allowable deductions	875
Interest paid on credit cards	380
Dividend and interest income earned	610
Sales taxes paid	2,470
Charitable contributions made	1,200
Capital losses realized	3,475
Interest paid on a car loan	570
Alimony paid by Ron to first wife	6,000
Social Security taxes paid	2,750
Property taxes paid	700
State income taxes paid	1,700

Given this information, how much taxable income will the Ballards have in 2005? (*Note*: Assume that Ron is covered by a pension plan where he works, the standard deduction amount for married filing jointly ($10,000) applies, and each exemption claimed is worth $3,200.)

LG4

7. Maureen and Bob O'Flaherty have been notified that they are being audited. What should they do to prepare for the audit?

APPLYING PERSONAL FINANCE • APPLYING PERSONAL FINANCE • APPLYING PERSONAL FINANCE • APPLYING PERSON

APPLYING PERSONAL FINANCE

Tax Relief!

Even though many were eliminated by the Tax Reform Act of 1986, tax shelters are still around. Beware, however, because some are legitimate, while others are not! American taxpayers have the right to lower their tax burdens, as long as they do it by legal means. This project will help you to learn about any tax shelters currently allowed by law.

Where can you go to find tax shelter opportunities? First, try the financial section of your newspaper. There may be advertisements or articles on tax shelters, such as tax-free bond funds. A bank is another source. Simply ask at "new accounts" if they can give you any tax shelter information. Another major source of new tax shelters is the brokerage houses that sell stocks, bonds, and other securities to the investing public. If you have access to a brokerage house, ask them for tax shelter information. Also, you might want to search for "tax shelters" on the Internet.

List the tax shelters you've found. Do any apply to you now, or are there any that you'd like to use in the future? Finally, pull up the IRS Web site at **http://www.irs.gov** and search for "abusive tax shelters" to determine if the tax shelters you have found are allowed by current tax laws.

CRITICAL THINKING CASES

LG2, 3   ## 3.1   The Aggarwals Tackle Their Tax Return

Sabash and Sue Aggarwal are a married couple in their early twenties living in Dallas. Sabash earned $33,550 in 2005 from his job as a sales assistant with Carson Corporation. During the year, his employer withheld $3,150 for income tax purposes. In addition, the Aggarwals received interest of $350 on a joint savings account, $750 interest on tax-exempt municipal bonds, and dividends of $400 on common stocks. At the end of 2005, the Aggarwals sold two stocks, A and B. Stock A was sold for $700 and had been purchased 4 months earlier for $800. Stock B was sold for $1,500 and had been purchased 3 years earlier for $1,100. Their only child, Rohn, age 2, received (as his sole source of income) dividends of $200 on stock of Kraft, Inc.

Although Sabash is covered by the Carson Corporation's pension plan, he plans to contribute $4,000 to a traditional deductible IRA for 2005. Here are the amounts of money paid out during the year by the Aggarwals:

Medical and dental expenses (unreimbursed)	$ 200
State and local property taxes	831
Interest paid on home mortgage	4,148
Charitable contributions	1,360
Total	$6,539

In addition, Sabash incurred some unreimbursed travel costs for an out-of-town business trip:

Airline ticket	$250
Taxis	20
Lodging	60
Meals (as adjusted to 50% of cost)	36
Total	$366

Critical Thinking Questions

1. Using the Aggarwals' information, determine the total amount of their itemized deductions. Assume that they'll use the filing status of married filing jointly, the standard deduction for that status is $10,000, and each exemption claimed is worth $3,200. Should they itemize or take the standard deduction? Prepare a joint tax return for Sabash and Sue Aggarwal for the year ended December 31, 2005, to give them the smallest tax liability. Use the appropriate tax rate schedule provided in Exhibit 3.3 to calculate their taxes owed.
2. How much have you saved the Aggarwals through your treatment of their deductions?
3. Discuss whether the Aggarwals need to file a tax return for their son.
4. Suggest some tax strategies the Aggarwals might use to reduce their tax liability for next year.

LG2, 3   ## 3.2   Joan Cavander: Bartender or Tax Expert?

Joan Cavander, who is single, goes to graduate school part-time and works as a bartender at the Twin Towers Supper Club in Atlanta. During the past year (2005), her gross income was $18,700 in wages and tips. She has decided to prepare her own tax return because she cannot afford the services of a tax expert. After preparing her return, she comes to you for advice. Here's a summary of the figures she has prepared thus far:

Gross income:	
Wages	$10,500
Tips	+ 8,200
Adjusted gross income (AGI)	$18,700
Less: Itemized deductions	− 2,300
	$16,400
Less: Standard deduction	− 5,000
Taxable income	$11,400

Joan believes that if an individual's income falls below $20,350, the federal government considers him or her "poor" and allows both itemized deductions and a standard deduction.

Critical Thinking Questions

1. Calculate Joan Cavander's taxable income, being sure to consider her exemption. Assume that the standard deduction for a single taxpayer is $5,000 and that each exemption claimed is worth $3,200.

2. Discuss with Joan her errors in interpreting the tax laws, and explain the difference between itemized deductions and the standard deduction.

3. Joan has been dating Sam Haley for nearly 4 years, and they are seriously thinking about getting married. Sam has income and itemized deductions identical to Joan's. How much tax would they pay as a married couple (using the filing status of married filing jointly and a standard deduction of $10,000) versus the total amount the two would pay as single persons (each using the filing status of single)? Strictly from a tax perspective, does it make any difference whether Joan and Sam stay single or get married? Explain.

Visit **http://www.thomsonedu.com/finance/gitman** for some additional Web-based exercises and hot links (with annotations) to a variety of resources relevant to the topics covered in this chapter.

PART 2 ▸ Managing Basic Assets

Chapter 4 Managing Your Cash and Savings
Chapter 5 Making Automobile and Housing Decisions

Managing Your Cash and Savings

LEARNING GOALS

LG1	❯	Understand the role of cash management in the personal financial planning process.	p. 102
LG2	❯	Describe today's financial services marketplace, both depository and nondepository financial institutions.	p. 104
LG3	❯	Select the checking, savings, electronic banking, and other bank services that meet your needs.	p. 106
LG4	❯	Open and use a checking account.	p. 114
LG5	❯	Calculate the interest earned on your money using compound interest and future value techniques.	p. 121
LG6	❯	Develop a savings strategy that incorporates a variety of savings plans.	p. 121
	❯		

LG1 · THE ROLE OF CASH MANAGEMENT IN PERSONAL FINANCIAL PLANNING

Establishing good financial habits involves managing cash as well as other areas of personal finance. In this chapter we'll focus on **cash management**—the routine, day-to-day administration of cash and near-cash resources, also known as *liquid assets*, by an individual or family. These assets are considered liquid because they're either held in cash or can be readily converted into cash with little or no loss in value.

In addition to cash, there are several other kinds of liquid assets, including checking accounts, savings accounts, money market deposit accounts, money market mutual funds, and other short-term investment vehicles. Exhibit 4.1 briefly describes some popular types of liquid assets and the representative rates of return they earned in the fall of 2006. As a rule, near-term needs are met using cash on hand, and unplanned or future needs are met using some type of savings or short-term investment vehicle.

In personal financial planning, efficient cash management ensures adequate funds for both household use and an effective savings program. The success of your financial plans depends on your ability to develop and follow cash budgets.

A good way to keep your spending in line is to make all household transactions (even fun money or weekly cash allowances) using a tightly controlled *checking account*. Write checks only at certain times of the week or month and, more important, avoid carrying your checkbook (or debit card) when you might be tempted to write checks (or make debits) for

cash management The routine, day-to-day administration of cash and near-cash resources, also known as *liquid assets*, by an individual or family.

157.5

EXHIBIT 4.1   Where to Stash the Cash

The wide variety of liquid assets available meets just about any savings or short-term investment need. Rates vary considerably both by type of asset and point in time, so shop around for the best interest rate.

REPRESENTATIVE RATES OF RETURN

Type	Fall 2006	Description
Cash	0%	Pocket money; the coin and currency in one's possession.
Checking account	0–1%	A substitute for cash. Offered by commercial banks and other financial institutions such as savings and loans and credit unions.
Savings account	1%	Money is available at any time but cannot be withdrawn by check. Offered by banks and other financial institutions.
Money market deposit account (MMDA)	1–2%	Requires a fairly large (typically $1,000 or more) minimum deposit. Offers check-writing privileges.
Money market mutual fund	4–5%	Savings vehicle that is actually a mutual fund (not offered by banks, S&Ls, and other depository institutions). Like an MMDA, it also offers check-writing privileges.
Certificate of deposit (CD)	2–4%	A savings instrument where funds are left on deposit for a stipulated period (1 week to 1 year or more); imposes a penalty for withdrawing funds early. Market yields vary by size and maturity; no check-writing privileges.
U.S. Treasury bill (T-bill)	5%	Short-term, highly marketable security issued by the U.S. Treasury (originally issued with maturities of 13 and 26 weeks); smallest denomination is $1,000.
U.S. savings bond (EE)	3–4%	Issued at a discount from face value by the U.S. Treasury; rate of interest is tied to U.S. Treasury securities. Long a popular savings vehicle (widely used with payroll deduction plans). Matures to face value in approximately 5 years; sold in denominations of $50 and more.

unplanned purchases. If you're going shopping, set a maximum spending limit beforehand—an amount consistent with your cash budget. This system not only helps you avoid frivolous, impulsive expenditures but also documents how and where you spend your money. Then, if your financial outcomes aren't consistent with your plans, you can better identify causes and take corrective actions.

Another aspect of cash management is establishing an ongoing savings program, an important part of personal financial planning. Savings are not only a cushion against financial emergencies, but a way to accumulate funds to meet future financial goals. You may want to put money aside so you can go back to school in a few years to earn a graduate degree, or buy a new home, or perhaps take a vacation. Savings will help you meet these specific financial objectives.

ⅠⅠ Concept Check

CHECK • CONCEPT CHECK • CONCEPT CHECK • CONCEPT CHECK • CONCEPT CHECK • CONCEPT CHECK • CONCEPT C

4-1	What is *cash management* and what are its major functions?
4-2	Give two reasons for holding liquid assets. Identify and briefly describe the popular types of liquid assets.

FINANCIAL ROAD SIGN

YOUR PRIVACY IS PROTECTED

The *Financial Modernization Act of 1999*, also known as the Gramm-Leach-Bliley Act, protects your personal financial information held by financial institutions. It has three principal parts:

1. Financial institutions must provide customers with a privacy notice—a clear, conspicuous, and accurate statement of their information-sharing practices.
2. Financial institutions must design, implement, and maintain safeguards to protect customer information.
3. Consumers are protected from individuals and companies that obtain their personal financial information under false pretenses—a practice known as "pretexting."

Source: "The Gramm-Leach-Bliley Act," *Privacy Initiatives,* http://www.ftc.gov/privacy/privacyinitiatives/glbact.html.

 Smart.Sites

To help you decide if Internet banks are for you, research them at Kiplinger—link at **http://www.thomsonedu.com/finance/gitman.**

 Smart.Sites

To learn more about credit unions and to find one in your area, click on "Consumer Information" at the Credit Union National Association Web site. Link to it at **http://www.thomsonedu.com/finance/gitman.**

Alison Green hadn't paid a visit to her bank for years. Her company paid her salary into her checking account each month by direct deposit, and she regularly did all her banking from her home computer—with the click of a mouse, she could check her account balances, pay her bills, even search for the best rates on savings instruments. And by pushing a few buttons, she was able to withdraw money from her U.S. bank account using an ATM in Paris!

The pace of change in the financial services industry is accelerating, thanks to advanced technology and less restrictive regulations. Consumers can now choose from many financial institutions competing for their business. No longer must you go to one place for your checking accounts, another for credit cards or loans, yet another for stock brokerage services. Today, financial institutions are expanding services and competitively pricing products by bundling different accounts. For example, if you have $25,000 worth of funds or securities in a Wells Fargo Portfolio Management Account, you're eligible for reduced commissions on stock trades, free checking, free bill-pay, a credit card, and free ATM debit card transactions. It's your choice: you can choose an institution like Wells Fargo that provides "one-stop shopping," or you can have accounts with a variety of financial service providers, depending on what's best for you.

The *financial services industry* as we know it today embraces all institutions that market various kinds of *financial products* (such as checking and savings accounts, credit cards, loans and mortgages, insurance, and mutual funds) and *financial services* (such as financial planning, securities brokerage, tax filing and planning, estate planning, real estate, trusts, and retirement). What 20–25 years ago was several distinct (though somewhat related) industries is now, in essence, one industry in which firms are differentiated more by organizational structure than by name or product offerings.

Types of Financial Institutions

Financial institutions can be classified into two broad groups—depository and nondepository—based on whether they accept deposits like traditional banks.

Depository Financial Institutions

The vast majority of financial transactions take place at *depository financial institutions*—commercial banks (both brick-and-mortar and Internet), savings and loan associations (S&Ls), savings banks, and credit unions. Although they're regulated by different agencies, depository financial institutions are commonly referred to as "banks" because of their similar products and services. What sets these institutions apart from others is their ability to accept deposits; most people use them for checking and savings account needs. These depository financial institutions are briefly described in Exhibit 4.2.

Nondepository Financial Institutions

Other types of financial institutions that offer banking services, but don't accept deposits like traditional banks, are considered *nondepository institutions*. Today you can hold a credit card issued by a stock brokerage firm or have an account with a mutual fund that allows you to write a limited number of checks.

- *Stock brokerage firms* offer several cash management options, including money market mutual funds that invest in short-term securities and earn a higher rate of interest than bank accounts, special "wrap" accounts, and credit cards.
- *Mutual funds*, discussed in detail in Chapter 13, provide yet another alternative to bank savings accounts. Like stockbrokers, mutual fund companies offer money market mutual funds.

Other nondepository financial institutions include life insurance and finance companies.

EXHIBIT 4.2   Depository Financial Institutions

Depository financial institutions differ from their nonbank counterparts, such as stock brokerages and mutual funds, in their ability to accept deposits. Most consumers use these institutions to meet their checking and savings account needs.

Institution	Description
Commercial bank	Offers checking and savings accounts and a full range of financial products and services; the only institution that can offer *non-interest-paying checking accounts (demand deposits)*. The most popular of the depository financial institutions. Most are traditional *brick-and-mortar bank*s, but **Internet banks**—online commercial banks—are growing in popularity due to their convenience, lower service fees, and higher interest paid on account balances.
Savings and loan association (S&L)	Channels the savings of depositors primarily into mortgage loans for purchasing and improving homes. Also offers many of the same checking, saving, and lending products as commercial banks. Often pays slightly higher interest on savings than do commercial banks.
Savings bank	Similar to S&Ls, but located primarily in the New England states. Most are *mutual* associations—their depositors are their owners and thus receive a portion of the profits in the form of interest on their savings.
Credit union	A nonprofit, member-owned financial cooperative that provides a full range of financial products and services to its *members*, who must belong to a common occupation, religious or fraternal order, or residential area. Generally small institutions when compared with commercial banks and S&Ls. Offer interest-paying checking accounts—called **share draft accounts**—and a variety of saving and lending programs. Because they are run to benefit their members, they pay higher interest on savings and charge lower rates on loans than do other depository financial institutions.

How Safe Is Your Money?

Today, the main reason that a bank goes out of business is its purchase by another bank. Almost all commercial banks, S&Ls, savings banks, and credit unions are federally insured by U.S. government agencies. The few that are not federally insured usually obtain insurance through either a state-chartered or private insurance agency. Most experts believe that these so-called privately insured institutions have less protection against loss than those that are federally insured. Exhibit 4.3 on page 106 lists the insuring agencies and maximum insurance amounts provided under the various federal deposit insurance programs.

Deposit insurance protects the funds you have on deposit at banks and other depository institutions against institutional failure. In effect, the insuring agency stands behind the financial institution and guarantees the safety of your deposits up to a specified maximum amount ($100,000 per depositor in the case of federal insurance).

Deposit insurance is provided to the *depositor* rather than a *deposit account*. Thus the checking *and* savings accounts of each depositor are insured and, *as long as the maximum insurable amount is not exceeded,* the depositor can have any number of accounts and still be fully protected. This is an important feature to keep in mind because many people mistakenly believe that the maximum insurance applies to *each* of their accounts. For example, a depositor with a checking account balance of $15,000 at a branch office of ABC bank, an MMDA of $35,000 at ABC bank's main office, and a $50,000 CD issued by ABC bank is entirely covered by the FDIC's deposit insurance of $100,000 per depositor. If the CD was for $75,000, however, the total for this depositor would be $125,000 and therefore not entirely covered. Purchasing the CD from another bank, which also provides $100,000 of deposit insurance, would fully protect all of this depositor's funds.

Now that banks are offering a greater variety of products, including mutual funds, it's important to remember that only deposit accounts, including certificates of deposit, are covered by

internet bank An online commercial bank.

share draft account An account offered by credit unions that is similar to interest-paying checking accounts offered by other financial institutions.

deposit insurance A type of insurance that protects funds on deposit against failure of the institution; can be insured by the FDIC and the NCUA.

EXHIBIT 4.3   Federal Deposit Insurance Programs

If your checking and savings accounts are at a federally insured institution, you are covered up to $100,000.

Savings Institution	Insuring Agency	Basic Insurance Amounts
Commercial bank	Federal Deposit Insurance Corporation (FDIC)	$100,000/depositor through the Bank Insurance Fund (BIF)
Savings and loan association	Federal Deposit Insurance Corporation (FDIC)	$100,000/depositor through the Savings Association Insurance Fund (SAIF)
Savings bank	Federal Deposit Insurance Corporation (FDIC)	$100,000/depositor through the Bank Insurance Fund (BIF)
Credit union	National Credit Union Administration (NCUA)	$100,000/depositor through the National Credit Union Share Insurance Fund (NCUSIF)

deposit insurance. *Securities purchased through your bank are not protected by any form of deposit insurance.*

As a depositor, it's possible to increase your $100,000 of deposit insurance if necessary by opening accounts in different depositor names at the same institution. For example, a married couple can obtain as much as $500,000 in coverage by setting up several accounts:

- One in the name of each spouse ($200,000 in coverage)
- A *joint* account in both names (good for another $100,000)
- *Separate trust or self-directed retirement (IRA, Keogh, etc.) accounts* in the name of each spouse (good for an additional $200,000)

In this case each depositor name is treated as a separate legal entity, receiving full insurance coverage—the husband alone is considered one legal entity, the wife another, and the husband and wife as a couple a third. The trust and self-directed retirement accounts are also viewed as separate legal entities.

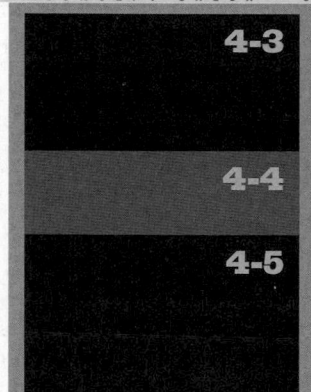

ⓘ Concept Check

CHECK • CONCEPT CHECK • CONCEPT CHECK • CONCEPT CHECK • CONCEPT CHECK • CONCEPT CHECK • CONCEPT

4-3   Briefly describe the basic operations and products and services offered by each of the following financial institutions: (a) commercial bank, (b) savings and loan association, (c) savings bank, (d) credit union, (e) stock brokerage firm, and (f) mutual fund.

4-4   What role does the FDIC play in insuring financial institutions? What other federal insurance program exists? Explain.

4-5   Would it be possible for an *individual* to have, say, six or seven checking and savings accounts at the same bank and still be fully protected under federal deposit insurance? Explain. Describe how it would be possible for a *married couple* to obtain as much as $500,000 in federal deposit insurance coverage at a single bank.

LG3   THE GROWING MENU OF CASH MANAGEMENT PRODUCTS

After meeting with an officer at his local bank, Ed Turner was confused. As a student on a tight budget, working to pay his way through college, he knew how important it was to plan his saving and spending, and he wanted to make the right decisions about managing his financial resources. By using a checking account comparison chart, like to the one in Exhibit 4.4,

Ed could compare information on daily balance requirements, service fees, interest rates, and services his bank offers to college students and others. As Exhibit 4.4 demonstrates, banks offer a variety of convenient checking account services.

Checking and Savings Accounts

People hold cash and other forms of liquid assets, like checking and savings accounts, for the convenience they offer in making purchase transactions, meeting normal living expenses, and providing a safety net, or cushion, to meet unexpected expenses or take advantage of unanticipated opportunities. Financial institutions compete to offer a wide array of products meeting every liquid-asset need.

The federal *Truth-in-Savings Act of 1993* helps consumers evaluate the terms and costs of banking products. Depository financial institutions must clearly disclose fees, interest rates, and terms—of both checking and savings accounts. The act places strict controls on bank advertising and what constitutes a "free" account. For example, banks cannot advertise free checking if there are minimum balance requirements or per-check charges. Banks must use a standard *annual percentage yield (APY)* formula that takes compounding (discussed later) into account when stating the interest paid on accounts. This makes it easier

---

EXHIBIT 4.4 | **Checking Accounts Comparison Chart**

Most banks offer a variety of checking account options, typically differentiated by minimum balances, fees, and other services.

ANYBANK USA

Features	College Checking	Custom Checking	Advantage Checking	Advantage Plus Checking
Minimum daily balance (to waive monthly service fee)	None	$1,000 in checking	$2,000 in checking, or $5,000 combined balance	$10,000 combined balance
Monthly service fee	$5 ($3.75 effective 9/1/07). No fee in summer (discontinued 9/1/08). $2 discount with a qualifying direct deposit of $100 or more.	$8 (No fee with direct deposit or direct debit)	$12 ($2 discount with direct deposit; no fee with Homeowner's Option)	$14 ($2 discount with direct deposit)
Interest	No	No	Yes	Yes
Online statements	Free	Free	Free	Free
Check safekeeping	Free	Free	Free	Free
Monthly check return	$3.00	$3.00	$3.00	Free
ATM & check card	Free	Free	Free	Free
Bank by phone	Free automated calls	Free automated calls	Free automated calls	Free banker-assisted calls
Overdraft protection	Credit card	Credit card	Credit card, line of credit account, and select deposit accounts	Credit card, line of credit account, and select deposit accounts
Direct deposit advance service	Not available	Yes, with a direct deposit of $100 a month or more	Yes, with a direct deposit of $100 a month or more	Yes, with a direct deposit of $100 a month or more

Go to **http://www .thomsonedu.com/finance/ gitman** for a link to save money by ordering your checks online.

for consumers to compare each bank's offerings. The law also requires banks to pay interest on a customer's full daily or monthly average deposit balance. Banks are prohibited from paying interest only on the lowest daily balance or paying no interest if the account balance falls below the minimum balance for 1 day. In addition, banks must notify customers 30 days before lowering rates on deposit accounts or certificates of deposit.

Checking Accounts

A checking account held at a financial institution is a **demand deposit,** meaning that the bank must permit these funds to be withdrawn when the account holder demands. You put money into your checking account by *depositing* funds; you withdraw it by *writing a check, using a debit card,* or *making a cash withdrawal.* As long as you have sufficient funds in your account, the bank, when presented with a valid check or an electronic debit, must immediately pay the amount indicated by deducting it from your account. Money held in checking accounts is liquid, so you can easily use it to pay bills and make purchases.

Regular checking is the most common type of checking account. It pays no interest, and any service charges can be waived if you maintain a minimum balance (usually between $750 and $1,500). Technically, only commercial banks can offer non-interest-paying regular checking accounts. S&Ls, savings banks, and credit unions also offer checking accounts; but these accounts, which must pay interest, are called *NOW (negotiable order of withdrawal) accounts* or, in the case of credit unions, *share draft accounts.* Demand deposit balances are an important type of cash balance, and using checks to pay bills or electronic debits to make purchases gives you a convenient payment record.

Savings Accounts

A savings account is another type of liquid asset available at commercial banks, S&Ls, savings banks, credit unions, and other types of financial institutions. Savings deposits are referred to as **time deposits** because they are expected to remain on deposit for longer periods of time than demand deposits. Because savings deposits earn higher rates of interest, savings accounts are typically preferable to checking accounts when the depositor's goal is to accumulate money for a future expenditure or to maintain balances for meeting unexpected expenses. Most banks pay higher interest rates on larger savings account balances. For example, a bank might pay 2.50 percent on balances up to $2,500, 2.75 percent on balances between $2,500 and $10,000, and 3.00 percent on balances of more than $10,000.

Although financial institutions generally have the right to require a savings account holder to wait a certain number of days before receiving payment of a withdrawal, most are willing to pay withdrawals immediately. In addition to withdrawal policies and deposit insurance, the stated interest rate and the method of calculating interest paid on savings accounts are important considerations in choosing the financial institution in which to place your savings.

Interest-Paying Checking Accounts

Depositors can choose from NOW accounts, money market deposit accounts, and money market mutual funds.

NOW Accounts. Negotiable order of withdrawal (NOW) accounts are checking accounts on which the financial institution pays interest. There is no legal minimum balance for a NOW, but many institutions impose their own requirement, often between $500 and $1,000. Some pay interest on any balance in the account, but most institutions pay a higher rate of interest for balances above a specified amount.

Money Market Deposit Accounts. Money market deposit accounts (MMDAs) are a popular offering at banks and other depository institutions and compete for deposits with money market mutual funds. MMDAs are popular with savers and investors due to their convenience and safety, because deposits in MMDAs, unlike those in money funds, are *federally insured.* Most banks require a minimum MMDA balance of $1,000 or more.

Depositors can use check-writing privileges or ATMs to access MMDA accounts. They receive a limited number of free monthly checks and transfers—usually six—but pay a fee on additional transactions. Although this reduces the flexibility of these accounts, most

demand deposit An account held at a financial institution from which funds can be withdrawn on demand by the account holder; same as a *checking account.*

time deposit A savings deposit at a financial institution; remains on deposit for a longer time than a demand deposit.

negotiable order of withdrawal (NOW) account A checking account on which the financial institution pays interest; NOWs have no legal minimum balance.

money market deposit account (MMDA) A federally insured savings account, offered by banks and other depository institutions, that competes with a money market mutual fund.

depositors view MMDAs as savings rather than convenience accounts and do not consider these restrictions a serious obstacle. Moreover, MMDAs pay the highest interest rate of any bank account on which checks can be written.

A major problem with the growing popularity of interest-paying checking accounts has been a rise in monthly bank charges, which can easily amount to more than the interest earned on all but the highest account balances. So the higher rates of interest offered by MMDAs can be misleading.

Money Market Mutual Funds. Money market mutual funds have become the most successful type of mutual fund ever offered. A **money market mutual fund (MMMF)** pools the funds of many small investors to purchase high-return, short-term marketable securities offered by the U.S. Treasury, major corporations, large commercial banks, and various government organizations. (Mutual funds are discussed in greater detail in Chapter 13.)

MMMFs generally pay interest at rates of 1 to 3 percent above those paid on regular savings accounts. Moreover, investors have instant access to their funds through check-writing privileges, although these must be written for a stipulated minimum amount (usually $500). The checks look like, and are treated like, any other check drawn on a demand deposit account; and, as with all interest-bearing checking accounts, you continue to earn interest on your money while the checks make their way through the banking system.

Asset Management Accounts

Perhaps the best example of a banking service offered by a nondepository financial institution is the **asset management account (AMA),** or *central asset account.* The AMA is a comprehensive deposit account that combines checking, investing, and borrowing activities and is offered primarily by brokerage houses and mutual funds. AMAs appeal to investors because they can consolidate most of their financial transactions at one institution and on one account statement.

A typical AMA account includes an MMDA with unlimited free checking, a Visa or MasterCard debit card, use of ATMs, and brokerage and loan accounts. Annual fees and account charges, such as a per-transaction charge for ATM withdrawals, vary; so it pays to shop around. AMAs have increased in popularity as more institutions have lowered minimum balance requirements to $5,000, and they pay higher interest rates on checking account deposits than banks do. Their distinguishing feature is that they automatically "sweep" excess balances—for example, those more than $500—into a higher-return MMMF daily or weekly. When the account holder needs funds to purchase securities or cover checks written on the MMDA, the funds are transferred back to the MMDA. If the amount of securities purchased or checks presented for payment exceeds the account balance, the needed funds are supplied automatically through a loan.

Although AMAs are an attractive alternative to a traditional bank account, they have some drawbacks. Compared with banks, there are fewer "branch" locations; however, AMAs are affiliated with ATM networks, making it easy to withdraw funds. ATM transactions are more costly, checks can take longer to clear, and some bank services, such as travelers' and certified checks, may not be offered. AMAs are not covered by deposit insurance, although these deposits are protected by the *Securities Investor Protection Corporation* (explained in Chapter 11) and the firm's private insurance.

Electronic Banking Services

The fastest-changing area in cash management today is electronic banking services. Whether you're using an ATM or checking your account balance online, electronic banking services make managing your money easier and more convenient. Electronic funds transfer systems allow you to conduct many types of banking business at any hour of the day or night.

Electronic Funds Transfer Systems

Electronic funds transfer systems (EFTSs) use the latest telecommunications and computer technology to electronically transfer funds into and out of your account. For example, your employer may use an EFTS to electronically transfer your pay from the firm's bank account directly into your personal bank account at the same or a different bank. This eliminates the

money market mutual fund (MMMF) A mutual fund that pools the funds of many small investors and purchases high-return, short-term marketable securities.

asset management account (AMA) A comprehensive deposit account, offered primarily by brokerage houses and mutual funds.

electronic funds transfer systems (EFTS) Systems using the latest telecommunications and computer technology to electronically transfer funds into and out of customers' accounts.

© CREATAS IMAGES/JUPITER IMAGES

employer's need to prepare and process checks and the employee's need to deposit them. Electronic transfer systems make possible such services as debit cards and ATMs, preauthorized deposits and payments, bank-by-phone accounts, and online banking.

Debit Cards and Automated Teller Machines. This form of EFTS uses specially coded plastic cards, called **debit cards,** to transfer funds from the customer's bank account (a debit) to the recipient's account. A debit card may be used to make purchases at any place of business set up with the point-of-sale terminals required to accept debit card payments. The personal identification number (PIN) issued with your debit card verifies that you are authorized to access the account.

Visa and MasterCard issue debit cards linked to your checking account that give you even more flexibility. In addition to using the card to purchase goods and services, you can use it at ATMs, which have become a popular way to make banking transactions. **Automated teller machines (ATMs)** are remote computer terminals that customers of a bank or other depository institution can use to make deposits, withdrawals, and other transactions such as loan payments or transfers between accounts—24 hours a day, 7 days a week. Most banks have ATMs outside their offices, and some place freestanding ATMs in shopping malls, airports, and grocery stores; at colleges and universities; and in other high-traffic areas to enhance their competitive position. If your bank belongs to an EFTS network, such as Cirrus, Star, or Interlink, you can get cash from the ATM of any bank in the United States or overseas that is a member of that network. (In fact, the easiest way to get foreign currency when you travel overseas is through an ATM on your bank's network! It also gives you the best exchange rate for your dollar.) Most banks charge a per-transaction fee of $1 to $4 for using the ATM of another bank, and some also charge when you use your ATM card to pay certain merchants.

Debit card use is increasing because these cards are convenient both for retailers, who don't have to worry about bounced checks, and for consumers, who don't have to write checks and can often get cash back when they make a purchase. ATM and other debit cards are accepted by supermarkets, gas stations, and convenience stores, and many other retail and service outlets. The convenience of debit cards may in fact be their biggest drawback: it can be easy to overspend. To avoid problems, make sure to record all debit card purchases immediately in your checkbook ledger and deduct them from your checkbook balance. Also be aware that if there's a problem with a purchase, you can't stop payment—an action you could take if you had paid by check or credit card.

Preauthorized Deposits and Payments. Two related EFTS services are *preauthorized deposits and payments*. They allow you to receive automatic deposits or make payments that occur regularly. For example, you can arrange to have your paycheck or monthly pension or Social Security benefits deposited directly into your account. Regular, fixed-amount payments, such as mortgage and consumer loan payments or monthly retirement fund contributions, can be preauthorized to be made automatically from your account. You can also preauthorize regular payments of varying amounts such as monthly utility bills. In this case, each month you would specify by phone the amount to be paid.

Charges for preauthorized payments vary from bank to bank. Typically, customers must maintain a specified minimum deposit balance and pay fees averaging 25 to 50 cents per transaction. This system better allows the customer to earn interest on deposits used to pay bills, and it's a convenient payment method that eliminates postage costs.

FINANCIAL ROAD SIGN

SMALL SAVINGS EQUAL LARGE GAINS

Think there are no other ways you can save money? When you're in a cash flow crunch and it's time for drastic action, you *can* save more if you really put your mind to it. Here's how.

- **Use a crash budget:** A crash budget works just like a crash diet—cut out all unnecessary spending, and don't buy on impulse. This works especially well for short periods.

- **The two-week rule:** Become an impulse saver, rather than an impulse buyer. If you want something, wait 2 weeks to get it.

Source: *A Working Woman's Guide to Financial Security,* "Planning for Financial Independence," http://www.urbanext.uiuc.edu, August 29, 2003.

---

debit cards Specially coded plastic cards used to transfer funds from a customer's bank account to the recipient's account to pay for goods or services.

automated teller machine (ATM) A remote computer terminal that customers of depository institutions can use to make basic transactions 24 hours a day, 7 days a week.

Smart Sites

Is an electronic bill presentment and payment (EBPP) service for you? Visit Paytrust through **http://www.thomsonedu .com/finance/gitman** to help you decide.

Bank-by-Phone Accounts. Bank customers can initiate various banking transactions by telephone, either by calling a customer service operator who handles the transaction or by using the keypad on a touch-tone telephone to instruct the bank's computer. After the customer provides a secret code to access his or her accounts, the system provides the appropriate prompts to perform various transactions, such as obtaining an account balance, finding out what checks have cleared, transferring funds to other accounts, and dispatching payments to participating merchants. To encourage banking by phone, many banks today charge no fee on basic account transactions or allow a limited number of free transactions per month.

Online Banking and Bill Payment Services

At the end of 2005, nearly 40 million households (a 27 percent increase over 2004) used some form of *online banking* services. The number has grown steadily as banks make online services easier to use and people become more comfortable using the Internet for financial transactions. Many individuals just check their balances, but more than half use the Internet to transfer funds as well. Thanks to improved Internet security procedures, most online bank services are delivered through the Internet although some may use direct dial-up connections with the customer's bank. Today most banks compete for your online banking business. It's in their best financial interests to do so. A recent study showed that the cost of a full-service teller transaction is about $1.10, an ATM transaction is about 30 cents, and an Internet transaction is about 1 cent.

An online banking service lets you access your bank's Web site from your computer at any time. After logging on with your personal identification code and password, you can review your current statement to check your balance and recent transactions. Then, you can transfer funds from one account to another or pay bills electronically. You can also download account information to money management software such as Quicken or Microsoft Money.

Although a computer-based bank-at-home system doesn't replace the use of an ATM to obtain cash or deposit money, it can save both time and postage when you're paying bills. Other benefits include convenience and the potential to earn higher interest rates and pay lower fees. Customers like being able to check their account balances at any time of the day or night, not just when their printed statement comes once a month.

Online banking services charge $5–$15 per month, which typically includes some bill payments. Some banks don't charge their customers for viewing accounts and transferring funds. But online banking doesn't always live up to its promises. You can't make cash deposits, checks may get lost in the mail, and you don't know when the funds will reach your account. The *Money in Action* box on page 112 provides more information to help you decide if online bill paying is right for you. Exhibit 4.5 on page 113 contains a checklist for choosing an online bill-paying service wisely.

Most consumers prefer the security of a bank with a physical presence and a variety of other banking options such as branches, ATMs, and phone services. Your current "traditional" bank probably offers online banking services. Another option is to open an account at an Internet bank that exists only online and has few or no physical locations. Because they don't incur branch costs, Internet banks can offer high interest rates on checking and savings accounts and CDs, attractive loan rates, and low fees and charges. However, only about 2 percent of all households that bank online choose these banks. Customers are concerned that Internet banks are less secure, and they find it inconvenient to deposit checks by mail. To counter these concerns, many Internet banks are moving to a "clicks-and-bricks" strategy, adding a physical presence such as ATM networks and staffed mini-branches with ATMs and videoconferencing stations.

Regulation of EFTS Services

The federal *Electronic Fund Transfer Act of 1978* delineates your rights and responsibilities as an EFTS user. Under this law, you cannot stop payment on a defective or questionable

ONLINE BILL PAYMENT: HOW AND WHY?

Do you hate writing checks? Online bill payment may be the solution.

If you want to receive bills by mail, then you can either pay bills directly at the biller's Web site or authorize a third-party consolidator to pay your bills. The drawback of paying at each biller's Web site is keeping track of the sites and corresponding user names and passwords. Third party consolidators may include your bank or a financial Web site such as bills.com (**http://www.bills.com**).

A third option eliminates all paperwork involved in bill payment. *Electronic bill presentment and payment (EBPP)* is offered by companies such as Paytrust (**http://www.paytrust.com**) or CheckFree (**http://www.mycheckfree.com**). These companies receive your bills and send you e-mail notification that a bill has arrived. You then go to the Web site to review the bill and arrange payment. EBPP services will also confirm that the payment has been made, remind you that an unpaid bill is due, and let you view and print a report of bill payments by date or expense category.

Here are some advantages of online bill payment:

- **Convenience:** You can pay all your bills at once from one Web site, without writing checks or buying stamps. You can access your bill-paying site while you travel or schedule payments up to 1 year ahead. Your bank will even cut a check for those who can't receive electronic funds, like your babysitter.

- **Organization:** EBPP services remind you if a due date is approaching and you haven't paid your bill. This feature can save you lots of money in late fees!

- **On-time guarantee:** Most services will cover late fees if a bill doesn't arrive on time.

- **Record keeping:** Many services save your payments so you can retrieve and print a record for the year (some go back several years). This is helpful at tax time.

- **Customization:** You can arrange automatic payment for bills whose amounts don't change, such as mortgage or car payments. With manual payments, you decide how much to pay and when.

- **Round-the-clock help:** E-mail help lines are available at any time, or you can call for help during normal business hours.

The disadvantages are:

- **Start-up issues:** The initial setup for any type of online bill payment—providing names, addresses, phone numbers, and account numbers for your payee list—may be time consuming, though some Web sites have lists of major billers. But once you've entered the information, you simply select the recipient, fill in the amount, and click the "pay" button. With EBPP there is a lag time of several billing cycles while you change the address on all your bills to that of the service.

- **Monthly fees:** Convenience isn't always free. Banks typically provide the service for free with a checking account, although some

require a minimum balance. Most other online payment services charge $5 to $15 to pay from 10 to 30 bills per month, with a per-bill fee of up to 50 cents for additional bills.

- **Float:** Most bill-paying services immediately withdraw funds from your account when you hit the pay button, so you lose the "float," the period between when you write a check and when the recipient cashes it, typically 3 to 10 days. However, some banks have changed this policy. Now the money stays in your bank account until payment is delivered.

- **Privacy and security:** These are always a concern when you give a third party your Social Security number and bank and credit card numbers. However, research suggests that most identity theft comes from mail that's stolen from garbage or mailboxes. So, eliminating the paper trail might reduce your risk of identity theft.

Save some trees and some stamps, and consider using online bill payment.

Critical Thinking Questions:

1. What are the three main types of online bill payment services?
2. What are some advantages and disadvantages of paying bills online?
3. Based on the information in this box, describe a situation when online bill payment would be appropriate. Describe another situation when online bill payment would not be the best solution.

Sources: Donna Rosato, "Why Are You Still Writing Checks? It's Never Been Easier or Cheaper to Do All Your Bill Paying Online," *Money*, January 1, 2004, p. 94; Jenny C. McCune, "Your Online Bill Payment Options," Bankrate.com, April 22, 2005, http://www.bankrate.com; Bruce Mohl, "Bank Sweetens Paying Bills Online," *Boston Globe*, February 14, 2006; Jean Chatzky, "Ending the Paper Trail: It Makes Sense that Banking and Paying Bills Online Saves Time—and Trees. But Who Knew It Could Protect You from Identity Theft?" *Money*, November 1, 2003, p. 176; Steve Bills, "Will Presentment Growth Enliven Online Bill Pay?" *American Banker*, February 2, 2005, p. 17.

Ch 13

1	d	14	a
2	e	15	c
3	c	16	e
4	c	17	a
5	b	18	d
6	b	19	e
7	b	20	a
8	d	21	c
9	d	22	a
10	d	23	c
11	e	24	d
12	b	25	b
13	a		

Ch 14

1	d	14	b
2	a	15	b
3	e	16	c
4	e	17	c
5	e	18	a
6	e	19	d
7	c	20	c
8	c	21	d
9	d	22	c
10	a	23	b
11	c	24	e
12	b	25	c
13	a		

1

Ch. 1   Test A

#			#	
1	d		14	b
2	c		15	e
3	d		16	a
4	d	? 17	b
5	c		18	d
6	e?		19	d
7	e		20	a
8	e		21	d
9	a		22	e
10	d		23	c
? 11	d		24	e
12	b		25	e
13	a			

Ch 2

#		#	
1	d	14	e
2	c	15	e
3	a	16	b
4	c	17	c
5	d	18	e
6	a	19	c
7	e	20	b
8	d	21	d
9	e	22	c
10	b	23	e
11	c	24	d
12	a	25	a
13	a		

EXHIBIT 4.5   Choosing an Online Bill-Paying Service

Before signing up with any online bill-paying service, use the following checklist to help you find the features you want and the security you need:

1. Check the Better Business Bureau for the company's reputation and any complaints that may have been lodged against it.
2. The service should provide you with written confirmation regarding its privacy policy, stating it will not share your personal information with anyone at any time.
3. Technological security is critical when handling sensitive financial information. Make sure the service offers secure data transmittal, as well as a firewall to protect information from hackers.
4. The company should perform background checks on its employees and guarantee your protection from losses due to fraud.
5. Know the company's policy for handling bills not paid due to its error. Will it help clear your credit record, pay any late fees, and compensate you for any out-of-pocket costs?

---

purchase, although individual banks and state laws have more lenient provisions. If there's an error, you must notify the bank within 60 days of its occurrence. The bank must investigate and tell you the results within 10 days. The bank can then take up to 45 more days to investigate the error but must return the disputed money to your account until the issue is resolved.

If you fail to notify the bank of the error within 60 days, the bank has no obligation under federal law to conduct an investigation or return your money. You must notify the bank immediately about the theft, loss, or unauthorized use of your EFTS card. Notification within 2 business days after you discover the card missing limits your loss to $50. After 2 business days, you may lose up to $500 (but never more than the amount that was withdrawn by the thief). If you don't report the loss within 60 days after your periodic statement was mailed, you can lose all the money in your account. When reporting errors or unauthorized transactions, it's best to notify your bank by telephone and follow up with a letter. Keep a copy of the letter in your file.

Many state regulations offer additional consumer protection regarding your use of EFTS. However, your best protection is to carefully guard the PIN used to access your accounts. Don't write the PIN on your EFTS card, and be sure to check your periodic statements regularly for possible errors or unauthorized transactions.

Other Bank Services

In addition to the services described earlier in this chapter, many banks offer other types of money management services, such as safe-deposit boxes and trust services.

- **Safe-deposit boxes:** A *safe-deposit box* is a rented drawer in a bank's vault. Boxes can be rented for $40–$85 per year (or more), depending on their size. When you rent a box, you receive one key to it, and the bank keeps another key. The box can be opened only when both keys are used. This arrangement protects items in the box from theft and serves as an excellent storage place for jewelry, contracts, stock certificates, titles, and other important documents. Keeping valuables in a safe-deposit box may also reduce your homeowner's insurance by eliminating the "riders" that are often needed to cover such items.
- **Trust services:** Bank trust departments provide investment and estate planning advice. They manage and administer the investments in a trust account or from an estate.

▌▌ Concept Check

4-6	Distinguish between a checking account and a savings account.
4-7	Define and discuss (a) demand deposits, (b) time deposits, (c) interest-paying checking accounts.
4-8	Briefly describe the key characteristics of each of the following forms of interest-paying checking accounts: (a) NOW account, (b) money market deposit account (MMDA), and (c) money market mutual fund (MMMF).
4-9	Describe the features of an asset management account (AMA), its advantages, and its disadvantages.
4-10	Briefly describe (a) debit cards, (b) banking at ATMs, (c) preauthorized deposits and payments, (d) bank-by-phone accounts, and (e) online banking and bill-paying services.
4-11	What are your legal rights and responsibilities when using EFTS?

LG4 MAINTAINING A CHECKING ACCOUNT

By the time Ben Adams started college, he had a thriving car-detailing business that earned him several hundred dollars per week. Some customers paid him in advance, some paid after the fact, and some forgot to pay at all. But by depositing each check or cash payment into his checking account, Ben was able to keep track of his earnings without complicated bookkeeping. A checking account is one of the most useful cash management tools you can have. It's a safe and convenient way to hold money and streamline point-of-sale purchases, debt payments, and other basic transactions. You can have regular or interest-paying checking accounts at commercial banks, S&Ls, savings banks, credit unions, and even brokerage houses through asset management accounts. For convenience, we'll focus on commercial bank checking accounts, although our discussion also applies to checking accounts maintained at other types of financial institutions.

Opening and Using Your Checking Account

Factors that typically influence the choice of where to maintain a checking account are convenience, services, and cost. Many people choose a bank based solely on convenience factors: business hours, location, number of drive-thru windows, and number and location of branch offices and ATMs. Ease of access is obviously an important consideration because most people prefer to bank near home or work. Although services differ from bank to bank, today most banks offer several types of accounts: debit, ATM, credit cards, and loans. Many banks also offer online and telephone banking and bill-paying services, safe-deposit box rental, provision for direct deposits and withdrawals, and mutual-fund sales.

After determining the banking services you need, evaluate the offerings of conveniently located, federally insured financial institutions. In addition to convenience and safety, consider interest rates, types of accounts (including special accounts that combine such features as credit cards, free checks, and reduced fees), structure and level of fees and charges, and quality of customer service.

The Cost of a Checking Account

Bank service charges have increased sharply due to deregulation and the growth of interest-paying checking accounts. Today few, if any, banks and other depository institutions allow unlimited free check-writing privileges. Most banks levy monthly and per-check fees when your checking account balance drops below a required minimum, and some may charge for checking no matter how large a balance you carry.

Usually, you must maintain a minimum balance of $500 to $1,000 or more to avoid service charges. Although some banks use the *average monthly* balance in an account to determine whether to levy a service charge, most use the *daily* balance procedure. This means that if your account should happen to fall just $1 below the minimum balance *just once* during the month, you'll be hit with the full service charge—even if your average balance is three times the minimum requirement.

Service charges take two forms: (1) a base service charge of, say, $7.50 a month, and (2) additional charges of, say, 25 cents for each check you write and 10 cents for each ATM or bank-by-phone transaction. Using these fees as an illustration, assume you write 20 checks and make 7 ATM transactions in a given month. If your balance falls below the minimum, you'll have to pay a service charge of $7.50 + (20 × $.25) + (7 × $.10) = $13.20.

In addition to the service charges on checking accounts, banks have increased most other check-related charges and raised the minimum balances required for free checking and waivers of specified fees. The charge on a returned check can be as high as $20 to $25, and stop-payment orders typically cost $20 to $35. Some banks charge fees for ATM or bank-by-phone transactions that exceed a specified number. Most also charge for using the ATM of another bank that's a member of the same network. It's not surprising that smart consumers use cost as the single most important variable in choosing where to set up a checking account.

Individual or Joint Account

Two people wishing to open a checking account may do so in one of three ways:

1. They can each open individual checking accounts (on which the other cannot write checks).
2. They can open a joint account that requires both signatures on all checks.
3. They can open a joint account that allows either one to write checks (the most common type of joint account).

One advantage of the joint account over two individual accounts is lower service charges. In addition, the account has rights of survivorship: for a married couple, this means that if one spouse dies, the surviving spouse, after fulfilling a specified legal requirement, can draw checks on the account. If account owners are treated as tenants in common rather than having rights of survivorship, the survivor gets only his or her share of the account. Thus, when you're opening a joint account, be sure to specify the rights you prefer.

General Checking Account Procedures

After you select the bank that meets your needs and has the type of account you want, it's a simple matter to open the account. The application form asks for basic personal information such as name, date of birth, Social Security number, address, phone, and place of employment. You'll also have to provide identification, sign signature cards, and make an initial deposit. The bank will give you a supply of checks to use until your personalized checks arrive.

After opening a checking account, follow these basic procedures:

- Always write checks in ink.
- Include the name of the person being paid, the date, and the amount of the check—written in both numerals and words for accuracy.
- Sign the check the same way as on the signature card you filled out when opening the account.
- Note the check's purpose on the check—usually on the line provided in the lower left corner. This information is helpful for both budgeting and tax purposes.

Make sure to enter all checking account transactions—checks written, deposits, point-of-sale debit purchases, ATM transactions, and preauthorized automatic payments and deposits—in the **checkbook ledger** provided with your supply of checks. Then, subtract the amount of each check, debit card purchase, ATM cash withdrawal, or payment, and add the amount of each deposit to the previous balance to keep track of your current account balance. Good transaction records and an accurate balance prevent overdrawing the account.

With each deposit, write a deposit slip (generally included with your checks and also available at your bank) listing the currency, coins, and checks being deposited. List checks by the *transit ID number* printed on the check, usually at the top right. Also properly endorse all checks that you're depositing. Federal regulations require your endorsement to be made in black or blue ink, within $1^1/_2$ inches of the check's trailing edge (left end of the check when viewed from the front) so as not to interfere with bank endorsements. If you don't comply, you'll still get your money but it may take longer.

To protect against possible loss of endorsed checks, it's common practice to use a special endorsement, such as "Pay to the order of XYZ Bank," or a restrictive endorsement, such as "For deposit only." If the way your name is written on the check differs from the way that you signed the signature card, you should sign your correct signature below your endorsement. To further ensure that the deposit is properly entered into your account, write your account number below your endorsement.

When depositing checks, you may encounter a delay in funds availability due to the time required for them to clear. To avoid overdrawing your account, know your bank's "hold" policy on deposits, which are capped by federal maximum funds-availability delays. It generally takes between 1 and 5 business days for funds to become available. For example, on a check drawn on another local bank, funds must be made available no later than the second business day after deposit. An out-of-town check, however, may take up to 5 business days to clear. Longer holds—up to 9 business days—can be applied by banks under special circumstances, such as when large amounts (over $5,000) are deposited in a given account within 1 day, or when the depositor has repeatedly overdrawn his or her account during the immediately preceding 6 months.

Overdrafts

When a check is written for an amount greater than the current account balance, the result is an **overdraft.** If the overdraft is proven intentional, the bank can initiate legal proceedings against the account holder. The action taken by a bank on an overdraft depends on the strength of its relationship with the account holder and the amount involved. In many cases, the bank stamps the overdrawn check with the words "insufficient balance (or funds)" and returns it to the party to whom it was written. This is often called a "bounced check." The account holder is notified of this action, and the holder's bank deducts a penalty fee of as much as $20 to $25 or more from his or her checking account. The depositor of a "bad check" may also be charged as much as $15 to $20 by his or her bank, which explains why merchants typically charge customers who give them bad checks $15 to $25 or more and often refuse to accept future checks from them.

When you have a strong relationship with your bank or arrange **overdraft protection,** the bank will pay a check that overdraws the account. In cases where overdraft protection has not been prearranged but the bank pays the check, the account holder is usually notified by the bank and charged a penalty fee for the inconvenience. However, the check does not bounce, and the check writer's creditworthiness is not damaged.

There are several ways to arrange overdraft protection. Many banks offer an overdraft line of credit, which automatically extends a loan to cover the amount of an overdraft. In most cases, however, the loans are made only in specified increments, such as $50 or $100, and interest (or a fee) is levied against the loan amount, not the actual amount of the overdraft. This can be an expensive form of protection, particularly if you do not promptly repay such a loan.

For example, if you had a $110 overdraft and the bank made overdraft loans in $100 increments, it would automatically deposit $200 in your account. If the bank charged 12 percent annually (or 1 percent per month) and you repaid the loan within a month, you would incur total interest of $2 ([$200 × 12 percent]/12). But remember, you paid interest on $90 ($200 − $110) you didn't need, and the annualized rate of interest on this overdraft loan is *21.8 percent* ([$2/$110] × 12)!

checkbook ledger
A booklet, provided with a supply of checks, used to maintain accurate records of all checking account transactions.

overdraft The result of writing a check for an amount greater than the current account balance.

overdraft protection
An arrangement between the account holder and the depository institution wherein the institution automatically pays a check that overdraws the account.

Another way to cover overdrafts is with an *automatic transfer program,* which automatically transfers funds from your savings account into your checking account in the event of an overdraft. Under this program, some banks charge both an annual fee and a fee on each transfer. Of course, the best form of overdraft protection is to employ good cash management techniques and regularly balance your checking account.

Stopping Payment

Occasionally it's necessary to **stop payment** on a check that has been issued because a good or service paid for by check is found to be faulty (some states prohibit you from stopping payment on faulty goods or services) or a check is issued as part of a contract that is not carried out. If your checks or checkbook are lost or stolen, there's no need to stop payment on them because you have no personal liability. Stopping payment in this case only incurs expense; it doesn't change your personal liability.

To stop payment on a check, you must notify the bank and fill out a form indicating the check number and date, amount, and the name of the person to whom it was written. You can initiate stop-payment orders online or by phone. Once you place a stop-payment order, the bank refuses payment on the affected check, and the check will be rejected if another bank presents it in the check-clearing process. Banks typically charge a fee ranging from $20 to $35 to stop payment on a check.

Monthly Statements

Once a month, your bank provides a statement—an itemized listing of all transactions in your checking account (checks written, ATM transactions, debit purchases, automatic payments, and deposits made). Also included are bank service charges and interest earned (see James C. Morrison's May 2007 bank statement in Exhibit 4.6 on page 118). Some banks include your original canceled checks with your bank statement, although as we move closer to a "paperless society," most are abandoning this practice. Banks that don't return canceled checks will provide photocopies of them on request, generally for a fee. Many banks now let you view canceled checks online, free of charge. It's important to review your monthly bank statement to verify the accuracy of your account records and reconcile differences between the statement balance and the balance shown in your checkbook ledger. The monthly statement is also a valuable source of information for your tax records.

Account Reconciliation

You should reconcile your bank account as soon as possible after receiving your monthly statement. The **account reconciliation** process, or *balancing the checkbook,* can uncover errors in recording checks or deposits, in addition or subtraction, and, occasionally, in the bank's processing of a check. It can also help you avoid overdrafts by forcing you to verify your account balance monthly. Assuming that neither you nor the bank has made any errors, discrepancies between your checkbook ledger account balance and your bank statement can be attributed to one of four factors.

1. Checks that you've written, ATM withdrawals, debit purchases, or other automatic payments subtracted from your checkbook balance haven't yet been received and processed by your bank and therefore remain outstanding.
2. Deposits that you've made and added to your checkbook balance haven't yet been credited to your account.
3. Any service (activity) charges levied on your account by the bank haven't yet been deducted from your checkbook balance.
4. Interest earned on your account (if it's a NOW or an MMDA account) hasn't yet been added to your checkbook balance.

Exhibit 4.7 on page 119 lists the steps to reconcile your checkbook each month.

The reverse side of your bank statement usually provides a form for reconciling your account along with step-by-step instructions. Worksheet 4.1 on page 120 includes an account reconciliation form that James Morrison completed for the month of May 2007 using the reconciliation procedures we have described. You can use the form to reconcile either regular or interest-paying checking accounts such as NOWs or MMDAs.

stop payment An order made by an account holder instructing the depository institution to refuse payment on an already issued check.

account reconciliation Verifying the accuracy of your checking account balance in relation to the bank's records as reflected in the bank statement, which is an itemized listing of all transactions in the checking account.

EXHIBIT 4.6 — A Bank Statement

Each month, you receive a statement from your bank or depository financial institution that summarizes the month's transactions and shows your latest account balance. This sample statement for May 2007 for James C. Morrison not only shows the checks that have been paid, but also lists all ATM transactions, point-of-sale transactions using his ATM card (the Interlink payments at Lucky Stores), and direct payroll deposits.

```
YOUR BANK                          #240
P.O. BOX 516   ANY CITY, USA    90000-0000

   JAMES C. MORRISON
   1765 SHERIDAN DRIVE              N        CALL (800) 222-0000
   YOUR CITY, STATE 12091           21       24 HOURS/DAY, 7 DAYS/WEEK
                                             FOR ASSISTANCE WITH
                                             YOUR ACCOUNT.

PAGE 1 OF 1      THIS STATEMENT COVERS: 4/30/07 THROUGH 5/29/07

PREMIUM          SUMMARY
ACCOUNT
                 PREVIOUS BALANCE       473.68    MINIMUM BALANCE    21.78
0123-45678       DEPOSITS             1,302.83+
                 WITHDRAWALS          1,689.02-
                 SERVICE CHARGES          7.50-
                 DIRECT DEPOSIT DISCOUNT   1.00+
                 NEW BALANCE             80.99

CHECKS AND     CHECK   DATE PAID   AMOUNT    CHECK   DATE PAID   AMOUNT
WITHDRAWALS     203      5/01       10.00     213      5/08       40.00
                204      4/30       15.00     214      5/09        9.58
                205      5/10      635.00     215      5/20       66.18
                206      5/08       25.00     216      5/20       64.92
                207      5/07       19.00     217      5/21       25.03
                208      5/07       50.00     218      5/21       37.98
                209      5/08       15.00     219      5/22       35.00
                210      5/10       83.00     220      5/22      105.00
                211      5/10       10.00     222*     5/22      100.00
                212      5/08       70.00     223      5/21       40.00
                                              224      5/29       40.82

               PREMIUM ACCOUNT FEE LESS $1.00 DISCOUNT   4/30     6.50
ATM
TRANSACTIONS   INTERLINK PURCHASE #572921 ON 04/30 AT    5/01    50.00
               LUCKY STORE NO 043
               WITHDRAWAL #08108 AT 00165A ON 05/04      5/06    20.00
               INTERLINK PURCHASE #807409 ON 05/11 AT    5/13    12.51
               LUCKY STORE NO 056
               WITHDRAWAL #01015 AT 00240C ON 05/17      5/17    20.00
               WITHDRAWAL #04792 AT 00167C ON 05/20      5/20    20.00
               WITHDRAWAL #04386 AT 00240D ON 05/21      5/21    40.00
               INTERLINK PURCHASE #880318 ON 05/28 AT    5/29    30.00
               LUCKY STORE #043

DEPOSITS                                        DATE POSTED   AMOUNT
               AVS RNT CAR SYST PAYROLL G2 000000035382   5/03   618.69
               AVS RNT CAR SYST PAYROLL G2 000000035382   5/17    83.39
               AVS RNT CAR SYST PAYROLL G2 000000035382   5/17   600.75

ATM            00165A: 249 PRIMROSE RD, ANY CITY, USA
LOCATIONS USED 00240C: 490 BROADWAY, ANY CITY, USA
               00167C: 1145 BROADWAY, ANY CITY, USA
               00240D: 490 BROADWAY, ANY CITY, USA
```

EXHIBIT 4.7   **Make That Checkbook Balance!**

Take the following steps to reconcile your account:

1. On receipt of your bank statement, arrange all canceled checks in ascending numerical order based on their sequence numbers or issuance dates. (Skip this step if your bank doesn't return canceled checks.)
2. Compare each check or its bank statement information with the corresponding entry in your checkbook ledger to make sure there are no recording errors. Check off in your checkbook ledger each check and any other withdrawals such as from ATMs, point-of-sale debit transactions, or automatic payments.
3. List the checks and other deductions (ATM withdrawals or debit purchases) still *outstanding*—that is, those deducted in your checkbook but not returned with your bank statement (see Step 2). Total their amount.
4. Compare the deposits indicated on the statement with deposits shown in your checkbook ledger. Total the amount of deposits still outstanding—that is, those shown in your checkbook ledger but not yet received by the bank. Be sure to include all automatic deposits and deposits made at ATMs in your calculations.
5. *Subtract* the total amount of checks outstanding (from Step 3) from your bank statement balance, and *add* to this balance the amount of outstanding deposits (from Step 4). The resulting amount is your *adjusted bank balance.*
6. Deduct the amount of any bank service charges from your checkbook ledger balance, and add any interest earned to that balance. Make sure that you include all service charges for the period, including those for any returned checks, stop payments, or new checks ordered. The resulting amount is your *new checkbook balance.* This amount should equal your adjusted bank balance (from Step 5). If it doesn't, check all addition and subtraction in your checkbook ledger, because you've probably made an error.

Special Types of Checks

In some circumstances sellers of goods or services may not accept personal checks because they can't be absolutely sure that the check is good. This is common for large purchases or when the buyer's bank is not located in the same area where the purchase is being made. A form of check that guarantees payment may be required instead: cashier's checks, traveler's checks, or certified checks.

cashier's check A check payable to a third party that is drawn by a bank on itself in exchange for the amount specified plus, in most cases, a service fee (of about $5).

traveler's check A check sold (for a fee of about 1.5 percent) by many large financial institutions, typically in denominations ranging from $20 to $100, that can be used for making purchases and exchanged for local currencies in most parts of the world.

certified check A personal check that is guaranteed (for a fee of $10 to $15 or more) by the bank on which it is drawn.

- **Cashier's check:** Anyone can buy a **cashier's check** from a bank. These checks are often used by people who don't have checking accounts. They can be purchased for the face amount of the check plus a service fee of about $5, although occasionally they're issued at no charge to bank customers. The bank issues a check payable to a third party and drawn on itself, not you—the best assurance you can give that the check is good.

- **Traveler's check:** Some large financial organizations—such as Citibank, American Express, MasterCard, Visa, and Bank of America—issue **traveler's checks,** which can be purchased at commercial banks and most other financial institutions, typically in denominations ranging from $20 to $100. A fee of about 1.5 percent is charged on their purchase. Properly endorsed and countersigned traveler's checks are accepted by most U.S. businesses and can be exchanged for local currencies in most parts of the world. Because they're insured against loss or theft by the issuing agency, they provide a safe, convenient, and popular form of money for travel.

- **Certified check:** A **certified check** is a personal check that the bank certifies, with a stamp, to guarantee that the funds are available. The bank immediately deducts the amount of the check from your account. There's normally a charge of $10 to $15 or more for this service.

James Morrison used this form to reconcile his checking account for the month of May 2007. Because line A equals line B, he has fully reconciled the difference between the $80.99 bank statement balance and his $339.44 checkbook balance. Accounts should be reconciled each month—as soon as possible after receiving the bank statement.

CHECKING ACCOUNT RECONCILIATION

For the Month of _____ May _____ , 20 _07_

Accountholder Name(s) _____ James Morrison _____

Type of Account _____ Regular Checking _____

1. Ending balance shown on bank statement _____ $ 80.99

Add up checks and withdrawals still outstanding:

Check Number or Date	Amount	Check Number or Date	Amount
221	$ 81.55		$
225	196.50		
Lucky—5/28	25.00		
ATM—5/29	40.00		
TOTAL	$ 343.05		

2. Deduct total checks/withdrawals still outstanding from bank balance _____ − $ 343.05

Add up deposits still outstanding:

Date	Amount	Date	Amount
5/29	595.00		
TOTAL	$ 595.00		

3. *Add* total deposits still outstanding to bank balance _____ + $ 595.00

A **Adjusted Bank Balance (1 − 2 + 3)** _____ $ 332.94

4. Ending balance shown in checkbook _____ $ 339.44

5. Deduct any bank service charges for the period (−$7.50 + $1.00) _____ − $ 6.50

6. Add interest earned for the period _____ + $ 0

B **New Checkbook Balance (4 − 5 + 6)** _____ $ 332.94

Note: Your account is reconciled when line A equals line B.

4-12 What are the key factors to consider when opening a checking account? Discuss the advantages and disadvantages of individual versus joint accounts.

4-13 Is it possible to bounce a check due to insufficient funds when the checkbook ledger shows a balance available to cover it? Explain what happens when a check bounces. Can you obtain protection against overdrafts?

4-14 Describe the procedure used to stop payment on a check. Why might you wish to initiate this process?

4-15 What type of information is found in the monthly bank statement, and how is it used? Explain the basic steps involved in reconciling an account.

4-16 Briefly describe each of these special types of checks:
a. Cashier's check
b. Traveler's check
c. Certified check

LG5, LG6 ESTABLISHING A SAVINGS PROGRAM

Alan Wilson's father started a savings account for his son when he was born, and every birthday he would add $50 or $100, depending on his cash flow. He told Alan that when he was ready to quit work, there would be a substantial sum available to help him retire. And there was. Alan now spends his days fishing and relaxing in the cabin he and his wife bought on Bluefish Lake, while most of his friends continue to work because they can't afford to retire.

An estimated 75 percent of American households have some money put away in savings, making it clear that most of us understand the value of saving for the future. The act of saving is a deliberate, well-thought-out activity designed to preserve the value of money, ensure liquidity, and earn a competitive rate of return. Almost by definition, *smart savers are smart investors.* They regard saving as more than putting loose change into a piggy bank; rather, they recognize the importance of saving and know that savings must be managed as astutely as any security.

After all, what we normally think of as "savings" is really a form of investment—a short-term, highly liquid investment—that's subject to minimal risk. Establishing and maintaining an ongoing savings program is a vital element of personal financial planning. To get the most from your savings, however, you must understand your savings options and how different savings vehicles pay interest.

Starting Your Savings Program

Careful financial planning dictates that you hold a portion of your assets to meet liquidity needs and accumulate wealth. Although opinions differ as to how much you should keep as liquid reserves, the consensus is that most families should have an amount equal to 3 to 6 months of after-tax income. Therefore, if you take home $3,000 a month, you should have between $9,000 and $18,000 in liquid reserves. If your employer has a strong salary continuation program covering extended periods of illness, or if you have a sizable line of credit available, the lower figure is probably adequate. If you lack one or both of these, however, the larger amount is more appropriate.

A specific savings plan must be developed to accumulate funds. Saving should be a priority item in your budget, not something that occurs only when income happens to exceed expenditures. Some people manage this by arranging to have savings directly withheld from their paychecks. Not only do direct deposit arrangements help your savings effort, they also enable your funds to earn interest sooner. Or you can transfer funds regularly to other financial institutions such as commercial banks, savings and loans, savings banks, credit unions, and even mutual funds. But the key to success is to establish a *regular* pattern of saving.

You should make it a practice to set aside an amount you can comfortably afford *each month,* even if it's only $50 to $100. (Keep in mind that $100 monthly deposits earning 4 percent interest will grow to more than $36,500 in 20 years.) Exhibit 4.8 lists 10 strategies you can use to increase your savings and build a nest egg.

You must also decide which savings products best meet your needs. Many savers prefer to keep their emergency funds in a regular savings or money market deposit account at an institution with federal deposit insurance. Although these accounts are safe, convenient, and highly liquid, they tend to pay relatively low rates of interest. Other important considerations include your risk preference, the length of time you can leave your money on deposit, and the level of current and anticipated interest rates.

Suppose that 1 year from now you plan to use $5,000 of your savings to make the down payment on a new car, and you expect interest rates to drop during that period. You should lock in today's higher rate by purchasing a 1-year certificate of deposit (CD). On the other hand, if you're unsure about when you'll actually need the funds or believe that interest rates will rise, you're better off with an MMDA or MMMF because their rates change with market conditions, and you can access your funds at any time without penalty.

Short-term interest rates generally fluctuate more than long-term rates, so it pays to monitor interest rate movements, shop around for the best rates, and place your funds in savings vehicles consistent with your needs. If short-term interest rates drop, you won't be able to reinvest the proceeds from maturing CDs at comparable rates. You'll need to reevaluate your savings plans and may choose to move funds into other savings vehicles with higher rates of interest but greater risk.

EXHIBIT 4.8   Ten Strategies to Build Your Nest Egg

Having trouble getting your savings program started? Here are 10 strategies to begin building your nest egg:

1. *Make saving a priority* when paying your bills. Write a check to yourself each month as if it were another invoice and deposit it in a savings account.
2. *Take a hard look at your spending habits* for places to cut back. Bring your lunch to work or school. Comparison shop. Carpool. Cut back on trips to the ATM.
3. *Set up a payroll deduction* and ask your employer to deduct money from your paycheck and have it deposited directly into your savings account. It's painless because you never see the money in your checking account.
4. *Banking your raise or bonus* is a perfect way to save. Keep your lifestyle where it is and put the difference in your savings account.
5. *Work a little harder* and avoid wasting time watching too much TV. Spend another 5 hours a week working and deposit the cash into your savings account.
6. *Keep making those loan payments,* and you'll feel rich when those obligations finally end. But keep writing those checks—only now it's for your savings account.
7. *Keep an eye on your returns* and know what kind of return you're getting on your savings account. If your bank is only paying you 2 or 3 percent, you might be able to add another percentage point or two by moving your money to an asset management account at a brokerage firm.
8. *Reinvest interest and dividends*—you won't miss the money, and your account will grow more rapidly. If you have a savings account, make sure the interest is reinvested rather than paid into your non-interest-bearing checking account. If you own stocks or mutual funds, virtually all offer dividend reinvestment plans.
9. *Set up a retirement plan* to make sure you contribute to your company's retirement program. Your contributions are tax deductible, and many employers match your contributions. Check out available individual retirement account options such as IRAs and 401(k)s (See Chapter 14).
10. *Splurge once in a while*—the boost you get will make saving money a little easier. All work and no play makes for a dull life, so once you've reached a savings goal, take some money and enjoy yourself.

Many financial planning experts recommend keeping a minimum of 10 to 25 percent of your investment portfolio in savings-type instruments in addition to the 3 to 6 months of liquid reserves noted earlier. Someone with $50,000 in investments should probably have a minimum of $5,000 to $12,500—and possibly more—in such short-term vehicles as MMDAs, MMMFs, or CDs. At times, the amount invested in short-term vehicles could far exceed the recommended minimum, approaching 50 percent or more of the portfolio. This generally depends on expected interest rate movements. If interest rates are relatively high, and you expect them to fall, you would invest in long-term vehicles in order to lock in the attractive interest rates. On the other hand, if rates are relatively low and you expect them to rise, you might invest in short-term vehicles so you can more quickly reinvest when rates do rise.

Earning Interest on Your Money

Interest earned is the reward for putting your money in a savings account or short-term investment vehicle, and it's important for you to understand how that interest is earned. But unfortunately, even in the relatively simple world of savings, not all interest rates are created equal.

The Effects of Compounding

Basically, interest can be earned in one of two ways. First, some short-term investments are sold on a *discount basis*. This means the security is sold for a price that's lower than its redemption value; the difference is the amount of interest earned. Treasury bills, for instance, are issued on a discount basis. Another way to earn interest on short-term investments is by *direct payment,* which occurs when interest is applied to a regular savings account. Although this is a simple process, determining the actual rate of return can be complicated.

The first complication is in the method used to set the amount and rate of **compound interest** earned annually. You've probably read or seen advertisements by banks or other depository institutions declaring that they pay daily, rather than annual, interest. To understand what this means, consider an example. Assume that you invest $1,000 in a savings account advertised as paying annual **simple interest** at a rate of 5 percent. With simple interest, the interest is paid only on the initial amount of the deposit. This means that if you leave the $1,000 on deposit for 1 year, you'll earn $50 in interest, and the account balance will total $1,050 at year end. In this case, the **nominal (stated) rate of interest** (the promised rate of interest paid on a savings deposit or charged on a loan) is 5 percent.

In contrast, the **effective rate of interest** is the annual rate of return that's *actually earned* (or *charged*) during the period the funds are held (or borrowed). You can calculate it with the following formula:

$$\text{Effective rate of interest} = \frac{\text{Amount of interest earned during the year}}{\text{Amount of money invested or deposited}}$$

In our example, because $50 was earned during the year on an investment of $1,000, the effective rate is $50/$1,000 or 5 percent, which is the same as the nominal rate of interest. (Notice in the above formula that it's interest earned during the *year* that matters; if you wanted to calculate the effective rate of interest on an account held for 6 months, you'd double the amount of interest earned.)

But suppose you can invest your funds elsewhere at a 5 percent rate, *compounded semiannually*. Because interest is applied to your account at midyear, you'll earn *interest on interest* for the last 6 months of the year, thereby increasing the total interest earned for the year. The actual dollar earnings are determined as follows:

First 6 months' interest	$= \$1{,}000 \times 0.05 \times 6/12 = \$25.00$
Second 6 months' interest	$= \$1{,}025 \times 0.05 \times 6/12 = \underline{\$25.63}$
Total annual interest	$\underline{\underline{\$50.63}}$

Interest is generated on a larger investment in the second half of the year because the amount of money on deposit has increased by the amount of interest earned in the first half

compound interest When interest earned in each subsequent period is determined by applying the *nominal (stated) rate of interest* to the sum of the initial deposit and the interest earned in each prior period.

simple interest Interest that is paid only on the initial amount of the deposit.

nominal (stated) rate of interest The promised rate of interest paid on a savings deposit or charged on a loan.

effective rate of interest The annual rate of return that is *actually earned* (or *charged*) during the period the funds are held (or borrowed).

($25). Although the nominal rate on this account is still 5 percent, the effective rate is 5.06 percent ($50.63/$1,000). As you may have guessed, *the more frequently interest is compounded, the greater the effective rate for any given nominal rate.* Exhibit 4.9 shows these relationships for a sample of interest rates and compounding periods. Note, for example, that with a 7 percent nominal rate, daily compounding adds one-fourth of a percent to the total return—not a trivial amount.

You can calculate the interest compounded daily by using a financial calculator similar to that described in Appendix E. Let's assume you want to invest $1,000 at 7 percent interest compounded daily. How much money will you have in the account at the end of the year? Using a calculator, we get $1,072.50. This value is clearly greater than the $1,070 that annual compounding would return. The effective interest rate would have been 7.25 percent ($72.50 interest earned/$1,000 initially invested), as noted in Exhibit 4.9.

Compound Interest Equals Future Value

Compound interest is the same as the *future value* concept introduced in Chapter 2. You can use the procedures described there to find out how much an investment or deposit will grow over time at a compounded rate of interest. For example, using the future value formula and the future value factor from Appendix A (see Chapter 2), you can find out how much $1,000 will be worth in 4 years if it's deposited into a savings account that pays 5 percent interest per year compounded annually:

$$\text{Future value} = \text{Amount deposited} \times \text{Future value factor}$$
$$= \$1,000 \times 1.216$$
$$= \underline{\$1,216}$$

You can use the same basic procedure to find the future value of an *annuity,* except you'd use the future value annuity factor from Appendix B (see Chapter 2). For instance, if you put $1,000 a year into a savings account that pays 5 percent per year compounded annually, in 4 years you will have:

$$\text{Future value} = \text{Amount deposited yearly} \times \text{Future value annuity factor}$$
$$= \$1,000 \times 4.310$$
$$= \underline{\$4,310}$$

A Variety of Ways to Save

During the past decade or so there has been a huge growth of savings and short-term investment vehicles, particularly for people of modest means. And because of the flexibility it provides, there'll always be a place in your portfolio for cash savings.

EXHIBIT 4.9   The Magic of Compounding

The effective rate of interest you earn on a savings account will exceed the nominal (stated) rate of interest if interest is compounded more than once a year (as are most savings and interest-paying accounts).

Nominal Rate	EFFECTIVE RATE				
	Annually	Semiannually	Quarterly	Monthly	Daily
3%	3.00%	3.02%	3.03%	3.04%	3.05%
4	4.00	4.04	4.06	4.07	4.08
5	5.00	5.06	5.09	5.12	5.13
6	6.00	6.09	6.14	6.17	6.18
7	7.00	7.12	7.19	7.23	7.25
8	8.00	8.16	8.24	8.30	8.33
9	9.00	9.20	9.31	9.38	9.42
10	10.00	10.25	10.38	10.47	10.52
11	11.00	11.30	11.46	11.57	11.62
12	12.00	12.36	12.55	12.68	12.74

Smart.Sites

At the T-bill page of Treasury Direct, you can learn about T-bills and then buy them online. Link at **http://www.thomsonedu.com/finance/gitman.**

Smart.Sites

Everything you always wanted to know about Series EE U.S. Savings Bonds—how to buy them, current rates, and answers to frequently asked questions—can be found through the link at **http://www.thomsonedu.com/finance/gitman.**

certificate of deposit (CD) A type of savings instrument issued by certain financial institutions in exchange for a deposit; typically requires a minimum deposit and has a maturity ranging from 7 days to as long as 7 or more years.

U.S. Treasury bill (T-bill) A short-term (3- or 6-month maturity) debt instrument issued at a discount by the U.S. Treasury in the ongoing process of funding the national debt.

Series EE bond A savings bond issued in various denominations by the U.S. Treasury.

Today, investors can choose from savings accounts, money market deposit accounts, money market mutual funds, NOW accounts, certificates of deposit, U.S. Treasury bills, Series EE bonds, and asset management accounts. We examined several of these savings vehicles earlier in this chapter. Now let's look at the three remaining types of deposits and securities.

Certificates of Deposit

Certificates of deposit (CDs) differ from the savings instruments discussed earlier in that CD funds (except for CDs purchased through brokerage firms) must remain on deposit for a specified period (from 7 days to as long as 7 or more years). Although it's possible to withdraw funds prior to maturity, an interest penalty usually makes withdrawal somewhat costly. The bank or other depository institution is free to charge whatever penalty it likes, but most require you to forfeit some interest. Banks, S&Ls, and other depository institutions can offer any rate and maturity CD they wish. As a result, a wide variety of CDs are offered by most banks, depository institutions, and other financial institutions such as brokerage firms. Most pay higher rates for larger deposits and longer periods of time. CDs are convenient to buy and hold because they offer attractive and highly competitive yields plus federal deposit insurance protection.

U.S. Treasury Bills

The **U.S. Treasury bill (T-bill)** is considered the ultimate safe haven for savings and investments. T-bills are issued by the U.S. Treasury as part of its ongoing process of funding the national debt. They are sold on a discount basis in minimum denominations of $1,000 and are issued with 3-month (13-week) or 6-month (26-week) maturities. The bills are auctioned off every Monday. Backed by the full faith and credit of the U.S. government, T-bills pay an attractive and safe return that is free from state and local income taxes.

T-bills are almost as liquid as cash because they can be sold at any time (in a very active secondary market) with no interest penalty. However, should you have to sell before maturity, you may lose some money on your investment if interest rates have risen, and you'll have to pay a broker's fee. Treasury bills pay interest on a *discount basis* and thus are different from other savings or short-term investment vehicles—that is, their interest is equal to the difference between the purchase price paid and their stated value at maturity. For example, if you paid $980 for a bill that will be worth $1,000 at maturity, you'll earn $20 in interest ($1,000 − $980).

An individual investor may purchase T-bills directly by participating in the weekly Treasury auctions or indirectly through a commercial bank or a securities dealer who buys bills for investors on a commission basis. T-bills may now be purchased over the Internet or by using a touch-tone phone (call 800-722-2678 and follow the interactive menu to complete transactions).

Outstanding Treasury bills can also be purchased in the secondary market through banks or dealers. This approach gives the investor a much wider selection of maturities, ranging from less than a week to as long as 6 months.

Series EE Bonds

Although issued by the U.S. Treasury on a discount basis, and free of state and local income taxes, **Series EE bonds** are quite different from T-bills. Savings bonds are *accrual-type securities,* which means that interest is paid when they're cashed in or before maturity, rather than periodically during their lives. The government does issue Series HH bonds; they have a 10-year maturity and are available in denominations of $500 to $10,000. Unlike EE bonds, HH bonds are issued at their full face value and pay interest semiannually at the current fixed rate.

Series EE bonds are backed by the full faith and credit of the U.S. government and can be replaced without charge in case of loss, theft, or destruction. Now also designated as "Patriot Bonds," in honor of September 11, 2001, they present an opportunity for all Americans to contribute to the government's war effort and save for their own futures as well. You can purchase them at banks or other depository institutions, or through payroll deduction plans. Issued in denominations from $50 through $10,000, their purchase price is a uniform 50 percent of the face amount (thus a $100 bond will cost $50 and be worth $100 at maturity).

Series EE bonds earn interest at a fixed rate for 30 years. Their long life lets investors use them for truly long-term goals like education and retirement. The higher the rate of interest being paid, the shorter the time it takes for the bond to accrue from its discounted purchase price to its maturity value. Bonds can be redeemed any time after the first 12 months, although redeeming EE bonds in less than 5 years results in a penalty of the last 3 months of interest earned. The fixed interest rate is set every 6 months in May and November and changes with prevailing Treasury security market yields. EE bonds increase in value every month and the fixed interest rate is compounded semiannually. To obtain current rates on Series EE bonds, call your bank, call 800-487-2663, or use the Web link for the savings bond site.

In addition to being exempt from state and local taxes, Series EE bonds give their holders an appealing tax twist: *Savers need not report interest earned on their federal tax returns until the bonds are redeemed.* Although interest can be reported annually (for example, when the bonds are held in the name of a child who has limited interest income), most investors choose to defer it. A second attractive tax feature allows partial or complete tax avoidance of EE bond earnings when proceeds are used to pay education expenses, such as college tuition, for the bond purchaser, a spouse, or another IRS-defined dependent. To qualify, the purchaser must be age 24 or older, and for 2005, have adjusted gross income below $76,200 for single filers and $121,850 for married couples. (These maximum income levels are adjusted annually.)

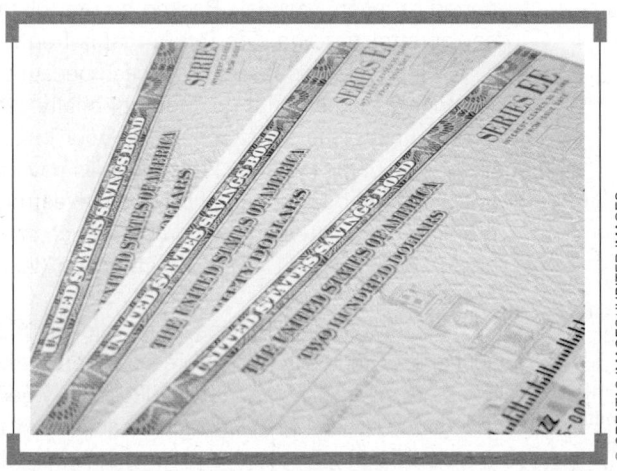

© CREATAS IMAGES/JUPITER IMAGES

▌▌ Concept Check

CHECK • CONCEPT CHECK • CONCEPT CHECK • CONCEPT CHECK • CONCEPT CHECK • CONCEPT CHECK • CONCEPT CHECK • CONCEPT

4-17	In general, how much of your annual income should you save in the form of liquid reserves? What portion of your investment portfolio should you keep in savings and other short-term investment vehicles? Explain.
4-18	Define and distinguish between the *nominal (stated) rate of interest* and the *effective rate of interest.* Explain why a savings and loan association that pays a nominal rate of 4.5 percent interest, compounded daily, actually pays an effective rate of 4.6 percent.
4-19	What factors determine the amount of interest you will earn on a deposit account? Which combination provides the best return?
4-20	Briefly describe the basic features of each of the following savings vehicles: (a) certificates of deposit, (b) U.S. Treasury bills, and (c) Series EE bonds.

SUMMARY

LG1 Understand the role of cash management in the personal financial planning process. Cash management plays a vital role in personal financial planning. It involves the administration and control of liquid assets—cash, checking accounts, savings, and other short-term investment vehicles. With good cash management practices, you'll have the necessary funds to cover your expenses and establish a regular savings program.

LG2 Describe today's financial services marketplace, both depository and nondepository financial institutions. Today's financial services marketplace is highly competitive and offers consumers expanded product offerings at attractive prices. Individuals and families continue to rely heavily on traditional depository financial institutions such as commercial banks, S&Ls, savings banks, and credit unions for most of their financial services needs. Nondepository financial institutions also offer some banking services such as credit cards and money market fund accounts with check-writing privileges. You should make sure your bank has federal deposit insurance and is financially sound. Most traditional depository institutions are federally insured for up to $100,000 per depositor name.

LG3 Select the checking, savings, electronic banking, and other bank services that meet your needs. Financial institutions provide a variety of accounts to help you manage your cash: regular checking accounts, savings accounts, and interest-paying checking accounts, such as NOW accounts, money market deposit accounts, and money market mutual funds. Asset management accounts offered by brokerage firms and mutual funds combine checking, investment, and borrowing activities and pay higher interest on deposits than do other more traditional checking accounts. Financial institutions also provide other money management services. Electronic funds transfer systems (EFTSs) use telecommunications and computer technology to electronically transfer funds. Popular EFTS services include debit cards, ATMs, preauthorized deposits and payments, bank-by-phone accounts, and online banking and bill-paying services. Today many banks also provide safe-deposit boxes, which serve as a storage place for valuables, important documents, and trust services.

LG4 Open and use a checking account. A checking account is a convenient way to hold cash and pay for goods and services. The sharp increase in bank service charges makes it important to evaluate different types of checking accounts and their service charges, minimum balance requirements, and other fees. You should understand how to write and endorse checks, make deposits, keep good checking account records, prevent overdrafts, and stop payment on checks. The account reconciliation, or checkbook balancing, process confirms the accuracy of your account records and monthly bank statement. Other special types of checks you may use occasionally include cashier's, traveler's, and certified checks.

LG5 Calculate the interest earned on your money using compound interest and future value techniques. Once you know the interest rate, frequency of compounding, and how the bank determines the balance on which interest is paid, you can calculate how much interest you'll earn on your money. Compound interest is the same as future value. Use future value and future value of an annuity formulas to find out how your savings will grow. The more often interest is compounded, the greater the effective rate for a given nominal rate of interest. Most banks use the actual balance, or day of deposit to day of withdrawl method to determine which balances qualify to earn interest; this is the most accurate and fairest method for depositors.

LG6 Develop a savings strategy that incorporates a variety of savings plans. Your savings strategy should include establishing a regular pattern of saving with liquid reserves of 3 to 6 months of after-tax income. The choice of savings products depends on your needs, your risk preference, the length of time you can leave money on deposit, and current and expected rates of interest. You may wish to put some of your savings into vehicles that pay a higher rate of interest than savings or NOW accounts, such as certificates of deposit, U.S. Treasury bills, and Series EE bonds.

FINANCIAL PLANNING EXERCISES

LG2, 3, 4

1. What type of bank serves your needs best? Visit the Web sites of the following institutions and prepare a chart comparing the services offered, such as traditional and online banking, investment services, and personal financial advice. Which one would you choose to patronize, and why?
   a. Bank of America (**http://www.bankofamerica.com**)—a nationwide full-service bank
   b. A leading local commercial bank in your area
   c. A local savings institution
   d. A local credit union

LG3

2. Suppose that someone stole your ATM card and withdrew $650 from your checking account. How much money could you lose according to federal legislation if you reported the stolen card to the bank: (a) the day the card was stolen, (b) 6 days after the theft, (c) 65 days after receiving your periodic statement?

LG2, 3, 4

3. You're getting married and are unhappy with your present bank. Discuss your strategy for choosing a new bank and opening an account. Consider the factors that are important to you in selecting a bank—such as the type and ownership of new accounts and bank fees and charges.

LG4

4. Determine the annual net cost of these checking accounts:
   a. Monthly fee $5, check-processing fee of 25 cents, average of 19 checks written per month
   b. Annual interest of 2.5 percent paid if balance exceeds $750, $8 monthly fee if account falls below minimum balance, average monthly balance $815, account falls below $750 during 4 months

LG4

5. *Use Worksheet 4.1.* Javier Rodriguez has a NOW account at the Third State Bank. His checkbook ledger lists the following checks:

Check Number	Amount
654	$206.05
658	55.22
662	103.00
668	99.00
670	6.10
671	50.25
672	24.90
673	32.45
674	44.50
675	30.00
676	30.00
677	111.23
678	38.04
679	97.99
680	486.70
681	43.50
682	75.00
683	98.50

Javier also made the following withdrawals and deposits at an ATM near his home:

Date	Amount	Transaction
11/1	$50.00	withdrawal
11/2	$525.60	deposit
11/6	$100.00	deposit
11/14	$75.00	withdrawal
11/21	$525.60	deposit
11/24	$150.00	withdrawal
11/27	$225.00	withdrawal
11/30	$400.00	deposit

Javier's checkbook ledger shows an ending balance of $286.54. He has just received his bank statement for the month of November. It shows an ending balance of $622.44; it also shows that he had earned interest for November of $3.28, a check service charge of $8 for the month, and another $12 charge for a returned check. His bank statement indicates the following checks have cleared: 654, 662, 672, 674, 675, 676, 677, 678, 679, and 681. ATM withdrawals on 11/1 and 11/14 and deposits on 11/2 and 11/6 have cleared; no other checks or ATM activities are listed on his statement, so anything remaining should be treated as outstanding. Use a checking account reconciliation form like the one in Worksheet 4.1 to reconcile Javier's checking account.

LG5, 6

6. If you put $5,000 in a savings account that pays interest at the rate of 4 percent, compounded annually, how much will you have in 5 years? (*Hint:* Use the *future value* formula.) How much interest will you earn during the 5 years? If you put $5,000 *each* year into a savings account that pays interest at the rate of 4 percent a year, how much would you have after 5 years?

LG5, 6

7. Bill and Betty Jacobs together earn approximately $42,000 a year after taxes. Through an inheritance and some wise investing, they also have an investment portfolio with a value of almost $90,000.
   a. How much of their annual income do you recommend they hold in some form of liquid savings as reserves? Explain.
   b. How much of their investment portfolio do you recommend they hold in savings and other short-term investment vehicles? Explain.
   c. How much, in total, should they hold in short-term liquid assets?

APPLYING PERSONAL FINANCE

Manage Your Cash!

What difference does it make where you keep your money? The returns are so low on checking and savings accounts that you certainly won't grow rich on their earnings! It's no wonder that many people tend to overlook the importance of managing their cash and liquid assets. This project will help you evaluate your cash management needs and the various financial service providers available so that you can select the one best suited to your needs.

First, spend some time making a list of your needs and preferences. Do you like to visit your banking institution in person, or would you rather do your banking electronically or by mail? Is a high yield important to you, or is your typical balance usually pretty low so that any earnings would be minimal? What other services might you need, such as a safe-deposit box, brokerage account, trust services, or financial and estate planning?

Next, go back through this chapter and review all the types of financial institutions and the services they provide. Then beside each need on your list, write down the institutions that would best meet that need. Is there one banking institution that would meet all your needs, or do you think you'd need several? After identifying the type or types that are appropriate for you, survey your community via the phone book, interviews with finance professionals, and other methods to identify the various financial institutions in your area. Look beyond your area as well, and consider what services are available over the Internet or from other regions of the country. Make a list of your top choices and find out more information concerning their services, products, and fees charged to help you decide where you'd like to do business. Bring your findings to class to compare and discuss with your classmates.

CRITICAL THINKING CASES

LG4, 5, 6

4.1 Amy Chan's Savings and Banking Plans

Amy Chan is a registered nurse who earns $3,250 per month after taxes. She has been reviewing her savings strategies and current banking arrangements to determine if she should make any changes. Amy has a regular checking account that charges her a flat fee per month, writes an average of 18 checks a month, and carries an average balance of $795 (although it has fallen below $750 during 3 months of the past year). Her only other account is a money market deposit account with a balance of $4,250. She tries to make regular monthly deposits of $50 to $100 into her money market account but has done so only about every other month.

Of the many checking accounts Amy's bank offers, here are the three that best suit her needs:

- *Regular checking, per-item plan:* $3 per month service charge plus 35 cents per check.
- *Regular checking, flat fee plan (the one Amy currently has):* Monthly fee of $7 regardless of how many checks written. With either of these regular checking accounts, she can avoid any charges by keeping a minimum daily balance of $750.
- *Interest checking:* Monthly service charge of $7; interest of 3 percent, compounded daily (refer to Exhibit 4.9). With a minimum balance of $1,500, the monthly charge is waived.

Amy's bank also offers certificates of deposit for a minimum deposit of $500; the current annual interest rates are 3.5 percent for 6 months, 3.75 percent for 1 year, and 4 percent for 2 years.

Critical Thinking Questions

1. Calculate the annual cost of each of the three accounts, assuming that Amy's banking habits remain the same. Which plan would you recommend and why?
2. Should Amy consider opening the interest checking account and increasing her minimum balance to at least $1,500 to avoid service charges? Explain your answer.
3. What other advice would you give Amy about her checking account and savings strategy?

LG4

4.2. Reconciling the Pattersons' Checking Account

Mike and Jennifer Patterson opened their first checking account at the American Bank on September 14, 2007. They've just received their first bank statement for the period ending October 5, 2007. The statement and checkbook ledger are shown in the following table.

Critical Thinking Questions

1. From this information, prepare a bank reconciliation for the Pattersons as of October 5, 2007, using a form like the one in Worksheet 4.1.
2. Given your answer to Question 1, what, if any, adjustments will the Pattersons need to make in their checkbook ledger? Comment on the procedures used to reconcile their checking account and their findings.
3. If the Pattersons earned interest on their idle balances because the account is a money market deposit account, what impact would this have on the reconciliation process? Explain.

MIKE & JENNIFER PATTERSON 2128 E. 51ST ST. DETROIT, MICHIGAN				THE AMERICAN BANK 800-000-0000 STATEMENT PERIOD SEPT. 6 – OCT 5, 2007
	Opening Balance	**Total Deposits for Period**	**Total Checks/Withdrawls for Period**	**Ending Balance**
	$ 0.00	$569.25	$473.86	$95.39
Date	**Withdrawls (Debits)**			**Deposits (Credits)**	**Balance**
Sept .14				$360.00	$360.00
Sept .15				97.00	457.00
Sept. 25	$45.20			9.25	421.05
Oct. 1				103.00	524.05
Oct. 1	3.00 BC				521.05
Oct. 4	65.90	$49.76	$45.00		360.39
Oct. 5	265.00				95.39

RT=Returned Check   DM=Debit Memo   BC=Bank Charges
FC=Finance Charges   CM=Credit Memo

Checkbook Ledger

Check Number	Date 2007	Details	✓	Check Amount	Deposit Amount	Account Balance
—	Sept. 14	Cash—gift from wedding			$360.00	$360.00
—	Sept. 15	Mike's wages from library			97.00	457.00
101	Sept. 24	Kroger's—groceries		$45.20		411.80
102	Sept. 27	Mich. Bell Telephone bill		28.40		383.40
—	Oct. 1	Mike's wages from library			103.00	486.40
103	Oct. 1	Univ. Bk. Sto.—college books		65.90		420.50
104	Oct. 1	Kmart—sewing material		16.75		403.75
105	Oct. 1	G. Heller—apartment rent		265.00		138.75
106	Oct. 2	Blue Cross—health insurance		17.25		121.50
107	Oct. 3	Kroger's—groceries		49.76		71.74
108	Oct. 4	Cash: gas, entertain., laundry		45.00		26.74
—	Oct. 5	Jennifer's salary—BDM Corp.			450.00	476.74

 MONEY ONLINE www.thomsonedu.com/finance/gitman

NLINE • MONEY ONLINE • MONEY ONLINE • MONEY ONLINE • MONEY ONLINE • MONEY ONLINE • MONEY ONLINE • MONEY ONLINE •

Visit **http://www.thomsonedu.com/finance/gitman** for some additional Web-based exercises and hot links (with annotations) to a variety of resources relevant to the topics covered in this chapter.

Making Automobile and Housing Decisions

LEARNING GOALS

LG1 · BUYING AN AUTOMOBILE

Buying an automobile is probably the first major expenditure many of us make. The car purchase is second only to housing in the amount of money the typical consumer spends. Because you'll buy a car many times during your life—most people buy one every 2 to 5 years—a systematic approach to selecting and financing a vehicle can mean significant savings. Before making any major purchase, whether it's a car, house, or large appliance, consider some basic guidelines to wise purchasing decisions.

- *Research* your purchase thoroughly, considering not only the market but also your personal needs.
- *Select* the best item for your needs.
- *Buy* the item after negotiating the best price and arranging financing on favorable terms. Be sure you understand all the terms of the sale before signing any contracts.
- *Maintain* your purchase and make necessary repairs promptly.

Exhibit 5.1 summarizes the steps in the car-buying process.

Choosing a Car

Sport utility vehicle (SUV) or pickup truck? Sedan, convertible, or coupe? Hybrid, diesel, or gas? Car buyers today have more choices than ever before, so more than one category of

EXHIBIT 5.1   10 Steps to Buying a Car

These 10 steps summarize the car-buying process discussed in this chapter.

1. Analyze how much car can you afford.
2. Choose the best way to pay for your new car—cash, financing, or lease. Consult your insurance agent to learn the annual premium on various cars. Those with high premiums are likely popular with thieves, have poor crash worthiness, or are considered sports cars likely to be driven more aggressively.
3. Select the right car for you in terms of size, performance, safety, and styling. Choose at least three "target cars" to consider buying.
4. Decide on a price based on dealer's cost for the car and options, plus a markup for the dealer's profit, minus rebates and incentives.
5. Test-drive the car at least once, both on local streets and on highways.
6. Get a used car inspected by a qualified independent mechanic.
7. Decide whether to trade in your used car or sell it yourself.
8. Begin negotiations with three or more dealers as necessary. Hold firm on your target price before closing the deal.
9. Review and sign contracts with the dealer's finance manager, avoiding pressure to buy unnecessary extras.
10. Consider alternate buying strategies such as Internet buying services, or faxing your offer to local dealerships for competitive bids.

Source: Adapted from Phil Read, "10 Steps to Buying a New Car: What Everyone Should Know," Edmunds.com, http://www.edmunds.com/advice.

vehicle may be of interest. A good way to start your research is by tapping into the many available sources of information about cars, their prices, features, and reliability. Industry resources include manufacturers' brochures and dealer personnel. Car magazines, such as *Car and Driver, Motor Trend,* and *Road and Track,* and consumer magazines, such as *Consumer Reports* and *Consumer Guide,* regularly compare and rate cars. In addition, *Consumer Reports* and *Kiplinger's Personal Finance* magazine publish annual buying guides that include comparative statistics and ratings on most domestic and foreign cars. Kiplinger's Personal Finanace also has an online Car Finder at **http://www.kiplinger.com/personalfinance/ tools/carfinder/.** *Consumer Reports* includes information on used cars in its guide, and offers a fee-based service called *Consumer Reports* Auto Price Service at **http://www.consumerreports .org/main/ aps/reports/questions.jsp,** that provides the list price and dealer cost on a new car, and its available options.

The Internet has made it especially easy to do your homework before ever setting foot in a dealer's showroom. In addition to finding online versions of automotive magazines, you can visit one of the many comprehensive Web sites for car shoppers, offering pricing and model information, as well as links to other useful sites. Don't forget the Web sites of the automobile companies themselves; for example, General Motors is online at **http://www .gm.com,** Toyota is at **http://www.toyota.com,** and so on. Once you've done the research, you'll be in a better position to negotiate with the dealer. (The *Money in Action* box on page 134 explores the online world of car buying.)

Although the main reason for buying a car is to have transportation, automobiles can also be viewed as status symbols, purchased as part of a hobby, or used as an investment. Whatever your motive, it's important to evaluate all of the following areas before buying a car. Knowing what you want and can afford before purchasing either a new or used car will prevent a slick auto salesperson from talking you into buying a car you don't need.

Affordability

Before shopping for a car, determine how much you can afford to spend. You'll need to calculate two numbers unless you can pay cash for the entire cost of the car:

- **Amount of down payment:** This money will come from savings, so be sure not to deplete your emergency fund.

CLICKING THE TIRES

Buying a new car is exciting—researching different types of cars and test driving the ones you like. Negotiating the deal can be more of a hassle. But now you can do much of your searching—and perhaps even buy the car—online.

Online research is increasingly popular; about 67 percent of car buyers do at least some Internet research before heading to the showroom, and 50 percent of new-car buyers said the Internet helped them decide which make/model to buy, according to the J.D. Power and Associates 2004 New Auto-shopper.com study.

One option for online car shopping, the manufacturer's Web site, is good for detailed information on the models. Another option, using independent Web sites, is best for pricing information. Most independent Web sites are comprehensive and include comparative information on new and used cars, reviews, notices of current rebates and incentives, and financing and insurance information. Sometimes you can even advertise your current car for sale.

Some independent Web sites, such as Edmunds (**http://www.edmunds.com**), Kelley Blue Book, (**http://www.kbb.com**), and Autobytel (**http://www.autobytel.com**), connect you to dealers in your area who then contact you by phone or e-mail. Dealers in turn pay the Web sites for the referrals. Other independent Web sites operate differently. AutoNation (**http://www.autonation.com**) owns dealerships and sells vehicles from its inventory, so much of the car-buying process is handled online. CarsDirect (**http://www.carsdirect.com**) has agreements with dealers to offer guaranteed price quotes, but you must go to the dealer to complete the transaction. A newcomer to online car buying, PriceGrabber.com (**http://www.pricegrabber.com**), offers a reverse auction. After you submit a request for a particular car, dealers bid against one another for a specified time. The dealer with the lowest bid at the end of the auction gets your contact information.

When shopping online, be aware that sometimes car-buying services don't deliver on their promises. Dealers may not contact you with a quote, or the price may change when you go to finalize the transaction. To get the best deal, visit several Web sites. Don't overlook your local dealers—they may match or beat the Internet offers.

Critical Thinking Questions

1. How has the Internet changed the way people buy cars? What key benefits does it offer?
2. Describe four methods of getting a price quote for a car.
3. What are the potential drawbacks to buying a car online?

Sources: Bob Tedeschi, "The World Wide Web Is Emerging as a Powerful Force in Car Sales, with Benefits for Manufacturers and Buyers," *New York Times*, September 16, 2002, p. C.5; Lisa Kalis and Dana White, "Kicking the Tires, from Afar and Online," *New York Times*, August 13, 2004, p. F10; Mark K. Solheim, "No-Hassle Car Buying," *Kiplinger's Personal Finance Magazine*, November 2005, p. 130.

- **Size of the monthly loan payment you can afford:** Analyze your available resources—for example, your other expenses, including housing—and your transportation requirements. Don't forget to include insurance. Your monthly car payment should be no more than 20 percent of your monthly net income.

Crunching the Numbers. You can also use the down payment and monthly payment amount to back into the total amount you can afford for a car. For example, suppose that you have $3,000 for a down payment, can pay $500 a month, and your bank is offering 4-year (48-month) car loans at 6 percent annual (6%/12 = 0.5 percent, monthly) interest. How much of a loan can you afford? Using a calculator and keystrokes shown in the margin, you'll find that you can pay off a loan of about $21,300. Add that to the $3,000 down payment, and you'll be able to afford a car costing $24,300. It pays to shop around for loans because their rates can differ by as much as 2 percent!

Operating Costs

The out-of-pocket cost of operating an automobile includes not only car payments but also insurance, license, fuel, oil, tires, and other operating and maintenance outlays. Some of these costs are *fixed* regardless of how much you drive; others are *variable*, depending on

CALCULATOR

INPUTS	FUNCTIONS
48	N
.5	I
500	PMT
	CPT
	PV
	Solution
	21,290.16

See Appendix E for details.

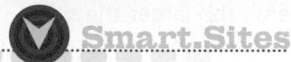

depreciation The loss in the value of an asset such as an automobile that occurs over its period of ownership; calculated as the difference between the price initially paid and the subsequent sale price.

the number of miles you drive. The biggest fixed cost is likely to be the *installment payments* associated with the loan or lease used to acquire the car; the biggest variable cost will probably be fuel.

Another purchase cost is **depreciation,** which is the loss in value that occurs over its period of ownership. In effect, depreciation is the difference between the price you paid for the car and what you can sell it for. If you paid $20,000 for an automobile that can be sold 3 years later for $14,000, the car will cost you $6,000 in depreciation. Although depreciation may not be a recurring out-of-pocket cost, it's an important operating expense that shouldn't be overlooked.

Gas, Diesel, or Hybrid?

Given today's high fuel prices, it's important to determine the type of fuel you prefer. If you're a "green" who's concerned about the environmental impact of the fuel your car uses, you may be interested only in a hybrid car. In this case, price differences may not matter. Although you'll want to consider fuel economy when car shopping, comparable gas-fueled, internal combustion engines and diesel-powered cars have similar fuel economy. Generally diesels are a bit noisier, have less acceleration and more power, and have longer engine lives than traditional gas-powered cars do.

Hybrids, which blend gas and battery power, have experienced rapid sales growth due to high gas prices and improved technology and availability. Although they're more economical and less polluting than gas- and diesel-powered vehicles, hybrids do have some disadvantages: high cost of battery replacement, more sluggish acceleration, generally higher repair costs, and typically higher initial purchase price. Clearly it's important to consider the differences between the costs and performance of differently fueled vehicles and decide on the vehicle you want before shopping for a specific new or used car.

New, Used, or "Nearly New"?

One decision you must make is whether to buy a new, used, or "nearly new" car. If you can't afford to buy a new car, the decision is made for you. Some people who can afford to buy a new car choose to buy a used car so they can have a better model—a used luxury car such as a BMW, Lexus, or Mercedes—rather than a less-expensive brand of new car such as a Chevrolet. With the increasing popularity of used cars, car dealers are trying to dispel the negative image associated with buying a used, or "pre-owned," car. You'll find used cars advertised in local or nearby city newspapers, publications like *AutoTrader,* and their Web sites. These provide an excellent source of information on used cars for sale. Exhibit 5.2 on page 136 offers advice for buying a used car.

Once you know what you want, shop at these places:

- **Franchise dealerships:** Offer the latest-model used cars, provide financing, and will negotiate on price. Be sure to research values before shopping.
- **Superstores:** AutoNation, CarMax, and similar dealers offer no-haggle pricing and a large selection. They certify cars and may offer a limited short-term warranty. May cost slightly more than at a dealer who will negotiate.
- **Independent used car lots:** Usually offer older (4 to 6 years) cars and have lower overhead than franchise dealers do. No industry standards, so be sure to check with the Better Business Bureau before buying.
- **Private individuals:** Generally cost less because there's no dealer overhead; may have maintenance records. Be sure seller has title to car.

Size, Body Style, and Features

Your first consideration should be what type of car you need. More than one style category may work for you. For example, a family of five can buy a mid-size or full-size sedan, station wagon, minivan, or compact or full-size SUV. When considering size, body style,

EXHIBIT 5.2   Don't Get Taken for a Ride

Thinking of buying a used car? Consider both advantages and disadvantages. Some *advantages* are

1. It's less expensive than a comparable new car, and the recent popularity of short-term car leases has increased the availability of late-model, attractively priced used cars.
2. It won't depreciate in value as quickly as a new car—purchasing a used car less than 18 months old often means saving the 20 to 25 percent depreciation in value typically experienced during the first 12 to 18 months of a car's life.
3. Because used cars are less expensive, buyers don't have to put down as much money as they would for a new car.
4. Today's used cars are more reliable. The quality and durability of well-maintained 2- to 4-year-old cars makes them more reliable and less expensive to maintain than the new cars of 10 years ago.
5. The *federal odometer disclosure law,* requiring sellers to give buyers a signed statement attesting that the mileage shown on the odometer of their used cars is accurate, protects consumers. Penalties for violating this law are stringent.

The main *disadvantage* of buying a used car is uncertainty about its mechanical condition. It might look good and have low mileage, but it could still have mechanical problems requiring future maintenance and repair expenditures. Having your prospective used car purchase checked by a reputable mechanic or independent inspection service is money well spent and could save you hundreds of dollars and much aggravation later on.

Smart Sites

IntelliChoice rates the certified pre-owned vehicle programs of manufacturers' dealers according to their inspection lists, warranties, title verification, availability of special financing, roadside assistance benefits, and return/exchange policies. Go to their Web site through **http://www .thomsonedu.com/finance/ gitman.**

and features, think about your needs, likes, and dislikes as well as the cost. In most cases there's a direct relationship between size and cost: In general, the larger the car, the more expensive it will be to purchase and to operate. Also consider performance, handling, appearance, fuel economy, reliability, repair problems, and the resale value of the car. And don't try to adapt your needs to fit the car you want—a two-passenger sports car may not be appropriate if you need the car for business or if you have children.

By listing all options you want before shopping for a new car, you can avoid paying for features you really don't need. Literally hundreds of options are available, ranging in price from a few dollars up to $2,000 or more, including automatic transmission, a bigger engine, air conditioning, high-performance brakes, a CD player, clock, power windows, power seats, electric door locks, leather seats, navigation systems, a rear window defroster, and special suspension. Some appearance-related options are two-tone or metallic paint, electric sunroof, special tires, sport wheels, and various interior and exterior trim packages.

Most cars have at least some options, but you can select additional optional features that provide a broad range of conveniences and luxuries—for a price. On new cars, a window sticker details each option and its price, but on a used car only close observation serves to determine the options. Window stickers quite often list standard features that might be considered optional on other models, and vice versa. When shopping for a new car, it's important to be sure that you're comparing comparably equipped models.

Reliability and Warranties

Assess the *reliability* of a car by talking with friends who own similar cars and reading objective assessments published by consumer magazines and buying guides such as *Consumer Reports.* Study the *warranty* offered by new car manufacturers, comparing those for cars that interest you. Significant differences may exist. Be sure to read the warranty booklet included with a new car to understand the warranty terms. Most warranties are void if the owner has not performed routine maintenance or has somehow abused the car.

On new cars, the manufacturer guarantees the general reliability and quality of construction of the vehicle for a specified period in a written warranty, obligating it to repair or replace, at little or no cost to the owner, any defective parts and/or flaws in workmanship. Today, most new car warranties cover a minimum of the first 3 years of ownership or 36,000 miles, whichever comes first, and some provide coverage for as long as 7 years or 70,000 miles. However, most warranties have limitations; for example, longer warranty periods may apply to only the engine and drive train. Auto manufacturers and private insurers also sell extended warranties and service contracts, sometimes called "buyer protection plans." Most experts consider these unnecessary and not worth their cost, given the relatively long initial warranty periods now being offered by most manufacturers.

Other Considerations

Here are some other considerations regarding affordability:

© STONE/GETTY IMAGES

- **Trading in or selling your existing car:** Although trading in is convenient, it's generally more financially advantageous to sell your old car outright. If you're willing to take the time, you can usually sell your car for more than the wholesale price typically offered by a dealer on a trade-in.
- **Fuel economy:** The *Environmental Protection Agency (EPA) mileage ratings* are especially useful on new vehicles, which carry a sticker indicating the number of miles per gallon each model is expected to get (as determined through EPA tests) for both city and highway driving. You can check out those ratings at **http://www.fueleconomy.gov.**
- **Safety features:** These features are likely to be similar in new cars due to government regulations, but older used cars may not have some features such as side-impact airbags. Don't forget to include *auto insurance costs,* which vary depending on make, model, safety features, and other factors (and are discussed in detail in Chapter 10).

The Purchase Transaction

Once you've determined what you can afford to spend and the features you desire, you're ready to begin car shopping. If you plan to buy a new car, visit all dealers with cars that meet your requirements. Look the cars over and ask questions—but don't make any offers until you've found two or three cars with the desired features that are priced within your budget. Also, if you can be flexible about the model and options you want, you can sometimes negotiate a better deal than if you're determined to have a particular model and options. Make an appointment to test-drive the cars you're interested in. Drive—then leave! You need time to evaluate the car yourself, without pressure to buy from the salesperson.

Comparison shopping is essential, because a dealer selling the same brand as another may give you a better deal. Be aware of the sales technique called *low-balling,* where the salesperson quotes a low price for the car to get you to make an offer, and then negotiates the price upward prior to your signing the sales contract. Exhibit 5.3 on page 138 lists some other factors to consider once you begin looking at cars.

Because low-balling, price haggling, and other high-pressure sales tactics can make car buying an unpleasant experience, many dealers have refocused their sales practices to emphasize customer satisfaction. Some manufacturers offer firm prices, so if you buy today, you can be sure that no one will get a better deal tomorrow. However, you should still research prices, as described in the next section, because a firm selling price doesn't guarantee the lowest cost.

Negotiating Price

Choosing among various makes, models, and options can make comparisons difficult, so the price you pay for a car, whether new or used, can vary widely. The more you narrow your choices to a particular car, the easier it is to get price quotes from dealers to make an "apples to apples" comparison.

The "sticker price" on a new car represents the manufacturer's *suggested retail price* for that particular car with its listed options. This price means very little. The key to negotiating a good price is knowing the *dealer's cost* for the car. The easiest and quickest way to find the dealer's invoice cost is going to the Edmunds and Kelley Blue Book Web sites mentioned in the *Money in Action* box on page 134, or by checking car-buying guides available at your library or bookstore.

EXHIBIT 5.3   Kicking the Tires

Start your examination of a car with an inspection of key points. Don't overlook the obvious:

- *How easy is it to get people and things into and out of the car?*
  Do the doors open easily?
  Is the trunk large enough for your needs?
  Does the car offer a pass-through or fold-down rear seat for larger items?
- *Comfort and visibility:*
  Are the seats comfortable?
  Can you adjust the driver's seat and steering wheel properly?
  What are the car's blind spots for a person of your height?
  Can you see all the gauges clearly?
  Can you reach the controls for the radio, CD player, heater, air conditioner, and other features easily while driving?
  Does it have the options you want?

Then take the car for a test drive.

- Set aside at least 20 minutes and drive it on highways and local roads.
- To test acceleration, merge into traffic getting onto the freeway and try passing another car.
- If possible, drive home and make sure the car fits into your garage—especially if you're interested in a larger SUV or truck!
- For a used car, test the heater and air conditioner. Then turn the fan off and listen for any unusual engine noises.
- Check out overall handling. Parallel park, make a U-turn, brake hard, and so on. Do the gears shift smoothly? If testing a standard transmission, try to determine if the clutch is engaging too high or too low, which might indicate excessive wear or a problem.

As soon as you return to the car lot, take notes on how well the car handled and how comfortable you felt driving it. This is especially important if you are testing several cars.

Before making an offer, prepare a worksheet with the cost versus the list price for the exact car you want. This will help you avoid high-pressure salesmanship and paying for options you don't want or need. Try to negotiate the lowest acceptable markup (3 to 4 percent for cars priced under $20,000; 6 to 7 percent for higher-priced models), push for a firm quote, and make it clear that you are comparison shopping. Don't let the salesperson pressure you into signing a sales contract or leaving a deposit until you're sure that you have negotiated the best deal. Good cost information will improve your bargaining position and possibly allow you to negotiate a price that is only several hundred dollars above the dealer's cost.

To research used car prices, you can check one of the popular price guides—the National Automobile Dealers Association (NADA) *Official Used Car Guide,* the *Kelley Blue Book,* or *Edmund's Used Car Prices*—available on the Internet or at your library or bank, and in the classified ads in your local newspaper.

If you want to avoid negotiating entirely, you can buy your car through a buying service, either by phone or over the Internet. These include independent companies, such as AutoVantage, Autobytel, AutoWeb, and Nationwide Auto Brokers, or services offered through credit unions, motor clubs, and discount warehouses such as Costco. Buying services work in a variety of ways. They may have an arrangement with a network of dealers to sell cars at a predetermined price above invoice, provide you with competitive bids from several local dealers, find the car you want and negotiate the price with the dealer, or place an order with the factory for a made-to-order car. The price for these services ranges from about $50 for a Costco membership to as much as $600, and results vary. You'll get a good price through a service—although you can't assume that it will be the best price.

Indifferent to race and gender, the Internet is leveling the car-buying playing field for women and minorities. The Internet's primary advantage for buyers is that subtle clues that might tip off the dealer to inflate the price—such as how much jewelry you wear, or what your body language is like—aren't visible.

It's best not to discuss your plan to finance the purchase or the value of your trade-in until you've settled the question of price. These should be separate issues. Salespeople will typically want to find out how much you can afford monthly and then offer financing deals with payments close to that amount. In the case of trade-ins, the dealer might offer you a good price for your old car and raise the price of the new car to compensate. The dealer may offer financing terms that sound attractive, but be sure to compare them with the cost of bank loans. Sometimes dealers increase the price of the car to make up for a low interest rate, or attractive financing may apply only to certain models. If you're interested in dealer financing, make sure the monthly payment quoted by the dealer's finance manager is just for the loan. Learn and compare the annual percentage rate (APR) with the rate quoted on a bank loan. Often financing charges include unneeded extras such as credit life insurance, accident insurance, an extended warranty, or a service package.

Manufacturers and dealers often offer buyers special incentives, such as rebates and cut-rate financing, particularly when car sales are slow. (Deduct rebates from the dealer's cost when you negotiate price.) You may have a choice between a rebate and low-cost financing. To determine which is the better deal, calculate the difference between the monthly payments on a market-rate bank loan and the special dealer loan for the same term. Multiply the payment difference by the loan maturity, in months, and compare it with the rebate. For example, assume the dealer offers either a $1,000 rebate or a 5 percent interest rate on a $10,000, 4-year loan. Your monthly payments would be $230 with dealer financing and $254 on a 10 percent bank loan with similar terms. The payment savings over the life of the loan are $1,152 ($24 per month × 48 months), which is greater than the $1,000 rebate. In this case you would be better off with the 5 percent loan.

Closing the Deal

Whether you're buying a new or used car, to make a legally binding offer you must sign a **sales contract** that specifies the offering price and all the conditions of your offer. The sales contract also specifies whether the offer includes a trade-in. If it does, the offering price will include both the payment amount and the trade-in allowance. Because this agreement contractually binds you to purchase the car at the offering price, be sure that you want and can afford the car before signing this agreement. To show that you're making an offer in good faith, you may be required to include a deposit of around $200 or more with the contract.

Once the dealer accepts your offer, you complete the purchase transaction and take delivery of the car. If you're not paying cash for the car, you can arrange financing through the dealer, at your bank, a credit union, or a consumer finance company. The key aspects of these types of installment loans, which can be quickly negotiated if your credit is good, are discussed in Chapter 7. Prior to delivery, the dealer is responsible for cleaning the car and installing any optional equipment. It's a good idea to make sure that all equipment you are paying for has been installed and that the car is ready for use before paying the dealer. When you pay, you should receive a title or appropriate evidence that you own the car.

Trade in Your Loan

Refinancing your auto loan can pay off—but only under particular circumstances. First, you need to have enough equity in the car to serve as collateral for what is essentially a used car loan. If you made a large down payment, or are well into a loan, you may be a candidate for refinancing. If you can cut your interest rate by at least two percentage points, without stretching the final payment date of your current loan, you could enjoy substantial savings.

Banks generally aren't interested in refinancing car loans, so online lenders such as E-Loan (**http://www.eloan.com**) and HSBC Auto Finance (**http://www.hsbcusa-autoloans.com**) get most of the business. If you're a member of a credit union, see what it can do for you.

sales contract An agreement to purchase an automobile that states the offering price and all conditions of the offer; when signed by the buyer and seller, the contract legally binds them to its terms.

Consider tapping a home equity line of credit if you own a home to pay off a high-interest auto loan. Unlike consumer loans, the interest paid on a home equity loan is tax deductible. Wherever you choose to refinance, you'll probably have to pay $5 to $50 for a title change listing the new lien holder. And forget about refinancing your auto loan if you have bad credit.

Traditionally, car loans extended 3 or 4 years, but loan terms are lengthening as buyers stretch to afford cars and SUVs that can top $40,000 or even $50,000. These loans typically carry higher interest rates—the average rate for a 4-year loan is about 6.5 percent compared with about 8 percent for a 72-month loan—than for shorter maturities, but monthly payments are lower. So far only a handful of banks and credit unions are offering 8-year loans, but many now offer 7-year loans. Today, 6-year loans account for about 30 percent of all new car loans, up from about 20 percent just 5 years ago. Long-term loans are most commonly used to buy high-end luxury vehicles and are not available for all vehicles. By the end of the loan term, you'll still be making payments on a vehicle that has used up most of its life and is practically worthless, a major downside of longer-term car loans.

▌▌ Concept Check

CHECK • CONCEPT CHECK • CONCEPT CHECK • CONCEPT CHECK • CONCEPT CHECK • CONCEPT CHECK • CONCEPT CHECK • CONCEPT

5-1 Briefly discuss how each of these purchase considerations would affect your choice of a car:

a. Affordability
b. Operating costs
c. Gas, diesel, or hybrid?
d. New, used, or "nearly new"?
e. Size, body style, and features
f. Reliability and warranty protection

5-2 Describe the purchase transaction process, including shopping, negotiating price, and closing the deal on a car.

LG2 LEASING A CAR

Don't worry about temperamental engines or transmissions—just get a new car. Put a small amount down, make easy payments. No wonder leasing is popular, accounting for about 35 percent of all vehicles sold today. When you **lease,** you (the lessee) receive the use of a car in exchange for monthly lease payments over a specified period, usually 2 to 4 years. Leasing appeals to a wide range of car buyers, even though the total cost of leasing is generally more than buying a car with a loan, and at the end of the lease you have nothing. The car—and the money you paid to rent it—is gone. So why do so many car buyers lease their cars? Reasons include rising new car prices, the nondeductibility of consumer loan interest, lower monthly payments, getting a more expensive car for the same monthly payment, and minimizing the down payment to preserve cash.

With all the advertisements promising low monthly lease payments, it's easy to focus on only the payment. Unlike a loan purchase, with a lease you're not paying for the whole car, only its use during a specified period. Leasing is a more complex arrangement than borrowing money to buy a car, and until you understand how leasing works, and compare lease terms with bank financing, you won't know if leasing is the right choice for you.

The Leasing Process

lease An arrangement in which the lessee receives the use of a car (or other asset) in exchange for making monthly lease payments over a specified period.

The first step is the same for leasing and purchasing: research car types and brands, comparison shop at several dealers, and find the car you want at the best price. Don't ask the dealer about leasing or any financing incentives until *after* you've negotiated the final price. Then compare the lease terms offered by the dealer to those of at least one independent leasing firm. As with a purchase, try to negotiate lower lease payments—a payment reduction of $20 a month saves nearly $1,000 on a 4-year lease. And don't reveal what you can afford to pay per month; doing so can lead you to a poor lease deal. Once you agree on leasing terms, be sure to get everything in writing.

About 80 percent of car lessees choose the **closed-end lease,** often called the *walk-away lease,* because at the end of its term you simply turn in the car, assuming that you have neither exceeded the preset mileage limit nor abused the car. This is the dominant type of lease used by consumers. Under the less popular **open-end (or finance) lease,** if the car is worth less than the estimated **residual value**—the remaining value of the car at the end of the lease term—you have to pay the difference. These leases are used primarily for commercial business leasing.

A commonly cited benefit of leasing is the absence of a down payment. However, today most leases require a "capital cost reduction," which is a down payment that lowers the potential depreciation and therefore your monthly lease payments. You may be able to negotiate a lower capital cost reduction or find a lease that doesn't require one.

The lease payment calculation is based on four variables:

1. The **capitalized cost** of the car (the price of the car you are leasing)
2. The forecast *residual value* of the car at the end of the lease
3. The **money factor,** or financing rate on the lease (similar to the interest rate on a loan)
4. The *lease term*

The *depreciation* during the lease term (which is what you are financing) is the capitalized cost minus the residual value. Dividing the sum of the depreciation and the sales tax (on the financed portion only) by the number of months in the lease term and adding the lessor's required monthly return (at the money factor) results in the monthly payment. (To convert the money factor to an annual percentage rate, multiply it by 2400. For example, a money factor of .00450 is the equivalent of paying interest at 10.8 percent on a loan.) The lower the capitalized cost and higher the residual value, the lower your payment. Residual values quoted by different dealers can vary, so check several sources to find the highest residual value to minimize depreciation.

Lease terms typically run 2 to 4 years. Terminating a lease early is often difficult and costly, so be reasonably certain that you can keep the car for the full lease term. The lease contract should outline any costs and additional fees associated with early termination. Early termination clauses also apply to cars that are stolen or totaled in an accident. Some leases require "gap insurance" to cover the lost lease payments that would result from early termination caused by one of these events.

Under most leases, you are responsible for insuring and maintaining the car. At the end of the lease, you are obligated to pay for any "unreasonable wear and tear." A good lease contract should clearly define what is considered unreasonable. In addition, most leases require the lessee to pay a disposition fee of about $150 to $250 when the car is returned.

Most auto leases include a **purchase option** (either a fixed price, the market price at the end of the lease term, or the residual value of the car) that specifies the price at which the lessee can buy the car at the end of the lease term. A lower residual results in a lower purchase price but raises monthly payments. Experts recommend negotiating a fixed-price purchase option, if possible.

The annual mileage allowance—typically, about 10,000 to 15,000 miles per year for the lease term—is another important lease consideration. Usually the lessee must pay between 10 and 25 cents per mile for additional miles. If you expect to exceed the allowable mileage, you would be wise to negotiate a more favorable rate for extra miles before signing the lease contract.

The Lease versus Purchase Analysis

To decide whether it is less costly to lease rather than purchase a car, you need to perform a *lease versus purchase analysis* to compare the total cost of leasing to the total cost of purchasing a car over equal periods. In this analysis, the purchase is assumed to be financed with an installment loan over the same period as the lease.

closed-end lease The most popular form of automobile lease, often called a *walk-away lease* because at the end of its term the lessee simply turns in the car, assuming the preset mileage limit has not been exceeded and the car hasn't been abused.

open-end lease An automobile lease under which the estimated *residual value* of the car is used to determine lease payments; if the car is actually worth less than this value at the end of the lease, the lessee must pay the difference.

residual value The remaining value of a leased car at the end of the lease term.

capitalized cost The price of a car that is being leased.

money factor The financing rate on a lease; similar to the interest rate on a loan.

purchase option A price specified in a lease at which the lessee can buy the car at the end of the lease term.

For example, assume that Mary Dixon is considering either leasing or purchasing a new Toyota Scion xA costing $15,000. The 3-year, closed-end lease she is considering requires a $1,500 down payment (capital cost reduction), a $300 security deposit, and monthly payments of $300, including sales tax. If she purchases the car, she will make a $2,500 down payment and finance the balance with a 3-year, 8 percent loan requiring monthly payments of $392. She will also have to pay 5 percent sales tax ($750) on the purchase, and she expects the car to have a residual value of $8,000 at the end of 3 years. Mary can earn 4 percent interest on her savings with short-term CDs. After filling in Worksheet 5.1, Mary concludes that purchasing is better because its *total cost* of $9,662 is $2,854 less than the $12,516 total cost of leasing—even though the monthly lease payment is $92 lower. Clearly, all else being equal, the least costly alternative is preferred.

Some Web sites can help you with your analysis. Intellichoice's lease area, **http://www.intellichoice.com/lease/finance_page/,** has links to a variety of auto lease deals and information. Or click on the "calculators" tab of Bankrate.com, **http://www.bankrate.com,** and go to the auto calculators section for several calculators to analyze a car purchase, including buy versus lease. You can quickly run several what-if scenarios to compare costs. The average cost per year of either owning or leasing is the highest in the first 2 years. Note also that the average cost of ownership is usually much lower if you own a vehicle for 4 years or more.

If you're fortunate enough to be able to pay cash for your car, you may still want to investigate leasing. Sometimes dealers offer such good lease terms that you can come out ahead by leasing and then investing the money you'd pay for the car. To compare the total cost of a cash purchase, simply take the cost of the car, including sales tax, add to it the opportunity cost of using all cash, and deduct the car's value at the end of the lease or loan period. At 4 percent per year on her savings, Mary's total cost of the car is as follows: $15,750 cost + $1,890 lost interest ($3 \times .04 \times \$15,750$) − $8,000 trade-in value = $9,640. In this case the cost of purchasing the car for cash is about the same as its purchase cost with financing, so Mary could do either.

When the Lease Ends

At the end of the lease, you'll be faced with a major decision. Should you return the car and walk away, or should you buy the car? If you turn in the car and move on to a new model, you may be hit with "excess wear and damage" and "excess mileage" charges and disposition fees. To minimize these, replace worn tires, get repairs done yourself, and document the car's condition before returning it. You may be able to negotiate a lower disposition fee. If you can't return the car without high repair charges or greatly exceeded mileage allowances, you may come out ahead by buying the car.

Whether the purchase option makes sense depends on the residual value. Sometimes, with popular cars, the residual value in your lease agreement is below the car's trade-in value. Buying the car then makes sense. Even if you want a different car, you can exercise the purchase option and sell the car on the open market and net $1,000 or more. If the reverse is true, and the residual is higher than the price of a comparable used car, just let the lease expire. Find your car's market value by looking in used car price guides and newspaper ads and comparing it with the residual value of your car.

This worksheet illustrates Mary Dixon's lease versus purchase analysis for a new Toyota Scion xA costing $15,000. The 3-year closed-end lease requires an initial payment of $1,800 ($1,500 down payment + $300 security deposit) and monthly payments of $300. Purchasing requires a $2,500 down payment, sales tax of 5 percent ($750), and 36 monthly payments of $392. The trade-in value of the new car at the end of 3 years is estimated to be $8,000. *Because the total cost of leasing of $12,516 is greater than the $9,662 total cost of purchasing, Mary should purchase rather than lease the car.*

AUTOMOBILE LEASE VERSUS PURCHASE ANALYSIS*

Name: Mary Dixon   Date: March 4, 2008

Item Description	Amount
LEASE	
1 Initial payment:	
a. Down payment (capital cost reduction)	$ 1,500
b. Security deposit	300 $ 1,800
2 Term of lease and loan (years)*	3
3 Term of lease and loan (months) (Item 2 × 12)	36
4 Monthly lease payment	$ 300
5 Total payments over term of lease (Item 3 × Item 4)	$ 10,800
6 Interest rate earned on savings (in decimal form)	.04
7 Opportunity cost of initial payment (Item 1 × Item 2 × Item 6)	$ 216
8 Payment/refund for market value adjustment at end of lease ($0 for closed-end leases) and/or estimated end-of-term charges	$ 0
9 Total cost of leasing (Item 1a + Item 5 + Item 7 + Item 8)	$ 12,516
PURCHASE	
10 Purchase price	$ 15,000
11 Down payment	$ 2,500
12 Sales tax rate (in decimal form)	.05
13 Sales tax (Item 10 × Item 12)	$ 750
14 Monthly loan payment (Terms: 12,500 , 36 months, 8 %)	$ 392
15 Total payments over term of loan (Item 3 × Item 14)	$ 14,112
16 Opportunity cost of down payment (Item 2 × Item 6 × Item 11)	$ 300
17 Estimated trade-in value of car at end of loan	$ 8,000
18 Total cost of purchasing (Item 11 + Item 13 + Item 15 + Item 16 − Item 17)	$ 9,662

DECISION

If the value of Item 9 is less than the value of Item 18, leasing is preferred; otherwise the *purchase alternative is preferred.*

---

*Note: This form is based on assumed equal terms (periods) for the lease and the installment loan, which is assumed to be used to finance the purchase.

❚❚ Concept Check

CHECK • CONCEPT CHECK • CONCEPT CHECK • CONCEPT CHECK • CONCEPT CHECK • CONCEPT CHECK • CONCEPT C

5-3   What are the advantages and disadvantages of leasing a car?

5-4   Given your personal financial circumstances, if you were buying a car today, would you probably pay cash, lease, or finance it, and why? Which factors were most important to you in making this decision?

Knowing when to buy your first home is not always clear-cut. There are many factors to consider before taking on such a large financial responsibility. In the remainder of this chapter, we'll explore some of these factors and discuss how to approach the home-buying process.

Because you have your own unique set of likes and dislikes, the best way to start your search for housing is to list your preferences and classify them according to whether their satisfaction is essential, desirable, or merely a "plus." This exercise is important for three reasons. First, it screens out housing that doesn't meet your minimum requirements. Second, it helps you recognize that you may have to make trade-offs because seldom will you find a single home that meets all your needs. Third, it will help you focus on those needs for which you are willing and able to pay.

Housing in America is diverse, and everybody's housing needs differ. Some people prefer quiet and privacy; others like the hustle and bustle of big-city life. The features you prefer vary as well, from gourmet kitchens to an extra bedroom for a home office. You'll find single-family homes, townhouses, condominiums, cooperative apartments, or many types of rental units that meet your needs.

From early 2001 through 2005, home prices in the United States rose rapidly. Between 2003 and 2005, the median sales price of existing single-family homes rose from $180,200 to $225,300. In early 2006 existing home prices were continuing to rise, although declines in sales of both existing and new homes were being forecast through 2007. In the first quarter of 2006, the median sales price of existing single-family homes dropped to $217,900 and pending home sales were declining. The housing market was cooling due to a growing inventory of new and unsold homes, escalating oil prices, and, most important, rising mortgage interest rates. The slow rise in mortgage rates that started in 2004 began to take its toll on the housing market late in 2005. Rates on conventional fixed-rate mortgages rose more than 0.50 percent during the final half of 2005. At that time the National Association of Realtors was forecasting increasing mortgage rates, slowing growth in home prices, and a leveling off in the number of homes sold through 2007.

Although housing prices and the number of home sales result from a variety of economic and behavioral factors, it's generally agreed that mortgage interest rates and home sales (and prices) are inversely related. Increasing interest rates tend to slow the volume (and prices) of home sales; and similarly, declines in mortgage rates tend to grow the number of home sales (and prices). For example between 2000 and 2004, mortgage rates dropped by more than 2.50 percent, annual home sales increased by about 30 percent, and prices grew at annual rates well in excess of 10 percent. The homeownership rate in the United States in early 2006 was fluctuating around a near-record high of 69 percent. However, as shown in Exhibit 5.4, prices vary widely from one part of the country to another.

What Type of Housing Meets Your Needs?

One of the first decisions you'll have to make is the type of housing unit that meets your needs. Several of the following may be suitable:

- **Single-family homes:** These are the most popular choice. They can be stand-alone homes on their own legally defined lots or *row houses* or *townhouses* that share a common wall. As a rule, single-family homes offer buyers privacy, prestige, pride of ownership, and maximum property control.

- **Condominiums:** The term **condominium,** or **condo,** describes a form of ownership rather than a type of building. Condominiums can be apartments, townhouses, or cluster housing. The condominium buyer receives title to an individual residential unit and joint ownership of common areas and facilities such as lobbies, swimming pools, lakes, and tennis courts. Buyers arrange their own mortgages and pay their own taxes for their units. They are assessed a monthly *homeowner's fee* for their proportionate share of common facility maintenance costs. The *homeowners' association* elects a board of managers to supervise the buildings and grounds. Condominiums generally

condominium (condo)
A form of direct ownership of an individual unit in a multiunit project in which lobbies, swimming pools, and other common areas and facilities are jointly owned by all property owners in the project.

EXHIBIT 5.4   Home Prices in Selected Metropolitan Areas

The median sales price of existing single-family homes varies widely from one part of the country to another—$96,800 in Buffalo, New York, $376,200 in Miami, Florida, and $613,100 in San Diego, California. Here are some other median home prices in selected cities.

Location	Median Price
Albuquerque, NM	$185,400
Atlanta, GA	$173,900
Austin, TX	$176,700
Baltimore, MD	$285,100
Baton Rouge, LA	$172,300
Boston, MA	$421,200
Charlotte, NC	$191,400
Chicago, IL	$278,500
Cincinnati, OH	$149,100
Columbia, SC	$145,100
Columbus, OH	$155,700
Dallas, TX	$153,900
Denver, CO	$255,200
Des Moines, IA	$147,800
Honolulu, HI	$640,000
Houston, TX	$152,700
Indianapolis, IN	$122,400
Las Vegas, NV	$319,100
Los Angeles, CA	$576,300
Minneapolis–St. Paul, MN	$233,000
New Orleans, LA	$178,000
New York, NY	$473,700
Oklahoma City, OK	$125,400
Orlando, FL	$271,700
Philadelphia, PA	$235,100
Phoenix, AZ	$272,200
Pittsburgh, PA	$120,300
Portland, OR	$283,400
Saint Louis, MO	$153,000
San Francisco, CA	$751,900
Syracuse, NY	$116,800
Toledo, OH	$115,800
Tucson, AZ	$247,300
Washington, DC	$443,400
Wichita, KS	$111,500

Source: National Association of Realtors®, Metropolitan Area Prices—2nd quarter 2006, http://www.realtor.org/Research.nsf/files/REL06Q1T.pdf August 30, 2006.

cost less than single-family, detached homes because they're designed for more efficient land use and lower construction costs. Many home buyers are attracted to condominiums because they don't want the responsibility of maintaining and caring for a large property. Exhibit 5.5 on page 147 lists some of the key things to check before buying a condominium.

- **Cooperative apartments:** In a **cooperative apartment,** or **co-op,** building, each tenant owns a share of the nonprofit corporation that owns the building. Residents lease their units from the corporation and pay a monthly assessment in proportion to ownership shares, based on the space they occupy. These assessments cover the cost of services, maintenance, taxes, and the mortgage on the entire building and are subject to change, depending on the actual costs of operating the building and the actions of the board of directors, which determines the corporation's policies. The cooperative owner

cooperative apartment (co-op) An apartment in a building in which each tenant owns a share of the nonprofit corporation that owns the building.

EXHIBIT 5.5   **Condo Buyer's Checklist**

It pays to carefully check out the various operating and occupancy features of a condo before you buy.

- Thoroughly investigate the developer's reputation—through local real estate brokers, banks, or the Better Business Bureau—whether the building is brand new, under construction, or being converted.
- Read the rules of the organization.
- Investigate the condo homeowners' association, the restrictions on condo owners, and the quality of the property management.
- Check the construction of the building and its physical condition. If the building is being converted to condos, ask to see an independent inspection firm's report on the building's condition.
- Insist that any planned changes in the property be detailed in writing.
- Talk to the occupants to see if they are satisfied with the living conditions.
- Determine how many units are rented; generally, owner-occupied units are better maintained.
- Determine if there is sufficient parking space.
- Watch for unusually low maintenance fees that may have to be increased soon.
- Consider the resale value.

For new developments, compare the projected monthly homeowner's fees with those of similar buildings already in operation. For older developments, check to see when capital improvements such as exterior painting and roof replacement were last made. Special assessments are usually levied on all unit owners for major costly improvements.

---

receives the tax benefits resulting from interest and property taxes attributable to his or her proportionate ownership interest. Drawbacks of co-op ownership include difficulty in obtaining a mortgage (because many financial institutions don't like taking shares of a corporation rather than property as collateral), rent increases to cover maintenance costs of vacant units, and the need to abide by the capital improvement decisions of the co-op board of directors, which increases the monthly assessment.

- **Rental units:** Some individuals and families choose to *rent* or *lease* their place of residence rather than own it. They may be just starting out and have limited funds for housing, or they may be uncertain where they want to live. Perhaps they like the short-term commitment and limited maintenance. The cost and availability of rental units varies from one geographic area to another. Rental units range from duplexes, fourplexes, and even single-family homes, to large, high-rise apartment complexes containing several hundred units. Renting does come with restrictions, however. You may not be allowed to have a pet or make changes to the unit's appearance.

The Rental Option

Many people choose to rent rather than buy their home. For example, young adults usually rent for one or more of the following reasons: (1) They don't have the funds for a down payment and closing costs, (2) they're unsettled in their jobs and family status, (3) they don't want the additional responsibilities associated with home ownership, or (4) they believe they can afford a nicer home later by renting now because housing market conditions or mortgage rates are currently unattractive. A big drawback of renting is that the payments are *not* tax deductible.

The Rental Contract/Lease Agreement

rental contract (lease agreement) A legal instrument that protects both the *lessor* and the *lessee* from an adverse action by the other party; it specifies the *amount* of the monthly payment, the payment *due date, penalties* for late payment, the *length* of the lease agreement, *deposit* requirements, *fair wear and tear* definitions and provisions, the distribution of *expenses, renewal* options and *early termination penalties*, and any *restrictions* on children, pets, subleasing or using the facilities.

When you rent an apartment, duplex, house, or any other type of residence, you'll be required to sign a **rental contract** or **lease agreement.** Although oral agreements are generally binding, a written contract is a legal instrument that better protects both the *lessor* (the person who owns the property) and the *lessee* (the person who leases the property). Because the rental contract binds you, the lessee, to various actions, be sure that you fully understand it before signing it. As a rule, the contract specifies the *amount* of the monthly payment, the payment *due date, penalties* for late payment, the *length* of the lease agreement, security and/or advance rent (*deposit*) requirements, *fair wear and tear* definitions and provisions, the distribution of *expenses, lease renewal* options and *early termination penalties*, and any *restrictions* on children, pets, subleasing, or using the facilities.

Most leases have a minimum term of either 6 months or 1 year and require payments at the beginning of each month. They may initially require a security deposit and/or payment of the last month's rent in advance as security against damages or violation of the lease agreement. If there's no serious damage, most of the deposit should be refunded to the lessee shortly after the lease expires; a portion of the deposit is sometimes retained by the lessor to cover the cost of cleaning and minor repairs, regardless of how clean and well kept the unit was. Because the landlord controls the deposit, a written statement describing any preexisting damage, *prior* to occupancy, may help the lessee avoid losing their entire deposit. Renters should also clarify who bears expenses such as utilities and trash collection and exactly what, if any, restrictions are placed on the use of the property. It's also a good idea for renters to check the renter-landlord laws in their state to fully understand their *rights* and responsibilities.

The Rent-or-Buy Decision

Owning a home is not always more costly on a monthly basis than renting, although there are many other factors to consider before making this important decision. The economics of renting or buying a place to live depends on three main factors: (1) housing prices and mortgage interest rates, (2) tax write-offs for homeowners, and (3) the increase or decrease in home values over time.

To choose the lowest-cost alternative, compare the cost of renting with the cost of buying, as illustrated by the rent-or-buy analysis in Worksheet 5.2 on page 148. Note that because the interest deduction nearly always exceeds the amount of the standard deduction ($5,000 for single and $10,000 for married filing jointly in 2005), the form assumes that the taxpayer will itemize deductions. Assume that you must decide between renting an apartment for $700 a month or buying a similar-sized, $100,000 condominium. Purchasing the condo involves a $15,000 down payment; an $85,000, 7-percent, 30-year mortgage with monthly mortgage payments of $566; $4,500 in closing costs; and property taxes, insurance, and maintenance. With renting, the only costs are the $700 monthly rental payment, an annual renter's insurance premium of $300, and the opportunity cost of interest lost on the required $700 security deposit. Assume that you're in the 25 percent ordinary income tax bracket and that you'll itemize deductions if you purchase the home. Substituting the appropriate values into Worksheet 5.2 and making the required calculations results in the total cost of each alternative.

The cost of renting in part A of Worksheet 5.2 is simply the annual rent (monthly rent multiplied by 12) plus the annual renter's insurance premium of $300 plus the opportunity cost of interest lost on the security deposit. This results in a total annual cost of $8,732. The annual cost of buying in part B includes mortgage payments, property taxes, homeowner's insurance, annual maintenance, and lost interest on the down payment and closing costs to arrive at $10,970.

Then, subtract the portion of the mortgage payment going to pay off the loan balance because it's not part of the interest cost. Subtract the tax savings derived from interest and property taxes to arrive at Item 11, the after-tax cost of home ownership, $8,140. But as a homeowner, you also enjoy the benefits of appreciation. Assuming a modest 3 percent inflation in the value of the home reduces the annual cost to $5,140. Buying appears better than renting because the total cost of renting is $3,592 ($8,732 − $5,140) a year more than the total cost of buying.

However, don't base the rent-or-buy decision solely on the numbers. Your personal needs and the general condition of the housing market are also important considerations. If you think you may want to move to a different city in a few years or if you're worried about job security, renting may make sense, even if the numbers favor buying. For some people, factors such as the need for privacy, the desire to personalize one's home, and the personal satisfaction gained from home ownership outweigh the financial considerations. In some housing markets a relative surplus of rental properties causes the cost of renting to be lower

CALCULATOR

INPUTS	FUNCTIONS
85000	PV
360	N
7	÷
12	=
	I
	CPT
	PMT
	Solution
	565.51

See Appendix E for details.

With this procedure for making the rent-or-buy decision, you should *rent* if the total cost of renting is less than the total cost of buying, and *buy* if the total cost of renting is more than the total cost of buying. In this example the rental option requires monthly payments of $700. The purchase option is a $100,000 condo, financed with a $15,000 down payment and an $85,000, 7-percent, 30-year mortgage, with additional closing costs of $4,500.

RENT-OR-BUY ANALYSIS

A. COST OF RENTING

1. Annual rental costs
   (12 × monthly rental rate of $ _700_) $ _8,400_

2. Renter's insurance   _300_

3. Opportunity cost of security deposit: $ _700_ × after-tax savings rate _4.5_%   _32_

   Total cost of renting (line A.1 + line A.2 + line A.3) $ _8,732_

B. COST OF BUYING

1. Annual mortgage payments (Terms: $ _85,000_ , _360_ months, _7_%) $ _6,792_
   (12 × monthly mortgage payment of $ _566_)

2. Property taxes   _2,000_
   (_2_ % of price of home)

3. Homeowner's insurance   _500_
   (_.5_% of price of home)

4. Maintenance   _800_
   (_.8_ % of price of home)

5. After-tax cost of interest on down payment and closing costs   _878_
   ($ _19,500_ × _4.5_ % after-tax rate of return)

6. Total costs (sum of lines B.1 through B.5) $ _10,970_

Less:

7. Principal reduction in loan balance (see note below) $ _842_

8. Tax savings due to interest deductions*   _1,488_
   (Interest portion of mortgage payments $ _5,950_ × tax rate of _25_%)

9. Tax savings due to property tax deductions*   _500_
   (line B.2 × tax rate of _25_%)

10. Total deductions (sum of lines B.7 through B.9)   _2,830_

11. Annual after-tax cost of home ownership $ _8,140_
    (line B.6 − line B.10)

12. Estimated annual appreciation in value of home   _3,000_
    (_3_ % of price of home)

    Total cost of buying (line B.11 − line B.12) $ _5,140_

Note: Find monthly mortgage payments using a calculator or from Exhibit 5.8. An easy way to approximate the portion of the annual loan payment that goes to interest (line B.8) is to multiply the interest rate by the size of the loan (in this case, $85,000 × .07 = $5,950). To find the principal reduction in the loan balance (line B.7), simply subtract the amount that goes to interest from total annual mortgage payments ($6,792 − $5,950 = $842).
* Tax-shelter items.

than the cost of owning a comparable house or condominium. You should look at the rent-or-buy decision over a timeline of several years, using different assumptions regarding rent increases, mortgage rates, home appreciation rates in the area, and the rate of return you can earn on the funds you can invest (if you rent) rather than use toward a down payment on a house (if you buy).

❚ Concept Check

5-5	In addition to single-family homes, what other forms of housing are available in the United States? Briefly describe each of them.
5-6	What type of housing would you choose for yourself now, and why? Why might you choose to rent instead of buy?
5-7	Why is it important to have a written lease? What should a rental contract include?

LG4 ⟩ HOW MUCH HOUSING CAN YOU AFFORD?

Buying a home obviously involves lots of careful planning and analysis. Not only must you decide on the kind of home you want (its location, number of bedrooms, and other features), you must also consider its cost, what kind of mortgage to get, how large a monthly payment you can afford, what kind of homeowner's insurance coverage to have, and so forth.

Buying a home (or any other major, big-ticket item) touches on many elements of personal financial planning. The money you use for a down payment will likely be drawn from your *savings program;* the homeowner's policy you choose is a part of your *insurance planning;* and your monthly mortgage payments will have an enormous impact on your *cash budget* and *tax plans*.

Sound financial planning dictates caution when buying a home or any other major item. Spending too much for a home or automobile can have a detrimental effect not only on your budget and lifestyle but also on your savings and investment plans and possibly even your retirement plans. Knowing how much housing you can afford goes a long way toward helping you achieve balanced financial goals.

Benefits of Owning a Home

Home ownership is important to most people, whether they own a detached home or a condominium. It offers the security and peace of mind derived from living in one's own home and the feeling of permanence and sense of stability that ownership brings. This so-called psychological reward is not the only reason people enjoy owning their home. There are also financial payoffs from home ownership:

- **Tax shelter:** As noted in Chapter 3, you can deduct both mortgage interest and property taxes when calculating your federal and, in most states, state income taxes, reducing your taxable income and thus your tax liability. The only requirement is that you itemize your deductions. This tax break is so good that people who have never itemized usually begin doing so after they buy their first house. Also, keep in mind that for the first 15 to 20 years of ownership (assuming a 30-year mortgage), most of your monthly mortgage payment is made up of interest and property taxes—in fact, during the first 5 to 10 years or so, these could well account for *85 to 90 percent of your total payment.* This allows you to write off nearly all of your monthly mortgage payment.
- **Inflation hedge:** Home ownership usually provides an inflation hedge because your home appreciates in value at a rate equal to or greater than the rate of inflation. From 2001 through 2005, the home became one of the best investments you could make, generating a far better return than stocks, bonds, or mutual funds. Many people bought homes simply for their investment value. The low inflation coupled with low mortgage rates resulted in rapid appreciation in home prices during that period. Whether a real estate market is "hot" or "cold" is literally a matter of supply and demand. Today, due to rising mortgage rates, housing demand is moderating and prices in most parts of the country are increasing at a rate about equal to or slightly below the rate of inflation.

© COMSTOCK IMAGE/JUPITER IMAGES

The Cost of Home Ownership

Although there definitely are some strong emotional and financial reasons for owning a home, there's still the question of whether you can afford to own one. There are two important aspects to the consideration of affordability: You must produce the down payment and other closing costs, and you must be able to meet the cash-flow requirements associated with monthly mortgage payments and other home maintenance expenses. In particular, you should consider these five items when evaluating the cost of home ownership to determine how much home you can afford: the down payment, points and closing costs, mortgage payments, property taxes and insurance, and maintenance and operating expenses.

The Down Payment

The first major hurdle is the **down payment.** Most buyers finance a major part of the purchase price of the home, but they're required by lenders to invest money of their own, called *equity*. The actual amount of down payment required varies among lenders, mortgage types, and properties. To determine the amount of down payment required in specific instances, lenders use the **loan-to-value ratio,** which specifies the maximum percentage of the value of a property that the lender is willing to loan. For example, if the loan-to-value ratio is 80 percent, the buyer will have to come up with a down payment equal to the remaining 20 percent.

Generally, first-time home buyers must spend several years accumulating enough money to afford the down payment and other costs associated with a home purchase. You can best accumulate these funds if you plan ahead, using future value techniques (presented in Chapters 2, 4, 11, and 14) to determine the monthly or annual savings necessary to have a stated amount by a specified future date. A detailed demonstration of this process is included in Chapter 11 (see Worksheet 11.1B). A disciplined savings program is the best way to obtain the funds needed to purchase a home or any other big-ticket item requiring a sizable down payment or cash outlay.

If you don't have enough savings to cover the down payment and closing costs, you can consider several other sources. You may be able to obtain some funds by withdrawing (subject to legal limitations) your contributions from your company's profit-sharing or thrift plan. Your IRA is another option; first-time homebuyers are permitted to withdraw $10,000 without penalty before age 59½. However, using retirement money should be a last resort because you must still pay income tax on retirement distributions. Thus, if you're in the 25 percent income-tax bracket, your $10,000 IRA withdrawal would net you only $7,500 ($10,000 − $2,500) for your down payment.

The Federal National Mortgage Association (known as "Fannie Mae") has several programs to help buyers who have limited cash for the down payment and closing costs. The "Fannie 3/2" program is available from local lenders. Borrowers who meet certain income criteria may qualify for a 95 percent loan-to-value mortgage and may obtain up to 2 percent of their 5 percent down payment from a public or nonprofit agency or relative. "Fannie 97" helps the homebuyer who can handle monthly mortgage payments but doesn't have cash for the down payment. It requires only a 3 percent down payment from the borrower's own funds, and the borrower needs to have only 1 month's mortgage payment in cash savings, or reserves, after closing.

As a rule, when the down payment is less than 20 percent, the lender will require the buyer to obtain **private mortgage insurance (PMI),** which protects the lender from loss if the borrower defaults on the loan. Usually PMI covers the lender's risk above 80 percent of the house price. Thus, with a 10 percent down payment, the mortgage will be a 90 percent loan, and mortgage insurance will cover 10 percent of the home's price. The cost of mortgage insurance is around 0.50 percent, ranging between 0.20 and 0.80 percent of the loan balance each

down payment A portion of the full purchase price provided by the purchaser when a house or other major asset is purchased; often called *equity*.

loan-to-value ratio The maximum percentage of the value of a property that the lender is willing to loan.

private mortgage insurance (PMI) An insurance policy that protects the mortgage lender from loss in the event the borrower defaults on the loan; typically required by lenders when the down payment is less than 20 percent.

year, depending on the size of your down payment. It can be included in your monthly payment, and the average cost ranges from about $40 to $70 per month. You should contact your lender to cancel the mortgage insurance once the equity in your home reaches 20 to 25 percent. Under federal law, PMI on most loans made on or after July 29, 1999, ends automatically once the mortgage is paid down to 78 percent of the original value of the house.

Points and Closing Costs

A second hurdle to home ownership relates to mortgage points and closing costs. **Mortgage points** are fees charged by lenders at the time they grant a mortgage loan. In appearance, points are like interest in that they are a charge for borrowing money. They're related to the lender's supply of loanable funds and the demand for mortgages; the greater the demand relative to the supply, the more points you can expect to pay. One point equals 1 percent of the amount borrowed. If you borrow $100,000 and loan fees equal 3 points, the amount of money you'll pay in points is $100,000 × .03 = $3,000.

Lenders typically use points as a way of charging interest on their loans. They can vary the interest rate along with the number of points they charge to create loans with comparable effective rates. For example, a lender might be willing to give you a 7 percent rather than an 8 percent mortgage if you're willing to pay more points; that is, you choose between an 8 percent mortgage rate with 1 point or a 7 percent mortgage rate with 3 points. If you choose the 7 percent loan, you'll pay a lot more *at closing* (although the amount of interest paid *over the life of the mortgage* may be considerably less).

Points increase the *effective rate of interest* on a mortgage. The amount you pay in points and the length of time you hold a mortgage determine the increase in the effective interest rate. For example, on an 8 percent, 30-year, fixed-rate mortgage, each point increases the annual percentage rate by about .11 percent if the loan is held for 30 years, .17 percent if held 15 years, .32 percent if held 7 years, and .70 percent if held 3 years. You pay the same amount in points regardless of how long you keep your home. So, the longer you hold the mortgage, the longer the period over which you amortize the points and the smaller the effect of the points on the effective annual interest rate.

According to IRS rulings, the points paid on a mortgage at the time a home is originally purchased are usually considered immediately tax deductible. The same points are *not* considered immediately tax deductible if they're incurred when *refinancing* a mortgage; rather, the amount paid in points must be written off (*amortized*) over the life of the new mortgage loan.

Closing costs are all expenses that borrowers ordinarily pay when a mortgage loan is closed and they receive title to the purchased property. Closing costs are like down payments: they represent money you must come up with *at the time you buy the house*. Closing costs are made up of such items as loan application and loan origination fees paid to the lender, mortgage points, title search and insurance fees, attorneys' fees, appraisal fees, and other miscellaneous fees for things such as mortgage taxes, filing fees, inspections, credit reports, and so on. As Exhibit 5.6 on page 152 shows, these costs can amount to 50 percent or more of the down payment. For example, with a 10 percent down payment on a $100,000 home, the closing costs, as shown in Exhibit 5.6, are nearly 70 percent of the down payment, or $6,625. Simple arithmetic indicates that this buyer will need nearly $17,000 to buy the house (the $10,000 down payment plus another $6,625 in closing costs).

Mortgage Payments

A monthly mortgage payment is determined using a fairly complex formula. Each mortgage payment is made up partly of principal repayment on the loan and partly of interest charges on the loan. However, as Exhibit 5.7 on page 152 shows, for most of the life of the mortgage the vast majority of each monthly payment goes to *interest*. The loan illustrated in the exhibit is a $100,000, 30-year, 7 percent mortgage with monthly payments of $665.30, for a total of $7,983.60 per year. Note that it is not until after the 21st year of this 30-year mortgage that the principal portion of the monthly loan payment exceeds the amount that goes to interest.

In practice, most mortgage lenders and realtors use their calculator to obtain monthly payments. Some of them still use *comprehensive mortgage payment tables*, which provide monthly payments for virtually every combination of loan size, interest rate, and maturity. Exhibit 5.8 on page 153 provides an excerpt from one such comprehensive mortgage payment table (with values rounded to the nearest cent). It lists the *monthly payments* associated with

mortgage points Fees (one point equals 1 percent of the amount borrowed) charged by lenders at the time they grant a mortgage loan; they are related to the lender's supply of loanable funds and the demand for mortgages.

closing costs All expenses (including mortgage points) that borrowers ordinarily pay when a mortgage loan is closed and they receive title to the purchased property.

EXHIBIT 5.6 | Closing Costs: The Hidden Costs of Buying a Home

The closing costs on a home mortgage loan can be substantial—as much as 5 to 7 percent of the price of the home. Except for the real estate commission (generally paid by the seller), the buyer incurs the biggest share of the closing costs and must pay them—in addition to the down payment—when the loan is closed and title to the property is conveyed.

Item	SIZE OF DOWN PAYMENT	
	20%	10%
Loan application fee	$ 200	$ 200
Loan origination fee	800	900
Points	1,600	2,700
Mortgage insurance	—	675
Title search and insurance	500	550
Attorneys' fees	400	400
Appraisal fees	150	150
Home inspection	250	250
Mortgage tax	575	650
Filing fees	25	25
Credit reports	25	25
Miscellaneous	100	100
Total closing costs	$4,625	$6,625

Note: Typical closing costs for a $100,000 home—2 points charged with 20 percent down, 3 points with 10 percent down. Actual amounts will vary by lender and location.

For most of the life of a mortgage loan, the vast majority of each monthly payment goes to interest and only a small portion goes toward principal repayment. Over the 30-year life of the 7 percent, $100,000 mortgage illustrated here, the homeowner will pay almost $140,000 in interest.

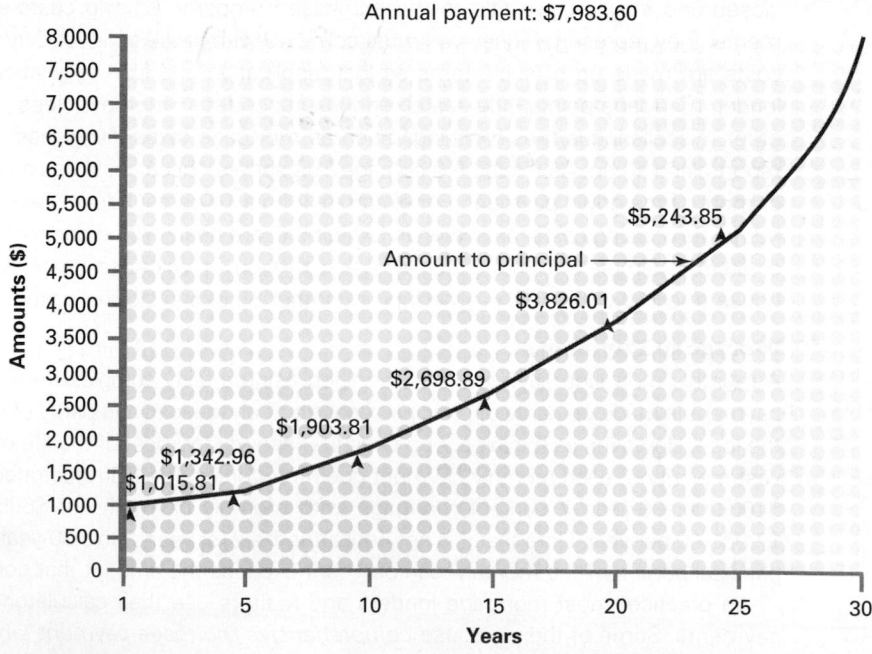

Annual payment: $7,983.60

Note: Dollar amounts noted on the graph represent the total amount of principal repaid from the $7,983.60 annual payment made during the given year.

<table>
<tr><td colspan="2">**CALCULATOR**</td></tr>
<tr><td>INPUTS</td><td>FUNCTIONS</td></tr>
<tr><td>90000</td><td>PV</td></tr>
<tr><td>360</td><td>N</td></tr>
<tr><td>6</td><td>÷</td></tr>
<tr><td>12</td><td>=</td></tr>
<tr><td></td><td>I</td></tr>
<tr><td></td><td>CPT</td></tr>
<tr><td></td><td>PMT</td></tr>
<tr><td></td><td>*Solution*</td></tr>
<tr><td></td><td>539.60</td></tr>
</table>

See Appendix E for details.

a $10,000, fixed-rate loan for selected maturities of 10 to 30 years, and various interest rates ranging from 5 to 11 percent. This table can be used to find the monthly payment for any size loan. Preferably, you can use a business calculator to quickly and precisely calculate monthly mortgage payments.

Suppose you'd like to use the mortgage payment tables to find the monthly loan payment on a $90,000, 6 percent, 30-year mortgage. Simply divide the amount of the loan ($90,000) by $10,000 and then multiply this factor (9.0) by the payment amount shown in Exhibit 5.8 for a 6 percent, 30-year loan ($59.96):

$$\$90,000/\$10,000 = 9.0 \times \$59.96 = \$539.64$$

The resulting monthly mortgage payment would be $539.64.

The calculator keystrokes shown in the margin can be used to more easily and precisely calculate mortgage payments. Note that the mortgage payment of $539.60 is more precise than the value calculated earlier using the table of monthly mortgage payments.

Affordability Ratios. The key issue regarding mortgage payments is *affordability*: How large a monthly mortgage payment can you afford, given your budget? This amount determines how much you can borrow to finance the purchase of a home.

To obtain a mortgage, a potential borrower must be "qualified"—demonstrate that he or she has adequate income and an acceptable credit record to reliably make scheduled loan payments. Federal and private mortgage insurers and institutional mortgage investors have certain standards they expect borrowers to meet to reduce the borrower's risk of default.

The most important affordability guidelines relate both *monthly mortgage payments and total monthly installment loan payments* (including the monthly mortgage payment and monthly payments on auto, furniture, and other consumer installment loans) *to monthly borrower gross income*. Customary ratios for a *conventional mortgage* stipulate that monthly mortgage payments cannot exceed 25 to 30 percent of the borrower's monthly *gross* (before-tax) income, and the borrower's total monthly installment loan payments (including the mortgage payment)

EXHIBIT 5.8   **A Table of Monthly Mortgage Payments (Monthly Payments Necessary to Repay a $10,000 Loan)**

The monthly loan payments on a mortgage vary not only by the amount of the loan, but also by the rate of interest and loan maturity.

| | | | LOAN MATURITY | | |
Rate of Interest	10 Years	15 Years	20 Years	25 Years	30 Years
5.0%	$106.07	$ 79.08	$ 66.00	$ 58.46	$ 53.68
5.5	108.53	81.71	68.79	61.41	56.79
6.0	111.02	84.39	71.64	64.43	59.96
6.5	113.55	87.11	74.56	67.52	63.21
7.0	116.11	89.88	77.53	70.68	66.53
7.5	118.71	92.71	80.56	73.90	69.93
8.0	121.33	95.57	83.65	77.19	73.38
8.5	123.99	98.48	86.79	80.53	76.90
9.0	126.68	101.43	89.98	83.92	80.47
9.5	129.40	104.43	93.22	87.37	84.09
10.0	132.16	107.47	96.51	90.88	87.76
10.5	134.94	110.54	99.84	94.42	91.48
11.0	137.76	113.66	103.22	98.02	95.24

Note: **To use:** (1) Divide amount of the loan by $10,000, (2) find the loan payment amount in the table for the specific interest rate and maturity, and (3) multiply the amount from Step 1 by the amount from Step 2.
Example: The monthly payment for a $98,000, 7.5 percent, 30-year loan would be (1) $98,000/$10,000 = 9.8; (2) the payment associated with a 7.5 percent, 30-year loan, from the table, is $69.93; (3) the monthly payment required to repay a $98,000, 7.5 percent, 30-year loan is 9.8 × $69.93 = $685.31.

cannot exceed 33 to 38 percent of monthly gross income. Because both conditions stipulate a range, the lender has some leeway in choosing the most appropriate ratio for a particular loan applicant.

Let's look at how these affordability ratios work. Assume that your monthly gross income is $4,500. Applying the lower end of the ranges (that is, 25 percent and 33 percent), we see that this income level supports mortgage payments of $1,125 a month ($4,500 × .25 = $1,125) *so long as total monthly installment loan payments do not exceed $1,500* ($4,500 × .33 = $1,500). If your nonmortgage monthly installment loan payments exceeded $375 (the difference between $1,500 and $1,125), your mortgage payment would have to be reduced accordingly, or the other installment loan payments reduced or paid off. For instance, if you had $500 in other installment payments, your maximum monthly mortgage payment would be $1,500 − $500 = $1,000.

Determining the largest mortgage for which you qualify is just the first step. You also need to consider your lifestyle needs. Will taking on the responsibility of a mortgage require you to forgo luxuries or radically change your spending habits? To see how buying a house affects your cash flow, revise your personal budget to include the costs of buying a home—monthly mortgage payments, utilities, maintenance, insurance—and so on. Only you can decide how much of your income you're willing to allocate to a mortgage. You may have to make some trade-offs, like choosing a lower-priced house with a smaller mortgage, to maintain greater financial flexibility.

Property Taxes and Insurance

Aside from loan costs, mortgage payments often include property tax and insurance payments. The mortgage payment therefore consists of *principal*, *interest*, property *taxes*, and homeowner's *insurance* (or **PITI** for short). Actually, that portion of the loan payment that goes for taxes and insurance is paid into an *escrow account*, where it accumulates until the lender pays property taxes and homeowner insurance premiums as due. Some lenders pay interest—typically at no higher than the regular savings rate—on escrow account balances. However, it's preferable to pay insurance and taxes yourself, if you have the financial discipline. This strategy provides greater cash flexibility and an opportunity to earn a higher rate of return on funds than the escrow account pays.

Because they're local taxes levied to fund schools, law enforcement, and other local services, the level of **property taxes** differs from one community to another. In addition, within a given community, individual property taxes will vary according to the *assessed value* of the real estate—the larger and/or more expensive the home, the higher the property taxes, and vice versa. As a rule, annual property taxes vary from less than .5 percent to more than 2 percent of a home's approximate market value. Thus the property taxes on a $100,000 home could vary from about $500 to more than $2,000 a year, depending on location and geographic area.

The other component of the monthly mortgage payment is **homeowner's insurance.** Its cost varies with such factors as the age of the house, location, materials used in construction, and geographic area. Homeowner's insurance is required by mortgage lenders and covers only the replacement value of the home and its contents and not the land. Annual insurance costs usually amount to approximately .25 to .5 percent of the home's market value, or from $250 to $500 for a $100,000 house. The types, characteristics, and features of homeowner's insurance policies are discussed in more detail in Chapter 10.

Maintenance and Operating Expenses

In addition to monthly mortgage payments, homeowners incur maintenance and operating expenses. Maintenance costs should be anticipated even on new homes. Painting, mechanical and plumbing repairs, and lawn maintenance, for example, are inescapable facts of home ownership. Such costs are likely to be greater for larger, older homes. Thus, although a large, established home may have an attractive purchase price, a new, smaller home may be a better buy in view of its lower maintenance and operating costs. Also consider the cost of operating the

FINANCIAL ROAD SIGN

ARE YOU READY TO BUY A HOME?

If you can answer yes to these questions, you're probably ready for home ownership:

1. Have you worked consistently for at least the last 2 years, demonstrating a steady income and job history? If not, can you explain any gaps?
2. Have you established a favorable credit profile with a track record of debts owed and repaid on time?
3. Have you saved money for a cash down payment and closing costs?
4. Are the monthly mortgage payments for the house you want within the lender's limits for both your gross monthly income and your total monthly installment debt?

Source: Reprinted with permission of Homestore, Inc. All rights reserved.

PITI Notation that refers to a mortgage payment including stipulated portions of *principal*, *interest*, property *taxes*, and homeowner's *insurance*.

property taxes Taxes levied by local governments on the *assessed value* of real estate for the purpose of funding schools, law enforcement, and other local services.

homeowner's insurance Insurance that is required by mortgage lenders and covers the replacement value of a home and its contents.

home, specifically the cost of utilities such as electricity, gas, water, and sewage. These costs have skyrocketed over the past 20 years and today are a large part of home owner-ship costs, so get estimates of utilities when evaluating a home for purchase.

Performing a Home Affordability Analysis

Worksheet 5.3 helps you determine your maximum home-purchase price, using your month-ly income and down payment amount after meeting estimated closing costs. In our example, the Renée and Edward Miller family has a combined annual income of $48,400, and savings of $22,500 for a down payment and closing costs. They estimate monthly property taxes and homeowner's insurance at $150 and expect the mortgage lender to use a 28 percent month-ly mortgage payment affordability ratio, to lend at an average interest rate of 7 percent on a 30-year (360-month) mortgage, and to require a 10 percent minimum down payment. The Millers' analysis shows they can afford to purchase a home for about $150,000.

Worksheet 5.3 walks us through the steps the Miller family took to reach this conclusion. Based on their monthly income and the 28 percent affordability ratio, their monthly payment could be $1,130 ($4,033 × .28), shown as Item 4. After deducting taxes and insurance, the max-imum monthly mortgage payment amount is $980 (Item 6). We can use the calculator key-strokes shown in the margin or the table in Exhibit 5.8 to find the Miller's maximum loan. Using Exhibit 5.8, a $10,000 loan for 30 years at 7 percent would result in a monthly payment of $66.53, as indicated in Item 9. Now, find out how much of a loan a payment of $980 would support:

$$\$10,000 \times \$980/\$66.53 = \$147,302 \text{ (Item 10)}$$

With a down payment of $15,000 and monthly income of $4,033, the Miller family can afford a home costing $162,302 (Item 13). The Millers then look at the maximum purchase price based on their $15,000 down payment , or $150,000 (Item 15). Their maximum home purchase price is the lower of Items 13 and 15, or $150,000 (Item 16) and is limited by the amount available for a down payment.

You can use Exhibit 5.9 on page 157 to quickly estimate the size of mortgage you can afford, based on various monthly mortgage payment and interest rate assumptions. First deter-mine the maximum monthly mortgage payment you can handle, then follow that line across to find the approximate size of the mortgage your payment will buy at each mortgage interest rate. (This figure assumes a 30-year, fixed-rate loan and does *not* include property taxes and homeowner's insurance.) For example, if you estimate that you have $1,000 available per month and the prevailing mortgage interest rate is 8 percent, you can afford a mortgage of about $136,000.

CALCULATOR

INPUTS	FUNCTIONS
980	PMT
360	N
7	÷
12	=
	I
	CPT
	PV
	Solution
	147,302

See Appendix E for details.

Ⅱ Concept Check

5-8   Briefly describe the various benefits of owning a home. Which one is most important to you? Which is least important?

5-9   What does the *loan-to-value ratio* on a home represent? Is the down payment on a home related to its loan-to-value ratio? Explain.

5-10   What are *mortgage points?* How much would a homebuyer have to pay if the lender wanted to charge 2.5 points on an $85,000 mortgage? When would this amount have to be paid? What effect do points have on the mortgage's rate of interest?

5-11   What are *closing costs,* and what items do they include? Who pays these costs, and when?

5-12   What are the most common guidelines used to determine the monthly mortgage payment one can afford?

5-13   Why is it advisable for the prospective homebuyer to investigate property taxes?

By using the following variables in the home affordability analysis form, the Millers estimate a maximum home purchase price of $150,000: their combined annual income of $48,400; the $22,500 available for a down payment and paying all closing costs; estimated monthly property taxes and homeowner's insurance of $150; the lender's 28 percent monthly mortgage payment affordability ratio; an average interest rate of 7 percent and expected loan maturity of 30 years; and a minimum down payment of 10 percent.

HOME AFFORDABILITY ANALYSIS*

Name: _Renée and Edward Miller_   Date: _July 12, 2008_

Item	Description	Amount
1	Amount of annual income	$ 48,400
2	Monthly income (Item 1 ÷ 12)	$ 4,033
3	Lender's affordability ratio (in decimal form)	.28
4	Maximum monthly mortgage payment (PITI) (Item 2 × Item 3)	$ 1,130
5	Estimated monthly prop tax and homeowner's ins payment	$ 150
?	Maximum monthly loan payment (Item 4 − Item 5)	$ 980
7	Approximate average interest rate on loan	7%
8	Planned loan maturity (years)	30
9	Monthly mortgage payment per $10,000 (using Item 7 and Item 8 and Table of Monthly Mortgage Payments in Exhibit 5.8 or a calculator)	$ 66.53
10	Maximum loan based on monthly income ($10,000 × Item ? ÷ Item 9)	$ 147,302
11	Funds available for making a down payment and paying closing costs	$ 22,500
12	Funds available for making a down payment (Item 11 × .77)	$ 15,000
13	Maximum purchase price based on available monthly income (Item 10 + Item 12)	$ 162,302
14	Minimum acceptable down payment (in decimal form)	.10
15	Maximum purchase price based on down payment (Item 12 ÷ Item 14)	$ 150,000
1?	Maximum home purchase price (lower of Item 13 and Item 15)	$ 150,000

*Note: This analysis assumes that $1/3$ of the funds available for making the down payment and paying closing costs are used to meet closing costs while the remaining $2/3$ are available for a down payment. This assumption means that closing costs will represent an amount equal to 50 percent of the down payment.

EXHIBIT 5.9   How Much Mortgage Will Your Payment Buy?

This table lets you quickly estimate the size of the mortgage you can afford based on the monthly mortgage payment and mortgage interest rate. It assumes a 30-year, fixed-rate loan. Remember that this amount is only for mortgage principal and interest; you must have funds available for paying property taxes and homeowner's insurance as well.

Monthly Mortgage Payment	Mortgage Interest Rate						
	5%	6%	7%	8%	9%	10%	11%
$ 500	$ 93,141	$ 83,396	$ 75,154	$ 68,142	$ 62,141	$ 56,975	$ 52,503
600	111,769	100,075	90,185	81,770	74,569	68,370	63,004
700	130,397	116,754	105,215	95,398	86,997	79,766	73,504
800	149,025	133,433	120,246	109,027	99,425	91,161	84,005
900	167,653	150,112	135,277	122,655	111,854	102,556	94,506
1,000	186,282	166,792	150,308	136,283	124,282	113,951	105,006
1,100	204,910	183,471	165,338	149,912	136,710	125,346	115,507
1,200	223,538	200,150	180,369	163,540	149,138	136,741	126,008
1,300	242,166	216,829	195,400	177,169	161,566	148,136	136,508
1,400	260,794	233,508	210,431	190,797	173,995	159,531	147,009
1,500	279,422	250,187	225,461	204,425	186,423	170,926	157,510

Note: **To use:** (1) Find the amount of monthly mortgage payment you can afford, to the nearest $100. Then find the current mortgage interest rate to the nearest percent. The approximate mortgage amount will be at the intersection of the two columns. (2) To estimate the mortgage size if the interest rate ends in .5 percent, add the mortgage amounts for the lower and higher mortgage interest rates and divide by 2. (3) To estimate the mortgage size for a payment ending in 50, add the mortgage amounts for the lower and higher monthly mortgage payments and divide by 2.

    Examples: (1) The estimated mortgage size if you have a monthly mortgage payment of $900 on a 30-year, 10 percent loan is $102,556. (2) To find the estimated mortgage size if you have a monthly mortgage payment of $900 and the mortgage interest rate is 9.5 percent, add the mortgage sizes for $900 at 9 percent and at 10 percent and divide by 2: ($111,854 + $102,556) ÷ 2 = $214,410 ÷ 2 = $107,205. (3) To find the estimated mortgage size if you have a monthly mortgage payment of $950 and the mortgage interest rate is 9 percent, add the mortgage sizes for $900 and $1,000 at 9 percent and divide by 2: ($111,854 + $124,282) ÷ 2 = $236,136 ÷ 2 = $118,068.

LG5   THE HOME-BUYING PROCESS

Are you in the market for your first home? Buying a home requires time, effort, and money. You'll want to educate yourself about available properties and prevailing prices by doing a systematic search and careful analysis. You'll also need a basic understanding of the role of a real estate agent, the mortgage application process, the real estate sales contract, and other documents required to close a deal.

Shop the Market First

Most people who shop the housing market rely on real estate agents for information, access to properties, and advice. Many of them also shop via the Internet, visiting various real estate sites to learn about available properties. Other sources of information, such as newspaper ads, are also widely used to find available properties. Occasionally a person seeking to buy or rent property will advertise his or her needs and wait for sellers to initiate contact.

    Today the Internet is a valuable resource for homebuyers. You can search an online real estate database; specify preferences such as location, price, and size; and obtain descriptions and color photos of all properties that meet your needs. Other systems allow buyers to use a touch-tone phone to get recorded descriptions of homes listed by a particular agency, or see and print descriptions and color photos of homes for sale using an electronic kiosk.

    Buying a home involves many factors, both financial and emotional, and the emotional factors often carry the greatest weight. As noted earlier, you must begin your home search project by figuring out what *you* require for your particular lifestyle needs—in terms of living space, style, and other special features. The property's location, neighborhood, and school

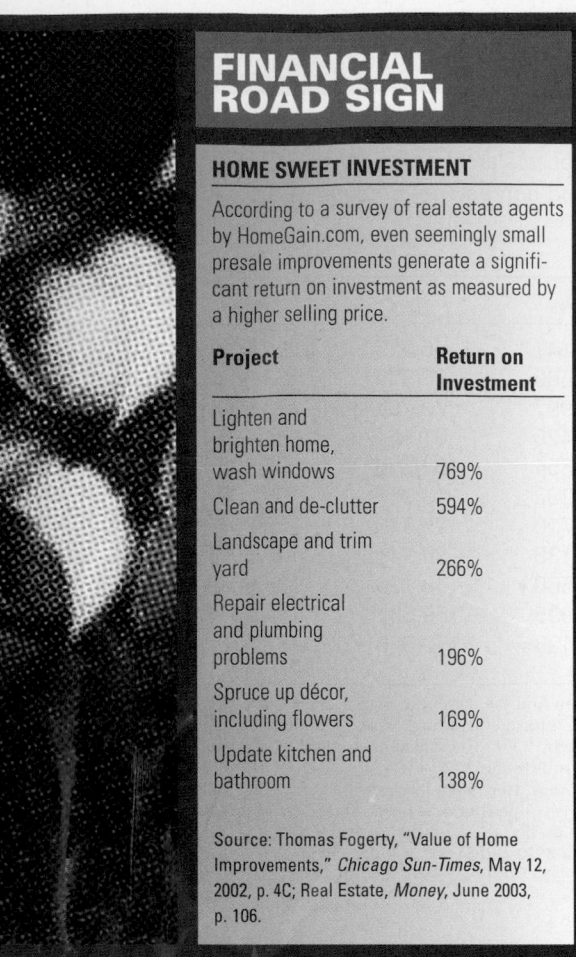
district are usually important considerations as well. It's helpful to divide your list into *necessary* features, such as the number of bedrooms and baths, and *optional*—but desirable—features, such as fireplaces, whirlpool tubs, and so on. And of course, an affordability analysis is a critical part of the housing search.

Keep an open mind as you start looking. You may find that you like a house that's far different from what you first thought you wanted. For example, you may begin your search looking for a one-story, contemporary ranch house with a pool, but fall in love with a two-story colonial with wonderful landscaping, no pool, and all the other features you want. Be flexible and look at a variety of homes in your price range. This can be invaluable in helping to define your wants and needs more clearly.

If you already own a house but want or need a larger or different type of home, you can either trade up or remodel it. You may choose to remodel it if you like your neighborhood and can make the desired changes to your current home. In some cases, the cost to remodel will be less than the transaction costs of buying another house. The best remodeling projects are those whose costs you can recover when you sell the house. Kitchen improvements, additional bathrooms, and family rooms tend to best enhance a home's market value. Although a swimming pool may give you pleasure, you may not recover its cost when you sell the house.

You're unlikely to find the "perfect" home at the "perfect" price, so you'll need to make some compromises. The greater your research and preparation, the better off you'll be. This should also help to reduce the *buyer's remorse* that can accompany a major purchase. Soon after signing the sales contract, homebuyers often question whether they did the right thing: Did I pay too much? Should I have negotiated harder? Is the location as good as I thought? Can I really afford the monthly payments? Can I manage without a pool, playroom, or workshop? These feelings are normal and usually disappear once you move in. One way to reduce buyer's remorse is to shorten the time between signing the sales contract and closing the deal.

Using an Agent

Most homebuyers rely on real estate agents because they're professionals who are in daily contact with the housing market. Once you describe your needs to an agent, he or she can begin to search for appropriate properties. Your agent will also help you negotiate with the seller, obtain satisfactory financing, and, although not empowered to give explicit legal advice, prepare the real estate sales contract.

Most real estate firms belong to a local **Multiple Listing Service (MLS),** a comprehensive listing, updated daily, of properties for sale in a given community or metropolitan area. A brief description of each property and its asking price are included, with a photo of the property. Only realtors who work for an MLS member firm have access to this major segment of the market.

Buyers should remember that *agents typically are employed by sellers.* Unless you've agreed to pay a fee to a sales agent to act as a buyer's agent, a realtor's primary responsibility, by law, is to sell listed properties at the highest possible prices. Agents are paid only if they make a sale, so some might pressure you to "sign now or miss the chance of a lifetime." But most agents will listen to your needs and work to match you with the right property, under terms that will benefit both you and the seller. Good agents recognize that their interests are best served when all parties to a transaction are satisfied.

Real estate commissions generally range from 5 to 6 percent for new homes and 6 to 7 percent for previously occupied homes or *resales*. It may be possible to negotiate a lower commission with your agent or to find a discount broker, or one who charges a flat fee. Commissions are paid only by the seller, but because the price of a home is often inflated by the size of the real estate commission—many builders are believed to factor commission costs into the prices of their new homes—the buyer probably absorbs some or even all of the commission. Of course, you may be able to find a suitable property that is "for sale by

Multiple Listing Service (MLS) A comprehensive listing, updated daily, of properties for sale in a given community or metropolitan area; includes a brief description of each property and its asking price with a photo and can be accessed only by realtors who work for an MLS member.

owner" and therefore eliminate the need for a realtor. This approach is generally not recommended due to the many legal and financial complexities of the real estate transaction.

Whereas traditional agents represent the seller's interests, *buyer's agents,* as the term implies, are hired by buyers to negotiate on their behalf. Commissions to buyer's agents are negotiated and may ultimately be paid by the seller. A *facilitator,* on the other hand, represents neither the buyer nor the seller but is typically paid by both parties to serve as a neutral intermediary between them.

Prequalifying and Applying for a Mortgage

Before beginning your home search, you may want to meet with one or more mortgage lenders to prearrange a mortgage loan. **Prequalification** can work to your advantage in several ways. You'll know ahead of time the specific mortgage amount that you qualify for—subject, of course, to changes in rates and terms—and can focus your search on homes within an affordable price range.

Prequalification also provides estimates of the required down payment and closing costs for different types of mortgages. It identifies in advance any problems, such as credit report errors, that might arise from your application, and allows you time to correct them. Finally, prequalification enhances your bargaining power with the seller of a house you want by letting her or him know that the deal won't fall through because you can't afford the property or obtain suitable financing. And since you've gone through the mortgage application process, the time required to close the sale should be relatively short.

There are many sources of mortgage loans, and you should begin investigating them while looking for a house. When you actually apply for a mortgage loan on a particular home, you'll need to give the lender information on your income, assets, and outstanding debts. Documents the lender may request include proof of your monthly income (paycheck stubs, W-2 forms, and so on), statements showing all debt balances (credit cards, car and education loans, bank lines of credit, and so on), lists of financial assets such as savings accounts and securities, several months' bank account statements, and at least 2 years' income tax returns. Financing your home is covered in detail later in this chapter.

The Real Estate Sales Contract

After selecting a home to buy, you must enter into a sales contract. State laws generally specify that to be enforceable in court, real estate buy-sell agreements must be in writing and contain certain information, including (1) names of buyers and sellers, (2) a description of the property sufficient for positive identification, (3) specific price and other terms, and (4) usually the signatures of the buyers and sellers. Real estate sales transactions often take weeks and sometimes months to complete. Because they involve a fair amount of legal work, they require expert assistance in preparation. Contract requirements help keep the facts straight and reduce the chance for misunderstanding, misrepresentation, or fraud.

Although these requirements fulfill the minimums necessary for court enforcement, in practice real estate sales contracts usually contain several other contractual clauses relating to earnest money deposits, contingencies, personal property, and closing costs. An **earnest money deposit** is the money you pledge to show good faith when you make an offer. If, after signing a sales contract, you withdraw from the transaction without a valid reason, you may forfeit this deposit. A valid reason for withdrawal would be stated in the contract as a contingency clause. With a **contingency clause,** you can condition your agreement to buy on such factors as the availability of financing, a satisfactory termite or other physical inspection of the property, or the advice of a lawyer or real estate expert. Generally speaking, your lawyer should review and approve all agreements before you sign them.

Closing the Deal

After you obtain financing and your loan is approved, the closing process begins. Although closing costs may climb into the thousands of dollars, homebuyers can often save significant amounts if they shop for financing, insurance, and other closing items rather than merely accepting the costs quoted by any one lender or provider of closing services.

prequalification The process of arranging with a mortgage lender, in advance of buying a home, to obtain the amount of mortgage financing the lender deems affordable to the home-buyer.

earnest money deposit Money pledged by a buyer to show good faith when making an offer to buy a home.

contingency clause A clause in a real estate sales contract that makes the agreement conditional on such factors as the availability of financing, property inspections, or obtaining expert advice.

The **Real Estate Settlement Procedures Act (RESPA)** governs closings on owner-occupied houses, condominiums, and apartment buildings of four units or fewer. This act reduced closing costs by prohibiting kickbacks made to real estate agents and others from lenders or title insurance companies. It also requires clear, advance disclosure of all closing costs to homebuyers. Lenders must give potential borrowers a U.S. Department of Housing and Urban Development booklet entitled *Settlement Costs and You: A HUD Guide for Homebuyers*. The booklet sets forth the specific requirements of RESPA, and can take much of the mystery out of the closing process. Exhibit 5.10 provides some tips to help you sail smoothly through the closing process.

Title Check

Numerous legal interests can exist in real estate simultaneously: for example, those of the owners, lenders, lien holders (such as an unpaid roofing contractor), and easement holders. Before taking title to a property, make sure that the seller (who is conveying title to you) actually has the legal interest he or she claims, and that the title is free of all liens and encumbrances (except those specifically referred to in the sales contract).

Although it's up to you to question the integrity of the title to the property you're buying, in most cases an attorney or title insurance company performs a **title check,** consisting of the necessary research of legal documents and courthouse records. The customary practices and procedures and costs vary widely throughout the country. Regardless of the specific custom in your area, be sure to make some form of title check an essential part of your closing process.

Closing Statement

A *closing statement*, provided to both buyer and seller at or before the actual closing, accounts for monies that change hands during the transaction. The statement reconciles the borrower's and seller's costs and shows how much the borrower owes and the seller receives from the transaction. Before closing a home purchase, you should be given an opportunity to review the closing statement and have your questions answered. Carefully and critically review the statement to make sure that it is accurate and consistent with the contractual terms of the transaction; if not, have the statement corrected before closing the deal.

Real Estate Settlement Procedures Act (RESPA) A federal law requiring mortgage lenders to give potential borrowers a government publication describing the closing process and providing clear, advance disclosure of all closing costs to homebuyers.

title check The research of legal documents and courthouse records to verify that the seller conveying title actually has the legal interest he or she claims, and that the title is free of all liens and encumbrances.

EXHIBIT 5.10 · 10 Things You Should Not Do Before Closing

The seller has accepted your offer to purchase, and your new home is officially under contract. Here are some tips to help you sail smoothly through the closing.

1. **Don't make a major purchase** even if you think your new house needs a new car in the driveway. Talk to your mortgage loan officer before making a major purchase.
2. **Don't change jobs;** banks like to see a consistent employment history.
3. **Don't give an earnest money deposit to a for-sale-by-owner seller;** instead, put it into a trust account to make sure the seller doesn't spend it.
4. **Don't let your emotions take over** by letting the seller's refusal to make a small repair kill the deal. Be realistic because no home is perfect, especially older homes.
5. **Don't forget to switch utilities** and apply for service at your new home. Do so as soon as you know your closing date.
6. **Don't forget about homeowner's insurance;** your lender will require an insurance binder for the new home prior to closing.
7. **Don't become best friends with the seller;** personality conflicts can cloud your judgment.
8. **Don't panic if the appraisal comes in low;** there are things you and your agent can do to correct the problem. Study your options.
9. **Don't go it alone;** it's the agent's duty to help you make it to the closing. Their commission depends on it.
10. **Don't ignore lender requirements;** make sure you know what's expected and take care of it. If your lender asks you for something, provide it immediately.

Source: From http://www.homebuying.about.com/cs/beforeyouclose/a/home-buying.htm, May 17, 2006.

Concept Check

CHECK • CONCEPT CHECK • CONCEPT CHECK • CONCEPT CHECK • CONCEPT CHECK • CONCEPT CHECK • CONCEPT C

5-14	Describe some of the steps homebuyers can take to improve the home-buying process and increase their overall satisfaction with their purchases.
5-15	What role does a real estate agent play in the purchase of a house? What is the benefit of the *Multiple Listing Service?* How is the real estate agent compensated, and by whom?
5-16	Why should you investigate mortgage loans and prequalify for a mortgage early in the home-buying process?
5-17	What information is normally included in a real estate sales contract? What is an *earnest money deposit?* What is a *contingency clause?*
5-18	Describe the steps involved in closing a home-purchase transaction.

LG6 FINANCING THE TRANSACTION

Earlier in the chapter, we saw that mortgage terms can dramatically affect the amount you can afford to spend on a home. The success of a real estate transaction often hinges on obtaining a mortgage with favorable terms. A **mortgage loan** is secured by the property: If the borrower defaults, the lender has the legal right to liquidate the property to recover the funds it is owed. Before you obtain such a loan, it's helpful to understand the sources and types of mortgages and their underlying economics.

Sources of Mortgage Loans

The major sources of home mortgages today are commercial banks, thrift institutions, and mortgage bankers or brokers; also, some credit unions make mortgage loans available to their members. Commercial banks are also an important source of *interim construction loans,* providing short-term financing during the construction process for individuals who are building or remodeling a home. After the home is completed, the homeowner obtains *permanent financing*, in the form of a standard mortgage loan, and uses the proceeds from it to repay the construction loan.

mortgage loan A loan secured by the property: If the borrower defaults, the lender has the legal right to liquidate the property to recover the funds it is owed.

mortgage banker A firm that solicits borrowers, originates primarily government-insured and government-guaranteed loans, and places them with mortgage lenders; often uses its own money to initially fund mortgages it later resells.

mortgage broker A firm that solicits borrowers, originates primarily conventional loans, and places them with mortgage lenders; the broker merely takes loan applications and then finds lenders willing to grant the mortgage loans under the desired terms.

Another way to obtain a mortgage loan is through a mortgage banker or mortgage broker. Both solicit borrowers, originate loans, and place them with traditional mortgage lenders as well as life insurance companies and pension funds. Whereas **mortgage bankers** often use their own money to initially fund mortgages they later resell, **mortgage brokers** take loan applications and then seek lenders willing to grant the mortgage loans under the desired terms. Mortgage bankers deal primarily in government-insured and government-guaranteed loans, whereas mortgage brokers concentrate on finding conventional loans for consumers. Most brokers also have ongoing relationships with different lenders, thereby increasing your chances of finding a loan even if you don't qualify at a commercial bank or thrift institution. Brokers can often simplify the financing process by cutting through red tape, negotiating more favorable terms, and reducing the amount of time to close the loan. Mortgage brokers earn their income from commissions and origination fees paid by the lender, costs that are typically passed on to the borrower in the points charged on a loan. The borrower must often pay application, processing, and document preparation fees to the lender at closing. Exhibit 5.11 on page 162 offers advice for finding a good mortgage broker. You may prefer to shop for a mortgage on your own or with your realtor, who is knowledgeable about various lenders and legally prohibited from collecting fees or kickbacks for helping to arrange financing.

Online Mortgage Resources

Shopping for the best mortgage rate and terms has become easier thanks to the Internet. Many sites allow you to search for the best fixed-rate or adjustable-rate mortgage in your

You've contracted to buy a property, and you have decided to use a mortgage broker to obtain a mortgage loan. Here are some tips to help you find a good mortgage broker.

- Get referrals from realtors, bankers, and other buyers.
- To help you get the best rate and terms, the broker should represent 10 or more lenders from around the United States.
- Investigate the firm and its reputation. Ask how many of their loan applications are actually funded; about 70 percent or more should result in closings.
- If your state licenses mortgage brokers, choose one who is licensed and has been in business for several years. Many brokers are certified by the National Association of Mortgage Brokers, although this is not a requirement.
- Request a written estimate of closing costs and an explanation of each cost.
- Avoid a broker who asks for up-front fees and promises to find you a loan.

Smart Sites

American Loan Search provides a list of online mortgage lenders in your area when you enter your state. The site also has a rate search engine to help you find a lender with the rate you want.
http://www.thomsonedu.com/finance/gitman.

area. HSH Associates, a mortgage consulting firm with a Web site at **http://www.hsh.com,** lists mortgages offered by banks, mortgage companies, and brokerage firms across the country, along with information on prevailing interest rates, terms, and points. Bankrate, **http://www.bankrate.com,** and similar sites also offer mortgage comparisons. Shopping via the Internet gives you great leverage when dealing with a lender. For example, if a local mortgage lender offers a 3-year adjustable-rate mortgage (ARM) with 1.20 points and a 6.75 percent rate, but a lender in a different state offers the same term with the same rate and only 1 point, you can negotiate with your local lender to get a better deal.

Although the Internet is still primarily a source of comparative information, online lenders such as E-Loan, **http://www.eloan.com,** a large online-only mortgage bank, hopes that homebuyers will choose to apply for and close a loan online. Or submit your information to LendingTree at **http://www.lendingtree.com;** within 24 hours you'll receive bids from four lenders interested in making your loan. Visit MSN Real Estate at **http://www.realestate.msn.com** for loan and general home-buying information.

Types of Mortgage Loans

There is no single way to classify mortgages. For our purposes, we'll group them in two ways: (1) terms of payment and (2) whether they're conventional, insured, or guaranteed.

There are literally dozens of different types of home mortgages from which to choose. The most common types of mortgage loans made today are fixed-rate and adjustable-rate mortgages. Let's take a closer look at their features, advantages, and disadvantages.

Fixed-Rate Mortgages

The **fixed-rate mortgage** still accounts for a large portion of all home mortgages. Both the rate of interest and the monthly mortgage payment are fixed over the full term of the loan. The most common type of fixed-rate mortgage is the *30-year fixed-rate* loan, although *10- and 15-year loans* are becoming more popular as homeowners recognize the advantages of paying off their loan over a shorter period of time. Due to the risks the lender assumes with a 30-year loan, it's usually the most expensive form of home financing.

Gaining in popularity is the *15-year fixed-rate* loan. Its chief appeal is that it is repaid twice as fast (15 years versus 30) and yet the monthly payments don't increase significantly. To pay off a loan in less time, the homeowner must pay more each month, but monthly payments don't have to be doubled to pay off the loan in half the time; rather, the monthly payment on a 15-year loan is generally only about 20 percent larger than the payment on a 30-year loan. The following table shows the difference in monthly payment and total interest paid for 30- and 15-year fixed-rate mortgages. In both cases the purchaser borrows $80,000 at a 7 percent fixed rate of interest:

fixed-rate mortgage
The traditional type of mortgage in which both the rate of interest and the monthly mortgage payment are fixed over the full term of the loan.

Term of Loan	Regular Payment	Total Interest Paid over Life of Loan
30 years	$532.24 per month	$111,606
15 years	$719.06 per month	$49,431

Perhaps the most startling feature is the substantial difference in the total amount of interest paid over the term of the loan. In effect, you can save *about $62,000* just by financing your home with a 15-year mortgage rather than over the traditional 30 years. Note that this amount of savings is possible even though monthly payments differ by only about $187. In practice, the difference in the monthly payment would be even less because 15-year mortgages are usually available at interest rates that are about half a percentage point below comparable 30-year loans.

Although the idea of paying off a mortgage in 15 years instead of 30 may seem like a good one, you should consider how long you plan to stay in the house. If you plan to sell the house in a few years, paying off the loan faster may not make much sense. In addition, the tax deductibility of mortgage interest makes a mortgage one of the least expensive sources of borrowing. If you can earn a higher rate of return than the rate of interest on a 30-year loan, you'd be better off taking the 30-year loan and investing the difference in the payment between it and the comparable 15-year loan.

Another way to shorten the mortgage term without committing to an initially shorter term is by regularly making extra principal payments, or when you have extra funds. If you can earn exactly the mortgage interest rate—7 percent annually in our example, you could take the 30-year loan and invest the $187 you save each month over the 15-year mortgage; and at any time, subtracting the sum of the saved mortgage payments and the interest earned on them from the outstanding 30-year mortgage balance would exactly equal the outstanding balance on the 15-year loan. In other words, you could use the 30-year loan to exactly replicate the 15-year loan. Because of this relationship, some people recommend "taking the 30-year loan and investing the savings over a comparable 15-year loan." Unfortunately, the success of this strategy depends on (1) your discipline to invest the difference every month and, more important, (2) an ability to consistently earn the mortgage interest rate on your investments. Because both of these conditions are unlikely, you're best off taking the mortgage that most closely meets your financial needs.

Some lenders offer other types of fixed-rate loans. **Balloon-payment mortgages** offer terms of 5, 7, or 10 years where the interest rate is fixed, typically at .25 to .5 percent below the 30-year fixed rate. The monthly payments are the same as for a 30-year loan at the given rate. When the loan matures, the remaining principal balance comes due and must be refinanced. Although the lower rate results in lower monthly payments, these loans do carry some risk because refinancing may be difficult, particularly if rates have risen.

Adjustable-Rate Mortgages (ARMs)

Another popular form of home loan is the **adjustable-rate mortgage (ARM).** The rate of interest, and therefore the size of the monthly payment, is adjusted based on market interest rate movements. The mortgage interest rate is linked to a specific *interest rate index* and is adjusted at specific intervals (usually once or twice a year) based on changes in the index. When the index moves up, so does the interest rate on the mortgage and, in turn, the size of the monthly mortgage payment increases. The new interest rate and monthly mortgage payment remain in effect until the next adjustment date.

The term of an ARM can be 15 or 30 years. Because the size of the monthly payments will vary with interest rates, there's no way to tell what your future payments will be. However, because the borrower assumes most or all of the interest rate risk in these mortgages, the *initial rate of interest* on an adjustable-rate mortgage is normally well below—typically by 2 to 3 percentage points—the rate of a standard 30-year fixed-rate loan. Of course, whether the borrower actually ends up paying less interest depends on the behavior of market interest rates during the term of the loan.

balloon-payment mortgage A mortgage with a single large principal payment due at a specified future date.

adjustable-rate mortgage (ARM) A mortgage on which the rate of interest, and therefore the size of the monthly payment, is adjusted based on market interest rate movements.

Features of ARMs. It's important for homebuyers to understand the basic features of an ARM:

- **Adjustment period:** Although the period of time between rate or payment changes is typically 6 months to 1 year, adjustment periods can range from 3 months to 3 or 5 years.
- **Index rate:** A baseline rate that captures the movement in interest rates, tied to 6-month U.S. Treasury securities, 6-month CDs, or the average cost of funds to savings institutions, commonly measured by the 11th Federal Home Loan Bank District Cost of Funds.
- **Margin:** The percentage points a lender adds to the index to determine the rate of interest on an ARM, usually a fixed amount over the life of the loan. Thus the rate of interest on an ARM equals the index rate plus the margin.
- **Interest rate caps:** Limits on the amount the interest rate can increase over a given period. *Periodic caps* limit interest rate increases from one adjustment to the next (typically lenders cap annual rate adjustments at 1 to 2 percentage points), and *overall caps* limit the interest rate increase over the life of the loan (lifetime interest rate caps are set at 5 to 8 percentage points). Many ARMs have both periodic and overall interest rate caps.
- **Payment caps:** Limits on monthly payment increases that may result from a rate adjustment—usually a percentage of the previous payment. If your ARM has a 5 percent payment cap, your monthly payments can increase no more than 5 percent from 1 year to the next—regardless of what happens to interest rates.

Because most ARMs are 30-year loans (360 payments), you can determine the initial monthly payment in the same manner as for any other 30-year mortgage. For example, for an $80,000 loan at 7.5 percent (5.5 percent index rate + 2 percent margin), we can use a calculator as shown in the margin or Exhibit 5.8 to find the first-year monthly payments of $559.44. Assuming a 1-year adjustment period, if the index rate rises to 7 percent, the interest rate for the second year will be 9 percent (7 percent + 2 percent = 9 percent). The size of the monthly payment for the next 12 months will then be adjusted upward to about $643.00. This process is repeated each year thereafter until the loan matures.

Beware of Negative Amortization. Some ARMs are subject to **negative amortization**—an increase in the principal balance resulting from monthly loan payments that are lower than the amount of monthly interest being charged. In other words, you could end up with a larger mortgage balance on the next anniversary of your loan than on the previous one. This occurs when the payment is intentionally set below the interest charge, or when the ARM has interest rates that are adjusted monthly—with monthly payments that adjust annually. In the latter case, when rates are rising on these loans, the current monthly payment can be less than the interest being charged, and the difference is added to the principal, thereby increasing the size of the loan.

ARMs with a cap on the dollar amount of monthly payments can also lead to negative amortization. For example, assume that the monthly payment on a 7.5 percent, 30-year, $80,000 loan is $560 with its next annual adjustment in 10 months. If, due to rising interest rates, the applicable rate increases to 9 percent, increasing the monthly payment to $640, negative amortization of $80 per month would occur. If no other interest rate change was to occur over the remaining 10 months until its next adjustment, the mortgage balance would be $80,800—the increase of $800 attributable to an $80 per month negative amortization over 10 months.

When considering an ARM, be sure to learn whether negative amortization could occur. Generally, loans without the potential for negative amortization are available although they tend to have slightly higher initial rates and interest rate caps.

Here are other types of ARMs lenders may offer:

- **Convertible ARMs** allow borrowers to convert from an adjustable-rate to a fixed-rate loan during a specified time period, usually any time between the 13th and 60th month. Although these loans seldom provide the lowest initial rate, they allow the borrower to convert to a fixed-rate loan if interest rates decline. A conversion fee of around $500 is

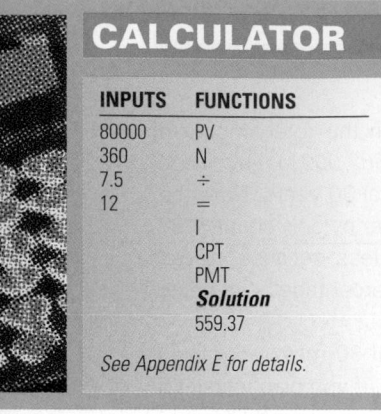

CALCULATOR

INPUTS	FUNCTIONS
80000	PV
360	N
7.5	÷
12	=
	I
	CPT
	PMT
	Solution
	559.37

See Appendix E for details.

adjustment period On an adjustable-rate mortgage, the period of time between rate or payment changes.

index rate On an adjustable-rate mortgage, the baseline index rate that captures interest rate movements.

margin On an adjustable-rate mortgage, the percentage points a lender adds to the *index rate* to determine the rate of interest.

interest rate cap On an adjustable-rate mortgage, the limit on the amount that the interest rate can increase each adjustment period and over the life of the loan.

payment cap On an adjustable-rate mortgage, the limit on the monthly payment increase that may result from a rate adjustment.

negative amortization When the principal balance on a mortgage loan increases because the monthly loan payment is lower than the amount of monthly interest being charged; some ARMs are subject to this undesirable situation.

convertible ARM An adjustable-rate mortgage loan that allows borrowers to convert from an adjustable-rate to a fixed-rate loan, usually at any time between the 13th and the 60th month.

typical, and the fixed rate is normally set at .25 to .5 percent above the going rate on fixed-rate loans at the time you convert.

- **Two-step ARMs** have just two interest rates, the first for an initial period of 5 to 7 years and a higher one for the remaining term of the loan.

Choosing an Index. The index on your ARM significantly affects the level and stability of your mortgage payments over the term of your loan. Lenders use short-term indexes such as the Six-Month Treasury Bill; LIBOR, the *London Inter Bank Offering Rate,* a base rate similar to the prime rate and used in the international marketplace; CD-based indexes; and the 11th Federal Home Loan Bank District Cost of Funds.

The most important difference between the indexes is their volatility. LIBOR and CD rates are volatile because they quickly respond to changes in the financial markets. The 11th Federal Home Loan Bank District Cost of Funds index is less volatile because it represents an average of the cost of funds to S&Ls in the District. It tends to lag other short-term rate movements, both up and down, and exhibits a fairly smooth pattern over time. To more fully understand how one index behaves relative to another, you may want to compare index rates over the past several years.

So what does this mean for the homebuyer considering an ARM? If your mortgage is tied to a LIBOR or CD index, you can expect sharper and more frequent upward and downward interest rate movements, while cost of funds indexes move more slowly in both directions. To choose which is better for you, consider the annual rate cap on the mortgage, the level of interest rates, and future interest rate expectations. If you have a low rate cap of 1 to 2 percentage points, and you think rates might go down, you may be comfortable with a more volatile index.

Some lenders offer special first-year "teaser" rates that are below the index rate on the loan. Be wary of lenders with very low rates. Ask them if the first-year rate is based on the index and verify the rate yourself. Be sure you can comfortably make the monthly mortgage payment when the interest rate steps up to the indexed rate.

Monitoring Your Mortgage Payments. You should carefully monitor your mortgage over its life. Always verify the calculation of your loan payment when rate or payment adjustments are made. To verify your payment amount, you need to know the index rate, the margin, and the formula used to adjust the loan; all are found in the loan agreement. Interest rates for the most commonly used indexes are readily available in the financial press and are published weekly in the real estate section of most newspapers. The loan formula tells you when the rate is set—for example, 45 days before the adjustment date—and the margin on the loan. You can use a handheld business calculator (as demonstrated earlier) to calculate the payment once you know the new rate, the number of years until the loan is paid off, and the current principal balance.

If you suspect you're being overcharged, call your lender and ask for an explanation of the rate and payment calculations. Special mortgage-checking services will review your ARM for a fee of about $70 to $100.

Fixed Rate or Adjustable Rate?

Fixed-rate mortgages are popular with homebuyers who plan to stay in their homes for at least 5 to 7 years and want to know what their payments will be. Of course, the current level of interest rates and your expectation about future interest rates will influence your choice of a fixed-rate or adjustable-rate mortgage. When the average interest rate on a 30-year mortgage loan was high, people chose adjustable-rate mortgages to avoid being locked into prevailing high rates. When interest rates are low, many homebuyers opt for fixed-rate mortgages to lock in these attractive rates. In such situations many homeowners with existing adjustable-rate mortgages refinance them with fixed-rate loans to take advantage of favorable current fixed rates.

Other Mortgage Payment Options

In addition to standard fixed-rate and adjustable-rate mortgage loans, some lenders offer variations designed to help first-time homebuyers:

two-step ARM An adjustable-rate mortgage with just two interest rates: one for the first 5 to 7 years of the loan, and a higher one for the remaining term of the loan.

- **Interest-only mortgages** are loans requiring the borrower to pay only the interest. The popularity of these mortgages has increased in response to the rapidly rising prices of the real estate boom occurring between 2001 and 2005. Rather than amortizing the loan into equal monthly payments over the term of the loan, the borrower merely pays the accrued interest each month. These mortgages allow the borrower, typically on more expensive properties, to make lower payments that are fully tax deductible. Most interest-only mortgages are offered as ARMs.
- **Graduated-payment mortgages** are loans offering low payments for the first few years, gradually increasing until year 3 or 5, then remaining fixed. The low initial payments appeal to people who are just starting out and expect their income to rise. If this doesn't occur, however, it could result in a higher debt load than the borrower can handle.
- **Growing-equity mortgages** are fixed-rate mortgages with payments that increase over a specific period. The extra funds are applied to the principal, so a conventional 30-year loan is paid off in about 20 years. However, you can accomplish the same thing without locking yourself into a set schedule by taking a fixed-rate mortgage that allows prepayments.
- **Shared-appreciation mortgages** are loans that have a below-market interest rate because the lender or other party shares from 30 to 50 percent of the appreciated value when the home is sold. This can be a useful tool if you absolutely can't afford the higher rates of a conventional loan; but keep in mind that with appreciation of only 2 percent per year for just 5 years, such a loan could cost you up to $5,000 in shared equity on a $100,000 property.
- **Biweekly mortgages** are loans on which payments equal to half of a regular monthly payment are made every 2 weeks rather than once a month. Because you make 26 payments (52 weeks/2), which is the equivalent of 13 monthly payments, the principal balance declines faster, and you pay less interest over the life of the loan. Once again, with most 30-year mortgages you can make extra principal payments at any time, without penalty. This may be preferable to committing to a biweekly loan that can charge an additional processing fee.
- **Buydowns** are a type of seller financing sometimes offered on new homes. A builder or seller arranges for mortgage financing with a financial institution at interest rates well below market rates—6 percent financing when the market rate of interest is around 7 or 7.5 percent. Typically the builder or seller subsidizes the loan for the buyer at a special low interest rate. However, the reduced interest rate may be for only a short period, or the buyer will pay for the reduced interest in the form of a higher purchase price.

Conventional, Insured, and Guaranteed Loans

A **conventional mortgage** is a mortgage offered by a lender who assumes all the risk of loss. To protect themselves, lenders usually require a down payment of at least 20 percent of the value of the mortgaged property. For lower down payments, the lender usually requires *private mortgage insurance (PMI)*, as described earlier in the chapter. High borrower equity greatly reduces the likelihood of default on a mortgage and subsequent loss to the lender. However, a high down payment requirement makes home buying more difficult for many families and individuals.

To promote home ownership, the federal government, through the Federal Housing Administration (FHA), offers lenders mortgage insurance on high loan-to-value ratio loans. These loans usually feature low down payments, below-market interest rates, few if any points, and relaxed income or debt ratio qualifications.

The **FHA mortgage insurance** program helps people buy homes even when they have very little money available for a down payment and closing costs. As of summer 2006, the up-front mortgage insurance premium for a 15- or 30-year mortgage was 1.5 percent of the loan amount—paid by the borrower at closing or included in the mortgage—plus another .5 percent annual renewal premium, paid monthly. Homebuyers who want a 15-year mortgage and make a down payment greater than 10 percent of the purchase price only pay the up-front fee. The FHA agrees to reimburse lenders for losses up to a specified maximum

interest-only mortgage
A mortgage that requires the borrower to pay only interest; typically used to finance the purchase of more expensive properties.

graduated-payment mortgage A mortgage that starts with unusually low payments that rise over several years to a fixed payment.

growing-equity mortgage Fixed-rate mortgage with payments that increase over a specific period. Extra funds are applied to the principal so the loan is paid off more quickly.

shared-appreciation mortgage A loan that allows a lender or other party to share in the appreciated value when the home is sold.

biweekly mortgage
A loan on which payments equal to half the regular monthly payment are made every 2 weeks.

buydown Financing made available by a builder or seller to a potential new-home buyer at well below market interest rates, often only for a short period.

conventional mortgage A mortgage offered by a lender who assumes all the risk of loss; typically requires a down payment of at least 20 percent of the value of the mortgaged property.

FHA mortgage insurance A program under which the Federal Housing Administration (FHA) offers lenders mortgage insurance on loans having a high loan-to-value ratio; its intent is to encourage loans to homebuyers who have very little money available for a down payment and closing costs.

amount if the buyer defaults. The minimum required down payment on an FHA loan is 3 percent of the sales price. The interest rate on an FHA loan is generally about .5 percent to 1 percent lower than that on conventional fixed-rate loans. Affordability ratios used to qualify applicants for these loans are typically less stringent than those used for conventional loans. The maximum mortgage amount the FHA can insure is based on the national *median* price of homes and varies depending on location. To learn more about FHA mortgages, visit **http://www.fha.com/home_purchase.cfm.**

Guaranteed loans are similar to insured loans, but better—if you qualify. **VA loan guarantees** are provided by the U.S. Veterans Administration to lenders who make qualified mortgage loans to eligible veterans of the U.S. Armed Forces and their unmarried surviving spouses. This program, however, does not require lenders or veterans to pay a premium for the guarantee. In many instances, an eligible veteran must pay only closing costs; in effect, under such a program, a veteran can buy a home with no down payment. (This can be done *only once* with a VA loan.) The mortgage loan—subject to a maximum of about $240,000 (as of summer 2006)—can amount to as much as 100 percent of a purchased property's appraised value. VA loans include a funding fee of about 2.2 percent on no down payment loans (the fee is lower if the down payment is 5 percent or more). The VA sets the maximum interest rate, which, like FHA loans, is usually about .5 percent below the rate on conventional fixed-rate loans. To qualify, the veteran must meet VA credit guidelines. You'll find more information at **http://www.homeloans.va.gov/pamphlet.htm.**

Refinancing Your Mortgage

After you've purchased a home and closed the transaction, interest rates on similar loans may drop. If rates drop by 1 to 2 percent or more, you should consider the economics of refinancing after carefully comparing the terms of the old and new mortgages, the anticipated number of years you expect to remain in the home, any prepayment penalty on the old mortgage, and the closing costs associated with the new mortgage.

Worksheet 5.4 on page 168 presents a form to use when analyzing the impact of refinancing. The data for the Philipatos family's analysis is shown. Their original $80,000, 10-year-old, 10 percent mortgage has a current balance of $72,750 and monthly payments of $702 for 20 more years. If they refinance the $72,750 balance at the prevailing rate of 7 percent, over the remaining 20-year life of the current mortgage, the monthly payment would drop to $564. The Philipatoses plan to live in their house for at least 5 more years. They won't have to pay a penalty for prepaying their current mortgage, and closing and other costs associated with the new mortgage are $2,400 after taxes. Substituting these values into Worksheet 5.4 reveals (in Item 7) that it will take the Philipatoses 23 months to break even with the new mortgage. Because 23 months is considerably less than their anticipated minimum 5 years (60 months) in the home, the economics easily support refinancing their mortgage under the specified terms.

There are two basic reasons to refinance—to reduce the monthly payment or to reduce the total interest cost over the term of the loan. If a lower monthly payment is the objective, the analysis is relatively simple: determine how long it will take for the monthly savings to equal your closing costs (see Worksheet 5.4).

If your objective is to reduce the total interest cost over the life of the loan, the analysis is more complex. The term of the new loan versus the existing loan is a critical element. If you refinance a 30-year loan that's already 10 years old, with another 30-year loan, you're extending the total loan maturity to 40 years. Consequently, even with a lower interest rate, you may pay more interest over the life of the newly extended loan. So, you should refinance with a shorter-term loan, ideally one that matures no later than the original loan maturity date. (The example in Worksheet 5.4 is prepared on this basis.)

Many homeowners want to pay off their loans more quickly to free up funds for their children's college education or for their own retirement. By refinancing at a lower rate and continuing to make the same monthly payment, a larger portion of each payment will go toward reducing the principal, so the loan will be paid off more quickly. Alternately, the borrower can make extra principal payments whenever possible. Paying only an additional $25 per month on a 30-year, 9 percent, $80,000 mortgage reduces the term to about 25 years and saves about $30,000 in interest.

VA loan guarantee A guarantee offered by the U.S. Veterans Administration to lenders who make qualified mortgage loans to eligible veterans of the U.S. Armed Forces and their unmarried surviving spouses.

Using this form, the Philipatoses find that by refinancing the $72,750 balance on their 10-year-old, $80,000, 10-percent, 30-year mortgage (which has no prepayment penalty and requires payments of $702 per month) with a 7-percent, 20-year mortgage requiring $564 monthly payments and $2,400 in total after-tax closing costs, it will take 23 months to break even. Because the Philipatoses plan to stay in their home for at least 60 more months, the refinancing is easily justified.

MORTGAGE REFINANCING ANALYSIS

Name __Demi and Nicholas Philipatos__   Date __September 6, 2008__

Item	Description		Amount
1	Current monthly payment (Terms: $80,000, 10%, 30 years)		$ 702
2	New monthly payment (Terms: $72,750, 7%, 20 years)		564
3	Monthly savings, pretax (Item 1 − Item 2)		$ 138
4	Tax on monthly savings [Item 3 × tax rate (25 %)]		35
5	Monthly savings, after-tax (Item 3 − Item 4)		$ 103
6	Costs to refinance:		
	a. Prepayment penalty	$ 0	
	b. Total closing costs (after-tax)	2,400	
	c. Total refinancing costs (Item 6a + Item 6b)		$ 2,400
7	Months to break even (Item 6c ÷ Item 5)		23

Some people consider the reduced tax deduction associated with a smaller mortgage interest deduction as a disadvantage of refinancing. Although the interest deduction may indeed be reduced because of refinancing, the more important concern is the amount of the actual after-tax cash payments. In this regard, refinancing with a lower-interest-rate mortgage (with all other terms assumed unchanged) will always result in lower after-tax cash outflows and is therefore economically appealing. Of course, as demonstrated in Worksheet 5.4, the monthly savings should be compared with the refinancing costs to make the final refinancing decision.

Because lenders offer new mortgage products regularly, carefully check all your options before refinancing. Remember that when you refinance, most lenders require you to have at least 20 percent equity in your home, based on a current market appraisal. Many financial institutions are willing to refinance their existing loans, often charging fewer points and lower closing costs than a new lender would charge, so be sure to check with your existing lender first.

❚❚ Concept Check

CHECK • CONCEPT CHECK • CONCEPT CHECK • CONCEPT CHECK • CONCEPT CHECK • CONCEPT CHECK • CONCEPT

5-19	Describe the various sources of mortgage loans. What role might a *mortgage broker* play in obtaining mortgage financing?
5-20	Briefly describe the two basic types of mortgage loans. Which has the lowest initial rate of interest? What is *negative amortization,* and which type of mortgage can experience it? Discuss the advantages and disadvantages of each mortgage type.
5-21	Differentiate among conventional, insured, and guaranteed mortgage loans.
5-22	What factors should you consider when deciding whether to refinance your mortgage to reduce the monthly payment? How can the refinancing decision be made?

SUMMARY

LG1 Implement a plan to research and select a new or used automobile. The purchase of an automobile, usually the second largest expenditure you'll make, should be based on thorough market research and comparison shopping. Important purchase considerations include affordability; operating costs; whether to buy a gas diesel, or hybrid fueled car; whether to buy a new versus a used or nearly new car; the type of car and its features; and its reliability and warranties. Knowing the dealer's cost is the key to negotiating a good price.

LG2 Decide whether to buy or lease a car. Before leasing a vehicle you should consider all the terms of the lease, including the annual mileage allowance and early termination penalties. The economics of leasing versus purchasing a car with an installment loan should not be considered until the price is set. The four components of the lease payment are the capitalized cost, residual value, money factor, and lease term.

LG3 Identify housing alternatives, assess the rental option, and perform a rent-or-buy analysis. A family can meet its housing needs in many different ways. In addition to single-family homes, there are condominiums, cooperative apartments, and rental units. Evaluate the advantages and disadvantages of each for your current lifestyle. Many people rent because they can't afford to buy a home; others choose to rent because it's more convenient for their lifestyle and economic situation. The rental contract, or lease agreement, describes the terms under which you can rent the property, including the monthly rental amount, lease term, restrictions, and so forth. A rent-or-buy analysis can help you choose the least costly alternative. Also consider qualitative factors, such as how long you plan to stay in an area, and perform the analysis over a several-year timeline.

LG4 Evaluate the benefits and costs of home ownership and estimate how much you can afford for a home. In addition to the emotional rewards, other benefits of home ownership are the tax shelter and inflation hedge it provides. Home ownership costs include the down payment, points and closing costs, monthly mortgage payments, property taxes and insurance, and normal home maintenance and operating expenses. Any of these can amount to a considerable sum of money. Carefully consider all of them to estimate how much you can afford to spend on a home.

LG5 Describe the home-buying process. Most people shopping for a home seek the help of a real estate agent to obtain access to properties and provide needed information and advice. The agents involved in the transaction split a 5 to 7 percent commission, paid by the seller, when the transaction is closed. Today the Internet is a valuable resource that allows homebuyers to conveniently search for suitable available properties. It's a good idea to prequalify yourself for a mortgage before starting to house hunt. A real estate sales contract is used to confirm in writing all terms of the transaction between buyer and seller. After a mortgage loan is approved, the loan is closed. A closing statement shows how much the borrower owes and the seller receives from the transaction.

LG6 Choose mortgage financing that meets your needs. Mortgage loans can be obtained from commercial banks, thrift institutions, or through a mortgage banker or mortgage broker. Although many types of mortgage loans are available, the most widely used are 30- and 15-year fixed-rate mortgages and adjustable-rate mortgages (ARMs). Sometimes interest rates will drop several years after closing, and mortgage refinancing will become attractive. The refinancing analysis considers the difference in terms between the old and new mortgages, any prepayment penalty on the old mortgage, closing costs, and how long you plan to stay in the home.

FINANCIAL PLANNING EXERCISES

LG1, 2

1. Janet Forrester has just graduated from college and needs to buy a car to commute to work. She estimates that she can afford to pay about $350 per month for a loan or lease and has about $2,000 in savings to use for a down payment. Develop a plan to guide her through her first car-buying experience, including researching car type, deciding whether to buy a new or used car, negotiating the price and terms, and financing the transaction.

LG2

2. *Use Worksheet 5.1.* Chris Svenson is trying to decide whether to lease or purchase a new car costing $18,000. If he leases, he'll have to pay a $600 security deposit and monthly pay-

ments of $425 over the 36-month term of the closed-end lease. If, on the other hand, he buys the car, he'll have to make a $2,400 down payment and will finance the balance with a 36-month loan requiring monthly payments of $515; he'll also have to pay a 6 percent sales tax ($1,080) on the purchase price, and he expects the car to have a residual value of $6,500 at the end of 3 years. Chris can earn 4 percent interest on his savings. Use the automobile lease versus purchase analysis form in Worksheet 5.1 to find the total cost of both the lease and the purchase and recommend the best strategy to Chris.

LG4   3. How much would you have to put down on a house costing $100,000 if the house had an appraised value of $105,000 and the lender required an 80 percent loan-to-value ratio?

LG4   4. Using the maximum ratios for a conventional mortgage, how big a monthly payment could the Bacon family afford if their gross (before-tax) monthly income amounted to $4,000? Would it make any difference if they were already making monthly installment loan payments totaling $750 on two car loans?

LG4   5. How much might a homebuyer expect to pay in closing costs on a $120,000 house with a 10 percent down payment? How much would the homebuyer have to pay at the time of closing, taking into account closing costs, down payment, and a loan fee of 3 points?

LG4   6. Find the *monthly* mortgage payments on the following mortgage loans using either your calculator or the table in Exhibit 5.8:
   a. $80,000/6.5 percent/30 years
   b. $105,000/8 percent/20 years
   c. $95,000/10.5 percent/15 years

LG3, 4   7. *Use Worksheet 5.2.* Rebecca Serra is currently renting an apartment for $625 per month and paying $275 annually for renter's insurance. She just found a small townhouse she can buy for $85,000. She has enough cash for a $10,000 down payment and $4,000 in closing costs. Her bank is offering 30-year mortgages at 7.5 percent per year. Rebecca estimated the following costs as a percentage of the home's price: property taxes, 2.5 percent; homeowner's insurance, .5 percent; and maintenance, .7 percent. She is in the 25 percent tax bracket. Using Worksheet 5.2, calculate the cost of each alternative and recommend the less costly option—rent or buy—to Rebecca.

LG4   8. *Use Worksheet 5.3.* Selena and Rodney Jackson need to calculate the amount they can afford to spend on their first home. They have a combined annual income of $47,500 and have $27,000 available for a down payment and closing costs. The Jacksons estimate that homeowner's insurance and property taxes will be $125 per month. They expect the mortgage lender to use a 30 percent (of monthly gross income) mortgage payment affordability ratio, to lend at an interest rate of 8 percent on a 30-year mortgage, and to require a 15 percent down payment. Based on this information, use the home affordability analysis form in Worksheet 5.3 to determine the highest-priced home the Jacksons can afford.

LG6   9. What would the monthly payments be on a $75,000 loan if the mortgage were set up as:
   a. A 15-year, 7 percent fixed-rate loan
   b. A 30-year adjustable-rate mortgage in which the lender adds a margin of 2.5 to the index rate, which now stands at 4.5 percent

   Find the monthly mortgage payments for the first year only.

LG6   10. *Use Worksheet 5.4.* Lee Yang purchased a condominium 4 years ago for $70,000, paying $504 per month on her $60,000, 9 percent, 25-year mortgage. The current loan balance is $56,920. Recently, interest rates dropped sharply, causing Lee to consider refinancing her condo at the prevailing rate of 6.5 percent. She expects to remain in the condo for at least 4 more years and has found a lender that will make a 6.5 percent, 21-year, $56,920 loan, requiring monthly payments of $415. Although there is no prepayment penalty on her current mortgage, Lee will have to pay $1,500 in closing costs on the new mortgage. She is in the 15 percent tax bracket. Based on this information, use the mortgage refinancing analysis form in Worksheet 5.4 to determine whether she should refinance her mortgage under the specified terms.

APPLYING PERSONAL FINANCE

How's Your Local Housing Market?

What's the best source of information about available housing in your community? The answer is a well-informed professional real estate agent whose business is helping buyers find and negotiate the purchase of the most suitable property at the best price. However, there's another readily available source of information: the local newspaper. Almost anything you want to know about the local housing scene can be found in the real estate section of the paper. For this project you'll gather information concerning your local housing market.

Review recent issues of your local newspaper and describe the market for both purchased homes and rental units. Look for useful information such as location, size of property, price or rent, lease requirements, and so forth. You should observe that the housing market is very fragmented, making good purchase and rent decisions more difficult. See if you can answer questions such as: What is the average size of a house or apartment in your community? What is the typical sales price or monthly rent per square foot? Is the purchase market competitive? How about the rental market? How great a difference exists in prices and rents between the most and least desirable areas of the community? Also check online for other sources of information, such as the county tax office, and try to find out how much property taxes and homeowner's insurance premiums average in your area. From your study of the local market, summarize its conditions and be prepared to participate in a class discussion of the local housing market.

CRITICAL THINKING CASES

LG1, 2

5.1 The McNeils' New Car Decision: Lease versus Purchase

Kevin and Brigit McNeil, a dual-income couple in their late twenties, want to replace their 7-year-old car, which has 90,000 miles on it and needs some expensive repairs. After reviewing their budget, the McNeils conclude that they can afford auto payments of not more than $350 per month and a down payment of $2,000. They enthusiastically decide to visit a local dealer after reading its newspaper ad offering a closed-end lease on a new car for a monthly payment of $245. After visiting with the dealer, test-driving the car, and discussing the lease terms with the salesperson, they remain excited about leasing the car, but decide to wait until the following day to finalize the deal. Later that day the McNeils begin to question their approach to the new car acquisition process and decide to carefully reevaluate their decision.

Critical Thinking Questions

1. What are some basic purchasing guidelines the McNeils should consider when choosing which new car to buy or lease? How can they get the information they need?
2. How would you advise the McNeils to research the lease-versus-purchase decision before visiting the dealer? What are the advantages and disadvantages of each alternative?
3. Assume the McNeils can get the following terms on a lease or a bank loan for the car, which they could buy for $17,000. This amount includes tax, title, and license fees.

   - **Lease:** 48 months, $245 monthly payment, 1 month's payment required as a security deposit, $350 end-of-lease charges; a residual value of $6,775 is the purchase option price at the end of the lease.
   - **Loan:** $2,000 down payment, $15,000, 48-month loan at 5 percent interest requiring a monthly payment of $345.44. They assume that the car's value at the end of 48 months will be the same as the residual value. Sales tax is 6 percent.

   They can currently earn interest of 3 percent annually on their savings. They expect to drive about the same number of miles per year as they do now.
   a. Use the format given in Worksheet 5.1 to determine which deal is best for the McNeils.
   b. What other costs and terms of the lease option might affect their decision?
   c. Based on the available information, should the McNeils lease or purchase the car? Why?

5.2 Evaluating a Mortgage Loan for the Schmidts

Elisa and Dominic Schmidt, both in their mid-twenties, have been married for 4 years and have two preschool-age children. Dominic has an accounting degree and is employed as a cost accountant at an annual salary of $42,000. They're now renting a duplex but wish to buy a home in the suburbs of their rapidly developing city. They've decided they can afford a $115,000 house and hope to find one with the features they desire in a good neighborhood.

The insurance costs on such a home are expected to be $800 per year, taxes are expected to be $2,500 per year, and annual utility bills are estimated at $1,440—an increase of $500 over those they pay in the duplex. The Schmidts are considering financing their home with a fixed-rate, 30-year, 7 percent mortgage. The lender charges 2 points on mortgages with 20 percent down and 3 points if less than 20 percent is put down (the commercial bank the Schmidts will deal with requires a minimum of 10 percent down). Other closing costs are estimated at 5 percent of the home's purchase price. Because of their excellent credit record, the bank will probably be willing to let the Schmidts' monthly mortgage payments (principal and interest portions) equal as much as 28 percent of their monthly gross income. Since getting married, the Schmidts have been saving for the purchase of a home and now have $24,000 in their savings account.

Critical Thinking Questions

1. How much would the Schmidts have to put down if the lender required a minimum 20 percent down payment? Could they afford it?
2. Given that the Schmidts want to put only $15,000 down, how much would closing costs be? Considering only principal and interest, how much would their monthly mortgage payments be? Would they qualify for a loan using a 28 percent affordability ratio?
3. Using a $15,000 down payment on a $115,000 home, what would the Schmidt's loan-to-value ratio be? Calculate the monthly mortgage payments on a PITI basis.
4. What recommendations would you make to the Schmidts? Explain.

5.3 Julie's Rent-or-Buy Decision

Julie Brown is a single woman in her late twenties. She is renting an apartment in the fashionable part of town for $900 a month. After much thought, she's seriously considering buying a condominium for $125,000. She intends to put 20 percent down and expects that closing costs will amount to another $5,000; a commercial bank has agreed to lend her money at the fixed rate of 7 percent on a 15-year mortgage. Julie would have to pay an annual condominium owner's insurance premium of $600 and property taxes of $1,200 a year (she's now paying renter's insurance of $550 per year). In addition, she estimates that annual maintenance expenses will be about 0.5 percent of the price of the condo (which includes a $30 monthly fee to the property owners' association). Julie's income puts her in the 25 percent tax bracket (she itemizes her deductions on her tax returns), and she earns an after-tax rate of return on her investments of around 4 percent.

Critical Thinking Questions

1. Given the information provided, use Worksheet 5.2 to evaluate and compare Julie's alternatives of remaining in the apartment or purchasing the condo.
2. Working with a friend who is a realtor, Julie has learned that condos like the one she's thinking of buying are appreciating in value at the rate of 3.5 percent a year and are expected to continue doing so. Would such information affect the rent-or-buy decision made in Question 1? Explain.
3. Discuss any other factors that should be considered when making a rent-or-buy decision.
4. Which alternative would you recommend for Julie in light of your analysis?

> **MONEY ONLINE** www.thomsonedu.com/finance/gitman

Visit **http://www.thomsonedu.com/finance/gitman** for some additional Web-based exercises and hot links (with annotations) to a variety of resources relevant to the topics covered in this chapter.

PART 3 ▸ Managing Credit

Chapter 6   Using Credit
Chapter 7   Using Consumer Loans

Using Credit

LEARNING GOALS

LG1	⊙	Describe the reasons for using consumer credit, and identify its benefits and problems.	p. 174
LG2	⊙	Develop a plan to establish a strong credit history.	p. 174
LG3	⊙	Distinguish among the different forms of open account credit.	p. 181
LG4	⊙	Apply for, obtain, and manage open forms of credit.	p. 190
LG5	⊙	Choose the right credit cards and recognize their advantages and disadvantages.	p. 200
LG6	⊙	Avoid credit problems, protect yourself against credit card fraud, and understand the personal bankruptcy process.	p. 200
	⊙		

\LG1, LG2   THE BASIC CONCEPTS OF CREDIT

Just say "Charge it." With those two little words and a piece of plastic, you can buy gas for your car, have a gourmet meal at an expensive restaurant, or furnish an apartment. It happens *several hundred million times a day* across the United States. Credit, in fact, has become an entrenched part of our everyday lives, and we as consumers use it in one form or another to purchase just about every type of good or service imaginable. Indeed, because of the ready availability and widespread use of credit, our economy is often called a "credit economy." And for good reason: by 2005, individuals in this country had run up almost *$2.2 trillion dollars* in consumer debt—and that *excludes* home mortgages.

Consumer credit is important in the personal financial planning process because of the impact it can have on (1) attaining financial goals and (2) cash budgets. For one thing, various forms of consumer credit can help you reach your financial objectives by enabling you to acquire some of the more expensive items in a systematic fashion, without throwing your whole budget into disarray. But there's another side to consumer credit: it has to be paid back! Unless credit is used intelligently, the "buy-now-pay-later" attitude can quickly turn an otherwise orderly budget into a budgetary nightmare and lead to some serious problems—even bankruptcy! So, really, the issue is one of moderation and affordability.

In today's economy, consumers, businesses, and governments alike use credit to make transactions. Credit helps businesses supply the goods and services needed to satisfy consumer demand. Business credit also provides higher levels of employment and helps raise our overall standard of living. Local, state, and federal governments borrow for various projects and programs that also increase our standard of living and create additional employment opportunities. Clearly, borrowing helps fuel our economy and enhance the overall quality of our lives. Consequently, *consumers in a credit economy need to know how to establish credit and how to avoid the dangers of using it improperly.*

Why Use Credit?

People typically use credit as a way to pay for goods and services that cost more than they can afford to take from their current income. This is particularly true for those in the 25 to 44 age group, who simply have not had time to accumulate the liquid assets required to pay cash outright for major purchases and expenditures. As people begin to approach their midforties, however, their savings and investments start to build up, and their debt loads tend to decline, which is really not too surprising when you consider that the median household net worth for those in the 45 to 54 age group is *about 80 percent more* than for those aged 35 to 44.

Whatever their age group, people tend to borrow for several major reasons:

- **To avoid paying cash for large outlays.** Rather than pay cash for large purchases such as houses and cars, most people borrow part of the purchase price and then repay the loan on some scheduled basis. Spreading payments over time makes big-ticket items more affordable, and consumers get the use of an expensive asset right away. Most people consider the cost of such borrowing a small price to pay for the immediate satisfaction they get from owning the house, car, or whatever it happens to be. In their minds, at least, the benefits of current consumption outweigh the interest costs on the loan. Unfortunately, while the initial euphoria of the purchase may wear off over time, the loan payments remain—perhaps for many more years to come.

- **To meet a financial emergency.** For example, people may need to borrow to cover living expenses during a period of unemployment, or to purchase plane tickets to visit a sick relative. As indicated in Chapter 4, however, using savings is preferable to using credit for financial emergencies.

- **For convenience.** Merchants as well as banks offer a variety of charge accounts and credit cards that allow consumers to charge just about anything—from gas and oil or clothes and stereos to doctor and dental bills and even college tuition. Further, in many places—restaurants, for instance—using a credit card is far easier than writing a check. Although such transactions usually incur no interest (at least initially), these credit card purchases are still a form of borrowing, because payment is not made at the time of the transaction.

- **For investment purposes.** As we'll see in Chapter 11, it's relatively easy for an investor to partially finance the purchase of many different kinds of investment vehicles with borrowed funds. In fact, *margin loans*, as they're called, amounted to nearly $220 billion in late 2005—a tidy sum, but down substantially from the $280 billion reached when the stock market peaked in March 2000.

Improper Uses of Credit

Many people use consumer credit to live beyond their means. Indeed, overspending is the biggest danger in borrowing, especially because it's so easy to do. Once hooked on "plastic," people may use their credit cards to make even routine purchases and don't realize they have overextended themselves until it's too late. Overspenders simply won't admit that they're spending too much. As far as they're concerned, they can afford to buy all those things because, after all, they still have their credit cards and can still afford to pay the minimum amounts each month.

Unfortunately, such spending eventually leads to mounting bills. And by making only the minimum payment, borrowers pay a huge price in the long run. Look at Exhibit 6.1, which shows the amount of time and interest charges required to repay credit card balances if you make only minimum payments of 3 percent of the outstanding balance. For example, if you carry a $3,000 balance—which is about *one-third* the national average—on a card that charges 15.0 percent annually, it would take you 14 years to retire the debt, and your interest charges would total *some $2,000—or more than 66 percent of the original balance!*

Incredibly, some cards offer even lower minimum payments of just 2 percent of the outstanding balance. While such small payments may seem like a good deal, clearly they don't work to your advantage and only increase the time and amount of interest required to repay the debt. For example, by making minimum 2 percent payments, it would take *more than 32 years* to pay off a $5,000 balance on a credit card that carries a 15 percent rate of interest. In contrast, as can be seen in Exhibit 6.1, that same $5,000 balance could be paid off in *just 16.4 years* if you had made 3 percent minimum payments. Just think, making an additional 1 percent payment can save you nearly 16 years of interest! That's why the federal banking regulators recently issued new guidelines stating that minimum monthly credit card payments should now cover at least 1 percent of the outstanding balance, plus all finance charges and any other fees.

To avoid the possibility of future repayment shock, keep in mind the following types of transactions for which you should *not* (routinely, at least) use credit: (1) to meet basic living expenses; (2) to make impulse purchases, especially expensive ones; and (3) to purchase nondurable (short-lived) goods and services. Except in situations where credit cards are used occasionally for convenience (such as for gasoline and entertainment) or payments on recurring credit purchases are built into the monthly budget, a good rule to remember when considering the use of credit is that *the product purchased on credit should outlive the payments.*

Unfortunately, people who overspend eventually arrive at the point where they must choose to either become delinquent in their payments or sacrifice necessities, such as food and clothing. If payment obligations aren't met, the consequences are likely to be a damaged credit rating, lawsuits, or even personal bankruptcy. Exhibit 6.2 lists some common signals that indicate it may be time to stop buying on credit. *Ignoring the telltale signs that you are overspending can only lead to more serious problems.*

Establishing Credit

The willingness of lenders to extend credit depends on their assessment of your creditworthiness—that is, your ability to promptly repay the debt. Lenders look at various factors in making this decision, such as your present earnings and net worth. Equally important, they look at your current debt position and your credit history. Thus, it's worth your while to do what you can to build a strong credit rating.

First Steps in Establishing Credit

First, open checking and savings accounts. They signal stability to lenders and indicate that you handle your financial affairs in a businesslike way. Second, use credit—open one or two charge accounts and use them periodically, even if you prefer paying cash. For example, get a Visa card and make a few credit purchases each month (don't overdo it, of course). You might pay an annual fee or interest on some (or all) of your account balances, but in the

---

EXHIBIT 6.1   Minimum Payments Mean Maximum Years

Paying off credit card balances at the minimum monthly amount required by the card issuer will take a long time and cost you a great deal of interest, as this table demonstrates. *The calculations here are based on a minimum 3 percent payment and 15.0 percent annual interest rate.*

Original Balance	Years to Repay	Interest Paid	Total Interest Paid as Percentage of Original Balance
$5,000	16.4	$3,434	68.7%
4,000	15.4	2,720	68.0
3,000	14.0	2,005	66.8
2,000	12.1	1,291	64.5
1,000	8.8	577	57.7

EXHIBIT 6.2   Some Credit Danger Signs

If one or more of these signs exist, take them as an indication that it's time to proceed with caution in your credit spending. Be prepared to revise and update your spending patterns, cut back on the use of credit, and be alert for other signs of overspending.

You may be headed for serious trouble if:

- You regularly use credit cards to buy on impulse.
- You postdate checks to keep them from bouncing.
- You regularly exceed the borrowing limits on your credit cards.
- You never add up all your bills, to avoid facing grim realities.
- You now take 60 or 90 days to pay bills you once paid in 30.
- You have to borrow just to meet normal living expenses.
- You often use one form of credit—such as a cash advance from a credit card—to make payments on other debt.
- You can barely make the minimum required payments on bills.
- You are using more than 20 percent of your take-home income to pay credit card bills and personal loans (excluding mortgage payments).
- You have no savings.
- You are so far behind on credit payments that collection agencies are after you.

process, you'll become identified as a reliable credit customer. Third, obtain a small loan, even if you don't need one. If you don't actually need the money, put it in a liquid investment, such as a money market account or certificate of deposit. The interest you earn should offset some of the interest expense on the loan; you can view the difference as a cost of building good credit. (It goes without saying that you should repay the loan promptly, perhaps even a little ahead of schedule, to minimize the difference in interest rates—don't pay off the loan too quickly, though, as lenders like to see how you perform over an extended period of time.) Keep in mind, your ability to obtain a large loan in the future will depend in part on how you managed smaller ones in the past.

Build a Strong Credit History

From a financial perspective, maintaining a strong credit history is just as important as developing a solid employment record! Don't take credit lightly, and don't assume that getting the loan or the credit card is the toughest part. It's not. That's just the first step; servicing it (i.e., making payments) in a prompt and timely fashion—month in and month out—is the really tough part of the consumer credit process. And in many respects, it's the most important element of consumer credit, as it determines your creditworthiness. By using credit wisely and repaying it on time, you're establishing a *credit history* that tells lenders you're a dependable, reliable, and responsible borrower.

The consumer credit industry keeps close tabs on your credit and your past payment performance (more on this when we discuss *credit bureaus* later in the chapter). So the better you do in being a responsible borrower, the easier it will be to get credit when and where you want it. The best way to build up a strong credit history and maintain your creditworthiness is to *consistently make payments on time*, month after month. Being late occasionally—say, two or three times a year—might label you a "late payer." When you take on credit, you have an *obligation* to live up to the terms of the loan, including how and when the credit will be repaid.

If you foresee difficulty in meeting a monthly payment, let the lender know, and usually arrangements can be made to help you through the situation. This is especially true with installment loans that require fixed monthly payments. If you have one or two of these loans and, for some reason or another, you encounter a month that's going to be really tight, the first thing you should try to do (other than trying to borrow some money from a family member) is

Smart.Sites

The American Banker's Association provides helpful information about shopping for credit and managing debt at its consumer education site. Link to it at **http://www .thomsonedu.com/finance/ gitman.**

debt safety ratio The proportion of total monthly consumer credit obligations to monthly take-home pay.

get an extension on your loan. Don't just skip a payment, because that's going to put your account into a *late status until you make up the missed payment*— in other words, until you make a *double* payment, your account/loan will remain in a late status, subject to a monthly late penalty. Trying to work out an extension with your lender obviously makes a lot more sense.

Here's what you do. Explain the situation to the loan officer and ask for an extension of one (or two) months on your loan. In most cases, so long as this hasn't occurred before, the extension is almost automatically granted. The maturity of the loan is formally extended for a month (or two), and the extra interest of carrying the loan for another month (or two) is either added to the loan balance or, more commonly, paid at the time the extension is granted (such an extension fee generally amounts to a fraction of the normal monthly payment). Then, in a month (or two), you pick up where you left off and resume your normal monthly payments on the loan. This is the most sensible way of making it through those rough times because it doesn't harm your credit record. Just don't do it too often.

To summarize, here are some things you can do to build a strong credit history:

- Use credit only when you can afford it and only when the repayment schedule fits comfortably into the family budget—in short, don't overextend yourself.
- Fulfill all the terms of the credit.
- Be *consistent* in making payments *promptly*.
- Consult creditors immediately if you cannot meet payments as agreed.
- Be truthful when applying for credit. Lies are not likely to go undetected.

How Much Credit Can You Stand?

Sound financial planning dictates that if you're going to use credit, you need a good idea of how much you can comfortably tolerate. The easiest way to avoid repayment problems and ensure that your borrowing won't place an undue strain on your monthly budget is to *limit the use of credit to your ability to repay the debt!* A useful *credit guideline* (and one widely used by lenders) is to make sure your monthly repayment burden doesn't exceed 20 percent of your monthly *take-home pay*. Most experts, however, regard the 20 percent figure as the *maximum* debt burden and strongly recommend **debt safety ratios** closer to 10 to 15 percent—perhaps even lower if you plan on applying for a new mortgage in the near future. Note that the monthly repayment burden here *does include* payments on your credit cards, but *excludes* your monthly mortgage obligation.

To illustrate, consider someone who takes home $2,500 a month. Using a 20 percent ratio, she should have monthly consumer credit payments of no more than $500—that is, $2,500 × .20 = $500. This is the maximum amount of her monthly disposable income she should have to use to pay off both personal loans and other forms of consumer credit (such as credit cards and education loans). This, of course, is not the maximum amount of consumer credit she can have outstanding—in fact, her total consumer indebtedness can, and likely would, be considerably larger. The key factor is that with her income level, her *payments* on this type of debt should not exceed $500 a month. (*Caution:* This doesn't mean that credit terms should be lengthened just to accommodate this guideline; rather, in all cases, it's assumed that standard credit terms apply.)

Exhibit 6.3 provides a summary of low (10 percent), manageable (15 percent), and maximum (20 percent) monthly credit payments for various income levels. Obviously, the closer your total monthly payments are to your desired debt safety ratio, the less future borrowing you can do. Conversely, *the lower the debt safety ratio, the better shape you're in, credit-wise, and the easier it should be for you to service your outstanding consumer debt.*

You can compute the debt safety ratio as follows:

$$\text{Debt safety ratio} = \frac{\text{Total monthly consumer credit payments}}{\text{Monthly take-home pay}}$$

EXHIBIT 6.3

Credit Guidelines Based on Ability to Repay

According to the debt safety ratio, the amount of consumer credit you should have outstanding depends on the monhtly payments you can afford to make.

Monthly Take-Home Pay	MONTHLY CONSUMER CREDIT PAYMENTS		
	Low Debt Safety Ratio (10%)	*Manageable* Debt Safety Ratio (15%)	*Maximum* Debt Safety Ratio (20%)
$1,000	$100	$150	$ 200
$1,250	$125	$188	$ 250
$1,500	$150	$225	$ 300
$2,000	$200	$300	$ 400
$2,500	$250	$375	$ 500
$3,000	$300	$450	$ 600
$3,500	$350	$525	$ 700
$4,000	$400	$600	$ 800
$5,000	$500	$750	$1,000

This measure is the focus of Worksheet 6.1, which you can use for keeping close tabs on your own debt safety ratio. It shows the impact that each new loan you take out, or credit card you sign up for, can have on this important measure of creditworthiness. Consider, for example, Jack and Sally Bicman. As seen in Worksheet 6.1, they have five outstanding consumer loans, plus they're carrying balances on three credit cards. All totaled, these eight obligations require monthly payments of almost $740, which accounts for about 1/5 of their combined take-home pay and gives them a debt safety ratio of 18 percent. And note toward the bottom of the worksheet that if the Bicmans want to lower this ratio to, say, 15 percent, they'll either have to get their monthly payments down to $615, or increase their take-home pay to over $4,900 a month.

The Special Credit Problems of Women

At one time, a woman stood little chance of getting credit on her own. In most lenders' minds, she was too much of a risk; even if she was gainfully employed, she might become pregnant and lose her job. Today, the Equal Credit Opportunity Act (ECOA) has removed most of these credit obstacles. Creditors cannot check into a woman's marital status or childbearing plans and, with two-income families, must consider the woman's income on the same basis as the man's, even if it's part-time employment.

Even with these and other protections, however, some women—especially those who are divorced or widowed—still have difficulty getting credit if they don't have their own credit history. The following steps can help overcome this problem:

- **Use your own name when filing a credit application.** Use your legal name, not a social title, such as Mrs. Thomas Watkins. A married woman can choose from several legal names; for example, if your maiden name is Joan Brown and you take your husband's name of Watkins, you can choose Joan Watkins or Joan Brown Watkins. Use your legal name consistently to build your own credit history.
- **Make sure any information reported to the credit bureau is in your name as well as your husband's.**
- **Consider retaining a credit file separate from your husband's when you marry.** This is true particularly if you have already established a good credit rating. You should notify creditors of your name change and intention to maintain your own file.

A worksheet like this one will help a household stay on top of their monthly credit card and consumer loan payments, as well as their *debt safety ratio*—an important measure of creditworthiness. The key here is to keep the debt safety ratio as low as (reasonably) possible; something that can be done by keeping monthly loan payments in line with monthly take-home pay.

MONTHLY CONSUMER LOAN PAYMENTS & DEBT SAFETY RATIO

Name _Jack & Sally Bicman_   **Date** _June 21, 2007_

■ Type of Loan*	Lender	Current Monthly (or Min.) Payment
• *Auto and personal loans*	1. GMAC	$360.
	2. Chase Bank	115.
	3.	
• *Education loans*	1. U.S. Dept. of Education	75.
	2.	
• *Overdraft protection line*	1. Chase Bank	30.
• *Personal line of credit*		
• *Credit cards*	1. MBNA Visa	28.
	2. Fidelity MC	31.
	3. Dillards	28.
	4.	
• *Home equity line*	1. Wash. Mutual	72.
TOTAL MONTHLY PAYMENTS		$739.

*__Note:__ List only those loans that require regular monthly payments.

■ Monthly Take-Home Pay	1. Jack	$1,855
	2. Sally	2,250.
TOTAL MONTHLY TAKE-HOME PAY		$4,105.

■ Debt Safety Ratio:

$$\frac{\text{Total monthly payments}}{\text{Total monthly take-home pay}} \times 100 = \frac{\$\ 739.}{\$\ 4,105.} \times 100 = \underline{18.0}\%$$

• *Changes needed to reach a new debt safety ratio*

    • New (target) debt safety ratio: _15.0_%

    1. At current take-home pay of $ ___4,105.___ ,
        total monthly payments must equal:

          Total monthly take-home pay × New (target) debt safty ratio**

$$\underline{\$\ 4,105.} \times \underline{0.15} = \underline{\$\ 615.75}$$
                                New Monthly Payments

    OR

    2. With current monthly payments of $ ___739.___
        total take-home pay must equal:

$$\frac{\text{Total monthly payments}}{\text{New (target) debt safety ratio}} \times 100 = \frac{\$\ 739.}{\$\ 0.15} = \underline{\$\ 4,926.67}$$
                                          New take-home pay

**__Note:__ Enter debt safety ratio as a decimal (e.g., 15% = 0.15).

6-1	Why do people borrow? What are some improper uses of credit?
6-2	Describe the general guidelines lenders use to calculate an applicant's maximum debt burden.
6-3	How can you use the *debt safety ratio* to determine whether your debt obligations are within reasonable limits?
6-4	What steps can you take to establish a good credit rating?

LG3 CREDIT CARDS AND OTHER TYPES OF OPEN ACCOUNT CREDIT

Open account credit is a form of credit extended to a consumer in advance of any transactions. Typically, a retail outlet or bank agrees to allow the consumer to buy or borrow up to a specified amount on open account. Credit is extended as long as the consumer does not exceed the established **credit limit** and makes payments in accordance with the specified terms. Open account credit issued by a retail outlet, such as a department store or oil company, is usually applicable only in that establishment or one of its locations. In contrast, open account credit issued by banks, such as *MasterCard* and *Visa* accounts, can be used to make purchases at a wide variety of businesses. For the rest of this chapter, we'll direct our attention to the various types and characteristics of open account credit; in Chapter 7 we'll look at various forms of single-payment and installment loans.

Having open account credit is a lot like having your own personal line of credit—it's there when you need it. But unlike most other types of debt, consumers who use open forms of credit can often avoid paying interest charges *if they promptly pay the full amount of their account balance*. For example, assume that in a given month you charge $75.58 on an open account at a department store. Sometime within the next month or so, you'll receive a **credit statement** from the store that summarizes recent transactions on your account. Now, if there are no other charges and the total account balance is $75.58, you can (usually) avoid any finance charges by paying the account in full before the next billing date.

Open account credit generally is available from two broadly defined sources: (1) financial institutions and (2) retail stores/merchants. *Financial institutions* issue general-purpose credit cards, as well as secured and unsecured revolving lines of credit and overdraft protection lines. Commercial banks have long been the major providers of consumer credit; and since deregulation, so have S&Ls, credit unions, major stock-brokerage firms, and consumer finance companies. *Retail stores and merchants* make up the other major source of open account credit. They provide this service as a way to promote the sales of their products, and their principal form of credit is the charge (or credit) card. Together, there are over 2 billion bank credit cards and retail charge cards outstanding today. Let's now take a look at these two forms of credit, along with *debit cards* and *revolving lines of credit*.

open account credit A form of credit extended to a consumer in advance of any transaction.

credit limit A specified amount beyond which a customer may not borrow or purchase on credit.

credit statement A monthly statement summarizing the transactions, interest charges, fees, and payments in a consumer credit account.

bank credit card A credit card issued by a bank or other financial institution that allows the holder to charge purchases at any establishment that accepts it.

Bank Credit Cards

Probably the most popular form of open account credit is the **bank credit card** issued by commercial banks and other financial institutions—Visa and MasterCard are the two dominant types. These cards allow their holders to charge purchases worldwide at literally millions of stores, restaurants, shops, and gas stations, as well as at state and municipal governments, colleges and universities, medical groups, and mail-order houses—not to mention the Internet, where they've become the currency of choice. They can be used to pay for almost anything—groceries, doctor bills, college tuition, airline tickets, and car rentals. Thousands of banks, S&Ls, credit unions, brokerage houses, and other financial services institutions issue Visa and MasterCard; and each issuer, within reasonable limits, can set its own credit terms and conditions. In recent years, several more big-league players have entered the field. Sears, for example, introduced the *Discover Card* (now a part of Morgan Stanley Dean Witter), and AT&T its *Universal Card* (which is actually just a special Visa or MasterCard).

Bank credit cards can be used to borrow money as well as buy goods and services on credit. Because of their potential for use in literally thousands of businesses and banks, they can be of great convenience and value to consumers. Individuals who use them, however, should be thoroughly familiar with their basic features.

Line of Credit

The **line of credit** provided to the holder of a bank credit card is set by the issuer for each card. It's the maximum amount that the cardholder can owe at any time. The size of the credit line depends on both the applicant's request and the results of the issuer's investigation of the applicant's credit and financial status. Lines of credit offered by issuers of bank cards can reach $50,000 or more, but for the most part they range from about $500 to $2,500. Although card issuers fully expect you to keep your credit within the specified limits, most won't take any real action unless you extend your account balance a certain percentage beyond the account's stated maximum. For example, if you had a $1,000 credit limit, you probably wouldn't hear a thing from the card issuer until your outstanding account balance exceeded, say, $1,200; that is, 20 percent above the $1,000 line of credit. On the other hand, don't count on getting off scot-free, because most card issuers assess *over-the-limit* fees whenever you go over your credit limit (more on this later).

Cash Advances

In addition to purchasing merchandise and services, the holder of a bank credit card can obtain a **cash advance** from any participating bank. Cash advances are loans on which interest begins to accrue immediately. They're transacted in the same way as merchandise purchases, except that they take place at a commercial bank or some other financial institution, and involve the receipt of cash (or a check) instead of goods and services. Another way to get a cash advance is to use the "convenience checks" you receive from the card issuer to pay for purchases. You can even use your credit card to draw cash from an ATM, any time of the day or night. Usually, the size of the cash advance from an ATM is limited to some nominal amount (perhaps $300), although the amount you can obtain from the teller window at a bank is limited only by the unused credit in your account. Thus, if you've used only $1,000 of a $5,000 credit limit, you can take out a cash advance of up to $4,000.

Interest Charges

With few exceptions, the *annual rate of interest* charged on bank credit cards in 2006 ranged from about 8 percent to over 20 percent (these exclude introductory rates). Keep in mind, however, that interest rates on credit cards were abnormally low during this period, in large part because market interest rates were at 40-year lows. That is, whereas rates in 2006 ranged from 8 to 20 percent, in the late 1990s the range was more like 14 or 15 percent to over 23 percent. Also, you'll find that most bankcards have one rate for merchandise purchases and a much higher rate for cash advances. For example, the rate on merchandise purchases might be, say, 12 percent, while the rate on cash advances could be 19½ or 20 percent. And when shopping for a credit card, watch out for those *special low introductory rates* that many banks offer. Known as "teaser rates," they're usually only good for the first 6 to 12 months. Then, just as soon as the introductory period ends, so do the low interest rates.

Most of these cards have variable interest rates that are tied to an index that moves with market rates. The most popular is the prime or **base rate;** the rate a bank uses as a base for loans to individuals and small or midsize businesses. These cards adjust their interest rate monthly or quarterly and usually have minimum and maximum rates. To illustrate, consider a bankcard whose terms are *prime plus 7.5 percent*, with a minimum of 10 percent and a maximum of 15½ percent. If the prime rate is 3½ percent, then the rate of interest charged on this card would be: 3.5 + 7.5 = *11.0 percent*. Given the widespread use of variable interest rates, bank cardholders should be aware that just as falling rates have brought down interest rates on credit cards, rising market rates are guaranteed to lead (and probably very quickly) to much higher interest charges!

Smart Sites

Which credit cards are best? The Citizens for Fair Credit Card Terms, a nonprofit consumer organization, offers free independent ratings that evaluate interest rates, fees, and benefits of leading cards. Go to their Web site at **http:// www.thomsonedu.com/ finance/gitman.**

line of credit The maximum amount of credit a customer is allowed to have outstanding at any point in time.

cash advance A loan that can be obtained by a bank credit cardholder at any participating bank or financial institution.

base rate The rate of interest a bank uses as a base for loans to individuals and small to midsize businesses.

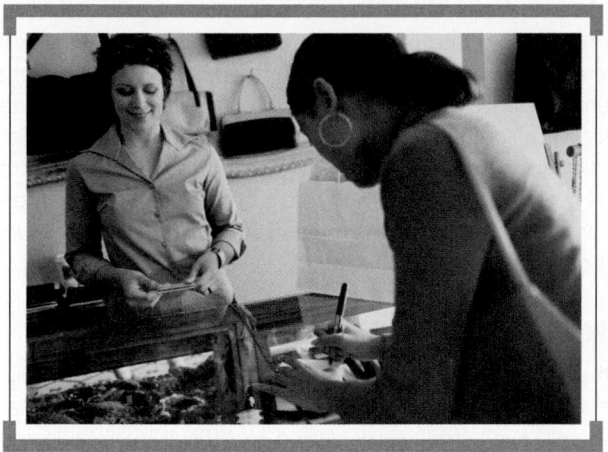

Generally speaking, *the interest rates on credit cards are higher than any other form of consumer credit*. But more and more banks—even the bigger ones—are now offering more competitive rates, especially to their better customers. Indeed, because competition has become so intense, a growing number of banks today are actually willing to negotiate their fees as a way to retain their customers. Whether this trend will have any significant impact on permanently reducing interest rates and fees remains to be seen, but at least most consumers would agree it's a step in the right direction.

Bank credit card issuers must disclose interest costs and related information to consumers *before* extending credit. In the case of purchases of merchandise and services, the specified interest rate may not apply to charges until after the **grace period.** During this short period, usually 20 to 30 days, you can pay your credit card bill in full and avoid any interest charges. Once you carry a balance—that is, when you don't pay your card in full during the grace period—the interest rate is usually applied to any unpaid balances carried from previous periods as well as to any new purchases made. Interest on cash advances, however, *begins the day the advance is taken out*.

Then There Are Those Other Fees

Besides the interest charged on bank credit cards, there are a few other fees you should be aware of. To begin with, many—though not all—bank cards charge *annual fees* just for the "privilege" of being able to use the card. In most cases, the fee is around $25 to $40 a year, though it can amount to much more for prestige cards. Sometimes, this annual fee is waived in the first year, but you'll be stuck with it for the second and every other year you hold the card. As a rule, the larger the bank or S&L, the more likely it is to charge an annual fee for its credit cards. What's more, many issuers also charge a *transaction fee* for each (non-ATM) cash advance; this fee usually amounts to about $5 per cash advance *or* 3 percent of the amount obtained in the transaction, whichever is more.

And now, more and more card issuers are coming up with new ways to sock it to you. These include late-payment fees, over-the-limit charges, foreign transaction fees, and balance transfer fees. For example, if you're a bit late in making your payment, at some banks you'll be hit with a late-payment fee—which is really a redundant charge because you're already paying interest on the unpaid balance. In a similar fashion, if you happen to go over your credit limit, you'll get hit with a charge for that, too (again, this is on top of the interest you're already paying). Critics really dislike this fee because they maintain it's hard for cardholders to know when they've hit their credit ceilings. Some card issuers today are even going so far as to slap you with a fee for *not using your credit card*—one bank, for example, charges a $15 fee to customers (cardholders) who don't use their credit cards in a 6-month period. The card issuers justify these charges by saying it costs money to issue and administer these cards, so they have a right to charge these fees if you don't use their cards. Of course, you have the right to let the issuer know what you think of these charges by canceling your card! Regardless of when or why any of these fees are levied, the net effect is that *they add to the true cost of using bank credit cards*.

Balance Transfers

grace period A short period of time, usually 20 to 30 days, during which you can pay your credit card bill in full and not incur any interest charges.

balance transfer A program that enables cardholders to readily transfer credit balances from one card to another.

A relatively new feature of bank credit cards is the ability to transfer balances from one card to another. Known as **balance transfers,** they have become a hot promotional feature in the ongoing credit card wars. That is, the card issuers make a big deal out of allowing you to transfer the balances from one or more (old) cards to their (new) card. The idea is to dump the old card(s) by putting everything, including current balances, on the issuer's (new) card. There are two potential advantages to these balance transfer programs. First, there's the convenience of being able to consolidate your credit card payments. And there's also the potential savings in interest that accompanies the transfer, as these deals usually come with very low (introductory) rates. But these transfers have their drawbacks, too. For starters, although you may benefit (initially) from a low rate on all transferred funds, the issuer will often charge a much higher rate on new purchases. On top of that, your monthly payment is usually applied first to the transferred balance and not the *new purchases*, which face the higher rate. In addition, some banks will also charge a flat fee on all transferred funds. For example, suppose that you transfer a balance of $5,000 to a card that imposes a 4 percent fee for the transfer. This would result in a charge of $200, and that's on top of any other interest charges! Finally, while many balance transfer programs may offer relatively low introductory rates, those low rates usually don't last very long.

Special Types of Bank Credit Cards

Bank credit cards sure aren't what they used to be. Today, in addition to standard, plain vanilla bankcards, you can obtain cards that offer rebates and special incentive programs, cards that are sponsored by nonprofit organizations, even credit cards aimed specifically at college and high school students. We'll now look at several of these special types of bank credit cards, including reward cards, affinity cards, secured credit cards, and student credit cards.

Reward Cards

One of the fastest-growing segments of the bankcard market is the **reward (co-branded) credit card,** which combines features of a traditional bank credit card with an incentive: cash, merchandise rebates, airline tickets, or even investments. Over 50 million cardholders carry Visa or MasterCard rebate cards, and new types are introduced almost every day. Here are some of the many incentive programs:

- **Frequent flyer programs.** In this program, the cardholder earns free frequent flyer miles for each dollar charged on his or her credit card. These frequent flyer miles can then be used with airline-affiliated programs for free tickets, first-class upgrades, and other travel-related benefits. Examples include Delta Sky Miles, American Airlines AAdvantage MasterCard, United Airlines Mileage Plus Visa Card, and American Express and Chase Travel Plus programs, with miles that can be used on any one of numerous airlines.
- **Automobile rebate programs.** General Motors offers a bank credit card that allows the cardholder to earn annual rebates of 5 percent for new car purchases or leases, up to specified limits. While the amount of the GM rebate depends on the model of car purchased (or leased), Citibank's Drivers Edge rebates 1 percent of your charges, up to $500 annually, for almost any new car you buy.
- **Other merchandise rebates.** An increasing number of companies are participating in bankcard reward programs, including, for example, Norwegian Cruise Line, Harrahs, NASCAR, Starbucks, Marriott Hotels, and Hard Rock Café. Some major oil companies also offer rebate cards, where the cardholder earns credit that can be applied to the purchase of the company's gasoline. Several regional phone companies even offer rebates on phone calls. (A good site for finding information about these and other rebate card offers is **http://www.cardtrak.com.**)

Are rebate cards a good deal? Well, yes and no. You should evaluate these cards carefully by looking at your usage patterns and working out the annual cost of the cards before and after the rebate, to see if they make sense for you. Don't get so carried away with the gimmick that you lose sight of the total costs. Most incentive cards carry higher interest rates than regular bankcards do. And as explains in the *Money in Action* box on our Web site **(http://www.thomsonedu.com/finance/gitman),** these cards work best for those who can use the rebates, charge a lot, and who don't carry high monthly balances.

Affinity Cards

Credit cards with a cause—that's the way to describe **affinity cards.** These cards are nothing more than standard Visa or MasterCards that are issued in conjunction with a sponsoring group—most commonly, some type of charitable, political, or professional organization. So named because of the bond between the sponsoring group and its members, affinity cards are sponsored by such nonprofit organizations as MADD, the American Association of Individual Investors, the American Wildlife Fund, AARP, and Special Olympics. In addition,

reward (co-branded) credit card A bank credit card that combines features of a traditional bank credit card with an additional incentive, such as rebates and airline mileage.

affinity cards A standard bank credit card issued in conjunction with some charitable, political, or other nonprofit organization.

they are issued by college and university alumni groups, labor organizations, religious and fraternal groups, and professional societies. In many cases, all you have to do is support the cause to obtain one of these cards (as in the case of MADD). In other cases, you'll have to belong to a certain group in order to get one of their cards (for example, be a graduate of the school or member of a particular professional group to qualify).

Why even bother to carry one of these cards? Unlike traditional bank cards, affinity cards make money for the group backing the card, as well as for the bank, because the sponsoring groups receive a share of the profits (usually 1/2 to 1 percent of retail purchases made with the card). So, for the credit cardholder, it's a form of "painless philanthropy." But to cover the money that goes to the sponsoring organization, the cardholder usually pays higher fees or higher interest costs. Even so, some may view these cards as a great way to contribute to a worthy cause. Others, however, may feel it makes more sense to use a traditional credit card and then write a check to their favorite charity.

Secured Credit Cards

You may have seen the ad on TV where the announcer says that no matter how bad your credit, you can still qualify for one of their credit cards. The pitch may sound too good to be true; and in some respects it is, because there's a catch. Namely, the credit is "secured"—meaning you have to put up *collateral* in order to get the card! These are so-called **secured, or collateralized credit cards** where the amount of credit is determined by the amount of liquid collateral you're able to put up. These cards are targeted at people with no credit, or bad credit histories, who don't qualify for conventional credit cards. Issued as Visa or MasterCard, except for the collateral, they're like any other credit card. To qualify, a customer must deposit a certain amount (usually $500 or more) into a 12- to 18-month certificate of deposit that the issuing bank holds as collateral. The cardholder then gets a credit line equal to the deposit. If the customer defaults, the bank has the CD to cover its losses. By making payments on time, it's hoped that these cardholders will establish (or reestablish) a credit history that may qualify them for a conventional (unsecured) credit card. Even though fully secured, these cards still carry annual fees and finance charges that are equal to, or greater than, those of regular credit cards.

Student Credit Cards

Some large banks, through their Visa and MasterCard programs, have special credit cards that target college students (and in some cases, even high school students). These **student credit cards** often come packaged with special promotional programs that are meant to appeal to this segment of the market—such as free music CDs, movie tickets, and the like. Some even offer special discounts on pizzas, clothing, computer software, and so on. Except for these features, there's really nothing unusual about these cards or their terms. Most simply require that you be enrolled in a 2- or 4-year college or university and have some source of income, whatever that may be. In contrast, they usually *do not require* any parental or guardian guarantees, nor do they require that you hold a full-time (or even part-time) job.

So what's in it for the card issuers? While they know that most college students don't earn much money, they also know that's likely to change after they graduate—which is why they're so willing to offer the cards. Their logic seems to be that you (students) obviously have some source of income and you're going to be spending money anyway, so why not spend it with one of their credit cards? From the student's perspective, these cards not only offer convenience but are also great for building up a solid credit history. Just *remember to use them responsibly*—that's the way to get the most from these cards or any other form of credit, for that matter!

Retail Charge Cards

Retail charge cards are the second largest category of credit card and are issued by department stores, oil companies, car rental agencies, and so on. These cards are popular

secured (collateralized) credit cards A type of credit card that's secured with some form of collateral, like a bank CD.

student credit card A credit card marketed specifically to college students.

retail charge card A type of credit card issued by retailers that allows customers to charge goods and services up to a preestablished amount.

with merchants because they build consumer loyalty and enhance sales; consumers like them because they offer a convenient way to shop. These cards carry a preset credit limit—a line of credit—that varies with the creditworthiness of the cardholder.

This form of credit is most common in department and clothing stores and other high-volume outlets, where customers are likely to make several purchases each month. Most large oil companies also offer charge cards that allow customers to buy gas and oil products, *but they're expected to pay for such purchases in full upon receipt of the monthly bill.* To promote the sale of their more expensive products, oil companies frequently offer revolving credit for use in purchasing items such as tires, batteries, and accessories. Many families have—and regularly use—five or six different retail charge cards. Interest on most retail charge cards is fixed at 1.5 to 1.85 percent monthly, or 18 to 22 percent per year. These cards are generally more expensive than bank credit cards.

Debit Cards

It looks like a credit card, it works like a credit card, it even has the familiar MasterCard and Visa credit card markings. But it's not a *credit* card—rather, it's a *debit* card. Simply put, a **debit card** provides direct access to your checking account and, thus, *works like writing a check.* For example, when you use a debit card to make a purchase, the amount of the transaction is charged directly to your checking account. Using a debit card isn't the same thing as buying on credit; it may appear that you're charging it, but actually *you're paying with cash.* Accordingly, there are no finance charges to pay.

Debit cards are becoming very popular, especially with consumers who want the convenience of a credit card but not the high cost of interest that comes with them. There are about 225 million debit cards in circulation in the United States today, which together account for about 60 percent of all credit/debit card transactions. They're accepted at most establishments displaying the Visa or MasterCard logo but function as an alternative to writing checks. If you use a debit card to make a purchase at a department store or restaurant, the transaction will show up on your next monthly *checking account* statement. Needless to say, to keep your records straight, you should enter debit card transactions directly into your checkbook ledger as they occur and treat them as withdrawals, or checks, by subtracting them from your checking account balance. Debit cards can also be used to gain access to your account through 24-hour teller machines or ATMs—which is the closest thing to a cash advance that these cards have to offer.

A big disadvantage of a debit card, of course, is that it doesn't provide a line of credit. In addition, it can cause overdraft problems if you fail to make the proper entries to your checking account or inadvertently use it when you think you're using a credit card. Also, some debit card issuers charge a transaction fee or a flat annual fee; and even some *merchants* may charge you for using your debit card. On the plus side, a debit card enables you to avoid the potential credit problems and high costs of credit cards. Further, it's as convenient to use as a credit card—in fact, if convenience is the major reason you use a credit card, you might want to consider switching to a debit card for at least some transactions, especially at outlets such as gas stations that give discounts for cash purchases and consider a debit card to be as good as cash.

Another difference between debit and credit cards that every cardholder should be aware of involves the level of protection for the user when a card is lost or stolen. When a credit card is lost or stolen, federal banking laws state that the cardholder is not liable for any fraudulent charges if the loss or theft is reported before that card is used. If reported after the card is used, the cardholder's maximum liability is $50. Unfortunately, *this protection does not extend to debit cards.* Instead, your liability resulting from a lost or stolen debit card is limited to $50 up to a maximum of $500, "depending on the circumstances of the loss." In practice, most banks provide the same level of protection for debit cards as for credit cards, but check with your bank to be sure. There are obviously some good points and bad points about debit cards, but as the accompanying *Money in Action* box explains, there may be times when you should be treating your debit card like a credit card.

debit card A card used to make transactions for *cash* rather than credit; replaces the need for cash or checks by initiating charges against the *checking* account.

WILL THAT BE A DEBIT OR CREDIT CARD?

The U.S. is saturated with literally millions of credit and debit cards. Young people are shifting to debit cards because these cards have no annual fee or monthly balances. You pay as you go. Debit card charges represent 60 percent of the transactions processed by Visa. You may not know that when you use your *debit* card, you don't have to choose debit and enter your PIN (PIN transaction). Instead, you can choose *credit* and sign the receipt (signature transaction). A 2004 MasterCard survey showed that 70 percent of people didn't realize that a debit card could be used for a signature transaction. Here are some benefits of choosing *credit* instead of *debit*:

- **Avoid fees:** Banks never charge for signature transactions, but 14 percent charge fees for PIN transactions.
- **Rewards points:** Some debit cards have rewards programs, but sometimes a signature transaction is required to earn points, or you may earn more points with a signature transaction than a PIN transaction.
- **Liability protection:** Signature transactions go through Visa or MasterCard networks that offer protection from fraudulent use. PIN transactions are processed through electronic funds transfer systems, such as NYCE or STAR, that don't offer liability protection.

One point to remember is that if you choose *debit* the money is removed from your account that day; but if you choose *credit* it will be two to three days before the money is deducted. In any case, it's important to keep your receipts and update your checkbook.

So, why would you ever use your PIN to complete a transaction? If you want cash back, then you should use your PIN. It's better to get cash back from a debit transaction than to use an ATM that doesn't belong to your bank. Both the ATM and your bank will charge fees that outweigh any benefit of signing for the transaction.

Critical Thinking Questions

1. What are the benefits to using a debit card over a credit card?
2. Explain why it is better to choose *credit* rather than *debit* when using a debit card.

Sources: Carolyn Bigda, "Debit or Credit? The Savvy Answer Is…," *Money*, October 2005, p. 40c; Robin Sidel, "American Express Tries to Find Its Place with a Younger Crowd," *Wall Street Journal*, September 22, 2005, p. A1; "Debit Cards," *Bankrate.com*, May 1, 2006.

Prepaid Cards

Tired of fumbling for change to buy a candy bar from a vending machine or to use a pay phone? Buy a **prepaid card** and your pockets won't jingle with coins anymore. These "smart cards" can now be used to purchase a variety of items—phone calls, meals in some employee cafeterias, vending machine snacks—and their use is increasing. You pay a fixed amount, which is then stored on either a magnetic strip or rechargeable microchip on the card. Each time you make a purchase, the amount is electronically deducted from the card. First used for public transportation fares in large cities, prepaid cards are now used by many companies. In fact, you might be carrying one yourself, as they have become popular on college campuses, where they're used to purchase meals, books, long-distance phone calls, and other items. The popularity of these "electronic purses" is increasing, as consumers and merchants alike find them convenient. And they're likely to become even more popular as the microchips that are being embedded in these smart cards today can be used not only to execute transactions but also to store such things as electronic plane tickets or theater tickets. It's also easier to control Internet fraud with them, as they have electronic readers that plug easily into your computer for authenticity verification.

Prepaid cards are a lot like *debit cards*. Each time you use one, you're actually debiting the amount purchased to what you have stored on the card (or in your checking account). But don't confuse prepaid cards with prepaid *credit cards*, which you can use again and again. With prepaid cards, once the card is used up, you either toss it or get it recharged—there's no line of credit here, no monthly bills with their minimum monthly payments.

prepaid card A plastic card with a magnetic strip or microchip that stores the amount of money the purchaser has to spend and deducts the value of each purchase.

Revolving Credit Lines

Revolving lines of credit are offered by banks, brokerage houses, and other financial institutions. These credit lines normally don't involve the use of credit cards. Rather, they're accessed by writing checks on regular checking accounts or specially designated credit line accounts. They are a form of open account credit and often represent a far better deal than credit cards, not only because they offer more credit but also because they can be a lot less expensive. And there may even be a tax advantage to using one of these other kinds of credit.

These lines basically provide their users with ready access to borrowed money (that is, cash advances) through revolving lines of credit. They're just as convenient as credit cards; all you have to do is write a check. The three major forms of open (non–credit card) credit are overdraft protection lines, unsecured personal lines of credit, and home equity credit lines.

Overdraft Protection

An **overdraft protection line** is simply a line of credit linked to a checking account that enables a depositor to overdraw his or her checking account up to a predetermined limit. These lines are usually set up with credit limits of $500 to $1,000, but they can be for as much as $10,000 or more. The consumer taps this line of credit by writing a check. If that particular check happens to overdraw the account, the overdraft protection line will automatically advance funds in an amount necessary to put the account back in the black. In some cases, overdraft protection is provided by *linking the bank's credit card to your checking account.* These arrangements act like regular overdraft lines, except when the account is overdrawn, the bank automatically taps your credit card line and transfers the money into your checking account. It's treated as a cash advance from your credit card, but the result is the same as a regular overdraft protection line; it automatically covers overdrawn checks.

Unfortunately, you never know for sure just how much a given check will overdraw your account (if in fact it does). The reason is that unless you write very few checks, the balance shown on your checkbook ledger will seldom be the same as the amount shown by the bank. To account for this, simply record the check in your checkbook ledger as you normally would, including the new balance after the check is written. If this overdraws your account—at least as far as your checkbook ledger is concerned—it won't be a problem, because you have an overdraft protection line to cover it. If your account is overdrawn, the bank will notify you in a matter of days and inform you that it has advanced funds to your checking account. The amount of the advance will be shown on the notice and should immediately be entered into your checkbook ledger as a *deposit.* Once an advance is made, a monthly repayment schedule is set up for systematically repaying the loan, along with all interest charges—generally with monthly payments being spread out over a period of 18 to 36 months.

It should be clear that if you're not careful, you can quickly exhaust this type of credit by writing a lot of overdraft checks. As with any line of credit, there's a limit to how much you can obtain. Be extremely careful with such a credit line, and *under no circumstances take it as a license to routinely overdraw your account!* Doing so on a regular basis is a signal that you're probably mismanaging your cash and/or living beyond your budget. It's best to view an overdraft protection line strictly as an *emergency* source of credit—and any funds advanced should be repaid as quickly as possible.

Unsecured Personal Lines

Another form of revolving credit is the **unsecured personal credit line,** which basically makes a line of credit available to an individual on an as-needed basis. In essence, it's a way of borrowing money from a bank, S&L, credit union, savings bank, or brokerage firm any time you wish, without going through all the hassle of setting up a new loan.

Here's how it works. Suppose you apply for and are approved for a personal line of credit at your bank. Once you've been approved and the credit line established, you'll be issued *checks* that you can write against it. If you need a cash advance, all you need to do is write a check (against your credit line account) and deposit it into your checking account. Or, if you need the money to buy some big-ticket item—say, an expensive stereo system—you can just make the credit line check out to the dealer and, when it clears, it will be charged against your

revolving line of credit
A type of open account credit offered by banks and other financial institutions that can be accessed by writing checks against demand deposit or specially designated credit line accounts.

overdraft protection line A line of credit linked to a checking account that allows a depositor to overdraw the account up to a specified amount.

unsecured personal credit line A line of credit made available to an individual on an as-needed basis.

unsecured personal credit line as an advance. (These credit line checks look and "spend" just like regular checks, but are not channeled through your normal checking account.) Personal lines of credit are usually set up for minimums of $2,000 to $5,000 and often amount to $25,000 or more. As with an overdraft protection line, once an advance is made, repayment is set up on a monthly installment basis. Depending on the amount outstanding, repayment is normally structured over a period of 2 to 5 years; to keep the monthly payments low, larger amounts of debt are usually given longer repayment periods.

Although these credit lines do offer attractive terms to the consumer, they come with their share of problems, perhaps the biggest of which is how easily cash advances can be obtained. These lines also normally involve *substantial* credit limits and are about as easy to use as credit cards. This combination can have devastating effects on a family's budget if it leads to overspending or excessive reliance on credit. To be safe, these lines should be used only for emergency purposes or to make *planned credit expenditures*. Systematic repayment of the debt should be built into the budget, and every effort should be made to ensure that using this kind of credit will not overly strain the family finances.

Home Equity Credit Lines

Here's a familiar situation. A couple buys a home for $185,000; some 10 years later, it's worth $265,000. The couple now has an asset worth $265,000 on which all they owe is the original mortgage, which may now have a balance of, say, $120,000. The couple clearly has built up a substantial amount of equity in their home: $265,000 − $120,000 = $145,000. But how can they tap that equity without having to sell their home? The answer is to obtain a **home equity credit line.** Such lines are much like unsecured personal credit lines except that the're *secured with a second mortgage on the home*. These lines of credit allow you to tap up to 100 percent (or more) of the equity in your home by merely writing a check. Although some banks and financial institutions allow their customers to borrow up to 100 percent of the *equity* in their homes—or, in some cases, even more—most lenders set their maximum credit lines at 75 to 80 percent of the *market value* of the home, which reduces the amount of money they'll lend.

Here's how these lines work. Recall the couple in our example that has built up equity of $145,000 in their home—equity against which they can borrow through a home equity credit line. Assuming they have a good credit record and using a 75 percent loan-to-market-value ratio, a bank would be willing to lend up to $198,750; that is, 75 percent of the value of the house is .75 × $265,000 = $198,750. Subtracting the $120,000 still due on the first mortgage, we see that our couple could qualify for a home equity credit line of a whopping $78,750. Note, in this case, that if the bank had been willing to lend the couple *100 percent of the equity* in their home, it would have given them a (much higher) credit line of $145,000, which is the difference between what the house is worth and what they still owe on it. Most lenders don't like to do this because it results in very large credit lines and, perhaps more important, it doesn't provide the lender with much of a cushion should the borrower default. Even worse, from the borrowers' perspective, it provides access to a lot of relatively inexpensive credit, which can lead some homeowners to overextend themselves and thus encounter serious debt service problems down the road—even bankruptcy or loss of their home!

Home equity lines also have a tax feature that you should be aware of—namely, the annual interest charges on such lines may be fully deductible for those who itemize. This is the only type of consumer loan that still qualifies for such tax treatment. According to the latest provisions of the tax code, a homeowner is allowed to *fully deduct the interest charges on home equity loans of up to $100,000*, regardless of the original cost of the house or use of the proceeds. Indeed, the only restriction is that *the amount of total indebtedness on the house cannot exceed its fair market value*—which is highly unlikely, because homeowners usually cannot borrow more than 75 to 80 percent of the market value of the house anyway. (Effectively, the interest on that portion of the loan that exceeds $100,000, or 100 percent of the market value of the house—whichever is lower—*cannot* be treated as a tax-deductible expense.) In our preceding example, the homeowners could take out the full amount of their credit line ($78,750), and every dime they paid in interest would be tax deductible. If they paid, say, $7,400 in interest, and if they were in the 28 percent tax bracket, this feature would reduce their tax liability by some $2,070—(i.e., $7,400 × .28)—given, of course, that they itemize their deductions.

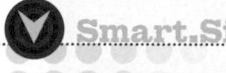

Smart Sites

If you need a home equity line of credit but your credit is not the best, Bankrate.com can point you to the best rates in your own state or suggest a more distant bank with a good deal. Visit their site by linking at **http://www.thomsonedu.com/finance/gitman.**

home equity credit line
A line of credit issued against the existing equity in a home.

Not only do home equity credit lines offer shelter from taxes, they're also among *the cheapest forms of consumer credit.* For example, while the average rate on standard credit cards in early 2006 was about 13.7 percent, the average rate on home equity credit lines was less than half that, or 6.2 percent. To see what that can mean to you as a borrower, assume you have $10,000 in consumer debt outstanding. If you had borrowed that money through a standard consumer loan at, say, 9.5 percent, you'd pay interest of $950 per year—none of which would be tax deductible. But borrow the same amount through a home equity credit line at 6.2 percent, and you'll pay only $620 in interest. That's all tax deductible though, so if you're in the 28 percent tax bracket, the after-tax cost to you would be $620 $\times$ (1 − .28) = $446. This is less than half the cost of the other loan! So, which would you rather pay for a $10,000 loan, $950 or $446? That's really not a tough decision, and it explains why these lines have become so popular and are today one of the fastest-growing forms of consumer credit.

Home equity credit lines are offered by a variety of financial institutions, from banks and S&Ls to major brokerage houses. All sorts of credit terms and credit lines are available, and most of them carry repayment periods of 10 to 15 years, or longer. Perhaps most startling, however, is the maximum amount of credit available under these lines—indeed, $100,000 figures are not at all unusual. And it's precisely because of the enormous amount of money available that this form of credit should be used with caution. *The fact that you have equity in your home does not mean that you have the cash flow necessary to service the debt that such a credit line imposes.* Remember that your house is the collateral. If you can't repay the loan, you could lose it! At the minimum, paying for major expenditures through a home equity credit line should be done only after you have determined that you can afford the purchase and the required monthly payments will fit comfortably within your budget. Equally important, don't be tempted to use a 15-year home equity credit line to finance, say, a new car that you may be driving for only 5 or 6 years—the last thing you want to be doing is paying for that car 8 to 10 years after you've traded it in. If a 15-year loan is the only way you can afford the car, then face it: you can't afford the car!

❚❚ Concept Check

6-5	What is *open account credit?* Name several different types of open account credit.
6-6	What is the attraction of *reward cards?*
6-7	How is the interest rate typically set on bank credit cards?
6-8	Many bank card issuers impose different types of fees; briefly describe three of these fees.
6-9	What is a *debit card?* How is it similar to a credit card? How does it differ?
6-10	Describe how *revolving credit lines* provide open account credit.
6-11	What are the basic features of a *home equity credit line?*

LG4 OBTAINING AND MANAGING OPEN FORMS OF CREDIT

Americans love to use their charge cards. In the year 2003 alone, they bought nearly *$2.2 trillion* in goods and services on credit. And this figure is rising as more places accept "plastic"; consumers find credit and debit cards more convenient than cash or checks, and the number of other benefits, like rebates and frequent flyer miles, continues to grow.

For the sake of convenience, people often maintain several different kinds of open credit. Nearly every household, for example, uses 30-day charge accounts to pay their utility bills, phone bills, and so on. In addition, most families have one or more retail charge cards and a couple of bank cards; some people, in fact, may have as many as 15 to 20 cards, or more. And that's not all—families can also have revolving credit lines in the form of overdraft protection or a home equity line. When all these cards and lines are totaled together, a family conceivably can have tens of thousands of dollars of readily available credit. It's easy to see why consumer credit has become such a popular way of making relatively routine purchases. Although open account credit can increase the risk of budgetary overload, these accounts can also serve as a useful way of keeping track of expenditures.

Opening an Account

What do retail charge cards, bank credit cards, and revolving lines of credit all have in common? *Answer*: They all require you to go through a formal credit application. Let's now look at how you'd go about obtaining open forms of credit, including the normal credit application, investigation, and decision process. We'll couch our discussion in terms of credit cards, but keep in mind that similar procedures apply to other revolving lines of credit as well.

The Credit Application

With over a billion credit cards in the hands of American consumers, you'd think that consumer credit is available to just about anyone. And it is—but you must apply for it. Applications are usually available at the store or bank involved. Sometimes they can be found at the businesses that accept these cards or obtained on request from the issuing companies. Exhibit 6.4 provides an example of a bank credit card application. As you can see, the type of information requested in a typical credit application covers little more than personal/family matters, housing, employment and income, and existing charge accounts. Such information is intended to give the lender insight about the applicant's creditworthiness. In essence, the lender is trying to determine whether the applicant has the *character* and *capacity* to handle the debt in a prompt and timely manner.

The Credit Investigation

Once the credit application has been completed and returned to the establishment issuing the card, it is subject to a **credit investigation.** The purpose is to evaluate the kind of credit risk you pose to the lender (the party issuing the credit or charge card). So be sure to fill out your credit application carefully. Believe it or not, they really do look at those things. The key items lenders look at are how much money you make, how much debt you have outstanding and how well you handle it, and how stable you are (for example, your age, employment history, whether you own or rent a home, and so on). Obviously, the higher your income and the better your credit history, the greater the chances of having your credit application approved.

During the credit investigation, the lender attempts to verify much of the information you've provided on the credit application—for obvious reasons, false or misleading information will almost certainly result in outright rejection of your application. For example, the lender may verify your place of employment, level of income, current debt load, debt service history, and so forth. Often, this can be done through one or two quick phone calls. If you've lived in the area for several years and have established relations with a local bank, a call to your banker may be all it takes to confirm your creditworthiness. If you haven't established such bank relations—and most young people have not—the lender is likely to turn to the local credit bureau for a *credit report* on you.

The Credit Bureau

A **credit bureau** is a type of reporting agency that gathers and sells information about individual borrowers. If, as is often the case, the lender doesn't know you personally, it must rely on a cost-effective way of verifying your employment and credit history. It would be far too expensive and time-consuming for individual creditors to confirm your credit application on their own, so they turn to credit bureaus that maintain fairly detailed credit files about you. Information in your file comes from one of three sources: creditors who subscribe to the

credit investigation An investigation that involves contacting credit references or corresponding with a credit bureau to verify information on a credit application.

credit bureau An organization that collects and stores credit information about individual borrowers.

EXHIBIT 6.4   An Online Credit Card Application

You can apply for many credit cards today right on the Internet. This credit application, like most, seeks information about the applicant's place of employment, monthly income, place of residence, credit history, and other financial matters that are intended to help the lender decide whether or not to extend credit.

Credit Card Application   YOUR BANK

Read Privacy Policy and Pricing and Terms for important information about rates, fees and other costs.

🔒 All application pages are secure.

* indicates a required field.

Application Information

Before completing the application, you should be able to answer "Yes" to the following statements by checking the boxes:

☐ Yes, my credit history is clear of bankruptcy.

☐ Yes, my credit history is clear of seriously delinquent accounts.

☐ Yes, I have NOT been denied credit within the last 6 months.

Personal Information

Name: Title   First* *(Required)*   M.I.   Last* *(Required)*

Residential Address Line 1:*   Unit/Apt #:

Residential Address Line 2:

City:*   **State:***

Zip Code:*   -   **Home Phone:***   -   -

Lived There:*   Years   Months

SSN:*   -   -

Date of Birth:*   /   /   (MM/DD/YYYY)

Mother's Maiden Name:*

E-mail Address:

Employment Information

(If retired, note previous employer. If self-employed, note nature of business.)

Employer:*   **Position:***

Worked There:*   years   months

Work Phone:*   -   -

Financial Information

Alimony, child support, or separate maintenance income need not be revealed if you do not wish it to be considered as a basis for repaying this obligation.

Annual Household Income:* $ ____ .00 *(Please do not use commas.)*

Please select the type(s) of bank account(s) you have:* ____

Select Residence:* ____

Monthly Rent or Mortgage:* $ ____ .00 *(Please do not use commas.)*

bureau, other creditors who supply information at your request, and publicly recorded court documents (such as tax liens or bankruptcy records).

Contrary to popular opinion, your credit file does *not* contain everything anyone would ever want to know about you—there's nothing on your lifestyle, friends, habits, or religious or political affiliations. Instead, most of the information is pretty dull stuff, and covers such things as:

- Your name, Social Security number, age, number of dependents, and current and previous addresses
- Your employment record, including current and past employers and salary data, if available
- Your credit history, including the number of loans and credit lines you have, number of credit cards issued in your name, your payment record, and account balances
- Public records data involving bankruptcies, tax liens, foreclosures, civil suits, and criminal convictions
- The names of firms and financial institutions that have recently requested copies of your file

While one late MasterCard payment probably won't make much of a difference on an otherwise clean credit file, a definite pattern of delinquencies (consistently being 30 to 60 days late with your payments) or a personal bankruptcy certainly will. Unfortunately, poor credit traits will stick with you for a long time, because delinquencies remain on your credit file for as long as 7 years and bankruptcies for 10 years. An example of an actual credit bureau report (or at least a part of one) is provided in Exhibit 6.5. It demonstrates the kind of information you can expect to find in one of these reports.

Local credit bureaus (there are about a thousand of them) are established and mutually owned by local merchants and banks. They collect and store credit information on people living within the community and make it available, for a fee, to members who request it. Local bureaus are linked together nationally through one of the "big three" national bureaus—Trans-Union, Equifax Credit Information Services, and Experian—each of which provides the mechanism for obtaining credit information from almost any place in the United States. Traditionally, credit bureaus did little more than collect and provide credit information; they did not analyze the information nor did they use it to make a final credit decision. In 2006, however, the three major credit bureaus announced that they had jointly developed a new credit-scoring system, called *VantageScore*, that would incorporate data from all three bureaus—Equifax, Experian, and TransUnion. Thus, for the first time, each of the three national bureaus began assigning uniform credit ratings to individual credit files. The new VantageScore system is supposed to simplify and enhance the credit granting process, because all three bureaus will now be reporting, among other things, the same credit score—although they're still obligated to report other credit scores, such as the widely used FICO scores. Of course, whether adding still another credit score to the four or five that already exist actually simplifies matters or not remains to be seen. (We'll examine credit scores and FICO scores in more detail below.)

Credit bureaus in the past were heavily criticized because of the large numbers of reporting errors they made and their poor record in promptly and efficiently correcting these errors. Fortunately, things have changed dramatically in recent years as the major credit bureaus have taken a more consumer-oriented approach, greatly improving their customer service and dispute resolution procedures, and making their reports easier to read. Many of these changes were formalized by a 1995 amendment to the Fair Credit Reporting Act that established industry guidelines for credit reporting procedures. According to this legislation, credit bureaus must provide you with low-cost copies of your own credit report, and they must have toll-free phone numbers. Disputes must be resolved in 30 days and take the consumer's documentation into account, not just the creditor's.

And since September 2005, all Americans are entitled to receive *a free copy of their credit report once a year*. To get your free report, go to the Web site set up by the Federal Trade Commission at **http://www.annualcreditreport.com** or call toll-free: 1-877-322-8228. You should ensure that your credit report accurately reflects your credit history. The best way to do that is to obtain a copy of your own credit report and then go through it carefully.

EXHIBIT 6.5   An Example of a Credit Bureau Report

Credit bureau reports have been revised and are now easier to understand. Notice that in addition to some basic information, the report deals strictly with credit information—including payment records, past-due status, and types of credit.

Your Credit Report as of 04/09/2007

This Credit Report is available for you to view for 30 days. If you would like a current Credit Report, you may order another from MyEquifax.

ID # XXXXXXXXXXXX

• **Personal Data**

John Q. Public
2351 N 85th Ave
Phoenix, AZ 85037

Social Security Number: 022-22-2222
Date of Birth: 1/11/1960

• **Previous Address(es):**

133 Third Avenue
Phoenix, AZ 85037

• **Employment History**

Cendant Hospitality FR

Location:	Employment Date:	Verified Date:
Phoenix, AZ	2/1/1989	1/3/2001

Previous Employment(s):

SOFTWARE Support Hospitality Franch

Location:	Employment Date:	Verified Date:
Atlanta, GA	1/3/2001	1/3/2001

• **Public Records**

No bankruptcies on file
No liens on file
No foreclosures on file

• **Collection Accounts**

No collections on file.

• **Credit Information**

Company Name	Account Number and Whose Account	Date Opened	Last Activity	Type of Account and Status	High Credit	Items as of Date Reported Terms	Balance	Past Due	Date Reported
Americredit Financial Services	40404XXXX JOINT ACCOUNT	03/1999	03/2000	Installment REPOSSESSION	$16933	$430	$9077	$128	2/2000

Prior Paying History
30 days past due 07 times; 60 days past due 05 times; 90+ days past due 03 times
INVOLUNTARY REPOSSESION AUTO

| Capital One | 412174147128XXXX INDIVIDUAL ACCOUNT | 10/1997 | 01/2001 | Revolving PAYS AS AGREED | $777 | 15 | $514 | | 01/2001 |

Prior Paying History
30 days past due 02 times; 60 days past due 1 times; 90+ days past due 00 times
CREDIT CARD

| Desert Schools FCU | 423325003406XXXX INDIVIDUAL ACCOUNT | 07/1997 | 06/1998 | Revolving PAYS AS AGREED | $500 | | $0 | | 07/1999 |

Prior Paying History
30 days past due 02 times; 60 days past due 00 times; 90+ days past due 00 times
ACCOUNT PAID   CLOSED ACCOUNT

• **Credit Inquiries**

Companies that Requested your Credit File

04/09/2001 EFX Credit Profile Online
06/30/2001 Automotive
01/18/2000 Desert Schools Federal C.U.
07/02/1999 Time Life, Inc.

FINANCIAL ROAD SIGN

KEEPING UP YOUR FICO SCORES

Raising your FICO score is a lot like losing weight: It takes time and there's no quick fix. But here are some tips you might want to follow to reach a high score:

- Pay your bills on time.
- If you've missed payments, get current and stay current.
- If you're having trouble making ends meet, contact your creditors and work out a payment plan.
- Keep credit card balances low.
- Pay off debt rather than moving it around.
- Don't open new credit cards just to increase your available credit.
- Reestablish your credit history if you've had problems in the past.

Source: http://www.myfico.com

If you do find a mistake, let the credit bureau know immediately—and by all means, put it writing; *then request a copy of the corrected file to make sure that the mistake has been eliminated.* Most consumer advisors recommend that you review your credit files annually. Here are the addresses, Web sites, and toll-free phone numbers for the three national credit bureaus:

- Equifax Credit Information Services
  P.O. Box 740241
  Atlanta, GA 30374
  http://www.equifax.com or phone 1-888-766-0008
- TransUnion LLC
  Consumer Disclosure Center
  P.O. Box 1000
  Chester, PA 19022
  http://www.tuc.com or phone 1-800-888-4213
- Experian (formerly TRW)
  National Consumer Assistance Center
  P.O. Box 2002
  Allen, TX 75013
  http://www.experian.com or phone 1-888-397-3742

The Credit Decision

Using the data provided by the credit applicant, along with any information obtained from the credit bureau, the store or bank must decide whether to grant credit. Very likely, some type of **credit scoring** scheme will be used to make the decision. An overall credit score is developed for you by assigning values to such factors as your annual income, whether you rent or own your home, number and types of credit cards you hold, level of your existing debts, whether you have savings accounts, and general credit references. Fifteen or 20 different factors or characteristics may be considered, and each characteristic receives a score based on some predetermined standard. For example, if you're 26 years old, single, earn $32,500 a year (on a job that you've had for only 2 years), and rent an apartment, you might receive the following scores:

1. Age (25–30)	5 points
2. Marital status (single)	−2 points
3. Annual income ($30–35 thousand)	12 points
4. Length of employment (2 yrs. or less)	4 points
5. Rent or own a home (rent)	0 points
	19 points

Based on information obtained from your credit application, similar scores would be assigned to another 10 to 15 factors.

In all cases, the stronger your personal traits or characteristics, the higher the score you'll receive. For instance, if you were 46 years old (rather than 26), you might receive 18 points for your age factor, being married rather than single would give you 9 points, and earning $75,000 a year would obviously be worth a lot more than earning $32,500! The idea is that the more stable you are *perceived* to be, the more income you make, the better your credit record, and so on, the higher the score you should receive. In essence, statistical studies have shown that certain personal and financial traits can be used to determine your creditworthiness. Indeed, the whole credit scoring system is based on extensive statistical studies, which identify the characteristics to look at and the scores to assign.

The biggest provider of credit scores is, by far, Fair Isaac & Co.—the firm that produces the widely used *FICO scores*. Unlike some credit score providers, *Fair Isaac uses only credit information in its calculations.* There's nothing in them about your age, marital status, salary, occupation, employment history, or where you live. Instead, FICO scores are derived from the following five major components (which are listed along with their respective weights): payment history (35 percent), amounts owed (30 percent), length of credit history

credit scoring A method of evaluating an applicant's creditworthiness by assigning values to such factors as income, existing debts, and credit references.

(15 percent), new credit (10 percent), and types of credit used (10 percent). FICO scores, which are reported by all three of the major credit bureaus, range from a low of 300 to a max of 850. In 2005, the distribution of FICO scores was as follows:

Less than 500	2%
500–599	13%
600–699	27%
700–749	18%
750–799	27%
800 or more	13%

Smart Sites

To learn more about FICO scores, including what's in your FICO score, what's not in it, and what you can do to improve it, visit the Fair Isaac & Co. Web site by linking at **http://www .thomsonedu.com/ finance/gitman.**

FICO scores are meant to be an indication of a borrower's credit risk; the higher the score, the lower the risk. While few, if any, credit decisions are based solely on FICO scores, you can be sure that higher scores are likely to result in lower interest rates on loans, and therefore, lower loan payments. For example, in early 2006, if you were taking out a 30-year, $150,000 fixed-rate mortgage, you could expect to borrow at an interest rate of around 6.10 percent, if you had a FICO score of 750–850, compared to 9.30 percent if your score was in the range of 500–560. That translates into monthly mortgage payments of around $910 a month versus $1,240 a month. Granted, a lot more goes into a credit decision than a simple credit score; but as you can see, it definitely pays to keep your FICO score as high as possible.

Computing Finance Charges

Because card issuers don't know in advance how much you'll charge on your account, they cannot specify the dollar amount of interest you will be charged. But they can—and must, according to the Truth in Lending Act—disclose the *rate of interest* they charge and their method of computing finance charges. This is the **annual percentage rate (APR),** the true or actual rate of interest paid, which must include all fees and costs and be calculated as defined by law. Remember, it's your right as a consumer to know—and the lender's obligation to tell you—the dollar amount of charges (where applicable) and the APR on any financing you consider.

The amount of interest you pay for open credit depends partly on the method the lender uses to calculate the balances on which they apply finance charges. Most bank and retail charge card issuers use one of four variations of the **average daily balance (ADB) method,** which applies the interest rate to the average daily balance of the account over the billing period. According to Bankcard Holders of America, a nonprofit consumer education organization, the most common method (used by an estimated 95 percent of bankcard issuers) is the *average daily balance including new purchases.* The other techniques are ADB excluding new purchases, two-cycle ADB including new purchases, and two-cycle ADB excluding new purchases. Balance calculations under each method are as follows:

- **ADB including new purchases.** For each day in the billing cycle, add the outstanding balance, including new purchases, and subtract payments and credits, then divide by the number of days in the billing cycle.
- **ADB excluding new purchases.** Same as first method, *excluding* new purchases.
- **Two-cycle ADB including new purchases.** Calculated like the first method, but using the average daily balance for both the current and previous billing cycles.
- **Two-cycle ADB excluding new purchases.** Same as the two-cycle method, but *excluding* new purchases.

annual percentage rate (APR) The actual or true rate of interest paid over the life of a loan; includes all fees and costs.

average daily balance (ADB) method A method of computing finance charges by applying interest charges to the average daily balance of the account over the billing period.

These different calculations can obviously affect a card's credit balance, and therefore the amount of finance charges you'll have to pay. Also be aware that the finance charges on two cards with the same APR but different methods of calculating balances may differ dramatically. It's important to know the method your card issuer uses. Most banks compute finance charges for a 1-month period, though some issuers (among them Discover Card) still use the *two-cycle average daily balance method.* The comparisons in Exhibit 6.6 show how the method used to calculate the ADB affects the amount of finance charges you pay. In the situation illustrated here, annual finance charges range from $66.00 to a high of $196.20—and note the procedure that's most widely used by credit card issuers results in finance charges of $132.00. Clearly, any way you look at it, carrying a balance on a credit card can be expensive.

Crunching the Numbers. Let's look at an example of how to calculate balances and finance charges under the most popular method, *the average daily balance including new purchases*. Assume that you have a LastBank Visa card with a monthly interest rate of 1.5 percent. Your statement for the billing period extending from October 10, 2007, through November 10, 2007—a total of 31 days—shows that your beginning balance was $582, you made purchases of $350 on October 15 and $54 on October 22, and you made a $25 payment on November 6. Therefore, the outstanding balance for the first 5 days of the period (October 11 through 15) was $582; for the next 7 days (October 16 through 22), it was $932 ($582 + $350); for the next 15 days (October 23 through November 6) it was $986 ($932 + $54); and for the last 4 days, it was $961 ($986 less the $25 payment). We can now calculate the average daily balance using the procedure shown in Exhibit 6.7 (page 198). Note that the outstanding balances are weighted by the number of days that the balance existed and then averaged (divided) by the number of days in the billing period. By multiplying the average daily balance of $905.42 by the 1.5 percent interest rate, we get a finance charge of $13.58.

Managing Your Credit Cards

Congratulations! You have applied for and been granted a bank credit card, as well as a retail charge card from your favorite department store. You carefully reviewed the terms of the credit agreement and have at least a basic understanding of how finance charges are computed for each account. Now you must manage your accounts efficiently, using the monthly statement to help you make the required payments on time as well as to track purchases and returned items.

The Statement

If you use a credit card, you'll receive monthly statements similar to the sample bank card statement in Exhibit 6.8 (page 199), showing billing cycle and payment due dates, interest rate, minimum payment, and all account activity during the current period. Retail charge cards have similar monthly statements, but without a section for cash advances. (Revolving line of credit lenders will also send you a monthly statement showing the amount borrowed, payments, and finance charges.) The statement summarizes your account activity: the previous balance (the amount of credit outstanding at the beginning of the month, not to be confused with past-due, or late, payments); new charges made during the past month (four in this case); any finance charges (interest) on the unpaid balance; the preceding period's payment; any other credits (such as those for returns); and the new balance (previous balance plus new purchases and finance charges, less any payments and credits).

EXHIBIT 6.6	Finance Charges for Different Balance Calculation Methods

The way a credit card issuer calculates the average daily balance on which the consumer pays finance charges has a big effect on the amount of interest you actually pay, as this table demonstrates.

Example: A consumer starts the first month with a zero balance and charges $1,000, of which he pays off only the minimum amount due (1/36 of balance due). The next month, he charges another $1,000. He then pays off the entire balance due. This same pattern is repeated three more times during the year. The interest rate is 19.8 percent.

	Finance Charges
Average daily balance (including new purchases):	$132.00
Average daily balance (excluding new purchases):	$ 66.00
Two-cycle average daily balance (including new purchases):	$196.20
Two-cycle average daily balance (excluding new purchases):	$131.20

Source: Based on data from Bankcard Holders of America, Salem, Virginia.

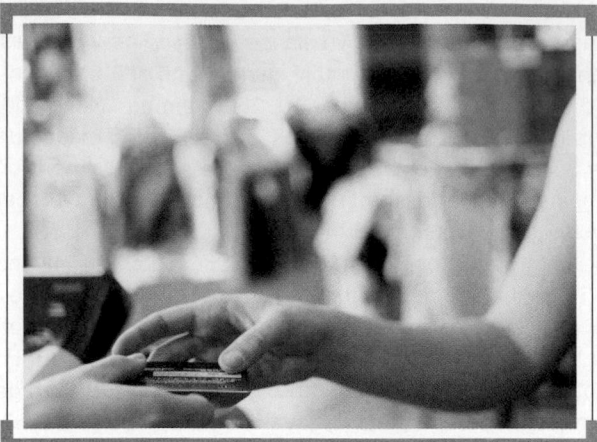

© PHOTONICA/GETTY IMAGES

Although merchandise and cash transactions are separated on the statement, the finance charge in each case is calculated at the rate of 1.5 percent per month (18 percent annually). While this procedure works fine for this illustration, it's a bit out of the ordinary, because most card issuers charge a higher rate for cash advances than for purchases. Note that the average daily balance method is used to compute the finance charge in this statement.

You should review your statements promptly each month. Save your receipts and use them to verify statement entries for purchases and returns *before* paying. If you find any errors or suspect fraudulent use of your card, first use the issuer's toll-free number to report any problems. Then always follow up *in writing* within 60 days of the postmark on the bill.

Payments

Credit card users can avoid *future* finance charges by paying the total new balance shown on their statement each month. For example, if the $534.08 total new balance shown in Exhibit 6.8 is paid by the September 21, 2007, due date, no additional finance charges will be incurred. (The cardholder, however, is still liable for the $4.40 in finance charges incurred to date.) If cardholders cannot pay the total new balance, they can pay any amount that is equal to or greater than the **minimum monthly payment** specified on the statement. If they do that, however, they will incur additional finance charges in the following month. Note that the account in Exhibit 6.8 has a minimum payment of 5 percent of the new balance, rounded to the nearest full dollar. As shown at the bottom of the statement, this month's minimum payment is $27.00 (i.e., $534.08 × .05 = $26.70 = $27.00). This $27.00 works out to be a *principal payment of $22.60*; that is, $27.00 − $4.40 (in interest charges) = $22.60. That's actually about 4¼ percent of the "new balance." Now if the new balance had been less than $200, the bank would have required a payment of $10 (which is the absolute minimum dollar payment), or of the total new balance, if less than $10. Cardholders who fail to make the minimum payment are considered in default on their account, and the bank issuing the card can take whatever action it deems necessary.

Returned Merchandise

When you return merchandise purchased with a credit card, the merchant will issue a *credit* to your account. The credit is handled like a purchase, but it appears on your statement as a *deduction* from the balance. If you purchase an item and have problems with it, you may not have to pay that part of your credit card bill if you have attempted in good faith to resolve the problem with the merchant. This protection is provided by the Fair Credit Billing Act. Of course, if the problem is resolved in the merchant's favor, you will ultimately have to pay.

Smart.Sites

Use About.com's Credit Card Calculators to find out how interest rate changes affect your balance, if debt consolidation makes sense, and answers to similar questions. Go to their Web site at **http://www .thomsonedu.com/finance/ gitman.**

minimum monthly pament In open account credit, a minimum specified percentage of the new account balance that must be paid in order to remain current.

EXHIBIT 6.7 — Finding the Average Daily Balance and Finance Charge

The average daily balance including new purchases is the method most widely used by credit card issuers to determine the monthly finance charge on an account:

	Number of Days (1)	Balance (2)	(1) × (2) (3)
	5	$582	$ 2,910
	7	$932	6,524
	15	$986	14,790
	4	$961	3,844
Total	31		$28,068

Average daily balance = $\frac{\$28,068}{31}$ = $905.42

Finance charge: $905.42 × .015 = $13.58

EXHIBIT 6.8   **A Bank Credit Card Monthly Statement**

Each month, a bank credit cardholder receives a statement that provides an itemized list of charges and credits as well as a summary of previous activity and finance charges.

Please detach the above portion and return it with your payment to insure proper credit.

Bank Card Statement

Retain this statement for your records.

Account Number	Name(s)		
123-XYZ-45678	Mr. Bill A. Bitshort Mrs. Bonnie R. Bitshort	8-24-07 Statement Date	09-21-07 Payment Due Date

ACCOUNT ACTIVITY

Previous Balance	203.64
Payments −	119.89
Credits −	.00
Subtotal	83.75
New Transaction +	445.93
Finance Charge +	4.40
Late Charge +	.00
NEW BALANCE	534.08

Credit Status
Your Credit Limit is:

2000.00

Your Available Credit is:

1465.92

FINANCE CHARGE CALCULATION

Amounts Subject to Finance Charge		This Month's Charge
A. *Average Daily Balance	293.25	4.40
B. *Cash Advance	.00	.00
C. *Loan Advance	.00	.00

ENTIRE BAL.	
1.5%	18.00%
Monthly Periodic Rate	Nominal Annual Rate
4.40	18.00%
Finance Charge	Annual Percentage Rate

*Finance Charges explained on reverse side

Mail Billing Inquiries to: Post Office Box 7890, Van Niles, California, 85258, or call   800/000-0000
For Inquiries on Past Due Accounts, Overlimits or Credit Line Increase, call   800/000-0000

Posted Mo./Day	Transaction Description or Merchant Name and Location		Purchase Mo./Day	Bank Reference Number	Purchases/ Advances/Debits	Payments Credits
8-08	AMERICA WEST AIRLINES	LOS ANGELES	07-25	850000008823395192	42.00	
8-13	HACIENDA MOTORS	COSTA MESA	08-05	015400018537022316	166.86	
8-15	RICOS RESTAURANT	PALM SPRG	08-10	114500018856161722	132.47	
8-12	PAYMENT—THANK YOU		08-11	4501000182MD02139		119.89
8-24	RENEES RESTAURANT	NEWPORT	08-13	114500068201632483	104.60	

Notice   See reverse side for important information

				Total Debits	Total Credits
MIN. PAYMENT: 27.00	NEW BALANCE: 534.08			445.93	119.89

▮▮ Concept Check

CHECK • CONCEPT CHECK • CONCEPT CHECK • CONCEPT CHECK • CONCEPT CHECK • CONCEPT CHECK • CONCEPT C

6-12	Describe *credit scoring* and explain how it's used (by lenders) in making a credit decision.
6-13	Describe the basic operations and functions of a *credit bureau*.
6-14	What is the most common method used to compute finance charges?
6-15	The monthly statement is a key feature of bank and retail credit cards. What does this statement typically disclose?

Does it seem that every week there's at least one new credit card application in your mailbox? Well, there's a good reason for that—each year, the 20,000 or so institutions and organizations that issue these cards mail out *over 4.8 billion* credit card applications! Every one of these unsolicited pieces of junk mail tries to give the impression that their offer is better than all the rest. It's easy to be overwhelmed by all these choices. And although we've discussed how credit cards and revolving lines of credit can simplify your life financially, we also made it clear that you can get into real trouble unless you use them wisely. That's why you should carefully shop around to choose the right credit cards for your personal situation, understand the advantages and disadvantages credit of cards, learn how to resolve credit problems, and know how to avoid the ultimate cost of credit abuse—bankruptcy.

Shop Around for the Best Deal

They say it pays to shop around, and when it comes to credit cards, that's certainly true. With all the fees and high interest costs, it pays to get the best deal possible. So, where do you start? Most credit experts suggest the first thing you should do is step back and take a look at yourself. What kind of "spender" are you, and how do you pay your bills? The fact is, no single credit card is right for everyone. If you pay off your card balance each month, you'll want a card that's different from the one that's right for someone who carries a credit balance from month to month and may only pay the minimum due.

Regardless of which category you fall into, there are basically four card features to look for:

- Annual fees
- Rate of interest charged on account balance
- Length of the grace period
- Method of calculating balances

Now, if you normally pay your account balance in full each month, get a card with *no annual fees and a long grace period*. The rate of interest on the card is irrelevant, since you don't carry account balances from month to month anyway.

In sharp contrast, if you don't pay your account in full, then look for cards that charge *a low rate of interest on unpaid balances*. The length of the grace period isn't all that important here, but obviously, other things being equal, you're better off with low (or no) annual fees. Sometimes, however, "other things aren't equal," and you have to decide between interest rates and annual fees. If you're not a big spender and don't build up big balances on your credit card (i.e., the card balance rarely goes above $400 or $500), then *avoid* cards with annual fees and get one with as *low* a rate of interest as possible. (*Note*: The above situation would probably apply to most college students—or at least it should.) On the other hand, if you do carry big balances (say, $1,000 or more), then you'll probably be better off *paying an annual fee* (even a relatively high one) *to keep the rate of interest on the card as low as possible*. For example, with a $2,000 average balance, your total yearly finance charges (including annual fees) will be *less* with a card that has, say, a $50 annual fee and an interest rate of 15 percent than with one that has no annual fee but charges a higher (19 percent) rate of interest.

The bottom line is—don't take the first credit card that comes along. Instead, get the one that's right for you. To do that, learn as much as you can about the credit cards you've been offered or are considering. Be sure to read (or at least review) the credit agreement, and look for information about annual fees, grace periods, interest rates, and how finance charges are calculated. Don't overlook all those other charges and fees you may be charged if you're ever late with a payment or go over your credit limit. Also,

FINANCIAL ROAD SIGN

SHOULD YOU SWITCH?

Shopping for a better deal on a credit card can be confusing because card issuers frequently change their offers. Here's how to figure out if it's time to switch.

1. Review your card terms about every 6 months. Visit the Web site of the card issuer to learn of current offers for new customers. If it's better than what you have, call the company and ask for the better deal. It may be willing to offer you the same terms to keep your business.
2. Compare offers from competing companies at one of the credit card sites mentioned in the chapter, like **http://www.bankrate.com.**
3. Know what you need. If you carry balances, you'll want a lower introductory rate. If you pay in full each month, look for ways to reduce fees or earn rewards.

if the local credit card deals aren't great, you might consider cards that are offered nationally. Many banks market their cards throughout the United States, and it may pay to check them out. To help you do that, look to publications like *Money* magazine and *Kiplinger's Personal Finance* magazine. They have Internet sites located at **http://www.money.com** and **http://www.kiplinger.com.** These magazines and Internet sites regularly publish information about banks and other financial institutions that offer low-cost credit cards nationally; an example is given in Exhibit 6.9.

One final point: Some people, it seems, spend a lot of time and energy shopping for deals, jumping from one card to another to take advantage of low introductory rates. Although a strategy like this may result in lower interest payments, it can backfire if the low rates rise significantly after the introductory period, or if you miss a payment. A wiser approach is to shop around, check for better deals from time to time, and then *direct the rest of your energy toward working to reduce (or even eliminate) any monthly balances.*

Avoiding Credit Problems

As more places accept credit cards, and as shopping online becomes more widely accepted, the volume of credit card purchases has grown tremendously—and so has the level of credit card debt. As a result, it's not unusual to find people using credit cards to solve cash-flow

EXHIBIT 6.9   Published Information about Bank Credit Card Terms

Information about low-cost credit cards is readily available in the financial media. Here's an example of what you can find online. Notice the report lists the *cards with the lowest rates* (probably best for people who regularly carry an account balance), *no-fee cards with the lowest rates* (probably best for people who pay their accounts in full each month), and the *best cash advance cards.*

LOW-INTEREST PREMIUM CARDS: *BEST IF YOU CARRY A BALANCE*

Issuer	Recent Rate (APR)	Cash-Advance Rate/Fee	Annual Fee	Late/Over Limit Fees	Grace Period
Pulaski Bank & Trust	7.99% F	7.99%/$0	$35	$29/$29	25 days
Amalgamated Bank of Chicago	9.75% V	9.75%/2.5%	$37	$25/$20	25 days
Blue Ball Nat. Bank	9.90% F	19.99%/3.0%	$0	$39/$39	25 days

NO-FEE CARDS WITH THE LOWEST RATES: *BEST IF YOU USUALLY PAY THE BALANCE EACH MONTH*

Issuer	Recent Rate (APR)	Cash-Advance Rate/Fee	Annual Fee	Late/Over Limit Fees	Grace Period
Blue Ball Nat. Bank	9.90% F	19.99%/3.0%	$0	$39/$39	25 days
Malvern Fed. Savings Bank	9.90% F	19.99%/3.0%	$0	$39/$39	25 days
MBNA America Bank	12.99% F	12.99%/3.0%	$0	$39/$39	25 days

RATES & LOW CASH ADVANCE FEES: *BEST IF YOU FREQUENTLY TAKE CASH ADVANCES*

Issuer	Recent Rate (APR)	Cash-Advance Rate/Fee	Annual Fee	Late/Over Limit Fees	Grace Period
Pulaski Bank & Trust	7.99% F	7.99%/$0	$35	$29/$29	25 days
Amalgamated Bank of Chicago	9.75% V	9.75%/2.5%	$37	$25/$20	25 days
MBNA America Bank	12.99% F	12.99%/3.0%	$0	$39/$39	25 days

As of January 10, 2006; rates are adjustable. Banks sometimes offer lower introductory rates. APRs: F = Fixed rate; V = Variable rate. Data compiled from various sources.

problems; even the most careful consumers occasionally find themselves with mounting credit card debt, especially after the year-end holiday buying season. The real problems occur when the situation is no longer temporary and the debt continues to increase. If overspending is not curtailed, the size of the unpaid balance may seriously strain the budget. Essentially, people who let their credit balances build up are *mortgaging their future*. By using credit, they're actually committing a part of their future income to make payments on the debt. Unfortunately, the more income that has to go just to make payments on charge cards (and other forms of consumer credit), the less there is available for other purposes.

The best way to avoid credit problems is to be disciplined when using credit. Reduce the number of cards you carry, and don't rush to accept the tempting preapproved credit card offers filling your mailbox. A wallet full of cards can work against you in two ways. Obviously, the ready availability of credit can tempt you to overspend and incur too much credit card debt. But there's another, less obvious, danger: when you apply for a loan, lenders look at the *total amount* of credit you have available as well as at the outstanding balances on your credit cards. If you have a lot of unused credit capacity, it may be harder to get a loan because of lender concerns that you could become overextended. So think twice before accepting a new credit card. You really don't need three or four bankcards. Two is the most financial advisors suggest you carry: perhaps one rebate card, if you charge enough to make the benefit worthwhile, and a low-rate card for purchases you want to repay over time. And should you decide to start using a new card (because their offer was just too good to pass up), then *get rid of one of your old cards*—physically cut up the old card and inform the issuer in writing that you're canceling your account.

Suppose that, despite all your efforts, you find that your credit card balances are higher than you'd like and you anticipate having problems reducing them to a more manageable level. The first thing you can do is stop making any new charges until you pay off (or pay down) the existing balances. Then, commit to a repayment plan. One good strategy is to pay off the highest-interest cards first, keeping the original payment rather than reducing it as your balance drops; or, even better, pay more than the minimum—even if it's just $10 more. You'd be surprised how much difference that makes.

You may also want to consider transferring your balances to a card with a low introductory rate and paying off as much as possible before the rate increases. Another option is to consolidate all your credit card debt and pay it off as quickly as possible using a lower-rate loan, such as a revolving personal line of credit. This can be a risky strategy, however. If you continue to be undisciplined about repaying your debts, you could end up with one big credit problem, rather than a bunch of small ones! Even worse, cleaning up your credit card debt may tempt you to start the credit card borrowing cycle all over again, putting you even farther behind than you were before.

Credit Card Fraud

Despite the efforts of law enforcement officials, there are still people out there who are doing their best to rip you off! In fact, plastic has become the vehicle of choice among crooks as a way of defrauding and stealing from both you and the merchants who honor credit cards. No doubt about it—credit card crime is a big business, with estimated losses of between $4 billion and $8 billion a year. Stolen account numbers are the biggest source of credit card fraud. Be especially careful where you use your credit card in cyberspace. Most, if not all, of the big-name sites are about as secure as they can get, but when you go to one of the less reputable sites, you may well be asking for trouble by giving them your credit card number!

Basically, "it's us against them," and the first thing you have to understand is that the credit card you're carrying around is a powerful piece of plastic. Be careful with it. To reduce your chances of being defrauded, here are some suggestions you should follow:

- Never, ever, give your account number to people or organizations *who call you*—no matter how legitimate it sounds, if you didn't initiate the call, don't give out the information!
- It's okay to give your account number over the phone (if you initiated the call) when order

ing or purchasing something from a major catalog house, airline, hotel, and so on, but don't do it for any other reason.

- Use the same precautions *when purchasing something over the Internet* with your credit card—don't do it *unless* you're dealing at the site of a major retailer who uses state-of-the-art protection against fraud and thievery.
- When paying for something *by check*, don't put your credit card account number on the check and don't let the store clerk do it—show the clerk a check guarantee card (if you have one), a driver's license, or some other form of identification—but *not* your Social Security number.
- Don't put your phone number or address (and certainly not your Social Security number) on credit/charge slips, even if the merchant asks for it—they're *not* entitled to it; but if the clerk insists, just scribble down any number you want.
- When using your card to make a purchase, *always keep your eye on it* (so the clerk can't make an extra imprint); if the clerk makes a mistake and wants to make another imprint, ask for the first imprint, and tear it up on the spot.
- Always draw a line on the credit slip through any blank spaces above the total, so the amount can't be altered.
- *Destroy* all carbons and old credit slips; and when you receive your monthly statement, be sure to *go over it promptly* to make sure there are no errors (if you find a mistake, call or send a letter immediately, detailing the error).
- If you lose a card or it's stolen, *report it to the card issuer immediately*—the most you're ever liable for with a lost or stolen card is $50 (per card), but if you report the loss *before* the card can be used, you won't be liable for any unauthorized charges (the phone number to call is listed on the back of your statement).
- Destroy old cards or those you no longer use.

 Smart.Sites

Safeguard your identity with the help of The Identity Theft Resource Center, where you'll find scam and consumer alerts, resources, information on current legislation, and more. Link to their site at **http://www .thomsonedu.com/finance/ gitman.**

personal bankruptcy A form of legal recourse open to insolvent debtors, who may petition a court for protection from creditors and arrange for the orderly liquidation and distribution of their assets.

Bankruptcy: Paying the Price for Credit Abuse

It certainly isn't an overstatement to say that during the 1980s and 1990s, *debt was in!* In fact, the explosion of debt that has occurred since 1980 is almost incomprehensible. The national debt rose from less than a trillion dollars when the 1980s began to about $8.5 trillion by 2006. Businesses also took on debt rapidly. And, not to be outdone, consumers were using credit like there was no tomorrow. So, it should come as no surprise that when you couple this heavy debt load with a serious economic recession (like the one we had in 2001–2003), you have all the ingredients of a real financial crisis. And that's just what happened, as personal bankruptcies soared—indeed, in 2002 alone, more than 1.5 million people filed for **personal bankruptcy.**

When too many people are too heavily in debt, a recession (or some other economic reversal) can come along and push many of them over the edge. But let's face it, the recession is not the main culprit here; the only way a recession can push you over the edge is if you're already sitting on it! The real culprit is excess debt. Some people simply abuse credit by taking on more than they can afford. Maybe they're pursuing a lifestyle beyond their means, or an unfortunate event—like the loss of a job—takes place.

Whatever the cause, sooner or later, these debtors start missing payments and their credit rating begins to deteriorate. Unless corrective actions are taken, this is followed by repossession of property and, eventually, even bankruptcy. These people have reached the end of a long line of deteriorating financial affairs. Households that cannot resolve serious credit problems on their own need help from the courts. Two of the most widely used legal procedures (employed by well over 95 percent of those who file for bankruptcy) are (1) the Wage Earner Plan and (2) straight bankruptcy.

Wage Earner Plan

The **Wage Earner Plan** (as defined in *Chapter 13* of the U.S. Bankruptcy Code) is a work-out procedure involving some type of debt restructuring—usually by establishing a debt repayment schedule that's more compatible to the person's income. It may be a viable alternative for someone who has a steady source of income, not more than $750,000 in secured debt and $250,000 in unsecured debt, and a reasonably good chance of being able to repay the debts in 3 to 5 years. A majority of creditors must agree to the plan, and interest charges, along with late-payment penalties, are waived for the repayment period. Creditors usually will go along with this plan because they stand to lose more in a straight bankruptcy. After the plan is approved, the individual makes periodic payments to the court, which then pays off the creditors. Throughout the process, the individual retains the use of, and keeps title to, all of his or her assets.

Straight Bankruptcy

Straight bankruptcy, which is allowed under *Chapter 7* of the bankruptcy code, can be viewed as a legal procedure that results in "wiping the slate clean and starting anew." *About 70 percent of those filing personal bankruptcy choose this route.* However, straight bankruptcy does not eliminate all the debtor's obligations, nor does the debtor necessarily lose all of his or her assets. For example, the debtor must make certain tax payments and keep up alimony and child-support payments but is allowed to retain certain payments from Social Security, retirement, veterans', and disability benefits. The debtor also may retain the equity in a home (up to $17,425), a car (up to $2,775), and other personal assets, such as clothing, books, and tools of his or her trade. These are minimums as established by federal regulations; generally, state laws are much more generous regarding the amount the debtor is allowed to keep. The choice of federal or state regulations would depend on the debtor's assets.

Using the Services of a Credit Counselor

Filing for bankruptcy is a serious step that should be taken only as a last resort. For one thing, it's going to stick with you for a long time (it will stay in your credit file for up to 10 years) and certainly won't help your chances of getting credit in the future. It often makes more sense to work problems out before they get so bad that bankruptcy is the only option. Some people can do that on their own but, in many cases, it may be a good idea to seek the help of a qualified *credit counselor*.

Credit counselors work with a family to set up a budget and may even negotiate with creditors to establish schedules for repaying debts. The counseling service will often go so far as to collect money from the debtor and distribute it to creditors. Some private firms, for a fee, will act as intermediaries between borrowers and creditors and provide counseling services. These counselors generally try to reduce the size of payments, the size of outstanding debt, or both. However, their fees can run as much as 20 percent of the amount owed.

Another option is a nonprofit agency, such as those affiliated with the nationwide network of *Consumer Credit Counseling Services* (CCCS) (800-388-2227). You'll get many of the services that private agencies provide, but at a lower cost. Of course, as with any financial advisor, you should check out a credit counselor's credentials, fees, services provided, and track record *before* using his or her services. But before even going to a credit counselor, try contacting your creditors yourself. You may be able to work out a deal on your own, especially if you have just a few lenders and need only 2 to 3 months to catch up. If, however, you have six or more creditors, you should probably see a credit counselor. Make sure to ask your counselor for *several debt-reduction options* appropriate for your financial situation. More important, face up to credit and debt problems as soon as they occur, and do everything possible to avoid ruining your credit record.

Wage Earner Plan An arrangement for scheduled debt repayment over future years that is an alternative to straight bankruptcy; used when a person has a steady source of income and there is a reasonable chance of repayment within 3 to 5 years.

straight bankruptcy A legal proceeding that results in "wiping the slate clean and starting anew"; most of a debtor's obligations are eliminated in an attempt to put the debtor's financial affairs in order.

credit counselor A professional financial advisor who assists overextended consumers in repairing budgets for both spending and debt repayment.

Concept Check

6-16	What are some key factors you should consider when choosing a credit card?
6-17	Discuss the steps you would take to avoid and/or resolve credit problems.
6-18	What's the biggest source of credit card fraud? List at least five things you can do to reduce your chances of being a victim of credit card fraud.
6-19	Distinguish between a *Wage Earner Plan* and *straight bankruptcy*.

« SUMMARY

LG1 **Describe the reasons for using consumer credit, and identify its benefits and problems.** Families and individuals use credit as a way to pay for relatively expensive items and, occasionally, to deal with a financial emergency. Consumer credit is also used simply because it's so convenient. Finally, it's used to partially finance the purchase of various types of investments. Unfortunately, while there are some definite positive aspects to using consumer credit, there are also some negatives. Most important, it can be misused to the point where people live beyond their means by purchasing goods and services they simply can't afford. Such overspending can get so bad that it eventually leads to bankruptcy.

LG2 **Develop a plan to establish a strong credit history.** Establishing a strong credit history is an important part of personal financial planning. Opening checking and savings accounts, obtaining one or two credit cards and using them judiciously, and taking out a small loan and repaying it on schedule are ways to show potential lenders that you can handle credit wisely. Be sure to use credit only when you're sure you can repay the obligation, make payments promptly, and notify a lender immediately if you can't meet payments as agreed. Using the debt safety ratio, you can calculate how much of your monthly take-home pay is going to consumer credit payments. One widely used credit capacity guideline is that total monthly consumer credit payments (exclusive of your mortgage payment) should not exceed 20 percent of your monthly take-home pay.

LG3 **Distinguish among the different forms of open account credit.** Open account credit is one of the most popular forms of consumer credit; it's available from various types of financial institutions and from many retail stores and merchants. Major types of open account credit include bank credit cards, retail charge cards, and revolving lines of credit, like overdraft protection lines, home equity credit lines, and unsecured personal lines of credit. Many financial institutions issue special types of credit cards, such as rewards cards, affinity cards, or secured credit cards. Instead of using only credit cards, a growing number of consumers are turning to debit cards, which give their users a way to write checks with plastic.

LG4 **Apply for, obtain, and manage open forms of credit.** Most types of revolving credit require formal application, which generally involves an extensive investigation of your credit background and an evaluation of your creditworthiness. This usually includes checking credit bureau reports. You should verify the accuracy of these reports regularly, and promptly correct any errors. The amount of finance charges, if any, due on consumer credit depends largely on the technique used to compute the account balance; the average daily balance method is the most common today. Managing your accounts involves understanding the monthly statement and making payments on time.

LG5 **Choose the right credit cards and recognize their advantages and disadvantages.** With so many different types of credit cards available, it pays to shop around to choose the best one for your needs. Consider your spending habits and then compare the fees, interest rates, grace period, and any incentives. If you pay off your balance each month, you'll want a card with low annual fees; if you carry a balance, a low interest rate is your best bet. Advantages of credit cards include interest-free loans, simplified recordkeeping, ease of making returns and resolving unsatisfactory purchase disputes, convenience and security, and use in emergencies. The disadvantages are the tendency to overspend and high interest costs on unpaid balances.

LG6 Avoid credit problems, protect yourself against credit card fraud, and understand the personal bankruptcy process. Avoiding credit problems requires self-discipline. Keep the number of cards you use to a minimum, and be sure you can repay any balances quickly. When credit card debt gets out of control, adopt a payment strategy to pay off the debt as fast as possible by looking for a low-rate card, paying more than the minimum payment, and not charging any additional purchases until the debt is repaid or substantially paid down. Another option is a consolidation loan. To protect yourself against credit card fraud, don't give out your card number unnecessarily, destroy old cards and receipts, verify your credit card transactions, and report a lost card or suspicious activity immediately. A solution to credit abuse, albeit a drastic one, is personal bankruptcy. Those who file for bankruptcy work out a debt restructuring program under Chapter 13's Wage Earner Plan or Chapter 7's straight bankruptcy. If you have serious problems in managing personal credit, a credit counselor may be able to help you learn to control spending and work out a repayment strategy.

FINANCIAL PLANNING EXERCISES

LG1   1. After graduating from college last fall, Janet Price took a job as a consumer credit analyst at a local bank. From her work reviewing credit applications, she realizes that she should begin establishing her own credit history. Describe for Janet several steps she could take to begin building a strong credit record. Does the fact that she took out a student loan for her college education help or hurt her credit record?

LG2   2. Brett Willard has a monthly take-home pay of $1,685; he makes payments of $410 a month on his outstanding consumer credit (excluding the mortgage on his home). How would you characterize Brett's debt burden? What if his take-home pay were $850 a month, and he had monthly credit payments of $150?

LG2   3. Calculate your own debt safety ratio. What does it tell you about your current credit situation and your debt capacity? Does this information indicate a need to make any changes in your credit use patterns? If so, what steps should you take?

LG2   4. *Use Worksheet 6.1.* Sandra Adams is evaluating her debt safety ratio. Her monthly take-home pay is $3,320. Each month, she pays $380 for an auto loan, $120 on a personal line of credit, $60 on a department store charge card, and $85 on her bank credit card. Complete Worksheet 6.1 by listing Sandra's outstanding debts, and then calculate her debt safety ratio. Given her current take-home pay, what is the maximum amount of monthly debt payments that Sandra can have if she wants her debt safety ratio to be 12½ percent? Given her current monthly debt payment load, what would Sandra's take-home pay have to be if she wanted a 12½ percent debt safety ratio?

LG4   5. Mary Maffeo has an overdraft protection line. Assume that her October 2007 statement showed a latest (new) balance of $862. If the line had a minimum monthly payment requirement of 5 percent of the latest balance (rounded to the nearest $5 figure), what would be the minimum amount she would have to pay on her overdraft protection line?

LG3   6. Don and Judy Nesbit have a home with an appraised value of $180,000 and a mortgage balance of only $90,000. Given that an S&L is willing to lend money at a loan-to-value ratio of 75 percent, how big a home equity credit line can Don and Judy obtain? How much, if any, of this line would qualify as tax-deductible interest if their house originally cost $100,000?

LG4 7. Sylvia Galano, a student at City Community College, has a balance of $380 on her retail charge card; if the store levies a finance charge of 21 percent per year, how much monthly interest will be added to her account?

LG4 8. Sanjiv Patel recently graduated from college and is evaluating two credit cards. Card A has an annual fee of $75 and an interest rate of 9 percent. Card B has no annual fee and an interest rate of 16 percent. Assuming that Sanjiv intends to carry no balance and pay off his charges in full each month, which card represents the better deal? If Sanjiv expected to carry a significant balance from one month to the next, which card would be better? Explain.

LG3, 4 9. Donna Wilson has several credit cards, on which she is carrying a total current balance of $12,500. She is considering transferring this balance to a new card issued by a local bank. The bank advertises that for a 2 percent fee, she can transfer her balance to a card that charges a 0 percent interest rate on transferred balances for the first 9 months. Calculate the fee that Donna would pay to transfer the balance, and describe the benefits and drawbacks of balance transfer cards.

LG4 10. Alan Bell recently received his monthly MasterCard bill for the period June 1–30, 2007, and wants to verify the monthly finance charge calculation, which is assessed at a rate of 15 percent per year and based on average daily balances including new purchases. His outstanding balance, purchases, and payments are as follows:

Previous balance:	$386		
Purchases:		Payments:	
June 4	$137	June 21	$35
June 12	78		
June 20	98		
June 26	75		

What is his average daily balance and the finance charge for the period? (Use a table like the one in Exhibit 6.7 for your calculations.)

LG3 11. Mark Strom is trying to decide whether to apply for a credit card or a debit card. He has $7,500 in a savings account at the bank and spends his money frugally. What advice would you have for Mark? Describe the benefits and drawbacks of each type of card.

LG4, 5 12. Jean Wong was reviewing her credit card statement and noticed several charges that didn't look familiar to her. Jean is unsure whether she should pay the bill in full and forget about the unfamiliar charges, or "make some noise." If some of these charges aren't hers, is she still liable for the full amount? Is she liable for any part of these charges, even if they're fraudulent?

LG1, 2 13. Rhett Weaver recently graduated from college and wants to borrow $50,000 to start a business, which he believes will produce a cash flow of at least $10,000 per year. As a student, Rhett was active in clubs, held many leadership positions, and did a lot of community service. He currently has no other debts. He owns a car worth about $8,000 and has $4,000 in a savings account. Although the economy is currently in a recession, economic forecasters expect the recession to end soon. If you were a bank loan officer, how would you evaluate Rhett's loan request within the context of the "5 C's of Credit"? Briefly describe each characteristic and indicate whether it has *favorable* or *unfavorable* implications for Rhett's loan request.

APPLYING PERSONAL FINANCE

How's Your Credit?

Establishing credit and maintaining your creditworthiness are essential to your financial well-being. Good credit allows you to obtain loans and acquire assets that you otherwise might not be able to attain. This project will help you to examine your credit.

If you've already established credit, get a copy of your credit report from one of the credit bureaus mentioned in this chapter. (If you've applied for a loan recently, your lender may already have sent you a copy of your credit report.) Carefully examine your report for any inaccuracies, and take the necessary steps to correct them. Then look over your report and evaluate your creditworthiness. If you feel you need to improve your creditworthiness, what steps do you need to take?

If you haven't yet established credit, find an application for a card such as Visa, MasterCard, or a department store or gasoline company credit card. Places to look might be at a department store, banking institution, gas station, or the Internet. Take it home and fill it out. Then look over your application and try to do a self-evaluation of your own creditworthiness. Based on the information you've provided, do you think you would qualify for the credit card? What do you see as your major strengths? What are your major weaknesses? Is there anything you can do about them?

CRITICAL THINKING CASES

LG2, 4

6.1 The Alvarados Seek Some Credit Card Information

Alberto and Sabina Alvarado are a newly married couple in their mid-twenties. Alberto is a senior at a state university and expects to graduate in the summer of 2008. Sabina graduated last spring with a degree in marketing and recently started working as a sales rep for the Alhambra Corporation. She supports both of them on her monthly salary of $2,500 after taxes. The Alvarados currently pay all their expenses by cash or check. They would, however, like to use a bank credit card for some of their transactions. Because neither Alberto nor Sabina knows how to apply for a credit card, they approach you for help.

Critical Thinking Questions

1. Advise the Alvarados on how to fill out a credit application.
2. Explain to them the procedure the bank will probably follow in processing their application.
3. Tell them about credit scoring and how the bank will arrive at a credit decision.
4. What kind of advice would you offer the Alvarados on the "correct" use of their card? What would you tell them about building a strong credit record?

LG2, 3, 4

6.2 Michelle Starts Over after Bankruptcy

A year after declaring bankruptcy and moving with her daughter back into her parents' home, Michelle Lamphere is about to get a degree in nursing. As she starts out in a new career, she also wants to begin a new life—one built on a solid financial base. Michelle will be starting out as a full-time nurse at a salary of $42,000 a year, and she plans to continue working at a second (part-time) nursing job with an annual income of $10,500. She'll be paying back $24,000 in bankruptcy debts and wants to be able to move into an apartment within a year and then buy a condo or house in 5 years.

Michelle won't have to pay rent for the time she lives with her parents. She also will have child care at no cost, which will continue after she and her daughter are able to move out on their own. While the living arrangement with her parents is great financially, the accommodations are "tight," and Michelle's work hours interfere with her parents' routines. Everyone agrees that one more year of this is about all the family can take. However, before Michelle is able to make a move, even into a rented apartment, she'll have to reestablish credit over and above paying off her bankruptcy debts. To rent the kind of place she'd like, she needs to have a good credit record for a year; to buy a home, she must sustain that credit standing for at least 3 to 5 years.

Critical Thinking Questions

1. In addition to opening checking and savings accounts, what else might Michelle do to begin establishing credit with a bank?
2. Although Michelle is unlikely to be able to obtain a major bank credit card for at least a year, how might she begin establishing credit with local merchants?
3. What's one way she might be able to obtain a bank credit card? Explain.
4. How often should Michelle monitor her credit standing with credit reporting services?
5. What general advice would you offer for getting Michelle back on track to a new life financially?

Visit **http://www.thomsonedu.com/finance/gitman** for some additional Web-based exercises and hot links (with annotations) to a variety of resources relevant to the topics covered in this chapter.

Using Consumer Loans

LG1	⊙	Know when to use consumer loans, and be able to differentiate between the major types.	p. 210
LG2	⊙	Identify the various sources of consumer loans.	p. 210
LG3	⊙	Choose the best loans by comparing finance charges, maturity, collateral, and other loan terms.	p. 217
LG4	⊙	Describe the features of, and calculate the finance charges on, single-payment loans.	p. 221
LG5	⊙	Evaluate the benefits of an installment loan.	p. 226
LG6	⊙	Determine the costs of installment loans, and analyze whether it is better to pay cash or take out a loan.	p. 226
	⊙		

ER 7 • CHAPTER 7 • CHAPTER 7 • CHAPTER 7 • CHAPTER 7 • CHAPTER 7 • CHAPTER 7 • CHAPTER 7 • CHAPTER 7

LG1, LG2 BASIC FEATURES OF CONSUMER LOANS

Several times in this book, we've discussed the different types of financial goals that individuals and families can set for themselves. These goals often involve large sums of money and may include such things as a college education or the purchase of a new car. One way to reach these goals is to systematically save the money. Another is to use a loan to at least partially finance the transaction. Consumer loans are important to the personal financial planning process because they can help you reach certain types of financial goals. You can work a major expenditure or purchase into a financial plan just as easily with a consumer loan as you can by saving. The key, of course, is to successfully manage the credit by keeping the amount of debt used and debt-repayment burden *well within your budget*!

Using Consumer Loans

As we saw in Chapter 6, using open or revolving credit can prove helpful to those who plan and live within their personal financial budgets. More important to the long-run achievement of personal financial goals, however, are single-payment and installment consumer loans. These long-term liabilities are widely used to finance goods that are far too expensive to buy from current income, to help with a college education, or to pay for certain types of nondurable items, such as expensive vacations. Of course, the extent to which this type of borrowing is used must be governed by personal financial plans and budgets.

These loans differ from open forms of credit in several ways, including the formality of their lending arrangements. That is, while open account credit results from a rather informal process, **consumer loans** are *formal, negotiated contracts* that specify both the terms for borrowing and the repayment schedule. What's more, an open line of credit can be used again and again, but consumer loans are one-shot transactions made for specific purposes. Because there's no revolving credit with a consumer loan, no more credit is available (from that particular loan) once it's paid off. Further, no credit cards or checks are issued with this form of credit. Finally, while open account credit is used chiefly to make repeated purchases of relatively low-cost *goods and services*, consumer loans are used mainly to *borrow money* to pay for big-ticket items.

Different Types of Loans

Although they can be used for just about any purpose imaginable, most consumer loans fall into one of these categories:

- **Auto loans.** Financing a new car, truck, SUV, or minivan is the single most common reason for borrowing money through a consumer loan. Indeed, auto loans account for about 35 percent of all consumer credit outstanding. Generally speaking, about 80 to 90 percent of the cost of a new vehicle (somewhat less with used cars) can be financed with credit; the buyer must provide the rest through a *down payment*. The loan is *secured* with the auto, meaning that the vehicle serves as **collateral** for the loan and can be repossessed by the lender should the buyer fail to make payments. These loans generally have maturities ranging from 36 to 60 months.

- **Loans for other durable goods.** Consumer loans can also be used to finance other kinds of *costly durable goods,* such as furniture, home appliances, TVs, home computers, recreational vehicles, and even small airplanes and mobile homes. These loans are also secured by the items purchased and generally require some down payment. Maturities vary with the type of asset purchased: 9- to 12-month loans are common for less costly items, such as TVs and stereos, whereas 10- to 15-year loans (or even longer) are normal with mobile homes.
- **Education loans.** Getting a college education is another important reason for taking out a consumer loan. Such loans can be used to finance either undergraduate or graduate studies, and special government-subsidized loan programs are available to students and parents. We'll discuss student loans in more detail in the following section.
- **Personal loans.** These loans are typically used for nondurable expenditures, such as an expensive European vacation or to cover temporary cash shortfalls. Many personal loans are *unsecured*, which means there's no collateral with the loan other than the borrower's good name.
- **Consolidation loans.** This type of loan is used to straighten out an unhealthy credit situation. When consumers overuse credit cards, credit lines, or consumer loans, and can no longer promptly service the debt, a consolidation loan may help control this deteriorating credit situation. By borrowing money from one source to pay off other forms of credit, borrowers can replace, say, five or six monthly payments that total $400 with one payment amounting to $250. *Consolidation loans are usually expensive, and people who use them must be careful to stop using credit cards and other forms of credit until they repay the loans. Otherwise, they may end up right back where they started.*

Student Loans

consumer loans Loans made for specific purposes using formally negotiated contracts that specify the borrowing terms and repayment.

collateral An item of value used to secure the principal portion of a loan.

Today, the annual cost of a college education ranges from about $10,000 to $12,000 at a state school to well over $35,000 or $40,000 at many private colleges. Many families, even those who started saving for college when their children were young, are faced with higher-than-expected bills. Fortunately, there are many types of financial aid programs available, including some federal programs described later, as well as state, private, and college-sponsored programs.

Certainly paying for a college education is one of the most legitimate reasons for going into debt. Although you could borrow money for college through normal channels—that is,

© JUPITER IMAGES

take out a regular consumer loan from your bank and use the proceeds to finance an education—there are better ways to go about getting education loans. That's because the federal government (and some state governments) have available several different types of subsidized educational loan programs. The federally sponsored programs are:

- Stafford loans (Direct and Federal Family Education Loans—FFEL)
- Perkins loans
- Parent Loans (PLUS)

The Stafford and Perkins loans have the best terms and are the foundation of the government's student loan program. PLUS (which stands for *Parent Loans for Undergraduate Students*) loans, in contrast, are *supplemental loans* for *undergraduate students* who demonstrate a need but, for one reason or another, don't qualify for Stafford or Perkins loans, or need more aid than they're receiving. Under this program, parents can take out loans to meet or supplement the costs of their children's college education, *up to the full cost of attendance*. Stafford and Perkins loans are made directly to students, but as just noted, PLUS loans are made to the parents or legal guardians of college students. Probably the best place to look for information about these and other programs is the Internet. For example, look up FASTWEB (which stands for *Financial Aid Search Through the WEB*). This site, which is free, not only provides details on all the major, and some of the not-so-major, student loan programs but also has a service that matches individuals with scholarships and loans, even going so far as to provide form letters to use in requesting more information. (The address for this Web site is **http://www.fastweb.com**.)

To see how student loans work, let's look at the Stafford loan program. (Except where noted, the other two federally subsidized programs have much the same standards and follow the same procedures as discussed here.) Stafford loans carry low, government-subsidized interest rates; most major banks as well as some of the bigger S&Ls and credit unions participate in the program. Actually, the loans are made directly by one of the participating banks or financial institutions (in the case of the Stafford FFEL loan program), although the student has no direct contact with the lending institution. Instead, the whole process—and it really is quite simple—begins with a visit to the school's financial aid office, where a financial aid counselor will help you determine your eligibility. To be eligible, you have to demonstrate a *financial need*, where the amount of your financial need is defined as the cost of attending school *less* the amount that can be paid by you or your family (in these programs, students are expected to contribute something to their educational expense, regardless of their income). You also have to be making *satisfactory progress in your academic program*, and you cannot be in default on any other student loans. (Each academic year, you'll have to fill out a Free Application for Federal Student Aid [FAFSA] statement that shows these qualifications are being met. The financial aid office will have the forms available in hard copy, or you can complete and submit the form on the Web at **http://www.fafsa.ed.gov**.) In effect, so long as you can demonstrate a financial need, are making satisfactory academic progress, and are not a deadbeat, you'll probably qualify for a Stafford loan.

To find advice on financing college (loans and scholarships) and helpful online calculators, check out The Princeton Review's financing section by linking at **http://www.thomsonedu .com/finance/gitman**.

Obtaining a Student Loan. All you have to do to obtain a (Stafford) loan is complete a simple application form, which is then submitted to *your school's financial aid office*. You do *not* have to deal with the bank (your school will submit all the necessary papers to the institution actually making the loan in the case of a FFEL loan, or directly to the federal government in the case of a Stafford Direct loan), and you won't be subject to credit checks—although with PLUS loans, the borrower (parent) may be subject to a credit judgment by the lender. The latest innovation in this procedure involves transmitting the application electronically to the necessary parties, thus reducing paperwork and speeding up the processing (see, for example, **http://www.staffordloan.com**). Most schools are converting to this method, if they haven't already done so.

Each program has specific loan limits. For example, with Stafford loans, you can borrow up to $2,625 per academic year for first-year studies, $3,500 for the second year, and $5,500 per academic year thereafter, up to a maximum of $23,000 for undergraduate studies—you can obtain even more if you can show that you're no longer dependent on your parents; that is, that you're an *independent* undergraduate student paying for your college education on your own. Graduate students can qualify for up to $8,500 per academic year. The maximum for both undergraduate and graduate loans combined is $138,500. There's no limit on the *number* of loans you can have, only on the maximum dollar amount that you can receive annually from each program.

Exhibit 7.1 compares the major loan provisions (i.e., borrower, interest rates, guarantee and/or origination fees, borrowing limits, and loan terms) of the three federally sponsored student loan programs—Stafford, Perkins, and PLUS loans.

Each year, right on through graduate school, a student can take out a loan from one or more of these government programs. Over time, that can add up to a lot of loans (indeed, the average graduating senior leaves school with more than $17,000 in student loans), and a substantial amount of debt—all of which have to be repaid. But here's another nice feature of these loans: in addition to carrying low (government-subsidized) interest rates, loan repayment doesn't begin until after you're out of school (for the Stafford and Perkins programs only—repayment on PLUS loans normally begins within 60 days of loan disbursement). In addition, interest doesn't begin accruing until you get out of school (except, of course, with PLUS loans, where interest starts accumulating with the first disbursement). While you're in school, the lenders will receive interest on their loans, but it's paid by the federal government! Once repayment begins, you start paying interest on the loans, which may be tax deductible, depending on your income.

Student loans are usually amortized with monthly (principal and interest) payments over a period of 5 to 10 years. To help you service the debt, if you have several student loans outstanding, you can *consolidate* the loans, at a single blended rate, and extend the repayment period to as far as 20 years. You also can ask for either: (1) an *extended repayment* for a longer term of up to 30 years; (2) a *graduated repayment schedule*, which will give you low payments in the early years and then higher payments later on; or (3) an *income-contingent*

EXHIBIT 7.1 Federal Government Student Loan Programs at a Glance

More and more college students rely on loans subsidized by the federal government to finance all or part of their educations. There are three types of federally subsidized loan programs, the basic loan provisions of which are listed here. These loans all have low interest rates and provide various deferment options and extended repayment terms. (*Note: Loan rates and terms shown here are for the 2005–2006 school year.*)

Loan Provisions	TYPE OF FEDERAL LOAN PROGRAM		
	Stafford Loans	Perkins Loans	PLUS Loans
1. Borrower	Student	Student	Parent
2. Interest rate	91-day T-bill rate + 1.7 (or 2.3) pts (4.7%–5.3%)	5.0%	91-day T-bill rate +3.1 pts (6.1%)
3. Guarantee and/or origination fees	Up to 4% of the amount of the loan	none	Up to 4% of the amount of the loan
4. Borrowing limits*	*Dependent students:* $23,000 (undergrad.); $65,000 (combined grad. and undergrad.) *Independent students:* $46,000 and $138,500	$20,000 (undergrad.); $49,000 (combined grad. & undergrad.)	*No dollar limit:* Yearly limit = total cost of undergrad. education less any financial aid.
5. Loan terms	10–30 years	10 years	10 years

*Stafford loans also have annual borrowing limits ranging from $2,625 for the freshman year to $18,500 per year in grad/professional school; likewise, Perkins loans have annual limits of $4,000 per year of undergraduate study and $6,000 per year of graduate school.
Source: Various student loan Web sites, including http://www.fastweb.com, http://www.staffordloan.com, and others; accessed January 2006.

repayment plan, with payments that fluctuate annually according to your income and debt levels. But no matter what you do, *take the repayment provisions seriously, because defaults will be reported to credit bureaus and become a part of your credit file!* What's more, due to recent legislation, you can't get out of repaying your student loans by filing for bankruptcy—no matter which Chapter you file under (7 or 13), *student loans are no longer dischargeable in a bankruptcy proceeding.*

Here are some things to keep in mind about student loans:

- Check with your school's financial aid office to see what programs are available and then apply early.
- Register on FASTWEB **(http://www.fastweb.com)** for scholarships, grants, and loans that will be matched to your background.
- Borrow no more than you need—remember, these loans eventually have to be repaid.
- Consider work-study as an alternative to borrowing.
- Become aware of loan forgiveness programs for selected occupations (military, law enforcement, Peace Corps, and so on).
- Take the loan repayment provisions seriously—defaults aren't taken lightly and can cause serious credit problems for you.
- Once you begin repaying the loans, take the interest deduction, up to the maximum allowed, on your (itemized) tax return.
- If you're having problems servicing the loans, contact the lender and see if some arrangements can be worked out (most lenders would rather work with you than have you default).

In addition to the government programs just described, there are other ways to pay for a college education. One of the most innovative is the so-called **529 College Savings Plan.** As explained in the *Money in Action* box on our Web site **(http://www.thomsonedu .com/finance/gitman)** these plans aren't based on borrowing money to pay for college, but rather on using a special tax-sheltered *savings and investment program.*

Single Payment or Installment Payments

Consumer loans can also be broken into categories based on the type of repayment arrangement—single-payment or installment. **Single-payment loans** are made for a specified period of time, at the end of which payment in full (principal plus interest) is due. They generally have maturities ranging from 30 days to a year; rarely do these loans run for more than a year. Sometimes single-payment loans are made to finance purchases or pay bills when the cash to be used for repayment is known to be forthcoming in the near future; in this case, they serve as a form of **interim financing.** In other situations, single-payment loans are used by consumers who want to avoid being strapped with monthly installment payments and choose instead to make one large payment at the end of the loan.

Installment loans, in contrast, are repaid in a series of fixed, scheduled payments rather than in one lump sum. The payments are almost always set up on a monthly basis, with each installment made up partly of principal and partly of interest. For example, out of a $75 monthly payment, $50 might be credited to principal and the balance to interest. These loans are typically made to finance the purchase of a good or service for which current resources are inadequate. The repayment period can run from 6 months to 6 years or more. Installment loans have become a way of life for many consumers. They're popular because they provide a convenient way to "buy now and pay later" in fixed monthly installments that can be readily incorporated into a family budget.

Fixed- or Variable-Rate Loans

Most consumer loans are made at fixed rates of interest—that is, the interest rate charged (as well as the monthly payment) remains the same over the life of the obligation. However, variable-rate loans are also being made with increasing frequency, especially on *longer-term installment loans.* As with an adjustable-rate home mortgage, the rate of interest charged on such loans changes periodically, in keeping with prevailing market conditions. If market interest rates go up, the rate of interest on the loan goes up accordingly, as does the monthly loan payment. These loans have periodic adjustment dates (for example, monthly, quarterly,

529 College Savings Plan A government-sponsored investment vehicle that allows earnings to grow free from federal taxes as long as they are used to meet college education expenses.

single-payment loan A loan made for a specified period, at the end of which payment is due in full.

interim financing The use of a single-payment loan to finance a purchase or pay bills in situations where the funds to be used for repayment are known to be forthcoming in the near future.

installment loan A loan that is repaid in a series of fixed, scheduled payments rather than a lump sum.

or semiannually), at which time the interest rate and monthly payment are adjusted as necessary. Once an adjustment is made, the new rate remains in effect until the next adjustment date (sometimes the payment amount remains the same, but the number of payments changes). Many variable-rate loans have caps on the maximum increase per adjustment period as well as over the life of the loan. Generally speaking, variable-rate loans are desirable *if interest rates are expected to fall* over the course of the loan; in contrast, fixed-rate loans are preferable *if interest rates are expected to rise.*

Whether the loans are fixed or variable, their cost tends to vary with market conditions. As a rule, when interest rates move up or down in the market, so will the cost of consumer loans. Inevitably, there will be times when *the cost of credit simply becomes too high to justify borrowing* as a way of making major purchases. So when market rates start climbing, you should ask yourself whether the cost is really worth it. Financially, you may be far better off delaying the purchase until rates come down.

Where Can You Get Consumer Loans?

Consumer loans can be obtained from a number of sources, including commercial banks, consumer finance companies, credit unions, S&Ls, sales finance companies, and life insurance companies—even brokerage firms, pawnshops, or friends and relatives. *Commercial banks* dominate the field and provide nearly half of all consumer loans. Second to banks are *consumer finance companies* and then *credit unions.* Together, about 75 percent of all consumer loans are originated by these three financial institutions! Interestingly, S&Ls are not much of a force in this market; they tend to focus on mortgage loans rather than consumer loans. (*Note:* The book's Web site (**http://www.thomsonedu.com/finance/gitman**) contains a table summarizing the types of loans, lending policies, costs, and services offered by the major providers of consumer loans.) Selection of a lender often depends on both the rate of interest being charged and how easily the loan can be negotiated. Of course, today, it's becoming easier than ever to obtain consumer loans online. Just go to Yahoo! and search for "installment loans," and you'll get literally hundreds of Web sites. Some of these sites will actually accept applications online; others offer a brief listing of their services, along with a toll-free phone number.

Commercial Banks

Because they offer various types of loans at attractive rates of interest, commercial banks are a popular source of consumer loans. One nice thing about commercial banks is that they typically charge lower rates than most other lenders, largely because they take only the best credit risks and are able to obtain relatively inexpensive funds from their depositors. The demand for their loans is generally high, and they can be selective in making consumer loans. Commercial banks usually lend only to customers with good credit ratings who can readily demonstrate an ability to make repayment according to the specified terms. They also give preference to loan applicants who are account holders. The fact that an applicant is already a good customer of the bank enhances his or her chances of being approved for the requested financing. Although banks prefer to make loans secured by some type of collateral, they also make unsecured loans to their better customers. The interest rate charged on a bank loan may be affected by the loan's size, terms, and whether it's secured by some type of collateral.

Consumer Finance Companies

consumer finance company A firm that makes secured and unsecured personal loans to qualified individuals; also called a *small loan company.*

Sometimes called *small loan companies,* **consumer finance companies** make secured and unsecured (signature) loans to qualified individuals. These companies do not accept deposits but obtain funds from their stockholders and through open market borrowing. Because they don't have the inexpensive sources of funds that banks and other deposit-type institutions do, their interest rates are generally quite high. Actual rates charged by consumer finance companies are regulated by interest-rate ceilings (or usury laws) set by the states in which they operate. The maximum allowable interest rate may vary with the size of the loan, and the state regulatory authorities may also limit the length of the repayment period. Loans made by consumer finance companies typically are for $5,000 or less and are secured by some type of collateral. Repayment is required in installments, usually within 5 years or less.

What does a consumer finance company like Household Finance offer its customers? Go to their site through **http://www.thomsonedu.com/finance/gitman** to check out the company's different credit cards and loans as well as its consumer education sections.

Consumer finance companies specialize in small loans to high-risk borrowers. These loans are quite costly, but they may be the only alternative for people with poor credit ratings. Due to the high rates of interest charged, individuals should consider this source only after exhausting other alternatives.

Credit Unions

A credit union is a cooperative financial institution, owned and controlled by the people ("members") who use its services. While only members can obtain installment loans and other types of credit from these institutions, credit unions can, if they so choose, offer membership to just about anyone they want, rather than to only certain groups of people. Because they're nonprofit organizations with minimal operating costs, credit unions charge relatively low rates on their loans. They make either unsecured or secured loans, depending on the size and type of loan requested. Generally speaking, membership in a credit union provides the most attractive borrowing opportunities available, because their interest rates and borrowing requirements are usually more favorable than other sources of consumer loans.

Savings and Loan Associations

Savings and loan associations (as well as savings banks) primarily make mortgage loans. They aren't major players in the consumer loan field, but S&Ls are permitted to make loans on such consumer durables as automobiles, televisions, refrigerators, and other appliances. They can also make certain types of home improvement and mobile-home loans, as well as some personal and educational loans. Rates of interest on consumer loans at S&Ls are fairly close to the rates charged by commercial banks; if anything, they tend to be a bit more expensive. Like their banking counterparts, the rates charged at S&Ls will, in the final analysis, depend on such factors as type and purpose of the loan, duration and type of repayment, and the borrower's overall creditworthiness.

Sales Finance Companies

Businesses that sell relatively expensive items—such as automobiles, furniture, and appliances—often provide installment financing to their customers. Because dealers can't afford to tie up their funds in installment contracts, they sell them to a **sales finance company** for cash. This procedure is often called "selling paper," because the merchants, in effect, are selling their loans to a third party. When the sales finance company purchases these notes, customers are usually notified to make payments directly to it.

The largest sales finance organizations are the **captive finance companies** owned by manufacturers of big-ticket items—automobiles and appliances. General Motors Acceptance Corporation (GMAC) and General Electric Credit Corporation (GECC) are just two examples of captive finance companies that purchase the installment loans made by the dealers of their products. Also, most commercial banks act as sales finance companies by buying paper from auto dealers and other businesses. The cost of financing through a sales finance company is generally higher than the rates charged by banks and S&Ls, particularly when you let the dealer do all the work in arranging the financing (dealers normally get a cut of the finance income, so it's obviously in their best interest to secure as high a rate as possible). That's certainly not true in all cases; however, as automakers today will frequently use interest rates on new car loans (or leases) as a marketing tool. They do this by dropping the rate of interest (*usually for selected models*) to levels that are well below the market—even 0 percent financing! Auto manufacturers use these loan rates (along with rebates) to stimulate sales by keeping the cost of buying a new car down. Clearly, cutting the cost of borrowing for a new car can result in big savings.

Life Insurance Companies

Life insurance policyholders may be able to obtain loans from their insurance companies. That's because certain types of policies not only provide death benefits but also have a savings function, so they can be used as collateral for loans. (*Be careful with these loans, however, as they could involve a tax penalty if certain conditions are not met.* A detailed discussion of life insurance is presented in Chapter 8.) Life insurance companies are required by law to make loans against the **cash value**—the amount of accumulated savings—of cer-

Do you think General Motors Acceptance Corporation just finances cars? Discover the full range of its services, from auto loans to home mortgages and insurance products, at their Web site. Go to **http://www.thomsonedu.com/finance/gitman.**

sales finance company A firm that purchases notes drawn up by sellers of certain types of merchandise, typically big-ticket items.

captive finance company A sales finance company that is owned by a manufacturer of big-ticket merchandise. GMAC is a captive finance company.

cash value (of life insurance) An accumulation of savings in an insurance policy that can be used as a source of loan collateral.

FINANCIAL ROAD SIGN

POTENTIAL FOR DISASTER

If you're faced with little or no alternative and must either lend or borrow money from a friend or family member, then do it carefully; here are some guidelines to follow.

- **Lend only money you can afford to give away:** Around 20 to 50 percent of these loans are never repaid.
- **Do it in a businesslike fashion:** Draw up a formal promissory note with specific terms.
- **Charge interest if the loan is not to be quickly repaid:** Make it around what you'd get in a savings account, but less than prevailing loan rates.
- **Both parties must understand this is a loan, not a gift:** Be specific about repayment terms.

tain types of life insurance policies. The rate of interest on this type of loan is stated in the policy and usually carries a variable rate that goes up and down with prevailing market conditions. Although you'll be charged interest for as long as the policy loan is outstanding, these loans don't have repayment dates—in other words, *you don't have to pay them back*. When you take out a loan against the cash value of your life insurance policy, you're really borrowing from yourself. Thus, the amount of the loan outstanding, plus any accrued interest, is deducted from the amount of coverage provided by the policy—*effectively lowering your insurance coverage* and endangering your beneficiaries with a lower payout should you die before repayment. The chief danger in life insurance loans is that they don't have a firm maturity date, so *borrowers may lack the motivation to repay them*. Also, many insurers put borrowed policies in a different (less attractive) investment return category, based on the lower cash value in the policy.

Friends and Relatives

Sometimes, rather than going to a bank or some other financial institution, you may know of a close friend or relative who's willing to lend you money. Such loans often are attractive because little or no interest is charged. The terms will, of course, vary depending on the borrower's financial needs; but they should be specified in some type of loan agreement that states the costs, conditions, and maturity date of the loan as well as the obligations of both borrower and lender. Not only does a written loan agreement reduce opportunities for disagreement and unhappiness, it also protects both borrower and lender should either of them die or if other unexpected events occur. *Still, given the potential for disagreement and conflict, borrowing from friends or relatives is not advisable*; consider doing so only when there are no other viable alternatives. Remember, a loan to or from a friend or family member is far more than a run of the mill banking transaction: the interest is emotional, and the risks are the relationship itself!

�II Concept Check

CHECK • CONCEPT CHECK • CONCEPT CHECK • CONCEPT CHECK • CONCEPT CHECK • CONCEPT CHECK • CONCEPT C

7-1	List and briefly discuss the five major reasons for borrowing money through a consumer loan.
7-2	Identify several different types of federally sponsored student loan programs.
7-3	As a college student, what aspects of these student loan programs appeal to you the most?
7-4	Define and differentiate between (a) fixed- and variable-rate loans and (b) a *single-payment loan* and an *installment loan*.
7-5	Compare the consumer lending activities of (a) *consumer finance companies* and (b) *sales finance companies*. Describe a *captive finance company*.
7-6	Discuss the role of (a) credit unions and (b) savings and loan associations in consumer lending. Point out any similarities or differences in their lending activities. How do they compare to commercial banks?

LG3 MANAGING YOUR CREDIT

Borrowing money to make major acquisitions—and, in general, using consumer loans—is a sound and perfectly legitimate way to conduct your financial affairs. From a financial planning perspective, you should ask yourself two questions when considering the use of a consumer loan: (1) does making this acquisition fit into your financial plans, and (2) does the required debt service on the loan fit into your monthly cash budget? Indeed, when *full consideration is given not only to the need for the asset or item in question but also to the repayment of the ensuing debt* sound credit management is the result. In contrast, if the expenditure in question will seriously jeopardize your financial plans or if repaying of the loan is likely to strain your cash budget, you should definitely reconsider the purchase! Perhaps it can be postponed, or you can liquidate some assets in order to come up with more down payment. You may even have to alter some other area of your financial plan in order to work in the expenditure. Whatever route you choose, the key point is to make sure that the debt will be fully compatible with your financial plans and cash budget *before* the loan is taken out and the money spent.

Shopping for Loans

Once you've decided to use credit, it's equally important that you shop around and evaluate the various costs and terms available. You may think the only thing you need do to make a sound credit decision is determine which source offers the lowest finance charge. But this could not be farther from the truth—for as we'll see below, finance charges are just one of the factors to consider when shopping for a loan.

Finance Charges

What's it going to cost me? That's one of the first things lots of people want to know when taking out a loan. And that's appropriate, because borrowers should know what they'll have to pay to get the money. Lenders are required by law to clearly state all finance charges and other loan fees. Find out the effective (or true) *rate* of interest you'll have to pay on the loan, and whether the loan carries a fixed or variable rate. Obviously, *as long as everything else is equal*, it's in your best interest to secure the least expensive loan. In this regard, ask the lender what the *annual rate of interest* on the loan will be, because it's easier (and far more relevant) to compare percentage rates on alternative borrowing arrangements than the dollar amount of the loan charges. This rate of interest, known as the *APR* (annual percentage rate), includes not only the basic cost of money but also any additional fees that might be required on the loan (APR is more fully discussed later). Also, if it's a variable-rate loan, find out what the interest rate is pegged to, how many "points" are added to the base rate, how often the loan rate can be changed, and if rate caps exist. Just as important, how will the lender make the periodic adjustments—will the *size* of the monthly payment change, or the *number* of monthly payments? To avoid any future shock, it's best to find out these things before making the loan.

Loan Maturity

Try to make sure that the size and number of payments will fit comfortably into your spending and savings plans. As a rule, the cost of credit increases with the length of the repayment period. Thus, to lower your cost, you should consider shortening the loan maturity—but only to the point where doing so won't place an unnecessary strain on your cash flow. Although a shorter maturity may reduce the cost of the loan, it also increases the size of the monthly loan payment. Indeed, finding a monthly loan payment you'll be comfortable with is a critical dimension of sound credit management. Fortunately, the personal computer provides an effective way of evaluating different loan configurations. Altering the loan maturity is just one way of coming up with an affordable monthly payment; there are scores of Web sites where you can quickly run through all sorts of alternatives to find the monthly payment that will best fit your monthly budget. (The "tools" section of most major financial services sites on the Internet have "calculators" that enable you to quickly and easily figure interest rates and monthly loan payments for all sorts of loans; generally, all you have to do is plug in a few key pieces of information, (like interest rate and loan term), hit "calculate," and the computer does the rest. For example, go to **http://www.finaid.org/calculators** and try out their "Loan Payments Calculator.")

Total Cost of the Transaction

When comparison shopping for credit, always look at the total cost of both the price of the item purchased *and* the price of the credit. Retailers often manipulate both sticker prices and

BORROWERS WHO ASK QUESTIONS GET THE BEST DEALS

For decades, the average borrower had just three questions: How much money can I borrow? What's my monthly payment? And when can I have the money? That approach allowed lenders to charge exorbitant interest rates and fees. Now, however, many consumers are wising up. They're asking more questions and comparing offers from lenders before committing.

Unfortunately, because some consumers don't ask the right questions, they fall victim to predatory lending—high-interest loans loaded with fees, prepayment penalties, and other abusive practices. Most predatory lending occurs in the subprime market, which is where consumers with limited or poor credit histories borrow money. In the subprime market, lenders charge higher interest rates. This practice is fair because lenders are assuming a bigger risk, but sometimes they charge more than necessary. Borrowers accept the terms because they don't have other options or don't know the loan terms are unfair.

To avoid predatory lending, you should ask certain questions before committing to a loan. Find out whether the lender is licensed by the state, and ask about the interest rate and other fees charged, the monthly payment, the principal balance, the length of the loan, and if there are prepayment penalties. Make sure all documents are correct and complete. You should receive a written statement outlining the loan terms. Read everything carefully, and ask questions as necessary. Never let anyone convince you to make a false statement or borrow more money than you can afford to repay. Most important, shop around and compare costs. Before committing to the loan, it's a good idea to consult a reputable consumer counselor or an attorney because they can help you identify any problems. You can find a counseling agency online or in the phone book. Be sure they're members of the National Foundation for Consumer Credit Counseling (**www.nfcc.org**) or the Association of Independent Consumer Credit Counseling Agencies (**www.aiccca .org**). The U.S. Trustee's Office (**www.usdoj.gov/ust**) also has a list of approved agencies. The cost for their advice should be no more than $50, depending on the assistance required.

Many state governments have laws to address predatory lending practices. Congress is also considering legislation to further protect consumers. There's some debate over whether states or the federal government should regulate the lending industry. Some lawmakers are concerned that the proposed federal legislation, which would preempt state laws, wouldn't adequately protect consumers. On the other hand, a federal law would impose consistency and make it easier for lenders to operate nationwide. Whatever the results of this debate, the best strategy is to be cautious when shopping for loans. Remember, if it sounds too good to be true, it probably is.

Critical Thinking Questions

1. Describe the relationship between predatory lending and the subprime market.
2. What steps can you take to protect yourself from predatory lending? What questions should you ask lenders?
3. What are state and federal governments doing to protect consumers against predatory lenders? Use the Web to find and summarize the latest regulations for your state and the nation.

Sources: Mary Branham Dusenberry, "Loans of Prey," *State News*, May 2006, p. 9; "Don't Be a Victim of Loan Fraud," *Homes & Communities*, U.S. Department of Housing and Urban Development, August 18, 2003, http://www.hud.gov; "20 Questions to Ask a Lender or Mortgage Broker," Department of Corporations, California's Investment and Financing Authority, January 9, 2006, http://www.corp.ca.gov; Kimberly Lankford, "Quality Credit Counseling," *Kiplinger.com*, May 2006.

interest rates, so you really won't know what kind of deal you're getting until you look at the total cost of the transaction. Along this line, comparing *monthly payments* is a good way to get a handle on total cost. It's a simple matter to compare total costs: *just add the amount put down on the purchase to the total of all the monthly loan payments*; other things being equal, the one with the lowest total is the one you should pick.

Smart Sites

At **http://www .thomsonedu.com/ finance/gitman** link to Bankrate to get the latest consumer loan rates, plus helpful guides on borrowing.

Collateral

Make sure you know up front what collateral (if any) you'll have to pledge on the loan and what you stand to lose if you default on your payments. Actually, if it makes no difference to you and if it's not too inconvenient, using collateral often makes sense. It may result in *lower* finance charges—perhaps half a percentage point or so.

Other Loan Considerations

Besides the preceding guidelines, here are some other questions you should ask: Can you choose a *payment date* that will be compatible with your spending patterns? Can you obtain the loan *promptly and conveniently?* What are the charges for late payments, and are they reasonable? Will you receive a refund on credit charges if you prepay your loan? Or will you have to pay prepayment penalties? Taking the time to look around for the best credit deal will pay off, not only in reducing the cost of such debt but also in keeping the burden of credit in line with your cash budget and financial plans. In the long run, you're the one who has the most to gain (or lose). *Thus you should see to it that the consumer debt you undertake does in fact have the desired effects on your financial condition.* As suggested in the *Money in Action* box on page 219, the lenders may not like the idea, but you're paying for the loan, so you might as well make the most of it!

Keeping Track of Your Consumer Debt

To stay abreast of your financial condition, it's a good idea to periodically take inventory of the consumer debt you have outstanding. You should do this at least once a year, and ideally every 3 or 4 months. To take inventory of what you owe, simply list all your outstanding consumer debt. Include *everything except your home mortgage*—installment loans, single-payment loans, credit cards, revolving credit lines, overdraft protection lines, even home equity credit lines.

You might find Worksheet 7.1 helpful in preparing a list of your debts. To use it, simply list the current monthly payment and the latest balance due for each type of consumer credit outstanding; then, total both columns to see how much you're paying each month and how large a debt load you have built up. Hopefully, when you've totaled all the numbers, you won't be surprised to learn just how much you really do owe.

A way to quickly assess your debt position is to compute your *debt safety ratio* (we looked at this ratio in Chapter 6) by dividing the total monthly payments (from the worksheet) by your monthly take-home pay. If 20 percent or more of your take-home pay is going to monthly credit payments, you're relying too heavily on credit; in contrast, if your debt safety ratio works out to 10 percent or less, you're in a strong credit position. *Keeping track of your credit and holding the amount of outstanding debt to a reasonable level is the surest way to maintain your creditworthiness.*

▮▮ Concept Check

7-7 What two questions should be answered before taking out a consumer loan? Explain.

7-8 List and briefly discuss the different factors to consider when shopping for a loan. How would you determine the total cost of the transaction?

Use a worksheet like this one to keep track of your outstanding credit, along with your monthly debt service requirements. Such information is a major component of sound credit management.

AN INVENTORY OF CONSUMER DEBT

Name _John & Mary Jergens_   Date _June 14, 2007_

Type of Consumer Debt	Creditor	Current Monthly Payment*	Latest Balance Due
Auto loans	1. GMAC	$ 342.27	$ 13,796
	2.		
	3.		
Education loans	1. U.S. Dept. of Education	117.00	7,986
	2.		
Personal installment loans	1. Chase Bank	183.00	5,727
	2. B of A	92.85	2,474
Home improvement loan			
Other installment loans	1.		
	2.		
Single-payment loans	1.		
	2.		
Credit cards (retail charge cards, bank cards, T&E cards, etc.)	1. MBNA Visa	42.00	826.
	2. Amex Blue	35.00	600
	3. Sears	40.00	1,600
	4.		
	5.		
	6.		
	7.		
Overdraft protection line	Hiland Schools Credit Union	15.00	310
Personal line of credit			
Home equity credit line	Wells Fargo	97.00	9,700
Loan on life insurance			
Margin loan from broker			
Other loans	1. Mom & Dad	—	2,500
	2.		
	3.		
	Totals	$ 964.12	$ 45,519

$$\text{Debt safety ratio} = \frac{\text{Total monthly payments}}{\text{Monthly take-home pay}} \times 100 = \frac{\$ \ 964.12}{\$5,200.00} \times 100 = \underline{18.5} \%$$

*Leave the space blank if there is **no** monthly payment required on a loan (e.g., as with a single-payment or education loan).

LG4   SINGLE-PAYMENT LOANS

Unlike most types of consumer loans, a single-payment loan is repaid in full with a single payment on a given due date. The payment usually consists of principal and all interest charges. Sometimes, however, interim interest payments may have to be made (for example, every quarter), in which case the payment at maturity is made up of principal plus any unpaid interest. Although installment loans are far more popular, single-payment loans still have their place in the consumer loan market.

Single-payment loans can be secured or unsecured and can be taken out for just about any purpose, from buying a new car to paying for a vacation. They're perhaps most useful when the funds needed for a given purchase or transaction are temporarily unavailable but are expected to be forthcoming in the near future. By helping you cope with a temporary cash shortfall, these loans can serve as a form of interim financing until more permanent arrangements can be made.

Single-payment loans can also be used to help establish or rebuild an individual's credit rating. Often, a bank will agree to a single-payment loan for a higher credit risk customer if an equal amount is deposited into an account at the bank, with both the loan and deposit having the same maturity. In this way, the bank has the principal of the loan fully secured and need only be concerned about the difference between the rate charged for the loan and the rate paid on the deposit.

Important Loan Features

When applying for either a single-payment or installment loan, you must first submit a **loan application,** an example of which is shown in Exhibit 7.2. Basically, the loan application gives the lending institution information about the purpose of the loan, whether it will be secured or unsecured, and the applicant's financial condition. The loan officer uses this document, along with other information (such as a credit report from the local credit bureau and income verification) to determine whether you should be granted the loan—here again, some type of *credit scoring* (as discussed in Chapter 6) may be used to make the decision. As part of the loan application process, you should also consider various features of the debt, the three most important of which are loan collateral, loan maturity, and loan repayment.

Loan Collateral

Most single-payment loans are secured by certain specified assets. For *collateral*, lenders prefer items they feel are readily marketable at a price that's high enough to cover the principal portion of the loan—for example, an automobile, jewelry, or stocks and bonds. If a loan is obtained to purchase some personal asset, that asset may be used to secure it. In most cases, lenders don't take physical possession of the collateral but instead file a **lien,** which is a legal claim that permits them to liquidate the collateral to satisfy the loan if the borrower defaults. The lien is filed in the county courthouse and is a matter of public record. If the borrowers maintain possession or title to *movable* property—such as cars, TVs, and jewelry—the instrument that gives the lenders title to the property in event of default is called a **chattel mortgage.** If lenders hold title to the collateral—or actually take possession of it, as in the case of stocks and bonds—the agreement giving them the right to sell these items in case of default is a **collateral note.**

Loan Maturity

As indicated earlier, the maturity, or term, on a single-payment loan is usually for a period of 1 year or less; it very rarely goes out to 2 years or longer. When you request a single-payment loan, be sure the term is long enough to allow you to obtain the funds to repay the loans, but not any longer than necessary. Don't stretch the maturity out too far, since the amount of the finance charges paid will increase with time. Because the loan is retired in a single payment, the lender must be assured that you'll be able to repay it even if certain unexpected events occur in the future. So, the term of your single-payment loan must be reconciled with your budget as well as with your ability to pay. If the money you plan to use for repayment will be received periodically over the term of the loan, an installment-type loan may be more suitable.

Loan Repayment

Repayment of a single-payment loan is expected at a single point in time: on its maturity date. Occasionally the funds needed to repay this type of loan will be received prior to maturity. Depending on the lender, the borrower might be able to repay the loan early and thus reduce the finance charges. Many credit unions permit early repayment of these loans with *reduced* finance charges. Commercial banks and other single-payment lenders, however, may not accept early repayments, or, if they do, they may charge a **prepayment penalty**

loan application An application that gives a lender information about the purpose of the loan, as well as the applicant's financial condition.

lien A legal claim permitting the lender, in case the borrower defaults, to liquidate the items serving as collateral to satisfy the obligation.

chattel mortgage A mortgage on personal property given as security for the payment of an obligation.

collateral note A legal note giving the lender the right to sell collateral if the borrower defaults on the obligation.

prepayment penalty An additional charge you may owe if you decide to pay off your loan prior to maturity.

EXHIBIT 7.2   A Consumer Loan Credit Application

A typical loan application, like this one, contains information about the persons applying for the loan, including source(s) of income, current debt load, and a brief record of employment.

CONSUMER CREDIT APPLICATION

LOAN INFORMATION

Amount Requested $	Purpose	Application Type ☐Individual ☐Joint

COLLATERAL INFORMATION

☐Motor Vehicle: Year_____ Make_____ Model_____ Miles_____
☐Personal Property   ☐Other (Describe)

APPLICANT INFORMATION

Name (Last, First, M.I.)	E-mail Address

Social Security # - -	Date of Birth / /	☐Married ☐Unmarried ☐Separated	# of Dependents

CO-APPLICANT INFORMATION

Name (Last, First, M.I.)	E-mail Address

Social Security # - -	Date of Birth / /	☐Married ☐Unmarried ☐Separated	# of Dependents

APPLICANT RESIDENCE INFORMATION

Address (Number, St, and Apt. or Lot # if applicable)	Telephone #
City, State, Zip Code	Time At Residence Years / Months /
Previous Address	Time At Residence Years / Months /

☐Rent ☐Live with Parents ☐Own ☐Other_____	Landlord or Mortgage Holder Name: Phone #:	Monthly Payment $

CO-APPLICANT RESIDENCE INFORMATION

Address (Number, St, and Apt. or Lot # if applicable)	Telephone #
City, State, Zip Code	Time At Residence Years / Months /
Previous Address	Time At Residence Years / Months /

☐Rent ☐Live with Parents ☐Own ☐Other_____	Landlord or Mortgage Holder Name: Phone #:	Monthly Payment $

APPLICANT EMPLOYMENT INFORMATION

Employer	Employer Telephone
Employer Address	Position

Gross Income: $	☐Weekly ☐Bi-weekly ☐Monthly	Time At Job Years / Months /

Other Income: $ Source	

Previous Employer & location	Previous Emp. Phone #
Position	Time At Job Years / Months /

CO-APPLICANT EMPLOYMENT

Employer	Employer Telephone
Employer Address	Position

Gross Income: $	☐Weekly ☐Bi-weekly ☐Monthly	Time At Job Years / Months /

Other Income: $ Source	Alimony, Child support, or separate maintenance income need not be revealed ifyou do not wish to have it considered as abasis for repaying this obligation.

Previous Employer & Location	Previous Emp. Phone #
Position	Time At Job Years / Months /

APPLICANT CREDIT REFERENCES

Creditor	Payment	Balance

CO-APPLICANT CREDIT REFERENCES

Creditor	Payment	Balance

☐Checking Bank Name_____ Acct#_____
☐Savings Bank Name_____ Acct#_____

☐Checking Bank Name_____ Acct#_____
☐Savings Bank Name_____ Acct#_____

AUTHORIZATION AND SIGNATURES

By signing this application, you promise that all information provided is true and complete. You also promise that you have revealed any pending lawsuits or unpaid judgements against you. You intend the lender and/or assignee to rely upon these promises in deciding whether to extend credit to you. You authorize a full investigation of your credit record and your employment history. You also authorize the seller and/or assignee to release information about your credit experience with them. You understand that the lender will retain this application whether or not it is approved. I understand that if the application is for a secured loan addit ional information may be required.

Applicant Signature	Date

Co-Applicant Signature	Date

on them. This penalty normally amounts to a set percentage of the interest that would have been paid over the remaining life of the loan. The Truth in Lending Act requires lenders to disclose in the loan agreement whether, and in what amount, prepayment penalties are charged on a single-payment loan.

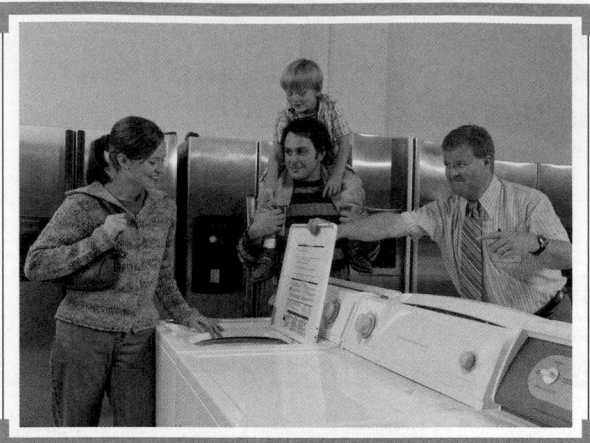
© STONE/GETTY IMAGES

Occasionally, an individual will borrow money using a single-payment loan, only to discover that he or she is short of money when the loan comes due—after all, making one big loan payment can cause a real strain on one's cash flow. Should this happen to you, don't just let the payment go past due; rather, *inform the lender in advance so a partial payment, loan extension, or some other arrangement can be made.* Under such circumstances, the lender will often agree to a **loan rollover,** in which case the original loan is paid off by taking out another loan. The lender will usually require that all the interest and at least part of the principal be paid at the time of the rollover. So, if you originally borrowed $5,000 for 12 months, the bank might be willing to lend you, say, $3,500 for another 6 to 9 months as part of a loan rollover. In this case, you'll have to "pay down" $1,500 of the original loan, along with all interest due. However, you can expect the interest rate on a rollover loan to go up a bit; that's the price you pay for falling short on the first loan. Also, you should not expect to get more than one, or at the most two, loan rollovers—a bank's patience tends to grow short after a while!

Finance Charges and the Annual Percentage Rate

As indicated in Chapter 6, lenders are required to disclose both the dollar amount of finance charges and the annual percentage rate (APR) of interest. A sample **loan disclosure statement** applicable to either a single-payment or installment loan can be seen in Exhibit 7.3. Note that such a statement discloses not only interest costs but also other fees and expenses that may be tacked onto the loan. Although disclosures like this one allow you to compare the various borrowing alternatives, you still need to understand the methods used to compute finance charges, because similar loans with the same *stated* interest rates may have different finance charges and APRs. The two basic procedures used to calculate the finance charges on single-payment loans are the *simple interest method* and the *discount method*.

Simple Interest Method

Interest is charged only on the *actual loan balance outstanding* in the **simple interest method.** This method is commonly used on revolving credit lines by commercial banks, S&Ls, and credit unions. To see how it's applied to a single-payment loan, assume that you borrow $1,000 for two years at a 12 percent annual rate of interest. On a single-payment loan, the actual loan balance outstanding for the two years will be the full $1,000, because no principal payments will be made until this period ends. With simple interest, the finance charge, F_s, is obtained by multiplying the *principal* outstanding by the stated annual rate of interest and then multiplying this amount by the term of the loan:

$$\mathbf{F_s = P \times r \times t}$$

where
F_s = finance charge calculated using simple interest method
P = principal amount of loan
r = stated annual rate of interest
t = term of loan, as stated in years (for example, t would equal 0.5 for a 6-month loan, 1.25 for a 15-month loan, and 2.0 for a 2-year loan)

loan rollover The process of paying off a loan by taking out another loan.

loan disclosure statement A document lenders are required to supply borrowers that states both the dollar amount of finance charges and the APR applicable to a loan.

simple interest method A method of computing finance charges in which interest is charged on the actual loan balance outstanding.

Crunching the Numbers. Substituting $1,000 for P, .12 for r, and 2 for t in the equation, we see that the finance charge, F_s, on this loan equals some $240 (i.e., $1,000 × .12 per year × 2 years). Because the size of the loan payment with this type of credit arrangement is found by adding the finance charges to the principal amount of the loan, you'd have to make a loan payment of $1,000 + $240 = $1,240 at maturity to retire this debt.

To calculate the true, or annual, percentage rate (APR) of interest on this loan, the average annual finance charge is divided by the average loan balance outstanding, as follows:

$$APR = \frac{\text{Average annual finance charge}}{\text{Average loan balance outstanding}}$$

The average annual finance charge is found by dividing the total finance charge by the life of the loan (in years). In our example, the result is $120 ($240/2). Because the loan balance outstanding remains at $1,000 over the life of the loan, the average loan balance outstanding is $1,000. Dividing the $120 average annual finance charge by the $1,000 average loan balance outstanding, we obtain an APR of 12 percent. Thus, the APR and the stated rate of interest are equivalent: they both equal 12 percent. *This is always the case when the simple interest method is used to calculate finance charges, regardless of whether loans are single-payment or installment.*

EXHIBIT 7.3   A Loan Disclosure Statement

The loan disclosure statement informs the borrower of all charges (finance and otherwise) associated with the loan and the annual percentage rate (APR). It also specifies the payment terms as well as the existence of any balloon payments.

FEDERAL TRUTH IN LENDING DISCLOSURE STATEMENT

Creditor: YOUR FAVORITE MORTGAGE CORPORATION
Borrower(s):

Account Number: 1111111

ANNUAL PERCENTAGE RATE	FINANCE CHARGE	Amount Financed	Total of Payments
The cost of your credit as a yearly rate	The dollar amount the credit will cost you	The amount of credit provided to you or on your behalf	The amount you will have paid after you have made all payments as scheduled
7.337 %	$ 205,017.52	$ 138,796.50	$ 343,814.02

Your payment schedule will be:

NUMBER OF PAYMENTS	AMOUNT OF PAYMENTS	WHEN PAYMENTS ARE DUE
359	$ 955.05	Monthly beginning 09/01 /01
1	951.07	Monthly beginning 08/01/31

Variable Rate: If checked, your loan contains a variable rate feature. Disclosures about the variable rate feature have been provided to you earlier.

Demand Feature: If checked, this obligation has a demand feature.

Insurance: You may obtain property insurance from anyone you want that is acceptable to the creditor.
    If checked, you can get insurance through Your Favorite Mortgage Corporation. You will pay $____ for 12 months hazard insurance coverage. You will pay $ ____for 12 months flood insurance coverage.

Security: You are giving a security interest in   property being purchased   property located at
1234 118TH STREET, NW, WASHINGTON, DC 20009
   Assignment of brokerage account and pledge of securities   Personal property: stocks and lease
   Assignment of life insurance policy   Other:
Late Charges: If a payment is late, you will be charged **5.000** % of the payment.

Prepayment: If you pay off early, you   may   will not have to pay a penalty. You   may   will not be entitled to a refund of part of the finance charge.

Assumption: Someone buying your house   may, subject to conditions, be allowed to   cannot assume the remainder of the mortgage on the original terms.

See your contract documents for any additional information about nonpayment, default, any required repayment in full before the scheduled date, prepayment refunds and penalties and assumption policy.

ACKNOWLEDGMENT
By signing below you acknowledge that you have received a completed copy of this Federal Truth in Lending Statement prior to the execution *of* any closing documents.

_____   _____
Borrower/Date of Acknowledgment   Borrower/Date of Acknowledgment

Source: http://www.in.gov/dfi/education/TILEX.htm.

Sometimes what you see is not what you get—such as when you borrow money through a discount loan and end up paying quite a bit more than the quoted rate.

Method	Stated Rate on Loan	Finance Charges	APR
Simple interest	12.0%	$240	12.0%
Discount	12.0	240	15.8

Discount Method

The **discount method** calculates total finance charges on the full principal amount of the loan, which is then subtracted from the amount of the loan. The difference between the amount of the loan and the finance charge is then disbursed (paid) to the borrower—in other words, finance charges are paid in advance and represent a discount from the principal portion of the loan. The finance charge on a single-payment loan using the discount method, F_d, is calculated in exactly the same way as for a simple interest loan:

$$F_d = F_s = P \times r \times t$$

Crunching the Numbers. Using the above formula, the finance charge, F_d, on the $1,000, 12 percent, 2-year, single-payment loan is, of course, the same $240 we calculated earlier. But, in sharp contrast to simple interest loans, the loan payment with a discount loan is the original principal amount of the loan, P, because the finance charges on the loan are deducted up front from the loan proceeds. Thus, for the $1,000 loan, the borrower will receive $760—which is found by subtracting the interest charges from the loan principal ($1,000 less $240)—and in 2 years will be required to pay back $1,000.

To find the APR on this discount loan, substitute the appropriate values into the APR equation cited above. For this 2-year loan, the average annual finance charge is $120 ($240/2). However, as mentioned, this is a discount loan, so the borrower will receive only $760. And because this is a single-payment loan, the average amount of money outstanding is also $760. When these figures are used in the APR equation, we find the true rate for this 12 percent discount loan is more like 15.8 percent ($120/$760). Clearly, the discount method yields a much higher APR on single-payment loans than does the simple interest method. Exhibit 7.4 contrasts the results from both methods for the single-payment loan example discussed here.

discount method A method of calculating finance charges in which interest is computed, then subtracted from the principal, and the remainder is disbursed to the borrower.

Concept Check

CHECK • CONCEPT CHECK • CONCEPT CHECK • CONCEPT CHECK • CONCEPT CHECK • CONCEPT CHECK • CONCEPT

7-9	What is a *lien*, and when is it part of a consumer loan?
7-10	When might you request a *loan rollover*?
7-11	Describe the two methods used to calculate the finance charges on a single-payment loan. As a borrower, which method would you prefer? Explain.

LG5, LG6 INSTALLMENT LOANS

Installment loans (known as ILs for short) differ from single-payment loans in that they require the borrower to repay the debt in a series of installment payments (usually monthly) over the life of the loan. Installment loans have long been one of the most popular forms of consumer credit—right up there with credit cards! Much of this popularity is due to how conveniently the loan repayment is set up; not surprisingly, most people find it easier on their checkbooks to make a series of small payments rather than one big one.

A Real Consumer Credit Workhorse!

As a financing vehicle, there are few things installment loans can't do—which explains, in large part, why this form of consumer credit is so widely used. They can be used to finance just about any type of big-ticket item imaginable. New car loans are the dominant type of IL, but this form of credit is also used to finance home furnishings, appliances and entertainment centers, camper trailers and other recreational vehicles, even expensive vacations. And, of course, more and more college students are turning to this type of credit as the way to finance their education.

Not only can they be used to finance all sorts of things, installment loans can also be obtained at many locations. You'll find them at banks and other financial institutions as well as at major department stores and merchants that sell relatively expensive products. Go into a home appliance store to buy a high-priced stereo, and chances are you'll be able to arrange for IL financing right there on the spot. These loans can be taken out for just a few hundred dollars, or they can involve thousands of dollars—indeed, ILs of $25,000 or more are common. What's more, they can be set up with maturities as short as 6 months or as long as 7 to 10 years, even 15 years!

Most installment loans are secured with some kind of collateral—for example, the car or home entertainment center you purchased with the help of an IL usually serves as collateral on the loan. Even personal loans used to finance things like expensive vacations can be secured—in these cases, the collateral could be securities, CDs, or some other type of financial asset. One rapidly growing segment of this market is ILs secured by second mortgages. These so-called *home equity loans* are similar to the home equity credit lines discussed in Chapter 6, except they involve a set amount of money loaned over a set period of time (often as long as 15 years), rather than a revolving credit line from which you can borrow, repay, and reborrow. Thus, if a borrower needs, say, $25,000 to help pay for an expensive new boat, he would simply take out a loan in that amount and *secure it with a second mortgage on his home*. This loan would be like any other IL in the sense that it's for a set amount of money and is to be repaid over a set period of time in monthly installments. Besides their highly competitive interest rates, a big attraction of *home equity loans* is that the interest paid on them usually can be taken as a tax deduction. So, borrowers get the double benefit of *low interest rates and tax deductibility*! As with home equity credit lines, however, failure to repay could result in the loss of your home.

Finance Charges, Monthly Payments, and APR

Earlier we discussed the simple interest and discount methods of determining finance charges on single-payment loans. In this section, we look at the use of simple and add-on interest to compute finance charges and monthly payments for installment loans (technically, discount interest can also be used with ILs; but because this is rare, we ignore it here). To illustrate, we'll use a 12 percent, $1,000 installment loan that is to be paid off in 12 monthly payments. As in the earlier illustration for single-payment loans, we assume interest is the only component of the finance charge; there are no other fees and charges.

Using Simple Interest

When simple interest is used with ILs, interest is charged only on the outstanding balance of the loan. Thus, as the loan principal declines with monthly payments, the amount of interest being charged also decreases. Because finance charges change each month, the procedure used to find the interest expense is mathematically complex. Fortunately, this isn't much of a problem in practice due to the widespread use of desktop computers/computer terminals, handheld financial calculators (which we'll illustrate later), and preprinted finance tables—an example of which is provided in Exhibit 7.5. Essentially, the tables show the *monthly payment* that would be required to retire an installment loan carrying a given simple rate of interest with a given term to maturity. Because these tables (sometimes referred to as *amortization schedules*) have interest charges built right into them, the monthly payments shown cover both principal and interest.

Noice that the loan payments shown in Exhibit 7.5 cover a variety of interest rates (from $7\frac{1}{2}$ to 18 percent) and loan maturities (from 6 to 60 months). The values in the table represent the monthly payments required to retire a $1,000 loan. Although it's assumed you're borrowing $1,000, you can use the table with any size loan. For example, if you're looking at a $5,000 loan, just multiply the monthly loan payment from the table by 5—that is, $5,000/$1,000 = 5; or, if you have, say, a $500 loan, multiply the loan payment by .5 ($500/$1,000 = .5). In many respects, this table is just like the mortgage loan payment schedule introduced in Chapter 5, except we use much shorter loan maturities here than with mortgages.

Here's how to use the table in Exhibit 7.5. Suppose we want to find the monthly payment required on our $1,000, 12 percent, 12-month loan. Looking under the 12-month column and across from the 12 percent rate of interest, we find a value of $88.85; that is the monthly payment it will take to pay off the $1,000 loan in 12 months. When we multiply the monthly payments ($88.85) by the term of the loan in months (12), the result is total payments of $88.85 × 12 = $1,066.20. The difference between the total payments on the loan and the principal portion represents the *finance charges on the loan*—in this case, $1,066.20 - $1,000 = interest charges of $66.20.

CALCULATOR

INPUTS	FUNCTIONS
12	N
12	I/Y
−1000	PV
	CPT
	PMT
	Solution
	88.85

See Appendix E for details.

Calculator Keystrokes. Instead of using a table like the one in Exhibit 7.5, you could just as easily have used a handheld financial calculator to *find the monthly payments on an IL.* Here's what you'd do: First, set the payments per year (P/Y) key to 12 to put the calculator in a monthly payment mode. Now, to find the monthly payment needed to pay off a 12 percent, 12-month, $1,000 installment loan, use the keystrokes shown here, where:

N = length of the loan, *in months*
I/Y = the *annual* rate of interest being charged on the loan
PV = the amount of the loan, entered as a *negative*

As seen, to pay off this IL, you'll have to make payments of $88.85 per month for the next 12 months.

From each monthly payment (of $88.85), a certain portion goes to interest and the balance is used to reduce the principal. Because the principal balance declines with each payment, the amount that goes to interest also *decreases* whereas the amount that goes to principal *increases.* Exhibit 7.6 illustrates this cash-flow stream. Because *monthly* payments are used with the loan, the interest column in Exhibit 7.6 is also based on a *monthly* rate of interest—that is, the annual rate is divided by 12 to obtain a monthly rate (12 percent per year/12 = 1 percent per month). This monthly rate is then applied to the outstanding loan balance to find the monthly interest charges in column 3. Because interest is charged only on the outstanding balance, *the annual percentage rate (APR) on a simple interest IL will always equal the stated rate*—in this case, 12 percent.

Add-on Method

Some installment loans, particularly those obtained directly from retail merchants or made at finance companies and the like, are made using the **add-on method.** Add-on loans are very expensive; indeed, they generally rank as one of the most costly forms of consumer credit, with APRs that are often well above rates charged even on many credit cards. With add-on interest, the finance charges are calculated using the *original* balance of the loan; this amount (the total finance charges) is then added on to the original loan balance to determine the total amount to be repaid. Thus, the amount of finance charges on an add-on loan can be found by using the familiar simple interest formula:

$$\mathbf{F = P \times r \times t}$$

add-on method A method of calculating interest by computing finance charges on the original loan balance and then adding the interest to that balance.

Given the $1,000 loan we've been using for illustrative purposes, the finance charges on a 12 percent, 1-year add-on loan would be

$$\mathbf{F = \$1,000 \times 12 \times 1 = \$120}$$

EXHIBIT 7.5

A Table of Monthly Installment Loan Payments (to Repay a $1,000, Simple Interest Loan)

You can use a table like this to find the monthly payments on a wide variety of simple interest installment loans. Although it's set up to show payments on a $1,000 loan, with a little modification you can easily use it with any size loan (the principal can be more or less than $1,000).

LOAN MATURITY

Rate of Interest	6 Months	12 Months	18 Months	24 Months	36 Months	48 Months	60 Months
7.5%	$170.33	$86.76	$58.92	$45.00	$31.11	$24.18	$20.05
8.0	170.58	86.99	59.15	45.23	31.34	24.42	20.28
8.5	170.82	87.22	59.37	45.46	31.57	24.65	20.52
9.0	171.07	87.46	59.60	45.69	31.80	24.89	20.76
9.5	171.32	87.69	59.83	45.92	32.04	25.13	21.01
10.0	171.56	87.92	60.06	46.15	32.27	25.37	21.25
10.5	171.81	88.15	60.29	46.38	32.51	25.61	21.50
11.0	172.05	88.50	60.64	46.73	32.86	25.97	21.87
11.5	173.30	88.62	60.76	46.85	32.98	26.09	22.00
12.0	172.50	88.85	60.99	47.08	33.22	26.34	22.25
12.5	172.80	89.09	61.22	47.31	33.46	26.58	22.50
13.0	173.04	89.32	61.45	47.55	33.70	26.83	22.76
14.0	173.54	89.79	61.92	48.02	34.18	27.33	23.27
15.0	174.03	90.26	62.39	48.49	34.67	27.84	23.79
16.0	174.53	90.74	62.86	48.97	35.16	28.35	24.32
17.0	175.03	91.21	63.34	49.45	35.66	28.86	24.86
18.0	175.53	91.68	63.81	49.93	36.16	29.38	25.40

EXHIBIT 7.6

Monthly Payment Analysis for a Simple Interest Installment Loan (Assumes a $1,000, 12 Percent, 12-Month Loan)

Part of each monthly payment on an installment loan goes to interest and part to principal. As the loan is paid down over time, less and less of each payment goes to interest, and more and more goes to principal.

Month	Outstanding Loan Balance (1)	Monthly Payment (2)	Interest Charges [(1) × 0.01] (3)	Principal [(2) − (3)] (4)
1	$1,000.00	$88.85	$10.00	$78.85
2	921.15	88.85	9.21	79.64
3	841.51	88.85	8.42	80.43
4	761.08	88.85	7.61	81.24
5	679.84	88.85	6.80	82.05
6	597.79	88.85	5.98	82.87
7	514.92	88.85	5.15	83.70
8	431.22	88.85	4.31	84.54
9	346.68	88.85	3.47	85.38
10	261.30	88.85	2.61	86.24
11	175.06	88.85	1.75	87.10
12	87.96	88.85	0.89	87.96
Total		$1,066.20	$66.20	$1,000.00

Note: Column 1 values for months 2 through 12 are obtained by subtracting the principal payment shown in column 4 for the preceding month from the outstanding loan balance shown in column 1 for the preceding month; thus, $1,000 − $78.85 = $921.15, which is the outstanding loan balance in month 2.

EXHIBIT 7.7 — Comparative Finance Charges and APRs (Assumes a $1,000, 12 Percent, 12-Month Installment Loan)

In sharp contrast to simple interest loans, the APR with add-on installment loans is much higher than the stated rate.

	Simple Interest	Add-on Interest
Stated rate on loan	12%	12%
Finance charges	$66.20	$120.00
Monthly payments	$88.25	$93.33
Total payments made	$1,066.20	$1,120.00
APR	12%	21.4%

Compared to the finance charges for the same loan on a simple interest basis ($66.20), the add-on loan is a lot more expensive—a fact that also shows up in monthly payments and APR. Keep in mind that both of these loans would be quoted as "12 percent" loans. Thus, you may think you're getting a 12 percent loan, but looks can be deceiving—especially when you're dealing with add-on interest! So, when you're taking out an installment loan, be sure to find out whether simple or add-on interest is being used to compute finance charges. And if it's add-on, you might want to consider looking elsewhere for the loan.

Crunching the Numbers. To find the monthly payments on an add-on loan, all you need to do is add the finance charge ($120) to the *original* principal amount of the loan ($1,000) and then divide this sum by the number of monthly payments to be made. In the case of our $1,000, one-year loan, this results in monthly payments of $93.33, found as follows:

$$\text{Monthly payments} = \frac{\$1,000 + \$120}{12} = \frac{\$1,120}{12} = \$93.33$$

As expected, these monthly payments are much higher than the ones with the simple interest loan ($88.85).

Because the actual rate of interest with an add-on loan is considerably higher than the stated rate, we must determine the loan's APR. That can easily be done with a financial calculator, as shown below. As you can see, the APR on this 12 percent add-on-loan is more like 21.4 percent. Clearly, when viewed from an APR perspective, this add-on loan is an expensive form of financing! (A rough but reasonably accurate rule of thumb is that the APR on an add-on loan is about *twice* the stated rate—thus, if the loan is quoted at an add-on rate of 9 percent, you're probably going to be paying a true rate that's closer to 18 percent.) This is because when add-on interest is applied to an installment loan, the interest included in each payment is charged on the *initial principal* even though the outstanding loan balance is reduced as installment payments are made. A summary of comparative finance charges and APRs for simple interest and add-on interest methods is presented in Exhibit 7.7.

CALCULATOR

INPUTS	FUNCTIONS
12	N
−1000	PV
93.33	PMT
	CPT
	I/Y
	Solution
	21.45

See Appendix E for details.

Calculator Keystrokes. Here's how you *find the APR on an IL* using a financial calculator. First, make sure the payments per year (P/Y) key is set to 12, so the calculator is in the monthly payment mode. Then, to find the APR on a $1,000, 12-month, 12 percent add-on IL, use the following keystrokes, where:

N = length of the loan, in months
PV = size of the loan, entered as a negative
PMT = size of the monthly IL payments

You'll find that the APR on the 12 percent add-on loan is a whopping 21.45 percent!

Federal banking regulations require that the exact APR (accurate to the nearest 0.25 percent) must be disclosed to borrowers. And note that not only interest, but also any other fees required to obtain a loan, are to be considered part of the finance charges and should be included in the computation of APR.

Prepayment Penalties

Another type of finance charge that's often found in installment loan contracts is the *prepayment penalty,* an additional charge you may owe if you decide to pay off your loan prior to maturity. When you pay off a loan early, you may find that you owe quite a bit more than expected, especially if the lender uses the **Rule of 78s** (or **sum-of-the-digits method**) to calculate the amount of interest paid and the principal balance to date. You might think that paying off a $1,000, 12 percent, 1-year loan at the end of 6 months would mean that you've paid about half of the principal and owe somewhere around $500 to the lender. Well, that's just not so with a loan that uses the rule of 78s! This method charges more interest in the early months of the loan, on the theory that the borrower has use of more money in the loan's early stages and should pay more finance charges in the early months and progressively less later. There's nothing wrong with that, of course; it's how all loans operate. But what's wrong is that the Rule of 78s front-loads an inordinate amount of interest charges to the early months of the loan, thereby producing a much higher principal balance than you'd normally expect (remember: the more of the loan payment that goes to interest, the less that goes to repayment of principal).

To see how this works, let's assume that we want to pay off the $1,000, 12 percent, 1-year add-on loan after 6 months. Using the Rule of 78s, of your $559.98 in total payments (that is, six payments at $93.33 each = 6 × $93.33 = $559.98), just $389.73 went to principal—all the rest went to interest. So, even though you've made payments for half of the life of the loan, you still owe more than 60 percent of the principal—the same loan under simple interest would have paid off $485 in principal after 6 months.

Credit Life Insurance

Sometimes, as a condition of receiving an installment loan, a borrower is required to buy **credit life insurance** and possibly **credit disability insurance.** Credit life (and disability) insurance is tied to a particular IL and provides insurance that the loan will be paid off if the borrower dies (or becomes disabled) before the loan matures. These policies essentially insure the borrower for an amount sufficient to repay the outstanding loan balance. The seller's (or lender's) ability to dictate the terms of these insurance requirements is either banned or restricted by law in many states. If this type of insurance is required as a condition of the loan, its cost must be added to the finance charges and included as part of the APR. From the borrower's perspective, credit life and disability insurance is not a good deal: *It's very costly and does little more than give lenders a lucrative source of income.* Not surprisingly, because it's so lucrative, some lenders aggressively push it on unsuspecting borrowers and, in some cases, even require it as a condition for granting a loan. The best advice is to avoid it if at all possible!

Buy on Time or Pay Cash?

When buying a big-ticket item, you often have little choice but to take out a loan—the acquisition (perhaps it's a new car) is just so expensive that you can't afford to pay cash. And even if you do have the money, you may still be better off using something like an IL *if the cash purchase would end up severely depleting your liquid reserves.* But don't just automatically take out a loan. Rather, take the time to find out if, in fact, that's the best thing to do. Such a decision can easily be made by using Worksheet 7.2, which considers the cost of the loan relative to the after-tax earnings generated from having your money in some type of short-term investment vehicle. It's assumed that the consumer has an adequate level of liquid reserves, and that these reserves are being held in some type of savings account. (Obviously, if this is not the case, there's little reason to go through the exercise because you have no choice but to borrow the money.) Essentially, it boils down to this: *If it costs more to borrow the money than you can earn in interest, then draw the money from your savings to pay cash for the purchase; if not, consider taking out a loan.*

To see how it works, consider this situation: You're thinking about buying a second car (a nice, low-mileage used vehicle) and after the normal down payment, you still need to come up with $12,000. This balance can be taken care of in one of two ways: (1) you can take out a 36-month, 10 percent IL (for a monthly payment of $387.24), or (2) you can pay

Rule of 78s (sum-of-the-digits method) A method of calculating interest that has extra-heavy interest charges in the early months of the loan.

credit life (or disability) insurance A type of life (or disability) insurance in which the coverage decreases at the same rate as the loan balance.

Using a worksheet like this, you can decide whether to buy on time or pay cash by comparing the (after-tax) cost of interest paid on a loan with the after-tax interest income lost by taking the money out of savings and using it to pay cash for the purchase.

BUY ON TIME OR PAY CASH

Name _John E. Jones_   Date _February 28, 2007_

■ Cost of Borrowing

1. Terms of the loan		
a. Amount of the loan	$12,000.00	
b. Length of the loan (in years)	3 yrs.	
c. Monthly payment	$ 387.24	
2. Total loan payments made		
(monthly loan payment × length of loan in months)		
$ _387.24_ per month × _36_ months		$ 13,940.64
3. Less: Principal amount of the loan		$ 12,000
4. Total interest paid over life of loan		
(line 2 — 3)		$ 1,940.64
5. Tax considerations:		
• Is this a home equity loan (where interest expenses can be deducted from taxes)?	☐ yes ☒ no	
• Do you itemize deductions on your federal tax returns?	☒ yes ☐ no	
• If you answered yes to BOTH questions, then proceed to line 6; if you answered no to *either one* or *both* of the questions, then proceed to *line 8* and use *line 4* as the after-tax interest cost of the loan.		
6. What federal tax bracket are you in?		
(use either 10, 15, 25, 28, 33, or 35%)	___%	
7. Taxes saved due to interest deductions		
(line 4 × tax rate, from line 6: $_____ ×____ %)		$ —
Total after-tax interest cost on the loan (line 4 − line 7)8.		$ 1,940.64

■ Cost of Paying Cash

9. Annual interest earned on savings (annual rate of interest earned on savings × amount of loan: _5_ % × 12,000.00)		$ 600.00
10. Annual after-tax interest earnings (line 9 × [1 − tax rate] — e.g., 1 − 28% = 72%: $ _600.00_ × _72_%)		$ 432.00
11. Total after-tax interest earnings over life of loan (line 10 × line 1b: $ _432.00_ × _3_ years)		$ 1,296.00

■ Net Cost of Borrowing

12. Difference in cost of borrowing vs. cost of paying cash (line 8 minus line 11)		$ 644.64

BASIC DECISION RULE: *Pay cash* if line 12 is positive; *borrow the money* if line 12 is negative.

Note: For simplicity, compounding is ignored in calculating *both* the cost of interest and interest earnings.

cash by drawing the money from a money fund (paying 5 percent interest today and for the foreseeable future). We can now run the numbers to decide whether to buy on time or pay cash—see Worksheet 7.2 for complete details. In this case, we assume the loan is a standard IL, where the interest does not qualify as a tax deduction, and that you're in the 28 percent tax bracket. The worksheet shows that by borrowing the money, you'll end up paying nearly $1,941 in interest (line 4), none of which is tax deductible. In contrast, by leaving your money on deposit in the money fund, you'll receive only $1,296 in interest, after taxes (see line 11). Taken together, we see the net cost of borrowing (line 12) is nearly $650—so you'll be paying over $1,900 to earn less than $1,300, which certainly doesn't make much sense! Clearly, it's far more cost-effective in this case to take the money from savings and pay cash for the car, because you'll save nearly $650.

Although $650 is a pretty convincing reason for avoiding a loan, sometimes the actual dollar spread between the cost of borrowing and interest earned is very small, perhaps only $100 or less. Being able to deduct the interest on a loan can lead to a relatively small spread, but it can also occur, for example, if the amount being financed is relatively small—say, you want $1,500 or $2,000 for a ski trip to Colorado. In this case, and so long as the spread stays small enough, you may decide it's still worthwhile to borrow the money in order to maintain a higher level of liquidity. Although this decision is perfectly legitimate when very small spreads exist, it makes less sense as the gap starts to widen.

❚❚ Concept Check

7-12	Briefly describe the basic features of an installment loan.
7-13	What is a home equity loan, and what are its major advantages and disadvantages?
7-14	Explain why a borrower is often required to purchase *credit life and disability insurance* as a condition of receiving an installment loan.
7-15	Define simple interest as it relates to an installment loan. Are you better off with add-on interest? Explain.
7-16	When does it make more sense to pay cash for a big-ticket item than to borrow the money to finance the purchase?

❮❮ SUMMARY

LG1 Know when to use consumer loans, and be able to differentiate between the major types. Single-payment and installment loans are formally negotiated consumer loan arrangements used mainly to finance big-ticket items. Most of these consumer loans are taken out as auto loans, loans for other durable goods, education loans, personal loans, and consolidation loans.

LG2 Identify the various sources of consumer loans. Consumer loans can be obtained from various sources, including commercial banks (the biggest providers of such credit), consumer finance companies, credit unions, S&Ls, sales finance (and captive finance) companies, life insurance companies (and other financial services organizations), and, finally, as a last resort, your friends and relatives.

LG3 Choose the best loans by comparing finance charges, maturity, collateral, and other loan terms. Before taking out a consumer loan, you should be sure the purchase is compatible with your financial plans and that you can service the debt without straining your budget. When shopping for credit, it's in your best interest to compare such loan features as finance charges (APRs), loan maturities, monthly payments, and collateral requirements and then to choose loans with terms that are fully compatible with your financial plans and cash budget.

LG4 Describe the features of, and calculate the finance charges on, single-payment loans. In a single-payment loan, the borrower makes just one principal payment (at the maturity of the loan), although there may be one or more interim interest payments. Such loans are usually made for 1 year or less, and they're normally secured by some type of collateral. A major advantage of the single-payment loan is that it doesn't require monthly payments and won't tie up the borrower's cash flow. Finance charges can be calculated using either the simple interest method—applying the interest rate to the outstanding loan balance—or the discount method—calculating the interest the same way as simple interest, but then deducting it from the loan principal and getting a higher APR.

LG5 **Evaluate the benefits of an installment loan.** In an installment loan, the borrower agrees to repay the loan through a series of equal installment payments (usually monthly) until the obligation is fully repaid; in this way, the borrower can receive a loan-repayment schedule that fits neatly into his or her financial plans and cash budget. This highly popular form of consumer credit can be used to finance just about any type of big-ticket asset or expenditure. Many ILs are taken out as home equity loans to capture tax advantages.

LG6 **Determine the costs of installment loans, and analyze whether it is better to pay cash or take out a loan.** Most single-payment loans are made with either simple or discount interest, whereas most ILs are made with either simple or add-on interest. When simple interest is used, the actual finance charge always corresponds to the stated rate of interest; in contrast, when add-on or discount rates are used, the APR is always more than the stated rate. In the end, whether it makes sense to borrow rather than to pay cash is a matter of which alternative costs less.

FINANCIAL PLANNING EXERCISES

LG3, 6 1. Assume that you've been shopping for a new car and intend to finance part of it through an installment loan. The car you're looking for has a sticker price of $15,000. Big A Autos has offered to sell it to you for $2,500 down and finance the balance with a loan that will require 48 monthly payments of $329.17; Cars-Are-Us will sell you exactly the same vehicle for $3,000 down plus a 60-month loan for the balance, with monthly payments of $268.45. Which of these two finance packages is the better deal? Explain.

LG3 2. *Use Worksheet 7.1.* Every 6 months, Neal Samuels takes an inventory of the consumer debts he has outstanding. His latest tally shows that he still owes $4,000 on a home improvement loan (monthly payments of $125); he is making $85 monthly payments on a personal loan with a remaining balance of $750; he has a $2,000, secured single-payment loan that's due late next year; he has a $70,000 home mortgage on which he's making $750 monthly payments; he still owes $8,600 on a new car loan (monthly payments of $375); he has a $960 balance on his Visa card (minimum payment of $40), a $70 balance on his Shell credit card (balance due in 30 days), and a $1,200 balance on a personal line of credit ($60 monthly payments). Use Worksheet 7.1 to prepare an inventory of Neal's consumer debt. Find his debt safety ratio given that his take-home pay is $2,500 per month; would you consider this ratio to be good or bad? Explain.

LG4 3. Robert Martino plans to borrow $8,000 for five years. The loan will be *repaid with a single payment after 5 years*, and the interest on the loan will be computed using the simple interest method at an annual rate of 8 percent. How much will Robert have to pay in 5 years? How much will he have to pay at maturity if he's required to make *annual interest payments* at the end of each year?

LG5, 6 4. Using the simple interest method, find the monthly payments on a $3,000 installment loan, given the funds are borrowed for 24 months at an annual interest rate of 14 percent. How much interest will be paid during the first year of this loan? (Use a monthly payment analysis similar to the one in Exhibit 7.6.)

LG4 5. Find the finance charges on a $7\frac{1}{2}$ percent, 18-month single-payment loan when interest is computed using the simple interest method. Find the finance charges on the same loan when interest is computed using the discount method. Determine the APR in each case.

LG4 6. Sally Gibbs has to borrow $4,000. First State Bank will lend her the money for 12 months through a single-payment loan at 13.5 percent discount; Home Savings and Loan will make

Using Consumer Loans

her a $4,000 single-payment, 12-month loan at 15 percent simple. Where should Sally borrow the money? Explain.

LG5, 6   7. Assuming that interest is the only finance charge, how much interest would be paid on a $5,000 installment loan to be repaid in 36 monthly installments of $166.10? What is the APR on this loan?

LG5, 6   8. After careful comparison shopping, Chris Jenkins decides to buy a new Nissan Maxima. With some options added, the car has a price of $29,500—including plates and taxes. Because he can't afford to pay cash for the car, he uses some savings and his old car as a trade-in to put down $9,500. He plans to finance the rest with a $20,000, 60-month loan at a simple interest rate of $9\frac{1}{2}$ percent.
    a. What will his monthly payments be?
    b. How much total interest will Chris pay in the first year of the loan? (Use a monthly payment analysis procedure similar to the one in Exhibit 7.6.)
    c. How much interest will Chris pay over the full (60-month) life of the loan?
    d. What is the APR on this loan?

LG5, 6   9. Justin Walton wants to buy a new high-end audio system for his car. The system is being sold by two dealers in town, both of whom sell the equipment for the same price: $2,000. Justin can buy the equipment from Dealer A, with no money down, by making payments of $119.20 a month for 18 months; he can buy the same equipment from Dealer B by making 36 monthly payments of $69.34 (again, with no money down). Justin is considering purchasing the system from Dealer B due to the lower payment. Find the APR for each alternative. What do you recommend?

LG5, 6   10. Joan Clark plans to borrow $5,000 and repay it in 36 monthly installments. This loan is being made at an annual add-on interest rate of $11\frac{1}{2}$ percent.
    a. Calculate the finance charge on this loan, assuming that the only component of the finance charge is interest.
    b. Use your finding in part **a** to calculate the monthly payment on the loan.
    c. Using a financial calculator, determine the APR on this loan.

LG6   11. ***Use Worksheet 7.2 to help Grace make this credit decision:*** Grace Hesketh wants to buy a home entertainment center. Complete with a big-screen TV, VCR, and sound system, the unit would cost $4,500. Grace has over $15,000 in a money fund, so she can easily afford to pay cash for the whole thing (the fund is currently paying 5.5 percent interest, and Grace expects that yield to hold for the foreseeable future). To stimulate sales, the dealer is offering to finance the full cost of the unit with a 36-month installment loan at 9 percent, simple. Grace wants to know: Should she pay cash for this home entertainment center or buy it on time? (*Note:* Assume Grace is in the 28 percent tax bracket and that she itemizes deductions on her tax returns.) Briefly explain your answer.
    a. Should she pay cash for this?
    b. Rework the preceding problem, assuming Grace has the option of using a 48-month, 9.5 percent *home equity loan* to finance the full cost of this entertainment center. Again, use Worksheet 7.2 to determine if Grace should pay cash or buy on time. Does your answer change from the one you came up with in part **a**? Explain.

LG5, 6   12. Due to a job change, Alex Rodriguez just relocated to the Pacific Northwest. He sold what furniture he had before he moved, so he's now shopping for new furnishings. At a local furniture store, he's found an assortment of couches, chairs, tables, and beds that he thinks would look great in his new two-bedroom apartment; the total cost for everything is $6,400. Because of moving costs, Alex is a bit short of cash right now, so he's decided to take out an installment loan for $6,400 to pay for the furniture. The furniture store offers to lend him the money for 48 months at an add-on interest rate of $8\frac{1}{2}$ percent. The credit union at Alex's firm also offers to lend him the money—they'll give him the loan at an interest rate of 12 percent, simple, but only for a term of 24 months.
    a. Compute the monthly payments for both of the loan offers.
    b. Determine the APR for both loans.
    c. Which is more important: low payments or a low APR? Explain.

APPLYING PERSONAL FINANCE

Making the Payments!

For many of us, new cars can be so appealing! We get bitten by the new car bug and think how great it would be to have a new car. Then we tell ourselves that we *really need* a new car because our old one is just a piece of junk waiting to fall apart in the middle of the road anyway. Of course, we don't have the money to purchase a new car outright, so we'll have to get a loan. That means car payments. Trouble is, car payments often turn out to be a lot less affordable *after* we actually get the loan than we thought they would be *before* we signed on the dotted line. And they tend to last way beyond the time the new car smell wears off. This project will help you understand how loan payments are determined and the obligation they place on you as the borrower.

Let's assume for this project that your parents have promised to make the down payment on a new car once you have your degree in hand. They have agreed to pay 30 percent of the cost of any car you choose as long as you are able to obtain a loan and make the payments on the remainder. Find the price of the vehicle you would like by visiting a car dealership or pulling up a Web site such as **http://www.edmunds.com**. Add another 4 percent to the price for tax, title, license, and so on, or ask a dealer to estimate these costs for you. Take 70 percent of the total to determine how much you'll have to finance from your car loan. Then find out what the going rate is for car loans in your area by calling or visiting your bank or by consulting a Web site such as **http://www.bankrate.com**. Calculate what your monthly payments would be at this rate if you financed the loan for 3, 5, and 6 years. How well do you think these car payments would fit into your budget? What kind of income would you have to make to comfortably afford these payments? If the payments are more than you thought they would be, what can you do to bring them down?

CRITICAL THINKING CASES

LG4

7.1 Financing Annette's Education

At age 19, Annette Peterson is in the middle of her second year of studies at a community college in San Diego. She has done well in her course work; majoring in prebusiness studies, she currently has a 3.75 grade point average. Annette lives at home and works part-time as a filing clerk for a nearby electronics distributor. Her parents can't afford to pay any of her tuition and college expenses, so she's virtually on her own as far as college goes. Annette plans to transfer to the University of Texas at Austin next year. (She has already been accepted.) After talking with her counselor, Annette feels she won't be able to hold down a part-time job and still manage to complete her bachelor's degree program at Texas in 2 years. Knowing that on her 22nd birthday she will receive approximately $35,000 from a trust fund left her by her grandmother, Annette has decided to borrow against the trust fund to support herself during the next 2 years. She estimates that she'll need $25,000 to cover tuition, room and board, books and supplies, travel, personal expenditures, and so on during that period. Unable to qualify for any special loan programs, Annette has found two sources of single-payment loans, each requiring a security interest in the trust proceeds as collateral. The terms required by each potential lender are as follows:
a. California State Bank will lend $30,000 at 8 percent discount interest. The loan principal would be due at the end of 2 years.
b. National Bank of San Diego will lend $25,000 under a 2-year note. The note would carry a 10 percent simple interest rate and would also be due in a single payment at the end of 2 years.

Critical Thinking Questions
1. How much would Annette (a) receive in initial loan proceeds and (b) be required to repay at maturity under the California State Bank loan?
2. Compute (a) the finance charges and (b) the APR on the loan offered by California State Bank.
3. Compute (a) the finance charges and (b) the APR on the loan offered by the National Bank of San Diego. How big a loan payment would be due at the end of 2 years?

4. Compare your findings in Questions 2 and 3, and recommend one of the loans to Annette. Explain your recommendation.
5. What other recommendations might you offer Annette relative to the disposition of the loan proceeds?

LG5,6 ## 7.2 Rob Gets His 4-Runner

Rob Lewis, a 27-year-old bachelor living in Charlotte, North Carolina, has been a high school teacher for 5 years. For the past 4 months, he's been thinking about buying a Toyota 4-Runner, but feels he can't afford a brand-new one. Recently, however, a friend, John McKenzie, has offered to sell Rob his fully loaded Toyota 4-Runner Ltd. John wants $22,500 for his SUV, which has been driven only 8,000 miles and is in very good condition. Rob is eager to buy the vehicle but has only $8,000 in his savings account at Tar Heel Bank. He expects to net $8,000 from the sale of his Chevrolet Camero, but this will still leave him about $6,500 short. He has two alternatives for obtaining the money:

a. Borrow $6,500 from the First National Bank of Charlotte at a fixed rate of 12 percent per annum, simple interest. The loan would be repaid in equal monthly installments over a 3-year (36-month) period.

b. Obtain a $6,500 installment loan requiring 36 monthly payments from the Charlotte Teacher's Credit Union at a 6.5 percent stated rate of interest. The add-on method would be used to calculate the finance charges on this loan.

Critical Thinking Questions

1. Using Exhibit 7.5 or a financial calculator, determine the required monthly payments if the loan is taken out at First National Bank of Charlotte.
2. Compute (a) the finance charges and (b) the APR on the loan offered by First National Bank of Charlotte.
3. Determine the size of the monthly payment required on the loan from the Charlotte Teacher's Credit Union.
4. Compute (a) the finance charges and (b) the APR on the loan offered by the Charlotte Teacher's Credit Union.
5. Compare the two loans and recommend one of them to Rob. Explain your recommendation.

MONEY ONLINE www.thomsonedu.com/finance/gitman

NLINE • MONEY ONLINE • MONEY ONLINE • MONEY ONLINE • MONEY ONLINE • MONEY ONLINE • MONEY ONLINE •

Visit **http://www.thomsonedu.com/finance/gitman** for some additional Web-based exercises and hot links (with annotations) to a variety of resources relevant to the topics covered in this chapter.

Natalie's off-campus apartment was broken into. Officer Tucker is creating a report of the stolen property while Natalie's friend Monica is trying to calm her down.

PART 4 > Managing Insurance Needs

Chapter 8 Insuring Your Life
Chapter 9 Insuring Your Health
Chapter 10 Protecting Your Property

Insuring Your Life

LG1	Explain the concept of risk and the basics of insurance underwriting.	p. 240
LG2	Discuss the primary reasons for life insurance and identify those who need coverage.	p. 242
LG3	Calculate how much life insurance you need.	p. 244
LG4	Differentiate among the various types of life insurance policies and describe their advantages and disadvantages.	p. 249
LG5	Choose the best life insurance policy for your needs at the lowest cost.	p. 259
LG6	Become familiar with the key features of life insurance policies.	p. 263

LG1 · BASIC INSURANCE CONCEPTS

As most people discover, life is full of unexpected events that can have far-reaching consequences. Your car is sideswiped on the highway and damaged beyond repair. A family member falls ill and can no longer work. A fire or other disaster destroys your home. Your spouse dies suddenly. Although most people don't like to think about possibilities like this, protecting yourself and your family against unforeseen events is part of sound financial planning. Insurance plays a central role in providing that protection. *Auto and homeowner's insurance*, for example, reimburses you if your car or home are destroyed or damaged. *Life insurance* helps replace lost income if premature death occurs, providing funds so that your loved ones can keep their home, maintain an acceptable lifestyle, pay for education, and meet other special needs. *Hospitalization and health insurance* covers medical costs when you get sick, and *disability insurance* protects your income while you're ill.

All of these types of insurance are intended *to protect you and your dependents from the financial consequences of losing assets or income when an accident, illness, or death occurs.* By anticipating the potential risks that your assets and income could be exposed to and weaving insurance protection into your financial plan, you lend a degree of certainty to your financial future. We'll begin this chapter by introducing important insurance concepts such as risk and underwriting before focusing on how to make decisions regarding life insurance. In Chapters 9 and 10, we'll discuss other important types of insurance, including health insurance and property insurance.

The Concept of Risk

An important concept in any discussion of insurance is *risk*. In insurance terms, risk is defined as uncertainty with respect to economic loss. Whenever you and your family have a financial interest in something—whether it's your life, health, home, car, or business—there's a risk of financial loss if that item is lost or damaged. Because such losses can be devastating to your financial security, you must devise strategies for anticipating and dealing with potential risks. These strategies include risk avoidance, loss prevention and control, risk assumption, and insurance.

Risk Avoidance

The simplest way to deal with risk is to avoid the act that creates it. For example, people who are afraid they might lose everything they own because of a lawsuit resulting from an automobile accident could avoid driving. Regarding life and health risks, avid skydivers or bungee jumpers might want to choose another recreational activity!

Although **risk avoidance** can be an effective way to handle some risks, it has its costs. People who avoid driving suffer considerable inconvenience, and the retired sky-diver may find she now suffers *more* stress, which can lead to different types of health risks. Risk avoidance is an attractive way to deal with risk only when the estimated cost of avoidance is less than the estimated cost of handling it in some other way.

Loss Prevention and Control

Generally, **loss prevention** can be defined as any activity that reduces the probability that a loss will occur (such as driving within the speed limit to lessen the chance of being in a car accident). **Loss control,** in contrast, is any activity that lessens the severity of loss once it occurs (such as wearing a safety belt or buying a car with air bags). Loss prevention and loss control should be important parts of the risk management program of every individual and family. In fact, insurance is a reasonable way of handling risk only when people use effective loss prevention and control measures.

Risk Assumption

With **risk assumption,** you choose to accept and bear the risk of loss. Risk assumption can be an effective way to handle many types of potentially small exposures to loss when insurance would be too expensive. (For example, the risk of having your *Personal Financial Planning* text stolen probably doesn't justify buying insurance.) It's also a reasonable approach for dealing with very large risks that you can't ordinarily prevent or secure insurance for (nuclear holocaust, for example). Unfortunately, people often assume risks unknowingly. They may be unaware of various exposures to loss or think that their insurance policy offers adequate protection when, in fact, it doesn't.

Insurance

An **insurance policy** is a contract between you (the insured) and an insurance company (the insurer) under which the insurance company agrees to reimburse you for any losses you suffer according to specified terms. From your perspective, *you are transferring your risk of loss to the insurance company.* You pay a relatively small amount (the insurance premium) in exchange for a promise from the insurance company that they'll reimburse you if you suffer a loss covered by the insurance policy.

Why are insurance companies willing to accept this risk? Simple. They combine the loss experiences of large numbers of people, and, by using statistical information known as *actuarial data*, they can estimate the risk of loss faced by the insured population. Losses for the entire group of policyholders are thus more predictable than for any one of the insureds individually. Insurance companies invest the amount they collect from premiums and, if the amount they pay out in losses and expenses is less than the sum of the premiums and the earnings on them, they make a profit. Therefore, accurately estimating the number and size of insured losses that will occur is critical for insurance companies.

risk avoidance To avoid an act that would create a risk.

loss prevention Any activity that reduces the probability that a loss will occur.

loss control Any activity that lessens the severity of loss once it occurs.

risk assumption The choice to accept and bear the risk of loss.

insurance policy A contract between the insured and the insurer under which the insurer agrees to reimburse the insured for any losses suffered according to specified terms.

Underwriting Basics

Insurance companies take great pains to decide whom they will insure and the applicable rates they will charge for premiums. This function is called **underwriting.** Underwriters design rate-classification schedules so that people pay premiums equal with their chance of loss. Through underwriting, insurance companies try to guard against *adverse selection*, which happens when only high-risk clients apply for and get insurance coverage.

Underwriting directly impacts an insurance company's chances of success. If underwriting standards are too high, people will be unjustly denied insurance coverage, and insurance sales will drop. On the other hand, if standards are too low, many insureds will pay less than their fair share based upon their potential for losses, and the insurance company's solvency may be jeopardized.

A basic problem facing insurance underwriters is how to select the best criteria for classifying the people they insure. Because there's no perfect relationship between available criteria and loss experience, some people invariably believe they're being charged more than they should be for their insurance. Insurers are always trying to improve their underwriting capabilities in order to set premium rates that will adequately protect policyholders against insolvency and yet be attractive and reasonable.

Because underwriting practices and standards also vary between insurance companies, you can often save money by shopping around for the company offering the most favorable underwriting policies for your specific characteristics and needs. To make an effective decision about any insurance product, therefore, you need a basic understanding of the different types of insurance available as well as insight into your own tolerance for risk when it comes to protecting your financial assets and your family. The discussion of life insurance that follows in this chapter, and succeeding chapters that discuss other types of insurance, will help you accomplish these goals.

❚❚ Concept Check

8-1	Discuss the role insurance plays in the financial planning process. Why is it important to have enough life insurance?
8-2	Define (a) *risk avoidance*, (b) *loss prevention*, (c) *loss control*, (d) *risk assumption*, and (e) an *insurance policy*. Explain their interrelationships, if any.
8-3	Explain the purpose of *underwriting*. What are some factors underwriters consider when underwriting a life insurance application?

LG2 WHY BUY LIFE INSURANCE?

Life insurance planning is an important part of every successful financial plan. Its primary purpose is to *protect your dependents from financial loss in the event of your untimely death*. It's an umbrella of protection for your loved ones, protecting the assets you've built up during your life and providing funds to help your family reach important financial goals even after you die.

Benefits of Life Insurance

Despite the importance of life insurance to sound financial planning, many people put off the decision to buy it. This happens partly because life insurance is associated with something unpleasant in many people's minds—namely, death. People don't like to talk about death or the things associated with it, so they often put off considering their life insurance needs. Life insurance is also intangible. You can't see, smell, touch, or taste its benefits—and those benefits mainly happen after you've died. However, life insurance does have some important benefits that should not be ignored in the financial planning process:

underwriting The process used by insurers to decide who can be insured and to determine applicable rates they will charge for premiums.

- **Financial protection for dependents.** If your family or loved ones depend on your income, what would happen to them after you die? Would they be able to maintain their current lifestyle, stay in your home, or afford a college education? Life insurance provides a financial cushion for your dependents, giving them a set amount of money after your death that they can use for many purposes. For example, your spouse may use your life insurance proceeds to pay off the mortgage on your home so your family can continue living there comfortably or set aside funds for your child's college education. In short, the most important benefit of life insurance is providing financial protection for your dependents after your death.

- **Protection from creditors.** A life insurance policy can be structured so that death benefits are paid directly to a named beneficiary rather than being considered as part of your estate. This means that even if you have outstanding bills and debts at the time of your death, creditors cannot claim the cash benefits from your life insurance policy, providing further financial protection for your dependents.

- **Tax benefits.** Life insurance proceeds paid to your heirs, as a rule, aren't subject to state or federal income taxes. Further, if certain requirements are met, policy proceeds can pass to named beneficiaries free of any *estate* taxes.

- **Vehicle for savings.** Some types of life insurance policies can serve as a savings vehicle, particularly for those who are looking for safety of principal. *Variable life policies*, which we'll discuss later in this chapter, are more investment vehicles than they are life insurance products. But don't assume that all life insurance products can be considered savings instruments. As we'll see later in this chapter, the comparison is often inappropriate.

Just like other aspects of personal financial planning, life insurance decisions can be made easier by following a step-by-step approach to answer the following questions:

1. Do you need life insurance?
2. If so, how much life insurance do you need?
3. Which type of life insurance is best given your financial objectives?
4. What factors should be considered in making the final purchase decision?

Do You Need Life Insurance?

The first question to ask when considering the purchase of life insurance is whether you need it. Not everyone does. Many factors, including your personal situation and other financial resources, play a role in determining your need for life insurance. Remember, the major purpose of life insurance is to provide financial security for your dependents in the event of your death. As we've discussed, life insurance provides other benefits, but they're all a distant second to this one.

Who needs life insurance? In general, life insurance should be considered if you have dependents counting on you for financial support. Therefore, a single adult who doesn't have children or other relatives to support may not need life insurance at all. Children also usually don't require insurance on their life.

Once you marry, your life insurance requirements should be reevaluated, depending on your spouse's earning potential and assets—such as a house—that you want to protect. The need for life insurance increases the most when children enter the picture, because young families stand to suffer the greatest financial hardship from the premature death of a parent. Even a non-wage-earning parent may require some life insurance to ensure that children are adequately cared for if the parent dies.

As families build assets, their life insurance requirements continue to change, both in terms of the amount of insurance needed and the type of policy necessary to meet their financial objectives and protect their assets. Other life changes will also affect your life insurance needs. For example, if you divorce or your spouse dies, you may need additional life insurance to protect your children. Once your children finish school and are on their own, the need for life insurance may drop. In later years, life insurance needs vary depending on the availability of other financial resources, such as pensions and investments, to provide for your dependents.

| 8-4 | Discuss some benefits of life insurance in addition to protecting family members financially after the primary wage earner's death. |
| 8-5 | Explain the circumstances under which a single college graduate would or would not need life insurance. What life-cycle events would change this initial evaluation, and how might they affect his or her life insurance needs? |

LG3 · HOW MUCH LIFE INSURANCE IS RIGHT FOR YOU?

After deciding that life insurance makes sense for your particular situation, you'll need to make more decisions to find the life insurance product that best fits your needs. First, you must determine how much life insurance you need for adequate coverage. Buying too much life insurance can be costly; buying too little may prove disastrous. To avoid these problems, you can use one of two methods to estimate how much insurance is necessary: the *multiple-of-earnings method* and the *needs analysis method*.

The **multiple-of-earnings method** takes your gross annual earnings and multiplies it by some selected (often arbitrary) number to arrive at an estimate of adequate life insurance coverage. The rule of thumb used by many insurance agents is that your insurance coverage should be equal to 5 to 10 times your current income. For example, if you currently earn $70,000 a year, using the multiple-of-earnings method you'd need between $350,000 and $700,000 worth of life insurance. Although simple to use, the multiple-of-earnings method fails to fully recognize the financial obligations and resources of the individual and his or her family. Therefore, the multiple-of-earnings method should be used only to roughly approximate life insurance needs.

A more detailed approach is the **needs analysis method.** The needs analysis method considers both the financial obligations and financial resources of the insured and his or her dependents. This method involves three steps, as shown in Exhibit 8.1:
1. Estimate the total economic resources needed if the individual were to die.
2. Determine all financial resources that would be available after death, including existing life insurance and pension plan death benefits.
3. Subtract available resources from the amount needed to calculate how much additional life insurance is required.

Step 1: Assess Your Family's Total Economic Needs

The first question the needs analysis method asks is: *What financial resources will my survivors need should I die tomorrow?* You should consider the following five items in answering this question:
1. **Income needed to maintain an adequate lifestyle.** If you died, how much money would your dependents need each month in order to live a comfortable life? Estimate this amount by looking at your family's current monthly budget, including expenses for housing costs, utilities, food, clothing, and medical and dental needs. Other expenses to consider include property taxes, insurance, recreation and travel, and savings. Try to take into account that the amount needed may change over time. For example, once children are grown, monthly household expenses should decrease substantially, but the surviving spouse may still need monthly support. Therefore, the survivor's life expectancy and the income required may also need to be considered.
2. **Extra expenses if the income producer dies.** These expenses include funeral costs and any expenses that might be incurred to replace services you currently provide. For example, a mother who doesn't work outside of the home still provides childcare, cooking, cleaning, and other services. If she were to die or have to return to work, these services might have to be replaced using the family's income. Because

multiple-of-earnings method A method of determining the amount of life insurance coverage needed by multiplying gross annual earnings by some selected number.

needs analysis method A method of determining the amount of life insurance coverage needed by considering a person's financial obligations and available financial resources *in addition to life insurance.*

EXHIBIT 8.1 How Much Life Insurance Do You Need?

The needs analysis method uses three steps to estimate life insurance needs.

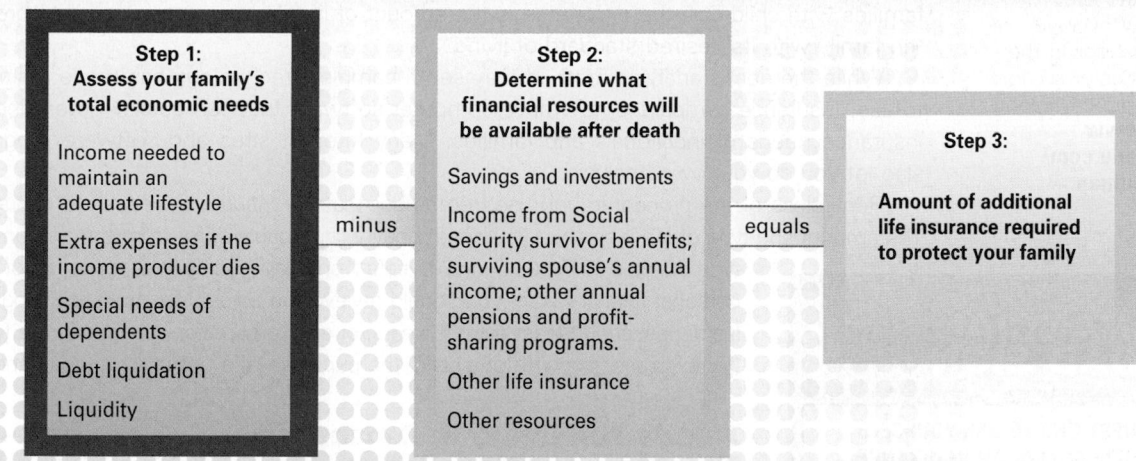

| Step 1:
Assess your family's total economic needs

Income needed to maintain an adequate lifestyle

Extra expenses if the income producer dies

Special needs of dependents

Debt liquidation

Liquidity | minus | Step 2:
Determine what financial resources will be available after death

Savings and investments

Income from Social Security survivor benefits; surviving spouse's annual income; other annual pensions and profit-sharing programs.

Other life insurance

Other resources | equals | Step 3:

Amount of additional life insurance required to protect your family |

such expenses can stretch a family budget to the breaking point, include them when you're estimating insurance needs.

3. **Special needs of dependents.** In addition to daily economic needs, you may want to provide for special needs of your dependents. These needs might include long-term nursing care for a disabled or chronically ill dependent, an emergency fund for unexpected financial burdens, or a college education fund for your children.

4. **Debt liquidation.** In the event of their death, most breadwinners prefer to leave their families relatively debt free. To accomplish this, it's necessary to calculate the average amount due for outstanding bills. This amount would include the balances on credit cards, department store accounts, and other similar obligations. In addition, some will want to leave enough money to allow their dependents to pay off the home mortgage.

5. **Liquidity.** After your death, it may take time for your dependents to be able to sell noncash assets. Real estate, for example, is difficult to convert to cash quickly. If a high percentage of your wealth is in nonliquid assets, the cash proceeds from life insurance can be used to pay the bills and maintain assets until they can be sold at a fair market value.

Step 2: Determine What Financial Resources Will Be Available after Death

After estimating the lifetime financial needs of dependents, the next step is to list all current resources that will be available for meeting those needs. For most families, money from savings, investments, and Social Security survivor's benefits make up the largest non-life-insurance financial resources. Additional resources include proceeds from employer-sponsored group life insurance policies and the death benefits payable from accumulated pension plans and profit-sharing programs. Another important source is income that can be earned by the surviving spouse or children. If the surviving spouse is skilled and readily employable, his or her earnings could be a family's largest available resource. Many families have real estate (in addition to their homes), jewelry, stocks, bonds, and other assets that can be liquidated to meet financial needs. After developing a complete list of available resources, you should make some reasonable estimate of their value. Although this step can be difficult due to the changing values of many assets, coming up with a set of reasonably accurate estimates is certainly within reach.

Estimate the amount of
life insurance your family
needs for financial secu-
rity with the Life
Insurance Coverage
Needs Analyzer in the
Learning Center section
their website by linking
to **http://www
.thomsonedu.com/
finance/gitman.**

Step 3: Subtract Resources from Needs to Calculate How Much Life Insurance You Require

Finally, subtract the total available resources from the total needed to satisfy all of the fam-ily's financial objectives. If available resources are greater than needs, no additional life insurance is required. If the resources are less than the needs—as is the case in most families with children—the difference is the amount of life insurance necessary to provide the family with its desired standard of living.

While the needs analysis method may seem complex, technology has made it simpler to use. Insurance companies now have computer software that can quickly determine the insurance needs of individuals and families. Many Internet sites and software programs also let you do your own analysis.

Regardless of the procedure you use, remember that *life insurance needs are not static.* The amount and type of life insurance you need today will probably differ from the amount and type suitable for you 10 or 20 years from now. As with other areas of your personal financial plan, you should review and adjust life insurance programs (as necessary) at least every 5 years, or after any major changes in the family (for example, the birth of a child, the purchase of a home, or a job change).

FINANCIAL ROAD SIGN

5 QUESTIONS TO ASK YOURSELF BEFORE BUYING AN INSURANCE POLICY

1. Am I sure that buying this policy is a necessary addition to my financial plan?
2. Have I compared the features of sev-eral policies?
3. Do I fully understand the policy I'm considering, including fees and poten-tial penalty costs?
4. Do I feel comfortable with the com-pany, agent, and product?
5. Have I reviewed the financial stability of the insurance company?

Needs Analysis in Action: The Benson Family

Let's take a closer look at how the needs analysis method works by con-sidering the hypothetical case of Bill and Joan Benson. Bill Benson is 37 and the primary breadwinner in the family; current earnings are $85,000. Bill and his wife Joan want to be sure that his life insurance policy will provide enough proceeds to take care of Joan and their two children, ages 6 and 8, if he should die. You can follow their analysis of needs and resources in Worksheet 8.1.

Financial Resources Needed after Death (Step 1)

Bill and Joan Benson review their budget and decide that monthly living expenses for Joan and the two children would be about $3,500 in current dollars while the children are still living at home, or $42,000 annually. After both children leave home, Joan, now 35, will need a monthly income of $3,000—or $36,000 a year—until she retires at age 65. At that point, the Bensons estimate Joan's living expenses would fall to $2,750 a month, or $33,000 annually. The life expectancy of a woman Joan's age is 87 years, so the Bensons calculate that Joan will spend about 22 years in retirement. Therefore, as shown in the first section of the worksheet, the total income necessary for the Bensons' living expenses over the next 52 years is $1,878,000.

Although Joan previously worked as a stockbroker, they planned for her to stay home until the children graduated from high school. The Bensons are concerned that her previous education may be somewhat outdated at that point, so they include $25,000 for Joan to update her education and skills. Bill and Joan also want to fund their children's college educa-tions. After researching the current cost of their state's pub-lic university, they decide to establish a college fund of $75,000 for this purpose. Last, they estimate final expenses of $15,000.

The Bensons use credit sparingly, so their outstanding debts are limited to a mortgage (with a current balance of $150,000), an automobile loan ($4,000), and miscellaneous charge accounts ($1,000). Bill and Joan, therefore, estimate that $155,000 would pay off all of their existing debts.

All of these estimates are shown in the top half of Bill and Joan's insurance calculations in Worksheet 8.1. Note that $2,148,000 is the total amount they estimate will be necessary to meet their financial goals if Bill were to die.

© STONE/GETTY IMAGES

LIFE INSURANCE NEEDS ANALYSIS METHOD

Insured's Name *Bill and Joan Benson* **Date** *April 12, 2008*

Step 1: Financial resources needed after death

1. Annual living expenses and other needs:

		Period 1	Period 2	Period 3	
a.	Monthly living expenses	$3,500	$3,000	$2,750	
b.	Net yearly income needed (a × 12)	$42,000	$36,000	$33,000	
c.	Number of years in time period	12	18	22	
d.	Total living need per time period (b × c)	$504,000	$648,000	$726,000	
TOTAL LIVING EXPENSES (add line d for each period):					$1,878,000

2. Special needs

a.	Spouse education fund	$25,000
b.	Children's college fund	$75,000
c.	Other needs	0
3. Final expenses (funeral, estate costs, etc.)		$15,000

4. Debt liquidation

a.	House mortgage	$150,000			
b.	Other loans	5,000			
c.	Total debt (4 a + 4 b)				$155,000
5. Other financial needs					0
TOTAL FINANCIAL RESOURCES NEEDED (add right column)					$2,148,000

Step 2: Financial resources available after death

1. Income

		Period 1	Period 2	Period 3	
a.	Annual Social Security survivor benefits	$38,400	0	0	
b.	Surviving spouse's annual income	0	$35,000	0	
c.	Other annual pensions and Social Security benefits	0	0	$27,000	
b.	Annual income	$38,400	$35,000	$27,000	
e.	Number of years in time period	12	18	22	
f.	Total period income (d × e)	$460,800	$630,000	$594,000	
g. TOTAL INCOME					$1,684,800
2.	Savings and investments				$65,000
3.	Other life insurance				$100,000
4.	Other resources				0
TOTAL FINANCIAL RESOURCES AVAILABLE (1g + 2 + 3 + 4)					$1,849,800

Step 3: Additional Life Insurance needed

Step 1: Total financial resources needed	$2,148,000
Step 2: Total financial resources available	$1,849,800
ADDITIONAL LIFE INSURANCE NEEDED	$298,200

Financial Resources Available after Death (Step 2)

If Bill died, Joan would be eligible to receive **Social Security survivor's benefits** for both herself and her children. Social Security survivor benefits are intended to provide basic, minimum support to families faced with the loss of their principal wage earner. The benefits are paid to unmarried children until age 18 (or 19 if they are still in high school) and nonworking surviving spouses until their children reach age 16. The surviving spouse will also receive individual survivor benefits upon turning 65. Limits are placed on the total amount of survivor's benefits that can be paid to a household, and if the surviving spouse returns to work, the amount of benefits will be reduced if earnings exceed certain limits. We'll discuss Social Security and its benefits in more detail in Chapter 14.

Joan and Bill visit the Social Security Administration's Web site for an estimate of the survivor benefits Joan will receive. Based on the number of years Bill has worked, his income, and the number of children they have, the Bensons estimate that Joan will receive approximately $3,200 a month, or $38,400 a year, in Social Security survivor benefits for herself and the children until the youngest child graduates from high school in 12 years.

In the 18 years between the time the children leave home and Joan retires, the Bensons expect Joan to be employed full-time and earn about $35,000 after taxes. After Joan turns 65, she'll receive approximately $2,250 a month ($27,000 a year) from Bill's survivor's benefits, her own Social Security benefits, and her own retirement benefits.

Joan will have some other resources available if Bill should die, however. The couple has saved $65,000 in a mutual fund, and Bill's employer provides a $100,000 life insurance policy for him. Adding these amounts to Joan's expected income means she'll have $1,849,800 in total resources available.

Additional Life Insurance Needed (Step 3)

How much life insurance should the Bensons buy for Bill in order to be sure Joan and the children will be adequately cared for? To find out, the Bensons subtract the total financial resources available—$1,849,800—from the total financial resources needed—$2,148,000. The difference is $298,200. So the additional life insurance Bill should buy to protect his family is about $300,000.

Of course, Bill and Joan will need to examine their insurance situation periodically as their children grow and the family's financial circumstances change. But, for now, they feel satisfied that they have a good estimate of the amount of additional life insurance they need to buy for Bill. They can now begin to consider which type of policy is best.

Life Insurance Underwriting Considerations

As we discussed earlier, insurance companies use a process called underwriting to determine whom they will insure and what they will charge for insurance coverage. Underwriting policies are particularly important to understand when choosing life insurance products, so let's briefly examine some of the factors life insurance underwriters consider.

Life insurance underwriting begins by asking potential insureds to complete an application designed to gather information about their risk potential. In other words, underwriters consider the likelihood that the insured will die while the life insurance policy is in effect. Underwriters use life expectancy figures to look at overall longevity for various age groups. They also consider specific factors related to the applicant's health. Someone who smokes, is obese, has a history of heart disease, or has a dangerous job or hobby is considered a greater risk than someone who doesn't. An applicant who has been charged with driving under the influence of drugs or alcohol or has had their driver's license suspended may also have higher risk factors.

All these factors are then used to determine whether to accept you and, based on your risk factors, what premium to charge. For example, someone in excellent health is usually considered "preferred" and pays the lowest premium. Other typical categories include standard, preferred smoker, and smoker. Those with special medical conditions— high cholesterol or diabetes, for example—fall into rated categories and pay considerably higher premiums if they're accepted.

Social Security survivor's benefits Benefits under Social Security intended to provide basic, minimum support to families faced with loss of their principal wage earners.

The bottom line: if you have any of the risks commonly considered in life insurance underwriting—such as obesity, heart disease, or a high-risk hobby or job—it's important to shop carefully and compare the cost implications of different types of insurance policies and the underwriting standards used by different companies.

❚❚ Concept Check

8-6	Discuss the two most commonly used ways to determine a person's life insurance needs.
8-7	Name and explain the most common financial resources needed after the death of a family breadwinner.
8-8	What are some factors underwriters consider when evaluating a life insurance application? Which, if any, apply to you or your family members?

LG4 WHAT KIND OF POLICY IS RIGHT FOR YOU?

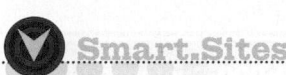
Smart Sites

At the site for the nonprofit Life and Health Insurance Foundation for Education, an insurance education organization, you'll find information to help you sort out your life insurance options. Link to them at **http://www.thomsonedu.com/finance/gitman.**

After determining the amount of life insurance you need to cover your family's financial requirements and considering how various underwriting policies might affect you, your next step is to decide on the type of insurance policy. Although a variety of life insurance products are available, three major types account for 90 to 95 percent of life insurance sales: term life, whole life, and universal life.

Term Life Insurance

Term life insurance is the simplest type of insurance policy. You purchase a specified amount of insurance protection for a set period. If you die during that time, your beneficiaries will receive the full amount specified in your policy. Term insurance can be bought for many different time increments, such as 5 years, 10 years, even 30 years. Depending on the policy, premiums can be paid annually, semiannually, or quarterly.

Types of Term Insurance

The most common types of term insurance are straight (or level) term and decreasing term.

Straight Term. A straight term life insurance policy is written for a set number of years, during which time the amount of life insurance coverage remains unchanged. The *annual premium* on a **straight term policy** may increase each year, as with *annual renewable term policies,* or remain level throughout the policy period, as with *level premium term policies.*

Exhibits 8.2 and 8.3 on page 250 list representative annual premiums for annual renewable term and level premium term life policies, respectively. (*Note*: The premiums are for nonsmokers; clearly, rates for similar smoker policies would be higher given the greater risk and generally shorter life expectancies of smokers than nonsmokers.) Until recently, annual renewable term premiums were less expensive in the early years but increased rapidly over time. These policies, however, aren't popular today. Because people now live longer, the rates for level premium term have fallen sharply and are well below those on annual renewable term from year 1 on, so they're a better value.

Decreasing Term. Because the death rate increases with each year of life, the premiums on annual renewable straight term policies for each successive period of coverage will also increase. As an alternative, some term policies *maintain a level premium* throughout all periods of coverage, but *the amount of protection decreases*. Such a policy is called a **decreasing term policy** because the amount of protection decreases over its life.

term life insurance
Insurance that provides only death benefits, for a specified period, and does not provide for the accumulation of cash value.

straight term policy A term insurance policy written for a given number of years, with coverage remaining unchanged throughout the effective period.

decreasing term policy
A term insurance policy that *maintains a level premium* throughout all periods of coverage, but *the amount of protection decreases*.

EXHIBIT 8.2

**Representative Annual Renewable Term Life Insurance Premiums:
$100,000 Policy, Preferred Nonsmoker Rates**

When you buy term life insurance, you're basically buying a product that provides life insurance coverage and nothing more. This table shows representative rates for several age categories and selected policy years; actual premiums increase every year. As you can see, females pay less than males for coverage, and premiums increase sharply with age.

Policy Year	AGE 25 Male	AGE 25 Female	AGE 40 Male	AGE 40 Female	AGE 60 Male	AGE 60 Female
1	$ 130	$ 119	$ 148	$ 139	$ 366	$ 252
5	$ 169	$ 147	$ 252	$ 219	$ 927	$ 562
10	$ 218	$ 187	$ 426	$ 368	$ 1,702	$ 1,080
15	$ 196	$ 176	$ 647	$ 507	$ 2,666	$ 1,313
20	$ 279	$ 259	$1,258	$1,054	$ 4,574	$ 2,989
Total Cost, 20 years	$3,777	$3,381	$9,871	$8,287	$38,457	$22,346

EXHIBIT 8.3

**Representative Level Premium Term Life Rates: $100,000 Preferred
Nonsmoker Policy**

This table shows annual, representative premiums for $100,000 of level premium term life insurance. Although level premium costs less than annual renewable term for the same period, you must requalify at the end of each term to retain the low premium.

Age	5 YEAR Male/Female	10 YEAR Male/Female	15 YEAR Male/Female	20 YEAR Male/Female
25	$102/$102	$81/$75	$89/$84	$103/$95
35	$102/$101	$81/$75	$90/$84	$103/$95
40	$121/$119	$96/$89	$111/$102	$132/$113
50	$176/$136	$183/$142	$237/$167	$259/$195
60	$358/$245	$380/$259	$475/$295	$555/$394

Decreasing term is used when the amount of needed coverage declines over time. For example, decreasing term policies are popular with homeowners who want a level of life insurance coverage that will decline at about the same rate as the balances on their home mortgages. Families with young children use these policies to ensure a sufficient level of family income while the kids are growing up. As they grow older, the amount of coverage needed decreases until the last child becomes independent and the need expires.

Again, remember that the type and length of term policy you choose affects the amount of premiums you'll pay over time. For a given person, the annual premium for a specified initial amount of coverage, say $250,000, would be lowest for straight term, higher for decreasing term, and highest for annual renewable term. The only reason that the premium on decreasing term is higher than the premium on straight term is that most major insurance companies don't offer decreasing term policies, so the small number of companies offering these policies operate in a less competitive market that allows them to charge high premiums. Of course, the death benefit on the decreasing term policy will by design decline during the policy's term.

Advantages and Disadvantages of Term Life

One of the biggest advantages of term life is cost. Term life usually offers lower initial premiums than other types of insurance, especially for younger people. Term life is an economical way to buy a large amount of life insurance protection over a given, relatively short period, making it particularly advantageous for covering needs that will disappear over time. For example, a family with young children can use term insurance to provide coverage until the children are grown.

The main disadvantage, however, is that term insurance offers only temporary coverage. Once the policy term expires, you must renew the policy. This can be a problem if you develop underwriting factors in the future that make it difficult to qualify for insurance.

However, some term life policies overcome part of this drawback by offering a **renewability** provision that gives you the option of renewing your policy at the end of its term without having to show evidence of insurability. A guaranteed renewable provision allows you to renew the policy even if you have become uninsurable due to an accident or other illness during the original policy period. Generally, term policies are renewable at the end of each term until the insured reaches age 65 or 70. However, the premium will still increase to reflect the greater chance of death at older ages.

Another option that can help overcome some of the limitations of term insurance is a **convertibility** provision. This lets you convert your term insurance policy to a comparable whole life policy at a future time. A whole life policy, as we'll discuss next, provides lifelong protection, eliminating the need to continually renew your life insurance. Convertibility is particularly useful if you need a large amount of relatively low-cost, short-term protection immediately but in the future expect to have greater income that will allow you to purchase permanent insurance. Convertibility options are standard on most term policies today, but many place specific limits on when the conversion can take place.

One way to overcome the drawback of having to pay increased premiums at the end of each term is to purchase a longer term policy. Recently, the insurance industry has started offering 30-year straight term policies that lock in a set premium. For example, a 35-year-old man who qualifies for preferred rates could lock in a $250,000 death benefit for 30 years in a row and pay only a set premium of $360 a year. As with all insurance policies, however, before signing up make sure that the rate is fully locked in for the duration of the policy.

Who Should Buy Term Insurance?

For most young families on limited budgets, the need for death protection greatly exceeds their need to save. If you fall into this category, guaranteed renewable and convertible term insurance should account for the largest portion of your insurance protection. These policies provide the most life insurance coverage for the least cost, thereby preserving financial resources for meeting immediate and future consumption and savings goals. Healthy older people with many other financial resources may also prefer to use term policies to meet specific coverage needs.

Whole Life Insurance

Unlike term insurance, which offers financial protection for only a certain period, **whole life insurance** is designed to provide ongoing insurance coverage during an individual's entire life. In other words, it's considered a permanent insurance product. In addition to death protection, whole life insurance has a *savings* feature, called **cash value,** that results from the investment earnings on paid-in insurance premiums. Thus, *whole life provides not only insurance coverage but also a modest return on your investment*. The idea behind cash value is to provide the insurance buyer with a tangible return while he or she also receives insurance coverage—the savings rates on whole life policies are normally *fixed* and *guaranteed* to be more than a certain rate (say, 4 to 6 percent). Exhibit 8.4 on page 252 illustrates how the cash value in a whole life policy builds up over time. Obviously, the longer the insured keeps the policy in force, the greater the cash value. Whole life can be purchased through several different payment plans, including continuous premium, limited payment, and single premium, all providing for accumulation of cash values.

The cash value of a policy increases over time to reflect the greater chance of death that comes with age. If policyholders cancel their contracts prior to death, that portion of the assets set aside to provide payment for the death claim is available to them. This right to a cash value is termed the policyholder's **nonforfeiture right.** Policyholders, by

---

renewability A term life policy provision allowing the insured to renew his or her policy at the end of its term without having to show evidence of insurability.

convertibility A term life policy provision allowing the insured to convert the policy to a comparable whole life policy.

whole life insurance Life insurance designed to offer ongoing insurance coverage over the course of an insured's entire life.

cash value The accumulated refundable value of an insurance policy; results from the investment earnings on paid-in insurance premiums.

nonforfeiture right A life insurance feature giving the whole life policyholder, on policy cancellation, the portion of those assets that were set aside to provide payment for the future death claim.

Here is an example of the projected cash value for an actual $200,000 whole life policy issued by a major life insurer to a male, age 30. For *each year* of the illustration, the difference between the $200,000 death benefit and the projected cash value represents the *death protection* offered by the insurer.

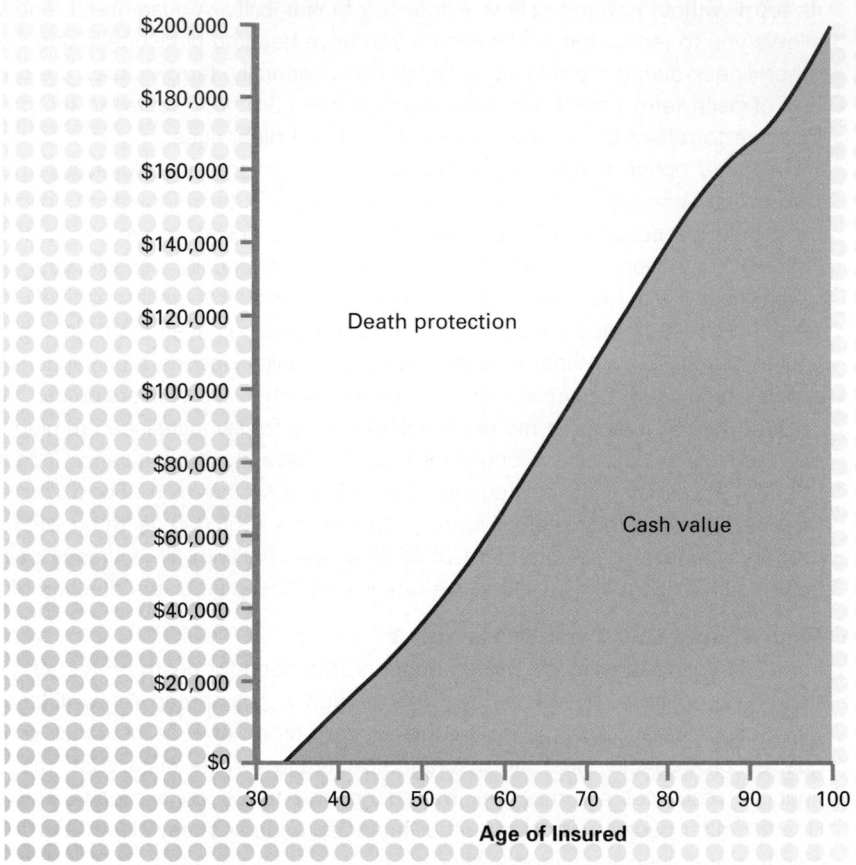

terminating their insurance contracts, forfeit their rights to death benefits. Likewise, the company must forfeit its right to keep all the monies paid by these policyholders for the future death benefit it is no longer required to pay.

Types of Whole Life Policies

Three major types of whole life policies are available: continuous premium, limited payment, and single premium. To get a feel for the costs of these policies, look at the representative rates shown in Exhibit 8.5.

Continuous Premium. Under a *continuous premium whole life* policy, or *straight life,* as it's more commonly called, individuals pay a level premium each year until they either die or exercise a nonforfeiture right. The earlier in life the coverage is purchased, the lower the annual premium. Life insurance agents often use this as a selling point to convince younger people to buy now. Their argument is that the sooner you buy, the less you pay *annually.* Of course, the sooner people purchase whole life, the longer they have coverage in force, but (all other things being equal) the *more* they pay in total. There are good reasons (such as securing needed protection, savings, and insurability) for many young people to buy whole life, but it should seldom be purchased by anyone simply because the annual premium will be lower now than if it's purchased later.

EXHIBIT 8.5 | Representative Whole Life Insurance Annual Premiums: $100,000 Policy, Preferred Nonsmoker Rates

As with any life insurance product, the older you are, the more expensive it is to buy whole life. Also, whole life is more costly than term because you're getting an investment/savings account, represented by the cash value column, in addition to life insurance coverage. Of course, the actual amount of cash value will depend on the actual dividend rate, which is subject to change (up or down) based on current market conditions.

	ANNUAL PREMIUM		PREMIUMS PAID THROUGH YEAR 20		TOTAL CASH VALUE AT YEAR 20*
Age	Male	Female	Male	Female	Male/Female
25	$ 988	$ 941	$19,760	$18,820	$ 30,894
30	$1,233	$1,188	$24,460	$23,760	$ 38,971
35	$1,473	$1,438	$29,460	$28,760	$ 46,223
40	$1,833	$1,788	$36,660	$35,760	$ 55,980
50	$2,816	$2,666	$55,425	$52,425	$ 76,225
60	$4,291	$3,899	$85,820	$77,980	$112,765

*Guaranteed cash value plus annual dividends at the assumed annual rate of 6.8 percent.

FINANCIAL ROAD SIGN

DOES INSURANCE COMPANY OWNERSHIP STRUCTURE AFFECT PREMIUMS?

Significant differences in insurance policy premiums can result, depending on the ownership structure of the life insurance company. Companies can be either **mutual companies** in which the policyholders effectively own the company or **stock companies** in which shareholders, who may or may not own policies, own the company.

- In a well-managed *mutual company*, like Northwestern Mutual, policyholders receive periodic dividends that either reduce premiums or pay them income.
- In a *stock company*, such as AIG, any dividends paid go directly to the shareholders.

Because of their differing ownership structures, **the stated premium for a stock company insurance policy should be lower than the stated premium on a comparable policy issued by a mutual company.**

Of the various whole life policies available, continuous premium/straight life offers the greatest amount of permanent death protection and the least amount of savings per premium dollar. This emphasis on *death protection* makes it the wisest choice to fill a permanent life insurance need.

Limited Payment. With a *limited payment whole life* policy, you're covered for your entire life but the premium payment is based on a specified period—for example, 20-pay life and 30-pay life require level premium payments for a period of 20 or 30 years. For stipulated age policies such as those paid up at age 55 or 65, you pay premiums until you reach the stated age. In all of these cases, on completion of the scheduled payments, *the insurance remains in force at its face value for the rest of the insured's life.*

Some insurance companies try to convince consumers to buy limited payment policies by stressing the "large" savings element that will develop and the fact that the policyholder won't have to pay premiums for his or her entire life. This logic fails on two points. First, for most people the primary purpose of whole life insurance is permanent protection against financial loss resulting from death, not the accumulation of savings. Second, even if people buy continuous premium whole life (straight life) policies, they need to pay the premium only as long as they wish to keep the policies in force for their full face value. If lifelong death protection is the primary aim of the life insurance policy, the insured should purchase continuous premium whole life instead of a limited payment policy. Because more continuous premium whole life insurance can be purchased with the same number of dollars as limited payment whole life, people who need whole life insurance are probably better off using straight life insurance to get the most from their life insurance dollars. Then, once their insurance needs are reduced, they can convert the policy to a smaller amount of paid-up life insurance. On the other hand, if people have life insurance already in force that is sufficient to protect against income loss, they can use limited payment policies as part of their savings or retirement plans.

Single Premium. Continuous premium and limited payment whole life policies represent methods of acquiring life insurance on an installment basis. In contrast, a *single premium whole life* policy is purchased with one cash premium payment at the inception of the contract, thus buying life insurance coverage for the rest of your life. The single premium policy has only limited usefulness in the life insurance programs of most families. However, because of its investment attributes, single premium life insurance, or *SPLI* for short, appeals to those looking for a *tax-sheltered investment vehicle.* Like any whole life insurance policy, interest/investment earnings within the policy are tax deferred. There is a catch, however: any cash withdrawals or loans taken against the SPLI cash value before you reach age 59$^1/_2$ are not only taxed as capital gains but also subject to the 10 percent penalty for early withdrawal.

Advantages and Disadvantages of Whole Life

The most noteworthy advantage of whole life insurance is that premium payments contribute toward building an estate, regardless of how long the insured lives. The face value of the policy is paid on death, or alternately the insured can borrow against it or withdraw cash value—which can be significant, as the final column of Exhibit 8.5 shows—when the need for insurance protection has expired.

A corresponding benefit of whole life (except SPLI) is that individuals who need insurance for an entire lifetime can budget their premium payments over a relatively long period, thus eliminating the problems of affordability and uninsurability often encountered with term insurance in later years.

Some people like whole life because the periodic payments force them to save regularly. There is also the favorable tax treatment afforded to accumulated earnings—because your earnings build up on a tax-sheltered basis, the underlying cash value of the policy also increases at a much faster rate than it otherwise would. Insurance experts also point out that the whole life policy offers other potentially valuable options in addition to death protection and cash value. Some of these options include the continuation of coverage after allowing the policy to lapse because premiums were not paid (nonforfeiture option) and the ability to revive an older, favorably priced policy that has lapsed (policy reinstatement). These and other options are discussed in a later section on life insurance contract features.

One disadvantage of whole life insurance is its cost. It provides less death protection per premium dollar than term insurance does. Contrast the premiums paid for various whole life products as shown with those paid for term insurance by comparing Exhibits 8.2, 8.3, and 8.5. You can readily see how much more expensive whole life is than term life. The reason for the difference? You pay extra for the savings/investment feature included with whole life.

Another frequently cited disadvantage of whole life is that it provides lower yields than many investment vehicles. Returns on most whole life insurance policies are just not very competitive. As with term insurance, the negative aspects of whole life often arise from misuse of the policy. In other words, a *whole life policy should not be used to obtain maximum return on investment.* However, if a person wishes to combine a given amount of death protection for the entire life of the insured (or until the policy is terminated) with a savings plan that provides a *moderate* tax-sheltered rate of return, whole life insurance may be a wise purchase.

One way to keep the cost of whole life down is to consider the purchase of *low-load* whole life insurance. Low-load products are sold directly by insurers to consumers, sometimes via a toll-free number or over the Internet, thereby eliminating sales agents from the transaction. With traditional whole life policies sold by an agent, sales commissions and marketing expenses account for between 100 and 150 percent of the first year's premium and between 20 and 25 percent of total premiums paid over the life of the policy. In comparison, only about 5 to 10 percent of low-load policy premiums go to cover selling and marketing expenses. As a result, cash values grow much more quickly. In one case a 50-year-old male was able to purchase a low-load policy with a $500,000 death benefit for an annual premium of $7,500. Within 5 years his cash surrender value was projected to be more than $36,000; a comparable, fully loaded policy was projected to produce only a $24,000 cash value.

Who Should Buy Whole Life Insurance?

Most families also need some amount of permanent insurance and savings, which a continuous premium whole life policy can satisfy. Some financial advisors recommend that you use cash value insurance to cover your *permanent need for insurance*—the amount your dependents will need regardless of the age at which you die. (Although term insurance is less expensive, you may not be able to buy term insurance as you get older, or it may be too expensive.) Such needs may include final expenses—funeral costs and estate taxes—and either the survivor's retirement need (Period 3 in Worksheet 8.1) or additional insurance coverage, whichever is less. This amount is different for every person. Using these guidelines, the Bensons in our earlier example would need about $147,000 in whole life insurance (in Worksheet 8.1: $15,000 final expenses [Step 1, line 3] plus about $132,000 of Period 3 living expenses [Step 1, line 1d for Period 3 minus Step 2, line 1f for Period 3, i.e., $726,000 − $594,000]) and about another $151,000 in term life (in Worksheet 8.1: about $298,000 [Step 3] minus about $147,000 permanent insurance calculated above). Limited payment whole life and single premium whole life policies should be purchased only when the primary goal is savings or additional tax-deferred investments and not protection against financial loss resulting from death.

Whole life may make sense in several other situations. For example, a family history of heart disease, cancer, or similar conditions may increase your risk of developing health problems and make it hard to qualify for term insurance at a later date. If you're already over 50, term life insurance may be too expensive. Or, perhaps you've "maxed out" your other tax-deferred savings options and want to buy cash value insurance to accumulate additional retirement funds.

Universal Life Insurance

Universal life insurance is another form of permanent cash value insurance that combines term insurance, which provides death benefits, with a tax-sheltered savings/investment account that pays interest, usually at competitive money market rates. The death protection (or pure insurance) portion and the savings portion are identified separately in its premium. This is referred to as *unbundling.* Exhibit 8.6 on page 256 shows representative annual outlays, premiums, and cash values for a $100,000 universal life policy.

Traditionally, for whole life insurance, you pay a premium to purchase a stated face amount of coverage in a policy with a *fixed cash-value schedule.* With universal life, part of your premium pays administrative fees, and the remainder is put into the cash value, or savings portion of the policy, where it earns a certain rate of return. This rate of earnings varies with market yields, but is guaranteed to be more than some stipulated minimum rate (say, 3 percent). Then, each month the cost of 1 month's term insurance is withdrawn from the cash value to purchase the required death protection. As long as there's enough in the savings portion to buy death protection, the policy will stay in force. Should the cash value grow to an unusually large amount, the amount of insurance coverage has to be increased in order for the policy to retain its favorable tax treatment (tax laws require that the death benefits in a universal life policy *must always exceed the cash value* by a stipulated amount).

The clear separation of the protection and savings elements in the universal policy has raised the question of whether this type of insurance is, in fact, whole life insurance. This question is important because the accumulation of cash values in whole life policies arises partly from interest credited to them. Under today's tax laws, *this accumulation occurs tax free as long as the cash value does not exceed the total premiums paid to the insurer.* But, if a whole life policy is surrendered for its cash value, and that cash value exceeds the premiums paid, then *the gain* is taxed. Due to an Internal Revenue Service ruling and federal legislation, universal life policies enjoy the same favorable tax treatment as do other forms of whole life insurance—that is, death benefits are tax-free and, prior to the insured's death, amounts credited to the cash value, including investment earnings, accumulate on a tax-deferred basis. The insurance company sends the insured an annual statement summarizing the monthly credits of interest and deductions of expenses.

universal life insurance
Permanent cash value insurance that combines term insurance (death benefits) with a tax-sheltered savings/investment account that pays interest, usually at competitive money market rates.

○○○○○○○○○○○

EXHIBIT 8.6 **Representative Universal Life Insurance Annual Outlays:**
$100,000 Policy, Preferred Nonsmoker Rates

Universal life premiums are lower than whole life and can vary over the policy's life. After deducting the cost of the death benefit and any administrative fees from your annual contribution, the rest goes into an accumulation account and builds at a variable rate—in this example, the current rate is 7.4 percent. The guaranteed rate, however, is only 4 percent, so your actual cash value may be less.

	ANNUAL OUTLAY		PREMIUMS PAID THROUGH YEAR 20		CASH SURRENDER VALUE AT YEAR 20*	
Age	Male	Female	Male	Female	Male	Female
25	$2,419	$2,358	$ 8,380	$ 7,160	$ 6,091	$ 5,048
30	$2,505	$2,425	$10,100	$ 8,500	$ 8,137	$ 6,176
35	$2,644	$2,534	$12,880	$10,680	$11,235	$ 8,453
40	$2,841	$2,682	$16,820	$13,640	$15,107	$11,399
50	$1,469	$1,146	$29,380	$22,920	$25,168	$20,074
60	$2,598	$1,992	$51,960	$39,840	$36,638	$32,633

*Based on an assumed annual rate of 7.4 percent.

A universal life insurance policy provides two types of death protection. The first type, known as Option A, provides a level death benefit. As the cash value increases, the amount of pure insurance protection *decreases*. The second type, Option B, provides a stated amount of insurance plus the accumulated cash value. Therefore, the death benefit at any time varies with the rate of earnings on the savings plan and will increase along with the accumulated cash value.

Advantages and Disadvantages of Universal Life

As with any insurance policy, universal life has its pros and cons. Among the advantages:

- **Flexibility.** The annual premium you pay can be increased or decreased from year to year, because the cost of the death protection *may be covered from either the annual premium or the accumulation account* (that is, cash value). If the accumulation account is adequate, you can use it to pay the annual premium. The death benefit also can be increased or decreased, and you can change from the level benefit type of policy to the cash value plus a stated amount of insurance. Note, however, that evidence of insurability is usually required if the death benefit is to be increased. This flexibility allows you to adapt the death benefit to your life-cycle needs—for example, increasing the death benefit when you have another child and decreasing it when your children are grown.

- **Savings feature.** A universal life insurance policy credits cash value at the "current" rate of interest. For example, the *current* rate of interest may be 4.5 percent, compared with a *guaranteed* minimum rate of 3 percent. Find out the benchmark used to determine the current rate of interest; the 90-day U.S. Treasury bill rate is often used.

Universal life's flexibility in making premium payments, although an attractive feature, is also one of its major drawbacks:

- **Changing premiums and protection levels.** A policyholder who economizes on premium payments in early years may find that he or she must pay higher premiums than originally planned in later policy years to keep the policy in force. Indeed, some policyholders buy universal life expecting their premiums to vanish once cash value builds to a certain level. All too often, however, the premiums never disappear altogether; or if they do, they reappear when interest rates fall below the rate in effect when the policy was purchased.

For more details about various life insurance products and policy types, turn to Insure.com's searchable database of over 3,000 articles on insurance topics by linking at **http://www.thomsonedu.com/finance/gitman.**

- **Charges or fees.** Universal life carries heavy fees compared to other policy types: the front-end load or commission on the first premium, the expense charge on each annual premium, investment expense charged by the insurer in determining the "current" rate of return, and other charges. Most states require the insurance company to issue an annual disclosure statement spelling out premiums paid, expenses and mortality costs, interest earned, and beginning and ending cash values.

Who Should Buy Universal Life Insurance?

Universal life is a suitable choice if you're looking for a savings vehicle with greater potential returns than a whole life policy offers. Its flexible nature makes it particularly useful for people who anticipate changes in their current need for death protection. For example, if you're recently married and expect to have children, a universal life policy will allow you to increase the death benefit as your family grows.

Other Types of Life Insurance

Besides term, whole life, and universal life, you can buy several other types of life insurance products, including variable life insurance, group life, and other special-purpose life policies such as credit life, mortgage life, and industrial life insurance. These insurance products serve diverse needs. Some may help you meet specific needs; others are simply alternatives to traditional types of life insurance.

Variable Life Insurance

Go to a variety of calculators and guides you can use to educate yourself about Prudential's life insurance products at **http://www.thomsonedu.com/finance/gitman.**

A **variable life insurance** policy goes further than whole and universal life policies in combining death benefits and savings. The policyholder decides how to invest the money in the savings (cash value) component. The investment accounts are set up just like *mutual funds,* and most firms that offer variable life policies let you choose from a full menu of different funds, ranging from money market accounts and bond funds to international investments or aggressively managed stock funds. Unlike whole or universal life policies, however, for variable life insurance *no minimum return is guaranteed.* Also, as the name implies, the amount of insurance coverage provided varies with the profits (and losses) generated in the investment account. Thus, in variable life insurance policies, the amount of death benefits payable is, for the most part, related to the policies' investment returns. Exhibit 8.7 on page 258 demonstrates how two possible investment return scenarios would affect the cash value and death benefits of a variable life insurance policy for a 45-year-old, nonsmoking male over a 20-year period.

Although all these features may sound great, it's important to know that variable life puts more emphasis on investments than any other life insurance product does. Indeed, many observers view variable life more as an investment vehicle than a life insurance policy—it's an investment product wrapped around just enough life insurance coverage to make it legal. If you want the benefits of higher investment returns, you must also be willing to assume the risks of reduced insurance coverage. Clearly, *you should use extreme care when buying variable life insurance.*

Group Life Insurance

Under **group life insurance,** one master policy is issued, and each eligible group member receives a certificate of insurance. Group life is nearly always term insurance, and the premium is based on the group's characteristics as a whole, rather than on those of any specific individual. Employers often provide group life insurance as a fringe benefit for their employees. However, just about any type of group (be it a labor union, a professional association, or an alumni organization) can secure a group life policy, as long as the insurance is only incidental to the reason for the group.

Accounting for about one-third of all life insurance in the United States, group life insurance is one of the fastest-growing areas of insurance. Many group life policies now offer coverage for dependents as well as group members. What's more, group life policies generally provide that if individual members leave the group, they may continue the coverage by converting their protection to individually issued whole life policies—and conversion normally doesn't require evidence of insurability, as long as it occurs within a specified period.

variable life insurance Life insurance in which the benefits are related to the returns being generated on the investments selected by the policyholder.

group life insurance Life insurance that provides a master policy for a group; each eligible group member receives a certificate of insurance.

Variable life insurance pays a death benefit related to the policy's investment returns. The cash value created over the life of the policy is also related to investment return. This table shows the effects of 6 percent and 12 percent annual returns over a 20-year period. Lower returns result in lower cash value and death benefits; higher returns result in higher cash value and death benefits.

Policy Year	Total Premiums Paid	6% RETURN		12% RETURN	
		Cash Value	Death Benefit	Cash Value	Death Benefit
1	$ 1,575	$ 995	$100,995	$ 1,064	$101,064
5	$ 8,705	$ 5,244	$105,244	$ 5,705	$105,705
10	$19,810	$10,592	$110,592	$15,365	$115,365
15	$33,986	$15,093	$115,093	$27,688	$127,688
20	$52,079	$17,080	$117,080	$43,912	$143,912

Of course, after conversion, the individual pays all premiums. Before buying additional coverage purchased through a group plan or converting a group policy to an individual one, it's important to compare rates. Often the premiums are more expensive than other readily available sources of term insurance.

As we noted in Chapters 1 and 2, availability of group coverage through employee benefit programs should be considered when developing a life insurance program. However, because of its potentially temporary nature and relatively low benefit amount (often equal to about 1 year's salary), it should fulfill only low-priority insurance needs. Only in rare cases should a family rely solely on group life insurance to fulfill its primary income-protection requirements.

Other Special-Purpose Life Policies

Use caution before buying one of these types of life insurance:

- **Credit life insurance.** Banks, finance companies, and other lenders generally sell **credit life insurance** in conjunction with installment loans. Usually credit life is a term policy of less than 5 years, with a face value corresponding to the outstanding balance on the loan. Although liquidating debts on the death of a family breadwinner is often desirable, it's usually preferable to do so through an individual's term or whole life insurance rather than buying a separate credit life insurance policy. This is because credit life is one of the most expensive forms of life insurance—and one you should therefore avoid.

- **Mortgage life insurance. Mortgage life insurance** is a term policy designed to pay off the mortgage balance on a home in the event of the borrower's death. As in the case of credit life, this need can usually be met less expensively by shopping the market for a suitable decreasing term policy.

- **Industrial life insurance.** Sometimes called **home service life insurance,** this whole life insurance is issued in policies with small face amounts, often $1,000 or less. Agents call on policyholders weekly or monthly to collect the premiums. The term *industrial* became popular when the policies were first sold primarily to low-paid industrial wage earners. Industrial life insurance costs a good deal more per $1,000 of coverage than regular whole life policies, primarily because of its high marketing costs. Even so, some insurance authorities believe that industrial life insurance offers the only practical way to deliver coverage to low-income families.

credit life insurance Life insurance sold in conjunction with installment loans.

mortgage life insurance A term policy designed to pay off the mortgage balance in the event of the borrower's death.

industrial life insurance (home service life insurance) Whole life insurance issued in policies with relatively small face amounts, often $1,000 or less.

Ⅱ Concept Check

8-9	What is *term life insurance?* Describe some common types of term life insurance policies.
8-10	What are the advantages and disadvantages of term life insurance?
8-11	Explain how *whole life insurance* offers financial protection to an individual throughout his or her life.
8-12	Describe the different types of whole life policies. What are the advantages and disadvantages of whole life insurance?
8-13	What is *universal life insurance?* Explain how it differs from whole life and *variable life insurance.*
8-14	Explain how *group life insurance* differs from standard term life insurance. What do employees stand to gain from group life?
8-15	Why should the following types of life insurance contracts be avoided? (a) *credit life insurance,* (b) *mortgage life insurance,* (c) *industrial life insurance (home service life insurance).*

LG5 · BUYING LIFE INSURANCE

Once you've evaluated your personal financial needs and become familiar with the basic life insurance options, you're ready to begin shopping for a life insurance policy. Exhibit 8.8 on page 260 summarizes the major advantages and disadvantages of the most popular types of life insurance we've discussed in this chapter.

Several factors should be considered in making the final purchase decision: (1) comparing the costs and features of competitive products, (2) selecting a financially healthy insurance company, and (3) choosing a good agent.

Compare Costs and Features

The cost of a life insurance policy can vary considerably from company to company, even for the same amount and type of coverage. By comparison shopping, you can save thousands of dollars over the life of your policy. For example, the total cost for a 10-year, $250,000, term life policy at preferred rates for a 25-year-old can range from $1,170 to over $2,000. Exhibit 8.9 on page 261 gives a quick overview of differences in the key features of various types of life insurance.

If you smoke or have a health problem, such as high cholesterol or high blood pressure, spending time to check out several companies can really pay off. Some companies are more willing to accept these risks than others are. They may even give you preferred rates if, within a certain period, you correct the problem. But, until you do your homework, you won't know which policy offers you the coverage you need at the lowest cost. If you have an unusual health problem or some other type of complication, an agent-sold policy may actually be cheaper than the low-cost alternatives.

It's not enough, however, to look only at current rates. You'll also need to ask how long the rates are locked in and find out about guaranteed rates—the maximum you can be charged when you renew. A guaranteed policy may cost another $20 a year, but you won't be hit with unexpected rate increases later. Know how long you need the coverage, and find the best rates for the total period; low premiums for a 5-year policy may jump when you renew for additional coverage. Also be sure you're getting the features you need, like the convertibility of term policies.

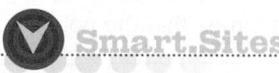

Smart.Sites

Discover how easy it is to get quotes on term life policies at QuickQuote's life insurance resource center—go to **http://www.thomsonedu.com/finance/gitman.**

Major advantages and disadvantages of the most popular types of life insurance are summarized here. They should be considered when shopping for life insurance.

Type of Policy	Advantages	Disadvantages
Term	Low initial premiums Simple, easy to buy	Provides only temporary coverage for a set period May have to pay higher premiums when policy is renewed
Whole life	Permanent coverage Savings vehicle: cash value builds as premiums are paid Some tax advantages on accumulated earnings	Cost: provides less death protection per premium dollar than term Often provides lower yields than other investment vehicles Sales commissions and marketing expenses can increase costs of fully loaded policy
Universal life	Permanent coverage Flexible: lets insured adapt level of protection and cost of premiums Savings vehicle: cash value builds at current rate of interest Savings and death protection identified separately	Can be difficult to evaluate true cost at time of purchase; insurance carrier may levy costly fees and charges
Variable life	Investment vehicle: insured decides how cash value will be invested	Higher risk

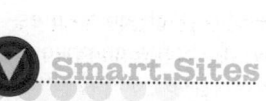

How satisfied are the customers of your prospective insurance company? The National Association of Insurance Commissioners site lets you see how many consumer complaints have been filed against each company. Link to them at **http://www .thomsonedu.com/ finance/gitman.**

Finally, be sure the policies you are comparing *have similar provisions and amounts.* In other words, don't compare a $100,000 term life policy from one company with a $150,000 universal life policy from another. Instead, *first decide how much and what kind of policy you want and then compare costs.* For similar cash value policies, you may find it useful to compare interest-adjusted cost indexes that are often shown on policy illustrations. The *surrender cost index* measures the policy's cost if you surrender it at a certain point, typically 10 or 20 years, assuming that premiums and dividends earn 5 percent interest. The *net payment cost index* is calculated in a similar way but assumes that the policy is kept in force.

Luckily, it's never been easier to gather the information that allows you to compare costs and features. Term life quote services, available over the phone or on the Internet, can streamline the selection process by providing you, free of charge, with the names of several companies offering the lowest-cost policies based on your specifications. For example, E Financial **(http://www.efinancial.com)**, Select Quote Insurance Services **(http:// www.selectquote.com)**, Insure.com **(http://www.insure.com)**, and Matrix Direct Insurance Services **(http://matrixdirect.com)** maintain databases of life insurance policy costs for various companies and will also act as your agent to buy the policy if you wish. Insure.com and Matrix Direct Insurance Services provide quotes for both term insurance and whole life. Also, don't overlook companies that sell directly to the public or offer low-load policies, such as Ameritas, Lincoln Benefit, and USAA.

EXHIBIT 8.9   Key Features of Various Types of Life Insurance

Differences in the key features of various types of life insurance are noted here. It's important to compare both costs and features when shopping for life insurance.

Feature	Term	Whole Life	Universal Life
Death protection	High	Moderate	Low to high
Coverage period	Temporary for set period	Ongoing	Ongoing
Costs	Low fixed premiums, no fees	High fixed premiums; may also be charged fees	Can vary from high to low; may also be charged fees
Return on investment?	None	Yes, moderate	Yes, return can vary
Tax advantages	No	Yes	Yes

FINANCIAL ROAD SIGN

WHAT TO EXPECT FROM A LIFE INSURANCE MEDICAL EXAM

If you're buying life insurance—especially large policies—you'll often be asked to take a medical exam before the insurance company approves your policy. Here's what you should know before taking an exam:

- Don't fudge your medical history—insurance companies can track down your medical background through insurance industry information clearinghouses.
- A paramedical professional will conduct the exam, which can sometimes be done at your home or office.
- Samples of blood, urine, and saliva may be taken to test for the presence of HIV antibodies, cholesterol, diabetes, and other medical issues. Blood pressure is also taken.
- If you're buying larger policies or are older than 40, an EKG, X-rays, or even a treadmill test may be required.
- For best results, avoid drinking alcoholic beverages and caffeinated beverages as well as smoking or chewing tobacco in the hours before the exam. Don't engage in strenuous exercise for at least 24 hours.

Sources: Adapted from "Life Insurance Health Exam," *Life Insurance In-Depth*, http://www .lifeinsuranceindepth.com/medical-exam.html, downloaded October 4, 2003; and "The Lowdown on Life Insurance Medical Exams," Money Central, http://moneycentral.msn.com, downloaded October 1, 2003, © insure.com.

Probably the fastest-growing source of life insurance quotes and policies in recent years is the Internet. You can not only obtain quick, real-time quotes but also buy insurance electronically. Buying on the Internet allows you to avoid dealing with insurance salespeople, and you can purchase the policies (usually term insurance only) on cost-effective terms. For example, one major life insurer offers discounts of up to 20 percent for term life policies purchased online. Of course, you'll still need a physical exam, but often the insurance company will send a qualified technician/nurse to your home or office to take a blood sample and other basic readings.

Select an Insurance Company

Selecting a life insurance company is an important part of shopping for life insurance. Besides looking for a firm that offers reasonably priced products, attractive contract features, and good customer service, it's vital to consider the financial health of any insurance firm before buying a life insurance policy. You want to be sure that the company will be around and have the assets to pay your beneficiaries should you die. Even before you die, however, your insurance company's financial stability is important. If the company fails, you may be forced to buy a new policy at less favorable rates.

To narrow your choices, age and size are useful indicators. Unless there's a good reason to do otherwise, you should probably limit the companies you consider to those that have been doing business for 25 years or more and that have annual premium volume of more than $100 million. These criteria will rule out a lot of smaller firms, but there are still plenty of companies left to choose from. You may also find that one company is preferable for your term protection and another for your whole life needs.

Factors to consider before making the final choice include the firm's reputation, financial history, commissions and other fees, and the specifics of their policy provisions. If you're choosing a company for a cash value life insurance policy, the company's investment performance and dividend history is also an important consideration.

How do you find all of this information? Luckily, private rating agencies have done much of the work for you. These agencies use publicly available financial data from insurance companies to analyze their debt structure, pricing practices, and management strategies in an effort to assess their financial stability. The purpose is to evaluate the insurance company's ability to pay future claims made by policyholders, known as their *claims paying ability*. In most cases insurance firms pay ratings agencies a fee for this rating service. The ratings agencies then give each insurance firm a "grade" based on their analysis of the firm's financial data.

The three biggest rating agencies are A.M. Best Company, Moody's Investor Service, and Standard & Poor's Corporation (S&P). Two smaller, but growing, rating agencies are Fitch Inc. and Weiss Ratings, Inc. Weiss does not charge a fee to the insurance firms it examines. Exhibit 8.10 provides detailed contact information for each of these agencies, including their Internet addresses. Basic rating information is often free of charge at these sites. You can also usually find these ratings on the insurance company's Web site, or you can ask your agent how the company is rated by Best, Moody's, and S&P.

Each rating agency uses its own grading system. When looking at these ratings, however, keep several things in mind. Except for Moody's and Weiss, the ratings agencies won't publish a firm's rating if the insurer requests that it be withheld. Obviously, an insurance firm receiving a low rating is more likely to suppress publication, something that can be viewed as a clear signal that it's an insurance company to avoid. Also, remember that a high rating doesn't ensure lasting financial stability. Even highly rated insurance firms can quickly encounter financial difficulties. In fact, in a recent report A.M. Best noted that fewer life insurers are receiving top ratings. It's a good idea, therefore, to check the ratings of your insurance carrier periodically even after you have purchased a policy.

Most experts agree that it's wise to purchase life insurance only from insurance companies that are assigned ratings by at least two of the major rating agencies and are consistently rated in the top two or three categories (say, Aaa, Aa1, or Aa2 by Moody's) by each of the major agencies from which they received ratings.

© TAXI/GETTY IMAGES

Choose an Agent

There's an old axiom in the life insurance business that life insurance is sold, not bought. Life insurance agents play a major role in most people's decision to buy life insurance. Unless you plan to buy all of your life insurance via the Internet, selecting a good life insurance agent is important because you'll be relying on him or her for guidance in making some important financial decisions. Don't assume that just because agents are licensed they are competent and will serve your best interests. Consider an agent's formal and professional level of educational attainment. Does the agent have a college degree with a major in business or insurance? Does the agent have a professional designation, such as Chartered Life Underwriter (CLU), Chartered Financial Consultant (ChFC), or Certified Financial Planner® (CFP®)? These designations are awarded only to those who meet certain experience requirements and pass comprehensive examinations in such fields as life and health insurance, estate and pension planning, investments, and federal income tax law.

Also observe how an agent reacts to your questions. Does the agent use fancy buzz-words and stock answers or instead listen attentively and, after some thought, logically answer your questions? These and other personal characteristics should be considered. In

EXHIBIT 8.10 — Major Insurance Rating Agencies

The three biggest insurance rating agencies are A.M. Best Company, Moody's Investor Services, and Standard & Poor's Corporation; Fitch Inc. and Weiss Ratings, Inc., are smaller but growing rating agencies. Contact information for each of these agencies is given here.

A.M. Best Company
Internet address: **http://www.ambest.com**
Phone: 908-439-2200
Top three grades: A++, A+, and A

Moody's Investor Services
Internet address: **http://www.moodys.com**
Phone: 212-553-0377
Top three grades: Aaa, Aa1, and Aa2

Standard & Poor's Corporation
Internet address: **http://www.standardandpoors.com**
Phone: 212-438-7280
Top three grades: AAA, AA+, and AA

Fitch Inc.
Internet address: **http://www.fitchratings.com**
Phone: 212-908-0500
Top three grades: AAA, AA+, and AA

Weiss Ratings, Inc.
Internet address: **http://www.weissratings.com**
Phone: 800-289-9222
Top three grades: A, A-, B

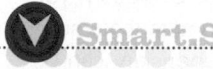

Smart Sites

Looking for an insurance agent? Try the site sponsored by the Independent Insurance Agents and Brokers of America, Inc., at **http://www .thomsonedu.com/ finance/gitman.**

most cases, you should talk with several agents and discuss the pros and cons of each agent with your spouse before committing yourself. Then, when you've decided, call and ask that agent to return for another visit.

When seeking a good life insurance agent, try to obtain recommendations from other professionals who work with agents. Bankers in trust departments, attorneys, and accountants who are specialists in estate planning are usually good sources. In contrast, be a bit wary of selecting an agent simply because of the agent's aggressiveness in soliciting your patronage.

II Concept Check

CHECK • CONCEPT CHECK • CONCEPT CHECK • CONCEPT CHECK • CONCEPT CHECK • CONCEPT CHECK • CONCEPT C

8-16	Briefly describe the steps to take when you shop for and buy life insurance.
8-17	Briefly describe the insurance company ratings assigned by A.M. Best, Moody's, and Standard & Poor's. Why is it important to know how a company is rated? What ratings would you look for when selecting a life insurance company? Explain.
8-18	What characteristics would be most important to you when choosing an insurance agent?

LG6 • KEY FEATURES OF LIFE INSURANCE POLICIES

When buying a life insurance policy, you are entering into a contract with the insurance company. The provisions in this contract spell out the policyholder's and the insurer's rights and obligations as well as the features of the policy being purchased. Unfortunately, there's no such thing as a standard life insurance policy. Each insurance company uses its own wording. Policies can also vary from state to state, depending on the law of the state where the policy is sold. Even so, certain elements are common in most life insurance contracts.

Life Insurance Contract Features

Key features found in most life insurance contracts are the beneficiary clause, settlement options, policy loans, premium payments, grace period, nonforfeiture options, policy reinstatement, and change of policy.

Beneficiary Clause

The **beneficiary** is the person who will receive the death benefits of the policy on the insured's death. All life insurance policies should have one or more beneficiaries. Otherwise, death benefits are paid to the deceased's estate and are subject to the often lengthy and expensive legal procedure of going through probate. An insured person is able to name both a *primary beneficiary* and various *contingent beneficiaries*. The primary beneficiary receives the entire death benefit if he or she is surviving when the insured dies. If the primary beneficiary does not survive the insured, the insurer will distribute the death benefits to the contingent beneficiary or beneficiaries. If neither primary nor contingent beneficiaries are living at the death of the insured, the death benefits pass to the estate of the insured and are distributed by the probate court according to the insured's will or, if no will exists, according to state law.

When naming the beneficiary, make sure the identification is clear. For example, a man could buy a policy and simply designate the beneficiary as "my wife." But, if he later divorces and remarries, there could be a controversy as to which "wife" is entitled to the benefits. Obviously, you should consider changing your named beneficiary if circumstances, such as marital status, change. The person you name as a beneficiary can be changed at any time as long as you didn't indicate an *irrevocable beneficiary* when you took out the policy. Thus, if your wishes change, all you need to do is notify the insurance company—easy to do, but also easy to forget.

Settlement Options

Insurance companies generally offer several ways of paying life insurance policy death proceeds. How the insurance benefits will be distributed can either be permanently established by the policyholder before his or her death or left up to the beneficiary when the policy matures on the insured's death.

- **Lump sum.** This is the most common settlement option, chosen by more than 95 percent of policyholders. The entire death benefit is paid in a single amount, allowing beneficiaries to use or invest the proceeds soon after death occurs.
- **Interest only.** The insurance company keeps policy proceeds for a specified time; the beneficiary receives interest payments, usually at some guaranteed rate. This option can be useful when there's no current need for the principal—for example, proceeds could be left on deposit until children go to college, with interest supplementing family income. Typically, however, interest rates paid by insurers are lower than those available on other savings vehicles.
- **Fixed-period.** The face amount of the policy, along with interest earned, is paid to the beneficiary over a fixed time period. For example, a 55-year-old beneficiary may need additional income until Social Security benefits start.
- **Fixed-amount.** The beneficiary receives policy proceeds in regular payments of a fixed amount until the proceeds run out.
- **Life income.** The insurer guarantees to pay the beneficiary a certain payment for the rest of his or her life, based on the beneficiary's sex, age when benefits start, life expectancy, policy face value, and interest rate assumptions. This option appeals to beneficiaries who don't want to outlive the income from policy proceeds and be dependent on others for support. An interesting variation of this settlement option is

beneficiary A person who receives the death benefits of a life insurance policy on the insured's death.

the *life-income-with-period-certain option,* whereby the company guarantees a specified number of payments that pass to a secondary beneficiary if the original beneficiary dies before the period ends.

The *Money in Action* box on page 266 contains useful advice about filing a life insurance claim when the insured dies.

Policy Loans

An advance made by a life insurance company to a policyholder against a whole life policy is called a **policy loan.** These loans are secured by the cash value of the life insurance policy. Although these loans do *not* have to be repaid, any balance plus interest on the loan remaining at the insured's death is *subtracted from the proceeds of the policy.* Typically policies offer either a fixed-rate loan or a rate that varies with market interest rates on high-quality bonds. Some policies let the insured choose whether the loans will be at fixed or variable rates. Take out a policy loan only if your estate is large enough to cover the accompanying loss of death proceeds if the loan is not repaid. Remember that life insurance is intended to provide basic financial protection for your dependents, and spending those proceeds prematurely defeats the purpose of life insurance. A word of caution: *Be careful with these loans; unless certain conditions are met, the IRS may treat them as withdrawals, meaning they could be subject to tax penalties.* If you're in any way unsure, consult your insurance agent or a tax advisor.

Premium Payments

All life insurance contracts have a provision specifying when premiums, which are normally paid in advance, are due. With most insurers, the policyholder may elect to pay premiums annually, semiannually, quarterly, or monthly. In most cases, insurance companies charge a fee if you decide to pay more often than annually.

Grace Period

The *grace period* permits the policyholder to retain full death protection for a short period (usually 31 days) after missing a premium payment date. In other words, you won't lose your insurance protection just because you're a little late in making the premium payment. If the insured dies during the grace period, the face amount of the policy less the unpaid premium is paid to the beneficiary.

Nonforfeiture Options

As discussed earlier, a *nonforfeiture option* gives a cash value life insurance policyholder some benefits even when a policy is terminated before its maturity. State laws require that all permanent whole, universal, or variable life policies (and term contracts covering an extended period) contain a nonforfeiture provision. Rather than taking a check in the amount of the policy's cash value, insurance companies usually offer the two options—*paid-up insurance* and *extended term insurance*—described here.

- **Paid-up insurance:** The policyholder receives a policy exactly like the terminated one, but with a lower face value. In effect, the policyholder uses the cash value to buy a new, single-premium policy. For example, a policy canceled after 10 years might have a cash value of $90.84 per $1,000 of face value, which will buy $236 of paid-up whole life insurance. The cash value continues to grow because of future interest earnings, even though the policyholder makes no further premium payments. This option is useful when a person's income and need for death protection declines—when he or she reaches age 60 or 65, for example—yet that person still wants some coverage.
- **Extended term insurance.** The insured uses the accumulated cash value to buy a term life policy for the same face value as the lapsed policy. The coverage period is based on the amount of term protection a single-premium payment (equal to the total cash value) buys at the insured's present age. This option usually goes into effect automatically if the policyholder quits paying premiums and gives no instructions to the insurer.

Policy Reinstatement

As long as a whole life policy is under the reduced paid-up insurance option or the extended term insurance option, the policyholder may reinstate the original policy by pay-

policy loan An advance, secured by the cash value of a whole life insurance policy, made by an insurer to the policyholder.

HOW TO FILE A LIFE INSURANCE CLAIM

Although no one likes to deal with paperwork immediately after a loved one's death, filing a life insurance claim should not be delayed. Life insurance proceeds can provide surviving family members with access to cash quickly so they can meet pressing needs.

First, identify the existence of all life insurance policies. Ideally, every person should leave clear instructions for their heirs concerning their life insurance that includes the policy itself and contact information for the insured's insurance agent or insurance company. If this information is available, call your loved one's agent or broker immediately. They can help you sort through the required paperwork and act as an intermediary with the insurance company.

Never assume that the deceased didn't have life insurance. It's always a good idea to check with current and former employers to see if group life insurance was provided. Many banks, credit unions, and credit card companies also offer free life insurance to their customers, so contact your relative's financial institutions as well. The deceased's lawyer, banker, or accountant may also know where the insured had his or her life insurance policy. If all else fails, write to the Missing Policy Service at the American Council of Life Insurers at 101 Constitution Avenue, NW, Washington, DC 20001-2133. For a nominal fee, the Council will contact 100 large insurance companies in an effort to locate life insurance information.

Once each insurance policy has been identified, contact the issuing insurance companies for the necessary forms to file a claim. Most insurance companies will ask each adult beneficiary to file a "proof of death" form and require you to provide at least one certified copy of the insured's death certificate. If the insured didn't specify a payment option when the policy was purchased, the beneficiaries will also be asked to specify how they wish to receive payments.

After you submit the paperwork, the insurance company will confirm that the policy is valid and process the settlement. If everything is in order, the beneficiaries should receive payment within a few weeks.

Critical Thinking Questions

1. Why is it important to file life insurance claims as soon as possible?
2. What are three approaches for finding out about a deceased loved one's insurance coverage?
3. What information is needed when filing an insurance claim?

Sources: Michelle Martin, "Making a Claim—How the Process Works," Insweb.com, http://www.insweb.com, September 28, 2003; Charles K. Plotnick and Stephan R. Leimberg, *How to Settle an Estate* (New York: Penguin Putnam Inc.), 1998, pp. 100–104, "Life Insurance Claims—Here's What to Do," Illinois Association of Insurance and Financial Advisors, http://www.iaifa.com, September 20, 2003.

ing all back premiums plus interest at a stated rate and by providing evidence that he or she can pass a physical examination and meet any other insurability requirements. *Reinstatement* revives the original contractual relationship between the company and the policyholder. Most often, the policyholder must reinstate the policy within a specified period (3 to 5 years) after the policy has lapsed. However, before exercising a reinstatement option, a policyholder should determine whether buying a new policy (from the same or a different company) might be less costly.

Change of Policy

Many life insurance contracts contain a provision that permits the insured to switch from one policy form to another. For instance, policyholders may decide they'd rather have paid-up at age 65 policies as opposed to their current continuous premium whole life policies. A change of policy provision would allow this change without penalty. When policyholders change from high- to lower-premium policies, they may need to prove insurability. This requirement reduces the possibility of adverse selection against the insurance company.

Other Policy Features

Along with the key contractual features described earlier, here are some other policy features to consider:

- **Multiple indemnity clause. Multiple indemnity clauses** increase the face amount of the policy, most often doubling or tripling it, if the insured dies in an accident. This benefit is usually offered to the policyholder at a small additional cost. Many insurance authorities dismiss the use of a multiple indemnity benefit as irrational. This coverage should be ignored as a source of funds when programming insurance needs because it offers no protection if the insured dies due to illness.

- **Disability clause.** A **disability clause** may contain a waiver-of-premium benefit alone or coupled with disability income. A *waiver-of-premium benefit* excuses the payment of premiums on the life insurance policy if the insured becomes totally and permanently disabled prior to age 60 (or sometimes age 65). Under the *disability income portion,* the insured not only is granted a waiver of premium but also receives a monthly income equal to $5 or $10 per $1,000 of policy face value. Some insurers will continue these payments for the life of the insured; others terminate them at age 65. Disability riders for a waiver of premium and disability income protection are relatively inexpensive and can be added to most whole life policies, but generally not to term policies.

- **Guaranteed purchase option.** The policyholder who has a **guaranteed purchase option** may purchase additional coverage at stipulated intervals without providing evidence of insurability. This option is frequently offered to buyers of a whole life policy who are under age 40. Increases in coverage usually can be purchased every 3, 4, or 5 years in sums equal to the amount of the original policy or $10,000, whichever is lower. This option should be quite attractive to individuals whose life insurance needs and ability to pay are expected to increase over a 5- to 15-year period.

- **Suicide clause.** Nearly all life insurance policies have a *suicide clause* that voids the contract if an insured commits suicide within a certain period, normally 2 years after the policy's inception. In these cases, the company simply returns the premiums that have been paid. If an insured takes his or her own life after this initial period has elapsed, the policy proceeds are paid without question.

- **Exclusions.** Although all private insurance policies exclude some types of losses, life policies offer broad protection. Other than the suicide clause, the only common exclusions are aviation, war, and hazardous occupation or hobby. However, a company would rarely be able to modify the premium charged or coverage offered should the insured take up, say, Formula One racing or hang gliding *after* a policy is issued.

- **Participation.** In a **participating policy,** the policyholder is entitled to receive *policy dividends* reflecting the difference between the premiums that are charged and the amount of premium necessary to fund the actual mortality experience of the company. When the base premium schedule for participating policies is established, a company estimates what it believes its mortality and investment experience will be and then adds a generous margin of safety to these figures. The premiums charged the policyholder are based on these overly conservative estimates.

- **Living benefits.** Also called *accelerated benefits*, this feature allows the insured to receive a percentage of his or her death benefits from a whole or universal life policy prior to death. Some insurers offer this option at no charge to established policyholders if the insured suffers a terminal illness expected to result in death within a specified period, such as 6 months to a year, or needs an expensive treatment, such as an organ transplant, to survive. These benefits can also be added as a *living benefit rider* that pays a portion of a policy's death benefit in advance, usually about 2 percent per month, for long-term healthcare, such as nursing home expenses. This rider can add an extra 5 to 15 percent to the normal life insurance premium, and benefits are capped as a percentage of the death benefit.

- **Viatical settlement.** Like a living benefits feature, this option allows a terminally ill insurance holder to get a percentage of the insurance policy for immediate use. But unlike the living benefits feature, this isn't done through the insurance company but

multiple indemnity clause A clause in a life insurance policy that typically doubles or triples the policy's face amount if the insured dies in an accident.

disability clause A clause in a life insurance contract containing a *waiver-of-premium benefit* alone or coupled with *disability income*.

guaranteed purchase option An option in a life insurance contract giving the policyholder the right to purchase additional coverage at stipulated intervals without providing evidence of insurability.

participating policy A life insurance policy that pays *policy dividends* reflecting the difference between the premiums that are charged and the amount of premium necessary to fund the actual mortality experience of the company.

rather through a third-party investor. The insured sells an interest in the life insurance policy to the investor, who then becomes the policy's beneficiary, and the insured receives a cash amount from the investor—most commonly 60 percent of the policy value; after the insured dies, the investor receives the balance from the policy. Approach viatical settlements carefully, because it means giving up all future claims on the life insurance policy and can also affect a patient's Medicare eligibility in some cases. Additionally, some viatical settlement companies—the firms that arrange the transfer between insureds and investors—have been scrutinized by government agencies for unethical practices.

❚❚ Concept Check

8-19	What is a *beneficiary*? A *contingent beneficiary*? Explain why it's essential to designate a beneficiary.
8-20	Explain the basic settlement options available for the payment of life insurance proceeds on a person's death.
8-21	What do *nonforfeiture options* accomplish? Differentiate between *paid-up insurance* and *extended term insurance*.
8-22	Explain the following clauses often found in life insurance policies: (a) *multiple indemnity clause,* (b) *disability clause,* and (c) *suicide clause.* Give some examples of common exclusions.
8-23	Describe what is meant by a *participating policy,* and explain the role of *policy dividends* in these policies.

SUMMARY

LG1 **Explain the concept of risk and the basics of insurance underwriting.** Adequate life insurance coverage is vital to sound personal financial planning because it not only protects what you've already acquired but also helps ensure the attainment of unfulfilled financial goals. The whole notion of insurance is based on the concept of risk and the different methods of handling it, including risk avoidance, loss prevention and control, risk assumption, and insurance (a cost-effective procedure that allows families to reduce financial risks by sharing losses). Through the underwriting process, insurance companies decide whom they consider an acceptable risk and the premiums to charge for coverage.

LG2 **Discuss the primary reasons for life insurance and identify those who need coverage.** Life insurance fills the gap between the financial resources available to your dependents if you should die prematurely and what they need to maintain a given lifestyle. Some policies provide only a death benefit; others also have a savings component. If you have children

or elderly relatives who count on your income to support them, you should include life insurance as one of several financial resources to meet their requirements. If you have no dependents, you probably don't need life insurance. Your life insurance needs change over your life cycle and should be reviewed regularly.

LG3 **Calculate how much life insurance you need.** There are several ways to determine the amount of life insurance a family should have. Although the multiple-of-earnings method is simple to use, most experts agree that the needs analysis method is the best procedure. It systematically considers such variables as family income, household and other expenses, special needs, final expenses, debt liquidation, and other financial needs, which are then compared with the financial resources available to meet these needs.

LG4 **Differentiate among the various types of life insurance policies and describe their advantages and disadvantages.** The three basic types of life insurance policies are term life, whole life, and universal life. Term life insurance provides a stipulated amount of death benefits, whereas whole life combines death benefits with a modest savings program, and universal life packages term insurance with a tax-sheltered savings/investment account that pays interest at competitive money market rates. Other types of life insurance include variable life, group life, credit life, mortgage life, and industrial life.

LG5 **Choose the best life insurance policy for your needs at the lowest cost.** To get as much coverage as possible from your insurance dollar, it's important not only to compare costs but also to buy the proper amount of life insurance and pick the right type of insurance policy. Beyond the cost and features of the insurance policy, carefully consider the financial stability of the insurer offering the policy, paying special attention to the ratings assigned by major rating agencies. The Internet has become an excellent resource for comparison shopping. In addition to selecting a company, you must also choose an agent who understands your needs.

LG6 **Become familiar with the key features of life insurance policies.** Some important contract features of life insurance policies you should become familiar with are the beneficiary clause, settlement options, policy loans, premium payments, grace period, nonforfeiture options, policy reinstatement, and change of policy. Other policy features include multiple indemnity and disability clauses, guaranteed purchase options, suicide clause, exclusions, participation, living benefits, and viatical settlements.

FINANCIAL PLANNING EXERCISES

LG2, 3, 4

1. **Use Worksheet 8.1.** Mildred Meyers is a 72-year-old widow who has recently been diagnosed with Alzheimer's disease. She has limited financial assets of her own and has been living with her daughter Janna for 2 years. Her only income is $850 a month in Social Security survivor's benefits. Janna wants to make sure her mother will be taken care of if Janna should die. Janna, 40, is single and earns $55,000 a year as a human resources manager for a small manufacturing firm. She owns a condo with a current market value of $100,000 and has a $70,000 mortgage. Other debts include a $5,000 auto loan and $500 in various credit card balances. Her 401(k) plan has a current balance of $24,500, and she keeps $7,500 in a money market account for emergencies. After talking with her mother's doctor, Janna believes that her mother will be able to continue living independently for another 2 to 3 years. She estimates that her mother would need about $2,000 a month to cover her living expenses and medical costs during this time. After that, Janna's mother will probably need nursing home care. Janna calls several local nursing homes and finds that it will cost about $5,000 a month when her mother enters a nursing home. Her mother's doctor says it is difficult to estimate her mother's life expectancy but indicates that with proper care some Alzheimer's patients can live 10 or more years after diagnosis. Janna also estimates that her personal final expenses would be around $5,000, and she'd like to provide a $25,000 contingency fund that would be used to pay a trusted friend to supervise her mother's care if Janna was no longer alive. Use Worksheet 8.1 to calculate Janna's total life insurance requirements and recommend the type of policy she should buy.

LG2, 3

2. **Use Worksheet 8.1.** Given your current personal financial situation, do you feel you need life insurance coverage? Why or why not? Use Worksheet 8.1 to confirm your answer and calculate how much additional insurance (if any) you might need to purchase.

LG2, 3, 4

3. **Use Worksheet 8.1.** Jim Henderson, 43, is a recently divorced father of two children, ages 9 and 7. He currently earns $95,000 a year as an operations manager for a utility company. The divorce settlement requires him to pay $1,500 a month in child support and $400 a month in alimony to his ex-wife. She currently earns $25,000 a year as a preschool teacher. Jim is now renting an apartment, and the divorce settlement left him with about $100,000 in savings and retirement benefits. His employer provides a $75,000 life insurance policy. Jim's ex-wife is currently the beneficiary listed on the policy. What advice would you give to Jim? What factors should he consider in deciding whether to buy additional life insurance at this point in his life? If he does need additional life insurance, what type of policy or policies should he buy? Use Worksheet 8.1 to help answer these questions for Jim.

LG4

4. Using the premium schedules provided in Exhibits 8.2, 8.3, and 8.5, how much in *annual* premiums would a 25-year-old male have to pay for $100,000 of annual renewable term, level premium term, and whole life insurance (assume a 5-year term or period of coverage)? How much would a 25-year-old woman have to pay for the same coverage? Consider a 40-year-old male (or female): Using annual premiums, compare the cost of 10 years of coverage under annual renewable and level premium term options and whole life insurance coverage. Compare the pluses and minuses of each type of policy in relation to their price differences.

LG2, 3, 4, 5

5. Monica and Manuel Juarez are a dual-career couple who just had their first child. Manuel, age 29, already has a group life insurance policy, but Monica's employer does not offer life insurance. A financial planner is recommending that the 25-year-old Monica buy a $250,000 whole life policy with an annual premium of $1,670—the policy has an assumed rate of earnings of 8 percent a year. Help Monica evaluate this advice and decide on an appropriate course of action.

LG2, 3, 4, 5

6. While at lunch with a group of coworkers, one of your friends mentions that he plans to buy a variable life insurance policy because it provides a good annual return and is a good way to build savings for his 5-year-old's college education. Another colleague says that she's adding coverage through the group plan's additional insurance option. What advice would you give them?

APPLYING PERSONAL FINANCE

Insure Your Life!

Providing for our loved ones in the event of our death is a serious concern for most of us. Trouble is, planning for such an event is not particularly pleasant, and most of us would just as soon put off thinking about it. This project will help you determine your current and future life insurance needs.

Life insurance can be put in place to provide income for your family, educate your children, or pay off debt. Life insurance can also be used in estate planning or to benefit a cause that's important to you. Make a list of your present life insurance needs and another list of what you expect your needs to be 10 years down the road. Estimate the dollar amount for each of your needs. Use Worksheet 8.1 to determine the amount of life insurance you need now and in the future. Consider the features of different types of life insurance. Which type of life insurance would be most appropriate for you? What would the cost be to provide these amounts of life insurance? You may use the premium schedules in this chapter or get actual quotes from an agent or off the Internet. Use these estimates to help you with your personal financial planning.

CRITICAL THINKING CASES

LG3, 4, 5

8.1 Lee Hsiah's Insurance Decision: Whole Life, Variable Life, or Term Life?

Lee Hsiah, a 38-year-old widowed mother of three children, ages 12, 10, and 4, works as a product analyst for Nestlé Purina PetCare Company. Although she's covered by a group life insurance policy at work, she feels, based on some rough calculations, that she needs additional protection. David Dustimer, an insurance agent from Siegfried Insurance, has been trying to persuade Lee to buy a $150,000, 25-year, limited payment whole life policy. However, Lee favors a variable life policy. To further complicate matters, Lee's father feels that term life insurance is more suitable to the needs of her young family. To resolve the issue, Lee has decided to consult Terry Patrick, a childhood friend who is now a professor of insurance at a nearby university.

Critical Thinking Questions
1. Explain to Lee the differences between a (a) whole life policy, (b) variable life policy, and (c) term life policy.

2. What are the major advantages and disadvantages of each type of policy?

3. In what way is a whole life policy superior to either a variable life or term life policy? In what way is a variable life policy superior? How about term life insurance?

4. Given the limited information in the case, which type of policy would you recommend for Ms. Hsiah? Defend and explain your recommendations.

LG3, 4, 5

8.2 The Kings Want to Know When Enough Is Enough

Dave and Karen King are a two-income couple in their early thirties. They have two children, ages 6 and 3. Dave's monthly take-home pay is $3,600, and Karen's is $4,200. The Kings feel that because they're a two-income family, they both should have adequate life insurance coverage. Accordingly, they are now trying to decide how much life insurance *each one of them* needs.

To begin with, they'd like to set up an education fund for their children in the amount of $120,000 to provide college funds of $15,000 a year—in today's dollars—for 4 years for each child. Moreover, if either spouse should die, they want the surviving spouse to have the funds to pay off all outstanding debts, including the $210,000 mortgage on their house. They estimate that they have $25,000 in consumer installment loans and credit cards. They also project that if either of them dies, the other probably will be left with about $10,000 in final estate and burial expenses.

Regarding their annual income needs, Dave and Karen both feel strongly that each should have enough insurance to replace their respective current income levels until the youngest child turns 18 (a period of 15 years). Although neither Dave nor Karen would be eligible for Social Security survivor's benefits, because they both intend to continue working, both children would qualify in the (combined) amount of around $1,800 a month. The Kings have amassed about $75,000 in investments, and they have a decreasing term life policy on each other in the amount of $100,000, which would be used to partially pay off the mortgage. Dave also has an $80,000 group policy at work and Karen a $100,000 group policy.

Critical Thinking Questions

1. Assume that Dave's gross annual income is $54,000, and Karen's is $64,000. Their insurance agent has given them a multiple earnings table showing that the earnings multiple to replace 75 percent of their lost earnings is 8.7 for Dave and 7.4 for Karen. Use this approach to find the amount of life insurance each should have if they want to replace 75 percent of their lost earnings.

2. Use Worksheet 8.1 to find the additional insurance needed on both Dave's and Karen's lives. (Because Dave and Karen hold secure, well-paying jobs, both agree that they won't need any additional help once the kids are grown; both also agree that they'll have plenty of income from Social Security and company pension benefits to take care of themselves in retirement. Thus, when preparing the worksheet, assume "funding needs" of zero in Periods 2 and 3.)

3. Is there a difference in your answers to Questions 1 and 2? If so, why? Which number do you think is more indicative of the King's life insurance needs? Using the amounts computed in Question 2 (employing the needs approach), what kind of life insurance policy would you recommend for Dave? For Karen? Briefly explain your answers.

> ## MONEY ONLINE   www.thomsonedu.com/finance/gitman

NLINE • MONEY ONLINE • MONEY ONLINE • MONEY ONLINE • MONEY ONLINE • MONEY ONLINE • MONEY ONLINE

Visit **http://www.thomsonedu.com/finance/gitman** for some additional Web-based exercises and hot links (with annotations) to a variety of resources relevant to the topics covered in this chapter.

Insuring Your Health

CHAPTER 9

LEARNING GOALS

LG1	●	Discuss why having adequate health insurance is important and identify the factors contributing to the growing cost of health insurance.	p. 272
LG2	●	Differentiate among the major types of health insurance plans and identify major private and public health insurance providers and their programs.	p. 274
LG3	●	Analyze your own health insurance needs and explain how to shop for appropriate coverage.	p. 278
LG4	●	Explain the basic types of medical expenses covered and policy provisions of health insurance plans.	p. 282
LG5	●	Assess the need for and features of long-term care insurance.	p. 289
LG6	●	Discuss the features of disability income insurance and how to determine your need for it.	p. 293
	●		

LG1 · THE IMPORTANCE OF HEALTH INSURANCE COVERAGE

The next best thing to good health is probably a good health insurance plan. In recent years, the price of medical treatment has risen dramatically. As a result, a serious illness or accident can involve not only physical pain from sickness and injury but also economic pain. A major illness can easily cost tens of thousands of dollars once you consider hospitalization and medical expenses as well as the loss of income while you recover. Even routine medical care such as doctors' office visits and healthcare screenings can quickly add up. Health insurance helps you pay for the costs associated with both routine and major medical care so that your financial accomplishments and plans are not seriously damaged or even destroyed.

Despite the financial importance of health insurance, however, many Americans remain underinsured or uninsured. According to the U.S. Census Bureau, nearly 16 percent of the population—over 46 million people—don't have health insurance. Young adults between 18 and 24 are even less likely to have health insurance: slightly more than 31 percent of individuals in that age group are covered by health insurance.

Why are so many uninsured? As Exhibit 9.1 shows, the cost of adequate health insurance has skyrocketed recently, increasing an average of 11.6 percent annually between 2000 and 2005—significantly faster than the 2.6 percent average annual inflation rate or the 2.8 percent average worker's annual wage growth during that same period. In 2005 the average annual premium for employer-sponsored plans was $4,024 for single coverage and $10,880 for family coverage. During that year, the average percentage of health care premiums paid by covered workers was 16 percent for single plans and 26 percent for family plans. Others got no help from their employers, or are unemployed, and have to foot the entire bill themselves.

Several health-related trends are behind the rising health insurance costs. First, recent advances in medical technology have resulted in advanced prescription drugs and new treatments. Although these advances are saving more lives than ever before, they also cost more to provide. The U.S. population is also aging, resulting in growing use of health-care services. A poor demand-and-supply distribution of healthcare facilities and services may be yet another factor. Administrative costs, excessive paperwork, increased regulation, and insurance fraud are also contributing to rising healthcare costs. When all of these factors are added together, insurance companies are finding it necessary to pass along rising healthcare costs to consumers by charging more for health insurance.

Still, as we've already noted, it can be very risky to go without adequate health insurance coverage. As with other types of insurance decisions, cost-effective health insurance depends on understanding the types of policies available and then matching them to your own specific medical needs.

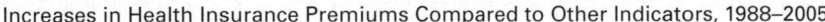

EXHIBIT 9.1   Historical Trends in Health Insurance Costs

As the chart shows, the year-to-year percentage change for health insurance premiums has been much higher than both the inflation rate and average workers' earnings.

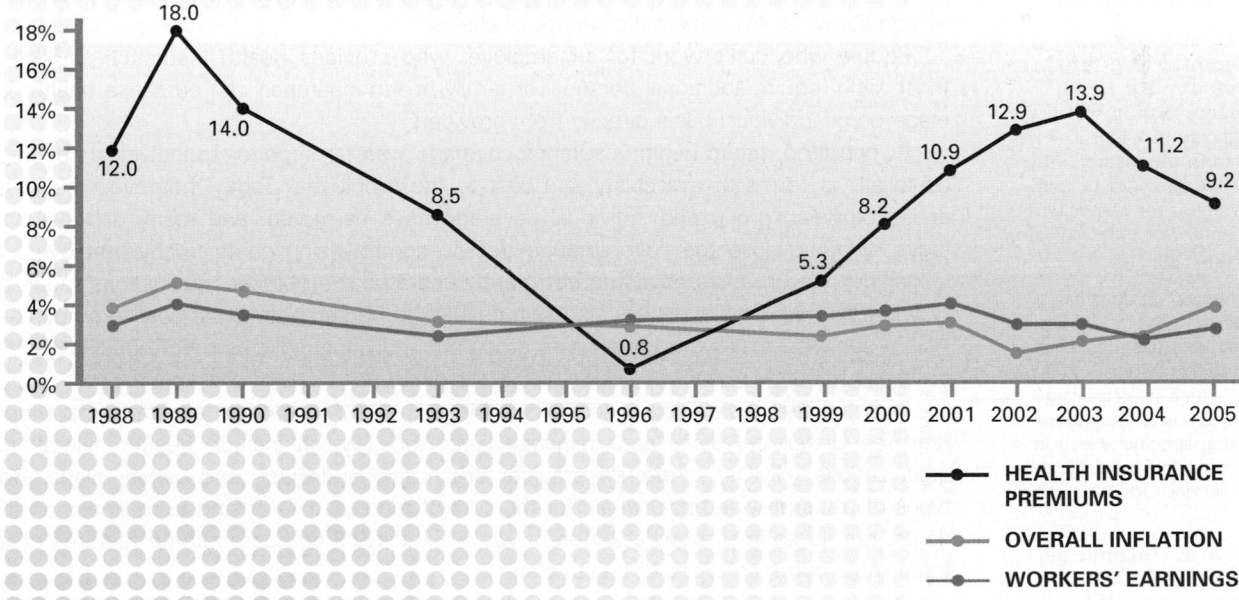

Increases in Health Insurance Premiums Compared to Other Indicators, 1988–2005

Source: "Employer Health Benefits 2005 Annual Survey," (#7315), The Henry J. Kaiser Family Foundation and Health Research and Educational Trust, September 2005. This information was reprinted with permission of the Henry J. Kaiser Family Foundation. The Kaiser Family Foundation, based in Menlo Park, California, is a nonprofit, independent national health care philanthropy and is not associated with Kaiser Permanente or Kaiser Industries.

9-1	Why should health insurance planning be included in your personal financial plan?
9-2	What factors have contributed to today's high costs of healthcare and health insurance?

LG2 · HEALTH INSURANCE PLANS

Smart.Sites

An excellent site for use in comparing the features of various health insurance plans and obtaining quotes from leading health insurance plans is eHealthInsurance. Link to it at **http://www .thomsonedu.com/finance/ gitman.**

group health insurance
Health insurance consisting of contracts written between a group, (employer, union, etc.) and the healthcare provider.

indemnity (fee-for-service) plan Health insurance plan in which the healthcare provider is separate from the insurer, who pays the provider or reimburses you for a specified percentage of expenses after a deductible.

managed care plan A healthcare plan in which subscribers/users contract with the provider organization, which uses a designated group of providers meeting specific selection standards to furnish healthcare services for a monthly fee.

health maintenance organization (HMO) An organization of hospitals, physicians, and other healthcare providers who have joined to provide comprehensive healthcare services to its members, who pay a monthly fee.

Health insurance coverage is available from two main sources: private and government-sponsored programs. Private health insurance pays for approximately 35 percent of all medical care expenditures in the United States, while government programs fund about 45 percent. Most of the remaining amount spent on medical care is paid for out of pocket by patients themselves.

Private Health Insurance Plans

Private companies sell a variety of health insurance plans to both groups and individuals. **Group health insurance** refers to health insurance contracts written between a group (such as an employer, union, credit union, or other organization) and the healthcare provider: a private insurance company, Blue Cross/Blue Shield plan, or a managed care organization. Typically, group plans provide comprehensive medical expense coverage and may also offer prescription drug, dental, and vision care service. The coverage provided by any given plan is subject to negotiation between the group and the insurer, and the group may offer several options for health insurance coverage.

If you work for an employer that has more than just a few employees, you'll probably have access to some type of group health plan. With the high cost of health insurance, most employers now require employees to pay part of the cost. Trade associations and professional groups may also offer group insurance to their members at attractive rates. Some groups choose to self-insure, which means that the employer or other group takes responsibility for full or partial payment of claims.

People who don't work for an employer who provides health insurance as well as those who require additional personal or family health insurance can purchase health coverage on an individual basis directly from providers.

At one time, group health insurance coverage was far superior to individual coverage, especially in terms of availability and cost to the employee. Today, however, the differences between group and individual coverage have narrowed, and many of the advantages of group coverage have disappeared. To control rising costs, many employers no longer provide universal coverage but merely underwrite employee applications much the way insurers do. Employers are also shifting a larger percentage of the cost to employees. As a result, you may want to compare group and individual policies before deciding which coverage to buy.

Most private health insurance plans fall into one of two categories: traditional *indemnity (fee-for-service) plans* and *managed care plans*, which include health maintenance organizations (HMOs), preferred provider organizations (PPOs), and similar plans. Both types of plans provide financial aid for the cost of medical care arising from illness or accidents, but do so in somewhat different ways. Exhibit 9.2 compares some features of the three most common types of health plans.

Traditional Indemnity (Fee-for-Service) Plans

With a traditional **indemnity (fee-for-service) plan,** the person or organization from which you obtain healthcare services is separate from your insurer. Your insurer either pays the health service provider directly or reimburses your expenses when you submit claims for medical treatment. Typically, indemnity plans pay 80 percent of the eligible healthcare expenses, while the insured pays the other 20 percent. The health insurance company will begin paying its share after you pay a deductible amount of expenses. The deductible can range from $100 to over $2,000. The lower your deductible, the higher your premium.

The amount the insurance company pays is commonly based on the usual, customary, and reasonable (UCR) charges—what the insurer considers to be the prevailing fees within your area, not what your doctor or hospital actually charges. If your doctor charges more than the UCR, you may be responsible for the full amount of the excess. UCR charges vary significantly among insurers, so you should compare your doctor's fees with what a plan pays. Some carriers offer indemnity plans wherein physicians who accept the insurance agree to accept the UCR payments set by the insurer.

Managed Care Plans

Today employers are moving away from traditional indemnity plans and adopting managed care plans. In a **managed care plan,** subscribers/users contract with and make monthly payments directly to the organization that provides the healthcare service. An insurance company may not even be involved, although today most major health insurance companies offer both indemnity and managed care plans. Managed care plan members receive comprehensive healthcare services from a designated group of doctors, hospitals, and other providers, who must meet the managed care provider's specific selection standards. Managed care plans use various strategies to provide cost-efficient medical care, such as controlling the amount of care provided and emphasizing prevention of illness.

With a managed care plan, the insured pays no deductibles and only a small fee, or co-payment, for office visits and medications. Most medical services—including preventive and routine care that indemnity plans may not cover—are fully covered when obtained from plan providers. Managed care plans include health maintenance organizations (HMOs), preferred provider organizations (PPOs), exclusive provider organizations (EPOs), and point-of-service plans (POS).

Health Maintenance Organizations. A **health maintenance organization (HMO)** is an organization of hospitals, physicians, and other healthcare providers who have joined to provide comprehensive

---

EXHIBIT 9.2   How the Most Common Types of Health Plans Compare

This table highlights some of the key differences among the three most common types of health plans.

Type	Choice of Service Providers	Premium Cost	Out-of-Pocket Costs	Annual Deductible
Indemnity	Yes	Low if high-deductible plan, high if low-deductible plan	Usually 20 percent of medical expenses plus deductible	Yes
HMO	No	Low	Low co-pay	No
PPO	Some	Higher than HMO	Low if using network providers, higher if provider is outside the network	No

group HMO An HMO that provides healthcare services *from a central facility;* most prevalent in larger cities.

individual practice association (IPA) A form of HMO in which subscribers receive services from physicians practicing *from their own offices and from community hospitals* affiliated with the IPA.

preferred provider organization (PPO) A health provider that combines the characteristics of the IPA form of HMO with an indemnity plan to provide comprehensive healthcare services to its subscribers within a network of physicians and hospitals.

exclusive provider organization (EPO) A managed care plan that is similar to a PPO, but reimburses members only when affiliated providers are used.

point-of-service (POS) plan A hybrid form of HMO that allows members to go outside the HMO network for care and reimburses them at a specified percentage of the cost.

Blue Cross/Blue Shield plans Prepaid hospital and medical expense plans under which healthcare services are provided to plan participants by member hospitals and physicians.

Medicare A health insurance plan administered by the federal government to help persons age 65 and over, and others receiving monthly Social Security disability benefits, to meet their healthcare costs.

healthcare services to its members. As an HMO member, you pay a monthly fee that varies according to the number of people in your family. You may also pay a co-payment of $5 to $20 each time you use some of the services provided by the HMO or fill a prescription. The services provided to HMO members include doctors' office visits, X-ray and laboratory services, preventive care, health screenings, hospital inpatient care and surgery, maternity care, mental health, and drug prescriptions. The advantages of HMO membership include a lack of deductibles, few or no exclusions, and not having to file insurance claims. The primary disadvantage is that HMO members can't always choose their physicians and may face limitations if they need care outside of the geographic area of their HMO.

There are two main types of HMOs: group and individual practice association. A **group HMO** employs a group of doctors to provide healthcare services to members *from a central facility*. Group HMO members obtain medical care from the doctors and other medical personnel who practice in this facility. Often, the group HMO's hospital facilities are located in the same facility. Group HMOs are most prevalent in larger cities.

An **individual practice association (IPA)** is the most popular type of HMO. IPA members receive medical care from individual physicians practicing *from their own offices and from community hospitals* that are affiliated with the IPA. As a member of an IPA, you have some choice of which doctors and hospitals to use.

Preferred Provider Organizations. A **preferred provider organization (PPO)** is a managed care plan that has the characteristics of both an IPA and an indemnity plan. An insurance company or provider group contracts with a network of physicians and hospitals that agree to accept a negotiated fee for medical services provided to the PPO customers. Unlike the HMO, however, a PPO also provides insurance coverage for medical services not provided by the PPO network, so you can choose to go to other doctors or hospitals. You will, however, pay a lower price for medical services provided by network doctors and hospitals.

Other Managed Care Plans. Besides the plans just described, you may encounter two other forms of managed care plans. An **exclusive provider organization (EPO)** contracts with medical providers to offer services to members at reduced costs, but reimburses members only when affiliated providers are used. Plan members who use a nonaffiliated provider must bear the entire cost. The **point-of-service (POS) plan** is a hybrid form of HMO that allows members to go outside of the HMO network for care. Payment for nonaffiliated physician services is similar to indemnity plan payments: the plan pays a specified percentage of the cost after your medical costs reach an annual deductible.

Blue Cross/Blue Shield Plans

In a technical sense, **Blue Cross/Blue Shield plans** are not insurance policies but rather prepaid hospital and medical expense plans. Today there are 38 independent local Blue Cross/Blue Shield organizations, all of them for-profit corporations.

Blue Cross contracts with hospitals that agree to provide specified hospital services to members of groups covered by Blue Cross in exchange for a specified fee or payment. Blue Cross also contracts for surgical and medical services. Blue Cross serves as the intermediary between the groups that want these services and the physicians who contractually agree to provide them. Today, many Blue Cross and Blue Shield plans have combined to form one provider, and they compete for business with other private insurance companies. Because Blue Cross/Blue Shield is a producer cooperative, payments for healthcare services are seldom made to the subscriber but rather directly to the participating hospital or physician.

Government Health Insurance Plans

In addition to health insurance coverage provided by private sources, federal and state agencies provide healthcare coverage to eligible individuals. About 25 percent of the U.S. population is covered by some form of government health insurance program.

Medicare

Medicare is a health insurance program administered under the Social Security Administration. It's primarily designed to help persons 65 and over meet their healthcare costs, but it also covers many people under 65 who receive monthly Social Security disability benefits. Funds for Medicare benefits come from Social Security taxes paid by covered workers and their employers. Traditionally, Medicare has provided two primary healthcare components, basic hospital insurance and supplementary medical insurance, and in 2006 began offering prescription drug coverage.

- **Basic hospital insurance**. This coverage (commonly called *Part A*) provides inpatient hospital services such as room, board, and other customary inpatient service for the first 90 days of illness. A deductible is applied during the first 60 days of illness. Coinsurance provisions, applicable to days 61 to 90 of the hospital stay, can further reduce benefits. Medicare also covers all or part of the cost of up to 100 days in posthospital extended-care facilities that provide skilled care, such as nursing homes. However, it doesn't cover the most common types of nursing home care—intermediate and custodial care. Medicare basic hospital insurance also covers some posthospital medical services such as intermittent nursing care, therapy, rehabilitation, and home healthcare. Medicare deductibles and coinsurance amounts are revised annually to reflect changing medical costs.

- **Supplementary medical insurance**. The **supplementary medical insurance (SMI)** program (commonly called *Part B*) covers the services of physicians and surgeons, as well as the costs of medical and health services such as X-rays, laboratory tests, prosthetic devices, rental of medical equipment, and ambulance transportation. It also covers some home health services (such as in-home visits by a registered nurse) and limited psychiatric care. Unlike the basic Medicare hospital plan, SMI is a *voluntary program* for which participants pay premiums, which are then matched with government funds. Anyone age 65 or over can enroll in SMI.

- **Prescription drug coverage**. The **prescription drug coverage** program (commonly called *Part D*), initiated January 1, 2006, is insurance covering both brand-name and generic prescription drugs at participating pharmacies. It's intended to provide protection for people who have very high drug costs. All Medicare recipients are eligible for this coverage, regardless of their income and resources, health status, or existing prescription expenses. There are several ways to get this coverage. Participants in this *voluntary program* pay a monthly fee and a yearly deductible, which was less than $250 in 2006. They also pay part of the cost of prescriptions, including a co-payment or coinsurance. The plan provides extra help—paying almost all prescription drug costs—for the 1 in 3 Medicare recipients with limited income and resources.

Although Medicare pays for many healthcare expenses for the disabled and those over 65, there are still gaps in its coverage. Many Medicare enrollees buy private insurance policies to fill in these gaps.

Medicaid

Medicaid is a state-run public assistance program that provides health insurance benefits only to those who are unable to pay for healthcare. Each state has its own regulations about who is eligible for Medicaid coverage and the types of medical services that are covered. Although Medicaid is primarily funded by each state, the federal government also contributes funds. About 40 million people receive Medicaid health benefits.

Workers' Compensation Insurance

Workers' compensation insurance is designed to compensate workers who are injured on the job or become ill through work-related causes. Although mandated by the federal government, each state is responsible for setting workers' compensation legislation and regulating its own program. Specifics vary from state to state, but typical workers' compensation benefits include medical and rehabilitation expenses, disability income, and scheduled lump-sum amounts for death and certain injuries, such as dismemberment. Employers bear nearly the entire cost of workers' compensation insurance in most states. Premiums are based on merit; employers who file the most claims pay the highest rates. People who are self-employed are required to contribute to workers' compensation for themselves and their employees.

What does Medicaid cover in your state? The Kaiser Family Foundation offers an online state-by-state explanation of these and other healthcare benefits. Go to their site through the link at **http://www.thomsonedu.com/finance/gitman.**

supplementary medical insurance (SMI) A *voluntary program* under Medicare (commonly called *Part B*) that provides payments for services not covered under *basic hospital insurance (Part A)*.

prescription drug coverage A *voluntary program* under Medicare (commonly called *Part D*) that is insurance covering both brand-name and generic prescription drugs at participating pharmacies. Participants pay a monthly fee and a yearly deductible and must pay part of the cost of prescriptions, including a co-payment or coinsurance.

Medicaid A state-run public assistance program that provides health insurance benefits only to those who are unable to pay for healthcare.

workers' compensation insurance Health insurance required by state and federal governments and nearly paid in full by employers in most states; it compensates workers for job-related illness or injury.

Concept Check

9-3	What are the two main sources of health insurance coverage in the United States?
9-4	What is *group health insurance*? Differentiate between group and individual health insurance.
9-5	Describe the features of traditional *indemnity (fee-for-service) plans* and explain the differences between them and *managed care plans*.
9-6	Briefly explain how an *HMO* works. Contrast *group HMOs*, *IPAs*, and *PPOs*.
9-7	Discuss the basics of the *Blue Cross/Blue Shield plans*.
9-8	Who is eligible for *Medicare* and *Medicaid* benefits? What do those benefits encompass?
9-9	What is the objective of *workers' compensation insurance*? Explain its benefits for employees who are injured on the job or become ill through work-related causes.

LG3 HEALTH INSURANCE DECISIONS

With all these options, how can you systematically plan your purchases of health insurance? As with other insurance decisions, you'll need to consider potential areas of loss, types of coverage and other resources available to you and your family, and any gaps in protection. Once you've done all three, you can choose a health insurance plan that's best for you.

Evaluate Your Healthcare Cost Risk

Most people need protection against two types of losses that can result from illness or accidents: (1) expenses for medical care and rehabilitation and (2) loss of income or household services caused by an inability to work. The cost of medical care can't be easily estimated; but in cases of long-term, serious illness, medical bills and related expenses can easily run into hundreds of thousands of dollars. An adequate amount of protection against these costs for most people would be at least $250,000 and, with a protracted disability, as high as $1 million. In contrast, lost income is relatively easy to calculate: it's a percentage of your (or your spouse's) current monthly earnings. Most people believe that 60 to 75 percent is sufficient.

A good health insurance plan considers more than financing medical expenses, lost income, and replacement services. It should also incorporate other means of risk reduction. Recall from Chapter 8 that you can deal with risk in four ways: risk avoidance, loss prevention and control, risk assumption, and insurance. So, in deciding on health insurance, you should consider these other ways of minimizing your risk:

Risk avoidance. Look for ways to avoid exposure to healthcare loss before it occurs. For example, people who don't take illegal drugs never have to worry about disability from overdose, people who refuse to ride on motorcycles avoid the risk of injury from

FINANCIAL ROAD SIGN

KEY QUESTIONS FOR CHOOSING A HEALTH INSURANCE PLAN

1. How much will it cost each month?
2. Are there deductibles I must pay before the insurance begins to help cover my costs?
3. What doctors, hospitals, and other medical providers are part of the plan?
4. Are there enough of the kinds of doctors I want to see?
5. If I use doctors outside a plan's network, how much more will I pay to get care?
6. Are there any limits to how much I must pay in case of major illness?

FINANCIAL ROAD SIGN

75% OF WORKERS TAKE MOST HEALTHCARE BENEFITS OFFERED BY EMPLOYERS

In its 2005 National Compensation Survey, the U.S. Department of Labor found that the following percentages of workers with access to their employer's healthcare plan took up each of the healthcare benefits listed here.

Benefit	Percentage of Workers Taking Benefit
Medical care	75%
Dental care	78
Vision care	75
Outpatient prescription drug coverage	75

Clearly, it's safe to say that when employer healthcare benefits are offered, about 75 percent of eligible employees take them.

Source: "National Compensation Survey: Employee Benefits in Private Industry in the United States, March 2005," U.S. Department of Labor, 2005, Table 6, p. 10.

this relatively dangerous means of transportation, and people who don't smoke in bed will never doze off and start a fire in their house.

- **Loss prevention and control.** People who accept responsibility for their own well-being and live healthier lifestyles can prevent illness and reduce high medical costs. Smoking, alcohol and drug dependency, improper diet, inadequate sleep, and lack of regular exercise contribute to more than 60 percent of all diagnosed illnesses. Eliminating some or all of these factors from your lifestyle can reduce your chances of becoming ill. Similarly, following highway safety laws, not driving while intoxicated, and wearing a seat belt helps prevent injury from car accidents.
- **Risk assumption.** Consider the risks you're willing to retain as you deal with health insurance decisions. Some risks pose relatively small loss potential; you can budget for them rather than insure against them. For example, choosing insurance plans with deductibles and waiting periods is a form of risk assumption because it's more economical to pay small losses from savings than to pay higher premiums to insure them.

Determine Available Coverage and Resources

As noted earlier, many employers offer some form of health insurance as an employee benefit. In some cases, the employer offers only one plan and pays for it either entirely or partially. If you work for an employer who provides health insurance this way, you should evaluate the plan's benefits and costs to determine if additional coverage—either for yourself or your dependents—will be necessary. Some employers offer their employees a choice among several types of plans. During an open-enrollment period each year, employees sign up for the health insurance plan they feel best suits their needs.

Some employers offer employees a *flexible-benefit ("cafeteria") plan* offering a choice of fringe benefits. Typically, the menu of benefits includes more than one health insurance option as well as life insurance, disability income insurance, and other benefits. As we discussed in Chapter 2, the employer specifies a set dollar amount it will provide, and employees choose a combination from these benefits, depending on their preferences and circumstances. If, after choosing your benefits from the menu offered, you decide you want or need additional insurance benefits, most employers will deduct the additional cost of providing them from your paycheck. However, before you make this decision, compare the cost and service offerings of coverage through your employer with that available from other sources.

Some employers offer consumer-directed health plans that go one step beyond a flexible-benefit plan. Typically, these plans combine a high-deductible health insurance policy with a tax-free **health reimbursement account (HRA),** a plan funded by employers for each participating employee. When the account is used up, you must pay the remaining deductible of the health insurance policy before insurance begins to pay. If you don't use the money by the end of the year, you can "roll over" the amount, and after several years of rolling it over, you can accumulate quite a bit of cash to pay for medical expenses. If you change jobs, the money stays with the employer. The Internal Revenue Service considers employer contributions to medical reimbursement accounts to be tax-free income.

Another similar type of account is the **health savings account (HSA).** The HSA is also a tax-free account, but the money is funded by employees, employers, or both to spend on routine medical costs. An HSA is also combined with a high-deductible insurance policy to pay for catastrophic care in case of major accident or illness, and—as with an HRA—can be rolled over each year. If you change jobs, the money in your HSA belongs only to you and is yours to keep. In addition to the HSA and HRA, there are many other consumer-directed health plans.

health reimbursement account An account into which employers place contributions that employees can use to pay for medical expenses. Usually combined with a high-deductible health insurance policy.

health savings account (HSA) A tax-free savings account funded by employees, employer, or both to spend on routine medical costs. Usually combined with a high deductible policy to pay for catastrophic care.

If your spouse is employed, then you should also evaluate his or her benefit package before making any decisions. You may, for example, already be covered under your spouse's group health insurance plan or be able to purchase coverage for yourself and family members at a cheaper rate than through your own employer's plan.

If you're laid off from or leave a job where you've had health benefits, you are legally eligible to continue your coverage for a period of 18 months under federal COBRA regulations (discussed later in the chapter). You'll be responsible for paying the full cost of the insurance if you decide to continue your coverage during this time, but you'll still pay group insurance rates that are often less expensive than buying individual insurance. However, you must arrange to continue your coverage before leaving your former employer.

Another important area of group coverage to consider is retiree benefits. The number of companies providing health insurance to retirees has decreased sharply, so you may not be able to count on receiving employer-paid benefits once you retire. Know what your options are to ensure continued coverage for both you and your family after you retire. Medicare will cover basic medical expenses, but you'll probably want to supplement this coverage with one of the 10 standard Medigap plans. These plans will cost from as little as $400 to as much as $6,500 per year for the typical 65-year-old, depending on coverage.

Supplementing traditional health insurance plans are several other possible sources of funds or services. As we'll discuss in Chapter 10, homeowner's and automobile insurance policies often contain limited amounts of medical expense protections. Your automobile policy, for example, may cover you if you're involved in an auto accident regardless of whether you're in a car, on foot, or on a bicycle when the accident occurs. In addition to Social Security's Medicare program, various other government programs help pay medical expenses. For instance, medical care is provided for people who've served in the armed services and were honorably discharged. Public health programs exist to treat communicable diseases, handicapped children, and mental health disorders.

Of course, you may still need or want to purchase additional medical insurance coverage on an individual basis. Private insurance companies sell a variety of indemnity and managed care plans to individuals. Well-known health insurance carriers are Aetna, CIGNA, and United Healthcare, among others. When buying health insurance—as with all types of insurance—you should buy plans from an insurance agent who will listen to your needs and give you well-thought-out responses to your questions. You should also research the carrier that will be providing your insurance. Look for a carrier that is rated highly by at least two of the major ratings agencies and that has a reputation for settling claims fairly and promptly. Avoid companies that have narrow and unusual legalistic claims practices. The National Committee for Quality Assurance (NCQA) is another source of information. This nonprofit, unbiased organization issues annual "report cards" that rate the service quality of various health plans.

Choose a Health Insurance Plan

After familiarizing yourself with the different health insurance plans and providers and reviewing your needs, you must choose one or more plans to provide coverage for you and your dependents. If you're employed, first review the various health insurance plans your company offers. If you can't get coverage from an employer, get plan descriptions and policy costs from several providers, including a group plan from a professional or trade organization, if available, for both indemnity and managed care plans. Then take your time and carefully read the plan materials to understand exactly what is covered, and at what cost. Next, add up what you've spent on medical costs over the past few years and what you might expect to spend in the future, so you can see what your costs would be under various plans.

How do you find health insurance if you've just graduated from college, don't yet have a job, and can no longer be covered by your parents' policy? Or maybe you're between jobs or need time to search out the best policy but don't want to be without protection. The *Money in Action* box on page 281 will help you with these situations.

FINANCIAL ROAD SIGN

FIVE WAYS TO SAVE ON HEALTH INSURANCE

1. Opt for a managed care plan.
2. If you're buying an indemnity plan, choose a higher deductible.
3. Buy group health insurance.
4. Buy while you're healthy.
5. Negotiate. If your health plan covers services you won't use, ask if you can eliminate them from your policy to lower your cost.

HEALTH INSURANCE: DON'T LEAVE SCHOOL WITHOUT IT

Although college graduates like to think of themselves as invincible, the truth is they're just as likely as anyone else to get sick or injured. A study by the Commonwealth Fund, a private fund that supports research on healthcare issues, found that 2 in 5 college graduates are without health insurance for part of the year after graduation. Many graduates find themselves without insurance as they search for a job. Others have jobs that don't offer health insurance, or there's a waiting period before the benefits take effect.

What can you do to fill in the gap if you find yourself without a group plan at work or in a waiting period for health insurance eligibility? The cheapest option is a short-term or temporary policy that provides up to 6 months, and sometimes 12 months, of major medical coverage. This option is best for those who'll be covered under a group plan in the near future. Premiums vary widely depending on the applicant's health, sex, age, and state of residence as well as on the deductible and co-pay. Short-term plans can start at $30 per month with a $2,500 deductible, but these plans don't cover preexisting conditions, pregnancy, or preventative care.

If you think your job search may take more than a year, or you accept a job that doesn't offer health insurance benefits, your best option is standard long-term coverage. You must be in good health to qualify for this insurance. Individual plans are typically more expensive than group coverage. Plans with high deductibles have monthly premiums starting at about $65. Plans with low deductibles can have monthly premiums from $150 and up, but a bonus of a long-term plan is that you're eligible to open a health savings account. This allows you to make tax-deductible contributions to the accounts and use the money, tax free, to pay for medical expenses.

To find an individual health insurance plan, search the Internet or contact a local insurance broker who specializes in individual health insurance. When choosing an individual health insurance plan, consider carefully the amount of the deductible you choose. Be careful of any plans advertising unusually low rates for the coverage that's offered since this may indicate that a company is fraudulent. Before you buy, contact your state insurance commission office to verify that a company is legitimate.

Even without a group plan through work, you may find group coverage through college alumni groups, religious and social organizations, trade or professional associations, and state business associations. Students covered under a parent's group plan can extend their coverage after they graduate. COBRA (Consolidated Omnibus Budget Reconciliation Act of 1985) requires that continuation of group coverage be offered to someone who loses insurance due to a qualifying event. Loss of dependent status is a qualifying event, and coverage may be extended up to 36 months. COBRA is usually the most expensive health insurance option, because you must pay the full premium, including the portion typically paid by the employer, but it's the best option for those with a preexisting condition. Many states are changing laws to allow coverage for older dependents. For example, New Jersey's law requires health insurers to cover dependents until age 30. However, to qualify you must sign up under COBRA 60 days from the existing policy's expiration date.

Critical Thinking Questions

1. What are the advantages and disadvantages of the various types of health insurance options available to recent graduates?

2. If you were graduating today and didn't have access to employer-sponsored health insurance, what option would be most attractive to you? Why?

3. Do you think most recent college graduates need health insurance? Why or why not?

Sources: Kimberly Lankford, "Nasty Surprise for the Class of '05," *Kiplinger's Personal Finance Magazine,* May 2005, p. 90; M. P. McQueen, "Health Insurers Must Cover Adult Children," Wall Street Journal, April 11, 2006, p. D1; Ann Tatko-Peterson, "Young Adults Could Pay Price for Being without Insurance," *Chicago Tribune Online Edition,* June 20, 2006, http://www.chicagotribune.com.

Smart Sites

What grade did your health plan get on its quality "report card" this year? The National Committee for Quality Assurance (NCQA) can tell you. Link at **http://www.thomsonedu.com/finance/gitman**.

You'll have to ask yourself some difficult questions to decide whether you want an indemnity or a managed care plan and then to choose the particular plan:

- **How important is cost compared with having freedom of choice?** You may have to pay more to stay with your current doctor if he or she is not part of a managed care plan you're considering. Also, you have to decide if you can live with the managed care plan's approach to healthcare.

- **Will you be reimbursed if you choose a managed care plan and want to see an out-of-network provider?** For most people, the managed care route is cheaper, even if you visit a doctor only once a year, because of indemnity plan "reasonable charge" provisions.

- **What types of coverage do you need?** Everyone has different needs; one person may want a plan with good maternity and pediatric care, whereas another wants out-patient mental health benefits. Make sure the plans you consider offer what you want.

- **How good is the managed care network?** Look at the participating doctors and hospitals to see how many of your providers are part of the plan. Check out the credentials of participating providers; a good sign is accreditation from the National Committee for Quality Assurance (NCQA). Are the providers' locations convenient for you? What preventive medical programs does it provide? Has membership grown? Talk to friends and associates to see what their experiences have been with the plan.

- **How old are you, and how is your health?** Many financial advisors recommend buying the lowest-cost plan—which may be an indemnity plan with a high deductible—if you're young and healthy.

After considering all of the coverage and resources available to you, consider where gaps in your health insurance coverage potentially lie and how best to fill them. Doing this requires an understanding of the features, policy provisions, and coverage provided by various insurance carriers and policies. We'll discuss these in detail in the next section.

⏸ Concept Check

CHECK • CONCEPT CHECK • CONCEPT CHECK • CONCEPT CHECK • CONCEPT CHECK • CONCEPT CHECK • CONCEPT CHECK • CONCEPT

9-10	Explain four methods for controlling the risks associated with healthcare expenses.
9-11	Explain what factors should be considered in evaluating available employer-sponsored health insurance plans.
9-12	Discuss possible sources of health insurance available to supplement employer-sponsored health insurance plans
9-13	Answer the five questions posed to help you choose a plan, based on your current situation. What type of plan do you think will best suit your needs?

LG4 MEDICAL EXPENSE COVERAGE AND POLICY PROVISIONS

So far, we've discussed the major types of health insurance plans, their providers, and the factors that should be considered in evaluating the need for health insurance. To evaluate different insurance plan options, however, you must be able to compare and contrast what they cover and how each plan's policy provisions may affect you and your family. By doing so, you can decide which health plan offers the best protection at the most reasonable cost. Worksheet 9.1 on page 284 provides a convenient checklist for comparing the costs and benefits of competing health insurance plans. You may want to refer to it while reading the following sections.

© PHOTONICA/GETTY IMAGES

Types of Medical Expense Coverage

The medical services covered vary from health plan to health plan. You can purchase narrowly defined plans that cover only what you consider the most important medical services or, if you can afford it and want the comfort of broader coverage, you can purchase insurance coverage to help you pay for most or all of your healthcare needs. Here are the medical expenses most commonly covered by health insurance.

Hospitalization

If you must spend time in the hospital, a *hospitalization insurance policy* will reimburse you for the cost of your stay. Hospitalization policies usually pay for a portion of (1) the hospital's daily semiprivate room rate, which typically includes meals, nursing care, and other routine services; and (2) the cost of ancillary services such as laboratory tests, X-rays, and medications you receive while hospitalized. Many hospitalization plans also cover some outpatient and out-of-hospital services once you're discharged, such as in-home rehabilitation, diagnostic treatment, and preadmission testing. Some hospitalization plans simply pay a flat daily amount for each day the insured is in the hospital, regardless of actual charges. Most policies set a limit on the number of days of hospitalization and the maximum dollar amount for ancillary services they will reimburse.

Surgical Expenses

Surgical expense insurance covers the cost of surgery in or out of the hospital. Usually, surgical expense coverage is provided as part of a hospitalization insurance policy or as a rider to such a policy. Most plans reimburse *reasonable and customary* surgical expenses based on a survey of surgical costs during the previous year. They may also cover anesthesia, nonemergency treatment using X-rays, and a limited allowance for diagnostic tests. Some plans still pay according to a *schedule of benefits,* reimbursing up to a fixed maximum for a particular surgical procedure. For example, the policy might state that you would receive no more than $1,500 for an appendectomy or $1,200 for diagnostic arthroscopic surgery on a knee. Scheduled benefits are often inadequate when compared with typical surgical costs. Most elective cosmetic surgeries, such as the proverbial "nose job" or "tummy tuck," are typically excluded from reimbursement unless they are deemed a medical necessity.

Physician Expenses

Physicians expense insurance, also called *regular medical expense,* covers the cost of visits to a doctor's office or for a doctor's hospital visits, including consultation with a specialist. Also covered are X-rays and laboratory tests performed outside of a hospital. Plans are offered on either a reasonable and customary or scheduled benefit basis. Sometimes, the first few visits with the physician for any single cause are excluded. This exclusion serves the same purpose as the deductible and waiting-period features found in other types of insurance. Often, these plans specify a maximum benefit per visit as well as a maximum number of visits per injury or illness.

major medical plan
An insurance plan designed to supplement the basic coverage of hospitalization, surgical, and physicians expenses; used to finance more catastrophic medical costs.

Major Medical Insurance

Major medical plans provide broad coverage for nearly all types of medical expenses resulting from either illnesses or accidents. As the name implies, the amounts that can be collected under this coverage are relatively large. Lifetime limits of $500,000, $1,000,000, or higher are common, and some policies have no limits at all. Because hospitalization, surgical, and physicians expense coverage meets the smaller medical costs, major medical is used to finance more catastrophic medical costs. Many people use major medical with a high deductible to protect them in case they have a catastrophic illness.

comprehensive major medical insurance A health insurance plan that combines, into a single policy, basic hospitalization, surgical, and physician expense coverage with major medical protection.

Comprehensive Major Medical Insurance

A **comprehensive major medical insurance** plan combines basic hospitalization, surgical, and physicians expense coverage with major medical protection into a single policy, usually with a low deductible. Comprehensive major medical insurance is often written

Here is a convenient checklist that you can use to compare the costs and benefits of competing healthcare plans.

	Company 1	Company 2	Company 3
PLAN TYPE (HMO, PPO, etc.)			
COSTS			
Premium per month			
Annual deductible: Per person/Per family			
Co-payment percent after deductible			
Co-pay or % coinsurance per office visit			
Co-pay or % coinsurance for "wellness" care			
COVERED MEDICAL SERVICES WITHIN NETWORK			
Inpatient hospital services			
Outpatient surgery			
Physician visits (in the hospital)			
Office visits (provider)			
Skilled nursing care			
Medical tests and X-rays			
Prescription drugs			
Mental healthcare			
Drug and alcohol abuse treatment			
Home healthcare visits			
Rehabilitation facility care			
Physical therapy			
Speech therapy			
Hospice care			
Maternity care			
Chiropractic treatment			
Preventive care and checkups			
Well-baby care			
Dental care			
Other covered services			
OTHER PROVISIONS			
Out-of-network coverage			
Medical service limits, exclusions, or preexisting conditions			
Requirements for utilization review, preauthorization, or certification procedures			

Source: Developed from information in *AHIP Guide to Health Insurance,* http://www.ahip.org/content/default.aspx?bc=41│329│351.

under a group contract. However, some efforts have been made to make this type of coverage available to individuals.

Dental Services

Dental insurance covers necessary dental care and some dental injuries sustained through accidents. (Expenses for accidental damage to natural teeth are normally covered under standard surgical expense and major medical policies.) Depending on the policy, covered services may include examinations, X-rays, dental cleanings, fillings, extractions, dentures, root canal therapy, orthodontics, and oral surgery. The maximum limit on most dental policies is often low—$1,000 to $2,500 per patient—so these plans don't fully protect against unusually high costs for dental work.

Obtained by Employer

An examination of every type of health insurance coverage available would fill a book twice the size of this one. The types of health plans already discussed are sufficient to meet the protection needs of most individuals and families. But insurance companies offer other options that provide limited protection against certain types of perils:

- *Accident policies* that pay a specified sum to an insured injured in a certain type of accident
- *Sickness policies*, sometimes called *dread disease policies*, that pay a specified sum for a named disease, such as cancer
- *Hospital income policies* that promise to guarantee a specific daily, weekly, or monthly amount as long as the insured is hospitalized

Before purchasing any of these or similar options, however, remember that sound insurance planning seldom dictates the purchase of these types of policies. Also be aware that the extra cost of purchasing these insurance options typically outweighs the limited coverage they provide. Accident and sickness policies, for instance, usually cover only one type of accident or illness, while hospital income policies generally exclude illnesses that could result in extended hospitalization or health conditions existing at the time of purchase.

The problem with buying policies that cover only a certain type of accident, illness, or financial need is that major gaps in coverage will occur. Clearly, the financial loss can be just as great regardless of whether the insured falls down a flight of stairs or contracts cancer, lung disease, or heart disease. Most limited-peril policies should be used only to supplement a comprehensive insurance program if the coverage is not overlapping.

Policy Provisions of Medical Expense Plans

To compare the health insurance plans offered by different insurers, evaluate whether they contain liberal or restrictive provisions. Generally, policy provisions can be divided into two groups: terms of payment and terms of coverage.

Terms of Payment

Four provisions govern how much your health insurance plan will pay: (1) deductibles, (2) the participation (coinsurance) clause, (3) the policy's internal limits, and (4) the coordination of benefits clause, if any.

Deductibles. Because major medical insurance plans are designed to supplement basic hospitalization, surgical, and physicians expense plans, those offered under an indemnity (fee-for-service) plan often have a relatively large *deductible,* typically $500 or $1,000. The **deductible** represents the initial amount that's *not* covered by the policy and is thus the insured's responsibility. Comprehensive major medical plans tend to offer lower deductibles, sometimes $100 or less. Most plans offer a calendar-year, all-inclusive deductible. In effect, this allows a person to accumulate the deductible from more than one incident of use. Some plans also include a *carryover provision* whereby any part of the deductible that occurs during the final 3 months of the year (October, November, and December) can be applied to the current year's deductible and can *also* be applied to the following calendar year's deductible. In a few plans the deductible is on a per-illness or per-accident basis. If you were covered by this type of policy with a $1,000 deductible and suffered three separate accidents in one year, each requiring $1,000 of medical expenses, you wouldn't be eligible to collect any benefits from the major medical plan.

Participation (Coinsurance). A **participation,** or **coinsurance, clause** stipulates that the company will pay some portion—say, 80 or 90 percent—of the amount of the covered loss in excess of the deductible rather than the entire amount. Coinsurance helps reduce the possibility that policyholders will fake illness and discourages them from incurring

deductible The initial amount *not* covered by an insurance policy and thus the insured's responsibility; it's usually determined on a calendar-year or on a per-illness or per-accident basis.

participation (coinsurance) clause A provision in many health insurance policies stipulating that the insurer will pay some portion—say, 80 or 90 percent—of the amount of the covered loss in excess of the deductible.

unnecessary medical expenses. Many major medical plans also have a *stop-loss provision* that places a cap on the amount of participation required. Without a stop-loss provision, a $1 million medical bill could leave the insured with, say, $200,000 of costs. Often such provisions limit the insured's participation to less than $10,000 and sometimes to as little as $2,000.

Internal Limits. Most major medical are written with **internal limits** that control the amounts paid for certain specified expenses—even if the claim *doesn't* exceed overall policy limits. Charges commonly subject to internal limits are hospital room and board, surgical fees, mental and nervous conditions, and nursing services. If an insured chooses an expensive physician or medical facility, he or she is responsible for paying the portion of the charges that are above a "reasonable and customary" level or beyond a specified maximum amount. The following example shows how deductibles, coinsurance, and internal limits constrain the amount a company is obligated to pay under a major medical plan.

Major Medical Policy: An Example. Assume that Frank Payne, a graduate student, has coverage under a major medical insurance policy that specifies a $500,000 lifetime limit of protection, a $1,000 deductible, an 80 percent coinsurance clause, internal limits of $350 per day on hospital room and board, and $2,000 as the maximum payable surgical fee. When Frank was hospitalized for 5 days to remove a small tumor, he incurred these costs:

Hospitalization: 5 days at $500 a day	$2,500
Surgical expense	1,800
Other covered medical expenses	1,800
Total medical expenses	$6,100

Because of the coinsurance clause in the policy, however, the maximum the company has to pay is 80 percent of the covered loss in excess of the deductible. Without internal limits, the company would pay $4,080 (.80 × [$6,100 − $1,000]). The internal limits further restrict the payment. Even though 80 percent of the $500-per-day hospitalization charge is $400, the most the company would have to pay is $350 per day. Thus Frank, the insured, becomes liable for $50 per day for 5 days, or $250. The surgical expense is below the $2,000 internal limit, so the 80 percent coinsurance clause applies and the insurer will pay $1,440 (.80 × $1,800). The company's total obligation is reduced to $3,830 ($4,080 − $250), and Frank must pay a total of $2,270 ($1,000 deductible + .20[$6,100 − $1,000] coinsurance + $250 excess hospital room and board charges). This example shows that although major medical insurance can offer large amounts of reimbursement, you may still be responsible for substantial payments.

Coordination of Benefits. Health insurance policies are not contracts of *indemnity*. This means that those insured can collect multiple payments for the same illness or accident unless health insurance policies include a **coordination of benefits provision.** This clause prevents you from collecting more than 100 percent of covered charges by collecting benefits from more than one policy. For example, many private health insurance policies coordinate benefit provisions with medical benefits paid under workers' compensation. In contrast, some companies widely advertise that their policies will pay claims regardless of other coverage the policyholder has. Of course, these latter types of insurance policies often charge more per dollar of protection. From the standpoint of insurance planning, using policies with coordination of benefits clauses can help you prevent coverage overlaps and, ideally, reduce your premiums.

Considering the complexity of medical expense contracts, the various clauses limiting payments, and coordination of benefits with other policies, one might expect that insurers often pay only partial claims and sometimes completely deny claims. If you make a claim and don't receive the payment you expected, don't give up. Exhibit 9.3 provides some guidelines on how you might go about getting your health insurance claims paid.

Terms of Coverage

Several contract provisions affect a health insurance plan's value to you. Some important provisions address (1) the persons and places covered, (2) cancellation, (3) preexisting conditions, (4) pregnancy and abortion, (5) mental illness, (6) rehabilitation coverage, and (7) continuation of group coverage.

internal limits A feature commonly found in health insurance policies that limits the amounts that will be paid for certain specified expenses—even if the claim *doesn't* exceed overall policy limits.

coordination of benefits provision A provision often included in health insurance policies to prevent the insured from collecting more than 100 percent of covered charges; it requires that benefit payments be coordinated if the insured is eligible for benefits under more than one policy.

EXHIBIT 9.3   How to Get Your Health Insurance Claims Paid

These guidelines will help you cut through red tape to get your health insurance claims paid:

1. *Treat your insurance claims almost like tax records.* Keep them, along with any supporting documentation, and keep them up to date. Set up a good filing system.

2. *List every claim, including the doctor's name, the date of the treatment, the type of treatment, the charge, and the date the claim was filed.* Photocopy it along with the bills or other supporting documents you submit and keep the copies in your file folder.

3. *Double-check your claim form for accuracy before filing it.* Make sure that all information is complete and correct; with computer processing, a typographic error or missing item could delay your claim or even cause it to be rejected.

4. *File all claims promptly, even if you don't think you are covered.* You need to file claims, usually within 6 to 12 months of the date of service, to meet your annual deductible.

5. *Review the company's Explanation of Benefits statement.* Within 30 days, you should receive a statement from your insurer telling you how much the insurance company will pay on the claim. If 30 days pass, and you haven't heard from the carrier, call or write.

6. *If a claim is rejected, don't take no for an answer.* Find out why the claim was denied, and supply additional information if required. The reason may be a misspelled name or transposed numbers or an incorrect diagnostic code. Properly documented appeals for covered services have a high likelihood of success.

7. *If your claim is not handled to your satisfaction, go directly to the company's claims supervisor or home office.* Sometimes a letter to the company president breaks the logjam. As a last resort, tell the company that you'll file a complaint with the state insurance department—and do it if necessary.

8. *Keep good records of utilization review approvals for hospital admissions or medical procedures.* You are ultimately responsible for getting these approvals, so be sure to allow enough time before your hospitalization and request written confirmation. If you have a chronic or life-threatening disease, it may be worth it to hire a private claims advocate to help you sort through your medical bills and insurance claims to figure out what you owe. Find one through the Alliance of Claims Assistance Professionals Web site, **http://www.claims.org.**

Sources: Michelle Andrews, "Don't Get Killed by Bills," *U.S. News & World Report,* August 25, 2003, p. 52; Josh Fischman, "Who'll Pay for the Doc You Want?" *U.S. News & World Report,* August 25, 2003, p. 50.

Persons and Places Covered. Some health insurance policies cover only the named insured; others offer protection to all family members. Of those that offer family coverage, some terminate benefits payable on behalf of children at age 18, and others continue them to age 24 as long as the child remains in school or is single. *If you are in this age group, you or your parents should check to see if you are covered under your parents' policy.* If not, sometimes by paying an additional premium, you can add such coverage. Some policies protect you only while you're in the United States or Canada; others offer worldwide coverage but exclude certain named countries.

Cancellation. Many health insurance policies are written to permit *cancellation* at any time at the insurer's option. Some policies explicitly state this; others don't. To protect yourself against premature cancellation, buy policies that specifically state that the insurer won't cancel coverage as long as premiums are paid.

preexisting condition clause A clause included in most individual health insurance policies permitting permanent or temporary exclusion of coverage for any physical or mental problems the insured had at the time the policy was purchased.

Preexisting Conditions. Most health insurance policies sold to individuals (as opposed to group/employer-sponsored plans) contain a **preexisting condition clause.** This means the policy might exclude coverage for any physical or mental problems you had at the time you bought it. In some policies, the exclusion is permanent; in others, it lasts only for the first year or two that the coverage is in force. Group insurance plans may also have preexisting condition clauses, but these tend to be less restrictive than those in individually written policies.

For an online primer explaining your rights under the Health Insurance Portability and Accountability Act (HIPAA), visit their site at **http://www.thomsonedu.com/finance/gitman.**

However, employees who have recently left a job or retired are covered by the **Health Insurance Portability and Accountability Act,** or **HIPAA.** This federal law, implemented in 1996, is designed to protect people's ability to get and continue health insurance after they leave a job or retire, even if they have a serious health problem. Under HIPAA, if you've already been covered by a health plan and you apply for new insurance, insurers cannot turn you down, charge you higher premiums, or enforce an exclusionary period because of your health status. HIPAA doesn't guarantee you group coverage, but it does protect your ability to buy individual health insurance even if you have a preexisting health condition.

Pregnancy and Abortion. Many individual and group health insurance plans include special clauses for medical expenses incurred through pregnancy or abortion. Some liberal policies pay for all related expenses, including sick-leave pay during the final months of pregnancy, whereas others pay for medical expenses that result from pregnancy or abortion complications but not for routine procedure expenses. In the most restrictive cases, the policy offers no coverage for any costs of pregnancy or abortion.

Mental Illness. Many health insurance plans omit or offer reduced benefits for treatment of mental disorders. For example, a health insurance policy may offer hospitalization benefits that continue to pay as long as you remain hospitalized—except for mental illness. It may restrict payment for mental illness to one-half the normally provided payment amounts and for a period not to exceed 30 days. Unfortunately, mental illness is the number one sickness requiring long-term hospital care. Because coverage for mental illness is an important insurance protection, check your policies to learn how liberal—or how restrictive—they are regarding this feature.

Rehabilitation Coverage. In the past, health insurance plans focused almost exclusively on reasonable and necessary medical expenses. If an illness or accident left an insured partially or totally disabled, no funds normally would be available to help the person retrain for employment and a more productive life. Now, though, many policies include *rehabilitation coverage* for counseling, occupational therapy, and even some educational or job-training programs. This is a good feature to look for in major medical and disability income policies.

Continuation of Group Coverage. Under the *Consolidated Omnibus Budget Reconciliation Act (COBRA),* passed by Congress in 1986, an employee who leaves the insured group voluntarily or involuntarily (except in the case of "gross misconduct") may elect to continue coverage for up to 18 months by paying premiums to his or her former employer on time (up to 102 percent of the company cost). The employee retains all benefits previously available, except for disability income coverage.

Similar continuation coverage is available for retirees and their families for up to 18 months or until they become eligible for Medicare, whichever occurs first. An employee's dependents may be covered for up to 36 months under COBRA under special circumstances, such as divorce or death of the employee. After COBRA coverage expires, most states provide for conversion of the group coverage to an individual policy regardless of the insured's current health and without evidence of insurability. Premium charges and benefits of the converted policy are determined at the time of conversion.

Cost Containment Provisions for Medical Expense Plans

Considering the continued inflation in medical costs, it's hardly surprising that insurers, along with employers that sponsor medical expense plans, are looking for ways to limit the costs incurred. Today, various cost containment provisions are included in almost all medical expense plans, both indemnity and managed care policies. These cost containment provisions include

- **Preadmission certification.** Requires you to receive approval from your insurer before entering the hospital for a scheduled stay. Such approval is not normally required for emergency stays.

Health Insurance Portability and Accountability Act (HIPAA) Federal law that protects people's ability to get and continue health insurance after they leave a job or retire, even if they have a serious health problem.

- **Continued stay review.** To receive normal reimbursement, the insured must secure approval from the insurer for any stay that exceeds the originally approved limits.
- **Second surgical opinions.** Many plans require second opinions on specific, nonemergency procedures and, in their absence, may reduce the surgical benefits paid. Most surgical expense plans now fully reimburse the cost of second opinions.
- **Waiver of coinsurance.** Because insurers can save money on hospital room and board charges by encouraging outpatient surgery, many now agree to waive the coinsurance clause and pay 100 percent of surgical costs for outpatient procedures. A similar waiver is sometimes applied to generic pharmaceuticals. For example, the patient may choose between an 80 percent payment for a brand-name pharmaceutical costing $35 or 100 percent reimbursement for its $15 generic equivalent.
- **Limitation of insurer's responsibility.** Many policies also have provisions limiting the insurer's financial responsibility to reimbursing only for costs that are considered "reasonable and customary." This provision can sometimes place limitations on the type and place of medical care for which the insurer will pay.

ⓘ Concept Check

9-14	Explain the differences between *hospitalization insurance* and *surgical expense insurance*.
9-15	What are the features of a *major medical plan*? Compare major medical to *comprehensive major medical insurance*.
9-16	Describe these policy provisions commonly found in medical expense plans: (a) deductibles, (b) coinsurance, (c) coordination of benefits, and (d) preexisting conditions.
9-17	What are the key provisions of the *Consolidated Omnibus Budget Reconciliation Act (COBRA)*? How do they relate to continuation of group coverage when an employee voluntarily or involuntarily leaves the group?
9-18	Explain the cost containment provisions commonly found in medical expense plans. How might the provision for second surgical opinions help an insurer contain its costs?

LG5 LONG-TERM CARE INSURANCE

Long-term care involves the delivery of medical and personal care, other than hospitalization, to persons with chronical medical conditions. Whether in a nursing home, in an assisted-living community, or through care provided in the patient's home, it can have major financial impact. A year's stay in a nursing home, for example, averages over $70,000, according to a 2006 publication of the Kaiser Commission on Medicaid and the Uninsured.

According to a recent Congressional Budget Office report, consumers pay about 25 percent of long-term care costs—over $50 billion annually—out of their own pockets. Government programs such as Medicare and Medicaid shoulder only about 38 percent of the total cost, and eligibility for their benefits is strictly defined. Major medical insurance plans also exclude most of the costs related to long-term care. When a person receiving nursing home care cannot afford to cover such a large personal expense out of pocket, the younger generation often ends up footing the bill.

Fortunately, special insurance policies are available to cover long-term care. Most are indemnity policies that pay a fixed dollar amount for each day you receive specified care either in a nursing home or at home. The decision to buy long-term care insurance is an important part of health insurance and retirement financial planning. Today, about 10 million individuals have long-term care insurance policies in force.

Most people purchase individual long-term care products either through organizations like the American Association of Retired Persons (AARP) or directly from the more than

long-term care The delivery of medical and personal care, other than hospital care, to persons with chronic medical conditions resulting from either illness or frailty.

110 insurance companies that offer them. Employer-sponsored long-term care insurance is also growing in popularity. Many businesses now offer some type of long-term care insurance to their employees. Usually, however, employees pay the full cost of premiums, although employer-sponsored plans can often cost less than purchasing long-term care on an individual basis. Whether you purchase long-term care insurance as an individual or through an employer-sponsored plan, however, it's important to evaluate policy provisions and costs.

Do You Need Long-Term Care Insurance?

The odds of needing more than 1 year of nursing home care before you reach age 65 are 1 in 33. On the other hand, the expense of a prolonged nursing home stay can cause severe financial hardship. How do you decide if you need long-term care insurance? Answer these questions:

- **Do you have a lot of assets to preserve for your dependents?** Because you must deplete most of your assets before Medicaid will pay for nursing home care, some financial advisors recommend that people over 65 whose net worth is more than $100,000 and income exceeds $50,000 a year consider long-term care insurance—*if* they can afford the premiums. The very wealthy, however, may prefer to self-insure.

- **Can you afford the premiums?** Premiums of many good-quality policies can be 5 to 7 percent of annual income or more. Such high premiums may cause more financial hardship than the cost of a potential nursing home stay. You may be better off investing the amount you'd spend in premiums; it would then be available for *any* future need, including long-term healthcare.

- **Is there a family history of disabling disease?** This factor increases your odds of needing long-term care. If there's a history of Alzheimer's, neurological disorders, or other potentially debilitating diseases, the need for long-term care insurance may increase.

- **Are you male or female?** Women tend to live longer and are more likely to require long-term care. They're also the primary caregivers for other family members, which may mean that when they need care, help won't be available.

- **Do you have family who can care for you?** The availability of relatives or home health services to provide care can reduce the cost of long-term care.

Long-Term Care Insurance Provisions and Costs

Whether you purchase long-term care insurance as an individual or through an employer-sponsored plan, it's important to understand what you're buying. Substantial variation exists between product offerings, so you must be especially careful to evaluate the provisions of each policy. Exhibit 9.4 summarizes the typical provisions of policies offered by leading insurers. Of course, policy provisions are important factors in determining the premium for each policy. Let's take a closer look at the most important policy provisions to consider in purchasing long-term care insurance.

- **Type of care.** Some long-term care policies offer benefits only for nursing home care, whereas others pay only for services in the insured's home, such as skilled or unskilled nursing care, physical therapy, homemakers, and home health aides. Because it's hard to predict whether a person might need to be in a nursing home, most financial planners recommend policies covering both. Many of these policies focus on nursing home care, and any expenses for healthcare in the insured's home are covered in a rider to the basic policy. Many policies also cover assisted-living, adult daycare and other community-care programs, alternative care, and respite care for the caregiver.

Long-term care insurers offer a wide range of provisions in their policies. A typical policy includes the following:

Services covered	Skilled, intermediate, and custodial care; home healthcare; adult day care (often)
Benefit eligibility	Physician certification/medically necessary
Daily benefit	$100–$300/day, nursing home; $50–$150/day, home healthcare
Benefit period	3–4 years
Maximum benefit period	5 years; unlimited
Waiting period	0–100 days
Renewability	Guaranteed
Preexisting conditions	Conditions existing 6–12 months prior to policy coverage
Inflation protection	Yes, for an additional premium
Deductibility periods	0, 20, 30, 90, 100 days
Alzheimer's disease coverage	Yes
Age limits for purchasing	40–84

- **Eligibility requirements.** Some important provisions determine whether the insured will receive payment for claims. These are known as *gatekeeper* provisions. The most liberal policies state that the insured will qualify for benefits as long as his or her physician orders the care. A common and much more restrictive provision pays only for long-term care that's medically necessary due to sickness or injury.

  One common gatekeeper provision requires the insured's inability to perform a given number of *activities of daily living (ADLs)* such as bathing, dressing, or eating. Some policies also provide care for cognitive impairment or when medically necessary and prescribed by the patient's physician. In the case of an Alzheimer's patient who remains physically healthy, inclusion of cognitive abilities as ADLs would be extremely important. Newer policies no longer require a certain period of nursing home care before covering home healthcare services.

- **Services covered.** Most policies today cover several levels of service in state-licensed nursing homes; specifically skilled, intermediate, and custodial care. *Skilled care* is needed when a patient requires constant attention from a medical professional, such as a physician or registered nurse. *Intermediate care* is provided when the patient needs medical attention or supervision but not the constant attention of a medical professional. *Custodial care* provides assistance in the normal activities of daily living, but no medical attention or supervision; a physician or nurse may be on call, however. Most long-term care policies also cover home care services, such as skilled or unskilled nursing care, physical therapy, homemakers, and home health aides provided by state-licensed or Medicare-certified home health agencies. Newer policies no longer require a certain period of nursing home care before covering home healthcare services.

- **Daily benefits.** Long-term care policies reimburse the insured for services incurred up to a daily maximum. For nursing home care policies, the daily maximums generally range from $100 to $300, depending on the amount of premium the insured is willing to pay. For combination nursing home and home care policies, the maximum home care benefit is normally half the nursing home maximum.

- **Benefit duration.** The maximum duration of benefits ranges from 1 year to the insured's lifetime. Lifetime coverage is expensive, however. Consumers should realize that the average stay in a nursing home is now about 2½ years. Most financial planners recommend the purchase of a policy with a duration of 3 to 6 years to give the insured protection for a longer-than-average period of care.

Confused about long-term care insurance coverage? The *Guide to Long-Term Care Insurance* at the America's Health Insurance Plans site—linked through **http://www.thomsonedu .com/finance/gitman**—will provide the answers.

- **Waiting period.** Even if the insured meets the eligibility requirements of his or her policy, he or she must pay long-term care expenses during the **waiting, or elimination, period.** Typical waiting periods are 90 to 100 days. Although premiums are much lower for policies with longer waiting periods, the insured must have liquid assets to cover his or her expenses during that period. If the insured is still receiving care after the waiting period expires, he or she will begin to receive benefits for the duration of the policy as long as its eligibility requirements continue to be met.

- **Renewability.** Most long-term care insurance policies now include a **guaranteed renewability** provision to ensure continued coverage for your lifetime as long as you continue to pay the premiums. This clause does not ensure a level premium over time, however. Nearly all policies allow the insurer to raise premiums if the claims experience for your peer group of policyholders is unfavorable. Watch out for policies with an **optional renewability** clause. These policies are renewable *only at the insurer's option.*

- **Preexisting conditions.** Many policies include a *preexisting conditions clause,* similar to those explained earlier, ranging from 6 to 12 months. On the other hand, many policies have no such clause, which effectively eliminates one important source of possible claim disputes.

- **Inflation protection.** Many policies offer riders that, for an additional premium, let you increase your benefits over time so that benefits roughly match the rising cost of nursing home and home healthcare. Most inflation protection riders let you increase benefits by a flat amount, often 5 percent, per year. Others offer benefits linked to the rise in the consumer price index (CPI). Most policies discontinue inflation adjustments after either 10 or 20 years. Inflation protection riders can add between 25 and 40 percent to the basic premium for a long-term care insurance policy.

- **Premium levels.** Long-term care insurance is rather expensive, and premiums vary widely among insurance companies. For example, a healthy 65-year-old may pay about $2,350 per year for a policy that pays for 4 years' care at $150 per day for nursing home care and $75 per day for home care, with a 90-day waiting period and a 5 percent inflation rider. The same coverage may cost a 50-year-old $1,150 per year, and a 79-year-old, $7,600 per year. Because of this marked rise in premium with age, some financial planners recommend buying long-term care insurance when you are fairly young.

How to Buy Long-Term Care Insurance

If you decide that you or a relative should have long-term care insurance, be sure to buy from a financially sound company (based on ratings from the major ratings agencies) that has experience in this market segment. Here are some additional guidelines to help you choose the right policy.

- **Buy the policy while you're healthy.** Once you have a disease, such as Alzheimer's or multiple sclerosis, or have a stroke, you become uninsurable. The best time to buy is when you're in your mid-fifties or sixties.

- **Buy the right types of coverage—but don't buy more coverage than you need.** Your policy should cover skilled, intermediate, and custodial care as well as adult day-care centers and assisted-living facilities. If you have access to family caregivers or home health services, opt for only nursing home coverage; if not, select a policy with generous home healthcare benefits. To reduce costs, increase the waiting period before benefits start; the longer you can cover the costs yourself, the lower your premiums. You may also choose a shorter benefit payment period; 3 years is a popular choice, but the average nursing home stay is about $2\frac{1}{2}$ years. Lifetime coverage increases the premium for a 65-year-old by as much as 40 percent.

- **Understand what the policy covers and when it pays benefits.** The amounts paid, benefit periods, and services covered vary among insurers. One rule of thumb is to buy a policy covering 80 to 100 percent of current nursing home costs in your area. Some policies pay only for licensed healthcare providers, whereas others include assistance with household chores. Know how the policy defines benefit eligibility.

waiting (elimination) period The period after an insured meets the policy's eligibility requirements, during which he or she must pay expenses out of pocket until the waiting period expires, and the insured begins to receive benefits.

guaranteed renewability Policy provision ensuring continued insurance coverage for the insured's lifetime as long as he or she continues to pay the premiums.

optional renewability Contractual clause allowing the insured to continue insurance *only at the insurer's option.*

CHECK • CONCEPT CHECK • CONCEPT CHECK • CONCEPT CHECK • CONCEPT CHECK • CONCEPT CHECK • CONCEPT CHECK • CONCEPT CH

9-19	Why should a consumer consider purchasing a *long-term care* insurance policy?
9-20	Describe the differences among long-term care policies regarding (a) type of care, (b) eligibility requirements, and (c) services covered. List and discuss some other important policy provisions.
9-21	Discuss some of the questions one should ask before buying long-term care insurance. What guidelines can be used to choose the right policy?

LG6 · DISABILITY INCOME INSURANCE

When a family member becomes sick for an extended period, the effect on the family goes beyond medical bills. The average chance of a person age 35 becoming disabled for 90 days or longer before age 65 is about 50 percent; this chance drops to about 32 percent—2.5 times greater than the chance of death at that age—at age 55. These percentages are far higher than the chance of dying, but although most Americans have life insurance, few have taken steps to protect their family should a serious illness or accident prevent them from working for an extended period.

The best way to protect against the potentially devastating financial consequences of a health-related disability is with disability income insurance. **Disability income insurance** provides families with weekly or monthly payments to replace income when the insured is unable to work due to a covered illness, injury, or disease. Some companies also offer disability income protection for a homemaker-spouse; such coverage helps pay for the services that the spouse would normally provide.

Almost all employers offer disability income insurance at advantageous rates. However, coverage is often voluntary, and you may have to pay the entire premium yourself. Group coverage is usually a good buy; however, premiums for employer-sponsored group coverage average $200 to $400 a year—about one-third less than the cost of comparable private coverage. A disadvantage is that if you change jobs, you may lose the coverage. The benefits from a group plan in which you pay the premiums are tax-free (unless paid through a flexible spending account). Be sure to run a needs analysis, as described in the instructions for Worksheet 9.2 on page 294, to be sure you have enough coverage for your needs.

Social Security offers disability income benefits, but you must be unable to do *any* job whatsoever to receive benefits. Benefits are payable only if your disability is expected to last at least 1 year (or to be fatal), and they don't begin until you've been disabled for at least 5 months. The actual amount paid is a percentage of your previous monthly earnings, with some statistical adjustments. The percentage is higher for people with low earnings. A 35-year-old who earns $20,000 and has dependents would receive about $1,300 per month (about 78 percent of earnings); if he or she earned $50,000, the amount rises to about $2,250 per month (54 percent of earnings).

The need for disability income coverage is great, yet generally ignored by the public. Although most workers receive some disability insurance benefits from their employer, in many cases the group plan falls short and pays only about 60 percent of salary for a limited period. The first step in considering disability income insurance is to determine the dollar amount your family would need (typically monthly) if an earner becomes disabled. Then you can buy the coverage you need or supplement existing coverage if necessary.

disability income insurance Insurance that provides families with weekly or monthly payments to replace income when the insured is unable to work due to a covered illness, injury, or disease.

Estimating Your Disability Insurance Needs

The main purpose of disability income insurance is to replace all (or most) of the income— that is, earnings—that would be lost if you became disabled and physically unable to hold a job. In essence, it should enable you to maintain a standard of living at or near your present level. To help decide how much disability income insurance is right for you, use Worksheet 9.2 to estimate your monthly disability benefit needs. Here is all you have to do:

1. **Calculate take-home pay.** Disability benefits are generally, but not always, tax-free, so you typically need to replace only your *take-home (after-tax) pay*. Benefits from employer-paid policies are fully or partially taxable. To estimate take-home pay, subtract income and Social Security taxes paid from your gross earned income (salary only). Divide this total by 12 to get your monthly take-home pay.

2. **Estimate the monthly amounts of disability benefits from government or employer programs:**
   a. *Social Security benefits.* Get an estimate of your benefits by calling 1-800-772-1213 for a *Personal Earnings and Benefit Estimate Statement*. An insurance agent may also have a computer program that can easily calculate it. The average Social Security disability benefit is estimated to range from about $1,300 to $2,700 per month for a wage earner with dependents, depending on age and income.
   b. *Other government program benefits* with disability benefits for which you qualify (armed services, Veterans Administration, civil service, the Federal Employees Compensation Act, state workers' compensation systems). There are also special programs for railroad workers, longshoremen, and people with black-lung disease.
   c. *Company disability benefits.* Ask your company benefits supervisor to help you calculate company-provided benefits, including sick pay or wage continuation plans (these are essentially short-term disability income insurance) and plans formally designated as disability insurance. For each benefit your employer offers, check on its tax treatment.
   d. *Group disability policy benefits.* A private insurer provides the coverage, and you pay for it, often through payroll deduction.

3. **Add up your existing monthly disability benefits.**

4. **Subtract your existing monthly disability benefits from your current monthly take-home pay.** The result shows the estimated monthly disability benefits you'll need to maintain your present after-tax income. Note that investment income and spousal income (if he or she is presently employed) are ignored because it's assumed this income will continue and is necessary to maintain your current standard of living. If your spouse is now unemployed but would enter the workforce if you ever became disabled, his or her estimated monthly income (take-home pay) could be subtracted from item 4 of Worksheet 9.2 to determine your net monthly disability benefit needs.

Worksheet 9.2 — Estimating Disability Income Insurance Needs

Using a worksheet like this makes the job of estimating disability benefit insurance needs a lot easier.

DISABILITY BENEFIT NEEDS

Name(s)_____ Date_____

1. Estimate current monthly *take-home pay* $_____
2. Estimate existing monthly benefits:
   a. Social Security benefits $_____
   b. Other government program benefits   _____
   c. Company disability benefits   _____
   d. Group disability policy benefits   _____
3. Total existing monthly disability benefits
   (2a + 2b + 2c + 2d) $_____
4. **Estimated monthly disability benefits needed ([1] − [3])** $_____

Disability Income Insurance Provisions and Costs

The scope and cost of your disability income coverage depends on its contractual provisions. Although disability income insurance policies can be complex, certain features are important: (1) definition of disability, (2) benefit amount and duration, (3) probationary period, (4) waiting period, (5) renewability, and (6) other provisions.

Definition of Disability

Disability policies vary in the standards you must meet to receive benefits. Some pay benefits if you're unable to perform the duties of your customary occupation—the *own occupation* (or "Own Occ") definition—whereas others pay only if you can engage in no gainful employment at all—the *any occupation* (or "Any Occ") definition. Under the "Own Occ" definition, a professor who lost his voice, but still could get paid to write or do research, would receive full benefits because he couldn't lecture, a primary function of his occupation. With a *residual benefit option,* you would be paid partial benefits if you can only work part-time or at a lower salary. The "Any Occ" definition is considerably less expensive because it gives the insurer more leeway in determining whether the insured should receive benefits.

Individual disability policies may contain a *presumptive disability* clause that supersedes the previously discussed definition of disability when certain types of losses occur. Loss of both hands, sight in both eyes, and hearing in both ears are examples where the insured may be *presumed* totally disabled and may receive full benefits even though he or she still can be employed in some capacity.

Benefit Amount and Duration

Most individual disability income policies pay a flat monthly benefit, which is stated in the policy, whereas group plans pay a fixed percentage of gross income. In either case, insurers normally won't agree to amounts of more than 60 to 70 percent of the insured's gross income. Insurers won't issue policies for the full amount of gross income because this would give some people an incentive to fake a disability (for example, "bad back") and collect more in insurance benefits than they normally would receive as take-home pay.

Monthly benefits can be paid for a few months or a lifetime. If you're ensured substantial pension, Social Security, or other benefits at retirement, a policy that pays benefits until age 65 is adequate. Most people, however, will need to continue their occupations for many more years and should consider a policy offering lifetime benefits. Many policies offer benefits for periods as short as 2 or 5 years. Although these policies may be better than nothing, they don't protect against the major financial losses associated with long-term disabilities.

Probationary Period

Both group and individual disability income policies are likely to include a probationary period, usually 7 to 30 days, which is a time delay from the date the policy is issued until benefit privileges are available. Any disability stemming from an illness, injury, or disease that occurs during the probationary period is *not* covered—even if it continues beyond this period. This feature keeps costs down.

Waiting Period

The waiting, or elimination, period provisions in a disability income policy are similar to those discussed for long-term care insurance. Typical waiting periods range from 30 days to 1 year. If you have an adequate emergency fund to provide family income during the early months of disability, you can choose a longer waiting period and substantially reduce your premiums, as shown in Exhibit 9.5 on page 296.

EXHIBIT 9.5   Disability Income Insurance Premium Costs

The cost of disability income insurance varies with the terms of payment as well as the length of the waiting period. Because they have longer life expectancies, women pay substantially higher rates than men do. This table shows premiums for basic disability income coverage for a 35-year-old that pays $2,000 per month in benefits, with guaranteed premiums to age 65. Any additional features, such as inflation riders, cost more.

Benefit Period	2 Years		5 Years		To Age 65		Lifetime	
Waiting Period	**Male**	**Female**	**Male**	**Female**	**Male**	**Female**	**Male**	**Female**
30 days	$698	$1,192	$922	$1,601	$1,284	$2,327	$1,402	$2,508
60 days	539	983	715	1,145	986	1,674	1,086	1,821
90 days	427	587	559	809	746	1,163	829	1,281
6 months	386	514	514	728	692	1,067	774	1,183
One year	358	464	475	660	638	972	718	1,086

With most insurers, you effectively can trade off an increase in the waiting period from, say, 30 days to 90 days for an increase in the duration of benefits from 5 years to age 65. In fact, as Exhibit 9.5 shows, the premium charged by this insurer for a policy covering a 35-year-old male with a 30-day waiting period and 2-year benefit period ($698) is about the same as one charged for benefits payable to age 65 with a 6-month waiting period ($692). Accepting this type of trade-off usually makes sense because the primary purpose of insurance is to protect the insured against a catastrophic loss, rather than smaller losses that are better handled through proper budgeting and saving.

Renewability

Most individual disability income insurance is either *guaranteed renewable* or *noncancelable.* As with long-term care policies, guaranteed renewability ensures that you can renew the policy until you reach the age stated in the clause, usually age 65. Premiums can be raised over time if justified by the loss experience of all those in the same class (usually based on age, sex, and occupational category). Noncancelable policies offer guaranteed renewability, but they also guarantee that future premiums will remain the same as those stated in the policy at issuance. Because of this stable premium guarantee, noncancelable policies generally are more expensive than those with only a guaranteed renewability provision.

Other Provisions

The purchasing power of income from a long-term disability policy that pays, say, $2,000 per month could be severely affected by inflation. In fact, a 3 percent inflation rate would reduce the purchasing power of this $2,000 benefit to less than $1,500 in 10 years. To counteract such a reduction, many insurers offer a *cost-of-living adjustment (COLA).* With a COLA provision, the monthly benefit is adjusted upward each year, often in line with the CPI, although these annual adjustments are often capped at a given rate, say, 8 percent. Although some financial advisors suggest buying COLA riders, others feel the 10 to 25 percent additional premium is not worth it with today's relatively low inflation rate.

Although the COLA provision applies only once the insured is disabled, the *guaranteed insurability option (GIO)* can allow you to purchase additional disability income insurance in line with inflation increases while you're still healthy. Under the GIO, the price of this additional insurance is fixed at the inception of the contract, and you don't have to prove insurability.

A *waiver of premium* is standard in disability income policies. If you're disabled for a minimum period, normally 60 or 90 days, the insurer will waive any future premiums that come due while you remain disabled. In essence, the waiver of premium gives you additional disability income insurance in the amount of your regular premium payment.

Remember that disability income insurance is just one part of your overall personal financial plan. You'll need to find your own balance between cost and coverage.

Smart.Sites

Want to learn more about disability income insurance? America's Health Insurance Plans offers a Guide to Disability Income Insurance. Link to it at **http://www.thomsonedu .com/ finance/gitman.**

9-22	What is *disability income insurance?* Explain the waiting period provisions found in such policies.
9-23	Describe both the liberal and strict definitions used to establish whether an insured is disabled.
	Why is benefit duration an important consideration when shopping for disability income coverage?

• SUMMARY • SUMMARY • SUMMARY • SUMMARY • SUMMARY • SUMMARY • SUMMARY • SUMMARY • SUMMARY • S

« SUMMARY

LG1 Discuss why having adequate health insurance is important and identify the factors contributing to the growing cost of health insurance. A serious illness or major injury can have devastating financial consequences, easily costing tens of thousands of dollars in medical care and lost income. Even routine medical care can be costly. Adequate health insurance protects you from having to pay all of these costs out of pocket. However, many Americans are uninsured or underinsured because the cost of health insurance has skyrocketed. Trends pushing medical expenses and health insurance higher include the growth of new drugs and treatments that save lives but also cost more to provide. Administrative costs, excessive paperwork, increased regulation, and insurance fraud are also contributing to rising costs.

LG2 Differentiate among the major types of health insurance plans and identify major private and public health insurance providers and their programs. Health insurance is available from both private and government-sponsored programs. Private health insurance plans include indemnity (fee-for-service) plans and managed care plans. Indemnity plans pay a share of healthcare costs directly to a medical provider, who is usually separate from the insurer. The insured pays the remaining amount. In a managed care plan, subscribers contract with and make monthly payments directly to the organization providing the health services. Examples of managed care plans include health maintenance organizations (HMOs) and preferred provider organizations (PPOs). Blue Cross/Blue Shield plans are prepaid hospital and medical expense plans. Federal and state agencies also provide health insurance coverage to eligible individuals. Medicare, Medicaid, and workers' compensation insurance are all forms of government health insurance plans.

LG3 Analyze your own health insurance needs and explain how to shop for appropriate coverage. From a health insurance perspective, most people need protection from two types of losses: (1) the cost of medical bills and other associated expenses and (2) loss of income or household services caused by an inability to work. A good healthcare plan should use risk avoidance, loss prevention and control, and risk assumption strategies to reduce risk and the associated need and cost of insurance. The best way to buy health insurance is to determine your current coverage and resources and then match your needs with the various types of coverage available. When shopping for health insurance, consider the cost of coverage, its availability as an employee benefit, the quality of both the agent and the insurer or managed care provider, and your own medical needs and care preferences.

LG4 Explain the basic types of medical expenses covered and policy provisions of health insurance plans. The basic types of medical expenses covered by insurance are hospitalization, surgical expenses, physicians expenses (nonsurgical medical care), and major medical insurance (which covers all types of medical expenses). Some health insurers offer comprehensive major medical policies that combine basic hospitalization, surgical, and physicians expense coverage with a major medical plan to form a single policy.

The most important provisions in medical insurance policies pertain to terms of payment, terms of coverage, and cost containment. How much your plan will pay depends on deductibles, participation (coinsurance), internal limits, and coordination of benefits. Terms of coverage encompass the persons and places covered, cancellation, preexisting conditions, pregnancy and abortion, mental illness, rehabilitation, and group coverage continuation. The most common cost containment provisions are preadmission certification, continued stay review, second surgical opinions, waiver of coinsurance, and limitations of insurer's responsibility.

LG5 **Assess the need for and features of long-term care insurance.** Long-term care insurance covers nonhospital expenses, such as nursing home care or home healthcare, caused by chronic illness or frailty. Coverage availability depends on provisions addressing type of care, eligibility requirements, services covered, renewability, and preexisting conditions. Terms-of-payment provisions include daily benefits, benefit duration, waiting period, and inflation protection. Premium levels result from differences in coverage and payment provisions, and they vary widely among insurance companies.

LG6 **Discuss the features of disability income insurance and how to determine your need for it.** The loss of family income caused by the disability of a principal wage earner can be at least partially replaced by disability income insurance. Disability insurance needs can be estimated by subtracting the amount of existing monthly disability benefits from current monthly take-home pay. Important coverage terms include the definition of disability, probationary period, renewability, guaranteed insurability, and waiver of premium. Provisions pertaining to benefit amount and duration, waiting period, and cost-of-living adjustments define the terms of payment. Because these policies are expensive, you should choose as long a waiting period as possible given your other available financial resources.

FINANCIAL PLANNING EXERCISES

LG2, 3, 4

1. John and Linda Carter have two children, ages 6 years and 5 months. Their younger child, Caleb, was born with a congenital heart defect that will require several major surgeries in the next few years to fully correct. John is employed as a salesperson for a major pharmaceutical firm, and Linda is a stay-at-home mother. John's employer offers employees a choice between two health benefit plans:

   • An indemnity plan that allows the Carters to choose health services from a wide range of doctors and hospitals. The plan pays 80 percent of all medical costs, and the Carters are responsible for the other 20 percent. There's a $500 per person deductible. John's employer will pay 100 percent of the cost of this plan for John, but the Carters will be responsible for paying $380 a month to cover Linda and the children under this plan.

   • A group HMO. If the Carters choose this plan, the company still pays 100 percent of the plan's cost for John, but insurance for Linda and the children will cost $295 a month. They'll also have to pay a $20 co-payment for doctors' office visits and prescription drugs. They will be restricted to using the HMO's doctors and hospital for medical services.

   Which plan would you recommend that the Carters choose? Why? What other health coverage options should the Carters consider?

LG2, 3, 4

2. David Chang was seriously injured in a snowboarding accident that broke both his legs and an arm. His medical expenses included 5 days of hospitalization at $900 a day, $6,200 in surgical fees, $4,300 in physician's fees (including time in the hospital and eight follow-up office visits), $520 in prescription medications, and $2,100 for physical therapy treatments. All of these charges fall within customary and reasonable payment amounts.

   a. If David has an indemnity plan with a $500 deductible that pays 80 percent of his charges and has a $5,000 stop-loss provision, how much will he have to pay out of pocket?

   b. What would David's out-of-pocket expenses be if he belonged to an HMO with a $20 co-pay for office visits?

c. Monthly premiums are $155 for the indemnity plan and $250 for the HMO. If he has no other medical expenses this year, which plan provides more cost-effective coverage for David? What other factors should he consider in deciding between the two plans?

LG1, 2, 3, 4   3. **Use Worksheet 9.1.** Sarah Connelly, a recent college graduate, has decided to accept a job offer from a nonprofit organization. She'll earn $34,000 a year but will receive no employee health benefits. She estimates that her monthly living expenses will be about $2,000 a month, including rent, food, transportation, and clothing. She has no health problems and expects to remain in good health in the near future. Using the Internet or other resources, gather information about three health insurance policies that Sarah could purchase on her own. Include at least one HMO. Use Worksheet 9.1 to compare the policies' features. Should Sarah buy health insurance? Why or why not? Assuming that she does decide to purchase health insurance, which of the three policies would you recommend and why?

LG5   4. Discuss the pros and cons of long-term care insurance. Does it make sense for anyone in your family right now? Why or why not? What factors might change this assessment in the future?

LG6   5. **Use Worksheet 9.2.** John Fitzmorris, a 35-year-old computer programmer, earns $72,000 a year. His monthly take-home pay is $3,750. His wife, Linda, works part-time at their children's elementary school but receives no benefits. Under state law, John's employer contributes to a worker's compensation insurance fund that would provide $2,250 per month for 6 months if John were disabled and unable to work.

a. Use Worksheet 9.2 to calculate John's disability insurance needs assuming that he won't qualify for Medicare under his Social Security benefits.

b. Based on your answer in part **a**, what would you advise John about his need for additional disability income insurance? Discuss the type and size of disability income insurance coverage he should consider, including possible provisions he might want to include. What other factors should he take into account if he decides to purchase a policy?

LG6   6. **Use Worksheet 9.2.** Do you need disability income insurance? Calculate your need using Worksheet 9.2. Discuss how you'd go about purchasing this coverage.

LG1, 2, 3, 4   7. Assess your current health insurance situation. Do you have any health insurance now? What does your policy cover? What is excluded? Are there any gaps that you think need to be filled? Are there any risks in your current lifestyle or situation that might make additional coverage necessary? If you were to purchase health insurance for yourself in the near future, what type of plan would you select, and why? What steps can you take to keep your health costs down?

APPLYING PERSONAL FINANCE

Insure Your Health!

Health care costs have increased dramatically in recent years, and many insurance providers have reduced their coverage, leaving the individual to foot more of the bill. In this project you'll examine your health insurance needs and determine the coverage that's appropriate for you.

First, make a list of the possible healthcare needs you're likely to have during the year. Be sure to include the potential accident risks to which you're typically exposed due to your lifestyle activities. Then, if you currently have health insurance, make a list of the coverages it provides, including deductibles, coinsurance amounts, prescription coverage, policy limits and exclusions, and so forth. Is your coverage adequate in light of your needs? Are there ways you can reduce your costs? If you don't currently have health insurance, research possible providers. Can you obtain insurance through your university, place of employment, or through an organization to which you belong? Do you qualify for insurance that may be provided by your state? Consider all of your feasible alternatives, the coverages that would be provided, and the cost of each.

CRITICAL THINKING CASES

LG2, 3, 4, 5, 6 **9.1 Evaluating Rick's Health Care Coverage**

Rick Lannefeld was a self-employed window washer earning approximately $700 per week. One day, while cleaning windows on the eighth floor of the First National Bank Building, he tripped and fell from the scaffolding to the pavement below. He sustained severe multiple injuries but miraculously survived the accident. He was immediately rushed to Mt. Sinai Hospital for surgery. He remained there for 60 days of treatment, after which he was allowed to go home for further recuperation. During his hospital stay, he incurred the following expenses: surgeon, $2,500; physician, $1,000; hospital bill for room and board, $250 per day; nursing services, $1,200; anesthetics, $600; wheelchair rental, $100; ambulance, $150; and drugs, $350. Rick has a major medical policy with LIC Corporation that has a $3,000 deductible clause, an 80 percent coinsurance clause, internal limits of $180 per day on hospital room and board, and $1,500 as a maximum surgical fee. The policy provides no disability income benefits.

Critical Thinking Questions

1. Explain the policy provisions as they relate to deductibles, coinsurance, and internal limits.
2. How much should Rick recover from the insurance company? How much must he pay out of his pocket?
3. Would any other policies have offered Rick additional protection? What about his inability to work while recovering from his injury?
4. Based on the information presented, how would you assess Rick's healthcare insurance coverage? Explain.

LG6 **9.2 Benito and Teresa Get a Handle on Their Disability Income Needs**

Benito Fernandez and his wife, Teresa, have been married for 2 years and have a 1-year-old son. They live in Detroit, where Benito works for Michigan Tool Company. He earns $3,200 per month, of which he takes home $2,300. As an employee of Michigan Tool, he and his family are entitled to receive the benefits provided by the company's group health insurance policy. In addition to major medical coverage, the policy provides a monthly disability income benefit amounting to 20 percent of the employee's average monthly take-home pay for the most recent 12 months prior to incurring the disability. (*Note*: Benito's average monthly take-home pay for the most recent year is equal to his current monthly take-home pay.) In case of complete disability, Benito would also be eligible for Social Security payments of $700 per month.

Teresa is also employed. She earns $700 per month after taxes by working part-time at a nearby grocery store. The store gives her no benefits other than Social Security. Should Benito become disabled, Teresa would continue to work at her part-time job. If she became disabled, Social Security would provide monthly income of $300. Benito and Teresa spend 90 percent of their combined take-home pay to meet their bills and provide for a variety of necessary items. They use the remaining 10 percent to fulfill their entertainment and savings goals.

Critical Thinking Questions

1. How much, if any, additional disability income insurance does Benito require to ensure adequate protection against his becoming completely disabled? Use Worksheet 9.2 to assess his needs.
2. Does Teresa need any disability income coverage? Explain.
3. What specific recommendations regarding disability income insurance would you give Benito and Teresa to provide adequate protection for themselves and their child?

> **MONEY ONLINE** www.thomsonedu.com/finance/gitman

Visit **http://www.thomsonedu.com/finance/gitman** for some additional Web-based exercises and hot links (with annotations) to a variety of resources relevant to the topics covered in this chapter.

Protecting Your Property

LEARNING GOALS

CHAPTER 10

LG1 ▶	Discuss the importance and basic principles of property insurance, including types of exposure, indemnity, and coinsurance.	p. 301
LG2 ▶	Identify the types of coverage provided by homeowner's insurance.	p. 305
LG3 ▶	Select the right homeowner's insurance policy for your needs.	p. 305
LG4 ▶	Analyze the coverage in a personal automobile policy (PAP) and choose the most cost-effective policy.	p. 313
LG5 ▶	Describe other types of property and liability insurance.	p. 322
LG6 ▶	Choose a property and liability insurance agent and company, and settle claims.	p. 323
▶		

0 • CHAPTER 10 • CHAPTER 10 • CHAPTER 10 • CHAPTER 10 • CHAPTER 10 • CHAPTER 10 • CHAPTER 10 • CHAPT

LG1 · BASIC PRINCIPLES OF PROPERTY INSURANCE

Suppose that a severe storm destroyed your home. Could you afford to replace it? Most people couldn't. To protect yourself from this and other similar types of property loss, you need property insurance. What's more, every day you face some type of risk of negligence. For example, you might be distraught over a personal problem and unintentionally run a red light, seriously injuring a pedestrian. Could you pay for the medical and other costs? Because consequences like this and other potentially negligent acts could cause financial ruin, having appropriate liability insurance is essential.

Property and liability insurance should be as much a part of your personal financial plans as life and health insurance. Such coverage protects the assets you've already acquired and safeguards your progress toward financial goals. **Property insurance** guards against catastrophic losses of real and personal property caused by such perils as fire, theft, vandalism, windstorms, and other calamities. **Liability insurance** offers protection against the financial consequences that may arise from the insured's responsibility for property loss or injuries to others.

People spend lots of money for insurance coverage, but few really understand what they're getting for their premium dollars. Even worse, the vast majority of people are totally unaware of any gaps, overinsurance, or underinsurance in their property and liability insurance policies. Inefficient or inadequate insurance protection is at odds with the objectives of personal financial planning, so it's important to become familiar with the principles of property and liability insurance.

property insurance
Insurance coverage that protects real and personal property from catastrophic losses caused by a variety of perils, such as fire, theft, vandalism, and windstorms.

liability insurance
Insurance that protects against the financial consequences that may arise from the insured's responsibility for property loss or injuries to others.

The basic principles of property and liability insurance pertain to types of exposure, indemnity, and coinsurance. We'll discuss each of these principles in the following sections.

Types of Exposure

Most individuals face two basic types of exposure: physical loss of property and loss through liability.

Exposure to Property Loss

Most property insurance contracts define the property covered and name the **perils**—the causes of loss—for which the insured will be compensated in case of a claim against their policy. As a rule, most property insurance contracts impose two obligations on the property owner: (1) developing a complete inventory of the property being insured and (2) identifying the perils against which protection is desired. Some property contracts limit coverage by excluding certain types of property and perils, while others offer more comprehensive protection.

Property Inventory. Do you know the value of all the property you own? If you're like most people, you don't, nor do you have an itemized property list for insurance purposes. Inventorying of property is part of the financial planning process. It is especially important in the case of a total loss—if your home is burned by fire, for example. All property insurance companies require you to show *proof of loss* when making a claim, and your personal property inventory, along with corresponding values at the time of inventory, can serve as evidence to satisfy the company. A comprehensive property inventory not only helps you settle a claim when a loss occurs but also serves as a useful guide for selecting the most appropriate coverage for your particular needs.

Most families have a home, household furnishings, clothing and personal belongings, lawn and garden equipment, and motor vehicles, all of which need to be insured. Fortunately, most homeowner's and automobile insurance policies provide coverage for these types of belongings. But many families also own such items as motorboats and trailers, various types of off-road vehicles, business property and inventories, jewelry, stamp or coin collections, furs, musical instruments, antiques, paintings, bonds, securities, and other items of special value, such as cameras, golf clubs, electronic equipment, and personal computers. Coverage for these belongings (and those that accompany you when you travel) often require special types of insurance.

To help policyholders prepare inventories, many insurance companies have easy-to-complete personal property inventory forms available. A partial sample of one such form is shown in Exhibit 10.1. These inventory forms can be supplemented with photographs or videos of household contents and belongings. For insurance purposes, a picture may truly be worth a thousand words. Regardless of whether inventory forms are supplemented with photographs or videotapes, *every effort should be made to keep these documents in a safe place,* where they can't be destroyed—such as a bank safe-deposit box. You might also consider keeping a *duplicate copy* with a parent or trusted relative. Remember, you may need these photographs and inventories if something serious does happen and you have to come up with an authenticated list of property losses.

Identifying Perils. Many people feel a false sense of security after buying insurance because they believe they're safeguarded against all contingencies. The fact is, however, that certain *perils* cannot be reasonably insured. For example, most homeowner's or automobile insurance policies limit or exclude damage or loss caused by flood (remember Hurricane Katrina in New Orleans in 2005), earthquake, mudslides, mysterious disappearance, war, nuclear radiation, and wear and tear. In addition, property insurance contracts routinely limit coverage based on the location of the property, time of loss, persons involved, and types of hazards to which the property is exposed. We'll explain these limitations further in later sections of this chapter.

Liability Exposures

We all encounter a variety of liability exposures daily. Driving a car, entertaining guests at home, or being careless in performing professional duties are some common liability risks.

peril A cause of loss.

EXHIBIT 10.1   A Personal Property Inventory Form

Using a form like this will help you keep track of your personal property, including date of purchase, original purchase price, and replacement cost.

Living Room

Stereo System

Brand	
Model	
Serial #	Date purchased
Purchase price $	Replacement cost $

Large Screen TV

Brand	
Model	
Serial #	Date purchased
Purchase price $	Replacement cost $

Compact Disc Player

Brand	
Model	
Serial #	Date purchased
Purchase price $	Replacement cost $

Home Theater System

Brand	
Model	
Serial #	Date purchased
Purchase price $	Replacement cost $

DVD Player

Brand	
Model	
Serial #	Date purchased
Purchase price $	Replacement cost $

Living Room

Article	Qty.	Date Purchase	Purchase Price	Replacement Cost
Air conditioners (window)				
Blinds/shades				
Bookcases				
Books				
Cabinets				
Carpets/rugs				
Chairs				
Chests				
Clocks				
Couches/sofas				
Curtains/draperies				
Fireplace fixtures				
Lamps/lighting fixtures				
Mirrors				
Pictures/paintings				
CDs				
Planters				
Stereo equipment				
Tables				
Television sets				
Other				
Other				

Loss exposures resulting from these activities are examples of **negligence**—failing to act in a reasonable manner or take necessary steps to protect others from harm. Even if you're never negligent and always prudent, someone might *think* you are the cause of a loss and bring a costly lawsuit against you. Losing the judgment could cost you thousands—or even millions—of dollars. A debt that size could force you into bankruptcy or financial ruin.

Fortunately, *liability insurance* coverage will protect you against losses resulting from these risks, *including the high legal fees* required to defend yourself against suits that may, or may not, have merit. It's important to include adequate liability insurance in your overall insurance program, either through your homeowner's and automobile policies or through a separate umbrella policy.

negligence Failing to act in a reasonable manner or take necessary steps to protect others from harm.

Principle of Indemnity

The **principle of indemnity** states that the insured may not be compensated by the insurance company in an amount exceeding the insured's economic loss. Most property and liability insurance contracts are based on this principle—although, as noted in Chapters 8 and 9, this *principle does not apply to life and health insurance*. Several important concepts related to the principle of indemnity include actual cash value, subrogation, and other insurance.

Actual Cash Value versus Replacement Cost

The principle of indemnity limits the amount an insured may collect to the **actual cash value** of the property: the replacement cost less the amount of physical depreciation. Some insurers guarantee replacement cost without taking depreciation into account—for example, most homeowner's policies will settle building losses on a replacement cost basis, if the proper type and amount of insurance is purchased. Without a replacement-cost provision, it's common practice to deduct the amount of depreciation to obtain the actual cash value. If an insured property is damaged, the insurer is obligated to pay no more than the property would cost new today (its replacement cost) less the amount of depreciation from wear and tear.

For example, assume that fire destroys two rooms of furniture that was 6 years old, with an estimated useful life of 10 years. Replacement cost is $5,000. Therefore, at the time of loss, the furniture was subject to an assumed physical depreciation of 60 percent (6 years ÷ 10 years)—in this case, $3,000. Because the actual cash value is estimated at $2,000 ($5,000 replacement cost minus $3,000 of depreciation), the maximum the insurer would have to pay is $2,000. Note that the original cost of the property has no bearing on the settlement.

Subrogation

After an insurance company pays a claim, its **right of subrogation** allows it to request reimbursement from either the person who caused the loss or that person's insurance company. For example, assume that you're in an automobile accident in which the other party damages your car. You may collect from your insurer or the at-fault party's insurer, but not from both (not for the same loss). Clearly, to collect the full amount of the loss from both parties would leave you better off after the loss than before it. This violates the principle of indemnity. Because the party who caused the accident (or loss) is ultimately responsible for paying the damages, your insurance company can go after the responsible party to collect its loss (the amount it paid out to you).

Other Insurance

Nearly all property and liability insurance contracts have an *other-insurance clause,* prohibiting insured persons from insuring their property with two or more insurance companies and collecting from multiple companies for the same loss. The other-insurance clause normally states that if a person has more than one insurance policy on a property, each company is liable for only a prorated amount of the loss based on its proportion of the total insurance covering the property. Without this provision, insured persons could use duplicate property insurance policies to actually profit from their losses.

Coinsurance

Coinsurance, a provision commonly found in property insurance contracts, requires policyholders to buy insurance in an amount equal to a specified percentage of the replacement value of their property, or the *policyholder* is required to pay for a proportional share of the loss. In essence, the coinsurance provision stipulates that if a property isn't properly covered, the property owner will become the "coinsurer" and bear part of the loss. If the policyholder has the stipulated amount of coverage (usually 80 percent of the value of the property), then the insurance company will reimburse him or her for covered losses, dollar for dollar, up to the amount of the policy limits. Assume, for example, that John and Mary have a fire insurance policy on their

---

principle of indemnity An insurance principle stating that an insured may not be compensated by the insurance company in an amount exceeding the insured's economic loss.

actual cash value A value assigned to an insured property that is determined by subtracting the amount of physical depreciation from its replacement cost.

right of subrogation The right of an insurer, who has paid an insured's claim, to request reimbursement from either the person who caused the loss or that person's insurer.

coinsurance In property insurance, a provision requiring a policyholder to buy insurance in an amount equal to a specified percentage of the replacement value of their property.

$200,000 home with an 80 percent coinsurance clause. The policy limits must equal or exceed 80 percent of the replacement value of their home. Further, assume that they ran short of money and decided to save by buying a $120,000 policy instead of $160,000 (80 percent of $200,000) as required by the coinsurance clause. If a loss occurred, the company would be obligated to pay only 75 percent ($120,000/$160,000) of the loss, up to the amount of the policy limit. Thus, on damages of $40,000, the insurer would pay only $30,000 (75 percent of $40,000). Obviously, you should closely evaluate the coinsurance clause of any property insurance policy so you won't have an unexpected additional burden in case of loss.

❙❙ Concept Check

CHECK • CONCEPT CHECK • CONCEPT CHECK • CONCEPT CHECK • CONCEPT CHECK • CONCEPT CHECK • CONCEPT C

10-1	Briefly explain the fundamental concepts related to property and liability insurance.
10-2	Explain the *principle of indemnity*. Are any limits imposed on the amount an insured may collect under this principle?
10-3	Explain the *right of subrogation*. How does this feature help lower insurance costs?
10-4	Describe how the *coinsurance* feature works.

LG2, LG3 HOMEOWNER'S INSURANCE

Although homeowner's insurance is often thought of as a single type of insurance policy, homeowners can choose from four different forms (HO-1, HO-2, HO-3, and HO-8). Two other forms (HO-4 and HO-6) meet the needs of renters and owners of condominiums (see Exhibit 10.2 on page 306). An HO-4 renter's policy offers essentially the same broad protection as an HO-2 homeowner's policy, but the coverage doesn't apply to the rented dwelling unit because tenants usually don't have a financial interest in the real property.

All HO forms are divided into two sections. Section I applies to the dwelling, accompanying structures, and personal property of the insured. Section II deals with comprehensive coverage for personal liability and for medical payments to others. The scope of coverage under Section I is least with an HO-1 policy and greatest with an HO-3 policy. HO-8 is a modified coverage policy for older homes, used to insure houses that have market values well below the cost to rebuild. The coverage in Section II is the same for all forms.

In the following paragraphs, we'll explain the important features of homeowner's forms HO-2 and HO-3, the most commonly sold policies. (As Exhibit 10.2 shows, HO-1 is a basic, seldom-used policy with relatively narrow coverage.) The coverage offered under the HO-2 and HO-3 forms is basically the same; the differences lie only in the number of perils against which protection applies.

Perils Covered

comprehensive policy
Property and liability insurance policy covering all perils unless they are specifically excluded.

Some property and liability insurance agreements, called **comprehensive policies,** cover all perils except those specifically excluded, whereas **named peril policies** name individual perils covered.

named peril policy
Property and liability insurance policy that individually names the perils covered.

Section I Perils

The perils against which the home and its contents are insured are shown in Exhibit 10.2. Coverage on household belongings is the same for the HO-2 and HO-3 forms, but coverage

EXHIBIT 10.2   **A Guide to Homeowner's Policies**

The amount of insurance coverage you receive depends on the type of homeowner's (HO) policy you buy. You can also obtain coverage if you're a renter or a condominium owner.

Form	Coverages*	Covered perils
Basic Form (HO-1)	A—$15,000 minimum; B—10% of A; C—50% of A; D—10% of A; E—$100,000; F—$1,000 per person	Fire, smoke, lightning, windstorm, hail, volcanic eruption, explosion, glass breakage, aircraft, vehicles, riot or civil commotion, theft, vandalism or malicious mischief
Broad Form (HO-2)	Minimum varies; other coverages in same percentages or amounts except D—20% of A	Covers all basic-form risks plus weight of ice, snow, sleet; freezing; accidental discharge of water or steam; falling objects; accidental tearing, cracking, or burning of heating/cooling/sprinkler system or appliance; damage from electrical current
Special Form (HO-3)	Minimum varies; other coverages in same percentages or amounts except D—20% of A	Dwelling and other structures covered against risks of direct physical loss to property except losses specifically excluded; personal property covered by same perils as HO-2 plus damage by glass or safety glazing material, which is part of a building, storm door, or storm window
Renter's Form (HO-4)	Coverages A and B—Not applicable C—Minimum varies by company D—20% of C E—$100,000 F—$1,000 per person	Covers same perils covered by HO-2 for personal property
Condominium Form (HO-6)	Coverage A—Minimum $1,000 B—Not applicable C—Minimum varies by company D—40% of C E—$100,000 F—$1,000 per person	Covers same perils covered by HO-2 for personal property
Modified Coverage Form (HO-8)	Same as HO-1, except losses are paid based on the amount required to repair or replace the property using common construction materials and methods	Same perils as HO-1, except theft coverage applies only to losses on the residence premises up to a maximum of $1,000; certain other coverage restrictions also apply

* Coverages:
A. Dwelling
B. Other structures
C. Personal property
D. Loss of use
E. Personal liability
F. Medical payments to others

on the house itself and other structures (for example, a detached garage) is comprehensive under HO-3 and a named peril in HO-2. Whether homeowners should buy an HO-2 or an HO-3 form depends primarily on how much they're willing to spend to secure the additional protection. The size of premiums for HO-2 and HO-3 policies can differ substantially among insurance companies; in some states, an HO-3 policy is the better buy because the premium differential is small. In other states, the HO-2 form has a much lower premium. Because of its more limited coverage, buying an HO-1 is not recommended.

Note in Exhibit 10.2 that the types of Section I perils covered include just about everything from fire and explosions to lightning and wind damage, to theft and vandalism; unfortunately, these are all perils to which any homeowner is exposed. Although the list of perils is extensive, some are specifically excluded from most homeowner's contracts—in particular, *most policies (even HO-2 and HO-3 forms) exclude earthquakes and floods.* Many areas of the country are not susceptible to earthquakes and floods, and homeowners in those areas shouldn't have to pay premiums for coverage they don't need. But even if you live in an area where the risk of an earthquake or a flood is relatively high, you'll find that *standard homeowner's policies do not provide protection against these perils* because the catastrophic nature of such events causes widespread and costly damage. As we'll see later in this chapter, you can obtain coverage for earthquakes and floods under a separate policy or a rider.

Section II Perils

The perils insured against under Section II of the homeowner's contract are the (alleged) negligence of an insured. The coverage is called *comprehensive personal liability coverage* because it offers protection against nearly any source of liability (major exclusions are noted later) resulting from negligence. It does not insure against other losses for which one may become liable, such as libel, slander, defamation of character, and contractual or intentional wrongdoing. For example, coverage would apply if you carelessly, but unintentionally, knocked someone down your stairs. If you purposely struck and injured another person, however, or harmed someone's reputation either orally or in writing, homeowner's liability coverage would not protect you.

Section II also provides a limited amount of medical coverage for persons other than the homeowner's family in certain types of minor accidents on or off the insured's premises. This coverage helps homeowners to meet their moral obligations and help deter possible lawsuits. The limited medical payment coverage pays irrespective of negligence or fault.

Factors Affecting Home Insurance Costs

Several influences have an impact on premiums for home and property insurance:

- **Type of structure.** Do you live in a home made from wood or brick? The construction materials used in your home affect the cost of insuring it. A home built from brick costs less to insure than a similar home of wood, yet the reverse is true when it comes to earthquake insurance—brick homes are more expensive to insure. The style and age of the house also contribute to its potential insurance risk, thereby affecting insurance costs.
- **Location of home.** Local crime rates, weather, and proximity to a fire hydrant all affect your home's insurance premium costs. If many claims are filed from your area, insurance premiums for all the homeowners there will be higher. Hailstorms and hurricanes will affect them, too.
- **Other factors.** If you have a swimming pool, trampoline, large dog, or other potentially hazardous risk factors on your property, your homeowner's premiums will be higher. Deductibles and the type and amount of coverage also affect the cost.

Property Covered

The homeowner's policy offers property protection under Section I for the dwelling unit, accompanying structures, and personal property of homeowners and their families. Coverage for certain types of loss also applies to lawns, trees, plants, and shrubs. However, the policy excludes structures on the premises used for business purposes (except incidentally), animals (pets or otherwise), and motorized vehicles not used in maintaining the premises (such as autos, motorcycles, golf carts, or snowmobiles). *Business inventory* (for example, goods held by an insured who is a traveling salesperson, or other goods held for sale) is not covered. Although the policy doesn't cover business inventory, it does cover *business property* (such as books, computers, copiers, office furniture, and supplies), typically up to a maximum of $2,500, while it is on the insured premises.

If you work at home, either full- or part-time, you may need to increase your policy's limits to protect your home office. This insurance is critical because damage to your home affects not only where you live but also your source of income. In many cases, adding a rider to your homeowner's policy can increase your home business limits to adequate levels for your computer and office equipment and provide additional limited liability coverage. The cost for these riders is low, about $75 per year, depending on what coverage you include. If you need greater protection, you should investigate a separate business owner's policy that offers broader coverage for business liability, all-risk protection for equipment, and business income protection if damage to your home results in lost income.

Personal Property Floater

As we'll see later in this chapter, policies limit the type and amount of coverage provided. Your homeowner's policy may not adequately protect your expensive personal property. To overcome this deficiency, you can either add the **personal property floater (PPF)** as an endorsement to your homeowner's policy or take out a separate floater policy. *The PPF provides either blanket or scheduled coverage of items not adequately covered in a standard homeowner's policy.*

A *blanket,* or *unscheduled, PPF* provides the maximum protection available for virtually all the insured's personal property. *Scheduled PPFs* list the items to be covered and provide supplemental coverage under a homeowner's contract. This coverage is especially useful for property valued at more than coverage C limits, and it includes loss, damage, and theft. Some popular uses of PPFs are for furs, jewelry, personal computers and peripheral equipment, photographic equipment, silverware, fine art and antiques, musical instruments, and stamp and coin collections. For example, you should itemize a diamond ring valued at $7,500 because it's worth more than the standard $1,000 coverage C allowance for jewelry theft. Generally, insurance companies require appraisals to determine value before scheduling items.

Renter's Insurance: Don't Move in Without It

If you live in an apartment (or some other type of rental unit), be aware that although the building you live in is likely to be fully insured, *your furnishings and other personal belongings are not.* As a renter (or even the owner of a condominium unit), you need a special type of HO policy to obtain insurance coverage on your personal possessions.

Consider, for example, Lois Weaver's predicament. She never got around to insuring her personal possessions in the apartment she rented in Denver. One wintry night, a water pipe ruptured and escaping water damaged her furniture, rugs, and other belongings. When the building owner refused to pay for the loss, Ms. Weaver hauled him into court—and lost. Why did she lose her case? Simple: *Unless a landlord can be proven negligent—and this one wasn't—he or she isn't responsible for a tenant's property.* The moral of this story is clear: once you've accumulated valuable personal belongings (from clothing and home furnishings to stereo equipment, TVs, computers, and DVD players), make sure they're adequately covered by insurance, even if you're only renting a place to live! Otherwise, you could risk losing everything you own.

Apparently many tenants don't realize this, because surveys show most of them aren't insured —although renter's insurance is available at reasonable rates. The policy, called Renter's Form HO-4, is a scaled-down version of homeowner's insurance; it covers the contents of a house, apartment, or cooperative unit, but not the structure itself. Owners of condominium units need Form HO-6; it's similar but includes a minimum of $1,000 in protection for any building alterations, additions, and decorations paid for by the policyholder. Like regular homeowner's insurance, HO-4 and HO-6 policies include liability coverage and protect you at home and away. For example, if somebody is injured and sues you, the policy would pay for damages up to a specified limit, generally $100,000, although some insurers go as high as $500,000.

personal property floater (PPF) An insurance endorsement or policy providing either blanket or scheduled coverage of expensive personal property not adequately covered in a standard homeowner's policy.

A standard renter's insurance policy covers furniture, carpets, appliances, clothing, and most other personal items, for their cash value at the time of loss. Expect to pay around $200 to $250 a year for about $15,000 in coverage, depending on where you live. For maximum protection, you can buy *replacement-cost insurance* (discussed again later in this chapter), which pays the actual cost of replacing articles with comparable ones, though some policies limit the payout to four times the cash value. You'll pay more for this—perhaps as little as another 10 percent, perhaps much more—depending on the insurer. Also, the standard renter's policy provides limited coverage of such valuables as jewelry, furs, and silverware. Coverage varies, although some insurers pay up to $1,000 for the loss of watches, gems, and furs and up to $2,500 for silverware. For larger amounts, you need an endorsement or a separate PPF policy, as discussed earlier.

Renter's insurance pays for losses caused by fire or lightning, explosion, windstorms, hail, theft, civil commotion, aircraft, vehicles, smoke, vandalism and malicious mischief, falling objects, building collapse, and the weight of ice and snow. Certain damages caused by water, steam, electricity, appliances, and frozen pipes are covered as well. Plus, if your residence can't be occupied because of damage from any of those perils, the insurer will pay for any increase in living expenses resulting from staying at a hotel and eating in restaurants. The liability coverage also pays for damages and legal costs arising from injuries or damage caused by you, a member of your family, or a pet, on or off your premises.

Coverage: What Type, Who, and Where?

We've discussed what types of property homeowner's policies cover. These policies also define the types of losses they cover and the persons and locations covered.

Types of Losses Covered

There are three types of property-related losses when misfortune occurs:

1. Direct loss of property
2. Indirect loss occurring due to loss of damaged property
3. Additional expenses resulting from direct and indirect losses

Homeowner's insurance contracts offer compensation for each type of loss.

Section I Coverage. When a house is damaged by an insured peril, the insurance company will pay reasonable living expenses a family might incur. One such covered expense would be the cost of renting alternative lodgings or accommodation while the insured's home is being repaired or rebuilt. Also, in many instances the insurer will pay for damages caused by perils other than those mentioned in the policy if a named peril is determined to be the underlying cause of the loss. Assume, for instance, that lightning (a covered peril) strikes a house while a family is away and knocks out power, causing $400 worth of food in the freezer and refrigerator to spoil. Insurance will pay for the loss even though temperature change (the direct cause) is not mentioned in the policy.

Section II Coverage. Besides paying successfully pursued liability claims against an insured, a homeowner's policy includes coverage for (1) the cost of defending the insured, (2) reasonable expenses incurred by an insured in helping the insurance company's defense, and (3) the payment of court costs. Because these costs apply even when the liability suit is found to be without merit, this coverage can save you thousands of dollars in attorney fees.

Persons Covered

A homeowner's policy covers the persons named in the policy and members of their families who are residents of the household. A person can be a resident of the household even while temporarily living away from home. For example, college students who live at school part of the year and at home during vacations are normally classified as household residents. Their parents' homeowner's policy may cover their belongings at school—

including such items as stereo equipment, TVs, personal computers, and microwave ovens. But there could be limits and exceptions to the coverage, so check the policy to find out what's covered. For example, some companies may consider a student living off-campus to be independent and therefore ineligible for coverage under his or her parents' insurance. The standard homeowner's contract also extends limited coverage to guests of the insured.

Locations Covered

Although some insurance contracts have territorial exclusions, most homeowner's policies offer coverage worldwide. Consequently, an insured's personal property is fully covered even if it is lent to the next-door neighbor or kept in a hotel room in Outer Mongolia. The only exception is property left at a second home, such as a beach house or resort condominium—where coverage is reduced to 10 percent of the policy limit on personal property—unless the loss occurs while the insured is residing there.

Homeowners and their families have liability protection for their negligent acts wherever they occur. This liability protection, however, doesn't include negligent acts involving certain types of motorized vehicles (such as large boats and aircraft), or those occurring in the course of employment or professional practice. It does include golf carts (when used for golfing purposes) and recreational vehicles such as snowmobiles and minibikes, provided they're used on the insured's premises.

Limitations on Payment

In addition to the principle of indemnity, actual cash value, subrogation, and other insurance features restricting the amount paid out under a property and liability insurance contract, replacement-cost provisions, policy limits, and deductibles influence the amount an insurance company will pay for a loss.

Replacement Cost

The amount necessary to repair, rebuild, or replace an asset at today's prices is the **replacement cost.** When replacement-cost coverage is in effect, a homeowner's reimbursement for damage to a house or accompanying structures is based on the cost of repairing or replacing those structures. This means the insurer will repair or replace damaged items without taking any deductions for depreciation. Exhibit 10.3 illustrates a replacement-cost calculation for a 2,400-square-foot home with a two-car garage.

Keep in mind, however, that for homeowners to be eligible for reimbursement on a full replacement-cost basis, they must keep their homes insured for at least 80 percent of the amount it would cost to build them today, not including the value of the land. In periods of inflation, homeowners must either increase their coverage limits on the dwelling unit every year or take a chance on falling below the 80 percent requirement. Alternatively, for a nominal cost homeowners can purchase an inflation protection rider that automatically adjusts the amount of coverage based on prevailing inflation rates. The inflation protection rider basically eliminates the chance of a coinsurance penalty. Without the rider, if the 80

replacement cost The amount necessary to repair, rebuild, or replace an asset at today's prices.

EXHIBIT 10.3 | Calculating Replacement Cost

Here's a typical example of how an insurance company calculates replacement cost. It would take $256,000 to fully replace this home today.

Dwelling cost: 2,400 sq. ft. at $85 per sq. ft.	$204,000
Extra features: built-in appliances, mahogany cabinets, 3 ceiling fans	10,600
Porches, patios: screened and trellised patio	3,700
Two-car garage: 900 sq. ft. at $35 per sq. ft.	31,500
Other site improvements: driveway, storage, landscaping	6,200
Total replacement cost	$256,000

percent condition isn't met, the coinsurance penalty kicks in; the maximum compensation for total or partial losses would thus be based on a specified percentage of loss. With the inflation protection rider, this wouldn't happen.

Contrary to popular opinion, replacement cost and actual cash value may not bear any relationship to a home's market value. Because replacement cost and actual cash value relate only to the physical structure and do not consider the influence of location, a home's market value can be in excess of its replacement cost or below its actual cash value. Even if a home is in an excellent state of repair, its market value may be lessened due to functional obsolescence within the structure. An example of functional obsolescence would be a house that doesn't have enough electrical power to run a dishwasher, microwave, and hair dryer at the same time. The HO-8 homeowner's form (for older homes) was adopted in partial response to this problem. A 2,200-square-foot home in an older neighborhood might have a market value, excluding land, of $95,000—although the replacement cost might be $160,000. The HO-8 policy solves this problem so homeowners don't have to buy more expensive coverage based on replacement cost. This policy covers property in full, up to the amount of the loss, or up to the property's market value, whichever is less.

Although coverage on a house is often on a *replacement-cost basis,* standard coverage on its contents may be on an *actual cash-value basis,* which deducts depreciation from the *current replacement cost* for claims involving furniture, clothing, and other belongings. Some policies offer, for a slight increase in premium, replacement-cost coverage on contents. For an additional premium of only about 5 to 15 percent more, you should seriously consider this option—and an inflation protection rider on the dwelling—when buying homeowner's insurance.

Policy Limits

In Section I of the homeowner's policy the amount of coverage on the dwelling unit (coverage A) establishes the amounts applicable to the accompanying structures (coverage B), the unscheduled personal property (coverage C), and the temporary living expenses (coverage D). Generally, the limits under coverage B, C, and D are 10, 50, and 10 to 20 percent, respectively, of the amount of coverage under A.

For example, if a house is insured for $150,000, the limits for coverage B, C, and D would be $15,000, $75,000, and $30,000 (that is, 10 percent of $150,000, 50 percent of $150,000, and 20 percent of $150,000). Each of these limits can be increased if it's insufficient to cover the exposure. Also, for a small reduction in premium, some companies will permit a homeowner to reduce coverage on unscheduled personal property to 40 percent of the amount on the dwelling unit.

Remember that homeowner's policies usually specify limits for certain types of personal property included under the coverage C category. These coverage limits are *within the total dollar amount* of coverage C and in no way act to increase that total. For example, the dollar limit for losses of money, bank notes, bullion, and related items is $200; securities, accounts, deeds, evidences of debt, manuscripts, passports, tickets, and stamps have a $1,000 limit. As mentioned earlier, loss from jewelry theft is limited to $1,000, and payment for theft of silverware, goldware, and pewterware has a $2,500 limit. Some policies also offer $5,000 coverage for home computer equipment. You can increase these limits by increasing coverage C.

In Section II the personal liability coverage (coverage E) often tops out at $100,000, and the medical payments portion (coverage F) normally has a limit of $1,000 per person. Additional coverage included in Section II consists of claim expenses, such as court costs and attorney fees, first aid and medical expenses, including ambulance costs, and damage to others' property of up to $500 per occurrence.

Although these are the most common limits, most homeowners need additional protection, especially liability coverage. In these days of high damage awards by juries, a $100,000 liability limit may not be adequate. The cost to increase the liability limit with most companies is nominal. For example, the annual premium difference between a

Smart Sites

You can obtain and compare premium quotes for homeowner's insurance by filling in a Quick Form and submitting it to obtain four quotes: **http://www.thomsonedu .com/finance/gitman.**

$100,000 personal liability limit and a $300,000 limit is likely to be only $50 to $100. You can also increase personal liability coverage with a personal liability umbrella policy, discussed later in the chapter.

Deductibles

Each of the preceding limits on recovery constrains the maximum amount an insurance company must pay under the policy. In contrast, *deductibles* limit what a company must pay for small losses. Deductibles help reduce insurance premiums because they do away with the frequent small loss claims that are proportionately more expensive to administer. The standard deductible in most states is $250 on the physical damage protection covered in Section I. However, choosing higher deductible amounts of $500 or $1,000 results in considerable premium savings—as much as 10 percent in some states. Deductibles don't apply to liability and medical payments coverage because insurers want to be notified of all claims, no matter how trivial. Otherwise, they could be notified too late to properly investigate and prepare adequate defenses for resulting lawsuits.

Homeowner's Premiums

For a basic package of protection—physical damage protection up to 80 percent of today's cost to rebuild, related coverage on other structures and personal property, personal liability ($100,000), and medical payments to others ($1,000 per person)—an insurer will quote you a premium. As you might expect, the size of insurance premiums vary widely depending on the insurance provider (company) and the location of the property (neighborhood/ city/state). It pays to shop around! When you're shopping, be sure to clearly state the type of insurance you're looking for and obtain and compare the cost, net of any discounts, offered by a number of agents or insurance companies. And remember, each type of property damage coverage is subject to a deductible of $250 or more.

Most people need to modify the basic package of coverage by adding an inflation rider and increasing the coverage on their homes to 100 percent of the replacement cost. Changing the contents protection from actual cash value to replacement cost and scheduling some items of expensive personal property may be desirable. Most insurance professionals also advise homeowners to increase their liability and medical payments limits. Each of these changes results in an additional premium charge.

At the same time, you can reduce your total premium by increasing the amount of your deductible. Because it's better to budget for, rather than insure, small losses, larger deductibles are becoming more popular. You may also qualify for discounts for deadbolt locks, monitored security systems, and other safety features, such as smoke alarms and sprinkler systems. Indeed, as explained in the *Money in Action* box on page 314, you can take many steps to keep your homeowner's insurance premiums lower.

⊪ Concept Check

CHECK • CONCEPT CHECK • CONCEPT CHECK • CONCEPT CHECK • CONCEPT CHECK • CONCEPT CHECK • CONCEPT

10-5	What are the *perils* most properties are insured for under various types of homeowner's policies?
10-6	What types of property are covered under a homeowner's policy? When should you consider adding a *PPF* to your policy? Are the following included in the coverage of a standard policy: (a) an African parrot, (b) a motorbike, (c) Avon cosmetics held for sale, and (d) Tupperware® for home use?
10-7	Describe (a) types of losses, (b) persons, and (c) locations that are covered under a homeowner's policy.
10-8	Describe *replacement-cost coverage* and compare this coverage to *actual cash value*. Which is preferable?
10-9	What are *deductibles?* Do they apply to either liability or medical payments coverage under the homeowner's policy?

Another asset involving major exposure to loss is the automobile. Damage to this asset, or negligence in its use, can result in significant loss. Indirect monetary losses to society also result from police and legal costs and from the lost productive capacity of capital and human resources. Fortunately, insurance can protect individuals against a big part of these costs.

Automobile insurance is actually a group of several types of coverage packaged together. You can adjust any coverage to suit your needs. Here we describe the major features of automobile insurance, starting with typical coverage of a private passenger automobile policy. We'll also explain how no-fault laws, in force in many states, typically affect reimbursement for losses caused by automobile accidents. Finally, we'll discuss auto insurance premiums and financial responsibility laws

Types of Auto Insurance Coverage

The **personal automobile policy (PAP)** is a comprehensive automobile insurance policy designed to be easily understood by the "typical" insurance purchaser. Made up of six parts, the policy's first four parts identify the coverage provided:

- Part A: Liability coverage
- Part B: Medical payments coverage
- Part C: Uninsured motorists coverage
- Part D: Coverage for damage to your vehicle

Part E pertains to your duties and responsibilities if you're involved in an accident, and Part F defines basic provisions of the policy, including the policy coverage period and the right of termination. We'll focus mostly on the types of coverage in Parts A through D of the policy.

You're almost sure to purchase liability, medical payments, and uninsured motorists protection. You may, however, choose *not* to buy protection against damage to your automobile if it's an older vehicle of relatively little value. On the other hand, if you have a loan against your car, you'll probably be required to have physical damage coverage—part D—at least equal to the loan amount.

Let's take a closer look at the coverage provided by parts A through D. Exhibit 10.4 on page 315 illustrates how the four basic parts of a PAP might be displayed in a typical automobile insurance policy. The premiums shown are for a 6-month period.

Part A: Liability Coverage

Most states require you to buy at least a minimum amount of liability insurance. As part of the liability provisions of a PAP, the insurer agrees to:

1. Pay damages for bodily injury and/or property damage for which you are legally responsible due to an automobile accident
2. Settle or defend any claim or suit asking for such damages

The provision for legal defense is important and could mean savings of thousands of dollars. Even if you're not at fault in an automobile accident, you may be compelled to prove your innocence in court, incurring expensive legal fees. Note, though, that the coverage is for a defense in civil cases only. It doesn't cover defense of criminal charges against the insured due to an accident (such as a drunk driver who's involved in an accident).

Besides reimbursing bodily injury and property damage, Part A of your insurance policy includes certain supplemental payments for items such as expenses incurred in settling the claim, reimbursement of premiums for appeal bonds, bonds to release attachments of the insured's property, and bail bonds required as a result of an accident. These supplemental payments are not restricted by the applicable policy limits.

Policy Limits. Although the insurance company provides both bodily injury and property damage liability insurance under Part A, it typically sets *a dollar limit up to which it will pay for damages from any one accident.* Typical limits are $50,000, $100,000, $300,000, and $500,000. You'd be well advised to consider no less than $300,000 coverage in today's

personal automobile policy (PAP) A comprehensive automobile insurance policy designed to be easily understood by the "typical" insurance purchaser.

KEEP YOUR HOMEOWNER'S PREMIUMS FROM GOING THROUGH THE ROOF

Everyone who pays monthly premiums for homeowner's insurance will tell you it's not cheap. But because most people can't afford to bear the risk of a catastrophic loss, such insurance is absolutely necessary. Fortunately, the industry is competitive so prices vary. The first step to keeping premiums down is to shop around. Major insurance companies are easily accessible by telephone and the Internet; these sources will provide an idea of price ranges. Some companies offer a 5 percent to 15 percent discount on a homeowner's policy if you also use them for auto insurance.

But there are factors other than cost to consider when selecting a policy. Ask friends or colleagues about companies they have done business with and their reputations for good service. If a claim is filed, do they pay right away or do they stall? Do they have a local office and an agent with whom you can meet personally, or does the company operate from a distant city?

After choosing a company, you can reduce your premiums even more by making certain decisions. If you have to choose between buying a new home or an older one,

be aware that the older home, although quaint, may cost more to insure due to antiquated heating and plumbing systems. Statistically, newer homes are less susceptible to fire and other hazards, so they cost less to insure. The closer your home is to a fire station, the lower your premium will be. A house near a fault line in California will cost more to insure than the same home in Montana. Frame and brick homes, because of their resistance to earthquake and wind damage, respectively, also reduce premiums. Avoiding areas prone to flooding saves several hundred dollars in flood insurance—a risk that homeowner's insurance doesn't cover.

Some insurers offer discounts if you install a sprinkler system or a burglar alarm. Other ways to reduce the risk of loss include installing multiple smoke detectors and fire extinguishers and using deadbolt locks to increase your security. Some companies offer lower premiums if residents in the house don't smoke, because smoking accounts for about 25,000 residential fires per year.

One way *not* to save money is to underinsure. It's imperative to get "guaranteed replacement-cost" coverage, not just actual cash value. Your insurance agent should be able to help you come up with the right figure. Make sure a company represen-

tative visits your home to measure and photograph it. Otherwise, it will be difficult to set appropriate replacement-cost amounts. You could find yourself overinsured or underinsured—either paying too much in premiums, or underprotected.

Replacement cost will likely be higher than actual cash value because the cost to build is usually higher than the cost to buy. Don't scrimp on liability coverage either— it's important to be covered for damages if someone who's injured on your property sues you.

In general, you should review your homeowner's insurance coverage every other year to establish that your premium is still competitive and ensure that your coverage is adequate to completely rebuild your home in case of a catastrophe.

Critical Thinking Questions

1. What should you look for when selecting a homeowner's insurance policy?
2. When purchasing a home, what factors should you consider to reduce your homeowner's insurance premiums? What improvements can you make to an existing home to take advantage of premium reduction programs?
3. Why isn't it cost-effective to underinsure your property?

Sources: "Lowering Your Homeowner's Insurance Premiums—Twelve Ways to Lower Your Homeowner's Insurance Cost," Claiminformation.com, http://www.claiminformation.com/homeownerpremiums.htm, downloaded December 2, 2003; Bobbie Sage, "Homeowner's Insurance Savings Checklist," PersonalInsure.com, http://www.personalinsure.about.com, downloaded December 2, 2003.

legal liability environment. Damage awards are increasing, and the insurer's duty to defend you *ends when the coverage limit has been exhausted*. It's very easy to "exhaust" $50,000 or $100,000, leaving you to pay any additional costs above the policy limit. So be sure to purchase adequate coverage—*regardless of the minimum requirements in your state.* Otherwise, you place your personal assets at risk. As Exhibit 10.4 shows, the Jones family obtained fairly high limits.

EXHIBIT 10.4 The Four Parts of a Personal Automobile Policy (PAP)

This automobile insurance statement for 6 months of coverage shows how the four major parts of a PAP might be incorporated. Notice that the premium for collision/comprehensive damage is relatively low due to the age and type of car (a 2002 Ford Taurus); these drivers also enjoyed a premium reduction of more than $130 for the 6 months due to having other insurance with the same provider, a car alarm system, and a good driving record.

ANYSTATE INSURANCE COMPANIES   **AUTO RENEWAL**

Anystate Automobile Insurance Company
1665 West Anywhere Drive
Yourtown, CA 91001   2002 Ford Taurus

POLICY NUMBER	PERIOD COVERED	DATE DUE	PLEASE PAY THIS AMOUNT
ABC-123-XYZ-456	MAY 26 2007 to NOV 26 2007	MAY 26 2007	$392

1 H -1582   A

Jones, Drew E. & Linda S.
240 E. Hazelwood St. # 50
Yourtown, CA 91004-0003

Coverages and Limits			Premiums
Part A	A	Liability	
		Bodily Injury 250,000/500,000	$219
		Property Damage 100,000	
Part B	M	Medical 5,000	14
Part C	U	Uninsured Motor Vehicle	
		Bodily Injury 100,000/300,000	27
Part D	G	500 Deductible Collision	102
	D-WG	500 Deductible Comprehensive	24
	H	Emergency Road Service	6

Amount Due $392

Your premium has already been adjusted by the following:

Premium Reductions

Multiple Line	22
Antitheft devices	40
Good driver	70

Your premium is based on the following ...
If not correct, contact your agent.

2002 Ford Taurus SES Sedan
Serial number: 4 ABCD12M3NP456789

Drivers of vehicle in your household ...
There are no male or unmarried female drivers under age 25.
Younger drivers included if rated on another car insured with us.

Ordinary use of vehicle ...
To and from work or school, more than 100 miles weekly.
Driven more than 7,500 miles annually. (National average is 10,000 miles annually.)

Source: Adapted from a major automobile insurance company quote.

Some insurers make so-called *split limits* of liability coverage available, with the first amount in each combination the per-individual limit and the second the per-accident limit. Some policy limit combinations for protecting individuals against claims made for **bodily injury liability losses** are $25,000/$50,000, $50,000/$100,000, $100,000/$300,000, $250,000/$500,000, and $500,000/$1,000,000. Because the Joneses purchased the $250,000/$500,000 policy limits, the maximum amount any one person negligently injured in an accident could receive from the insurance company would be $250,000. Further, the total amount the insurer would pay to all injured victims in one accident would not exceed $500,000. If a jury awarded a claimant $80,000, the defendant whose insurance policy limits were $50,000/$100,000 could be required to pay $30,000 out of his or her pocket ($80,000 award – $50,000 paid by insurance). For the defendant, this could mean loss of home, cars, bank accounts, and other assets. In many states, if the value of these assets is too little to satisfy a claim, the defendant's wages may be garnished (taken by the court and used to satisfy the outstanding debt).

The policy limits available to cover **property damage liability losses** are typically $10,000, $25,000, $50,000, and $100,000. In contrast to bodily injury liability limits, property damage limits are stated as a per-accident limit, without specifying limits applicable on a per-item or per-person basis.

Persons Insured. Two basic definitions in the PAP determine who is covered under Part A: insured person and covered auto. Essentially, an *insured person* includes you (the named insured) and any family member, any person using a covered auto, and any person or organization that may be held responsible for your actions. The *named insured* is the person named in the declarations page of the policy. The spouse of the person named is considered a named insured if he or she resides in the same household. Family members are persons related by blood, marriage, or adoption and residing in the same household. An unmarried college student living away from home usually is considered a family member. *Covered autos* are the vehicles shown in the declarations page of your PAP, autos acquired during the policy period, any trailer owned, and any auto or trailer used as a temporary substitute while your auto or trailer is being repaired or serviced. An automobile that you lease for an extended time can be included as a covered automobile.

The named insured and family members have Part A liability coverage regardless of the automobile they are driving. However, for persons other than the named insured and family members to have liability coverage, they must be driving a covered auto.

When a motorist who is involved in an automobile accident is covered under two or more liability insurance contracts, the coverage *on the automobile* is primary and the other coverage is secondary. For example, if Dan Slater, a named insured in his own right, was involved in an accident while driving Diana Bauer's car (with permission), a claim settlement exceeding the limits of Diana's liability policy would be necessary before Dan's liability insurance would apply. If Diana's insurance had lapsed, Dan's policy would then offer primary protection (but it would apply to Dan only and not to Diana).

Part B: Medical Payments Coverage

Medical payments coverage insures a covered individual for reasonable and necessary medical expenses incurred within 3 years of an automobile accident, in an amount not to exceed the policy limits. It provides for reimbursement even if other sources of recovery, such as health or accident insurance, also make payments. What's more, in most states the insurer reimburses the insured for medical payments even if the insured proves that another person was negligent in the accident and receives compensation from that party's liability insurer.

As with liability insurance, discussed earlier, and uninsured motorists insurance, detailed in the following section, a person need not be occupying an automobile when the accidental injury occurs to be eligible for benefits. Injuries sustained as a pedestrian, or on a bicycle in a traffic accident, are covered too. (Motorcycle accidents are normally not covered.) Part B insurance also pays on an excess basis. For instance, if you're a passenger in a friend's automobile during an accident and suffer $8,000 in medical

bodily injury liability losses A PAP provision that protects the insured against claims made for bodily injury

property damage liability losses A PAP provision that protects the insured against claims made for damage to property expenses, you can collect under his medical payments insurance up to his policy limits. Further, you can collect (up to the amount of your policy limits) from your insurer the amount exceeding what the other medical payments provide. Of course, you may also collect from the liability insurance of another person involved in the accident if that person can be shown to have been at fault. You may also be able to collect from your health insurance policy.

Policy Limits. Medical payments insurance usually has per-person limits of $1,000, $2,000, $3,000, $5,000, or $10,000. Thus an insurer could conceivably pay $60,000 or more in medical payments benefits for one accident involving a named insured and five passengers. Most families are advised to buy the $5,000 or $10,000 limit because even though they may have other health insurance available, they can't be sure their passengers are as well protected. Having automobile medical payments insurance also reduces the probability that a passenger in your auto will sue you and try to collect under your liability insurance coverage (in those states that permit it).

Persons Insured. Coverage under an automobile medical payments insurance policy applies to the named insured and family members who are injured while occupying an automobile (whether owned by the named insured or not) or when struck by an automobile or trailer of any type. Part B also applies to any other person occupying a covered automobile.

Part C: Uninsured motorist coverage. Uninsured motorists coverage is available to meet the needs of "innocent" victims of accidents who are negligently injured by uninsured, underinsured, or hit-and-run motorists. Nearly all states require uninsured motorists insurance to be included in each liability insurance policy issued. The insured is allowed, however, to reject this coverage in most of these states. Because there are about 25 million uninsured drivers, and many others meet only minimum insurance coverage requirements, rejecting uninsured motorists coverage is not a good idea. In many states a person may also collect if the negligent motorist's insurance company is insolvent. With uninsured motorists insurance, an insured is legally entitled to collect an amount equal to the sum that could have been collected from the negligent motorist's liability insurance, had such coverage been available, up to a maximum amount equal to the policy's stated *uninsured motorists limit.*

Three points must be proven to receive payment through uninsured motorists insurance: (1) another motorist must be at fault, (2) the motorist has no available insurance or is underinsured, and (3) damages were incurred. As property damage is not included in this coverage in most states, with uninsured motorists coverage, you can generally collect only for losses arising from bodily injury. If the motorist and insurer can't agree on the settlement terms of a claim under uninsured motorists coverage, the motorist can seek an attorney to negotiate the claim. If a mutually agreeable settlement still can't be worked out, the insured has the right to have the case arbitrated by a neutral third party. In most cases, the accident victim and the insurer are then bound to accept the arbitrator's decision.

Policy Limits. Uninsured motorists insurance is fairly low in cost (usually around $50 to $75 per year). Because the cost of this coverage is low compared to the amount of protection it provides, drivers should purchase at least the minimum available limits of uninsured motorists insurance. The Joneses purchased $100,000/$300,000 coverage for just $54 per year ($27 per 6 months).

Persons Insured. Uninsured motorists protection covers the named insured, family members, and any other person occupying a covered auto.

Underinsured Motorists Coverage. In addition to *uninsured motorists,* in some states for a nominal premium you can obtain protection for *underinsured motorists.* This coverage, called **underinsured motorists coverage,** protects the insured against damages caused by being in an accident with an underinsured motorist who is found liable. Because most states require minimum levels of liability coverage, underinsured motorists

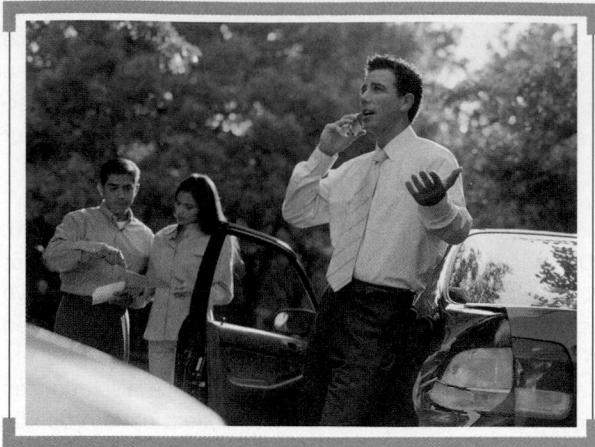

© GETTY IMAGES

insurance has become increasingly popular. *This optional coverage can be purchased for both bodily injury and property damage.* If an at-fault driver causes more damage to you than the limit of her liability, your insurance company makes up the difference (up to the limits of your coverage) and then goes after the negligent driver for the deficiency. For example, if you have underinsured motorists coverage of $50,000 for bodily injury and incur medical expenses of $40,000 because of an accident caused by an at-fault insured driver with the minimum compulsory bodily injury limits of $25,000, your insurer will cover the $15,000 gap ($40,000 medical expenses − $25,000 liability limit of at-fault driver). Clearly, this optional coverage, if available in your state, should be considered when purchasing an automobile insurance policy.

Part D: Coverage for Physical Damage to a Vehicle

This part of the PAP provides coverage for damage to your auto. The two basic types of coverage are collision and comprehensive (or "other than collision").

Collision Insurance. Collision insurance is automobile insurance that pays for collision damage to an insured automobile *regardless of who is at fault*. The amount of insurance payable is the actual cash value of the loss in excess of your deductible. Remember that *actual cash value is defined as replacement cost less depreciation*. So, if a car is demolished, the insured is paid an amount equal to the car's depreciated value minus any deductible.

Lenders typically require collision insurance on cars they finance. In some cases, especially when the auto dealer is handling the financing, it will try to sell you this insurance. *Avoid buying automobile insurance from car dealers or finance companies.* Buy such insurance from your regular insurance agent and include collision insurance as part of your full auto insurance policy (PAP). A full-time insurance agent is better able to assess and meet your insurance needs. The collision provision of your insurance policy often fully protects you, even in a rental car, so you may not need to purchase expensive supplemental collision insurance when renting a car. Be sure to check what rental car coverage your PAP provides. Also, when you charge your car rental to your credit card, collision insurance may be offered.

When purchasing collision insurance, deductibles between $50 and $1,000 may be available. Selecting a higher deductible, as did the Joneses, will reduce your premium.

Comprehensive Automobile Insurance. Comprehensive automobile insurance protects against loss to an insured automobile caused by any peril (with a few exceptions) *other than collision*. The maximum compensation provided under this coverage is the actual cash value of the automobile. This broad coverage includes, but is not limited to, damage caused by fire, theft, glass breakage, falling objects, malicious mischief, vandalism, riot, and earthquake. Contrary to popular belief, the automobile insurance policy normally does *not* cover theft of personal property left in the insured vehicle. The off-premises coverage of the homeowner's policy may cover such a loss if the auto was locked when the theft occurred.

No-Fault Automobile Insurance

No-fault automobile insurance is a system that reimburses the parties involved in an accident without regard to negligence. Each insured party is compensated by his or her own company, regardless of which party caused the accident. In return, legal remedies and payments for pain and suffering are restricted. Under the concept of *pure* no-fault insurance, the driver, passengers, and injured pedestrians are reimbursed by the insurer of the car for economic losses stemming from bodily injury. The insurer doesn't have to cover claims for losses to other motorists who are covered by their own policies.

collision insurance Automobile insurance that pays for collision damage to an insured automobile *regardless of who is at fault.*

comprehensive automobile insurance Coverage that protects against loss to an insured automobile caused by any peril (with a few exceptions) *other than collision.*

no-fault automobile insurance Automobile insurance that reimburses the parties involved in an accident without regard to negligence.

Unfortunately, advocates of no-fault forget that liability insurance isn't intended to be the primary system for compensating injured parties. Its sole purpose is to protect the assets of the insured—not to pay losses, *per se,* a concept that applies to all liability insurance. State laws governing no-fault insurance vary widely as to both the amount of no-fault benefits provided and the degree to which restrictions for legal actions apply. Most states provide from $2,000 to $10,000 in personal injury protection and restrict legal recovery for pain and suffering to cases where medical or economic losses exceed some threshold level, such as $500 or $1,000. In all states recovery based on negligence is permitted for economic loss exceeding the amount payable by no-fault insurance.

Automobile Insurance Premiums

The cost of car insurance depends on many things, including your age, where you live, the car you drive, your driving record, the coverage you have, the amount of your deductible, and so forth. Consequently, car insurance premiums—even for the same coverage—vary all over the map. If you're fortunate enough to live in a low-premium state, such as Maine, Iowa, Vermont, or Idaho, you're probably relatively satisfied with the cost of your car insurance; if on the other hand you're in one of the more expensive states, like New York, Louisiana, Rhode Island, or Maryland, you may well be feeling the pinch of rapidly increasing auto insurance rates.

You may think that auto insurance rates rise every year. That's not always the case. For example, of the 47 states surveyed by Insurance.com for the Insurance.com 2005 Auto Insurance Pricing Report, 21 states actually saw their auto insurance rates fall, and the national average actually fell slightly. According to the report, in 2005 the average U.S. household paid $2,302 for auto insurance each year, which is a 2 percent decrease, or nearly $60 savings from 2004. This information was collected from nearly 9 million auto insurance quotes provided by Insurance.com to its consumers in 2004 and 2005.

Factors Affecting Premiums

Factors that influence how auto insurance premiums are set include (1) rating territory, (2) amount of use the automobile receives, (3) personal characteristics of the driver, (4) type of automobile, and (5) insured's driving record.

- **Rating territory.** Rates are higher in geographic areas where accident rates, number of claims filed, and average cost of claims paid are higher. Rates reflect auto repair costs, hospital and medical expenses, jury awards, and theft and vandalism in the area. Even someone with a perfect driving record will be charged the going rate for the area where the automobile is garaged. Exhibit 10.5 on page 320 gives some helpful tips for protecting your vehicle wherever you live. Some jurisdictions prohibit the use of rating territories, age, and sex factors because they believe these factors unfairly discriminate against the urban, the young, and the male.

- **Use of the automobile.** Drive less, pay less! Low annual miles translate into a smaller probability of being in an accident, so you pay lower rates. Rates are also lower if the insured automobile isn't usually driven to work or is driven less than 3 miles one way. Premiums rise slightly if you drive more than 3 but fewer than 15 miles to work and increase if your commute exceeds 15 miles each way.

- **Drivers' personal characteristics.** The insured's age, sex, and marital status can also affect automobile insurance premiums. Insurance companies base the premium differentials on the number of accidents involving certain age groups. For example, drivers aged 25 and under make up only about 15 percent of the total driving population but are involved in nearly 30 percent of auto accidents, and 26 percent of all fatal accidents. Male drivers are involved in a larger percentage of fatal crashes, so unmar-

EXHIBIT 10.5   Top 10 Ways to Prevent Auto Theft

1. Invest in and install a good antitheft device.
2. Take any packages that are in plain sight with you.
3. Turn off the car and remove keys from the ignition when leaving the car unattended.
4. Close windows and lock your doors.
5. Park in well-lit, heavily traveled areas, and keep your driveway light on all night when at home.
6. Etch the VIN (vehicle identification number) in the windows and other major parts of your car, thus making the car harder to resell on the black market.
7. Keep any spare keys on your person, not in your car.
8. Remove any portable electronics such as cell phones, car stereos, and PDAs when you park.
9. Park your car in a garage and lock the garage door, if one is available to you.
10. Make your car harder to tow by parking between other cars, turning the wheels toward the curb, and putting on the emergency brake.

Sources: Adapted from "Top 10 Ways to Prevent Auto Theft," Insurance.com, http://auto.insurance.com/profiles_insights/hot_topics/article_0902_3.asp, accessed February 6, 2004; and "10 Tips to Avoid Auto Crime," Insurance Corporation of British Columbia, http://www.icbc.com/Crime-Fraud/autocr_thefta_tentip.html, accessed February 12, 2004.

---

ried males age 29 or under, and married males under age 25, pay higher premiums than older individuals do. Females over age 24, and married females of any age, are exempt from the youthful operator classification and pay lower premiums.

- **Type of automobile.** Insurance companies charge higher rates for automobiles classified as intermediate-performance, high-performance, and sports vehicles, and for rear-engine models. Some states even rate four-door cars differently from two-door models. If you're thinking of buying, say, a Corvette or a Porsche, be prepared for some hefty insurance rates.

- **Driving record.** The driving records—traffic violations and accidents—of those insured and the people who live with them affect premium levels. More severe traffic convictions—driving under the influence of alcohol or drugs, leaving the scene of an accident, homicide or assault arising from the operation of a motor vehicle, and driving with a revoked or suspended driver's license—result in higher insurance premiums. Any conviction for a moving traffic violation that results in the accumulation of points under a state point system also may incur a premium surcharge. In most states, accidents determined to be the insured's fault also incur points and a premium surcharge.

Many states place drivers with multiple traffic violations in an **automobile insurance plan** (formerly called an *assigned-risk plan*), providing automobile insurance to those refused regular coverage. The automobile insurance plan generally offers less coverage for a higher premium. Even with high premiums, however, insurers lost billions of dollars on this type of business in a recent 5-year period.

Driving Down the Cost of Car Insurance

Comparison shopping for car insurance can really pay off, yet only about one-third of car owners shop around for auto coverage. One of the best ways to reduce the cost of car insurance is to take advantage of the discounts auto insurers offer. Taken together, such discounts can knock 5 to 50 percent off your annual premium. Exhibit 10.6 summarizes some of the discounts offered by top auto insurance companies. Some give overall *safe-driving* (accident-free) discounts, and most give youthful operators lower rates if they've had *driver's training*. Some states have laws requiring insurers to offer lower premiums to any driver, young or old, who has taken driver's training. High school and college students may also receive *good-student* discounts for maintaining a B average or making the dean's list at their school.

Can you save money on your insurance by using a direct underwriter? Get a quote from Geico Direct and compare it with your current policies and premiums. Link to their site at **http://www.thomsonedu.com/finance/gitman.**

automobile insurance plan An arrangement providing automobile insurance to drivers who have been refused regular coverage under normal procedures.

Nearly all insurance companies give discounts to families with two or more automobiles insured by the same company (the *multicar* discount). Most insurers also offer discounts to owners who install *antitheft devices* in their cars. Likewise, some insurers offer *nonsmoker* and *nondrinker* discounts. Other companies specialize in insuring only certain portions of the population. For example, some insurers accept only persons who are educators or executives; others accept only government employees. Although not offering discounts in the normal sense, through more selective underwriting these companies are able to reduce losses and operating expenses, resulting in lower premiums.

Clearly, it's to your advantage to look for and use as many of these discounts as you can. Take another look at the auto insurance statement in Exhibit 10.4, and you'll see that the insured reduced his overall cost of coverage by 25 percent by qualifying for just three of the discounts (labeled "Premium Reductions"). Another effective way to drive down the cost of car insurance is to *raise your deductibles* (as discussed earlier in this chapter). This frequently overlooked tactic can dramatically affect the cost of your insurance premium. For example, the difference between a $100 deductible and a $500 deductible may be as much as 25 percent on collision coverage and 30 percent on comprehensive coverage; request a $1,000 deductible, and you may save as much as 45 to 50 percent on both collision and comprehensive coverage.

Financial Responsibility Laws

financial responsibility laws Laws *requiring motorists to buy a specified minimum amount of automobile liability insurance,* or to provide other proof of comparable financial responsibility.

Annual losses from automobile accidents in the United States run into billions of dollars. For this reason, most states have **financial responsibility laws** whereby motorists *must buy a specified minimum amount of automobile liability insurance,* or provide other proof of comparable financial responsibility. These laws attempt to force motorists to be financially responsible for the damage they cause due to automobile accidents, although the required limits are low in most states—well below what you should carry.

Financial responsibility laws fall into two categories. *Compulsory auto insurance laws* require motorists to show evidence of insurance coverage *before* receiving their license plates. Penalties for not having liability insurance include fines and suspension of your driver's

---

EXHIBIT 10.6   Are You a Good Auto Insurance Risk?

Many insurance companies offer discounts for auto safety equipment and good driving habits. Here are some items that will buy you insurance discounts:

Antitheft devices. Many insurance companies offer a discount only if you have an active or passive disabling alarm system or alarm-only system. Check with your insurer for specific devices they'll discount for.

Antilock brakes (ABS). Antilock braking systems can help prevent the loss of control in sudden braking situations.

Restraint systems. Air bags, dual air bags, and seat belts are now common in most late-model vehicles. Having all three may qualify you for the highest discount level.

Driver training. For teenage drivers who successfully complete training with a certified instructor.

Good student discount. Awarded to teenagers with a B average or better.

Accident prevention course. Discounts for approved accident prevention courses with presentation of a completion certificate.

Good driver. A good driver has a license for more than 3 years in the United States, and not more than 2 violation points on his or her driving record for either an accident and/or moving violation. Also no DWI, DUI, manslaughter, or gross negligence in an accident within the past 7 years.

Multiple policies: Discounts offered for having more than one vehicle and/or a homeowner's insurance policy with the same company.

Carpool: Discount for participating in a shared-vehicle car pool.

Electronic fund transfer (EFT). Pay your policy in full through EFT.

Sources: Adapted from "Discounts," at http://www.cheap-auto-car-insurance-quotes.com/discounts.htm, February 9, 2004; and "Discounts" at http://www.4-insurance-auto.com/discounts/discounts.php, February 9, 2004.

license. The second category requires motorists to show evidence of their insurance coverage only *after* being involved in an accident. If they then fail to demonstrate compliance with the law, their registrations and driver's licenses are suspended. This law has been criticized because it allows negligent motorists to have one "free" accident. Although motorists who aren't able to fulfill their financial responsibility lose their driving privileges, victims may never recover their losses.

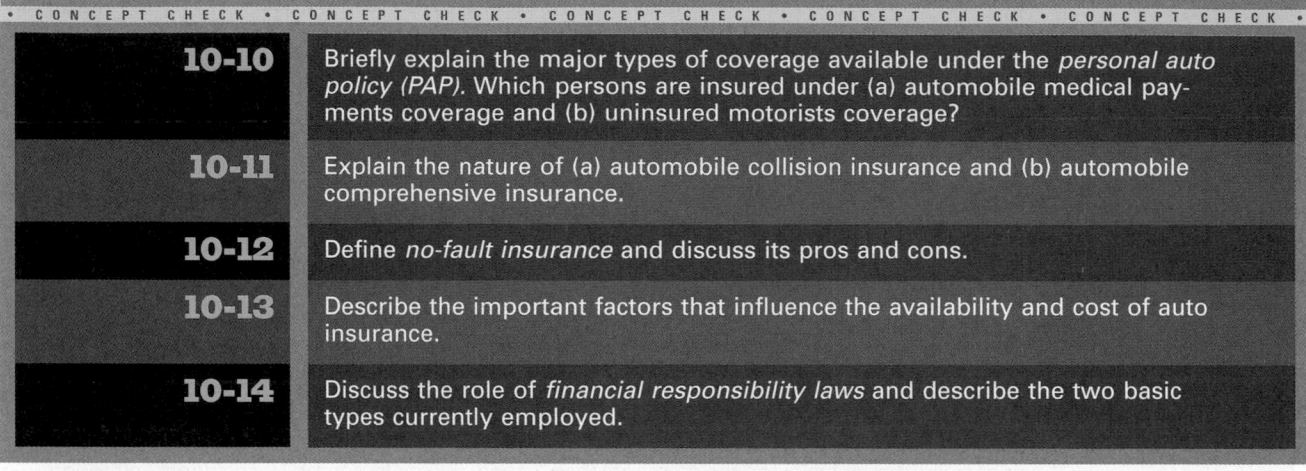

⑪ Concept Check

10-10	Briefly explain the major types of coverage available under the *personal auto policy (PAP)*. Which persons are insured under (a) automobile medical payments coverage and (b) uninsured motorists coverage?
10-11	Explain the nature of (a) automobile collision insurance and (b) automobile comprehensive insurance.
10-12	Define *no-fault insurance* and discuss its pros and cons.
10-13	Describe the important factors that influence the availability and cost of auto insurance.
10-14	Discuss the role of *financial responsibility laws* and describe the two basic types currently employed.

LG5 · OTHER PROPERTY AND LIABILITY INSURANCE

Homeowner's and automobile insurance policies represent the basic protection needed by most families, but other types of insurance, such as property and liability coverage, may be appropriate for some people. Among those discussed here are popular forms of supplemental property insurance coverage—earthquake insurance, flood insurance, and other forms of transportation insurance—as well as the personal liability umbrella policy.

Supplemental Property Insurance Coverage

Because homeowner's policies exclude certain types of damage, you may want to consider some of the following types of supplemental coverage.

- **Earthquake insurance.** Although most people think of California when earthquakes are mentioned, areas in other states are also subject to this type of loss. Very few homeowners buy this coverage because these policies typically carry a 15 percent deductible on the replacement cost of a home damaged or destroyed by earthquake. So even though the premiums are relatively inexpensive, you have to pay a lot out of pocket before you can collect on the policy.
- **Flood insurance.** Before 1968, most private insurers regarded floods as an uninsurable peril because the risk couldn't be spread among people not located in flood-prone areas. But in 1968, the federal government established a subsidized flood insurance program in cooperation with private insurance agents, who can now sell this low-cost coverage to homeowners and tenants living in designated communities. The flood insurance program also encourages communities to initiate land-use controls to reduce future flood losses.
- **Other forms of transportation insurance.** In addition to automobile insurance, you may wish to insure other types of vehicles, such as mobile homes, recreational vehicles, or boats.

Personal Liability Umbrella Policy

Persons with moderate to high levels of income and net worth may want to take out a **personal liability umbrella policy.** It provides added liability coverage for homeowner's and automobile insurance as well as additional coverage not provided by either of those policies. Umbrella policies often include limits of $1 million or more. Some also provide added amounts of coverage for a family's major medical insurance.

Because middle- and upper-income individuals are logical targets for liability claims, umbrella protection provides a desirable, added layer of coverage. The premiums are usually quite reasonable for the broad coverage offered—$150 to $300 a year for as much as $1 million in coverage. Although the protection is comprehensive, it does contain some exclusions. The insured party must already have relatively high liability limits ($100,000 to $300,000) on their homeowner's and auto coverage in order to purchase a personal liability umbrella policy.

Do you need the extra protection a personal liability umbrella policy provides? The answer is yes if you have sizable assets that could be seized to pay a judgment against you that is not fully covered by your homeowner's and automobile policies. But you may also need this coverage if you rent your home to others, have house sitters, or hire unbonded help such as gardeners or babysitters, because you're responsible for any injuries they incur or cause. You may also need this coverage if you work from home and clients visit you at your home office.

⏸ Concept Check

10-15	Briefly describe the following supplemental property insurance coverage: (a) earthquake insurance, (b) flood insurance, and (c) other forms of transportation insurance.
10-16	What is a *personal liability umbrella policy?* Under what circumstances might it be a wise purchase?

LG6 · BUYING INSURANCE AND SETTLING CLAIMS

If you're thinking about buying property and liability insurance, the first step is to develop an inventory of exposures to loss and arrange them from highest to lowest priority. Losses that lend themselves to insurance protection are those that seldom occur but are potentially substantial—for example, damage to a home and its contents, or liability arising from a negligence claim. Somewhat less important, but still desirable, is insurance to cover losses that could disrupt a family's financial plans, even though the losses might not result in insolvency. Such risks include physical damage to automobiles, boats, and other personal property of moderate value. Lowest-priority exposures can be covered by savings or from current income; some personal property of minor value, such as an old auto, may not merit coverage—at least as far as collision insurance is concerned.

personal liability umbrella policy An insurance policy providing excess liability coverage for homeowner's and automobile insurance as well as additional coverage not provided by either policy.

captive agent An insurance agent who represents only one insurance company and is more or less an employee of that company.

independent agent An insurance agent who may place coverage with any company with which he or she has an agency relationship, as long as the insured meets that company's underwriting standards.

Property And Liability Insurance Agents

There's more to buying property insurance than simply signing applications for homeowner's and automobile insurance, and a good agent can make the process much easier. Most property insurance agents fall into either the captive or independent category. A **captive agent** represents only one insurance company and is more or less an employee of that company. Allstate, Nationwide, and State Farm are major insurance companies that market their products through captive agents. In contrast, **independent agents** typically represent between 2 and 10 different insurance companies. These agents may place your coverage with any of the companies they have an agency relationship with, as long as you meet the underwriting standards of that company. Some well-known companies that operate through independent agents include The Hartford, Unitrin Kemper, Chubb, and Travelers. Either type of agent can serve your needs well and should take the time to:

- Review your total property and liability insurance exposures
- Inventory property and identify exposures
- Determine appropriate covered perils, limits, deductibles, and floater policies

Because of large variations in premiums and services, it pays to comparison shop.

Property insurance agents who meet various experiential and educational requirements, including passing a series of written examinations, qualify for the *Chartered Property and Casualty Underwriter (CPCU)* or *Certified Insurance Counselor (CIC)* designation. Another alternative to consider is companies that sell directly to the consumer through an 800 number or online. Generally, their premiums are lower. Examples of direct sellers are Amica, Erie, Geico, and USAA.

Property and Liability Insurance Companies

Selecting an agent is an important step when purchasing property and liability insurance, but you should ask questions about the company, including its financial soundness, its claims-settlement practices, and the geographic extent of its operations (this could be important if you're involved in an accident 1,000 miles from home). As with any form of insurance, you should check the company's ratings (see Chapter 8) and stick with those rated in the top categories. The agent should be a good source of information about the technical aspects of a company's operations; friends and acquaintances often can provide insight into its claims-settlement policy. The Internet offers lots of information about various property and liability insurance products. Many insurance companies now have elaborate home pages on the Web containing basic information about the provider and its products, directions to local agents, or calculators to crunch the numbers and generate sample premiums.

Settling Property and Liability Claims

Generally speaking, insurance companies settle claims promptly and fairly—especially life and healthcare claims. But in settling property and liability claims, there is some claimant–insurer disagreement. In this section, we'll review the claims-settlement process and the people who participate in it. First, though, let's consider what you should do immediately following an accident.

First Steps Following an Accident

After an accident, record the names, addresses, and phone numbers of all witnesses, drivers, occupants, and injured parties, along with the license numbers of the automobiles involved. Never leave the scene of an accident, even if the other party says it's OK. In many states, leaving the scene is a criminal offense unless there's a special provision for reporting non-injury accidents. Immediately notify law enforcement officers and your insurance agent of the accident. Never discuss liability at the scene of an accident, or with anyone other than the police and your insurer. Before it can be determined whom, if anyone, is legally liable for an accident, the requisites of liability must be established. It's the duty of the police to assess the probability of a law violation and maintain order at the scene of an accident—not to make judgments about liability.

Steps in Claims Settlement

If you're involved in an accident, one of the first things to decide is whether you want to file a claim. Most experts agree that unless it's a very minor or insignificant accident, the best course of action is to file a claim. Be aware, though, that if you've made several claims, the insurance company may decide to drop you after settling the current one. The claims settlement process typically involves these steps:

FINANCIAL ROAD SIGN

STRATEGIES TO AVOID LIABILITY

Understanding liability can help you avoid it. Here are some practical strategies you can use.

- **Understand what causes liability:** Educate yourself through books and seminars or by consulting with those in a position to advise you.
- **Develop your own safety program.** Dedication to personal safety and that of others you're responsible for will reduce the risk of injuries and thus of liability. Regular auto or equipment inspections will keep you a step ahead.
- **Carry adequate liability insurance.** It doesn't prevent liability, but it may protect your home, savings, and property if a claim or lawsuit is brought against you. At the very least, insurance can spare you the high cost of a legal defense.

FINANCIAL ROAD SIGN

1. **Notice to your insurance company.** You must notify your insurance company that a loss (or potential for loss) has occurred. Timely notice is extremely important.
2. **Investigation.** Insurance company personnel may talk to witnesses or law enforcement officers and gather physical evidence to determine whether the claimed loss is covered by the policy, and they'll check to make sure that the date of the loss falls within the policy period. If you delay filing your claim, you hinder the insurer's ability to check the facts. All policies specify the period within which you must give notice. Failure to report can result in losing your right to collect.
3. **Proof of loss.** This proof requires you to give a sworn statement. You may have to show medical bills, submit an inventory, and certify the value of lost property (for example, a written inventory, photographs, and purchase receipts). You may also have to submit an employer statement of lost wages and, if possible, physical evidence of damage (X-rays if you claim a back injury; a broken window or pried door if you claim a break-in and theft at your home). After reviewing your proof of loss, the insurer may (1) pay you the amount you asked for, (2) offer you a lesser amount, or (3) deny that the company has any legal responsibility under the terms of your policy.

If the amount is disputed, most policies provide for some form of claims arbitration. You hire a third party, the company hires a third party, and these two arbitrators jointly select one more person. When any two of the three arbitrators reach agreement, their decision binds you and the company to their solution. When a company denies responsibility, you do not get the right of arbitration. In such cases the company is saying the loss does not fall under the policy coverage. You must then either forget the claim or bring in an attorney or, perhaps, a public adjustor (discussed next).

Claims Adjustment

Usually the first person to call when you need to file a claim is your insurance agent. If your loss is relatively minor, the agent can quickly process it and, in fact, often gives you a check right on the spot. If your loss is more complex, your company will probably assign a claims adjustor to the case. A **claims adjustor** is an insurance specialist who works for the insurance company, as an independent adjustor, or for an adjustment bureau. The adjustor investigates claims, looking out for the company's interests—which might very well be to keep you, its customer, satisfied. However, many claimants are out to collect all they can from insurance companies, which they think have "deep pockets." Thus adjustors walk a fine line: they must diligently question and investigate, while at the same time offering service to minimize settlement delays and financial hardship. To promote your own interest in the claim, cooperate with your adjustor and answer inquiries honestly—keeping in mind that the company writes the adjustor's paycheck.

claims adjustor An insurance specialist who works for the insurance company, as an independent adjustor, or for an adjustment bureau, to investigate claims.

� Concept Check

CHECK • CONCEPT CHECK • CONCEPT CHECK • CONCEPT CHECK • CONCEPT CHECK • CONCEPT CHECK • CONCEPT C

10-17	Differentiate between *captive* and *independent insurance agents*. What characteristics should you look for in an insurance agent and an insurance company when you're buying property or liability insurance?
10-18	Briefly describe key aspects of the claims-settlement process, explaining what to do after an accident, the steps in claim settlement, and the role of *claims adjustors*.

« SUMMARY

LG1 **Discuss the importance and basic principles of property insurance, including types of exposure, indemnity, and coinsurance.** Property and liability insurance protects against the loss of real and personal property that can occur from exposure to various perils. Such insurance also protects against loss from lawsuits based on alleged negligence by the insured. The principle of indemnity limits the insured's compensation to the amount of economic loss. The coinsurance provision requires the policyholder to buy insurance coverage that equals a set percentage of the property's value to receive full compensation under the policy's terms.

LG2 **Identify the types of coverage provided by homeowner's insurance.** Most homeowner's insurance policies are divided into two sections. Section I covers the insured's dwelling unit, accompanying structures, and personal property. Section II provides comprehensive coverage for personal liability and medical payments to others. The most commonly sold homeowner's policies (Forms HO-2 and HO-3) cover a broad range of perils, including damage from fire or lightning, windstorms, explosions, aircraft, vehicles, smoke, vandalism, theft, freezing, and so on. Personal property coverage is typically set at 50 percent of the coverage on the dwelling.

LG3 **Select the right homeowner's insurance policy for your needs.** Everyone should have some form of homeowner's insurance, whether you own a single-family house or a condominium, or rent an apartment. Renter's insurance covers your personal possessions. Except for the house and garage, which are covered on a replacement-cost basis, homeowner's or renter's insurance normally reimburses all losses on an actual cash-value basis, subject to applicable deductibles and policy limits. For an additional premium, you can usually obtain replacement-cost coverage on personal belongings. In Section I, internal limits are set for various classes of property. You may wish to increase these limits if you have valuable property. One way to do so is with a personal property floater (PPF). Because the

standard Section II liability limit is only $100,000, it's a good idea to buy additional liability coverage, generally available at minimal cost. To reduce premiums, choose a policy with a higher deductible.

LG4 **Analyze the coverage in a personal automobile policy (PAP) and choose the most cost-effective policy.** Automobile insurance policies usually protect the insured from loss due to personal liability, medical payments, uninsured (and underinsured) motorists, collision (property damage to the vehicle), and comprehensive coverage (which applies to nearly any other type of noncollision damage a car might suffer, such as theft or vandalism). Where you live, type of car, driving record, how much you drive, and your personal characteristics influence the policy premium cost. Most automobile insurers offer discounts for good driving records, safety and antitheft devices, driver's training courses, and so on. Other ways to reduce premiums are through higher deductibles and eliminating collision coverage if your car is old.

LG5 **Describe other types of property and liability insurance.** Besides the major forms of homeowner's and automobile insurance, you can get other property and liability coverage, including supplemental property insurance coverage—earthquake insurance, flood insurance, and other forms of transportation insurance (mobile-home, recreational vehicle, and boat insurance)—and personal liability umbrella policies.

LG6 **Choose a property and liability insurance agent and company, and settle claims.** Before buying property and liability coverage, evaluate your exposure to loss and determine the coverage needed. Also carefully select your insurance agent and insurance company to obtain appropriate coverage at a reasonable price. Equally important, make sure the agent and company you deal with have reputations for fair claims-settlement practices. Before filing a claim, decide whether the amount of damage warrants a claim. Document all claims properly and file promptly. If you have a complex loss claim, expect your insurer to assign a claims adjustor to the case.

FINANCIAL PLANNING EXERCISES

LG1 1. Assume Marcus Browning had a homeowner's insurance policy with $100,000 of coverage on the dwelling. Would a 90 percent coinsurance clause be better than an 80 percent clause in such a policy? Give reasons to support your answer.

LG2 2. Last year Steve and Jessica Morgan bought a home with a dwelling replacement value of $250,000 and insured it (via an HO-3 policy) for $210,000. The policy reimburses for actual cash value and has a $500 deductible, standard limits for coverage C items, and no scheduled property. Recently, burglars broke into the house and stole a 2-year-old television set with a current replacement value of $600 and an estimated useful life of 8 years. They also took jewelry valued at $1,850 and silver flatware valued at $3,000.

a. If the Morgans' policy has an 80 percent coinsurance clause, do they have enough insurance?

b. Assuming a 50 percent coverage C limit, calculate how much the Morgans would receive if they filed a claim for the stolen items.

c. What advice would you give the Morgans about their homeowner's coverage?

LG3 3. Vickie Korte's luxurious home in the suburb of Broken Arrow, Oklahoma, was recently gutted in a fire. Her living and dining rooms were completely destroyed, and the damaged personal property had a replacement price of $27,000. The average age of the damaged personal property was 5 years, and its useful life was estimated to be 15 years. What is the maximum amount the insurance company would pay Vickie, assuming that it reimburses losses on an actual cash-value basis?

LG3 4. Doris and Ed Barnow, both graduate students, moved into an apartment near the university. Doris wants to buy renter's insurance, but Ed thinks they don't need it because their furniture isn't worth much. Doris points out that, among other things, they have some expensive computer and stereo equipment. To help the Barnows resolve their dilemma, suggest a plan for deciding how much insurance to buy, and give them some ideas for finding a policy.

LG4 5. Robert Taylor has a personal automobile policy (PAP) with coverage of $25,000/$50,000 for bodily injury liability, $25,000 for property damage liability, $5,000 for medical payments, and a $500 deductible for collision insurance. How much will his insurance cover in each of the following situations? Will he have any out-of-pocket costs?

a. He loses control and skids on ice, running into a parked car and causing $3,785 damage to the unoccupied vehicle and $2,350 damage to his own car.

b. He runs a stop sign and causes a serious auto accident, badly injuring two people. The injured parties win lawsuits against him for $30,000 each.

c. Taylor's wife borrows his car while hers is being repaired. She backs into a telephone pole and causes $450 damage to the car.

APPLYING PERSONAL FINANCE

Insure Your Property!

Adequate property insurance is a vital part of financial planning. It helps protect our hard-earned investments in a home, car, or other property. This project will help you determine your property insurance needs.

List the property for which you'd need insurance coverage. Your list may include such things as a home, car, boat, motorcycle, or household items. Beside each entry, list the insurance you currently have in place on each. Then examine the depth of coverage of your policies. Is this coverage adequate? What are its exclusions and limits? What are the costs? Can you do something to lower these costs? If you don't have coverage, or if your coverage is inadequate, research various policies. If you rent a place to live, do you have renter's insurance? If not, tally up what it would cost you to replace all your household items and then find several quotes for renter's insurance.

CRITICAL THINKING CASES

LG2, 3

10.1 The Salvatis' Homeowner's Insurance Decision

Rodrigo and Anita Salvati, ages 30 and 28, were recently married in Chicago. Rodrigo is an electrical engineer with Geophysical Century, an oil exploration company. Anita has a master's degree in special education and teaches at a local middle school. After living in an apartment for 6 months, the Salvatis have negotiated the purchase of a new home in a rapidly growing Chicago suburb. Republic Savings and Loan Association has approved their loan request for $180,000, which represents 90 percent of the $200,000 purchase price. Before closing the loan, the Salvatis must obtain homeowner's insurance for the home. The Salvatis currently have an HO-4 renter's insurance policy, which they purchased from Rodrigo's tennis partner, Kelly Duvall, who is an agent with Kramer's Insurance Company. To learn about the types of available homeowner's insurance, Rodrigo has discussed their situation with Kelly, who has offered them several homeowner's policies for their consideration. He has recommended that the Salvatis purchase an HO-3 policy because it would provide them with comprehensive coverage.

Critical Thinking Questions

1. What forms of homeowner's insurance are available? Which forms should the Salvatis consider?
2. What are the perils against which the home and its contents should be insured?
3. Discuss the types of loss protection provided by the homeowner's policies under consideration.
4. What advice would you give the Salvatis regarding Kelly's suggestion? What coverage should they buy?

LG4

10.2 Auto Insurance for Cheryl Weisbach

Cheryl Weisbach of Phoenix, Arizona, is a divorced 40-year-old loan officer at the Frontier National Bank of Arizona; she has a 16-year-old son. She has decided to use her annual bonus as a down payment on a new car. One Saturday afternoon in late December, she visits Chuck Thomas's Auto Mall and buys a new car for $28,000. To obtain insurance on the car, Cheryl calls her agent, Jane Cunningham, who represents Farmers Insurance Company, and explains her auto insurance needs. Jane says she'll investigate the various options for her. Three days later, Cheryl and Jane get together to review her coverage options. Jane offers several proposals, including various combinations of the following coverages: (a) basic automobile liability insurance, (b) uninsured motorists coverage, (c) automobile medical payments insurance, (d) automobile collision insurance, and (e) comprehensive automobile insurance.

Critical Thinking Questions

1. Describe the key features of these insurance coverages.
2. Are there any limitations on these coverages? Explain.
3. Indicate the persons who would be protected under each type of coverage.
4. What kind of insurance coverages would you recommend that Ms. Weisbach purchase? Explain your recommendation.

> **MONEY ONLINE** www.thomsonedu.com/finance/gitman

Visit **http://www.thomsonedu.com/finance/gitman** for some additional Web-based exercises and hot links (with annotations) to a variety of resources relevant to the topics covered in this chapter.

PART 5 ▶ Managing Investments

Investment Planning

CHAPTER 11 • CHAPTER 11 • CHAPTER 11 • CHAPTER 11 • CHAPTER 11 • CHAPTER 11 • CHAPTER 11 • CHAPTER 11

LG1 THE OBJECTIVES AND REWARDS OF INVESTING

People invest their money for all sorts of reasons. Some do it as a way to accumulate the down payment on a new home; others do it as a way to supplement their income; still others invest to build up a nest egg for retirement. Actually, the term *investment* means different things to different people; that is, while millions of people *invest* regularly in securities like stocks, bonds, and mutual funds, others *speculate* in commodities or options. **Investing** is generally considered to take a long-term perspective and is viewed as a process of purchasing securities wherein stability of value and level of return are somewhat predictable. **Speculating,** on the other hand, is viewed as a short-term activity that involves the buying and selling of securities in which future value and expected return are highly uncertain. Obviously, speculating is far riskier than investing.

If you're like most investors, at first you'll probably keep your funds in some type of savings vehicle (as described in Chapter 4). Once you have *sufficient savings*—for emergencies and other purposes—you can begin building up a *pool of investable capital*. This often means making sacrifices and doing what you can to *live within your budget*. Granted, it's far easier to spend money than to save it, but if you're really serious about getting into investments, you'll have to accumulate the necessary capital! In addition to a savings and capital accumulation program, it's also important to have adequate *insurance coverage* to provide protection against the unexpected (we discussed different kinds of insurance in Chapters 8, 9, and 10). For our purposes here, we'll assume that you're ade-

investing The process of placing money in some medium such as stocks or bonds in the expectation of receiving some future benefit.

speculating A form of investing in which future value and expected returns are highly uncertain.

quately insured and that the cost of insurance coverage is built into your family's monthly cash budget. Ample insurance and liquidity (cash and savings) with which to meet life's emergencies are two *investment prerequisites* that are absolutely essential to developing a successful investment program. Once these conditions are met, you're ready to start investing.

How Do I Get Started?

Contrary to what you may believe, there's really nothing magical about the topic of investments—in fact, as long as you have the capital to do so, it's really quite easy to get started in investing. The terminology may seem baffling at times, and some of the procedures and techniques quite complicated. But don't let that mislead you into thinking there's no room for the small, individual investor. Nothing could be farther from the truth! As we'll see in this and the next two chapters, individual investors can choose from a wide array of securities and investment vehicles. What's more, opening an investment account is no more difficult than opening a checking account.

How, then, do you get started? First, you need some money—not a lot; $500 to $1,000 will do, although $4,000 or $5,000 would be better (and remember, this is *investment capital* we're talking about here—money you've accumulated above and beyond any basic emergency savings). Besides the money, you need knowledge and know-how. Never invest in something you're not sure about—that's the quickest way to lose money. Instead, learn as much as you can about the market, different types of securities, and various trading strategies. This course you're taking on personal finance is a good start, but you may want to do more. For one thing, you can become a regular reader of publications such as *Money*, *The Wall Street Journal*, *Barron's*, and *Forbes* (we'll review these and other sources of information later in this chapter). Also try to stay current with major developments as they occur in the market; start following the stock market, interest rates, and developments in the bond market.

We strongly suggest that, after you've learned a few things about stocks and bonds, you set up a portfolio of securities on paper and make *paper trades* in and out of your portfolio, for 6 months to a year, to get a feel for what it's like to make (and lose) money in the market. Start out with an imaginary sum of, say, $50,000 (as long as you're going to dream, you might as well dream big). Then keep track of the stocks and bonds you hold, record the number of shares bought and sold, dividends received, and so on. Throughout this exercise, be sure to use actual prices (as obtained from *The Wall Street Journal* or your local newspaper) and keep it as realistic as possible. If you have access to a computer, you might want to use one of the *portfolio tracking* programs offered at such sites as **http://www.quicken.com** or **http://moneycentral.msn.com;** you'll find some powerful Internet sites out there that make it easy to track the behavior of a portfolio of securities. The advantage to creating a paper portfolio is clear: if you're going to make mistakes in the market, you're much better off doing so on paper. Also, if your parents, relatives, or friends have done a lot of investing, talk to them! Find out what they have to say about investing, pick up some pointers and possibly even learn from their mistakes. Eventually, you'll become familiar with the market and be comfortable with how things are done there. When that happens, you'll be ready to take the plunge.

At that point, you'll also need a way to invest—more specifically, a broker and some investment vehicle in which to invest. As we'll see later in this chapter, the stockbroker is the party through whom you'll be buying and selling stocks, bonds, and other securities. If your relatives or friends have a broker they like and trust, have them introduce you to him or her. Or, visit several of the brokerage firms in your community; talk to one of their brokers about your available investment funds and your investment objectives.

As a beginning investor with limited funds, it's probably best to confine your investment activity to the basics. Stick to stocks, bonds, and mutual funds. Avoid getting fancy, and certainly don't try to make a killing every time you invest—that will only lead to frustration, disappointment, and very possibly, heavy losses. Further, *be patient!* Don't expect the price of the stock to double overnight, and don't panic when things don't work out as expected in the short run (after all, security prices do occasionally go down). Finally, remember that you don't need spectacular returns in order to make a lot of money in the market. Instead, be consistent and let the concept of compound interest work for you. Do that, and you'll find that just $2,000 a year invested at the fairly conservative rate of 10 percent will grow to well over $100,000 in 20 years! While the type of security you invest in is a highly personal decision, you might want to seriously consider some sort of mutual fund as your first investment (see Chapter 13). Mutual funds provide professional management and diversification that individual investors—especially those with limited resources—can rarely obtain on their own.

The Role of Investing in Personal Financial Planning

Buy a car, build a house, enjoy a comfortable retirement—these are goals we'd all like to attain some day and, in many cases, they're the centerpieces of well-developed financial plans. As a rule, a financial goal such as building a house is not something we pay for out of our cash reserves; the cost (in most cases, even the down payment) is simply too great to allow for that. Instead, we must accumulate the funds over time—which is where investment planning and the act of investing enter into the personal financial planning process. By investing our money, we are letting it work for us.

It all starts with an objective—a particular financial goal you'd like to achieve within a certain period of time. Take the case of the Thompsons. Shortly after the birth of their first child, they decided to start building a college education fund. After doing some rough calculations, they concluded they'd need to accumulate about $60,000 over the next 18 years to have enough money for their daughter's education. Simply by setting that objective, the Thompsons created a well-defined, specific financial goal. The purpose is to meet their child's educational needs and the amount of money involved is $60,000 in 18 years. But how do they reach their goal? First, they must decide where the money will come from. While part of it will come from the return (profit) on their investments, they still have to come up with the *investment capital*.

Coming Up with the Capital

So far, the Thompsons know how much money they want to accumulate ($60,000), and how long they have to accumulate it (18 years). The only other thing they need to determine at this point is the *rate of return* they feel they can earn on their money. Having taken a financial planning course in college, the Thompsons know that the amount of money they'll have to put into their investment program largely depends on *how much they can earn from their investments*—the higher their rate of return, the less they'll have to put up. Let's say they feel comfortable using a 9 percent rate of return. That's a fairly conservative number—one that won't require them to put all or most of their money into a bunch of high-risk investments—and they're reasonably certain they'll be able to reach that level of return, *on average*, over the long haul. It's important to use some care in coming up with a projected rate of return. Don't saddle yourself with an unreasonably high rate, as that will simply reduce the chance of reaching your targeted financial goal.

Probably the best way of arriving at a reasonable projection is to look at what the market has done over the past 10 to 15 years, and then use the average return performance over that period as your estimate—or, if you want to be a bit more conservative, knock a point or two off the market's return. To help you in this regard, take a look at the statistics in the following table; they show the average annual returns on stocks, bonds, and U.S. Treasury bills over various holding periods of from 5 to 15 years.

Holding Periods	Stock Returns (as measured by the DJIA)	High-Grade Corp. Bond Returns	Stocks and Bonds Together (50/50)	Returns on Short-Term U.S. Treasury Bills	Stocks, Bonds, and T-Bills Combined (1/3–1/3–1/3)
5 years: 2001–2005	2.01%	5.87%	3.94%	2.23%	3.37%
10 years: 1996–2005	9.76%	6.16%	7.96%	3.78%	6.57%
15 years: 1991–2005	12.30%	7.26%	9.78%	4.03%	7.86%

One of the first things you'll notice is the abnormally low returns generated by stocks over the 5-year period from 2001 to 2005. This was the result of a nasty bear market that started in 2000 and ran until late 2002. Fortunately, 5-year stock returns of only 2 percent just don't happen very often; the last time it did was in the early 1970s. So it wouldn't seem sensible to use such low returns as the basis for forecasting future returns. Instead, consider using one of the other two holding periods—they both produce returns that are within a point or two of each other, and are more representative of long-term returns in the market. Indeed, using the 10- to 15-year returns as viable standards of market performance, it's clear that unless you had put just about everything into short-term U.S. Treasury bills, generating an average return of around 8 to 10 percent (or even more) was well within the reach of most investors. Of course, there's no guarantee these returns will happen again in the next 10 to 15 years, but at least the past does give us a basis—or "handle"—for making projections into the future.

Now, returning to our problem at hand, there are two ways of coming up with the capital needed to reach a targeted sum of money: (1) you can make a lump-sum investment right up front and let that amount grow over time, or (2) you can set up a systematic savings plan and put away a certain amount of money each year. Worksheet 11.1 is designed to help you find the amount of investment capital you'll need to reach a given financial goal. It employs the *compound value* concept discussed in Chapter 2 and is based on a given financial target (line 1) and a projected average rate of return on your investments (line 2). You can use this worksheet to find either a required lump-sum investment (part A), or an amount that will have to be put away each year in a savings plan (part B). For our purposes, we'll assume the Thompsons have $7,500 to start with (this comes mostly from gifts their daughter received from her grandparents). Since they know they'll need a lot more than that to reach their target, the Thompsons decide to use part B of the worksheet to find out how much they'll have to save annually.

The first thing to do is find the future value of the $7,500 initial investment—the question here is: How much will that initial lump-sum investment grow to over an 18-year period? Using the compound value concept and the appropriate "future value factor" (from Appendix A), we see, in line 7, that this deposit will grow to some $35,400. That's nearly 60 percent of the targeted $60,000 that we already have covered. Thus, by subtracting the terminal value of the initial investment (line 7) from our target (line 1), we find the amount that must be generated from some sort of annual savings plan—see line 8. (*Note:* If you were starting from scratch, you'd enter a zero in line 5, and the amount in line 8 would be equal to the amount in line 1.) Again, using the appropriate future value factor (this time from Appendix B), we find the Thompsons will have to put away/invest just $600 a year (actually $596) to reach their target of $60,000 in 18 years. That is, the $596 a year will grow to $24,600, which, when added to the $35,400 that the initial $7,500 will grow to, equals the Thompsons' targeted financial goal of $60,000. (By the way, they can also reach their target by making a lump-sum investment right up front of $12,712—try working out part A of the worksheet on your own, and see if you can come up with that number.) As you might have suspected, the last few steps in the worksheet can just as easily be done on a good handheld calculator. That is, after determining the size of the nest egg (as in step 8, for example), you can use a financial calculator to find the amount of money that must be put away each year to fund the nest egg.

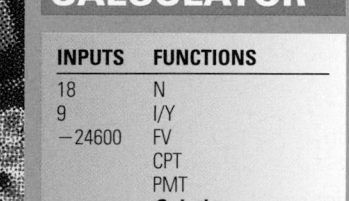

CALCULATOR

INPUTS	FUNCTIONS
18	N
9	I/Y
−24600	FV
	CPT
	PMT
	Solution
	595.62

See Appendix E for details.

Calculator Keystrokes. You can use a financial calculator to *find the annual payments necessary to fund a target amount* by first putting the calculator in the *annual compounding* mode. Then, to determine the amount of money that must be put away each year, at a 9 percent rate of return, to accumulate $24,600 in 18 years, make the keystrokes shown here, where:

N = number of *years* in investment horizon
I/Y = expected average *annual* rate of return on investments
FV = the targeted amount of money you want to accumulate, entered as a *negative*

A value of $595.62 should appear in the calculator display, which is the amount of money that must be put away each year to reach the targeted amount of $24,600 in 18 years. (*Note:* The calculator keystrokes take you from Steps 8 to 10 in Worksheet 11.1. You can also do steps 5 to 7 on the calculator by letting **N** = 18; **I/Y** = 9.0; **PV** = −7,500; and then solving for **(CPT)FV.** Try it—you should come up with a number fairly close to the amount shown on line 7 of Worksheet 11.1).

An Investment Plan Provides Direction

Now that the Thompsons know how much they have to save each year, their next step is deciding how they'll save it. It's probably best to follow some type of *systematic routine*—for example, build a set amount of savings each month or quarter into the household budget, and then stick with it. But whatever procedure is followed, keep in mind that all we're doing here is accumulating the required investment capital. That money still has to be put to work in some kind of investment program, and that's where an investment plan enters the picture. An **investment plan** is nothing more than a simple—preferably written—statement explaining how the accumulated investment capital will be invested in order to reach the targeted goal. In the Thompsons' case, their capital accumulation plan calls for a 9 percent rate of return as a target they feel they can achieve. Now they need to find a way to obtain that 9 percent return on their money—meaning they have to specify, in general terms at least, the kinds of investment vehicles they intend to use. *When completed, an investment plan is a way of translating an abstract investment target* (in this case, a 9 percent return) *into a specific investment program.*

What Are Your Investment Objectives?

Some people buy securities for the protection they provide from taxes (that's what tax shelters are all about). Others want to have money put aside for that proverbial rainy day or, perhaps, to build up a nice retirement nest egg. *Your goals tend to set the tone for your investment program, and they play a major role in determining how conservative (or aggressive) you're likely to be in making investment decisions.* In a very real way, they provide a purpose for your investments. Given that you have adequate savings and insurance to cover any emergencies, the most frequent investment objectives are to (1) enhance current income, (2) save for a major purchase, (3) accumulate funds for retirement, and (4) seek shelter from taxes.

Current Income

The idea here is to put your money into investments that will enable you to supplement your income. In other words, it's for people who want to live off their investment income. A secure source of high current income, from dividends or interest, is the principal concern of such investors. Retired people, for example, often choose investments offering high current income—at low risk. Another common reason for seeking supplemental income is that a family member requires extended costly medical care. Even after insurance, such recurring costs can heavily burden a family budget without this vital income supplement.

Major Expenditures

People often put money aside, sometimes for years, to save up enough to make just one major expenditure. Here are the most common ones:

- The down payment on a home
- Money for a child's college education
- Some capital for going into business
- An expensive (perhaps once-in-a-lifetime) vacation
- The purchase of a very special, expensive item
- Funds for retirement (discussed in the next section)

Whatever your goal, the idea is to set your sights on something and then go about building your capital with that objective in mind. It sure makes the act of investing more pleasurable. Once you know about how

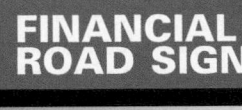

You can use a worksheet like this one to find out how much money you must come up with to reach a given financial goal. This worksheet is based on the same future value concepts we first introduced in Chapter 2.

DETERMINING AMOUNT OF INVESTMENT CAPITAL

Financial goal: *To accumulate $60,000 in 18 years for the purpose of meeting the cost of daughter's college education.*

1. Targeted Financial Goal (see Note 1)	$ 60,000
2. Projected Average Return on Investments	9.0%
A. Finding a Lump-Sum Investment:	
3. Future Value Factor, from Appendix A	
■ based on _____ years to target date and a projected average return on investment of _____	
4. Required Lump-Sum Investment (See Note 3)	
■ line 1 ÷ line 3	$
B. Making a Series of Investments over Time	
5. Amount of Initial Investment, if any (see Note 2)	$ 7,500
6. Future Value Factor, from Appendix A	
■ based on __18__ years of target date and a projected average return on investment of __9%__	4.72
7. Terminal Value of Initial Investment (See Note 3)	
■ line 5 × line 6	$ 35,400
8. Balance to Come from Savings Plan	
■ line 1 − line 7	$ 24,600
9. Future Value Annuity Factor, from Appendix B	
■ based on __18__ years to target date and a projected average return on investment of __9%__	41.3
10. Series of Annual Investments Required over Time (See Note 3)	
■ line 8 ÷ line 9	$ 596

Note 1: The "targeted financial goal" is the amount of money you want to accumulate by some target date in the future.

Note 2: If you're starting from scratch (i.e., there is no initial investment enter zero on line 5, skip lines 6 and 7, and then use the total targeted financial goal (from line 1) as the amount to be funded from a savings plan; now proceed with the rest of the worksheet.

Note 3: Alternatively, lines 4, 7, and 10 can all be determined with a good handheld calculator (one with a time-value function).

---

much money you're going to need to attain one of these goals (following a procedure like the one illustrated in Worksheet 11.1), you can specify the types of investment vehicles you intend to use. For example, you might follow a low-risk approach by making a single lump-sum investment in a high-grade bond that matures the same year you'll need the funds; or you could follow a riskier investment plan that calls for investing a set amount of money over time in something like a growth-oriented mutual fund (where there's little assurance of the investment's terminal value). Of course, for some purposes—such as the down payment on a home or a child's education—you'll probably want to accept a lot less

investment plan A statement—preferably written—that specifies how investment capital will be invested to achieve a specified goal.

risk than for others, as attaining these goals should not be jeopardized by the types of investment vehicles you choose to employ.

Retirement

Accumulating funds for retirement is *the single most important reason for investing.* Too often, though, retirement planning occupies only a small amount of our time, because we tend to rely heavily on employers and Social Security for our retirement needs. As many people learn too late in life, that can be a serious mistake. A much better approach is to review the amounts of income you can realistically expect to receive from Social Security and your employee pension plan, and then decide, based on your retirement goals, *whether they'll be adequate to meet your needs.* You'll probably find that you'll have to supplement them through personal investing. Obviously, the earlier in life you make this assessment, the greater your opportunity to accumulate the needed funds. (Retirement plans are discussed in Chapter 14.)

Shelter from Taxes

As we explained in Chapter 3, federal income tax law doesn't treat all sources of income equally. For example, if you own real estate—either directly or through some pooling arrangement—you may be able to take depreciation deductions against certain other sources of income, thereby reducing the amount of your final taxable income. This tax write-off feature can make real estate an attractive investment vehicle for some investors, even though its pretax rate of return may not appear very high. The goal of sheltering income from taxes is a legitimate one that, for some investors, often goes hand in hand with the goals of saving for a major outlay or for retirement. Clearly, if you can avoid paying taxes on the income from an investment, you will, all other things considered, have more funds available for reinvestment during the period.

Different Ways to Invest

After establishing your investment objectives, you can use a variety of investment vehicles to fulfill those goals. In this section we'll briefly describe various types of investment vehicles, though for our purposes here—and in the next two chapters—we'll limit our discussion to securities that are popular with (and widely used by) individual investors.

Common Stock

Common stocks are basically a form of *equity*— as an investment, they represent an ownership interest in a corporation. Each share of stock symbolizes a fractional ownership position in a firm; for example, one share of common stock in a corporation that has 10,000 shares outstanding would denote a 1/10,000 ownership interest in the firm. A share of stock entitles the holder to equal participation in the corporation's earnings and dividends, an equal vote, and an equal voice in management. From the investor's perspective, the return to stockholders comes from dividends and/or appreciation in share price. Common stock has no maturity date and, as a result, remains outstanding indefinitely (discussed in Chapter 12).

Bonds

In contrast to stocks, *bonds* are *liabilities*—they're IOUs of the issuer. The bondholder actually loans money to the issuer. Governments and corporations issue bonds that pay a stated return, called *interest.* When an individual invests in a bond, he or she receives a stipulated interest income, typically paid every 6 months, plus the return of the principal (face) value of the bond at maturity. For example, if you purchased a $1,000 bond that paid 10 percent interest in semiannual installments, you could expect to receive $50 every 6 months (that is, 10% × 0.5 years × $1,000) and at maturity recover the $1,000 face value of the bond. Of course, a bond can be bought or sold prior to maturity at a price that can differ from its face value because bond prices, like common stock prices, do fluctuate in the marketplace (discussed in Chapter 12).

Preferreds and Convertibles

These are forms of *hybrid securities* in that each has the characteristics of both stocks and bonds; they're a cross between the two. *Preferred securities* are issued as stock and, as such, represent an equity position in a corporation. Unlike common stock, however, preferreds have a stated (fixed) dividend rate, payment of which is given preference over dividends to holders of common stock. Like bonds, preferred stocks are usually purchased for the current income (dividends) they pay. A *convertible security*, in contrast, is a special type of fixed-income obligation (usually a bond, but sometimes a preferred stock) that carries a conversion feature permitting the investor to convert it into a specified number of shares of common stock. Convertible securities, therefore, provide the fixed-income benefits of a bond (interest) while offering the price appreciation (capital gains) potential of common stock. (Convertibles are briefly discussed in Chapter 12.)

Mutual Funds

An organization that invests in and professionally manages a diversified portfolio of securities is called a *mutual fund*. A mutual fund sells shares to investors, who then become part owners of the fund's securities portfolio. Most mutual funds issue and repurchase shares at a price that reflects the underlying value of the portfolio at the time the transaction is made. Mutual funds have become popular with individual investors because they offer not only a wide variety of investment opportunities but also a full array of services that many investors find particularly appealing (discussed in Chapter 13).

Real Estate

Investments in *real estate* can take many forms, ranging from raw land speculation to limited-partnership shares in commercial property, even real estate mutual funds. The returns on real estate come from rents, capital gains, and certain tax benefits. For various reasons (including some lingering fears from the bear market of 2000–2002), real estate has become a popular form of investing in the past 4 or 5 years that has, in fact, rewarded investors with some pretty attractive returns. (Various types of real estate investments are discussed in Chapter 13).

Ⅱ Concept Check

11-1	Briefly discuss the relationship between *investing* and personal financial planning.
11-2	What's the difference between an *investment plan* and a capital accumulation plan?
11-3	Why is it important to have one or more investment objective(s) when embarking on an investment program?

LG2 SECURITIES MARKETS

It takes more than money to be a successful investor. As anyone who's found success in the market will tell you, *there is no substitute for being an informed investor!* Among other things, that means you must understand the institutions, mechanisms, and procedures involved in making security transactions. We looked at some investment fundamentals earlier; for the rest of this chapter, we'll examine different securities markets and market transactions, sources of investment information, online investing, and ways to manage your investment holdings.

The term **securities markets** generally describes the place where stocks, bonds, and other financial instruments are traded. Securities markets can be broken into two parts: capital markets and money markets. The *capital market* is where long-term securities like stocks and banks are traded; the *money market* is the marketplace for short-term, low-risk credit instruments with maturities of 1 year or less, like U.S. Treasury bills, commercial paper, negotiable certificates of deposit, and so on. Both types of markets provide a vital mechanism for bringing the buyers and sellers of securities together. Some of the more popular money market securities were discussed in Chapter 4, where we looked at short-term investment vehicles. In this chapter we consider the capital markets.

securities markets The marketplace in which stocks, bonds, and other financial instruments are traded.

Primary or Secondary Markets

Securities markets can also be divided into primary and secondary segments. In the *primary market* new securities are sold to the public—where one party to the transaction is always the issuer. In contrast, old (outstanding) securities are bought and sold in the *secondary market*—here the securities are "traded" between investors. A security is sold in the primary market just once, when it's originally issued by the corporation or some governmental body, like a state or municipality. Subsequent transactions, in which securities are sold by one investor to another, take place in the secondary market. As a rule, when people speak of the securities markets, they're referring to the secondary market, because it's where the vast majority of security transactions occur.

Primary Markets

When a corporation sells a new issue to the public, several financial institutions participate in the transaction. To begin with, the corporation will probably use an *investment banking firm*, which specializes in *underwriting* (selling) new security issues. The investment banker will give the corporation advice on pricing and other aspects of the issue and will either sell the new security itself or arrange for a *selling group* to do so. The selling group is normally made up of several brokerage firms, each responsible for selling a certain portion of the new issue. On very large issues, the originating investment banker brings in other underwriting firms as partners and forms an *underwriting syndicate* in order to spread the risks associated with underwriting and selling the new securities.

A potential investor in a new issue must be given a **prospectus,** which is a document describing the firm and the issue. Certain federal agencies are responsible for ensuring that all the information included in a prospectus accurately represents the facts. Investors frequently have trouble purchasing new security issues because all the shares have been sold—often before the official sale date. Also, if the new shares are sold using rights or warrants, the ability to purchase the new securities will be somewhat restricted, because only the holders of these rights or warrants can buy the stock.

Secondary Markets

The secondary markets permit investors to execute transactions among themselves—it's the marketplace where an investor can easily sell his or her holdings to someone else. Included among the secondary markets are the various *securities exchanges*, in which the buyers and sellers of securities are brought together for the purpose of executing trades. Another major segment of the market is made up of those securities that are listed and traded on the *NASDAQ market*, which employs an all-electronic trading platform to execute trades. Finally, there is the *over-the-counter (OTC)* market that deals in smaller, unlisted securities. We'll cover each of these markets in more detail.

Broker Markets and Dealer Markets

By far, the vast majority of trades made by small individual investors take place in the secondary market, so we'll focus on it for the rest of this chapter. When you look at the secondary market *on the basis of how securities are traded*, you'll find you can essentially divide the market into two segments: broker markets and dealer markets. Exhibit 11.1 shows the structure of the secondary market in terms of broker or dealer markets. As you can see, the *broker market* consists of national and regional "securities exchanges," whereas the *dealer market* is made up of both the NASDAQ market and the OTC market.

Before we look at these markets in more detail, it's important to understand that probably *the biggest difference in the two markets is a technical point about how the trades are executed*. That is, when a trade occurs in a *broker market* (on one of the so-called securities exchanges), the two sides to the transaction, the buyer and the seller, are brought together and the trade takes place at that point: Party A sells his or her securities directly to the buyer, Party B. In a sense, with the help of a *broker*, the securities change hands right there on the floor of the exchange. In contrast, when trades are made in one of the *dealer markets*, the buyer and seller are never brought together directly; instead, their buy/sell orders are executed separately through *securities dealers*, who act as *market*

prospectus A document made available to prospective security buyers that describes the firm and a new security issue.

EXHIBIT 11.1 **Broker and Dealer Markets**

On a typical trading day, the secondary market is a beehive of activity, where literally billions of shares change hands daily. This market consists of two parts—the broker market and the dealer market—and as can be seen, each of these markets is made up of various exchanges and trading venues.

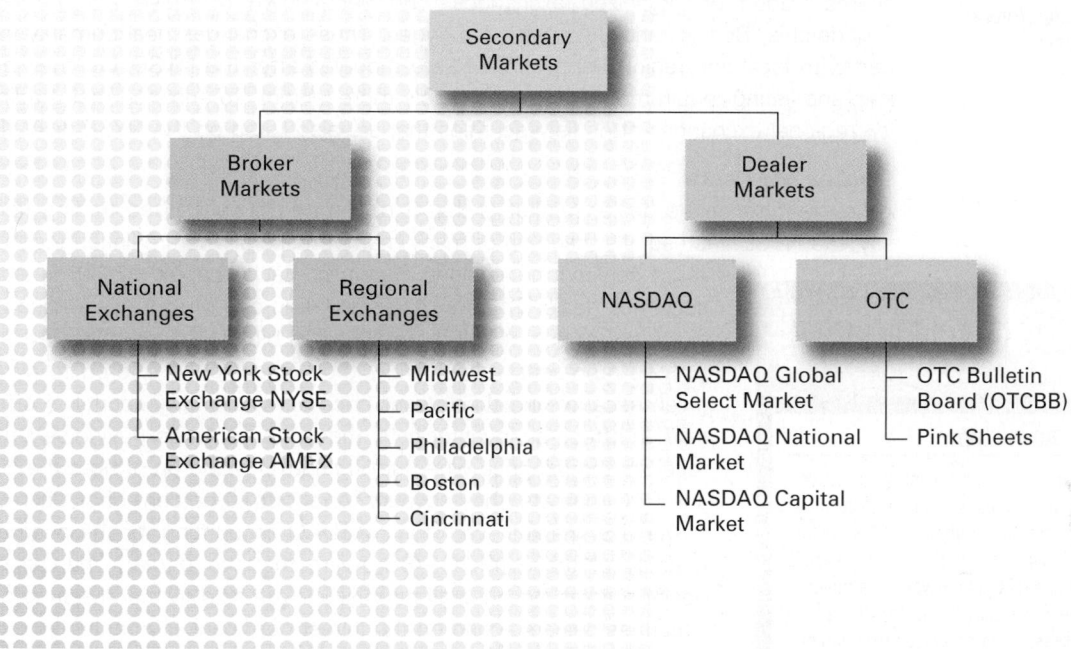

Secondary Markets
- Broker Markets
  - National Exchanges
    - New York Stock Exchange NYSE
    - American Stock Exchange AMEX
  - Regional Exchanges
    - Midwest
    - Pacific
    - Philadelphia
    - Boston
    - Cincinnati
- Dealer Markets
  - NASDAQ
    - NASDAQ Global Select Market
    - NASDAQ National Market
    - NASDAQ Capital Market
  - OTC
    - OTC Bulletin Board (OTCBB)
    - Pink Sheets

makers. Essentially, two separate trades are made: Party A sells his or her securities (in, say, the XYZ Corp.) to one dealer, and Party B buys his or her securities (in the same XYZ Corp.) from another, or possibly even the same, dealer. Thus, there is always a dealer (market maker) on one side of the transaction.

Broker Markets

When you think of the stock market, if you're like most individual investors, the first name to come to mind is the New York Stock Exchange (NYSE). Actually, the NYSE is a part of the broker market—indeed, it's their biggest player! Also included in this market is the American Stock Exchange (AMEX), another *national exchange*, as well as several so-called *regional exchanges*. One thing these exchanges have in common is that all the trading

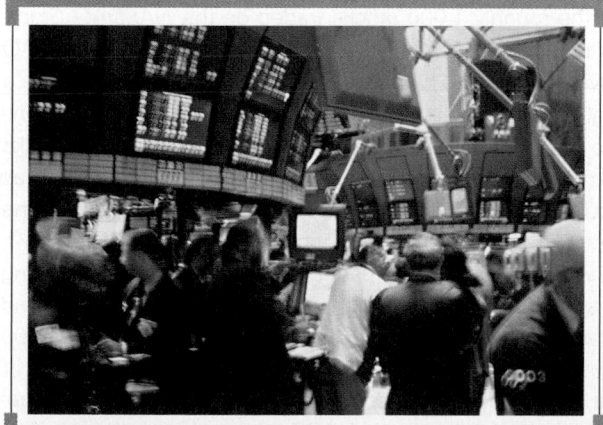

takes place on centralized trading floors. These exchanges account for about 60 percent of the *total dollar volume* of all shares traded in the U.S. stock market.

The NYSE is one of two national exchanges in the United States, and is in fact, the biggest securities exchange in the world. Known as "the big board," the NYSE lists over *350 billion* shares of stock that, at year-end 2005, had a market value of some *$13.3 trillion*. It has stringent listing requirements; still in 2006, more than 2,700 firms from around the world listed their shares on the NYSE. The AMEX is the second largest stock exchange in terms of number of listed companies, but when it comes to the dollar volume of trading, the AMEX is actually smaller than the largest regional exchange (the Midwest in Chicago). It is home to about 700 listed stocks and handles about 4 percent of the

© NONSTOCK/JUPITER IMAGES

total annual dollar volume of shares traded on all U.S. securities exchanges. In contrast, the NYSE handles around 90 percent of all common shares traded on organized exchanges, so the AMEX is nowhere near the NYSE in size or stature. Even so, the AMEX has created a strong market niche for itself through the listing and trading of the popular exchange-traded funds, or ETFs (a lot like index funds; we'll discuss ETFs in Chapter 13).

Besides the NYSE and AMEX, a handful of so-called *regional exchanges* are part of the broker market. The number of securities listed on each of these exchanges typically ranges from about 100 to 500 companies. As a group, they handle around 6 percent of all shares traded on organized exchanges. The best-known of these are the Midwest, Philadelphia, Boston, and Cincinnati exchanges. These exchanges deal primarily in securities with local and regional appeal. Most are modeled after the NYSE, but their membership and listing requirements are considerably more lenient. To enhance their trading activity, regional exchanges often list securities that are also listed on the NYSE or AMEX.

Dealer Markets

A key feature of the dealer market is that it doesn't have centralized trading floors, like say, the NYSE. Instead, it's made up of many market makers who are linked together via a mass telecommunications network. Each market maker is actually a securities dealer who makes a market in one or more securities by offering to either buy or sell them at stated bid/ask prices. (The **bid** and **ask prices** represent, respectively, the highest price offered to purchase a given security and the lowest price at which the security is offered for sale. In effect, an investor pays the ask price when *buying* securities and receives the bid price when *selling* them.) Made up of both the NASDAQ and OTC markets, they account for about 40 percent of all shares traded in the U.S. market—with the NASDAQ accounting for the overwhelming majority of those trades. (Be aware that the *primary market* is also a dealer market, because all new issues are sold to the investing public by securities dealers acting on the investment banker's behalf.)

The biggest dealer market, hands down, is made up of a select list of stocks that are listed and traded on the *National Association of Securities Dealers Automated Quotation System*, or just *NASDAQ*, for short. Founded in 1971, NASDAQ had its origins in the OTC market, but today is considered *a totally separate entity that's no longer a part of the OTC market*. In fact, in 2006, the SEC formally recognized NASDAQ as a "listed exchange," giving it pretty much the same stature and prestige as the NYSE. To be traded on NASDAQ, all stocks must have at least two market makers, although the bigger, more actively traded stocks—like, Cisco—will have many more than that. These dealers electronically post all their bid/ask prices so that when investors place (market) orders, they're immediately filled at the best available price.

NASDAQ sets various listing standards, the most comprehensive of which are for the 2,000 or so stocks traded on the *NASDAQ National Market (NNM)* and the roughly 1,000 stocks traded on the *NASDAQ Global Select Market* (created in 2006, this market is reserved for the biggest and bluest NASDAQ stocks). Stocks included on these two markets are all actively traded and, in general, have a *national following*. These securities are widely quoted, and the trades, all executed electronically, are just as efficient as they are on the floor of the NYSE. Indeed, the big-name stocks traded on the NASDAQ Global Select Market, and to some extent on the NNM, receive as much national visibility and are as liquid as those traded on the NYSE. As a result, just as the NYSE has its list of big-name players (like ExxonMobil, GE, Citigroup, Wal-Mart, Pfizer, IBM, Procter & Gamble, Coca-Cola, Home Depot, and UPS), so too does NASDAQ—including names like Microsoft, Intel, Cisco Systems, Dell, eBay, Google, Yahoo!, Apple, Starbucks, and Staples. (The *NASDAQ Capital Market* is yet another NASDAQ market; it includes about 600 or 700 stocks that, for various reasons, aren't eligible for the NNM.)

The other part of the dealer market is made up of securities that trade in the *over-the-counter (OTC) market*. This market is separate from NASDAQ, and includes mostly small companies that either can't or don't wish to comply with NASDAQ listing require-

bid price The price at which one can sell a security.

ask price The price at which one can purchase a security.

ments. They trade on either the *OTC Bulletin Board (OTCBB)* or in the so-called *Pink Sheets*. The OTCBB is an electronic quotation system that links the market makers who trade the shares of small companies. The Bulletin Board is regulated by the SEC, which, among other things, requires all companies traded on this market to file audited financial statements and comply with federal securities law. In sharp contrast, the OTC Pink Sheets represent the *unregulated* segment of the market, where the companies aren't even required to file with the SEC. Actually, this market is broken into two tiers. The biggest is populated by all those small and many times questionable companies that provide little or no information about their operations, while the top (albeit smallest) tier is reserved for companies that choose to provide audited financial statements and other required information. While the name comes from the color of paper these quotes used to be printed on, the Pinks today use an electronic quotation system. Even so, liquidity is often minimal or almost nonexistent; and the market, especially the bottom tier, is littered with scores of nearly worthless stocks—definitely not a market for the uninitiated!

Foreign Securities Markets

In addition to those in the United States, more than 100 other countries worldwide have organized securities exchanges. Indeed, actively traded markets can be found not only in the major industrialized nations like Japan, Great Britain, Germany, and Canada, but also in emerging economies. In terms of market capitalization (total market value of all shares traded), the New York Stock Exchange is the biggest stock market in the world, followed by the Tokyo stock market and then the NASDAQ market. After these three markets comes the London market, then Paris, Frankfurt, and Toronto. Other major exchanges are located in Sydney, Zurich, Hong Kong, Singapore, Rome, and Amsterdam. Besides these markets, you'll find developing markets all over the globe—from Argentina and Armenia to Egypt and Fiji; from Iceland, Israel, and Malaysia to New Zealand, Russia, and Zimbabwe. Surely, as these and other markets begin to develop, they'll open up opportunities not only for investors in those countries but also for U.S. investors willing to go offshore in search of returns.

Regulating the Securities Markets

Several laws have been enacted to regulate the activities of various participants in the securities markets and provide for adequate and accurate disclosure of information to potential and existing investors. State laws, regulating the sale of securities within state borders, typically establish procedures that apply to the sellers of securities doing business within the state. The most important and far-reaching securities laws, however, are those enacted by the federal government:

- **Securities Act of 1933.** This act was passed by Congress to ensure full disclosure of information with respect to new security issues and to prevent a stock market collapse similar to the one that occurred during 1929–1932. The act requires the issuer of a new security to file a registration statement containing information about the new issue with the **Securities and Exchange Commission (SEC),** an agency of the U.S. government established to enforce federal securities laws.
- **Securities Exchange Act of 1934.** One of the most important pieces of securities legislation ever passed, this act expanded the scope of federal regulation and formally established the SEC as the agency in charge of the administration of federal securities laws. The act gives the SEC power to regulate organized securities exchanges and the OTC market by extending disclosure requirements to outstanding securities. It requires the stock exchanges and the stocks traded on them to be registered with the SEC.
- **Investment Company Act of 1940.** This act protects those purchasing investment company (mutual fund) shares. It established rules and regulations for investment companies and formally authorized the SEC to regulate the companies' practices and procedures. It requires the investment companies to register with the SEC and to fulfill certain disclosure requirements. The act was amended in 1970 to prohibit investment companies from paying excessive fees to their advisors as well as charging excessive commissions to purchasers of company shares.

Securities and Exchange Commission (SEC) An agency of the federal government that regulates the disclosure of information about securities and generally oversees the operation of the securities exchanges and markets.

- **The Sarbanes-Oxley Act of 2002.** This act (known as "SOX") is viewed as the most sweeping piece of securities legislation in decades. Its purpose is to eliminate corporate fraud as related to accounting practices and other information released to investors. Among other things, SOX requires an annual evaluation of internal controls and procedures for financial reporting; it also requires the top executives of the corporation, as well as its auditors, to certify the accuracy of its financial statements and disclosures. What's more, it prohibits audit/accounting firms from engaging in consulting activities with its clients and establishes ethical guidelines for financial officers and security analysts. The law also establishes a five-member oversight board to monitor the accounting industry and its standards of performance.

- **Other significant federal legislation.** The *Maloney Act of 1938* provides for the establishment of trade associations for the purpose of self-regulation within the securities industry; this act led to the creation of the **National Association of Securities Dealers (NASD),** which is made up of all brokers and dealers who participate in the OTC market. The NASD is a self-regulatory organization that polices the activities of brokers and dealers to ensure that its standards are upheld. The SEC supervises NASD activities, thus further protecting investors from fraudulent activities. *The Securities Investor Protection Act of 1970* created the SIPC (Securities Investor Protection Corp.), an organization that protects investors against the financial failure of brokerage firms, much as the FDIC protects depositors against bank failures (we'll examine the SIPC later in this chapter).

Bull Market or Bear?

The general condition of the market is termed as either *bullish* or *bearish*, depending on whether securities prices are rising or falling over extended periods. Changing market conditions generally stem from changing investor attitudes, changes in economic activity, and certain governmental actions aimed at stimulating or slowing down the economy. Prices go *up* in **bull markets;** these favorable markets are normally associated with investor optimism, economic recovery, and growth. In contrast, prices go *down* in **bear markets,** which are normally associated with investor pessimism and economic slowdowns. These terms are used to describe conditions in the bond and other securities markets as well as the stock market. For example, the bond market is considered bullish when interest rates fall, causing bond prices to rise; on the other hand, a bear market in bonds exists when bond prices fall (which occurs when rates rise). As a rule, investors can earn attractive rates of return during bull markets and only low (or negative) returns during bear markets. Market conditions are difficult to predict and usually can't be identified until after they exist.

Over the past 50 or so years, stock market behavior has been generally bullish, reflecting the growth and prosperity of the economy. Exhibit 11.2 shows the five biggest bull markets since the Second World War, the longest of which lasted 125 months—from November 1990 through March 2000. Interestingly, the 1990–2000 bull market is probably as well known for *how it ended* as it is for the returns it generated. That record-breaking bull market ended abruptly in the spring of 2000 when a nearly record-breaking bear market took over. Indeed, after increasing nearly fourfold during the 1990s, the market (as measured by the Dow Jones Industrial Average—DJIA) gave back nearly 40 percent of those gains over the next 3 years. As it turned out, this bear market (which ran from early 2000 to late 2002) was one of the worst in the last 75 years and only the fourth time in the DJIA's 108-year history that the index fell 3 years in a row. (An interesting take on this market can be found in the *Money in Action* box on our Web site—**http://www.thomsonedu .com/finance/gitman**—see the article entitled, "Anatomy of a Market Meltdown.") Clearly, the 10-year bull market was something special; but so was the bear market that followed, as it had to deal with far more than old-fashioned speculation and overenthusiasm. It also had to cope with the 9/11 attack on America, terrorism, war, and various accounting and corporate scandals, not to mention a weak economy. No wonder this bear of a market lasted for nearly 3 years! (The most recent bull market, which started in October 2002 and was still going strong in February 2006, is not included in the graph. It's up just over 50 percent—not enough to make the cut.)

National Association of Securities Dealers (NASD) An agency made up of brokers and dealers in over-the-counter securities that regulates OTC market operations.

bull market A market condition normally associated with investor optimism, economic recovery, and expansion; characterized by generally rising securities prices.

bear market A condition of the market typically associated with investor pessimism and economic slowdown; characterized by generally falling securities prices.

EXHIBIT 11.2

The Five Biggest Bull Markets Since the Second World War (as Measured by Changes in the DJIA)

Most stock prices will go up in a bull market, so it's hard to lose money—although not impossible, because not all stocks will appreciate in value during such markets. One of the biggest bull markets on record started in November 1990 and ended in March 2000, with one of the worst bear markets on record.

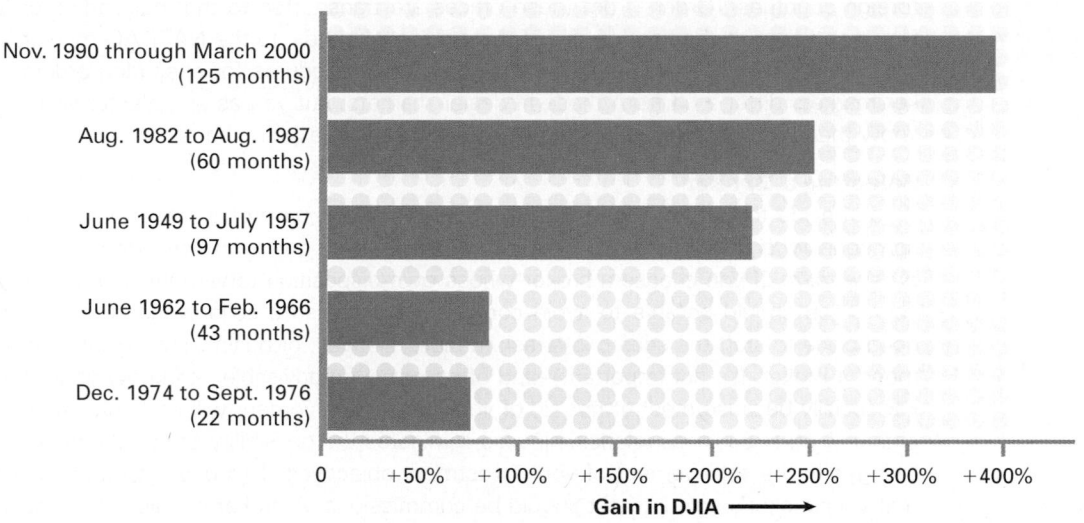

ⓘ Concept Check

11-4	How does a primary market differ from a secondary market? Where are most securities traded—in the primary or secondary market?
11-5	What is the difference between the New York Stock Exchange and the American Stock Exchange?
11-6	What are *regional exchanges*, and what role do they play?
11-7	Describe the operations of the NASDAQ market; compare it with an exchange, like the NYSE.
11-8	What are NASDAQ and the National Market System? How does it differ from the OTCBB?
11-9	Explain the difference between a *bull market* and a *bear market*. How would you characterize the current state of the stock market?

LG3 MAKING TRANSACTIONS IN THE SECURITIES MARKETS

In many respects, dealing in the securities markets almost seems like operating in another world—one with all kinds of unusual orders and strange-sounding transactions. Actually, making securities transactions is relatively simple once you understand the basics—in fact, you'll probably find it's no harder than using a checking account! Making money in the market isn't all that easy, but making transactions is.

Stockbrokers

Stockbrokers, or **account executives** and **financial consultants,** as they're also called, buy and sell securities for their customers. Although deeply ingrained in our language, the term *stockbroker* is really somewhat of a misnomer; such an individual helps you to buy and sell not only stocks but also bonds, convertibles, mutual funds, options, and many other types of securities. Brokers must be licensed by the exchanges and must abide by the strict ethical guidelines of the exchanges and the SEC. They work for brokerage firms and in essence are there to execute the orders placed. The largest stockbrokerage firm, Merrill Lynch, has brokerage offices in virtually every major U.S. city (and many foreign countries). Orders from these offices are transmitted to the main office of Merrill Lynch and then to the floor of one of the stock exchanges, to the NASDAQ market, or the OTC, where they're executed. As we saw earlier, procedures for executing orders in broker markets differ a bit from those in dealer markets; but you as an investor would never know the difference because you'd place your order in exactly the same way.

Selecting a Broker

If you decide to start investing with a so-called *full-service broker*, it's important to select someone *who understands your investment objectives and who can effectively help you pursue them*. If you choose a broker whose own disposition toward investing is similar to yours, you should be able to avoid conflict and establish a solid working relationship. A good place to start the search is to ask friends, relatives, or business associates to recommend a broker. It's not important—and often not even advisable—to know your stockbroker socially because most, if not all, of your transactions/orders will probably be placed by phone. A strict business relationship also eliminates the possibility of social concerns interfering with the achievement of your investment objectives. This doesn't mean, of course, that your broker's sole interest should be commissions. A broker should be far more than just a salesperson; *a good broker is someone who's more interested in your investments than his or her commissions*. Should you find you're dealing with someone who's always trying to get you to trade your stocks, or who's pushing new investments on you, then by all means, dump that broker and find a new one!

Full-Service, Discount, and Online Brokers

Just a few years ago, there were three distinct types of brokers—full-service, discount, and online—and each occupied a well-defined market niche. Today, the lines between these three types of brokers are blurred. Most brokerage firms, even the more traditional ones, now offer online services to compete with the increasingly popular online firms. And many discount brokers now offer services once available only from a full-service broker—like research reports for clients. The traditional **full-service broker** offers investors a full array of brokerage services, including investment advice and information, execution of securities transactions, holding securities in safekeeping, online brokerage services, and margin loans. Such services are fine for investors who want such help—and are willing to pay for it. In contrast, investors who simply want to execute trades and aren't interested in obtaining all those brokerage services should consider either a *discount broker* or *online broker*. **Discount brokers** tend to have low-overhead operations and offer fewer customer services than full-service brokers do. Those with the very lowest commissions, offering hardly any of the normal broker services other than executing trades, are called *deep discounters*. Many discount brokers, however, do provide research and other services, but charge higher commissions. Transactions are initiated by calling a toll-free number—or visiting the broker's Web site—and placing the desired buy or sell order. The brokerage firm then executes the order at the best possible price and confirms the transaction details by phone, e-mail, or regular mail. Depending on the transaction size, *discount brokers can save investors from 30 to 80 percent of the commissions charged by full-service brokers*. The investor who doesn't need the research and advisory help available from full-service brokers may find discount brokers especially attractive.

With the technology that's available to almost everyone today, it's not surprising that investors can just as easily trade securities online as on the phone. All you need is an **online broker** (also called *Internet* or *electronic brokers*) and you, too, can execute

stockbroker (account executive, financial consultant) A person who buys and sells securities on behalf of clients and gives them investment advice and information.

full-service broker A broker who, in addition to executing clients' transactions, offers a full array of brokerage services.

discount broker A broker with low overhead who charges low commissions and offers little or no services to investors.

online broker Typically a discount broker through which investors can execute trades electronically/online through a commercial service or on the Internet; also called *Internet broker* or *electronic broker.*

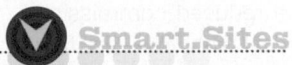
trades electronically. The investor merely accesses the online broker's Web site to open an account, review the commission schedule, or see a demonstration of available transaction services and procedures. Confirmation of electronic trades can take as little as 10 seconds and most occur within 1 minute. Online investing is increasingly popular, particularly among affluent young investors who enjoy surfing the Web—so popular, in fact, that it has prompted virtually every traditional full-service broker (and many discount brokers) to offer online trading to their clients. The rapidly growing volume of business done by discount and online brokers attests to their success. Today, many banks and savings institutions are making discount and online brokerage services available to depositors who wish to buy stocks, bonds, mutual funds, and other investment vehicles. Some of the major full-service, discount, and online brokers are listed here:

Type of Broker		
Full-Service	**Discount**	**Online**
A.G. Edwards	American Express Brokerage	AccuTrade
Edward Jones	Charles Schwab	Ameritrade
Morgan Stanley	J.D. Seibert	E*Trade
Merrill Lynch	Muriel Siebert	Fidelity Brokerage Services
Prudential Financial	Vanguard Brokerage Services	Scotttrade
UBS Financial	York Securities	TD Waterhouse

Brokerage Services

Discount or online brokers offer little more than execution of trades, but that's certainly not the case with full-service brokers. These brokers offer their clients a wide variety of brokerage services. For that reason, selecting a good *brokerage firm* is often just as important as choosing a good broker, because not all brokerage firms provide the same services. Try to select a broker you'd like to work with and whose *firm provides the types of services you're looking for*. Many brokerage firms, for example, provide all sorts of free information, ranging from stock and bond guides to research reports on specific securities or industries. Some have a research staff that periodically issues analyses of economic, market, industry, or company behavior and events, and relates them to its recommendations for buying or selling certain securities. As a brokerage firm client, you can expect to receive monthly bulletins discussing market activity and possibly even a recommended investment list. You'll also receive an *account statement* describing all your transactions for the period, commission charges, interest charges, dividends and interest received, the securities you currently hold, and your account balances.

Most brokerage offices provide up-to-the-minute stock price quotations and world news. Stock price information can be obtained either from the quotation board (a large screen that electronically displays security transactions within minutes of their occurrence) or from the computerized telequote system. World news, which can significantly affect the stock market, is obtained from a newswire service. Most offices also have a reference library the firm's clients can use. Another valuable service offered by most major brokerage firms is the automatic transfer of surplus cash left in a customer's account into one of the firm's money funds, thereby allowing the customer to earn a return on temporarily idle funds. Brokerage houses will also hold your securities for you, as protection against their loss; the securities kept in this way are said to be held in *street name*. Some of these same services are also offered by discount brokerages.

Brokerage Fees

Brokerage firms receive commissions for executing buy and sell orders for their clients. Brokerage commissions are said to be *negotiated*, meaning they're not fixed. In practice, however, most firms have *established fee schedules* that they use with small transactions (on larger, mostly institutional trades, commissions actually are negotiated). Although these fees aren't really negotiated, they do differ from one brokerage firm to another; so it pays to shop around. If you're an "active trader," generating a couple thousand dollars (or more) in annual commissions, then by all means try to negotiate a reduced commission schedule with your broker. Chances are, they'll probably agree to a deal with you—the fact is, brokers much prefer active traders to buy-and-hold investors, because traders generate a lot more commissions. Generally speaking, brokerage fees on a round lot of common stock will amount to roughly 2 to 4 percent of the transaction value. (As a rule, at full-service brokerage firms, the broker gets to keep about 40 percent of the commission and the brokerage firm gets the rest.)

Because there are so many discount brokers today, there is greater variation in fees charged and services offered. The way commissions are calculated also varies; some firms base them on the dollar value of the transaction, some on the number of shares, and some use both. Exhibit 11.3 provides a list of representative commissions at eight discount and online brokerage firms. (Note: Many discount brokers, especially the larger ones, also offer online brokerage services, so there's a good deal of overlap here.) The firms with higher commissions generally offer more services; similarly, many discounters charge clients extra for research services.

Brokerage commissions on *bond transactions* differ from those on stock transactions. Brokerage firms typically charge a minimum fee of $25 to $30, regardless of the number of bonds involved. For multiple bond transactions, the brokerage cost per $1,000 corporate bond typically amounts to around $10. Commission schedules for other securities, such as mutual funds and options, differ from those used with stocks and bonds (we'll look at some of these in the next two chapters). The magnitude of brokerage commissions is obviously an important consideration when making security transactions, because these fees tend to raise the overall cost of purchasing securities and lower the overall proceeds from their sale.

EXHIBIT 11.3 — Comparison of Discount and Online Brokers' Commissions

They say it pays to shop around, and that advice certainly applies when it comes to selecting a broker. Just look at the different commissions these brokers charge to execute essentially the same trade—to trade 500 shares of a $50 stock, for example, the commission ranges from $9.95 (or 0.1 percent of the trade) to $170.00 (0.7 percent of the trades) at the listed discount and online brokers, and as high as $399.00 at one of the major full-service brokers.

| Firm* | Broker-Assisted Commissions | | Online Commissions |
	100 Shares at $50/Share ($5,000)	500 Shares at $50/Share ($25,000)	500 Shares at $50/Share ($25,000)
A.B. Watley (OLB)	$9.95 (0.2%)	$9.95 (0.1%)	$9.95 (0.1%)
AccuTrade (OLB)	30.00	68.00	29.95 (0.12%)
Charles Schwab (DB)	80.00 (1.6%)	170.00 (0.7%)	19.95
Fidelity Brokerage Services (OLB)	55.00	111.00	19.95
Scottrade (OLB)	27.00	27.00	7.00
Muriel Siebert (DB)	45.00	75.00	14.95
T. Rowe Price Brokerage (DB)	50.00	150.00	19.95
Vanguard Brokerage Serv. (DB)	50.00	70.00	25.00
Avg. of 55 Discount (DB) and Online (OLB) brokerage firms	$33.77 (0.7%)	$54.09 (0.2%)	$20.21 (0.1%)
Highest broker	$80.00	$150.00	$29.95
Lowest broker	$9.95	$9.95	$9.95
Major full-service firm	$99.90 (2.0%)	$399.00 (1.6%)	—

* *Note:* **DB** after the firm name indicates fees and commissions as a discount broker; **OLB** indicates fees and commissions as an online broker; the parenthetical numbers after the commissions represent the weight of the commission as *a percentage of the dollar value of the trade.*

Source: Adapted from Jean Henrich, "The 2006 Discount Broker Survey," *AAII Journal*, February 2006; and other sources.

Odd or Round Lots

Security transactions can be made in either odd or round lots. An **odd lot** consists of fewer than 100 shares of stock, while a **round lot** represents a 100-share unit or multiples thereof. The sale of 400 shares of stock would be considered a round-lot transaction, but the purchase of 75 shares would be an odd-lot transaction; trading 250 shares of stock would involve two round lots and an odd lot. Because the purchase or sale of odd lots requires additional processing and the assistance of a specialist (an *odd-lot dealer*), an added fee—known as an *odd-lot differential*—is often tacked on to the normal commission charge, driving up the costs of these small trades. Indeed, the relatively high cost of an odd-lot trade is why it's best to deal in round lots whenever possible.

Investor Protection

As a client, you're protected against the loss of securities or cash held by your broker by the **Securities Investor Protection Corporation (SIPC)**—a nonprofit corporation authorized by the Securities Investor Protection Act of 1970 to protect customer accounts against the financial failure of a brokerage firm. Although subject to SEC and congressional oversight, the SIPC is *not an* agency of the U.S. government.

SIPC insurance covers each account for up to $500,000 (of which up to $100,000 may be in cash balances held by the firm). Note, however, that SIPC insurance does not guarantee that the dollar value of the securities will be recovered. It ensures only that *the securities themselves will be returned*. So, what happens if your broker gives you bad advice and you lose a lot of money on an investment? SIPC won't help you; it's not intended to insure you against bad investment advice, stock market risk, or broker fraud. If you do have a dispute with your broker, first discuss the situation with the managing officer at the branch where you do your business. If that doesn't help, then write or talk to the firm's compliance officer and contact the securities office in your home state. If you still aren't satisfied, you may have to take the case to **arbitration,** a process whereby you and your broker present the two sides to the argument before an arbitration panel, which then decides how the case will be resolved. If it's *binding* arbitration, and it usually is, you have no choice but to accept the decision—you cannot go to court to appeal your case. Many brokerage firms, in fact, require you to resolve disputes by going to binding arbitration. So, before you open an account, check the brokerage agreement to see if it contains a binding arbitration clause.

Executing Trades

For most individual investors, a securities transaction involves placing a buy or sell order, usually by phone or on the Net, and later getting confirmation that it has been completed. These investors have no idea what happens to their orders. In fact, a lot goes on—and very quickly—once the order is placed. It has to, because on a typical day, the NYSE alone executes approximately *3.0 million* trades, and many more occur on the NASDAQ, AMEX, and the rest of the market. In most cases, if the investor places a market order (which we will explain later), it should take *less than 2 minutes* to place, execute, and confirm a trade.

The process starts with a phone call to the broker, who then transmits the order via sophisticated telecommunications equipment to the stock exchange floor, the NASDAQ market, or the OTC Bulletin Board, where it's promptly executed. Confirmation that the order has been executed is transmitted to the originating broker and then to the customer. Once the trade takes place, the investor has 3 (business) days to "settle" his or her account with the broker—that is, to pay for the securities.

As we noted earlier, investors can also use their PCs to execute online securities trades. There are more than 75 online brokers, including AccuTrade, Netvest, E-Trade, Wells Fargo Investments, and Charles Schwab, all of whom are there to execute investor trades promptly, efficiently, and at low cost. In an online trade, your order goes by modem from your computer to the brokerage computer, which checks the type of order and confirms that it's in compliance with regulations. It is then transmitted to the exchange floor or a NASDAQ (or OTC) dealer for execution. The time for the whole process, including a confirmation that's sent back to your computer, is usually 1 minute or less.

odd lot A quantity of fewer than 100 shares of a stock.

round lot A quantity of 100 shares of stock, or multiples thereof.

Securities Investor Protection Corporation (SIPC) A nonprofit corporation, created by Congress and subject to SEC and congressional oversight, that insures customer accounts against the financial failure of a brokerage firm.

arbitration A procedure used to settle disputes between a brokerage firm and its clients; both sides present their positions to a board of arbitration, which makes a final and often binding decision on the matter.

Types of Orders

Investors may choose from several different kinds of orders when buying or selling securities. The type of order chosen normally depends on the investor's goals and expectations regarding the given transaction. The three basic types of orders are the market order, limit order, and stop-loss order.

Market Order

An order to buy or sell a security at the best price available at the time it's placed is a **market order.** It's usually the quickest way to have orders filled, because market orders are executed as soon as they reach the trading floor. In fact, on small trades of less than a few thousand shares, it takes only about 10 seconds to fill a market order once it hits the trading floor! These orders are executed through a process that attempts to allow *buy orders* to be filled at the lowest price and *sell orders* at the highest, thereby providing the best possible deal to both the buyers and sellers of a security. Because of how quickly market orders are transacted, the investor can be sure that the price at which the order is completed will be very close to the market price that existed when it was placed.

Limit Order

An order to buy at a specified price (or lower), or sell at a specified price (or higher) is known as a **limit order.** The broker transmits a limit order to a *specialist* dealing in the given security on the floor of the exchange. The order is executed as soon as the specified market price is reached and all other such orders with precedence have been filled. For example, assume you place a limit order to buy 100 shares of a stock at a price of $20, even though the stock is currently selling at $20.50. Once the specialist has cleared all similar orders received before yours, and the market price of the stock is still at $20 or less, he or she will execute the order. Although a limit order can be quite effective, it can also cost you money! If, for instance, you wish to buy at 20 or less and the stock price moves from its current $20.50 to $32 while you're waiting, your limit order will have caused you to forgo an opportunity to make a profit of $11.50 ($32.00 − $20.50) per share. Had you placed a market order, this profit would have been yours.

Stop-Loss Order

An order to *sell a stock* when the market price reaches or drops below a specified level is called a **stop-loss,** or **stop order.** Used to protect the investor against rapid declines in stock prices, the stop order is placed on the specialist's book and activated when the stop price is reached. At that point, the stop order becomes a *market order* to sell. This means that the stock is offered for sale at the prevailing market price, which could be less than the price at which the order was initiated by the stop. For example, imagine that you own 100 shares of DEF, which is currently selling for $25. Because of the high uncertainty associated with the price movements of the stock, you decide to place a stop order to sell at $21. If the stock price drops to $21, your stop order is activated and the specialist will sell all your DEF stock at the best price available, which may be $18 or $19 a share. Of course, if the market price increases, or stays at or about $25 a share, nothing will have been lost by placing the stop-loss order.

Margin Trades and Short Sales

When you're ready to buy securities, you can do so by putting up your own money, or by borrowing some of the money. *Buying on margin*, as it's called, is a practice that allows investors to use borrowed money to make security transactions. Margin trading is closely regulated and is carried out under strict *margin requirements* set by the Federal Reserve Board. These requirements specify the amount of *equity* an investor must put up when buying stocks, bonds, and other securities. The most recent requirement is 50 percent for common stock, which means that at least 50 percent of each dollar invested must be the investor's own; the remaining 50 percent may be borrowed.

FINANCIAL ROAD SIGN

TYPES OF LIMIT ORDERS

With a limit order, you set the price you want, as well as the time period you want the order to remain outstanding; here are some choices:

- **Fill-or-kill order.** Execute the order immediately (at the specified price or better), or else cancel it.
- **Day order.** Order that expires at the end of the day, even if it hasn't been executed.
- **Good-till-canceled (GTC) order.** Order that will remain open indefinitely, until it's either executed or canceled.
- **All-or-none order.** Order to buy or sell a *specified quantity* of stocks (at a given price, or better), the order to remain open until executed, either for the day or till canceled.

---

market order An order to buy or sell a security at the best price available at the time it is placed.

limit order An order to either buy a security at a specified or lower price, or to sell a security at or above a specified price.

stop-loss (stop order) An order to sell a stock when the market price reaches or drops below a specified level.

The use of margin allows you to increase the return on your investment when stock prices increase. A major attribute of margin trading is that it allows you to *magnify your returns*—that is, you can use margin to reduce your equity in an investment and thereby magnify the returns from invested capital when security prices go up. For example, assume you buy 100 shares of stock that goes from $50 to $70 a share —that's a $2,000 profit from a $5,000 investment, which translates into a 40 percent return on investment (i.e., $2,000 profit/$5,000 investment = 40 percent). However, if that trade had been made on 50 percent margin (so you put up only $2,500 of the $5,000 and borrow the rest), your return would amount to twice that amount, or a whopping 80 percent (i.e., $2,000 profit/$2,500 investment = 80 percent). Now if the price of the stock in our example had fallen from $50 to $30 a share, the return on your investment would have been a *negative* 40 percent (without the margin) or a *negative* 80 percent (with margin). Clearly, the use of margin magnifies both profits and losses! And if the price of the stock in our example continues to drop, you'll eventually reach the point where your equity in the investment will be so low that the brokerage house will require you to either provide more collateral or else it will liquidate the investment.

Investors can go long or short when they trade stocks. By far, the vast majority of trades are *long transactions*, like the margin trade just illustrated; that is, they're made in anticipation of *stock prices going up*, so the investor can make money by buying low and selling high. A **short sale** transaction, in contrast, is made in anticipation of a decline in the price of a stock. When an investor sells a security short, the broker borrows the security and then sells it on behalf of the short seller's account—short sellers actually *sell securities they don't own*. The borrowed shares must, of course, be replaced in the future and if the investor can repurchase the shares at a lower price, a profit will result.

For example, if an investor short-sells 100 shares of stock at $50 a share, and then some time later, *after the price of the stock has dropped*, she buys them back at, say, $30 a share, she'll generate a profit of $20 a share, or $2,000 (i.e., sell at $50—buy back at $30 = $20 × 100 shares = $2,000). Of course, the investor will have to make a margin deposit (equal to 50 percent of the value of the stock when the short sale was made), so even a short transaction will require the investor to come up with some capital before the trade can be made! The objective of a short sale is to take advantage of a *drop in price* by first selling high and then buying low—just like the old adage, "buy low, sell high," except in reverse. And while decreasing prices are good news to short-sellers, the worst thing that can happen to them is for the price of the stock to go up. Make no mistake about it, *both margin trades and short sales involve a lot of risks, so it's important that you become thoroughly familiar with these techniques before using them!*

short sale A transaction that involves selling borrowed securities with the expectation that they can be replaced at a lower price at some future date; made in anticipation of a decline in the security's price.

�III Concept Check

CHECK • CONCEPT CHECK • CONCEPT CHECK • CONCEPT CHECK • CONCEPT CHECK • CONCEPT CHECK • CONCEPT C

11-10	Why does the selection of a broker play such an important role in the purchase of securities?
11-11	Describe the role that *discount brokers* play in carrying out security transactions. To whom are their services especially appealing?
11-12	What are *online brokers*, and what kind of investors are most likely to use them?
11-13	What is the SIPC, and how does it protect investors?
11-14	What is *arbitration*? Does SIPC require the use of arbitration in investor disputes?
11-15	Name and describe three basic types of orders.
11-16	Why might an investor buy securities on margin?
11-17	What is a *short sale*? Explain the logic behind it.

Face it: Some people know more about investing than others. As a result, they may use certain investment vehicles or tactics that aren't even in another investors' vocabulary. Investor know-how, in short, defines the playing field. It helps determine how well you'll meet your investment objectives. Being knowledgeable about investments is important, because a key element to successful investing is *knowing how to achieve decent rates of return without taking unnecessary risks*.

Basing investment decisions on sound information is at the heart of any successful investment program. There's simply no substitute for being informed when it comes to making investment decisions. While it can't guarantee success, it can help you avoid unnecessary losses—as happens all too often when people put their money into investment vehicles they don't fully understand. Such results aren't too surprising, because these investors violate the first rule of investing: *Never start an investment program, or buy an investment vehicle, unless you're thoroughly familiar with what you're getting into!* Before making any major investment decision, thoroughly investigate the security and its merits. Formulate some basic expectations about its future performance, and gain an understanding of the sources of risk and return. This can usually be done by reading the popular financial press and referring to other print or Internet sources of investment information.

Here are the four types of investment information you should try to follow:

- **Economic developments and current events.** To help you evaluate the underlying investment environment
- **Alternative investment vehicles.** To keep you abreast of market developments
- **Current interest rates and price quotations.** To monitor your investments and stay alert for developing investment opportunities
- **Personal investment strategies.** To help you hone your skills and stay alert for new techniques as they develop

In the end, the payoff of an informed approach to investing is both an improved chance of gain and a reduced chance of loss. While there are many sources of investment information, you, as a beginning investor, should concentrate on the common ones, such as annual stockholders' reports, the financial press, brokerage reports, advisory services, investment advisors, and of course, as we'll see, the Internet.

Annual Stockholders' Reports

Every publicly traded corporation is required to provide its stockholders and other interested parties with **annual stockholders' reports.** These documents contain a wealth of information about the companies, including balance sheets, income statements, and other summarized statements for the latest fiscal year, plus several prior years. Annual reports usually describe the firm's business activities, recent developments, and future plans and outlook. Financial ratios describing past performance are also included, along with other relevant statistics. In fact, annual reports offer a great deal of insight into the company's past, present, and future operations. You can obtain them for free directly from the companies, through a brokerage firm, or at most large libraries; with today's technology, most companies are also posting their annual reports on the Internet, so now you can obtain them online.

Here are some suggestions to help you get the most information when reading an annual report:

annual stockholders' report A report made available to stockholders and other interested parties that includes a variety of financial and descriptive information about a firm's operations in the recent past.

- **Start with the highlights or selected financial data sections.** These provide a quick overview of performance by summarizing key information, such as the past 2 years' revenues, net income, assets, earnings per share (EPS), and dividends. EPS has the most effect on the stock's price, so watch it closely.
- **Read the chief executive's letter.** But read it with a careful eye, looking for euphemisms like "a slowing of growth," meaning a "drop in earnings."

- **Move on to the discussion of operations in management's discussion and analysis.** This section provides information on sales, earnings, debt, inventory levels, litigation, taxes, and so on.
- **Review the financial statements, including the notes.** These will tell you about the company's financial condition and performance. Look for trends in sales, costs, profit, cash position, and net working capital.
- **Read the auditor's report.** This statement from the independent accountants who review the numbers has two paragraphs when everything is fine; a third paragraph or phrases like "except for" or "subject to" means there may be problems you need to understand.

The Financial Press

The most common source of financial news is the local newspaper. The newspapers in many larger cities often devote several pages to business news and information. Of course, big-city papers, like *The New York Times*, provide even more information. Other, more specific sources of financial news include *The Wall Street Journal*, *Barron's*, *Investor's Business Daily*, and the "Money" section of *USA Today*. These are all national publications that include articles on the behavior of the economy, the market, various industries, and individual companies. The most comprehensive and up-to-date coverage of financial news is provided Monday through Saturday by *The Wall Street Journal*. Other excellent sources of investment information include magazines, such as *Money*, *Forbes*, *Fortune*, *Business Week*, *Smart Money*, and *Kiplinger's Personal Finance*. (Today, of course, the Internet is rapidly becoming a major source of information for investors; we'll discuss this source in more detail later in this chapter.)

Economic Data

Summaries and analyses of economic events can be found in all the sources just mentioned. Economic data include news items related to government actions and their effects on the economy; political and international events as they pertain to the economy; and statistics related to economic activity, price levels, interest rates, the federal budget, and taxes.

Market Data

Usually presented in the form of averages, or indexes, *market data* describe the general behavior of the securities markets. The averages and indexes are based on the price movements of a select group of securities over an extended period. They're used to capture the overall performance of the market as a whole. You would want to follow one or more of these measures *to get a feel for how the market is doing over time* and, perhaps, an indication of what lies ahead. The absolute level of the index at a specific time (or on a given day) is far less important than *what's been happening to that index over a given period*. The most commonly cited market measures are those calculated by Dow Jones, Standard & Poor's, the New York Stock Exchange, and NASDAQ. These measures are all intended to track the behavior of the stock market, particularly NYSE stocks (Dow, S&P, and NYSE averages all follow stocks on the big board). In addition, several averages and indexes follow the action in other markets, including the bond, commodities, and options markets, and even the markets for mutual funds, real estate, and collectibles. However, because all these other averages and indexes aren't followed nearly as much as those of stocks, we'll concentrate here on stock market performance measures.

Dow Jones Industrial Averages. The granddaddy of them all and probably the most widely followed measure of stock market performance is the **Dow Jones Industrial Average (DJIA).** Actually, the Dow Jones averages, which began in 1896, are made up of four parts: (1) an industrial average, the DJIA, which is based on 30 stocks; (2) a transportation average based on 20 stocks; (3) a utility average based on 15 stocks; and (4) a composite average based on all 65 industrial, transportation, and utility stocks. (The Dow also provides several other market measures, including the DJ Global Titans 50 and the DJ STOXX 50). Most of the stocks in the DJIA are picked from the NYSE; but a few NASDAQ

Dow Jones Industrial Average (DJIA) The most widely followed measure of stock market performance; consists of 30 blue-chip stocks listed mostly on NYSE.

shares are in there, such as Intel and Microsoft. Although these stocks are intended to represent a cross section of companies, there's a strong bias toward blue chips, which is a major criticism of the Dow Jones Industrial Average. However, the facts show that as a rule, the DJIA behavior closely reflects that of other broadly based stock market measures—with the possible exception of NASDAQ. Exhibit 11.4 lists the 30 stocks in the DJIA, along with some important dates in its life.

Standard & Poor's Indexes. The **Standard & Poor's (S&P) indexes** are similar to the Dow Jones averages to the extent that they're both used to capture the overall performance of the market. However, some important differences exist between the two meas-

---

EXHIBIT 11.4 — The Dow Jones Industrial Average

The DJIA is made up of 30 of the bluest of blue-chip stocks and has been closely followed by investors for the past 100 years or so.

The 30 Stocks in the DJIA (as of September 2006)

Aluminum Co. of Amer.	ExxonMobil	McDonald's
Altria Group	General Electric	Merck
American International Group	General Motors	Minnesota M&M (3M)
American Express	Hewlett-Packard	Microsoft
AT&T	Home Depot	Pfizer
Boeing	Honeywell	Procter & Gamble
Caterpillar	IBM	United Technologies
Citigroup	Intel	Verizon
Coca-Cola	J.P. Morgan Chase	Wal-Mart
DuPont	Johnson & Johnson	Walt Disney

Some Important Dates for the Dow

May 26, 1896	The Dow Jones Industrial Average makes its debut; originally made up of just 12 stocks (of the 12 stocks that originally made up the DJIA, only GE is still on the list).
January 12, 1906	Closes above 100 for the first time.
October 28, 1929	The infamous "1929 crash"; Dow drops 38.33 points in one day.
November 14, 1972	Closes above 1,000 for the first time.
August 12, 1982	Closes at 776.92, as the market bottoms out and the Great Bull Market of the 1980s and 1990s is born.
October 19, 1987	The market crashes; the DJIA closes at 1,738.74, for a record 1-day drop of 508 points (23 percent).
November 21, 1995	Closes above 5,000 for the first time.
October 27, 1997	Stocks plunge as the market falls 554 points (a new record) to 7,161.15.
March 29, 1999	Closes above 10,000 for the first time.
January 14, 2000	Closes at all-time high of 11,722.98, as the bull market that started in 1982 reaches the end of the road; a couple months later, the worst bear market since the Depression begins.
September 10, 2001	Closes the day before 9/11 at 9,605.51; the market closes after 9/11 for the rest of the week. Opens the following Monday to a 700-point loss.
October 9, 2002	Closes at 7,286.27 as the bear market that started $2\frac{1}{2}$ years earlier bottoms out; over the course of those $2\frac{1}{2}$ years, the Dow drops 4,436.71 points (or 37.8 percent).
October 3, 2006	Closes at 11,727.34, which sets a new all-time high, surpassing by just 4 points the previous high set nearly 6 years earlier on January 14, 2000; then, a couple of weeks later, on October 14, 2006, the Dow closes above the 12,000 mark for the first time.

ures. For one thing, the S&P uses a lot more stocks; the popular S&P 500 composite index is based on 500 different stocks, whereas the DJIA uses only 30. What's more, the S&P index is made up of all large NYSE stocks, as well as some major AMEX and NASDAQ stocks, so there's not only more issues in the S&P sample but also a greater breadth of representation. And, finally, there are some technical differences in the mathematical procedures used to compute the two measures; the Dow Jones is an *average*, whereas the S&P is an *index*. Despite of these technical differences, movements in these two measures are, in fact, *highly correlated*; as a result, they're used in much the same way.

The four most widely followed S&P indexes are (1) the S&P 500, (2) the *MidCap 400*, (3) the *SmallCap 600*, and (4) the composite *S&P 1500* made up of the S&P 500, 400, and 600 indexes. The MidCap index is made up of 400 medium-sized companies—those with market values ranging, for the most part, from about $500 million to $3 billion, or more; the SmallCap index consists of small companies, with market caps of around $500 million or less. The S&P has a much lower value than the DJIA—for example, in February 2006, the Dow stood at over 11,000, whereas the S&P index of 500 stocks was just over 1,275. Now this doesn't mean that the S&P consists of less valuable stocks; rather, the disparity is due solely to the different methods used to compute the measures.

The NYSE, NASDAQ, and Other Market Indexes. The most widely followed exchange-based indexes are those of the New York Stock Exchange (NYSE) and NASDAQ. The **NYSE index** includes all the stocks listed on the "big board," and provides a measure of performance in that market. Behavior in the NASDAQ market is also measured by several indexes, the most comprehensive of which is the *NASDAQ Composite index*, which is calculated using virtually all the stocks traded on NASDAQ. In addition, there's the *NASDAQ 100 Index*, which tracks the price behavior of the biggest 100 (nonfinancial) firms traded on NASDAQ—companies like Microsoft, Intel, Oracle, Cisco, Staples, and Dell. The NASDAQ Composite is often used as a benchmark in assessing the price behavior of *high-tech* stocks. This index is far more volatile than either the Dow or the S&P and way outperformed other market measures from 1995 to 1999—before taking a big dive in 2000, 2001, and 2002.

Besides the major indexes just described, there are a couple of other measures of market performance, one of which is the **Wilshire 5000 index.** Although this index originally covered some 5,000 stocks, today that number is up to more like 6,000 or 7,000 stocks. Whatever the number, it's estimated that the Wilshire index reflects the *total market value of 98–99 percent of all publicly traded stocks in this country*. In essence, it shows what's happening in the stock market as a whole—the dollar amount of market value added or lost as the market moves up and down. In this index, one point is worth $1 *billion* (vs. about 1 cent in the DJIA). Thus, the Wilshire can be used not only to track the behavior of the U.S. stock market but also to give you a pretty accurate reading as to the size of our market on any given day. For example, in February 2006, the Wilshire index stood at about 12,995. Because this index is in billions of dollars, that translates into a total market value of some $13 *trillion!!* Another widely followed measure is the *Russell 2000*, which tracks the behavior of 2,000 relatively small companies and is widely felt to be a fairly accurate measure of the small-cap segment of the market.

Industry Data

Local newspapers, *The Wall Street Journal*, *Barron's*, and various financial publications regularly contain articles and data about different industries. For example, Standard & Poor's *Industry Surveys* provides detailed descriptions and statistics for all the major industries; on a smaller scale, *Business Week* and other magazines regularly include indexes of industry performance and price levels. Other industry-related data can be obtained from industry trade associations, one example of which is the American Petroleum Institute.

Company Data

Articles about new developments and the performance of companies are included in local newspapers, *The Wall Street Journal*, *Barron's*, and most investment magazines. The prices of the securities of all listed companies and the most active over-the-counter stocks

NYSE index An index of the performance of all stocks listed on the New York Stock Exchange.

Wilshire 5000 index An index of the total market value of the 6,000 to 7,000 or so most actively traded stocks in this country.

are quoted daily in *The Wall Street Journal*, *Investor's Business Daily*, and *USA Today*, and weekly in *Barron's*. Many daily newspapers also contain stock price quotations, though in the smaller ones the listing may be selective; in some cases, only stocks of local interest are included.

Stock Quotes

To see how price quotations work and what they mean, consider the quotes that appear daily (Monday–Saturday.) in *The Wall Street Journal*. As we'll see, the quotations provide not only current prices, but a great deal of additional information as well. A portion of the NYSE stock quotations from *The Wall Street Journal* is presented in Exhibit 11.5, (We'll look at stock quotes here, briefly discuss bond prices in Chapter 12, and then cover mutual fund quotes in Chapter 13.) Let's use the quotations for *Nike* stock, which trades under the symbol *NKE*, for purposes of illustration. These quotes appeared on February 14, 2006, and are for trades that occurred the day before, on February 13. A glance at the quotes shows that stocks, like most other securities, are stated in dollars and cents.

Starting with the first two columns on the left (in Exhibit 11.5) and then working our way across, we see that, over the past 52 weeks, Nike hit a high of $91.54 a share, and a low of $75.10. Next is the company name, Nike B; the B behind the name indicates that it's *Nike's Class B common shares* that are listed and traded on the NYSE. (The company also has some Class A stock outstanding, but they're closely held by the company founders and a few others and aren't publicly traded.) Following that, we see that NKE paid an annual cash dividend of $1.24 a share, providing shareholders with a dividend yield of 1.5 percent (found by dividing the dividend of $1.24 by the closing price of $84.28). The next entry is the P/E ratio, which is the current market price divided by the per-share earnings for the most recent 12-month period (these are known as "trailing P/Es"); as can be seen, NKE is trading at a P/E of 17 times earnings—a nice solid multiple. That's followed by the number of shares traded, where the trades are listed in round lots (of 100 shares). Thus, the actual number of Nike shares traded was 11,891 × 100 = *1,189,100 shares*. Finally, we see that Nike's closing price (on the final trade of the day) was $84.28, which was 19 cents lower (−0.19) than the price at which the stock had ended the day before, when it closed at $84.47. Basically the same quotation system is used for NASDAQ *Global Market* and *National Market* shares. That's not the case, however, for AMEX and small NASDAQ/OTC stocks, where you may get little more than the stock's name and symbol, share volume, closing price, and change in price; and even then, such information is provided for only a limited number of the larger companies (like the 20 biggest AMEX firms).

FINANCIAL ROAD SIGN

LET THE BUYER BEWARE!

For better or worse, analysts' reports are widely used by investors. Most of the reports provide valuable insights, but some are really bad! In particular, beware of an analyst who:

- Downplays bad news.
- Claims a company is unaffected by the economy.
- Shrugs it off when a major customer leaves a company.
- Insists the departure of a top executive won't hurt the company.
- Declares the cost to launch a new product will be low.
- Gives instant approval of a merger.
- Insists that a company that has struggled for years will have a bright future.

Brokerage Reports

Reports produced by the research staffs of major (full-service) brokerage firms provide still another important source of investor information. These reports cover a wide variety of topics, from economic and market analyses to industry and company reports, news of special situations, and reports on interest rates and the bond market. Reports on certain industries or securities prepared by the house's back-office research staff may be issued regularly and contain lists of securities within certain industries classified as to the type of market behavior they are expected to exhibit. Brokerage houses also regularly issue reports, prepared by their security analysts, on specific securities, including among other things their recommendations for the type of investment returns expected and whether to buy, hold, or sell specific securities.

Advisory Services

Some subscription advisory services—available both in print and online—provide information and recommendations on various industries and specific securities. The services normally cost from $50 to several hundred dollars a year. Although these costs may be tax deductible, only the most active investors will find them worthwhile because you can usually

EXHIBIT 11.5 — Listed Stock Quotes

This list summarizes one day's trading activity and price quotes for a group of stocks traded on the New York Stock Exchange. Note that in addition to the latest stock prices, a typical stock quote conveys an array of other information.

52-WEEK HI	LO	STOCK (DIV)	YLD %	PE	VOL 100s	CLOSE	NET CHG
29.34	12.95	NewMrkt(US)	...	12	1242	29.31	0.25
62.72	34.90	NewmtMin .40	.7	55	74208	54.09	–0.71
9.65	5.46	NewpkRes	...	43	3495	8.13	–0.10
18.24	13.94	NewsCp A .12e	.8	...	37929	15.80	0.04
18.63	14.76	NewsCp B .10e	.6	29	10574	16.60	–0.06
59.94	22.88	Nexen s .20g	...	...	5925	48.83	–1.39
42.97	35.76	Nicor 1.86	4.6	15	1913	40.65	–0.01
23.40	12.98	Nidec ADS s .05	.3	...	408	18.34	–1.50
91.54	75.10	Nike B 1.24	1.5	17	11891	84.28	–0.19
16.60	8.61	99cOnlyStr lf	...	29	2393	10.38	–0.12
25.97	19.85	Nippon ADS .27e	1.2	...	3555	21.67	–0.18
25.50	19.51	NiSource .92	4.5	18	10105	20.50	–0.15
29.37	9	Nissin ADS s .06e	.3	...	55	20.20	–0.90
84.96	48.81	Noble Crp x .16	.2	34	26684	72.93	–0.46
48.75	30.90	NobleEngy s .20	.5	15	13501	40.99	–1.35
19.94	14.52	Nokia .88e	4.9	...	77512	17.95	–0.04
20.46	11.65	NmuraHldg .20e	1.1	...	5704	17.90	–0.44
56.68	28.60	NrdcAmTkr 4.47e	12.9	12	4508	34.76	–0.92
42.90	24.45	Nordstm .34	.8	23	10180	40.51	–0.39
50.17	29.60	NorflkSo .64f	1.3	16	19343	48.27	–0.73
124.90	75.90	Norsk 3.10e	2.8	...	301	112.42	–3.14
12.35	7.82	NrtlInvr ADS	...	...	24	9.25	–0.26
3.60	2.26	NortelNtwks	...	cc	198182	2.97	0.01

Callout labels:
- High and low prices for previous 52 weeks
- Company name and annual dividends per share for past 12 months
- Dividend yield (dividends as percentage of share price)
- Price/earnings ratio: $\left(\dfrac{\text{market price}}{\text{earnings per share}} \right)$
- Net change in price from previous day
- Closing (final) price for the day—this is also the price used to compute dividend yield and the P/E ratio
- Share volume, in hundreds

Source: *The Wall Street Journal*, February 14, 2006.

review such materials (for free) at your broker's office, at university and public libraries, or online. Probably the best-known investment advisory services are those provided by Standard & Poor's, Moody's Investors Service, and Value Line Investment Survey. Each offers an array of services. Both Standard & Poor's and Moody's publish manuals containing historical facts and financial data on thousands of corporations, broken down by industry groups. Standard & Poor's publishes a monthly stock guide and bond guide, each summarizing the financial conditions of a few thousand issues; Moody's also publishes stock and bond guides. Some reports are also prepared weekly, like Standard & Poor's *Outlook*.

Separate reports on specific companies are another valuable type of subscription service. An example of one such stock report is given in Exhibit 11.6. This report, prepared by Standard & Poor's, presents a concise summary of a company's financial history, current finances, and future prospects; similar stock reports are also available from *Value Line* and *Morningstar*. Recommended lists of securities, broken down into groups based on investment objectives, constitute still another type of service. Besides these popular subscription services, many *investment letters*, which periodically advise subscribers on buying and selling securities, are available. Finally, by subscribing to weekly chart books, investors may also obtain graphs showing stock prices and volume over extended periods. (We'll discuss online services a little later in this chapter.)

Investment Advisors

Successful investors often establish themselves as professional investment advisors. In this capacity, they attempt to develop investment plans consistent with the financial objectives of their clients. You can obtain the services of a professional money manager in several ways: (1) you can hire an *independent investment advisor* (but they're usually pretty expensive and prefer to deal with well-heeled clients); (2) you can go to the *trust department of a major bank* (many offer their investment services to the general public at reasonable cost, and you don't have to die or have a trust account to obtain such services—all you have to do is enter into a simple *agency agreement*); (3) if you deal with a full-service brokerage firm, you can check with your broker to see if they offer fee-based *wrap accounts* (in these portfolio management accounts, your brokerage firm takes over the full-time management of your investments, in return for a flat annual fee—but watch out, that annual fee can get pretty hefty); or (4) you might consider the services of a *financial planner* (preferably a *fee-based* planner who has a strong track record in the field of *investments*).

If you're thinking of using a professional money manager, the best thing to do is shop around—look at the kind of returns he or she has been able to generate (in good markets and bad), and don't overlook the matter of cost—find out up front how much you'll have to pay and what the fee is based on. Annual fees for advisory services, which may involve the complete management of the client's money, are likely to range from about 1 percent to as much as 2 or 3 percent of assets under management. Equally important, find out if the advisor has a specialty and, if so, make sure it's compatible with your investment objectives; for example, don't go to a financial planner who specializes in high-risk limited partnerships or high-cost variable annuities if you're not interested in those kinds of investment.

ⓘ Concept Check

11-18	Briefly discuss the four basic types of information that you, as an investor, should try to follow.
11-19	What role do market averages and indexes play in the investment process?
11-20	Briefly describe the *DJIA, S&P 400, S&P 500, NASDAQ Composite, Russell 2000,* and *Wilshire 5000* indexes; which segments of the market does each track?

EXHIBIT 11.6   An S&P Stock Report

An S&P report like this one provides a wealth of information about the operating results and financial condition of the company and is an invaluable source of information to investors.

Stock Report | August 19, 2006 | NYS Symbol: **NKE** | NKE is in the S&P 500

STANDARD &POOR'S

NIKE Inc.

S&P Recommendation `HOLD` ★★★☆☆

Price	12-Mo. Target Price	Investment Style
$76.71 (as of Aug 18, 2006)	$90.00	Large-Cap Growth

GICS Sector Consumer Discretionary
Sub-Industry Footwear

Comment NIKE is the world's leading designer and marketer of high-quality athletic footwear, athletic apparel, and accessories.

Key Stock Statistics (Source S&P, Vickers, company reports)

52-Wk Range	$91.54–75.52	S&P Oper. EPS 2007E	5.55	P/E on S&P Oper. EPS 2007E	13.8	Dividend Rate/Share	$1.24
Trailing 12-Month EPS	$5.28	S&P Oper. EPS 2008E	5.90	Common Shares Outstg. (M)	255.4	Yield (%)	1.62
Trailing 12-Month P/E	14.5	S&P Core EPS 2007E	5.55	Market Capitalization(B)	$14.689	Beta	0.52
$10K Invested 5 Yrs Ago	$16,665	S&P Core EPS 2008E	5.90	Institutional Ownership (%)	84	S&P Credit Rating	A+

Price Performance

30-Week Mov. Avg. ··· 10-Week Mov. Avg. -- **GAAP Earnings vs. Previous Year** Volume Above Avg. STARS
12-Mo. Target Price — Relative Strength — ▲ Up ▼ Down ► No Change   Below Avg. ★

2003   2004   2005   2006

Options: ASE, CBOE, P, Ph

Analysis prepared by **Mark S. Basham** on August 07, 2006, when the stock traded at **$ 77.92**.

Qualitative Risk Assessment

LOW	**MEDIUM**	HIGH

Our risk assessment reflects what we see as NKE's strong financial and operating metrics, offset by an increasingly competitive global marketplace and prospects for slowing consumer spending in the U.S.

Quantitative Evaluations

S&P Quality Ranking A+

D	C	B-	B	B+	A-	A	**A+**

Relative Strength Rank MODERATE

31

LOWEST = 1   HIGHEST = 99

Revenue/Earnings Data

Revenue (Million $)

	1Q	2Q	3Q	4Q	Year
2006	3,862	3,475	3,613	4,005	14,955
2005	3,562	3,148	3,308	3,721	13,740
2004	3,025	2,837	2,904	3,487	12,253
2003	2,796	2,515	2,401	2,985	10,697
2002	2,614	2,337	2,260	2,682	9,893
2001	2,637	2,199	2,170	2,483	9,489

Earnings Per Share ($)

2006	1.61	1.14	1.24	1.27	5.28
2005	1.21	0.97	1.01	1.30	4.48
2004	0.98	0.66	0.74	1.13	3.51
2003	0.81	0.57	0.47	0.92	2.77
2002	0.75	0.48	0.46	0.77	2.46
2001	0.77	0.44	0.35	0.60	2.16

Fiscal year ended May. 31. Next earnings report expected: Mid September. EPS Estimates based on S&P Operating Earnings; historical GAAP earnings are as reported.

Dividend Data (Dates: mm/dd Payment Date: mm/dd/yy)

Amount ($)	Date Decl.	Ex-Div. Date	Stk. of Record	Payment Date
0.310	11/18	12/08	12/12	01/03/06
0.310	02/21	03/09	03/13	04/03/06
0.310	05/15	06/08	06/12	07/03/06
0.310	08/14	09/07	09/11	10/02/06

Dividends have been paid since 1984. Source: Company reports.

Highlights

➤ We expect 7.2% sales growth in FY 07, driven by contributions from recent acquisitions, momentum at Nike Golf, and international growth in the Americas and Asia-Pacific regions. We project that U.S. apparel and footwear sales will post low to mid-single digit sales gains, a slight decrease from our earlier expectations, as we expect retailers will become more cautious when replenishing inventories.

➤ We look for FY 06 operating margins to narrow slightly, as greater operating efficiencies derived by improved sourcing, and supply chain upgrades are more than offset by stock option expense and World Cup related marketing and promotion initiatives. Raw material costs should experience continued moderate pressure.

➤ The company announced in mid-2006 a new four year, $3 billion stock repurchase program. We expect the diluted share count to decline by 4% to 5% in each year of the program. Also aiding comparisons should be the absence of an $0.11 per share charge related to an arbitration award that was included in FY 06 results.

Investment Rationale/Risk

➤ At 15X our calendar 2006 EPS estimate of $5.30, NKE recently traded near the market multiple of the S&P 500. We think this is warranted by our expectations that consumer spending on footwear is likely to moderate. Europe remains soft, but consumer spending there is likely to accelerate, we think. Our different outlooks for consumer spending in Europe and the U.S. reflects the different points at which the two regions are in the economic cycle.

➤ Risks to our recommendation and target price include an economic slowdown domestically and a decline in consumer sentiment. International risks include economic weakness, supply disruptions, and unfavorable currency fluctuations.

➤ Our 12-month target price of $90 is equal to 17X our calendar 2006 EPS estimate of $5.30, nearer to the lower end of the 14X-26X range in which the stock has traded over the past five years. Our target price is based on our DCF analysis that assumes a WACC of 9.9%, and growth ranging from 9% to a perpetuity growth rate after 20 years of 3%.

Please read the Required Disclosures and Analyst Certification on the last page of this report.
Redistribution or reproduction is prohibited without written permission. Copyright ©2006 The McGraw-Hill Companies, Inc.

The McGraw-Hill Companies

EXHIBIT 11.6   An S&P Stock Report *continued*

Stock Report | August 19, 2006 | NYS Symbol: **NKE**

NIKE Inc.

**STANDARD
&POOR'S**

Quantitative Evaluations

S&P Fair Value Rank   4+

| 1 | 2 | 3 | 4 | 5 |

LOWEST   HIGHEST

Based on S&P's proprietary quantitative model, stocks are ranked from most overvalued (1) to most undervalued (5).

Fair Value Calculation $76.40

Analysis of the stock's current worth, based on S&P's proprietary quantitative model suggests that NKE is fairly valued

Investability Quotient Percentile

100

LOWEST = 1   HIGHEST = 100

NKE scored higher than 100% of all companies for which an S&P Report is available.

Volatility

| LOW | AVERAGE | HIGH |

NKE has had Low price volatility over the past year.

Technical Evaluation   BEARISH

Since July, 2006, the technical indicators for NKE have been BEARISH.

Insider Activity

| UNFAVORABLE | NEUTRAL | FAVORABLE |

Expanded Ratio Analysis

	2006	2005	2004	2003
Price/Revenue	1.35	1.71	2.00	1.71
Price/EBITDA	0.85	10.91	13.57	12.34
Price/Pretax Income	9.45	12.61	16.87	16.31
Price/Net Income	14.54	19.36	25.87	24.75
Total Shares Outstg (M)	263.8	270.3	269.7	267.6

Figures based on calendar year-end price

Key Growth Rates and Averages

Past Growth Rate (%)	1 Year	3 Years	5 Years	9 Years
Sales	8.84	11.85	10.19	5.71
Net Income	14.89	23.90	10.67	11.71

Ratio Analysis (Annual Avg.)				
Net Margin (%)	9.31	8.61	9.96	7.98
LTD of Capitalization (%)	Nil	7.78	9.90	10.49
Return on Equity (%)	23.34	22.71	26.60	21.65

Company Financials

Per Share Data ($) Year Ended May. 31	2006	2005	2004	2003	2002	2001	2000	1999	1998	1997
Tangible Book Value	22.46	19.54	16.27	14.44	12.78	11.53	10.11	10.28	9.81	9.28
Cash Flow	6.35	5.43	4.44	3.66	7.01	2.88	2.75	2.25	1.98	3.15
Earnings	5.28	4.48	3.51	2.77	2.46	2.16	2.07	1.57	1.35	2.68
S&P Core Earnings	5.12	4.28	3.35	2.62	2.32	2.05	NA	NA	NA	NA
Dividends	0.90	0.90	0.68	0.52	0.48	0.48	0.48	0.48	0.44	0.35
Payout Ratio	17%	20%	19%	19%	20%	22%	23%	31%	33%	13%
Calendar Year	2005	2004	2003	2002	2001	2000	1999	1998	1997	1996
Prices:High	91.54	92.43	68.54	64.28	60.06	57.00	66.94	52.69	76.38	64.00
Prices:Low	75.10	65.81	42.38	38.53	35.50	25.81	38.75	31.00	37.75	31.75
P/E Ratio:High	17	21	20	26	24	26	32	34	57	24
P/E Ratio:Low	14	15	12	16	14	12	19	20	28	12

Income Statement Analysis (Million $)										
Revenue	14,955	13,740	12,253	10,697	9,893	9,489	8,995	8,777	9,553	9,187
Operating Income	23,912	2,151	1,802	1,485	1,291	1,212	1,150	1,054	1,049	1,518
Depreciation	282	257	252	239	224	197	188	198	185	138
Interest Expense	Nil	39.7	40.3	42.9	47.6	58.7	45.0	44.0	60.0	52.3
Pretax Income	2,142	1,860	1,450	1,123	2,035	921	919	745	653	1,295
Effective Tax Rate	35.0%	34.9%	34.8%	34.1%	17.2%	36.0%	37.0%	39.5%	38.7%	38.5%
Net Income	1,392	1,212	946	740	1,686	590	579	451	400	796
S&P Core Earnings	1,346	1,148	897	698	632	559	NA	NA	NA	NA

Balance Sheet & Other Financial Data (Million $)										
Cash	954	1,388	828	634	576	304	254	198	109	445
Current Assets	7,359	6,351	5,512	4,680	4,158	3,625	3,596	3,265	3,533	3,831
Total Assets	9,870	8,794	7,892	6,714	6,443	5,820	5,857	5,248	5,397	5,361
Current Liabilities	2,623	1,999	2,009	2,015	1,836	1,787	2,140	1,447	1,704	1,867
Long Term Debt	Nil	687	682	552	626	436	470	386	379	296
Common Equity	6,285	5,644	4,782	3,991	3,839	3,495	3,136	3,335	3,262	3,156
Total Capital	6,286	6,332	5,464	4,543	4,465	3,931	3,607	3,721	3,641	3,452
Capital Expenditures	334	257	214	186	283	318	420	384	506	466
Cash Flow	1,674	1,469	1,198	979	1,909	787	767	645	585	934
Current Ratio	2.8	3.2	2.7	2.3	2.3	2.0	1.7	2.3	2.1	2.1
% Long Term Debt of Capitalization	Nil	10.9	12.5	12.1	14.0	11.1	13.0	10.4	10.4	8.6
% Net Income of Revenue	9.3	8.8	7.7	6.9	17.0	6.2	6.4	5.1	4.2	8.7
% Return on Assets	14.9	14.5	12.9	11.3	27.5	10.1	10.4	8.5	7.4	17.1
% Return on Equity	23.3	23.2	21.6	18.9	46.0	17.8	17.9	13.7	12.5	28.5

Data as orig reptd.; bef. results of disc opers/spec. items. Per share data adj. for stk. divs.; EPS diluted. E-Estimated. NA-Not Available. NM-Not Meaningful. NR-Not Ranked. UR-Under Review.

The McGraw-Hill Companies

Not that many years ago, online investing focused on finding the lowest transaction cost at one of the few discount brokers offering cheap electronic trades. Today, the Internet is a major force in the investing environment. It has opened the world of investing to individual investors, leveling the playing field and providing access to tools and market information formerly restricted to professionals. Not only can you trade all types of securities online, you can also find a wealth of information, from real-time stock quotes to securities analysts' research reports. So instead of weeding through mounds of paper, investors can quickly sort through vast databases to find appropriate investments, monitor their current investments, and make securities transactions—all without leaving their computers. Clearly, the Internet's power as an investing tool is alluring. Do-it-yourself investing is now possible for the average investor, even novices who have never before bought stock. However, online investing also carries risks. The Internet requires investors to exercise the same—and possibly more—caution as they would if they were getting information from and placing orders with a human broker. You don't have the safety net of a live broker suggesting that you rethink your trade. Online or off, the basic rules for smart investing are still the same: *know what you're buying, from whom, and at what level of risk.*

How can you successfully navigate through this cyberinvesting universe? You probably already have the technology you need: a computer, modem, and an Internet service provider (ISP). Open your Web browser, and you're ready to explore the multitude of investing sites. Typically one site includes a combination of resources for novice and sophisticated investors alike. For example, if you're on line, go to the home page for *E*Trade*, a major online brokerage firm **(http://www.etrade.com).** With a few clicks of the mouse, you can learn about E*Trade's services, open an account, or place an order to trade securities. You can also get a quick overview of recent market activity, obtain price quotes and research reports, or use their services to track a whole portfolio of securities. You can also use their site to select stocks, bonds, and mutual funds, get advice on retirement planning and saving for college, go to their Knowledge Center to learn about the markets, even do your banking at the *E*Trade Bank.*

Online Investor Services

As the E*Trade Web site reveals, the Internet offers a full array of online investor services, from up-to-the-minute stock quotes and research reports to charting services and portfolio tracking. When it comes to investing, you name it and you can probably find it online! Unfortunately, although many of these are truly high-quality sites offering valuable information, many others are pure garbage, so be careful when entering the world of online investing. But even if you confine yourself to the quality sites, the fact is, all this information can be overwhelming and even intimidating. It takes time and effort to use the Net wisely. Let's now review the kinds of investor services you can find online, starting with investor education sites.

Investor Education

The Internet offers a wide array of tutorials, online classes, and articles to educate the novice investor. Even experienced investors will find sites that expand their investing knowledge. Although most good investment-oriented Web sites include many educational resources, here are a few good sites featuring *investment fundamentals:*

- *The Motley Fool* **(http://www.fool.com)** *Fool's School* has sections on fundamentals of investing, mutual fund investing, choosing a broker, investment strategies and styles, lively discussion boards, and more.
- America Online (AOL) *Money Basics* (developed with *Smart Money* magazine and for subscribers only) offers Investing 101, which covers basic investment theory, risk management, asset categories, and taxes. Other departments include building and managing your portfolio, investment strategies, and personal finance topics.
- Zacks Investment Research **(http://www.zacks.com),** a free site from *The Wall Street Journal,* is an excellent starting place to learn what the Internet can offer investors.

- NASDAQ **(http://www.nasdaq.com)** has an Investor Resource section that helps with financial planning and choosing a broker.

Other good educational sites include leading personal finance magazines like *Money* **(http://money.cnn.com)**, *Kiplinger's Personal Finance Magazine* **(http://www.kiplinger.com)**, and *Smart Money* **(http://www.smartmoney.com)**.

Investment Tools

Once you're familiar with the basics of investing, you can use the Internet to develop financial plans and set investment goals, find securities that meet your investment objectives, analyze potential investments, and organize your portfolio. Many of these tools, once used only by professional money managers, are free to anyone who wants to go online. You'll find financial calculators and worksheets, screening and charting tools, and portfolio trackers at the Web sites of large brokerage firms, as well as other financial sites. You can even set up a personal calendar to notify you of forthcoming earnings announcements and receive alerts when one of your stocks has hit a predetermined price target.

Investment Planning. Online calculators and worksheets can help you find answers to your financial planning and investing questions. With them, you can figure out how much to save each month for a particular goal, such as the down payment for your first home, a college education for your children, or to be able to retire by the time you reach 55. For example, Fidelity **(http://www.fidelity.com)** has a wide selection of planning tools that deal with such topics as investment growth, college planning, and retirement planning. One of the best sites for financial calculators is *Kiplinger's Personal Finance* **(http://www.kiplinger.com)**. Go to their personal finance page, click on "Tools," and you'll find over 100 calculators dealing with everything from stocks, bonds, and mutual funds to retirement planning, home buying, and taxes. The site's investment-related calculators, for example, show the tax and return difference between selling a stock before or after 1 year, your current yield from dividends, how currency exchange rates affect foreign stock transactions, how fees and costs affect your mutual fund purchases, how to find the yield to maturity on a bond, whether a taxable or tax-exempt bond provides a better return, and more.

FINANCIAL ROAD SIGN

TIPS FOR SUCCESSFUL ONLINE TRADES

Before submitting an online stock trade, follow these tips to protect yourself from common problems:

- Do your own research.
- Don't believe everything you read on the Internet.
- Know how to place and confirm your order before you begin trading.
- Verify the stock symbol of the security you wish to buy (or sell).
- Use limit orders.
- Don't get carried away with the ease of online trading. It's easy to churn your account—which often translates into higher costs, lower returns, and more taxes.
- Double-check orders for accuracy. Review the confirmation notice to make sure each trade was completed according to your instructions.

Investment Research and Screening. One of the best investor services offered online is the ability to conduct in-depth research on stocks, bonds, mutual funds, and other types of investment vehicles. Go to a site like **http://www.kiplinger.com,** click on "personal finance," then the "investing" tab, and you can obtain literally dozens of pages of financial and market information about a specific stock or mutual fund. For example, you can find historical and forecasted information about a firm's earnings, earnings per share, dividend yields, growth rates, and more in both tabular and graphic formats; you can also track the behavior of a specific stock relative to a market index, or to one or more of its major competitors. And many of these sites have links back to the company itself, so with a few mouse clicks, you can obtain the company's annual report, detailed financial statements, and historical summaries of a full array of financial and market ratios.

Besides the types of research information just described, investors can also use various *online screening tools* to identify attractive and potentially rewarding investment vehicles. Most major sites, like Quicken, Morningstar, or MSN Money Central, offer screening tools. These tools enable you to quickly sort through huge databases of stocks and mutual funds to find those that meet specific characteristics, such as stocks with low or high P/E multiples, small market capitalizations, high dividend yields, specific revenue growth, and low debt-to-equity ratios. For mutual funds you might specify a certain type of fund, a particular industry or geographical sector, and low fees. You answer a series of questions to specify the type of stock or fund you're looking for, perfor-

Smart.Sites

For a one-stop financial portal, head to MSN MoneyCentral Investor by linking to it at **http://www.thomsonedu.com/finance/gitman.** You'll find good educational articles, research, interactive tools like Research Wizard, and a portfolio tracker.

mance criteria you desire, cost parameters, and so on. The screen then provides a list of stocks (or funds) that have met the standards you've set. You can then do more research (as already described) on the listed stocks (or mutual funds) to decide on those you want to further pursue.

Portfolio Tracking. Almost every investment-oriented Web site includes *portfolio-tracking tools.* Simply enter the number of shares held and the symbol for those stocks or mutual funds you wish to follow, and the tracker automatically updates the value of your portfolio in real time. What's more, you can usually click on one of the provided links and quickly obtain detailed information about each stock or mutual fund in your portfolio. But be careful; the features, quality, and ease of using these portfolio trackers varies widely, so check several to find the one that meets your needs. Quicken.com, MSN MoneyCentral **(http://investor.msn.com),** and E*Trade **(http://www.etrade.com)** all have portfolio trackers that are easy to set up and use. Quicken's tracker, for example, alerts you whenever an analyst changes the rating on one of your stocks or funds and tells you how well you're diversified among the major asset classes or sectors you hold.

Online Trading

As discussed earlier, trading stocks (and other securities) online has become popular among investors—if for no other reason than the rock-bottom cost of executing such trades. Face it, it's an easy, convenient, and low-cost way of trading securities. But for some investors, the attraction of trading stocks online is so compelling that they become day traders. The opposite of buy-and-hold investors with a long-term perspective, **day traders** buy and sell stocks quickly throughout the day. They hope their stocks will continue to rise in value for the short time they own them—sometimes just seconds or minutes—so they can make quick profits. True day traders don't own any stocks overnight—hence the term *day trader*—because they believe the chance of prices changing radically overnight (from the close on one day to the open on the next) can lead to large losses. While day trading is not illegal or unethical, *it is highly risky.* To compound their risk, day traders usually buy on margin to earn even higher returns. But as we've seen, margin trading also increases the risk of larger losses. Day traders typically incur major financial losses when they start trading. Some never reach profitability. Day traders also have high expenses for brokerage commissions, training, and computer equipment. By some estimates, they must make a 50 to 60 percent profit just to break even on fees and commissions.

day trader An investor who buys and sells stocks (and other securities) rapidly throughout the day in hopes of making quick profits.

❚❚ Concept Check

HECK • CONCEPT CHECK • CONCEPT CHECK • CONCEPT CHECK • CONCEPT CHECK • CONCEPT CHECK • CONCEPT CH

11-21	Describe the Internet's impact on the world of investing.
11-22	What are some products and services that you, as an individual investor, can now obtain online?
11-23	Briefly describe several types of online investment tools, and note how they can help you become a better investor.
11-24	What is *day trading*, and how is it different from the more traditional approach to investing?

LG6 • MANAGING YOUR INVESTMENT HOLDINGS

portfolio A collection of securities assembled for the purpose of meeting common investment goals.

As we've seen, buying and selling securities is not difficult; the hard part is finding securities that will provide the kind of return you're looking for. Like most individual investors, in time you too will be buying, selling, and trading securities with ease. Eventually, your investment holdings will increase to the point where you're managing a whole portfolio of securities. In essence, a **portfolio** is a collection of investment vehicles assembled to meet a common investment goal. For instance, Bill Hansen's investment portfolio is made up of 150 shares of Cisco Systems, 200 shares of Nike, 100 shares of Wal-Mart Stores, 300 shares of Medtronic, 400 shares of P. F. Chang's China Bistro, and 20 American Greetings convertible bonds. But a portfolio is far more than a collection of investments! For a portfolio breathes life into your investment program; *it's an investment philosophy that provides guidelines for carrying out your investment program*. A portfolio, in effect, combines your personal and financial traits with your investment objectives to give some structure to your investments.

Seasoned investors often devote lots of attention to constructing diversified portfolios of securities. Such portfolios consist of stocks and bonds selected not only for their returns but also for their combined risk-return behavior. The idea behind **diversification** is that by combining securities with dissimilar risk-return characteristics, you can produce a portfolio of reduced risk and more predictable levels of return. In recent years, investment researchers have shown that you can achieve a noticeable reduction in risk simply by diversifying your investment holdings. For the small investor with a moderate amount of money to invest, this means that *investing in several securities rather than a single one should be beneficial*. The payoff from diversification comes in the form of reduced risk without a significant impact on return. For example, Joan Rainer, who has all of her $30,000 portfolio invested in just one stock (Stock A), might find that by selling two-thirds of her holdings and using the proceeds to buy equal amounts of Stocks B and C, she'll continue to earn the same level of return—say, 12 percent—while greatly decreasing the associated risk. Professional money managers emphasize that investors should not put all their eggs in one basket but instead should hold portfolios that are diversified across a broad segment of businesses.

Building a Portfolio of Securities

In developing a portfolio of investment holdings, it's assumed that diversification is a desirable investment attribute that leads to improved return and/or reduced risk. Again, as emphasized previously, holding a variety of investments is far more desirable than concentrating all your investments in a single security or industry (for example, a portfolio made up of nothing but auto stocks, such as GM, Ford, and DaimlerChrysler, would hardly be well diversified). Of course, when you first start investing, you probably won't be able to do much, if any, diversifying because of insufficient investment capital. However, as you build up your investment funds, your opportunities (and need) for diversification will increase dramatically. Certainly, by the time you have $10,000 to $15,000 to invest, you should start to diversify your holdings. To get an idea of the kind of portfolio diversification employed by investors, look at the following numbers; they show the types of investments held by *average individual investors*:

Type of Investment Product	Percentage of Portfolio (January 2006)
Stocks and stock funds	67%
Bonds and bond funds	11%
Short-term investments (CDs, money mkt. dep. accts., etc.)	22%
Total	100%

This portfolio reflects the results of a monthly asset allocation survey conducted by the *American Association of Individual Investors*, and it shows the portfolio holdings of a typical individual investor. Whether this is what your portfolio should look like depends on various factors, including your own needs and objectives.

Investor Characteristics

To formulate an effective portfolio strategy, begin with an honest evaluation of your own financial condition and family situation. Pay particular attention to variables like these:

diversification The process of choosing securities with dissimilar risk-return characteristics in order to create a portfolio that provides an acceptable level of return and an acceptable exposure to risk.

- Level and stability of income
- Family factors
- Investment horizon
- Net worth
- Investment experience and age
- Disposition toward risk

These are the variables that set the tone for your investments. They determine the kinds of investments you should consider and how long you can tie up your money. For your portfolio to work, it must be tailored to meet your personal financial needs. Your income, family responsibilities, relative financial security, experience, and age all enter into the delicate equation that yields a sound portfolio strategy.

The size and certainty of an investor's employment income has a significant bearing on portfolio strategy. An investor with a secure job is more likely to embark on a more aggressive investment program than is an investor with a less-secure position. Income taxes bear on the investment decision as well. The higher an investor's income, the more important the tax ramifications of an investment program become. For example, municipal bonds normally yield about 25 to 30 percent less in annual interest than corporate bonds, because the interest income on municipal bonds is tax free. On an after-tax basis, however, municipal bonds may provide a superior return if an investor is in a tax bracket of 28 percent or higher.

An individual's investment experience also influences the appropriateness of an investment strategy. Normally, investors assume higher levels of investment risk gradually over time. It's best to "get your feet wet" in the investment market by slipping into it slowly rather than leaping in head first. Investors who make risky initial investments very often suffer heavy losses, damaging the long-run potential of the entire investment program. A cautiously developed investment program will likely provide more favorable long-run results than an impulsive, risky one. Finally, investors should carefully consider risk. High-risk investments have not only high return potential but also high risk of loss. Remember, by going for the home run (via a high-risk, high-return investment), the odds of striking out are much higher than by going for a base hit (a more conservative investment posture). A good rule to remember is that *an investor's exposure to risk should never exceed his or her ability to bear that risk!*

Investor Objectives

After developing a personal financial profile, the investor's next question is: "What do I want from my portfolio?" This seems like an easy question to answer. Ideally, we would all like to double our money every year by making low-risk investments. However, the realities of the highly competitive investment environment make this outcome unlikely, so the question must be answered more realistically. There's generally a trade-off between earning a high current income from an investment and obtaining significant capital appreciation from it. An investor must choose one or the other; it's hard to obtain both from a single investment vehicle. It's possible, of course, in a *portfolio*, to have a *balance* of both income and growth (capital gains); but most often that involves "tilting" the portfolio one direction (e.g., toward income) or the other (toward growth). The price of having high appreciation potential in the portfolio is low current income potential.

The investor's needs may determine which avenue to choose. For instance, a retired investor whose income depends partly on his or her portfolio will probably choose a lower-risk, current-income-oriented approach out of the need for financial survival. In contrast, a high-income, financially secure investor may be much more willing to take on risky investments in hopes of improving his or her net worth. Likewise, a young investor with a secure job may be less concerned about current income and more able to bear risk. This type of investor will likely be more capital-gains oriented and may choose speculative investments. As an investor approaches age 60, the desired level of income likely rises as retirement approaches. The more senior investor will be less willing to bear risk and will want to keep what he or she has, because these investments will soon be needed as a source of retirement income.

Asset Allocation and Portfolio Management

A portfolio must be built around an individual's needs, which in turn depend on income, family responsibilities, financial resources, age, retirement plans, and ability to bear risk. These needs shape one's financial goals. But to create a portfolio geared to those goals, you need to develop an **asset allocation** strategy. Basically, all that asset allocation involves is a decision on *how to divide your portfolio among different types of securities*. For example, what portion of your portfolio will be devoted to short-term securities, longer bonds and bond funds, and common stocks and equity funds? In asset allocation, the emphasis is on *preserving capital*. The idea is to position your assets in such a way that you can protect your portfolio from potential negative developments in the market, while still taking advantage of potential positive developments. Asset allocation is one of the most overlooked yet most important aspects of investing. There's overwhelming evidence that over the long run, *the total return on a portfolio is influenced far more by its asset allocation plan than by specific security selections*.

Asset allocation deals in broad categories and *does not tell you which individual securities to buy or sell*. It might look something like this:

Type of Investment	Asset Mix
Short-term securities	5%
Longer bonds	
(7-to 10-year maturities)	20%
Equity funds	75%
Total Portfolio	100%

As you can see, all you're really doing here is deciding how to cut up the pie. You still have to decide which particular securities to invest in. Once you've decided that you want to put, say, 20 percent of your money into intermediate-term (7- to 10-year) bonds, your next step is to select those specific securities. For ideas on how to start your own portfolio, even if you don't have a lot of money, see the nearby *Money in Action* box.

After establishing your asset allocation strategy, you should check it regularly for two reasons: first, to make sure that your portfolio is in line with your desired asset mix; and second, to see if that mix is still appropriate for your investment objectives. Here are some reasons to reevaluate your asset allocations:

- A major change in personal circumstances—marriage, birth of a child, loss of a spouse from divorce or death, child graduating from college, loss of job, or family illness, for example—that changes your investment goals.
- The proportion of an asset rises or falls considerably, changing your target allocation for that class by more than, say, 5 percent.
- You're close to reaching a certain goal (such as saving for your child's college or for your retirement).

Periodically, you may find it necessary to *rebalance* your portfolio—that is, to reallocate the assets in your portfolio. For example, suppose that your asset allocation plan calls for 75 percent equities and the stock market falls so that stocks represent only 65 percent of your total portfolio. If you're still bullish on the (long-term) market and stocks are still appropriate for your portfolio, you may view this as a good time to buy stocks and, in so doing, bring your portfolio back up to 75 percent in equities. If your personal goals change, or if you think the market may not recover in the near future, you may decide to change your percentages so as to hold fewer stocks. But don't be too quick to rebalance every time your portfolio gets a little out of whack; you must allow for some variation in the percentages, as market fluctuations may make it impossible to constantly maintain exact percentages. And don't forget the costs from commissions or sales charges and tax considerations.

asset allocation A plan for dividing a portfolio among different classes of securities in order to preserve capital by protecting the portfolio against negative market development.

HOW TO BUILD A PORTFOLIO WHEN YOU'RE JUST STARTING OUT

After setting aside funds for emergencies and developing long-term goals and an investment strategy, you're now ready to start investing. You know you'll need to have an asset allocation plan that includes stocks, bonds, and cash. But where do you go from here?

If you have a limited amount of money to invest, it's best to start with a balanced mutual fund. You can invest in many of these funds with $1,000 or less. Mutual funds, with a mix of stocks and bonds, can diversify assets with just one investment. Look for a fund with lower-than-average fees (average is 1.11 percent) and a strong track record. This investment strategy is appropriate for those with limited knowledge of investing or little time to research and monitor investments. The main disadvantage to this approach is that you don't control the asset mix.

If you have more risk tolerance and a longer time horizon, you can invest in a stock index fund, such as Standard & Poor's 500, as the core of your portfolio. Investing in this type of fund will cost about $1,000, or as little

as $250 if the investment is in an IRA. Because these funds are composed only of stocks, they're riskier than a balanced fund—but over time, you should be able to ride the market's ups and downs. You should still diversify your portfolio with additional assets, such as a bond fund, to minimize your risk.

With more experience, you may choose to add either sector funds (investments restricted to a particular sector of the market, such as a particular industry or sector of the economy) or specific stocks and bonds to your investments. This also requires more time and effort on your part—know about the companies you're investing in, and make sure you diversify among different economic sectors. Also make sure you have a mix of large- and small-cap and international and domestic stocks.

If you'd like to invest in an individual stock, but have limited funds, dividend reinvestment plans (DRPs), offered by about 1,000 companies, are a good option. After you own at least one share of stock, dividends are automatically reinvested in more shares, and you can buy additional stock directly from the company—usually without a fee.

Whatever assets you choose, review your holdings regularly and rebalance your portfolio, even when it's doing well; some investment categories outperform others, so the asset allocation percentages shift. This exposes you to more or less risk than you intended. Rebalancing the portfolio involves buying or selling assets to bring them back to their original allocation.

Remember to invest regularly in your funds or stocks, every month or pay period if possible. Be patient and stick with your investment strategy, even if returns aren't as high as you'd like. Unless you hold your investments for a while, transaction costs and taxes will wipe out profits. With the market's volatility, you're bound to have down periods. Remember you chose this plan for the long term, so being consistent should pay off over time.

Critical Thinking Questions

1. Under what circumstances would a balanced mutual fund be the best option for investment?
2. What factors should you keep in mind when purchasing a stock fund or individual stocks?
3. Why is rebalancing a portfolio important?

Sources: Katy Marquardt, "The Beauty of Balance," *Kiplinger's Personal Finance Magazine*, July 2006, p. 50; Amey Stone, "A Five-Step Investing Plan for '05," *Business Week Online*, January 4, 2005; Walter Updegrave, "Stocks vs. Funds?" *CNNMoney.com*, January 6, 2006, from http://money.cnn.com; Joshua Kennon, "All About Dividends," July 6, 2006, from http://beginnersinvest.about.com.

Security selection and portfolio management are recurring activities that become an almost routine part of your investment program. You receive an interest or dividend check, and you have to find a place to put it; you add new capital to your investment program, or one of the Treasury notes you're holding matures, and you have to decide what to do with the money. These events occur quite regularly, so you're likely to be faced with a series of little (and sometimes not so little) investment decisions over time. This, in short, is portfolio management: the initial construction and ongoing administration of a collection of securities and investments.

Portfolio management involves the buying, selling, and holding of various securities in order to meet a set of predetermined investment needs and objectives. To give you an idea

Copyright 2003 by Randy Glasbergen.
www.glasbergen.com

GLASBERGEN

"I have 40% of my portfolio invested in fire.
I think it's the technology of the future."

of portfolio management in action, Exhibit 11.7 provides examples of four portfolios, each developed with a particular financial situation in mind. Notice that in each case the asset allocation strategies and portfolio structures change with the different financial objectives. The first one is the *newlywed couple*; in their late twenties, they earn $58,000 a year and spend just about every cent. They have managed to put away some money, however, and are quickly beginning to appreciate the need to develop a savings program. Next there is the *two-income couple*; in their early forties, they earn $115,000 a year and are concerned about college costs for their children, ages 17 and 12. Next is the *divorced mother*; she is 34, has custody of her children, ages 7 and 4, and receives $40,000 a year in salary and child support. Finally, we have the *older couple*; in their mid-fifties, they're planning for retirement in 10 years, when the husband will retire from his $95,000-a-year job.

Keeping Track of Your Investments

Keeping track of your investment holdings is essential to a well-managed securities portfolio. Just as you need investment objectives to provide direction for your portfolio, so too do you need to *monitor* it by keeping informed about what your investment holdings consist of, how they've performed over time, and whether they've lived up to your expectations. Sometimes investments fail to perform the way you thought they would. Their return may be well below what you'd like, or you may even have suffered a loss. In either case, it may be time to sell the investments and put the money elsewhere. A monitoring system for keeping track of your investments should allow you to identify such securities in your portfolio. It should also enable you to stay on top of the holdings that are performing to your satisfaction. Knowing when to sell and when to hold can significantly affect the amount of return you're able to generate from your investments—certainly it will help you keep your money fully invested.

You can use a tool like Worksheet 11.2 to keep an inventory of your investment holdings. All types of investments can be included on this worksheet—from stocks, bonds,

---

EXHIBIT 11.7   Four Model Portfolios

The type of portfolio you put together will depend on your financial and family situation as well as on your investment objectives. Clearly, what is right for one family may be totally inappropriate for another.

Family Situation	Portfolio
Newlywed couple	80 to 90 percent in common stocks, with three-quarters of that in mutual funds aiming for maximum capital gains and the rest in growth-and-income or equity-income funds 10 to 20 percent in a money market fund or other short-term money market securities
Two-income couple	60 to 70 percent in common stocks, with three-quarters of that in blue chips or growth mutual funds and the rest in more aggressive issues or mutual funds aiming for maximum capital gains 25 to 30 percent in discount Treasury notes whose maturities correspond with the bills for college tuition 5 to 10 percent in money market funds or other short-term money market securities
Divorced mother	40 to 50 percent in money market funds or other short-term money market securities 50 to 60 percent in growth and income mutual funds
Older couple	60 to 70 percent in blue-chip common stocks, growth funds, or value funds 25 to 30 percent in municipal bonds or short- and intermediate-term discount bonds that will mature as the couple starts needing the money to live on 5 to 10 percent in CDs and money market funds

and mutual funds to real estate and savings accounts. To see how it works, consider the investment portfolio that has been built up over the last 18 years or so by John and Mary Maffeo, a two-income couple in their early fifties. As Worksheet 11.2 reveals, John and Mary hold common and preferred stock in five companies, three bond issues, two mutual funds, some real estate, and two savings accounts. In addition to the type and description of the investment vehicles, the worksheet contains the dates the investments were made (the purchase date is needed for tax purposes), the original amount of the investment, the amount of annual income currently being earned from it, and its latest market value. (Using such a worksheet in conjunction with an *online portfolio tracker* would give an investor plenty of information about the performance of his or her portfolio—the *worksheet* providing long-term information from the date of purchase of an asset, and the *online portfolio tracker* providing year-to-date or annual returns.)

Worksheet 11.2 lists all the investments John and Mary held as of December 2007, regardless of when they were purchased. In contrast, any securities/ investments sold during the year (2007) would not be included. A report like this should be prepared at least once a year; when completed, it provides a quick overview of your investment holdings and lets you know where you stand at a specific time. Note that the Maffeos earn almost $4,500 a year from their investments and that—thanks largely to their investments in a couple of stocks and stock funds—their holdings have grown from around $100,000 to more than $460,000! In fact, they have only one security that's not doing too well—Pall Corp. All the rest are quite profitable.

Worksheet 11.2 | Keeping Tabs on Your Investment Holdings

A worksheet like this one will enable you to keep track of your investment holdings and identify investments that aren't performing up to expectations.

AN INVENTORY OF INVESTMENT HOLDINGS

Name(s): John & Mary Maffeo   Date: December 2007

Type of Investment	Description of Investment Vehicle	Date Purchased	Amount of Investment (Quote — $ Amount)	Amount of Annual Income from Dividends, Interest, etc.	Latest Market Value (Quote — $ Amount)	Comments/ Planned Actions
Common stock	250 shares—McDonald's	12/8/90	8.25–$2,062	$230	25.14 (now 1,000 shs.)–$25,140	A keeper
Common stock	300 shares–Disney	10/20/92	15–$4,500	$190	20.00 (now 900 shs.)–$18,000	Another keeper
Common stock	400 shares–Pall Corp.	4/10/93	23.50–$9,400	$145	18.50 (now 400 shs.)–$7,400	DUMP IT!
Common stock	150 shares–Intel	8/11/95	8.50–$1,275	$96	28.00 (now 1,200 shs.)–$33,600	Doing great.
Preferred stock	100 shares–Dupont pf 4.50	1/26/89	50.75–$5,075	$450	62.25–$6,225	
Corporate bond	$5,000–Pacific Telephone 7¼–17	8/19/92	75½–$3,775	$363	94¾–$4,738	
Corporate bond	$7,000–Texaco 5¾–17	2/27/87	39¼–$2,748	$402	94½–$6,615	
Treasury bond	$6,000–U.S. Treasury 7½–15	10/4/95	62–$3,720	$450	102–$6,120	
Mutual fund	1,300 shares–Vanguard Health Care	6/16/89	9.08–$11,800	$120	108.50–$141,050	A great fund!!
Mutual fund	725 shares–Clipper fund	12/12/92	17.72–$12,850	$994	79.80–$57,855	Stay with it...
Real estate	Four-plex at 1802 N. 75 Ave.	9/16/87	$140,000–$28,000	N/A	(est.) $250,000–$138,000	Time to sell?
Savings	1-year/6.5% CD at First National Bank	6/10/00	N/A–$10,000	$650	N/A–$10,000	
Savings	Money fund at Paine Webber	3/13/95	N/A–$7,200	$340	N/A–$7,200	
	Totals		$102,369	$4,430	$461,943	

Instructions: List number of shares of *common and preferred stock* purchased as part of the description of securities held; then put the price paid *per share* under the "Quote" column and total amount invested (number of shares × price per share) under the "$ Amount" column. Enter the principal (par) value of all bonds held in place of number of shares: "$ Amount" column for bonds = principal value of bonds purchased × quote (for example, $5,000 × .755 = $3,775). List *mutual funds* as you did for stock. For *real estate*, enter total market value of property under "Quote" column and amount actually invested (down payment and closing costs) under "$ Amount." Ignore the "Quote" column for *savings* vehicles. For "Amount of Income" column, list total amount received from dividends, interest, and so on (for example, dividends per share × number of shares held). Under "Latest Market Value," enter market price as of the date of this report. The latest market value for real estate is entered as an estimate of what the property would likely sell for (under "Quote") and the estimated amount of equity the investor has in the property (under "$ Amount").

11-25	Explain why it might be preferable for a person to invest in a *portfolio* of securities rather than in a single security.
11-26	Briefly describe the concept of *asset allocation* and note how it works.
11-27	Discuss the role of asset allocation in portfolio management.
11-28	What, if anything, can be gained from keeping track of your investment holdings?

RY • SUMMARY • SUMMARY • SUMMARY • SUMMARY • SUMMARY • SUMMARY • SUMMARY • SUMMARY • SUMMARY •

« SUMMARY

LG1 **Discuss the role that investing plays in the personal financial planning process and identify several different investment objectives.** Investing plays an important part in personal financial planning; it's the vehicle through which many of your financial goals can be reached. Your investment activities should be based on a sound investment plan that's linked to an ongoing savings plan. Most people invest their money to enhance their current income, accumulate funds for a major expenditure, save for retirement, or shelter some of their income from taxes.

LG2 **Distinguish between primary and secondary markets, as well as broker and dealer markets.** Stocks, bonds, and other long-term securities are traded in the capital, or long-term, markets. Newly issued securities are sold in the primary markets, whereas transactions between investors occur in the secondary markets; the secondary market can be further divided into broker and dealer markets. Broker markets are made up of various securities exchanges, like NYSE and AMEX, as well as some smaller regional exchanges. In contrast, the dealer market is where you'll find both the NASDAQ markets (like the NASDAQ Global Select and National Markets) as well as the OTC markets (i.e., the OTCBB and Pink Sheets).

LG3 **Explain the process of buying and selling securities and recognize the different types of orders.** The securities transaction process starts when you call and place an order with your broker, who then transmits it via sophisticated telecommunications equipment to the floor of the stock exchange or the OTC market, where it's promptly executed and confirmed. Investors can buy or sell securities in odd or round lots by simply placing one of the three basic types of orders: a market order, limit order, or stop-loss order.

LG4 **Develop an appreciation of how various forms of investment information can lead to better investing skills and returns.** Becoming an informed investor is essential to developing a sound investment program. Vital information about specific companies and industries, the securities markets, the economy, and different investment vehicles and strategies can be obtained from such sources as annual stockholders' reports, brokerage and advisory service reports, the financial press, and the Internet. Various averages and indexes, such as the DJIA, the Standard & Poor's indexes, and the NYSE, and NASDAQ indexes, provide information about daily market performance. These averages and indexes not only measure performance in the overall market but also provide standards of performance.

LG5 **Gain a basic understanding of the growing impact of the computer and the Internet on the field of investments.** The computer and the Internet have empowered individual investors by providing information and tools formerly available only to investing professionals. The savings they offer in time and money are huge. Investors get the most current information, including real-time stock price quotes, market activity data, research reports, educational articles, and discussion forums. Tools such as financial planning calculators, stock-screening programs, and portfolio tracking are free at many sites. Buying and selling securities online is convenient, simple, inexpensive, and fast.

LG6 **Describe an investment portfolio and how you'd go about developing and managing a portfolio of securities.** While an investment portfolio represents a collection of the securities/investments you hold, it also gives focus and purpose to your investing activities. Developing a well-diversified portfolio of investment holdings enables an investor to not only achieve given investment objectives, but also enjoy reduced exposure to risk and a more predictable level of return. To develop such a portfolio, the investor must carefully consider his or her level and stability of income, family factors, financial condition, experience and age, and disposition toward risk. Designing an asset allocation strategy, or mix of securities, that's based on these personal needs and objectives is also an important part of portfolio management. You should monitor your investment portfolio regularly to measure its performance and make changes as required by return data and life-cycle factors.

FINANCIAL PLANNING EXERCISES

LG1

1. **Use Worksheet 11.1** Erin Coates is a young career woman who's now employed as the managing editor of a well-known business journal. While she thoroughly enjoys her job and the people she works with, what she would really like to do is open a bookstore of her own. She would like to open her store in about 8 years and figures she'll need about $50,000 in capital to do so. Given that she thinks she can make about 10 percent on her money, use Worksheet 11.1 to find the following:

    a. How much would Erin have to invest today, in one lump sum, to end up with $50,000 in 8 years?

    b. If she's starting from scratch, how much would she have to put away annually to accumulate the needed capital in 8 years?

    c. How about if she already has $10,000 socked away; how much would she have to put away annually to accumulate the required capital in 8 years?

    d. Given Erin now has an idea of how much she has to save, briefly explain how she could use an *investment plan* to help her reach her objective.

LG4

2. Assume that the following quote for Financial Learning Systems (a NYSE stock) appeared in the Thursday, August 10 issue of *The Wall Street Journal:*

    29.62   17.75   FinLrnSys 1.64   5.5   24   2779   29.70   0.32

    Given this information, answer the following questions:

    a. On what day did the trading activity occur?

    b. At what price did the stock sell at the end of the day on Wednesday, August 9?

    c. What is the stock's price/earnings ratio? What does that indicate?

    d. What is the last price at which the stock traded on the date quoted?

    e. How large a dividend did the company pay in the current year? What's the stock's dividend yield?

    f. What are the highest and lowest prices at which the stock traded during the latest 52-week period?

    g. How many shares of stock were traded on the day quoted?

    h. How much, if any, of a change in price took place between the day quoted and the immediately preceding day? At what price did the stock close on the immediately preceding day?

LG4

3. Here are three pairs of stocks. Look at each pair and select the security you'd like to own, given that you want to *select the one that's worth more money.* Then, *after* making all three of your selections, use *The Wall Street Journal* or some other source to find the latest market value of the two securities in each pair.

    a. 50 shares of Berkshire Hathaway (stock symbol BRKA) or 150 shares of Coca-Cola (stock symbol KO). (Both are listed on the NYSE.)

    b. 100 shares of WD-40 (symbol WDFC—a Nasdaq National Market issue) or 100 shares of Nike (symbol NKE—a NYSE stock).

    c. 150 shares of Wal-Mart (symbol WMT) or 50 shares of Sears (symbol S). (Both are listed on the NYSE.)

    How many times did you pick the one that was worth more money? Did the price of any of these stocks surprise you? If so, which one(s)? Does the price of a stock represent its value? Explain.

LG3

4. Assume that Cecile Higgins places an order to buy 100 shares of Kodak; explain how the order will be processed if it's a market order. Would it have made any difference if it had been a limit order? Explain.

5. Sarah Jordan wants to buy 300 shares of PepsiCo, which is currently selling in the market for $45 a share. Rather than liquidate all her savings, she decides to borrow through her broker. Assume the margin requirement on common stock is 50 percent. If the stock rises to $60 a share by the end of the year, show the kind of profit (in dollars) and return (in percentages) Sarah would earn if she makes the investment with 50 percent margin; contrast this to what she'd make if she uses no margin.

6. Which of the following would offer the best return on investment? Assume that you buy $5,000 in stock in all three cases; also, ignore interest and transaction costs in all your calculations.
   a. Buy a stock at $80 without margin, and sell it at $120 one year later.
   b. Buy a stock at $32 with 50 percent margin, and sell it 1 year later at $41.
   c. Buy a stock at $50 with 75 percent margin, and sell it in 1 year at $65.

7. How much profit (if any) would Buster Summers make if he short-sold 300 shares of stock at $75 a share and the price of the stock suddenly tumbled to $60?

8. Given that Humphrey Dog Toys Inc.'s stock is currently selling for $50 a share, calculate the amount of money that Elmer D. will make, or lose, on each of the following transactions (assume that all transactions involve 100 shares of stock, and ignore brokerage commissions).
   a. He short-sells the stock and then repurchases the borrowed shares at $60.
   b. He buys the stock and then sells it some time later at $60.
   c. He short-sells the stock and then repurchases the borrowed shares at $35.

9. Assume that an investor short-sells 500 shares of stock at a price of $65 a share, making a 50 percent margin deposit. A year later, she repurchases the borrowed shares at $45 a share.
   a. How much of her own money did the short-seller have to put up to make this transaction?
   b. How much money did the investor make, or lose, on this transaction?
   c. What rate of return did she make on her *invested capital* (see part a)?

10. Why do you suppose that large, well-known companies such as Oracle, Starbucks, and Nextel prefer to have their shares traded on the NASDAQ rather than on one of the major listed exchanges, such as the NYSE (for which they'd easily meet all listing requirements)? What's in it for them? What would they gain by switching over to NYSE?

11. Using a resource like *The Wall Street Journal* or *Barron's* (either in print or online), find the latest values for each of the following market averages and indexes, and indicate how each has performed over the past 6 months:
    a. DJIA
    b. Dow Jones Global Titans 50
    c. S&P 500
    d. NYSE Composite
    e. NASDAQ Composite
    f. S&P MidCap 400
    g. Wilshire 5000
    h. Russell 2000

12. Using the stock quotations in Exhibit 11.5, find the 52-week high and low for Nordstrom's common stock (the department store chain). How much does the stock pay annually in dividends, and what is its latest dividend yield? How many shares of Nordstrom's changed hands (were traded), what was the closing price, and at what P/E ratio was the stock trading? There are 23 stocks listed in Exhibit 11.5; which one had the highest price/earnings ratio? The largest share volume (i.e., number of shares traded)? And the biggest change in price? Which three stocks had the highest dividend yields, and which three had the highest closing prices?

13. Using the S&P report in Exhibit 11.6, find the following information as it pertains to Nike:
    a. What was the amount of revenues (that is, sales) the company generated in 2005?
    b. What were the latest annual dividends per share and dividend yield?
    c. What were the earnings (per share) projections for 2006?
    d. What were the number of common shareholders?
    e. What was the book value per share and earnings per share in 2005?
    f. Where is the stock traded?

g. How much long-term debt did the company have in 2005?

h. When was the company formed, and who is the chairman?

i. What was the company's effective tax rate in 2005?

14. ***Use Worksheet 11.2*** to help Rebecca and Andrew Cook, a married couple in their early 30s, evaluate their securities portfolio, which includes these holdings:

a. *Adams Express* (NYSE—stock symbol: ADX): 100 shares bought in December 1994 for $18 per share (stock had a 3-for-2 split in 2000, so the Cooks now own 150 shares of ADX).

b. *Fannie Mae* (NYSE—stock symbol: FNM): 250 shares purchased in December 1995 for $24.25 per share (stock had a 4-for-1 stock split in 1996, so the Cooks now own 1000 shares of FNM).

c. *Bed Bath and Beyond* (NASDAQ—stock symbol: BBBY): 150 shares purchased in 1997 at $8.75 per share (stock has since had *two* 2-for-1 stock splits, so the Cooks now own 600 shares of BBBY).

d. *Starbucks* (NASDAQ—stock symbol: SBUX): 200 shares purchased in 1998 at $15.25 per share (stock split 2 for 1 in 1999, 2001, and 2005, so the Cooks now own 1,600 shares of SBUX).

e. The Cooks also have $8,000 in a 3-year *bank CD* that pays 6.15 percent annual interest.

1. Based on the latest quotes obtained from *The Wall Street Journal*, or elsewhere, complete Worksheet 11.2.

2. What's the total amount the Cooks invested in these securities, the annual income they now receive, and the latest market value of their investments?

APPLYING PERSONAL FINANCE • APPLYING PERSONAL FINANCE • APPLYING PERSONAL FINANCE • APPLYING PERSONA

APPLYING PERSONAL FINANCE

Research Your Investments!

Investing involves making informed decisions and researching companies and industries ahead of time, before plunking down your hard-earned money! An excellent source of information about a company is from the company itself, particularly its annual report to stockholders. In this project, you'll examine the annual stockholders' report of a company in which you are interested.

The annual report is a document that provides financial and operating information about a company to its owners, the stockholders. Obtain a copy of the latest annual report of the company you are researching. Copies can be found in many public and college libraries, local brokerage offices, or the company's Web site. Carefully study the annual report and prepare a *Corporate Profile* of the firm you selected. Include the following:

a. Name of the company, its ticker symbol, and the exchange on which it trades.

b. Current market price of the stock and its percentage change from 1, 3, and 5 years ago. Try to find a chart of its stock price.

c. Location of its corporate headquarters, names of its officers, and percentage of inside ownership.

d. Brief description of the company, including its major products or services.

e. Brief history of the company.

f. Major competitors.

g. Sales and profit summaries.

h. Other relevant financial ratios and measures.

i. Recent developments and future plans.

Based on your findings, would you consider this company for a potential investment? Why or why not?

CRITICAL THINKING CASES • CRITICAL THINKING CASES • CRITICAL THINKING CASES • CRITICAL THINKING CASE

CRITICAL THINKING CASES

11.1 The Thomsons Struggle with Two Investment Goals

Like a lot of married couples, Steve and Barbara Thomson are trying their best to save for two important investment objectives: (1) an education fund to put their two children through college and (2) a retirement nest egg for themselves. They want to have set aside $40,000 per child by the time each one starts college. Given that their children are now 10 and 12 years old, Steve and Barbara have 6 years remaining for one child and 8 for the other. As far as their retirement plans are concerned, the Thomsons both hope to retire in 20 years when they reach age 65. Both Steve and Barbara work, and together they currently earn about $90,000 a year.

Six years ago, the Thomsons started a college fund by investing $6,000 a year in bank CDs. That fund is now worth $45,000—enough to put one child through an in-state college. They also have $50,000 that they received from an inheritance invested in several mutual funds and another $20,000 in a tax-sheltered retirement account. Steve and Barbara feel they'll easily be able to continue putting away $6,000 a year for the next 20 years. In fact, Barbara thinks they'll be able to put away even more, particularly after the children are out of school. The Thomsons are fairly conservative investors and feel they can probably earn about 8 percent on their money. (Ignore taxes for the purpose of this exercise.)

Critical Thinking Questions

1. *Use Worksheet 11.1* to determine whether the Thomsons have enough money right now to meet their childrens' educational needs. That is, will the $45,000 they've accumulated so far be enough to put their children through school, given they can invest their money at 8 percent? Remember, they want to have $40,000 set aside for each child by the time each one starts college.
2. Regarding their retirement nest egg, assuming that no additions are made to either the $50,000 they now have in mutual funds or the $20,000 in the retirement account, how much would these investments be worth in 20 years, given they can earn 8 percent?
3. Now, if the Thomsons can invest $6,000 a year for the next 20 years and apply all of that to their retirement nest egg, how much would they be able to accumulate given their 8 percent rate of return?
4. How do you think the Thomsons are doing with regard to meeting their twin investment objectives? Explain.

LG6 11.2 Col Takes Stock of His Securities

Col Thomas is 32 years old, single, and works as a designer for a major architectural firm. He is well paid and over time has built up a sizable portfolio of investments. He considers himself an aggressive investor and, because he has no dependents to worry about, likes to invest in high-risk/high-return securities. His records show the following:

1. In 1999, Col bought 200 shares of eBay (NASDAQ; symbol: EBAY) at $9 a share—the stock has since split 2 for 1 *three times*, and 3 for 1 *once*, so he now owns 4,800 shares of the stock.
2. In 1999 he bought 250 shares of WD-40 Co. (NASDAQ; symbol: WDFC) at $21 a share.
3. In 1997, Col bought 200 shares of Franklin Resources (NYSE; symbol: BEN) at $52 a share— Col now owns 400 shares, because the stock has since split 2 for 1.
4. In early 1999, he bought 450 shares of Fisher Scientific (NYSE; symbol: FSH) at $17.50 a share.
5. Also in 1999, Col bought 400 shares of P. F. Chang's China Bistro (NASDAQ; symbol: PFCB) at $12.50 a share—Col now owns 800 shares of the stock, because it split 2 for 1 in 2002.
6. He has $12,000 in a 3 percent money market mutual fund.

Every 3 months or so, Col prepares a complete, up-to-date inventory of his investment holdings.

Critical Thinking Questions

1. **Use a form like Worksheet 11.2** to prepare a complete inventory of Col's investment holdings. (*Note:* Look in the latest issue of *The Wall Street Journal* or pull up an online source such as **http://finance.yahoo.com** to find the most recent closing price of the five stocks in Col's portfolio.)
2. What is your overall assessment of Col's investment portfolio? Does it appear that his personal net worth is improving because of his investments?
3. Based on the worksheet you prepared in Question 1, do you see any securities that you think Col should consider selling? What other investment advice might you give Col?

> **MONEY ONLINE** www.thomsonedu.com/finance/gitman

Visit **http://www.thomsonedu.com/finance/gitman** for some additional Web-based exercises and hot links (with annotations) to a variety of resources relevant to the topics covered in this chapter.

Investing in Stocks and Bonds

LG1	●	Describe the various types of risks to which investors are exposed, as well as the sources of return.	p. 373
LG2	●	Know how to search for an acceptable investment, based on risk, return, and yield.	p. 373
LG3	●	Discuss the merits of investing in common stock and be able to distinguish among the different types of stocks.	p. 381
LG4	●	Become familiar with the various measures of performance and how to use them in putting a value on stocks.	p. 381
LG5	●	Describe the basic issue characteristics of bonds and note how these securities are used as investment vehicles.	p. 395
LG6	●	Distinguish between the different types of bonds, gain an understanding of how bond prices behave, and know how to compute different measures of yield.	p. 395
	●		

LG1, LG2 THE RISKS AND REWARDS OF INVESTING

Most rational investors are motivated to buy or sell securities based on its expected (or anticipated) return—buy if the return looks good, sell if it doesn't. Of course, it's a lot more complex than that, but this statement pretty much describes the role that *return* plays in the investment decision-making process. But a security's return is just part of the story; you can't consider the return on an investment without also looking at its *risk*—the chance that the actual return from an investment may differ from (i.e., fall short of) what was expected. Generally speaking, you'd expect riskier investments to provide higher levels of return. Otherwise, what incentive is there for an investor to risk his or her capital? These two concepts (risk and return) are of vital concern to investors, so, before taking up the issue of investing in stocks and bonds, let's look more closely at the risks of investing and the various components of return. Equally important, we'll see how these two components can be used together to find potentially attractive investment vehicles.

The Risks of Investing

As we've noted, when selecting investments, you should look at potential returns and the level of perceived risk to which the investment is exposed. Just about any type of investment is subject to some risk—some investment types more than others. The basic types of investment risk are business risk, financial risk, market risk, purchasing power risk, interest rate risk, liquidity risk, and event risk. Obviously, other things being equal, you'd like to reduce your exposure to these risks as much as possible.

Business Risk

When investing in a company, you may have to accept the possibility that the firm will fail to maintain sales and profits, or even to stay in business. Such failure is due either to economic or industry factors or, as is more often the case, to poor management decisions. In a general sense, this is **business risk;** it may be thought of as the degree of uncertainty surrounding the firm's earnings and subsequent ability to meet principal and interest payments on time. Companies that are subject to high degrees of business risk may experience wide fluctuations in sales, have widely erratic earnings, and can, in fact, experience substantial operating losses every now and then.

Financial Risk

Financial risk relates to the amount of debt used to finance the firm. Look to the company's balance sheet to get a handle on a firm's financial risk. As a rule, companies that have little or no long-term debt are fairly low in financial risk. This is particularly so if a company has a healthy earnings picture as well. The problem with debt financing is that it creates principal and interest obligations that have to be met regardless of how much profit the company is generating. As with business risk, financial risk can lead to failure (as in the case of bankruptcy), or a rate of return that's far below your expectations.

Market Risk

Market risk results from the behavior of investors in the securities markets. The fact is, prices of stocks and bonds will sometimes change even though business and financial risks, and other intrinsic factors, stay about the same. Such changes may have little to do with the securities themselves but instead are due to changes in political, economic, and social conditions or in investor tastes and preferences. Essentially, market risk is reflected in the *price volatility* of a security—the more volatile the price of a security, the greater its perceived market risk.

Purchasing Power Risk

Possible changes in price levels within the economy also result in risk. In periods of rising prices (inflation), the purchasing power of the dollar declines. This means that a smaller quantity of goods and services can be purchased with a given number of dollars. An awareness of **purchasing power risk** and changes in purchasing power allows investors to select investments that are best suited for a given price-level environment. In general, investments whose values tend to move with general price levels (like stocks or real estate) are most profitable during periods of rising prices, whereas those providing fixed returns (like bonds) are preferred during periods of low or declining price levels/inflation.

Interest Rate Risk

Fixed-income securities, which include notes, bonds, and preferred stocks, offer investors a fixed periodic return and, as such, are most affected by **interest rate risk.** As interest rates change, the prices of these securities fluctuate, decreasing with rising interest rates and increasing with falling rates. For example, the prices of fixed-income securities drop when interest rates increase, in order to give investors rates of return that are more competitive with those securities offering higher levels of interest income. Changes in interest rates are due to fluctuations in the supply of or demand for money. These fluctuations are caused by various economic actions of the government or the interactions of business firms, consumers, and financial institutions.

Liquidity Risk

The risk of not being able to liquidate (i.e., sell) an investment conveniently and at a reasonable price is called **liquidity (or marketability) risk.** The liquidity of a given investment vehicle is important because it gives investors a safety valve in case they ever have to get out. In general, investment vehicles traded in *thin markets*, where supply and demand are small, tend to be less liquid than those traded in *broad markets*. However, to

business risk The degree of uncertainty associated with a firm's earnings and subsequent ability to pay interest and dividends.

financial risk A type of risk associated with the mix of debt and equity financing used by the issuing firm.

market risk A type of risk associated with the price volatility of a security.

purchasing power risk A type of risk, resulting from possible changes in price levels, that can significantly affect investment returns.

fixed-income securities Securities such as bonds, notes, and preferred stocks that offer purchasers fixed periodic income.

interest rate risk A type of risk, resulting from changing market interest rates, that mainly affects fixed-income securities.

liquidity (or marketability) risk A type of risk associated with the inability to liquidate an investment conveniently and at a reasonable price.

be liquid, an investment not only must be easily salable but also must be so *at a reasonable price*. The liquidity of an investment can generally be enhanced merely by cutting its price. For example, a security recently purchased for $1,000 wouldn't be viewed as highly liquid if it could be sold only at a significantly reduced price, such as $500. Vehicles such as mutual funds, common stocks, or U.S. Treasury securities are generally highly liquid; others, such as an isolated parcel of raw land in rural Georgia, are not.

Event Risk

More than just a buzzword used by the financial media, **event risk** is real, and it can directly and dramatically affect investment return. Event risk occurs when something substantial happens to a company and that event, in itself, has a sudden impact on the company's financial condition. Event risk goes beyond business and financial risk, and it doesn't necessarily mean the company or market is doing poorly. Instead, it involves a largely (or totally) unexpected event that has a significant and usually immediate effect on the underlying value of an investment. A good example of event risk was the action by the Food and Drug Administration several years ago to halt the use of silicone breast implants. The share price of Dow Chemical—the dominant producer of this product—was quickly affected (negatively) by this single event! Event risk can take many forms, although fortunately its impact tends to be confined to specific companies, securities, or market segments.

The Returns from Investing

Any investment vehicle—be it a share of stock, a bond, a piece of real estate, or a mutual fund—has just two basic sources of return: *current income* and *capital gains*. Some investments offer only one source of return (for example, non-dividend-paying stocks provide only capital gains), but many others offer both income and capital gains, which together make up what's known as the *total return* from an investment. Of course, where both elements of return are present, the relative importance of each will vary among investments. For example, whereas current income is more important with bonds, capital gains are usually a larger portion of total return for common stocks.

Current Income

Current income is generally received with some degree of regularity over the course of the year. It may take the form of dividends on stock, interest from bonds, or rents from real estate. People who invest to obtain income look for investment vehicles that will provide regular and predictable patterns of income. Preferred stocks and bonds, which are expected to pay known amounts at specified times (quarterly or semiannually, for example), are usually viewed as good income investments.

Capital Gains

The other type of return available from investments is capital appreciation (or growth), which is reflected as an increase in the market value of an investment vehicle. Capital gains occur when you're able to sell a security for more than you paid for it, or when your security holdings go up in value. Investments that provide greater growth potential through capital appreciation normally have lower levels of current income, because the firm achieves its growth by reinvesting its earnings instead of paying dividends to the owners. Many common stocks, for example, are acquired for their capital gains potential.

Interest-on-Interest: Another Source of Return

Question: When does an 8 percent investment end up yielding only 5 percent? Answer: Probably more often than you think! Of course, it can happen when investment performance fails to live up to expectations. But it can also happen even when everything goes right. That is, so long as at least part of the return from an investment involves the periodic receipt of current income (such as dividends or interest payments), that income has to be *reinvested* at a given rate of return in order to achieve the yield you thought you had going into the investment. To see why that's so, consider an investor who buys an 8 percent U.S. Treasury bond and holds it to maturity, a period of 20 years. Each year the bondholder

event risk The risk that some major, unexpected event will occur, leading to a sudden, substantial change in the value of an investment.

receives $80 in interest, and at maturity, the $1,000 in principal is repaid. There's no loss in capital, no default; everything is paid right on time. Yet this sure-fire investment ends up yielding only 5 percent. Why? Because the investor failed to reinvest the annual interest payments he was receiving. By not plowing back all the investment earnings, the bondholder failed to earn any *interest-on-interest*.

Take a look at Exhibit 12.1. It shows the three elements of return for an 8 percent, 20-year bond: (1) the recovery of principal, or capital gain, if any is earned; (2) periodic interest income; and (3) the interest-on-interest earned from reinvesting the periodic interest payments. Observe that because the bond was originally bought at par ($1,000), you start off with an 8 percent investment. *Where you end up depends on what you do with the profits (interest earnings) from this investment.* If you don't reinvest the interest income, you'll end up on the 5 percent line.

To move to the 8 percent line, you have to earn interest-on-interest from your investments. Specifically, because you started out with an 8 percent investment, that's the rate of return you have to earn when reinvesting your income. The rate of return you start with, in effect, is the required, or minimum, reinvestment rate. Put your investment profits to work at that rate, and you'll get the rate of return you set out to; fail to do so, and your return will decline accordingly. Keep in mind that even though we used a bond in our illustration, as long as current income is part of an investment's return, *this same principle applies to any type of long-term investment vehicle*. It's just as relevant to common stocks and mutual funds as it is to long-term bond instruments. This notion of earning interest-on-interest is what the market refers to as a *fully compounded rate of return*. It's an important concept because you can't start reaping the full potential from your investments until you start earning a fully compounded return on your money.

Thus, if periodic investment income is a part of your investment return, the reinvestment of that income and interest-on-interest are matters you're going to have to deal with. In fact, *interest-on-interest is a particularly important element of return for investment programs involving a lot of current income*. This is so because, in contrast to capital gains, current income has to be reinvested by the individual investor. (With capital gains, the investment vehicle itself is doing the reinvesting, all automatically.) It follows, then, that if your investment program tends to lean toward income-oriented securities, then interest-on-interest—and the continued reinvestment of income—will play an important role in defining the amount of investment success you have. Of course, *the length of your investment horizon* also plays a key role in defining the amount of interest-on-interest embedded in a security's return. In particular, *long-term investments* (like 20-year bonds) are subject to a lot more interest-on-interest than short-term investments—like, for example, 6-month T-bills, or dividend-paying stocks that you hold for only 2 or 3 years.

The Risk-Return Trade-Off

Generally speaking, the amount of risk associated with a given investment vehicle is directly related to its expected return. This universal rule of investing means that if you want a higher level of return, you'll probably have to accept greater exposure to risk. Thus investors should expect to be compensated for taking higher levels of risk by earning higher rates of return. But while higher risk generally is associated with higher levels of return, this relationship doesn't necessarily work in the opposite direction. That is, you can't just invest in a high-risk security and expect to automatically earn a high rate of return. Unfortunately, it doesn't work that way—risk simply isn't that predictable!

Because most people are believed to be risk averse—they dislike taking risks—some incentive for taking risks must be offered. If a low-risk investment offered the same return as a high-risk one, investors would naturally opt for the former—or, put another way, investors would choose the investment with the least risk for a given level of return. The

EXHIBIT 12.1   Three Elements of Return for an 8 Percent, 20-Year Bond

As seen here, the long-term return from an investment (in this case, a bond) is made up of three parts: recovery of capital, current income, and interest-on-interest; of the three components, interest-on-interest is particularly important, *especially for long-term investments.*

relationship between risk and return is shown in Exhibit 12.2, which generalizes the risk-return trade-off for some popular investment vehicles. Note that it's possible to receive a positive return for zero risk, such as at point A; this is sometimes referred to as the **risk-free rate of return,** which is often measured by the return on a short-term government security, such as a 90-day Treasury bill.

What Makes a Good Investment?

In keeping with the preceding risk-return discussion, it follows that the value of any investment depends on the amount of return it's expected to provide relative to the amount of perceived risk involved. This basic rule applies to any type of investment vehicle, be it stocks, bonds, convertibles, options, real estate, or commodities. In this respect, they should all be treated the same.

Future Return

risk-free rate of return
The rate of return on short-term government securities, such as Treasury bills, that is free from any type of risk.

In the field of investments, the only return that matters is *expected future return.* Aside from the help they can provide in getting a handle on future income, past returns are of little value to investors—after all, it's not what the security did last year that matters, but what it's expected to do next year.

EXHIBIT 12.2   The Risk-Return Relationship

For investments, there's generally a direct relationship between risk and return: the more risk you face, the greater the return you should expect from the investment.

Smart.Sites

When you come across an investing term you don't understand, the online glossary at InvestorWords can help. Link at **http://www .thomsonedu.com/finance/ gitman.**

Earlier, we defined returns as being made up of current income and capital gains. To get an idea of the future return on an investment, we must *formulate expectations of its future current income and future capital appreciation*. To illustrate, assume you're thinking of buying some stock in Rose Colored Glasses, Inc. (RCG). By reviewing several financial reports, you've estimated the future dividends and price behavior of RCG as follows:

Expected average annual dividends, 2007–2009	$2.15 a share
Expected market price of the stock, 2009	$95.00 a share

Because the stock is now selling for $60 a share, the difference between its current and expected future market price ($95 − $60) represents the amount of *capital gains* you can expect to receive over the next 3 years—in this case, $35 a share. The projected future price, along with expected average annual dividends, gives you an estimate of the *stock's future income stream;* what you need now is a way to measure *expected return*.

Approximate Yield

Finding the exact rate of return on an investment involves a complex mathematical procedure—one that's hard to determine without using a handheld financial calculator (which we'll demonstrate below). There is, however, a fairly easy way to obtain a reasonably close estimation of expected return, and that is to compute an investment's *approximate yield*. While this measure is only an approximation, it's useful when dealing with forecasted numbers (that are subject to some degree of uncertainty anyway); and as such, it's usually considered to be "close enough." Moreover, the measure considers not only current income and capital gains, but interest-on-interest as well. As such, *approximate yield provides a measure of the fully compounded rate of return* from an investment and, in so doing, represents a viable measure of expected return performance.

The method for finding the approximate yield on an investment is shown in the following equation. If you briefly study the formula, you will see it's really not as formidable as it may first appear. All it does is relate (1) average current income and (2) average capital gains to the (3) average amount of the investment.

$$
\text{Approximate yield} = \frac{\text{Average annual current income} + \left[\dfrac{\text{Future price of investment} - \text{Current price of investment}}{\text{Number of years in investment period}} \right]}{\left[\dfrac{\text{Current price of investment} + \text{Future price of investment}}{2} \right]}
$$

$$
= \frac{\text{CI} + \left[\dfrac{\text{FP} - \text{CP}}{\text{N}} \right]}{\left[\dfrac{\text{CP} + \text{FP}}{2} \right]}
$$

where

CI = *average* annual current income (amount you expect to receive annually from dividends, interest, or rent)

FP = expected future price of investment

CP = current market price of investment

N = investment period (length of time, in years, that you expect to hold the investment)

Crunching the Numbers. To illustrate, let's use the Rose Colored Glasses example again. Given the average annual dividends (CI) of $2.15, current stock price (CP) of $60, future stock price (FP) of $95, and an investment period (N) of 3 years (you expect to hold the stock from 2007 through 2009), you can use this equation to find the expected approximate yield on RCG as follows:

$$
\text{Approximate yield} = \frac{\$2.15 + \left[\dfrac{\$95 - \$60}{3} \right]}{\left[\dfrac{\$60 + \$95}{2} \right]}
$$

$$
= \frac{\$2.15 + \left[\dfrac{\$35}{3} \right]}{\left[\dfrac{\$155}{2} \right]}
$$

$$
= \frac{\$2.15 + \$11.67}{\$77.50} = \frac{\$13.82}{\$77.50}
$$

$$
= \underline{17.8\%}
$$

In this case, if your forecasts of annual dividends and capital gains hold up, an investment in Rose Colored Glasses should provide a return of around 17.8 percent per year.

Calculator Keystrokes. You can easily find the *exact* return on this investment by using a handheld financial calculator. Here's what you do: First, put the calculator in the *annual compounding* mode. Then, to find the expected return on a stock that you buy at $60 a share, hold for 3 years (during which time you receive average annual dividends of $2.15 a share), and then sell at $95, use the keystrokes shown in the margin, where:

N = number of *years* you hold the stock
PV = the price you pay for the stock (entered a *negative* number)
PMT = *average* amount of dividends received *each year*
FV = the price you expect to receive when you *sell* the stock (in 3 years)

You'll notice there is a difference in the computed yield measures (17.8 percent with the approximate procedure vs. 19.7 percent here); that's to be expected, since one is only an approximate measure of performance, whereas this is an exact, and more accurate, measure.

Whether you should consider RCG a viable investment candidate depends on how this level of expected return stacks up to the amount of risk you must assume. Suppose you've decided the stock is moderately risky. To determine whether the expected rate of return on this investment will be satisfactory, you can compare it to some benchmark. One of the best is the rate of return you can expect from a *risk-free* security, such as a *U.S. Treasury bill*. The idea is that the return on a *risky* security should be greater than that available on a risk-free security (this is the concept underlying the graph in Exhibit 12.2). If, for example, U.S. T-bills are yielding 5 or 6 percent, then you'd want to receive considerably more—perhaps 12 to 15 percent—to justify your investment in a moderately risky security like RCG. In essence, the 12 to 15 percent is your **desired rate of return**—it's the minimum rate of return you feel you should receive in compensation for the amount of risk you must assume. *An investment should be considered acceptable only if it's expected to generate a rate of return that meets (or exceeds) your desired rate of return.* In the case of RCG, the stock *should be considered a viable investment candidate*, because it more than provides the minimum or desired rate of return. In short, even after factoring in the perceived exposure to risk, the stock still generates a sufficiently attractive expected return—one that comfortably *exceeds* the amount you desire, based on the risks involved.

desired rate of return
The minimum rate of return an investor feels should be earned in compensation for the amount of risk assumed.

ⓘ Concept Check

CHECK • CONCEPT CHECK • CONCEPT CHECK • CONCEPT CHECK • CONCEPT CHECK • CONCEPT CHECK • CONCEPT

12-1	Describe the various types of risk to which investors are exposed.
12-2	What is meant by the risk-return trade-off? What is the *risk-free rate of return*?
12-3	Briefly describe the two basic sources of return to investors.
12-4	What is interest-on-interest, and why is it such an important element of return?
12-5	What is the *desired rate of return,* and how would it be used to make an investment decision?

Common stocks appeal to investors for various reasons. To some, investing in stocks is a way to hit it big if the issue shoots up in price; to others, it's the level of current income they offer. In fact, given the stock market's size and diversity, it's safe to say that no matter what the investment objective, common stocks are available to fit the bill. Not surprisingly, common stocks are a popular form of investing used by literally millions of individuals and a variety of financial institutions.

The basic investment attribute of a share of common stock is that it enables the investor to participate in the profits of the firm, which is how it derives its value Every shareholder is, in effect, a part owner of the firm and, as such, is entitled to a piece of its profit. But this claim on income has limitations, for common stockholders are really the **residual owners** of the company, meaning they're entitled to dividend income and a prorated share of the company's earnings only after all of the firm's other obligations have been met. Equally important, as residual owners, *holders of common stock have no guarantee that they'll ever receive any return on their investment.*

Common Stocks as a Form of Investing

Given the nature of common stocks, when the market is strong, investors can generally expect to benefit from steady price appreciation. A good example is the performance in 1999, when the market, as measured by the Dow Jones Industrial Average (DJIA), went up more than 25 percent. Unfortunately, when markets falter, so do investor returns. Look at what happened over the 3-year period from early 2000 through late 2002, when the market (again, as measured by the DJIA) fell some 38 percent. Excluding dividends, that means a $100,000 investment would have declined in value to a little over $60,000.

Make no mistake, the market does have its bad days; and sometimes those bad days seem to go on for months. It may not always seem that way, but those bad days *really are the exception rather than the rule.* That was certainly the case over the 50-year period from 1956 through 2005, when the Dow went down (for the year) just 16 times. That's only about 30 percent of the time; the other 70 percent, the market was up—anywhere from around 2 percent on the year to nearly 40 percent! True, there's some risk and price volatility (even in good markets), but that's the price you have to pay for all that upside potential. Consider, for example, the behavior of the market from 1982 through early 2000. Starting in August 1982, when the Dow stood at 777, this market saw the DJIA climb nearly 11,000 points to a high of 11,723, reached in January 2000. This turned out to be one of the longest bull markets in history, as the DJIA grew (over 18 years) at an annual rate of nearly 17 percent.

Unfortunately, all that came to a screeching halt in early 2000, when each of the three major market measures peaked—the Dow at 11,723, the NASDAQ at 5,048, and the S&P 500 at 1,527. Over the course of the next 32 months, through September 2002, these market measures fell flat on their collective faces:

- The Dow fell 38 percent.
- The S&P dropped 49 percent.
- The NASDAQ fell 77 percent.

This turned out to be one of the worst bear markets in recent history and clearly had a devastating effect on investor returns. Take a look at Exhibit 12.3, which tracks the behavior of the DJIA and the NASDAQ Composite over the 10-year period ending in early 2006, and you'll quickly get a feel for just how volatile this market was! Fitting, isn't it, that one of the biggest bull markets on record would be followed by one of the worst bear markets ever? Even so, as the exhibit shows, despite all those market gyrations, both the Dow and the NASDAQ—which track two totally different segments of the market—ended up at about the same point: they both doubled in value over the course of the decade.

residual owners
Shareholders of the company; they are entitled to dividend income and a share of the company's profits only after all of the firm's other obligations have been met.

One of the greatest bull markets in history began on August 12, 1982, with the Dow at 777. It continued through the 1980s and into the 1990s. But it all ended in early 2000, when the market went from a rip-snorting bull to a full-fledged bear—one that lasted until late 2002, when the bulls took over again.

Source: Based on market data from various sources, including *Morningstar* and *Business Week*, March 2, 2006.

Issuers of Common Stock

Shares of common stock can be issued by any corporation in any line of business. All corporations have stockholders, but not all of them have publicly traded shares. The stocks of interest to us in this book are the so-called *publicly traded issues*—the shares that are readily available to the general public and that are bought and sold in the open market. Aside from the initial distribution of common stock when the corporation is formed, subsequent sales of additional shares may be made through a procedure known as a *public offering*. In a public offering, the corporation, working with its underwriter, simply offers the investing public a certain number of shares of its stock at a certain price. Exhibit 12.4 depicts the announcement for such an offering. Note in this case that *Advanced Micro Devices (AMD)* is offering 14,096,000 shares of stock at a price of $35.20 per share. The new issue of common stock will provide this NYSE-traded company with nearly $500 million in new capital. When issued, the new shares will be commingled with the outstanding shares (they're all the same class of stock), and the net result will be an increase in the number of shares outstanding—after the new stocks are issued, the company will have about 418 million shares of stock outstanding.

Voting Rights

The holders of common stock normally receive *voting rights*, which means that for each share of stock held, they receive one vote. In some cases, common stock may be designated as nonvoting at the time of issue, but this is the exception rather than the rule. Although different voting systems exist, the small stockholders need not concern themselves with them because, regardless of the system used, their chances of affecting corporate control with their votes are quite slim.

Corporations have annual stockholders' meetings, at which time new directors are elected and special issues are voted on. Because most small stockholders can't attend these meetings, they can use a proxy to assign their votes to another person, who will vote for them. A **proxy** is a written statement assigning voting rights to another party.

proxy A written statement used to assign a stockholder's voting rights to another person, typically one of the directors.

Here the company—Advanced Micro Divices—is issuing over 14 million shares of stock at a price of $35.20 per share. For this manufacturer of microprocessors and memory chips, the new issue will mean nearly *half a billion dollars* in fresh capital.

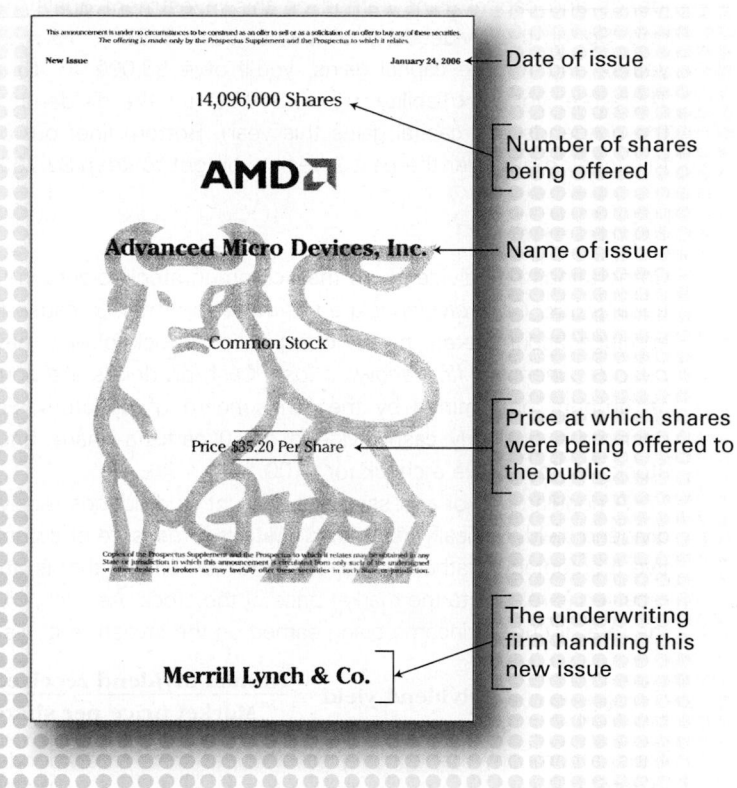

This announcement is under no circumstances to be construed as an offer to sell or as a solicitation of an offer to buy any of these securities. The offering is made only by the Prospectus Supplement and the Prospectus to which it relates.

New Issue   January 24, 2006 — Date of issue

14,096,000 Shares — Number of shares being offered

AMD

Advanced Micro Devices, Inc. — Name of issuer

Common Stock

Price $35.20 Per Share — Price at which shares were being offered to the public

Copies of the Prospectus Supplement and the Prospectus to which it relates may be obtained in any State or jurisdiction in which this announcement is circulated from only such of the undersigned or other dealers or brokers as may lawfully offer these securities in such State or jurisdiction.

Merrill Lynch & Co. — The underwriting firm handling this new issue

Source: *The Wall Street Journal*, February 2, 2006.

Basic Tax Considerations

Common stocks provide income in the form of dividends, usually paid quarterly, and/or capital gains, which occurs when the price of the stock goes up over time. From a tax *rate* perspective, it really makes no difference whether the investment return comes in the form of dividends or long term capital gains—today, they're both taxed at the same rate of 15 percent, or less (it's 5 percent for those filers in the 10 percent and 15 percent tax brackets).

The appeal of cash dividends took a giant leap forward in 2003, when the federal tax code was changed to reduce the tax on dividends. Cash dividends formerly were taxed as ordinary income, meaning they could be taxed at rates as high as 39 percent. For that reason, many investors viewed cash dividends as an unattractive source of income, especially since capital gains (when realized) were taxed at much lower preferential rates. Now, *both dividends and capital gains are taxed at the same low, preferential rate.* That, of course, makes dividend-paying stocks far more attractive, even to those investors in the higher tax brackets. (See Chapter 3 for details on taxes and tax rates.)

There's one slight difference between the taxes due on dividends and capital gains: that is, there is no tax liability on any capital gains until the stock is actually sold (*paper gains*—that is, any price appreciation occurring on stock that you still own—accumulate tax-free). Taxes are due on any dividends and capital gains in the year in which the dividends are received or the stock is actually sold. So if you received, say, $125 in dividends in 2007, you'd have to include that income on your 2007 tax return.

Here's how it works: Assume that you just sold 100 shares of common stock for $50 per share. Also assume the stock was originally purchased 2 years ago for $20 per share and that during each of the past 2 years, you received $1.25 per share in cash dividends. For tax purposes, you would have received cash dividends of $125 (i.e., $1.25/share × 100 shares) *both* this year and last, plus you would have generated a capital gain, that is taxable this year, of $3,000 ($50/share − $20/share) × 100 shares. Now, let's say you're in the 33 percent tax bracket. Even though you're in one of the higher brackets, both the dividends and capital gains earned on this investment qualify for the lower 15 percent tax rate. So, on the dividends, you'll pay taxes of $125 × .15 = $18.75 (for each of the past 2 years), and for the capital gains, you'll owe $3,000 × .15 = $450 (for this year only). Therefore, your tax liability will be $18.75 (for the dividends last year), plus $468.75 (for the dividends and capital gains this year). Bottom line: out of the $3,250 you earned on this investment over the past 2 years, you get to keep $2,762.50, after taxes.

Dividends

Corporations pay dividends to their common stockholders in the form of cash and/or additional stock. *Cash dividends* are the most common. Because firms can pay dividends from earnings accumulated in previous periods, stockholders may receive dividends *even in periods when the firm shows a loss*. Cash dividends are normally distributed quarterly in an amount determined by the firm's board of directors. For example, if the directors declared a quarterly cash dividend of 50 cents a share, and you owned 200 shares of stock, you'd receive a check for $100.

A popular way of assessing the amount of dividends received is to measure the stock's dividend yield. Basically, **dividend yield** is a measure of common stock dividends on a relative (percentage), rather than absolute (dollar) basis—that is, the dollar amount of dividends received is related to the market price of the stock. As such, dividend yield is an indication of the rate of current income being earned on the investment. It's computed as follows:

$$\text{Dividend yield} = \frac{\text{Annual dividend received per share}}{\text{Market price per share of stock}}$$

Thus, a company that annually pays $2 per share in dividends and whose stock is trading at $50 a share will have a dividend yield of 4 percent ($2/$50 = .04). Dividend yield is widely used by income-oriented investors looking for (reasonably priced) stocks with a long and sustained record of regularly paying higher-than-average dividends.

Occasionally the directors may declare a stock dividend as a supplement to or in place of cash dividends. **Stock dividends** are paid in the form of additional shares of stock. That is, rather than receiving cash, shareholders receive additional shares of the company's stock—say, 1/10 of a share of new stock for each share owned (as in a *10 percent stock dividend*). Although they often satisfy the needs of some investors, stock dividends really have no value, because they represent the receipt of something already owned. For example, if you owned 100 shares of stock in a company that declared a 10 percent stock dividend, you'd receive 10 new shares of stock. Unfortunately, you'll be no better off after the stock dividend than you were before. That's because all stockholders will receive a 10 percent increase in the number of shares they own, so the relative ownership position of all shareholders will remain the same. Moreover, the total market value of the shares owned is (roughly) the same after the stock dividend as before. Why is that so? Because the price of the stock usually falls in direct proportion to the size of a stock dividend. Thus, in this example, a drop in price will bring the total market value of 110 shares (after the stock dividend) to about the same as the total market value of the 100 shares that existed before the dividend. Clearly, under such circumstances, the investors are right back where they started from: they've received nothing of value.

Some Key Measures of Performance

Professional money managers and seasoned investors use a variety of financial ratios and measures when making common stock investment decisions. They look at such things as

dividend yield The percentage return provided by the dividends paid on common stock.

stock dividends New shares of stock distributed to existing stockholders as a supplement to or substitute for cash dividends.

dividend yield (mentioned earlier), book value, return on equity, and earnings per share to get a feel for the investment merits of a particular stock. In short, they use these and other ratios to help them decide whether to invest in a particular stock. Fortunately, most of the widely followed ratios can be found in published reports—like those produced by *Value Line* or Standard & Poor's (see Exhibit 11.6 in Chapter 11 for an example of an S&P stock report)—so you don't have to compute them yourself. Even so, if you're thinking about buying a stock, or already have some common stock, there are a few measures of performance you'll want to keep track of: book value (or book value per share), net profit margin, return on equity, earnings per share, price/earnings ratio, and beta.

Book Value

The amount of stockholders' equity in a firm is measured by **book value.** This accounting measure is determined by subtracting the firm's liabilities and preferred stocks from the value of its assets. Book value indicates the amount of stockholder funds used to finance the firm. For example, assume Rose Colored Glasses (RCG) had assets of $5 million, liabilities of $2 million, and preferred stock valued at $1 million. The book value of the firm's common stock would be $2 million ($5 million − $2 million − $1 million). If the book value is divided by the number of shares outstanding, the result is *book value per share*. If RCG had 100,000 shares of common stock outstanding, its book value per share would be $20 ($2,000,000/100,000 shares). Because of the positive impact it can have on the firm's growth, you'd like to see book value per share steadily increasing over time; also, look for stocks whose market prices are comfortably above their book values.

Net Profit Margin

As a yardstick of profitability, **net profit margin** is one of the most widely followed measures of corporate performance. Basically, this ratio relates the firm's net profits to its sales, providing an indication of how well the company is controlling its cost structure. The higher the net profit margin, the more money the company earns. Look for a relatively stable—or even better, an increasing—net profit margin.

Return on Equity

Another very important and widely followed measure, **return on equity** (or **ROE,** for short), reflects the firm's overall profitability. It captures, in a single ratio, the amount of success the firm is having in managing its assets, operations, and capital structure. Return on equity is important because it directly and significantly affects the profits, growth, and dividends of the firm. The better the ROE, the better the company's financial condition and competitive position. Look for a stable or increasing ROE, and watch out for a falling ROE, as that could spell trouble.

Earnings per Share

With stocks, the firm's annual earnings are usually measured and reported in terms of **earnings per share (EPS).** Basically, EPS translates total corporate profits into profits on a per-share basis and provides a convenient measure of the amount of earnings available to stockholders. Earnings per share is found by using this simple formula:

$$\text{EPS} = \frac{\text{Net profit after taxes} - \text{Preferred dividends paid}}{\text{Number of shares of common stock outstanding}}$$

For example, if RCG reported a net profit of $350,000, paid $100,000 in dividends to preferred stockholders, and had 100,000 shares of common outstanding, it would have an EPS of $2.50 [($350,000 − $100,000)/100,000]. Note that preferred dividends are *subtracted* from profits because they must be paid before any monies can be made available to common stockholders. Stockholders follow EPS closely because it represents the amount the firm has earned on behalf of each outstanding share of common stock. Here, too, look for a steady rate of growth in EPS.

Price/Earnings Ratio

When the prevailing market price of a share of common stock is divided by the annual earnings per share, the result is the **price/earnings (P/E) ratio,** which is viewed as an

book value The amount of stockholders' equity in a firm; determined by subtracting the company's liabilities and preferred stock from its assets.

net profit margin A key measure of profitability relating a firm's net profits to its sales; shows the rate of return the company is earning on its sales.

return on equity (ROE) ROE captures the firm's overall profitability; it is important due to its impact on the firm's growth, profits, and dividends.

earnings per share (EPS) The return earned on behalf of each share of common stock; calculated by dividing all earnings remaining after paying preferred dividends by the number of common shares outstanding.

price/earnings (P/E) ratio A measure of investors' confidence in a given security; calculated by dividing market price per share by earnings per share.

READING BETWEEN THE LINES OF AN ANNUAL REPORT

Annual reports offer a wealth of information to anyone interested in investing in or working for a company. The SEC requires any publicly held company to submit a report at the end of the fiscal year describing the key events of the past year and future outlook for the company, along with a complete set of financial statements. Sometimes the term *annual report* refers to a glossy, colorful brochure; sometimes it refers to the 10K (the Form 10K contains more detailed information). The annual report is sent to all shareholders, but it can also be obtained at no charge from the company or SEC Web sites, or at your local library. So, once you have the annual report, how do you make sense of all the information it contains? Here are some pointers:

- Fancy isn't better. Don't let all the glossy pages, wonderful updates, and lovely photos color your thinking. They mean little or nothing if the financial statements reflect declining performance.
- Start at the end. Check the auditor's opinion to see if the financial statements conform with "generally accepted accounting principles." In recent years there were several accounting scandals at firms such as Enron, WorldCom, Tyco, and

Arthur Andersen that resulted in billions of dollars in losses. In response to these scandals, Congress passed the Sarbanes-Oxley Act of 2002. This act established new accountability standards for companies and their independent auditors. One intended result is an annual report that more accurately reflects a company's financial state.

- Read the footnotes. Do this before looking at the financial statements themselves. Footnotes reveal key information about the financial statements, such as whether an increase or decrease in profits was largely due to an accounting change or a one-time event. If there's a change in accounting methods, consider whether the change was made to hide poor performance. The footnotes disclose other important details such as lawsuits.
- Focus on the management discussion and analysis. This in-depth discussion gives you a clear picture of what the company does and how it has performed over the past year. The information in this section of the report should correspond to the financial statements. While management tends to put a positive spin on performance, it is a bad sign if any serious problems facing the company are ignored.
- Dear Stockholder . . . . The chairman's letter to stockholders should

summarize key events of the past year. It should tell you how the company has performed and give reasons for this performance. The letter should also discuss the company's future and any regulatory or economic trends that may affect it. Watch out for phrases like "except for" or "in spite of," which could signal problems.

- Numbers, please. Now delve into the financial statements themselves, looking at trends in sales, profits, expenses, inventory and debt levels, cash flow, and more. Compare your company to industry norms. Investors tend to be most concerned with the net earnings per share that is presented on the income statement, but this figure can be misleading. Companies can boost earnings by selling off an asset or trimming some area of the budget. The cash-flow statement gives a clearer picture of the company's financial standing. There's little a company can do to manipulate these numbers—the company either has the cash or it doesn't.

Critical Thinking Questions

1. What is the purpose of an annual report? Describe the major components.
2. How might the earnings per share figure mislead investors?
3. What is the independent auditor's role in the annual report?

Sources: Based on "Fundamental Analysis," Investopedia.com, July 10, 2006, from http://www.investopedia.com/university/fundamentalanalysis; and Jane Bryant Quinn, "How to Read an Annual Report" (free reprint from International Paper Company), July 10, 2006, from http://websites.quincy.edu/~jschlepp/anrpread.html; "Sarbanes-Oxley Act of 2002," Wikipedia, July 10, 2006, from http://en.wikipedia.org.

indication of investor confidence and expectations. The higher the price/earnings multiple, the more confidence investors are presumed to have in a given security. In the case of RCG, whose shares are currently selling for $30, the price/earnings ratio is 12 ($30 per share/$2.50 per share). This means that RCG stock is selling for 12 times its earnings. P/E ratios are important to investors because they reveal how aggressively the stock is being priced in the market. Watch out for very high P/Es—that is, P/Es that are way out of line with the market—because that could indicate the stock is being overpriced (and thus might be headed for a big drop in price). P/E ratios are not static, but tend to move with the market: when the market's soft, a stock's P/E will be low, and when things heat up in the market, so will the stock's P/E.

Beta

A stock's **beta** is an indication of its *price volatility;* it shows how responsive the stock is to the market. In recent years, using betas to measure the *market risk* of common stock has become widely accepted; as a result, published betas are now available from most brokerage firms and investment services. The beta for a given stock is determined by a statistical technique that relates the stock's historical returns to the market. The market (as measured by something like the S&P index of 500 stocks) is used as a benchmark of performance, and it always has a beta of 1.0. From there, everything is relative: low-beta stocks—those with betas of less than 1.0—have low price volatility (their prices are relatively stable), while high-beta stocks—those with betas of more than 1.0—are considered to be highly volatile. In short, the higher a stock's beta, the riskier it's considered to be. Stock betas can be either positive or negative, though the vast majority are positive, meaning the stocks move in the same general direction as the market.

Actually, beta is an *index* of price performance that's interpreted as a percentage response to the market. If RCG has a beta of, say, 0.8, it should rise (or fall) only 80 percent as fast as the market—if the market goes up by 10 percent, RCG should go up only 8 percent (10 percent × .8). In contrast, if the stock had a beta of 1.8, it would go up or down 1.8 times as fast—the price of the stock would rise higher and fall lower than the market. Clearly, other things being equal, if you're looking for a relatively conservative investment, you should stick with low-beta stocks; on the other hand, if it's capital gains and price volatility you're after, then go with high-beta securities.

Types of Common Stock

Common stocks are often classified on the basis of their dividends or their rate of growth in EPS. Some popular types of common stock are blue-chip, growth, tech stocks, income, speculative, cyclical, defensive, mid-cap, and small-cap stocks.

Blue-Chip Stocks

Blue chips are the cream of the common stock crop; these stocks are unsurpassed in quality and have a long and stable record of earnings and dividends. They're issued by large, well-established firms that have impeccable financial credentials—firms like GE, Wal-Mart, Citigroup, Microsoft, United Parcel Service, and Abbott Labs. These companies hold important, if not leading, positions in their industries and often determine the standards by which other firms are measured. Blue chips are particularly attractive to investors who seek high-quality investment outlets offering decent dividend yields and respectable growth potential. Many use them for long-term investment purposes and, because of their relatively low-risk exposure, as a way of obtaining modest but dependable rates of return on their investment dollars. Blue-chip stocks are popular with a large segment of the investing public and, as a result, are often relatively high priced, especially when the market is unsettled and investors become more quality conscious.

Growth Stocks

Stocks that have experienced, and are expected to continue experiencing, consistently high rates of growth in operations and earnings are known as **growth stocks.** A good growth stock might exhibit a *sustained* rate of growth in earnings of 15 to 20 percent (or more) over a period when common stocks are averaging only 6 to 8 percent. Starbucks, Lowe's, Medtronic, Nike, Symantec, and Boston Scientific are all prime examples of growth stocks. These stocks often pay little or nothing in dividends, because the firm's rapid growth potential requires that its earnings be retained and reinvested. The high growth expectations for these stocks usually cause them to sell at relatively high P/E ratios, and they typically have betas in excess of 1.0. Because of their potential for

beta An index of the price volatility for a share of common stock; a reflection of how the stock price responds to market forces.

blue-chip stock A stock generally issued by companies expected to provide an uninterrupted stream of dividends and good long-term growth prospects.

growth stock A stock whose earnings and market price have increased over time at a rate well above average.

dramatic price appreciation, they appeal mostly to investors who are seeking capital gains rather than dividend income.

Tech Stocks

Over the past 10 or 15 years, *tech stocks* have become such a dominant force in the market that they deserve to be put in a class all their own. **Tech stocks** basically represent the technology sector of the market and include all those companies that produce or provide technology-based products and services such as computers, semiconductors, data storage devices, computer software and hardware, peripherals, Internet services, content providers, networking, and wireless communications. There are literally thousands of companies that fall into the tech stock category, including everything from very small firms providing some service on the Internet to huge multinational companies. These stocks would likely fall into either the *growth stock* category (described earlier) or the *speculative stock* class (discussed next), although some of them are legitimate *blue chips*. Tech stocks may offer the potential for attractive (and in some cases, phenomenal) returns, but they also involve considerable risk and (for the most part anyway) are probably most suitable for the more risk-tolerant investor. Included in the tech stock category are some big names—Microsoft, Cisco Systems, SanDisk, Applied Materials, and Dell—as well as many not-so-big names, such as Multimedia Games, MTC Technologies, Quality Systems, ANSYS, and SigmaTron International.

Income Stocks versus Speculative Stocks

Stocks whose appeal is based primarily on the dividends they pay out are known as **income stocks.** They have a fairly stable stream of earnings, a large portion of which is distributed in the form of dividends. Income shares have relatively high dividend yields and, thus, are ideally suited for investors seeking a relatively safe and high level of current income from their investment capital. An added (and often overlooked) feature of these stocks is that, unlike bonds and preferred stock, holders of income stock can expect *the amount of dividends paid to increase over time*. Examples of income stock include Washington Mutual, Oneok, Verizon Communications, ConAgra Foods, and FPL Group. Because of their low risk, these stocks commonly have betas of less than 1.0.

Rather than basing their investment decisions on a proven record of earnings, investors in **speculative stocks** gamble that some new information, discovery, or production technique will favorably affect the firm's growth and inflate its stock price. For example, a company whose stock is considered speculative may recently have discovered a new drug or located a valuable resource, such as oil. The value of speculative stocks and their P/E ratios tend to fluctuate widely as additional information about the firm's future is received. Betas for speculative stocks are nearly always well in excess of 1.0. Investors in speculative stocks should be prepared to experience losses as well as gains, since *these are high-risk securities*. They include companies like Sirius Satellite Radio, Dreamworks Animation, FoxHollow Technologies, Liberty Media, and NitroMed.

Cyclical Stocks or Defensive Stocks

Stocks whose price movements tend to follow the business cycle are called **cyclical stocks.** This means that when the economy is in an expansionary stage (recovery or expansion), the prices of cyclical stocks increase; during a contractionary stage (recession or depression), they decline. Most cyclical stocks are found in the basic industries—automobiles, steel, and lumber, for example—which are generally sensitive to changes in economic activity. Investors try to purchase cyclical stocks just before an expansionary phase and sell just before the contraction occurs. Because they tend to move with the market, these stocks always have positive betas. Caterpillar, Genuine Parts, Alcoa, Timken, Lear, Lennar, and Navistar International are all examples of cyclical stocks.

The prices and returns from **defensive stocks,** unlike those of cyclical stocks, are expected to remain stable during periods of contraction in business activity. For this rea-

tech stock A stock that represents the technology sector of the market.

income stock A stock whose appeal is the dividends it pays out; offers dividend payments that can be expected to increase over time.

speculative stock Stock that is purchased on little more than the hope that its price per share will increase.

cyclical stock Stock whose price movements tend to parallel the various stages of the business cycle.

defensive stock Stock that tends to exhibit price movements contrary to movements in the business cycle.

son, they're often called *countercyclical*. The shares of consumer goods companies, certain public utilities, and gold mining companies are good examples of defensive stocks. Because they're basically income stocks, their earnings and dividends tend to hold their market prices up during periods of economic decline. Betas on these stocks are quite low and occasionally even negative. Bandag, Checkpoint Systems, Weis Markets, Extendicare, and WD-40 are all examples of defensive stocks.

Mid-Caps and Small-Caps

In the stock market, a stock's size is based on its market value—or, more commonly, on what's known as its *market capitalization* or *market cap*. A stock's market cap is found by multiplying its market price by the number of shares outstanding. Generally speaking, the market can be broken into three major segments, as measured by a stock's market "cap":

> Small-cap—Stocks with market caps of less than $1 billion
> Mid-cap—Market caps of $1 billion to $4 or $5 billion
> Large-cap—Market caps of more than $4 or $5 billion

In addition to these three segments, another is reserved for the *really small* stocks, known as *micro-caps*. Many of these stocks have market caps well below $100 million (some as low as $10–$15 million), and should be used only by investors who fully understand the risks involved and can tolerate such risk exposure.

Of the three major categories, the large-cap stocks are the real biggies—the Wal-Marts, GEs, and Microsofts of the world. Many of these are considered to be blue-chip stocks, and, although there are far fewer large-cap stocks than any of the other market cap categories, these companies account for about 80 to 90 percent of the total value of all U.S. equity markets. Just because they're big, however, doesn't mean they're better. Indeed, both the small- and mid-cap segments of the market tend to hold their own with, or even outperform, large stocks over time.

Mid-cap stocks are a special breed that offers investors some very attractive return opportunities. They provide much of the sizzle of small-stock returns, but without all the price volatility. At the same time, because these are fairly good-sized companies, and many of them have been around for a long time, they offer some of the safety of the big, established stocks. Among the ranks of the mid-caps are such well-known companies as Tootsie Roll, Barnes & Noble, Petsmart, Liz Claiborne, and the Cheesecake Factory, in addition to some not-so-well-known names. Although these securities offer a nice alternative to large stocks without all the drawbacks and uncertainties of small-caps, they're probably most appropriate for investors who are willing to tolerate a bit more risk and price volatility.

Some investors consider small companies to be in a class by themselves. They believe these firms' stocks hold especially attractive return opportunities—and in many cases, this has turned out to be true. Known as **small-cap stocks,** these companies generally have annual revenues of less than $250 million; because of their size, spurts of growth can dramatically affect their earnings and stock prices. Sanderson Farms, K-Swiss, Jos. A. Bank Clothiers, Pier 1 Imports, and Tuesday Morning are just some of the better-known small-cap stocks. Now although some small-caps (Sanderson Farms, for example) are solid companies with equally solid financials, that's definitely not the case with most of them! Because many of these companies are so small, they don't have a lot of stock outstanding, and their shares aren't widely traded. What's more, small company stocks have a tendency to be "here today and gone tomorrow." Some of these stocks may hold the potential for high returns, but investors should also be aware of the very high risk exposure that comes with many of them.

Market Globalization and Foreign Stocks

Besides investing in many of the different types of stocks already mentioned, a growing number of American investors are turning to foreign markets as a way to earn attractive returns. Ironically, as our world is becoming smaller, our universe of investment opportunities is growing by leaps and bounds! Consider, for example, that in 1970 the U.S. stock market accounted for fully *two-thirds of the world market*. In essence, our stock market was twice

mid-cap stock A stock whose total market value falls somewhere between $1 billion and $4 or $5 billion.

small-cap stock A stock with a total market value of less than $1 billion.

as big as all the rest of the world's stock markets *combined*. That's no longer true, for in 2005 the U.S. share of the world equity market had dropped to less than 50 percent.

Foreign stocks can offer not only attractive return opportunities, but because the returns in most foreign markets are not highly correlated with ours, they can also add some stability (reduced risk) to investor portfolios. Among the various ways of investing in foreign shares, two stand out: mutual funds and American Depository Shares (ADSs). Without a doubt, the best and easiest way to invest in foreign markets is through *international mutual funds* (we'll discuss such funds in Chapter 13). An alternative to mutual funds is to buy *ADSs (or American Depository Shares)*. ADSs (or ADRs, as they're also known) are *denominated in dollars and are traded directly on U.S. markets* (like the NYSE). They're just like common stock, except that each ADS represents a specific number of shares in a specific foreign company. The shares of more than 1,000 companies from some 50 foreign countries are traded on U.S. exchanges as ADSs—companies like Sony, Nestlé, Ericsson Telephone, Nokia, Teva Pharmaceuticals, Norsk Hydro, Huaneng Powers, and Grupo Televisa, to mention just a few. ADSs are a great way to invest in foreign stocks because their prices are quoted in dollars, not British pounds, Swiss francs, or euros. What's more, all dividends are paid in dollars.

Investing in Common Stock

There are three basic reasons for investing in common stock: (1) to use the stock as a warehouse of value, (2) to accumulate capital, and (3) to provide a source of income. Storage of value is important to all investors, because nobody likes to lose money. However, some investors are more concerned about it than others, and they put safety of principal first in their stock selection process. These investors are more quality conscious and tend to gravitate toward blue chips and other low-risk securities. Accumulation of capital generally is an important goal to individuals with long-term investment horizons. These investors use the capital gains and dividends that stocks provide to build up their wealth. Some use growth stocks for such purposes; others do it with income shares; still others use a little of both. Finally, some people use stocks as a source of income; to them, a dependable flow of dividends is essential. High-yielding, good-quality income shares are usually their preferred investment vehicle.

Advantages and Disadvantages of Stock Ownership

Ownership of common stock has both advantages and disadvantages. Its advantages are threefold. First, the potential returns, in the form of both dividend income and price appreciation, can be substantial. Second, many stocks are actively traded (there are literally thousands of such actively traded stocks), making them a highly liquid form of investment—meaning they can be quickly bought and sold. Finally, they involve no direct management (or unusual management problems), and market/company information is usually widely published and readily available.

Risk, the problem of timing purchases and sales, and the uncertainty of dividends are all disadvantages of common stock ownership. Although potential common stock returns may be high, the risk and uncertainty associated with the actual receipt of that return is also great. Even though careful selection of stocks may reduce the amount of risk to which the investor is exposed, the risk-return trade-off still exists. In other words, high returns on common stock are not guaranteed; they may or may not occur depending on numerous economic, industry, and company factors. When it comes to common stock, not even dividends are guaranteed. If things turn bad, the company can always shut off the stream of dividends, and with no legal ramifications. Finally, there's the timing of purchases and sales—human nature being what it is, we don't always do it right. Take a common stock that's loaded with uncertainty, add in our lack of accurate foresight, and you have the perfect recipe for making mistakes. Unfortunately, all too many investors purchase a stock, hold it for a period of time during which the price drops, and then sell it below the original purchase price—that is, at a loss. The proper strategy, of course, is to buy low and sell high; but the problem of predicting price movements makes it difficult to implement such a plan.

Making the Investment Decision

The first step in investing is to know *where* to put your money; the second is to know *when* to make your moves. The first question basically involves matching your risk and return objectives with the available investment vehicles. Essentially, *a stock (or any investment vehicle for that matter) should be considered a viable investment candidate only as long as it promises to generate a sufficiently attractive rate of return* and, in particular, one that fully compensates you for any risks you have to take. Thus, if you're considering the purchase of a stock, you should expect to earn more than what you can get from T-bills or high-grade corporate bonds. The reason: stocks are riskier than bills or bonds, so you deserve more return. Indeed, if you can't get enough return from the security to offset the risk, then you shouldn't invest in the stock!

Putting a Value on Stock

No matter what kind of investor you are or what your investment objectives happen to be, sooner or later you'll have to face one of the most difficult questions in the field of investments: *How much are you willing to pay for the stock*? To answer this question, you have to put a value on the stock. As noted earlier in this chapter, we know that the value of a stock depends on its expected stream of future earnings. Once you have a handle on the expected stream of future earnings, you can use that information to find the *expected rate of return on the investment*. If the expected return from the investment exceeds your desired or minimum rate of return, you should make the investment—in effect, you should be willing to pay the current or prevailing market price. If the return you expect from the investment is less than your desired rate of return, you should not buy the stock (at its current market price) because it's currently "overpriced," so you won't be able to earn your desired rate of return.

So, how do you go about finding a stock that's right for you? The answer is by doing a little digging and crunching a few numbers. Here's what you'd want to do: First, find a company you like and then take a look at how it has performed *over the past 3 to 5 years*. Find out what kind of growth rate (in sales) it has experienced, if it has a strong ROE and has been able to maintain or improve its profit margin, how much it has been paying out to stockholders in the form of dividends, and so forth. This kind of information is readily available in publications like *Value Line* and *S&P Stock Reports* (which we discussed in Chapter 11) or online at a number of sites. The idea is to find stocks that are financially strong, have done well in the past, and continue to be market leaders or hold prominent positions in a given industry or market segment. Looking at the past is only the beginning, however; what's really important to stock valuation is the *future!*

So, let's turn our attention to the expected future performance of a stock. The idea is to assess the *outlook* for the stock, thereby *gaining some insight about the benefits to be derived from investing in it*. Of particular concern are future dividends and share price behavior. As a rule, it doesn't make much sense to go out more than 2 or 3 years—5, at the most—because the accuracy of most forecasts begins to deteriorate rapidly after that. So, using a 3-year investment horizon, you'd want to forecast annual dividends per share for each of the next 3 years, *plus* the future price of the stock at the end of the 3-year holding period (obviously, if the stock price is projected to go up over time, you'll have some capital gains). You can try to generate these forecasts yourself, or you can look to a publication like *Value Line* to obtain projections (*Value Line* projects dividends and share prices 3 to 5 years into the future). After projecting dividends and share price, you can use the approximate yield equation, or a handheld calculator, to determine the expected return from the investment.

Crunching the Numbers. To see how that can be done, consider the common shares of Nike, Inc., the world's leading designer and marketer of high-quality athletic footwear, apparel, and accessories. According to several financial reporting services, the company has very strong financials; its sales have been growing at around 10 to 12 percent per year for the past 5 years, it has a net profit margin of more than 10 percent, and its ROE is around 27 percent. Thus, historically, the company has performed well and is definitely a market leader in its field. In March of 2006, the stock was trading at around $85 a share and was paying annual dividends at the rate of $1.24 a share. One major financial service was projecting dividends to go up to about $1.65 a share within the next 3 to 5 years; they were also estimating the price of the stock could rise to as high as $140 a share within 3 years.

Using the projections obtained above, and given current dividends (in 2006) of $1.24 a share, we could expect dividends of, say, $1.38 a share next year (2007), $1.50 a share the year after (2008), and $1.65 a share in 2009—assuming, of course, that dividends do in fact grow as estimated. Now, because the approximate yield equation uses "average annual current income" as one of the inputs, let's use the midpoint of our projected dividends ($1.50 a share) as a proxy for average annual dividends. Because this stock is currently trading at $85 a share, has a projected future price of $140 a share, and we have a 3-year investment horizon, we can find our expected return as follows:

$$\text{Approximate yield (Expected return)} = \frac{\$1.50 + \left[\dfrac{\$140 - \$85}{3}\right]}{\left[\dfrac{\$140 + \$85}{2}\right]}$$

$$= \frac{\$1.50 + \$18.33}{\$112.50} = \underline{17.63\%}$$

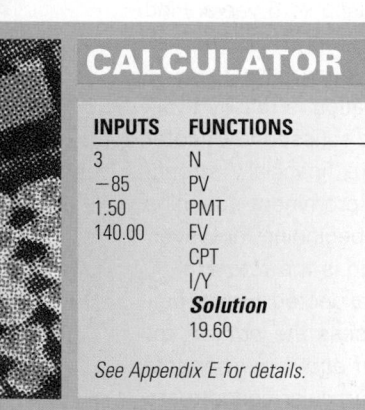

CALCULATOR

INPUTS	FUNCTIONS
3	N
−85	PV
1.50	PMT
140.00	FV
	CPT
	I/Y
	Solution
	19.60

See Appendix E for details.

Calculator Keystrokes. You can use a handheld financial calculator—set in the *annual compounding mode*—to find the expected return on a stock that you purchase at $85 a share, hold for 3 years (during which time you receive average annual dividends of $1.50 a share), and then sell at $140 per share. Simply use the keystrokes shown in the margin, where

N = number of *years* you hold the stock
PV = the price you pay for the stock (entered as a *negative* value)
PMT = average amount of dividends received each *year*
FV = the price you expect to receive when you sell the stock (in 3 years)

The expected return (of 19.6 percent) is a bit higher here, but even so, it's still reasonably close to the return we computed using the approximate yield method (of 17.6 percent).

Thus, if Nike's stocks performs as expected, it should give us a return of around 18 or 19 percent. In today's market, that would be a very attractive return, and one that likely will *exceed* our required rate of return (which probably should be around 12 to 15 percent). If that's the case, then this stock most definitely *should* be considered a viable investment candidate. According to our standards, the stock is currently undervalued and thus, should be seriously considered as a possible addition to our portfolio.

The Investment Club Approach to Stock Valuation

BetterInvesting (formerly known as the National Association of Investors Corporation) functions as the organizational and educational clearinghouse for the thousands of *investment clubs* scattered all over the United States. Its mission is to provide sound investment information, education, and support to its nearly 200,000 members, who collectively belong to some 18,000 investment clubs nationwide. Among the many investment products and services that BetterInvesting makes available to investors are a number of *stock valuation worksheets*. The procedures used in these worksheets are similar to those we described earlier, except they employ a set 5-year investment horizon, and the user follows a formatted series of steps to come up with a value for the stock. For example, the *Stock Selection Worksheet* is broken into five parts: (1) a graphic analysis of sales, earnings, and price; (2) an evaluation of management; (3) a price-earnings history; (4) an evaluation of the stock's risk-reward; and (5) the stock's 5-year potential. It's an informative guide for the beginning investor, covering all the key elements of stock valuation in a single, (relatively) simple-to-use worksheet. Essentially, it takes the stock's appreciation potential over a 5-year period and adds that to its dividend yield to arrive at the stock's expected return. Thus, it looks at both forecasted dividends and capital gains as the foundation of its stock valuation process. To obtain one of these worksheets, go to the *BetterInvesting* Web site at **http://www.betterinvesting.org,** click on "Stocks," then "Software/ Worksheets," and pick one (or more) of their *Stock Evaluation Worksheets*—you have four worksheets to choose from, including the Stock Check List, Selection Guide, Selection Guide & Report, and Comparison Guide. And while you're there, you might also want to look at their Portfolio Management Worksheets.

Timing Your Investments

Once you find a stock that you think will give you the kind of return you're looking for, you're ready to deal with the matter of timing your investment. As long as the prospects for the market and the economy are positive, the time may be right to invest in stocks. On the other hand, sometimes investing in stocks makes no sense at all. In particular, *don't* invest in stocks if:

- You feel *very strongly* that the market is headed down in the short run. If you're absolutely certain the market's in for a big fall (or will continue to fall, if it's already doing so), then wait until the market drops, and buy the stock when it's cheaper.
- You feel uncomfortable with the general tone of the market—it lacks direction, or there's way too much price volatility to suit you. For example, this became a problem before and after the October 1987 crash, when computer-assisted trading started taking over the market. The result was a stock market that behaved more like a commodities market, with an intolerable amount of price volatility. When this happens, fundamentals go out the window, and the market simply becomes too risky. In this case, do what the pros do, and wait it out on the sidelines. (See the *Money in Action* box on our Web site **http://www.thomsonedu.com/finance/gitman** for suggestions on deciding when to *sell* a stock.)

Be Sure to Plow Back Your Earnings

Unless you're living off the income, the basic investment objective with stocks is the same as it is with any other security: to earn an attractive, fully compounded rate of return. This requires regular reinvestment of dividend income. And there's no better way to accomplish such reinvestment than through a **dividend reinvestment plan (DRP).** The basic investment philosophy at work here is that if the company is good enough to invest in, it's good enough to reinvest in. In a dividend reinvestment plan, shareholders can sign up to have their cash dividends automatically reinvested in additional shares of the company's common stock—in essence, it's like taking your cash dividends in the form of more shares of common stock. The idea is to put your money to work by building up your investment in the stock. Such an approach can have a tremendous impact on your investment position over time, as seen in Exhibit 12.5.

Today, over 1,000 companies (including most major corporations) have DRPs, and each one gives investors a convenient and inexpensive way to accumulate capital. Stocks in most DRPs are acquired free of any brokerage commissions, and most plans allow *partial participation*. That is, rather than committing all their cash dividends to

dividend reinvestment plan (DRP) A program whereby stockholders can choose to take their cash dividends in the form of more shares of the company's stock.

EXHIBIT 12.5   Cash or Reinvested Dividends

Participating in a dividend reinvestment plan is a simple yet highly effective way of building up capital over time. Over the long haul, it can prove to be a great way of earning a fully compounded rate of return on your money.

Situation: Buy 100 shares of stock at $25 a share (total investment $2,500); stock currently pays $1 a share in annual dividends. Price of the stock increases at 8 percent per year; dividends grow at 5 percent per year.

Investment Period	Number of Shares Held	Market Value of Stock Holdings	Total Cash Dividends Received
Take Dividends in Cash			
5 years	100	$ 3,672	$ 552
10 years	100	$ 5,397	$1,258
15 years	100	$ 7,930	$2,158
20 years	100	$11,652	$3,307
Participate in a DRP			
5 years	115.59	$ 4,245	$0
10 years	135.66	$ 7,322	$0
15 years	155.92	$12,364	$0
20 years	176.00	$20,508	$0

these plans, participants may specify a portion of their shares for dividend reinvestment and receive cash dividends on the rest. Some plans even sell stocks to their DRP investors at below-market prices—often at discounts of 3 to 5 percent. Most plans also credit fractional shares to the investors' accounts. Shareholders can join these plans simply by sending the company a completed authorization form. Once in the plan, the number of shares you hold will begin to accumulate with each dividend date. There's a catch, how-ever—even though these dividends take the form of additional shares of stock, *reinvested dividends are taxable, in the year they're received, just as if they had been received in cash.*

❚❚ Concept Check

CHECK • CONCEPT CHECK • CONCEPT CHECK • CONCEPT CHECK • CONCEPT CHECK • CONCEPT CHECK • CONCEPT

12-6 From a tax perspective, would it make any difference to an investor whether the return on a stock took the form of dividends or capital gains? Explain.

12-7 What's the difference between a cash dividend and a *stock dividend?* Which would you rather receive?

12-8 Define and briefly discuss each of these common stock measures: (a) *book value,* (b) *ROE,* (c) *earnings per share* (EPS), (d) *price/earnings (P/E) ratio,* and (e) *beta.*

12-9 Briefly discuss some of the different types of common stock. Which types would be most appealing to you, and why?

12-10 What are *dividend reinvestment plans,* and how do they fit into a stock invest-ment program?

In contrast to stocks, *bonds are liabilities*—they're nothing more than publicly traded IOUs where the bondholders are actually *lending money* to the issuer. Bonds are often referred to as *fixed-income securities* because the debt service obligations of the issuer are fixed— that is, the issuing organization agrees to pay a *fixed amount of interest periodically and to repay a fixed amount of principal at or before maturity*. Bonds normally have face values of $1,000 or $5,000, and maturities of 10 to 30 years or more.

Why Invest in Bonds?

Like many other types of investment vehicles, bonds provide investors with two kinds of income: (1) They provide a generous amount of current income, and (2) they can often be used to generate substantial amounts of capital gains. The current income, of course, is derived from the interest payments received periodically over the life of the issue. Indeed, this regular and highly predictable source of income is a key factor that draws investors to bonds. But these securities can also produce capital gains, which occurs whenever market interest rates fall. A basic trading rule in the bond market is that *interest rates and bond prices move in opposite directions:* when interest rates rise, bond prices fall; and when they drop, bond prices rise. Thus, it's possible to buy bonds at one price and, if interest rate conditions are right, to sell them sometime later at a higher price. Of course, it's also possible to incur a capital loss should market rates move against the investor. Taken together, the current income and capital gains earned from bonds can lead to highly competitive investor returns.

Bonds are also a highly versatile investment outlet. They can be used conservatively by those who seek high current income, or aggressively by those who actively go after capital gains. Although bonds have long been considered as attractive investments by those going after high levels of current income, it's only been since the advent of volatile interest rates that they've also become recognized for their capital gains potential and as trading vehicles. Finally, because of the general high quality of many bond issues, they can also be used for the preservation and long-term accumulation of capital. In fact, some individuals, regularly and over the long haul, commit all or a good deal of their investment funds to bonds because of this single attribute.

Bonds versus Stocks

Although bonds definitely do have their good points—low risk and high levels of current income, along with *desirable diversification properties*—they also have a significant downside: their *comparative* returns. The fact is, *relative to stocks*, there's a big sacrifice in returns when investing in bonds—which, of course, is the price you pay for the even bigger reduction in risk! But just because there's a deficit in long-term returns, it doesn't mean that bonds are always the underachievers. Consider, for example, what's happened over the past 20 years or so: Starting in the 1980s, fixed-income securities held their own and continued to do so through the early 1990s, only to fall far behind for the rest of the decade. But then along came a nasty bear market in stocks (2000–2002) and the impact was nothing short of spectacular. The net results of all this can be seen in Exhibit 12.6, which tracks the comparative returns of stocks (via the S&P 500) and bonds (using the Lehman Bros. Long Bond Index) from 1996 through 2005. While bonds held up pretty well over the first half of the 1990s, by 1996, stocks were clearly beginning to outpace bonds by ever-increasing margins. And the spread continued to widen through early 2000; so much so, in fact, that for the decade as a whole (January 1990 through December 1999), long-term bonds produced average annual returns of 8.7 percent, whereas stocks turned in average returns of 18.2 percent. That difference meant that a $10,000 investment in bonds would have led to a terminal value of some $23,000, versus more than $53,000 for stocks.

That's a high opportunity cost to pay for holding bonds, and it prompted some market observers to question whether bonds should have *any place at all* in an investment portfolio.

EXHIBIT 12.6 | Comparative Performance of Stocks and Bonds: 1996–2005

This graph shows what happened to $10,000 invested in bonds over the 10-year period from January 1996 through December 2005, versus the same amount invested in stocks. Clearly, while stocks held a commanding lead through early 2000, the ensuing bear market erased virtually all of that. As a result, stocks and bonds finished the period at ending (or "terminal") values that were less than $3,500 apart.

Avg. Annual Returns	Amt. to which a $10,000 investment will grow
STOCKS	
9.07 %	$23,831
BONDS	
7.44 %	$20,489

Source: *Morningstar Principia for Mutual Funds,* December 31, 2005.

FINANCIAL ROAD SIGN

WHO NEEDS LONG BONDS?

As a rule, you'd expect longer-term bonds to provide higher yields, and they usually do. But that doesn't necessarily mean they're the best investment. It's long been common knowledge in the bond market that for most individual investors, intermediate-term bonds is the place to be. The reason: *Intermediate-term bonds (those with maturities of 7 to 10 years) typically deliver about 80 percent, or more, of the returns obtained from long bonds (with maturities of 25 to 30 years), but at roughly half the risk.* The perfect risk-return trade-off: you give up a little return for a much bigger cut in risk.

They reasoned that since market interest rates had dropped so low, bonds really didn't have much to offer, other than relatively low returns. But the market experts overlooked one tiny detail: it wasn't bonds that would prove to be the problem, it was stocks! For, as Exhibit 12.6 shows, the bear market had such a devastating effect on stocks that by 2003, the differential returns between these two segments of the market all but evaporated. Indeed, over the 10-year period from January 1996 through December 2005, stocks outperformed bonds by only 1.6 percentage points (9.07 percent versus 7.44 percent). The net result was a terminal value of just over $23,800 for stocks, compared to nearly $20,500 for bonds.

Most investors would agree that's a very low price to pay for *the level of stability that bonds bring to a portfolio!* The fact is, bond returns are far more stable than stock returns, and they possess *excellent portfolio diversification properties.* Except for the most aggressive of investors, bonds can contribute a lot to your portfolio. As a general rule, adding bonds to a portfolio will—*up to a point*—have a much bigger impact on (lowering) risk than it will on return! Face it: you don't buy bonds for their high returns (except when you think interest rates are heading down); rather, you buy them for their current income and the stability they bring to a portfolio. And that's still true, even today.

Basic Issue Characteristics

A bond is a negotiable, long-term debt instrument that carries certain obligations on the part of the issuer. Unlike the holders of common stock, bondholders have no ownership or equity position in the issuing firm or organization. This is so because bonds are debt, and the bondholders, in a roundabout way, are only lending money to the issuer.

As a rule, bonds pay interest every 6 months. The amount of interest paid is a function of the **coupon,** which defines the annual interest that the issuer will pay to the bond-holder. For instance, a $1,000 bond with an 8 percent coupon would pay $80 in interest every year ($1,000 × .08 = $80), generally in the form of two $40 semiannual payments. The principal amount of a bond, also known as *par value*, specifies the amount of capital that must be repaid at maturity—so there's $1,000 of principal in a $1,000 bond.

Of course, debt securities regularly trade at market prices that differ from their principal (or par) values. This occurs whenever an issue's coupon differs from the prevailing market rate of interest; in essence, the price of an issue will change until its yield is compatible with prevailing market yields. Such behavior explains why a 7 percent issue will carry a market price of only $825 when the market yield is 9 percent; the drop in price is necessary to raise the yield on this bond from 7 percent to 9 percent. Issues with market values lower than par are known as *discount bonds* and carry coupons that are less than those on new issues. In contrast, issues with market values above par are called *premium bonds* and have coupons greater than those currently being offered on new issues.

Types of Issues

A single issuer may have any number of bonds outstanding at a given time. In addition to their coupons and maturities, bonds can be differentiated from one another by the type of collateral behind them. In this regard, the issues can be viewed as having either junior or senior standing. *Senior bonds are secured obligations*, because they're backed by a legal claim on some specific property of the issuer that acts as *collateral* for the bonds. Such issues include **mortgage bonds,** which are secured by real estate, and **equipment trust certificates,** which are backed by certain types of equipment and are popular with railroads and airlines. *Junior bonds*, on the other hand, are backed only with a promise by the issuer to pay interest and principal on a timely basis. There are several classes of *unsecured* bonds, the most popular of which is known as a **debenture.** Issued as either notes (with maturities of 2 to 10 years) or bonds (maturities of more than 10 years), debentures are totally unsecured in the sense that there's no collateral backing them up—other than the issuer's good name. But in the final analysis, even in the world of corporate finance, that's all that matters!

Sinking Fund

Another provision that's important to investors is the **sinking fund,** which stipulates how a bond will be paid off over time. Not all bonds have these requirements; but for those that do, a sinking fund specifies the annual repayment schedule to be used in paying off the issue and indicates how much principal will be retired each year. Sinking fund requirements generally begin 1 to 5 years after the date of issue and continue annually thereafter until all or most of the issue has been paid off. Any amount not repaid by maturity (which might equal 10 to 25 percent of the issue) is then retired with a single balloon payment.

Call Feature

Every bond has a **call feature,** which stipulates whether a bond can be called (that is, retired) before its regularly scheduled maturity date and, if so, under what conditions. Basically, there are three types of call features:

- A bond can be *freely callable*, which means the issuer can prematurely retire the bond at any time.
- A bond can be *noncallable*, which means the issuer is prohibited from retiring the bond prior to maturity.

coupon Feature on a bond that defines the annual interest income the issuer will pay the bondholder.

mortgage bond A bond secured by a claim on real assets, such as a manufacturing plant.

equipment trust certificate A bond secured by certain types of equipment, such as railroad cars and airplanes.

debenture An unsecured bond issued on the general credit of the firm.

sinking fund A bond provision specifying the annual repayment schedule to be used in paying off the issue.

call feature A feature included in bond issues that allows the issuer to retire the security prior to maturity.

- The issue could carry a *deferred call*, which means the issue cannot be called until after a certain length of time has passed from the date of issue. In essence, the issue is noncallable during the deferment period and then becomes freely callable thereafter.

Call features are normally used to replace an issue with one that carries a lower coupon; in this way, the issuer benefits by being able to realize a reduction in annual interest cost. In an attempt to compensate investors who have their bonds called out from under them, a *call premium* (usually equal to about 6 months to 1 year of interest) is tacked onto the par value of the bond and paid to investors, along with the issue's par value, at the time the bond is called. For example, if a company decides to call its 12 percent bonds some 15 years before they mature, it might have to pay $1,090 for every $1,000 bond outstanding (a call premium equal to 9 months' interest—$120 × .75 = $90—would be added to the par value of $1,000).

Although this might sound like a good deal, it's really not. The only party that benefits from a bond refunding is the issuer. The bondholder may indeed get a few extra bucks when the bond is called; but in turn, she loses a source of high current income—for example, the investor may have a 10 percent bond called away at a time when the best she can do in the market is maybe 7 or 8 percent. To avoid this, stick with bonds that are either *noncallable* or that have long *call-deferment periods*, meaning they can't be called for refunding (or any other purpose) until the call-deferment period ends.

The Bond Market

One thing that really stands out about the bond market is its size—the U.S. bond market is huge and getting bigger almost daily. Indeed, from a $250 billion dollar market in 1950, it has grown to the point where, in 2006, the amount of bonds outstanding in this country exceeded $25 *trillion*! Given such size, it's not surprising that today's bond market offers securities to meet just about any type of investment objective and suit virtually any type of investor, no matter how conservative or aggressive. For convenience, the bond market is usually divided into four segments, according to type of issuer: Treasury, agency, municipal, and corporate.

Treasury Bonds

Treasury bonds (sometimes called *Treasuries* or *governments*) are a dominant force in the bond market and, if not the most popular, certainly are the best known. The U.S. Treasury issues bonds, notes, and other types of debt securities (such as the Treasury bills discussed in Chapter 4) as a means of meeting the federal government's ever-increasing needs. All Treasury obligations are of the highest quality (backed by the full faith and credit of the U.S. government), a feature that, along with their liquidity, makes them extremely popular with individual and institutional investors, both here and abroad. U.S. Treasury securities are traded in all of the world's major markets, from New York to London to Tokyo.

Treasury notes are issued with maturities of 2, 3, 5, and 10 years, whereas *Treasury bonds* carry 20- and 30-year maturities. (Note that while the Treasury is authorized to issue these securities, it hasn't issued 20-year bonds in over 20 years [the last one came out in January 1986]; and only recently, in February 2006, did it resume issuing 30-year bonds.) The Treasury issues its securities at regularly scheduled auctions, the results of which are widely reported by the financial media. It's through this auction process that the Treasury establishes the initial yields and coupons on the securities it issues. All Treasury notes and bonds are sold in minimum denominations of $1,000, and although interest income is subject to normal federal income tax, *it is exempt from state and local taxes*. Also, the Treasury today issues only *noncallable* securities—the last time the U.S. Treasury issued callable debt was in 1984.

In 1997, the Treasury began issuing its newest security, the **Treasury inflation-indexed bond,** or **TIPS** as they're also known, which stands for "Treasury Inflation-Protected Securities." These securities—which are issued with maturities, of 5, 10, or 20 years—give investors the opportunity to stay ahead of inflation by periodically adjusting their returns for any inflation that has occurred. That is, if inflation is running at an annual rate of, say, 3 percent, then at the end of the year the par (or maturity) value of your bond will increase by 3 percent (actually, the adjustments to par value are done every 6 months). Thus,

Treasury bond A U.S. Treasury obligation that has a maturity of more than 10 years and pays interest semi-annually.

Treasury inflation-indexed bond (TIPS) A type of Treasury security that provides protection against inflation by adjusting investor returns for the annual rate of inflation.

the $1,000 par value will grow to $1,030 at the end of the first year and, if the 3 percent inflation rate continues for the second year, the par value will once again move up, this time from $1,030 to $1,061 (or $1,030 × 1.03). Unfortunately, the coupons on these securities are set very low, as they're meant to provide investors with so-called *real (inflation-adjusted) returns*. So one of these bonds might carry a coupon of only 3¹/₂ percent (when regular T-bonds are paying, say, 6¹/₂ or 7 percent). But there's an upside even to this: the actual *size of the coupon payment will increase over time as the par value on the bond goes up*. For investors who are concerned about inflation protection, these securities may be just the ticket.

Agency Bonds

Agency bonds are an important segment of the U.S. bond market. Although issued by political subdivisions of the U.S. government, *these securities are not obligations of the U.S. Treasury*. An important feature of these securities is that they customarily provide yields comfortably above the market rates for Treasuries and, therefore, offer investors a way to increase returns with little or no real difference in risk. Some actively traded and widely quoted agency issues include those sold by the Federal Farm Credit Bank, the Federal National Mortgage Association (or "Fannie Maes," as they're more commonly known), the Federal Land Bank, the Student Loan Marketing Association, and the Federal Home Loan Bank. Although these issues aren't the direct obligations of the U.S. government, some actually do carry government guarantees and thus effectively represent the full faith and credit of the U.S. Treasury. Moreover, some have unusual interest-payment provisions (interest is paid monthly in a few instances and yearly in one case), and, in some cases, the interest is exempt from state and local taxes.

Municipal Bonds

Municipal bonds are the issues of states, counties, cities, and other political subdivisions, such as school districts and water and sewer districts. They're unlike other bonds in that their interest income is usually free from federal income tax (which is why these issues are known as *tax-free bonds*). Note, however, that the same tax-free status does not apply to any capital gains that may be earned on these securities—that is, such gains are subject to the usual federal taxes. A tax-free yield is probably the most important feature of municipal bonds and is certainly a major reason why individuals invest in them. Exhibit 12.7 shows what a taxable bond (like a Treasury issue) would have to yield to equal the take-home yield of a tax-free municipal bond. It demonstrates how the yield attractiveness of municipal bonds varies with an investor's income level; clearly, the higher the individual's tax bracket, the more attractive municipal bonds become.

agency bond An obligation of a political subdivision of the U.S. government.

municipal bond A bond issued by state or local governments; interest income is usually exempt from federal taxes.

EXHIBIT 12.7   Table of Taxable Equivalent Yields

Tax-exempt securities generally yield less than fully taxable obligations; because of that, you have to be in a sufficiently high tax bracket (25 percent or more) to make up for the yield shortfall.

	TO MATCH A TAX-FREE YIELD OF:					
	5%	6%	7%	8%	9%	10%
Tax Bracket*	**You Must Earn This Yield on a Taxable Investment:**					
10%	5.55%	6.66%	7.77%	8.88%	10.00%	11.11%
15	5.88	7.06	8.24	9.41	10.59	11.76
25	6.67	8.00	9.33	10.67	12.00	13.33
28	6.94	8.33	9.72	11.11	12.50	13.89
33	7.46	8.96	10.45	11.94	13.43	14.92
35	7.69	9.23	10.77	12.31	13.85	15.38

*Federal tax rates in effect on January 1, 2006.

As a rule, the yields on municipal bonds are (almost always) lower than the returns available from fully taxable issues. So unless the tax effect is sufficient to raise the yield on a municipal to a level that equals or exceeds the yields on taxable issues, it obviously doesn't make sense to buy municipal bonds. You can determine the return a fully taxable bond would have to provide in order to match the after-tax return on a lower-yielding tax-free issue by computing what's known as a municipal's *fully taxable equivalent yield:*

$$\text{Fully taxable equivalent yield} = \frac{\text{Yield on municipal bond}}{1 - \text{Tax rate}}$$

For example, if a certain municipal bond offered a yield of 6 percent, an individual in the maximum 35 percent federal tax bracket would have to find a fully taxable bond with a yield of more than 9 percent to reap the same after-tax return: that is, 6 percent / (1 − .35) = 6 percent / .65 = 9.23 percent.

Municipal bonds are generally issued as **serial obligations,** meaning that the issue is broken into a series of smaller bonds, each with its own maturity date and coupon rate. Thus, instead of the bond having just one maturity date 20 years from now, it will have a series of, say, 20 maturity dates over the 20-year time frame. Because such a diversity of municipal bonds is available, investors must also be careful to assess their quality to ensure that the issuer won't default. Although it may not seem that municipal issuers would default on either interest or principal payments, it does occur! Investors should be especially cautious when investing in **revenue bonds,** which are municipal bonds serviced from the income generated by specific income-producing projects, such as toll roads. Unlike issuers of so-called **general obligation bonds**—which are backed by the full faith and credit of the municipality—the issuer of a revenue bond is obligated to pay principal and interest *only if a sufficient level of revenue* is generated. General obligation municipal bonds, in contrast, are required to be serviced in a prompt and timely fashion regardless of the level of tax income generated by the municipality.

Corporate Bonds

The major nongovernmental issuers of bonds are corporations. The market for **corporate bonds** is customarily subdivided into several segments, which include *industrials* (the most diverse of the group), *public utilities* (the dominant group in terms of volume of new issues), *rail and transportation bonds*, and *financial issues* (banks, finance companies, and so forth). The corporate bond market offers the widest range of issue types. There are *first mortgage bonds, convertible bonds* (discussed below), *debentures, subordinated debentures*, and *income bonds*, to mention just a few. Interest on corporate bonds is paid semiannually, and sinking funds are common. The bonds usually come in $1,000 denominations and are issued on a term basis with a single maturity date. Maturities usually range from 5 to 10 years, up to 30 years or more. Many of the issues—particularly the longer-term bonds—carry call provisions that prohibit prepayment of the issue during the first 5 to 10 years. Corporate issues are popular with individuals because of their relatively high yields.

The Special Appeal of Zero Coupon Bonds

In addition to the standard bond vehicles already described, investors can also choose from several types of *specialty issues*—bonds that, for the most part, have unusual coupon or repayment provisions. That's certainly the case with **zero coupon bonds,** which, as the name implies, are bonds issued without coupons. To compensate for their lack of coupons, these bonds are sold at a deep discount from their par values and then increase in value over time, at a compound rate of return, so at maturity they're worth much more than their initial investment. Other things being equal, the cheaper the bond, the greater the return you can earn (for example, whereas a 10 percent bond might sell for $239, an issue with a 6 percent yield will cost a lot more—say, $417).

Because they have no coupons, these bonds pay nothing to the investor until they mature. In this regard, zero coupon bonds are like the Series EE savings bonds we discussed in Chapter 4. Strange as it may seem, this is the main attraction of zero coupon bonds. Because there are no interest payments, investors need not worry about reinvest-

serial obligation An issue that is broken down into a series of smaller bonds, each with its own maturity date and coupon rate.

revenue bond A municipal bond serviced from the income generated by a specific project.

general obligation bond A municipal bond backed by the full faith and credit of the issuing municipality.

corporate bond A bond issued by a corporation.

zero coupon bond A bond that pays no annual interest but sells at a deep discount to its par value.

ing coupon income twice a year; instead, the fully compounded rate of return on a zero coupon bond is virtually guaranteed at the rate that existed when the issue was purchased. For example, in early 2006, good-grade (corporate) zero coupon bonds with 20-year maturities were available at yields of around 8 percent; thus, for just a little over $200, investors could buy a bond that would be worth five times that amount, or $1,000, when it matures in 20 years. Best of all, they would be *locking in* an 8 percent compound rate of return on their investment capital for the full 20-year life of the issue. Because of their unusual tax exposure (even though the bonds don't pay regular yearly interest, the IRS treats the annually accrued interest as taxable income), zeros should be used only in tax-sheltered investments, such as individual retirement accounts (IRAs), or be held by minor children who are likely to be taxed at low rates, if at all.

Zeros are issued by corporations, municipalities, and federal agencies; you can even buy U.S. Treasury notes and bonds in the form of zero coupon securities. During the 1980s, major brokerage houses packaged U.S. Treasury securities as zeros and sold them to the investing public in the form of unit investment trusts. These securities became so popular with investors that the Treasury decided to eliminate the middleman and "issue" its own form of zero coupon bond, known as *Treasury STRIPS*, or *STRIP-Ts*, for short. Actually, the Treasury doesn't issue zero coupon bonds; instead, *they allow government securities dealers to take regular coupon-bearing notes and bonds in stripped form*, which can then be sold to the public as zero coupon securities. Essentially, the coupons are stripped from the bond, repackaged, and then sold separately as zero coupon bonds. For example, a 10-year Treasury bond has 20 semiannual coupon payments, plus one principal payment—each of these 21 cash flows can be repackaged and sold as 21 different zero coupon securities, with maturities ranging from 6 months to 10 years.

Convertible Bonds

Another popular type of specialty issue is the convertible bond. Found only in the corporate market, these issues are a type of *hybrid security* because they possess the features of both corporate bonds and common stocks. That is, they're initially issued as debentures (i.e., unsecured debt) but carry the provision that, within a stipulated time period, *they may be converted into a certain number of shares of the issuing company's common stock.*

The key element of any convertible issue is its **conversion privilege,** which stipulates the conditions and specific nature of the conversion feature. First, it states exactly when the bond can be converted. Sometimes there'll be an initial waiting period of 6 months to perhaps 2 years after the date of issue, during which time the issue cannot be converted. The *conversion period* then begins, after which the issue can be converted at any time. Technically it's the *bondholder* who has the right to convert the bond into common stock, but more commonly the issuing firm will initiate the conversion by calling the issue. From the investor's point of view, the most important item of information is the **conversion ratio,** which specifies the number of shares of common stock that the bond can be converted into. For example, a $1,000 convertible bond might stipulate a conversion ratio of 20, meaning that you can "cash in" one convertible bond for 20 shares of the company's stock.

Given the significance of the price behavior of the underlying common stock to the value of a convertible security, one of the most important measures to a convertible bond investor is conversion value. In essence, **conversion value** is an indication of what a convertible issue would trade for *if it were priced to sell based on its stock value.* Conversion value is easy to find: simply multiply the conversion ratio of the issue by the current market price of the underlying common stock. For example, a convertible that carried a conversion ratio of 20 would have a conversion value of $1,200 if the firm's stock traded at a current market price of $60 per share (20 × $60 = $1,200). Unfortunately, convertible issues seldom trade precisely at their conversion value; rather, they invariably trade at **conversion premiums,** which means the convertibles are priced in the market at more than their conversion values. For example, a convertible that traded at $1,400 and had a conversion value of $1,200 would have a conversion premium of $200 (that is, $1,400 − $1,200 = $200). Convertible securities appeal to investors who want *the price potential of a common stock along with the downside risk protection of a corporate bond.* This two-sided feature is critical with convertibles and is virtually impossible to match with straight common stock or straight debt.

conversion privilege
The provision in a convertible issue that stipulates the conditions of the conversion feature, such as the conversion period and conversion ratio.

conversion ratio A ratio specifying the number of shares of common stock into which a convertible bond can be converted.

conversion value A measure of what a convertible issue would trade for if it were priced to sell based on its stock value.

conversion premium
The difference between a convertible security's market price and its conversion value.

Bond Ratings

Bond ratings are like grades: A letter grade is assigned to a bond, which designates its investment quality. Ratings are widely used and are an important part of the municipal and corporate bond markets. The two largest and best-known rating agencies are Moody's and Standard & Poor's. Every time a large, new corporate or municipal issue comes to the market, a staff of professional bond analysts determine its default risk exposure and investment quality. The financial records of the issuing organization are thoroughly examined and its future prospects assessed. The result of all this is the assignment of a bond rating at the time of issue that indicates *the ability of the issuing organization to service its debt in a prompt and timely manner.* Exhibit 12.8 lists the various ratings assigned to bonds by each of the two major agencies. Except for slight variations in designations (Aaa versus AAA, for example), the meanings and interpretations are basically the same. Note that the top four ratings (Aaa through Baa; or AAA through BBB) designate *investment-grade bonds*—such ratings are highly coveted by issuers because they indicate financially strong, well-run companies or municipalities. The next two ratings (Ba/B; or BB/B) are where you'll find most **junk bonds;** these ratings mean that although the principal and interest payments on the bonds are still being met, the risk of default is relatively high, as the issuers generally lack the financial strength found with investment-grade issues. While junk bonds—or *high-yield bonds*, as they're also known—are popular with some investors, it should be understood that these are highly speculative securities. They may offer high rates of return, but they also involve substantial amounts of risks; in particular, there's a very real likelihood that the issue may encounter some difficulties.

Once a new issue is rated, the process doesn't stop there. Older, outstanding bonds are also regularly reviewed to ensure that their assigned ratings are still valid. Most issues will carry a single rating to maturity, but it's common for some to undergo revision. Finally,

junk bond Also known as *high-yield bonds*, these are highly speculative securities that have received low ratings from Moody's or Standard & Poor's.

EXHIBIT 12.8 Moody's and Standard & Poor's Bond Ratings

Agencies like Moody's and Standard & Poor's rate corporate and municipal bonds; the ratings provide an indication of the bonds' investment quality (particularly regarding an issue's default risk exposure).

BOND RATINGS*

Moody's	S&P	Description
Aaa	AAA	*Prime-Quality Investment Bonds*—This is the highest rating assigned, denoting extremely strong capacity to pay.
AaA A	AA A	*High-Grade Investment Bonds*—These are also considered very safe bonds, though they're not quite as safe as Aaa/AAA issues; double-A-rated bonds (Aa/AA) are safer (have less risk of default) than single-A-rated issues.
Baa	BBB	*Medium-Grade Investment Bonds*—These are the lowest of the investment-grade issues; they're felt to lack certain protective elements against adverse economic conditions.
Ba B	BB B	*Junk Bonds*—With little protection against default, these are viewed as highly speculative securities.
Caa Ca C	CCC CC C D	*Poor-Quality Bonds*—These are either in default or very close to it; they're often referred to as "Zombie Bonds."

*Some ratings may be modified to show relative standing within a major rating category; for example, Moody's uses numerical modifiers (1, 2, 3), whereas S&P uses plus (+) or minus (−) signs.

although it may appear that the issuing firm or municipality is receiving the rating, it's actually the individual issue that is being rated. As a result, a firm (or municipality) can have different ratings assigned to its issues; the senior securities, for example, might carry one rating and the junior issues a slightly lower rating. Most bond investors pay careful attention to ratings, because they can affect comparative market yields—specifically, *the higher the rating, the lower the yield of an obligation*, other things being equal. Thus, whereas an A-rated bond might offer an 8 percent yield, a comparable AAA issue would probably yield something like 7.25 or 7.50 percent.

Pricing a Bond

Unlike stocks, the vast majority of bonds—especially corporate and municipal bonds—rarely change hands in the secondary markets. As a result, except for U.S. Treasury and some agency issues, bonds aren't widely quoted in the financial press, not even in the *Wall Street Journal*. So, rather than looking at how bonds are quoted, let's look at how they're priced in the marketplace. Regardless of the type, *all bonds are priced as a percentage of par*, meaning that a quote of, say, 85 translates into a price of 85 percent of the bond's par value. In the bond market, 1 point = $10, so a quote of 85 does not mean $85, but, rather, $850. This is so because market convention assumes that bonds carry par values of $1,000; thus a bond quote of 85 means the price is really $850, or 85 percent of $1,000. Also keep in mind that the price of any bond is always related to the issue's coupon and maturity—those two features are always a part of any listed price because of their effect on the price of a bond. (We'll talk more about the impact of coupons and maturities on bond behavior later in this chapter.)

In the corporate and municipal markets, bonds are priced in decimals, using three places to the right of the decimal point. Thus a quote of 87.562, as a percentage of a $1,000 par bond, converts to a price of $875.62; similarly, a quote of 121.683 translates into a price of $1.21683 \times \$1,000 = \$1,216.83$. In contrast, U.S. Treasury and agency bond quotes are stated in *thirty-seconds of a point* (where, again, 1 point = $10). For example, you might see the price of a T-bond listed at, say, 94:16. Translated, that means the bond is being priced at $94^{16}/_{32}$, or $94^{1}/_{2}$ percent of par—in other words, it's being priced at $945.00. With government bonds, the figures to the right of the colon (:) show the number of thirty-seconds embedded in the price. Consider another bond that's trading at 141:08. This bond is being priced at $141^{8}/_{32}$, or 141.25 percent of par. Thus, if you wanted to buy, say, 15 of these bonds (with a par value of $15,000), you'd have to pay $21,187.50 (i.e., $1.4125 \times \$15,000$).

Bond Prices and Yields

The price of a bond is a function of its coupon, maturity, and the movement of market interest rates. *When interest rates go down, bond prices go up, and vice versa*. The relationship of bond prices to market rates is captured in Exhibit 12.9. The graph serves to reinforce the *inverse* relationship between bond prices and market interest rates; note that *lower* rates lead to *higher* bond prices. The exhibit also shows the difference between premium and discount bonds. A **premium bond** is one that sells for more than its par value, which occurs whenever market interest rates drop below the coupon rate on the bond; a **discount bond,** in contrast, sells for less than par and is the result of market rates being greater than the issue's coupon rate. So the 10 percent bond in our illustration traded as a premium bond when market rates were at 8 percent, but as a discount bond when rates stood at 12 percent.

When a bond is first issued, it's usually sold to the public at a price that equals, or is very close to, its par value. Likewise, when the bond matures—some 15, 20, or 30 years later—it will once again be priced at its par value. But what happens to the price of the

premium bond A bond that has a market value higher than par.

discount bond A bond with a market value lower than par.

A bond sells at its par value as long as the prevailing market interest rate remains the same as the bond's coupon (for example, when both coupon and market rates equal 10 percent). But when market rates drop, bond prices rise, and vice versa; moreover, as a bond approaches its maturity, the issue price always moves toward its par value, no matter what happens to interest rates.

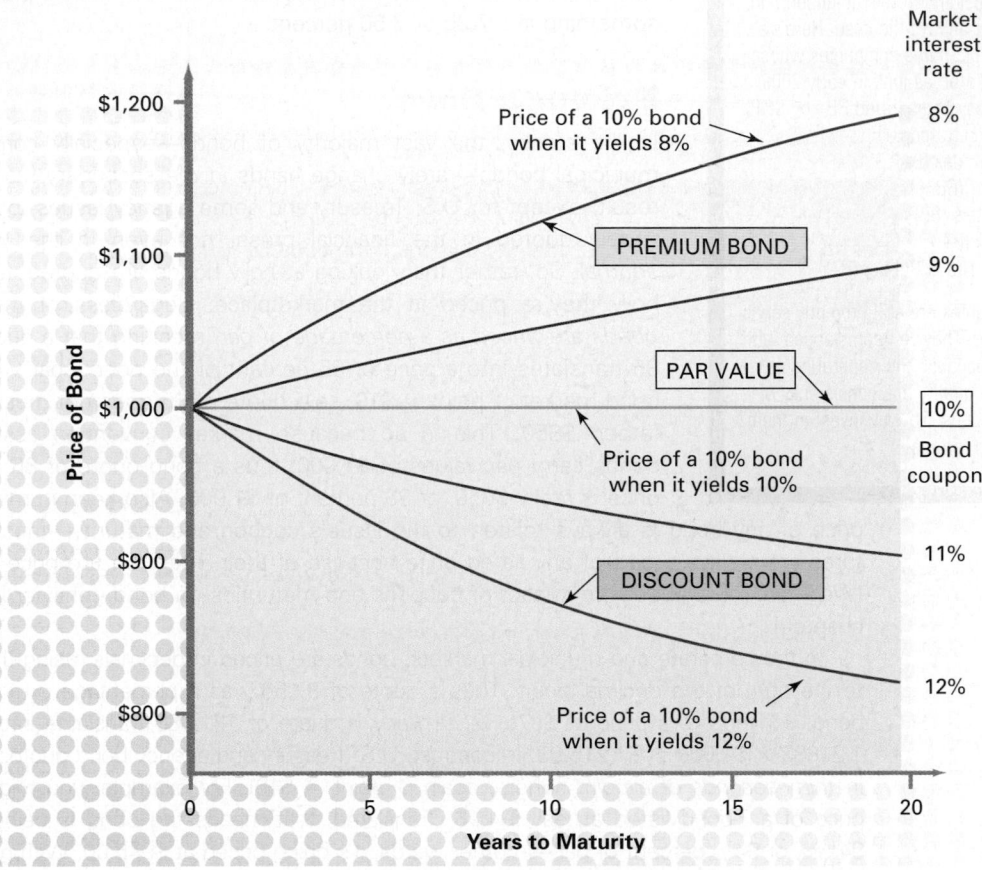

bond in between is of considerable concern to most bond investors. In this regard, we know that how much bond prices move depends not only on the *direction* of change in interest rates but also on the *magnitude* of such changes; for the greater the moves in interest rates, the greater the swings in bond prices. But there's more, for bond prices will also vary according to the coupon and maturity of the issue—that is, bonds with *lower coupons* and/or *longer maturities* will respond more vigorously to changes in market rates and undergo *greater price swings*. It should be obvious, then, that if interest rates are moving up, the investor should seek high coupon bonds with short maturities, because this will cause minimal price variation and *preserve as much capital as possible*. In contrast, if rates are heading down, that's the time to be in long-term bonds—if you're a speculator looking for lots of capital gains, then go with long-term, *low coupon bonds*, but if you're trying to lock in a high level of coupon (interest) income, then stick with long-term, *high coupon* bonds that offer plenty of call protection (which you can get from issues that are noncallable or have extended call-deferment periods).

Current Yield and Yield to Maturity

The *yield* on a bond is the rate of return you'd earn if you held the bond for a stated period of time. The two most commonly cited bond yields are current yield and yield to maturity.

Current yield reflects the amount of annual interest income the bond provides relative to its current market price. Here's the formula for current yield:

$$\text{Current yield} = \frac{\text{Annual interest income}}{\text{Market price of bond}}$$

As you can see, the current yield on a bond is basically the same as the dividend yield on a stock. Assume, for example, that a 9 percent bond with a $1,000 face value is currently selling for $910. Because annual interest income would amount to $90 (i.e., 0.09 × $1,000) and the current market price of the bond is $910, its current yield would be 9.89 percent ($90/$910). This measure of yield would be of interest to *investors seeking current income*; other things being equal, the higher the current yield, the more attractive a bond would be to such an investor.

The annual rate of return a bondholder would receive *if he held the issue to its maturity* is captured in the bond's **yield to maturity.** This measure captures both the annual interest income and the recovery of principal at maturity; it also includes the impact of interest-on-interest and therefore provides a fully compounded rate of return. If a bond is purchased at its face value, its yield to maturity will equal the coupon, or stated, rate of interest. If it is purchased at a discount, its yield to maturity will be greater than the coupon rate because the investor will receive, in addition to annual interest income, the full face value of the bond even though he paid something less than par—in effect, the investor will earn some capital gains on the investment. Of course, if the bond is purchased at a premium, the opposite will be true: the yield to maturity on the issue will be less than its coupon rate because the transaction will involve a capital loss—that is, the investor will pay more for the bond than she will get back at maturity.

You can find the yield to maturity on a bond by using the *approximate yield* formula introduced earlier in this chapter. Actually, using a handheld financial calculator (which we'll demonstrate soon) results in a yield to maturity that's a bit more accurate and is, in fact, very close to the measure used in the market; the only difference is that market participants normally use semiannual compounding in their calculations, whereas we use annual compounding. (Bonds are normally priced in the market using semiannual compounding, because the vast majority of U.S. bonds pay interest semiannually. Actually, using semiannual rather than annual compounding is more of a technical matter that's of concern primarily to large institutional bond investors. The fact is, the difference in yields using annual versus semiannual compounding usually amounts to no more than 5 or 6 basis points—where 1 basis point = 1/100 of 1 percent. Now that might be a big deal to the big guys, but not to the small individual investor. So we'll stick with annual compounding here, though we'll show how you can use your handheld calculator to find yield to maturity on a semiannual basis. There's a bit of good news in all this: you'll find the approximate yield formula produces yield measures that are much closer to their actual yields than what we saw with stocks! So, with bonds anyway, the approximate yield measure does give you a fairly close approximation of the bond's actual yield to maturity.)

Thus, employing the approximate yield approach for now, by setting the future price *(FP)* of the investment equal to the bond's face value ($1,000), you can use the following version of the equation to find the *approximate yield to maturity on a bond*:

current yield The amount of current income a bond provides relative to its market price.

yield to maturity The fully compounded rate of return a bondholder would earn if she held it to maturity.

$$\text{Approximate yield to maturity} = \frac{CI + \left[\dfrac{\$1,000 - CP}{N}\right]}{\left[\dfrac{CP + \$1,000}{2}\right]}$$

As you'll recall, CI equals annual current income (or annual interest income, in the case of a bond), CP stands for current price (of the bond), and N is the investment period (the number of years to maturity).

Crunching the Numbers. Now, assume you're contemplating the purchase of a $1,000, 9 percent bond with 15 years remaining to maturity, and that the bond currently trades at a price of $910. Given CI = $90, CP = $910, and N = 15 years, the approximate yield to maturity on this bond will be:

$$\text{Approximate yield to maturity} = \frac{\$90 + \left[\dfrac{\$1,000 - \$910}{15}\right]}{\left[\dfrac{\$910 + \$1,000}{2}\right]}$$

$$= \frac{\$90 + \left[\dfrac{\$90}{15}\right]}{\left[\dfrac{\$1,910}{2}\right]} = \underline{10.05\%}$$

This is above both the 9 percent stated (coupon) rate and the 9.89 percent current yield, because the bond is purchased at a discount from its face value. (Note that had the bond been selling at $1,090, it would have had a current yield of 8.26 percent and an approximate yield to maturity of 8.04 percent—both below the 9 percent coupon rate; such behavior would occur because the bond was selling at a premium price.)

Calculator Keystrokes. You can also *find the yield to maturity on a bond* by using a financial calculator; here's what you'd do. With the calculator in the *annual mode*, to find the yield to maturity on our 9 percent (annual pay coupon), 15-year bond that's currently trading at $910, use the keystrokes shown here, where:

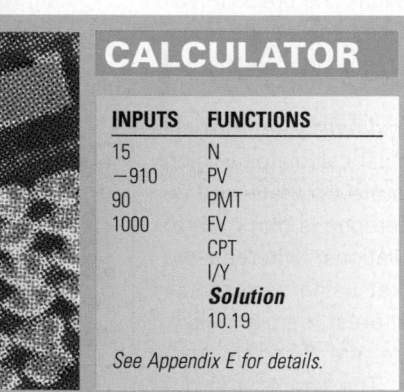

CALCULATOR

INPUTS	FUNCTIONS
15	N
−910	PV
90	PMT
1000	FV
	CPT
	I/Y
	Solution
	10.19

See Appendix E for details.

N = number of *years* to maturity
PV = the current market price of the bond [entered as a *negative*]
PMT = the size of the annual coupon payments [in *dollars*]
FV = the par value of the bond

A value of 10.19 should appear in the calculator display—thus, 10.19 percent is the bond's yield to maturity using annual compounding and, as can be seen, it's very close to the approximate yield of 10.05 percent that we just computed.

You can also use your handheld calculator to find the slightly more accurate *yield to maturity based on semiannual compounding.* Here's how: Keeping the calculator in the *annual mode, multiply* the number of years to maturity by 2 (to obtain the number of 6-month periods to maturity), and *divide* the coupon by 2 (to determine the size of the semiannual coupon payments). Now, input the data, as appropriate—let **N** = 15 × 2 = **30**, **PMT** = 90/2 = **45**, **PV** = −910; and **FV** = 1,000; then hit **CPT I/Y** and you should end up with **5.09**, which is the semiannual yield; double that (5.09 × 2) and you'll have **10.18 percent**, *the bond's yield to maturity using semiannual compounding.* Notice in this case that the difference in the annual (10.19 percent) versus semiannual (10.18 percent) yield to maturity is just 1 basis point!

Yield to maturity measures are used by investors to assess the underlying attractiveness of a bond investment. The higher the yield to maturity, the more attractive the investment, other things being equal. *If a bond provided a yield to maturity that equaled or exceeded an investor's desired rate of return, it would be considered a worthwhile investment candidate*, because it would promise a yield that should adequately compensate the investor for the level of risk involved.

12-11	What's the difference between a secured bond and an unsecured bond?
12-12	Are *junk bonds* and *zero coupon bonds* the same? Explain. What are the basic tax features of a tax-exempt *municipal bond*?
12-13	What is a convertible bond, and why do investors buy convertible securities?
12-14	Describe the *conversion privilege* on a convertible security. Explain how the market price of the underlying common stock affects the market price of a convertible bond.
12-15	Explain the system of bond ratings used by Moody's and Standard & Poor's.
12-16	What effects do market interest rates have on the price behavior of outstanding bonds?

SUMMARY • SUMMARY • SUMMARY • SUMMARY • SUMMARY • SUMMARY • SUMMARY • SUMMARY • SUMMARY • SU

« SUMMARY

LG1 **Describe the various types of risks to which investors are exposed, as well as the sources of return.** Although investing offers returns in the form of current income and/or capital gains, it also involves risk; the basic types of investment risk are business risk, financial risk, market risk, purchasing power risk, interest-rate risk, liquidity risk, and event risk—all of which combine to affect the level of return from an investment.

LG2 **Know how to search for an acceptable investment, based on risk, return, and yield.** The value, and therefore the acceptability, of any investment is a function of the amount of return it's expected to produce relative to the amount of perceived risk involved in the investment. Investors are entitled to be compensated for the risks they must accept in an investment; therefore, the more risk there is in an investment, the more return you should expect to earn. This risk-return trade-off is generally captured in the "desired rate of return," which is that rate of return you feel you should receive in compensation for the amount of risk you must assume. As long as the expected return on an investment (the return you *think* you'll earn) is greater than the desired rate of return (the return you *should* earn), it should be considered an acceptable investment candidate—one worthy of your attention.

LG3 **Discuss the merits of investing in common stock and be able to distinguish among the different types of stocks.** Common stocks are a popular form of investing that can be used to meet just about any investment objective—from capital gains or current income to some combination of both. Investors can choose from blue chips, growth, or tech stocks; income, speculative, cyclical, or defensive stocks; and small- or mid-cap stocks. If they're so inclined, they can even buy foreign stocks by investing in ADRs (American Depository Receipts).

LG4 **Become familiar with the various measures of performance and how to use them in putting a value on stocks.** The value of a share of stock is largely based on performance measures—dividend yield, book value, net profit margin, return on equity (ROE), earnings per share, price/earnings (P/E) ratio, and beta. Investors look at these measures to gain insights about a company's financial condition and operating results, and ultimately, to obtain the input needed to measure the expected return on the stock.

LG5 **Describe the basic issue characteristics of bonds and note how these securities are used as investment vehicles.** Bonds are another popular form of investing; they're often referred to as fixed-income securities because the debt service obligations of the issuer are fixed. The coupon that the bond carries defines the amount of annual interest income that the investor will receive over time, while the par value defines the amount of capital to be repaid at maturity. Bonds may be issued with or without collateral, and most bonds allow the issuer to retire the issue before its maturity. As investment vehicles, bonds can be used to generate either current income or capital gains (which occur when market rates go down).

LG6 **Distinguish between the different types of bonds, gain an understanding of how bond prices behave, and know how to compute different measures of yield.** Bonds are the publicly issued debt of corporations and various levels of government (from the U.S. Treasury and various agencies of the U.S. government to state and local—municipal—governments). Regardless of the issuer, the price of a bond moves inversely with market interest rates—the lower the market rate, the higher the price of the bond. There are basically two ways to measure the yield performance of a bond: one is current yield, which looks only at the coupon income on a bond; the other is yield to maturity, which provides a fully compounded rate of return that considers not only interest income but also capital gains (or loss) and interest-on-interest.

FINANCIAL PLANNING EXERCISES

LG1, 2

1. What makes for a good investment? Use the approximate yield formula, or a financial calculator, to rank these investments according to their expected returns:
   a. Buy a stock for $45 a share, hold it for 3 years, then sell it for $75 a share (the stock pays annual dividends of $3 a share).
   b. Buy a security for $25, hold it for 2 years, then sell it for $60 (current income on this security is zero).
   c. Buy a 1-year, 12 percent note for $950 (assume that the note has a $1,000 par value and that it will be held to maturity).

LG3, 4

2. Selected financial information about Engulf and Devour, Inc., is as follows:

Total assets	$20,000,000
Total liabilities	$8,000,000
Total preferred stock	$3,000,000
Total annual preferred stock dividends	$240,000
Net profits after tax	$2,500,000
Number of shares of common stock outstanding	500,000 shares
Current market price of common stock	$50.00 a share
Annual common stock dividends	$2.50 a share

Using the company's financial information, compute the following:
   a. The stock's dividend yield
   b. Book value per share
   c. Earnings per share
   d. P/E ratio

LG3, 4

3. Assume that you've just inherited $350,000 and have decided to invest a big chunk of it ($250,000 to be exact) in common stocks. Your objective is to build up as much capital as you can over the next 15 to 20 years, and you're willing to tolerate a "good deal" of risk.
   a. What *types* of stocks (for example, blue chips, income stocks, and so on) do you think you'd be most interested in, and why? Select at least three types of stocks and briefly explain the rationale for each.
   b. Would your selections change if you were dealing with a smaller amount of money—say, only $50,000? What if you were a more risk-adverse investor?

LG3, 4

4. This is an *Online Investing* question that requires access to the Internet. Once you're online, go to the *BetterInvesting* Web site at **http://www.betterinvesting.org**, click on the "Stocks" tab from the menu along the top, and then select "Software/Worksheets." Under the list of Worksheets, click on the *Stock Selection Guide*, and then download or print it out. Now, pick a stock of your choice, or one that's been assigned by your instructor. (*Hint:* Choose a company that's been publicly traded for at least 5 to 10 years, and *avoid* public utilities, banks, and other

financial institutions.) Next, obtain a recent S&P or *Value Line* report on the stock you've selected, or stay online and go to a financial Web site, like **http://finance.yahoo.com**, to obtain financial and market information about your company. Use that information to complete the Stock Selection Guide, **especially page 2 of the guide.** What value did you come up with for the "Average Total Annual Return Over the Next 5 years"—the bottom line of the report? Discuss your findings. Do you think your stock would make a good investment candidate? Explain.

LG3, 4   5. An investor is thinking about buying some shares of FinComm-I at $60 a share. She expects the price of the stock to rise to $100 a share over the next 3 years. During that time, she also expects to receive annual dividends of $3 per share. Given that the investor's expectations (about the future price of the stock and the dividends it pays) hold up, what rate of return can the investor expect to earn on this investment? (*Hint:* Use either the approximate yield formula or a financial calculator to solve this problem.)

LG3, 4   6. A company has total assets of $2.5 million, total liabilities of $1.8 million, and $200,000 worth of 8 percent preferred stock outstanding. What is the firm's total book value? What would its book value per share be if the firm had 50,000 shares of common stock outstanding?

LG3, 4   7. The Med Online Co. recently reported net profits after taxes of $15.8 million. It has 2.5 million shares of common stock outstanding and pays preferred dividends of $1 million a year. The company's stock currently trades at $60 per share.
   a.   Compute the stock's earnings per share (EPS).
   b.   What's the stock's P/E ratio?
   c.   Determine what the stock's dividend yield would be if it paid $1.75 per share to common stockholders.

LG3, 4   8. The price of Consolidated Everything is now $65. The company pays no dividends. Mr. M. Bags expects the price 4 years from now to be $105 a share. Should Mr. B. buy Consolidated E. if he desires a 15 percent rate of return? Explain.

LG5, 6   9. An investor in the 28 percent tax bracket is trying to decide which of two bonds to select: one is a 6.5 percent U.S. Treasury bond selling at par; the other is a municipal bond with a 5.25 percent coupon, which is also selling at par. Which of these two bonds should the investor select? Why?

LG5, 6   10. Describe and differentiate between a bond's (a) current yield and (b) yield to maturity. Why are these yield measures important to the bond investor? Find the yield to maturity of a 20-year, 9 percent, $1,000 par value bond trading at a price of $850. What's the current yield on this bond?

LG5, 6   11. Which of these three bonds offers the highest current yield? Which one has the highest yield to maturity?
   a.   A 9.5 percent, 20-year bond quoted at 97.750
   b.   A 16 percent, 15-year bond quoted at 164.625
   c.   A 5.25 percent, 18-year bond quoted at 54.000

LG5, 6   12. Find the current yield of a 10 percent, 25-year bond that's currently priced in the market at $1,250. Now, use a financial calculator to find the yield to maturity on this bond (use annual compounding). What's the current yield and yield to maturity on this bond given that it trades at $1,000? How about if it's priced at $750? Comment on your findings.

LG5, 6   13. A 25-year, zero coupon bond was recently quoted at 12.500. Find the current yield and yield to maturity of this issue, given the bond has a par value of $1,000. (Assume annual compounding for the yield-to-maturity measure.)

LG5, 6   14. Assume that an investor pays $850 for a long-term bond that carries a $7\frac{1}{2}$ percent coupon. During the next 12 months, interest rates drop sharply, and the investor sells the bond at a price of $962.50.
   a.   Find the current yield that existed on this bond at the beginning of the year. What was it by the end of the 1-year holding period?

b. Compute the return on this investment using the approximate yield formula and a 1-year investment period.

LG5, 6 15. Find the conversion value of a convertible bond that carries a conversion ratio of 24, given that the market price of the underlying common stock is $55 a share. Would there be any conversion premium if the convertible bond had a market price of $1,500? If so, how much?

LG5, 6 16. A certain 6 percent convertible bond (maturing in 20 years) is convertible into 20 shares of the company's common stock. The bond has a par value of $1,000 and is currently trading at $800; the stock (which pays a dividend of 75 cents a share) is currently trading in the market at $35 a share. Use this information to answer these questions:
a. What is the current yield on the convertible bond? What is the dividend yield on the company's common stock? Which provides more current income: the convertible bond or the common stock? Explain.
b. What is the bond's conversion ratio? Its conversion price?
c. What is the conversion value of this issue? Is there any conversion premium in this issue? How much?
d. What is the (approximate) yield to maturity on the convertible bond?

LG3, 4, 5, 6 17. Using the resources available at your campus or public library, work the following problems. (*Note*: Show your work for all your calculations.)
a. Select any two *common* stocks, and determine the dividend yield, earnings per share, and P/E ratio for each.
b. Select any two *bonds*, and determine the current yield and yield to maturity of each.
c. Select any two *convertible debentures*, and determine the conversion ratio, conversion value, and conversion premium for each.

APPLYING PERSONAL FINANCE

What's Your Type?

In this chapter, we learned that common stock is often placed into various categories—blue chip, growth, income, and so forth—and referred to by its size, such as large-, mid-, or small-cap. In this project, you'll examine and compare the returns on various types of common stock.

Common comparisons include:

- Large-cap vs. mid- or small-cap
- Blue chip vs. speculative
- Growth vs. income
- Growth vs. value

Pick any two combinations from the list above, and then select a stock to represent each of the categories included in your choices. For all four of your stocks, obtain information on:

- The company's growth in earnings (EPS)
- Growth in dividends per share
- Dividend yield
- Price/earnings ratio
- The stock's beta

In addition, use the formula given in this chapter to compute each stock's approximate yield for the past year, based on what the stock is trading for today versus the price it sold for a year ago. Be sure to include any dividends paid over the past 12 months. You can obtain this information from financial newspapers or from online sources, such as **http://finance.yahoo.com.**

Compare and contrast the performance and characteristics of the stocks you've chosen. Based on your findings, does the type of stock you own make a difference? Which type or types are the most suitable for your investment purposes?

CRITICAL THINKING CASES

LG3, 5

12.1 The Jordons' Problem: What to Do with All That Money?

A couple in their early thirties, Allen and Sandra Jordon, recently inherited $90,000 from a relative. Allen earns a comfortable income as a sales manager for Smith and Johnson, Inc., and Sandra does equally well as an attorney with a major law firm. Because they have no children and don't need the money, they've decided to invest all of the inheritance in stocks, bonds, and perhaps even some money market instruments. However, because they're not very familiar with the market, they turn to you for help.

Critical Thinking Questions

1. What kind of investment approach do you think the Jordons should adopt—that is, should they be conservative with their money or aggressive? Explain.

2. What kind of stocks do you think the Jordons should invest in? How important is current income to them (that is, dividends or interest income)? Should they be putting any of their money into bonds? Explain.

3. Construct an investment portfolio that you feel would be right for the Jordons; invest the full $90,000. Put actual stocks, bonds, and/or convertible securities in the portfolio; also, if you like, you may put up to one-third of the money into short-term securities such as CDs, Treasury bills, money funds, or MMDAs. Select any securities you want, so long as you feel they'd be suitable for the Jordons. Make sure that the portfolio consists of six or more different securities; use the latest issue of *The Wall Street Journal* or an online source such as **http://finance.yahoo.com** to determine the market prices of the securities you select. Show the amount invested in each security, along with the amount of current income (from dividends and/or interest) that will be generated from the investments. Briefly explain why you selected these particular securities for the Jordons' portfolio.

LG3, 5

12.2 Kathy Decides to Try Her Hand at Investing

Kathy Karras is a 26-year-old management trainee at a large chemical company. She is single and has no plans for marriage. Her annual salary is $34,000 (placing her in the 15 percent tax bracket), and her monthly expenditures come to approximately $1,500. During the past year or so, Kathy has managed to save around $8,000, and she expects to continue saving at least that amount each year for the foreseeable future. Her company pays the premium on her $35,000 life insurance policy. Because Kathy's entire education was financed by scholarships, she was able to save money from the summer and part-time jobs she held as a student. Altogether, she has a nest egg of nearly $18,000, out of which she'd like to invest about $15,000. She'll keep the remaining $3,000 in a bank CD that pays 3 percent interest and will use this money only in an emergency. Kathy can afford to take more risks than someone with family obligations can, but she doesn't wish to be a speculator. She simply wants to earn an attractive rate of return on her investments.

Critical Thinking Questions

1. What investment options are open to Kathy?

2. What chance does she have of earning a satisfactory return on her investments if she invests her $15,000 in (a) blue-chip stocks, (b) growth stocks, (c) speculative stocks, (d) corporate bonds, or (e) municipal bonds?

3. Discuss the factors you would consider when analyzing these alternate investment vehicles.

4. What recommendation would you make to Kathy regarding to her available investment alternatives? Explain.

> **MONEY ONLINE** www.thomsonedu.com/finance/gitman

Visit **http://www.thomsonedu.com/finance/gitman** for some additional Web-based exercises and hot links (with annotations) to a variety of resources relevant to the topics covered in this chapter.

Investing in Mutual Funds and Real Estate

LEARNING GOALS

LG1	◉	Describe the basic features and operating characteristics of a mutual fund.	p. 412
LG2	◉	Differentiate between open- and closed-end funds, as well as exchange-traded funds, and discuss the various types of fund loads and charges.	p. 412
LG3	◉	Discuss the types of funds available to investors and the different kinds of investor services offered by mutual funds.	p. 423
LG4	◉	Gain an understanding of the variables that should be considered when selecting funds for investment purposes.	p. 431
LG5	◉	Identify the sources of return and calculate the rate of return earned on an investment in a mutual fund.	p. 431
LG6	◉	Understand the role that real estate plays in a diversified investment portfolio, along with the basics of investing in real estate, either directly or indirectly.	p. 439
	◉		

CHAPTER 13 • CHAPTER 13 • CHAPTER 13 • CHAPTER 13 • CHAPTER 13 • CHAPTER 13 • CHAPTER 13 • CHAPTER 13 • C

LG1, LG2 MUTUAL FUNDS: SOME BASICS

Sound investment planning involves finding investment vehicles with risk-return characteristics that are compatible with your financial objectives. In this chapter we'll look beyond stocks and bonds and consider two other types of investment products that enjoy widespread use among individual investors: mutual funds and real estate. Both of these investment outlets offer risk-return opportunities that you may not be able to obtain from stocks or bonds. For example, investors interested in receiving the benefits of professional portfolio management, but who don't have the funds to purchase a diversified portfolio of securities, may find mutual fund shares attractive. Other investors may be drawn to real estate either because of its perceived return potential or perhaps to obtain some preferential tax treatment. Let's now take a closer look at both of these investments, starting with mutual funds.

A mutual fund is basically a financial services organization that receives money from its shareholders and invests those funds on their behalf in a diversified portfolio of securities. Thus, when investors buy shares in a mutual fund, they actually become *part owners of a widely diversified portfolio of securities*. In an abstract sense, a mutual fund can be thought of as the *financial product* that's sold to the public by an investment company. That is, the investment company builds and manages a portfolio of securities and sells ownership interests—shares of stock—in that portfolio through a vehicle known as a mutual fund. This concept underlies the whole mutual fund structure and is depicted in Exhibit 13.1. For individual investors today, mutual funds are without a doubt the investment vehicle of choice. The fact is, more people invest in mutual funds than any other type of investment product. Mutual funds are popular because they offer not only a variety of interesting investment opportunities but also a wide array of services that many investors find appealing. They're an easy and convenient way to invest—one that's especially suited to beginning investors and those with limited investment capital.

The Mutual Fund Concept

The first mutual fund in this country was started in Boston in 1924. By 1940, 68 mutual funds were in operation, and by 1980 there were 564. But that was only the beginning, for the next 25 years saw unprecedented growth in the mutual fund industry, as assets under management grew to some $9.2 trillion by January 2006. Indeed, by year-end 2005, *there were nearly 8,000 publicly traded mutual funds.* (Actually, counting duplicate or multiple fund offerings from the same portfolio, more like *21,000 funds were available*—such duplication occurs because sometimes two or three versions of the same fund are offered, with each "fund" having a different type of load charge or fee structure.) To put that number in perspective, *there are more mutual funds in existence today than there are stocks listed on the New York and American exchanges combined!* The fund industry has grown so much, in fact, that it is now *the largest financial intermediary* in this country—ahead of even banks.

EXHIBIT 13.1	The Basic Mutual Fund Structure

A mutual fund brings together the funds from many individual investors and uses this pool of money to acquire a diversified portfolio of stocks, bonds, and other securities.

Mutual Fund Shareholders

Investors purchase shares in the mutual fund.

Mutual Fund

Money managers select and purchase securities.

Mutual Fund's Diversified Portfolio of Securities

Mutual funds are big business in the United States and, indeed, all over the world. As of June 2005, more than 91 million individuals in 54 million U.S. households owned mutual funds. That's 47.5 percent of all U.S. households! Clearly, mutual funds appeal to a lot of investors—investors from all walks of life and all income levels. And they all share one view: they've decided, for one reason or another, to turn the problems of security selection and portfolio management over to professional money managers. Questions of which stock or bond to select, when to buy, and when to sell have plagued investors for about as long as there have been organized securities markets. Such concerns lie at the heart of the mutual fund concept and are largely behind the growth in funds. The fact is, many people simply lack the time, the know-how, or the commitment to manage their own securities, so they turn to others. And most often, that means mutual funds.

Pooled Diversification

The mutual fund concept is based on the simple idea of turning the problems of security selection and portfolio management over to professional money managers. A mutual fund combines the investment capital of many people with similar investment goals and invests the funds in a wide variety of securities. Investors receive shares of stock in the mutual fund and, through the fund, enjoy much wider investment diversification than they could otherwise achieve. Indeed, a single mutual fund commonly holds literally hundreds of different stocks or bonds—some funds, in fact, have over 1,000 different holdings! For example, as of year-end 2005, Fidelity Contrafund held some 530 different securities, while the Dreyfus GNMA fund had over 1,100 holdings. Clearly, for all but the super-rich, that's far more diversification than most investors could ever hope to attain. Yet each investor who owns shares in a fund is, in effect, a part owner of that fund's diversified portfolio of securities.

Regardless of the fund size, as the securities held by it move up and down in price, the market value of the mutual fund shares moves accordingly. And when the fund receives dividend and interest payments they too are passed on to the mutual fund shareholders and distributed on the basis of prorated ownership. For example, if you own 1,000 shares of stock in a mutual fund and that represents, say, 1 percent of all shares outstanding, you would receive 1 percent of the dividends paid by the fund. When a security held by the fund is sold for a profit, the capital gain is also passed on to fund shareholders. The whole mutual fund idea, in fact, rests on the concept of **pooled diversification** and works very much like insurance, whereby individuals pool their resources for the collective benefit of all contributors.

Why Invest in Mutual Funds?

Mutual funds can be used by individual investors in various ways. One investor may buy a fund because of the substantial capital gains opportunities it provides; another may buy a totally different fund not for its capital gains, but for its current income. Whatever kind of income a fund provides, individuals tend to use these investment vehicles for one or more of these reasons: (1) to achieve diversification in their investment holdings, (2) to obtain the services of professional money managers, (3) to generate an attractive rate of return on their investment capital, and (4) for the convenience they offer.

Diversification

Certainly, as we just saw, diversification is a primary motive for investing in mutual funds. This ability to diversify allows investors to sharply reduce their exposure to risk by indirectly investing in several types of securities and companies rather than just one or two. If you have only $500 or $1,000 to invest, you obviously won't achieve much diversification on your own. But if you invest that money in a mutual fund, you'll end up owning part of a well-diversified portfolio of securities.

Professional Management

Another major appeal of a mutual fund is the professional management it offers. Of course, management is paid a fee from the fund's earnings, but the contributions of a full-time expert manager should be well worth the cost. These pros know where to look for return, and how to avoid unnecessary risk; at the minimum, their decisions should result in better returns than the average individual investor can achieve.

pooled diversification
A process whereby investors buy into a diversified portfolio of securities for the collective benefit of individual investors.

Financial Returns

Although professional managers *may* be able to achieve better returns than small investors can generate, the relatively high purchase fees, coupled with the management and operating costs, tend to reduce the returns actually earned on mutual fund investments. But the mutual fund industry hasn't attracted millions of investors by generating substandard returns. Quite the contrary; over the long haul, mutual funds have provided relatively attractive returns. Look at Exhibit 13.2. It shows the average return performance on a variety of mutual funds and suggests the kind of returns investors were able to achieve over the 12-year period from January 1994 through 2005. With such return potential, it's easy to see why investors are so anxious to put their money into mutual funds.

Convenience

Mutual fund shares can be purchased from various sources, which is another reason for their appeal. Mutual funds make it easy to invest, and most don't require much capital to get started. They're relatively easy to acquire, they handle all the paperwork and recordkeeping, their prices are widely quoted, and it's usually possible to deal in fractional shares. Opening a mutual fund account is about as easy as opening a checking account. Just fill in a few blank spaces, send in the minimum amount of money, and you're in business!

EXHIBIT 13.2	Comparative Performance of Mutual Funds for the 12-year period through 2005

The type of fund you invest in has a lot to do with the kind of return you can expect. For example, had you put $10,000 in a typical health care fund in January 1994, that investment would have grown to over $50,000 by year-end 2005; in contrast, had you invested the same $10,000 in a typical high-grade bond fund, it would have grown to less than $18,000.

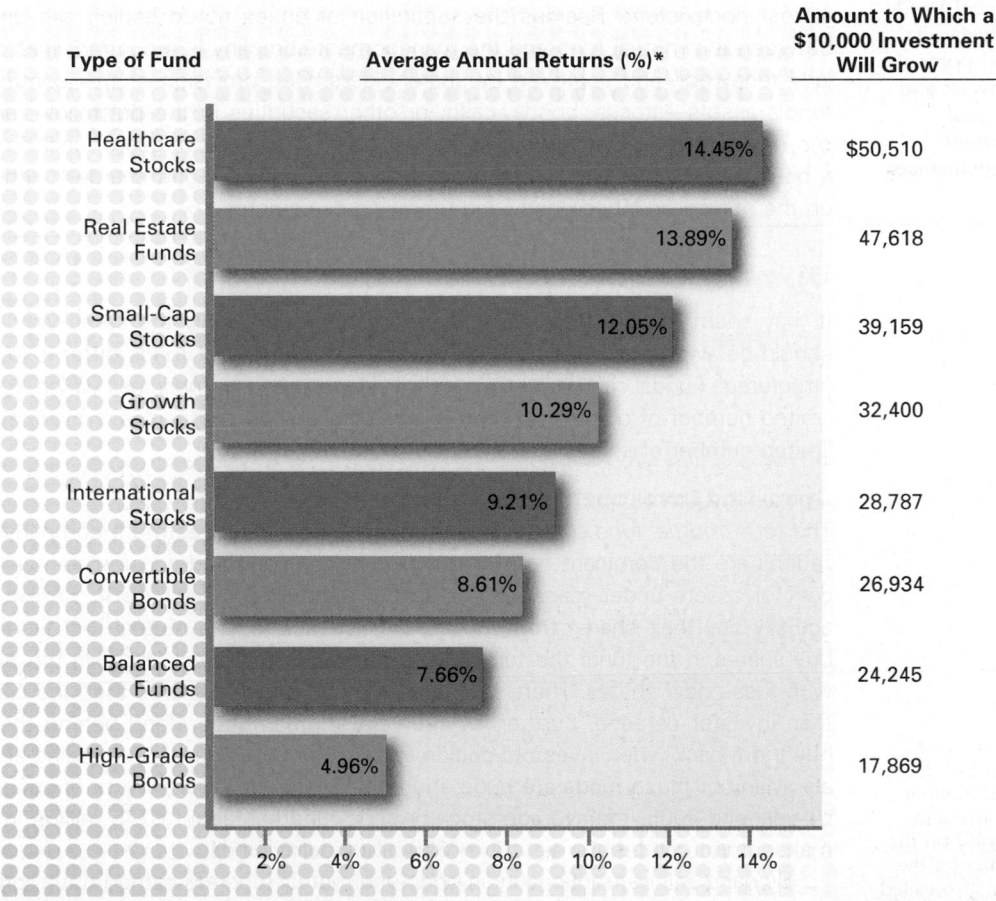

Type of Fund	Average Annual Returns (%)*	Amount to Which a $10,000 Investment Will Grow
Healthcare Stocks	14.45%	$50,510
Real Estate Funds	13.89%	47,618
Small-Cap Stocks	12.05%	39,159
Growth Stocks	10.29%	32,400
International Stocks	9.21%	28,787
Convertible Bonds	8.61%	26,934
Balanced Funds	7.66%	24,245
High-Grade Bonds	4.96%	17,869

Assumes reinvestment of all dividends and capital gains distributions.
Source: *Morningstar*, December 2005.

How Mutual Funds Are Organized and Run

Although it's tempting to think of a mutual fund as a monolithic entity, that's really not the case. Various functions—investing, recordkeeping, safekeeping, and others—are split among two or more companies. Besides the fund itself, which is organized as a separate corporation or trust and *is owned by the shareholders*, there are several other major players:

- The *management company* runs the fund's daily operations. These are the firms we know as Fidelity, Vanguard, T. Rowe Price, Dreyfus, and so forth; they create the funds in the first place. Usually, the management firm also serves as investment advisor.
- The *investment advisor* buys and sells the stocks or bonds and otherwise oversees the portfolio. Usually, three parties participate in this phase of the operation: the *money manager*, who actually runs the portfolio and makes the buy and sell decisions; *securities analysts*, who analyze securities and look for attractive investment candidates; and *traders*, who try to buy and sell big blocks of securities at the best possible price.
- The *distributor* sells the fund shares, either directly to the public or through certain authorized dealers (such as major brokerage houses and commercial banks). When you request a prospectus and sales literature, you deal with the distributor.
- The *custodian* physically safeguards the securities and other assets of a fund, without taking an active role in the investment decisions. To discourage foul play, an independent party (a bank, in most cases) serves in this capacity.
- The *transfer agent* executes transactions, keeps track of purchase and redemption requests from shareholders, and maintains other shareholder records.

All this separation of duties is designed for just one thing—to protect the mutual fund investor/shareholder. Obviously, you can always lose money if your fund's stock or bond holdings go down in value. But that's really the only risk of loss you face, because the chance of ever losing money from fraud or a mutual fund collapse is actually quite low—almost nonexistent. Besides the separation of duties noted earlier, the only formal link between the mutual fund and the management company is a contract that must be regularly renewed—and approved by shareholders. One provision of this contract is that the fund's assets—stocks, bonds, cash, or other securities in the portfolio—*can never be in the hands of the management company*. As still another safeguard, each fund must have a board of directors, or trustees, elected by shareholders and charged with keeping tabs on the management company and renewing its contract.

Open-End versus Closed-End

It may seem that all mutual funds are organized in roughly the same way, but investors should be aware of some major differences. One way that funds differ is in how they are structured. Funds can be set up either as *open-end companies*, which can sell an unlimited number of ownership shares, or as *closed-end companies*, which can issue only a limited number of shares.

Open-End Investment Companies

The term *mutual fund* commonly denotes an open-end investment company. Such organizations are the dominant type of investment company and account for well over 95 percent of assets under management. In an **open-end investment company,** investors actually buy their shares from, and sell them back to, the mutual fund itself. When they buy shares in the fund, the fund issues new shares of stock and fills the purchase order with these new shares. There's no limit to the number of shares the fund can issue, other than investor demand. Further, all open-end mutual funds stand behind their shares and buy them back when investors decide to sell. So there's never any trading among individuals. Many of these funds are huge and hold billions of dollars' worth of securities. Indeed, by year-end 2005, the average stock or bond fund had about $775 million in assets under management, and there were over 850 billion-dollar funds.

Buy and sell transactions in an open-end mutual fund are carried out at prices based on the current value of all the securities held in the fund's portfolio. This is known as the

open-end investment company A firm that can issue an unlimited number of shares that it buys and sells at a price based on the current market value of the securities it owns; also called a mutual fund.

fund's **net asset value (NAV);** it is calculated at least once a day and represents the underlying value of a share of stock in a particular fund. NAV is found by taking the total market value of all securities held by the fund, subtracting any liabilities, and dividing the result by the number of shares outstanding. For example, if on a given day the market value of all the securities held by the XYZ mutual fund equaled some $10 million, and if XYZ on that day had 500,000 shares outstanding, the fund's net asset value per share would amount to $20 ($10,000,000/500,000 = $20). This figure would then be used to derive the price at which the fund shares could be bought and sold. (As we'll see later, NAV is generally included in the fund's quoted price and indicates the price at which an investor can *sell* shares—or, the price an investor would pay to *buy no-load funds*.)

Closed-End Investment Companies

The term *mutual fund* is supposed to be used only with open-end funds, but as a practical matter, it's regularly used with closed-end investment companies as well. Basically, **closed-end investment companies** operate with a fixed number of shares outstanding and do *not* regularly issue new shares of stock. In effect, they have a capital structure like that of any other corporation, except that the corporation's business happens to be investing in marketable securities. Like open-end funds, closed-end investment companies have enjoyed remarkable growth in the past decade or so. That is, while only 34 of these funds existed in 1980, by year-end 2005 there were more than 600 closed-end funds with total net assets of nearly $280 billion—still just a fraction of the $9.2 trillion invested in open-end funds. Shares in closed-end investment companies are actively traded in the secondary market, just like any other common stock; but unlike open-end funds, *all trading is done between investors in the open market*. The fund itself plays no role in either buy or sell transactions; once the shares are issued, the fund is out of the picture. By far, most closed-end investment companies are traded on the New York Stock Exchange; a few are on the American Exchange, and occasionally some are traded in the NASDAQ market or on some other exchange.

Many investment advisors who run closed-end funds also manage open-end funds, often with similar investment objectives. So, why would they do that? Because these are two different animals. It may not appear so, but some major differences exist between open- and closed-end funds. To begin with, because closed-end funds have a fixed amount of capital to work with, they don't have to worry about stock redemptions or new money coming into the fund. So, they don't have to be concerned about keeping cash on hand to meet redemptions. Equally important, because closed-end funds don't have new money flowing in all the time, they don't have to worry about finding new investments. Instead, they can concentrate on a set portfolio of securities and do the best job they can in managing them. But that puts added pressures on the money managers, because their investment styles and fund portfolios are closely monitored and judged by the market. That is, the share prices of closed-end companies are determined not only by their net asset values but also by general supply and demand conditions in the market. As a result, depending on the market outlook and investor expectations, closed-end companies generally trade at a *discount* or *premium* to their NAVs.

Exchange-Traded Funds

Combine some of the operating characteristics of an open-end fund with some of the trading characteristics of a closed-end fund, and you'll end up with something called an *exchange-traded fund*. Technically, an **exchange-traded fund (ETF)** is a type of mutual fund that trades as a listed security on one of the stock exchanges (mostly the AMEX). Actually, all ETFs thus far (through 2005) have been structured as *index funds*, set up to match the performance of a certain market segment; they do this by owning all or a representative sample of the stocks (or bonds) in a targeted market segment or index (we'll examine traditional index funds in more detail later in this chapter). Thus ETFs offer the professional money management of traditional mutual funds and the liquidity of an exchange-traded stock.

net asset value (NAV) The current market value of all the securities the fund owns, less any liabilities, on a per-share basis.

closed-end investment company An investment company that issues a fixed number of shares, which are themselves listed and traded like any other share of stock.

exchange-traded fund (ETF) A mutual fund that trades as a listed security (principally on the AMEX); usually structured as an index fund that's set up to match the performance of a certain market segment.

Even though ETFs are like closed-end funds (they're traded on listed exchanges), *they are in reality open-end mutual funds*, where the number of shares outstanding can be increased or decreased in response to market demand. That is, while ETFs can be bought or sold like any other stock, *the ETF distributor can also create new shares or redeem old shares.* This is done to prevent the fund from trading at (much of) a premium or discount, thereby avoiding a big pitfall of closed-end funds. By year-end 2005, more than 225 ETFs were traded on U.S. markets—together accounting for more than $300 billion in assets under management. These funds cover a wide array of domestic and international stock indexes and submarkets, as well as a handful of U.S. Treasury and corporate bond indexes. The biggest and oldest ETFs (dating back to 1993) are based on the S&P 500 and are known as *Spiders* (SPDRs). In addition, there are *Qubes* (based on the NASDAQ 100, this is the most actively traded ETF—in fact, it's the most actively traded stock in the world), Diamonds (based on the DJIA), and ETFs based on dozens of international markets (from Australia and Canada to Germany, Japan, and the United Kingdom). Just about every major U.S. index, in fact, has its own ETF, along with lots of minor indexes covering specialized market segments. The net asset values of ETFs are set at a fraction of the underlying index value at any given time. For example, if the S&P 500 Index stands at, say, 1,164.46, the ETF on that index will trade at around $116.50 (or about 1/10 of the index); likewise, the ETF on the Dow is set at 1/100 of the DJIA (so when it's at, say, 10,449.30, the ETF will trade at around 104.50).

ETFs combine many advantages of closed-end funds with those of traditional (open-end) index funds. That is, like closed-end funds, ETFs can be bought and sold at *any time of the day*; you can by place an order through your broker (and pay a standard commission just like you would with any other stock). In contrast, you *cannot* trade a traditional open-end fund on an intraday basis, because all buy and sell orders for these funds are filled at the end of the trading day, at closing prices. What's more, because ETFs are passively managed, they offer all the advantages of any index fund: low costs, low portfolio turnover, and low taxes. The fund's tax liability is kept low because ETFs rarely distribute any capital gains to shareholders; you could hold one of these things for decades and never pay a dime in capital-gains taxes (at least not until you sell the shares).

Some Important Cost Considerations

When you buy or sell shares in a *closed-end* investment company, or in *EFTs* for that matter, you pay a commission just as you would with any other types of listed or OTC common stock transaction. This isn't so with *open-end* funds, however. In particular, the cost of investing in an open-end mutual fund depends on the types of fees and load charges that the fund levies on its investors.

Load Funds

Most open-end mutual funds are so-called **load funds,** because they charge a commission *when the shares are purchased* (such charges are often referred to as *front-end loads*). Front-end loads can be fairly substantial and amount to as much as 8½ percent of the *purchase price* of the shares. The fact is, however, very few funds today charge the maximum; instead, many funds charge commissions of only 2 or 3 percent—such funds are known as **low-load funds.** The good news on front-end load funds is that there's normally no charge or commission to pay when you *sell* your shares! Occasionally, however, you'll run into funds that charge a commission—or a so-called *redemption fee*—when you sell your shares. Known as **back-end load funds,** they may charge as much as 7¼ percent of the value of the shares sold, although back-end loads tend to decline over time and usually disappear altogether after 5 or 6 years. The purpose of such charges is to discourage investors from trading in and out of the funds over short periods of time.

No-Load Funds

Some open-end investment companies charge you nothing at all to buy their funds; these are known as **no-load funds.** Relatively few pure no-loads are available; less than 30 percent of the funds sold today are true no-loads, and all the rest charge some type of load or fee. Even funds that don't have front-end loads (and so may appear as no-loads)

load fund A fund that charges a fee at time of purchase.

low-load fund A fund that has a low purchase fee.

back-end load A commission charged for redeeming fund shares.

no-load fund A fund on which no transaction fees are charged.

can have back-end load charges that you must pay when selling your fund shares—or something called a 12(b)-1 fee, which you'd pay for as long as you hold your shares.

12(b)-1 Fees

Also known as *hidden loads*, **12(b)-1 fees** have been allowed by the SEC since 1980 and were originally designed to help no-load funds cover their distribution and marketing expenses. Not surprisingly, the popularity of these fees spread rapidly among fund distributors, so they're now used by nearly 70 percent of all open-end mutual funds. The fees are assessed annually and can amount to as much as 1 percent of assets under management. In good markets and bad, they're paid right off the top—and that can take its toll. Consider, for instance, $10,000 in a fund that charges a 1 percent 12(b)-1 fee. That translates into an annual charge of *$100 a year*, certainly a significant amount of money.

The latest trend in mutual fund fees is the so-called *multiple-class sales charge.* You'll find such arrangements at firms like American Express, Dreyfus, Merrill Lynch, MFS, Scudder, Putnam, and others. The way it works is that the mutual fund will issue different classes of stocks on the same fund or portfolio of securities. So, rather than having just one class of stock outstanding, there might be three of them: Class A shares might have normal (modest) front-end loads; Class B stock might have no front-end loads, but substantial back-end loads along with maximum annual 12(b)-1 fees; and Class C shares might carry a small back-end load and modest 12(b)-1 fees. In other words, you choose your own poison.

In trying to bring some order to fund charges and fees, the SEC instituted a series of caps on mutual fund fees. According to the latest regulations, a mutual fund cannot charge more than 8.5 percent in *total sales charges and fees*, and that includes front- and back-end loads as

well as 12(b)-1 fees. So, if a fund charges a 5 percent front-end load and a 1 percent 12(b)-1 fee, it can charge a maximum of only 2.5 percent in back-end load charges—otherwise, it will violate the 8.5 percent cap. The SEC also set a 1 percent cap on annual 12(b)-1 fees and, perhaps more significantly, stated that true "no-load" funds cannot charge more than 0.25 percent in annual 12(b)-1 fees (if they do, they have to drop the no-load label in their sales and promotional material).

Management Fees

The **management fee** is the cost you incur to hire the professional money managers to run the fund's portfolio of investments. These fees are also assessed annually and usually range from less than 0.5 percent to as much as 3 or 4 percent of assets under management. All funds—whether they're load or no-load, open- or closed-end—have these fees; and, like 12(b)-1 fees, they bear watching, because high management fees will take their toll on performance. As a rule, the size of the management fee is totally unrelated to the fund's performance—you'll pay the same amount whether it's been a winning year or a real loser. In addition to these management fees, some funds may charge an *exchange fee* whenever an investor transfers money from one fund to another within the same fund family and/or an *annual maintenance fee* to help defer the costs of providing service to low-balance accounts.

Keeping Track of Fund Fees and Loads

Critics of the mutual fund industry have come down hard on the proliferation of fund fees and charges. Fortunately, steps have been taken to bring fund fees and loads out into the open. For one thing, fund charges are more widely reported now than they were in the past. Most notably, today you can find detailed information about the types and amounts of fees and charges on just about any mutual fund by going to one of the dozens of Web sites that report on mutual funds, including Quicken.com, Kiplinger.com, Morningstar.com, Yahoo! (at **http://finance.yahoo.com**), and a host of others. Or you could use the mutual

12(b)-1 fee A fee, charged annually that's supposed to be used to offset the promotion and selling expenses.

management fee A fee paid to the professional money managers who administer a mutual fund's portfolio.

fund quotes that appear daily in (most) major newspapers and in *The Wall Street Journal*. For example, take a look at *The Wall Street Journal* quotations in Exhibit 13.3; right after the (abbreviated) name of the fund, you'll often find the letters "r," "p," and "t." If you see an "r" behind a fund's name, it means that the fund charges some type of *redemption fee*, or back-end load, when you sell your shares. The use of a "p," in contrast, means the fund levies a *12(b)-1 fee*. Finally, a "t" indicates funds that charge *both* redemption fees and 12(b)-1 fees. The quotations, of course, tell you only the *kinds* of fees charged by the funds; they don't tell you how much is charged. To get the specifics on the amount charged, you'll have to turn to other sources, like a favorite Web site. What's more, these quotes *tell you nothing about the front-end loads*, if any, charged by the funds. Again, to find out if a particular fund charges a front-end load, you'll have to turn to a Web site or some other source.

EXHIBIT 13.3   Mutual Fund Quotes

Open-end mutual funds are listed separately from other securities and have their own quotation system; an example is shown here in quotes from *The Wall Street Journal*. Note that these securities are also quoted in dollars and cents and that the quotes include not only the fund's NAV but also year-to-date (YTD) and 3-year returns. Also included as part of the quotes is an indication of whether the fund charges redemption and/or 12(b)-1 fees.

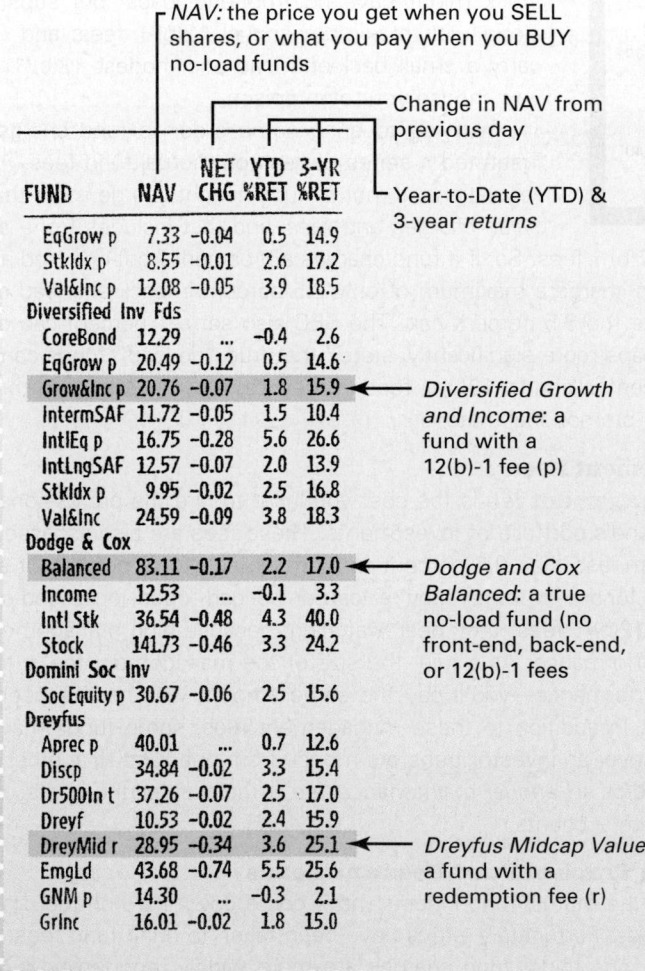

Source: *The Wall Street Journal*, March 8, 2006.

In addition to the public sources just noted, the mutual funds themselves are required by the SEC to *fully disclose* all of their fees and expenses in a standardized, easy-to-understand format. Every fund prospectus must contain, right up front, a fairly detailed *fee table*, much like the one illustrated in Exhibit 13.4. Notice that this table has three parts. The first specifies all *shareholder transaction costs*. This section tells you what it's going to cost to buy and sell shares in the mutual fund. The next section lists all *annual operating expenses* of the fund. Showing these expenses as a percentage of average net assets, the fund must break out management fees, those elusive 12(b)-1 fees, and any other expenses. The third section gives the *total cost over time* of buying, selling, and owning the fund. This part of the table contains both transaction and operating expenses and shows what the total costs would be over hypothetical 1-, 3-, 5-, and 10-year holding periods. To ensure consistency and comparability, the funds must follow a rigid set of guidelines when presenting the example costs.

Buying and Selling Funds

Buying and selling shares of *closed-end investment companies*, or *ETFs*, is no different from buying shares of common stock. The transactions are executed through brokers or dealers who handle the orders in the usual way. They're subject to the normal transaction costs, and because they're treated like any other listed or OTC stock, their shares can even be margined or sold short.

The situation is considerably different, however, with *open-end funds*. There are several ways of acquiring such shares, depending on whether the fund is load or no-load. Regardless of type, however, the fund is required to provide you with basic information about its operations. According to SEC rules, investors now have the choice of buying into a mutual fund based on a brief (2- to 6-page), concise, readable document called a *fund profile*, or of requesting a more detailed *prospectus* from the fund company. The fund profile is designed to tell you (in plain English and in a standardized format) the most important things you need to know about a fund (for example, its investment objectives, principal risks, fees and expenses, etc.) without overwhelming you with lots of unnecessary legalese. Likewise, the fund prospectuses are now far more user friendly as they, too, must be simplified and downsized (by removing all the irrelevant boiler plates); they must be written in plain English, as well.

Should you want more information than provided in either the profile or prospectus, you can always request a copy of the fund's *Statement of Additional Information*, which contains detailed information on the fund's investment objectives, portfolio composition, management, and past performance. Whether it's the fund profile (which should be good enough for most investors), the fund's prospectus, or its Statement of Additional Information, the bottom line is these publications should be required reading for anybody who's thinking about investing in a mutual fund.

In the case of load funds, investors buy shares in the fund from a broker or through salespeople employed by the funds—not surprisingly, many of these funds carry substantial load charges. Most brokerage firms are authorized to sell shares in a variety of load funds; this is the easiest and most convenient way of buying funds for investors who have established brokerage accounts. Sometimes, however, the fund may not be sold through brokerage houses, in which case the investor would deal directly with the fund's commissioned salespeople—individuals employed by the mutual fund for the sole purpose of selling its shares.

If you happen to be interested in a no-load, or perhaps even a low-load fund, you may be pretty much on your own. You'll have to write or call the mutual fund directly (most have toll-free numbers) to obtain information. You'll then receive an order form and instructions on how to buy shares; no salesperson will ever call on you. To complete the transaction, you simply mail your check, along with the completed

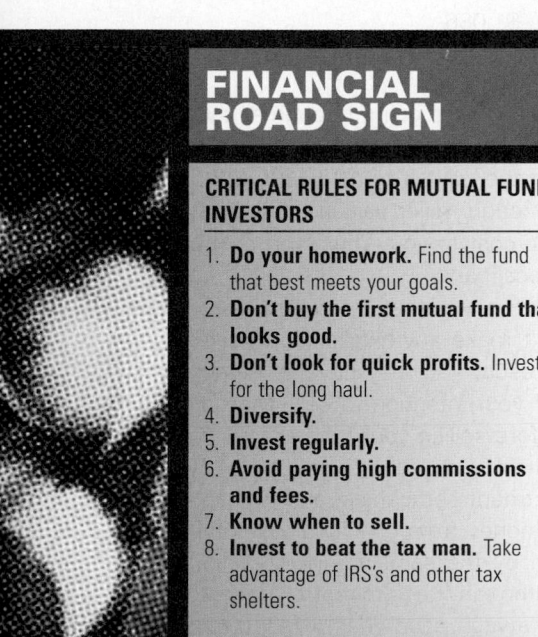

EXHIBIT 13.4   A Mutual Fund Fee Table

The SEC requires mutual funds to fully disclose load charges, redemption fees, and annual expenses in a three-part table like the one shown here. The table must be conspicuously placed near the front of the prospectus, not hidden somewhere in the back.

Fee Table

The following table describes the fees and expenses that are incurred when you buy, hold, or sell shares of the fund.

Shareholder Fees (paid by the investor directly)

Maximum sales charge (load) on purchases (as a % of offering price)	3.00%
Sales charge (load) on reinvested distributions	None
Deferred sales charge (load) on redemptions	None
Exchange fees	None
Annual account maintenance fee (for accounts under $2,500)	$12.00

Annual fund operating expenses (paid from fund assets)

Management fee	0.45%
Distribution and service (12b-1) fee	None
Other expenses	0.20%
Total annual fund operating expenses	0.65%

Example

This example is intended to help an investor compare the cost of investing in different funds. The example assumes a $10,000 investment in the fund for 1, 3, 5, and 10 years and then a redemption of all fund shares at the end of those periods. The example also assumes that an investment returns 5 percent each year and that the fund's operating expenses remain the same. Although actual costs may be higher or lower, based on these assumptions an investor's costs would be:

1 year	$364
3 years	$502
5 years	$651
10 years	$1,086

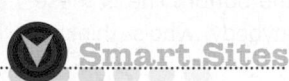
Smart Sites

Unlike many mutual fund Web sites, FundAlarm focuses on when to sell the funds you own rather than what funds to buy. Link to the site at **http://www.thomsonedu.com/finance/gitman.**

order form, to the mutual fund or its designated agent. Before going through all that, however, check with your bank; if it's a major (good-sized) commercial bank, it may be authorized to sell a wide variety of mutual funds. During the past 5 to 10 years, a lot of big mutual funds have arranged to sell their products through major banking and other financial institutions around the country—and at no added cost to you. Thus, you may be able to find just the fund you're looking for right in your local bank.

Selling shares in a fund is also a do-it-yourself affair, whether the fund is load or no-load. Because brokers and salespeople usually don't make anything on fund *sales*, they have little motivation to execute sell orders. As a result, you may have to redeem your fund shares by directly notifying the mutual fund of your intention to sell. The fund then buys the shares back and mails you a check. But before selling your fund shares this way, check to see if the fund offers you the ability to switch funds either by phone or over the Internet. This service is available from several investment companies, and it enables you to simply pick up the phone (or go online) to move money from one fund to another—the only constraint is that the funds must be managed by the same family of funds. Most companies charge little or nothing for these shifts, although funds that offer free exchange privileges often limit the number of times you can switch each year. (We'll discuss this service in more detail later in the chapter, when we cover *conversion privileges*.)

❚ Concept Check

CHECK • CONCEPT CHECK • CONCEPT CHECK • CONCEPT CHECK • CONCEPT CHECK • CONCEPT CHECK • CONCEPT C

13-1	What is a mutual fund? Why are diversification and professional management so important to mutual funds?
13-2	Who are the key players in a typical mutual fund organization?
13-3	What's the difference between an open-end fund and an exchange-traded fund?
13-4	What's the difference between a load fund and a no-load fund?
13-5	What is a *12(b)-1* fund? Can such a fund operate as a no-load fund?
13-6	Briefly describe a *back-end load*, a *low load*, a *hidden load*. How can you tell what kind of fees and charges a fund has?

LG3 ❘ TYPES OF FUNDS AND FUND SERVICES

Some mutual funds specialize in stocks and others in bonds; some funds have maximum capital gains as their investment objective, and some seek high current income. Some funds will appeal to speculators, and others primarily to income-oriented investors. Every fund has a particular investment objective, some of the more common ones being capital appreciation, income, tax-exempt income, preserving investment capital, or some combination thereof. Disclosure of a fund's investment objective is required by the SEC, and each fund is expected to do its best to conform to its stated investment policy and objective.

Categorizing funds according to their investment policies and objectives is widely practiced in the mutual fund industry because it tends to reflect similarities not only in how the funds manage their money but also in their risk and return characteristics. Some popular types of mutual funds include growth, aggressive growth, value, equity-income, balanced, growth-and-income, bond, money market, index, sector, socially responsible, international, and asset allocation funds. Let's now look at these funds to see what they are and what they have to offer investors. After we do that, we'll look at the kinds of investor services these funds offer.

Types of Funds

Growth Funds

The objective of a *growth fund* is simple—capital appreciation. Long-term growth and capital gains are the primary goals of such funds, and as a result they invest principally in common stocks with above-average growth potential. Due to the uncertain nature of their investment income, growth funds involve a fair amount of risk exposure. They're usually viewed as long-term investment vehicles that are most suitable for the aggressive investor who wants to build capital and has little interest in current income.

Aggressive Growth Funds

These are the so-called performance funds that tend to increase in popularity when the markets heat up. *Aggressive growth funds* are highly speculative investment vehicles that seek large profits from capital gains; in many ways, they're really an extension of the growth fund concept. Many are fairly small (with average assets under management of less than $300 million), and their portfolios consist mainly of high-flying common stocks. Also known as "capital appreciation" funds, they often buy stocks of small, unseasoned companies, stocks with relatively high price/earnings multiples, and stocks whose prices are highly volatile. Some of these funds even go so far as to use leverage in their portfolios (that is, they buy stocks on margin by borrowing part of the purchase price). All this is designed, of course, to yield big returns. However, aggressive growth funds are also highly speculative and are perhaps the most volatile of all the fund types. When the markets are good, these funds do well; when the markets are bad, they typically experience substantial losses.

Value Funds

Value funds confine their investing to stocks considered to be *undervalued* by the market; that is, the funds look for stocks that are fundamentally sound but have yet to be discovered and as such remain undervalued by the market. These funds hold stocks as much for their underlying intrinsic values as for their *growth potential.* In stark contrast to growth funds, value funds look for stocks with relatively low P/Es, high dividend yields, and moderate amounts of financial leverage. They prefer undiscovered companies that offer the potential for growth, rather than those that are already experiencing rapid growth. Value investing isn't easy! It involves extensive evaluation of corporate financial statements and any other documents that will help fund managers *uncover value (i.e., investment opportunities) before the rest of the market does* (that's the key to getting the low P/Es). And the approach seems to work. For even though value investing is generally regarded as being *less risky* than growth investing (lower P/Es, higher dividend yields, and fundamentally stronger companies all translate into reduced risk exposure), the long-term returns to investors in value funds are quite competitive with those earned from growth or even aggressive growth funds. Thus, value funds are often viewed as a viable alternative for relatively conservative investors who are looking for the attractive returns that common stocks have to offer, yet want to keep share price volatility and investment risk in check.

Equity-Income Funds

Equity-income funds emphasize current income, which they provide by investing primarily in high-yielding common stocks. Preserving capital is also a goal of these funds; so is increasing capital gains, although it's not their primary objective. These funds invest heavily in high-grade common stocks, some convertible securities and preferred stocks, and occasionally even junk bonds or certain types of high-grade foreign bonds. They like securities that generate hefty dividend yields, but also consider potential price appreciation over the longer haul. In general, because of their emphasis on dividends and current income, these funds tend to hold higher-quality securities that are subject to less price volatility than seen in the market as a whole. They're generally viewed as a fairly low-risk way of investing in stocks.

Balanced Funds

Balanced funds are so named because they tend to hold a balanced portfolio of both stocks and bonds, and they do so to generate a well-balanced return of current income and long-term capital gains. In many ways, they're like equity-income funds, except that balanced funds usually put much more into fixed-income securities; generally they keep around 30 to 40 percent of their portfolios in bonds, sometimes more. The bonds are used principally to provide current income, and stocks are selected mainly for their long-term growth potential. The funds can, of course, tilt the emphasis in their security holdings one way or the other. Clearly, the more the fund leans toward fixed-income securities, the more income-oriented it will be. Balanced funds tend to confine their investing mainly to high-grade securities and are therefore usually considered a relatively safe form of investing, one that can earn you a competitive rate of return without a lot of price volatility.

Growth-and-Income Funds

Like balanced funds, *growth-and-income funds* seek a balanced return made up of current income and long-term capital gains, but they put greater emphasis on growth of capital. Moreover, unlike balanced funds, growth-and-income funds put most of their money into equities—it's not unusual for these funds to have 80 to 90 percent of their capital in common stocks. They tend to confine most of their investing to high-quality issues, so you can expect to find lots of growth-oriented blue-chip stocks in their portfolios, along with a fair amount of high-quality income stocks. One big appeal of these funds is the fairly substantial return many of them have been able to generate over the long haul. But then, these funds do involve a fair amount of risk, if for no other reason than their emphasis on stocks and capital gains. Growth-and-income funds are most suitable for investors who can tolerate their risk and price volatility.

Bond Funds

As their name implies, *bond funds* invest in various kinds of fixed-income securities. Income is their primary investment objective, although they don't ignore capital gains. There are three important advantages to buying shares in bond funds rather than investing directly in bonds. First, bond funds generally are more liquid; second, they offer a cost-effective way of achieving a high degree of diversification in an otherwise expensive investment vehicle (most bonds carry minimum denominations of $1,000 to $5,000, or more); and third, bond funds will automatically reinvest interest and other income, thereby allowing the investor to earn fully compounded rates of return. There are more than 6,000 publicly traded bond funds, which together have over $1.5 *trillion* worth of bonds under management.

Bond funds are usually considered a fairly conservative form of investment, but they're not totally without risk, because the prices of the bonds held in the funds' portfolios will fluctuate with changing interest rates. Although many of the funds are basically conservative, a growing number are increasingly aggressive—in fact, much of the growth that bond funds have experienced in the recent past can be attributed to this new investment attitude. Thus, no matter what your tastes, you'll find a full menu of bond funds available, including these:

- **Government bond funds,** which invest in U.S. Treasury and agency securities.
- **Mortgage-backed bond funds,** which put their money into various types of mortgage-backed securities issued by agencies of the U.S. government (such as GNMA issues). These funds appeal to investors not only because they provide diversification and a more affordable way to get into these securities but also because they have a provision that allows investors (if they so choose) to reinvest the *principal* portion of the monthly cash flow—thereby enabling them to preserve, rather than consume, their capital.
- **High-grade corporate bond funds,** which invest chiefly in investment-grade securities rated triple-B or better.
- **High-yield corporate bond funds,** which are risky investments that buy *junk bonds* for the yields they offer.
- **Convertible bond funds,** which invest primarily in (domestic and possibly foreign) securities that can be converted or exchanged into common stocks; by investing in convertible bonds and preferreds, the funds offer investors some of the price stability of bonds, along with the capital appreciation potential of stocks.
- **Municipal bond funds,** which invest in tax-exempt securities and are suitable for investors looking for tax-free income. Like their corporate counterparts, municipals can also come out as either high-grade or high-yield funds. A special type of municipal bond fund is the so-called *single-state* fund, which invests in the municipal issues of only one state, thus producing (for residents of that state) interest income that's *fully* exempt from federal taxes as well as state (and possibly even local/city) taxes.
- **Intermediate-term bond funds,** which invest in bonds with maturities of 7 to 10 years, or less, and offer not only attractive yields but also relatively low price volatility; shorter (2- to 5-year) funds are also available and can be used as substitutes for money market investments by investors looking for higher returns on their money, especially when short-term rates are way down.

Money Market Mutual Funds

With the introduction of the very first *money fund* in 1972, the concept of investing in a portfolio of short-term money market instruments caught on like wildfire. The reason for their popularity is quite simple: money funds gave investors with modest amounts of capital access to the higher-yielding end of the money market, where many instruments require minimum investments of $100,000 or more. Today, there are about 900 publicly traded money funds that, together, hold nearly $2.1 *trillion* in assets.

Actually, there are several different kinds of money market mutual funds. **General-purpose money funds** essentially invest in any and all types of money market investment vehicles, from Treasury bills to corporate commercial paper and bank certificates of deposit. They invest their money wherever they can find attractive short-term returns. Most money funds are of this type. The **tax-exempt money fund** limits its investments to tax-exempt municipal securities with very short (30- to 90-day) maturities. Because their income is free from federal income tax, they appeal predominantly to investors in high tax brackets. **Government securities money funds** were established as a way of meeting investors' concern for safety. These funds eliminate any risk of default by confining their investments to Treasury bills and other short-term securities of the U.S. government or its agencies (such as the Federal National Mortgage Association).

Money funds are highly liquid investment vehicles that are very low in risk because they're virtually immune to capital loss. However, the interest income they produce tends to follow interest rate conditions, and as such, the returns to shareholders are subject to the ups and downs of market interest rates. (Money funds were discussed more fully in Chapter 4, along with other short-term investment vehicles.)

Index Funds

"If you can't beat 'em, join 'em." That saying pretty much describes the idea behind *index funds*. Essentially, an index fund is a type of mutual fund that buys and holds a portfolio of stocks (or bonds) equivalent to those in a market index like the S&P 500. An index fund that's trying to match the S&P 500, for example, would hold the same 500 stocks that are held in that index, in exactly (or nearly) the same proportion. Rather than trying to beat the market, as most actively managed funds do, *index funds simply try to match the market*—that is, to match the performance of the index on which the fund is based. They do this through low-cost investment management; in fact, in most cases, the whole portfolio is run almost entirely by a computer that matches the fund's holdings with those of the targeted index. Besides the S&P 500, several other market indexes are used, including the S&P MidCap 400, Russell 2000, and Wilshire 5000, as well as value stock indexes, growth stock indexes, international stock indexes, and even bond indexes.

The approach of index funds is strictly buy and hold. About the only time there's a change to the portfolio of an index fund is when the targeted market index alters its "market basket" of securities. A pleasant by-product of this buy-and-hold approach is that the funds have extremely low portfolio turnover rates and, therefore, very little in *realized* capital gains. As a result, aside from a modest amount of dividend income, these funds produce very little taxable income from year to year, which leads many high-income investors to view them as a type of tax-sheltered investment. In addition to their tax shelter, these funds provide something else. That is, as boring as the whole idea may sound, by simply trying to match the market, index funds actually produce *highly competitive returns* for investors! The fact is, it's very tough to consistently outperform the market, so the index funds don't even try. The net result is that on average, index funds tend to produce better returns than most other types of stock funds do. Granted, every now and then the fully managed funds will have a year (or two) when they outperform index funds, but those are the exception rather than the rule!

Sector Funds

As the name implies, a *sector fund* restricts its investments to a particular sector of the market. These funds concentrate their investment holdings in the one or more industries that make up the targeted sector. For example, a *healthcare* sector fund would confine its investments to those industries that make up this segment of the market: drug companies, hospital management firms, medical suppliers, and biotech concerns. Its portfolio would then consist of promising growth stocks from those industries. The underlying investment objective of sector funds is *capital gains*. In many ways, they're similar to growth funds and should be considered speculative. The idea behind sector funds is that the really attractive returns come from small segments of the market. So, rather than diversifying the portfolio across wide segments of the market, you can put your money where the action is. Some popular sector funds are those that concentrate their investments in real estate (REITs), technology, financial

At Index Funds.com, you'll find a wealth of resources, articles, and a Fund Screener to search based on expense ratio, returns, net assets, or other criteria. **http://www .thomsonedu.com/finance/ gitman.**

general-purpose money fund A money fund that invests in virtually any type of short-term investment vehicle.

tax-exempt money fund A money fund that limits its investments to short-term tax-exempt municipal securities.

government securities money fund A money fund that limits its investments to short-term securities of the U.S. government and its agencies.

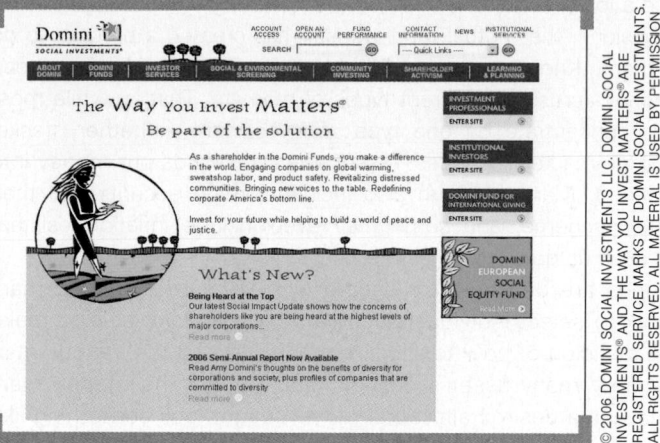

services, natural resources, electronics, telecommunications, and, of course, healthcare.

Socially Responsible Funds

For some, investing is far more than just cranking out some financial ratios. To these investors, the security selection process doesn't end with bottom lines, P/E ratios, growth rates, and betas; rather, it also includes the *active, explicit consideration of moral, ethical, and environmental issues*. The idea is that social concerns should play just as big a role in the investment decision as profits and other financial matters. Not surprisingly, a number of funds today cater to such investors; known as **socially responsible funds,** they actively and directly incorporate morality and ethics into the investment decision. These funds consider only what they view as socially responsible companies for inclusion in their portfolios—if a company doesn't meet certain moral, ethical, or environmental tests, they simply won't consider buying the stock, no matter how good the bottom line looks. Generally speaking, these funds abstain from investing in companies that derive revenues from tobacco, alcohol, or gambling; are weapons contractors; or operate nuclear power plants. The funds also tend to favor firms that produce "responsible" products and services, have strong employee relations, have positive environmental records, and are socially responsive to the communities in which they operate.

International Funds

In searching for higher yields and better returns, American investors have shown increased interest in foreign securities. Sensing an opportunity, the mutual fund industry was quick to respond with a proliferation of so-called **international funds**—a type of mutual fund that does all or most of its investing in foreign securities. Just look at the number of international funds around today versus a few years ago. In 1985, there were only about 40 of these funds; by 2005, that number had grown to nearly 2,500. The fact is, many people would like to invest in foreign securities but simply don't have the experience or know-how. International funds may be just the ticket for such investors. Technically, the term *international fund* is used to describe a type of fund that *invests exclusively in foreign securities*, often confining the fund's activities to specific geographical regions (such as Mexico, Australia, Europe, or the Pacific Rim). In contrast, there's another class of international funds, known as *global funds*, that invest not only in foreign securities *but also in U.S. companies*—usually multinational firms. As a rule, global funds provide more diversity and, with access to both foreign and domestic markets, can go wherever the action is.

These funds attempt to take advantage of international economic developments in two ways: (1) by capitalizing on changing foreign *market conditions*, and (2) by positioning themselves to benefit from *devaluation of the dollar*. They do so because they can make money not only from rising share prices in a foreign market, but—perhaps just as important—from a falling dollar (which in itself produces capital gains to American investors in foreign securities and international funds). Many of these funds, however, try to protect their investors from currency exchange risks by using various types of *hedging strategies*. That is, by using foreign currency options and futures (or some other type of derivative product), the fund tries to eliminate (or reduce) the effects of currency exchange rates.

Asset Allocation Funds

Studies have shown that the most important decision an investor can make concerns where to allocate his or her investment assets. This is known as *asset allocation*, and, as we saw in Chapter 11, involves deciding how you're going to divide your investments among different types of securities. For example, what portion of your money will be devoted to money market securities, what portion to stocks, what portion to bonds? Asset allocation deals in broad terms and doesn't address individual security selection. Even so, as strange as it may sound, asset allocation has been found to be a far more important determinant of total returns on a well-diversified portfolio than individual security selection

---

If socially responsible funds appeal to you, the Social Investment Forum is a good first stop. **http://www .thomsonedu.com/ finance/gitman.**

---

socially responsible fund
A fund that invests only in companies meeting certain moral, ethical, and/or environmental tests.

international fund A mutual fund that does all or most of its investing in foreign securities.

has. Because a lot of individual investors have a tough time making asset allocation decisions, the mutual fund industry has created a product to do the job for them. Known as *asset allocation funds*, these funds spread investors' money across all different types of markets. That is, while most mutual funds concentrate on one type of investment—whether stocks, bonds, or money market securities—asset allocation funds put money into all these markets. Many of them also include foreign securities in their asset allocation scheme, and some may even include inflation-resistant investments such as gold or real estate.

These funds are designed for people who want to hire fund managers not only to select individual securities for them but also to make the strategic decision of how to allocate money among the various markets. Here's how many asset allocation funds work. The money manager will establish a desired allocation mix—it might look something like this: 50 percent of the portfolio goes to U.S. stocks, 10 percent to foreign securities, 30 percent to bonds, and 10 percent to money market securities. Securities are then purchased for the fund in this proportion, and the overall portfolio maintains the desired mix. Actually, each segment of the fund is managed almost as a separate portfolio, so securities within, say, the stock portion are bought, sold, and held as the market dictates. Now, here's what really separates asset allocation funds from the rest of the pack: *As market conditions change over time, the asset allocation mix also changes.* So, if the U.S. stock market starts to soften, funds will be moved out of stocks to some other area; as a result, the stock portion of the portfolio may drop to, say, 35 percent and the foreign securities portion may increase to 25 percent. Of course, there's no assurance that the money manager will make the right moves at the right time, but that's the idea behind these funds.

Services Offered by Mutual Funds

Ask most investors why they buy a particular mutual fund, and they'll probably tell you that the fund offers the kind of income and return they're looking for. Now, no one would question the importance of return in the investment decision, but there are other reasons for investing in mutual funds, not the least of which are the valuable services they provide. Some of the most sought-after *mutual fund services* are automatic investment and reinvestment plans, regular income programs, conversion privileges, and retirement programs.

Automatic Investment Plans

It takes money to make money, and for an investor that means being able to accumulate the capital to put into the market. Unfortunately, that's not always the easiest thing to do. Enter mutual funds, with a program that makes savings and capital accumulation as painless as possible. The **automatic investment plan** allows fund shareholders to automatically funnel fixed amounts of money *from their paychecks or bank accounts* into a mutual fund. It's very much like a payroll deduction plan that treats savings a lot like insurance coverage—that is, just as insurance premiums are automatically deducted from your paycheck (or bank account), so too are investments to your mutual fund.

This fund service has become popular because it allows shareholders to invest without having to think about it. Just about every major fund group offers some kind of automatic investment plan. To enroll, a shareholder simply fills out a form authorizing the fund to transfer a set amount (usually it has to be a minimum of $25 to $100 per period) from your bank account or paycheck at regular intervals—typically monthly or quarterly. Once enrolled, you'll be buying shares in the funds of your choice every month or quarter (most funds deal in fractional shares); of course, if it's a load fund, you'll still have to pay normal

automatic investment plan An automatic savings program that enables an investor to systematically channel a set amount of money into a given mutual fund.

sales charges on your periodic investments. You can get out of the program anytime you like, without penalty, by simply contacting the fund. Convenience may be the chief advantage of these plans, but they make solid investment sense, because one of the best ways of building up a sizable amount of capital is to systematically add *funds to your investment program over time*. The importance of making regular contributions to your investment program cannot be overstated—it ranks right up there with compound interest!

Automatic Reinvestment Plans

This plan is one of the real draws of mutual funds, and it's offered by just about every open-ended mutual fund. Whereas automatic investment plans deal with money shareholders put into a fund, automatic *reinvestment* plans deal with the dividends and other distributions the funds pay to their shareholders. Much like the dividend reinvestment plans we looked at with stocks, the **automatic reinvestment plans** of mutual funds enable you to keep all your capital fully employed. Through this service, dividend and capital gains income is *automatically used to buy additional shares in the fund*, and in so doing, enables the investor to earn a fully compounded rate of return. Keep in mind, however, that even though you reinvest your dividends and capital gains, the IRS still treats them as cash receipts and taxes them in the year that they're paid.

The important point is that by plowing back profits (reinvested dividends and capital gains distributions), investors can put their profits to work in generating even more earnings. Indeed, the effects of these plans on total accumulated capital over the long haul can be substantial. Exhibit 13.5 shows the long-term impact of one such plan. (These are the actual performance numbers for a *real* mutual fund—Fidelity Low-Priced Stock, in this case.) In the illustration, we assume that the investor starts with $10,000 and, except for reinvesting dividends and capital gains distributions, *adds no new capital over time*. Even so, the initial investment of $10,000 grew to nearly $135,000 over the 15-year period from 1991 to 2005 (which, by the way, amounts to a fully compounded rate of return of 18.84 percent). Clearly, so long as care is taken in selecting an appropriate fund, *attractive benefits can be derived from the systematic accumulation of capital offered by automatic reinvestment plans*.

Regular Income

Automatic reinvestment plans are great for the long-term investor, but how about the investor who's looking for a steady stream of income? Once again, mutual funds have a service to meet the need. It's called a **systematic withdrawal plan,** and it's offered by most open-ended funds. Once enrolled in one of these plans, you'll automatically receive a predetermined amount of money every month or quarter. To participate, shareholders are usually required to have a minimum investment of $5,000 to $10,000, and the size of the withdrawal must usually be $50 or more per month. Depending on how well the fund is doing, the annual return generated by the fund may actually be greater than the withdrawals, thus allowing the investor not only to receive regular income but also to enjoy an automatic accumulation of *additional* shares in the plan. On the other hand, if the fund isn't performing well, the withdrawals could eventually deplete the original investment.

Conversion Privileges

Sometimes investors find it necessary to switch out of one fund and into another; for example, their investment objectives may change, or the investment environment itself may have changed. **Conversion (or exchange) privileges** conveniently and economically meet the needs of these investors. Investment companies that offer a number of different funds to the investing public—known as *fund families*—usually provide conversion privileges that enable shareholders to easily move from one fund to another; this can be done either by phone or on the Internet. The only limitation is that the investor must confine the switches to the same *family* of funds. For example, an investor can switch from a Dreyfus growth fund to a Dreyfus money fund, or to its income fund, or to any other fund managed by Dreyfus. Most fund families, especially the bigger ones, offer investors a full range of investment products as part of providing one-stop mutual fund shopping. Whether you want an equity fund, a bond fund, or a money fund, these fund families have something for you.

automatic reinvestment plan A plan that allows share owners to elect to have dividends and capital gains distributions reinvested in additional fund shares.

systematic withdrawal plan A plan offered by mutual funds that allows shareholders to be paid specifiedamounts of money each period.

conversion (exchange) privileges A feature that allows investors to switch from one mutual fund to another within a family of funds.

EXHIBIT 13.5 Effects of Reinvesting Income

Reinvesting dividends and/or capital gains can have tremendous effects on your investment position. This graph shows the results of a hypothetical investor who initially invested $10,000 and, for a period of 15 years, reinvested all dividends and capital gains distributions in additional fund shares. (No adjustment has been made for any income taxes payable by the shareholder—which would be appropriate so long as the fund was held in, say, an IRA or Keogh account.)

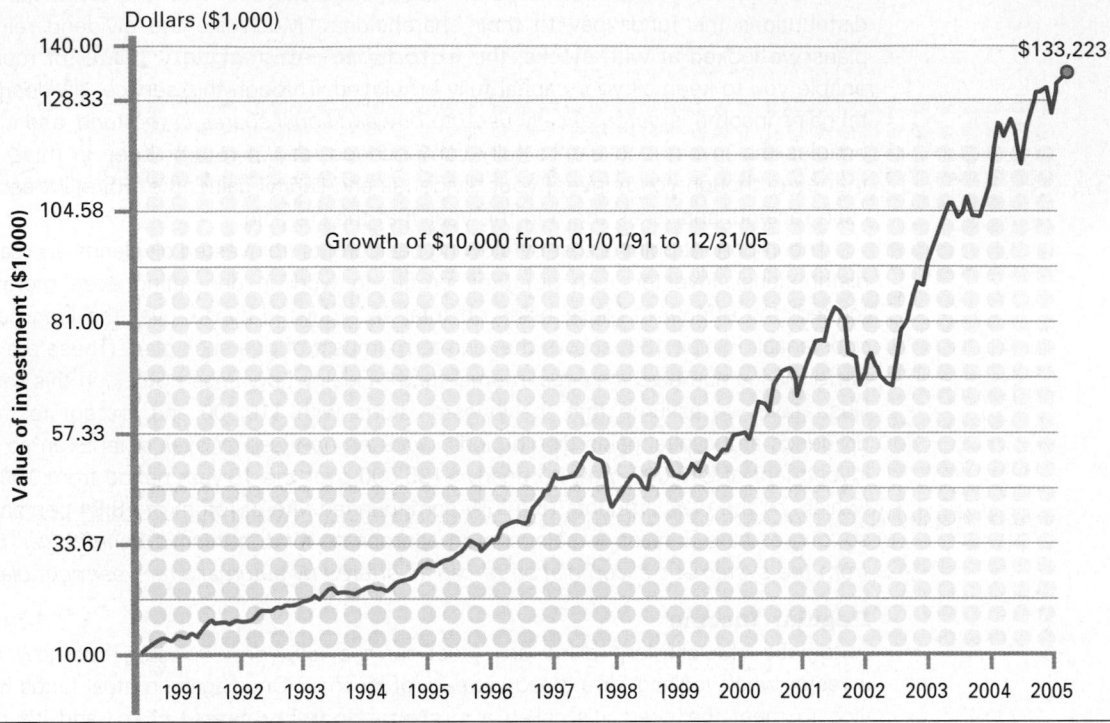

Source: *Morningstar Principia for Mutual Funds*, December 31, 2005.

Conversion privileges are attractive because they permit investors to manage their holdings more aggressively by allowing them to move in and out of funds as the investment environment changes. Unfortunately, there's one major drawback; although you never see the cash, the exchange of shares from one fund to another is regarded, for tax purposes, as a sale followed by the purchase of a new security. As a result, if any capital gains exist at the time of the exchange, the investor is liable for the taxes on that profit.

Retirement Plans

Government legislation permits self-employed individuals to divert part of their income into self-directed *retirement plans*. And all working Americans, whether they're self-employed or not, are allowed to establish individual retirement accounts—either in the form of a standard tax-deductible IRA, or the newest type of retirement account, the Roth IRA (all of which we'll look at in the next chapter). Today all mutual funds provide a special service that allows individuals to quickly and easily set up tax-deferred retirement programs as either IRA or Keogh accounts—or, through their place of employment, to participate in a qualified tax-sheltered retirement plan, such as a 401(k). The funds set up the plans and handle all the administrative details so that the shareholders can take full advantage of available tax savings.

▐▌ Concept Check

13-7	What's the difference between a growth fund and a balanced fund?
13-8	What's an international fund, and how does it differ from a global fund?
13-9	What's an asset allocation fund? How do these funds differ from other types of mutual funds?
13-10	If growth, income, and capital preservation are the primary objectives of mutual funds, why do we bother to categorize them by type?
13-11	What are fund families? What advantages do these families offer investors?
13-12	What are automatic reinvestment plans, and how do they differ from automatic investment plans?

LG4, LG5 MAKING MUTUAL FUND INVESTMENTS

Suppose you're confronted with this situation: You have money to invest and are trying to select the right place to put it. You obviously want to pick a security that not only meets your idea of an acceptable risk but also generates an attractive rate of return. The problem is that you have to choose from literally thousand of securities. Sound like a "mission impossible"? Well, that's what a typical investor is up against when trying to select a suitable mutual fund. But perhaps if you approach the problem systematically, it may not be so formidable after all. For as we'll see, it is possible to whittle down the list of alternatives by matching your investment needs with the investment objectives of the funds.

The Selection Process

When it comes to mutual funds, one question that every investor has to answer is: Why invest in a mutual fund to begin with; why not just go it alone (that is, buy individual stocks and bonds directly)? For beginning investors, or investors with little capital, the answer is pretty simple—mutual funds provide far more diversification than such investors could ever get on their own, plus they get the help of professional money managers, and at a very reasonable cost to boot.

For more seasoned, better-heeled investors, the answers are probably a bit more involved. Certainly, the diversification and professional money management come into play, but there are other reasons. The competitive returns offered by mutual funds have to be a factor with many investors, and so do the services they provide. A lot of well-to-do investors have simply decided that they can get better returns over the long haul by carefully selecting mutual funds than by trying to invest on their own. So they put all, or a big chunk, of their money into funds. Many of these investors will use part of their capital to buy and sell individual securities on their own, and they'll use the rest *to buy mutual funds that invest in areas they don't fully understand or aren't well informed about*—for example, they'll use mutual funds to get into foreign markets or as the way to buy mortgage-backed securities. For more on the question of which way to go—mutual funds or individual securities—see the *Money in Action* box on our Web site **(http://www.thomsonedu.com/finance/ gitman.com).**

After deciding to use mutual funds, the investor then has to decide which funds to buy. The selection process itself (especially regarding the *types* of funds to purchase) obviously plays an important role in defining the amount of success you'll have with mutual funds. It means putting into action all you know about investing to gain as much return as possible from an acceptable level of risk. Given that you have an asset allocation strategy in place, and you're trying to select funds compatible to your targeted mix, the selection process begins with an assessment of your own investment needs; this sets the tone for your investment program. Obviously, you'll want to select from those thousands of funds the one or two (or three or four) that will best meet your investment needs.

Objectives and Motives for Using Funds

Selecting the right investment means finding those funds that are most suitable to your investment needs. *The place to start is with your own investment objectives*. In other words, why do you want to invest in a mutual fund, and what are you looking for in a fund? Obviously, an attractive rate of return would be desirable, but there's also the matter of ensuring a tolerable amount of risk exposure. Face it, some investors are more willing to take risks than others are, and this is certainly an important ingredient in the selection process. More than likely, when looking at your own risk temperament in relation to the various types of mutual funds available, you'll discover that certain types of funds are more appealing to you than others. For instance, aggressive growth or sector funds will probably *not* be attractive to individuals wishing to avoid high exposure to risk.

Another important factor in the selection process is the intended use of the mutual fund. That is, do you want to invest in mutual funds as a way of *accumulating capital* over an extended time, to *speculate* with your money in the hopes of generating high rates of return, or to *conserve your capital* by investing in low-risk securities where preservation of capital is as important, or more so, than return on capital. This is helpful information, because it helps you to focus on exactly what you're trying to do with your investment dollars. Finally, there's the matter of the services provided by the fund. If you're particularly interested in some services, be sure to look for them in the funds you select. Having assessed what you're looking for in a fund, you can now look at what the funds have to offer.

What Funds Have to Offer

The ideal mutual fund would achieve maximum capital growth when security prices rise, provide complete protection against capital loss when prices decline, and achieve high levels of current income at all times. Unfortunately, such funds don't exist. Instead, just as each individual has a set of investment needs, each fund has its own *investment objective*, its own *manner of operation*, and its own *range of services*. These three parameters are useful in helping you assess investment alternatives. But where does the investor look for such information? One obvious place is the fund's *profile* (or its prospectus), where information on investment objectives, portfolio composition, management, and past performance can be obtained. In addition, publications such as *The Wall Street Journal*, *Barron's*, *Money*, *Fortune*, and *Forbes* provide all sorts of useful data and information about mutual funds. These sources publish a wealth of operating and performance statistics in a convenient, easy-to-read format. Services are also available that provide background information and assessments on a wide variety of funds. Among the best in this category are *Morningstar's Mutual Funds* (see Exhibit 13.6), and *Value Line Mutual Fund Survey* (these reports are similar to its stock reports, but they apply to mutual funds). And, of course, all sorts of performance statistics are available on the Internet. For example, there are scores of free finance Web sites, like **http://finance.yahoo.com,** where you can obtain historical information on a fund's performance, security holdings, risk profile, load charges, and purchase information. Or you can buy, usually at reasonable prices, quarterly or annually updated software from organizations like *Morningstar* or the American Association of Individual Investors (AAII).

Whittling Down the Alternatives

At this point, fund selection becomes a process of elimination as you weigh your investment needs against the types of funds available. Many funds can be eliminated from consideration simply because they don't meet these needs. Some may be too risky; others

EXHIBIT 13.6 Mutual Fund Information

Investors who want in-depth information about the operating characteristics, investment holdings, and market performance of mutual funds can usually find what they're looking for in publications like *Morningstar Mutual Funds*, or, as shown here, from computer-based information sources like *Morningstar's Principia*.

Data through November 30, 2005. For internal and/or client reporting purposes only.

Fidelity Low-Priced Stk

	Ticker	Load	NAV	Yield	Total Assets	Mstar Category
	FLPSX	Closed	$41.30	0.5%	$36,517 mil	Mid-Cap Blend

Governance and Management

Stewardship Grade: B

Portfolio Manager(s)

Joel Tillinghast has managed this fund since its inception. Not only is he one of the most experienced managers in the group, he also is one of the best. Tillinghast receives research support from a team of small-cap analysts and from Fidelity's industry analysts, but he does much of the research on his own. He was named Morningstar's Domestic Equity Fund Manager of the Year for 2002.

Strategy

This fund focuses on companies with share prices of $35 or less, but that is a marketing gimmick. Manager Joel Tillinghast buys mostly smaller-cap fare with reasonable valuations and solid growth prospects. He spreads the portfolio across hundreds of holdings. Tillinghast is also willing to devote a substantial chunk of the portfolio to foreign issues and larger-cap stocks, and will let cash build if he can't find enough good investment opportunities. The fund closed to new investors on Dec. 31, 2003.

Historical Profile

Return: High
Risk: Below Avg
Rating: ★★★★★ Highest

81% 89% 98% 94% 80% 85% 91% 86% 88%

Investment Style
Equity
Stock %

▼ Manager Change
▼ Partial Manager Change
Growth of $10,000
— Investment Values of Fund
— Investment Values of S&P 500

59.0 / 43.6 / 32.4 / 24.0 / 17.0 / 10.0

Performance Quartile (within Category)

History

	1994	1995	1996	1997	1998	1999	2000	2001	2002	2003	2004	11-05	
	16.00	18.50	21.35	25.13	22.85	22.64	23.12	27.42	25.17	34.98	40.25	41.30	NAV
	4.81	24.89	26.89	26.73	0.53	5.08	18.83	26.71	-6.18	40.85	22.24	6.72	Total Return %
	3.49	-12.64	3.94	-6.62	-28.05	-15.96	27.93	38.59	15.91	12.18	11.37	1.85	+/-S&P 500
	8.40	-6.03	7.71	-5.52	-18.58	-9.64	1.34	27.31	8.35	5.26	5.77	-5.05	+/-S&P Mid 400
	0.55	1.46	1.33	1.34	0.81	0.67	0.75	0.70	0.11	0.08	0.35	0.37	Income Return %
	4.26	23.43	25.56	25.39	-0.28	4.41	18.08	26.01	-6.29	40.77	21.89	6.35	Capital Return %
	10	65	14	56	83	83	21	2	8	23	8	65	Total Rtn % Rank Cat
	0.09	0.23	0.24	0.28	0.20	0.15	0.16	0.16	0.03	0.02	0.12	0.26	Income $
	2.05	1.24	1.66	1.58	1.94	1.19	3.43	1.54	0.54	0.44	2.09	2.62	Capital Gains $
	1.13	1.11	1.04	1.01	0.95	1.08	0.80	1.00	0.97	1.01	0.97	0.94	Expense Ratio %
	0.51	1.31	1.46	1.36	1.10	0.52	0.58	0.92	0.34	0.05	0.15	0.57	Income Ratio %
	54	65	79	45	47	24	15	44	26	23	28	24	Turnover Rate %
	2,355	3,350	5,664	10,691	9,195	6,646	6,834	12,429	15,104	26,725	35,976	36,517	Net Assets $mil

Performance 11-30-05

	1st Qtr	2nd Qtr	3rd Qtr	4th Qtr	Total
2001	3.94	12.90	-7.30	16.48	26.71
2002	6.97	-0.27	-16.98	5.93	-6.18
2003	-6.04	21.31	8.50	13.88	40.85
2004	5.86	1.24	0.20	13.83	22.24
2005	-0.97	3.11	4.49		

Trailing	Total Return%	+/- S&P 500	+/-S&P Mid 400	%Rank Cat	Growth of $10,000
3 Mo	0.74	-2.13	-2.68	76	10,074
6 Mo	7.82	1.94	-2.31	65	10,782
1 Yr	10.97	2.53	-5.48	61	11,097
3 Yr Avg	20.87	8.78	1.69	16	17,659
5 Yr Avg	18.49	17.85	8.44	1	23,357
10 Yr Avg	16.15	6.87	1.91	3	44,688
15 Yr Avg	18.95	7.23	2.60	1	135,041

Tax Analysis	Tax-Adj Rtn%	%Rank Cat	Tax-Cost Rat	%Rank Cat
3 Yr (estimated)	20.05	16	0.68	66
5 Yr (estimated)	17.32	2	0.99	60
10 Yr (estimated)	14.09	7	1.77	60

Potential Capital Gain Exposure: 35% of assets

Rating and Risk

Time Period	Load-Adj Return %	Morningstar Rtn vs Cat	Morningstar Risk vs Cat	Morningstar Risk-Adj Rating
1 Yr	10.97			
3 Yr	20.87	+Avg	Avg	★★★★
5 Yr	18.49	High	-Avg	★★★★★
10 Yr	16.15	High	-Avg	★★★★★
Incept	17.44			

Other Measures	Standard Index S&P 500	Best Fit Index Mstar Small Core
Alpha	6.5	1.5
Beta	1.15	0.85
R-Squared	81	93
Standard Deviation	12.72	
Mean	20.87	
Sharpe Ratio	1.41	

Portfolio Analysis 07-31-05

Share change since 04-05 Total Stocks:986	Sector	PE	Tot Ret%	% Assets
DR Horton	Consumer	9.0	18.44	2.79
⊖ Safeway	Consumer	17.8	18.28	1.73
⊕ Health Management Associ	Health	17.1	3.90	1.53
Petroleo Brasileiro ADR	Energy	12.0	74.91	1.38
⊕ MBNA	Financial	16.1	-2.85	1.33
⊕ PacifiCare Health System	Health	22.5	52.23	1.24
⊖ Lafarge	Ind Mtrls	19.1	8.90	1.13
⊕ Next	Financial	—	—	1.09
⊕ SunGard Data Systems	Business	—	—	1.07
Lincare Holdings	Health	19.4	0.63	1.00
PMI Group	Financial	10.7	-2.40	0.96
⊕ Constellation Brands A	Goods	18.4	1.57	0.94
Renal Care Group	Health	25.7	30.45	0.91
⊕ CVS	Consumer	21.3	20.57	0.87
⊖ Unumprovident	Financial	13.2	24.70	0.86
⊕ Barratt Developments	Business	—	—	0.80
Metro	Consumer	—	—	0.64
Hon Hai Precision Indust	Hardware	—	—	0.64
Computer Sciences	Business	19.0	-10.89	0.64
⊖ Career Education	Consumer	16.8	-6.75	0.63

Current Investment Style

Value Blnd Growth — Large/Mid/Small

Market Cap	%
Giant	5.2
Large	13.6
Mid	48.5
Small	24.0
Micro	8.8

Avg $mil: 2,475

Value Measures		Rel Category
Price/Earnings	13.50	0.80
Price/Book	1.90	0.88
Price/Sales	0.71	0.65
Price/Cash Flow	6.32	0.88
Dividend Yield %	1.24	1.06

Growth Measures	%	Rel Category
Long-Term Erngs	12.99	1.05
Book Value	9.44	1.07
Sales	8.07	1.07
Cash Flow	4.01	0.48
Historical Erngs	14.16	0.92

Profitability	%	Rel Category
Return on Equity	17.68	1.20
Return on Assets	9.09	1.14
Net Margin	10.27	0.99

Sector Weightings	% of Stocks	Rel S&P 500	3 Year High Low	
⟳ Info	7.01	0.34		
Software	1.16	0.32	3	1
Hardware	4.73	0.46	7	5
Media	0.62	0.17	2	1
Telecom	0.50	0.16	1	1
Service	60.18	1.31		
Health	12.45	0.98	14	9
Consumer	21.90	2.66	25	18
Business	9.28	2.40	12	9
Financial	16.55	0.79	19	16
Mfg	32.82	0.98		
Goods	8.47	0.98	11	8
Ind Mtrls	16.54	1.36	18	15
Energy	7.17	0.77	7	2
Utilities	0.64	0.19	1	0

Composition

● Cash	10.5
● Stocks	87.9
● Bonds	0.0
● Other	1.6
Foreign (% of Stock)	26.6

Morningstar's Take by Laura Pavlenko Lutton 10-03-05

Fidelity Low-Priced Stock is sailing ahead, but the headwinds are stiff.

This small-blend fund is one of the mutual fund industry's most-successful offerings. With $37 billion in assets, it's one of the largest funds around, and manager Joel Tillinghast has consistently delivered peer-beating returns. The offering's five- and 10-year records are among the best in its peer group and have been achieved amid modest volatility.

The question becomes then, can this fund sustain its winning streak? On one hand, it appears unlikely. The fund's girth is a disadvantage because Tillinghast must often spend months building a relatively tiny position in the portfolio, and should a stock go south, it would be nearly impossible for him to unload it without driving the price lower. The fund's bulk has also pushed Tillinghast to expand the portfolio to include more than 1,000 stocks, which dilutes the effect of his best picks.

Still, although this fund is facing tougher circumstances, we wouldn't count it out just yet. Tillinghast has curbed the fund's risk profile by owning hundreds of stocks, yet the fund is no index-hugger. (Its overlap with the Russell 2000 Index is low.) Tillinghast's conviction in his picks is another plus. The fund's turnover is among the lowest in the small-blend category, and that helps keep its bloat ratio--a Morningstar measure that multiplies an offering's turnover rate by the average days' trading volume of its top 25 holdings--below that of many other prominent smaller-cap funds. We're also somewhat encouraged by Fidelity's recent commitment to significantly expand its small-cap research team. We believe the team has been understaffed for some time, and given the fund's size, Tillinghast needs and deserves all the support he can get.

In the end, we think Tillinghast's job has gotten much harder in recent years, and it's likely the fund won't perform as well. But we still think this fund's prospects are better than many of its peers'.

Address:	82 Devonshire Street, Boston MA 02109 800-343-3548
Web Address:	www.fidelity.com
Inception:	12-27-89
Advisor:	Fidelity Management & Research (FMR)
Subadvisor:	Multiple Subadvisors
NTF Plans:	Fidelity Retail-NTF, CommonWealth NTF

Minimum Purchase:	Closed	Add: —	IRA: —
Min Auto Inv Plan:	Closed	Add: —	
Sales Fees:	No-load, 1.50%R		
Management Fee:	0.74%		
Actual Fees:	Mgt:0.74%	Dist: —	
Expense Projections:	3Yr:$303	5Yr:$525	10Yr:$1166
Income Distrib:	Semi-Annually		

M⟳RNINGSTAR Mutual Funds

Source: *Morningstar Principia*, Release Date: December 31, 2005.

may be unsuitable as a storehouse of value. So, rather than trying to evaluate thousands of different funds, you can use a process of elimination to narrow the list down to two or three *types* of funds that best match your investment (and asset allocation) needs.

From here, you can whittle the list down a bit more by introducing other constraints. For example, because of cost considerations, you may want to deal only in no-load or low-load funds (more on this later), or you may be seeking certain services that are important to your investment goals.

Now we're ready to introduce the final (but certainly not the least important) element in the selection process: *the fund's investment performance*. Useful information includes (1) how the fund has performed over the past 5 to 7 years; (2) the type of return it has generated in good markets as well as bad; (3) the level of dividend and capital gains distributions, which is an important indication not only of how much current income the fund distributes annually but also of the fund's *tax efficiency* (as a rule, funds with low dividends and low asset turnovers expose their shareholders to taxes and have higher tax-efficiency ratings); and (4) the level of investment stability the fund has enjoyed over time (or, put another way, the amount of volatility/risk in the fund's return). By evaluating such information, you can identify some of the more successful mutual funds—those that not only offer the investment objectives and services you seek but also provide the best payoffs. And while you're doing this, you might want to consider some of the fund facts listed in Exhibit 13.7. Also keep in mind that this discussion deals with the mutual fund selection process in general. You should also understand the role of mutual funds in various types of company-sponsored retirement programs, such as 401(k) plans. So you might want to look at the *Money in Action* box, which addresses how to select mutual funds for a retirement account. In Chapter 14 on retirement planning, we'll discuss selecting mutual funds and other types of investment vehicles to include in both company-sponsored and self-directed retirement programs.

Stick with No Loads or Low Loads

There's a long-standing "debate" in the mutual fund industry regarding load funds and no-load funds. The question is, do load funds add value? And if not, why pay the load charges? As it turns out, the results generally don't support load funds. Rather than producing superior returns, load fund returns generally don't seem any better than the returns from no-load funds. In fact, the funds with abnormally high loads and 12(b)-1 fees often

Smart Sites

MAXfunds offers investors an entertaining and educational site to help make better investing decisions. It also covers lesser-known and smaller funds. Link to it at **http://www .thomsonedu.com/finance/ gitman.**

Mutual funds are meant to give investors a simple yet effective way of buying into the stock and bond markets. Unfortunately, fund investing isn't always as simple as it looks. So, here are a few fund facts every investor should keep in mind when making mutual fund investments.

- Stock funds that get hit hard in market crashes aren't necessarily bad investments.
- Even great funds have bad years now and then.
- Most stock (and bond) funds fail to beat the market.
- You don't need a broker to buy mutual funds.
- A fund that doesn't charge a sales commission isn't necessarily a no-load fund.
- If you own more than a dozen different funds, you probably own too many.
- Mutual fund names are often misleading.
- Bond funds with high yields don't necessarily produce high returns.
- Money market funds are not risk-free (you never know what kind of return you're going to earn with these things).
- If the market crashes, it will probably be too late to sell your fund shares (the damage likely will already have been done).
- Even bad funds sometimes rank as top performers.

MONEY IN ACTION

FINDING FUNDS FOR YOUR 401(K)

There may be no such thing as a free lunch, but there is such a thing as free money—in your company 401(k) plan. Most eligible workers contribute to their company-provided 401(k) retirement savings plans, with its matching contributions. The advantage of the 401(k) over other forms of retirement savings is that contributions are made with pretax dollars, and the money in the account grows tax deferred. Many employees don't give much thought to 401(k) investments, but it's important to carefully choose the mutual funds for a 401(k) based on an overall investment strategy.

The first step is to determine how much money you'll invest in your 401(k). It's a good idea to contribute at least enough money to take full advantage of your employer's matching contributions. Most employers offer 50 cents for every dollar you contribute, up to 6 percent of your salary. Next you should determine your asset allocation based on your risk tolerance and your years to retirement. Then you need to choose mutual funds from among those offered by the 401(k) that match your strategy.

There are several factors to consider. The fund should have better-than-average returns and ideally perform in the top 25 percent of funds, expenses should be low because they're taken as a percentage of your return, the fund's management should have a good track record, and the fund should be of a reasonable size so that the manager can move in and out of stock efficiently. If you think you might not pay enough attention to your investment, you might consider a target retirement fund. Such funds don't require as much attention because your investment is diversified based on your target retirement date. If you don't like many of the funds offered by your company's 401(k) plan, it's still wise to contribute to the plan to take advantage of the tax-deferred growth and your employer's matching contribution. A broad-based index fund is a good choice in this situation. You can then invest in other assets outside the 401(k) that are more appealing to you.

Remember to diversify your assets when planning your contributions to your 401(k). Your investments should include mutual funds with large- and small-cap stocks, as well as domestic and foreign funds. You should allocate no more than 10 percent of your portfolio to employer stock.

You'll need investments outside of your 401(k) to meet your retirement goals because the limits on contributions to a 401(k) won't provide enough savings for retirement. It's also a good idea to have outside investments for tax purposes. After-tax dollars can be invested in a Roth IRA, but the money grows tax free and withdrawals are tax free, while money withdrawn from a 401(k) plan is taxed. Make sure that the assets in your 401(k) and your other investments complement one another and don't overlap. In combination, your 401(k) and your other investments should satisfy your asset allocation goals. The Fix your mix tools at CNNMoney (**http://money .cnn.com,** click on "Calculators" at the bottom of the home page, then on "Asset Allocator") and RiskGrades (**http://www.riskgrades .com**) can help you determine the right asset mix. Most 401(k) plans offer investment advice, or you can consult with an independent financial adviser. Remember to review and rebalance your holdings yearly to maintain your allocations.

Critical Thinking Questions

1. What steps should you take when investing in your company's 401(k)?
2. Why is it important to diversify between your 401(k) and your other investments?
3. Why is it always a good idea to contribute to your company's 401(k)?

Sources: Penelope Wang, "The 401(k) Solution," CNNMoney.com, April 27, 2005, http://money.cnn.com; Paul J. Lim, "Birthday Bash!" *U.S. News & World Report*, January 16, 2006, p. 38–41; "Money 101 Lesson 23 401(k)s," July 11, 2006, http://money.cnn.com/pf/101/lessons/23/.

produce returns that are far *less* than what you can get from no-loads! And, because of compounding, the differential returns tend to widen with longer holding periods.

That shouldn't be surprising, though, because big load charges and/or 12(b)-1 fees do nothing more than *reduce your investable capital*, thus reducing the amount of money you have working for you. In fact, the only way a load fund can overcome this handicap is to *produce superior returns*—which is no easy thing to do, year in and year out. Granted, a handful of load funds have produced attractive returns over extended periods, but they're the exception rather than the rule.

Obviously, it's in your best interest to pay close attention to load charges (and other fees) whenever you're considering an investment in a mutual fund. As a rule, to maximize returns, *you should seriously consider sticking to no-load funds, or low-loads* (funds with total load charges, including 12(b)-1 fees, of 3 percent or less). At the very least, you should consider a more expensive load fund *only* if it has a much better performance record (and offers more return potential) than a less expensive fund. There may well be times when the higher costs are justified; but far more often, you're better off trying to minimize load charges. That shouldn't be all that hard to do, however; there are literally thousands of no-load and low-load funds to choose from, and they come in all types and sizes.

Getting a Handle on Mutual Fund Performance

If you were to believe all the sales literature, you'd think there was no way you could go wrong by investing in mutual funds. Just put your money into one of these funds and let the good times roll! Unfortunately, the hard facts of life are that *when it comes to investing, performance is never guaranteed.* And that applies just as much to mutual funds as it does to any other form of investing. Perhaps even more so, because with mutual funds, the single variable driving a fund's market price and return behavior is the performance of the fund's portfolio of securities.

Measuring Fund Performance

Basically, any (open- or closed-end) mutual fund has three potential sources of return: (1) dividend income, (2) capital gains distribution, and (3) change in the fund's share price. Depending on the type of fund, some will derive more income from one source than another; for example, we'd normally expect income-oriented funds to have higher dividend income than capital gains distributions do. Mutual funds regularly publish reports that recap investment performance. One such report is *The Summary of Income and Capital Changes*; an example is provided in Exhibit 13.8. This statement gives a brief overview of the fund's investment activities, including expense ratios and portfolio turnover rates. Of interest to us here is the top part of the report (from "Net asset value, beginning of period" through "Net asset value, end of period"—lines 1 to 10). This part reveals the amount of dividend income and capital gains distributed to the shareholders, along with any change in the fund's net asset value.

Dividend income (see line 7 of Exhibit 13.8) is the amount derived from the dividend and interest income earned on the security holdings of the mutual fund. When the fund receives dividends or interest payments, it passes these on to shareholders in the form of dividend payments. The fund accumulates all the current income it has received for the period and then pays it out an a prorated basis. Because the mutual fund itself is tax exempt, any taxes due on dividend earnings are payable by the individual investor. For funds that are not held in tax-deferred accounts, like IRAs or 401(k)s, the amount of taxes due on dividends will depend on the source of such dividends. That is, *if these distributions are derived from dividends earned on the fund's common stock holdings, then they're subject to the preferential tax rate of 15 percent or less.* But, if these distributions are derived from interest earnings on bonds, dividends from real estate investment trusts (REITs), or dividends from most types of preferred stocks, then such dividends do *not qualify for the preferential tax treatment,* but instead are taxed as ordinary income (see Chapter 4 for details).

Capital gains distributions (see line 8) work on the same principle as dividends, except that they're derived from the *capital gains actually earned* by the fund. (From a tax perspective, if the capital gains are long term, they qualify for the preferential tax rate of 15 percent, or less; if not, they're treated as ordinary income.) Note that these (capital gains) distributions apply only to *realized* capital gains—that is, where the securities holdings were actually

EXHIBIT 13.8   **A Summary of Income and Capital Changes**

The return on a mutual fund is made up of (1) the (net) investment income the fund earns from dividends and interest and (2) the realized and unrealized capital gains the fund earns on its security transactions. Mutual funds provide such information to their shareholders in a standardized format (like the statement here) that highlights, among other things, key income, expense, and capital gains information.

	2007	2006	2005
1. **Net asset value, beginning of period:**	$24.47	$27.03	$24.26
2. **Income from investment operations:**			
3. Net investment income	$ .60	$ .66	$ .50
4. Net gains on securities (realized and unrealized)	6.37	(1.74)	3.79
5. Total from investment operations	6.97	(1.08)	4.29
6. **Less distributions:**			
7. Dividends from net investment income	($ .55)	($ .64)	($ .50)
8. Distributions from realized gains	(1.75)	(.84)	(1.02)
9. Total distributions	(2.30)	(1.48)	(1.52)
10. **Net asset value, end of period:**	$29.14	$24.47	$27.03
11. **Total return:**	28.48%	(4.00%)	17.68%
12. **Ratios/supplemental data:**			
13. Net assets, end of period ($000)	$307,951	$153,378	$108,904
14. Ratio of expenses to average net assets	1.04%	0.85%	0.94%
15. Ratio of net investment income to average net assets	1.47%	2.56%	2.39%
16. Portfolio turnover rate*	85%	144%	74%

* *Portfolio turnover rate* measures the number of shares bought and sold by the fund against the total number of shares held in the fund's portfolio; a high turnover rate (for example, over 100 percent) would mean the fund has been doing a lot of trading.

sold and capital gains actually earned. *Unrealized* capital gains (or paper profits) are what make up the third and final element in a mutual fund's return, *for when the fund's securities holdings go up or down in price, its net asset value moves accordingly*. This change (or movement) in the net asset value (NAV) is what makes up the unrealized capital gains of the fund. It represents the profit that shareholders would receive (and are entitled to) if the fund were to sell its holdings.

Crunching the Numbers. A simple but effective way of measuring performance is to describe mutual fund returns based on the three major sources of return noted earlier—dividends earned, capital gains distributions received, and change in share price. These payoffs can be converted to a convenient return figure by using the standard *approximate yield* formula that was first introduced in Chapter 12. The calculations necessary for finding such a return measure can be shown by using the 2007 figures from Exhibit 13.8. Referring to the exhibit, we can see that this hypothetical no-load fund paid $.55 per share in dividends and another $1.75 in capital gains distributions; also, its price (NAV) at the beginning of the year (that is, at year-end 2006) of $24.47 rose to $29.14 by the end of the year (see lines 1 and 10, respectively). Putting this data into the familiar approximate yield formula, we see that the hypothetical mutual fund provided an annual rate of return of 26.0 percent.

$$\text{Approximate yield} = \frac{\text{Dividends and capital gains distributions} + \left[\dfrac{\text{Ending price} - \text{Beginning price}}{\text{1-year time period}}\right]}{\left[\dfrac{\text{Ending price} + \text{Beginning price}}{2}\right]}$$

$$= \frac{(\$.55 + \$1.75) + \left[\dfrac{\$29.14 - \$24.47}{1}\right]}{\left[\dfrac{\$29.14 + \$24.47}{2}\right]}$$

$$= \frac{\$2.30 + \$4.67}{\$26.80} = \frac{\$6.97}{\$26.80} = \underline{\underline{26.0\%}}$$

CALCULATOR

INPUTS	FUNCTIONS
1	
−24.47	PV
2.30	PMT
29.14	FV
	CPT
	I/Y
	Solution
	28.48

See Appendix E for details.

Calculator Keystrokes. You can just as easily find the *exact return* on this investment with a handheld financial calculator. Here's what you'd do: Using *annual compounding*, to find the return on this mutual fund in 2007, we use the same input data as above; namely, we start with a price at the beginning of the year of $24.47, add in total dividends and capital gains distributions of $2.30 a share (i.e., $.55 + $1.75), and then using a year-end price of $29.14, we punch the keystrokes shown in the margin, where:

N = number of *years* you hold the fund
PV = the *initial* price of the fund (entered as a *negative*)
PMT = *total* amount of dividends and capital gains distributions received
FV = the *ending* price of the fund

Note that our computed return (of 28.48 percent) is exactly the same as the "Total Return" shown on line 11 of Exhibit 13.8—that's because this is basically the same procedure that the mutual funds must use to report their return performance. The approximate yield measure (26.0 percent) may be close to the actual return, but clearly it's not close enough for fund-reporting purposes.

What about Future Performance?

There's no question that approximate yield and return on investment are simple, yet highly effective measures that capture all the important elements of mutual fund return. Unfortunately, looking at past performance is one thing, but how about the future? Ideally, we'd want to evaluate the same three elements of return over the future much like we did for the past. The trouble is, when it comes to the future performance of a mutual fund, it's difficult—if not impossible—to get a handle on what the future holds as far as dividends, capital gains, and NAV are concerned. The reason: a mutual fund's future investment performance is directly linked to the future makeup of its securities portfolio, which is impossible to predict. It's not like evaluating the expected performance of a share of stock, where you're focusing on one company. With mutual funds, investment performance depends on the behavior of many different stocks and bonds.

So, where do you look for insight into the future? Most market observers suggest you do two things. First, carefully consider the *future direction of the market as a whole*. This is important, because the behavior of a well-diversified mutual fund tends to reflect the general tone of the market. So, if the feeling is that the market is going to be generally drifting up, that should bode well for the investment performance of mutual funds. Second, take a good hard look at the past performance of the mutual fund itself; it's a good way to see how successful the fund's investment managers have been. The success of a mutual fund rests largely *on the investment skills of the fund managers*. So, when investing in a mutual fund, look for consistently good performance, in up as well as down markets and over extended periods (5 to 7 years, or more). Most important, check to see if the same key people are still running the fund. Although past success is certainly no guarantee of future performance, a strong team of money managers can have a significant bearing on the level of fund returns. Put another way, when you buy a mutual fund, you're buying a formula (investment policy + money management team) that has worked in the past, in the expectation that it will work again in the future.

13-13	What are the most common reasons for buying mutual funds?
13-14	Briefly describe the steps in the mutual fund selection process.
13-15	Why does it pay to invest in no-load funds rather than load funds? Under what conditions might it make sense to invest in a load fund?
13-16	Identify three potential sources of return to mutual fund investors, and briefly discuss how each could affect total return to shareholders.
13-17	Which would you rather have: $100 in dividend income or $100 in capital gains distribution? $100 in realized capital gains or $100 in unrealized capital gains?
13-18	How important is general market behavior in affecting the price performance of mutual funds?

LG6 · INVESTING IN REAL ESTATE

For many years, investing in real estate was quite lucrative. Real estate, it seemed, was one of the few investment vehicles that just couldn't go wrong—everybody was making money in real estate and, according to all the self-proclaimed "experts," there was no end in sight. Of course, as with any investment, the market for real estate fluctuates over time, and investors must do their homework before making real estate investments. When the economy is growing and inflation is relatively high, as it was in the 1970s and early 1980s, real estate prices are also strong. In the early 1990s, however, the market weakened, primarily because of a slowdown in economic activity. But that didn't last long, as real estate values began to climb again in the mid-1990s, buoyed by a return to economic growth and low rates of interest on loans. Another factor was the collapse of the stock market in 2000–2002, prompting investors to look for other ways to generate returns. Encouraged by the increasing values of their homes, many investors turned to various types of real estate investments.

© ICONICA/GETTY IMAGES

Real estate includes everything from homes and raw land to different types of income-producing properties such as warehouses, commercial and retail space, office and apartment buildings, and condominiums. Investments in real estate can take several forms. For example, investors can buy land or property directly, or they may prefer to invest in real estate securities, such as real estate mutual funds (discussed earlier in this chapter), real estate investment trusts (REITS), mortgages, stocks of real-estate-related companies, or real estate limited partnerships. A principal reason for including real estate in your investment portfolio is that it *provides greater diversification properties than does holding just stocks or bonds. That's because real estate typically exhibits less volatility than stocks do and it doesn't move in tandem with stocks.* Before deciding to buy real estate for your portfolio, however, it's essential for you to evaluate such issues as the outlook for the national economy, interest rate levels, supply and demand for space, and regional considerations. Then you must choose the right properties or investment vehicles for your investment needs—and manage them well.

Some Basic Considerations

Investing in real estate takes time and should always be based on a careful analysis of the facts. As with any investment, you must look at the future cash flow you expect to realize from the property, and compare it to the returns obtainable from alternative investment vehicles (such as stocks, bonds, and mutual funds). Obviously, don't put your money into real estate if you think you can earn more in some other type of equally risky investment.

Current income and capital gains are important sources of return for real estate investors, but measuring such returns involves more than just counting rent receipts. Taxes, cash flow, and the use of leverage are all important in real estate investments. We'll now briefly describe the basic factors affecting the value of real estate investments, including cash flow and taxes, appreciation in value, and the use of leverage.

Cash Flow and Taxes

An investor's *cash flow*, or annual after-tax earnings, depends not only on the revenues generated from a particular piece of property but also on depreciation and taxes. Certain types of real estate provide large depreciation write-offs that tend to lower the taxable income of certain (*qualified*) investors. Since the physical condition of real estate in general tends to deteriorate over time, depreciation gives the property owner an allowance for this decline in value. In short, depreciation is a bookkeeping entry that's considered an expense for tax purposes, even though it involves no actual outflow of cash. Depreciation can result in lower taxes; for this reason, it's viewed as a *tax shelter*. But there's a catch: depreciation can be used only up to a certain amount, and only by investors who meet certain income qualifications, as we'll explain next.

First, keep in mind that for tax purposes, real estate is considered a *passive* investment, no matter how actively involved you are in managing the property. So, the amount of expenses *(including depreciation)* that can be written off is generally limited to the amount of income generated by this and any other passive investments owned by the taxpayer/investor. For example, if you owned some apartments that generated $25,000 a year in rental income, and (in the absence of any other passive investments) you had mortgage interest and other operating expenses (such as property taxes and minor repairs) of, say, $20,000 annually, you may be able to write off up to $5,000 in depreciation ($25,000 income − $20,000 other expenses). However, if your *adjusted gross income* is less than $100,000 a year, you may be able to write off even more depreciation—specifically, as much as $25,000 in losses on *rented real estate* can be used to offset the ordinary income of people who "actively participate" in the rental activity of the buildings *and* whose adjusted gross income is less than $100,000. (This provision is phased out at $150,000.) In this example, if you had $90,000 in adjusted gross income and $15,000 in depreciation expense, $5,000 of it could be written off against the remaining $5,000 of net rental income. The other $10,000 could be charged directly against your ordinary income, thereby reducing your taxable income and your taxes. Because of its effect on taxes, *depreciation is considered an important component of real estate investments*. Since depreciation and taxes are such important elements in measuring cash flow, an individual investor should employ a tax consultant to evaluate proposed real estate investments.

Appreciation in Value

Most types of real estate—everything from raw land to various forms of income-producing properties—have experienced significant growth in value over time. An investment evaluation of a proposed piece of real estate, therefore, should include not only the recurring cash flows from the property (for example, rents) but also expected changes in property values (that is, price appreciation). In many cases, such appreciation has a much bigger impact on rate of return than does the net annual cash flow from the property. So, if the market price of the real estate is expected to increase by $100,000, that price appreciation should be treated as capital gains and included as part of the return from the investment (minus, of course, the capital gains taxes paid).

Use of Leverage

A big attraction for investing in real estate is the high degree of financial leverage it permits. Basically, leverage involves using borrowed money to magnify returns. Because real estate is a tangible asset, investors can borrow as much as 75 to 90 percent of its cost. As a result, if the profit rate on the investment is greater than the cost of borrowing, then the return on a leveraged investment will be *proportionally greater* than the return generated from an unleveraged investment.

For example, imagine that you're considering a real estate investment costing $100,000—like the one in Exhibit 13.9. Let's assume that you can purchase the property in one of two ways: you can either pay cash for it, or you can put up $10,000 of your own money and borrow the remaining $90,000 at, say, 10 percent annual interest. If the property earns $13,000 per year after all expenses, including property taxes and depreciation, *but before interest and income taxes are deducted*, then the leveraged investment will provide a much better rate of return than the cash deal, as seen in Exhibit 13.9. Notice that in the no-leverage case, your return on investment will be 9.36 percent, but with leverage, you stand to make a return of 28.80 percent!

Because some of the leveraged investment is made with borrowed money, the return on investment in Exhibit 13.9 reflects *only your investment in the property*—that is, the amount of money that you put up to buy it. So, even though the leveraged investment provides *less in earnings after taxes*, it has a lower investment base. The net result is a *higher return on investment*. By leveraging your investment, you'll get a bigger bang from your investment dollars. Note from this example, however, that when no borrowing is involved, you have no risk of default. But, when you use leverage, minimum earnings before interest and taxes of $9,000 are necessary to pay the interest and thereby avoid default. The risk that comes with leverage must therefore be considered along with the potential benefits. Indeed, many people have been driven into bankruptcy because they used too much leverage.

Speculating in Raw Land

Investing in real estate can take several forms. One approach that's popular with many investors is to *speculate in raw land*. In this approach, *which is often viewed as highly risky*, investors seek to generate high rates of return by investing in property *they hope* will undergo dramatic increases in value. The key to such speculation is to isolate areas of potential population growth and/or real estate demand (ideally, before anyone else does) and purchase property in these areas in anticipation of their eventual development. Undeveloped acreage with no utilities or improvements is often purchased by land speculators either to hold for future development or to sell, as is, at a higher price later. Speculation in raw land often occurs near an area where some type of new development is anticipated. Raw land

---

EXHIBIT 13.9   Using Leverage in Real Estate Investments

Although earnings after taxes are lower with the leveraged investment, the return on investment is considerably higher because the investor puts a lot less of his or her own money into the deal.

	No Leverage		Leverage
Owner investment	$100,000		$ 10,000
Borrowed money	0		90,000
Total investment	$100,000		$100,000
Earnings before interest and income taxes*	$ 13,000		$ 13,000
Less: Interest	0	(.10)($90,000) =	9,000
Earning before taxes	13,000		$ 4,000
Less: Income taxes (assumed 28% rate)	3,640		1,120
Earnings after taxes	$ 9,360		$ 2,880

$$\text{Return on investment} = \frac{\text{Earnings after taxes}}{\text{Amount of owner investment}} = \frac{\$9,360}{\$100,000} = \underline{9.36\%} \qquad \frac{\$2,280}{\$10,000} = \underline{28.80\%}$$

---

*All expenses, including property taxes and depreciation, are assumed to have been deducted from earnings.

speculation, due to the high degree of uncertainty involved, should be reserved for real estate investors who recognize and can accept the inherent risks.

Investing in Income Property

One of the most popular forms of real estate investment is **income (or income-producing) property** which includes commercial and residential properties. Investments in income properties offer both attractive returns and tax advantages for investors. The purchased real estate is leased to tenants to generate income from rent. And although the primary purpose of investing in income property is to produce an attractive annual cash flow, certain types of strategically located income properties also offer attractive opportunities for appreciation in value. Before buying income property, be sure you know what you're getting into. The owner of income property is responsible for leasing the units and maintaining the property. This means fixing leaky roofs and appliances, painting and other repairs, cleaning after a tenant leaves, and similar responsibilities.

Calculating the value of income-producing property requires estimating the annual net operating income, or the NOI as it's called. *NOI equals gross rental income less an allowance for vacancies and bad debts, and all operating expenses, like property (but not income) taxes, insurance, maintenance, and so on.* Once you have a property's NOI, you can apply a *cap rate* (representing the expected annual rate of return on the property) to arrive at an estimated value for the property. A typical cap rate for income property is around 9 or 10 percent. For example, assume you're thinking about buying an office building that generates an estimated $50,000 per year in NOI. Given a 9 percent cap rate, that property would have an estimated value of some $555,000 (i.e., $50,000/.09 = $555,555).

Commercial Properties

The commercial property category consists of many types of properties, including office buildings, industrial space, warehouses, retail space (from freestanding stores to strip shopping centers to malls), and hotels. The risks and returns on commercial real estate investments are tied to business conditions and location. The value of commercial property, especially retail businesses, is enhanced by a location in a high-traffic area. Because commercial properties call for professional management and involve significant expenses, investing in this category of income property is generally the domain of more seasoned (often professional) real estate investors.

Residential Properties

First-time investors often choose income-producing *residential properties*, such as apartments and smaller multifamily buildings. This category of income property is available in various sizes, prices, and types, ranging from duplexes and quadriplexes to large apartment buildings. Aside from purchase and financing cost considerations, major factors influencing the profitability of these investments are the occupancy rates—the percentage of available space rented over the year—and maintenance and management costs. Other factors to consider are the neighborhood where the units are located, local regulations regarding tenants, and supply and demand trends for the type of property.

Homes as Investment Vehicles

Single-family homes can also serve as investment vehicles. As we learned in Chapter 5, owning a home provides tax advantages, such as the ability to deduct interest paid on a mortgage and a capital gains exemption when you sell the home. Besides being a primary residence, second homes can be treated as investment properties. If the second home is for personal use, such as for family vacations, and you rent the unit for less than 14 days, interest payments on the mortgage are also tax deductible on the first $1 million of debt. Different tax laws apply when you've rented the home for more than 14 days. Then the home is considered an investment property, and applicable expenses (mortgage interest, maintenance, etc.) must be allocated proportionally based on the days the property was rented. Only the expenses for the investment portion of the property are deductible.

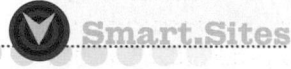 **Smart Sites**

If you want to invest in real estate without the hassle of buying property, consider a real estate investment trust (REIT). Learn more about these closed-end trusts at Invest in REITs by linking to their site at **http://www/thomsonedu.com/finance/gitman.**

income (or income-producing) property
Real estate purchased for leasing or renting to tenants in order to generate ongoing monthly/annual income in the form or rent receipts.

Another way to use a single-family home as an investment property is "flipping houses," or buying and selling quickly for profit. Often investors buy houses that require renovations to increase their value. These renovations can range from minor repairs such as fresh paint and carpet to new kitchens and bathrooms; they can involve extensive remodeling that includes structural changes, like adding a master bedroom suite. For example, you might buy a house that's structurally sound but needs cosmetic work— some fresh paint, better landscaping, a new kitchen, carpet, and bathroom fixtures. After upgrading the property, you try to sell it for a far higher price than you paid, including the cost of the upgrades. Flipping houses requires having a good sense of the local market, understanding the types of improvements that add value, and knowing which upgrades you can do yourself and when you should call in professionals.

Other Ways to Invest in Real Estate

What if the idea of owning and managing property doesn't appeal to you? Or maybe you don't have enough money to buy income property outright. Another way to own real estate is by purchasing specialized securities. For example, you can buy shares in a *real estate mutual fund* (discussed earlier in this chapter). Or you can buy stock in *publicly traded real-estate-related companies*. These include residential homebuilders, construction companies, mortgage lenders, home improvement retailers, property managers, real estate brokerage firms, and engineering companies. Let's now look at three other options: *real estate investment trusts (REITs), mortgage-backed securities (MBSs),* and *real estate limited partnerships, or limited liability companies.*

Real Estate Investment Trusts

A **real estate investment trust (REIT)** is a type of closed-end investment company that invests money in various types of real estate and real estate mortgages. A REIT is like a mutual fund in that it sells shares of stock to the investing public and uses the proceeds, along with borrowed funds, to invest in a portfolio of real estate investments. The investor therefore owns part of the real estate portfolio held by the real estate investment trust. REITs appeal to investors because they offer the benefits of real estate ownership—both capital appreciation and current income—without the headaches of property management.

REITs have become popular with investors who want to diversify their portfolios, because they have relatively low correlations with other market sectors, such as common stocks and bonds. They also provide attractive dividend yields—well above the yields on common stocks. (In fact, historically, about 65 percent of the total return from REITs comes from their dividends.) REITS have also produced highly competitive returns. In fact, according to the National Association of Real Estate Investment Trusts, compound annual returns from REITs (dividends plus stock price appreciation) for the period 1975 to 2005 was 13.8 percent, compared to 8.8 percent for the DJIA, 10.9 percent for the NASDAQ Composite, and 12.7 percent for the S&P 500.

Like any investment fund, each REIT has certain stated investment objectives, which should be carefully considered before acquiring shares. Here are three basic types of REITs:

- **Equity REITs.** They own and operate income-producing real estate, such as apartments, office buildings, shopping centers, and hotels.
- **Mortgage REITs.** These make both construction and mortgage loans to real estate investors.
- **Hybrid REITs.** They invest in both income-producing properties and mortgage loans.

Real estate investment trusts (REITs) An investment company that accumulates money, by selling shares to investors, in order to invest it in various forms of real estate, including mortgages; similar to a mutual fund, but REITs invest only in specific types of real estate or real-estate-related products.

Equity REITS produce both attractive current yields and the potential to earn attractive capital gains as their properties appreciate in value. In contrast, mortgage REITS tend to be more income oriented; they emphasize the high current yields they generate by investing in debt. In 2005 there were some 200 REITs in existence, together holding more than $465 billion in real estate assets. Equity REITs dominated, accounting for 77 percent of the market, followed by mortgage REITs at 19 percent. The income earned by a REIT isn't taxed, but *the income distributed to owners is designated and taxed as ordinary income.* While dividends on common stocks normally are taxed at preferential rates (of 15 percent or less), this is not the case with REITs, whose cash dividends are treated as ordinary income and taxed accordingly.

Mortgage-Backed Securities

Mortgage-backed securities (MBSs) offer yet another alternative. These securities represent ownership in a pool of mortgage loans, typically on residential properties. Government agencies, such as the Government National Mortgage Association (GNMA) and the Federal National Mortgage Association (FNMA), issue most of the MBSs. Also known as *mortgage pass-throughs*, most MBSs are actively traded and offer returns of about 1 to 2 percent above similar low-risk securities. Investors receive monthly income from the principal and interest on the underlying individual mortgages. The income stream, which is taxed as ordinary income, depends on interest-rate levels and prepayments of pool mortgages. Most MBSs require a $25,000 minimum investment.

Real Estate Limited Partnerships or Limited Liability Companies

Special-purpose syndicates organized to invest in real estate are another type of real estate investment. These can be structured as limited partnerships (LPs) or limited liability companies (LLCs). With LPs, the managers assume the role of *general partner*, which means their liability is unlimited, and the other investors are *limited partners* who are legally liable only for the amount of their initial investment. In recent years, the LLC has become a more popular way to form these entities. Rather than general and limited partners, the LLC has a managing member and other members—neither of which have any liability. Some states allow single-number LLCs. Investors buy *units* in an LP or LLC; a unit represents an ownership position. Real estate LPs and LLCs are riskier investment categories than REITs and MBSs are and they appeal to more affluent investors who can afford the typical unit cost of $100,000 or more.

⏸ Concept Check

CHECK • CONCEPT CHECK • CONCEPT CHECK • CONCEPT CHECK • CONCEPT CHECK • CONCEPT CHECK • CONCEPT CHECK • CONCEPT

13-19	Define and briefly discuss the role of each of these factors in evaluating a proposed real estate investment: a. Cash flow and taxes b. Appreciation in value c. Use of leverage
13-20	Why is speculating in raw land considered a high-risk venture?
13-21	Describe the major categories of income property, and explain the advantages and disadvantages of investing in income property. How can a single-family home be used to generate income?
13-22	How do these securities allow investors to participate in the real estate market? a. Stock in real-estate-related companies b. Mortgage-backed securities (MBSs) c. Real estate limited partnerships or limited liability companies
13-23	Briefly describe the basic structure and investment considerations associated with a real estate investment trust (REIT). What are the three basic types of REITs?

◀◀ SUMMARY

LG1 Describe the basic features and operating characteristics of a mutual fund. Mutual fund shares represent ownership in a diversified, professionally managed portfolio of securities; many investors who lack the time, know-how, or commitment to manage their own money turn to mutual funds as an investment outlet. By investing in mutual funds, shareholders benefit from a level of diversification and investment performance they might otherwise find difficult to achieve.

LG2 Differentiate between open- and closed-end funds, as well as exchange-traded funds, and discuss the various types of fund loads and charges. Investors can buy either open-end funds, which can issue an unlimited number of shares, or closed-end funds, which have a fixed number of shares outstanding and which trade in the secondary markets like any other share of common stock. Investors also can buy exchange-traded funds, or ETFs, which are structured like index funds and operate much like open-end funds but trade in the market like closed-end funds. There's a cost, however, to investing in mutual funds (and other types of professionally managed investment products). Mutual fund investors face a full array of loads, fees, and charges, including front-end loads, back-end loads, annual 12(b)-1 charges, annual management fees, and so forth. Some of these costs are one-time charges (like front-end loads); but others, like 12(b)-1 and management fees are paid annually.

LG3 Discuss the types of funds available to investors and the different kinds of investor services offered by mutual funds. Each fund has an established investment objective that determines its investment policy and identifies it as a certain type of fund. Some popular types of funds are growth, aggressive growth, value, equity-income, balanced, growth-and-income, bond, money market, index, sector, socially responsible, asset allocation, and international funds. The different categories of funds have different risk-return characteristics and are important variables in the fund selection process. Many investors buy mutual funds not just for but their investment returns, but to take advantage of the various investor services they offer, such as automatic investment and reinvestment plans, systematic withdrawal programs, low-cost conversion and phone-switching privileges, and retirement programs.

LG4 Gain an understanding of the variables that should be considered when selecting funds for investment purposes. The fund selection process generally starts by assessing your own needs and wants; this sets the tone for your investment program and helps you decide on the types of funds to consider. Next, look at what the funds have to offer, particularly regarding the fund's investment objectives and investor services—here, narrow down the alternatives by aligning your needs with the types of funds available. From this list of funds, conduct the final selection tests: fund performance and cost—other things being equal, look for high performance and low costs.

LG5 Identify the sources of return and calculate the rate of return earned on an investment in a mutual fund. The investment performance of mutual funds is largely a function of the returns the money managers are able to generate from their securities portfolios; generally speaking, strong markets translate into attractive returns for mutual fund investors. Mutual funds have three basic sources of return: (1) dividends, (2) capital gains distributions, and (3) changes in the fund's NAV (accruing from unrealized capital gains). Both the approximate yield and total return measures recognize these three elements and provide a simple yet effective way of measuring the annual rate of return from a mutual fund.

LG6 Understand the role that real estate plays in a diversified investment portfolio, along with the basics of investing in real estate, either directly or indirectly. Investing in real estate—be it raw land, income property (such as office buildings, apartments, and retail space), or even homes—provides an opportunity to earn attractive returns and further diversify an investment portfolio. Investors can buy property directly or invest in several types of real estate securities. Speculating in raw land is a high-risk type of real estate investment. Income-producing property, on the other hand, offers attractive returns from income and price appreciation as well as certain tax advantages. Buying single-family homes and fixing them up to sell at a higher price is another way to invest in real estate. Investors not wishing to own real estate directly can invest indirectly through real estate mutual funds, as well as the common shares of real-estate-related companies, real estate investment trusts (REITs), mortgage-backed securities (MBSs), or real estate limited partnerships or limited liability companies. REITs, which are closed-end investment companies that invest in real estate, are the most popular type of real estate security and have a track record of solid returns.

FINANCIAL PLANNING EXERCISES

LG4
1. Contrast *mutual fund ownership* with *direct investment in stocks and bonds*. Assume that your class is going to debate the merits of investing through mutual funds versus investing directly in stocks and bonds. Develop some pro and con arguments for this debate, and be prepared to discuss them in class. If you had to choose a side, which one would it be? Explain.

LG2
2. Using the mutual fund quotes in Exhibit 13.3, and assuming that you can buy these funds at their quoted net asset values, how much would you have to pay to buy each of the following funds?
   a. Diversified Equity Growth Fund (EqGrow)
   b. Domini Social Equity Fund (Soc Equity)
   c. Dodge & Cox International Stock Fund (Intl Stk)
   d. Dreyfus S&P 500 Index Fund (Dr500In)
   e. Dreyfus Growth & Income Fund (GrInc)

   According to the quotes, which of these five funds have 12(b)-1 fees? Which have redemption fees? Are any of them no-loads? Which fund has the highest year-to-date return? Which has the lowest? Which fund has the highest 3-year return? The lowest?

LG2, 3
3. Imagine that you've just inherited $20,000 from a rich uncle. Now you're faced with the problem of deciding how to spend it. You could make a down payment on a condo—or better yet, on that Corvette that you've always wanted. Or, you could spend your windfall more profitably by building a mutual fund portfolio. Let's say that after a lot of soul searching, you decide to do the latter: build a mutual fund portfolio. Your task is to develop a $20,000 mutual fund portfolio—use actual funds and actual quoted prices, invest as much of the $20,000 as you possibly can, and be specific! Briefly describe the portfolio you end up with, including the investment objectives you're trying to achieve.

LG4
4. For *each pair* of funds listed here, select the fund that would be the *least* risky; briefly explain your answer:
   a. Growth versus growth-and-income
   b. Equity-income versus high-grade corporate bonds
   c. Intermediate-term bonds versus high-yield municipals
   d. International versus balanced

LG3
5. What investor service is most closely linked to the notion of a fund family? If a fund is not part of a family of mutual funds, can it still offer a full range of investor services? Explain. Using a source such as *The Wall Street Journal*, or perhaps your local newspaper, find two examples of fund families; list some of the mutual funds they offer.

LG3
6. Using a source like *Barron's, Forbes, Money*, or *Morningstar*, along with any of the online sites, select five mutual funds—(a) a growth fund, (b) an index fund, (c) a sector fund, (d) an international fund, and (e) a high-yield corporate bond fund—that you feel would make good investments. Briefly explain why you selected each of the funds.

LG5
7. About a year ago, Dave Kidwell bought some shares in the Hi-Flyer Mutual Fund. He bought the stock at $24.50 a share, and it now trades at $26.00. Last year the fund paid dividends of 40 cents a share and had capital gains distributions of $1.83 a share. Using the approximate yield formula, what rate of return did Dave earn on his investment? Repeat the calculation using a handheld financial calculator. Would he have made a 20 percent rate of return if the stock had risen to $30 a share?

LG2, 3   8. Describe an ETF and explain how these funds combine the characteristics of open- and closed-end funds. Looking in the Vanguard family of funds, which of their funds would most closely resemble a "Spider" (SPDR)? In what respects are the Vanguard fund (that you selected) and Spiders the same; how are they different? If you could invest in only one of them, which would it be? Explain.

LG5   9. A year ago, the Full-Bore Growth Fund was being quoted at an NAV of $21.50 and an offer price of $23.35; today it's being quoted at $23.04 (NAV) and $25.04 (offer). Use the approximate yield formula, or a handheld financial calculator, to find the rate of return on this load fund; it was purchased a year ago, and its dividends and capital gains distributions over the year totaled $1.05 a share. (*Hint:* You, as an investor, buy fund shares at the offer price and sell at the NAV.)

LG5   10. Here is the per-share performance record of the East Coast Growth-and-Income fund for 2007 and 2006:

	2007	2006
1. **Net asset value, beginning of period:**	$58.60	$52.92
2. **Income from investment operations:**		
3. Net investment income	$1.39	$1.35
4. Net gains on securities (realized and unrealized)	8.10	9.39
5. Total from investment operations	9.49	10.74
6. **Less distributions:**		
7. Dividends from net investment income	($ .83)	($1.24)
8. Distributions from realized gains	(2.42)	(3.82)
9. Total distributions	(3.25)	(5.06)
10. **Net asset value, end of period:**	$64.84	$58.60

Use this information to find the rate of return earned on the East Coast G-&-I fund in 2006 and in 2007. What is your assessment of the investment performance of this fund for the 2006–2007 period?

LG6   11. Assume that you've just inherited $ 100,000 and wish to use all or part of it to make a real estate investment.
   a. Would you invest directly in real estate, or indirectly through something like a REIT? Explain.
   b. Assuming that you decided to invest directly, would you invest in income-producing property or speculative property? Why? Describe the key characteristics of the types of income-producing or speculative property you would seek.
   c. What financial and nonfinancial goals would you establish before beginning the search for suitable property?
   d. If you decide to invest in real estate indirectly, which type(s) of securities would you buy, and why?

   12. Pam Flores is thinking about investing in some residential income-producing property, which she can purchase for $200,000. Pam can either pay cash for the full amount of the property or put up $50,000 of her own money and borrow the remaining $150,000 at 8 percent interest. The property is expected to generate $30,000 per year after all expenses but *before* interest and income taxes. Assume that Pam is in the 28 percent tax bracket. Calculate her annual profit and return on investment assuming that she (a) pays the full $200,000 from her own funds, or (b) borrows $150,000 at 8 percent. Then discuss the effect, if any, of leverage on her rate of return.

   13. Using the *Find a REIT* section of the *Invest in REITs* site, **http://www.investinreits.com/findaREIT/findareit.cfm**, select two publicly traded real estate investment trusts in different property categories. Using information you can find on the REIT's Web site and other Internet sites, prepare a comparison that includes
   a. The type of REIT (equity, mortgage, or hybrid) each represents.
   b. The type and quality of the properties they hold.
   c. Each REIT's financial performance and management track record.

Based on your analysis, in which REIT would you invest? Explain why, including how it does or doesn't meet your investment objectives.

14. Using Yahoo! Finance, or another investor information portal, find three real-estate-related stocks. Evaluate them as potential additions to your portfolio. Do you think they provide the same degree of diversification as other forms of real estate investments? Explain.

APPLYING PERSONAL FINANCE

The Feeling's Mutual!

Mutual funds offer convenience, diversification, and the services of professional money managers and analysts. Mutual funds can be particularly appealing for small investors who don't have a lot of money and for those who are new to investing. This project will help you learn more about the various types of mutual funds and how to pick the funds that best suit your investment objectives.

Assume that you've just received a windfall of $25,000 and would like to invest it all in mutual funds. There are several ways to segment mutual funds, but for this project, use these eight categories:

1. Growth
2. Value
3. Equity-income
4. Bond
5. Balanced
6. Index
7. Socially responsible
8. International

Pick three or four categories that you believe best meet your financial needs and risk tolerance, and then select one fund from each category. You are strongly encouraged to use some of the online sources and other references mentioned in this chapter to help you make your selections. For each fund, find the following information:

a. Name of fund, its ticker symbol, the fund manager, and the tenure of the fund manager.
b. Category and size of the fund—try to find the *Morningstar* style box.
c. Loads, fees, and other charges; minimum investment required.
d. Performance of the fund over the past 1, 3, and 5 years. Compare the fund's performance to at least two or three other funds in its category, and to an appropriate index over these same periods.
e. How much did the fund pay out last year in dividends and in short- and long-term capital gains distributions?
f. What was the approximate yield on the fund last year? (You may have to compute this yourself using the approximate yield formula or a handheld calculator, and by finding its price 1 year ago from a source such as **http://finance.yahoo.com.**)
g. What services does the fund offer, such as automatic reinvestment plans or phone switching?
h. Briefly explain why you selected the fund and how it meets your investment objectives.

CRITICAL THINKING CASES

LG1, 3, 4   13.1 Dave's Dilemma: Common Stocks or Mutual Funds?

Dave Brubaker has worked in the management services division of Ace Consultants for the past 5 years. He currently earns an annual salary of about $65,000. At 33, he's still a bachelor and has accumulated about $60,000 in savings over the past few years. He keeps his savings in a money market account, where it earns about 3 percent interest. Dave wants to earn "a bigger bang for his buck" and thus is contemplating withdrawing $50,000 from his money market account and investing it in the stock market. He feels that such an investment can easily earn more than 3 percent. Marlene Bellamy, a close friend, suggests that he invest in mutual fund shares. Dave has approached you, his broker, for advice.

Critical Thinking Questions

1. Explain to Dave the key reasons for purchasing mutual fund shares.
2. What special fund features might help Dave achieve his investment objectives?
3. What types of mutual funds would you recommend to Dave?
4. What recommendations would you make regarding Dave's dilemma about whether to go into stocks or mutual funds? Explain.

LG3, 4

13.2 Marge Ponders Mutual Funds

Marge Simmons is the director of a major charitable organization in Springfield, Ohio. A single mother of one young child, she earns what could best be described as a modest income. Because charitable organizations aren't known for their generous retirement programs, Marge has decided it would be best for her to do a little investing on her own. She'd like to set up a program to supplement her employer's retirement program and, at the same time, provide some funds for her child's college education (which is still 12 years away). Although her income is modest, Marge feels that with careful planning, she could probably invest about $250 a quarter, and hopefully increase this amount over time. She now has about $15,000 in a bank savings account, which she's willing to use to kick off this program. In view of her investment objectives, she isn't interested in taking a lot of risk. Because her knowledge of investments extends to savings accounts, series EE bonds, and a little bit about mutual funds, she approaches you for some investment advice.

Critical Thinking Questions

1. In view of Marge's long-term investment goals, do you think mutual funds are an appropriate investment vehicle for her?
2. Do you think she should use her $15,000 savings to start off a mutual fund investment program?
3. What type of mutual fund investment program would you set up for Marge? In your answer, discuss the types of funds you'd consider, the investment objectives you'd set, and any investment services (such as withdrawal plans) you'd seek. Would taxes be an important consideration in your investment advice? Explain.
4. Do you think some type of real estate investment would make sense for Marge, and if so, what type would you suggest? Which would make more sense for Marge: flipping homes or a REIT? Explain.

> ## MONEY ONLINE www.thomsonedu.com/finance/gitman

NLINE • MONEY ONLINE • MONEY ONLINE • MONEY ONLINE • MONEY ONLINE • MONEY ONLINE • MONEY ONLINE

Visit **http://www.thomsonedu.com/finance/gitman** for some additional Web-based exercises and hot links (with annotations) to a variety of resources relevant to the topics covered in this chapter.

PART 6 ▶ Retirement and Estate Planning

Chapter 14 Planning for Retirement
Chapter 15 Preserving Your Estate

Planning for Retirement

LG1	❯	Recognize the importance of retirement planning, and identify the three biggest pitfalls to good planning.	p. 452
LG2	❯	Estimate your income needs in retirement and your retirement income.	p. 452
LG3	❯	Explain the eligibility requirements and benefits of the Social Security program.	p. 460
LG4	❯	Differentiate among the types of basic and supplemental employer-sponsored pension plans.	p. 464
LG5	❯	Describe the various types of self-directed retirement plans.	p. 464
LG6	❯	Choose the right type of annuity for your retirement plan.	p. 476
	❯		

LG1, LG2 AN OVERVIEW OF RETIREMENT PLANNING

Do you know your life expectancy? Well, if you're in your late teens or early twenties, you'll probably live another 60 or 70 years. While this prospect may sound delightful, it also brings into focus the need for careful retirement planning. After all, you may only work for about 40 of those years—perhaps less—and spend 20 or more years in retirement. The challenge, of course, is to do it in style—and that's where retirement planning comes into play! But to enjoy a comfortable retirement, you must *start now*—for one of the biggest mistakes people make in retirement planning is waiting too long to begin.

Accumulating adequate retirement funds is a daunting task that takes careful planning. Like budgets, taxes, and investments, retirement planning is vital to your financial well-being and is a critical link in your personal financial plans. Even so, it's difficult for most people under the age of 30 to develop a well-defined set of retirement plans. There are just too many years to go until retirement and too many uncertainties to deal with: inflation, Social Security, family size, the type of pension you'll receive—*if any*—and how much money you will have when you're ready to retire. Yet, it's just this kind of uncertainty that makes retirement planning so important. To cope with uncertainty, you must plan for various outcomes, and monitor and modify your plans as your hopes, abilities, and personal finances change.

Role of Retirement Planning in Personal Financial Planning

The financial planning process would be incomplete without *retirement planning*. Certainly no financial goal is more important than achieving a comfortable standard of living in retirement. In many respects, retirement planning captures the very essence of financial planning. It is forward looking (perhaps more so than any other aspect of financial planning), affects both your current and future standard of living, and, if successful, can be highly rewarding and contribute significantly to your net worth.

Okay, it's important; so where do you start? Well, as with most aspects of financial planning, you need a goal or an objective—that is, the first step in retirement planning is to set *retirement goals* for yourself. Take some time to define the things you want to do in retirement, the standard of living you hope to maintain, the level of income you'd like to receive, and any special retirement goals you may have (like buying a retirement home in Arizona, or taking an around-the-world cruise). Such goals are important because *they give direction to your retirement planning*. Of course, like all goals, they're subject to change over time as the situations and conditions in your life change.

Once you know what you want out of retirement, the next step is to establish the *size of the nest egg* you're going to need to achieve your retirement goals. How much money will you need to retire the way you'd like? The final step is to formulate an *investment program* that enables you to build up your required nest egg. This usually involves creating some type of systematic savings plan (putting away a certain amount of money each year) and identifying the types of investment vehicles that will best meet your retirement needs. This phase of your retirement program is closely related to two other aspects of financial planning—investment and tax planning.

Investments and investment planning (see Chapters 11 through 13) are the vehicles for building up your retirement funds. They're the active, ongoing part of retirement planning in which you manage and invest the funds you've set aside for retirement. It's no coincidence that a major portion of most individual investor portfolios is devoted to building up a pool of funds for retirement. Taxes and tax planning (see Chapter 3) are also important because a major objective of sound retirement planning is to legitimately shield as much income as possible from taxes and, in so doing, maximize the accumulation of retirement funds.

The Three Biggest Pitfalls to Sound Retirement Planning

Human nature being what it is, people often get a little carried away with the amount of money they want to build up for retirement. Face it, having a nest egg of $4 million or $5 million would be great, but it's beyond the reach of most people. Besides, you don't need that much to live comfortably in retirement. So set a more realistic goal. But when you set that goal, remember: it's not going to happen by itself; you have to do something to bring it about. And this is precisely where things start to fall apart. Why? Because when it comes to retirement planning, people tend to make three big mistakes:

- They start too late.
- They put away too little.
- They invest too conservatively.

Many people in their twenties, or even thirties, find it hard to put money away for retirement. Most often, that's because they have other, more pressing financial concerns—such as buying a house, retiring a student loan, or paying for child care. The net result is that they *put off retirement planning until later in life*—in many cases, until they're in their late thirties or forties. Unfortunately, the longer people put it off, the less they're going to have in retirement. Or, they're not going to be able to retire as early as they'd hoped. Even worse, once people start a retirement program, *they tend to be too skimpy and put away too little*. Although this, too, may be due to pressing family needs, all too often it boils down to lifestyle choices. They'd rather spend for today than save for tomorrow. So they end up putting maybe $1,000 a year into a retirement plan when, with a little more effective financial planning and family budgeting, they could easily afford to save two or three times that amount.

On top of all this, many *people tend to be far too conservative* in the way they invest their retirement money. Too often, people fail to achieve the full potential of their retirement programs because they treat them more like savings accounts than investment vehicles! The fact is, they place way too much of their retirement money into *low-yielding*, fixed-income securities such as CDs and Treasury notes. You should *never speculate* with something as important as your retirement plan, but you don't have to totally avoid risk. There's nothing wrong with following an investment program that involves a reasonable amount of risk, so long as it results in a correspondingly higher level of return. Caution is fine, but being overly cautious can be very costly in the long run. Indeed, a low rate of return can have an enormous impact on the long-term accumulation of capital and, in many cases, may mean the difference between just getting by or enjoying a comfortable retirement.

Compounding the Errors

All three of these pitfalls become even more important when we introduce *compound interest*. Why is that so? Because *compounding essentially magnifies the impact of these mistakes*. To illustrate, consider the first variable—starting too late. If you were to start a retirement program at age 35 by putting away $2,000 a year, it would grow to more than $150,000 by the time you're 65, when invested at an average rate of return of 6 percent. Not a bad deal, considering your total out-of-pocket investment over this 30-year period is only $60,000. But look at what you end up with if you start this investment program just 10 years earlier, at age 25: that same $2,000 a year will grow to over $300,000 by the time you're 65. Think of it—for another $20,000 ($2,000 a year for an extra 10 years), you can double the terminal value of your investment! Of course, it's not the extra $20,000 that's doubling your money; rather, it's *compound interest* that's doing most of the work.

And the same holds true for the rate of return you earn on the investments in your retirement account. Take the second situation just described—starting a retirement program at 25. Earning 6 percent means a retirement nest egg of over $300,000; increase that rate of return to 10 percent (a reasonable investment objective), and your retirement nest egg will be worth nearly $900,000! *You're still putting in the same amount of money*, but because your money is working harder, you end up with a much bigger nest egg. Of course, when you seek higher returns (as you would when going from 6 percent to 10 percent), that generally means you also have to take on more risks. But that may not be as much of a problem as it appears, because in retirement planning, *the one thing you have on your side is time* (unless you start your plan very late in life). And the more time you have, the less of a burden risk becomes. That is, the more time you have, the easier it is to recover from those temporary market setbacks.

On the other hand, if you simply cannot tolerate the higher risks that accompany higher returns (and, certainly, some people can't), then stay away from the higher-risk investments. Rather, stick to safer, lower-yielding securities and find some other ways to build up your nest egg. For instance, contribute more each year to your plan or extend the length of your investment period. The only other option—and not a particularly appealing one—is to accept that you won't be able to build up as big a nest egg as you had thought and, therefore, will have to accept a lower standard of living in retirement. All else being the same, it should be clear that the more you sock away each year, the more you're going to have at retirement. That is, put away $4,000 a year, rather than $2,000, and you're going to end up with twice as much money at retirement.

The combined impact of these three variables is seen in Exhibit 14.1. Note that it's really *the combination of these three factors* that determines the amount you'll have at retirement. Thus, you can offset the effects of earning a lower rate of return on your money by increasing the amount you put in each year or by lengthening the period over which you build up your retirement account—meaning that you start your program earlier in life (or work longer and retire later in life). The table shows that *there are several ways of getting to roughly the same result*; that is, knowing the kind of nest egg you'd like to end up with, you can pick the combination of variables (period of accumulation, annual contribution, and rate of return) that you're most comfortable with.

Estimating Income Needs

Retirement planning would be much simpler if we lived in a static economy. Unfortunately (or perhaps fortunately), we don't, so, both your personal budget and the general state of the economy will change considerably over time. All of which makes accurate forecasting of retirement needs difficult at best. Even so, it's a necessary task, and you can handle it in one of two ways. One strategy is to plan for retirement over *a series of short-run time frames*. A good way to do this is to state your retirement income objectives as a percentage of your present earnings. For example, if you desire a retirement income equal to 80 percent of your final take-home pay, you can determine the amount necessary to fund this need. Then, every 3 to 5 years, you can revise and update your plan.

Alternately, you can follow *a long-term approach* in which you actually formulate the level of income you'd like to receive in retirement, along with the amount of funds you must amass to achieve that desired standard of living. Rather than addressing the problem in a series of short-run plans, this approach goes 20 or 30 years into the future—to the time when you'll retire—to determine how much saving and investing you must do today to achieve your long-run retirement goals. Of course, if conditions or expectations should happen to change dramatically in the future (as they very likely could), it may be necessary to make corresponding alterations to your long-run retirement goals and strategies.

Determining Future Retirement Needs

To illustrate how future retirement needs and income requirements can be formulated, let's consider the case of Jack and Lois Spellman. In their mid-thirties, they have two children and an annual income of about $60,000 before taxes. Up to now, Jack and Lois have given only passing thought to their retirement. But even though it's still some 30 years away, they recognize it's now time to seriously consider their situation to see if they'll be able to pursue a retirement lifestyle that appeals to them. Worksheet 14.1 provides the basic steps to follow in determining retirement needs. This worksheet shows how the Spellmans have estimated their retirement income and determined the amount of investment assets they must accumulate to meet their retirement objectives.

Jack and Lois began by determining what their *household expenditures* will likely be in retirement. Their estimate is based on maintaining a "comfortable" standard of living—one

---

EXHIBIT 14.1 — Building Up Your Retirement Nest Egg

The size of your retirement nest egg will depend on when you start your program (period of accumulation), how much you contribute each year, and the rate of return you earn on your investments. As this table shows, you can combine these variables in several ways to end up with a given amount at retirement.

AMOUNT OF ACCUMULATED CAPITAL FROM

Accumulation Period*	Contribution of $2,000/year at These Average Rates of Return				Contribution of $5,000/year at These Average Rates of Return			
	4%	6%	8%	10%	4%	6%	8%	10%
10 yrs. (55 yrs. old)	$ 24,010	$ 26,360	$ 28,970	$ 31,870	$ 60,030	$ 65,900	$ 72,440	$ 79,690
20 yrs. (45 yrs. old)	59,560	73,570	91,520	114,550	148,890	183,930	228,810	286,370
25 yrs. (40 yrs. old)	83,290	109,720	146,210	196,690	208,230	274,300	365,530	491,730
30 yrs. (35 yrs. old)	112,170	158,110	226,560	328,980	280,420	395,290	566,410	822,460
35 yrs. (30 yrs. old)	147,300	222,860	344,630	542,040	368,260	557,160	861,570	1,355,090
40 yrs. (25 yrs. old)	190,050	309,520	518,100	885,160	475,120	773,790	1,295,260	2,212,900

* Assumes retirement at age 65; parenthetical figure, therefore, is the age at which the person would start his or her retirement program.

that isn't extravagant, yet allows them to do the things they'd like to in retirement. A simple yet highly effective way to derive an estimate of expected household expenditures is to base it on the current level of such expenses. Assume that the Spellmans' annual household expenditures (*excluding savings*) currently run about $42,000 a year—this information can be readily obtained by referring to their most recent income and expenditures statement. Making some obvious adjustments for the different lifestyle they'll have in retirement—their children will no longer be living at home, their home will be paid for, and so on—the Spellmans estimate that they should be able to achieve the standard of living they'd like in retirement at an annual level of household expenses equal to about 70 percent of the current amount. Thus, *based on today's dollars*, their estimated household expenditures in retirement will be $42,000 × .70 = $29,400. (This process is summarized in steps A through D in Worksheet 14.1.)

Worksheet 14.1   Estimating Future Retirement Needs

A worksheet like this will help you define your income requirements in retirement, the size of your retirement nest egg, and the amount you must save annually to achieve your retirement goals.

PROJECTING RETIREMENT INCOME AND INVESTMENT NEEDS

Name(s) __Jack & Lois Spellman__   Date __June 2007__

I. Estimated Household Expenditures in Retirement (Note 1):

A. Approximate number of years to retirement	30
B. Current level of annual household expenditures, excluding savings	$ 42,000
C. Estimated household expenses in retirement as a *percentage of current expenses*	70%
D. Estimated annual household expenditures in retirement (B × C)	$ 29,400

II. Estimated Income in Retirement (Note 1):

E. Social security, annual income	$ 13,000
F. Company/employer pension plans, annual amounts	$ 9,000
G. Other sources, annual amounts	$ 0
H. Total annual income (E + F + G)	$ 22,000
I. Additional required income, or annual shortfall (D − H)	$ 7,400

III. Inflation Factor (Note 2):

J. Expected average annual rate of inflation over the period to retirement	5%
K. Inflation factor (in Appendix A): Based on _30_ years to retirement (A) and an expected average annual rate of inflation (J) of _5%_	4.32
L. Size of inflation-adjusted annual shortfall (I × K)	$ 32,000

IV. Funding the Shortfall (Note 2):

M. Anticipated return on assets *after* retirement	10%
N. Amount of retirement funds required—size of nest egg (L ÷ M)	$ 320,000
O. Expected rate of return on investments *prior* to retirement	8%
P. Compound interest factor (in Appendix B): Based on _30_ years to retirement (A) and an expected rate of return on investments of _8%_	113.3
Q. Annual savings required to fund retirement nest egg (N ÷ P)	$ 2,824

Note 1: Parts I and II are prepared in terms of current (today's) dollars.

Note 2: Alternatively, parts III and IV can be computed with a good handheld calculator (one that has a time-value function).

FINANCIAL ROAD SIGN

BEAT THE RETIREMENT CLOCK

Here are some tips that'll help you make the most of your retirement planning:

- Know how much you'll need to retire in comfort.
- Think about where you want to live and the cost of living in those locations.
- Find out about your Social Security benefits.
- Learn about your employer's pension or profit-sharing plan.
- Put money into an IRA.
- Don't cash out your retirement plan every time you change jobs; instead, roll it over to an IRA or some other tax-sheltered program.

 Smart.Sites

Want an online approach to determine how much you'll need to retire? Use the T. Rowe Price Retirement Income Calculator, to help you figure it out. Go to **http://www.thomsonedu .com/finance/gitman.**

Estimating Retirement Income

The next question is: Where will the Spellmans get the money to meet their projected household expenses of $29,400 a year? They've addressed this problem by estimating what their *income* will be in retirement—again *based on today's dollars*. Their two basic sources of retirement income are Social Security and employer-sponsored pension plans. Using today's retirement tables, they estimate that they'll receive about $13,000 a year from Social Security (as we'll see later in this chapter, you can receive an estimate directly from the Social Security Administration of what your future Social Security benefits are likely to be when you retire) and another $9,000 from their employer pension plans, for a total projected annual income of $22,000. When comparing this figure to their projected household expenditures, it's clear the Spellmans will be facing an annual shortfall of $7,400 (see steps E through I in Worksheet 14.1). This is the amount of additional retirement income they must come up with; otherwise, they'll have to reduce the standard of living they hope to enjoy in retirement.

At this point, we need to introduce the *inflation factor* to our projections in order to put the annual shortfall of $7,400 in terms of retirement dollars. Here we assume that both income and expenditures will undergo approximately the same average annual rate of inflation, causing the shortfall to grow by that rate over time. In essence, 30 years from now, the annual shortfall is going to amount to a lot more than $7,400. How large this number becomes will, of course, depend on what happens to inflation. Assume that the Spellmans think inflation, on average, over the next 30 years will amount to 5 percent—that's a bit on the high side by today's standards, but the Spellmans decide to use it anyway since they'd rather overestimate the effects of inflation than underestimate them. Using the compound value table from Appendix A, we find that the *inflation factor* for 5 percent and 30 years is 4.32; multiplying this inflation factor by the annual shortfall of $7,400 gives the Spellmans an idea of what that figure will be by the time they retire: $7,400 × 4.32 = $31,970, or nearly $32,000 a year (see steps J to L in Worksheet 14.1). Thus, based on their projections, the shortfall should amount to about $32,000 a year when they retire 30 years from now. *This is the amount they'll have to come up with through their own supplemental retirement program.*

Funding the Shortfall

The final two steps in the Spellmans' estimation process are to determine (1) *how big the retirement nest egg must be* to cover the projected annual income shortfall, and (2) *how much to save each year* to accumulate the required amount by the time they retire. To find out how much money they need to accumulate by retirement, they must estimate the rate of return they think they'll be able to earn on their investments *after* they retire. This will tell them how big their nest egg will have to be by retirement in order to eliminate the expected annual shortfall of $32,000. Let's assume that this rate of return is estimated at 10 percent, in which case the Spellmans must accumulate $320,000 by retirement. This figure is found by *capitalizing* the estimated shortfall of $32,000 at a 10 percent rate of return: $32,000 ÷ .10 = $320,000 (see steps M and N). Given a 10 percent rate of return, such a nest egg will yield $32,000 a year: $320,000 × .10 = $32,000. And so long as the capital ($320,000) remains untouched, it will generate the same amount of annual income for as long as the Spellmans live and can eventually become a part of their estate.

Now that the Spellmans know how big their nest egg has to be, the final question is: How are they going to accumulate such an amount by the time they retire? For most people, that means setting up a *systematic savings plan* and putting away a certain amount *each* year. To find out how much must be saved each year to achieve a targeted sum in the future, we can use the table of annuity factors in Appendix B. The appropriate interest factor is a function of the rate of return one can (or expects to) generate and the length of the investment period. In the Spellmans' case, there are 30 years to go until retirement, meaning that the length of their investment period is 30 years. If they feel they'll be able to earn an average rate of return of 8 percent on their investments over this 30-year period, they'll want to use an 8-percent, 30-year interest factor; from Appendix B, we see that this equals 113.3. Because the Spellmans must accumulate $320,000 by the time they retire, *the amount they'll have to save each year* (over the next 30 years) can be found by *dividing* the amount they need to accumulate by the appropriate interest factor; that is, $320,000 ÷ 113.3 = $2,824 (see steps O to Q in Worksheet 14.1).

Calculator Keystrokes. As you might have suspected, the last few steps in the worksheet can just as easily be done on a good handheld financial calculator. Consider, for example, *Part III, the inflation-adjusted annual shortfall.* With the calculator in the *annual mode*, you can determine how big the current annual shortfall of $7,400 will grow in 30 years, given an average annual inflation rate of 5 percent. by using these keystrokes, where:

N = number of *years* to retirement
I/Y = *expected* annual rate of inflation
PV = the amount of additional required annual income (Line I in W/S 14.1), entered as a *negative*

Hit **CPT (FV)** and you should end up with an answer **(FV)** equal (or very close) to $31,982.37 (see step L in Worksheet 14.1).

Now, take a look at *Part IV, funding the shortfall* (step Q in W/S 14.1). Again, with the calculator in the *annual mode*, to find the amount that must be put away annually to fund a $320,000 retirement nest egg in 30 years, given an expected return of 8 percent, use the keystrokes shown here, where:

N = number of *years* over which the retirement nest egg is to be accumulated
I/Y = *expected* annual return on invested capital
FV = the size of the targeted nest egg, entered as a *negative*

A value of 2,824.78 should appear in the calculator display, indicating the amount that must be put away annually to reach a target of $320,000 in 30 years.

The Spellmans now know what they must do to achieve the kind of retirement they want: *Put away $2,824 a year and invest it at an average annual rate of 8 percent over the next 30 years.* If they can do that, they'll have their $320,000 retirement nest egg in 30 years. Of course, they could have been more aggressive in their investing and assumed an average annual rate of 10 percent—in which case they'd either end up with a bigger nest egg at retirement or could get away with saving less than $2,824 a year. Now, how they actually invest their money so as to achieve the desired 8 (or 10) percent rate of return will, of course, depend on the investment vehicles and strategies they use. All the worksheet tells them is how much money they'll need, not how they will get there; it's at this point that investment management enters the picture.

The procedure outlined here admittedly is a bit simplified and does take a few shortcuts, but considering the amount of uncertainty imbedded in the long-range projections being made, it does provide a viable estimate of retirement income and investment needs. The procedure certainly is far superior to the alternative of doing nothing! One important simplifying assumption in the procedure, though, is that it ignores the income that can be derived from the *sale of a house*. The sale of a house not only offers some special tax features (see Chapter 3), but can generate a substantial amount of cash flow as well. Certainly, if inflation does occur in the future (and it will!), it will very likely drive up home prices right along with the cost of everything else. Many people sell their homes around the time they retire and either move into smaller houses (often in Sun Belt retirement communities) or decide to rent in order to avoid all the problems of homeownership. Of course, the cash flow from the sale of a house can substantially affect the size of the retirement nest egg. However, rather than trying to factor it into the forecast of retirement income and needs, we suggest that you *recognize* the existence of this cash-flow source in your retirement planning and consider it as a cushion against all the uncertainty inherent in retirement planning projections.

Online Retirement Planning

Like many other aspects of our life, retirement planning has become easier with the Internet. Indeed, with the hundreds of Web sites that offer online retirement planning, the Internet has literally brought retirement planning to our doorsteps! For example, *Smartmoney.com* has its "Retirement Worksheets," *Quicken.com* offers a "Retirement Planner," and *Bloomberg.com* has its "Retirement Calculator." At most of these Web sites, all you do is answer a few key questions about expected inflation, desired rate of return on investments, and current levels of income and expenditures, and the computer determines the size of any income shortfall, the amount of retirement funds that must be accumulated over time, and different ways to achieve the desired retirement nest egg. *An attractive feature of most of these Web sites is the ability to easily run through a series of what-if exercises.* By just punching a few buttons, you can change one or more key variables to see their effect on the size of your retirement nest egg and the amount of money you must put away annually. For example, you can find out what would happen if you failed to achieve the desired rate of return on your investments.

Sources of Retirement Income

As seen in Exhibit 14.2, other than earnings generated from full- or part-time jobs, the three principal sources of income for retired people are Social Security, assets (income-producing types, such as savings, stocks, and bonds), and pension plans. For the average retiree, these categories will account for about 80 percent of total retirement income. Just about every retired worker receives Social Security income, about 65 to 85 percent obtain at least some of their income from savings or

EXHIBIT 14.2 — Sources of Income for the Average Retiree

Social Security is the single largest source of income for the average U.S. retiree. This source alone is larger than the amount the average retiree receives from pension plans and personal wealth/investment assets *combined*.

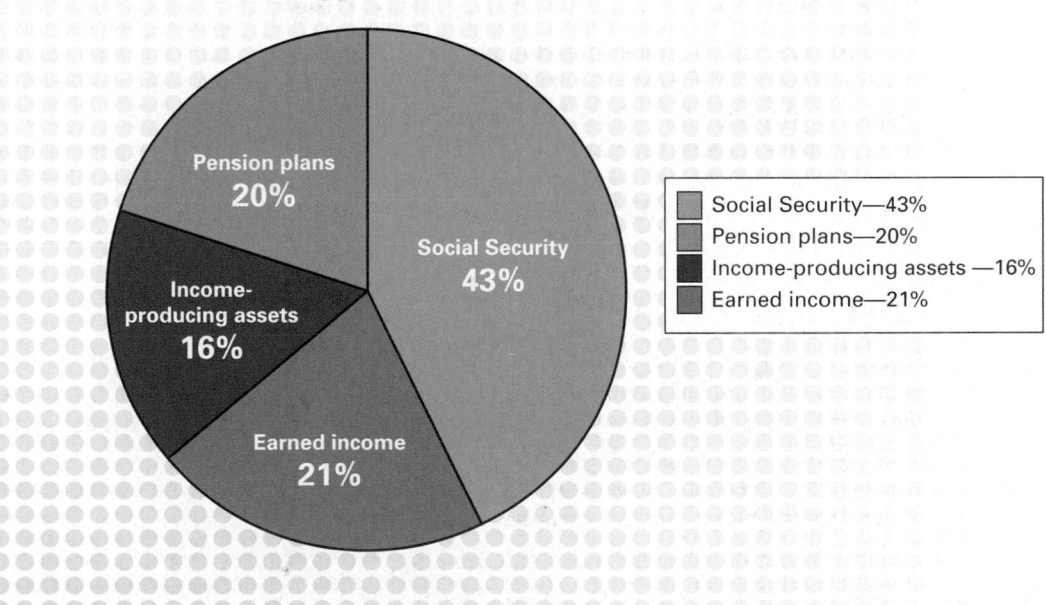

- Social Security—43%
- Pension plans—20%
- Income-producing assets —16%
- Earned income—21%

Source: Employee Benefit Research Institute 2003 Report.

investment assets, and, surprisingly, only about half (40 to 55 percent) receive benefits from some type of employer-provided pension plan. Interestingly, earned income accounts for about 20 percent of the average retiree's income—more than the amount derived from investments and other forms of income-producing assets. Clearly, either because they have to or they want to, a substantial number of individuals continue to work in retirement as a way to supplement their other sources of income. Now, keep in mind that these are *sources* of retirement income and not dollar amounts. The *amount* of income retired individuals will receive will, of course, vary from amounts that are barely above the poverty line to six-figure incomes. The amount received in retirement depends on a number of variables, the most important of which is the level of preretirement earnings. Obviously, the more individuals make before they retire, the more they'll receive in Social Security benefits and from company-sponsored pension plans—and, very likely, the greater the amount of income-producing assets they'll hold. In this chapter, we'll examine Social Security and various types of pension plans and retirement programs. We'll also look briefly at an investment vehicle designed especially for retirement income: the *annuity*.

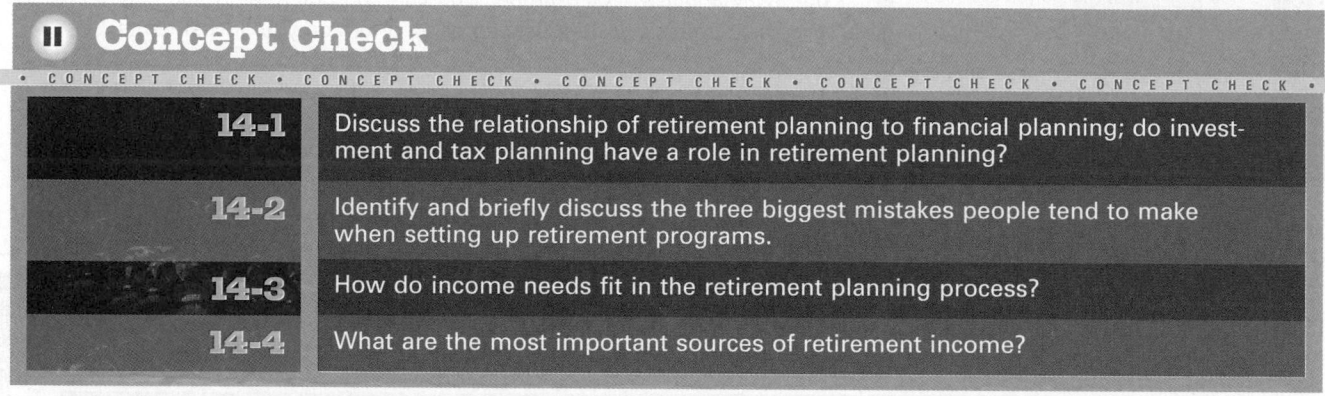

⓫ Concept Check	
14-1	Discuss the relationship of retirement planning to financial planning; do investment and tax planning have a role in retirement planning?
14-2	Identify and briefly discuss the three biggest mistakes people tend to make when setting up retirement programs.
14-3	How do income needs fit in the retirement planning process?
14-4	What are the most important sources of retirement income?

LG3 SOCIAL SECURITY

The Social Security Act of 1935 was landmark legislation. It created a basic retirement program for working Americans at all income levels, and it established several other social programs, all administered under the auspices of the *Old Age, Survivor's, Disability, and Health Insurance (OASDHI) program*. Some of the other services include supplementary security income (SSI), Medicare, unemployment insurance, public assistance, welfare services, and provision for black lung benefits. In this section we give primary attention to the old age and survivor's portion of the act, because it bears directly on retirement planning. We discuss the disability and health/Medicare benefits of Social Security in Chapter 9.

Coverage

As mandated by Congress, Social Security coverage today extends to nearly all gainfully employed workers. Only two major classes of employees are now exempt from *mandatory* participation in the Social Security system: (1) federal *civilian* employees who were hired before 1984 and are covered under the Civil Service Retirement System and (2) employees of state and local governments who have chosen not to be covered (although most of these employees are covered through *voluntary participation* in Social Security). Certain marginal employment positions, such as newspaper carriers under age 18 and full-time college students working in fraternity and sorority houses, are also exempt. By far, the largest number of workers in these excluded classes are employees of state and local governments. These groups aren't forced to participate, because the federal government is not empowered to impose a tax on state and local governments.

To obtain Social Security benefits, an application must be filed with the Social Security Administration, which then determines the applicant's eligibility for benefits based on whether he or she has had enough quarters (3-month periods) of participation in the system. To qualify for full retirement benefits, nearly all workers today must be employed in a job covered by Social Security for at least 40 quarters, or 10 years. These quarters need not be consecutive. Once this 40-quarter requirement is met, the worker becomes fully insured and remains eligible for retirement payments even if he or she never works again in covered employment.

The surviving spouse and dependent children of a *deceased worker* are also eligible for monthly benefits if the worker was fully insured at the time of death or, in some special cases, if certain other requirements are met. Workers may be considered fully insured if they had six quarters of coverage during the 3-year period preceding the time of death.

Social Security Payroll Taxes

The cash benefits provided by Social Security are derived from the payroll (FICA) taxes paid by covered employees and their employers. The tax rate in 2006 was 7.65 percent—this is the amount paid by employees, and an equal amount was paid by employers. Self-employed people are also covered by Social Security; in 2006, they had to pay the total rate of 15.3 percent (that is, 7.65 percent × 2). Because there are no employers to share the burden, self-employed people have to pay the full amount themselves.

Whether the individual is an employee or self-employed, the indicated tax rate stays in effect only until the employee reaches a maximum *wage base*, which increases each year. For 2006, basic Social Security taxes were paid on the first $94,200 of wages earned or self-employed income. Thus, the maximum Social Security tax paid by an employee in 2006 was $7,206 ($94,200 × .0765) and by the *self-employed* was $14,213 ($94,200 × .1530). Note that starting in 1991, a second tax was added to cover the rising costs of Medicare. Now, once the Social Security wage base is passed, the new, higher Medicare wage base kicks in and employees are subject to a tax rate of 1.45 percent *on all earnings* over $94,200, whereas the added earnings of the self-employed are taxed at the rate of 2.9 percent.

Social Security Retirement Benefits

Basic Social Security benefits that are important to retired people and their dependents include (1) old-age benefits and (2) survivor's benefits. Both programs provide extended benefits to covered workers and their spouses; in this section, we'll briefly describe the major provisions of each program.

Old-Age Benefits

Workers who are fully covered (that is, who have worked the required 40 quarters under Social Security) may receive old-age benefits for life once they reach full retirement age. For anyone born in 1960 or later, the Social Security Administration defines "full retirement age" as age 67. (If you were born before 1960, your full retirement age is between 65 and 67, and can be calculated at **http://www.ssa.gov.** For our discussions here, we'll use 67 as the full retirement age.) Workers who elect to retire early—at age 62—will receive reduced benefits, currently 70 to 80 percent of the full amount (again, depending on when they were born). If the retiree has a spouse age 67 or older, the spouse may be entitled to benefits equal to one-half of the amount received by the retired worker. The spouse may also elect early receipt of reduced benefits at age 62. For retirement planning purposes, it seems reasonable to expect Social Security to provide the average retired wage earner (who is married) with perhaps 40 to 60 percent of the wages he or she was earning in the year before retirement—assuming, of course, that the retiree has had a full career working in covered employment. Social

Security, therefore, should be viewed as *a foundation for your retirement income*. By itself, *it's insufficient to allow a worker and spouse to maintain their preretirement standard of living!* (The estimated amount of Social Security benefits is be covered in the next section.)

In two-income families, both the husband and wife may be eligible for full Social Security benefits. When they retire, they can choose to receive their benefits in one of two ways: each can (1) take the full benefits to which each is entitled from his or her account or (2) take the husband and wife benefits of the higher-paid spouse. If each takes his or her own full share, there are no spousal benefits; if they take the husband and wife benefits of the higher-paid spouse, they effectively receive 1.5 shares. Obviously, two-income couples should select the option that provides the greatest amount of benefits.

Survivor's Benefits

If a covered worker dies, the spouse can receive survivor's benefits from Social Security. These benefits include a small lump-sum payment of several hundred dollars, followed by monthly benefit checks. The lump-sum amount is paid automatically upon application. To be eligible for monthly payments, the surviving spouse generally must be at least 60 years of age or have a dependent and unmarried child of the deceased worker in his or her care. (To qualify for *full* benefits, the surviving spouse must be at least 67 years of age; reduced benefits are payable between ages 60 and 67.) If the children of a deceased worker reach age 16 before the spouse reaches age 60, the monthly benefits cease and do not resume until the spouse turns 60. This period during which survivor's benefits are not paid is sometimes called the *widow's gap*. (As we saw in Chapter 8, Social Security survivor's benefits play a key role in life insurance planning.)

How Much Are Monthly Social Security Benefits?

The amount of Social Security benefits to which an eligible person is entitled is set by law and defined according to a fairly complex formula. But you don't need to worry about doing the math yourself; the Social Security Administration has a computerized service that does the benefits estimating for you. Indeed, the government is required by law to provide all covered workers with a *Social Security Statement*. The book's Web site (**http://www.thomsonedu.com/finance/gitman**) contains an example of this statement, which is sent out annually and is supposed to arrive about 3 months before the covered worker's birthday. (You can also request a statement by going to the Social Security Administration Web site: **http://www.ssa.gov.**) "Your Social Security Statement" lists the year-by-year Social Security earnings you've been credited with, and shows (in today's dollars) what benefits you can expect under three scenarios: (1) if you retire at age 62 and receive 80 percent of the full benefit (or less, depending on your age), (2) the full benefit at age 65 to 67 (depending on your year of birth), and (3) the increased benefit (of up to 8 percent per year) that's available if you delay retirement until age 70. The statement also estimates what your children and surviving spouse would get if you die, and how much you'd receive monthly if you became disabled.

A Range of Benefits

Using information provided by the Social Security Administration, we can show the *current level of benefits* (for someone who retired in 2006); this is done in Exhibit 14.3. The benefits, *as of 2006*, are for a retired worker, a retired worker and nonworking spouse, and a two-income couple for low, medium (average), and high career income levels (a *high* income worker is one whose annual earnings equaled or exceeded the maximum Social Security tax base). Bear in mind that the figures illustrated in the exhibit represent amounts that the beneficiaries will receive in the *first year* of their retirement. Those amounts will, of course, be adjusted upward each year with subsequent increases in the cost of living.

Note that the benefits shown in Exhibit 14.3 *may be reduced* if the Social Security recipient is *under age 66 and still gainfully employed*—perhaps in a part-time job. In particular, given full retirement age is 67, retirees aged 62 through 66 are subject to a so-called earnings test that effectively limits the amount of income they can earn before they start

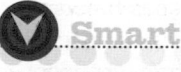
Smart.Sites

Do you qualify for Social Security benefits, and if so, how much will you get? The Social Security Administration's Web site has the answers. Link at **http://www.thomsonedu.com/finance/gitman.**

The Social Security benefits listed here are illustrations of initial, *first-year benefits*, given "full retirement age" is 66. As time passes, the beneficiary will receive correspondingly higher benefits as the cost of living goes up. For example, the maximum benefit payable to someone who retired in 1980 was $572 a month; by 2006 those benefits had grown to $2,053 a month.

Latest Benefits (2006)	Career Earnings Level		
	Low	Average	Maximum
Retired worker, age 66	$ 836	$1,381	$2,053
Retired worker, age 62	669	1,105	1,642
Family benefits:			
Retired worker and spouse, both 66	1,254	2,072	3,080
Retired worker and spouse, both 62	1,004	1,657	2,463
Two-income couple[a]			
Both retire at 66	1,672	2,762	4,106
Both retire at 62	1,338	2,210	3,284

[a] *Both* in the same career income category and *both* eligible for normal benefits at their career income levels.
Source: Based on data from Social Security Administration, http://www.ssa.gov, 2006.

losing some (or all) of their Social Security benefits. In 2006, that limit was $12,480 per year (this earnings limit rises annually with wage inflation). The rule states that if you're a Social Security recipient aged 62 through 66, you'll lose $1 in benefits for every $2 you earn above the earnings test amount. So if you earned, say, $16,000 a year at a part-time job, you'd lose $1,760 in annual Social Security benefits—that is, $16,000 − $12,480 = $3,520 ÷ 2 = $1,760. That's $147 a month you'd lose simply because you hold a job that pays you more than the stipulated maximum. Not a very fair deal! But at least it applies only to early retirees. *And once you reach "full retirement age," the earnings test no longer applies, so you can earn any amount without penalty.* (Keep in mind that the age 67 cutoff applies only to those recipients born *after 1960*; if you were born prior to that year, your cutoff will fall somewhere between ages 65 and 67, depending on your year of birth.) In contrast to earned income, there never have been any limits on so-called unearned income derived from such sources as interest, dividends, rents, or profits on securities transactions—a retiree can receive an unlimited amount of such income with no reduction in benefits.

Taxes on Benefits

Even though Social Security "contributions" are made in after-tax dollars, you may actually have to pay taxes (again) on at least some of your Social Security benefits. Specifically, as the law now stands, *Social Security retirement benefits are subject to federal income taxes if the beneficiary's annual income exceeds one of the following base amounts:* $25,000 for a single taxpayer, $32,000 for married taxpayers filing jointly, and zero for married taxpayers filing separately. In determining the amount of income that must be counted, the taxpayer starts with his or her *adjusted gross income* as defined by current tax law (see Chapter 3) and then adds all nontaxable interest income (such as income from municipal bonds) plus a stipulated portion of the Social Security benefits received. Thus, if for single taxpayers the resulting amount is between $25,000 and $34,000, 50 percent of Social Security benefits are taxable. If income exceeds $34,000, 85 percent of Social Security benefits is subject to income tax. If the combined income of married taxpayers filing joint returns is between $32,000 and $44,000, 50 percent of the Social Security benefits is taxable. The percentage of benefits taxed increases to 85 percent when their combined income exceeds $44,000.

14-5	What benefits are provided under the Social Security Act, and who is covered?
14-6	What is the "earnings test," and how does it affect Social Security retirement benefits?
14-7	Does Social Security coverage relieve you of the need to do some retirement planning on your own?

LG4, LG5 PENSION PLANS AND RETIREMENT PROGRAMS

Accompanying the expansion of the Social Security system, there's been a corresponding growth in employer-sponsored pension and retirement plans. In 1940, when the Social Security program was in its infancy, fewer than 25 percent of the workforce had the benefit of an employer-sponsored plan. Today, better than 50 percent of all wage earners and salaried workers (in both the private and public sectors) are covered by some type of employer-sponsored retirement or profit-sharing plan.

In 1948, the National Labor Relations Board (NLRB) ruled that pensions and other types of insurance programs are legitimate subjects for collective bargaining. In response, many employers established new pension plans or liberalized the provisions of existing ones to meet or anticipate union demands. Qualified pension plans (discussed later) allow firms to deduct for tax purposes their contributions to employee retirement programs. Even better, the employees can also deduct these contributions from their taxable income; the participants are thus able to build up their own retirement funds on a tax-deferred basis. Eventually, of course, when the funds are paid out as benefits, the employees will have to pay taxes on this income.

Government red tape, however, has taken a toll on pension plans. In particular, the **Employee Retirement Income Security Act of 1974** (sometimes referred to as **ERISA** or the *Pension Reform Act*), established to protect employees participating in private employer retirement plans, has actually led to a reduction in the number of new retirement plans started among firms, especially the smaller ones. Indeed, the percentage of workers covered by company-sponsored plans has fallen dramatically since the late 1970s. It's estimated that today, *in the private sector*, only about 40 percent of all full-time workers *are covered by company-financed plans*—even worse, only about one-third (or less) of the part-time labor force is covered. In contrast, *there has been a significant increase in salary-reduction forms of retirement plans* (discussed later). In addition to ERISA, the widespread availability of Keogh plans, individual retirement arrangements (IRAs), and other programs has lessened the urgency for small firms (and bigger ones as well) to offer their own company-financed pension plans.

Now fast forward some 30 years. In an attempt to curb some of the increasingly serious funding problems occurring in private pension plans, Congress passed, and the President signed into law, the **Pension Protection Act of 2006.** One of the major provisions of this Act is that it will force those employers that provide traditional pension plans to their employees (with their defined monthly retirement benefits) to shore up these programs by pumping in tens of billions of dollars in *additional* contributions over the next 7 to 10 years. While the purpose of this provision was to enhance the financial integrity of corporate defined benefit plans—by requiring, among other things, that they be fully funded within 7 years—the net result, in the opinion of experts, is more likely to be a continued exodus away from traditional defined benefit plans to defined contribution (salary reduction) plans, thereby exacerbating the flood of employers already moving away from the traditional plans. At the same time, however, the law encourages employees to

Employee Retirement Income Security Act (ERISA) A law passed in 1974 to ensure that workers eligible for pensions actually receive such benefits; also permits uncovered workers to establish individual tax-sheltered retirement plans.

Pension Protection Act A federal law passed in 2006 intended to shore up the financial integrity of private traditional (defined benefit) plans, and at the same time, encourage employees to make greater use of salary reduction (defined contribution) plans.

make use of various salary reduction (defined contribution) plans, like 401(k)s and IRAs, by setting higher contribution limits, and perhaps most important, by making it easier for companies to automatically enroll workers into company-sponsored savings plans, rather than relying on the current system that leaves the option with the worker; the employees, of course, will still have the right to opt out of the programs if they so wish. This latter measure, which many believe could end up being the most significant part of the legislation, is aimed at substantially raising the participation rate among workers in various types of corporate savings plans. Fortunately, there's still another provision of the law that's intended to help employees manage their pension accounts by easing the rules limiting the amount and types of investment advice that mutual funds and savings plan operators can give directly to employees. Previously, such advice was barred all together because of conflict of interest concerns, a situation that too often left the workers with little or no investment advice at all.

Employer-Sponsored Programs: Basic Plans

Employers can sponsor two types of retirement programs—*basic plans*, in which employees automatically participate after a certain period of employment, and *supplemental plans*, which are mostly voluntary programs that enable employees to increase the amount of funds being set aside for retirement. We'll look first at some key characteristics of basic plans. Apart from financing, there are certain features of employer-sponsored pension plans that you should become familiar with, including participation requirements, contributory obligations, benefit rights, and methods of computing benefits.

Participation Requirements

In most pension plans, employees must meet certain criteria before being eligible for participation. Most common are requirements relating to years of service, minimum age, level of earnings, and employment classification. Years of service and minimum-age requirements are often incorporated into retirement plans in the belief that a much higher labor turnover rate applies to both newly hired and younger employees. Therefore, to reduce the administrative costs of the plans, employees in these categories are often excluded— at least initially—from participation. Once these (or any other) participation requirements are met, the employee automatically becomes eligible to participate in the program.

Not everyone who participates in a pension plan, however, will earn *the right to receive retirement benefits*. Pension plans impose certain criteria that must be met before the employee can obtain a nonforfeitable right to a pension, known as **vested rights.** As the law now stands, *full vesting* rights are required after only 3 to 6 years of employment. More specifically, companies must now choose between two vesting schedules. One, the so-called *cliff vesting*, requires full vesting after no more than 3 years of service—but you obtain no vesting privileges until then. It's sort of a "zero-one" proposition; there are no vesting privileges at all for the first 3 years, and then suddenly you're fully vested. Once vested, you're entitled to everything that's been paid in so far (your contributions *plus* your employer's) and everything that will be contributed in the future. Under the alternate procedure, the so-called *graded schedule*, vesting takes place gradually over the first 6 years of employment. At the minimum, after 2 years you'd have a nonforfeiture right to at least 20 percent of the benefits, with an additional 20 percent each year thereafter until you're 100 percent vested after 6 years. Note, however, that these are minimum standards, and employers can grant more favorable vesting terms.

To illustrate the vesting process, assume that a medium-sized firm offers a plan in which full vesting of benefits occurs after 3 years. The plan is contributory, with employees paying 3 percent of their salaries and the employer paying an amount equal to 6 percent of the salaries. Under this plan, employees cannot withdraw the contributions made by the employer until they reach retirement age, usually 65. The plan provides annual benefits in the amount of $11 per year of service for each $100 of an employee's final monthly earnings—the amount earned during the final month in the employ of the firm. Therefore, an employee who worked a minimum of 3 years for the firm would be eligible for a retirement benefit from that company even if he or she left the company at, say, age 30.

vested rights Employees' nonforfeitable rights to receive benefits in a pension plan based on their own and their employer's contributions.

However, because of inflation, the value of the benefit for a worker who leaves the firm long before retirement age would be very small. Consequently, the employee might be better off simply withdrawing his or her own contributions (which always vest immediately) and terminating participation in the plan at the same time he or she leaves the employer. Of course, any worker who leaves the firm before accumulating the required years of service would be entitled only to a return of his or her own contributions to the plan (plus nominal investment earnings). *And whenever you terminate employment, resist the urge to spend the money you have built up in your retirement account! Over time, that can have a devastating effect on your ability to accumulate retirement capital. Instead, when you take money out of one retirement account, roll it over into another one.*

What's Your Contribution?

Whether you, as an employee, must make payments toward your own pension depends on the type of plan you're in. If you belong to a **noncontributory pension plan,** the employer pays the total cost of the benefits—you don't have to pay a thing. Under a **contributory pension plan,** the employer and the employee share the cost. Today the trend is toward contributory plans. In addition, nearly all plans for employees of federal, state, and local governments require a contribution from the employee. In contributory plans, the employee's share of the costs is often between 3 and 10 percent of annual wages and is typically paid through a payroll deduction. Probably the most common arrangement is for the employer to match the employee's contribution—the employee puts up half the annual contribution and the employer puts up the other half. When employees who've participated in a contributory retirement plan terminate employment before retirement, they're legally entitled to some benefit, based on the amount of their own contributions. Usually this benefit is a cash lump sum, but in some cases it can be taken as a monthly payment at retirement. Whether departing employees receive any benefit from the *employer's* contributions depends on the plan's benefit rights.

Defined Contributions or Defined Benefits

The method used to compute benefits at retirement is explained in detail in every retirement plan. The two most commonly used methods are the defined contribution plan and the defined benefits plan. A **defined contribution plan** specifies the amount of contribution that both the employer and employee must make. At retirement, the worker is awarded whatever level of monthly benefits those contributions will purchase. Although such factors as age, income level, and the amount of contributions made to the plan have a great deal to do with the amount of monthly benefits received at retirement, probably no variable is more important than the level of *investment performance* generated on the contributed funds.

A defined contribution plan promises nothing at retirement except the returns the fund managers have been able to obtain. The only thing that's defined is the amount of contribution that the employee and/or employer have to make (generally stated as a percentage of the employee's income). The benefits at retirement depend totally on investment results. Of course, the investment managers follow a certain standard of care, so some protection is provided to the plan participants (indeed, most of the investing is confined to high-quality investment vehicles). Even so, that still leaves a lot of room for variability in returns. There'll be a big difference in retirement benefits for someone who's in a fund that's earned 6 percent versus someone who's in a fund that's earned 12 percent.

Under a **defined benefits plan,** the formula for computing benefits, not contributions, is stipulated in the plan provisions. These benefits are paid out regardless of how well (or poorly) the retirement funds are invested. If investment performance falls short, the employer has to make up the difference to come up with the benefits agreed to in the plan. This type of plan allows employees to determine before retirement how much their monthly retirement income will be. Often the number of years of service and amount of earnings are prime factors in the formula. For example, workers might be paid 2.5 percent of their final 3-year average annual salary for each year of service. Thus, the *annual* benefit to an employee whose final 3-year average annual salary was $65,000 and who was with the company for 20 years would be $32,500 (2.5 percent × $65,000 × 20 years).

noncontributory pension plan A pension plan in which the employer pays the total cost of the benefits.

contributory pension plan A pension plan in which the employee bears part of the cost of the benefits.

defined contribution plan A pension plan specifying the contributions that both employer and employee must make; *it makes no promises concerning the size of the benefits at retirement.*

defined benefits plan A pension plan in which the formula for computing benefits is stipulated in its provisions.

Other types of defined benefits plans may simply pay benefits based on (1) a consideration of earnings excluding years of service, (2) a consideration of years of service excluding earnings, or (3) a flat amount with no consideration given to either earnings or years of service. Many defined benefits plans also increase retirement benefits periodically to help retirees keep up with the cost of living. In periods of high inflation, these increases are essential to maintain retirees' standards of living. Today, nearly 50 million people (workers and retirees) are covered by defined benefits plans. However, while the number of *people covered* by such plans continues to rise, the number of (private sector) *defined benefit plans in existence* has steadily declined, from about 115,000 plans in 1985 to less than 35,000 today. In fact, for the first time ever, there are now more assets held in defined contribution plans than there are in traditional (defined benefit) pension plans! And as noted above (see the Pension Protection Act of 2006), *it's very likely that this shift to defined contribution plans will only accelerate in the coming years.*

Regardless of the method used to calculate benefit amounts, the employee's basic concern should be with the percentage of final take-home pay the plan is likely to produce at retirement. A pension is usually thought to be good if, when combined with Social Security, it will result in a monthly income equal to about 70 to 80 percent of preretirement net earnings. To reach this goal, however, today's employees must take some responsibility, because *there's a growing trend for companies to switch from defined benefits plans to defined contribution programs.* In 1975, about 85 percent of all plans were defined benefits plans; today, fewer than half are. Companies don't like the idea of being faced with undefined future pension liabilities—after all, the pension/retirement payments that don't come from investment earnings have to be made up from company earnings, and that means lower profits. So more and more companies are avoiding these problems by changing to defined contribution plans—indeed, there are far more defined contribution plans today than there are defined benefits plans. And in cases where the firms are sticking with their defined benefits plans, the benefits are often so meager that they don't come close to the desired 70 to 80 percent income target. (Some of the defined contribution plans don't either.)

In either case, *the employee is being forced to assume more responsibility for ensuring the desired level of postretirement income.* The logic from the company's perspective is that if obtaining a comfortable standard of living in retirement is a worthwhile objective, the employee should be willing to help achieve it. That might mean participating in a company-sponsored supplemental retirement plan or possibly even setting up your own self-directed program (we'll look at both supplemental and self-directed plans later). All this means that where you end up in retirement will depend, more than ever, on what *you've* done, rather than on what your employers have done. *Very likely, you're the one who is going to control not only how much goes into the company's retirement programs, but where it goes as well.*

Cash-Balance Plans

One of the newest types of employer-sponsored retirement programs is the so-called **cash-balance plan.** Essentially, a cash-balance plan is like a traditional defined benefits plan, with features similar to defined contribution plans. As with traditional pension plans, the company funds the pension (the employee pays nothing into the plan); it also controls the investments and guarantees a benefit payout at retirement. And as with a defined contribution plan, the company contributions are based on a percentage (say, 4 or 5 percent) of the employee's current salary; most important, the company sets up a separate "account" for each employee that shows how much has been accumulated in the account at any given time. In a cash-balance plan, the account is guaranteed by the company to earn a given minimum rate of return—which might be a fixed percentage rate (of perhaps 4 or 5 percent) on a variable rate of return, linked to something like T-bills. That's it; that's

cash-balance plan An employer-sponsored retirement program that combines features of defined contribution and defined benefit plans and is well suited for a mobile workforce.

all the company guarantees. So, unlike traditional pension plans, your retirement benefits are in no way linked to the salary you'll be making when you retire. Instead, at retirement, you receive whatever the cash balance of your account happens to be, either in the form of a lump-sum payment or as a stream of fixed annuity payments over time.

Given the low guaranteed earnings rate, there's little doubt that the retirement benefits of cash-balance plans will turn out to be less—and perhaps substantially so—than what would have been paid under traditional plans (where the benefits are linked to how much the employee was making at the time of his or her retirement). But there's a big upside to these plans, particularly for younger employees—*the accounts are portable.* This means that when employees leave a firm, they can roll their accounts into their new employer's cash-balance plans or into an IRA. Indeed, the portability of cash-balance plans makes them better suited than traditional pension plans to meet the needs of an increasingly mobile workforce.

Qualified Pension Plans

The Internal Revenue Code permits a corporate employer making contributions to a **qualified pension plan** to deduct from taxable income its contributions to the plan. As a result, the employees on whose behalf the contributions are made don't have to include these payments as part of their taxable income until the benefits are actually received. Further, in contributory plans, *the employee can also shelter his or her contributions from taxes.* In other words, such contributions aren't counted as part of taxable income in the year that they're made; but instead they act to reduce the amount of taxable income reported to the IRS and therefore lead to lower taxes for the employee.

Still another tax advantage of these plans is that any and all investment income is allowed to accumulate tax free; as a result, investment capital can build up quicker. Yet, despite all these tax benefits, many firms still believe that the costs of regulation exceed any benefits that might result and therefore choose to forgo the procedures required for having a plan qualified. Probably the biggest disadvantage of nonqualified pension plans from the employee's perspective is that any contributions made to *contributory* plans are fully taxable and, as such, are treated just like any other type of income—in other words, the contributions are made on an after-tax basis and thus are *not* sheltered from taxes.

Employer-Sponsored Programs: Supplemental Plans

In addition to basic retirement programs, many employers offer supplemental plans. These plans are often *voluntary* and enable employees not only to increase the amount of funds being held for retirement but also to enjoy attractive tax benefits. There are three basic types of supplemental plans: profit-sharing, thrift and savings, and salary reduction plans.

Profit-Sharing Plans

Profit-sharing plans enable employees to participate in the earnings of their employer. A **profit-sharing plan** may be qualified under the IRS and become eligible for essentially the same tax treatment as other types of pension plans. An argument supporting the use of profit-sharing plans is that they encourage employees to work harder because the employees benefit when the firm prospers. From the firm's perspective, a big advantage of profit-sharing plans is that they impose no specific levels of contribution or benefits by the employer. When profits are low, the firm makes smaller contributions to the plan, and when profits are high, it pays more.

To give some continuity to these programs, many employers establish minimum and maximum amounts to be paid as contributions to profit-sharing plans, regardless of how low or high corporate earnings are. Contributions to profit-sharing plans can be invested in certain types of fixed-interest products, stocks and bonds, or in many cases, securities issued by the employing firm itself. Employees who receive the firm's securities may actually benefit twice. When profits are good, larger contributions are made to the profit-sharing plan, *plus* the price of the shares already owned is likely to increase.

Some major firms offer *voluntary profit-sharing plans* that invest heavily in their own stock. It's common in many of these cases for long-term career employees to accumulate several hundred thousand dollars worth of the company's stock. And we're not talking

qualified pension plan A pension plan that meets specified criteria established by the Internal Revenue Code.

profit-sharing plan An arrangement in which the employees of a firm participate in the company's earnings.

IS YOUR PENSION PLAN AT RISK?

In 2005 a financially troubled United Airlines terminated its pension plan, leaving workers with significantly reduced benefits. The pilot who was promised $140,000 a year instead earns $28,000 a year in retirement. Delta Airlines is set to follow suit. It's not just underfunded plans that are in jeopardy; companies such as Verizon, Sears, and IBM have also moved to freeze their pension plans. In such situations, how do you avoid losing your retirement savings?

First, it's important to distinguish between plans that are frozen and those that are terminated. Plans that are terminated are typically taken over by the Pension Benefit Guaranty Corporation (PBGC), a government-run insurer that guarantees private sector pensions up to certain limits. PBGC took over United's pension plan when executives proved that the airline couldn't remain in business unless the plan was terminated. To find out if your pension plan is covered by PBGC, check your company's Summary Plan Description. Although cases such as United and Delta gather lots of media attention, the odds of a company defaulting on a pension

plan aren't so high. What seems increasingly likely is that a pension plan will be frozen. Hewitt Associates, a human resources firm, expects that 16 percent of large employers are likely to freeze pension plans in 2006. Companies are freezing pension plans to eliminate this large liability from their books and stay competitive with companies that don't have pension plans to fund. If a plan is frozen, employees may collect any benefits earned up to that point; but the size of the pension won't grow. Instead of pension plans, companies are offering 401(k) plans. Many companies that freeze pension plans contribute a percentage of an employee's salary to the 401(k) plan in compensation—IBM is offering to contribute 4 percent. When a plan is frozen, if the 401(k) earns an 8 percent annual return, workers up to the age of 53 might be better off than if the plan was never frozen.

Whether the pension plan is frozen or terminated, you need to have other retirement savings. The fact is that many young workers won't stay with the same company until retirement. Contribute to the company 401(k)—you can take it with you when you move to another company.

If you do retire with a pension, you need to be careful that the choices *you* make don't lead to reduced benefits. The amount of your yearly payout could vary by thousands of dollars depending on retirement age and the number of years on the job. The combination of a higher salary and more years of service can significantly boost your pension. In one scenario, a person who retires at age 58 might draw a pension of $21,000 a year; but if this same person waited until age 60 to retire, the payout would be about $39,000 a year. In this case it certainly pays to work 2 more years. The human resources department at your company or your retirement benefits manager can help you with projections to determine the right scenario for you.

Critical Thinking Questions

1. Describe what happens when a company defaults on its pension plan. What role does the PBGC play?
2. Why are companies freezing pension plans? How does this affect workers?
3. How can you maximize the amount of your pension in retirement?

Sources: Walter Updegrave, "Could You Bust Your Own Pension?" *Money*, July 2005, p. 25–26; Ellen E. Schultz and Theo Francis, "How Safe Is Your Pension?" *Wall Street Journal*, January 12, 2006, p. D1; Walter Updegrave, "Pensions: The Big Chill," *Money*, March 2006, p. 25; Jeanne Sahadi, "Some May Profit from Pension Freezes." CNNMoney.com, March 9, 2006, http://money.cnn.com.

about highly paid corporate executives here; rather, these are just average employees who had the discipline to consistently divert a portion of their salary to the company's profit-sharing plan. *There is a very real and important downside to this practice, however*—if the company should hit hard times, not only could you face salary cuts (or even worse, the loss of a job), but the value of your profit-sharing account will likely take a tumble as well. Just look at what happened to employees in the tech sector during the 2000–2002 bear market!

thrift and savings plan A plan to supplement pension and other fringe benefits; the firm contributes an amount equal to a set proportion of the employee's contribution.

salary reduction, or 401(k), plan An agreement by which part of a covered employee's pay is withheld and invested in some form of investment; taxes on the contributions and the account earnings are deferred until the funds are withdrawn.

Thrift and Savings Plans

Thrift and savings plans were established to supplement pension and other fringe benefits. Most plans require the employer to make contributions to the savings plan in an amount equal to a set proportion of the amount contributed by the employee. For example, an employer might match an employee's contributions at the rate of 50 cents on the dollar up to, say, 6 percent of salary. Thus, an employee making $40,000 a year could pay $2,400 into the plan annually, and the employer would kick in another $1,200. These contributions are then deposited with a trustee, who invests the money in various types of securities, including stocks and bonds of the employing firm. With IRS-qualified thrift and savings plans, the *employer's* contributions and earnings on the savings aren't included in the *employee's* taxable income until he or she withdraws these sums. Unfortunately, this attractive tax feature doesn't extend to the employee's contributions, so any money put into one of these savings plans is still considered part of the employee's taxable income— subject to regular income taxes.

Thrift and savings plans usually have more liberal vesting and withdrawal privileges than do pension and retirement programs. Often the employee's right to the employer's contributions becomes nonforfeitable immediately upon payment, and the total savings in the plan can be withdrawn by giving proper notice. Employees who terminate participation in such a plan, however, are frequently prohibited from rejoining it for a specified period, such as 1 year. An employee who has the option should seriously consider participating in a thrift plan. The returns are usually pretty favorable, especially when you factor in the *employer's* contributions.

Salary Reduction Plans

Another type of supplemental retirement program—and certainly the most popular judging by employee response—is the **salary reduction plan,** or the **401(k) plan** as it's more popularly known. Our discussion here centers on 401(k) plans, but similar programs are available for employees of public, nonprofit organizations. Known as *403(b) plans* or *457 plans*, they offer many of the same features and tax-shelter provisions as 401(k) plans. (Workers at public schools, colleges, universities, nonprofit hospitals, and similar organizations have 403(b) plans; state or local government workers probably have a 457 plan, as do employees at some tax-exempt organizations.) Today, more and more companies are cutting back on their contributions to traditional (defined benefits) retirement plans. They're turning instead to 401(k) plans, a type of defined contribution plan. More than 80 percent of all companies with more than 200 employees now offer 401(k) plans. In 2003, the amount of assets held in 401(k) plans exceeded $2 trillion, up from just $300 billion in 1990.

A 401(k) plan basically gives employees the option to divert part of their salary to a company-sponsored, tax-sheltered savings account. In this way, the earnings diverted to the savings plan accumulate tax free. Taxes must be paid eventually, but not until the employee starts drawing down the account at retirement, presumably when he or she is in a lower tax bracket. In 2006, an individual employee could put as much as $15,000 (up to 25 percent of salary, to this maximum) into a tax-deferred 401(k) plan. (Contribution limits for 403(b) and 457 plans are the same as those for 401(k) plans.)

To see how such tax-deferred plans work, consider an individual who earned, say, $75,000 in 2006, and would like to contribute the maximum allowable—$15,000—to the 401(k) plan where she works. Doing so reduces her taxable income to $60,000 and, assuming she's in the 28 percent tax bracket, lowers her federal tax bill by some $4,200 (i.e., $15,000 × .28). Such tax savings will offset a good portion—28 percent—of her contribution to the 401(k) savings plan. In effect, she'll add $15,000 to her retirement program with only $10,800 of her own money; the rest will come from the IRS via a reduced tax bill. What's more, all the *earnings* on her savings account will accumulate tax free as well.

These plans are generally viewed as attractive *tax shelters* that offer not only substantial tax savings but also a way to save for retirement. As long as you can afford to put the money aside, *you should seriously consider joining a 401(k)/403(b)/457 plan if one is offered at your place of employment.* This is especially true considering the matching features offered by many of these plans. That is, a special attraction of 401(k) plans is that the firms offering them can sweeten the pot by matching all or a part of the employee's contributions. Most companies that offer 401(k) plans have some type of matching contributions program, often putting up 50 cents (or more) for every dollar contributed by the employee. Such matching plans give both tax and savings incentives to individuals and clearly enhance the appeal of 401(k) plans. (Matching contributions by employers are far less common with 403(b) plans and virtually non-existent with 457 plans.)

And now, another kind of 401(k) plan is being offered by a growing number of firms. This new retirement savings option, which first became available in January 2006, is the so-called *Roth 401(k)*. It's just like a traditional 401(k), except for one thing: *All contributions to Roth 401(k) plans are made in after-tax dollars*. That means there are no tax savings to be derived from the annual employee contributions; if you earn, say $75,000 a year and want to put $15,000 into your Roth 401(k), you'll end up paying taxes on the full $75,000. That's the bad news; now the good news. Because all contributions are made in after-tax dollars, *there are no taxes to be paid on plan withdrawals (in other words, they're tax free)*, provided you're at least $59\frac{1}{2}$ and have held the account for 5 years or more. Like traditional 401(k) plans, Roth 401(k)s also have a contribution cap of $15,000 (in 2006). And that limit applies to *total contributions to both types of 401(k) plans combined*, so you can't put $15,000 into a traditional 401(k) plan and then put another $15,000 into a Roth 401(k). You can also have employer matches with the Roth plans, although technically those matches will accumulate in a separate account that will be taxed as ordinary income at withdrawal. Essentially, *employer* contributions represent tax-free income to employees, so they'll pay taxes on that income, plus any account earnings, when the funds are withdrawn—as with a traditional 401(k). One final point: because of the tax differences in traditional versus Roth 401(k) plans, all earnings generated in the *employee's account* accumulate on a *tax-free basis* in Roth plans; they accumulate on a *tax-deferred basis* in traditional 401(k) plans.

Both Roth and traditional 401(k) plans typically offer their participants various investment options, such as equity and fixed-income mutual funds, company stock, and other interest-bearing vehicles, such as bank CDs or similar insurance company products. Indeed, the typical 401(k) has about 10 choices, and some plans have as many as 20 or more. Today, the trend is toward giving plan participants more options and providing seminars and other educational tools to help employees make informed retirement plan decisions.

Evaluating Employer-Sponsored Pension Plans

When participating in a company-sponsored pension plan, you're entitled to certain benefits in return for meeting certain conditions of membership—which may or may not include making contributions to the plan. Whether your participation is limited to the firm's basic plan or includes one or more of the supplemental programs, *it's vital that you take the time to acquaint yourself with the various benefits and provisions* of these retirement plans. And be sure to familiarize yourself not only with the basic plans (even though participation is mandatory, you ought to know what you're getting for your money) but also with any (voluntary) supplemental plans you may be eligible to join.

So, how should you evaluate these plans? Most experts agree that although a typical company-sponsored pension plan has many aspects (some of which are a bit complex and difficult to evaluate), you can get a pretty good handle on essential plan provisions and retirement benefits by taking a close look at these features:

- **Eligibility requirements.** Precisely what are they, and if you're not already in the plan, when will you be able to participate?

- **Defined benefits or contributions.** Which one is defined? If it's the benefits, exactly what formula is used to define them? Pay particular attention to how Social Security benefits are treated in the formula. If it's a defined contribution program, do you have any control over how the money is invested? If so, what are your options? *What you'd like to have*: lots of attractive no-load stock/equity mutual funds to choose from; *what you don't need:* a bunch of low-yielding investment options, such as bank CDs, money market mutual funds, or fixed annuities.

- **Vesting procedures.** Does the company use a cliff or graded procedure, and precisely when do you become fully vested?

- **Contributory or noncontributory.** If the plan is contributory, how much comes from you and how much from the company; and what's the total of this contribution as a percentage of your salary? If it's noncontributory, what is the company's contribution as a percentage of your salary?

- **Retirement age.** What's the normal retirement age, and what provisions are there for *early retirement*? What happens if you leave the company before retirement? Are the pension benefits *portable*—that is, can you take them with you if you change jobs?

- **Voluntary supplemental programs.** How much of your salary can you put into one or more of these plans, and what—if anything—is matched by the company? Remember, these are like defined contribution plans, so nothing is guaranteed as far as benefits are concerned.

Getting answers to these questions will help you determine where you stand and what, if any, improvements need to be made in your retirement plans. As part of this evaluation process, try to determine, as best as you can, *a rough estimation of what your benefits are likely to be at retirement*—you'll need to make some projections about future income levels, investment returns, and so on, but it's an exercise well worth taking (before you start cranking out the numbers, check with the people who handle employee benefits at your work place; they'll often give you the help you need). Then, using a procedure similar to what we did with Worksheet 14.1, you can estimate what portion of your retirement needs will be met from your company's basic pension plan. If there's a shortfall—*and there likely will be*—it will indicate the extent to which you need to participate in some type of company-sponsored supplemental program, such as a 401(k) plan, or (alternatively) how much you're going to have to rely on your own savings and investments to reach the standard of living you're looking for in retirement. *Such insights will enable you to more effectively dovetail the investment characteristics and retirement benefits of any company-sponsored retirement plans you're entitled to with the savings and investing that you do on your own.*

Self-Directed Retirement Programs

In addition to participating in company-sponsored retirement programs, individuals can set up their own tax-sheltered retirement plans. There are two basic types of self-directed retirement programs: *Keogh* and *SEP plans*, which are for self-employed individuals, and *individual retirement arrangements (IRAs)*, which can be set up by almost anyone.

Keogh and SEP Plans

Keogh plans were introduced in 1962 as part of the Self-Employed Individuals Retirement Act, or simply the Keogh Act. Keogh plans allow self-employed individuals to set up tax-deferred retirement plans for themselves and their employees. Like contributions to 401(k) plans, payments to Keogh accounts may be taken as deductions from taxable income. As a result, they reduce the tax bills of self-employed individuals. The maximum contribution to this tax-deferred retirement plan in 2006 was $44,000 per year, or 25 percent of earned income, whichever is less.

Any individual who's self-employed, either full- or part-time, is eligible to set up a Keogh account. They can also be used by individuals who hold full-time jobs and moonlight part-time—for instance, the engineer who has a small consulting business on the side or the accountant who does tax returns at night and on weekends. If the engineer, for example, earns $10,000 a year from his part-time consulting business, he can contribute

Keogh plan An account to which self-employed persons may make specified payments, which may be taken as deductions from taxable income; earnings also accrue on a tax-deferred basis.

25 percent of that income ($2,500) to his Keogh account and, in so doing, reduce both his taxable income and the amount he pays in taxes. Further, he's still eligible to receive full retirement benefits from his full-time job and to have his own IRA (but as we'll see, contributions to his IRA may not qualify for tax shelter).

Keogh accounts can be opened at banks, insurance companies, brokerage houses, mutual funds, and other financial institutions. Annual contributions must be made at the time the respective tax return is filed or by April 15 of the following calendar year (for example, you have until April 15, 2007, to contribute to your Keogh for 2006). Although a designated financial institution acts as custodian of all the funds held in a Keogh account, *actual investments held in the account are directed completely by the individual contributor*. These are self-directed retirement programs; the *individual* decides which investments to buy and sell (subject to a few basic restrictions).

Income earned from the investments must be reinvested in the account. This income also accrues tax free. All Keogh contributions and investment earnings must remain in the account until the individual turns 59½, unless he or she becomes seriously ill or disabled. Early withdrawals for any other reason are subject to 10 percent tax penalties. However, the individual is *not required* to start withdrawing the funds at age 59½; the funds can stay in the account (and continue earning tax-free income) until the individual is 70½. The individual *must* then begin withdrawing funds from the account—unless he or she continues to be gainfully employed past the age of 70½ [technically, participants in a Keogh plan must start receiving distributions from the plan by April 1 of the year following the *latter of:* (1) the year in which they turn 70½ or (2) the year in which they retire]. Of course, once an individual starts withdrawing funds (upon or after turning 59½), all such withdrawals are treated as ordinary income and subject to normal income taxes. Thus the taxes on all contributions to and earnings from a Keogh account will eventually have to be paid—a characteristic of any tax-*deferred* (as opposed to tax-*free*) program.

A program that's similar in many ways to the Keogh account is something called a *simplified employee pension plan*—or SEP-IRA for short. It's aimed at small business owners, particularly those with *no employees*, who want a plan that's simple to set up and administer. SEP-IRAs *can be used in place of Keoghs*, and although they're simpler to administer, they have the same annual contribution caps as a Keogh account—that is, $44,000 per year, or 25 percent of earned income, whichever is less.

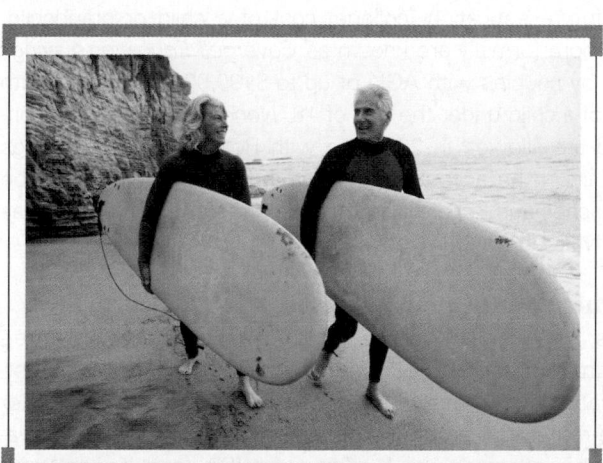

© CORBIS IMAGES/JUPITER

Individual Retirement Arrangements (IRAs)

Some people mistakenly believe that an IRA is a specialized type of investment. It's not. An **individual retirement arrangement (IRA),** or individual retirement *account*, as it's more commonly known, is virtually the same as any other investment account you open with a bank, credit union, stockbroker, mutual fund, or insurance company, except that it's clearly designated as an IRA. That is, the form you complete designates the account as an IRA and makes the institution its trustee. That's all there is to it. Any gainfully employed person (and his or her spouse) can have an IRA account, although the type of accounts a person can have and the tax status of those accounts depend on several variables. All IRAs, however, have one thing in common: they're designed to encourage retirement savings for individuals.

The whole IRA landscape was altered dramatically in 1997–1998, with the introduction of *Roth IRAs*. The individual now has a full menu of IRAs to choose from, including these:

individual retirement arrangement (IRA) A retirement plan, open to any working American, to which a person may contribute a specified amount each year.

• **Traditional (deductible) IRA,** which can be opened by anyone without a retirement plan at his or her place of employment, *regardless of income level*, or by couples filing jointly who, even if they are covered by retirement plans at their places of employment, have adjusted gross incomes of less than $70,000 (or single tax payers with

AGIs of less than $50,000). Individuals who qualify may make tax-deductible contributions of up to $4,000 a year to their accounts (an equal tax-deductible amount can be contributed by a nonworking spouse). This maximum annual contribution increases to $5,000 in 2008 and beyond (and there's a catch-up contribution of an additional $1,000 per year that individuals age 50 or older can make). All account earnings grow tax free until withdrawn, when ordinary tax rates apply (though a 10 percent penalty normally applies to withdrawals made before age 59½).

- **Nondeductible (after-tax) IRA,** which is open to anyone, regardless of their income level or whether they're covered by a retirement plan at their workplace. Contributions of up to $4,000 a year in 2006, rising (as with the traditional IRA) to $5,000 in 2008, can be made to this account; but they're *made with after-tax dollars* (that is, the contributions are not tax deductible). However, *the earnings do accrue tax free and are not subject to tax until they are withdrawn*, after the individual reaches age 59½ (funds withdrawn before age 59½ may be subject to the 10 percent penalty).

- **Roth IRAs** are a lot like *Roth 401(k)s*, which we discussed earlier. Roth IRAs are the newest kid on the block (available only since 1998); they can be opened by couples filing jointly with adjusted gross incomes of up to $150,000 (singles up to $95,000), whether or not they have other retirement or pension plans. But the neatest part of the Roth IRA is its tax features—although the annual contributions of up to $4,000 a person in 2006, rising (as with the traditional IRA) to $5,000 in 2008, are made with nondeductible/after-tax dollars, all earnings in the account grow tax free. And *all withdrawals from the account are also tax free, as long as the account has been open for at least 5 years and the individual is past the age of 59½*. In other words, as long as these conditions are met, you won't have to pay taxes on any withdrawals you make from your Roth IRA!

Key features and provisions of all three of these IRAs are outlined in Exhibit 14.4.

Regardless of the type, and notwithstanding the conditions just described, penalty-free withdrawals (of up to $10,000) are generally allowed from an IRA as long as the funds are being used for first-time home purchases, qualifying educational costs, certain major medical expenses, or other qualified emergencies. Also, with both the traditional/deductible and nondeductible IRAs, you must start making withdrawals from your account once you reach age 70½—although *this requirement does not apply to Roth IRAs*. Finally, in addition to the three retirement-based IRAs, 1998 also brought us the so-called *Education IRA*, which can be set up and used to meet the future education (college) cost of a child or grandchild. Specifically, these accounts, which more formally are known as *Coverdell Education Savings Accounts* (or ESAs), can be opened by couples with AGIs of up to $190,000 (or singles with AGIs up to $95,000) for the benefit of a child under the age of 18. *Nondeductible* annual contributions of up to $2,000 per child are allowed in 2006. As with Roth IRAs, the earnings grow tax free as long as they remain in the account, and all withdrawals (which must be made by the time the beneficiary reaches age 30) are also made tax free and penalty free, as long as the funds are used for qualifying education expenses.

Self-Directed Accounts and Their Investment Vehicles

IRAs are like Keogh and SEP plans; they're *self-directed accounts*—meaning you are free to make almost any kind of investment decision you want. Actually, as with any investment, an individual can be conservative or aggressive in choosing securities for an IRA (or Keogh), though the nature of these retirement programs generally favors a more conservative approach. In fact, conventional wisdom favors funding your IRA (and Keogh) with *income-producing assets*; this would also suggest that if you're looking for capital gains, it's best to do so *outside* your retirement account. The reasons are twofold: (1) growth-oriented securities are by nature *more risky*, and (2) you *cannot write off losses* from the sale of securities held in an IRA (or Keogh) account. This doesn't mean, however, that it would be totally inappropriate to place a good-quality growth stock or mutual fund in a Keogh or IRA—in fact, many advisors contend that growth investments should always have a place in your retirement account due to their often impressive performance and ability to counteract inflation. Such investments may pay off handsomely, because they can appreciate totally free of taxes.

EXHIBIT 14.4   Qualifying for an IRA

In 1998, the ground rules for opening an IRA changed dramatically with the introduction of the new Roth IRAs. Individuals can now select from three types of individual retirement accounts.

Deductible IRA

- For 2006, annual contributions of up to $4,000 by a working taxpayer and $4,000 by a nonworking spouse are fully deductible if the taxpayer is not covered by an employer's pension plan or has adjusted gross income of less than $50,000 a year on a single taxpayer return or $70,000 on a joint return. The maximum annual contribution will increase to $5,000 in 2008, and an additional $1,000 per year catch-up contribution can be made by those age 50 or older.

- Partial tax-deductible contributions are available to joint filers with AGIs (in 2006) of $70,000 to $80,000, and to single filers with AGIs (in 2006) of $50,000 to $60,000—essentially, the deductible contribution is reduced at higher levels of AGI and phases out completely at AGI of $60,000 for single taxpayers and $80,000 for joint returns.

- The nonworking spouse of a taxpayer covered by a deductible IRA can also contribute from $4,000 (in 2006) to $5,000 (in 2008) per year to a fully deductible IRA, provided the couple's AGI is $150,000 or less.

After-Tax IRA

- Working taxpayers who fail to qualify for deductible IRAs, and their nonworking spouses, can make annual non-deductible IRA contributions of up to $4,000 each in 2006, rising (as outlined previously) to $5,000 in 2008.

Roth IRA

- A working taxpayer with AGI of up to $95,000 on a single return or $150,000 on a joint return can make nondeductible contributions of up to $4,000 (in 2006) to $5,000 (in 2008).

- The contribution phases out at $110,000 single and $160,000 joint; partial contributions are available to single filers with AGIs of $95,000–$110,000 and to joint filers with AGIs of $150,000–$160,000.

- A nonworking spouse can make after-tax contributions of up to $4,000 per year (in 2006) to $5,000 per year (in 2008) to a Roth IRA with AGI of $150,000 or less on a joint return.

In the end, of course, *it's how much you have in your retirement account that matters, not how your earnings were made along the way.* Also, no matter what type of investment vehicle you use, keep in mind that once you place money in an IRA, it's meant to stay there for the long haul. Like most tax-sheltered retirement programs, there are restrictions on when you can withdraw the funds from an IRA. Specifically, as noted earlier, any funds withdrawn from an IRA prior to age 59½ are subject to a 10 percent tax penalty, on top of the regular tax paid on the withdrawal. (Note, however, that you can avoid the 10 percent tax penalty and still start withdrawals before age 59½ by setting up a systematic withdrawal program that essentially pays you equal amounts over the rest of your life expectancy; obviously, unless you have a substantial amount of money in your IRA, the annual payments under this program are likely to be pretty small.) In addition, when you move your IRA account to a new firm (this is known as a rollover), the transfer is subject to a *20 percent withholding tax* if the proceeds from the transfer are paid to you directly. The rule is very clear on this: if you take possession of the funds (even for just a few days), you'll be hit with the withholding tax. So, the best way to handle IRA rollovers is to *arrange for the transfer of funds from one firm to another.*

So, should you contribute to an IRA or not? Obviously, so long as you qualify for either a traditional/tax-deductible IRA or a Roth IRA (see Exhibit 14.4), you should seriously consider making the maximum payments allowable. There are no special recordkeeping requirements or forms to file, and the IRA continues to be an excellent vehicle for sheltering income from taxes. Probably the biggest decision you'll have to make is which IRA is right for you—the traditional or the Roth? (*Hint*: The Roth is probably most appropriate for people in their thirties or forties.)

ⓘ Concept Check

14-8	Which basic features of employer-sponsored pension plans should you be familiar with?
14-9	Under which procedure will you become fully vested most quickly—cliff or graded vesting?
14-10	What is the difference between a *profit-sharing plan* and a *salary reduction*, or *401(k), plan?*
14-11	Why is it important to evaluate and become familiar with the pension plans and retirement benefits offered by your employer?
14-12	Briefly describe the tax provisions of *401(k) plans* and *Keogh plans.*
14-13	Describe and differentiate between Keogh plans and *individual retirement arrangements*; what's the difference between a *nondeductible IRA* and a *Roth IRA?*

LG6 · ANNUITIES

An annuity is just the opposite of life insurance. As we pointed out in Chapter 8, life insurance is the systematic accumulation of an estate that is used for protection against financial loss resulting from premature death. In contrast, an **annuity** is the systematic *liquidation* of an estate in such a way that it provides protection against the economic difficulties that could result from outliving personal financial resources. The period during which premiums are paid toward the purchase of an annuity is called the **accumulation period;** correspondingly, the period during which annuity payments are made is called the **distribution period.**

Under a pure life annuity contract, a life insurance company will guarantee regular monthly payments to an individual for as long as he or she lives. These benefits are composed of three parts: principal, interest, and survivorship benefits. The *principal* consists of the premium amounts paid in by the *annuitant* (person buying the annuity) during the accumulation period. *Interest* is the amount earned on these funds between the time they're paid and distributed. The interest earnings on an annuity accrue (that is, accumulate) tax free—but note that while the earnings in an annuity accumulate on a tax-sheltered basis, the amounts paid into an annuity are all made with *after-tax dollars* (that is, no special tax treatment is given to the capital contributions). The portion of the principal and interest that has not been returned to the annuitant before death is the **survivorship benefit.** These funds are available to those members of the annuity group who survive in each subsequent period. By using mortality tables and estimated investment returns, life insurance companies can calculate for a group of annuitants of a given age the amount of monthly payment they can guarantee to each individual without prematurely depleting the total amount accumulated. Consequently, the risk of outliving one's income is eliminated.

Classification of Annuities

Annuities may be classified according to several key characteristics, including payment of premiums, disposition of proceeds, inception date of benefits, and method used in calculating benefits. Exhibit 14.5 illustrates this classification system.

Single Premium or Installments

There are two ways to pay the premiums when you purchase an annuity contract: you can make one large (lump-sum) payment up front or pay the premium in installments. The **single-premium annuity contract** usually requires a *minimum investment* of anywhere from $2,500 to $10,000, with $5,000 the most common figure. These annuities

---

annuity An investment product, created by life insurance companies, that provides a series of payments over time.

accumulation period The period during which premiums are paid for the purchase of an annuity.

distribution period The period during which annuity payments are made to an annuitant.

survivorship benefit On an annuity, the portion of premiums and interest that has not been returned to the annuitant before his or her death.

single-premium annuity contract An annuity contract purchased with a lump-sum payment.

EXHIBIT 14.5 Types of Annuity Contracts

Annuity contracts vary according to how you pay for the annuity, how the proceeds are disbursed, how earnings accrue, and when you receive the benefits.

have become popular, primarily because of their attractive tax features. They're often purchased just before retirement as a way of creating a future stream of income. In these circumstances, the individual normally purchases an **immediate annuity,** in which case the stream of monthly benefits begins immediately—the first check arrives a month or so after purchase. Sometimes the cash value of a life insurance policy is used at retirement to acquire a single-premium annuity. This is an effective use of a life insurance policy: you get the insurance coverage when you *need* it the most (while you're raising and educating your family) and then a regular stream of income when you can probably *use* it the most (after you've retired).

Although most *group* annuity policies are funded with single premiums, many *individuals* still buy annuities by paying for them in installments. With these so-called **installment-premium annuity contracts,** set payments, starting as low as $100, are made at regular intervals (monthly, quarterly, or annually) over an extended period of time. Sometimes, these annuities are set up with a fairly large initial payment (of perhaps several thousand dollars), followed by a series of much smaller installment payments (of, say, $250 a quarter). This approach would be used to purchase a **deferred annuity,** a type of contract in which cash benefits are deferred for several years (note that single premiums can also be used to purchase deferred annuities). A big advantage of *installment-premium deferred annuities* is that your savings can build up over time, *free of taxes*. With no taxes to pay, you have more money working for you and can build up a bigger retirement nest egg—of course, you'll have to pay taxes on your earnings eventually, but not until you start receiving benefit payments from your annuity.

Installment-premium contracts also carry an important *life insurance provision*, which stipulates that if an annuitant dies before the distribution period begins, the annuitant's beneficiaries will receive the market value of the contract or the amount invested, whichever is greater (note that single-premium annuities contain similar life insurance provisions, as long as the payout of benefits is deferred to some future date). In addition, the annuitant can terminate an installment-premium contract at any time, or simply stop paying the periodic

immediate annuity An annuity in which the annuitant begins receiving monthly benefits immediately.

installment-premium annuity contract An annuity contract purchased through periodic payments made over time.

deferred annuity An annuity in which benefit payments are deferred for a certain number of years.

installments and take a paid-up annuity for a reduced amount. One potential advantage of purchasing an installment-type annuity relatively early in life is that scheduled benefits are based on mortality rates in effect when the contract was purchased. Even if the mortality rate increases, as it normally does with the passage of time, the annuitant won't be required to pay the higher premium stipulated in contracts issued later.

Deposition of Proceeds

All annuities revolve around the basic pay-now, receive-later concept, and therefore allow individuals to prepare for future cash needs, like planning for retirement, while obtaining significant tax benefits. When the annuity is distributed, you can take a lump-sum payment or, as is more often the case, you can *annuitize* the distribution by systematically parceling out the money into regular payments over a defined or open-ended period. Because most people choose to annuitize their proceeds (which is how an annuity is intended to be used), let's look at the most common annuity disbursement options:

life annuity with no refund (pure life) An option under which an annuitant receives a specified amount of income for life, regardless of the length of the distribution period.

- **Life annuity with no refund (pure life).** The annuitant receives a specified amount of income for life, whether the disbursement period turns out to be 1 year or 50 years. The estate or family receives no refunds when the annuitant dies. This results in the largest monthly payments of any of the distribution methods, because the issuer (a life insurance company) doesn't have to distribute the principal, if any, to the annuitant's heirs.

guaranteed-minimum annuity An annuity that provides a guaranteed minimum distribution of benefits.

life annuity, period certain A type of guaranteed-minimum annuity that guarantees the annuitant a stated amount of monthly income for life; the insurer agrees to pay for a minimum number of years.

- **Guaranteed-minimum annuity (life annuity with refund).** In this type of contract, the benefits (future cash flows) aren't limited to the annuitant only, but may extend to named beneficiaries. There are two forms of this annuity. With a **life annuity, period certain,** the annuitant gets a guaranteed monthly income for life, with the added provision that the insurance company will pay the monthly benefits for a minimum number of years (5 or 10, for example). If the annuitant dies soon after the distribution begins, his or her beneficiaries receive the monthly benefits for the balance of the "period certain." With a **refund annuity,** if the annuitant dies, the designated beneficiary receives monthly payments (or in some cases, a lump-sum cash refund) until the total purchase price of the annuity has been refunded.

refund annuity A guaranteed-minimum annuity that, on the annuitant's death, makes monthly payments to the beneficiary until the total price of the annuity is refunded.

- **Annuity certain.** This type of annuity pays a set amount of monthly income for a specified number of years, thereby filling a need for monthly income that will expire after a certain length of time. An annuitant selecting a 10-year annuity certain receives payments for 10 years after retirement, regardless of whether he or she lives for 2 or 20 more years. For example, a widow, age 52, could use a 10-year annuity certain contract to provide income until she reaches age 62 and can apply for Social Security benefits.

annuity certain An annuity that provides a specified monthly income for a stated number of years, without consideration of any life contingency.

Fixed versus Variable Annuity

fixed-rate annuity An annuity in which the insurance company agrees to pay a guaranteed rate of interest on your money.

When you put your money into an annuity, the premium is invested on your behalf by the insurance company, much as a mutual fund invests the money you put into it. From the time you pay the first (or only) annuity premium until it's paid back to you as a lump sum or as an annuitized monthly benefit, you'll earn a rate of return on your investment. How that rate of return is figured determines whether you own a fixed or variable annuity. In a **fixed-rate annuity** the insurance company safeguards your principal and agrees to pay a guaranteed minimum rate of interest over the life of the contract—which often amounts to little more than prevailing money market rates existing when you bought the contract. These are conservative, very low-risk annuity products that essentially promise to return *the original investment plus interest* when the money is paid out to the annuitant (or any designated beneficiaries). Unlike bond mutual funds, fixed annuities don't fluctuate in value when interest rates rise or fall; so your principal is always secure. These *interest-earning annuities*, as they're also called, are ideally suited for the cautious investor who likes the secure feeling of knowing what his or her monthly cash flow will be.

variable annuity An annuity in which the monthly income provided by the policy varies based on the insurer's actual investment experience.

Imagine an investment vehicle that lets you move between stocks, bonds, and money funds and, at the same time, accumulate profits tax free. That, in a nutshell, is a variable annuity. With a **variable annuity** contract, the amount that's ultimately paid out to the annuitant varies with the investment results obtained by the insurance company—*nothing*

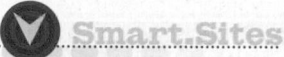
is guaranteed, not even the principal! When you buy a variable annuity, *you decide* where your money will be invested, based on your investment objectives and tolerance for risk; you can usually choose from stocks, bonds, money market securities, or some combination thereof. Insurance companies typically offer five or six stock and bond funds, as well as money market investments for short-term safety; some companies even offer a relatively exotic fleet of alternatives, ranging from zero coupon bonds to real estate and foreign securities. As an annuity holder, you can stay put with a single investment for the long haul; or, as with most variable annuities, you can aggressively play the market by switching from one fund to another. Obviously, when the market goes up, investors in variable annuities do well; but when the market falters, the returns on these policies can go down as well.

Although there's nothing to keep you from staying with market-sensitive variable annuities during both the accumulation and distribution periods, in most cases *you can convert to a fixed annuity at distribution.* What you do, in effect, is use the cash value in your variable annuity to buy a paid-up fixed annuity. In this way, you use a *variable annuity during the accumulation period* to build up your capital as much as possible, and then switch to a *fixed annuity for the distribution period* to obtain a certain, well-defined stream of future income.

FINANCIAL ROAD SIGN

ARE ANNUITIES RIGHT FOR YOU?

You may want to consider annuities if you:

- Have contributed the maximum to your 401(k) plans and IRAs, but want more tax-deferred investment gains.
- Prefer investing in mutual funds over individual securities.
- Will keep the annuity for several years, at least until you reach $59\frac{1}{2}$.
- Are in a 28 percent or higher tax bracket today, but expect to be in a lower tax bracket in retirement.
- Are unconcerned that your heirs must pay ordinary income taxes on any appreciation.
- Desire a "guaranteed" income for life in retirement.

Source: Adapted from "Annuities: What's to Like?" *The Motley Fool*, http://www.fool.com.

Sources and Costs of Annuities

Annuities are administered by life insurance companies, so it's no surprise that they're also the leading sellers of these financial products. Annuities can also be purchased from stock brokers, mutual fund organizations, banks, and financial planners. When you buy an annuity, the cost will vary with the annuitant's age at issue, the annuitant's age when payments begin, the method used to distribute benefits, the number of lives covered, and the annuitant's sex. Exhibit 14.6 provides some real-life examples of the lump-sum costs of two types of immediate annuities. Notice the substantial differences among the companies' premiums. These differences confirm the need to shop around before making an annuity purchase. Note also that in every category the cost to females is higher than the cost to males, because of the lower mortality rates among women.

In addition, as with mutual funds, there are some annual fees you should be aware of. In particular, be prepared to pay insurance fees of 1 percent or more—and that's on top of annual management fees of perhaps 1 to 2 percent paid on variable annuities. That's a total of 2 to 3 percent—or more— taken right off the top, year after year. And then there's also a *contract charge* (or maintenance fee) that's deducted annually to cover various contract-related expenses; these fees usually run from about $30 to $60 per year. Obviously, these fees can drag down returns and reduce the advantage of tax-deferred income. Finally, most annuities charge hefty *penalties for early withdrawal;* meaning that in order to get out of a poorly performing annuity, you'll have to forfeit a chunk of your money.

Investment and Income Properties of Annuities

A major attribute of most types of annuities is that they're a source of income that can't be outlived. Although individuals might be able to create a similar arrangement by simply living off the interest or dividends from their investments, they'd find it difficult to systematically liquidate their principal so that the last payment would coincide closely (or exactly) with their death. Another advantage is that the income earned in an annuity is allowed to accumulate tax free, so it's a form of *tax-sheltered investment.* Actually, the income from an annuity is *tax deferred*, meaning that taxes on the earnings will have to be paid when the annuity is liquidated.

Annuity costs vary not only by the type of annuity and the beneficiary's sex and age but also by the company selling the contract. Clearly, it pays to shop around. Here are some costs actually quoted by four life insurance companies; note that it would cost a 55-year-old male about 22 percent less to buy a life annuity contract from Company 2 than from Company 3.

Life Annuity with No Refund

	Male				Female		
Company	55	65	75		55	65	75
1	$13,110	$11,170	$8,510		$13,930	$12,280	$9,700
2	11,820	10,250	8,010		12,450	11,140	8,980
3	15,020	11,970	8,420		16,510	13,440	9,580
4	12,900	10,960	8,480		13,660	11,860	9,270

Life Annuity—10 Years Certain

	Male				Female		
Company	55	65	75		55	65	75
1	$13,400	$11,840	$10,170		$14,070	$12,660	$10,770
2	12,050	10,800	9,390		12,560	11,440	9,870
3	N/A	N/A	N/A		N/A	N/A	N/A
4	13,190	11,570	9,940		13,790	12,200	10,300

Shelter from taxes is an attractive investment attribute, but there's a hitch. You may be faced with a big tax penalty if you close out or withdraw money from an annuity before it's time. Specifically, the IRS treats annuity withdrawals like withdrawals from an individual retirement account, meaning that except in cases of serious illness, *anybody who takes money out before reaching age 59½ will incur a 10 percent tax penalty*. So, if you're under age 59½ and in the 28 percent tax bracket, you'll end up paying a 38 percent tax rate on any funds withdrawn from an annuity. (The IRS views withdrawals *as taxable income* until the account balance falls to the amount of original paid-in principal—then any further withdrawals are tax free.) Barring some type of serious illness, about the only way to tap your account penalty free before you're 59½ is to *annuitize*. Unfortunately, the annuity payments must be spread out over your estimated remaining life span, which means the size of each monthly payment could be pretty small. All of which only reinforces the notion that *an annuity should always be considered a long-term investment*. Assume that it's a part of your retirement program (that's the way the IRS looks at it) and that you're getting in for the long haul.

From an investment perspective, the returns generated from an annuity can, in some cases, be a bit disappointing. For instance, as we discussed earlier, the returns on *variable annuities* are tied to returns in the money and capital markets; even so, they're still no better than what you can get from other investment vehicles—indeed, they're often lower, due in part to higher annuity fees. And keep in mind, these differential returns aren't due to tax features, because in both cases returns were measured on a before-tax basis. But *returns from annuities are tax sheltered*, so that makes those lower returns a lot more attractive. If you're considering a variable annuity, go over it much like you would a traditional mutual fund: look for superior past performance, proven management talents, and the availability of attractive investment alternatives that you can switch in and out of. And *pay particular attention to an annuity's total expense rate*. For although these products have a (bad) reputation for being heavily loaded with fees and charges, it's possible to find annuities with both above-average performance as well as relatively low fee structures. That's the combination you're looking for.

One final point: If you're seriously considering buying an annuity, be sure to read the contract carefully and see what the guaranteed rates are, how long the initial rate applies, and if there's a bailout provision. (A *bailout provision* allows you to withdraw your money free of any surrender fees, if the rate of return on your annuity falls below a specified minimum level. Of course, even if you exercise a bailout provision, you may still have to face a tax penalty for early withdrawal—unless you transfer the funds to another annuity through what's known as a *1035 exchange.*) Just as important, because *the annuity is only as good as the insurance company that stands behind it*, check to see how the company is rated by Best's, Standard & Poor's, or Moody's. It's important to make sure that the insurance company itself is financially sound before buying one of its annuity products. See Chapter 8 for more discussion on these insurance ratings and how they work.

▮▮ Concept Check

CHECK • CONCEPT CHECK • CONCEPT CHECK • CONCEPT CHECK • CONCEPT CHECK • CONCEPT CHECK • CONCEPT C

14-14	What is an *annuity*? Briefly explain how an annuity works and how it differs from a life insurance policy.
14-15	Which one of the annuity distribution procedures will result in the highest monthly benefit payment?
14-16	What is a *fixed-rate annuity*, and how does it differ from a *variable annuity*? Does the type of contract (fixed or variable) have any bearing on the amount of money you'll receive at the time of distribution?
14-17	Which type of contract (fixed or variable) might be most suitable for someone who wants a minimum amount of risk exposure?
14-18	How do variable annuity returns generally compare to mutual fund returns? Can you explain why there would be any difference in returns?

SUMMARY • SUMMARY • SUMMARY • SUMMARY • SUMMARY • SUMMARY • SUMMARY • SUMMARY • SUMMARY • SU

◀◀ SUMMARY

LG1 **Recognize the importance of retirement planning, and identify the three biggest pitfalls to good planning.** Retirement planning plays a vital role in the personal financial planning process. It's based on many of the same principles and concepts of effective financial planning, including establishing financial goals and strategies, using savings and investment plans, and using certain insurance products, such as annuities. The three biggest pitfalls to sound retirement planning are starting too late, not saving enough, and investing too conservatively.

LG2 **Estimate your income needs in retirement and your retirement income.** Rather than address retirement planning in a series of short-run (3- to 5-year) plans, it's best to take a long-term approach and look 20 to 30 years into

the future to determine how much saving and investing you must do today to achieve the retirement goals you've set for tomorrow. Implementing a long-term retirement plan involves determining future retirement needs, estimating retirement income from known sources (such as Social Security and company pension plans), and deciding how much to save and invest each year to build up a desired nest egg.

LG3 **Explain the eligibility requirements and benefits of the Social Security program.** Social Security is the foundation for the retirement programs of most families; except for a few exempt classes (mostly government employees), almost all gainfully employed workers are covered by Social Security. Upon retirement, covered workers are entitled to certain monthly benefits, as determined mainly by the employee's earning history and age at retirement.

LG4 Differentiate among the types of basic and supplemental employer-sponsored pension plans.
Employer-sponsored pension and retirement plans provide a vital source of retirement income to many individuals. Such plans can often spell the difference between enjoying a comfortable standard of living in retirement or a bare subsistence. In *basic* retirement programs, all employees participate after a certain period of employment. These plans can be defined contribution or defined benefits plans. There are also several forms of *supplemental* employer-sponsored programs, including profit-sharing plans, thrift and savings plans, and perhaps most popular, salary reduction plans such as 401(k) plans.

LG5 Describe the various types of self-directed retirement plans. In addition to company-sponsored retirement programs, individuals can set up their own self-directed tax-sheltered retirement plans; it's through such plans that most individuals can build up the nest eggs they'll need to meet their retirement objectives. The basic types of self-directed retirement programs are Keogh and SEP plans for self-employed individuals as well as various forms of IRAs, which any salary or wage earner can set up.

LG6 Choose the right type of annuity for your retirement plan. Annuities are also an important source of income for retired people. Basically, an annuity is an investment vehicle that allows investment income to accumulate on a tax-deferred basis; it provides for the systematic liquidation (payout) of all invested capital and earnings over an extended period. There's a wide variety of annuities, including single-payment and installment-premium, fixed and variable, and immediate and deferred; there are also different payout options.

FINANCIAL PLANNING EXERCISES

LG2

1. DeShawn Thomas, a 25-year-old personal loan officer at First State Bank, understands the importance of starting early when it comes to saving for retirement. She has designated $3,000 per year for her retirement fund and assumes she'll retire at age 65.
   a. How much will she have if she invests in CDs and similar money market instruments that earn 4 percent on average?
   b. How much will she have if she invests in equities instead and earns 10 percent on average?
   c. DeShawn is urging her friend, Mark Randolph, to start his plan right away, too, because he's 35. What would his nest egg amount to if he invested in the same manner as DeShawn and he, too, retires at age 65? Comment on your findings.

LG2

2. *Use Worksheet 14.1* to help Al and Linda Gonzales, who'd like to retire while they're still relatively young—in about 20 years. Both have promising careers, and both make good money. As a result, they're willing to put aside whatever is necessary to achieve a comfortable lifestyle in retirement. Their current level of household expenditures (excluding savings) is around $75,000 a year, and they expect to spend *even more* in retirement; they think they'll need about 125 percent of that amount (*note*: 125 percent equals a multiplier factor of 1.25). They estimate that their Social Security benefits will amount to $20,000 a year in today's dollars, and they'll receive another $35,000 annually from their company pension plans. They feel that future inflation will amount to about 3 percent a year; they also think they'll be able to earn about 12 percent on their investments before retirement and about 8 percent afterward. Use Worksheet 14.1 to find out how big their investment nest egg will have to be and how much they'll have to save annually to accumulate the needed amount within the next 20 years.

LG3

3. Many critics of the Social Security program feel that participants are getting a substandard investment return on their money. Discuss why you agree or disagree with this viewpoint.

LG3

4. Use Exhibit 14.3 to determine the amount of Social Security retirement benefits that Elwood Cheeseater would receive annually if he had a high (that is, "maximum") level of career earnings, is age 62, has a dependent wife (also age 62), and has a part-time job that pays him $24,000 a year. If Elwood also receives another $47,500 a year from a company

pension and some tax-exempt bonds that he holds, will he be liable for any tax on his Social Security income? Explain.

LG4
5. Diane Fein has just graduated from college and is considering job offers from two companies. Although the salary and insurance benefits are similar, the retirement programs are not. One firm offers a 401(k) plan that matches employee contributions with $.25 for every $1 contributed by the employee, up to a $10,000 limit. The other has a contributory plan that allows employees to contribute up to 10 percent of their annual salary through payroll deduction and matches it dollar for dollar. The plan vests fully after 5 years. Because Diane is unfamiliar with these plans, explain the features of each to her so she can make an informed decision.

LG4
6. John Yee is an operations manager for a large manufacturer. He earned $68,500 in 2006 and plans to contribute the maximum allowed to the firm's 401(k) plan. Assuming that John is in the 28 percent tax bracket, calculate his taxable income and the amount of his tax savings. How much did it actually cost John on an after-tax basis to make this retirement plan contribution?

LG3, 4
7. At what age would you like to retire? What type of lifestyle do you envision (for example, where do you want to live, do you want to work part-time, and so on)? Discuss the steps you think you should take to realize this goal.

LG3, 4
8. Describe the three basic types of IRAs (traditional, Roth, and nondeductible), including their respective tax features and what it takes to qualify for each. Which is most appealing to you personally? Explain.

LG3, 4
9. Dave Jones is in his early thirties and is thinking about opening an IRA; however, he can't decide whether to open a traditional/deductible IRA or a Roth IRA, so he turns to you for help.
   a. To support your explanation, you decide to *run some comparative numbers on the two types of accounts*; for starters, use a 25-year period to show Dave what contributions of $4,000 per year will amount to (after 25 years), given he can earn, say, 10 percent on his money. Will the type of account he opens have any impact on this amount? Explain.
   b. Given Dave is in the 30 percent tax bracket (and will remain there for the next 25 years), determine the annual and total (over 25 years) tax savings he'll enjoy from the $4,000-a-year contributions to his IRA; contrast the (annual and total) tax savings he'd generate from a traditional IRA with those from a Roth IRA.
   c. Now, fast-forward 25 years. Given the size of Dave's account in 25 years (as computed in part **a**), assume he takes it all out in one lump sum. If he's still in the 30 percent tax bracket, how much will he have, *after taxes*, with a traditional IRA as compared with a Roth IRA? How do the taxes computed here compare with those computed in part **b**? Comment on your findings.
   d. Based on the numbers you computed earlier, as well as any other factors, what kind of IRA would you recommend to Dave? Explain. Would knowing that maximum contributions are scheduled to increase to $5,000 per year make any difference in your analysis? Explain.

LG6
10. Explain how buying a variable annuity is much like investing in a mutual fund. Do you, as a buyer, have any control over the amount of investment risk to which you're exposed in a variable annuity contract? Explain.

LG6
11. Briefly explain why annuities are a type of tax-sheltered investment. Do you have to give up anything to obtain this tax-favored treatment? (*Hint:* Age 59½)

LG6
12. Why is it important to check an insurance company's financial ratings when buying an annuity? Why should you look at past performance when considering the purchase of a variable annuity?

LG4
13. Briefly describe the main characteristics of defined contribution and defined benefits pension plans, and discuss how they differ from cash-balance plans. In each of these plans, does the employee or employer bear the risk of poor investment performance?

14. Use Exhibit 14.3 to determine the annual Social Security benefit for Chester Atherton, assuming that he has an "average" career earnings level. Chester is 65 years old and earns $18,000 a year at a part-time job. (Note that Chester is already at "full retirement age," since he was born well before 1960.) What would Chester's annual benefit be if he were only 62 years old?

15. **Use Worksheet 14.1** to assist Linda Bailey with her retirement planning needs. She plans to retire in 15 years, and her current household expenditures run about $50,000 per year. Linda estimates that she'll spend 80 percent of that amount in retirement. Her Social Security benefit is estimated at $15,000 per year, and she'll receive $12,000 per year from her employer's pension plan (both in today's dollars). Additional assumptions include an inflation rate of 4 percent and a rate of return on retirement assets of 9 percent a year before retirement and 6 percent afterward. Use Worksheet 14.1 to calculate the required size of Linda's retirement nest egg and the amount that she must save annually over the next 15 years to reach that goal.

16. What are the main differences between fixed-rate and variable annuities? Which type is more appropriate for someone who is 60 years old and close to retirement?

APPLYING PERSONAL FINANCE

Your Ideal Retirement Plan!

Many people have little or no money set aside for their retirement. Those who do may find their retirement funds insufficient for maintaining their desired standard of living during retirement. In this project, you'll contemplate the type and features of a retirement program that would best meet your needs.

Looking back over this chapter, review the features of both employer-sponsored and self-directed retirement programs. Depending on your career, you may actually have both kinds. Develop an outline of your ideal retirement plan or plans (*be realistic*), being sure to consider these issues:

1. Would the plan be contributory or noncontributory?
2. Stated as a *percentage* of your base salary, how much would be put into your retirement plan each year? Remember that there are certain allowable limits.
3. What would be the eligibility and vesting provisions? Would your plan be portable? Under what conditions?
4. What would be the earliest retirement age? Would there be provisions for early retirement?
5. Would your plan be a defined contribution or a defined benefit plan? You could also have a combination of the two types.
6. Would the plan be qualified?
7. Would you want a voluntary supplemental plan as part of your program? If you could have only one supplemental plan, what would it be?

What would be the advantages and disadvantages of your ideal plan? This research will help you understand the retirement benefits you may have with your current job or of job offers you may receive in the future.

CRITICAL THINKING CASES

14.1 Comparing Pension Plan Features: Which Plan Is Best?

Mary Maloney and Ellen Saperstein are neighbors in Kansas City. Mary works as a systems engineer for United Foods Corporation, while Ellen works as an executive assistant for U.S. Steel and Castings. Both are married, have two children, and are well paid. Before Mary and Ellen joined their respective companies, there had been some employee unrest and strikes. To counteract these problems, their firms had developed job enrichment and employee motivation programs. Of particular interest are the portions of these programs dealing with pensions and retirement.

United Foods Corp., Mary's company, has a contributory plan by which 5 percent of the employees' annual wages is deducted to meet the cost of the benefits. The firm contributes an amount equal to the employee contribution. The plan uses a 5-year graded vesting procedure; it has a normal retirement age of 60 for all employees, and the benefits at retirement are paid according to a defined contribution plan.

Although U.S. Steel and Castings, Ellen's company, has a minimum retirement age of 60, it provides an extension period of 5 to 6 years before compulsory retirement. Employees (full-time, hourly, or salaried) must meet participation requirements. Further, in contrast to the United Foods plan, the U.S. Steel and Castings program has a noncontributory feature. Annual retirement benefits are computed according to the following formula: 2 percent of the employee's final annual salary for each year of service with the company is paid upon retirement. The plan vests immediately.

Critical Thinking Questions

1. Discuss the features of the retirement plans offered by United Foods Corp. and U.S. Steel and Castings.
2. Which plan do you think is more desirable? Consider the features, retirement age, and benefit computations as just explained. Which plan do you think could be subject to a conversion to a cash-balance plan sometime in the future? Explain. Include in your answer the implications for the employee's future retirement benefits.
3. Explain how you would use each of these plans in developing your own retirement program.
4. What role, if any, could annuities play in these retirement programs? Discuss the pros and cons of using annuities as a part of retirement planning.

LG2, 4, 5

14.2 Evaluating Lydia Sanchez's Retirement Prospects

Lydia Sanchez is 57 years old and has been widowed for 13 years. Never remarried, she has worked full-time since her husband died—in addition to raising her two children, the youngest of whom is now finishing college. After being forced back to work in her forties, Lydia's first job was in a fast-food restaurant. Eventually, she upgraded her skills sufficiently to obtain a supervisory position in the personnel department of a major corporation, where she's now earning $58,000 a year.

Although her financial focus for the past 13 years has, by necessity, been on meeting living expenses and getting her kids through college, she feels she can now turn her attention to her retirement needs. Actually, Lydia hasn't done too badly in that area either. Due to some shrewd investing of the proceeds from her husband's life insurance policy, Lydia has accumulated the following investment assets:

Money market securities, stocks, and bonds	$72,600
IRA and 401(k) plans	$47,400

Other than the mortgage on her condo, the only other debt she has is $7,000 in college loans.

Lydia would like to retire in 8 years and recently hired a financial planner to help her come up with an effective retirement program. He has estimated that for her to live comfortably in retirement, she'll need about $37,500 a year (in today's dollars) in retirement income.

Critical Thinking Questions

1. After taking into account the income Lydia will receive from Social Security and her company-sponsored pension plan, the financial planner has estimated that her investment assets will need to provide her with about $15,000 a year to meet the balance of her retirement income needs. Assuming a 6 percent after-tax return on her investments, how big of a nest egg will Lydia need to earn that kind of income?
2. Given she can invest the money market securities, stocks, and bonds (the $72,600) at 5 percent after taxes, and the amount she's now accumulated in her tax-sheltered IRA and 401(k)—the $47,400—at 9 percent, how much will Lydia's investment assets be worth in 8 years, when she retires?
3. Lydia's employer matches her 401(k) contributions dollar for dollar, up to a maximum of $3,000 a year. If she continues to put $3,000 a year into that program, how much more will she have in 8 years, given a 9 percent rate of return?
4. What would you advise Lydia about her ability to retire in 8 years, as she hopes to?

Visit **http://www.thomsonedu.com/finance/gitman** for some additional Web-based exercises and hot links (with annotations) to a variety of resources relevant to the topics covered in this chapter.

Preserving Your Estate

LEARNING GOALS

LG1	▶	Describe the role of estate planning in personal financial planning and identify the seven steps involved in the process.	p. 487
LG2	▶	Recognize the importance of preparing a will and other documents to protect you and your estate.	p. 493
LG3	▶	Explain how trusts are used in estate planning.	p. 503
LG4	▶	Determine whether a gift will be taxable and use planned gifts to reduce estate taxes.	p. 506
LG5	▶	Calculate federal taxes due on an estate.	p. 509
LG6	▶	Use effective estate planning techniques to minimize estate taxes.	p. 512
	▶		

CHAPTER 15 • CHAPTER 15 • CHAPTER 15 • CHAPTER 15 • CHAPTER 15 • CHAPTER 15 • CHAPTER 15 • CHAPT

LG1 · PRINCIPLES OF ESTATE PLANNING

Like it or not, no one lives forever. Although this thought may depress you, safeguarding the future of the people you care about is one of the most important aspects of financial planning. Unless you develop plans and take steps during your lifetime to accumulate, preserve, and distribute your wealth on your death, chances are that your heirs and beneficiaries will receive only part of your estate. The rest will go (often unnecessarily) to taxes and various administrative costs. This process, called *estate planning*, requires knowledge of wills, trusts, and taxes.

Understanding these components and their interrelationships will help you minimize estate shrinkage after your death, while still achieving your lifetime personal financial goals. Also, keep in mind that not only wealthy people but also individuals of modest or moderate means need to plan their estates. Those who start saving for retirement early are likely to have sizable retirement accounts. Without proper planning, taxes could consume much of what's left in those accounts after your death.

Estate planning is the process of developing a plan to administer and distribute your assets after death in a manner consistent with your wishes and the needs of your survivors, while minimizing taxes. This process helps people accumulate enough capital to meet college education costs and other special needs, provide financial security for family members after the death of the head of household, take care of themselves and their family during a long-term disability, and provide for a comfortable retirement. However, estate

estate planning The process of developing a plan to administer and distribute your assets after death in a manner consistent with your wishes and the needs of your survivors, while minimizing taxes.

planning goes beyond financial issues. It also includes plans to manage your affairs if you become disabled and a statement of your personal wishes for medical care should you become unable to make them clear yourself.

As with other financial planning activities, a major objective of estate planning is to eliminate or minimize tax exposure. Doing so, of course, increases the amount of your estate that ultimately is passed on to your heirs and beneficiaries. Estate planning is closely related to insurance and retirement planning. Certainly the most important reason for buying life insurance is to provide for your family in the event of your premature death. Likewise, a principal challenge of effective retirement planning is to achieve a comfortable standard of living in retirement, while preserving as much of your accumulated wealth as possible. This not only reduces the chances of you (or your spouse) outliving your financial resources but also leaves an estate that can be passed on to your heirs and designated beneficiaries according to your wishes.

Planning occurs in every estate. The estate owner and his or her professional counselors control some parts of the plan, and federal and state governments may control other parts of the plan. If an individual fails to plan, state and federal laws will control the disposition of assets and determine who bears the burden of expenses and taxes. Indeed, the taxes may be higher due to the lack of planning. People who wish to plan their estates must systematically uncover problems in several important areas and solve them. Exhibit 15.1 lists the major types of problems and their associated causes or indicators. In later sections, we'll discuss techniques to avoid or minimize these problems.

Who Needs Estate Planning?

Estate planning should be part of everyone's financial plan, whether they're married or single, have five children or none. For example, married couples who own many assets jointly and have designated beneficiaries for assets such as retirement funds and life insurance policies may think that they don't need wills. However, a will covers many other important details, such as naming an executor to administer the estate and a guardian for children, clarifying how estate taxes will be paid, and distributing property that doesn't go directly to a joint owner.

EXHIBIT 15.1   **Potential Estate Planning Problems and Major Causes or Indicators**

Careful estate planning can prevent many problems that arise when settling an estate. The first step toward preventing problems is an awareness and understanding of their major causes or indicators.

Problem	Major Cause or Indicator
• Excessive transfer costs	Taxes and estate administrative expenses higher than necessary.
• Lack of liquidity	Insufficient cash. Not enough assets that are quickly and inexpensively convertible to cash within a short period of time to meet tax demands and other costs.
• Improper disposition of assets	Beneficiaries receive the wrong asset, or the proper asset in the wrong manner or at the wrong time.
• Inadequate income at retirement	Capital insufficient or not readily convertible to income-producing status.
• Inadequate income, if disabled	High medical costs, capital insufficient or not readily convertible to income-producing status, difficulty in reducing living standards.
• Inadequate income for family at estate owner's death	Any of the above causes.
• Insufficient capital	Excessive taxes, inflation, improper investment planning.
• Special problems	A family member with a serious illness or physical or emotional problem, children of a prior marriage, beneficiaries who have extraordinary medical or financial needs, beneficiaries who can't agree on how to handle various estate matters, business problems or opportunities.

Smart Sites

What should you do first when someone close to you dies? Download the University of Pittsburgh Medical Center's comprehensive guide, "When a Loved One Dies," to help you through these difficult times. Link to the site at **http://www.thomsonedu.com/finance/gitman.**

Partners who aren't married and single persons will discover that estate planning is especially important, particularly if they own a home or other assets that they want to leave to specific individuals or to charity. Unmarried couples need to put extra effort into their estate plans. They may need to make special arrangements to be sure they can indeed leave assets to a partner.

The two main areas of estate planning are *people planning and asset planning.*

People Planning

People planning means anticipating the psychological and financial needs of those people you love and providing enough income or capital or both to ensure a continuation of their way of life. People planning also means keeping Mother's cameo brooch in the family and out of the pawnshop, or preserving the business that Granddad started in the early 1900s. People planning is especially important for individuals with children who are minors; children who are exceptionally artistic or intellectually gifted; children or other dependents who are emotionally, mentally, or physically handicapped; and spouses who can't or don't want to handle money, securities, or a business.

Minor children cannot legally handle large sums of money or deal directly with real estate or securities. Custodial accounts, guardianships, or trusts will provide administration, security, financial advice, and the legal capacity to act on behalf of minors. Few children are exceptionally artistic or intellectually gifted, but those who are often need—or should have—special (and often expensive) schooling, travel opportunities, or equipment. Emotionally, mentally, or physically handicapped children (and other relatives) may need nursing, medical, or psychiatric care. Clearly, outright gifts of money or property to those who can't care for themselves are foolishly inappropriate. These individuals may need more (or less) than other children. An individual who gives all of his or her children equal shares may not be giving them equitable shares.

How many of us have handled hundreds of thousands of dollars? Think of the burden we place on others when we expect that a spouse who can't—or doesn't want to—handle such large sums of money or securities will do so. This is particularly burdensome when the assets being handled are his or her only assets. Engaging in people planning demonstrates a high degree of caring. People planning also involves talking about estate planning with your loved ones, as the *Money in Action* box on page 490 explains.

Asset Planning

From the standpoint of wealth alone, estate planning is essential for anyone—single, widowed, married, or divorced—with an estate exceeding the "applicable exclusion amount," which is $2,000,000 for the years 2006–2008 and increases to $3,500,000 in 2009. (Note that the 2001 Tax Act provides for the complete repeal of the estate tax in 2010; of course, this is subject to change by the legislature at any time.) When an estate involves a closely held business, estate planning is essential to stabilize and maximize its asset and income-producing values, both during the owner's lifetime and at the owner's death or disability. Likewise, estate planning is essential to avoid the special problems that occur when an estate owner holds title to property in more than one state; these problems include incurring attorneys' fees in each state and being taxed on the same assets by more than one state.

The estate planning process gets more complicated if you're part of a blended family or have special requests. With careful planning, you can be sure that your assets will go to the desired beneficiaries.

Why Does an Estate Break Up?

Quite often, when people die, their estates die with them—not because they've done anything wrong, but because they haven't done

---

FINANCIAL ROAD SIGN

EXCUSES, EXCUSES, EXCUSES!

It's easy to put off estate planning. After all, who wants to think about dying? Don't let any of these excuses keep you from moving forward.

- I don't have time.
- Thinking about death is morbid.
- I don't have enough assets to need estate planning.
- I'm too young to need a will.
- I have no kids/I'm not married.
- My spouse and I can't agree on a guardian for our children.
- My life insurance policy takes care of my estate planning.
- It costs too much.

Without an estate plan, your relatives will be left with a messy situation, will have no guidance as to your wishes, and could owe more taxes than necessary. The state will appoint a guardian for your children and decide who gets which assets. Accidents and disease can strike at any age. And life insurance is just one component of an estate plan; you need to look at the other areas, such as tax planning and end-of-life planning.

HAVING "THE TALK"—THE ADULT VERSION

Remember when your parents sat you down to have "The Talk?" Now it's your turn, but this time the talk is about money, their wills, and other estate planning matters. These discussions are uncomfortable for both parties. Children don't want to appear nosy or as if they're trying to get their hands on their inheritance. Parents may not want to burden their children or may simply feel their finances are none of their children's business. Still, it's critical to have this talk, for both your sakes.

There are a couple of ways you might approach the subject. You can start by mentioning your own retirement investments or estate planning. Or you might use a personal event, such as the death of a relative, or a magazine article on retirement planning to spark the conversation. If all else fails, take the direct approach. Tell them you care about them and want to help them, but you need to know their wants and needs. If after every attempt your parents still don't want to have the talk, respect their privacy. Recommend a reputable financial adviser, and make sure they follow through. You can find a financial adviser through The National Association of Personal Financial Advisers (www.napfa.org) or the Financial Planning Association (www.fpanet.org).

Once you've decided to have the talk, there are several topics for the discussion.

1. *Where do they keep their important documents?* You need to know where to locate birth and marriage certificates, the names of financial and legal advisers, insurance policies, lists of bank accounts and investments, passwords for any online accounts, and a letter of last instructions. It's a good idea for your parents to keep this information in one notebook with its location known to you.

2. *Will they have enough money to live on?* Because people are living longer, retirement savings must stretch 30 to 35 years. Financial planners recommend keeping some investments (at least 25 percent) in stocks throughout retirement to ensure enough growth so that the retiree can live on the interest and preserve the principal as a financial cushion. Dividend-paying stocks are a good option since they tend to be less volatile than other stocks.

3. *What are their plans in the event of illness?* Do your parents want to remain at home as long as possible, or would they consider an assisted living community or nursing care? Do they have long-term care insurance? Are there durable powers of attorney, so that someone can make financial decisions and pay the bills if they cannot? Do they have living wills outlining their wishes regarding the kind of care and life-prolonging procedures they prefer in the event of hospitalization? While on the subject of health issues, review your parents' prescription drug benefit plans and supplemental health insurance for adequate coverage.

4. *Have they written wills or established any trusts?* Where can you find these documents? Wills should be reviewed every 3 to 5 years or with any major change in their life situation. Encourage your parents to share their intentions. What may be clear to them while they're writing their wills may not be so apparent to their heirs. For example, sometimes parents leave different sums of money to each of their children. It's a good idea for the parents to explain their intentions to avoid surprises that can lead to rifts in the family after they're gone.

5. *What are their wishes with regard to funeral and burial arrangements?*

Don't try to accomplish everything at once. A series of conversations will be necessary to cover all the various topics. When having these talks with your parents, it's important for you to include all siblings so that no one feels left out and the burden doesn't fall to one person. Finally, let your parents know they're in control, and always respect their wishes.

Critical Thinking Questions

1. Why is it important to discuss end-of-life issues with family members?
2. Describe three ways you might begin a conversation about estate planning and end-of-life issues with your parents.
3. When discussing retirement and estate plans with your parents, what specific information should you obtain?

Sources: Walter Updegrave, "Your Family's Money," *Money*, July 2006, p. 72; Clint Willis, "Have 'The Talk' with Your Parents," *Money*, April 1, 2005, p 69; Marc Hogan, "Parents' Day in the Sun," *Business Week Online*, May 11, 2006, InfoTrac College Edition.

anything. There are numerous forces that, if unchecked, tend to shrink an estate, reduce the usefulness of its assets, and frustrate the objectives of the person who built it. These include death-related costs, inflation, lack of liquidity, improper use of vehicles of transfer, and disabilities.

1. **Death-related costs.** When someone dies, the estate incurs certain types of death-related costs. For example, medical bills for a final illness and funeral expenses are good examples of *first-level death-related costs. Second-level death-related costs* consist of fees for attorneys, appraisers, and accountants along with probate expenses—so-called administrative costs, federal estate taxes, and state death taxes. Most people also die with some current bills unpaid, outstanding long-term obligations (such as mortgages, business loans, and installment contracts), and unpaid income taxes and property taxes.

2. **Inflation.** Death-related costs are only the tip of the estate-impairment iceberg. Failure to continuously reappraise and rearrange an estate plan to counter the effects of inflation can impair the ability of assets—liquid, real, and personal property and investments—to provide steady and adequate levels of financial security.

3. **Lack of liquidity.** Insufficient cash to cover death costs and other estate obligations has always been a major factor in estate impairment. Sale of the choicest parcel of farmland or a business that's been in the family for generations, for instance, often has undesirable psychological effects on the heirs. The outcome can be a devastating financial and emotional blow.

4. **Improper use of vehicles of transfer.** Assets are often put into the hands of beneficiaries who are unwilling or unable to handle them. Improper use of vehicles of transfer may pass property to unintended beneficiaries or to the proper beneficiaries in an improper manner or at an incorrect time. For example, spendthrift spouses or minors may be left large sums of money outright in the form of life insurance, through joint ownership of a savings account, or as the beneficiaries of an employee fringe benefit plan.

5. **Disabilities.** A prolonged and expensive disability of a family wage earner is often called a *living death.* Loss of income due to disability is often coupled with a massive financial drain caused by the illness itself. The financial situation is further complicated by inadequate management of currently owned assets. This not only threatens the family's financial security but also quickly diminishes the value of the estate.

What Is Your Estate?

Your estate is your property—whatever you own. Your **probate estate** consists of the real and personal property you own in your own name that can be transferred at death according to the terms of a will, or under intestate laws if you have no valid will. The probate estate is distinct from the gross estate (a tax law term that may encompass a considerably larger amount of property). Your **gross estate** includes all the property—both probate and nonprobate—that might be subject to federal estate taxes at your death. Life insurance, jointly held property with rights of survivorship, and property passing under certain employee benefit plans are common examples of nonprobate assets that might be subject to federal (and state) estate taxes.

You also may provide for property that's not probate property and won't be part of your estate for federal estate tax purposes yet will pass to your family and form part of their financial security program. There are two types of such assets. One is *properly arranged* life insurance. For instance, you could give assets to your daughter to allow her to purchase, pay the premiums for, and be the beneficiary of a policy on your life. At your death, the proceeds wouldn't be included as part of your estate. The other type of financial asset that falls into this category is *Social Security*. Social Security payments to a surviving spouse and minor children generally are neither probate assets nor subject to any federal (or state) estate taxes. Because of the freedom from administrative costs and taxes, this category of assets provides unique and substantial estate planning opportunities.

probate estate The real and personal property owned by a person that can be transferred at death.

gross estate All property that might be subject to federal estate taxes on a person's death.

The Estate Planning Process

The estate planning process consists of seven important steps, as summarized in Exhibit 15.2. First, you must assess your family situation, evaluating its strengths and weaknesses, and set estate planning goals. Next, gather comprehensive and accurate data on all aspects of the family. Exhibit 15.3 summarizes the data that professionals require to prepare detailed estate plans. Most professional estate planners provide forms to help their clients compile this information. Then, you should take inventory and determine the value of your estate. Next, you must designate beneficiaries of your estate's assets, estimate estate transfer costs, and formulate and implement your plan. The final step is ongoing: review your estate plan periodically—at least every 3 to 5 years, and revise it as circumstances dictate. Key events that should also trigger a review include the death or disability of a spouse or family member, moving to another state, changing jobs, getting married or divorced, having children, or acquiring new assets.

The objective of estate plans, of course, is to maximize the usefulness of people's assets during their lives and to achieve their personal objectives after their deaths. Once the plan has been implemented, however, you must reevaluate it regularly. An estate plan is good only as long as it fits the needs, desires, and circumstances of the parties involved. As these elements change, you must modify your estate plan. Marriage or remarriage, divorce, the birth of a child, a change of job or location, and substantial changes in income, health, or living standards are the types of events that indicate a need for a review. Even if none of these occur, you should automatically review life insurance needs at least once every 2 years and perform a full estate audit at least once every 3 to 5 years (or whenever there has been a major change in the federal or state death-tax laws). Due to the general complexity of the laws relating to estate transfer, the assistance of estate planners, life insurance professionals, certified financial planners (CFP®s), chartered financial consultants (ChFCs), accountants, and attorneys is often necessary in the planning and evaluation process. Given the individual nature of estate planning, we cannot include specific guidelines in this chapter.

EXHIBIT 15.2 Steps in the Estate Planning Process

The estate planning process consists of seven important steps, listed here in the order they would be performed.

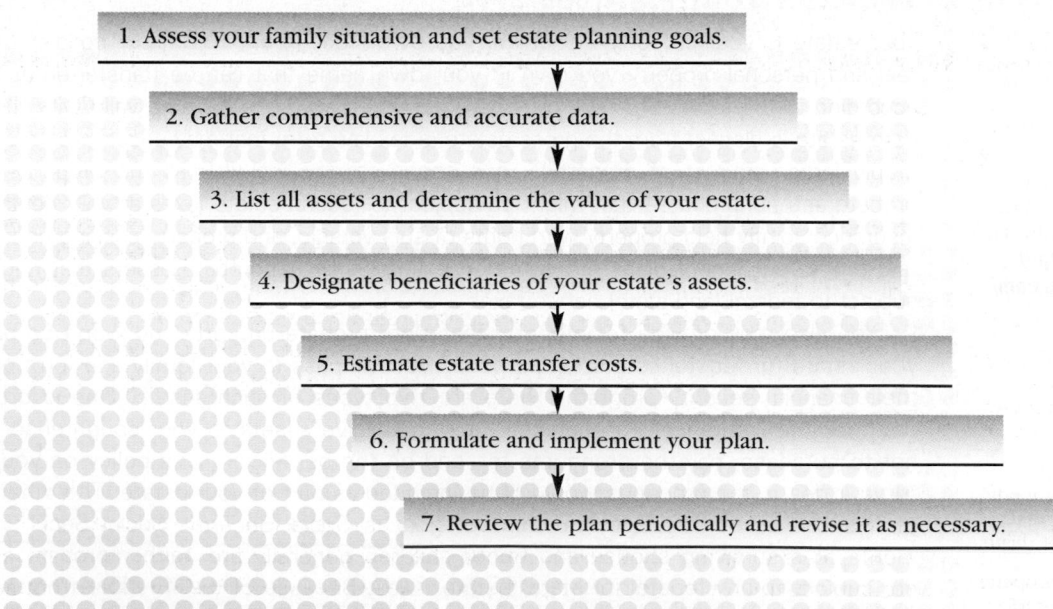

1. Assess your family situation and set estate planning goals.

2. Gather comprehensive and accurate data.

3. List all assets and determine the value of your estate.

4. Designate beneficiaries of your estate's assets.

5. Estimate estate transfer costs.

6. Formulate and implement your plan.

7. Review the plan periodically and revise it as necessary.

EXHIBIT 15.3   Data Needed for Estate Planning

The second step in developing an effective estate plan involves gathering comprehensive and accurate data about you and your family. The types of data required by estate planners include the following:

Personal data:	Names, addresses, phone numbers, birth dates, marital status, marital agreements, wills, trusts, custodianships, trust beneficiary, gifts or inheritances, Social Security numbers, and military service
Property:	Classification, title, indebtedness, date and manner of acquisition, value of marketable securities and their locations
Life insurance:	Name of insured, kinds of policies, amounts, insurance companies, agents' names and addresses
Health insurance:	Medical insurance company, policy numbers and benefits; disability income insurance
Business interest:	Name, address, ownership, desired survivorship control; names, addresses, and phone numbers of business attorney and accountant
Employee benefits:	Group insurance plans, pension benefits
Family income:	Income of client, spouse, income tax information
Family finances:	Budget information, investment preferences, capital needs, other objectives
Other data:	Retirement: planned retirement age, potential sources of retirement income; disability: required amount, sources; upon death: expected sources of income for heirs
Liabilities:	Listing of liabilities, creditors, amounts, whether insured or secured
Authorization for information:	Life insurance, executor

▮▮ Concept Check

CHECK • CONCEPT CHECK • CONCEPT CHECK • CONCEPT CHECK • CONCEPT CHECK • CONCEPT CHECK • CONCEPT C

15-1	Discuss the importance and goals of estate planning. Explain why estates often break up. Distinguish between the *probate estate* and the *gross estate*.
15-2	Briefly describe the steps involved in the estate planning process.

LG2   THY WILL BE DONE...

will A written and legally enforceable document expressing how a person's property should be distributed on his or her death.

As the Robbins family learned, having an up-to-date will is an important aspect of personal financial planning and estate planning. Without it, you have no assurance that your assets will be divided according to your desires. A **will** is a written, legally enforceable expression or declaration of a person's wishes concerning the disposition of his or her property on death. Unfortunately, about 70 percent all Americans do not have valid wills. The importance of a valid will becomes very apparent when we examine what happens when someone dies without one.

Absence of a Valid Will: Intestacy

intestacy The situation that exists when a person dies without a valid will.

testator A person whose will directs the disposition of property at his or her death.

Suppose that Frederick Robbins had died without a valid will, in a situation called **intestacy.** State intestacy laws "draw the will the decedent failed to make" to determine the disposition of the probate property of persons who have died intestate. These statutes set forth certain preferred classes of survivors. Generally, the decedent's spouse is favored, followed by the children and then other offspring. If the spouse and children or other offspring, such as grandchildren or great-grandchildren, survive, they will divide the estate, and other relatives will receive nothing. If no spouse, children, or other offspring survive, the deceased's parents, brothers, and sisters will receive a share of the estate.

Exhibit 15.4 gives an example of how a typical intestate estate is distributed. After paying debts and taxes and deducting state-defined family exemptions, that individual's separately owned property would be distributed in the order and percentages shown. Where property goes to the state due to the absence of a will, the property is said to *escheat to the state*. If a person without relatives dies with a valid will, his or her property will probably go to friends or to charity rather than to the state.

Aside from having lost control of the disposition of the property, the person who dies intestate also forfeits the privileges of naming a personal representative to guide the disposition of the estate, naming a guardian for persons and property, and specifying which beneficiaries would bear certain tax burdens. Estate planning and a valid will may also minimize the amount of estate shrinkage through transfer taxes. Having a valid will—regardless of the estate size—is a critical element in the personal financial planning process.

Preparing the Will

A will allows a person, called a **testator,** to direct the disposition of property at his or her death. The testator can change or revoke a will at any time before his or her death. On the death of the testator, the will becomes operative.

Will preparation, or drafting, varies in difficulty and cost, depending on individual circumstances. In some cases, a two-page will costing $150 may be adequate; in others, a complex document costing $1,500 or more may be necessary. A will must not only effectively accomplish the objectives specified for distributing assets but also take into consideration income, gift, and estate tax laws. Will preparation also requires a knowledge of corporate, trust, real estate, and securities laws. Note that a will, important as it is, may be ineffective or misstate the testator's estate plan if it doesn't consider and coordinate assets passing outside its limits.

Smart Sites

For a "Crash Course in Wills & Trusts" and general estate-planning advice, visit the award-winning site of Michael T. Palermo, an attorney and CFP®. Link through **http://www.thomsonedu .com/finance/gitman.**

EXHIBIT 15.4	Distribution of a Typical Intestate Estate

If a person dies intestate (without a valid will), the estate is distributed according to established state laws of intestate succession. This summary is based on Utah's probate code.

Survivors	Distribution*
Spouse and offspring—children, grandchildren, etc.—not of the surviving spouse	The first $50,000 plus 50% of the balance to the surviving spouse and the other 50% of the balance to the decedent spouse's offspring by right of representation (the spouse's share is reduced by any nonprobate transfers to him or her)
Spouse and no offspring or decedent's offspring all by the surviving spouse	100% to surviving spouse
No spouse but offspring	To decedent's descendants per capita at each generation
No spouse and no offspring, but parent(s)	To parent or parents equally
No spouse, no offspring, no parents, but generation	To parents' descendants per capita at each offspring of parents
No spouse, no offspring, no parents, and no offspring of parents, but grandparents or offspring of grandparents	Divided half to maternal grandparents (or their offspring, if neither survives) and half to the paternal grandparents (or their offspring, if neither survives). If one side predeceased and there are no offspring, the other side takes all.
None of the above	The intestate estate passes to the state for the benefit of the state school fund.

* Because intestate laws vary from state to state, the actual distribution of assets may differ from that shown here; however, the Utah Probate Code is based on the Uniform Probate Code that has been adopted, at least in part, by 18 states.

A properly prepared will should meet these three important requirements:

- Provide a plan for distributing the testator's assets according to his or her wishes, the beneficiaries' needs, and federal and state dispositive and tax laws
- Consider the changes in family circumstances that might occur after its execution
- Be unambiguous and complete in describing the testator's desires

By following these general guidelines, the testator generally can develop a satisfactory will.

Will drafting, no matter how modest the estate size, should not be attempted by a layperson. The complexity and interrelationships of tax, property, domestic relations, and other laws make the homemade will a potentially dangerous document. Nowhere is the old adage, "He who serves as his own attorney has a fool for a client," more true. Few things may turn out more disastrous in the long run than the do-it-yourself will.

Common Features of the Will

There's no absolute format that must be followed when preparing a will, but most wills contain similar distinct sections. Exhibit 15.5 on page 496, which presents the will of John Steven Fabian, includes generalized examples of each of these clauses. Refer to the exhibit as you read these descriptions of the clauses. *These clauses must be tailored to individual needs and circumstances by an attorney familiar with the testator's situation.*

- **Introductory clause.** An introductory clause, or preamble, normally states the testator's name and residence; this determines the county that will have legal jurisdiction and be considered the testator's domicile for tax purposes. The revocation statement nullifies old and forgotten wills and *codicils*—legally binding modifications of an existing will.
- **Direction of payments.** This clause directs the estate to make certain payments of expenses. As a general rule, however, the rights of creditors are protected by law, and such a clause is largely useless.
- **Disposition of property.** Fabian's will has three examples of clauses dealing with disposition of property:
    1. *Disposition of personal effects:* A testator may also make a separate detailed and specific list of personal property and carefully identify each item, and to whom it is given, as an informal guide to help the executor divide the property. (This list generally should not appear in the will itself, because it's likely to change frequently.)
    2. *Giving money to a specifically named party:* Be sure to use the correct legal title of a charity.
    3. *Distribution of residual assets after specific gifts have been made:* Bequests to close relatives (as defined in the statute) who die before the testator will go to the relative's heirs unless the will includes other directions. Bequests to nonrelatives who predecease the testator will go to the other residual beneficiaries.
- **Appointment clause.** Appointment clauses name the *executors* (the decedent's personal representatives who administer the estate), guardians for minor children, and trustees and their successors.
    - **Tax clause.** In the absence of a specified provision in the will, so-called *apportionment statutes* of the testator's state will allocate the burden of taxes among the beneficiaries. The result may be an inappropriate and unintended reduction of certain beneficiaries' shares or adverse estate tax effects. Earlier statutes tended to charge death taxes on the residual of the estate, but today the trend is toward statutes that charge each beneficiary based on his or her share of the taxable estate. Because the spouse's share and the portion going to a charity are deducted from the gross estate before arriving at the taxable estate, neither is charged with taxes.
    - **Simultaneous death clause.** This clause describes what happens in the event of simultaneous death. The

© CORBIS

EXHIBIT 15.5   A Representative Will for John Steven Fabian

John Steven Fabian's will illustrates the eight distinct sections of most wills.

The Last Will and Testament of John Steven Fabian

Section 1 — Introductory Clause

I, John Steven Fabian, of the city of Chicago, state of Illinois, do, hereby make my last will and revoke all wills and codicils made prior to this will.

Section 2 — Direction of Payments

Article 1: Payment of Debts and Expenses

I direct payment out of my estate of all just debts and the expenses of my last illness and funeral.

Section 3 — Disposition of Property

Article 2: Disposition of Property

I give and bequeath to my wife, Sally Warren Fabian, all my jewelry, automobiles, books, and photography equipment, as well as all other articles of personal and household use.

I give to the Chicago Historical Society the sum of $100,000.

All the rest, residue, and remainder of my estate, real and personal, wherever located, I give in equal one-half shares to my children, Charles Elliot and Lara Sue, their heirs and assigns forever.

Section 4 — Appointment Clause

Article 3: Nomination of Executor and Guardian

I hereby nominate as the Executor of this Will my beloved wife, Sally Warren Fabian, but if she is unable or unwilling to serve then I nominate my brother, Winston James Fabian. In the event both persons named predecease me, or shall cease or fail to act, then I nominate as Executor in the place of said persons, the Northern Trust Bank of Chicago, Illinois.

If my wife does not survive me, I appoint my brother, Eugene Lawrence Fabian, Guardian of the person and property of my son, Charles Elliot, during his minority.

Section 5 — Tax Clause

Article 4: Payment of Taxes

I direct that there shall be paid out of my residuary estate (from that portion which does not qualify for the marital deduction) all estate, inheritance, and similar taxes imposed by a government in respect to property includable in my estate for tax purposes, whether the property passes under this will or otherwise.

Section 6 — Simultaneous Death Clause

Article 5: Simultaneous Death

If my wife and I shall die under such circumstances that there is not sufficient evidence to determine the order of our deaths, then it shall be presumed that she survived me. My estate shall be administered and distributed in all respects in accordance with such assumption.

Section 7 — Execution and Attestation Clause

In witness thereof, I have affixed my signature to this, my last will and testament, which consists of five (5) pages, each of which I have initialed, this 15th day of September, 2008.

John Steven Fabian

Section 8 — Witness Clause

Signed, sealed, and published by John Steven Fabian, the testator, as his last will, in the presence of us, who, at his request, and in the presence of each other, all being present at the same time, have written our names as witnesses.

(Note: Normally the witness signatures and addresses would follow this clause.)

assumption that the spouse survives is used mainly to permit the marital deduction, which offers a tax advantage. Other types of clauses are similarly designed to avoid double probate of the same assets—duplication of administrative and probate costs. Such clauses require that the survivor live for a certain period, such as 30 or 60 days, to be a beneficiary under the will.

- **Execution and attestation clause.** Every will should be in writing and signed by the testator at its end as a precaution against fraud. Many attorneys suggest that the testator also initial each page after the last line or sign in a corner of each page.
- **Witness clause.** The final clause helps to affirm that the will in question is really that of the deceased. All states require two witnesses to the testator's signing of the will—except for Vermont, which requires three. Most states require witnesses to sign in the presence of one another, after they witness the signing by the testator. Their addresses should be noted on the will. If the testator is unable to sign his or her name for any reason, most states allow the testator to make a mark and to have another person (properly witnessed) sign for him or her.

Requirements of a Valid Will

To be valid, a will must be the product of a person with a sound mind, there must have been no *undue influence* (influence that would remove the testator's freedom of choice), the will itself must have been properly executed, and its execution must be free from fraud.

1. **Mental capacity.** You must be of "sound mind" to make a valid will. This means that you:
   a. Know what a will is and are aware that you are making and signing one.
   b. Understand your relationship with persons for whom you would normally provide, such as a spouse or children.
   c. Understand what you own.
   d. Are able to decide how to distribute your property and have knowledge of the persons who would generally be expected to receive the estate (even though the testator is not required to leave anything to them); generally, such capacity is presumed.

   Setting aside a will requires clear and convincing proof of mental incapacity, and the burden of proof is on the person contesting the will.
2. **Freedom of choice.** When you prepare and execute your will, you must not be under the undue influence of another person. Threats, misrepresentations, inordinate flattery, or some physical or mental coercion employed to destroy the testator's freedom of choice are all types of undue influence.
3. **Proper execution.** To be considered properly executed, a will must meet the requirements of the state's wills act or its equivalent. It must also be demonstrable that it is in fact the will of the testator. Most states have statutes that spell out who may make a will (generally any person of sound mind, age 18 or older but 14 in Georgia and 16 in Louisiana), the form and execution the will must have (most states require a will to be in writing and signed by the testator at the logical end), and requirements for witnesses. Generally, a beneficiary should not serve as a witness. Although the will is otherwise valid, about 60 percent of the states penalize the beneficiary-witness in some way, such as limiting the beneficiary-witness' bequest to the intestate share that he or she would receive.

Most states now provide for a *self-proving will* that states in the attestation clause that the correct formalities for will execution were observed. A self-proving will eliminates the need to have the witnesses sign, after the testator's death, a declaration verifying their signatures and that of the testator. This saves time, money, and often lots of inconvenience to the executor.

Changing or Revoking the Will: Codicils

As life circumstances change, so should your will. Because a will is inoperative until the testator's death, the testator can change it at any time, as long as he or she has the mental capacity. In fact, periodic revisions should occur, especially on these events:

- His or her (or the beneficiaries') health or financial circumstances change significantly
- Births, deaths, marriages, or divorces alter the operative circumstances
- The testator moves to a state other than where the will was executed
- An executor, trustee, or guardian can no longer serve
- Substantial changes occur in the tax law

Only the testator can change a will. By reviewing your will regularly, you can be sure that it accurately reflects your current wishes.

Changing the Will

To make minor changes to an existing will, the testator draws up a **codicil.** This simple and convenient legal means of modifying a will is often a single-page document reaffirming all the existing provisions in the will except the one to be changed. The codicil should be executed and witnessed in the same formal manner as a will.

When a will requires substantial changes, a new will is usually preferable to a codicil. In addition, if a gift in the original will is removed, it may be best to make a new will and destroy the old, even if substantial changes aren't required. This avoids offending the omitted beneficiary. Sometimes, however, the prior will should not be destroyed even after the new will has been made and signed. If the new will fails for some reason (because of the testator's mental incapacity, for example), the prior will may qualify. Also, a prior will could help to prove a "continuity of testamentary purpose"—in other words, that the latest will (which may have provided a substantial gift to charity) continued an earlier intent and wasn't an afterthought or the result of an unduly influenced mind.

Revoking the Will

When he remarried, Frederick Robbins might have wanted to change his will significantly. In that case, he'd have been better off revoking his will and writing a new one, rather than doing a series of codicils. A will may be revoked either by the testator or automatically by the law. A testator can revoke a will in one of four ways:

1. Making a later will that expressly revokes prior wills
2. Making a codicil that expressly revokes all wills earlier than the one being modified
3. Making a later will that is inconsistent with a former will
4. Physically mutilating, burning, tearing, or defacing the will with the intention of revoking it

The law automatically modifies a will under certain circumstances, which vary from state to state but generally center on divorce, marriage, birth or adoption, and murder. In many states, if a testator becomes divorced after making a will, all provisions in the will relating to the spouse become ineffective. If a testator marries after making a will, the spouse receives that portion of the estate that would have been received had the testator died without a valid will. If a testator did not provide for a child born or adopted after the will was made (unless it appears that such lack of provision was intentional), the child receives that share of the estate not passing to the testator's spouse that would have been given to him or her had the deceased not had a will. Finally, almost all states have some type of slayer's statute forbidding a person who commits murder from acquiring property as the result of the deed.

Safeguarding the Will

In most cases, you should keep your original will in a safe-deposit box, with copies in a safe and accessible place at home and with the attorney who drafted it. Although some authorities and many attorneys recommend leaving the original will with the attorney who

---

FINANCIAL ROAD SIGN

WILL-WRITING POINTERS

Here are some tips to help you write your will in a way that will prevent problems later:

- **Take stock.** Compile lists of your assets, outstanding debts, and family members and other beneficiaries.
- **Evaluate your findings.** Take your time considering how to distribute your assets equitably.
- **Consider taxes.** A carefully designed will and estate plan can reduce the taxes your heirs will owe.
- **Talk about your will and your intentions.** Letting family members know what you're leaving them and why could avoid hard feelings afterward.
- **Create a trust.** Evaluate whether trusts make sense for estate administration and to reduce estate taxes.
- **Be reasonable.** You don't have to divide everything equally among your children, but strive for fairness in asset distribution. Again, explain the rationale behind your decisions.
- **Spread the wealth.** Try to bequeath something to all those with a valid interest in your estate. Otherwise they might try to contest the will.
- **Review and update regularly.** Life circumstances change, and your will may no longer be appropriate.
- **Leave more than money.** An ethical will that discusses the values you hope to have left your survivors can be a wonderful gift to will in addition to one that deals with possessions.

---

codicil A document that legally modifies a will without revoking it.

drafted it, this may make it awkward for the executor to exercise the right to choose his or her own attorney. Further, it may discourage the estate owner from changing the will or engaging a new attorney even if he or she moves out of the state in which the will is drawn.

Worksheet 15.1 on page 500 contains an executor's checklist of documents and information that should be kept in a safe-deposit box. If each spouse has a separate safe-deposit box, the couple may want to keep their wills in each other's boxes. Some states provide for *lodging* of the will, a mechanism for filing and safekeeping it in the office of the probate court (also called *orphan's* or *surrogate's court*). In those states, this procedure satisfies the need to safeguard the will.

Letter of Last Instructions

People often have thoughts they want to convey and instructions they wish others to carry out that aren't appropriate to include in their wills. For example, Frederick Robbins might have explained why he chose Carolyn as his executor rather than choosing her brother. A **letter of last instructions** is the best way to communicate these suggestions or recommendations. It's typically an informal memorandum separate from the will. (This letter of last instructions should contain no bequests, because it has no legal standing.) It's best to make several copies of the letter, keeping one at home and the others with the estate's executor or attorney, who can deliver it to beneficiaries at the appropriate time.

A letter of last instructions might provide directions regarding such items as:

1. Location of the will and other documents
2. Funeral and burial instructions (often a will is not opened until after the funeral)
3. Suggestions or recommendations as to the continuation, sale, or liquidation of a business (it's easier to freely suggest a course of action in such a letter than in a will)
4. Personal matters that the testator might prefer not to be made public in the will, such as statements that might sound unkind or inconsiderate but would be valuable to the executor (for example, comments about a spendthrift spouse or a reckless son)
5. Legal and accounting services (executors are free, however, to choose their own counsel—not even testators can bind them in that selection)
6. An explanation of the actions taken in the will, which may help avoid litigation (for instance, "I left only $1,000 to my son, Ramon, because . . ." or "I made no provisions for my oldest daughter, Melissa, because . . .")
7. Suggestions on how to divide the personal property

Administration of an Estate

letter of last instructions An informal memorandum separate from a will and containing suggestions or recommendations for carrying out a decedent's wishes.

probate process The court-supervised process of liquidation that occurs when a person dies.

executor The personal representative of an estate designated in the decedent's will.

administrator The personal representative of the estate appointed by the court if the decedent died intestate.

When people die, they usually own property and owe debts. Often, they'll have claims (accounts receivable) against other persons. A process of liquidation called the **probate process,** similar to that used in dissolving a corporation, might be required. In this process, money owed the decedent is collected, creditors (including tax authorities) are satisfied, and what remains is distributed to the appropriate individuals and organizations. A local court generally supervises the probate process through a person designated as an **executor** in the decedent's will, or if the decedent died intestate (without a valid will), through a court-appointed **administrator.**

An executor or administrator, sometimes called the *decedent's personal representative*, must collect the decedent's assets, pay debts or provide for payment of debts that aren't currently due, and distribute any remaining assets to the persons entitled to them by will or by the intestate law of the appropriate state. Estate administration is important for many reasons. The executor or administrator becomes the decedent's legal representative, taking care of such matters as collecting bank accounts and other contracts, releasing liability, and creating clear title to make real estate marketable. Due to the importance of the estate administration process, you should select executors who are not only familiar with the testator's affairs but also can effectively handle the responsibilities of being an executor.

This checklist itemizes the various documents and information that the executor may need to effectively carry out the terms of the will. These items should be kept in a safe-deposit box.

CHECKLIST FOR EXECUTORS

Name (Testator) _____ Date _____

_____ 1. Marriage certificates (including prior marriages)
_____ 2. Your will and trust agreements
_____ 3. Life insurance policies or certificates
_____ 4. Your Social Security numbers
_____ 5. Military discharge papers

_____ 6. Bonds, stocks, and securities
_____ 7. Real estate deeds
_____ 8. Business agreements
_____ 9. Automobile titles and insurance policies
_____ 10. Property insurance policies
_____ 11. Tax Information
_____ 12. Letter of last instructions

List all checking and savings account numbers, bank addresses, and locations of safe-deposit boxes:

_____ _____ _____

_____ _____ _____

List names, addresses, and phone numbers of property and life insurance agents:

_____ _____ _____

List names, addresses, and phone numbers of attorney and accountant:

_____ _____ _____

List names, addresses, and phone numbers of (current or last) employer. State retirement date, if applicable. Include employee benefits booklets:

_____ _____ _____

List all debts owed to *and* by you, including names and account numbers:

_____ _____ _____

List the names, addresses, telephone numbers, and birth dates of your children and other beneficiaries (including charities):

_____ _____ _____

_____ _____ _____

Source: Based on Stephan R. Leimberg, Stephen N. Kandell, Ralph Gano Miller, Morey S. Rosenbloom, and Timothy C. Polacek, *The Tools & Techniques of Estate Planning*, 14th ed. (Upper Saddle River, NJ: Prentice Hall, 2006); Fidelity Investments Estate Planning Action Center, http://www.fidelity.com; enotes, Wills, http://law.enotes.com/everyday-law-encyclopedia/wills; Metropolitan Life Insurance Company, The Executor's Checklist, http://www.metlife.com.

Other Important Estate Planning Documents

In addition to your will and the letter of last instructions, you should have several other documents to protect yourself and your family: a power of attorney, a living will, a durable power of attorney for healthcare, and an ethical will.

power of attorney Legal document that authorizes another person to take over one's financial affairs and act on his or her behalf.

living will A document that precisely states the treatments a person wants if he or she becomes terminally ill.

durable power of attorney for healthcare A written power of attorney authorizing an individual to make healthcare decisions on behalf of the principal when the principal is unable to make such decisions. Also called *advanced directive for healthcare*.

ethical will An informal personal statement left for family, friends, and community that shares your values, blessings, life's lessons, and hopes and dreams for the future. Also called *legacy statement*.

right of survivorship The right of surviving joint owners of property to receive title to the deceased joint owner's interest in the property.

Power of Attorney

If you're incapacitated by a serious illness, a **power of attorney** allows you to name as your agent the person you consider best suited to take over your financial affairs—perhaps a spouse or other relative. Although this is a simple document, it transfers enormous power to your designated appointee, so be sure you can rely on the person you choose to manage your finances responsibly. If you have investments, your power of attorney should include language that covers powers of investment on your behalf. You may want to clear your power of attorney with the brokerage firms and mutual funds where you have accounts.

Living Will and Durable Power of Attorney for Healthcare

Had Frederick Robbins lingered in a coma with little or no hope of recovery, his family could have faced difficult decisions regarding his medical care. He hadn't prepared a *living will* or *durable power of attorney for healthcare* to guide them as to his preferences. These documents address another important aspect of estate planning: determining the medical care you wish to receive, or *not* receive, if you become seriously ill and are unable to give informed consent. The **living will** states, precisely, the treatments that you want and to what degree you wish them continued. You must be as specific as possible so that your wishes are clear; otherwise, a living will might be put aside because it is too vague. For example, you should define what you mean by "terminal illness." Each state has its own form for a living will, and you can usually complete it yourself.

Many experts prefer the **durable power of attorney for healthcare,** often called *advanced directives for healthcare,* instead of the living will; some advise having both to reinforce each other. Through the durable power of attorney for healthcare, you authorize an individual (your *agent*) to make healthcare decisions for you if you're unable to do so either temporarily or permanently. Unlike the living will, it applies in any case where you cannot communicate your wishes, not just when you're terminally ill. You can limit the scope of the durable power of attorney and include specific instructions for the desired level of medical treatment. You should spend some time making these decisions and then review your ideas and philosophy concerning these matters with your family and the person you designate as your agent. These documents, copies of which should be held by your designated agent and your doctor, can make it easier for your family to deal with these difficult issues.

Ethical Wills

In addition to a traditional will that covers the distribution of tangible assets, today many people also prepare **ethical wills** to leave family, friends, and community a personal statement of values, blessings, life's lessons, and hopes and dreams for the future. Sometimes called *legacy statements*, ethical wills are informal documents, usually added to formal wills and read at the same time. They offer a way to share your morals, business ethics, life experiences, family stories and history, and more with future generations. They can take various forms, such as handwritten letters or journals, personal essays written on a computer, or even videotaped or audiotaped conversations.

Writing an ethical will can be a daunting project and may perhaps be even more difficult than writing a regular will. Experts suggest dividing it into smaller steps. You might prepare a list of questions about the impact of certain experiences on shaping your life and values, how you want to be remembered, the lessons you wish to pass on to your family and friends, and any other important messages.

It's a good idea to review your ethical will with the lawyer who handles your estate planning. An ethical will that can be interpreted in a way that seems to contradict the intentions of the formal will may lead to a challenge of the formal will.

What about Joint Ownership?

Many people take title to property jointly either through a *joint tenancy* or as *tenants by the entirety*. The two forms of joint ownership have these characteristics:

1. The interest of a decedent passes directly to the surviving joint tenant(s) [that is, to the other joint owner(s)] by operation of the law and is free from the claims of the decedent's creditors, heirs, or personal representatives. This is called the **right of survivorship.**

2. A **joint tenancy** may consist of any number of persons. The joint owners don't have to be related. A **tenancy by the entirety,** on the other hand, can exist only between husband and wife.
3. In the case of joint tenancy, each joint tenant can unilaterally sever the tenancy. This is not the case with a tenancy by the entirety, which can be severed only by mutual agreement, divorce, or conveyance by both spouses to a third party. In some states a tenancy by the entirety can exist only with respect to real property; other don't recognize such tenancies at all.
4. The co-owners have equal interests.

Joint tenancy, the more common form of joint ownership, offers a sense of family security, quick and easy transfer to the spouse at death, exemption of jointly owned property from the claims of the deceased's creditors, and avoidance of delays and publicity in the estate-settlement process. The key disadvantage of joint tenancy is the inability to control jointly owned property by a will, so that the first joint owner to die cannot control the property's disposition and management on his or her death. Another disadvantage is the potential for higher tax costs often incurred in creating and severing a joint tenancy.

For example, a father who purchases and pays for property and places it in his own and his daughter's name is making a gift to her of one half of the value. On the termination of the tenancy, if the daughter receives the entire proceeds (for example, on the sale of a jointly owned home), the father is making a *second* gift to her—of *his* half-interest in the property. In both situations, he will have gratuitously transferred an interest to her that she did not have before. Fortunately, because federal gift tax law doesn't tax most interspousal transfers, the problem won't arise on a federal level between a married couple (although some states may tax such gifts). The property passes to the surviving spouse tax free, but larger estate taxes could be due when the second spouse dies—if the estate is worth more than $2 million (in 2008). Because most people believe the advantages of joint ownership of major assets, such as a home or automobile, far outweigh the potential disadvantages, it's commonly used by married couples.

You should also be familiar with two other forms of ownership: *tenancy in common* and *community property.*

Tenancy in Common

A third common form of co-ownership is called **tenancy in common.** There is *no right of survivorship*, and each co-owner can leave his or her share to whomever he or she desires. Thus the decedent owner's will controls the disposition of the decedent's partial interest in the asset. If the decedent dies without a will, the intestate succession laws of the state where the property is located will determine who inherits the decedent's interest. Tenancy in common interests can be unequal; a property owned by three co-owners could be apportioned such that their respective shares are 50 percent, 30 percent, and 20 percent of the property.

Community Property

Just as tenancy by the entirety is a special form of marital property co-ownership found only in common-law states (that is, states that trace their property law to England), community property is a form of marital property co-ownership based on Roman law and found primarily in the Southwestern states, which had a Spanish or French influence.

Community property is all property acquired by the effort of either or both spouses during marriage while they reside in a community property state. For example, wages and commissions earned and property acquired by either spouse while living in a community property state are automatically owned equally by both spouses, even if only one was directly involved in acquiring the additional wealth. Property acquired before marriage or by gift or inheritance can be maintained as the acquiring spouse's separate property.

By agreement, which typically must be in writing to be enforceable, the couple can change community property into separate property, and vice versa. Each spouse can leave his or her half of the community property to whomever he or she chooses, so there's *no right of survivorship* inherent in this form of ownership.

joint tenancy A type of ownership by two or more parties, with the survivor(s) continuing to hold all such property on the death of one or more of the tenants.

tenancy by the entirety A form of ownership by husband and wife, recognized in certain states, in which property automatically passes to the surviving spouse.

tenancy in common A form of joint ownership under which there is *no right of survivorship*, and each co-owner can leave his or her share to whomever he or she desires.

community property All marital property co-owned equally by both spouses while living in a community property state.

15-3	What is a *will?* Why is it important? Describe the consequences of dying *intestate*.
15-4	Describe the basic clauses normally included in a will and the requirements regarding who may make a valid will.
15-5	How can changes in the provisions of a will be made legally? In what four ways can a will be revoked?
15-6	Explain these terms: (a) *intestacy*, (b) *testator*, (c) *codicil*, (d) *letter of last instructions*.
15-7	What is meant by the *probate process?* Who is an *executor*, and what is the executor's role in estate settlement?
15-8	Describe briefly the importance of these documents in estate planning: (a) *power of attorney*, (b) *living will*, (c) *durable power of attorney for health-care*, and (d) *ethical will*.
15-9	Define and differentiate between *joint tenancy* and *tenancy by the entirety*. Discuss the advantages and disadvantages of joint ownership. How does *tenancy in common* differ from joint tenancy?
15-10	What is the *right of survivorship?* What is *community property*, and how does it differ from joint tenancy regarding this right?

LG3 · TRUSTS

Trusts, another important tool for estate planning, facilitate the transfer of property and the income from that property to another party. Although trusts were once considered estate planning techniques only for the wealthy, today even those of modest means use trusts to their advantage in estate planning. This change is attributed to rising real estate values, the bull markets of the 1980s and 1990s, and marketing by estate planning attorneys. Also, as people live longer and are more likely to marry more than once, they need ways to protect and manage assets.

> **trust** A legal relationship created when one party transfers property to a second party for the benefit of third parties.

A **trust** is a legal relationship created when one party, the **grantor** (also called the *settlor, trustor,* or *creator*), transfers property to a second party, the **trustee** (an organization or individual), for the benefit of third parties, the **beneficiaries,** who may or may not include the grantor. The property placed in the trust is called *trust principal* or *res* (pronounced "race"). The trustee holds the legal title to the property in the trust and must use the property and any income it produces solely for the benefit of trust beneficiaries. The trust generally is created by a written document.

> **grantor** A person who creates a trust and whose property is transferred into it. Also called *settlor, trustor,* or *creator*.

The grantor spells out the substantive provisions (such as how to allocate the property in the trust and how to distribute income) and certain administrative provisions. A trust may be *living* (funded during the grantor's life) or *testamentary* (created in a will and funded by the probate process). It may be *revocable* or *irrevocable*. The grantor can regain property placed into a revocable trust and alter or amend the terms of the trust. The grantor cannot recover property placed into an irrevocable trust during its term.

> **trustee** An organization or individual selected by a *grantor* to manage and conserve property placed in trust for the benefit of the *beneficiaries*.

Let's now look at how trusts solve various estate planning problems.

> **beneficiaries** Those who receive benefits—property or income—from a trust or from the estate of a decedent; may or may not include the *grantor*.

Why Use a Trust?

Trusts are designed for various purposes. The most common motives are to attain income and estate tax savings and manage and conserve property over a long period.

Income and Estate Tax Savings

Under certain circumstances, a grantor who is a high-bracket taxpayer can shift the burden of paying taxes on the income produced by securities, real estate, and other investments to a trust itself or to its beneficiary, both of whom are typically subject to lower income tax rates than the grantor is. However, the *Tax Reform Act of 1986* severely limited a person's ability to shift income in this way. Specifically, with certain types of trusts, the beneficiary must be more than 14 years of age; otherwise, the income from the trust is taxed at the same rate as the beneficiary's parents. In addition to possible income tax benefits, impressive *estate tax* savings are possible because the appreciation in the value of property placed into such a trust can be entirely removed from the grantor's estate and possibly benefit several generations of family members without incurring adverse federal estate tax consequences.

Managing and Conserving Property

Minors, spendthrifts, and those who are mentally incompetent need asset management for obvious reasons. However, busy executives and others who can't or don't want to spend the countless hours necessary to handle large sums of money and other property often use trusts to relieve themselves of those burdens. The trustee assumes the responsibility for managing and conserving the property on behalf of the beneficiaries. In some cases, management by the trustee is held in reserve in case a healthy and vigorous individual is unexpectedly incapacitated and becomes unable or unwilling to manage his or her assets.

Selecting a Trustee

Five qualities are essential in a trustee. He or she must

1. Possess sound business knowledge and judgment
2. Have an intimate knowledge of the beneficiary's needs and financial situation
3. Be skilled in investment and trust management
4. Be available to beneficiaries (specifically, this means that the trustee should be young enough to survive the trust term)
5. Be able to make decisions impartially

A corporate trustee, such as a trust company or bank that has been authorized to perform trust duties, may be best able to meet these requirements. A corporate trustee is likely to have investment experience and will not impose the problems created by death, disability, or absence. Unlike a family member, a corporate trustee is impartial and obedient to the directions of the trust instrument. Such objectivity adds value if there are several beneficiaries. On the other hand, a corporate trustee may charge high fees or be overly conservative in investments, be impersonal, or lack familiarity with and understanding of family problems and needs. Often a compromise involves appointing one or more individuals and a corporate trustee as co-trustees.

Common Types and Characteristics of Trusts

Although there are various types of trusts, the most common are the *living trust*, the *testamentary trust*, and the *irrevocable life insurance trust*, each of which is described in the following sections. Exhibit 15.6 describes seven other popular trusts.

Living Trusts

living (inter vivos) trust
A trust created and funded during the grantor's lifetime.

A **living (inter vivos) trust** is one created and funded during the grantor's lifetime. It can be either revocable or irrevocable and can last for a limited period or continue long after the grantor's death. These come in two forms, revocable and irrevocable.

revocable living trust
A trust in which the grantor reserves the right to revoke the trust and regain trust property.

Revocable Living Trust. The grantor reserves the right to revoke the trust and regain trust property in a **revocable living trust.** For federal income tax purposes, grantors of these

EXHIBIT 15.6   Seven Popular Trusts

Trusts shift assets (and thus appreciation) out of one's estate while retaining some say in the future use of the assets. The drawback is that trusts can be cumbersome and expensive to arrange and administer. Here are brief descriptions of seven popular trusts:

- **Credit shelter trust.** Most common trust for estate planning; couples with combined assets worth more than the "applicable exclusion amount" can gain full use of each partner's exclusion by having that amount placed in a bypass trust, that is, one that bypasses the surviving spouse's taxable estate. It's called a *credit shelter trust* because the taxes are calculated using a method called the *unified credit*. The surviving spouse is usually given the right to all the trust income and, in an emergency, even has access to the principal. So if the first death occurred in the year 2008, the trust would be funded with assets worth $2,000,000.

- **Qualified terminable interest property (QTIP) trust.** Usually set up in addition to a *credit shelter trust* to ensure that money stays in the family; it receives some or all of the estate assets over the applicable exclusion amount ($2,000,000 in 2008). Assets left outright to a spouse who remarries could be claimed by the new spouse. The survivor receives all income from the property until death, when the assets go to the persons chosen by the first spouse to die. Estate taxes on QTIP trust assets can be delayed until the second spouse dies. Also useful for couples with children from prior marriages.

- **Special needs trust.** An irrevocable trust established for the benefit of a person with disabilities. It is designed to provide extra help and life enrichment without reducing state and federal government help to the beneficiary.

- **Minor's section 2503(c) trust.** Set up for a minor, often to receive tax-free gifts. However, assets must be distributed to the minor by the time he or she turns 21.

- **Crummey trust.** Used to make tax-free gifts up to the annual exclusion amounts to children; unlike a *minor's section 2503(c) trust*, these funds don't have to be distributed at age 21. However, the beneficiary can withdraw the funds placed into the trust for a limited time (for example, for up to 30 days), after which the right to make a withdrawal ceases. (The annual exclusion amount is the annual amount that can be given each year without being subject to gift tax—for example, $12,000 in 2008.)

- **Charitable lead (or income) trust.** Pays some or all of its income to a charity for a period of time. Then, the property is distributed to noncharitable beneficiaries. Grantor gets immediate income tax deduction based on expected future payout to charity.

- **Charitable remainder trust.** Similar to a *charitable lead trust*, except that income goes to taxable beneficiaries (for example, the grantor or the grantor's children) and the principal goes to a charity when the trust ends.

trusts are treated as owners of the property in the trust—in other words, just as if they held the property in their own names—and are therefore taxed on any income produced by the trust.

Revocable living trusts have three basic advantages:

1. Management continuity and income flow are ensured even after the grantor's death. No probate is necessary, because the trust continues to operate after the death of the grantor just as it did while he or she was alive.
2. The trustee assumes burdens of investment decisions and management responsibility. For example, an individual may want to control investment decisions and management policy as long as he or she is alive and healthy but sets up a trust to provide backup help in case he or she becomes unable or unwilling to continue managing the assets.
3. The terms and the amount of assets placed into the trust do not become public knowledge, as they would during the probate process.

The principal disadvantages of these trusts include the fees charged by the trustee for managing the property placed into the trust and the legal fees charged for drafting the trust instruments.

Irrevocable Living Trust.

Grantors who establish an **irrevocable living trust** relinquish title to the property they place in it and give up the right to revoke or terminate the trust. (The grantor may retain the income from certain types of irrevocable trusts.) Such trusts have all the advantages of revocable trusts plus the potential for reducing taxes. Disadvantages of such a trust relate to the fees charged by trustees for managing assets placed in it, possible gift taxes on assets placed into it, in some cases the grantor's complete loss of the trust property and any income it may produce, and the grantor's forfeiture of the right to alter the terms of the trust as circumstances change.

Living Trusts and Pour-Over Wills.

A will can be written so that it "pours over" designated assets into a previously established revocable or irrevocable living trust. The trust may also be named beneficiary of the grantor's insurance policies. The **pour-over will** generally contains a provision passing the estate—after debts, expenses, taxes, and specific bequests—to an existing living trust. The pour-over will ensures that the property left out of the living trust, either inadvertently or deliberately, will make its way into the trust (that is, "pour over" into it). The trust contains provisions for administering and distributing those assets (together with insurance proceeds payable to the trust). Such an arrangement provides for easily coordinated and well-administered management of estate assets.

Testamentary Trust

A trust created by a decedent's will is called a **testamentary trust.** Such a trust comes into existence only after the will is probated. A court order directs the executor to transfer the property to the trustee to fund the trust. This type of trust provides no tax savings for the grantor, because he or she continues to own the property until his or her death.

Irrevocable Life Insurance Trust

A wealthy individual can establish an **irrevocable life insurance trust** in which the major asset of the trust is life insurance on the grantor's life. To avoid having the proceeds of the policy included in the grantor's estate, the independent trustee usually acquires the policy. The terms of the trust enable the trustee to use the proceeds to pay the grantor's estate taxes and to take care of the grantor's spouse and children.

irrevocable living trust A trust in which the grantor relinquishes the title to the property placed in it and gives up the right to revoke or terminate the trust.

pour-over will A provision in a will that provides for the passing of the estate—after debts, expenses, taxes, and specific bequests—to an existing living trust.

testamentary trust A trust created by a decedent's will and funded through the probate process.

irrevocable life insurance trust An irrevocable trust in which the major asset is life insurance on the grantor's life.

gift tax A tax levied on the value of certain gifts made during the giver's lifetime.

❙❙ Concept Check

CHECK • CONCEPT CHECK • CONCEPT CHECK • CONCEPT CHECK • CONCEPT CHECK • CONCEPT CHECK • CONCEPT

15-11	Describe the basic trust arrangement, and discuss typical reasons for establishing trusts. What essential qualities should a trustee possess?
15-12	What is a *living (inter vivos) trust?* Distinguish between a *revocable living trust* and an *irrevocable living trust.*
15-13	Explain each of these terms: (a) *grantor,* (b) *trustee,* (c) *beneficiary,* (d) *pour-over will,* (e) *testamentary trust,* and (f) *irrevocable life insurance trust.*

LG4 FEDERAL UNIFIED TRANSFER TAXES

estate tax A tax levied on the value of property transferred at the owner's death.

unified rate schedule A graduated table of rates applied to all taxable transfers; used for *both* federal gift and estate tax purposes.

Federal tax law establishes a **gift tax** on the value of certain gifts made during one's lifetime and an **estate tax** on "deathtime" gifts. For decades, the gift tax and estate tax gave similar treatment to wealth transfers, whether the transfer was during life (a gift) or at death (part of an estate). Indeed, these taxes are still officially part of what is called the Uniform Transfer Tax within the Internal Revenue Code. While the tax rate is the same for gifts and estates and is known as the **unified rate schedule** (see the graduated table of rates in Exhibit 15.7), the difference in the applicable exclusion amount will make large gifts more expensive than estate transfers between now and 2010.

The *Economic Growth and Tax Relief Reconciliation Act of 2001 (EGTRRA)* has greatly complicated estate planning for wealthy families because it initially increases the amount that can pass free of estate taxes; temporarily eliminates the estate tax altogether for the year 2010; and then, in 2011, returns the tax to what it would have been had the act never been passed. In addition, EGTRRA makes gift taxes more costly than estate taxes; the amount that can pass tax free, called the *applicable exclusion amount,* is frozen at $1 million for gifts, while it increases in increments from $1 million in 2002 to $3.5 million for estates in 2009.

Consider these two examples:

1. Fred gives his daughter a $4,000,000 taxable gift in 2008. Gift taxes equal $1,335,000.
2. Mary dies in 2008 and leaves her son a $4,000,000 estate. The estate tax equals $900,000.

Due to the difference in the respective applicable exclusion amounts (see Exhibit 15.8 on page 508), in the previous examples the gift tax is $435,000 higher than the estate tax— even though the transferred amount is the same.

Because of the 2001 Tax Act, many estate planners recommend against giving sizable lifetime gifts. Many planners expect Congress to revisit this area of the law to "fix" the estate tax so that it doesn't disappear for the year 2010 only to reappear the following year for estates over $1 million. The fix is likely to include having the estate applicable exclusion amount set permanently (well, as permanent as things get in tax law) at $4 million, perhaps with that amount being indexed for inflation.

EXHIBIT 15.7	Federal Unified Transfer Tax Rates

This *unified rate schedule* defines the amount of federal gift and estate taxes that estates of various sizes would have to pay; it incorporates the rates passed in the *Economic Growth and Tax Relief Reconciliation Act of 2001*. Rates and amounts remain the same through 2009 for estates worth up to $2,000,000. Estates under the exclusion amount pay no federal tax; anything over that amount is currently taxed at 45 to 50 percent. The exclusion amount increases annually from $2,000,000 in 2006 to $3,500,000 in 2009 (see Exhibit 15.8 on page 508). From 2007 to 2009, the top tax rates for estates worth more than $2,000,000 decrease slightly as shown here.

Taxable Estate Value		Tentative Tax		
More Than	But Not More Than	Base Amount	+ Percent	On Excess Over
$ 0	$ 10,000	$ 0		
10,000	20,000	1,800	20%	$ 10,000
20,000	40,000	3,800	22	20,000
40,000	60,000	8,200	24	40,000
60,000	80,000	13,000	26	60,000
80,000	100,000	18,200	28	80,000
100,000	150,000	23,800	30	100,000
150,000	250,000	38,800	32	150,000
250,000	500,000	70,800	34	250,000
500,000	750,000	155,800	37	500,000
750,000	1,000,000	248,300	39	750,000
1,000,000	1,250,000	345,800	41	1,000,000
1,250,000	1,500,000	448,300	43	1,250,000
1,500,000	2,000,000	555,800	45	1,500,000
Top rate, 2006				
2,000,000		780,800	46	2,000,000
Top rate, 2007–2009				
2,000,000		780,800	45	2,000,000
2010	Repealed for estates. The maximum rate for gifts is 35% starting at $500,000.			
2011 and beyond	Returns to pre-2001 tax law levels unless otherwise modified by Congress.			

Source: Adapted from material in John C. Bost, *Estate Planning and Taxation*, 14th ed. (Dubuque, IA: Kendall Hunt, 2006).

The *Economic Growth and Tax Relief Reconciliation Act of 2001* increased the applicable exclusion amount on a scheduled basis over the period from 2002 to 2009, with a complete repeal of the estate tax in 2010. This table shows the step-up in the exclusion amount from 2006 through repeal in 2010. Also shown are the unified tax credit amounts over the 2006 to 2011 period.

Year	Unified Tax Credit—Estates	Applicable Exclusion Amount—Estates	Unified Tax Credit—Gifts	Applicable Exclusion Amount—Gifts
2006	$780,800	$2,000,000	$345,800	$1,000,000
2007	$780,800	$2,000,000	$345,800	$1,000,000
2008	$780,800	$2,000,000	$345,800	$1,000,000
2009	$1,455,800	$3,500,000	$345,800	$1,000,000
2010	Estate tax repealed for 2010		$330,800	$1,000,000
2011	$345,800	$1,000,000	$345,800	$1,000,000

Gifts and Taxes

Gifting can be a good way to transfer property to a beneficiary before you die. However, most transfers will be subject to gift taxes. There's no gift tax on services that one person performs for another, nor is the rent-free use of property a taxable transfer. A tax may be payable on cash gifts, gifts of personal or real property, and both direct and indirect gifts. For example, if a father makes the mortgage payments on his adult son's home, the payment is an indirect gift from father to son. In fact, almost any shifting of financial advantage in which the recipient does not provide full consideration in money or money's worth may be considered a gift. For example, suppose that your father gave you a summer home valued at $175,000 in exchange for $125,000. This type of transaction is called a *bargain sale*. The $50,000 excess value received over the consideration paid is treated as a gift. Of course, if you didn't pay your dad anything for the house, the gift would be equal to its market value ($175,000).

Usually a gift is considered to be made *when the donor relinquishes dominion and control over the property or property interest transferred*. For example, if a mother places cash in a bank account held jointly with her son, no gift is made until the son makes a withdrawal. Until then the mother can completely recover the entire amount placed in the account. So, when parents place property into a revocable trust for their children, no gift occurs because they haven't relinquished control over the assets placed in it. But if they later make the trust irrevocable and thereby relinquish their right to control the gift, the transfer will be considered a completed gift.

Is It Taxable?

Not everything that's transferred by an individual is subject to a gift tax. Annual exclusions, gift splitting, charitable deductions, and marital deductions are all means of reducing the total amount for tax purposes.

annual exclusion Under the federal gift tax law, a deduction of up to $12,000 per donee (through 2007 and indexed for inflation) for gifts by any donor to any number of donees in a given calendar year.

gift splitting A method of reducing gift taxes; a gift given by one spouse, with the consent of the other spouse, can be treated as if each had given one-half of it.

- **Annual exclusions.** The gift tax law allows a person to give gifts up to a specified annual amount—$12,000 per calendar year (through 2007 and indexed for inflation)—to any number of donees. For example, a person could give gifts of $12,000 each to 30 recipients, for a total of $360,000, without using up any of the donee's applicable exclusion amount (and of course not paying any gift tax). Further, the ability to give tax-free gifts of $12,000 per donee renews annually. This annual exclusion applies only for gifts given with "no strings attached."
- **Gift splitting.** In this method of reducing gift taxes, a gift given by one spouse, with the consent of his or her spouse, can be treated as if each had given one-half of it.
- **Charitable deductions.** There's no limit on the amount that can be given—with no gift tax—to a qualified charity (one to which deductible gifts can be made for income tax

purposes). Therefore, people could give their entire estates to charity and receive gift tax deductions for the total amount. There would be no federal gift taxes, regardless of the type or amount of assets transferred.

- **Marital deductions.** Federal law permits an unlimited deduction for gift tax and estate tax purposes on property given or left to a spouse who is a U.S. citizen. Special rules apply for transfers to a spouse who is not a U.S. citizen. These prevent tax avoidance if the noncitizen spouse returns to his or her native country, where the bequest would then escape taxation in the United States.

Reasons for Making Lifetime Gifts

Estate planners recommend gift giving for these tax-related reasons:

- **Gift exclusion.** As noted earlier, a single individual can give any number of donees up to $12,000 each year with no tax costs to either the donees or the donor.
- **Gift tax exclusion escapes estate tax.** Fortunately, property that qualifies for the annual exclusion is not taxable and is thus free from gift and estate taxes. Estate tax savings from this exclusion can be significant. Regardless of a gift's size—and even if it's made within 3 years of the donor's death—it's typically not treated as part of the donor's gross estate. However, the taxable portion of lifetime gifts (technically called *adjusted taxable gifts*) pushes up the rate at which the donor's estate will be taxed.
- **Appreciation in value.** Generally, the appreciation on a gift, from the time it's made, is excluded from the donor's estate. Suppose that Larry gives his son, Steve, a gift of stock worth $25,000 in 2006. When Larry dies 2 years later, the stock is worth $60,000. The amount subject to transfer taxes will be $13,000—the amount of the gift that exceeded the $12,000 annual exclusion when the gift was made. None of the appreciation would be subject to gift or estate taxes.
- **Credit limit.** Because of the credit that's used to offset otherwise taxable gifts, gift taxes don't have to be paid on cumulative lifetime gifts up to the applicable exclusion amount of $1,000,000 (note that the applicable exclusion amount for gifts doesn't increase over the years); see Exhibit 15.8. To the extent that the credit is used against lifetime gift taxes, it's not available to offset estate taxes.
- **Impact of marital deduction.** The transfer tax marital deduction allows one spouse to give the other spouse an unlimited amount of money or other property entirely tax free without reducing the applicable exclusion amount that can be transferred to others tax free.

❚❚ Concept Check

CHECK • CONCEPT CHECK • CONCEPT CHECK • CONCEPT CHECK • CONCEPT CHECK • CONCEPT CHECK • CONCEPT C

15-14	What is a gift, and when is a gift made? Describe the following terms as they relate to federal gift taxes: (a) *annual exclusion*, (b) *gift splitting*, (c) *charitable deduction*, and (d) *marital deduction*.
15-15	Discuss the reasons estate planners cite for making lifetime gifts. How and in what ways might gift giving help reduce estate shrinkage?

LG5 CALCULATING ESTATE TAXES

Estate taxes may be generated when property is transferred at the time of death, so one goal of effective estate planning is to minimize the amount of estate taxes paid. The federal estate tax is levied on the transfer of property at death. The tax is measured by the value of the property that the deceased transfers (or is deemed to transfer) to others. The phrase "deemed to transfer" is important because the estate tax applies not only to transfers that a deceased actually makes at death but also to certain transfers made during the person's lifetime. In other words, to thwart tax-avoidance schemes, the estate tax is imposed on

© STONE/GETTY IMAGES

certain lifetime gifts that essentially are the same as dispositions of property made at death.

Although most gifts made during one's life are not part of the decedent's gross estate, there are some exceptions. A major exception pertains to life insurance if the owner is also the insured. If the owner-insured gives away the policy within 3 years of his or her death, the proceeds will be included in the insured's gross estate.

For example, 2 years before his death, Max gives his son, Eric, a $1 million term insurance policy on Max's life. At the time of the gift, Max was in good health, and the value of the term insurance policy for gift tax purposes was clearly less than the annual exclusion amount. Therefore, Max did not have to file a gift tax return. Because Max died within 3 years of gifting the life insurance policy, the $1 million proceeds amount is included in his gross estate for estate tax purposes. Had Max outlived the transfer by more than 3 years, the proceeds would not have been included in his gross estate.

Computing the Federal Estate Tax

The computation of federal estate taxes involves six steps:

1. Determine the *gross estate*, the total of all property in which the decedent had an interest and that is required to be included in the estate.
2. Find the *adjusted gross estate* by subtracting from the gross estate any allowable funeral and administrative expenses, debts, and other expenses incurred during administration.
3. Calculate the *taxable estate* by subtracting any allowable marital deduction or charitable deduction from the adjusted gross estate.
4. Compute the *estate tax base*. After determining the value of the taxable estate, any "adjusted taxable gifts"—which are the taxable gifts (gifts above the annual exclusion) made after 1976—are added to the taxable estate. The unified tax rate schedule—the one applicable to gift taxes, shown in Exhibit 15.7—is then applied to determine a *tentative tax on estate tax base*.
5. After finding the tentative tax, subtract any gift taxes the decedent paid on certain gifts and the **unified tax credit** (described below). The result is the total death taxes.
6. Determine the *federal estate tax due*. Certain credits are allowed against the total death taxes, which result in a dollar-for-dollar reduction of the tax. The dominant credit is the state death-tax credit. After reducing the total death taxes by any eligible credits, the federal estate tax due is payable by the decedent's executor, generally within 9 months of the decedent's death.

You can use Worksheet 15.2 to estimate federal estate taxes. The worksheet depicts the computations for a hypothetical situation involving a death in 2007, when the applicable exclusion of $2 million applies. Note that the applicable exclusion amount is not subtracted from the gross estate. The worksheet is useful in following the flow of dollars from the gross estate to the federal estate tax due.

Over the period from 1997 to 2009, the *Taxpayer Relief Act of 1997* and *Economic Growth and Tax Relief Reconciliation Act of 2001* increased the amount that can pass free of transfer taxes. Exhibit 15.8 shows the applicable exclusion amount for estates and the unified credit—the credit that's applied against the tentative tax. The tentative tax is calculated on the estate tax base. Using the rates shown in Exhibit 15.7, you can determine the tentative tax on an estate. For a taxable estate of $2 million in the year 2007, no tax is owed because the unified tax credit for that year is $780,800, which exactly matches the tentative tax on $2 million (calculated using Exhibit 15.7). If the taxable estate in 2007 is $2,200,000, the tentative tax is $870,800, and the estate tax is $90,000 ($870,800 tentative tax − $780,800 unified credit). Notice that a taxable estate of $2,200,000 is $200,000

unified tax credit The credit that can be applied against the *tentative tax on estate tax base*.

This worksheet is useful in determining federal estate tax due. Note that taxes are payable at the marginal tax rate applicable to the estate tax base (line 7), which is the amount that exists before the tax-free exclusion is factored in.

COMPUTING FEDERAL ESTATE TAX DUE

Name: *Mary Widow*   Date: *June 10, 2007*

Line	Computation	Item	Amount	Total Amount
1		Gross estate		$ 4,600,000
2	Subtract sum of:	(a) Funeral expenses	$ 6,000	
		(b) Administrative expenses	25,000	
		(c) Debts	130,000	
		(d) Other expenses	0	
		Total		(161,000)
3	Result:	Adjusted gross estate		$ 4,439,000
4	Subtract sum of:	(a) Marital deduction	—	
		(b) Charitable deduction	—	
		Total		(0)
5	Result:	Taxable estate		$ 4,439,000
6	Add:	Adjusted taxable gifts (post-1976)		$ 0
7	Result:	Estate tax base		$ 4,439,000
8	Compute:	Tentative tax on estate tax base[a]		$ 1,878,350
9	Subtract sum of:	(a) Gift tax payable on post-1976 gifts	$ —	
		(b) Unified tax credit[b]	780,800	
		Total		(780,800)
10	Result:	Federal estate tax due		$ 1,097,550

[a] Use Exhibit 15.7 to calculate the tentative tax:

$780,800 + [45\% \times (\$4,439,000 - \$2,000,000)] = \$780,800 + (45\% \times \$2,439,000) = \$1,878,350$.

[b] Use Exhibit 15.8 to determine the appropriate unified credit.

above the applicable exclusion amount, so the excess is taxed at the marginal rate of 45 percent. Hence the tax owed is $90,000 (.45 × $200,000).

Worksheet 15.2 factors the unified credit for the year 2007 into the calculation at line 9b. The $780,800 shown on that line is equal to the tentative tax on an estate tax base of $2 million. If the tentative tax shown on line 8 is less than the unified credit available for the decedent's year of death, no federal estate tax is due.

⏸ Concept Check

CHECK · CONCEPT CHECK · CONCEPT CHECK · CONCEPT CHECK · CONCEPT CHECK · CONCEPT CHECK · CONCEPT C

15-16 Explain the general nature of the federal estate tax. How does the *unified tax credit* affect the amount of estate tax owed?

15-17 Explain the general procedure used to calculate the *federal estate tax due*.

As with income taxes, you can minimize the estate taxes owed by applying appropriate tax-avoidance strategies. The federal tax laws described earlier present both problems and opportunities for you and your estate planner. Judicious use of certain tax-oriented strategies will minimize estate shrinkage and maximize financial security. Two basic techniques of estate planning are dividing your estate and deferring income to minimize income taxes and leave a larger amount to accumulate for the estate. Life insurance is another estate planning tool.

Dividing

Each time you create a new tax paying entity, you'll save income taxes and stimulate estate accumulation. Here are some popular techniques:

1. **Giving income-producing property to children, either outright or in trust.** Because each child can receive a specified amount of unearned income each year, some income tax savings may be realized each year even by persons who are not in high tax brackets.
2. **Establishing a corporation.** Incorporation may permit individuals in high tax brackets, such as doctors or other professionals, to save taxes by accumulating income in a manner subject to relatively lower income tax rates.
3. **Properly qualifying for the federal estate tax marital deduction.** This marital deduction allows an individual to pass—estate tax free—unlimited amounts to a spouse, taking full advantage of both spouses' unified credits. Properly qualifying in some estates may mean something less than fully qualifying. That is, in some circumstances an advisor will properly recommend passing less than an individual's entire estate to the surviving spouse.

Deferring

Progressive tax rates (rates that increase as the amount of income or size of the estate increases) penalize taxpayers whose maximum earnings (or estates) reach high peaks. This makes it harder to gain and maintain financial security. Techniques to minimize the total tax burden by spreading income over more than one tax year or deferring the tax to a later period—so the taxpayer can invest the tax money for a longer time—apply to estate planning as well as income tax planning. Here are some examples:

1. **Nonqualified deferred-compensation plans** for selected individuals in corporate businesses and private contractors.
2. **Making installment sales** instead of cash sales to spread the taxable gain over several years.
3. **Private annuities,** which are arrangements whereby one person transfers property to another, usually a younger family member. This recipient promises in return to pay an annuity to the original owner for as long as he or she lives. The income tax attributable to such an annuity can thereby be spread over several years. Further, when the original owner dies, the property transferred is not part of the transferrer's estate, and the annuity's value drops to zero.
4. **Qualified pension and profit-sharing plans** that allow tax deferral on the income and gains from investments.
5. **Government Series EE bonds**—because their earnings can be treated as taxable income at maturity rather than yearly as earned.
6. **Stocks that pay no or low dividends** but have high price appreciation because they invest retained earnings in profitable projects.
7. **Life insurance policies** in which lifetime growth is not taxed and death values are income tax free. If the insured survives, earnings inherent in policy values become taxable only as received, so the tax on any gain can be deferred over a lifetime.
8. **Depreciable real estate** that yields high write-offs in years when the estate owner is earning high levels of taxable passive income.

9. **Installment payment of federal estate taxes** applicable to a business interest that equals or exceeds 35 percent of the adjusted gross estate. Payments can be spread over as many as 14 years with only the interest being paid on the unpaid tax during the first 4 years.
10. **Possible elimination of the estate tax** in the near future, or at least additional significant increases in the applicable exclusion amount. (We'll discuss this topic in more detail below.)

Life Insurance as an Estate Planning Tool

Life insurance can be a valuable component of your estate plan. A policy can be purchased for an annual premium of from 3 to 6 percent of the face (death) value of the policy. If someone other than the insured owns the policy, the proceeds of such insurance can pass to the decedent's beneficiaries free of income tax, estate tax, inheritance tax, and probate costs. For example, the trustee of an irrevocable life insurance trust might be selected to apply for and own the policy. After the insured's death, the trustee uses the insurance proceeds for the benefit of the surviving family members, who in turn might use them to pay death taxes, debts, administrative expenses, or other family expenses such as college costs, mortgage balances, and other major expenditures. What's more, whole life and universal life insurance policies are an attractive form of loan collateral. As we pointed out in Chapters 7 and 8, some lending institutions and other creditors require borrowers to obtain enough life insurance to repay them if borrowers die before fully repaying their loans.

Future of the Estate Tax

The estate tax law passed in 2001 raised the applicable exclusion amounts and decreased the transfer tax rates, with a complete repeal of the estate tax taking place in 2010 but lasting for just one year. The estate tax springs back to life for decedents dying in 2011 or later with a taxable estate exceeding $1 million. While it's likely that Congress will revisit the estate tax issue before then, it's too early to predict what the future holds.

As we've learned in this chapter, estate planning goes beyond minimizing taxes. It is the best way to take care of the people you love, help charitable organizations, transfer property, and spell out your wishes if you die or become disabled. Regardless of what happens to the estate tax in the future, estate planning will continue to be a key component of personal financial planning.

❙❙ Concept Check

15-18   The two basic techniques of estate planning are (1) dividing your estate and (2) deferring income to minimize taxes. Describe and discuss each of these techniques.

≪ SUMMARY

LG1   **Describe the role of estate planning in personal financial planning and identify the seven steps involved in the process.** Estate planning involves accumulating, preserving, and distributing an estate in order to most effectively achieve an estate owner's personal goals. The seven major steps to estate planning are (1) assess the family situation and set estate planning goals, (2) gather comprehensive and accurate data, (3) list all assets and determine estate value, (4) designate beneficiaries of estate's assets, (5) estimate estate transfer costs, (6) formulate and implement a plan, and (7) review the plan periodically and revise it as necessary.

LG2   **Recognize the importance of preparing a will and other documents to protect you and your estate.** A person who dies without a valid will forfeits important privileges, including the right to decide how property will be distributed at death and the opportunity to select who will administer the estate and bear the burden of estate taxes and administrative expenses. The will should provide a clear and unambiguous expression of the testator's wishes, be flexible enough to encompass possible changes in family circumstances, and give proper regard to minimizing income, gift, and estate taxes. A will is valid only if properly executed by a person of sound mind. Once drawn up, wills can be changed by codicil or be fully revoked. The executor, named in the will, is responsible for collecting the decedent's assets, paying his or her debts and taxes, and distributing any remaining assets to the beneficiaries in the prescribed fashion. In addition to the will, other important estate planning documents include the letter of last instructions, power of attorney, living will, durable power of attorney for healthcare, and an ethical will.

LG3 **Explain how trusts are used in estate planning.** The trust relationship arises when one party, the grantor, transfers property to a second party, the trustee, for the benefit of a third party, the beneficiary. There are several types of trusts, but each is designed primarily for one or both of these reasons: to save income and estate taxes and to manage and conserve property over a long period.

LG4 **Determine whether a gift will be taxable and use planned gifts to reduce estate taxes.** Gifts of cash, financial assets, and personal or real property made during the donor's lifetime are subject to federal taxes. A gift of $12,000 per year (through 2007 and indexed for inflation) to each recipient is excluded from the donor's gift tax calculation. Generally, donations to qualified charities and gifts between spouses are also excluded from the gift tax.

LG5 **Calculate federal taxes due on an estate.** Federal estate taxes are a levy on the transfer of assets at death. They are unified (coordinated) with the gift tax—which imposes a graduated tax on the transfer of property during one's lifetime—so that the rates and credits are the same for both. Today, because of the 2001 Tax Act, the gift tax exclusion amount stays at $1 million, and the estate tax exclusion amount is rising from $2 million in 2006 to $3,500,000 in 2009, will be eliminated in 2010, and drops to $1 million in 2011. (Congress is likely to reconsider estate taxes before then.) Once federal estate taxes are computed, certain credits are allowed, and the resulting amount is payable in full generally within 9 months of the decedent's death.

LG6 **Use effective estate planning techniques to minimize estate taxes.** Most well-defined estate plans use two estate planning techniques. Dividing involves the creation of new tax entities. Deferring gives an individual the use of money that would otherwise have been paid in taxes. Life insurance proceeds can be used to pay estate taxes or to provide heirs with funds for specific purposes.

FINANCIAL PLANNING EXERCISES

LG1   1. Generate a list of estate planning objectives that apply to your personal family situation. Be sure to consider the size of your potential estate as well as people planning and asset planning.

LG2   2. Renée and Steve Burrows are in their mid-thirties and have two children, ages 8 and 5. They have combined annual income of $95,000 and own a house in joint tenancy with a market value of $310,000, on which they have a mortgage of $250,000. Steve has $100,000 in group term life insurance and an individual universal life policy for $150,000. However, the Burrowses haven't prepared their wills. Steve plans to do one soon, but they think that Renée doesn't need one because the house is jointly owned. As their financial planner, explain why it's important for both Steve and Renée to draft wills as soon as possible.

LG2   3. Prepare a basic will for yourself, using the guidelines presented in the text; also prepare your brief letter of last instructions.

LG2   4. Your best friend has asked you to be executor of his estate. What qualifications do you need, and would you accept the responsibility?

LG2, 3   5. Joe Phillips, 48 and a widower, and Amy Parsons, 44 and divorced, were married 5 years ago. Joe has two children, and Amy has one (from their prior marriages). Their estate totals $1.4 million, including a house valued at $475,000, a vacation home in the mountains, investments, antique furniture that's been in Amy's family for many years, and jewelry belonging to Joe's first wife. Discuss how they could use trusts as part of their estate planning, and suggest some other ideas for them to consider when preparing their wills and related documents.

LG4, 5   6. ***Use Worksheet 15.2.*** When Jim Levitt died in 2007, he left an estate valued at $3,650,000, as follows: $10,000 to the local hospital, $60,000 to his alma mater, and the remainder to his three adult children. Death-related costs and expenses were $6,800 for funeral expenses, $40,000 paid to attorneys, $5,000 paid to accountants, and $30,000 paid to the trustee of his living trust. In addition, there were debts of $115,000. Use Worksheet 15.2 and Exhibits 15.7 and 15.8 to calculate the federal estate tax due on his estate.

LG6   7. Summarize any recent legislation affecting estate taxes, and briefly describe its impact on estate planning. Explain why getting rid of the estate tax doesn't eliminate the need for estate planning.

APPLYING PERSONAL FINANCE

Prepare Your Will!

If you die without a valid will, the laws of your state will determine what happens to your property. That may be fine with people who have few assets, but it's not fine for people who care what happens to their property, and it's certainly not fine for people with dependents. In this project, you'll consider what your current will should contain and what changes you should make to your will based on your future circumstances.

Look back through this chapter and review the common features of a will. Then write your own will, based on the sample clauses and examples of a representative will given in the text. List the property that you currently have or expect to have in the future, and name a beneficiary for each. Be sure to name your personal representative, and charge him or her with disposing of your estate according to your wishes. If you have children or expect to have children, or if you have other dependents such as an elderly parent or disabled sibling, be sure to name a guardian and a backup guardian for them. Also prepare a letter of last instructions to convey any personal thoughts or instructions that you feel cannot be properly included in your will. Remember, this exercise should help you think about the orderly disposition of your estate, which is the final act in implementing your personal financial plans.

CRITICAL THINKING CASES

LG2   ## 15.1 A Long-Overdue Will for Theo

In the late 1970s Theo Pappadopolus, originally from Greece, migrated to the United States, where he is now a citizen. A man of many talents and deep foresight, he has built a large fleet of ocean-going oil tankers during his stay in the United States. Now a wealthy man in his sixties, he resides in Palm Springs, Florida, with his second wife, Veronica, age 35. He has two sons, who are both high school seniors. For some time, Theo has considered preparing a will to ensure that his estate will be properly distributed if some unforeseen tragedy or natural cause takes his life. A survey of his estate—all legally owned by him—reveals the following:

Ranch in Amarillo, Texas	$ 800,000
Condominium in San Francisco	400,000
House in Palm Springs	600,000
Franchise in ice cream stores	2,000,000
Stock in Seven Seas International	5,000,000
Shares in Fourth National Bank	1,000,000
Corporate bonds	3,000,000
Other assets	200,000
Total assets	$13,000,000

In addition to $1 million for their education and welfare, he'd like to leave each of his sons 20 percent of his estate. He wishes to leave 40 percent of the estate to his wife. The rest of the estate is to be divided among relatives, friends, and charitable institutions. He has scheduled an appointment for drafting his will with his attorney and close friend, Leonard Wiseman. Theo would like to appoint Leonard and his cousin, Plato Jones, as coexecutors of his estate. If one of them predeceases Theo, he'd like his bank, Fourth National Bank, to act as coexecutor.

Critical Thinking Questions

1. Does Theo really need a will? Explain why or why not. What would happen to his estate if he were to die without a will?
2. Explain to Theo the common features that need to be incorporated into a will.
3. Is a living trust an appropriate part of his estate plan? How would a living trust change the nature of Theo's will?
4. What options are available to Theo if he decides later to change or revoke the will? Is it more difficult to change a living trust?
5. What duties will Leonard Wiseman and Plato Jones have to perform as coexecutors of Theo's estate?

LG4, 5

15.2 Estate Taxes on Philip Colburn's Estate

Philip Colburn of Arlington Heights, Delaware, was 65 when he retired in 1998. His wife of 35 years passed away shortly thereafter. Her will left everything to Philip. Although her estate was valued at $1,750,000, there was no estate tax due because of the 100 percent marital deduction. Their only child, Mark Colburn, is married to Alice; they have four children, two in college and two in high school. When Philip died in 2007, his home was valued at $650,000, his vacation cabin on a lake was valued at $285,000, his investments in stocks and bonds at $890,000, and his pension funds at $645,000 (Mark was named beneficiary). Philip also owned a life insurance policy that paid proceeds of $500,000 to Mark. He left $60,000 to his church and $25,000 to his high school to start a scholarship fund in his wife's name. The rest of the estate was left to Mark. Funeral costs were $5,000. Debts and expenses totaled $90,000. In 2001, Philip made a gift of XYZ stock worth $170,000 jointly to Mark and Alice. Because of the two $10,000 annual exclusions (allowed in 2001) and the unified credit, no gift taxes were due. Use Worksheet 15.2 to guide your calculations as you complete these exercises.

Critical Thinking Questions

1. Compute the value of Philip's *probate estate*.
2. Compute the value of Philip's *gross estate* at the time of his death.
3. Determine the total allowable deductions.
4. Calculate the *estate tax base*, taking into account the gifts given to Mark and Alice (remember the annual exclusions).
5. Use Exhibit 15.7 to determine the *tentative tax on estate tax base*.
6. Subtract the appropriate *unified tax credit* (Exhibit 15.8) for 2007 from the *tentative tax on estate tax base* to arrive at the *federal estate tax due*. Note that there is no credit for gift tax payable on post-1976 gifts because no gift taxes had to be paid.
7. Comment on the estate shrinkage experienced for Philip's estate. What might have been done to reduce this shrinkage? Explain.

> **MONEY ONLINE** www.thomsonedu.com/finance/gitman

ONLINE • MONEY ONLINE • MONEY ONLINE • MONEY ONLINE • MONEY ONLINE • MONEY ONLINE • MONEY ONLINE

Visit **http://www.thomsonedu.com/finance/gitman** for some additional Web-based exercises and hot links (with annotations) to a variety of resources relevant to the topics covered in this chapter.

APPENDIX A

Table of Future Value Factors

Instructions: To use this table, find the future value factor that corresponds to both a given time period (year) and an interest rate. To illustrate, if you want the future value factor for 6 years and 10 percent, move across from year 6 and down from 10 - percent to the point at which the row and column intersect: 1.772. Other illustrations: For 3 years and 15 percent, the proper future value factor is 1.521; for 30 years and 8 percent, it is 10.062.

							Interest Rate					
Year	2%	3%	5%	6%	8%	9%	10%	12%	15%	20%	25%	30%
1	1.020	1.030	1.050	1.060	1.080	1.090	1.100	1.120	1.150	1.120	1.250	1.300
2	1.040	1.060	1.102	1.120	1.166	1.190	1.210	1.254	1.322	1.440	1.562	1.690
3	1.061	1.090	1.158	1.190	1.260	1.290	1.331	1.405	1.521	1.728	1.953	2.197
4	1.082	1.130	1.216	1.260	1.360	1.410	1.464	1.574	1.749	2.074	2.441	2.856
5	1.104	1.160	1.276	1.340	1.469	1.540	1.611	1.762	2.011	2.488	3.052	3.713
6	1.126	1.190	1.340	1.420	1.587	1.670	1.772	1.974	2.313	2.986	3.815	4.827
8	1.172	1.260	1.477	1.590	1.851	1.990	2.144	2.476	3.059	4.300	5.960	8.157
10	1.219	1.340	1.629	1.790	2.159	2.360	2.594	3.106	4.046	6.192	9.313	13.786
12	1.268	1.420	1.796	2.010	2.518	2.810	3.138	3.896	5.350	8.916	14.552	23.298
15	1.346	1.560	2.079	2.390	3.172	3.640	4.177	5.474	8.137	15.407	28.422	51.185
20	1.486	1.810	2.653	3.210	4.661	5.600	6.727	9.646	16.366	38.337	86.736	190.047
25	1.641	2.090	3.386	4.290	6.848	8.620	10.834	17.000	32.918	95.395	264.698	705.627
30	1.811	2.420	4.322	5.740	10.062	13.260	17.449	29.960	66.210	237.373	807.793	2619.936
35	2.000	2.810	5.516	7.690	14.785	20.410	28.102	52.799	133.172	590.657	2465.189	9727.598
40	2.208	3.260	7.040	10.280	21.724	31.410	45.258	93.049	267.856	1469.740	7523.156	36117.754

Note: All factors are rounded to the nearest 1/1000 as shown to agree with values used in the text.

APPENDIX B

Table of Future Value Annuity Factors

Instructions: To use this table, find the future value of annuity factor that corresponds to both a given time period (year) and an interest rate. To illustrate, if you want the future value of annuity factor for 6 years and 10 percent, move across from year 6 and down from 10 percent to the point at which the row and column intersect: 7.716. Other illustrations: For 3 years and 15 percent, the proper future value of annuity factor is 3.472; for 30 years and 8 percent, it is 113.282.

							Interest Rate					
Year	2%	3%	5%	6%	8%	9%	10%	12%	15%	20%	25%	30%
1	1.000	1.000	1.000	1.000	1.000	1.000	1.000	1.000	1.000	1.000	1.000	1.000
2	2.020	2.030	2.050	2.060	2.080	2.090	2.100	2.120	2.150	2.200	2.250	2.300
3	3.060	3.090	3.152	3.180	3.246	3.270	3.310	3.374	3.472	3.640	3.813	3.990
4	4.122	4.180	4.310	4.380	4.506	4.570	4.641	4.779	7.993	5.368	5.766	6.187
5	5.204	5.310	5.526	5.630	5.867	5.980	6.105	6.353	6.742	7.442	8.207	9.043
6	6.308	6.460	6.802	6.970	7.336	7.520	7.716	8.115	8.754	9.930	11.259	12.756
8	8.583	8.890	9.549	9.890	10.637	11.030	11.436	12.300	13.727	16.499	19.842	23.858
10	10.950	11.460	12.578	13.180	14.487	15.190	15.937	17.549	20.304	25.959	33.253	42.619
12	13.412	14.190	15.917	16.870	18.977	20.140	21.384	24.133	29.001	39.580	54.208	74.326
15	17.293	18.600	21.578	23.270	27.152	29.360	31.772	37.280	47.580	72.035	109.687	167.285
20	24.297	26.870	33.066	36.780	45.762	51.160	57.274	72.052	102.443	186.687	342.945	630.157
25	32.030	36.460	47.726	54.860	73.105	84.700	98.346	133.333	212.790	471.976	1054.791	2348.765
30	40.567	47.570	66.438	79.060	113.282	136.300	164.491	241.330	434.738	1181.865	3227.172	8729.805
35	49.994	60.460	90.318	111.430	172.314	215.700	271.018	431.658	881.152	2948.294	9856.746	32422.090
40	60.401	75.400	120.797	154.760	259.052	337.870	442.580	767.080	1779.048	7343.715	30088.621	120389.375

Note: All factors are rounded to the nearest 1/1000 as shown to agree with values used in the text.

APPENDIX C

Table of Present Value Factors

Instructions: To use this table, find the present value factor that corresponds to both a given time period (year) and an interest rate. To illustrate, if you want the present value factor for 25 years and 7 percent, move across from year 25 and down from 7 percent to the point at which the row and column intersect: .184. Other illustrations: For 3 years and 15 percent, the proper present value factor is .658; for 30 years and 8 percent, it is .099.

						Interest Rate						
Year	2%	3%	5%	7%	8%	9%	10%	12%	15%	20%	25%	30%
1	.980	.971	.952	.935	.926	.917	.909	.833	.870	.893	.800	.769
2	.961	.943	.907	.873	.857	.842	.826	.797	.756	.694	.640	.592
3	.942	.915	.864	.816	.794	.772	.751	.712	.658	.579	.512	.455
4	.924	.888	.823	.763	.735	.708	.683	.636	.572	.482	.410	.350
5	.906	.863	.784	.713	.681	.650	.621	.567	.497	.402	.328	.269
6	.888	.837	.746	.666	.630	.596	.564	.507	.432	.335	.262	.207
8	.853	.789	.677	.582	.540	.502	.467	.404	.327	.233	.168	.123
10	.820	.744	.614	.508	.463	.422	.386	.322	.247	.162	.107	.073
12	.789	.701	.557	.444	.397	.356	.319	.257	.187	.112	.069	.043
15	.743	.642	.481	.362	.315	.275	.239	.183	.123	.065	.035	.020
20	.673	.554	.377	.258	.215	.178	.149	.104	.061	.026	.012	.005
25	.610	.478	.295	.184	.146	.116	.092	.059	.030	.010	.004	.001
30	.552	.412	.231	.131	.099	.075	.057	.033	.015	.004	.001	*
35	.500	.355	.181	.094	.068	.049	.036	.019	.008	.002	*	*
40	.453	.307	.142	.067	.046	.032	.022	.011	.004	.001	*	*

*Present value factor is zero to three decimal places.

Note: All factors are rounded to the nearest 1/1000 as shown to agree with values used in the text.

APPENDIX D

Table of Present Value Annuity Factors

Instructions: To use this table, find the present value of annuity factor that corresponds to both a given time period (year) and an interest rate. To illustrate, if you want the present value of annuity factor for 30 years and 7 percent, move across from year 30 and down from 7 percent to the point at which the row and column intersect: 12.409. Other illustrations: For 3 years and 15 percent, the proper present value of annuity factor is 2.283; for 5 years and 8 percent, it is 3.993; for 30 years and 8 percent, it is 11.258.

						Interest Rate						
Year	2%	3%	5%	7%	8%	9%	10%	12%	15%	20%	25%	30%
1	.980	.971	.952	.935	.926	.917	.909	.893	.870	.833	.800	.769
2	1.942	1.913	1.859	1.808	1.783	1.759	1.736	1.690	1.626	1.528	1.440	1.361
3	2.884	2.829	2.723	2.624	2.577	2.531	2.487	2.402	2.283	2.106	1.952	1.816
4	3.808	3.717	3.546	3.387	3.312	3.240	3.170	3.037	2.855	2.589	2.362	2.166
5	4.713	4.580	4.329	4.100	3.993	3.890	3.791	3.605	3.352	2.991	2.689	2.436
6	5.601	5.417	5.076	4.767	4.623	4.486	4.355	4.111	3.784	3.326	2.951	2.643
8	7.326	7.020	6.463	5.971	5.747	5.535	5.335	4.968	4.487	3.837	3.329	2.925
10	8.983	8.530	7.722	7.024	6.710	6.418	6.145	5.650	5.019	4.192	3.570	3.092
12	10.575	9.954	8.863	7.943	7.536	7.161	6.814	6.194	5.421	4.439	3.725	3.190
15	12.849	11.938	10.380	9.108	8.560	8.061	7.606	6.811	5.847	4.675	3.859	3.268
20	16.352	14.878	12.462	10.594	9.818	9.129	8.514	7.469	6.259	4.870	3.954	3.316
25	19.524	17.413	14.094	11.654	10.675	9.823	9.077	7.843	6.464	4.948	3.985	3.329
30	22.396	19.601	15.373	12.409	11.258	10.274	9.427	8.055	6.566	4.979	3.995	3.332
35	24.999	21.487	16.378	12.948	11.655	10.567	9.844	8.176	6.617	4.992	3.998	3.333
40	27.356	23.115	17.159	13.332	11.925	10.757	9.779	8.244	6.642	4.997	3.999	3.333

Note: All factors are rounded to the nearest 1/1000 as shown to agree with values used in the text.

APPENDIX E
Using a Financial Calculator

Important Financial Keys on the Typical Financial Calculator

The important financial keys on a typical financial calculator are depicted and defined below. On some calculators the keys may be labeled using lowercase characters for "N" and "I". Also, "I/Y" may be used in the place of the "I" key.

CPT — Compute Key; Used to initiate financial calculation once all values are input
N — Number of Periods
I — Interest Rate per Period
PV — Present Value
PMT — Amount of Payment; Used only for annuities
FV — Future Value

The handheld financial calculator makes it easy to calculate time value. Once you have mastered the time value of money concepts using tables, we suggest you use such a calculator. For one thing, it becomes very cumbersome to use tables when calculating anything other than annual compounding. For another, calculators rather than tables are used almost exclusively in the business of personal financial planning.

You don't want to become overly dependent on calculators, however, because you may not be able to recognize a nonsensical answer in the event that you accidentally push the wrong button. The important calculator keys are shown and labeled in the above exhibit. Before using your calculator to make the financial computations described in this text, be aware of the following points.

1. The keystrokes on some of the more sophisticated and expensive calculators are menu-driven: after you select the appropriate routine, the calculator prompts you to input each value; a compute key (CPT) is not needed to obtain a solution.
2. Many calculators allow the user to set the number of payments per year. Most of these calculators are preset for monthly payments—12 payments per year. Because we work primarily with annual payments—one payment per year—it is important to make sure that your calculator is set for one payment per year. Although most calculators are preset to recognize that all payments occur at the end of the period, it is important to make sure your calculator is in the END mode. Consult the reference guide that accompanies your calculator for instructions for setting these values.
3. To avoid including previous data in current calculations, always clear all registers of your calculator before inputting values and making each computation.
4. The known values can be punched into the calculator in any order; the order specified in this and other calculator use demonstrations included in this text results merely from convenience and personal preference.

CALCULATOR

INPUTS	FUNCTIONS
5000	PV
6	N
10	I
	CPT
	FV
	Solution
	8,857.81

CALCULATOR

INPUTS	FUNCTIONS
6	N
10	I
26140	FV
	CPT
	PMT
	Solution
	3,387.94

Calculator Keystrokes. Let's go back to the future value calculation on page 53, in which we're trying to calculate the future value of $5,000 at the end of 6 years invested at 10 percent. Here are the steps to solve the problem with a calculator:

1. Punch in 5000 and press PV.
2. Punch in 6 and press N.
3. Punch in 10 and press I.
4. To calculate the future value, press CPT and then FV. The future value of 8,857.81 should appear on the calculator display.

On many calculators, this value will be preceded by a minus sign, which is a way of differentiating cash inflows from outflows. For our purposes, this sign can be ignored.

To calculate the yearly savings (the amount of an annuity), let's continue with the example on pages 53 and 54. This time, you're given the interest rate of 10 percent, the number of periods is 6, and the future value is $26,140. Your job is to solve the equation for the annuity. The steps using the calculator are:

1. Punch in 6 and press N.
2. Punch in 10 and press I.
3. Punch in 26140 and press FV.
4. To calculate the yearly payment or annuity, press CPT and then PMT.

The annuity of 3,387.94 should appear on the calculator display. Again, a negative sign can be ignored.

A similar procedure is used to find present value of a future sum or an annuity, except you would input the FV or PMT and press CPT and then PV to calculate the desired result. To find the equal annual future withdrawals from an initial deposit, the PV would be input and you would solve for the PMT by pressing CPT and then PMT.